International Directory of
COMPANY
HISTORIES

International Directory of

COMPANY

HISTORIES

VOLUME 8

Editor
Paula Kepos

St James Press

Detroit   London   Washington D.C.

The paper used in this publication meets the minimum requirements of American National Standard for Information Sciences— Permanence Paper for Printed Library Materials, ANSI Z39.48-1984.

This book is printed on recycled paper that meets Environmental Protection Agency Standards.

Library of Congress Catalog Number: 89-190943

British Library Cataloguing in Publication Data

International directory of company histories. Vol. 8
I. Paula Kepos
338.7409

ISBN 1-55862-323-X

Printed in the United States of America
Published simultaneously in the United Kingdom

I(T)P™

The trademark **ITP** is used under license.

Cover photograph courtesy of the London Stock Exchange.

10 9 8 7 6 5 4 3 2 1

CONTENTS _____

Company Histories

PREFACE _____

International Directory of Company Histories provides detailed information on the development of the world's largest and most influential companies. To date, *Company Histories* has covered more than 1600 companies in eight volumes.

Inclusion Criteria

Most companies chosen for inclusion in *Company Histories* have achieved a minimum of US$500 million in annual sales. Some smaller companies are included if they are leading influences in their industries or geographical locations. State-owned companies that are important in their industries and that may operate much like public or private companies also are included. Wholly owned subsidiaries are presented if they meet the requirements for inclusion.

St. James Press does not endorse any of the companies or products mentioned in this book. Companies that appear in *Company Histories* were selected without reference to their wishes and have in no way endorsed their entries. The companies were given the opportunity to participate in the compilation of the articles by providing information or reading their entries for factual accuracy, and we are indebted to many of them for their comments and corrections. We also thank them for allowing the use of their logos for identification purposes.

Entry Format

Each entry in this volume begins with a company's legal name, the address of its headquarters, its telephone number and fax number, and a statement of public, private, state, or parent ownership. A company with a legal name in both English and the language of its headquarters country is listed by the English name, with the native-language name in parentheses.

Also provided are the company's earliest incorporation date, the number of employees, and the most recent sales figures available, which are for fiscal year 1992 unless otherwise noted. Sales figures are given in local currencies with equivalents in U.S. dollars. For some private companies, sales figures are estimates. The entry lists the exchanges on which a company's stock is traded, as well as the company's principal Standard Industrial Classification codes. American spelling is used, and the word ''billion'' is used in its American sense of a thousand million.

Sources

The histories were compiled from publicly accessible sources such as general and academic periodicals, books, annual reports, and material supplied by the companies themselves. *Company Histories* is intended for reference use by students, business people, librarians, historians, economists, investors, job candidates, and others who want to learn more about the historical development of the world's most important companies.

Cumulative Indexes

An Index to Companies and Persons provides access to companies and individuals discussed in the text. Beginning with Volume 7, an Index to Industries allows researchers to locate companies by their principal industry.

ABBREVIATIONS FOR FORMS OF COMPANY INCORPORATION

A.B.	Aktiebolaget (Sweden)
A.G.	Aktiengesellschaft (Germany, Switzerland)
A.S.	Atieselskab (Denmark)
A.S.	Aksjeselskap (Denmark, Norway)
A.Ş.	Anomin Şirket (Turkey)
B.V.	Besloten Vennootschap met beperkte, Aansprakelijkheid (The Netherlands)
Co.	Company (United Kingdom, United States)
Corp.	Corporation (United States)
G.I.E.	Groupement d'Intérêt Economique (France)
GmbH	Gesellschaft mit beschränkter Haftung (Germany)
H.B.	Handelsbolaget (Sweden)
Inc.	Incorporated (United States)
KGaA	Kommanditgesellschaft auf Aktien (Germany)
K.K.	Kabushiki Kaisha (Japan)
LLC	Limited Liability Company (Middle East)
Ltd.	Limited (Canada, Japan, United Kingdom, United States)
N.V.	Naamloze Vennootschap (The Netherlands)
OY	Osakeyhtiöt (Finland)
PLC	Public Limited Company (United Kingdom)
PTY.	Proprietary (Australia, Hong Kong, South Africa)
S.A.	Société Anonyme (Belgium, France, Switzerland)
SpA	Società per Azioni (Italy)

ABBREVIATIONS FOR CURRENCY

DA	Algerian dinar	Dfl	Netherlands florin
A$	Australian dollar	NZ$	New Zealand dollar
Sch	Austrian schilling	N	Nigerian naira
BFr	Belgian franc	NKr	Norwegian krone
Cr	Brazilian cruzado	RO	Omani rial
C$	Canadian dollar	P	Philippine peso
DKr	Danish krone	Esc	Portuguese escudo
E£	Egyptian pound	SRls	Saudi Arabian riyal
Fmk	Finnish markka	S$	Singapore dollar
FFr	French franc	R	South African rand
DM	German mark	W	South Korean won
HK$	Hong Kong dollar	Pta	Spanish peseta
Rs	Indian rupee	SKr	Swedish krona
Rp	Indonesian rupiah	SFr	Swiss franc
IR£	Irish pound	NT$	Taiwanese dollar
L	Italian lira	B	Thai baht
¥	Japanese yen	£	United Kingdom pound
W	Korean won	$	United States dollar
KD	Kuwaiti dinar	B	Venezuelan bolivar
LuxFr	Luxembourgian franc	K	Zambian kwacha
M$	Malaysian ringgit		

International Directory of
COMPANY
HISTORIES

A.G. Edwards, Inc.

A.G. Edwards, Inc.

One North Jefferson
St. Louis, Missouri 63103
U.S.A.
(314) 289-3000
Fax: (314) 289-2333

Public Company
Incorporated: 1967 as A.G. Edwards & Sons, Inc.
Employees: 9,487
Sales: $1.1 billion
Stock Exchanges: New York Amex
SICs: 6211 Security Brokers & Dealers; 6719 Holding
   Companies Nec

In a field dominated and often warped by the glamour of New York's Wall Street, A.G. Edwards, Inc., owes its success as an investment brokerage to the traditional midwestern virtues of hard work, thrift, and pragmatism. Founded in St. Louis, Missouri, more than 100 years ago, Edwards is the United States' largest brokerage firm headquartered outside New York and the fifth-largest overall, as measured by number of retail offices.

Retail investment brokerage is the heart and soul of A.G. Edwards. Benjamin Franklin Edwards III, the company's president and a fourth-generation member of its founding family has maintained the firm's longstanding commitment to serve the small investor while shunning both the latest Wall Street fads and the marketing of in-house investment packages. A.G. Edwards, Inc., does not trade stocks on its own or offer cut-rate services or search the globe for the next potential merger of corporate giants; it advises individual investors on what to do with their money, and very little else. The reward for this single-minded conservatism has been steady growth and virtual immunity from the bloodshed and panic that periodically overwhelm the high fliers on Wall Street.

Benjamin Franklin Edwards is the great-grandson of Albert Gallatin Edwards, the founder of A.G. Edwards and himself the son of Ninian W. Edwards, an important figure in the early history of the state of Illinois. Born October 15, 1812, Albert Gallatin Edwards was named (with remarkable prescience, as events proved) after U.S. Secretary of the Treasury Albert Gallatin, an influential advocate of fiscal conservatism in Washington, D.C. Young Edwards was born in Kentucky and grew up in Illinois, of which his father was territorial governor and

later state governor and senator after its admission to the Union in 1818. After graduating from West Point in 1832, A. G. Edwards served briefly with the U.S. Army's first permanent cavalry unit, based south of St. Louis. There he met and in 1835 married Louise Cabanne, a member of one of the oldest St. Louis families. He subsequently resigned from the Army to work for the local wholesaling firm of William L. Ewing.

With ties to leading families in Missouri, Illinois, and Kentucky, Edwards, not surprisingly, prospered in the world of trade. William Ewing specialized in the supply of goods to stores throughout the southwestern United States, a role for which its St. Louis location rendered the company well suited. Albert Edwards brought to the firm a number of important political connections, most notably with a rising Illinois attorney named Abraham Lincoln. Edwards's older brother, Ninian Wirt Edwards, had followed his father into Illinois politics, where he enjoyed little success but became a fixture in the capital city's social and political circles. Ninian's wife, Elizabeth, was a member of the powerful Todd family of Kentucky, and her cousin, John Todd Stuart, became the law partner of Abraham Lincoln in 1839. The Edwardses were soon close friends of Lincoln—so close, in fact, that the future president married the sister of Elizabeth Todd in the home of Ninian Edwards in 1842. Whether Mary Todd was a good love match for Abe Lincoln has long been a subject of debate, but she was certainly a political asset, as Lincoln would later be of great help economically to the Edwards family.

When the Civil War erupted in 1861, Albert Edwards proved loyal to the party of his in-law President Lincoln, staunchly defending the Union cause in a state torn between factions of both parties. Edwards was involved in the defeat of Confederate troops at St. Louis early in the war, and in 1861 he was made a brigadier general in the Missouri State Militia and later bank examiner for the state of Missouri. On April 9, 1865, Edwards was appointed assistant Secretary of the Treasury by Lincoln, who was assassinated six days later. Edwards's job was to oversee the Sub-Treasury Bank in St. Louis, a regional depository similar to today's Federal Reserve Banks. He would continue as assistant secretary throughout the administrations of four subsequent presidents, retiring in 1887 at the age of 75 with a solid reputation in the financial community of St. Louis.

Edwards's retirement was brief, however. Less than a year later he formed a partnership with his eldest son, Benjamin Franklin Edwards, to buy and sell stocks, bonds, and similar investment instruments. Because banks were then among the heaviest traders in securities, Albert Edwards's strong ties with the St. Louis banking community would be invaluable to the new brokerage house of A.G. Edwards & Sons (AGE). The company soon announced that it would become the first St. Louis broker to handle transactions on the New York Stock Exchange (NYSE) for local banks. By thus allying itself more closely with banking interests and the NYSE, AGE escaped involvement with the briefly fashionable St. Louis Mining and Stock Exchange, where heavily leveraged mining stocks were traded like poker chips until the markets' sudden collapse in the early 1890s. When the Exchange closed for good during the depression of 1893, it took with it many local brokerage companies, but AGE suffered only minor losses. This was the first of many occasions on which AGE's conservative investment policy would save it from the worst of the markets' cyclical downturns.

Albert G. Edwards died in 1892 at age 80, leaving the brokerage business in the hands of George Lane Edwards, the founder's second son, who was born in 1869. George Edwards would serve as managing partner of the firm from 1891 to 1919, at which time his brother Albert Ninian Edwards took over. With the recovery of the St. Louis economy in the late 1890s, AGE increased its trading on the NYSE, buying a seat on the exchange for $29,500 in 1898 and two years later opening its first New York office. A year later, AGE was instrumental in the creation of the St. Louis Stock Exchange, which enjoyed immediate popularity; trade volume reached a peak in 1902 of $44 million that would not be exceeded until the salad days of the late 1920s. Federal regulation of the wilder financial schemes cooled market activity in the intervening years, during which time AGE built on its blue chip reputation and quietly prospered.

The nature of the investment business changed radically after World War I. The widespread sale during the war of government "Liberty Bonds" introduced the concept of financial markets to millions of private citizens who previously had been content to leave their savings in bank accounts or hold it as hard cash. In the booming 1920s this trend was greatly accelerated and brokers like AGE adjusted accordingly, shifting an increasing amount of their attention from banks and wealthy speculators to the mass retail market of small investors. Under the direction of managing partner Albert N. Edwards, AGE added its first brokers devoted solely to the soliciting of new individual investors, of whom the firm gained countless numbers as the bull market of the 1920s roared toward its catastrophic conclusion. Stock speculation became a hobby and passion for millions of Americans who ten years before did not know Wall Street from Main Street, many of them trading stocks for which they paid margins as low as ten percent of the current price.

Fortunately for AGE, St. Louis brokerage houses kept their margin requirements higher than the New York firms, thus softening the pain of October 24, 1929, when the stock market crash wiped out many investors and began ten years of national depression. AGE came through the crisis of 1929 in relatively good condition, its largest single loss only $5,000 (on an account of $1 million), but the years following were bleak. Not only had the great crash soured a whole generation of Americans on the notion of stock investments, it brought the entire securities industry under a cloud of suspicion for its role in the calamity. Again, the brunt of this criticism was felt in New York, while regional firms such as AGE were correctly perceived as having acted more responsibly toward their customers. Indeed, when the NYSE reorganized its governing body in the late 1930s in an effort to convince the U.S. Securities and Exchange Commission (SEC) that it had addressed past regulatory lapses, it named AGE's own William McChesney Martin, Jr., as its first president. Martin was AGE's first floor broker and only 31 at the time, but his status as an outsider and a man of integrity combined to make him the ideal candidate. He remained president of the Exchange until 1941, when he joined the Army.

In St. Louis, meanwhile, AGE was now led by Presley W. Edwards, son of Benjamin Edwards and grandson of founder Albert Edwards. This latest Edwards faced a brutal business environment in the 1930s—"Every day you went home exhausted from doing nothing," he was quoted as saying in AGE's official company history—but the lean years forced AGE to adopt the thrift and assiduity that later made the company's fortunes. Presley Edwards foresaw that AGE's future lay in the direction of small branch offices, but his plans were blocked by America's entry into World War II in 1941. A boon for most American businesses, the war only continued the Depression's long freeze in the securities markets, and AGE's retail expansion did not get underway until the 1950s.

Renewed investor confidence and the strong postwar economy allowed AGE to increase its number of branch offices to 11 in five states by 1957, which jumped to 19 by 1960 and then quickly to 44 only five years later. AGE had been the first brokerage house outside New York to install a computer back in the 1940s, and its sophisticated approach to data management helped the company coordinate the activities of its widely scattered and generally small branch offices. At the head of this 300-man brokerage force was Benjamin Franklin Edwards III, who joined his great-grandfather's company in 1956 and ten years later was its president at the age of 33. Rather surprisingly, the combined handicaps of youth, great responsibility, and family expectations did not deter Benjamin Edwards III; as of 1993, he remained the chief executive officer (CEO) of a company far larger than his forebears would have thought possible, and has been cited numerous times as one of the outstanding CEOs in the securities business.

When Benjamin Edwards took over the top spot at AGE in 1965, the nation's economy was booming and brokerage houses expanding on every front. The question for AGE was not whether to expand but in what direction; as a midsized regional player in the securities industry the company could have embarked on any number of different paths. Edwards and his staff conducted a two-year study of AGE's strengths and weaknesses relative to the emerging marketplace, concluding in 1968 that they should continue what they were already doing but on a larger scale. As Benjamin Edwards later described in *Investor's Daily,* "We ended up with a model that called for the delivery of financial services of value to a 'mass/class' market through a network of retail branches acting as agents of the customer. [The brokers'] allegiance was to clients, not to us."

Central to Edwards's declaration are the terms "mass/class" and "allegiance." By "mass/class" Edwards meant that his brokerage force would concentrate its energies on the mass of individual investors, the "little people" of middle America, and only incidentally pursue the wealthy, "class" investor. That meant continuing to open more retail offices in small communities around the country—from 44 in the mid-1960s to 450 in 1992—and staffing them with a higher proportion of brokers than the average Wall Street outlet. It also meant largely ignoring the big-money deal making that came to be known on Wall Street as investment banking. AGE has always done its share of stock underwriting, but it did not get caught up in the exotic corporate deals of the 1980s simply because its clients were not corporations and because Benjamin Edwards maintained a healthy skepticism toward get-rich-quick schemes of all kinds.

The second key term of Edwards's statement quoted in *Investors Daily,* "allegiance," is harder to define but probably more fundamental to AGE's success. All brokers claim to be acting on behalf of their clients, and it would be easy to dismiss Edwards's statement as routine puffery if not for the fact that AGE's history appears to confirm its truth. AGE has long made it a policy not to trade stocks on its own account, just as it has not marketed its own investment packages to clients. Either step can easily divide the "allegiance" of a broker between the welfare of his customers and the making of money for the corporation, eventually destroying the relationship of trust between client and broker on which AGE has built its reputation. For the same reason, AGE has refused to lure top brokers away from other firms with bonuses and high salaries and encourages its own brokers to maintain annual sales figures about 30 percent lower than the industry average. Freed from the pressure to earn high commissions, AGE brokers are more likely to consider the interests of their clients instead of looking to make the maximum number of trades possible in every eight-hour day. As compensation, AGE lets the brokers keep approximately ten percent more in commission than is standard in the industry.

The result of AGE's "goody two-shoes" philosophy, as Edwards humorously characterized it in the *New York Times,* has been a tradition of loyalty from customers and employees alike. When the company suffered large losses in the industry shakeout of the early 1970s, AGE employees responded to management's frank call for help by working four-day weeks and cutting overall costs by 17 percent in a matter of months. Brokers tend to stay at AGE for its low-pressure approach to sales and closely knit, supportive environment. "There's less politicking here and more teamwork," commented one senior broker when interviewed for the company's profile in *The 100 Best Companies to Work for in America,* which appeared in 1983.

Customer loyalty was tested severely in the period following the SEC's 1975 decision to deregulate commission rates. Soon "discount houses" appeared in the securities business, offering to transact trades at prices substantially lower than those charged by full-service houses like AGE. Such discounters appealed directly to small investors from whom AGE earned the bulk of its revenues and should have taken a significant piece of market share; but it appeared that the discounters did not adversely affected AGE's business, even though the latter refused to lower its commission rates. Indeed, the period from 1975 to 1990 saw the greatest expansion in AGE history, offices increasing from 100 to more than 400 and employees from 2,000 to over 8,000. Clearly, the company's several hundred thousand customers valued the knowledge and experience of AGE brokers more than the dollars they would have saved by using a discounter, which typically offers no client counseling. AGE's

success in the face of such direct competition confirmed the company's long-held belief that when it comes to money handling, customers desire above all a broker whom they know and trust.

The most dramatic demonstration of AGE's independence from Wall Street fashions—and the strength derived from such independence—was provided by the market crash in October of 1987. The 1980s had seen a phenomenal rise in the deal making power of investment bankers, many of whom earned enormous fees for engineering mergers, acquisitions, and leveraged buyouts that were often undercapitalized and sometimes fraudulent, as in the cases of Michael Milken and Ivan Boesky. The market crash destroyed this glitter-and-greed atmosphere, and in its wake about 18 percent of the industry's employees had lost their jobs by 1991. By contrast, AGE, since it does not trade its own account, sustained minor losses in the crash and in the following years *increased* its work force by 33 percent—much to the satisfaction of Benjamin Edwards, who later told the *St. Louis Post-Dispatch* that his Wall Street counterparts had "wanted to be macho at the lunch table. The ego was gratified if you had the big numbers."

Since then AGE has been the firm with the big numbers: tremendous growth in every category, bottom-line earnings that make its competitors green with envy and, most remarkable for a company expanding so quickly, no long-term debt to speak of. In recognition of his firm's success, Benjamin Edwards was named one of the industry's top three executives no fewer than six times in the 1980s; and waiting in the wings to continue the family tradition at AGE are his sons Benjamin Edwards IV and Scott P. Edwards. AGE celebrated its 100th anniversary in 1987, and it seemed quite possible that its 200th would be celebrated in 2087 by a young man with blond hair and boyish features named Benjamin Edwards VII.

Principal Subsidiaries: A.G. Edwards & Sons, Inc.

Further Reading:

A.G. Edwards: A Heritage of Serving Investors, St. Louis, MO: A.G. Edwards & Sons, Inc., 1991, revised edition, 1993.
Friedman, Amy, "Positive Prospects," *Financial Services Weekly,* June 11, 1990.
Gallagher, Jim, "Sitting Pretty: Being 'Out in the Sticks' Saved Edwards," *St. Louis Post-Dispatch,* April 1, 1991.
Levering, Robert, Milton Moskowitz, and Michael Katz, *The 100 Best Companies to Work for in America,* Reading, MA: Addison-Wesley, 1983.
Rogers, Doug, "A.G. Edwards Matches Profit with Stock Price Performance," *Investor's Daily,* June 6, 1991.
Scott, Mac, "Edwards Quietly Climbs Ranks of Wall Street," *St. Louis Business Journal,* January 6–12, 1992.
Wayne, Leslie, "Where the Brokers Are Still Smiling," *New York Times,* November 26, 1989.

—Jonathan Martin

A. Schulman, Inc.

3550 West Market Street
Akron, Ohio 44333
U.S.A.
(216) 666-3751
Fax: (216) 668-7204

Public Company
Incorporated: 1928
Employees: 1,587
Sales: $732.17 million
Stock Exchanges: NASDAQ
SICs: 2821 Plastic Materials & Resins

A relatively small plastics manufacturer, A. Schulman is something of an anomaly in an industry dominated by huge diversified companies. The company concentrates on producing special plastic resins and compounds. Unlike its larger competitors—BASF, Himont, Dow, Hoechst, Monsanto, and Quantum—which derive profit from small margins on massive production runs of common plastics, A. Schulman produces high margin, special-use plastics that demand the employment of special technologies and production methods. As a result of its technological innovation, A. Schulman avoids direct competition with specialty plastics divisions of larger companies.

The company was founded by Alex Schulman, who established a rubber brokerage in Akron, Ohio, in 1928. Working out of a small shop, Schulman purchased and resold wholesale and scrap rubber, which his customers would refashion into a variety of rubber products. While Schulman cultivated a clientele, the business remained small. The largest consumers of rubber were tire makers, automobile companies, and hose manufacturers. These companies purchased raw virgin rubber on a huge scale, providing few large sales opportunities for Schulman's enterprise.

In 1930, just as Schulman's business became stable, the nation was plunged into the Great Depression. Demand for most products, including rubber, fell precipitously. Before rubber stocks were depleted, prices nosedived, eliminating demand for used rubber. A few years later, when rubber became scarce, this demand recovered, providing some support to Schulman's business and enabling him to realize a small margin on his sales. The A. Schulman Company recovered from the Depression slowly, as Alex Schulman's business depended almost entirely on the successes and resources of his customers. Fortunately, Schulman was not crushed by fluctuations in the broader rubber market or larger final markets, as were many tire, automobile, and hose manufacturers.

By the late 1930s and early 1940s, the onset of war in Europe and then in the Pacific caused industrial demand for rubber to increase. Rubber was an important war commodity, and sources of rubber were limited. As a result, a premium was placed on companies that could recycle scrap rubber, producing a useful product from waste. A. Schulman and several other companies in the scrap rubber business were placed under the authority of a war production board that had responsibility for coordinating efficient production of essential commodities and setting prices. Often, Schulman did not know who his customers ultimately were. While it took a few months to gain footing, Schulman's company went into full production, supplying mulched rubber for recasting into tires, window seals, and numerous other products.

The scarcity of rubber during the war helped to accelerate the development of substitute and synthetic rubber products. The most important of these is what we know today as plastic, which was extremely useful in small castings, exhibiting many of the same resilient and durable qualities as rubber. Although the primary ingredient in plastic was petroleum, also a crucial and limited war commodity, plastic like rubber could be recycled. As the war progressed, A. Schulman began to accept scrap plastic for chipping and shipment to casting mills. By the end of the war, A. Schulman had doubled its product line to include scrap rubber and scrap plastic. In 1950, having heard some convincing arguments from a young salesman named William Zekan, Schulman realized he stood on the threshold of a new industry.

Schulman hired Zekan in 1937 after meeting him on the golf course of the Rosemont Country Club, where the 18-year old Zekan worked as a caddie. Although Zekan started at A. Schulman as an office boy, earning less than he could as a caddie, he stayed with the business and was promoted to salesman just before he enlisted in the army at the outbreak of the war. Zekan returned to the company after his tour, and in 1947 he was tapped by Schulman to head his New York sales office. Here the shy and reserved Zekan learned the art of sales. He honed his skills of persuasion, and later told *Chemical Week,* "The customer is going to buy, everything being equal, from the guy that he likes the best." Zekan performed exceptionally well in New York, and when he was called back to Akron in 1953, it was to take the number two position under Alex Schulman.

Schulman and Zekan developed a new strategy during this period to abandon the scrap markets and move the company into the plastics manufacturing business. Rather than molding its own products, A. Schulman would draw on its substantial reputation as a raw product supplier and concentrate on making plastic compounds. This product is manufactured in the form of pellets, smaller than peanuts. By applying heat, these pellets could be extruded or molded into many types of finished products.

The company grew considerably during the 1950s, mostly on the strength of cheap oil as well as the increasing number of applications for plastic. For the first time, automobile manufacturers began molding plastic parts for cars, including dashboards, interior side panel trim, and window insulation.

Searching for new growth markets, Schulman established a network of small plants in Britain, France, and Germany. There he hoped to get in on the ground floor of emerging industries in postwar Europe. The company later established a plant in Canada that served various plastics consumers in that country, including the automotive industry.

Alex Schulman died in 1962, and his will specified that Zekan should succeed him as president of the company. For his part, Zekan had become so deeply involved with executive decisions under Schulman that, despite the founder's sudden death, the transition to new leadership was smooth.

The 1960s were a period of strong growth for A. Schulman. It was during the decade after Schulman's death that the company began to really define its place in the industry. The company began to produce plastics, albeit in smaller quantities than competitors, with special characteristics. Often the tolerances of these products were specified in advance of manufacture by the customer. The company then instructed its laboratories to design a plastic to meet those specifications. Thus, with the employment of technology, A. Schulman was able to offer a limited quantity of plastics that could outperform other plastics.

As a major player in this vital niche market, A. Schulman was somewhat insulated from the competition elsewhere in the industry. Because A. Schulman dealt in a unique family of products, it was able to sell on quality and not price. This produced a new sales philosophy which, Zekan later told *Forbes,* was "We don't talk price, we talk quality."

The company's ability to build such a strong position in the market led Zekan to consider expansion. Rather than just the addition of production facilities, Zekan was concerned with innovations in his product line. Unable to adequately fund technological research internally, he went forward with plans to take the company public in 1972.

In 1973 an Arab-Israeli war triggered an oil embargo against the United States that caused the price of petroleum to skyrocket. For plastics producers like A. Schulman, this meant temporary shortages of raw materials and necessary price increases. While these price increases were ultimately passed along to the consumer, the net effect was a serious recession that forced many companies in the plastics industry to go out of business. A. Schulman remained insulated from much of this activity because it produced a product defined by quality and technology rather than simply by price. Nonetheless, the company did suffer some reverses due to the onset of recession.

By 1977 inflationary pressure had stabilized, but a second oil crisis two years later caused additional price shocks that continued to cut into demand. By 1982, automobile manufacturers had entered a prolonged period of serious financial trouble. Because they were large consumers of specialty plastics, A. Schulman's growth continued to lag. Hoping to tie its products to growing companies in the automotive industry, A. Schulman began cultivating relationships with Japanese plastics manufacturers,

with the intention of gaining supply contracts with Japanese car makers.

The timing was perfect. Several companies, including Honda and Toyota, began building large production facilities in the United States during this time. In 1988, A. Schulman established a joint venture with Japan's largest chemical company, the Mitsubishi Kasei Vinyl Company, and set up a new plastics plant at Bellevue, Ohio. With the help of Mitsubishi Kasei, A. Schulman concluded numerous supply contracts with Honda, Nissan, and Toyota.

The addition of new customers forced A. Schulman to modernize and expand its production facilities. The company spent $33 million to expand worldwide capacity by 25 percent. Still, the company avoided becoming overly reliant on only a few customers in a single industry. The company's five largest accounts comprised less than ten percent of sales.

Zekan had a hands-on leadership style and a genuine love of selling. He kept the reins of the company tightly in his hands, prompting some critics to fear that this concentration of power could leave a void in management. But A. Schulman had a highly capable second tier of management that would be put to the test and would ultimately rise to the challenge in 1989, when Zekan, aged 69, underwent surgery for treatment of cancer. It was at this juncture that Zekan promoted three senior managers in preparation for his retirement. One of these was Terry Haines, who was named president, while Zekan remained chairperson and CEO.

However, retirement never came. Zekan remained in charge of the company until his death in January, 1991. Haines remained president and took on the duties of CEO as well. Robert Stefanko, who ran the finance department, was elected chairperson. With the death of Bill Zekan, A. Schulman lost the last link to its founder. But it also marked the beginning of a new era.

The modern A. Schulman's primary line of business remains engineering and manufacturing specialty plastic compounds that are made at seven plants in North America and Europe, each equipped with its own laboratory. These products include PVC for automobile window seals, special polyethylene films for shopping bags and agricultural crop covers, and polypropylene film for packaging candy bars, snack food, cosmetics, and textiles. The company's plastics may also be found in patio furniture, lawn sprinklers, garden and pool equipment, toys, and games.

In its merchant sales business, A. Schulman purchases production overruns and surplus stocks of plastic materials and resells them directly to customers through its marketing operations as a broker. Finally, as a distributor, A. Schulman sells plastic products of other companies, including Akzo nylon resins, Enichem neopropene elastomers, Exxon polypropylene and Epsilon polypropylene.

While the company had shunned growth by acquisition for nearly its entire existence, A. Schulman took over the French plastics company Diffusion Plastique in August, 1991. Initial integration of the business was difficult but ultimately successful. In addition, the company's joint venture with Mitsubishi Kasei posted its first profit in 1992. That year A. Schulman posted its tenth consecutive record for annual net income and was ranked 12th on the *Fortune 500* list of companies with highest total return over ten years, averaging 37.2 percent. Maintaining very little debt, a unique line of products, and a diversified customer base, A. Schulman is well positioned to maintain steady rates of growth.

Principal Subsidiaries: Sunprene Company (70%); N.V. A. Schulman Plastics, S.A. (Belgium); A. Schulman, Inc., Ltd. (UK); A. Schulman GmbH., (Germany); A. Schulman Canada Ltd. (Canada); A. Schulman A.G. (Switzerland); A. Schulman S.A. (France); A. Schulman Plastics S.A. (France).

Further Reading:

A. Schulman Inc., Akron, OH: A. Schulman Inc.

A. Schulman Inc. Annual Reports, Akron, OH: A. Schulman Inc., 1989, 1990, 1991, and 1992.

"A. Schulman Inc., Plastics Supplier Profits from Foreign Affairs," *Barron's,* November 19, 1990.

"A Plastics Play on the Dollar's Dip, *Fortune,* November 11, 1985.

"Pssst! Plastics," *Barron's,* April 7, 1986.

"Schulman: A Timely Switch to Plastics," *Chemical Week,* July 9, 1986.

"You Just Work Your Heart Out," *Forbes,* March 5, 1990.

"Zekan's Rise from Office Boy to Chief Executive," *Chemical Week,* July 13, 1988.

—John Simley

ADVANTA

ADVANTA Corp.

300 Welsh Road
Horsham, Pennsylvania 19044
U.S.A.
(215) 657-4000
Fax: (215) 784-8075

Public Company
Incorporated: 1974 as Teachers Service Organization, Inc.
Employees: 1,082
Assets under management: $4.5 billion
Stock Exchanges: NASDAQ
SICs: 6141 Personal Credit Institutions; 6159 Miscellaneous
  Business Credit Institutions; 6153 Short-Term Business
  Credit Institutions, Except Agricultural; 6162 Mortgage
  Bankers & Loan Correspondents; 7359 Equipment Rental
  & Leasing, Nec

ADVANTA Corp. originates, services and sells credit card and
home equity loans. It also provides equipment leasing for small
businesses and offers credit life, disability, and unemployment
insurance to its credit card holders. From a family-run credit
union issuing loans primarily to nurses and teachers, the company pioneered the no-fee credit card in the 1980s and moved
into the 1990s as a relatively small but highly profitable niche
business, depending on gold cards for the bulk of its success.
Though credit risks affecting card lenders skyrocketed from the
mid-1980s on, ADVANTA entered the 1990s with strong
growth and signs of continued success.

ADVANTA's roots reach back to a family business that financed educational programs. In 1951 J. R. Alter, a former
Philadelphia schoolteacher, founded the Philadelphia Teachers
Service Organization, Inc., in the Olney section of Philadelphia.
The example of J. R. Alter and his wife, also a schoolteacher,
influenced their son, Dennis Alter, who also became a schoolteacher and eventually served as chairman and CEO of the
much-expanded family business. In the 1960s Dennis Alter
taught English at Benjamin Franklin High School for three
years while moonlighting as executive vice president and director of TSO. J. R. Alter retired in 1971. His son finished graduate
school and assumed the post of president and chief executive
officer of the company.

After 20 years in business, TSO maintained a modest profile,
with a net worth of $300,000 in 1971. The bulk of business
consisted of loans by mail, primarily to school teachers, nurses,

and other affinity groups via endorsements by their professional
and trade organizations. Its lending activities included second
mortgage loans, unsecured installment loans, and home equity
installment loans. The company also operated consumer finance
subsidiaries in Pennsylvania, New Jersey, and Florida.

Dennis Alter worked quickly to change TSO from a sleepy
credit union into a national consumer finance company. One of
his first steps was to lure James T. Dimond, a former Fidelity
Bank of Philadelphia senior vice president, to TSO as president
and chief operating officer. Dimond's banking expertise contributed to TSO's next strategic move: its 1982 acquisition of
Colonial National Bank in Wilmington, Delaware, for $2.1
million. With its $9 million in assets, Colonial became TSO's
primary resource for lending and funding management.

As part of the acquisition transaction, Colonial divested its
commercial loan portfolio and thus moved outside the Bank
Holding Company Act's definition of a bank, becoming what
Banking Expansion Reporter called a "Nonbank Bank" in a
September 1982 article. Though Colonial no longer made commercial loans, it serviced 30,000 depositors from all 50 states,
accounting for $525 million in deposits by 1986. Even as a so-
called nonbank, Colonial drew new customers to TSO because
of banking benefits such as FDIC-insured deposits. In addition,
exploitation of communications technology enabled clients to
reap the benefits of Colonial's banking without ever going near
the bank. Loans and deposits were managed via WATS long-
distance telephone lines, wire transfers, mail, nationwide automated teller machines, debit and credit cards, and checks. With
such branchless banking, Colonial could potentially provide
TSO customers with more personalized service than traditional
bank service. "The corner branch of a local bank may seem far
more distant and less responsive than our customer service
personnel," said Alter in an August 4, 1986, *American Banker*
article.

TSO also developed a special unit, Colonial National Leasing,
Inc. to lease computers, telephone and medical equipment,
industrial machinery, and other tools to professionals and small
businesses. In 1987 TSO acquired Leasetech Inc., an Atlanta-
based equipment leasing organization.

With its unusual features—a "nonbank bank" organizing
"branchless banking"—Colonial helped TSO realize unusual
growth. From 1982 to 1986, TSO's net income grew at a
compound annual rate of 113 percent, while assets grew at a
compound annual rate of 63 percent. Gross revenue for 1985
was $67.8 million, representing an 87 percent increase over the
$36.2 million revenue of 1984.

Success in the early 1980s, however, was only a preface to the
virtual explosion of growth that was set in motion by the 1983
introduction of credit cards. By 1985, card receivables topped
installment loans—$169 million versus $167 million at year-
end. While installment loans grew 25 percent in 1985, card
outstandings jumped by more than 250 percent. In 1986 *Money*
magazine, *USA Today*, and the Consumer Credit Card Rating
Service all rated TSO's premium cards in their top categories.
TSO, in turn, put 350,000 cards in circulation, assuming 89th
place on the national charts. By 1991 the company derived 70
percent of its revenues from its Visa and MasterCard customers.

TSO's credit card strategy involved loans to the general public, as opposed to its previous practice of lending to select affinity groups. At year end, the general public accounted for 67 percent of card receivables in 1985, up from 17 percent the year before; they also accounted for 22 percent of installment loans, up from less than one percent. Driven by aggressive marketing to foster nationwide deposits and loans, the company relied on direct mail, telemarketing, newspaper ads, and radio and television spots. Institutional deposits were promoted by telephone marketing and certificate of deposit quotes on the Telerate Service. With high rates to attract deposits, longer-term loans to draw installment-loan borrowers, and very competitive rates on premium credit cards, TSO expanded operations at a hefty rate.

Lending to the general public, however, represented substantial credit risk as well as quick growth. In order to best protect itself, the company invested in sophisticated marketing research, enlisting several services to provide in-depth demographic data on precise areas of the country. The company only targeted potential customers of a very specific profile: usually college-educated, ages 20 to 44, with above-average incomes. "You cannot apply to ADVANTA [TSO's name after 1988]. They have to pick you as a customer who has these two characteristics: high credit quality and high usage patterns," said First Boston's Allerton Smith in a September 15, 1992, article for *Financial World*. Once a potential customer was selected, however, the offer was unusually attractive. It often consisted of mostly no-fee credit cards with better-than-average interest rates and attractive credit lines, according to company spokeswoman Deborah Dove in a January 31, 1992, *Investor's Business Daily* article. By 1992, 80 percent of the company's credit-card offerings were gold cards, reflecting the high-end emphasis of the company's marketing research efforts.

Even with the support of extensive market research, credit-card lending proved a risky business in the mid-1980s, giving rise to some skepticism regarding TSO's stability. Not only was the company portfolio relatively new and untested, but mounting consumer debt had reached frightening heights. Credit-card defaults doubled during 1986, to 4.2 percent of charges outstanding. "Consumers cannot continue to carry the debt they have, and if we have an economic slowdown early next year, which I think we will, we could see a lot of problems," said Nancy Bush, analyst with Butcher & Singer, Inc., in a December 8, 1986, *Philadelphia Business Journal* article. That year, Moody's graded a BA3 to $50 million in subordinated debentures offered by TSO, while Standard & Poor's ranked them B+. Likewise, TSO's common stock fell from an $18.50 high in April to $13.50 in December.

One buffer against credit-card risks was TSO involvement in other financial services, including consumer installment loans, equipment leasing, credit life and disability insurance, and residential mortgage services. Such a wide range of services was partly responsible for the company's 1985 name change from Teachers Service Organization, Inc. (TSO) to the more inclusive TSO Financial Corp. In 1986 the company acquired ADVANTA Mortgage Corp. USA (formerly Apex Financial Corp.) for $7.5 million. TSO's mortgage banking rapidly expanded nationwide and capitalized on home equity loans that grew in popularity after mid-1980s tax reform cut the personal deductions allowed on credit-card charges.

Starting in 1988, TSO began securitizing its growing home equity loan assets and credit-card receivables, pooling the loan balances into securities for sale to investors. Over the years, that financial strategy became one of ADVANTA's (TSO's name as of 1988) fundraising specialties. In May 1989, for example, the company announced that Colonial National and ADVANTA Mortgage had placed with institutional investors $31.1 million of Class A certificates representing fractional ownership interests in ADVANTA Second Mortgage Trust 1989-1. The certificates were insured by Financial Guaranty Insurance Corp. and were rated "AAA" by Standard & Poor's and "Aaa" by Moody's. On August 29, 1990, Colonial sold $250 million in credit-card-backed notes, marking its 10th asset securitization deal. William Kaiser, senior vice president of ADVANTA Mortgage, estimated in a June 12, 1991, *Business Wire* article that the company had securitized over $550 million in home equity loans since 1988 and intended to continue the practice on a regular basis. In May 1992 ADVANTA continued funding its credit portfolio by tapping the securitization market, completing two private placements with a combined value of about $332 million. In June of that same year, the company issued certificates in a $100 million home equity loan securitization deal. The announcement was notable on several accounts: it was ADVANTA's first transaction insured by MBIA, and it employed an innovative form of securitization with both fixed and variable components, increasing the company's funding flexibility and broadening its investor base, according to a June 1992 article in *Global Guaranty*. ADVANTA not only applied, but broadened securitization techniques.

In the late 1980s the company continued to grow. In August 1987 it delved back into familiar territory, acquiring Educational Credit Corporation (ECC) from Pacific Financial Asset Management Corp. ECC loan programs included competitive rates and long-term repayment plans to accommodate escalating costs of education aggravated by reductions in federal tuition assistance. That same year, the company acquired the remaining stock of LeaseComm Financial Corp., of which it previously held 21 percent equity interest. By 1988, since its primary focus was no longer on educators, TSO stockholders voted to change the company name to ADVANTA Corp.

In addition to a change of name, 1988 brought a change of fortune, as ADVANTA posted its first loss—$9 million—since it was founded in 1951. After an initial loss of $6.1 million in the fourth quarter of 1987, Dennis Alter commented in a February 10, 1988, *PR Newswire* report that "the decline in earnings . . . is due, in large part, to an earlier decision to restructure the company's balance sheet to achieve a more balanced asset portfolio. We believe this restructuring will significantly strengthen ADVANTA."

Along with financial restructuring, chairman and CEO Dennis Alter recruited a new management team to help refocus the company. In June 1987 James T. Dimond resigned as chief operating officer, to be replaced by Richard A. Greenawalt, former president of Transamerica Financial Corporation in Los Angeles. Before that he had been with Citicorp for 15 years, as chairman and chief executive of Citicorp Person-to-Person Inc., and president and chief executive of Citicorp Retail Services Inc., New York. In March 1988 Dennis R. Eickhoff joined the company as president of its ADVANTA Mortgage Corp. USA subsidiary. Eickhoff had served since 1983 as president and chief executive officer of Gibraltar MoneyCenter, Inc., the San Diego-based $1 billion second mortgage subsidiary of Gibraltar Financial Corporation. With the expertise of its new management, ADVANTA exited the installment loan business and focused on credit cards and secured lending products.

ADVANTA also began more aggressively promoting its stock, undertaking a new investor relations campaign in the early 1990s. Convincing investors to buy into high stock prices proved challenging, as 50 percent of the company's 9.13 million outstanding shares were controlled by insiders. Dennis Alter himself held 41 percent of the company's outstanding stock, or 3.8 million shares. Consequently, the float—the number and value of shares tradable—was small. ADVANTA enlisted the help of Prudential-Bache Securities and First Boston Corp., two of Wall Street's big players, to provide analyst coverage and consulting services. In September 1990 Hambrecht & Quist analyst Dirk Godsey valued ADVANTA stock at $18 to $23 a share, with strong potential for the future, according to a September 17, 1990, article in *Philadelphia Business Journal*. His assessment was confirmed in July 1991, when Prudential Securities Research, Inc., analyst Larry Eckenfelder named ADVANTA Corp. his "single best idea" in the financial services industry and repeated his buy recommendation on the stock.

Eckenfelder almost proved mistaken when the stock price of ADVANTA and other credit card companies fell on worries over a November 1991 Senate vote to cap interest rates on consumer credit cards. After a 52-week high of $38.50 on Nov. 13, ADVANTA dropped $9.25 to $29.25 over the next two days. Even after the Senate's quick shelving of the rate ceiling, ADVANTA shares remained well below their November peak. Nevertheless, the remoteness of the legislation combined with ADVANTA's outstanding growth record—the company registered 40 percent compound growth in cards outstanding between 1987 and 1990—to make ADVANTA shares a good investment, according to Gordon Matthews in a December 17, 1991, feature for *The American Banker*.

With its experienced management team and focus on a profitable niche business, ADVANTA moved into the 1990s with excellent prospects. By January 30, 1992, its stock had more than recovered from the 1991 scare, closing at 39⅜. From the beginning of 1991 to the beginning of 1992, stock rose 245 percent, according to the January 1992 *Investor's Business Daily*. The company had also realized a broad portfolio, with a 1991 revenue breakdown of 70 percent from credit cards, 20 percent from home equity loans, five percent from equipment leasing, and five percent from its credit insurance business. To expand its leasing program, ADVANTA introduced the Access to Capital Equipment (ACE) card in January 1993. The service was designed to augment leasing services with such features as deferred payment, adjustable payment schedules, and a simplified application process.

With roughly one percent of the U.S. credit-card market in 1991, ADVANTA had plenty of room for continued growth. In April 1992 its board approved a share-for-share dividend of Class B common for each old common (now Class A Common) share outstanding, doubling the number of common shares out-

standing to 22.2 million and increasing the float for new investors. "This plan is designed to increase the company's flexibility in financing future growth and to promote management continuity," said Dennis Alter in an April 13, 1992, *National Mortgage News* article. Indeed, ADVANTA Corp. appears to be entering the latter half of the 1990s in healthy condition, as it recently announced a company record $17.2 million in net income for the second quarter of 1993.

Principal Subsidiaries: Colonial National Bank USA; ADVANTA Mortgage Corp. USA; ADVANTA Leasing Corp.; ADVANTA Life Insurance Co.

Further Reading:

"ADVANTA Corp. Announces Year End Earnings," *PR Newswire*, February 10, 1988.
"ADVANTA Corp. Subsidiaries Place $31.1 Million of Class A Home Equity Loan Certificates," *PR Newswire*, May 2, 1989.
"ADVANTA Sells ABS Debt, Will Service Daiwa Placement," *American Banker-Bond Buyer*, May 25, 1992, p. 3.
"ADVANTA Subsidiaries Complete $91 Million Home Equity Loan Securitization," *Business Wire*, June 12, 1991.
Chesler, Caren, "Advanta's Alter and Greenawalt: Turning Technology Into Credit Card Marketing Machine," *Investor's Business Daily*, January 14, 1993.
Foust, Dan, "TSO Gets Credit for Three-Year's Rapid Growth," *Philadelphia Business Journal*, December 8, 1986, p. 5.
Groc, Isabelle, "ADVANTA: Credit Where Credit Is Due," *Financial World*, September 15, 1992, p. 16.
Jones, John A., "ADVANTA Picks Its Prospects In No-Fee Credit Card Market," *Investor's Business Daily*, November 3, 1992, p. 32.
Kramer, Farrell, "ADVANTA Rebounds From Rate-Cap Scare," *Investor's Business Daily*, January 31, 1992, p. 1.
Mandzy, Orest, "TSO Unit Buys Leasetech," *American Banker*, August 3, 1987, p. 3.
Matthews, Gordon, "STOCKS: ADVANTA Gets Thumbs Up Despite a Brief Downturn," *The American Banker*, December 17, 1991, p. 16.
"MBIA to Insure $100 million ADVANTA Securitization Deal," *American Banker-Bond Buyer*, June 15, 1992, p. 7.
Newman, Joseph A., Jr., "Greenawalt Named President of TSO," *American Banker*, October 7, 1987, p. 18.
——, "TSO Welcomes Long-distance/Nationwide Customer With System That Could Make Walk-in Banking Passe," *American Banker*, August 4, 1986, p. 24.
"'Nonbank Banks' Continue to Attract Interest," *Banking Expansion Reporter*, November 15, 1982, p. 4.
Pae, Peter, "Advanta Finds Edge With Careful Customer Screening," *Wall Street Journal*, April 8, 1993.
Roberts, William L., "'Proactive' ADVANTA Trumpets Value of Stock," *Philadelphia Business Journal*, September 17, 1990, p. 14.
"Top Financial Corp. Changes Name To ADVANTA Corp." *PR Newswire*, January 28, 1988.
"TSO Financial Acquires Educational Credit Corporation," *PR Newswire*, August 25, 1987.
"TSO Financial Negotiating Possible Sale," *PR Newswire*, June 4, 1987.
"TSO-Financial; TSO Reports Financial Results," *Business Wire*, February 4, 1987.
Voorhees, N. J., "New Leasing Card Speeds Financing of Commercial Equipment," *Business Wire*, January 13, 1993.

—Kerstan Cohen

Albany International Corp.

P.O. Box 1907
Albany, New York 12201-1907
U.S.A.
(518) 445-2200
Fax: (518) 445-2264

Public Company
Incorporated: 1895 as Albany Felt Company
Employees: 5,726
Sales: $561.1 million
Stock Exchanges: New York
SICs: 2299 Textile Goods Nec

Albany International Corp. plays a key role in papermaking as the world's leading designer and producer of paper machine clothing—large, continuous belts of custom designed and engineered fabrics that are installed on paper machines to carry paper stock through the three primary stages of the paper production process. With facilities in 11 countries, the company controls 20 percent of the paper machine clothing market; the company's closest competitor claims a 13 percent market share. Albany International also produces auxiliary equipment for cleaning, conditioning, and de-watering fabrics on the paper machine, as well as some unrelated industrial fabric applications.

The machine clothing comes in fabric sizes more than 30 feet wide and 200 feet long and has a useful life of one to 15 months, depending on the type of clothing and its use. A paper machine may require one million dollars of clothing a year and is needed for making all paper, from the finest writing paper to tissue to containerboard.

Demand for the paper machine clothing is dependent on the health of the papermaking industry. According to *Fortune* magazine, U.S. paper manufacturing grew by only about three percent a year in the 1990s. In order to maintain healthy growth, Albany International spent as much as three percent of sales on research and development of new products, a very high rate for the industry. Because of its technological advances and its reputation for producing quality materials, it has grown to become the world leader in market share.

Albany International has been an innovator in paper machine clothing technology, developing many specialty materials and even licensing competitors to produce them. In order to follow the history of Albany International, it is helpful to understand more about the role of Albany's products in production of paper.

There are three major phases to paper production—forming, pressing and drying—and each phase requires different clothing for the gigantic papermaking machines, some of which are as long as a football field.

During the forming stage, a thin mixture of about two percent wood pulp and 98 percent water is sent through the machine, riding on the machine clothing. As the clothing moves, it works almost like a strainer, with water draining out and pulp fibers remaining on top of the clothing. This phase reduces the water content to about 83 percent, and it is at this phase that the paper's characteristics are set. The forming fabrics last from two to four months.

During the pressing stage, the paper is carried on the press fabric through rollers which, like a wringer washer, squeeze water out until the paper is 60 percent water. The pressing fabric must be capable of absorbing large amounts of water, then quickly getting rid of that water through pressure, centrifugal force, or vacuum. The pressing paper also influences the finish of the paper because the paper is still mostly water when it enters this phase and the rollers exert great pressure. A press fabric lasts only one to three months. Ideally, as much water as possible is removed at this stage, as the last phase requires high energy usage.

In the drying stage, the paper rides the drying clothing around huge heated cylinders so that most of the remaining water evaporates. Drying fabric can last nine to fifteen months. According to Albany International, the use of paper machine clothing worldwide is about 35 percent forming clothing, 45 percent pressing clothing, and 20 percent dryer clothing. The company estimated that 85 percent of the fabrics it produced in the 1990s had not even existed 10 years before. Of course the technology had changed quite a bit since the company's early days, when its name was Albany Felt Company and it was producing only press felts made from wool.

Albany Felt Company was incorporated in 1895 by Parker Corning, James W. Cox, Jr., and Selden E. Marvin, with a total investment of $40,000. Corning's father, Erastus, who was a banker and industrialist, may have been the person who thought of starting the company because of a variety of circumstances: the feltmaker from the nearby F.C. Huyck & Sons had been released from employment and was available for hire; the Huyck mill had burned down in 1894; and Parker's father thought the paper machine felt business might be just the project his son needed after his graduation from Yale in 1895.

Parker Corning became vice-president of Albany Felt Company, and partner James Cox served as president from 1895 to 1918, when Corning succeeded him. Two years later, Corning bought Cox's shares, thus securing control of 72 percent of the company shares. Marvin, president of Albany Savings Institution and Corning's uncle by marriage, died in 1899.

Cox managed a 30-person staff the first year. Within six years, Albany Felt had outgrown its original site and the company built a new plant on a six-acre lot in Menands, a town near Albany. A staff of 150 worked at this new building, constructed to withstand the tremendous vibrations of the felt-making machines. By 1907 the president's salary had been raised to $5,000 a year, and the vice president's to $4,000.

In 1908 the Albany Company expanded its markets to Europe, Canada, Japan, and Mexico. The company continued to prosper in the 1920s and even during the Depression of the 1930s. Its facilities did not expand beyond the Albany area, however, until 1945, when it acquired a mill in North Monmouth, Maine. This plant was used to expand the company's production of flannel for baseball uniforms. Albany Felt also produced felts for other purposes. It became the leading producer in the United States and the world of Sanforized Blankets; Sanforizing is a patented process invented by Sanford Cluett for preshrinking cloth.

In 1952 Albany Felt became an international company when it established Albany Felt Company of Canada. This led to growth in its worldwide market. The firm's president, Lewis R. Parker, also saw great opportunity in the South. During his tenure Albany Felt built a new mill in St. Stephen, South Carolina.

Parker died in 1957, and John C. Standish, who had been hired in 1921 as a feltmaker, became president. Under his leadership, Albany Felt became the pacesetter in the design and manufacture of needled press felts and moved into dryer fabric manufacture and development. In 1961 Standish became chairman of the board. Under the presidency of Everett C. Reed, Standish's successor at that position, the 1960s proved to be a decade of growth, diversification, and innovation for Albany International. It developed an innovative forming fabric that was actually multi-layered and more efficient than the woven metal wire cloth that papermakers had been using prior to the 1960s. This became the standard for the industry. (Currently, Albany International maintains forming fabrics plants in the United States, Canada, Mexico, Australia, Norway, Sweden, Finland, Germany, the Netherlands, and France.)

Albany International produced dryer fabrics in the 1960s, with its introduction of an open-mesh synthetic fabric for the third section of the paper machine. Heavy canvas cotton and asbestos had been the standard drying clothing until Albany introduced a monofilament fabric from which water evaporated more quickly, lowering energy costs and allowing the machine to be operated at higher speeds.

That same decade, it acquired Woven Belting Co. of Buffalo, as well as wire and plastics companies. It also acquired a felt company in France to gain entrance to the felt market there. By 1966 Albany Felt employed 2,500 people and had 19 plants in six countries. In 1969 the company bought Nordiskafilt in Sweden, as well as mills in England and Brazil. It also built new mills in Holland, Finland, and Australia.

The company successfully defended itself from a hostile takeover in the late 1960s. In 1944 Clark Estates Inc., an investment company, had purchased a large block—32 percent—of Albany stock. In 1967 Clark sold its shares to Deering Milliken. That company's head, Roger Milliken, soon informed Albany Felt that it was sending tender offers to stockholders in order to acquire a 51 percent share of the company. Six Albany directors, however, owned 42 percent of the shares, and they in-

formed shareholders that they did not think purchase by Deering Milliken was in the company's best interests. A syndicate of directors and a local businessman offered stockholders the option of selling their shares to this syndicate at whatever price Deering Milliken offered. Deering Milliken tendered at $27 per share, then $37, and finally $50. Most shares that were tendered were purchased by this syndicate.

In 1968 the company, still under control of the management syndicate, engineered the purchases of Appleton Wire Works Corp., International Wire Works Corp., and Crellin Plastics in exchange for shares of Albany stock. Under state law, however, the company needed shareholder permission to increase the number of capital shares. Deering Milliken was unable to muster enough votes to block approval, and with the increased shares created, Milliken's stake dropped from 32 percent ownership to 20 percent. In 1972 Milliken sold its Albany International shares in a public offering.

In 1969 Albany Felt was renamed Albany International to reflect its new identity with facilities and markets around the world. In the 1970s Albany International moved its offices from the plant it had occupied since 1902 to Fernbrook, a former estate. During this decade, Albany also launched a new division called Albany Engineered Systems to produce auxiliary equipment to maintain and improve clothing performance. Albany Engineered Systems manufactured high-pressure showers for keeping the clothing clean; drainage elements such as vacuum foils blades; doctor blades for removing the paper sheet from the roll on the machine; and vacuum systems for improving water removal.

In the 1980s Albany developed and patented an on-machine seamed press fabric that was safer, quicker, and easier to install than previous press fabrics. This saved paper companies time and money since it substantially reduced the length of time that the machine had to be shut down for installation of a new pressing cloth.

In 1983 Albany International became a private company through a leveraged buyout by a group of its managers. They sold all of the businesses that were not related to papermaking, including a division that produced tennis ball covers and another that made plastic tubes. Albany International's status as a private company was short-lived, though. Four years later, with record sales of $402 million, it once again was listed on the New York Stock Exchange.

By the late 1980s, the company had begun to diversify again as research into new fabrics for its core business led to the production of synthetic fabrics for other applications. Company researchers developed a synthetic goose down that the company called Primaloft, which they claimed had all the advantages of goose down and none of the disadvantages. Goose down provides great protection against frigid temperatures but when wet absorbs 160 percent of its weight, while some other synthetics absorb as much as 1000 percent their weight. According to Albany International, Primaloft, which it developed for the U.S. Army, maintains its warmth even when damp and absorbed only 30 percent of its weight after being submerged for half an hour. Some leading manufacturers of winterwear, sleeping bags, and clothing for mountaineering now use Primaloft in their products.

Albany International had supplied material for America's space shuttle program since the 1970s. In 1989 Albany International further expanded its involvement in such high technology manufacturing, selling a lightweight, noncombustible insulation material used in automotive, plastics, and aerospace applications.

Using technology developed while engineering fabrics, the company also came out with a high-speed industrial door that rolls up and down like a window shade and is used in airports and carwashes. The subsidiary, Nomafa Door Division, has factories in four countries.

In late 1989 Albany International moved its headquarters back to its roots—the 450,000-square-foot factory complex with its various additions—that Albany Felt had occupied almost 90 years before in Menands. Four million dollars later, it had been transformed into contemporary, efficient office space. A new, multi-million dollar press fabric facility was erected in 1988 across the river in East Greenbush.

The company reported a relatively unsuccessful year in 1990, citing the poor state of the world economy and its own high overhead costs. It initiated a cost reduction program, reducing its salaried work force by about 10 percent and cutting other operational costs. That same year, it started up a new fabrics plant in Sondrum, Sweden, replacing the Nordiskafilt plant three miles away. It also built new plants in Finland and the Netherlands. In addition, the company acquired Wallbergs Fabriks A.B., a paper machine clothing maker founded in 1823 in Halmstad, Sweden.

During the 1990s the papermaking industry was consolidating globally, increasing the competition and consolidation within the paper machine clothing industry as well. However, as the largest clothing supplier, Albany International said that it would benefit from consolidation in both industries, reasoning that large papermaking concerns would find it more efficient to work with one company that could supply clothing for all three phases.

The world's papermaking industry remained depressed in 1991 and 1992, and Albany International's sales reflected this, as they rose only slightly. The company continued to put substantial resources into research and development. The American paper industry had a goal of manufacturing 40 percent of all U.S. paper from recycled fibers by 1995, and to achieve this goal, Albany International worked closely with its customers in the paper industry as well as with makers of paper machines.

In 1993 Albany International strengthened its position in the market for dryer clothing by acquiring Mount Vernon Group for $51 million. This company, with plants in North Carolina and South Carolina, produced clothing for forming, pressing, and drying; by acquiring it, Albany moved from third place to second in the dryer cloth market.

While the world economy remained sluggish well into the 1990s, Albany International anticipates that once the economy picks up, it will be in a strong position because of its reputation as a manufacturer of quality materials and an innovator in fabric technology.

Principal Subsidiaries: Albany International Research Co.; Press Fabrics Division; Albany/Mount Vernon Dryer Fabrics Division; Engineered Fabrics Division; Albany International Canada, Inc.; Nordiskafilt A.B. (Sweden and Germany); Wallbergs Fabriks A.B. (Sweden); Oy Fennofelt A.B. (Finland); Albany International Ltd.(England); Albany International B.V. (Netherlands); Albany International S.A. (France); Martel Catala S.A. (France); Albany International Pty. Ltd.; (Australia); Albany International Feltros e Telas Interiais Ltda. (Brazil); Albany International S.A. de C.V. (Mexico); Nomafa Division (U.S., Sweden, France).

Further Reading:

Albany International Corp. Annual Reports, 1989–92.
Albany International: A History, Albany, NY: Albany International Corporation.
Nulty, Peter, "Growing Fast on the 500s Fringe," *Fortune*, April 24, 1989, p. 72.

—Wendy J. Stein

Alberto-Culver Company

2525 Armitage Avenue
Melrose Park, Illinois 60160
U.S.A.
(708) 450-3000
Fax: (708) 450-3354

Public Company
Incorporated: 1955
Employees: 7,300
Sales: $1.09 billion
Stock Exchanges: New York
SICs: 2844 Toilet Preparations; 2099 Food Preparations Nec;
   7319 Advertising Nec

Perhaps best known for its Alberto VO5 product line, Alberto-Culver Company also markets a range of toiletry, grocery, and household brands. Alberto-Culver has done well as a small, family-run company in an industry of giants primarily through introducing new products and aggressively advertising them.

Alberto-Culver Company dates back to the 1950s. Under the harsh, hair-frying lights of Hollywood motion picture studios, word was spreading about a product named after the chemist who invented it: Alberto VO5 Conditioning Hairdressing. With a unique water-free, five-oil formula, VO5 had been developed at the request of studios and had proven successful at rescuing hair from dryness and damage. In 1955 Leonard H. Lavin borrowed $400,000 and bought the small beauty supply firm that manufactured VO5. This regional Los Angeles-based company also made more than 100 other products, but Alberto VO5 made up 85 percent of its sales. After buying the firm, Lavin dropped its other products, relocated to Chicago, and concentrated on VO5. He was just 36 years old at the time and his wife, Bernice, joined the company as secretary-treasurer. The Alberto-Culver Company had five employees on the production line and two employees in sales for its first year of operation.

The first television commercial for VO5 ran in Pennsylvania in 1955. It marked the company's first year of operation and the start of a company mainstay—aggressive marketing. In three years, sales were more than $5 million. By 1958 Alberto VO5 Conditioning Hairdressing had raced to the top of its category, outselling many sizable competitors. In 1956 and 1959 some other products were added to the line, and TRESemme—a regional line of hair colors—was purchased. TRESemme has

since grown to include a best-selling professional mousse. Then in 1961 and 1962, Alberto VO5 Hair Spray and Alberto VO5 Shampoo were introduced and, along with Alberto VO5 Conditioning Hairdressing, became the financial cornerstones of the company.

The 1960s were a time of explosive growth. The company went public in 1961, trading stock over the counter. A new plant and corporate offices were built in Melrose Park, Illinois, in 1960, and a plant opened in Canada in 1961. That same year, an international division was formed to sell products in Mexico, England, Australia, Guatemala, and elsewhere. Company sales surged to $25 million in 1961, then boomed to $61 million in 1962. By 1963 Alberto-Culver was ranked second among advertisers of hair care products. The results were evident: in 1964 sales were still climbing, exceeding more than $100 million. Company stock was listed on the New York Stock Exchange in 1965.

Other products were introduced in the mid-1960s. Consort Hair Spray was the first product of its kind made specifically for men. New Dawn Hair Color was the first shampoo-in permanent hair color on the retail market. The first feminine deodorant spray, FDS, was introduced in 1966 and has been a leader in that product category ever since—despite a dip in sales following the hexachlorophene scare of the early 1970s. Kleen Guard Furniture Polish went on sale in 1966, and new manufacturing operations were initiated in Mexico and Puerto Rico. By 1967 Alberto-Culver Company had more than 2,000 employees and sold products in more than 65 countries.

Alberto-Culver acquired several companies toward the end of the 1960s. The first was SugarTwin, a low-calorie sugar substituted sold regionally as part of Alberto-Culver's Food Service Division. The company slashed SugarTwin's calories in half and released it into national distribution, along with Brown SugarTwin, the first low-calorie granulated brown sugar replacement. These items are credited with much of the growth of the food sector of Alberto-Culver. With the federal ban on cyclamates and the conversion to a saccharin formula, SugarTwin's double-digit growth slowed, but it remained a profitable brand for the company.

In 1969 Alberto-Culver acquired Milani Foods and Sally Beauty Company, Inc. Milani represented a range of food products sold to restaurants, hospitals, and other institutions. Milani came to be operated out of Alberto-Culver's Food Service Division and marketed about 400 items, including food bases, beverages, soups, and dressings. Sally Beauty Company was not unlike Alberto VO5: a concept with a lot of promise. At the time Alberto-Culver purchased it, Sally Beauty consisted of one store and nine independent franchises that sold professional products for hair stylists and barbers. The franchises were closed, and Alberto-Culver developed a new merchandising strategy. This eventually bloomed into more than 1,000 company-owned and -operated outlets. Located largely in shopping centers, with some 40 outlets in the United Kingdom, Sally Beauty Supply stores offer thousands of salon products and appliances to professionals as well as retail customers.

Alberto-Culver had another significant first in 1972: it won the fight for 30-second commercials. By buying standard 60-second slots, then dividing them to run two separate commercials for different products, the company caused an uproar. Networks balked and ad agencies scoffed, but before long, the 30-second commercial was an industry standard.

Alberto-Culver's hair care line seemed to reach its peak in the early 1970s. Sales were down in 1974, although company products were being sold in more than 100 countries, and a new food plant had been built in Melrose Park. Earnings were hard-hit at this time by OPEC (Organization of Petroleum Exporting Countries) price increases that impacted petroleum-based raw material costs. After a decade of dizzying growth, the slump was alarming. As a result, money was redirected into new products.

Meanwhile, Alberto-Culver Company had developed an ethnic hair care line, TCB. It was launched in 1975 with eight products and grew to include 36 products considered leaders in domestic retail and professional markets as well as selling solidly abroad. The first 60-second hot oil deep conditioner, Alberto VO5 Hot Oil Treatment, was introduced in 1976 and became the country's number one selling brand. Static Guard, the first anti-static spray, was presented that same year and became a best-seller. Then in 1977, Alberto VO5 Hair Spray became the first nationally advertised premium brand to introduce an aerosol free of chlorofluorocarbons, chemicals which deplete the earth's ozone layer. According to Lavin, the company preferred to develop original products rather than copy products already on the market, a strategy that would require heavy investment to promote over competitors. Alberto-Culver has thus earned a reputation for innovation and for spending generously to promote the products it develops.

Another aspect of Alberto-Culver's comeback effort was the 1977 acquisition of the John A. Frye Shoe Company. Then a maker of western leather boots, Frye grew to include hand-sewn men's shoes and belts as well as products for women and children. In the 1980s Frye boots were nearly staple items, and by 1981 Frye accounted for 19 percent of Alberto-Culver's revenues. Following its established recipe for success, the company took Frye's regional name recognition and aggressively advertised and distributed its products. In 1980 Phillippe of California was acquired, along with its line of handbags. Phillippe underwent the same transformation as Frye, including the addition of a line of small leather accessories; within a year Phillippe was contributing 5 percent of the company's total sales. However, Frye and Phillippe of California were both sold by 1986 after accumulating $16 million in losses over three years. Alberto-Culver has since stayed away from fashion and concentrated on its core toiletries business.

A high degree of brand loyalty continued to make the Alberto VO5 and hair-care products line a stable one. In 1982 it represented about a third of total Alberto-Culver sales. Research and marketing efforts were paying off in the company's other divisions. In 1983 Mrs. Dash—the first herb and spice alternative to salt—was introduced and went on to dominate sales in its category. This set the tone for a series of new ''healthy'' products in the Household/Grocery Products Division, including the first all-natural butter-flavor powder, Molly McButter, released in 1987, and Papa Dash, a light salt, very low-sodium blend introduced in 1991.

Also performing well in the mid-1980s was Sally Beauty Company, which boasted 145 outlets by 1983, making it the nation's largest wholesaler of barber and beauty supplies. That same year, Alberto-Culver acquired Indola Cosmetics B.V., a prominent Dutch firm well known throughout Europe for products used by professional hairdressers. At first financially unsuccessful, Indola was extensively revamped, and its line was expanded to include all aspects of salon service, such as perms, hair colors, and specialty products. In 1990 it began to perform better and was making a fresh entrance into markets in Spain, Australia, and the Far East.

Alberto-Culver's sales improved in 1984, when they topped $400 million. Compared to such hair-industry giants as Procter & Gamble and Bristol-Myers, Alberto-Culver was tiny, but tough. Unable to compete with the industry Goliaths in the areas of promotion, advertising, sales force, and recoverable losses, Alberto-Culver has had to rely on sharp-wittedness and timing. In addition to its many firsts in products, the company distinguished itself as an innovator in advertising. After championing the 30-second commercial, Alberto-Culver again entered the ring to fight for the 15-second commercial. This battle actually led to a threatened class action antitrust suit against the larger station group owners in broadcasting who refused to carry the split 30-second commercials. The suit was dropped when the restrictions against the ads were dropped. This was a significant win for companies of Alberto-Culver's size, which are pinched by the high advertising costs that larger firms can more easily afford.

While still largely a family-owned company in 1986—the Lavin family controlling about 45 percent of the stock—Alberto-Culver went public, offering a new class of common stock with reduced voting rights. Lavin had his eye on several possible acquisitions. When sales topped $500 million in 1987, Alberto-Culver joined ranks with the *Fortune* 500. It was a leap of 37 percent in net income and a sign the company was on the right track. Sally Beauty was thriving at this time, with 470 stores and successful overseas sales, making it the largest international beauty supply company in the world.

Extending its tradition for niche-building, Alberto-Culver introduced its Bold Hold Styling Line in 1988. Targeted at teens, the products include Scrunch Spritz, Frizz Taming Mousse, and Mega Gel, all helping to achieve the latest in hair-styling trends. Meanwhile, the company's overseas sales and profits were reaching record levels. That same year, company founder Leonard Lavin relinquished the title of president and chief operating officer to his son-in-law Howard Bernick, then the company's chief financial officer; Lavin remained chairman and chief executive officer. Bernick joined Alberto-Culver in 1977. His wife, Carol Bernick, is Lavin's daughter and head of the company's New Products Division.

In 1990 the strongest growth area for Alberto-Culver continued to be international sales and the Sally stores, which grew to nearly 900 outlets that year. The company enjoyed a very solid market in Canada and England. As the domestic economy forced retailers to cut back on inventory levels, the marketplace at home was more competitive than ever. Because of the expense of opening new stores, Alberto-Culver slowed the Sally store openings in 1990. In 1989 175 stores that had been owned and operated as Safeway Stores were purchased and converted. In 1990 the company said it would be opening only about 75 stores.

The Papa Dash Lite Salt introduced in 1991 was the first to meet the government's low-sodium guidelines. Containing no potassium chloride, Papa Dash uses an agglomeration technology to bond real salt molecules onto the surface of tiny carbohydrate particles, thus providing the taste of salt without the excess sodium.

Alberto-Culver was ranked 396th in the *Fortune* 500 that year in 1991. Also that year, the company agreed to drop the "ozone friendly" label from its aerosol hair products, which, while containing no ozone-depleting chlorofluorocarbons, do feature other propellants such as propane and isobutane, which are harmful to the atmosphere. Without admitting wrongdoing or inaccuracy, the company paid $50,000 in costs as part of a settlement with ten state attorneys general. Alberto-Culver purchased Cederroth International AB, a producer of health and hygiene goods, in 1991.

When sales rose again in 1992, and profits improved considerably in the toiletries and household/grocery divisions, Alberto-Culver Company attributed its decision to plump up advertising spending that year to a desire to overcome the weak market. Alberto-Culver crossed the billion dollar mark in sales that year and proved that its premise of strong support for strong products is the key to long-term growth.

Principal Subsidiaries: Alberto-Culver International, Inc.; Draper Daniels Media Services, Inc.; Sally Beauty Company, Inc.; Cederroth International AB.

Further Reading:

"Alberto-Culver Co.," *Insiders' Chronicle,* July 22, 1991, p. 3.

"Alberto-Culver Co.," *New York Times,* September 11, 1991, p. D4.

"Alberto-Culver Co.," *Wall Street Journal,* July 23, 1992, p. B4.

"Alberto-Culver Wins Split-30 Battle, Drops Antitrust Suit," *Broadcasting,* March 19, 1984, p. 42.

"Alberto to Modify Labels," *New York Times,* August 7, 1991, p. D19.

Appelbaum, Cara, "Alberto VO5, Graying at the Temples, Gets a Younger Look," *Adweek's Marketing Week,* January 28, 1991, p. 12.

Braham, James, "Leonard Lavin," *Industry Week,* August 18, 1986, p. 48.

Crown, Judith, "Alberto Clipped by VO5 Pricing Strategy," *Crain's Chicago Business,* August 19, 1991, p. 1.

Freeman, Laurie, "Alberto Gambles on Prestige Haircare Line," *Advertising Age,* April 14, 1986, p. 22; "Knack for Niches," *Advertising Age,* April 18, 1988, pp. 70–74.

Furman, Phyllis, "Ethnic Haircare Marketers Battling for Share," *Advertising Age,* March 2, 1987, p. S2.

"Green Settlement," *Wall Street Journal,* August 6, 1991, p. B6.

Hoggan, Karen, "Alberto Bounces Back," *Marketing,* May 24, 1990, p. 2.

Hoppe, Karen, "Alberto-Culver's Leonard Lavin, An Industry Original," *Drug & Cosmetic Industry,* August 1988, p. 26.

Kentouris, Chris, "Alberto-Culver Sees Gains in Toiletries," *Women's Wear Daily,* October 31, 1989, p. 16.

Kuhn, Susan, "The Hidden Allure of Alberto-Culver," *Fortune,* May 20, 1991, p. 3.

Loeffelholz, Suzanne, "Lavin's Coat of Many Colors," *Financial World,* February 21, 1989, pp. 26–27.

McCarthy, Michael, "Alberto-Culver Continues Its Spending Ways," *Adweek Eastern Edition,* August 3, 1992, p. 4.

Norris, Floyd, "Disparity in Stock of Alberto-Culver," *New York Times,* May 29, 1990, p. D12.

O'Toole, John, "Second Splits: Advertising," *Atlantic,* June 1984, p. 30.

"Papa Dash Lite Salt," *Fortune,* May 6, 1991, p. 81.

Parr, Jan, "How Often Matters, Not How Long," *Forbes,* August 25, 1986, p. 139.

Pitzer, Mary, "An Acid Test for Antitakeover Laws," *Business Week,* September 28, 1987, p. 31.

"The Regrooming of Alberto-Culver," *Financial World,* February 15, 1982, pp. 25–26.

Teitelbaum, Richard, "Carol L. Bernick," *Fortune,* May 21, 1990, p. 158.

—Carol Keeley

Allegheny
Ludlum
C O R P O R A T I O N

Allegheny Ludlum Corporation

1000 Six PPG Place
Pittsburgh, Pennsylvania 15222-5479
U.S.A.
(412) 394-2800
Fax: (412) 394-3033

Public Company
Incorporated: 1938 as Allegheny Ludlum Steel Corporation
Employees: 5,400
Sales: $1.03 billion
Stock Exchanges: New York Philadelphia
SICs: 3312 Steel Works, Blast Furnaces (including Coke
  Ovens) & Rolling Mills; 3316 Cold-Rolled Steel Sheet,
  Strip & Bars; 3322 Malleable Iron Foundries; 3325 Steel
  Foundries Nec; 5051 Metal Service Centers & Offices

Allegheny Ludlum Corporation is one of the largest manufacturers of specialty steel and other specialty metals in the United States. Stainless steel, by far the principal product line of Allegheny Ludlum, accounts for about 80 percent of its total sales and ranks it among the three largest manufacturers of the specialty metal. Silicon electrical steel and other specialty alloys compose the remainder of the corporation's product lines, accounting for about 16 percent and 4 percent of total sales, respectively. The niche the company has carved in the specialty steel market has withstood the deleterious effects of the historically cyclical steel market and survived mounting foreign competition by keeping a technological step ahead of its competitors, increasing productivity and efficiency and maintaining a broad market base.

Allegheny Ludlum's genesis can be traced to the 1938 merger of Allegheny Steel Company of Brackenridge, Pennsylvania, and Ludlum Steel Company of Watervliet, New York. Both companies were manufacturers of specialty steel, and each desired facilities the other possessed; for example, Allegheny wanted to enter the bar business, and Ludlum wished to get into the flat business. Consequently, the merger produced scarcely any duplication of facilities and enabled the newly formed corporation, named Allegheny Ludlum Steel Corporation (ALSC), to move to the forefront of the specialty steel market by virtue of the combined product lines of the two companies. W. F. Detwiler, a former night-shift apprentice for Allegheny Steel Company, became the corporation's first chairman of the

board, and Hiland G. Batcheller, president of Ludlum Steel Company, was appointed its president.

At the completion of ALSC's first full year of operation in 1940, the demand for specialty steel had shown a steady increase for the past decade. ALSC reported more than $37 million in sales for the year, 58 percent of which were made in the final quarter. The United States' entry into World War II took the steady increase of the market to unprecedented heights. As the demand for jet airplanes and armaments spiraled upward, research engineers at ALSC intensified their search for metal materials that would answer the growing demand. ALSC developed heat-resisting alloys for use in the construction of aircraft turbine engines. By 1944 the number of employees had ballooned to 17,000, almost three times the number at the outbreak of the war. Sales had climbed to more than $114 million, and ALSC parlayed this wartime-induced success toward an $80 million expansion and modernization program in 1946. The expansion program focused on increasing ALSC's production capacities of stainless steel—which had more than quadrupled in use since 1920—and the burgeoning demand for flat-rolled silicon electrical steel, used in the manufacture of electrical transformers and communication equipment.

The 1950s, a decade of vast growth for the steel industry as a whole, occasioned only a marginal gain in sales for ALSC. At the conclusion of 1950, sales were just below $190 million and by the end of the decade had grown to only $230 million. But during those ten years, ALSC's sales figures fluctuated wildly, reaching a peak of $286 million in 1956 and a nadir of $170 million two years earlier. Although part of the blame for the vacillating sales was attributed to slackening demand, ALSC nevertheless remained steadfast to its long-term policy of expansion and modernization. By 1956 it had spent more than $100 million on such programs since the merger of Allegheny Steel and Ludlum Steel and continued to fund further programs. ALSC's capacity for melting and refining special steel alloys was doubled in 1956, and, in the same year, $30 million to be spent over a two year period was allotted for expanding its production of stainless, electrical, and other high alloy specialty steels.

At this time, ALSC also made improvements in production efficiency and the quality of its products by installing the steel industry's first semi-automated system for hot working steel. Instead of having to manually set the measurements each time a slab of steel passed through a rolling mill—a process that could take up to 15 passes to achieve the desired thickness and shape—the semi-automated system required only one operator to insert a card containing the specifications for the slab into the system and then push a button. This procedure greatly diminished the chances of error since the measurements were dictated by a computer, and consequently the quality of the formed steel product was improved.

Having now firmly established itself as one of the leading specialty steels manufacturers in the United States, ALSC began to turn to foreign markets as the backlog demand dating from World War II began to ebb. It was a direction the steel industry as a whole followed by the mid-1960s, but in 1960 ALSC became one of the first U.S. steel companies to engage in overseas steel manufacturing investments. In a bid to capitalize on the rapid growth of specialty steel sales in the European Common Market area, ALSC formed a Belgian company in partnership with Evence Coppee & Cie., of Brussels, and Société Anonyme Metallurgique d'Esperance-Longdoz, to produce and sell specialty steel.

ALSC also expanded once again on the home front. After posting sales of $292 million in 1964, its highest since 1956, the corporation invested $28 million in new plants and equipment, focusing its efforts on the conversion from open hearth furnaces for silicon-steel production to basic-oxygen furnaces in 1966.

Two acquisitions in the late 1960s augured a change of market focus for ALSC. In 1967 the company acquired True Temper Corporation, a maker of sporting goods and garden tools. This acquisition, which represented a significant diversification of ALSC's product line, was followed in 1969 by the acquisition of Jacobsen Manufacturing Co., a maker of power lawn mowers, garden tractors, and snow blowers.

In early 1970 Allegheny Ludlum Steel Corporation changed its name to Allegheny Ludlum Industries Inc. (ALI). As a consequence of the name change, the specialty steel operation became a division of ALI but continued to bear the ALSC name. As quoted in the *Wall Street Journal,* a company spokesperson stated the name change "would reflect the changing nature of the business of Allegheny Ludlum." Indeed, the 1970s, a horrendous decade for the steel industry, marked the decline of the specialty steel market as a major focus of ALI. By the end of 1970, a third of ALI's sales came from non-steel items.

Then, in early 1972, ALI reached outside of the steel industry for a new president and chief operating officer (COO). Robert J. Buckley, who had held various positions in industrial management, was selected to lead ALI into a more diversified future. The announcement by ALI in the *Wall Street Journal* of Buckley's selection as president and COO, reiterated the company's movement, articulated two years earlier, toward a more diversified product line. When questioned about the specific duties Buckley would assume as president, a spokesperson for the corporation stated Buckley would "run the day-to-day operations of Allegheny Ludlum Industries, which includes more than just a steel company." The qualifying statement clearly underscored ALI's decision to branch out and aggressively pursue markets other than specialty steel.

Still, by 1974, ALSC continued to be the major money earner for the parent company. Specialty steel accounted for 70 percent of the corporation's sales, producing over $500 million in revenue, but Buckley had already decided by 1973 to dispose of the specialty steel operation. He began to actively pursue buyers for a minority equity position in the subsidiary, but by 1976 he had found no satisfactory offers.

At this time, in the mid-1970s, the steel market was plummeting. If there ever was a time to exit the steel market, now was such a time. The steel industry was severely hampered by undercutting its own demand projections, slow world-wide economic growth, massive oil price increases, and increased foreign competition. By the end of the decade, ALSC had begun to feel the brunt of the harsh economic times. In 1978 Buckley engaged investment bankers to attempt to sell the specialty steel unit. The bar division had been spun off in 1976 as a leveraged

buyout to existing management. When the bankers had no success in finding a buyer, Richard P. Simmons was asked and received approval to try to put together his own buyout, while the bankers continued their efforts to find a buyer for the specialty steel operation.

Simmons, president of the steel division and executive vice-president of ALI, began working for ALSC in 1953 as a metallurgist. Six years later, he left ALSC and worked for two steel companies before returning to ALSC in 1968 to become vice-president of manufacturing. After becoming president of ALSC in 1972, he merged manufacturing plants, reduced staff, established cost control systems, and formulated the strategies that would carry the steel company into the next decade.

In 1980 Simmons and Clint W. Murchinson, Jr., a Dallas financier who owned the Dallas Cowboys football team and held investments in petroleum and broadcasting properties, began negotiations for the sale of ALSC. By the end of the year, an agreement had been reached. As part of the deal, Simmons agreed to leave ALI and become president of the spun off specialty steel operation. In late December of 1980, the sale of the corporation for approximately $195 million was approved by ALI shareholders, but then, during final arrangements between Murchinson, Simmons, and the managers of the specialty steel subsidiary who held an invested interest in the sale, negotiations stalled due to last-minute disagreements, and Murchinson withdrew his offer.

As quickly as the deal fell through, however, it was revived when a wealthy Pittsburgh industrialist, George W. Tippins, entered the scene at the behest of Simmons. Tippins filled the void created by Murchinson's departure by offering the necessary financial backing to enable the sale of ALSC for the same amount offered by Murchinson—and exactly the same terms agreed to by both partners—to the private ownership of Tippins, Simmons, and 16 of his managers. The unexpected withdrawal of Murchinson's offer and the sale to the group headed by Tippins occurred virtually overnight. It is interesting to note that this 1980 leveraged buyout was the second-largest at that point in time, and it was completed without investment bankers.

With Tippins as chairman of the board and Simmons as president and chief executive officer, ALSC braced itself for yet another downturn in the steel market. Large U.S. steel companies suffered disastrous losses—nearly $6 billion over a two-year period—during the early 1980s. Outdated facilities and inefficient production processes, as well as a decreasing demand for steel, were to blame for the losses. For years, steel manufacturers had looked toward raising prices rather than improving their productivity as a source for ameliorating their profits, and by 1983 their practices had begun to severely affect them. ALSC's largest competitor, Crucible Steel, went out of business during this difficult period, as did several other specialty steel producers. This was the most challenging time experienced by the steel industry, including specialty steel, going back to the Great Depression of the 1930s. Nevertheless, ALSC posted a profit for every quarter and every year.

The impact of foreign steel companies on U.S. steel manufacturers was also one of the other major contributors to the ills of the steel industry during the 1980s. The increasing rate of foreign subsidized steel imports entering the U.S. market and the practice of foreign steel companies selling steel in the United States at prices below the cost of production in the U.S. market—referred to as "dumping"—took its toll on the industry. Although the effect of foreign steel manufacturers had been felt years before, the U.S. steel industry began lobbying in earnest by the late 1970s for government intervention. In late 1984 their pleas were answered by the introduction of voluntary restraint agreement (VRA) curbs on illegally dumped and subsidized steel imports. The VRAs, in effect for five years and then subject to renewal, would restrict steel imports from 29 countries to just under a fifth of the U.S. market. The steel industry, ALSC included, used this grace period to finance capital-spending projects, totaling more than $6.5 billion in a five-year period, in an effort to modernize their facilities and make them more efficient. The VRAs also aided ALSC by offering a respite from foreign competition at a time when imports were surging into the specialty steel market. Even during the period when VRAs were in effect, record input levels of specialty steel continued.

In 1985 Robert P. Bozzone, an employee of ALSC since 1955, succeeded Simmons as president of the company. Simmons remained as chief executive officer and a year later became the chairman of the board, replacing Tippins. The corporation remained financially healthy at this time, posting a profit every quarter since its buy out from ALI. Sales stood at $716 million by 1985, and ALSC's survival through the economic slide was attributed to its focus on product lines ignored by the big steel companies as well as its modern facilities that increased worker production. In 1986 ALSC changed its name to Allegheny Ludlum Corporation. A year later, sales topped $1 billion, and in May the corporation went public.

By the end of the decade, sales were hovering around $1.2 billion and VRAs had been extended for another two-and-a-half years, giving ALC additional incentive to boost its capital-spending projects by $25 million. Buoyed by a U.S. stainless steel market that had more than doubled over the past two decades, ALC entered the 1990s as another recession loomed on the horizon. Yet ALC was able to record profits, albeit at lower levels than previous years, throughout the downturn by adhering to the corporate strategies that had carried the company through decades of cyclical ups and downs since 1938. Since going private in 1980, Allegheny Ludlum has earned 15 percent on total capital employed, a record matched by few metals companies.

By this time, ALC produced stainless steel and other specialty steel for a wide variety of uses beyond traditional markets. Its products were used in the production of stainless steel skis, home cookware, personal computer diskettes, Gillette's Sensor razor, and in the creation of Biosphere 2, the scientific experiment that attempted to replicate a self-sustaining environment in a hermetically sealed complex. The search for new applica-

tions and markets for its products and the practice of eschewing overdependence on cyclical customers—both hallmarks of ALC's history—enabled the corporation to remain stable during an economic period that rocked many other steel companies.

Another linchpin of ALC's survival has been its efforts toward seeking innovative technology to improve efficiency and lower production costs, a characteristic that continued into the 1990s. In 1992 ALC completed construction of the first prototype casting machine to produce stainless and carbon steel products from molten steel. The casting machine, called COILCAST and developed in cooperation with a company in Linz, Austria, would eliminate the need for several stages of the production process, thereby improving the efficiency of production and lowering costs. When commercialized, it would provide a continuing advantage for Allegheny Ludlum over its competition.

Although the steel industry is fraught with many ills and has experienced a turbulent history, ALC has remained comparatively stable throughout its history and has continued to grow by pursuing objectives established at its inception. The markets for Allegheny Ludlum's stainless steel grow at an annual rate of approximately five percent. Thus, it describes itself as a cyclical growth company. Its strategies for remaining cost competitive, finding special niches, increasing exports, and being sensitive to customer needs have kept Allegheny Ludlum in good standing. Based on history, dedication to technology, and focus on specialty materials, and with continuity and large ownership positions of key managers, Allegheny Ludlum would likely remain one of the most successful metals companies in the world.

Principal Subsidiaries: ALstrip, Inc.

Further Reading:

"Allegheny Ludlum Merger Details," *Steel,* May 23, 1938, p. 26.
Andersen, D. F., "Steel Industry History: Riddled With Changes," *American Metal Market,* July 21, 1989, p. 25.
Chakravraty, Subrata N., "A Farewell to Steel," *Forbes,* December 8, 1980, pp. 36–37.
Contavespi, Vicki, "It's a Good Thing the Steel Industry Worked So Hard in the 1980s to Prepare for the Next Recession," *Forbes,* January 6, 1992, p. 166.
Graham, Thomas C., "Steel Industry Has Gone Far, But There is Much to Be Done," *American Metal Market,* July 21, 1989, pp. 1 and 31.
Petzinger, Thomas Jr., "Allegheny Ludlum's Steel Operations Sold," *Wall Street Journal,* December 29, 1980, p. 4.
"A Politician's Promise," *The Economist,* July 29, 1989, pp. 54–56.
Russel, Mark, "Small Steelmakers Finding Profitable Market Niches," *Wall Street Journal,* January 8, 1987, p. 6.
"Sorting out What's Left at Allegheny Ludlum," *Business Week,* December 1, 1980, p. 49.
"Steel Mills Head Into Push-Button Era," *Business Week,* January 12, 1957, pp. 80–82.

—Jeffrey L. Covell

ALLIANTTECHSYSTEMS

Alliant Techsystems, Inc.

5901 Lincoln Drive
Edina, Minnesota 55436
U.S.A.
(612) 939-2000
Fax: (612) 939-2480

Public Company
Incorporated: September 28, 1990
Employees: 4,200
Sales: $1.0 billion
Stock Exchanges: New York
SICs: 3489 Ordnance and Accessories Nec; 3483
   Ammunition, Except for Small Arms

Alliant Techsystems is the product of a corporate spin-off of defense-related businesses that had been acquired or built up by Honeywell Inc. over a period of 50 years. Having become an independent company only in 1990, the majority of Alliant's existence has been spent as a set of divisions of Honeywell Inc., which had made its name making buttons, switches, appliances and other industrial and consumer electronics products.

Honeywell's entrance into the defense industry came in 1941, when the war in Europe and Japan's occupation of China convinced the Roosevelt Administration to begin preparations for the possibility that the United States might be dragged into the conflict. At the time, the company—then called Minneapolis-Honeywell—was one of the few American manufacturers with the work force, facilities, tooling, and expertise to produce precision instruments and controls for the military.

Minneapolis-Honeywell's first military contracts were for an automatic system for releasing payloads at high altitudes for precision bombing. The company's chairman, Harold Sweatt, assigned the company's heating regulator division to develop the system. The company's volume of military business expanded rapidly after the Japanese attack on Pearl Harbor and, as Roosevelt had feared, the United States was drawn into the war. During the course of the hostilities, the Minnesota-based firm turned out turbo engine regulators and complex automatic ammunition firing control devices, among other items, and served as the only American manufacturer of tank periscopes.

At the end of the war, Sweatt was determined to keep Minneapolis-Honeywell thoroughly in the electronic controls business.

The most lucrative customer at the time was the Pentagon, which was gearing up for cold war hostilities with the Soviet Union. These circumstances drew Minneapolis-Honeywell even deeper into the stable and lucrative government contracting business. In addition, research dollars provided for Pentagon projects were almost always applicable to commercial projects. The formula worked in reverse, as well. Minneapolis-Honeywell purchased the Micro Switch division of First Industrial in 1950. The company's switches were used to operate relays in vending machines and other manually operated devices, but soon found military applications in battle tanks, artillery, and guided missile systems.

Minneapolis-Honeywell's brief association with the radar powerhouse Raytheon, coupled with their subsequent computer venture Datamatic, firmly established the company's reputation as a high-technology electronics manufacturer. It led to increased activity in aviation control systems and the company's eventual participation in the manned space program.

In 1964, after shortening its name to Honeywell, the company opted out of the competition for major defense and NASA projects. Honeywell simply wasn't in a position to compete economically with the likes of industry giants such as Boeing, General Electric, or General Dynamics. Instead, Honeywell concentrated on working as a subcontractor within a narrow range of electronics systems. Honeywell's profitable defense systems businesses, however, created public relations difficulties. Headquartered in the politically liberal state of Minnesota, Honeywell endured a series of protests launched by groups opposed to American involvement in the Vietnam war.

During the Nixon and Ford Administrations, as the war effort in Vietnam wound down, defense budgets were scaled back. This produced less work for Honeywell's defense businesses and later caused the company to scale back its operations. In 1982 chairman James Renier carried out a corporate downsizing that claimed 3,500 jobs. With this restructuring, Honeywell abandoned its adversarial position in the marketplace with regard to IBM, and later sold off much of its computer manufacturing assets.

The break to Honeywell came in 1986 and 1988 when its defense businesses recorded tremendous losses, stemming from huge cost overruns. Unable to collect for these losses, and penalized for late delivery of products under contract, Renier decided to immediately reduce Honeywell's exposure to Pentagon projects. Initially Renier attempted to reposition much of the government defense business toward commercial aviation and flight control markets. In the short run, this strategy appeared effective. The company's defense and aerospace operations comprised nearly half of Honeywell's total income, and a significant portion of its total profits.

Renier, however, was determined to refocus Honeywell on its core commercial operations. While profitable, the defense businesses—specifically the Defense & Marine Systems division—were not as profitable or promising as other groups in the company. Defense operations, it was felt, were diluting the company's profitability. In addition, the lessening in tensions between the United States and the Soviet Union raised increasing questions about the long-term viability of involvement in the defense market.

Renier decided to organize the Defense & Marine Systems and Test Instruments divisions and the Signal Analysis Center into a separate corporate entity. This new entity would operate as an independent subsidiary until it could be sold, hopefully to another defense contractor. After several months, however, no company stepped forward with an acceptable bid. Eager to dispense of the low-margin division and get on with the business of running Honeywell, Renier decided to distribute shares in the division to Honeywell shareholders. To do this, the division would have to be prepared for life as an independent corporation.

Renier offered the chairmanship of the new company to Toby G. Warson, a former naval commander and CEO of Honeywell's subsidiary in the United Kingdom. Completing the management team were Kenneth Jenson, a former executive in the division, and Dean Fjestul, the head of finance for Honeywell Europe. With his management team in place, it came time to choose a new name (Renier asked that the new company not borrow the venerable Honeywell name). The team eventually settled upon the name Alliant Techsystems. This name was based on the word alliance which, it was felt, accurately described the relationship it hoped to maintain with the Defense Department.

After a distribution of one Alliant share for every four Honeywell shares, Alliant began business as an independent company in October 1990. It entered the market with a 50-year history, 8,300 employees, and a position as the Pentagon's 17th largest contractor. Its operations were divided into four main units: precision armament, ordnance, marine, and information storage systems. At the time of the company's creation, Alliant consisted of two groups, six divisions and two operations, representing tremendous bureaucracy and redundancy. One of Warson's first actions as chairman was to consolidate work functions among the company's various fiefdoms and, in the process, eliminate 800 administrative jobs.

Within months the operation had been streamlined into a manufacturing and materials arm and an engineering and technology center. Sales were handled by four market groups that were organized in the same fashion the Defense Department is aligned. In another important move, Warson used the company's entire first quarter operating income to pay for Alliant's restructuring costs and get it operating under lower debt. Still, Alliant was saddled with a $14 million charge for legal and administrative costs, $30 million in severance payments, a $165 million loan from Honeywell, and a $60 million dividend payment to Honeywell. This brought the new company's debt to equity ratio to a precarious 1.4:1.

With 1989 earnings of $53.8 million on sales of $1.14 billion, it seemed that Alliant was off to a difficult start. But the company gained its independence only three months after the Iraqi army's invasion of Kuwait. Suddenly, the dynamics of Pentagon work changed drastically. The invasion, coupled with the evaporation of the Soviet military threat because of the collapse of communism, forced American military strategists to focus their combat planning on a new type of enemy, the well-armed third world

dictator. Battling this type of opponent did not require nuclear weapons or new weapons platforms.

With the demise of the Soviet military machine, the Bush Administration increasingly turned to lower-cost improvements in existing weapons systems, those necessary to battle armies such as Iraq's. Alliant was perfectly suited for this approach to modernization. In 1990 Warson told *Industry Week,* "If you look at the U.S. defense budget, it's clear that the major new weapons systems—for instance the B-2 bomber, the advanced tactical fighters, new tanks and submarines—are in trouble. The Pentagon is looking for ways to enhance existing systems and to improve the performance of the individual soldier. And that's the market we're in."

Warson noted that budget constraints were likely to preclude the Army from replacing its aging Abrams tanks. Instead, he suggested that the Pentagon would opt instead to upgrade the weapons by equipping them with the new 120mm ammunition that Alliant made. By and large, the company's products were cheap and effective. And because ammunition, a large part of Alliant's production, had to be continually replaced, the company was assured of a more stable market than airplane, rocket, and submarine builders could enjoy.

As the confrontation in Kuwait became a shooting war and Operation Desert Shield was transformed into Desert Storm, more than 1,300 Alliant workers represented by the Teamsters went out on strike in a dispute over wages, benefits, and the term of another contract. These workers, who manufactured 25mm shells for the Bradley Fighting Vehicle, were quickly replaced by managers who struggled to keep production running.

The strike, a notably unpopular one because of the timing, was short-lived, however, as both sides managed to resolve the dispute and get back to work. Alliant served the war effort well, turning out 120mm uranium-tipped anti-tank shells, 30mm bullets for the A-10 Warthog and Apache helicopter, and a variety of other ordnance. In addition, Alliant was the sole manufacturer of Mk 46 and Mk 50 anti-submarine torpedoes, although none were employed during the war.

Alliant continued to gain momentum after the war in Kuwait was over. Warson carried out a successive wave of consolidations, mostly within the management ranks, dropping a further 800 employees by October 1991. In addition, the number of layers of management were cut from 14 to seven. This enabled the company to compete more efficiently for the dwindling number of Pentagon contracts for new weapons systems.

The one weak spot in Alliant's organization was the company's Metrum Information Storage division. Metrum, Alliant's only non-munitions unit, manufactured data recording and storage devices. While half of Metrum's sales were to commercial customers, the unit suffered from numerous production setbacks that forced the company to write off millions of dollars. The Metrum division was eventually sold. Still, Warson made tremendous progress in clearing up Alliant's balance sheet by 1992. With interest payments under control, and a manageable debt of $148 million, it was expected that Alliant would manage to work its debt off the books by 1994.

With a strong financial position, Warson hoped to broaden the company's markets by acquiring another company or establishing a joint venture. His first effort in this direction met a swift rebuke. Warson proposed merging the Stamford, Connecticut-based Olin Corporation's ordnance division into those of Alliant, and had even sealed the $68 million agreement when the Federal Trade Commission became involved, opposing the sale on the basis that the combination would leave the Pentagon with only one supplier of specialized munitions.

Warson and his colleagues at Olin argued that the market could only support one manufacturer. Far from conspiring to gouge the Pentagon with monopoly pricing, Warson argued that by preventing the two companies from realizing economies of scale under reduced orders, the Pentagon would in fact be shelling out more for its ammunition. Despite gaining the support of the Army for its case, Alliant called off its proposed merger in December 1992.

Eventually, softening defense budgets proved too light to sustain Alliant's business. Unable to affect further consolidation, Alliant further cut its work force—already down to 5,600—by 1,700 employees. Alliant also scaled back production of its Adam land mine, disposal AT-4 infantry weapon and Mk 46 torpedo.

With the savings from these curtailed operations, Alliant expected to raise margins against declining sales, down from $1.1 billion in 1992 to only $800 million in 1993. Further military defense budget reductions are likely, however, under the Clinton Administration. Alliant thus faces a challenging period for the immediate future as it seeks to carve out a place in a shrinking market.

Further Reading:

''Alliant to Cut 30% of Work Force; Posts Loss of $90 Million,'' *Wall Street Journal*, January 28, 1993, p. B4.

''At Military Contractor, Strikers Face Winter's Chill and Neighbors' Wrath,'' *New York Times*, February 16, 1991, p. 10.

''FTC Seeks to Block Merger of Defense Firms,'' *Washington Post*, November 7, 1992, p. C1.

''Honeywell Board OKs Spin-off of Defense Units,'' *Electronic News*, October 1, 1990, p. 6.

''Honeywell Defense Business Can't Find Buyer; Spin-off Set,'' *Electronic News*, July 30, 1990, p. 27.

''Linkage Plan of Olin, Alliant is Called Off,'' *Wall Street Journal*, December 9, 1992, p. A4.

''Precision Pick on Target,'' *Barron's*, June 17, 1991, pp. 44–45.

''Sink or Swim,'' *Forbes*, October 14, 1991, pp. 66–71.

''Toby Warson Dives For Profits,'' *Industry Week*, December 3, 1990, pp. 35–38.

—John Simley

American Cyanamid

One Cyanamid Plaza
Wayne, New Jersey 07470
U.S.A.
(201) 831-2000
Fax: (201) 831-3151

Public Company
Incorporated: July 22, 1907
Employees: 36,432
Sales: $3.816 billion
Stock Exchanges: New York London Basle Amsterdam
  Frankfurt Geneva Lausanne Zurich
SICs: 2834 Pharmaceutical Preparations; 2879 Agricultural
  Chemicals Nec; 3842 Surgical Appliances & Supplies;
  2899 Chemical Preparations Nec; 8731 Commercial
  Physical Research; 2836 Biological Products Except
  Diagnostic; 2821 Plastics Materials & Resins

When William Bell became president of American Cyanamid in 1922, he is reported to have said ''even a fool could see what we need is diversification.'' Thus began a prolonged program designed to vary the company's products and services. Once solely a manufacturer of fertilizer, American Cyanamid now makes products as diverse as Pine Sol cleaner and L'Air du Temps perfume.

American Cyanamid was founded in 1907 by Frank Washburn, a Cornell-educated civil engineer. Cyanamid is a compound of lime, carbide, and nitrogen that is suitable for use in fertilizer. Washburn had been a consultant to a nitrate operation in Chile and had also built three dams in the southern United States. Intent on discovering new industrial uses for hydro-electric power, he saw the perfect opportunity in a revolutionary new way of extracting nitrogen from the air through use of an electric arc. He bought the North American rights to this process, as well as the rights to a new method of binding nitrogen, carbide, and lime. For Washburn, the beauty of these new methods of producing cyanamid lay in the fact that they required large amounts of electricity. He had originally planned to build his first plant and the dam it would require in Alabama, but his hydro-electric project became increasingly controversial. For this reason, the first Cyanamid facility was built in Ontario, Canada, its power supplied by Niagara Falls.

The first carload of cyanamid rolled out of the plant on December 4, 1909. After seven years of producing only this product, Washburn traded holdings in American Cyanamid for stock in Ammo-Phos, a company owned by James Duke (of Duke University). This arrangement provided American Cyanamid with an inexpensive supply of phosphoric acid. Phosphoric acid, combined with the nitrogen in cyanamid, produces ammonium phosphate, a good plant food.

The demand for American Cyanamid's products came almost exclusively from those people engaged in producing agricultural products. Farmers were especially affected by the poor economy that followed World War I. American Cyanamid's sales suffered as a result. The once-busy Ontario plant began to operate at 14 percent of its previous capacity. Washburn became seriously ill in 1921 and died the following year. His successor, a Quaker lawyer named William Bell, did not have an easy job ahead of him.

When Bell became head of American Cyanamid in 1922, the company had two principal raw materials: calcium cyanamid and phosphate rock, which were combined to form products for use in agriculture. The challenge for Bell was to find uses for these materials in less cyclical industries. Fortunately for American Cyanamid, while the economic aftermath of World War I had reduced the demand for fertilizers, it had increased the demand for cyanide, which had formerly been supplied by Germany. At the time, cyanide was principally used in the extraction of gold and silver from their ores. American Cyanamid began to manufacture cyanide from cyanamid, thereby broadening its market by supplying mining companies with a necessary chemical. The company also started to produce hydrocyanic acid, an important ingredient in the vulcanization of rubber.

By the mid-1920s American Cyanamid's expansion of its line of products, along with a revival in the fertilizer industry, launched the company into a period of growth. In the first three or four years of Bell's leadership the company had pursued a conservative policy of vertical diversification; that is, it concentrated on finding new markets for the same basic material, cyanamid. However, during the 1920s, general improvement in the economy, coupled with an increase in the value of American Cyanamid's securities, enabled the company to embark on a slightly more aggressive plan of diversification. American Cyanamid, a public company, began to exchange its common stock for holdings in other companies. Some of the first companies acquired in this way were Kalbfleish (heavy chemicals), Selden (sulfuric acid), and Calco (dyes). In retrospect, Lederle Labs, acquired in 1930, was the company's most important acquisition.

The period between the post-war deflation and the crash of the U.S. stock market in 1929 was a time of expansion for many companies. American Cyanamid, with a total of 30 subsidiaries, was one of the most diversified companies in the chemical industry. Chemical companies as a whole weathered the Depression well in comparison with other businesses. In the mid-1930s, direct sales to consumers in drugs and plastics helped to offset the sharp decline in the industrial demand for American Cyanamid's products.

With the onset of World War II American Cyanamid's fortunes improved considerably. The war cut off trade between American companies and their European suppliers so American Cyanamid enjoyed an expanded domestic market. The bulk of the company's business, however, was from the government. American Cyanamid's most important contributions to the war effort came from their pharmaceutical division, which supplied typhus vaccine, gangrene anti-toxin, and dried blood plasma to the armed forces. A subsidiary, Davis and Geck, was a major supplier of surgical sutures.

American Cyanamid received its share of commendations for its part in the war effort; however, questions were raised about the size of the company's financial rewards. In 1942 the parent company was charged with a violation of anti-trust laws and fined $453,461, a large fine considering that American Cyanamid's net profit for the previous year was a little more than $5.6 million. Bell, writing in the company's annual report, was reticent in discussing the affair, but he did hint that Calco (a subsidiary that produced dyes) was involved, and that a member of the board of directors had been indicted.

The company had a good year in 1950 when its sales increased from $237 million to $322 million. This increase in sales was largely due to a series of breakthroughs made by Lederle Labs. In 1947 Lederle researchers succeeded in synthesizing vitamin B. In 1948 they discovered Aureomayacin, an antibiotic that was used to treat pneumonia. By 1953 they were producing tetracycline, one of the first broad-spectrum antibiotics. An oral polio vaccine went on the market in 1954. The demand for Lederle's vaccines and antibiotics was such that new plants were built to keep up with the demand, both at home and abroad. In 1957, for instance, plants to manufacture Lederle's antibiotics were built in England, Brazil, and Argentina. Growth was slow during the 1950s for many of Cyanamid's products, and overseas pharmaceutical sales were important to the company's financial stability. At times Lederle accounted for almost half of the company's profits.

During the 1950s the leadership of American Cyanamid changed four times. William Bell died in 1950 and his replacement died within the year. Kenneth Towe took over, but in 1957 he moved to the position of chairman of the board. While the top executives were busy switching places, the workers were frequently on strike. There were four work stoppages in 1954 alone.

In the early 1960s American Cyanamid received increased attention from the press because of its new corporate headquarters in Wayne, New Jersey. Its major divisions are scattered around New York, New Jersey, and Connecticut, and it has subsidiaries in countries all around the world. Industry analysts have remarked, however, on the remarkable coordination that existed within the company.

The 1960s was not a particularly good decade for American Cyanamid or the larger chemical industry. In 1967 American Cyanamid suffered a major setback when it was convicted on the charge of restraint of trade. Along with Pfizer and Bristol-Myers, American Cyanamid was accused of conspiring to monopolize the marketing and manufacturing of tetracycline from 1953 to 1961. The company finally paid a fine of $48.5 million, which represented more than 50 percent of the net profit for that year.

Despite its legal difficulties and conservative fiscal policies, the decade had some bright spots. In the 1960s, part of the formula for Breck hair conditioner was discovered in the textile labs, while the chemical basis for an anti-tuberculosis drug was discovered by chemists working on products for the rubber industry.

For American Cyanamid, the 1970s began with a slump in profits. Industrial sales were down, in part due to a series of prolonged strikes in the rubber and automobile industries. As petroleum companies diversified into chemicals, an overcrowded market developed that depressed chemical prices at a time when inflation had increased operating expenses.

During the 1970s Lederle Labs continued to carry the company. The consumer products division, which had a number of lucrative brands, began to lose a portion of its market share. The best-selling Breck Shampoo was overtaken by Johnson's Baby Shampoo and Prell; Davis and Geck had once led the market in sutures, but it fell behind products of rival Johnson and Johnson.

The company was also affected by unfavorable publicity from labor disputes and environmental abuses. In 1973 the Georgia State Water Quality Control Board forced Cyanamid to stop dumping sulfuric acid in the Wilmington and Savannah rivers, a practice that the state charged was killing fish. When workers at the Bound Brook, New Jersey, plant charged in 1978 that employee health was being compromised by exposure to carcinogens, they found management unsympathetic. 1,300 workers decided to strike in order to protest health hazards at the plant only to be told by plant manager Eldon Knape that "we don't run a health spa." When the company decided that exposure to lead compounds at the Willow Island, Virginia, pigments plant might cause birth defects, women of child-bearing age in the plant were ordered to quit, accept demotion, or be sterilized. A large amount of adverse publicity resulted from this last incident after five women admitted they had themselves sterilized in order to keep their jobs.

Whereas the strategy of American Cyanamid had once been to diversify, the strategy of the 1980s was to eliminate unprofitable product lines. President George Sella sold the Formica and titanium divisions because their markets were too cyclical. Sella put a greater emphasis on research as well. The increase in research and development began in 1979 and began to show results. Lederle Labs continued its status as a leading company in the American Cyanamid family, racking up more than 40 percent of Cyanamid's earnings some years.

In the mid-1980s American Cyanamid move increasingly into pharmaceuticals via purchases and joint ventures. It bought 49.9 percent of Langford Labs, a Canadian company specializing in veterinary biologicals, and signed an agreement to jointly develop and market veterinary products with Enzon. It bought Acufex Microsurgical, a medical equipment manufacturer for $19 million, Storz Instrument for $100 million, and then, in mid-1986, formed a medical devices division. The firm signed a $7.5 million agreement with Britain's Celltech Ltd. to produce a new generation of monoclonal antibodies. Researchers hoped to use the antibodies to deliver cancer drugs directly to affected sights in the body. The two firms planned to eliminate the parts of the antibodies not involved in delivering the drugs, improving their effectiveness and lessening allergic reactions.

Cyanamid moved into other high-tech areas it believed would grow in the future. In 1986 it bought 75 percent of Applied Solar Energy from Chesebrough-Pond for $38 million. At the same time, the firm was moving out of the lower-tech chemical businesses it had been engaged in for years. Its calcium carbonate business was sold to Iowa Limestone, while its dicalcium phosphate business went to Occidental Chemical and its lead chemical plant went to Cookson America. Cyanamid sold its phosphate rock processing plants to International Minerals and Chemical and its lead chemical business to Anzon Industries.

Since consumer products were less cyclical than its chemical business, the firm invested in expanding them, rolling out Pine-Sol spray cleaner and three new products in the Combat insecticide line.

As the restructuring progressed and the U.S. economy grew, profits for 1987 climbed to $275.6 million from $202.5 million in 1986. In 1988 Cyanamid formed a biotechnology research and development consortium with six firms to focus on fermentation technology. The following year the firm made its biggest investment yet in biotechnology when it acquired Praxis Biologics, a vaccine manufacturer, for $238 million in stock. The purchase brought Cyanamid products like Praxis' meningitis vaccine into the Cyanamid fold. Cyanamid was already putting its biotech expertise to work through work on herbicides and growth hormones for cows.

In 1990 the company took a major step toward making drugs and agricultural products its most important focus when it sold the product lines in its Shulton consumer products unit to various buyers. The Old Spice toiletries division was sold to Procter & Gamble for over $300 million. Clorox Co. bought Combat Insecticide and Pine-Sol cleanser for $465 million, a price many industry analysts believed to be an excellent deal for Cyanamid.

Many of the Shulton products were leading brands or had high name recognition, but with total sales of $600 million a year, the division was far too small to compete effectively against consumer products giants like Procter & Gamble. Shulton had an operating margin of about eight percent, while the medical division had a 17.5 percent margin. The medical division accounted for about 50 percent of 1990's $4.5 billion in sales, a healthy figure but still small compared to the medical divisions of rivals such as Bristol-Myers Squibb. Agricultural products sales were also booming, as the U.S. farm economy picked up and Cyanamid's newest insecticides and herbicides proved popular.

In 1991, with the U.S. chemical industry in a prolonged downturn, Cyanamid consolidated its chemicals business into a separate division called Cytec Industries, based in West Patterson, New Jersey. The company's chemicals business pulled in 1991 sales of $1.1 billion, with profits of about $30 million.

To help increase its presence in the drug market, Cyanamid bought 53.5 percent of Immunex Corp. in 1992. Immunex, a California biotech company, was strong in anti-cancer research, and Cyanamid soon combined Immunex's anti-cancer division with its own. Sales for 1992 reached a record of $5.27 billion, with revenue of $395 million.

In 1993 Albert J. Costello, a chemist with 36 years of experience at Cyanamid, was named to succeed Sella. At the same time, the Clinton administration's attack on drug prices cast new uncertainties on Cyanamid's strategy of emphasizing drug sales. Cyanamid and other drug companies reacted by sending lobbyists to Washington to persuade lawmakers they were not the villains behind rising medical costs.

With the 1993 announcement that it would sell Cytec to its shareholders, Cyanamid virtually finished its transformation from a chemical to a drug and agricultural products company. American Cyanamid now awaits the outcome of the health care reform struggle, which is certain to have a significant impact on the company.

Principal Subsidiaries: Acufex Microsurgical, Inc.; Cyanamid Inter-American Corp.; Cyanamid International Corp.; Cyanamid Metals Corp.; Cyanamid International Sales Corp.; Cyanamid Overseas Corp.; Davis & Geck, Inc.; Glendale Protective Technologies, Inc.; Jacqueline Cochran, Inc.; Lederle Parenterals, Inc.; Lederle Piperacillin, Inc.; La Prairie, Inc.; Shulton, Inc.; Toiletries, Inc. The company also lists subsidiaries in the following countries: Australia, Bermuda, Brazil, Canada, Costa Rica, France, India, Italy, Japan, Korea, Mexico, The Netherlands, Netherlands Antilles, Pakistan, Peru, Philippines, Portugal, Switzerland, United Kingdom, Venezuela, and West Germany.

Further Reading:

American Cyanamid Annual Report, Wayne, NJ: American Cyanamid, 1992.
McMurray, Scott, "American Cyanamid names Costello," *Wall Street Journal,* February 18, 1993.
Ramirez, Anthony, "P&G Agrees to Purchase Part of American Cyanamid," *Wall Street Journal,* June 14, 1990.
Roman, Monica, "Cyanamid's Rx: More Drugs, Fewer Consumer Products," *Business Week*, July 16, 1990.

—updated by Scott M. Lewis

American National Insurance Company

One Moody Plaza
Galveston, Texas 77550
U.S.A.
(409) 763-4661
Fax: (409) 766-6502

Public Company
Incorporated: 1905
Employees: 7,500
Sales: $1.32 billion
Stock Exchanges: NASDAQ
SICs: 6311 Life Insurance; 6321 Accident & Health
    Insurance; 66331 Fire, Marine & Casualty Insurance

American National Insurance Company is one of the 100 largest life insurance companies in the United States in terms of insurance in force, providing personal life insurance and related financial services to more than seven million policy owners in 49 states, the District of Columbia, Guam, Puerto Rico, and American Samoa. Directly and through its subsidiaries, American National offers a broad line of coverage, including individual life, health, and disability insurance; group life and health insurance; personal lines of property and casualty insurance; and credit insurance. The company also offers a variety of mutual funds.

American National Insurance Company traces its origins to the entrepreneurial spirit of William Lewis Moody, Jr., a Texan with diverse business interests who prospered in the cotton and banking industries during the latter part of the nineteenth century before turning his attention to insurance in the early 1900s. In 1904—at a time when the insurance industry was dominated by large east coast companies writing most of the life insurance policies in Texas—the 39-year-old Moody became president of American National Insurance and Trust Company of Houston and relocated that company's headquarters to Galveston, where Moody's family owned a bank.

The following year Moody organized and became president of American National Insurance Company, which then took over $800,000 worth of insurance policies covered by American National Insurance and Trust. Chartered as a life insurance company with $100,000 of capital and $20,000 surplus, Ameri-

can National Insurance Company began operating with ten employees in the original Moody Bank building in Galveston. Initially American National paid no dividends because Moody, who held controlling interest in American National, believed that during a company's early years all profits should go towards financing future growth.

Moody's plans for growth paid off, and within five years American National's assets had risen to more than $1 million. Between 1905 and 1910 American National's insurance in force also rose considerably—from $2.1 million to $22 million—and in 1911 the company paid its first dividend. The following year the company's home office workforce had expanded to 70 employees, while the number of American National field representatives totaled more than 700. In 1913, to accommodate its growing workforce, American National moved into a new 11-story office building, initially claiming two of its floors.

American National's premium revenues increased rapidly during the 1920s, with the deadly influenza epidemic of 1918–1919 fresh in the memories of potential customers. American National's growth was also fueled by a stream of acquisitions, and by 1928 the company had absorbed 27 other insurance companies and was employing 500 persons in its home office.

During the decade of the 1920s American National's assets increased over 400 percent—compared to the national average for insurance companies at the time of 160 percent—climbing from $7.3 million to $38 million, while insurance in force leaped from about $100 million to more than $600 million.

Largely as a result of its carefully selected investment portfolio, American National weathered the worst of the Great Depression without laying off employees or suffering annual losses. In 1933, with the nation's banks closed, American National continued to meet its financial obligations as policyholders paid small weekly premiums in cash.

Between 1930 and 1935—the worst years of the Depression for most businesses—American National's assets grew by 37 percent, while its capital and surplus funds nearly doubled, rising from $6 million to $11.5 million. During that same period American National's insurance in force declined only about three percent, or at half the rate of the insurance industry as a whole. The company's insurance sales picked up in 1936, and by 1939 American National had assets of $82 million while insurance in force totaled $777 million.

At the onset of World War II, the company's assets and sales grew dramatically during the early 1940s, and in 1942 American National became the first Texas insurance company to claim $100 million in assets. Two years later the company's insurance in force passed the billion dollar mark. During the war, American National was a significant financial contributor to the military efforts of the United States, purchasing about $33 million worth of government war bonds.

In 1950 American National made its first major diversification move, entering the accident insurance field through the purchase of Commonwealth Life and Accident Insurance Company of St. Louis, Missouri. That year the company also entered the health, hospitalization, and credit insurance fields through acquisitions of other companies operating out of St. Louis and

Dallas. By the end of 1950, American National had $2 billion worth of insurance in force.

In 1954, after nearly 50 years of running the company he founded, W. L. Moody died. Moody left behind a business legacy which included control of American National, as well as ownership of newspapers, hotels, and businesses operating in the fields of banking, printing, and ranching. Before his death, Moody's assets were used to establish a family trust, as well as the Moody Foundation, with the latter holding a controlling interest in American National as well as responsibility for future distribution of nonprofit grants. Moody's daughter, Mary Moody Northen, succeeded her father as president of American National. The company continued to prosper under Northen, and by 1959 American National's insurance in force had grown to $5 billion.

However, during the late 1950s the Moody Foundation's four-member board became deadlocked on numerous issues, with Shearn and Robert Moody, great-grandsons of W. L. Moody, opposing the two other board members. Texas state officials responded to the foundation feud by increasing the board's size and adding non-family members, beginning a long battle between Shearn Moody and non-family foundation trustees.

In 1961, Mary Moody Northen retired, and American National's presidency and chair passed out of the Moody family to W. L. Volger, executive vice-president since 1944. Two years later, R. A. Forbush took over the presidency of the company, whose assets which had grown to more $1 billion.

Under the leadership of Forbush and Volger, American National made several moves to expand the company's business activities. In March, 1967, American National acquired Securities Management & Research, Inc. (SM&R), the investment management company of Citadel, Inc.'s mutual fund. With the acquisition of SM&R, which became American National's first major wholly owned subsidiary, the company entered the investment oriented financial services field and began offering mutual funds under the name American National Growth Fund, Inc. One month after acquiring SM&R, American National also entered the savings and loan field by acquiring a majority interest in Southern California Financial Corporation, a holding company based in Los Angeles with control over Southern California Savings & Loan Association and $200 million in assets.

In December, 1967, American National—in another strategic acquisition—purchased controlling interest in Trans World Life Insurance Company of New York, the only state in which American National was not already licensed to operate. Between 1967 and 1968 American National also extended its operations beyond the United States and was licensed to operate in Western Europe.

The acquisitions and expansion moves helped boost revenues, and by 1968 American National had $10 billion worth of insurance in force. In 1969 Phil B. Noah, an executive vice president since 1962, became president and chairperson of American National. American National continued to expand its life insurance operations that year by acquiring Equitable Insurance Company of Texas, which became American National Life Insurance Company of Texas (ANTEX), American National's

second major subsidiary. During its initial years under American National's control, the operations of ANTEX were focused primarily in the areas of credit life and accident and health insurance.

By 1969 American National's home office work force had grown to more than 1,000 employees while field representatives included more than 7,000 agents and office workers. In response to the growth of its workforce, during the late 1960s American National began construction of its 20-story American National Tower in Galveston. The new headquarters was completed in 1971.

In 1970 Glendon E. Johnson was named president and assumed the additional duties of chairperson in 1973. That year American National created a third principal subsidiary, American National Property and Casualty Company (ANPAC), based in Springfield, Missouri. Designed to broaden the scope of coverage available to its customers, ANPAC was licensed in 40 states and chartered to handle multiple lines of insurance, including automobile and homeowners policies. Between 1973 and 1974 American National also expanded its activities in New York and acquired complete control of Trans World Life.

During the early 1970s Shearn Moody filed a lawsuit aimed at ousting Moody Foundation trustees accused of allowing American National to make large, low collateral loans to Las Vegas gambling casinos. Shearn Moody won the suit, and in 1973 his family regained control of the Moody Foundation. However, Shearn Moody's battles with the law and the foundation board continued into the next two decades. During the late 1980s he was convicted of mail fraud and improperly taking money from the Moody Foundation, and was subsequently voted off the foundation board. In 1990 the conviction was overturned.

In 1976 American National took over control of Standard Life & Accident Insurance Company, a unit of Standard Life Corporation based in Oklahoma. Standard Life & Accident Insurance, which had filed for bankruptcy and had been charged with securities fraud prior to being acquired, became American National's fourth major wholly owned subsidiary. The following year Orson C. Clay assumed the presidency of American National.

Late in 1980 American National sold Trans World Life to a Mutual of Omaha Insurance Company subsidiary. During this time American National created its fifth major subsidiary, American National General Insurance Company. American National General was chartered to handle most lines of property and casualty insurance and like ANPAC, was based in Springfield, Missouri.

In 1981 the subsidiary ANTEX discontinued its credit insurance operations and became active in the business of reinsuring ordinary life and individual annuity policies written by other companies. That year SM&R began offering its American National Money Market Fund. The following year the leadership of American National was returned to the Moody family when Robert Moody was named as chair of American National's board of directors. American National doubled the size of its credit insurance operations in 1986 when it acquired the operations of World Service Life Insurance Company of Colorado and two of its affiliates. American National's total assets climbed above the $3 billion mark in 1986, and by 1987 the company's insurance in force had grown to more than $25 billion.

In 1987 American National acquired the universal and life insurance operations of American Health & Life Insurance Company. The following year the company purchased three Primerica Corporation insurance companies—Pennsylvania Life Insurance Company, Executive Fund Life Insurance Company, and Trans Pacific Life Insurance Company—specializing in various kinds of individual life, accident, and health insurance.

Between 1985 and 1988 ANTEX wrote no new insurance policies, turning its attention to the acquisition of business through the assumption of reinsurance agreements, including two large blocks of individual life and annuity contracts which were acquired during this time. In 1989 ANTEX resumed writing individual life insurance polices and also began marketing individual accident and health insurance.

In 1989 American National's annual revenues exceeded $1 billion for the first time, and one year later the company's insurance in force topped $30 billion. Pushing sales upward during the early 1990s were acquisitions of life insurance business and a marketing diversification program. In 1990 ANTEX significantly expanded its direct policy writing activities after entering into the association group health market, with health, accident, and hospitalization coverage offered under an agreement with an outside sales agency and group polices sold through the National Business Association.

In 1990 American National also acquired American Security Life Insurance Company, a Texas life insurer licensed in 31 states. American Security Life was sold the following year after American National assumed the former company's insurance portfolio.

In 1991 Robert Moody assumed the additional duties of chief executive officer. That year the company expanded its investment fund sales channels when SM&R began a new marketing program and expanded its distribution outlets to include banks, savings and loan associations, and credit unions. In an effort to broaden its insurance sales force, in 1992 American National began recruiting non-career insurance agents, association groups, bank affiliates, auto dealers, and other groups to sell its insurance products.

In June, 1992, American National expanded its distribution channels further, paying $41.1 million to acquire Garden State Life Insurance Company, a direct-response insurance company based in New Jersey. Licensed to do business in 49 states, Garden State's activities included television and direct mail marketing of term life insurance policies with a face amount of $100,000 or more.

Largely as a result of its increasingly diversified sales and marketing efforts, in 1992 American National saw significant financial gains. In July, 1992, American National sold the insurance portfolio of Commonwealth Life and Accident Insurance Company for $14.2 million. Net income for the year rose $40 million to $168 million, while revenues increased better than ten percent, climbing from $1.1 billion to $1.3 billion. Assets exceeded the $5 billion mark for the first time in 1992, while life insurance in force swelled by almost 20 percent, climbing to more than $37 billion.

American National entered 1993 having paid annual dividends for 82 consecutive years, and raised its dividend 19 straight years. In terms of industry measuring sticks, in 1993 the company received A.M. Best Company's top rating (A-double-plus) and held $156 in assets for every $100 in liabilities, which was one of the better assets-to-liability ratios in the insurance field.

Moving towards the mid-1990s, the company planned to continue expansion efforts through the purchase of insurance companies and blocks of insurance business. As a result of its diversified sales force and marketing techniques which were substantially expanded in the early-1990s, American National expected to reap continued growth in revenues and assets, while it remained guardedly optimistic about the ramifications of proposed national health care programs on health insurance premiums and the company's overall operations.

Principal Subsidiaries: American National Life Insurance Company of Texas; Garden State Life Insurance Company; Standard Life and Accident Insurance Company; American National Property and Casualty Company; American National General Insurance Company; American Printing Company; ANREM Corporation; Securities Management & Research, Inc.

Further Reading:

The Archives: American National Insurance Company, Galveston Island, Texas, Galveston, Texas: American National Insurance Company.

Hackett, George, with Daniel Shapiro, "In Galveston, Moody's Blues: A Saga of Sex, Violence and Money, Texas style," *Newsweek,* February 2, 1987.

History of American National, Galveston, Texas: American National Insurance Company, 1975.

Norman, James R., "Texas Gothic," *Forbes,* October 22, 1990, pp. 345–349.

—Roger W. Rouland

American Residential Mortgage Corporation

11119 North Torrey Pines Road
La Jolla, California 92037-1009
U.S.A.
(619) 535-4900
Fax: (619) 535-4939

Wholly Owned Subsidiary of American Residential Holding
* Corporation*
Incorporated: 1983 as ICA Mortgage Corporation
Employees: 1,300
Sales: $5.50 billion
Stock Exchanges: NASDAQ
SICs: 6162 Mortgage Bankers and Loan Correspondents

American Residential Mortgage Corporation, a wholly owned
subsidiary of American Residential Holding Corporation, is one
of the leading residential mortgage lenders and servicers in the
United States. Founded in 1983, San Diego-based American
Residential grew to more than 50 branches in 17 states and
funded over 250,000 home loans by the end of its first decade.

American Residential began as the mortgage division of a large
California savings and loan, the Imperial Savings Association
(ISA). John M. Robbins, Jr., a ten-year veteran of the mortgage
banking industry, was chosen to develop and serve as president
of the subsidiary ICA Mortgage Corporation. The new division
experienced significant growth in its first few years. By 1986,
ICA Mortgage Corporation originated $4.2 billion in home
loans, and although 1986 was considered a banner year for most
mortgage companies, ICA Mortgage Corporation continued its
impressive performance over the following years, with originations totaling $3.7 billion in 1988 and $3.2 billion in 1989.

During this time, however, new ownership of the mortgage
corporation's parent company brought new priorities, including
a shift to high-yield, high-risk investments. Suddenly, the ICA
Mortgage Corporation seemed out of place. In late 1987, ISA
announced that it would sell the mortgage division to First
Nationwide Bank, a San Francisco-based savings and loan that
was part of the Ford Motor Company's financial services division. The sale was finalized in 1987, and while the purchase
price was not disclosed, it was estimated to be about $65
million. The following year, ICA Mortgage Corporation

changed its name to American Residential Mortgage Corporation to avoid confusion with its former parent, ISA.

First Nationwide's ownership of American Residential, however, was brief. In a 1991 interview in *Mortgage Banking,*
Robbins recalled that First Nationwide offered American Residential a buyout opportunity in August 1989. First Nationwide
wished to sell in order to focus on an internal mortgage operation and considered American Residential as representing a
duplication of efforts.

About the same time, the New York investment firm of Welsh,
Carson, Anderson, and Stowe began considering mortgage servicing as a potential investment. According to Janet Reilley
Hewitt in *Mortgage Banking,* ''Nothing in particular triggered
the interest other than the turmoil in the thrift industry.'' In
addition, several partners at Welsh Carson had backgrounds in
data processing and viewed mortgage servicing as a process that
would allow them to increase their technology in this field.
Thomas E. McInerney, general partner at Welsh Carson, noted
in *Mortgage Banking* that American Residential's firm commitment to technology as an essential part of the business, as
demonstrated in a state-of-the-art computer system, was an appealing aspect of the company. In May 1990, the senior management of American Residential and Welsh Carson bought
American Residential from First Nationwide for an undisclosed
price. Welsh Carson became the majority investor, and Robbins
remained as president and CEO. According to McInerney in
Mortgage Banking, Robbins and his managers continued to run
the company; for his part, Robbins reflected that becoming an
owner ''tends to make decision making more conservative.''

Following the buyout, American Residential faced some difficulties. First Nationwide had retained servicing rights to American Residential's loans, and Robbins noted in the *San Diego
Business Journal* that the payroll was sometimes hard to meet.
Low interest rates helped American Residential by boosting
business. More significant, however, was the ability of the management team, most of whom had been together since the early
days as an ISA subsidiary, to move American Residential pro-
ductively through yet another transformation.

In November 1990, American Residential successfully negotiated a warehouse line (a credit line to fund originations) from
six of the nation's largest banks. According to *Mortgage Banking,* American Residential faced quite a challenge: ''In the
midst of one of the worst credit crunches in recent history, in the
midst of a significant housing slump, there probably could not
have been a tougher time to be a new, independent, mortgage
banking company looking for a warehouse line.'' Despite these
difficult circumstances, six banks, including The First National
Bank of Chicago and The Bank of New York, established a
credit line of $270 million to fund originations for American
Residential.

After securing funds for originations, American Residential
turned to establishing a servicing portfolio to replace the one it
lost when it was sold by First Nationwide. In April of 1991, the
corporation entered into an agreement to purchase loan servicing contracts for $3.4 billion in loans from Resolution Trust
Corporation (RTC), the savings and loan liquidator. Ironically,
the loan servicing contracts of came from ISA, then under RTC

conservatorship. As part of the arrangement, American Residential received contracts as well as 175 employees. The deal was implemented in several phases, continuing into 1992.

American Residential also won a contract to assist with RTC auctions of properties from the real estate portfolios of failed savings and loans to prequalified, targeted low- to middle-income households. In competitive bidding drawing more than three thousand applicants, American Residential was one of only two companies selected for national contracts. The company provides a range of functions for customers, including aiding the loan application process, prequalifying buyers, analyzing property, and coordinating the closing. In addition, American Residential counsels prospective home buyers on a number of issues regarding home ownership, including types of loans, insurance, taxes, the qualifying process, and the importance of maintaining a good credit history. American Residential's numerous regional branches enabled the corporation to provide staff in many of the cities in which auctions were held. Jim Gilcrest, executive vice president of American Residential, explained in the *San Diego Daily Transcript* that American Residential's involvement in this program reflected a long standing philosophy of the company, that of promoting home ownership among a wide range of consumers: "This is an exciting program that links business practicality with social purpose. We're proud to be part of a project team that will make the dream of homeownership a reality for thousands of Americans."

The year 1992 was remarkable for American Residential. Originations totaled $5.5 billion, up from $2.9 billion in 1991, while the company expanded its service portfolio to $9.7 billion. In addition, net income was increased by 49 percent.

American Residential planned an initial public offering (IPO) of its stock in March of 1992. Because a number of other IPOs were on the market at that time, however, the corporation delayed its stock offering until August. The sale raised more than $37 million, which was used to expand the company's mortgage origination capabilities and to acquire additional loan servicing portfolios. According to the company, nearly every employee of American Residential owned stock in 1992.

American Residential Mortgage Corporation, which sold additional shares of stock in early 1993, was poised to continue its growth through the 1990s, demonstrating several strengths. Having numerous offices across the country allowed American Residential to withstand regional slumps. Robbins was regarded as an innovative leader who spearheaded the idea for private ownership. And the management team, whose style and strategies have been praised in *Mortgage Banking,* have clearly weathered difficult changes in the past and seem ready to face challenges in the future.

Further Reading:

American Residential Holding Corporation Annual Report, La Jolla, CA: American Residential Holding Corporation, 1992.
Bogan, Christopher, and John Robbins, "Steal This Idea," *Mortgage Banking,* December 1992, pp. 55–61.
" 'Corporate Profiles': American Residential." *San Diego Daily Transcript,* January 11, 1993, p. C9.
Hewitt, Jane Reilley, "A New Venture," *Mortgage Banking,* May 1991, pp. 10–18.
Hock, Sandy, "American Residential to Buy Imperial Mortgage Services." *San Diego Business Journal,* May 6, 1991, 4; "Robbins Helps Mortgage Company Rise from the Ashes." *San Diego Business Journal,* August 19, 1991, p. 10; "American Residential Completes Second Phase of RTC Purchases," *San Diego Business Journal,* December 9, 1991, p. 14; "American Residential Postpones Its IPO: Launch Depends on Market." *San Diego Business Journal,* May 18, 1992, p. 3.
"La Jolla Firm to Underwrite Loans for RTC-Auctioned Homes." *San Diego Daily Transcript,* January 22, 1992, p. B1.

—Michelle L. McClellan

Amoskeag Company

4500 Prudential Center
Boston, Massachusetts 02199-4599
U.S.A.
(617) 262-4000
Fax: (617) 262-9625

Public Company
Incorporated: July 1, 1831 as the Amoskeag Manufacturing
    Company
Employees: 17,300
Sales: $1.25 billion (1992)
Stock Exchanges: NASDAQ
SICs: 2211 Broadwoven Fabric Mills—Cotton; 2221
    Broadwoven Fabric Mills—Manmade Fiber and Silk; 2273
    Carpets and Rugs; 2261 Finishers of Broadwoven Fabrics
    of Cotton; 2262 Finishers of Broadwoven Fabrics of
    Manmade Fiber & Silk; 4011 Railroads—Line-Haul
    Operating

Amoskeag Company is a holding and operating company, whose main revenue (98 percent) is derived from its control of approximately 81 percent of the common shares of Fieldcrest Cannon, Inc. In an unusual twist, Fieldcrest Cannon and Amoskeag came to an agreement in mid-1993 to merge the two companies and allow a Fieldcrest Cannon subsidiary to purchase all of Amoskeag's outstanding stock for $40 per share. This would, in turn, make Amoskeag a wholly owned subsidiary of Fieldcrest Cannon. Although Amoskeag was incorporated in its present form in 1965, its roots go back to the end of the 18th century. When it was incorporated in 1831, the Amoskeag Manufacturing Company was already an important player in the American Industrial Revolution.

In 1793 Judge Samuel Blodgett began constructing locks and canals on the Merrimack River just south of Concord, New Hampshire, at the Amoskeag Falls to utilize the river's power to operate textile mills. The first actual mill was built on the site in 1804 by Benjamin Pritchett. This was taken over by the Amoskeag Cotton and Wool Manufactory in 1810. Several other mills were built around that time, but the entire project foundered in 1825, partly because of its inaccessibility to markets.

In 1822 Francis Cabot Lowell effectively harnessed the Merrimack at Lowell, Massachusetts. Using plans he had brought back from Manchester, England, he and his partners turned Lowell into the cutting-edge textile manufacturing town in the United States. The 25-mile Middlesex Canal—actually completed in 1804—connected Lowell with the port city of Boston. These events in Lowell, just a few miles downstream from Amoskeag, helped reenergize the Amoskeag undertaking. Several investors from Boston took over the mills in 1825, and Samuel Slater applied the technology he had learned in Manchester to the mills. By 1831 the ownership of the mills was reorganized, and the Amoskeag Manufacturing Company was incorporated on July 1 of that year. Control of the mills remained in Boston, as was true of almost all the large textile mills in New England. The directorates interlocked to a remarkable degree; directors of seemingly competing mills sat on each other's boards.

Manufacturing at Amoskeag was not restricted to textiles, although that was their main business. Guns and rifles, locomotives, fire engines, and even the rotating gun turret for the Civil War ironclad *Monitor* were manufactured there. Amoskeag's manpower needs increased to the point that starting about 1838, the company built a company town, Manchester, New Hampshire, on the site. By the 1880s, the Amoskeag textile mills were the largest in the world, extending one and one half miles on both sides of the Merrimack. The mills were also very profitable. When Thomas Jefferson Coolidge became treasurer in 1876, he reported to the shareholders that ''you have received in dividends for forty-two years an average of 11 per cent a year, and if to that is added the increase of the quick capital, the Company has earned 15 per cent per annum, without taking into consideration the money spent on the plant.'' Coolidge, who was treasurer of the company for a total of 16 years between 1876 and 1898, went on to become president of the board of directors until 1911. He is credited with more than tripling Amoskeag's industrial capacity. In 1883 there were 171,000 spindles used in cloth production; by 1912 that number had risen to nearly 670,000. The total output at that time came to about 470 miles of cloth per day.

From about 1906 on, much of the day-to-day direction of the company was placed in the hands of Frederic C. Dumaine, who was treasurer of the company until 1939 and then served as president from 1939 to 1946. He was also chairman of the board from 1946 until his death in 1951. Dumaine was a financial strategist who guided Amoskeag through the economic downturn that hit the textile industry around 1925 and through the Depression, including the eventual closing of the mills. In 1939 Dumaine's son, F. C. ''Buck'' Dumaine, replaced his father as treasurer. Buck had started work at the mills in 1914 and retired from his position as director of Amoskeag in 1992.

With the exception of a few years before the United States' entry into World War I, Amoskeag continued to be extremely profitable. During the war, it was a major supplier of uniforms, barracks bags, and other textiles to the military. Immediately after the war, company income soared, due to pent-up consumer demand and steep price increases. The mills employed almost 18,000 workers in 1921, and the company piled up sizable financial reserves during this period. In the mid-1920s, however, there was a marked decline in sales, particularly of ginghams—an Amoskeag mainstay. This decline affected mills throughout New England, although companies in the South continued to see modest gains in output. Dumaine foresaw a long period of decline and reported his prediction to the directors. The company realized that it could either use its reserves to ride out hard times or begin the painful process of closing the mills.

Under Dumaine's leadership, Amoskeag Manufacturing Company reorganized as a holding company, or trust, and changed its name to Amoskeag Company in 1925. The new company established a trust, Amoskeag Manufacturing Company, to operate the mills. According to economist Alan R. Sweezy in a 1938 issue of *Quarterly Journal of Economics,* a large part of the reserves that had been built up over the years were then transferred to the holding company and were withheld from operation. The mills had just enough money to operate, but there were no funds for maintenance of the plant and little for upkeep and replacement of machinery. Spare parts were taken from machines that had been shut down. Gross sales slid from $33 million in 1926 to $10.2 million in 1932, the worst year of the Depression. At the same time, Amoskeag was able to get tax abatements from a panicked Manchester, and the company cut wages until they almost matched those in Southern textile mills. By 1935, with losses mounting, the trustees recommended that the mills be liquidated.

A bankruptcy court in Boston decreed that the liquidation could take place. Arthur Black, the master appointed by the federal court to oversee the bankruptcy proceedings, noted, "The Trust was rich and had no creditors. It was under no obligation to stand idly by while the accumulation of a hundred years was eaten up in a losing operation. It was right to set the plant on its own legs to win or lose. It was right to withdraw $18,000,000 from the risks of mill operation." Nonetheless, several criticisms were leveled at the Amoskeag Company in the aftermath of its pullout. According to critics, the company refused to change with the times. While gingham was going out of style, Amoskeag clung to this traditional part of its line. The possibility of moving production into sheets and bedding was turned down. In addition, employees who demonstrated that the factories could easily expand its small rayon production and regain profitability were ignored.

The effects of the Amoskeag pullout would have been devastating to the economy of Manchester, and all of southern New Hampshire, therefore business leaders and citizens of the city collected $5 million in pledges to buy the factories in late 1936. The slogan of their door-to-door campaign was "say it with subscriptions." Despite the poor condition of the mills, newly formed Amoskeag Industries, Inc. attracted diverse industries to the factories, which were 60 percent leased by September, 1939. According to Tamara K. Hareven in her book *Amoskeag: Life and Work in an American Factory City,* until the mills shut down, Manchester had been in many ways a company town. Virtually no new industry could be established in the city without Amoskeag's cooperation since the company controlled most of the industrial land. Control over the city's economic life also gave it influence over politics; company officials and managers often served as aldermen.

Even though Amoskeag Company had exited the textile business, it was cash rich. Added to the money already in Amoskeag Company, there was the $5 million from the sale of the mills. Beginning in the late-1940s and 1950s, Amoskeag Company

began to invest in transportation, particularly railroads. The company's aim during that period was to consolidate the fragmented New England railroad system. Investments included the Bangor and Aroostook Railroad Company; the Boston and Maine; the Delaware and Hudson; the Maine Central; and the New York, New Haven, and Hartford railroads. Amoskeag also invested in the Middlesex and Boston Street Railway, the Springfield Street Railway, and the Worcester Bus Company. Because of competition from trucking and the deindustrialization of New England, the plan to consolidate railroads in the region proved unrealistic. Most of Amoskeag's rolling assets were sold up until 1981 when it divested itself of the Springfield operation.

Only Bangor and Aroostook Railroad Company, of which the company took control in 1969, was still owned by Amoskeag in the mid-1990s. The railroad, founded in 1891, owns and operates about 420 miles of road running north from Searsport to Madawaska on the Canadian border. It mainly services lumber, paper, and pulp mills in the area. The line does not transport passengers. In 1992 its revenues, including warehousing and distribution business of its subsidiary, Logistics Management Systems, Inc., came to $27.5 million.

Amoskeag also owned Avis, Inc. from 1958 to 1965 and Fanny Farmer from 1962 to 1984. In 1953 Amoskeag bought Fieldcrest Mills from Marshall Field & Co., marking its reentry into the textile business, and in 1965 Amoskeag Company became incorporated under Delaware law. By the early 1990s, Fieldcrest Cannon (Cannon Mills were acquired in 1986) accounted for 98 percent of Amoskeag Company's sales revenues. However, because sales of bedding and related products and carpeting are sensitive to economic conditions, the company experienced decreased revenues in three out of five years from 1987 to 1992. Most of Fieldcrest Cannon's customers are department, chain, specialty, and other stores dealing in domestic goods. In 1992 Wal-Mart Stores, Inc. was Fieldcrest Cannon's largest single customer, accounting for about 13 percent of sales. Of the company's 17,300 employees, 16,950 work for Fieldcrest Cannon. While Amoskeag Company lacks diversity, Fieldcrest Cannon, its main component, has proved profitable. There is no apparent reason why that should not continue to be the case. Both companies should benefit from their forthcoming reversed relationship.

Principal Subsidiaries: Fieldcrest Cannon, Inc. (81%); Bangor and Aroostook Railroad Company; Logistics Management Systems, Inc.

Further Reading:

"Amoskeag Comeback," *Business Week,* September 2, 1939, p. 21.
"Amoskeag: Court Imposes Death Sentence on Huge Textile Plant," *Newsweek,* August 1, 1936, p. 30.
Hareven, Tamara K., and Randolph Langenbach, *Amoskeag: Life and Work in an American Factory City,* New York: Pantheon, 1978.
One Hundred Fiftieth Annual Report: 1831–1981, Boston: Amoskeag Company, 1981.
"Payroll Rescue," *Business Week,* April 17, 1937, p. 29.
Sweezy, Alan R., "The Amoskeag Manufacturing Company," *Quarterly Journal of Economics,* May 1938, pp. 473–512.
"Taps for Amoskeag," *Business Week,* July 25, 1936, p. 36.

—Kenneth F. Kronenberg

Apogee Enterprises, Inc.

7900 Xerxes Avenue South, Suite 1800
Bloomington, Minnesota 55431-1159
U.S.A.
(612) 835-1874
Fax: (612) 835-3196

Public Company
Incorporated: 1949 as Harmon Glass Company, Inc.
Employees: 5,358
Sales: $572.45 million
Stock Exchanges: NASDAQ
SICs: 1793 Glass and Glazing Work; 3211 Flat Glass; 3231
    Products of Purchased Glass; 3479 Metal Coating and
    Allied Services; 7536 Automotive Glass Replacement
    Shops

A leader in glass fabrication and installation, Apogee Enterprises, Inc. consists of four divisions—Commercial Construction, Window Fabrication, Glass Fabrication, and Installation and Distribution—that are run almost as autonomous businesses. This intrapreneurial, laissez-faire structure, which is further defined by 22 operating units and more than 200 individual profit centers, has been the shaping force for the company since its inception in 1949 as an auto glass replacement business. Through its 237 Harmon Glass stores spread over 35 states, Apogee's longstanding Installation division ranks as the nation's second largest retail chain of automotive glass service centers; the division, which posted $165 million in sales for fiscal 1993, is strengthened by a nationwide Harmon Glass Network that allows for further geographic expansion. However, Apogee is perhaps better known for its 20-year-old Commercial Construction Division, which garnered $248 million in 1993 revenues. Since 1987, this division, led by Harmon Contract, has ranked as the number one domestic designer and installer of skyscraper curtainwalls (the aluminum framing system that holds high-performance glass in place). Other important units of Apogee include Glass Fabrication's Viracon, the nation's largest manufacturer of architectural glass, and Window Fabrication's Wausau Metals, a key provider of custom windows to commercial and institutional markets.

Apogee traces its origins to July 1949, when a truck driver and part-time glass installer founded the Harmon Glass Company in Minneapolis by convincing another installer and a used car salesman to pool $3,000 and launch their own service business. The idea was the brainchild of Harold Burrows, who reasoned that if the businesses to which he delivered windshields were too busy to answer their phones, there must be room in the market for some competition. Burrows, was right. Harmon kept busy by day replacing windshields for used car dealers and, by night, installing protective screens, or implosion plates, for television sets using the same auto glass supplied by its wholesalers. First-year sales for the company totaled a modest, but respectable $50,000. The partners found they could increase profits for the television business after persuading one of their suppliers to omit the manufacturing logo on the perimeter of its shields, thus saving Harmon the time and waste involved in cutting and scrapping this otherwise good glass. The supplier's only counter request was that each new order be prepaid. Lacking the necessary cash, the three sought financing early in 1950 from the St. Paul lawyer who had incorporated the business and his partner, Russ Baumgardner.

Although he described himself as a young, struggling lawyer, Baumgardner nonetheless could afford the $10,000 required by the original partners. More importantly, Baumgardner possessed sound money management skills as well as an interest in fledgling enterprises, in part the result of post-law school employment with his father, the owner of a Washington, D.C.-based investment company. Baumgardner quickly became engrossed in Harmon Glass and was placed on the payroll for a token $20-a-week salary. His enjoyment was cut short, however, when he learned that one of the partners, the former car salesman, was embezzling from the company. Nearly $7,000 was missing; there was literally no equity left. The crisis was solved when Baumgardner and the other two partners supplied $5,000 in emergency cash and forced the salesman to relinquish his company stock.

Shortly thereafter, Burrows's sole remaining partner died. To salvage the company, Baumgardner purchased the stock of both departed partners and thereby obtained 70 percent ownership. He then decided that because Burrows performed 90 percent of the work for Harmon Glass, a 30 percent stake was unfair, and so sold Burrows, another 20 percent of the business for $100. The now legendary story was later analyzed in the company history, entitled *Windows of Opportunity*: "Perhaps he did it unwittingly, but in making the offer to Burrows, Baumgardner established the pattern for what would become one of the company's most enduring values: providing employees with a sense of ownership in their work, one of the most important underpinnings to the entrepreneurial verve that later became a company hallmark." Inevitably, Baumgardner was forced to choose between what he expected to be a mediocre law career and what he knew to be the difficult management of a promising, but nevertheless uncertain business. Initially, he chose the former, until Burrows, pleaded with him to remain a partner for at least another year. By 1953, Baumgardner's ultimate decision had already begun to prove a wise one. During that year, Detroit automakers converted to curved windshields that, among other things, created storage problems for traditional wholesalers but opened opportunities for quick-acting retailers prepared to branch into wholesaling. Through an exclusive shipping arrangement with Shatterproof Glass of Detroit, Harmon Glass soon had control of 40 percent of new windshield supply in Minnesota (the wholesaling venture eventually became a subsidiary named The Glass Depot). Ten years later, because of such coups and because of a strong customer service commitment, Baumgardner and Burrows, owned a thriving business.

Reflecting on this early period, Baumgardner noted, "We became mavericks in the glass business. The industry was a little slow when it came to recognizing opportunity, so we started looking for niches in the market that nobody else wanted.'' In July 1955, the company launched Hiawatha Glass to perform commercial window glazing. The venture proved particularly successful when it began to focus on producing edged glass for display cases and store counters, eventually becoming the nation's largest manufacturer in this niche market. By the end of the decade, Harmon and its subsidiaries had blossomed into a million dollar growth company with 60 employees.

Following Burrows's surprise retirement in 1963, Baumgardner invited three valued executives—Don Goldfus, Larry Niederhofer, and Don Eichler—to become principal shareholders with him, going so far as to arrange loans for each of them to purchase the company stock. The 1960s proved to be a period of rapid expansion for the company. In 1966, Harmon Glass branched beyond Minnesota for the first time, opening a store in Des Moines, Iowa. This move came upon the heels of the purchase of Gopher Glass Company, which raised Harmon's total Twin Cities outlets to nine.

Baumgardner's management of the company had always been in keeping with his overall business philosophy: invest employees with responsibility and trust, allow them room to grow and learn from their mistakes, refrain from interfering, and expect good results in the long run. Yet, by the mid-1960s, the rapid growth of the company had caused organizational problems that effectively thwarted the easy implementation of this philosophy. Realizing this, Baumgardner decided to remodel his company, which now performed a variety of services, after Minnesota's largest and arguably most dynamic public company, 3M. By October 1967 he instituted a divisional organization defined by distinct profit centers that truly placed decision-making in the hands of those most attuned to the customers and the markets. In the winter of 1968, Apogee (a name that originated with an investment club to which Baumgardner once belonged and a term suggestive of the space age) was formed as a holding company to coordinate operations. Later that year, Apogee learned that a Wausau, Wisconsin, manufacturer of custom windows was up for sale for $2 million. Cash-poor and with 1967 sales of just $2.7 million, Apogee was an unlikely buyer. Yet, the opportunity for growth was tempting, and Niederhofer and Baumgardner negotiated a deal that amounted to a leveraged buyout in an era when such creative financing was extremely rare. The company closed the decade on an ambitious note by launching Viracon, one of the first regional glass fabricators for architectural and automotive markets. Groundbreaking for the $1.2 million-facility was begun in April 1970 near Owatonna, Minnesota.

By 1971, with five-year average increases in revenues and earnings of 34 percent and 45 percent, respectively, Apogee represented a particularly hot prospect for an initial stock offering. The company, therefore, went public in June with 190,000 shares of over-the-counter (OTC) stock that netted better than $1.9 million for the company. Unfortunately for short-term investors, Apogee stock proceeded to drop by more than 75 percent; almost seven years transpired before the original selling price was surpassed. Generally falling OTC prices and a string of poor earnings reports reflective of price-cutting in the auto glass installation industry contributed to the stock's dismal performance. However, Baumgardner turned the severe downswing, which had little relation to Apogee's future prospects, into a benefit for his employees by establishing a stock purchasing incentive program in 1973.

Also that year an event even more important to the company's development took place. This was the hiring of contract glazing expert Gerald Anderson to redirect the company's stagnant contract unit, responsible for installing glass and window frames for new construction projects. Prior to Anderson's hiring, Apogee's largest contract project, handled through Harmon Glass, was a $40,000 job. A $350,000 project had been bid around the time of his arrival, but there was little hope of being awarded the contract, for Harmon's reputation was still limited largely to auto installation. Anderson succeeded in both landing and fulfilling the major project at a profit. Furthermore, he went on to win a $750,000 office center contract from Dayton Hudson Corporation in 1973 by offering a full-service bid for not only the glazing, but the curtainwall as well as certain design and engineering aspects. In so doing, he outshone his glazing competitors, who had theretofore restricted themselves to glass production and installation. The contract glazing unit grew rapidly under Anderson's direction—pre-tax profits and sales doubled in 1974 and 1975—and soon distinguished itself from Harmon Glass with the name Harmon Contract. Its strong performance helped compensate for highly unusual employee theft, bad debt, and mafia related problems of some of Apogee's Florida auto outlets, problems that resulted in losses of at least $700,000. Later, a major turnaround of the Florida operations helped the unit become one of Apogee's most successful to date.

Other important developments of the 1970s included Wausau Metals' acquisition of Milco Specialties, a Michigan manufacturer of double-hung and sliding windows. Under Wausau's wing, Milco expanded its $35,000 backlog to $1 million in the first year by expanding its offering to eight separate window lines. Shortly thereafter, Wausau expanded one of its niche businesses, specialty windows for hospitals, by acquiring a bankrupt venetian blind-maker; this Wausau unit, named Nanik Venetian Blind, has blossomed into a four-company window coverings group that has consistently outperformed most of Apogee's other business units. In 1979, Wausau itself captured special attention by landing its largest contract ever, a window contract for AT&T's world headquarters in New York.

By the early 1980s, Apogee had completed a fundamental shift from a simple auto glass business, which at that time represented slightly over ten percent of revenue, to a well-rounded glass competitor in a number of lucrative markets. Window fabrication for a booming office construction industry was Apogee's most obvious source of momentum, for it then provided roughly half of all corporate earnings on just one-fourth of total sales. Closely related to this division's success was the steadily rising Commercial Construction division. Fueling both divisions—aside from the construction boom—was the 1980 acquisition of Interstate Glass of South Bend, Indiana, for $3.6

million. Interstate's $7 million in sales as a multiservice provider, as well as its proximity to Chicago, accelerated Harmon Contract's transformation from a regional to a national curtainwall concern. Within the decade, Harmon opened offices in 15 major U.S. cities. The core Harmon strategy was to penetrate markets where construction was strong while investing little in overhead; when these markets later fizzled, Harmon could then retreat and fortify elsewhere, with minimal adverse effect. Consequently, sales grew at rates regularly in excess of 30 percent.

The pursuit of sales volume, in fact, became the chief goal of several regional managers, leading to low-margin contracts and the dangerous sacrifice of profits. The results of this trend were reflected in uncharacteristically low division earnings in 1984 and 1985. A reorientation towards less volume and higher margins, along with an emphasis on expanded design and engineering services for its clientele, helped Harmon Contract's operating income rebound by 60 percent (on a 19 percent increase in sales) in fiscal 1986. Within the next two years, Harmon had not only become Apogee's largest and most thriving business, it had also succeeded in becoming the nation's largest curtainwall contractor, this despite only a four percent share of the curtainwall market. Apogee celebrated its fortieth anniversary on a high note, boasting sales and earnings growth rates, compounded since the beginning, of 26 percent and 28 percent, respectively.

After an illustrious career, Baumgardner retired in 1988, and Donald Goldfus, a veteran manager, was installed as the new chairperson and CEO. Goldfus soon focused on creating a greater international presence for Apogee; his opening of a Harmon Contract office in London, expected to be the reigning commercial construction market of the 1990s, augured well for the company's future, as did aggressive actions on other Apogee fronts, including the rapid widening, via acquisitions, of the auto glass business.

Although the early 1990s were less than satisfying for the company because of the economic recession (earnings were cut almost in half from 1991 to 1992, and were then halved again in 1993), Apogee has maintained strong positions in all of its markets. Furthermore, it has continued to seek out new opportunities to augment its commercial construction work through such recent market entries as detention and security systems for convenience stores, military bases, corporate offices, and prisons. After its July 1991 acquisition of Norment Industries—a leading contractor in the security industry, with 1990 revenues of $39 million—Apogee acquired two related businesses, Airteq and EMSS. With first-quarter earnings tripling and order backlogs up by 47 percent, fiscal 1994 promised to be a turn-

around year for the company. Perhaps Goldfus and Anderson were fittingly optimistic, then, when in their 1993 report they chose to move beyond a dour analysis of the "raw numbers" to an inspiring roundtable discussion of Apogee's numerous accomplishments and strengths, practically all of which hearken back to Baumgardner's original vision: employee ownership and unparalleled service.

Principal Subsidiaries: Apogee Sales Corporation; Empire State Auto & Plate Glass, Inc. (66.7%); Glass & Metal Distributors, Inc.; Glass Depot, Inc.; Harmon Contract U.K., Ltd.; Harmon Glass Co.; Harmon Glass of Florida, Inc.; Harmon Glass of Indiana, Inc.; Marcon Coatings, Inc. (50%); Norshield Corporation; Randell Thomas Glass Co., Inc. (55%); Savanna Glass Co. (67%); Viracon/Curvlite Inc.; Viratec Thin Films Inc.; Viratec True Vue, Inc.; Wausau Metals Corporation; W.S.A., Inc.; W.S.A. Europe, Inc.

Further Reading:

"Apogee Earnings $918,000 for Quarter," *Star Tribune,* June 23, 1993, p. 5D.
"Apogee Expects Break-Even Results," *Star Tribune,* June 12, 1992, p. 4D.
"Apogee Expects Reduced Earnings," *Star Tribune,* January 29, 1993, p. 3D.
"Apogee's Pathway to Growth," *Mergers & Acquisitions,* March-April 1989, p. 198.
Cook, James, "The Niche-Seeker," *Forbes,* June 13, 1988, p. 74.
Gross, Steve, "To Other Firms, Apogee Profits Panefully High," *Star Tribune,* January 9, 1983, pp. 1D, 7D.
Hammond, Ruth, "Glass Appeal: Why Apogee Enterprises Is All It's Cracked up to Be," *Corporate Report Minnesota,* June 1985, pp. 98–108.
Meyers, Mike, "Apogee Conducts a Winning Score," *Star Tribune,* July 21, 1988, pp. 1D, 5D.
Moskal, Brian S., "The No-Klutz Theory," *Industry Week,* December 12, 1983, pp. 19–20.
Rutigliano, Anthony J., "Apogee: Lets Managers Grow Their Own Businesses," *Management Review,* September 1987, pp. 28–33.
Saunders, Laura, "Making and Keeping Niches," *Forbes,* December 6, 1982, pp. 116, 120.
Smith, Geoffrey, "Feasting on Crumbs," *Forbes,* December 24, 1979, pp. 61–63.
Troxell, Thomas N., Jr., "Rebuilding Profits: Apogee Gains from Stress on Design, Not Cost," *Barron's,* January 20, 1986, pp. 49–50.
Youngblood, Dick, "Clear Opportunity: Apogee's Reputation for Quality Pushes up Its Earnings as Key Market Declines," *Star Tribune,* May 15, 1988, pp. 1–2D.
——, "Apogee Tightens Its Belt in a Tougher Market," *Star Tribune,* May 8, 1991, pp. 1–2D.

—Jay P. Pederson

Arvin Industries, Inc.

One Noblitt Plaza
Box 3000
Columbus, Indiana 47202-3000
U.S.A.
(812) 379-3000
Fax: (812) 379-3688

Public Company
Incorporated: 1921 as Indianapolis Pump and Tube
    Company
Employees: 16,002
Sales: $1.89 billion
Stock Exchanges: New York Midwest
SICs: 3714 Motor Vehicle Parts and Accessories; 3479 Metal
    Coating and Allied Services; 8734 Testing Laboratories;
    3355 Aluminum Rolling and Drawing

Arvin Industries, Inc. is an international manufacturing company supplying automotive parts and related products and services in more than 100 countries. Arvin is the world's leading independent producer of automotive exhaust systems and catalytic converters as well as a major manufacturer of ride control products. The company also produces tire valves, pressure gauges, and related products.

Arvin traces its roots to an Indiana partnership formed in 1919 to produce tire pumps. After a frustrating experience fixing a flat tire, Quintin G. Noblitt, a mechanical engineer and inventor, told a former business colleague, Frank H. Sparks, that he could make a reliable tire pump if Sparks could sell it. Sparks said he could, and the Indianapolis Air Pump Company—the earliest predecessor of Arvin Industries—was born.

Noblitt recruited a third partner, Albert G. Redmond, to oversee the company's production of tire pumps, and the three partners each agreed to contribute $1,000 in initial capital. The company then rented an empty grocery storm room for $10 month, supplying a make-shift factory with second-hand machinery. By the end of its first year, the partnership showed a profit of more than $10,000.

The company's eventual name arose from its brief relationship with Richard Hood Arvin, a former arms and ammunition salesman who had invented a heating device for Ford automobiles. In 1920 Arvin, who had applied for patents for his heater but

lacked the capital to manufacture it, offered his product to Indianapolis Air Pump. Arvin granted the young company exclusive marketing rights for his heater, and in return, Indianapolis Air Pump agreed to manufacture it. As a result, the Arvin Heater Company was formed in 1920 with Arvin, Noblitt, Sparks, and Redmond becoming sole stockholders.

In 1921 Indianapolis Air Pump leaped into the national arena when Sparks secured a contract to produce tire pumps for Ford Motor Company. That same year the company began experimenting with a tube manufacturing process that led to a company name change in December of 1921, when the partnership was incorporated as the Indianapolis Pump and Tube Company. Noblitt was named president, and Sparks was appointed secretary of the new corporation, which established headquarters in Indianapolis.

In the spring of 1922 Ford Motor Company informed Sparks that it was planning to manufacture its own tire pumps, and soon afterward Redmond sold his interest in Indianapolis Pump and Tube to his two partners. Arvin sold his stake in Arvin Heater Company to Noblitt and Sparks, and the heater company was consolidated into Indianapolis Pump and Tube. That same year the company secured a contract to provide tire pumps for Chevrolet, and that same year Ford, after a short-lived attempt to manufacture its own tire pumps, returned its business to Indianapolis Pump & Tube. With sales expanding, in 1923 the company constructed its first new factory in Greenwood, Indiana, and closed its manufacturing facilities in Indianapolis. As more gas stations began offering free air during the early 1920s, the company's tire pump business began to suffer. In response, it began diversification efforts and in 1924 introduced a new foot accelerator pedal for automobiles and a cast-iron heater for Ford, Chevrolet, and Dodge vehicles.

Also that year, Indianapolis Pump and Tube purchased the Dan Patch Novelty Company of Connerville, Indiana, producers of a line of wheeled toys. Noblitt quickly developed a new ball bearing wheel for the Dan Patch coaster wagon, while production of most other toy products was discontinued. In 1925 the company separated its heater business from its tube operations and established a plant in Columbus to produce metal heaters, cast-iron manifold heaters, and a new product, automobile jacks. Tire pumps and tubing production was isolated in Greenwood, while coaster wagon production remained at Connerville until the company purchased a building in Seymour, Indiana, and moved its toy manufacturing operations there.

In 1927 the Indianapolis Pump and Tube's name was changed to Noblitt-Sparks Industries, Inc. By that time Arvin hot-air heaters were being manufactured for every make of car on the market. In 1928 Noblitt-Sparks installed its first nickel-plating units in its Columbus plant and began producing additional automotive parts, including brake levers, hub caps, and bent steel tubing. With annual sales soaring towards $3 million, in the spring of 1928 the company went public and was listed on the Chicago Stock Exchange.

In 1929 Noblitt-Sparks began manufacturing a muffler for Studebaker and Ford. Other new automotive products that year included a rear-vision mirror and the first Arvin hot-water automobile heater. The company's line of toys was also expanded to include wheelbarrows and scooters. The stock market crash of October 1929 had little initial effect on the company's sales, which swelled to nearly $5 million by the end of that year. As the company entered the 1930s, hot-air heater sales were falling, while hot-water automobile heaters were rising in popularity. Capitalizing on its work with heaters, in 1930 the company developed a fan-forced electric room heater and moved into the arena of household products.

By 1931 Noblitt-Sparks began to feel the effects of the Great Depression. In a series of retrenchment moves that year, the company discontinued production of toys, closed its Seymour plant, and moved its corporate headquarters from Indianapolis to Columbus, Indiana. Those cost-cutting steps did little to keep sales from plummeting, though, and in 1931 the company suffered its first deficit, losing $100,000. Losses were trimmed slightly in 1932, the last unprofitable year in the company's history.

In 1933 Noblitt-Sparks entered the car radio field, and two years later the first Arvin home radio was introduced. In 1934 the company purchased facilities in Franklin, Indiana, and the following year began manufacturing automobile parts there. During the mid-1930s the muffler became the company's number one automotive product, helping to propel profits to more than $1 million for the first time.

Sparks left the company in 1937 to devote his time to a career in education and public administration. He went on to become president of Wabash College, governor of the New York Stock Exchange, and president of the Council for Financial Aid to Education. By the time of the company's 1937 introduction of its three-way car heater—with heater, foot warmer, and defroster—Noblitt-Sparks Industries was regarded as the largest manufacturer of trade-name car heaters in the field. The company had also expanded its home radio offerings to include 33 models. With product lines expanding, total annual sales topped the $10 million mark for the first time in 1937.

In 1938 recessionary conditions developed, and Noblitt-Sparks reduced its line of radios to nine popular table models. The following year economic conditions improved, and the company added carburetor silencers to its automotive product line. Before the decade closed, Noblitt-Sparks was listed on the New York Stock Exchange. In 1940 Noblitt-Sparks opened a new factory in Columbus, where it began manufacturing metal outdoor furniture and dinette sets. That same year, the company introduced an under-seat automobile heater and a motor-driven defroster unit. In 1940 the company also began supplying Sears, Roebuck & Co. with home radios.

In 1941 Noblitt-Sparks began producing its first private-brand merchandise. Such production was brought to a quick halt after the United States entered World War II late that year, and by 1942 all production efforts were geared toward the war effort. During the war Noblitt-Sparks produced a wide range of military products, including chemical and incendiary bombs, rocket-launching tubes, steel containers, fire extinguishers, anti-tank mine parts, radio communications equipment, and parts for military vehicles. In 1944 the company purchased a former furniture plant in North Vernon, Indiana, and began producing boxes for the bombs being made at its Columbus plant.

In December of 1945, Quintin Noblitt became the company's first chairman, and Glenn W. Thompson became president. To facilitate its re-entry into civilian markets, in 1946 Noblitt-Sparks began a three-year factory expansion program. At the same time the company also began focusing on the development of consumer products and electrical appliances. Some of these new products included electric irons and metal ironing tables, record changers, waffle cookers, laundry tubs, AM/FM radios, and electric room heaters. Late in 1949 Noblitt-Sparks began production of its first television set.

In 1950 the company changed its name to Arvin Industries, Inc., in order to take advantage of the "Arvin" name, which by that time was on numerous company products. In 1954 Q. G. Noblitt died, having watched his company grow from a one-room tire pump business into national corporation with better than $50 million in annual sales. Thompson succeeded Noblitt as chairman while remaining president. Arvin introduced a color television set in 1954, but a year later the company bowed out of the television business after deciding there was too little profit margin in the field. In 1955 Arvin established a research and engineering department to foster the development of new products. One year later the company began marketing its patented Arvinyl, a vinyl-to-metal sheet laminate; by 1960 the company was the largest laminator in the country.

During the 1950s Arvin introduced dozens of new non-automotive products, including numerous electrical appliances, a broad range of indoor and outdoor furniture, and a line of home fans and heater products. In 1959 Arvin entered the primary home electric heat field, introducing a line of baseboard, cable, and panel heating units. In a major step to boost automotive sales, in 1959 Arvin also entered the exhaust system replacement market.

In 1960 Eldo H. Stonecipher became president, while Thompson remained chairman. Under the Stonecipher-Thompson reign Arvin began an acquisitions and plant expansion program and in 1961 purchased Lok-Products Company, a leading manufacturer of suspended ceiling systems. That same year the company established its first plant outside of Indiana—an automotive parts factory in Tennessee. During the remainder of the decade Arvin Industries established automotive manufacturing facilities in Tennessee, Alabama, and Kentucky, and electronics plants in Hong Kong and Taipei, Taiwan.

In 1962 Arvin entered the advance electronics field by acquiring Westgate Laboratory, Inc. (renamed Arvin Systems, Inc.), an original design and development corporation specializing in electronics, optics, and communications. In 1963, with built-in heaters becoming standard equipment for most cars, the company ceased production of its Arvin heater. Arvin Industries moved into the international arena in 1963, when it acquired half interests in Waller K.K., a Tokyo corporation producing radio components, and Arvin-Standard Ltd., an auto exhaust system manufacturing plant in Canada.

Laminating operations were expanded in 1966, when Arvin Industries acquired Roll Coater, Inc.; the company gave Arvin the capability of coating materials in coil as well as sheet form. The following year Arvin acquired Federal Tool Engineering Company (renamed Arvin Automation, Inc.), a producer of automated welding equipment and machinery, semiconductor components, and reed switches. Thompson retired at the end of the decade and was succeeded as chairman by Stonecipher, while Eugene I. Anderson became president.

During the first half of the 1970s Arvin continued its drive to internationalize and expand its manufacturing and distribution facilities. In 1970 a national distribution center for automotive replacement parts was constructed in Indianapolis, and between 1972 and 1974 Arvin completed several other new facilities, including automotive parts plants in Arkansas and Missouri, a coil-coating facility in Indiana, and an electric housewares plant in Mississippi. In 1973 the company also sold its Hong Kong production facility and consolidated radio manufacturing operations in Taiwan.

Acquisitions during the early-1970s included the 1971 purchase of Data Magnetics Corporation, a prominent producer of magnetic recording heads and video recording devices. In 1972 Arvin bought General Tubes Limited of Toronto (later renamed Arvin North American Automotive of Canada), a manufacturer of automotive tubing and aftermarket exhaust pipes. During the next few years General Tubes' operations were converted to produce original exhaust pipe equipment. In 1973 Arvin expanded into South America with the formation of Arvin do Brazil S.A., a joint venture designed to produce exhaust system parts for the South American market. In 1973 Arvin also acquired Diamond Electronics, a leading producer of electronic process control monitoring equipment.

In 1974 Stonecipher resigned as chairman and was succeeded by Anderson, who continued as president. That same year Arvin sold Lok-Products and acquired Echo Science Corporation, a producer of magnetic video tape systems and digital magnetic tape recorders. After 15 years of engineering work in the area of automobile emission controls, Arvin produced its first catalytic converter in 1974.

During the latter half of the 1970s Arvin's activities were increasingly focused on research and product development. In 1976 Arvin debuted ARVEX, a new process for fabricating fiberglass-reinforced thermoplastic parts on traditional metal-working presses. Two years later Arvin completed an exhaust products testing and development center in Walesboro, Indiana. The company also acquired Calspan Corporation of Buffalo, New York, a well-known research and development company specializing in avionics, acoustics, electronics, thermal research, ground transportation systems, and energy systems. In 1980 Arvin's Calspan won a three-year, $95.6 million U.S. Air Force contract to manage wind tunnel facilities in Tennessee.

In 1981 James K. Baker became president and chief executive officer of Arvin Industries. That same year Echo Science Corporation was sold. In 1982 Arvin began production of stainless steel tubular manifolds and acquired the nation's largest manufacturer of evaporative coolers, McGraw Edison Company's International Metals Products Division (renamed ArvinAir). Arvin's sales in 1982 exceeded the half-billion dollar mark for the first time.

Between 1983 and 1984 Arvin's Calspan Corporation was awarded a number of government contracts, including a management contract for the wind tunnel facilities at Ames Research Center in California. In addition, a joint venture between Calspan and Dynalectron Corporation during this period was awarded a service contract for the U.S. Army's White Sands Missile Range in New Mexico.

During the mid-1980s Baker began guiding the company into global markets through joint ventures and acquisitions designed to enhance Arvin's international sales of automotive products. In 1984 Arvin and Bosal International of Germany formed the joint venture Bosal Industries, GmbH, to supply catalytic converters and tubular products to the European market. That same year Arvin's joint venture in Brazil was restructured with a new parts supplier, COFAP, and Arvin also purchased Ap de Mexico, S.A. de C.V., a manufacturer of exhaust systems for the Mexican auto industry.

In 1985 Arvin began consolidating operations and moved all of its automotive aftermarket parts production and distribution activities to a new Kentucky facility. Consumer housewares activities were consolidated that year into ArvinAir's operations. In 1986 Anderson retired as chairman and was succeeded by Baker, who quickly stepped up Arvin's international strategy with an increased focus on acquisitions. In 1986 Arvin purchased Maremont Corporation, a leading producer of original and replacement shock absorbers and exhaust systems with nearly $500 million in annual sales. That same year Arvin acquired the Canadian-based Schrader Automotive, the world's largest producer of tire valves. Looking to capitalize on the growing number of Japanese auto-makers with operations in the United States, Arvin also formed a joint venture with Sango Co., Ltd., to produce exhaust systems for foreign-turned-domestic North American automobile manufacturers.

In 1987 Loren K. Evans was elected president of Arvin. That same year the company acquired Systems Research Laboratories, Inc., a leading applied research and development services company specializing in aero-systems. Sales in 1987 jumped to $1.3 billion as profits climbed to $47.6 million. In March of 1988 Arvin announced plans to restructure its American automotive business and consolidate exhaust system operations into Maremont, which had became a subsidiary.

In 1988 Maremont purchased Amortext, a French manufacturer of shock absorbers, and Arvin acquired Cheswick, Ltd., and Bainbridge Silencers, Ltd., two leading European producers of original and replacement exhaust systems with facilities in the United Kingdom, the Netherlands, and Spain. Arvin's tire valve product line was also expanded in 1988 when Schrader Automotive and Neotech Industries, Inc. (renamed Sentronics Ltd.) agreed to jointly develop and distribute electronic pressure measurement devices.

Arvin continued to implement the game plan announced in 1987, a key element of which was to establish automotive operations in all major assembly capitals of the world. Furthering that end, in 1989 Arvin acquired a 75 percent stake in AP Amortiguadores, S.A. (APA), a leading European manufacturer of shock absorbers and MacPherson struts, located in Spain. Arvin also continued to restructure its U.S. operations, closing two exhaust plants in 1989 and selling Arvin Electronics. Efforts to make labor costs competitive helped pay dividends for Arvin and by 1989 union employees at all of Arvin's

U.S. original equipment exhaust plants had agreed to wage reductions. In 1989 the company's sales surpassed the $1.5 billion mark for the first time, having grown nearly four-fold during the course of the decade.

In 1990 Baker was named chairman of the U.S. Chamber of Commerce for 1990–91. Arvin itself entered the 1990s continuing its push to globalize. In 1990 Arvin-Tubemakers Pty. Ltd. was formed to expand production of original equipment exhaust systems in Australia. To strengthen its original equipment auto parts business in Europe, Arvin purchased the French engine-manifold and exhaust-tube production business of Tubauto S.A. (renamed Cheswick France S.A.). A ride control research and development center in Pamplona, Spain, was also completed in 1990.

In 1991 ArvinAir was sold, and after nearly a decade of revamping and expanding its business, Arvin provided only auto-related products. Evans was named vice-chairman that year, and Bryon O. Pond became president. In 1991 Arvin began assembly of catalytic converters in Born, Holland, and completed a new research and development center for exhaust systems in Warton, England. A two-year strike at Arvin's North Vernon site was resolved in 1991, with employees agreeing to accept wage cuts.

In 1992 Arvin and Schmitz & Brill, a German automotive exhaust systems parts manufacturer, formed a joint venture to serve European automakers. That same year Arvin's Calspan and Space Industries International, Inc., a Houston-based commercial space research company, reached an agreement, which was completed in July of 1993, to merge their operations into a new company with Arvin holding approximately 70 percent of the new venture.

As Arvin entered 1993, its exhaust systems and ride controls systems business held strong positions in the North American and European markets. Arvin planned to continue establishing operations in major assembly capitals of the world and, as a leading independent producer of catalytic converters, to capitalize on the need for converters to meet new European Community air quality standards and emission regulations. The company also continued research and development activities on electronic muffler systems, electronic ride control products, and on-dash tire pressure gauges.

Principal Subsidiaries: Maremont Corporation; Maremont Exhaust Products, Inc.; Gabriel Ride Control Products, Inc.; AVM, Inc.; Gabriel Europe, Inc.; A.P. Mexico; Roll Coater, Inc.; Schrader Automotive, Inc.; Arvin Finance Corporation; Arvin Automotive of Canada; Arvin Industries Deutschland GmbH; Schmitz & Brill GmbH; Arvin International Holdings Inc.; Arvin International U.K. PLC; Arvin Cheswick International B.V. (Netherlands); A.P.A., S.A. (Spain); Cheswick Spain; Arvin France.

Further Reading:

Amberg-Vajdic, Melinda, ''Arvin Profits Are Testament to Company's Keen Strategy,'' *Indianapolis Business Journal,* November 2, 1992, sec. 1, p. 4.

Barrett, Amy, ''Beating the Odds: How Beleaguered Arvin Industries Learned to Play the Game,'' *Financial World,* December 11, 1990, pp. 30–32.

Byrne, Harlan S., ''Arvin Industries Inc.: It Pushes an Overhaul of Its Auto-Parts Business,'' *Barron's,* September 18, 1989, pp. 62–63.

Coons, Coke, *Arvin. . . The First Seventy Years,* Columbus, IN: Arvin Industries, Inc., 1989.

Dobie, Maureen, ''Acquisition Fever: Arvin Makes Quick Transition Towards Replacement Parts Market,'' *Indianapolis Business Journal,* September 22, 1986, sec. 1, p. 12.

Holzinger, Albert G., ''A Strategy For Growth,'' *Nation's Business,* June 1990, pp. 38–40.

Johnston, Phil, ''Arvin Industries: Stockholders Applaud,'' *Indiana Business,* November 1987, p. 50.

Maturi, Richard J., ''Acquiring for Growth: Contributions by Newcomers Could Help Arvin Earn $2.80 a Share,'' *Barron's,* April 27, 1987, pp. 53–54.

Nulty, Peter, ''Arvin Industries: A Quick Course in Going Global,'' *Fortune,* January 13, 1992, p. 64.

Parent, Tawn, ''*Fortune* 500s Share Secrets of the Far East,'' *Indianapolis Business Journal,* November 30, 1992, p. 1A.

—Roger W. Rouland

 **THE AUSTIN COMPANY**

The Austin Company

3650 Mayfield Road
Cleveland, Ohio 44121
U.S.A.
(216) 382-6600
Fax: (216) 291-6684

Private Company
Incorporated: 1904 as The Samuel Austin & Son Company
Employees: 2,100
Sales: $2.23 billion (1992)
SICs: 8712 Architectural Services; 8711 Engineering
Services

From roots extending back well into the nineteenth century, The Austin Company has grown into one of the largest and most sophisticated design, engineering, and construction companies in the world. With 40 offices in ten countries on five continents, including eight regional operating units in the United States, the Cleveland-based company boasts a history of world records for building size and technological innovation. Austin's triumphs include the design, engineering, and construction of the world's largest industrial facility to date, the Boeing Company's manufacturing and assembly complex in Everett, Washington. Moreover, in 1992–93, Austin constructed the Asia and Pacific Trade Center in Osaka, Japan, one of the world's largest international exhibition facilities.

The Austin story begins with a young English carpenter who came to America in 1872 to find work rebuilding Chicago after that city's great fire. The carpenter, Samuel Austin, never made it to Chicago. When he arrived in the United States, he chose to work in Cleveland, building residences with a contractor and, over the course of the next six years, building a reputation of solid workmanship. He then set off to carry on his work alone, meeting with enough success to build a shop for his business in 1880.

A contract to construct a new savings bank building in 1889 marked Samuel Austin's debut into commercial work. Industry executives who banked in the new Broadway Savings Bank admired Austin's work and soon offered him work to construct their factories. In 1895 Austin won the contract to build Cleveland's first electric lamp factory; a series of contracts from the National Electric Lamp Association soon followed. Also in

1895, when the Western Mineral Wool Company decided to branch out and begin production in Chicago, it called on Samuel Austin to build their factory. The Western Mineral Wool contract represented Austin's first work outside of Cleveland. Ironically, the work was in the same location—Chicago—that he had originally intended to reach after emigrating to America 23 years earlier.

When Samuel Austin's son, Wilbert J. Austin, graduated from the Case School of Applied Sciences (now part of Case Western Reserve University) in 1904 with a degree in engineering, the father and son established The Samuel Austin & Son Company. Wilbert Austin brought to the business the innovative concept of combining full-service engineering and construction into one operation. This approach came to be known as "The Austin Method" and would distinguish the firm throughout the United States and eventually across the world.

The Austin Method transformed the traditional process of contracting by including in one contract the responsibility for the architecture, engineering, and construction of an entire project. By integrating these three services into one process, the Austin Method enabled the contractor to complete the project in a more timely fashion, thus saving the client both time and money. Armed with the prototype concept of an integrated engineering and construction contract, Samuel Austin & Son began its long history of firsts that carried the company to national and international prominence.

In 1907 Samuel Austin & Son built the first reinforced concrete structure in Cleveland for the H. Black Company. The building initially housed the region's largest women's clothing factory, the Wooltex Cloak Company, then served as offices for a series of tenants, including Tower Press, Inc., a printing company. (The Black Company building, located on Superior Avenue, was designated a Cleveland landmark in 1963.)

In 1911 Samuel Austin & Son engineered and constructed the first campus-type, industrial research facility for the National Electric Lamp Association. This facility is now known as Nela Park, General Electric's principal research complex, located in suburban East Cleveland. A contract for the design and construction of another large lamp manufacturing plant about one mile away accompanied the contract for the research complex. Since these two contracts were the two largest that Samuel Austin & Son had worked on to date, the Company moved its offices closer to the sites, specifically to Euclid and Noble Roads, where the company's headquarters remained until 1960.

While applying their new design and construction methodology on these two projects, the Austins developed a keener awareness of the economic problems of planning new industrial plants. In 1916, then, Austin & Son introduced standard building designs for the quick delivery of prefabricated packaged industrial building concepts. Refining and standardizing the Austin Method, the company enjoyed successes in factories of all types in New England, the Midwest, and the West Coast. Samuel Austin & Son was incorporated as The Austin Company in 1916, which soon opened district offices across the country to handle scores of new contracts. The Austin Company had gained a national reputation.

With its stature established, Austin strove over the succeeding decades to become one of the nation's leading architectural, engineering, and construction organizations. To that end, Austin branched into design and construction services for a variety of different industries, researched and developed cutting-edge engineering and construction concepts, and continually innovated new kinds of building concepts.

One of the earliest and longest-running lines of business that Austin diversified into was the defense industry. Many of the plants that had been designed and built earlier by Austin were producing arms for the Allies during World War I. When the United States entered the war in 1917, an enormous demand emerged virtually overnight for additional war materials. Manufacturers immediately turned to Austin for new facilities.

The Austin Company's involvement in these and other industries remained constant across the decades, continuing on beyond the lives of its founders. By the end of 1940, both Samuel Austin and Wilbert J. Austin had died. Under the leadership of the new president, George A. Bryant, however, Austin continued its work in war plants as well as other, non-defense, industries. During World War II, according to *The Austin Story,* Austin designed and constructed crucial facilities for the war, including "mammoth aircraft production plants, military airports, air force training stations and naval facilities" for the U.S. Government and "a variety of industrial defense plants" for private industry. Austin also constructed chemical-processing plants for the defense industry during the war. Austin's work for the government in its war efforts resumed in the early 1990s.

As innovators in the design and construction of automated distribution centers for use by the retail-merchandising and manufacturing industries, Austin in 1990 developed the U.S. Army's Eastern Distribution Center in New Cumberland, Pennsylvania. That 1.6-million-square-foot facility was designed to deliver supplies to military installations in the United States, Europe, and the Middle East. It fulfilled crucial logistical functions during the Persian Gulf War in 1991.

Austin's contribution to U.S. defense efforts has been largely the result of its success, based on technological developments, in a host of civilian industries. The fields of industry in which Austin has achieved leadership in facilities design and construction are few, but each is important. Austin has followed a policy of expansion into only a limited number of industries, such as aviation, broadcasting, food processing, newspaper publishing, and pharmaceutical manufacturing. At the same time, Austin has developed expertise in operations centers, research and development centers, automated distribution centers, computer-controlled manufacturing and processing plants, and "intelligent" office buildings.

Austin's work in aviation stemmed from government contracts garnered during the First World War, when Austin built aviation support facilities at many of the nation's airports. Following the war, Austin continued its work in aviation. In the late 1920s, Austin designed and constructed hangars, maintenance facilities, and administration and terminal buildings, including those for the Cleveland Municipal Airport (now Cleveland Hopkins International Airport). Under the direction of Wilbert

Austin, who had succeeded his father as company president in 1925 when Samuel Austin became chairman, the company perfected the original canopy door for wide-span hangars. Austin's new hangar design became the prototype for many succeeding hangar-door designs.

Moreover, an enduring business relationship with the Boeing Company, begun in the mid-1920s, led to a world record in building size in the early 1990s. Austin began constructing facilities for the Boeing Company in 1924; during 1966–67, Austin designed and constructed a 2.2-million-square-foot facility to assemble the 747 jumbo jet. In 1991 Austin was awarded a contract from Boeing to expand that Everett, Washington, manufacturing plant for the production of the new 777 aircraft; with the addition of 1.7 million square feet in mid-1993, the plant became the largest-volume industrial structure in the world to date.

This world record of building size was not Austin's first, however. In 1927 the company erected what was then the world's largest building, a manufacturing plant for the Oakland Motor Car Company in Pontiac, Michigan. Austin has continued its work in the automotive industry since that time. In 1930 an historically significant international contract called for a $60 million integrated automobile manufacturing complex and workers' city located in the Soviet town of Gorki. The project incorporated infrastructure to accommodate 50,000 people.

In addition to the automobile industry, Austin has distinguished itself in design and construction for the communications industry. The company designed Hollywood's first sound stages and film studios in the 1920s, NBC's famous Radio City of the West in Hollywood in 1938, and 50 of the first 75 local television stations that went on the air across the country after World War II.

Austin's experience in newspaper publishing dates back to 1921, when it created the *Warren Tribune*'s newspaper production plant. *The Austin Story* recounts that in 1959, the newspaper publishing trade journal, *Editor & Publisher*, credited one of Austin's creations as "probably the most efficiently laid out plant ever constructed for a major newspaper in the United States." Austin's client list has more than 100 of the country's leading dailies, including The Austin Company's hometown newspaper, the *Cleveland Plain Dealer*.

Austin's expertise in engineering cutting-edge buildings has manifested itself also in operations centers and research and development centers. While Austin has designed computer operating centers for public utilities and airlines, its most significant computer facilities have been sophisticated computer data processing centers for institutions of finance. Notable earlier experience in this area accrued to Austin as a result of its design and construction of the largest computer center in Ohio during the mid-1960s, a six-story facility completed in 1964 for Cleveland Trust, subsequently absorbed into Society Corporation. More recently, Austin designed and constructed a 180,000-square-foot computer center in Cleveland in 1991 for Society Corporation, parent of Society National Bank. This center processed all of the bank's collections of data.

Advanced research centers represent a similarly complex area of building design. Austin has gained experience in such facilities through its work for clients in the industries of food, petroleum, and pharmaceuticals, among several others. In 1992 Austin completed one of the world's largest pharmaceutical research centers for the Upjohn Company, located in Kalamazoo, Michigan.

The design and construction of these complex structures, as well as the company's reputation in serving such a broad range of industries, were a direct result of Austin's long-standing practice of researching and innovating new building technologies. During the late 1920s and 1930s, construction of vast automotive and farming implements factories demanded immense tonnages of riveted steel. Austin saw an opportunity to improve the assembly of steel-framed plants, and launched experiments into steel fabrication using electric-arc welding.

In 1928 The Austin Company designed and constructed at its own expense the Upper Carnegie Building using arc welding technology developed by the Lincoln Electric Company. The Upper Carnegie was the world's first commercial building with an all-welded steel structural framework. Across the street from the Upper Carnegie, Austin constructed the prestigious Carnegie Medical Building, using similar technology in 1931.

Austin's research achievements are diverse and numerous. 1929, for instance, marked the beginning of research that led to the design of the world's first "controlled-conditions" building, for the Simmonds Saw and Steel Company at Fitchburg, Massachusetts. This factory, from which windows were entirely eliminated, made possible the control of all internal environmental conditions—temperature, humidity, light, and sound. In the late 1930s, Austin pioneered the installation of fluorescent lighting in industrial buildings and championed the efficiency of single-story factories. When business slowed during the 1930s, Austin intensified its research and diversified its business. It established a division in 1933 devoted to the design and construction of insulated steel structures. The division eventually produced packaged, pre-fabricated, porcelain-enamel service stations for major oil corporations across the nation.

Beginning in 1980, Austin also gained considerable experience in building computer-controlled logistics facilities such as automated distribution centers. By the early 1990s, Austin had assumed a position as a leader in the design and construction of such facilities; its clientele included both the U.S. Army and the U.S. Postal Service.

Finally, Austin can boast of having engineered one of the most sophisticated "intelligent" buildings in the world, the Information Systems Building for the Salt River Project public utility in Phoenix, Arizona. In an "intelligent" building, every operation and function is completely computerized, automated, and electronically controlled. Austin has built similar facilities in other locations such as Los Angeles and Madrid, Spain, as well.

While The Austin Company ownership remained stable throughout most of its lifetime, in the 1980s its corporate identity began to shift. In 1984 the National Gypsum Company, a gypsum wallboard manufacturer, acquired Austin. National Gypsum underwent a leveraged buyout in 1988, after fending off take-over bids from The Wickes Cos. of Santa Monica, Drexel Burnham Lambert Inc., and Ivan F. Boesky. National Gypsum thus became a centerpiece of the largest insider trading lawsuits ever filed by the Securities and Exchange Commission against brokers and investment bankers.

National Gypsum filed for voluntary bankruptcy in 1990. Austin was not included in the bankruptcy filing, however. In March 1993 a bankruptcy court judge confirmed National Gypsum's reorganization plan, thus preparing NGC to emerge from bankruptcy. As part of the reorganization plan, a trust was established to pay the claims of thousands of plaintiffs who had sued National Gypsum and other former asbestos manufacturers for injuries allegedly derived from asbestos. The trust became the legal owner of The Austin Company's stock, as well as insurance policies intended to compensate the asbestos claimants. Austin now operates independently as a private company under the trust.

The Austin Company currently has two specialized divisions, Austin Consulting and Austin Process, as well as a general contracting subsidiary, Ragnar Benson Inc. Austin Consulting provides services to clients in the area of manufacturing and logistics operations. Austin Process offers engineering and construction services for the process industries, particularly in the fields of agrichemicals, chemicals, fermentation, food processing, petrochemicals, and pharmaceuticals. Ragnar Benson, Inc., a subsidiary of Austin, provides general contracting and construction management services for clients. RBI projects include commercial buildings, facilities for public power utilities, corporate headquarters, and manufacturing plants.

Internationally, Austin maintains permanent offices in Japan, Australia, Belgium, Canada, Mexico, the Netherlands, Spain, and the United Kingdom. Associated companies operate in Argentina, Brazil, and Italy. Internationally, Austin has won six major contracts in Japan since 1990. Most recently, an Austin-Japanese consortium won the bid to construct a wing of the Asia and Pacific Trade Center at Osaka, which, after completion, will house one of the world's largest international trading facilities. Austin has maintained an office in Tokyo since 1972, and since then has gradually built credibility among major Japanese corporations and the Japanese government. Austin hopes to continue expanding its international operations while maintaining its stature in the U.S. marketplace.

Principal Subsidiaries: Ragnar Benson Inc.; Austin Australia Pty. Ltd.; Austin Belgium; The Austin Company Limited (Canada); The Austin Company (Japan); Austin de Mexico S.A.; Austin Nederland B.V. (The Netherlands); The Austin Company S.A. (Spain); The Austin Co. of U.K. Ltd. (United Kingdom).

Further Reading:

"Austin, designer of PD plant, molds city's skyline," *The Plain Dealer,* January 5, 1992.
The Austin Story, Cleveland: The Austin Company, May 11, 1993.
"Bankruptcy Court Judge Confirms Reorganization," *Wall Street Journal,* March 10, 1993, p. A4.
The Challenge of Change, Rosemont, IL: Austin Consulting, 1991.
Company Overview: Historical Milestones, Cleveland: The Austin Company, 1990.
Creators of Facilities for Global Competition, Cleveland: The Austin Company, 1993.
Facilities for Tomorrow's Global Marketplace, Cleveland: The Austin Company, 1993.

Holden, Ted and Zachary Schiller, ''Building a Doorway to Japan,'' *Business Week,* December 31, 1990, p. 50.

Paltrow, Scot J., ''The Anatomy of 3 Alleged Insider Deals,'' *Los Angeles Times,* September 9, 1988, part IV, p. 1.

''4 Companies Agree to Settle Asbestos Case in Maryland,'' *New York Times,* July 6, 1992, p. D2.

—Nicholas S. Patti

Bank of America

BankAmerica Corporation

555 California Street
San Francisco, California 94104
U.S.A.
(415) 622-3456
Fax: (415) 622-7915

Public Company
Incorporated: 1904 as Bank of Italy
Employees: 54,369
Assets: $180.64 billion
Stock Exchanges: New York Pacific Midwest
SICs: 6712 Bank Holding Companies; 6021 National
    Commercial Banks

When BankAmerica merged with Security Pacific Corporation in 1992, it became the nation's second-largest bank. This merger of the California banks was the largest merger in the history of banking and created an institution with nearly $190 billion in assets and $150 billion in deposits.

The Bank of America was founded in 1904 as the Bank of Italy. Its credo was radical at the time: to serve ''the little fellows.'' From its humble beginnings in a former tavern, the Bank of America grew to become a force that revolutionized U.S. banking. With deregulation, however, its traditional emphasis on the general consumer created problems for the bank.

Amadeo Peter Giannini, founder of today's BankAmerica, became one of the most important figures in 20th-century American banking. Giannini, an Italian immigrant, was seven when his father died. By age 21, he had earned half ownership of his stepfather's produce business. He married into a wealthy family, and profits from the produce business, combined with shrewd real estate investments in San Francisco, enabled him to retire at age 31.

His retirement was brief. When his father-in-law died, he left a sizable estate, including a directorship of a small San Francisco savings bank. When Giannini failed to convince the board of this bank that the poor but hardworking people who had recently come to the West Coast were good loan risks, he resigned his position and set out to start his own bank—a bank for ''people who had never used one.''

The year, 1904, was an inauspicious one; an up-and-down economy and the financial irresponsibility of many banks during this period gave banking such a bad name that the government was eventually prompted to create the Federal Reserve system, in 1917. But Giannini's bank was atypical. His policy of lending money to the average citizen was unheard of in the early 1900s, when most banks lent only on a wholesale basis to commercial clients or wealthy individuals.

Giannini raised capital for his new bank, called the Bank of Italy, by selling 3,000 shares of stock, mostly to small investors, none of whom were allowed to own more than 100 shares. Although Giannini never held a dominant share of stock, the extreme loyalty of these and subsequent stockholders allowed him to rule the bank as though it were closely held. His innovative policies made the Bank of Italy and its successor, the Bank of America, the most controversial bank in the United States. The nation watched with wary eyes as he created a system of branch banking that made the Bank of America the world's largest bank in a mere 41 years.

During the famous San Francisco earthquake of 1906 Giannini rescued $80,000 in cash before the bank building burned by hiding it in a wagon full of oranges and bringing it to his house for safekeeping. With this money he reopened his bank days before any other bank and began making loans from a plank-and-barrel counter on the waterfront, urging demoralized San Franciscans to rebuild an even better city.

Giannini's original vision led naturally to branch banking. Expense made it difficult for small depositors to travel long distances to a bank, so Giannini decided his bank would go to them, with numerous well-placed branches. Accordingly, the Bank of Italy bought its first branch, a struggling San Jose bank, in 1909.

Giannini made up the rules as he went; he was not a banker, and his was the first attempt ever at branch banking. Going his own way included loudly denouncing the ''big interests,'' and he repeatedly offended influential members of the financial community, including local bankers, major Californian bankers, and many state and federal regulators, who were already uncertain about how to handle an entirely new kind of banking. Some did support Giannini's vision though, including William Williams, an early California superintendent of banks, and the Crocker National Bank, which lent money to a subsidiary of the Bank of Italy expressly for acquiring branch banks.

The bank grew rapidly; in 1910 it had assets of $6.5 million. By 1920, assets totaled $157 million, far outstripping the growth of any other California bank and dwarfing its onetime benefactor, Crocker National. Further expansion was stymied, however, by the state of California and by the new Federal Reserve system, which did not allow member banks to open new branches. Giannini shrewdly sidestepped this regulation by establishing separate state banks for southern and northern California (in addition to the Bank of Italy) as well as another national bank, and putting them all under the control of a new holding company, BancItaly. Finally, in 1927 California regulations were changed to permit branch banking, and Giannini consolidated his four banks into the Bank of America of California.

With California conquered, Giannini turned to the national scene. He believed that a few large regional and national banks would come to dominate American banking by using branches, and he intended to blaze the trail. He already owned New York's Bowery and East River National Bank (as well as a chain of banks in Italy); next he established Bank of America branches in Washington, Oregon, Nevada, and Arizona, again before branch banking was explicitly permitted.

Federal regulators, objecting to Giannini's attempts to dictate the law, took exception to some of his practices. In response, Giannini created another holding company in 1928, to supplant BancItaly. The new company was called Transamerica, to symbolize what Giannini hoped to accomplish in banking.

Giannini knew he needed a Wall Street insider to help him realize his dream of nationwide branch banking, and he thought Elisha Walker, the head of Blair and Company, and old-line Wall Street investment-banking firm, was just the man. So, in 1929, the year Bank of America passed the $1 billion mark in assets, Transamerica bought Blair.

A year later, Giannini consolidated his two banking systems into the Bank of America National Trust and Savings Association, under the control of Transamerica. Sixty years old and in poor health, he relinquished the presidency to Walker, retired for the second time, and went to Europe to recuperate. It was again a short retirement. His stay ended abruptly in 1931, when he received news that Walker was trying to liquidate Transamerica.

Giannini headed straight for California, where three-quarters of the bank's stockholders remained. What followed was one of the most dramatic proxy fights in U.S. history. Giannini crisscrossed California, holding stockholder meetings in town halls, gymnasiums, courthouses, and other public spaces. A poor public speaker, he hired orators to drive home the message that Walker and eastern interests, the dreaded "big guys" Giannini had battled against for years, were trying to ruin the bank. The campaign succeeded and the stockholders returned control of the Bank of America to Giannini.

The bank had suffered, though. By the end of 1932, deposits had shrunk to $876 million, from a high of $1.16 billion in 1930. No dividend was paid that year, for the first time since 1905, and the battle had cost Giannini his New York banks. Depositor confidence had to be rebuilt.

Giannini's presence seemed to be just the right thing. By 1936 Bank of America was the fourth-largest banking institution in the United States (and the second-largest savings bank) and assets had grown to $2.1 billion. The bank continued to innovate, instituting a series of new loans called Timeplan installment loans. Timeplan included real estate loans, new and used car financing, personal credit loans from $50 to $1,000, home appliance financing, and home-improvement loans, all industry firsts.

As the Bank of America became more influential, Giannini took on bigger and bigger foes, among them the Federal Reserve, Wall Street, the Treasury Department, the Securities and Exchange Commission (SEC), Hans Morgenthau, and J.P. Morgan Jr. Eventually, the enmity Giannini aroused in his war against the Establishment cost the bank its chance for nationwide branch banking. The beginning of the end came in 1937, when the Federal Reserve made its first attempt to force Transamerica and Bank of America to separate.

World War II brought tremendous growth to the Bank of America. As people and businesses flocked to California during the war, the bank more than doubled in size: in 1945, with assets of $5 billion, it passed Chase Manhattan to become the world's largest bank.

As California began to rival New York as the most populous state, Bank of America continued to expand. Giannini continued to battle, and win, against the big interests, until his death in 1949. From radical outsider to the leader of what *Business Week* called the "new orthodoxy" of banking—the trend toward serving average consumers—Giannini's was one of the most innovative careers in 20th-century banking.

He was succeeded as president of Transamerica by his son, Lawrence Mario, long a top official at the bank. He continued in his father's tradition, but for only three years; he succumbed to lifelong health problems in 1952.

Following the deaths of the Gianninis, Bank of America slowly made itself over. New chief Clark Beise moved to decentralize operations, encouraging branch managers to assume more responsibility for their branches. This approach paid off with tremendous growth; by 1960, assets totaled $11.9 billion. The bank continued to innovate. In 1959, it was the first bank to fund a small-business investment company. It was also the first U.S. bank to adopt electronic and computerized recordkeeping; by 1961, operations were completely computerized. Other new programs included student loans, an employee loan-and-deposit plan that let workers transact bank business through their offices (a response to increased competition from credit unions), and the first successful credit card, BankAmericard, the predecessor of Visa.

In addition, Bank of America stepped up its international presence, becoming one of only four U.S. banks with significant impact on international lending. It also began to pursue wholesale accounts, to supplement its traditional retail base. Finally, in 1957, the Federal Reserve forced Transamerica to separate from Bank of America, an event the two institutions had anticipated.

Bank of America's efforts to become a "department store of finance" in the late 1950s and early 1960s marked the last significant period of innovation in the bank's history until the 1980s. It was a time when the bank strove to sell the widest variety of banking services to the widest possible market. Beise felt there was more room for innovation, saying in 1959 "there are new frontiers to develop," but warning that "we are constantly fighting against the attitude of entrenched success." It was a battle that the Bank of America lost, as it eventually became a conservative, stodgy, and inflexible institution.

In 1968, BankAmerica Corporation was created as a holding company to hold the assets of Bank of America N.T. & S.A. and to help the bank expand and better challenge its archrival, Citibank. This came just before banking deregulation, which affected Bank of America more adversely than was predicted.

Bank of America's branch banking system was a major problem, since it gave the bank the highest overhead in the banking industry.

Through this period the retail division provided 50 percent of the bank's profits. It was not until interest rates exploded in the 1970s that the bank's bulk of low-interest-bearing mortgages became damaging, as it was for many savings and loans.

As the largest bank in the world, the Bank of America was a natural target for groups with statements to make during the 1960s. It became the first major employer in California to sign a statement of racial equality in hiring. At the time, the Bank of America had more than 3,500 minority employees—more than 10 percent of its workforce. The bank also responded to complaints from women's groups by creating a $3.8 million fund for training female employees in 1974, and set itself the goal of a 40 percent-female workforce.

By 1970, Bank of America had established a $100 million loan fund for housing in poverty-stricken areas, and purchased municipal bonds that other California banks wouldn't touch. This was in keeping with the tradition Giannini had established when he bought rural school bonds and bonds for the Golden Gate Bridge at a time when no other bank would buy such issues.

A. W. ''Tom'' Clausen succeeded Rudy Peterson as chief executive officer (CEO) in 1971. He presided over Bank of America's last tremendous growth spurt—assets jumped 50 percent (to $60 billion) just between 1973 and 1975. Bank of America was the only one of the 20 largest U.S. banks to average 15 percent growth between 1971 and 1978; its seemingly unstoppable growth earned its management great praise during the 1970s.

When Clausen left Bank of America in 1981 to head the World Bank, Bank of America had $112.9 billion in assets. Clausen was replaced by 40-year-old Samuel Armacost. Soon the Bank of America began to fall apart. Energy loans, shipping loans, farming loans (Bank of America was the largest agricultural lender in the world) and loans to Third World countries all started to go bad. Bank of America, whose large deposit base had traditionally made it exceptionally liquid but had also given it trouble in maintaining proper capital reserves, was ill prepared to meet the crisis. Suddenly, the biggest bank in the world had no money. It could not even raise capital in the stock market because its stock price had plummeted at a time when most bank stocks were rising.

Armacost started a general campaign to cut costs. The bank dropped a third of its 3,000 corporate clients, sold subsidiaries and its headquarters building, closed 187 branches, and began to lay off employees, something it had never done before. In 1986, the wounded BankAmerica became the target of a takeover bid from a company half its size. First Interstate Bancorp offered $2.78 billion for the nation's second-largest banking group. A few days after this bid was made public in early October, Armacost resigned and was replaced by none other than Tom Clausen, the man many blamed for BankAmerica's troubles in the first place. Clausen resisted the takeover, but Joe Pinola, Interstate's chairman, was determined, and by the end of October had sweetened the deal to $3.4 billion. Clausen was equally determined to prevent BankAmerica's takeover. He rejected First Interstate's bid and battened down the hatches for a hostile assault. In the end, Clausen was able to rally shareholders behind him and thwart First Interstates' plans.

In 1987, BankAmerica set about restructuring its operations. Clausen sold nonessential assets—including the Charles Schwab discount securities brokerage and Bank of America's Italian subsidiary—and refocused the bank's attention on the domestic market. New services, including advanced automated teller machines and extended banking hours, lured Californian customers back. In addition, the bank went after the corporate business it had neglected in the early 1980s. Clausen cut back substantially on staff, cleaned up the nonperforming loans in Bank of America's portfolio, and hired a number of exceptional managers to execute BankAmerica's new directives. By the end of 1988, the bank was in the black again. Though still plagued by a good deal of exposure to Third World debt, BankAmerica was able to record a profit of $726 million, its first in three years.

By 1989, BankAmerica's recovery was so strong that it was able to declare its first dividend since the fourth quarter of 1985. Industry analysts called the recovery the biggest turnaround in the history of U.S. banking. Retail operations were expanded in Nevada with the acquisition of Nevada First Bank, and in Washington with the purchase of American Savings Financial Corp. by the subsidiary Seafirst Corp., the largest bank in the Pacific Northwest. During this year, BankAmerica was the first major bank in California to announce that it would open all its branches on Saturdays and extend weekday hours for greater consumer convenience.

In 1990, BankAmerica showed further evidence of its recovery by announcing that its revenues exceeded $1 billion for the first time. Industry analysts theorized that the bank had the cleanest loan portfolio of the nation's big banks. Acquisitions included Woodburn State Bank of Oregon, Western Savings and Loan branches in Arizona, and Benjamin Franklin and MeraBank Federal Savings, the largest S&Ls in Oregon and Arizona, respectively. The bank also opened a new international branch in Milan, Italy.

In 1990, BankAmerica surpassed Chase Manhattan to become the second-largest bank holding company in the nation. Also, in keeping with the bank's policy of community responsibility, it began an Environmental Program that included activities directed toward saving paper and other materials through recycling, and energy and water conservation.

Seeking to expand its operations beyond its branches in seven western states, the bank added branches in two more states with the 1991 acquisitions of ABQ and Sandia Federal Savings banks of New Mexico, and Village Green National Bank in Houston. Another purchase was a subsidiary of GNA Securities that had operated an investment program in the bank's branches since 1988. The program, called Bank of America Investment Services, offered mutual funds and tax-deferred annuities. In spite of the nation's economic recession at this time as well as higher deposit insurance premiums and higher credit losses and nonaccruals, BankAmerica was able to post its third straight year of record earnings—more than $1 billion.

Expanding services to customers continued with the opening of full-service branches in grocery stores in southern California. In addition, to allow customers access to money anytime and anywhere, the bank opened several hundred new Versateller ATMs for a total of 2,300 in nine states.

After nine months of preparation, the merger of BankAmerica Corp. and Security Pacific Corp. became final on April 22, 1992. The merger was part of a national trend of bank consolidation that sought to strengthen troubled and even healthy institutions. For BankAmerica, the merger offered an opportunity to become more efficient and save money—an estimated $1.2 billion annually within the next three years. The merger also helped the bank expand into new markets and geographic locations. By the end of 1992, consumer banking services were provided in ten western states, trust and consumer financial services were provided nationwide, and commercial and corporate banking operations were located in 35 countries worldwide.

Acquisition activity continued with the purchase of Sunbelt Federal Savings, which held 111 branches in 76 cities in Texas; HonFed, the largest thrift in Hawaii; and Valley Bank of Nevada, which made BankAmerica the largest depository institution in that state. However, the persistent national recession, combined with a recession in the state of California, caused a decline in earnings reported for 1992.

Domestic expansion continued in 1993 with the acquisition of First Gibraltar of Texas and with an agreement to make a $1 million equity investment in Founders National Bank, the only African-American-owned bank on the West Coast. Additional overseas expansion occurred when BankAmerica received approval from the People's Bank of China to upgrade its Guangzhou representative office into a full-service branch, the first U.S. bank to have such a branch. Consolidation of consumer and commercial finance units was undertaken, and one year after the merger, the bank had consumer operations in much of the United States, wholesale offices in 37 nations, retail branches in ten western states, and consumer finance company operations in 43 states.

As BankAmerica moved into the mid-1990s, it planned to continue many of the policies it had begun in the 1980s. They included the development of new products and services for consumers; geographic diversification into such fast-growing economies as Asia and Latin America, which would enable the bank to better withstand the economic cycles of the domestic market; community investments; environmental programs; and loans to students and those with low income. BankAmerica also continued to hope for changes in laws and regulations that would allow interstate banking and more effective competition with non-bank institutions providing similar financial services. Such legislation would create new markets for which BankAmerica was poised to serve.

Principal Subsidiaries: Bank of America NT&SA; Bank of America Alaska, N.A.; Bank of America Arizona; Bank of America FSB; Bank of America Idaho, N.A.; Bank of America Nevada; Bank of America New Mexico, N.A.; Bank of America Oregon; Bank of America Texas, N.A.; Seafirst Corp. Seattle-First National Bank.

Further Reading:

BankAmerica Corporation Annual Reports, San Francisco: BankAmerica Corporation, 1991 and 1992.
"BankAmerica Corp.," *Wall Street Journal,* February 4, 1993, p. B6.
BankAmerica Environmental Progress Report, BankAmerica Corporation, 1992.
Bank of America Milestones, 1989–93.
Hector, Gary, *Breaking the Bank: The Decline of BankAmerica,* Boston, MA: Little, Brown, 1988.
James, Marquis, and James, Bessie R., *Biography of a Bank: The Story of Bank of America, N.T. & S.A.,* New York, NY: Harper, 1954.
"New BankAmerica Debuts," *BankAmerican,* April 22, 1992, p. 1.
Zuckerman, Sam, "B of A Adopting SecPac's Orphan NonBank Units," *American Banker,* April 6, 1993, p. 1.

—updated by Dorothy Kroll

Beech Aircraft Corporation

P.O. Box 85
Wichita, Kansas 67201-0085
U.S.A.
(316) 676-7111
Fax: (316) 676-8286

Wholly Owned Subsidiary of Raytheon Corporation
Incorporated: 1932
Employees: 10,900
Sales: $1.10 billion
SICs: 3721 Aircraft; 3728 Aircraft Parts & Equipment Nec;
  3761 Guided Missiles & Space Vehicles

Best known for its line of Beechcraft propeller and jet airplanes, Beech Aircraft Corporation is one of several American manufacturers of small aircraft. Beech competes with Cessna, Piper, and Lear for shares of such markets as private pilots, small air taxi services, corporate customers, and military forces. In addition, Beech manufactures a variety of aircraft parts and special systems for larger companies, principally McDonnell-Douglas.

The company's founder, Walter Herschel Beech, began his interest in aviation as a boy, when he constructed a glider out of wood and his mother's newest bed sheets. Later employed as an automobile salesman, Beech took his first powered flight in a Curtiss biplane in 1914 at the age of 23. He took to the skies himself and learned dogfighting maneuvers when he joined the Army Signal Corps aviation section in 1917.

After his discharge in 1920, Beech employed his army flying skills as a barnstormer until he joined the Swallow Airplane Company in Wichita as a test pilot and salesman in 1921. Although he did well and was promoted to general manager of the operation after just two years, Beech left the company when Swallow refused to pursue construction of a metal, rather than wooden, airplane.

Beech and another local aviator named Lloyd Stearman decided to start their own business and formed the Travel Air Company. In 1925 the pair convinced aircraft builder Clyde Cessna, who had given up on the trade, to join the partnership. Travel Air began as a very successful venture. The company's planes garnered numerous awards for their design and won many flight competitions—often when piloted by Walter Beech. Early designs were powered by Curtiss-Wright engines, marking the

beginning of an important business relationship. However, a conflict arose between Beech and Cessna, the company's president. Although Travel Air was recording decent sales from its line of biplanes, Cessna was determined that the company should immediately begin work on a new single-wing design. Unable to win agreement from Beech, Cessna set up his own shop and built the craft himself.

Cessna later demonstrated his monoplane for Beech, who conceded that Cessna had produced an excellent craft and agreed to have Travel Air begin manufacturing the planes. Cessna's early designs led to the Travel Air Woolaroc and Mystery S, which won the company further acclaim in competitions and races. Cessna continued to have differences with Beech and Stearman, however, and in 1927 elected to leave the partnership. He later established his own business, though he continued to deal with Beech regularly.

By 1929, Travel Air had turned out a thousand airplanes. The venture proved so successful that the partners were invited to make Travel Air part of the powerful Curtiss-Wright Corp., which represented the surviving business interests of aviation pioneer Glenn Curtiss and the Wright Brothers. Travel Air merged with Curtiss-Wright in 1930, and as part of the deal, Beech was asked to serve as president of the company. The year also marked Beech's marriage to Olive Ann Mellor, who had been working as the office manager for Travel Air. Mrs. Beech continued to work with her husband, now in the capacity of business advisor, at which she proved highly adept, having thoroughly learned about the aircraft industry.

Curtiss-Wright fell on extremely difficult times later that year, principally as a result of the Great Depression. Meanwhile Beech, as president of the company, had been relegated to piloting a desk in panic-stricken New York City, and he longed for an opportunity to get back to building airplanes. In 1932, when the Depression was at its worse, Beech resigned from Curtiss-Wright and returned to Wichita. He established the Beech Aircraft Company in April of that year, convincing a number of former Travel Air employees to join him.

Working out of leased space in the shuttered Cessna factory, Beech and his team of workers set out to build a five-seat luxury sedan biplane with an enclosed cabin, a recessed upper wing, and a top speed of 200 miles per hour. Finally, on November 4, 1932, Beech rolled out his first airplane, the Model 17. Beech spent the following year promoting his new design at air shows and in competitions. After receiving orders for several dozen of the craft, Beech negotiated a lease of his original Travel Air factory from Curtiss-Wright and moved his operation to the larger building.

As the country slowly climbed out of the Depression, demand for aircraft began to recover. To cover as much of the market as possible, Beech created several variations of the Model 17, featuring different Wright engines and load capacities, and ranging in top speed from 150 to 240 miles per hour. The Staggerwing, as the Model 17 had become known, was produced in ever greater quantities during the latter half of the 1930s. Cash flow provided from this successful model enabled Beech to begin work on his second design, a radically different twin-engine monoplane called the Model 18.

The seven-seat Model 18, or Twin Beech, had even more impressive duration and payload characteristics than the Model 17. After winning several more aircraft competitions, the 243 mile-per-hour Twin began to invite interest from the U.S. Army and Navy. As hostilities in Europe set the stage for a large-scale war, the Roosevelt Administration began preparations for wartime supplies and production. The armed services ordered several Model 17s and 18s for use as transports and for bomber and gunnery training duty in 1939.

In 1940, when Britain and France declared war on Germany, the army and navy flooded Beech with new aircraft orders. Employment at the Beech factory skyrocketed from 235 employees to more than 2,000. After the United States became directly involved in the war in 1941, Beech was called into action as one of America's major aircraft manufacturers. In addition to the Models 17 and 18, Beech turned out a wood-frame training plane—so constructed to conserve aluminum for combat aircraft—called the AT-10.

Beech's largest military aircraft never went into production. The XA-38 "Grizzly," a twin-engine ground attack aircraft, was cancelled as the war drew to a close. By the end of the war in 1945, however, Beech had turned out 7,400 military aircraft and its employment stood at 14,000. The company was awarded five Army/Navy "E" citations for excellence in efficiency under the War Production Board. As many as 90 percent of all American war pilots were trained in Beech-built aircraft.

The end of the war also spelled the end of huge military orders. Beech began concentrating on reentering the commercial and civilian markets, planning for this conversion well before the war's end. Within months of its conclusion Beech was on the market with improved versions of the Model 17 and 18. In 1947 the company rolled out its first new basic design in ten years, the Model 35 Bonanza. This plane was an all-metal four-seater with a distinctive V-tail which replaced the conventional T-tail of other designs. Beech received hundreds of orders for this new design before it was rolled out, confirming the existence of a pent-up demand for private aircraft. The Bonanza was Beech's smallest design, perfect for the profitable winged "family sedan" market that was emerging for competitors such as Cessna and Piper.

Despite churning out more than 1,000 Bonanzas in 1947, the small aircraft market proved unable to keep Beech's wartime work force fully occupied. The company's roles were trimmed until they reached 2,200 in 1949. In addition, the flood of civilian aircraft into the market quickly overran demand. Beech now faced very soft market conditions and had few alternatives but to quickly retool for other more profitable products. During the immediate postwar years, Beech manufactured corn harvesters and a variety of aluminum parts for other manufacturers in order to maintain its factory space and a core of skilled employees.

In the meantime Walter Beech turned his attention back to new aircraft designs to take the place of the venerable but aging Models 17 and 18. Beech attempted to follow other airplane builders, including Boeing, Convair, and Douglas, into the commercial market, where they had succeeded in winning major sales of ever larger aircraft. Beech, on the other hand, focused

on a market niche by building smaller commuter-type aircraft to be used for the hundreds of shorter airline routes being charted. Beech's entry was the Model 34 Twin Quad, a 20-passenger, V-tail plane. In 1949, after two years of failed sales efforts, the program was canceled.

On December 2, 1948, Beech rolled out a new single-engine trainer called the Model 45 Mentor, and eight months later began work on the Model 50 Twin Bonanza. While the Mentor became the new standard trainer for the U.S. Air Force, Navy, and numerous foreign military organizations, the Model 50 was snapped up by industrial customers for use as an executive craft. With the eruption of hostilities in Korea, the army once again became a big customer, using the rugged Model 50 as a utility plane, and ordering $50 million worth of new aircraft. As the hostilities turned into war, Beech Aircraft was once again brought into the military fold, producing training craft and a variety of parts for other manufacturer's planes. Under military specifications, Beech dabbled with jet-powered models, but never received a production order.

On November 29, 1950, Walter Beech died suddenly of a heart attack. He was succeeded by his wife, Olive Ann, who became one of the first female chief executives in American business. In August of 1956 Olive Ann Beech revived the Travel Air name as the moniker for her company's Model 95, a twin-engine plane designed to fill the gap between the Model 35 and Model 50 Bonanzas. The Bonanza Twins subsequently evolved into a third design, introduced in 1959, called the Model 65 Queen Air. During the 1950s Beech also became involved with NASA space exploration projects. The company was asked to pursue development of cryogenic systems that would permit liquified hydrogen and oxygen to be used as rocket fuels. Beech set up a facility in Boulder, Colorado, to research and build these systems, and began supplying cryogenic apparatus with the Gemini project.

Beech had also established a second factory at Liberal, Kansas, where a new airplane, the Model 23 Musketeer was produced in 1963. By this time, Beech had expanded its product line by introducing its Model 33 Debonair and twin-engine Model 55 Baron series. In 1964 Beech rolled out its most enduring design since the Model 17, a corporate turboprop called the Model 90 King Air. This was followed in 1968 by the 17-seat Beechcraft C99, which represented Beech's reentry into the commuter airline market. That year Olive Ann Beech turned the presidency of Beech Aircraft over to Frank E. Hedrick, while she remained as chairman and CEO.

As the space program accelerated toward the July 1969 manned moon landing, Beech cryogenic devices were employed aboard Apollo space craft for propulsion systems, air and electrical supply, and even manufacturing water. Beech's work for NASA drew it closer to a major aerospace contractor, the newly merged McDonnell-Douglas company, which built the Apollo command module. It also led Beech into a series of Defense Department projects to build missiles, target drones, and other implements.

In the late 1960s the avionics engineer Bill Lear and Beech's crosstown rival, Cessna, launched new product extensions that threatened to seriously undermine Beech's position in the market—private jets. Unable to fund development of a jet and with almost no time to get one in the air, Frank Hedrick sealed a deal with Britain's Hawker-Siddeley Group that would allow Beech to manufacture and market that company's HS-125, originally designed by DeHavilland. Hedrick won an agreement to sell the proven model under license for five years as the BH-125.

In 1975, after five years of poor sales and despite Beech's excellent marketing network, Beech and Hawker-Siddeley agreed not to renew their arrangement. While Lear, Cessna, and Dassault prevailed in the private jet business, the BH-125 enabled Beech to enter and exit the market with no development or wind-up costs. Those that remained in the market had yet to earn a decent return on their jet products.

Beech suffered the first of numerous product liability setbacks in 1971 when an FAA study identified problems with control locks on the Model 55. Problems identified were quickly rectified, but the process inspired a battery of personal injury lawyers to launch wrongful death suits against all small aircraft manufacturers, including Beech.

The litigation costs affected Beech less than a downturn in the market. In 1973, unable to secure credit for additional development and production, Hedrick sought out a merger of Beech with Grumman Corp., a deep-pocketed defense contractor. Grumman hoped to use Beech to lessen its overall dependence on the government for its business. Grumman, however, had serious financial difficulties of its own, stemming from problems with its F-14 Tomcat. When demand for its aircraft began to recover, Beech called off merger talks. Within a year Beech was back in trouble. At that time an OPEC oil embargo plunged the United States into a serious energy crisis that resulted in, among other things, the cancellation of aircraft purchasing.

The company sputtered along for three more years before Hedrick again actively sought a merger for Beech. He approached General Dynamics Corp., another defense contractor, several times larger than Grumman, with the same proposal. General Dynamics saw the benefits of diversification into civilian businesses, but as talks progressed, that company's share price began to slip while Beech's rose. For the second time, Hedrick abandoned a merger.

After allowing its agreement with Hawker-Siddeley to lapse, Beech invested heavily in its 8- to 15-seat King Air turboprop. In light of the energy crisis, this was a strategic move. Turboprop planes were slower than jets, but were much more economical to operate. Thus, customers chose craft like the King Air over jets from Lear, Cessna, and Falcon. When demand for turboprops began to wane, however, Beech once again found itself unable to finance the development of new products, and was locked out of an increasingly tight credit market. Hedrick began looking once again for a corporate suitor with a deep commitment to aviation.

In 1980 Hedrick settled on the Raytheon Company, a Massachusetts-based manufacturer of avionics and missile systems, and one of the earliest developers of radar systems. As a primary Pentagon contractor, Raytheon had access to billions of dollars in cash flow. For Raytheon, the $800 million acquisition of Beech represented a chance to diversify its customer base. Hedrick joined the board of Raytheon in January of 1981, and

was succeeded as president of Beech Aircraft by Edward C. Burns. Olive Ann Beech continued to serve as the company's chairman.

A year after Raytheon took over Beech, the general aviation market crashed, due mainly to a recession and the emergence of a strong market for used aircraft. Nevertheless, Raytheon allowed Beech to sink tremendous amounts of development money into a highly experimental aircraft called the Starship. The plane, constructed mainly out of special plastic composites, featured two rear-mounted pusher propellers and other design features that made the Starship appear to be oriented backwards. And, while it flew in a wind tunnel, there was no guarantee the craft would actually work.

In 1983 Hedrick, Burns, and Mrs. Beech retired. Linden Blue served as president for a year and was succeeded by James A. Walsh. During this time, Beech delivered the first of its newly pressurized Model 1900 airliners. Laid out for 19 passengers—because federal law requires that 20 have a flight attendant—the 1900 became a popular short-run airplane for numerous small airlines. The 1900 airliner separated Beech from its traditional rivals as the company found itself competing in a new market, populated by small airliner manufacturers such as Fairchild, Short, and Canadair.

Beech made its second entry into the jet market by purchasing the marketing rights, and later production rights, of the Diamond jet from Mitsubishi Heavy Industries. But from 1986 to 1989, Beech managed to sell only 62 of its "Beechjets." The company began to regain its footing in the jet market in 1988, when it began production of its Beechjet 400A, an improved version of the Mitsubishi Diamond.

In 1987, Beech Aircraft agreed to retrofit more than 5,000 Bonanzas that were inadvertently certified by the Federal Aviation Administration (FAA). The two-year retrofit, covering every V-tail Bonanza built since 1950, was initiated by Beech and the company absorbed the costs. Meanwhile the Starship continued to drain Beech of its profits, although the company won a huge contract from the Pentagon. In partnership with McDonnell-Douglas and Quintron, Beech surprised its competitors, Cessna and Lear, by winning a billion-dollar bid to supply 180 T1-A Jayhawk tanker trainers to the air force. The Jayhawk, a military version of the 400A Beechjet, helped to bolster its civilian counterpart's place in the market.

In 1990, Beech recorded its best year, turning out 433 aircraft and collecting $1.1 billion in sales. As a result, Max Bleck, who had succeeded Walsh as president of Beech in 1987, was promoted to president of Raytheon. He was replaced at Beech by Jack Braly. Also in 1990 the Starship won certification. While a fine aircraft, the Starship was expensive and, in an era of corporate cost-cutting, it could prove difficult to sell. In 1992, Beech's 60th anniversary year, the company turned out its 50,000th aircraft. That same year, however, a sales slump, attributed to a ten percent federal luxury tax, caused the company to cut back production and lay off 180 administrative staff.

By virtue of its 1900 and Jayhawk projects, Beech remains the largest of the small aircraft manufacturers, though Cessna builds more private aircraft. It offers a complete line of advanced aircraft, from the single-engine Bonanza, to the twin-

engine Baron and Super King Air series, to the futuristic Starship. The bulk of Beech's recent success, however, lies with its
Beechjet and 1900 airliner. Barring any severe depression in
small aircraft markets, Beech is likely to retain its leading
position in this sector of the aviation industry.

Principal Subsidiaries: Beech Holdings, Inc.; Beechcraft East;
Hangar One Company; Hedrick Beechcraft Company; United
Beechcraft Company; Beech Aerospace Services, Inc.; Beech
Acceptance Corporation; Travel Air Insurance Company;
BeechPower, Inc.

Further Reading:

Atchison, Sandra D., "Why Beech Is Floating on Cloud 9," *Business
    Week,* March 19, 1990, pp. 128–129.
Beech Aircraft Corporation: 1932–1992, 60 Years of Excellence,
    Wichita, KS: Beech Aircraft Corporation, 1992.
"Beech Layoffs," *Aviation Week & Space Technology,* April 13, 1992,
    p. 11.
"Beech Makes Its Move," *Forbes,* February 1, 1970, p. 48.
"Control Lock Design On Beech Plane Called Cause of 3 Accidents,"
    Wall Street Journal, December 29, 1971, p. 9.
"General Dynamics and Beech Aircraft End Merger Talks," *Wall
    Street Journal,* November 7, 1977, p. 8.
Grangier, Marc, "The Story of a Beechcraft Dynasty—From the King
    Air 90 to the King Air 400," *Interavia,* February 1976, pp. 135–38.
"Grumman Corp., Beech Aircraft End Merger Discussions," *Wall
    Street Journal,* October 5, 1973, p. 9.
"Hedrick's Familiar Quotations," *Forbes,* April 17, 1978, pp. 93–94.
"Highflier in High Heels," *Forbes,* August 1, 1964, pp. 30–31.
A Historical Overview of Beech Aircraft Corporation, Wichita, KS:
    Beech Aircraft Corporation, 1993.
Irving, Robert R., "How Beech Aircraft Tracks New Technologies,"
    Iron Age, December 10, 1979, pp. 43–45.
Phillips, Edward H., *Beechcraft, Pursuit of Perfection,* Eagan, MN:
    Flying Books, 1992.
Raytheon Company Annual Report, Lexington, MA: Raytheon Com-
    pany, 1992.
Walter Herschel Beech—Air Pioneer, Wichita, KS: Beech Aircraft
    Coporation.

—John Simley

Bemis Company, Inc.

222 S. Ninth St., Suite 2300
Minneapolis, Minnesota 55402
U.S.A.
(612) 376-3000
Fax: (612) 376-3180

Public Company
Incorporated: 1885 as Bemis Bro. Bag Co.
Employees: 7,733
Sales: $1.18 billion
Stock Exchanges: New York
SICs: 2671 Paper Coated and Laminated—Packaging; 2673
Bags: Plastics, Laminated, and Coated; 3089 Plastics
Products, nec; 3565 Packaging Machinery

Bemis Company, Inc. is a leading provider of flexible packaging and specialty coated and graphics products. Markets include the food, agribusiness, printing, graphic arts, medical, and chemical industries. Bemis' flexible packaging business, which generated $858 million in 1992 revenues, comprises everything from paper bags for pet food to see-through resealable cheese packaging and cold-temperature resistant packaging for frozen vegetables. Roughly 70 percent of all Bemis packaging is for the food industry. Its clientele includes such giants as Philip Morris, ConAgra, General Mills, Inc., Pillsbury, and Archer-Daniels-Midland. Processed meats, cheeses, confections, rice, flour, and breads are among those markets in which Bemis holds a dominant position. The company owes much of its reputation as a leader to its versatility as a packaging printer; measured by the number of individual printing impressions it makes annually, Bemis ranks as the world's largest printer in the packaging industry.

The corporation's other main line of business, specialty coated and graphics products, accounted for 27 percent of 1992 sales but 34 percent of its operating profits. Several analysts agree that this business, devoted to manufacturing pressure-sensitive label stock and other products for many of the same markets as the packaging division, is likely to generate the fastest growth during the 1990s.

Judson Moss Bemis founded the company in St. Louis in 1858. Born in Fitchburg, Massachusetts in 1833, Judson Moss Bemis spent part of his early childhood in New York state. He and his family moved to Illinois in 1838. Bemis flexed his entrepreneurial bent at an early age while working in Chicago as a shipping clerk and dabbling regularly in assorted enterprises, including real estate investment. Determined to launch a permanent business of his own, he contacted his cousin, Simeon Farwell, owner of a modestly successful bag factory. After touring Farwell's factory a few times, Bemis decided to enter the industry himself, with St. Louis as his headquarters. His cousin, though unable to invest money in the new venture, was willing to supply the necessary machinery for start-up operations in exchange for one-third ownership. Thus, at twenty-five, Bemis became his own boss, launching J. M. Bemis and Company, Bag Manufacturers with a pooled investment of $4,000.

The city of St. Louis soon proved an especially fortunate choice, for it had lately become the hub of trade for points both north and south along the Mississippi River and also benefited from tributary traffic stemming from the Missouri and the Illinois Rivers. Until 1866, when H. and L. Chase (considered the country's first bag company) opened a branch factory in St. Louis, Bemis had no serious competition. Indeed, there were at that time few bag manufacturers in any part of the country and none that offered the type of mechanized printing Bemis was planning. In order to overcome lingering skepticism among his customers that the neatly printed, machine-sewn, cotton bags were as sturdy as the more commonplace hand-sewn ones, Bemis guaranteed all his bags against ripping. The company's staff of four was soon filling orders and, after Bemis had sent circulars to most of the city's flour millers, the factory was operating at capacity. Inexpensive, custom-printed Bemis bags saved millers the time-consuming, messy task of stenciling and also appealed to the average consumer, long accustomed to buying flour in cumbersome wooden barrels.

By the end of its first year, the company was only marginally profitable, despite producing bags at the rate of 4,000 per day, and the owner was in desperate need of additional help and capital. Coincidentally, Simeon Farwell had written Bemis asking if a Harvard-educated relative, Edward J. Brown, might be able to come to St. Louis and work at the factory on a trial basis. Bemis agreed, provided that Brown become an equal partner in the business. Brown's diligence as a salesperson and bill collector noticeably enhanced the company's growth, but not to the point that it could sustain three partners; within two years, it was decided that Farwell should bow out.

The company's name then became Bemis and Brown, reflecting its two owners. With the advent of the Civil War, business accelerated, though bank failures and currency fluctuations created numerous headaches for the firm. A premium of 5–15 percent was being charged for Missouri state bank currency by Eastern exchanges at this time. In an effort to obtain the best possible exchange rates for his raw materials, Bemis directed Brown to open an office in Boston, their principal East Coast market. The company also gained an advantage from its entry into the sale of raw cotton, a commodity whose price skyrocketed during the war. Profits from this sideline business helped finance the growth of the company, which began to focus increasingly on burlap production, first of gunnysacks, made from secondhand bags used to ship linseed from Calcutta, and then original burlap sacks, made from imported jute fiber.

In 1867, Bemis's elder brother, Stephen A. Bemis, joined the firm. By 1870, Stephen had become a partner and was responsible for overseeing both manufacturing and selling in St. Louis. Judson Moss Bemis was thus able to join Brown in Boston, where he could more closely involve himself with commodity purchases and the financing of operations. Ultimately unhappy with his partner's managerial style, Bemis requested in 1873 that Brown state his conditions for relinquishing his part-ownership of the business. As biographer William C. Edgar wrote, "So great was Mr. Bemis's faith in the future of the business he had founded that although the sum must have seemed enormous to him . . . he did not hesitate to buy Mr. Brown's share of it for the figure he asked—three hundred thousand dollars."

Now named Bemis Bro. and Company (later changed to Bemis Bro. Bag Co.), the bag manufacturer was steadily outshining its competition. By the early 1880s, with still just one factory, it ranked second in volume in the nation to an older, four-factory rival. Prodigious growth via geographic expansion would make Bemis number one in the world by the close of the nineteenth century.

Significantly, Bemis' first branch factory was opened in 1881 in Minneapolis, the city destined to become the company's modern-day headquarters. The evolution of agriculture and the advent of railroad networks had transformed the milling trade into a vital national industry. Minneapolis, the Mill City, had become the industry's new mecca with the rise of Pillsbury, General Mills, and other major concerns.

After its expansion into Minneapolis, Bemis established bag factories in Omaha (1887); New Orleans (1891); Superior, Wisconsin (1896); San Francisco (1897); Indianapolis (1900); Memphis (1900); Kansas City (1903); Seattle (1905); Houston (1906); and Winnipeg (1906). In addition, the company began operation in 1896 of a bleachery in Indianapolis for finished bag goods, and opened a cotton mill near Jackson, Tennessee, in 1900. The company-sponsored village that arose by the mill was eventually dubbed Bemis. This last development was designed to augment the production of the Home Cotton Mills, which had been established in 1870 as a separate corporation, incorporated in 1885, and taken over by Bemis in 1902.

Judson Moss Bemis's son, A. Farwell Bemis, assumed the presidency upon his father's retirement in 1909. In the foreword to Edgar's biography of his father, A. Farwell Bemis wrote that his father's "most remarkable quality of all was his progressiveness, the pioneering instinct. To the very end, progress was what interested him, the latest machine, the latest way. . . ." Although Bemis had already retired, save for his service as a director, this instinct was certainly evident when the company's principals ventured into jute manufacturing in 1913 through the Angus Jute Company of Calcutta. At the time, Judson Moss Bemis recognized the commodity burlap as particularly valuable, a material that was "king of its kind."

Even more forward-thinking than this joint development was Bemis's entry a year later, at a time when textiles were practically the only packaging materials being used, into paper milling and paper bag manufacturing. Paper packaging continued to grow under the leadership of Judson S. Bemis, who followed A. Farwell Bemis. The emerging paper packaging industry was

to become the company's bread-and-butter business, particularly during and immediately after World War II. At that time the scarcity of cotton and burlap coincided with a steadily mounting production of paper, particularly in the South. Interestingly, other raw material shortages during the war led to the development of polyethylene, a highly versatile substance that would soon carry the company to its next technological plateau: plastic film packaging. Successfully leading the company through the World War II years and on into the start of its involvement with plastics and pressure-sensitive materials was F. Gregg Bemis. A grandson of the founder, F. Gregg Bemis managed the company from 1940 to 1960.

Although Bemis still continued to produce cotton and burlap in the 1950s and 1960s, its central product base had shifted decidedly toward paper, plastics, and custom-made packaging machinery. In 1952 the company made a firm commitment to research and development with the construction of its own research laboratory and pilot plant in Minneapolis. Seven years later, it inaugurated a long-range growth program to broaden its product lines and seek out new, compatible markets.

Heady growth under Judson (Sandy) Bemis, another grandson of the founder, characterized the 1960s. It was also during this decade that the company consolidated its headquarters in Minneapolis. By 1965, to reflect the company's growing diversity, the name was officially changed from Bemis Bro. Bag Company to Bemis Company, Inc. In 1966 Bemis common stock was listed on the New York Stock Exchange. Between 1959 and 1969 some 20 acquisitions were made. One of them, Curwood, Inc., launched Bemis into a leadership position in coated and laminated films it retains today. MACtac, established in 1959, also has shown excellent growth as a pressure-sensitive materials supplier. Among other acquisitions of the period that remain a part of the company today, Hayssen Manufacturing Company has been a particularly successful one. Acquired in 1966 to broaden the company's offering of packaging machinery, Hayssen today produces several types of state-of-the-art equipment that are compatible with many Bemis packaging materials. Yet many of the acquisitions of this era proved to be a poor fit with the company's key businesses. According to Pamela Sherrid in a 1975 *Forbes* article, "a multitude of nowhere diversifications" persisted within the company, endangering its long-term health.

In 1978 Howard Curler was named Bemis' new CEO. With Curler's appointment, the restructuring of Bemis began in earnest. Curler's relationship with Bemis originated in 1965, when Curwood, Inc.—then a small manufacturer of film packaging for cheese and other perishable foods he had co-founded—was acquired by the larger firm. He stayed on as head of his company, which became a leader in polymer manufacture and the related technologies of extrusion, coating, laminating, metallizing, and printing. Following his appointment as head of Bemis, Curler continued to focus on these areas, as well as pressure-sensitive materials, while divesting the company of its textile, publication printing, vinyl wall covering, and other extraneous operations. Within four years, more than $100 million worth of businesses were sold. Curler also launched a $140 million capital expenditure program in 1980, in effect betting close to half of the company's assets to become a first-class producer, rather than converter, of sophisticated multi-layer films for high-margin, specialty food products.

By 1990, if not earlier, Curler's bet had paid off. A *Barron's* report that year declared Bemis a company "with few peers in the field of flexible packaging," noting that "in almost any area of film or plastic packaging, Bemis is either a major player or staking out a position." Heavy capital investment has continued to distinguish Bemis during the early 1990s under Curler's protégé, CEO John Roe (son-in-law of Sandy Bemis). Acquisitions that place Bemis in a dominant market position have also been emphasized. For example, the purchase of Milprint in late 1990 made the company a leading supplier in printer packaging for the candy industry. Likewise, the acquisition of Princeton Packaging in February 1993 placed Bemis at the top in bread packaging. Clearly Bemis seems to have regained its stride, building upon its preeminence in the milling industry of former days with a host of enviable competencies in the complex food markets of present times.

Principal Subsidiaries: Accraply, Inc.; Curwood, Inc.; Hayssen Manufacturing Company; MacKay Gravure Systems, Inc.; Mankato Corp.; Milprint, Inc.; Morgan Adhesives Co. (86.9%)

Further Reading:

"Bemis—A Century of Bag Making History," *Industrial Supply Expediter,* November 1962, pp. 1–2.

Bemis Company, Inc. Annual Report, Minneapolis: Bemis Company, Inc., 1992.

"Bemis May Acquire Packaging Firm," *Star Tribune,* December 5, 1992, p. 2D.

Byrne, Harlan S., "Bemis Co.: Packaging Maker Finds the New Year a Pleasant Surprise," *Barron's,* April 9, 1990, pp. 59–60.

——, "Bemis Co.: Good Things Come in Its Flexible Packaging," *Barron's,* August 5, 1991, pp. 33–34.

Edgar, William C., *Judson Moss Bemis: Pioneer,* Minneapolis: Bellman Company, 1926.

Guide to Bemis Company, Minneapolis: Bemis Company, Inc., 1988.

"In Brief," *Star Tribune,* February 12, 1993, p. 3D.

Paul, Herb, "Bemis Researchers Find New Products," *Minneapolis Star,* September 16, 1955.

Sherrid, Pamela, "Wake-up Time at Bemis," *Forbes,* June 21, 1982, pp. 50, 54.

Walden, Gene, "Bemis Company, Inc.," *The 100 Best Stocks to Own in America,* 2nd ed., Chicago: Dearborn Financial Publishing, 1991.

"With a Little Bit of Luck," *Forbes,* December 15, 1975, p. 27.

—Jay P. Pederson

Beneficial Corporation

P.O. Box 911
Wilmington, Delaware 19899
U.S.A.
(302) 798-0800
Fax: (302) 781-3044

Public Company
Incorporated: 1929 as Beneficial Finance Corporation
Employees: 8,500
Sales: $1.81 billion
Stock Exchanges: Boston Midwest New York Philadelphia
   Pacific
SICs: 6141 Personal Credit Institutions; 6162 Mortgage
   Bankers & Correspondents; 6021 National Commercial
   Banks; 6719 Holding Companies Nec

Beneficial Corporation is one of the oldest and largest consumer finance companies in the United States. Involved in sales finance, mortgages, banking, and insurance, Beneficial opened its first office, the Beneficial Loan Society, in 1914 in Elizabeth, New Jersey. In its early years, the company loaned money to consumers who could not get loans from banks. The loans, which were often used to buy such durable goods as appliances and furniture, were then paid back in installments. The first office allowed consumers to borrow up to $300. By 1924 Beneficial had 80 offices, making $13 million a year in loans, each averaging less than $100. In 1929 the firm was reorganized as Beneficial Finance Corporation.

Consumer finance was a risky field, dependent on market conditions and the vagaries of state law. Nonetheless, Beneficial managed to slowly expand during the difficult years of the Great Depression and World War II through careful attention to its customer base of middle-class borrowers. Beneficial salespeople offered customers personalized service, getting to know the names and ages of customers' children and taking other steps that made customers feel more comfortable than if they were applying for a loan at a bank.

The U.S. economy boomed after the war, as did Beneficial, fueled by pent-up consumer demand. In the mid-1950s the firm began diversifying. In 1954 it began a ''fly now—pay later'' plan with Pan American World Airways. Soon after, it formed a subsidiary that financed leased computers and other office equipment. Consumer finance remained a fickle field, and when

Canada reduced the allowable rate on small loans, Beneficial closed 22 offices there and stopped making certain kinds of loans. By the late 1950s Beneficial was expanding rapidly. It moved quickly into Alaska and Hawaii when they became states and opened more than 60 offices in 1959. Beneficial eventually had 1,200 offices in the United States and Canada, making loans averaging $370.

In 1960 Beneficial became the first U.S. consumer finance company to enter the British market. The British government had just relaxed its formerly tight controls over consumer credit, the economy was in a period of growth, and consumer durables were widely available for the first time since World War II. The British market was intensely competitive, however. It already had about 1,250 finance companies, with 12 of them controlling nearly 70 percent of the market. British consumers were also less enamored of installment buying; 25 percent of cars were bought on installment, for example, versus 64 percent in the United States.

In 1961 Beneficial bought Western Auto Supply Co., a 4,500-store retail chain. The customers who bought Western's hardware were largely the same industrial and clerical workers that took out loans with Beneficial.

By 1964 Beneficial had 1,600 loan offices and made 1.7 million loans worth about $950 million. Interest rates were rising, reaching an effective rate of 18 percent by late 1965, and Beneficial's profits rose with them. Beneficial decided to expand by buying Spiegel Inc., a Chicago-based mail-order merchandiser. Spiegel, with $300 million in annual sales, sold 90 percent of its goods on credit and made most of its profits from the interest. Beneficial thus viewed Spiegel as a source of new customers for its lending business; Spiegel's customers were mostly the same people who used Beneficial and Western Auto.

Beneficial viewed its acquisitions as a way to compensate for the increasing competition in the lending business. But by 1966 this diversification strategy began going awry. Interest rates had risen so high that consumers stopped taking on debt, and sales at Spiegel and Western Auto plummeted, multiplying Beneficial's problems. Western Auto was largely a franchise operation; when its sales slumped, other retailers began offering attractive franchise pacts, and Western lost many dealers. Meanwhile, giant J.C. Penney entered the mail-order market in 1966, further hurting Spiegel. Beneficial itself did better than its two subsidiaries. Its capital came from long-term debt acquired during lower interest rates, and its loans were already at close to the legal maximum rate, so its customers were not scared off by a rise in rates.

The situation began improving by the end of 1967 as consumers began returning to the credit market. To boost Spiegel's profits, management tightened credit, brought out special interest catalogues, removed certain items from its catalogue, and started a shopping club. To strengthen Western Auto, Beneficial bought Midland International, an electronic equipment supplier, for 55,000 shares of stock.

Beneficial itself continued to grow; by 1968 the firm had 1,770 offices in every state but Delaware. Revenue for 1968 was $238.6 million. It had 262 offices in California alone and 141 in New York. The firm also had 234 offices in Canada, 24 in

Australia, and eight in England. Beneficial was the number two firm in the consumer loan industry. It had more offices than Household Finance, the leader, but Household had an average $950,000 in receivables per office, while Beneficial had only $550,000. To catch up, Beneficial began pushing bigger loans. The maximum size of loans was regulated by law in most states, however. Most of Beneficial's loans were to families making around $7,500 a year, taking out an average loan of around $690 for a period of 36 months. Approximately 75 percent of loans were secured by liens on autos or chattel mortgages on household goods.

To bring more customers into its offices, the firm began offering on-the-spot tax refunds in 1970 through its Benevest Inc. subsidiary. Customers whose taxes were prepared by Benevest were given their refunds in cash by the company, which was reimbursed when the customer's state or federal tax refund arrived. The refunds increased Benevest's tax preparation business but also provided an opening to sell customers other financial services.

In 1970 the firm changed its name to Beneficial Corporation. Interest rates were again rising, meaning that it cost Beneficial more to get the money it loaned. Since the maximum interest Beneficial could charge was often set by law, higher interest rates meant lower earnings as well as less borrowing, as consumers again became wary. By 1973 the short-term interest rate situation had worsened, and large banks like Chase Manhattan Corporation were buying personal loan companies in an attempt to diversify. The economy was in recession, and loan defaults increased. On the positive side, Beneficial was cutting its operating expenses by switching to on-line computer systems, while the size of the average loan was growing.

As interest rates fell in the following years, Beneficial recovered. It had record profits of $100.4 million in 1976 on revenue of $1.743 billion. The volume of consumer loans was increasing, and Beneficial's insurance operations were growing. Banks were still entering Beneficial's niche, however, and to counterattack the firm began offering Visa and Master Charge credit cards through its wholly owned People's Bank & Trust Co. of Wilmington, Delaware. M. W. Caspersen became chairman and chief executive in 1976, at the age of 35.

Profits took a hit in 1977, however, due to losses at Midland International. Consumer loans accounted for less of its profits—56 percent in 1977—while insurance grew to 35 percent. The average size of Beneficial loans continued to grow, reaching $1,348 in 1977, up from $962 in 1973. The average payback period extended to 45 months. Beneficial's two primary insurers, the Central National Life Insurance Company of Omaha and American Centennial Insurance Co., offered a wide range of coverage from life to property. Beneficial entered reinsurance in 1977, lured by potentially quick profits from high interest rates. The firm also liked reinsurance because risk is divided among many insurers. Further, because reinsurance claims are often delayed by litigation, premiums can be collected and invested without having to pay claims for years.

Beneficial entered the leasing field in 1977, when it bought Parliament Leasing, which leased hospital and medical equipment. Beneficial also bought a small consumer finance firm in West Germany for $40 million in receivables. The firm bought First Texas Financial Corp., a savings and loan, in 1978. The following year, Beneficial purchased Capital Financial Services Ltd. in Columbus, Ohio, and Southwestern Investment Co. in Amarillo, Texas, for a combined total of $184.3 million. To avoid anti-trust laws, Beneficial made an agreement with the U.S. Department of Justice to sell some of its offices. In 1980 Beneficial sold 138 offices in 12 states to a subsidiary of Barclays Bank International Ltd.

The consumer loan industry again fell on hard times in 1979 as a recession caused personal bankruptcies to increase 60 percent, while interest rates soared. Beneficial's recently purchased savings and loans were also hurting, losing $800,000 in 1980. Beneficial's purchases had cost more than $300 million. To raise cash it sold Spiegel to a German company for $52 million, a sale that freed Beneficial from most of Spiegel's formidable $441 million debt. Spiegel's retailing division had not been doing well, posting profits of only $10.8 million in 1980. Beneficial also moved into the profitable second-mortgage loan business, along with many other finance companies.

By its own admission, Beneficial had known very little about reinsurance when it entered the field in 1977, so it hired ten managing general agents to handle it through American Centennial Insurance. But one of the agents defrauded the company, diverting millions of dollars in premiums while distributing the risk to fraudulent or insolvent reinsurers. Two other agents, Beneficial later claimed, grossly under-reported losses likely to be claimed from programs they wrote. As a result, Beneficial was forced to put $200 million into the reinsurance operation in the early 1980s. Even so, the firm made $101.2 million in 1985 on revenues of $2.1 billion. But in 1986 its reinsurance losses forced the writeoff of another $260 million, creating a loss of nearly $50 million for the year.

The reinsurance debacle damaged Beneficial's credit rating and forced down the price of its stock. Alleghany Corporation, a New York-based financial services and industrial company, bought three percent of Beneficial and announced plans to buy more. The firm's management responded by announcing that Beneficial was looking for a buyer. Beneficial stock rose 50 percent amid various takeover rumors.

Its reinsurance woes obscured Beneficial's underlying strengths. It had $7 billion in receivables and an 11 percent spread between the cost of its money and the rate it could charge consumers. In addition, its second mortgage and credit card loan programs were also doing well. Given these strengths, management soon decided to sell off Beneficial's troubled operations rather than the entire corporation.

The sale of American Centennial Insurance was complicated by regulatory hurdles stemming from the insurer's poor financial condition. The deal nevertheless went through, leaving Beneficial free to pursue its core businesses. By 1990 the firm was the third-largest issuer of second mortgages in the United States and had $8.4 billion in assets. It charged 14 percent interest for second mortgages and 23 percent for unsecured personal loans. Beneficial also was expanding into Europe, opening offices in Dresden and Leipzig, both in the former East Germany.

To find potential clients, Beneficial bought customer bills from retailers and used automated telemarketing. With many banks and thrifts weakened by bad loans, Beneficial was able to buy consumer loans worth $863 million in 1991, adding to its rapidly growing receivables portfolio. Income for 1992 would have been $148.4 million but was lowered by a charge of $98.6 million, much of it for foreclosed real estate, particularly in southern California. But due to its return to conservative lending practices in the mid-1980s, Beneficial largely avoided the huge real estate losses that hurt many lenders, including rival Household Finance.

With the approach of the mid-1990s, Beneficial was in a more solid position than it had been in many years. It continued its focus on middle-income consumers, starting new ventures aimed at them, including the Personal Mortgage Corporation and FlashTax, Inc.

Further Reading:

"Benefits for Beneficial," *Forbes,* October 15, 1965.

Gordon, Mitchell, "Beneficial Corp. to Ring up Record High Net This Year," *Barron's,* October 30, 1978.

"Harder Than It Looks," *Forbes,* January 15, 1967.

Hays, Laurie, "Reinsurance Woes Threatening Beneficial," *Wall Street Journal,* September 2, 1986; "Beneficial Bid to Sell Unit Faces Hurdles," *Wall Street Journal,* January 19, 1987.

Kantrow, Yvette D., "Beneficial Gains by Lending to the People Banks Shun," *American Banker,* February 19, 1992.

"Luring Clients With On-the-Spot Tax Refunds," *Business Week,* December 20, 1969.

Nathan, Leah J., "Beneficial Could Give Lending a Good Name Again," *Business Week,* October 22, 1990.

Pacey, Margaret D., "Beneficial Finance: Number Two in the Personal Loan Field Is Also Trying Harder," *Barron's,* April 8, 1968.

"Personal Loan Companies Could Use Some Help," *Financial World,* November 28, 1973.

"Selling Spiegel to Prepare for a Future in Banking," *Business Week,* July 6, 1981.

Spragins, Ellyn E., "Beneficial: On the Block and Loving It," *Business Week,* September 8, 1986.

"U.S. Lender Seeks to Cash In," *Business Week,* October 31, 1959.

—Scott M. Lewis

BIC Corporation

500 BIC Drive
Milford, Connecticut 06460
U.S.A.
(203) 783-2000
Fax: (203) 783-2081

Public Subsidiary of Societe BIC, S.A. (63%)
Incorporated: 1958 as Waterman-BIC Pen Corporation
Employees: 2,400
Sales: $417.4 million
Stock Exchanges: New York
SICs: 3951 Pens and Mechanical Pencils; 3999
  Manufacturing Industries, Nec; 3421 Cutlery

BIC Corporation is the country's leading manufacturer of disposable ballpoint pens and cigarette lighters. It is also an industry leader in the production of disposable shavers. Producing inexpensive, quality products promoted through aggressive advertising campaigns, BIC has steadily increased its marketshare in the United States, maintaining 60 percent of the ballpoint pen market and 45 percent of the disposable shaver market in 1992. After moving into sporting goods with a leading brand of sailboards in the late 1980s, the company also strengthened its position in stationery goods by purchasing Wite-Out Products, Inc. in 1992.

The company was founded by Marcel Bich, who left his job as production manager for an ink company in 1945 to set up his own business outside of Paris, manufacturing parts for fountain pens and mechanical pencils. During this time ballpoint pens, although still very expensive, were becoming popular in Europe, and the first ballpoint pens were introduced in the United States, selling for $12.50 each at New York's Gimbel's Department Store.

First Bich expanded his business to include the manufacture of plastic barrels for ballpoint pen companies, and then, in 1949, he introduced his own line of ballpoint pens. Called BICs—using the phonetic spelling of Bich's name—the pens were of a simple design, nonretractable with clear plastic barrels, and sold for around 19 cents each. While early ballpoint pens were known to clog and leak, Bich's pens proved reliable and achieved immediate success in Europe with annual sales exceeding $5 million by 1955. Bich then turned his attention to marketing his products in the United States.

The Waterman Pen Company in Seymour, Connecticut, was founded by Lewis E. Waterman, an American insurance salesperson and part-time inventor, who developed the first practical fountain pen in 1884. At one time, Waterman Pen was the world's leading maker of fountain pens. In the 1950s, however, with the growing popularity of ballpoint pens, the company had begun to falter. In 1958, Bich agreed to purchase 60 percent of the company for $1 million. When the true financial condition of the company became known, Bich was able to acquire the remaining 40 percent for nothing. The company was renamed the Waterman-BIC Pen Corporation, and its headquarters was moved to Milford, Connecticut.

The inexpensive BIC pens did not catch on as quickly in the United States as they had in Europe, probably because the U.S. market had been flooded with shoddy pens by other companies. The leading brand in the "over-a-dollar" pen market was made by the PaperMate pen company, purchased in 1955 by The Gillette Company. Bich's U.S. managers urged him to make a more expensive ballpoint to compete with PaperMate, but Bich resisted. He reportedly told his advisers, "Waterman is 100 percent mine. You are going to do what you are told."

In the early 1960s Waterman-BIC launched an aggressive television advertising campaign that boasted that BIC pens would write "First Time, Every Time." To prove that a 29¢ BIC pen would perform as well as pens costing several times more, the commercials showed BIC pens still working after being drilled through wallboard, shot from guns, fire-blasted, and strapped to the feet of ice skaters. In another effort to establish a market in the United States, Waterman-BIC distributed its pens for sale in grocery stores and small shops near schools where students congregated, rather than in the department stores that carried more expensive pens.

After a rocky start, Waterman-BIC established itself as the largest maker of ballpoint pens in the United States. By 1967, the company was turning out nearly 500 million pens annually, accounting for nearly 60 percent of the U.S. market. In 1972, *Time* reported that "Baron Bich has done for ballpoints what Henry Ford did for cars: he has produced a cheap but serviceable model." In 1974, a reporter for *Forbes* wrote, "From the start, Bich concentrated on the cheap end of the market—but with a difference. Where his competitors were turning out junk, Bich made a reliable pen that could command a premium, but still cheap price. . . . By the time his competitors figured out how to build an equally good pen for the price, Bich had a lock on the market."

In 1971, Waterman-BIC became the BIC Pen Corporation, more accurately reflecting its business. However, that name soon became outdated as the company embarked on its first diversification.

In 1970, Gillette purchased the S. T. Dupont Company, a prestigious French manufacturer whose principal product was luxury cigarette lighters that sold for hundreds of dollars. During this time Dupont explored the possibilities of marketing a disposable lighter, developing an inexpensive disposable lighter called Cricket, which it introduced in the United States in 1972. Later that year, *Time* reported that BIC was test marketing a disposable lighter that could provide 3,000 lights before wearing out. BIC introduced this lighter in 1973.

To compete with Gillette, which was solidly entrenched as the market leader, BIC again turned to creative television advertising. A series of commercials soon showed sensuous women urging cigarette smokers to "Flick My BIC," a phrase perceived as having sexual connotations, that soon became a part of the national lexicon. Writing about network censors in *The Best Thing On TV: Commercials,* Jonathan Price remarked, "They absolutely do not see sex in advertising if it's blatant. . . . They can find sex in a garage mechanic talking about shock absorbers. But let somebody say, 'Flick my Bic,'—this is beautifully obscene—everyone nods their heads and lets that go, because . . . well, we know you can't possibly mean that, that would be obscene. . . .''

BIC also slashed the wholesale price of its lighters so they sold at retail for less than one dollar. This action set off a fierce price war with Gillette. But by the end of 1978, BIC had surpassed Cricket, and in 1984, Gillette acknowledged defeat. It pulled Cricket from the market and later sold the brand to Swedish Match Corporation, which licensed the lighter for distribution in the United States. At the time, BIC controlled about 65 percent of the market for disposable lighters.

During the time that BIC and Gillette were battling over disposable lighters, the companies were also going head-to-head for a new segment of Gillette's traditional business, disposable shavers. King C. Gillette had invented the safety razor in 1903, and the company he founded dominated the market for the next 70 years. Then in 1975, BIC's parent corporation, the French Societe BIC, S.A., introduced a disposable plastic shaver in Europe. Anticipating that BIC would next bring out the shaver in the United States, Gillette quickly introduced its own disposable razor dubbed "Good News!" in 1976, a full year before the BIC shaver made its American debut. However, Gillette seriously underestimated the demand for disposable razors. Furthermore, it was not eager to see customers switch from its reusable razor systems to its disposables, since Good News! cost more to make and sold for less than the company's replacement blades. Therefore, Gillette spent very little on advertising.

BIC, however, advertised heavily, again relying on catchy television commercials. In one series of commercials, people were blindfolded and shaved by professional barbers, using either the BIC Shaver or Gillette's nondisposable Trac II razor. According to the ads, 58 percent of the participants claimed that there was no difference between the BIC shave and the Gillette shave. Gillette leaders were incensed by the ads and asked the three major television networks not to run the commercials unless BIC could document its claims.

By the end of 1979, Gillette and BIC each controlled about 50 percent of the market for disposables, which had grown to represent 20 percent of the total market for wet-shave razors. Disposables were especially popular among teenagers, and women appreciated the BIC Lady Shaver, the first razor specially designed and marketed with them in mind. Within ten years, Gillette would stop advertising its disposables to concentrate on its razor systems and replacement blades.

In 1982, with revenues approaching $220 million, BIC acknowledged its expanding status as a leading maker of lighters and shavers by dropping "pen" from its name to officially become BIC Corporation. By then BIC had also taken a tentative step into sports equipment. In 1982, the company introduced the BIC Sailboard, which quickly became the North American market leader. However, in 1985 the company was forced to stop selling the sailboard in the United States when a U.S. District Court ruled that BIC had infringed on a patent owned by Windsurfing International. BIC reintroduced the sailboard to the U.S. market when the patent expired in 1987.

Having weathered fierce competitive battles for three decades, BIC faced perhaps its most serious threat in April 1987 when the *New York Times* reported that at least three people had died because BIC lighters had malfunctioned. The newspaper also reported that the company agreed to pay $3.2 million in damages to a Pennsylvania woman who claimed her lighter ignited in a pocket while she was on a camping trip.

The Pennsylvania case was the first involving BIC to go to trial, and the *Times* reported that although "claims began to trickle in soon after Bic introduced its throwaway lighters in 1972, . . . the company has until recently been able to keep the cases quiet by settling them out of court." The newspaper stated that BIC had settled more than 20 cases for amounts ranging from $5,000 to almost $500,000. During the trial, design engineers testified that BIC lighters occasionally leaked, and debris could cause the shut-off valve to fail. There were also reports of BIC lighters flaring up while they were being used or accidentally igniting while lying on overheated automobile dashboards.

At the time, lighters accounted for about 40 percent of BIC's revenues, and the day the story appeared, BIC stock fell 25 percent, from $32 to $24 per share. For a week, the company stonewalled, refusing to provide information or answer questions about the allegations amid rumors that thousands of lawsuits had been brought against the company and that a New Jersey congressperson was threatening to hold hearings on the safety of BIC lighters. Eventually, the company changed its tactics and revealed that there were 42 lawsuits then pending. BIC maintained that most of the incidents were caused by user negligence. Also acknowledging that a woman had died in an accident involving one of its lighters, BIC reassured the public that it had discontinued the model that was involved in the accident.

As a result of BIC management's candor, the company's stock began to regain value. Although it stumbled again briefly in September following the airing of the ABC television program "20/20," which featured a story on lighter safety, the stock was back to $31 per share by October. Bruno Bich, Marcel's son, who became president of the U.S. subsidiary in 1982, later told *Investor Relations* that, "With hindsight we should have given out more information and done it faster to avoid the inaccuracies and exaggerations that appeared in the press."

According to BIC, the company has defended itself in more than 50 lawsuits involving lighters between 1988 and 1993, losing only three. In one of those, however, a jury in Creek County, Oklahoma, found BIC responsible for injuries to three children severely burned while playing with a lighter, awarding

$22 million in actual and punitive damages. The lighter allegedly exploded when it was dropped while lit. Attorneys for the children argued that the lighter should have been more child resistant; BIC argued that the children should have been better supervised.

In its 1992 annual report, the company said it was "vigorously appealing the verdict." The annual report went on to say, "The legal expenses of defending product liability claims involving lighters continue to be heavy. However, as a result of our longstanding philosophy to vigorously defend these claims, and our success in doing so, the number of lawsuits continues to decline." The first adverse decision resulted in a $1,000 verdict, and the second verdict that went against BIC has been reversed and remanded for a new trial following BIC's successful appeal.

Also that year, BIC introduced a lighter with a "child resistant" catch, reportedly the result of a seven-year, $21 million development program. The patented Child Guard lighter required that a safety latch be moved to the side and up before it would light. The latch slid back into place automatically after each use. The Consumer Product Safety Commission has also adopted a child-resistant standard for disposable lighters that will become effective in July 1994.

However, the issue of safety became even more convoluted in 1992 when a U.S. Court of Appeals in Philadelphia ruled that manufacturers of products completely safe when used as intended may also have an obligation to make the product safe in unconventional circumstances. The ruling involved a case in which a three-year-old child took a BIC lighter from his father's pants pocket and set fire to an infant's bedclothes. The case, Griggs v. BIC Corp., was remanded to a lower court that had originally dismissed the case. In light of a subsequent decision by the Pennsylvania court, BIC is expected to re-file its motion for summary judgment.

During this time BIC attempted a further diversification by launching a line of inexpensive, pocket-sized perfume "spritzers" in 1989. Marketed under the name Parfum BIC, the fragrances were first introduced by Societe BIC, S.A., in Europe, where they were sold alongside other BIC products. Analysts were skeptical whether U.S. consumers would accept an inexpensive French perfume since part of the appeal of French perfumes lay in their image as luxurious and expensive. Despite an ad campaign that *Advertising Age* estimated as costing $22 million, touting the fragrances as "Paris in your pocket," Parfum BIC lasted less than a year in the United States. Sales of the fragrances lasted longer in Europe, but were eventually dropped overseas as well in 1991.

In 1992, BIC purchased Wite-Out Products, Inc., the second largest maker of correction fluids for office use in the United States. The correction fluid was subsequently reintroduced as BIC Wite-Out. The company also changed the name of its Writing Instruments division to Stationery Products, indicating an intention to market an expanded line of stationery related products, while continuing to expand its successful lines of pens, lighters, and shavers. The company reported its highest ever sales and earnings in 1992, and moved its trading from the American Stock Exchange to the New York Stock Exchange. Recent corporate literature has reaffirmed the company's intent to produce "excellent consumable products at the lowest possible price."

Principal Subsidiaries: BIC Sport, Inc.

Further Reading:

"Are the Talents Transferable?" *Forbes,* April 1, 1974, p. 62.
Armstrong, Jeffrey D., "BIC Corp.: 'The Stock Will Strengthen as the Issue of Lighter Safety Fades,' " *Barron's,* October 12, 1987, p. 69.
"Bich the Ballpoint King," *Fortune,* August 15, 1969, p. 122.
Cooper, Wendy, "The Case of the Exploding Lighters," *Institutional Investor,* December 1987, p. 209.
"Discovering the Potential in BIC," *Business Week,* July 30, 1979, p. 65.
"Extinguished: Gillette Puts Out Its Cricket," *Time,* October 15, 1984, p. 93.
Flax, Steven, "Why Bic Got Flicked," *Forbes,* September 27, 1982, p. 38.
"Gillette Challenges Bic to Verify Its Ad Claims," *Business Week,* March 19, 1979, p. 32.
"Going Bananas Over Bic, *Time,* December 18, 1972, p. 93.
Hayes, Linda Snyder, "Gillette Takes the Wraps Off," *Fortune,* February 25, 1980, p. 148.
"An Igniting Controversy," *Time,* April 20, 1987, p. 56.
Ingrassia, Lawrence, "Gillette Holds Its Edge By Endlessly Searching For a Better Shave," *Wall Street Journal,* December 10, 1992, p. A1.
King, Resa W., "Will $4 Perfume Do the Trick for Bic?" *Business Week,* June 20, 1988, p. 89.
Langway, Lynn, "Razor Fighting," *Newsweek,* November 22, 1976, p. 103.
Moskowitz, Daniel, "Courts Tackle Safety Liability in Product Design," *Washington Post,* February 8, 1993, p. WB11.
"Scents and Sensibility," *Time,* May 20, 1991, p. 47.
Sloan, Pat, "Bic Pulls Fragrances After Flickering Sales," *Advertising Age,* March 12, 1990, p. 77.
——, "$22M Campaign Urges: Spritz Your Bic," *Advertising Age,* February 20, 1989, p. 3.
"Starting To Click; Mainstay Products Help BIC Mark Profit Gains," *Barron's,* June 23, 1986, p. 52
Warner, Liz, "Bic Scents a Quick Killing," *Marketing,* June 30, 1988, p. 1.
"Waterman-Bic Pen Corp.: On the Ball with the Ball-point," *Nation's Business,* December 1970, p. 72.
Welles, Chris, "The War of the Razors," *Esquire,* February 1980, p. 29.

—Dean Boyer

Block Drug Company, Inc.

257 Cornelison Avenue
Jersey City, New Jersey 07302-9988
U.S.A.
(201) 434-3000
Fax: (201) 434-5739

Incorporated: 1970
Employees: 3,300
Sales: $562.9 million
Stock Exchanges: NASDAQ
SICs: 3843 Dental Equipment & Supplies; 2843 Surface
   Active Agents; 2844 Toilet Preparations; 2834
   Pharmaceutical Preparations

Block Drug Company, Inc., develops and manufactures a variety of pharmaceutical products, including dental care, oral hygiene and professional dental care products (which accounted for about 66 percent of total net sales in 1992); consumer products (which made up about 20 percent); and ethical pharmaceutical products (14 percent). Block's most popular products include Polident denture cleanser and Poli-Grip dental adhesives; BC headache powders and tablets; Nytol sleeping pills; Tegrin medicated shampoo; 2000 Flushes, an automatic in-tank toilet bowl cleaner; and medical relief products that help treat problems such as hemorrhoids and psoriasis. Block Drug is a family-run business in its third generation. With a very closed and private history, the company went public in 1970 and remains solidly profitable: sales more than doubled from 1983 to 1992. Block's products are sold in 125 countries.

While Block Drug Company, Inc., was incorporated in 1970, the history of the company can be traced back to 1907 when Alexander Block, a Russian immigrant, opened a small drug store on Fulton Street in Brooklyn, New York. By 1915 he turned wholesaler, and by 1925 he was in the drug manufacturing business, acquiring a 50 percent interest in Wernet's Dental Manufacturing Company.

Continuing to grow through acquisitions in the 1930s, Block entered the dental care products business, which would be the company's most profitable over the years. In 1931 Block bought Antikamnia Remedy Company, a small drug and dental care products company, as well as Pycopay toothbrush and Romilar cough syrup. During this period Block also developed Polident dental powder, which eventually spawned brands including Poli-Grip denture adhesive.

Heavily advertised brand names and slightly differentiated products became Block's trademark for success. In the 1950s, Block was a pioneer in the use of network television commercials, which succeeded in making his products household names. This led to huge growth and new products; for example, he built an entire family of products around the Polident name. An ex-product manager at Block once commented that Block Drug "could hide in the bushes, then . . . push a button and TV would sell the product."

After Alexander Block died in 1953, his son Leonard took over the company. He has run the operation since, keeping earnings and sales growth at around ten percent per year. Commentators have noted that while Block does not have the capital to compete directly with the large pharmaceutical companies like Warner-Lambert, its innovative advertising has meant safe niche markets alongside the bigger brand names.

By 1966 Block was spending $10.5 million annually to advertise its very successful Polident denture cleanser against fierce competition. Warner-Lambert had introduced Efferdent denture cleanser tablets, which reportedly gained 20 percent of the market in its West Coast debut. In response to this move, Block stepped up advertising in 1966, with the company delivering 1.5 billion messages (twice as many as in 1965) in an attempt to reach the denture wearer who watched television.

Block developed a slightly differentiated product, Polident "tablets" for the "portable denture wearer," and also developed new decorator boxes. The new tablets took 15 percent of the entire denture cleanser market by the end of 1965 and had expanded the total denture cleanser market volume by 25 percent. The ad campaign by Polident (twice the amount of money spent on the 1964 Democratic presidential campaign) also included a Block version of Efferdent, called SteraKleen.

The late 1960s were a period of growth for Block Drug. Income increased from $4.8 million in 1967 to $6.6 million for the year ending March 31, 1971. The drug products segment of the business went from nine percent to 29 percent of total business, while dental care products fell from 85 to 65 percent of the total. Foreign sales and television and radio ad expenditures were both on the rise.

In 1970 Block Drug incorporated, and the following year the company went public, putting 275,000 shares of common stock on the market. Revenues rose by seven percent in fiscal year 1971 and net income jumped eight percent over the same period. International sales in 125 foreign countries had 15 percent of the business in 1971. Television was still the company's favored advertising vehicle, with Polident the most advertised Block product in 1971. Polident lost ground to competitor Efferdent, holding a 36 percent market share compared to Efferdent's 40 percent. Block's other leading products, including Nytol, held their own, and Block added a medicated soap to the Tegrin shampoo line.

In the early 1970s the company was able to cut distribution costs of spot and network commercials by 35 percent by using video tape rather than film. Block turned to Advertel, a tape company in Toronto, to distribute Block commercials, whatever the original production medium, and hence reduce the costs of duplicating. For a company that relied so heavily on television advertising, this outsourcing of distribution was an important breakthrough in cost reduction.

In 1972 Block's advertising reputation was dealt a blow when the federal government and the National Association of Broadcasters asked Block to downplay its promotion of sleeping pills. The government asked that Block's Nytol (along with J. B. Williams Company's Sominex and Whitehall Labs' Sleep-Eze) ads show sleeping pills as an aid to, rather than a direct cause of, sleep. The ads were modified to comply with the request.

Block's sales began to stagnate in the early to mid–1970s as larger competitors such as Procter & Gamble and Warner-Lambert entered its markets. Some attributed Block's problems to an apparent move away from TV advertising into other merchandising and marketing activities, in which the company couldn't compete effectively with the giants. It was also noted that Block needed other strategies, such as more aggressive new product development. According to Melvin Kopp, Block's controller, "Our products must constantly be replaced by newer products. We fell behind on that."

Block kept Polident and Tegrin competitive by spending more advertising dollars per sales dollar, especially on television. In 1976, for example, Block spent $30 million, or 23 percent of its sales, on advertising, while Procter & Gamble, with the largest total advertising budget in the industry, spent $445 million, or eight percent of sales; Warner-Lambert spent 15 percent of its sales on advertising.

While sales of dental care products declined domestically, sales abroad increased from ten percent of net income in 1971 to 26 percent of net income in 1973. One concern over the denture cleanser market was that the market was becoming saturated and that there would be a reduced number of people who use dentures as dental hygiene improved during the 1960s and 1970s.

More advertising battles followed as the struggle between Polident and Efferdent continued. Block brought suit against Warner-Lambert, charging that Warner-Lambert "falsely and deceptively" disparaged Polident tablets in its ads. Block withdrew the suit when Warner-Lambert agreed to revise the contested spot.

Block ran into advertising trouble of its own in 1977. The Federal Trade Commission (FTC) ordered Block to stop what it considered false and misleading advertising, taking exception to Block's claims that users of Poli-Grip or Super Poli-Grip could eat such foods as apples or corn-on-cob without difficulty. The FTC also stated that Block didn't have reliable scientific evidence to substantiate the claim that its new Extra Effervescent Polident denture cleanser would clean better than Warner-Lambert's Extra Strength Efferdent.

In the 1980s Block aggressively pursued its niche marketing strategy, including a successful campaign to revive the popularity of powdered pain killers. Targeting the southern United States, where powdered pain killers have retained popularity, Block marketed a "better-tasting," granulated pain killer

through folksy ads; soon the "fast-acting powders," as they were known, became available throughout the United States. Sales of powders more than doubled between 1980 and 1986.

The company reorganized its front office in the late 1980s. In 1988 Leonard Block, chairman, was named senior chairman of the board, a newly created post. He was succeeded by James A. Block, who had been president of the company; Thomas Block was named president.

Block's advertising made news once again in the late 1980s as the company developed a new line of commercials for its Super Poli-Grip product. The company sought to develop TV spots with the "real touch," a new trend in product endorsement. This approach involved using an average "Joe" or "Jane" who used the product to speak on its behalf. To develop the Poli-Grip TV spots, Block spent two years—with the help of commercial casting consultants—to find an ideal "real" candidate to promote their new Super Poli-Grip denture adhesive: a woman between the ages of 35 and 50 who was physically active and attractive, wore dentures, *and* used the Poli-grip line.

Block continued to expand into new product areas and to market other companies' products. As part of a joint venture with Chemex Pharmaceuticals, Inc., Block Drug marketed Chemex's Actinex Cream, designed to treat pre-malignant skin lesions. Relying on its expertise in dental products, Block also contracted to market Ciba-Geigy Corporation's Habitrol nicotine skin patch, a smoking cessation aid, to dental professionals. Habitrol was the leading nicotine patch, with sales of about $350 million.

Block's sales grew by 12 percent in 1992, and its profits increased by 10 percent. A public company, Block nevertheless remains a family affair: Block family members hold three top positions with the company, while the family controls 100 percent of the company's voting stock and 50 percent of the non-voting stock. Block is generally risk-averse, preferring to keep a good portion of its retained earnings in the form of long-term bonds, which generate increasing amounts of tax-free income. The company's taxes have been generally kept low by the location of major subsidiaries in tax sanctuaries like Ireland and Puerto Rico.

Principal Subsidiaries: Block Drug Company Reed and Carnick Division.

Further Reading:

Alsop, Ronald, "Folksy Ads Help in Reviving Old-Time Headache Powders," *Wall Street Journal,* June 19, 1986.
"Block Drug Co.'s Ads For Denture Products Are Cited by FTC Aide," *Wall Street Journal,* October 28, 1977.
"Block Drug Exec Tallies Savings in Shift to Tape," *Advertising Age,* February 15, 1971.
"Block Drug Introduces Instant Mildew Stain Remover," *Spray-Technology-and-Marketing,* January 1992.
"Block Drug Unit Goes to McAdams," *Advertising Age,* August 10, 1970.
"Block Drug Will Sell Ciba-Geigy's Nicotine Skin-Patch to Dentists," *Wall Street Journal,* September 30, 1992.
"Block Gives Grey BC; SSC&B Picks Up New Products," *Advertising Age,* January 1, 1973.

"Block Struggles To Regain Winning Formula of Old," *Advertising Age,* August 19, 1974.

Giges, Nancy, "Block, W-L Cold-Fighters Bow," *Advertising Age,* July 23, 1984.

"Just Itching For Sales: Tegrin Shampoo Cuts Price, Rethinks Ad Strategy," *Advertising Age,* May 18, 1992.

"New Chip At The Old Block?" *Forbes,* May 29, 1978.

Phalon, Richard, "In Anonymity They Thrive: An Incomparable Sense of Niche Marketing and Shrewd Tax Strategy Make Low-Profile Block Drug One of the Pharmaceutical Industry's Most Reliable Growth Companies," *Forbes,* December 25, 1989.

"$10,500,000 Ad Campaign Boosts Block's Polident," *Advertising Age,* May 16, 1966.

"Three Sleep Aid Makers Agree to Tone Down Ads," *Advertising Age,* June 12, 1972.

—John A. Sarich

Boise Cascade Corporation

One Jefferson Square
P.O. Box 50
Boise, Idaho 83728
U.S.A.
(208) 384-6161
Fax: (208) 384-7224

Public Company
Incorporated: 1931 as Boise Payette Lumber Company
Employees: 19,619
Sales: $3.71 billion
Stock Exchanges: New York Midwest Pacific
SICs: 2421 Lumber: Rough, Sawed or Planed; 2436
   Plywood, Softwood; 2621 Uncoated Paper; 2653
   Stationery & Office Supplies; 5031 Corrugated & Solid
   Fiber Boxes; 5112 Newsprint Paper

Boise Cascade Corporation has grown from a small local lumber company into a major manufacturer and distributor of forest products, ranging from paper to building materials. It also supplies office products to large companies. The company owns 2.8 million acres of timberland in North America and holds long-term leases or licenses on an additional 3.3 million acres.

The firm was established under the name Boise Cascade Corportion in 1957 through the merger of the Boise Payette Lumber Company and the Cascade Lumber Company of Yakima, Washington. Boise Payette had been one of Idaho's top lumber producers since its formation in the 1930s; however, the building boom following World War II had seriously depleted its timberlands. The Cascade Lumber Company had been in operation since 1902, when it was founded by George S. Rankin, the owner of several other businesses in the Yakima Valley. Rankin had been joined in this new venture by a business associate, Fred V. Pennington, and other individuals experienced in lumber operations in the Midwest. Initially, Cascade owned timberland at the headwaters of the Yakima River, which it had purchased for $100,000, and also operated several retail lumber yards in the area in addition to its Yakima mill. These yards were closed in 1914 and consolidated into one lumber yard at the Yakima sawmill, which continued operating even after the merger with Boise Payette.

Robert V. Hansberger, who had joined Boise Payette in 1956 as president, saw the merger of the two companies as an opportu-

nity for Boise Payette to replenish its timber supply. More importantly, combining the resources of the two firms would enable the resulting company to build a base of raw materials large enough to allow it to expand beyond lumber production into the manufacture of paper and pulp products.

In 1958 the company, now known as Boise Cascade, built a kraft pulp and paper mill in Wallula, Washington, and corrugated container plants at both Wallula and Burley, Idaho. The paper and pulp area grew rapidly over the next five years with further expansion of the company's paper and wood production capacity. In spite of this success, Hansberger and his management team recognized how vulnerable the company was because of the cyclical nature of the wood and paper industries. They decided to diversify into other areas as a hedge against possible downturns in demand for its forest products.

Since joining the company, Hansberger had filled the company's top management ranks with graduates of the country's leading business schools. He permitted these executives to operate independently and expand the company's operating divisions as they saw fit. By 1969 Boise Cascade had completed over 30 mergers and acquisitions and had become the third-largest forest products company in the United States. Its operations now encompassed such diverse activities as residential and mobile home construction, recreational vehicle production, publishing, and cruise management.

One of the company's major interests during the mid-1960s was the field of real estate speculation and recreational land development. In 1967 alone, Boise Cascade acquired U.S. Land Company, Lake Arrowhead Development Company, and Pacific Cascade Land Company, and amassed real estate holdings of 126,000 acres in more than 12 states, with the majority of the land in California. Hoping to sell this property to large investors, the company met with little success and was forced to revise its strategy and develop the land itself into residential and recreational areas.

Although the company experienced greater success with this approach and sales were brisk, the new business division encountered several unanticipated problems. For example, Boise Cascade became a prime target for a growing ecological movement, particularly on the West Coast, which was concerned about the impact of the company's plans on the environment. Activist groups often hampered the company's efforts to gain approval for its developments from local planning agencies. Another major setback resulted from a series of lawsuits brought against Boise Cascade by the California attorney general. These legal actions were filed in response to complaints from prospective buyers about the tactics used by the company's salesmen, many of whom had been inherited in the course of the company's acquisitions of realty projects. The suits were eventually settled at a cost of $59 million.

In addition to these problems, Boise Cascade also experienced serious cash flow difficulties related to its land development business. In this industry, the developer was responsible for paying the costs of constructing a community's sewer and water systems. These costs, typically, were high and had to be paid immediately, yet the developer was unable to collect its revenues until up to seven years after its sales were made. In an attempt to infuse the firm with fresh capital to fund the land development business on an ongoing basis, Boise Cascade acquired Ebasco in 1969. Ebasco and it subsidiaries were in the engineering and construction business and provided engineering services to major utilities. It was particularly attractive to Boise Cascade because it was rich with cash. It held millions of dollars worth of Latin American bonds, payable in U.S. dollars, that had been gained through the sale of Ebasco's utility operations in Argentina, Brazil, Chile, Colombia, and Costa Rica. By 1970 it was clear the company's land development business was in serious trouble, accumulating losses that placed the entire organization in jeopardy.

Upon the 1968 purchase of Princess Cruises, the company shifted its marketing efforts away from independent travel agencies, which had originally spurred the growth of the cruise line. Instead, it instituted a direct mail campaign that was developed internally and proved less effective in generating business. As a result, the cruise line went from profits to losses within a matter of months.

In an attempt to reverse its losses, Boise Cascade wrote off a significant portion of its real estate holdings and divested its residential housing operation, along with other assets judged to be inadequate performers or lying too far outside the company's core business areas. In light of the lead-development reversals, Robert Hansberger, the architect of the company's rapid growth, resigned in 1972 and was replaced as president and chief executive officer by John Fery. Fery had been hired as Hansberger's assistant in 1957 and had ascended to executive vice-president and director within ten years.

After taking the helm, Fery immediately placed tighter controls on the company's internal management structure. He began selling off additional subsidiaries, including several Latin American investments gained in the Ebasco purchase, in order to reduce debt and refocus the firm's energies on forest products. As a result of these measures, Boise Cascade moved from a $171 million net loss to a $142 million net profit in just one year. Fery also instituted a five-year, billion-dollar capital spending program that was intended to help reduce the company's dependence on areas with correlating demand cycles, such as lumber and plywood, in favor of businesses with higher and more consistent growth potential. Fery's strategy placed greater emphasis on the manufacture of products for the construction industry and on paper products that could be marketed directly to end users in business form printing, data processing, and publishing.

This initiative propelled Boise Cascade into the 1980s as a specialized and efficient manufacturer of forest products and owner of timberland. By 1982 the company encountered sluggish demand for its products on two key fronts. The housing industry was badly depressed, reducing the demand for building products. The company's pulp and paper operation, intended to help Boise Cascade weather downturns in its other markets, experienced similar problems as industrial firms cut back expenditures in response to the weakening economy. Over the next two years, the firm closed a number of inefficient or unprofitable mills and consolidated its marketing operations. In 1987 Boise Cascade sold its consumer packaging division, which had manufactured containers for various products, and a chain of retail building materials centers that had been acquired from Edwards Industries in 1979. Labor contracts with union employees were renegotiated in an attempt to reduce the company's overall cost structure.

At this time, the Federal Trade Commission accused Boise Cascade of violating the Robinson-Patman Act and the Federal Trade Commission (FTC) Act. In its suit, filed in 1980, the FTC claimed that the company had purchased office products for resale to commercial users and retailers at prices below those available to competitors. The FTC subsequently issued a cease and desist order to the firm in 1986. However, in 1988, an appeals court reversed this directive, determining that the FTC had not effectively substantiated its claim that the company's purchasing practices had adversely affected competition. The case was re-argued before the FTC, resulting in a renewed finding of violation, which was under appeal in 1991.

When the paper industry rebounded in 1986, Boise Cascade and other manufacturers began construction to increase both production and capacity to meet the demand. By 1990, however, this response to the market upswing resulted in an oversupply of paper and excess industry capacity that caused prices and profits to drop. Boise Cascade again found itself vulnerable to the peaks and valleys of another cyclical industry.

Although periods of recession were not new to Boise Cascade, the severity of this economic slump, coupled with the company's large investment in facility renovation and expansion, presented formidable challenges unrivaled in the company's history. Within the paper industry, the grades of paper most severely affected by the recession were newsprint and uncoated business and printing papers—the two grade categories in which Boise Cascade was most heavily committed. To make matters worse, preservation limits on the harvesting of timber in the Pacific Northwest, where the company maintained a greater presence than its competitors, reduced the supply of timber and consequently negatively affected operating costs. Expansion costs, especially the company's $550 million modernization program at its International Falls, Minnesota, paper mill, which was funded by borrowed money, raised its debt level, adding to the economic woes of the company. Boise Cascade's office products division also felt the brunt of the recession, suffering substantial losses in sales and profits

To mitigate losses during the downturn, Boise Cascade formulated a business plan in 1990 to respond to the debilitating economic situation. The company decided to retain only those mills that could be upgraded to compete on a worldwide basis, to lessen its dependence on timber in the Pacific Northwest, and to sell assets that did not fit within its new strategic plan.

By the following year, the nation was still mired in a recession, and the paper industry continued to suffer from an oversupply of paper. Conditions at Boise Cascade were not much better. Facing its most difficult year ever, Boise experienced a drop in sales from 1990 levels; operating costs continued to rise due to timber supply reductions in the Pacific Northwest. The company, however, continued to invest heavily toward the expansion and modernization of its facilities, spending $2.2 billion on such programs over a three-year period. The combination of lower prices, increased operating costs, and the high interest payments stemming from capital investment projects, resulted in a net loss of over $79 million, a considerable drop from a profit of $267 million two years earlier. In an effort to streamline the company, Boise Cascade announced the sale of $250 million of assets it no longer deemed strategically prudent to own. In July of 1991, Boise Cascade sold its 50 percent interest in Durapack AG, a corrugated container manufacturer in Europe, for $50 million. Also in 1991, the company sold 29,500 acres of timberland in western Oregon and by January of 1992 had sold the wholesale segment of its office products distribution business.

Despite its efforts to recover from the downturn, Boise Cascade suffered even greater losses in 1992. Sales dropped to $3.7 billion from nearly $4 billion in 1991, and the company recorded a net loss of $227 million. Still plagued by the same problems that had affected the company since the beginning of the recession in 1989, Boise Cascade responded by expanding its production of specialized papers and increasing the breadth of its office products distribution business. After divesting its wholesale operations, the company expanded its commercial distribution channels by opening new facilities in South Carolina and Florida, and acquired an existing office products distribution business in Minnesota. A year earlier, Boise Cascade attempted to tap into the growing trend for recycled products by converting its Vancouver, Washington, mill into a recycled white paper facility. But none of these endeavors could wrest Boise Cascade from the grip of the recession.

As Boise Cascade entered 1993, the economic picture began to brighten. Demand for its paper products started to increase and the company's loss for the first quarter was down to $12 million from $43 million during the first quarter of 1992. With the national economy on the mend, and five years of extensive expansion and modernization behind it, Boise Cascade's prospects for the future were more optimistic than they were several years ago. Whether the company would be able to achieve a successful recovery and turn losses into profits depended largely on whether the billions of dollars spent on new and existing facilities would realize anticipated profits in the immediate future.

Principal Subsidiaries: Boise Cascade Canada Limited; Boise Cascade Office Products Corporation; Boise Southern Company; Oxford Paper Company.

Further Reading:

Benoit, Ellen, "Late Bloomer in the Forest," *Financial World,* September 8, 1987.

"Boise Cascade Shifts Toward Tighter Control," *Business Week,* May 15, 1971.

"Cinderella," *Forbes,* November 15, 1972.

Downs, Tim, "New Uncoated Free-Sheet Capacity Starts Up at Boise's I-Falls Mill," *Pulp & Paper,* May 1991, p. 98.

Heiman, Grover, "Getting Back to Basics," *Nation's Business,* January 1983.

Moskowitz, Milton, Michael Katz, and Robert Levvering, eds., *Everybody's Business: An Almanac,* San Francisco, CA: Harper & Row, 1980.

Richards, Bill, "Boise Cascade May Be Out of the Woods in First Period," *Wall Street Journal,* April 12, 1993, p. B4.

Taylor, John H., "Fery on the Defensive," *Forbes,* November 12, 1990, pp. 52–58.

"Will Quality Tell?," *Forbes,* July 15, 1970.

—Sandy Schusteff
updated by Jeffrey L. Covell

Brenntag AG

Humboldtring 15
Postfach 10 03 52
D-45403 Muelheim an der Ruhr
Germany
49208 494-0
Fax: 49208 494-698

Subsidiary of Stinnes AG
Incorporated: 1874 as the Philipp Muehsam Company
Employees: 2,800
Sales: DM 3 billion
SICs: 5169 Chemicals & Allied Products Nec; 8640
   Chemical Industry; 8999 Services, Nec; 6120 Wholesale
   Distribution of Fuels, Ores, Metals & Industrial Materials.

Brenntag AG is Europe's largest distributor of industrial chemicals. A multibillion dollar company and affiliate of Germany's largest transportation and distribution firm, Stinnes AG, Brenntag is headquartered in the small city of Muelheim on the Ruhr River, the country's most industrialized corridor. Also a global leader in the distribution of chemicals, the company has 33 supply centers in Europe and 48 in the United States, its most important non-European market.

Brenntag has been in continuous operation since it was founded in 1874. The early 1870s were a propitious time for establishing new businesses in Germany, which had recently been unified after a series of bloody wars. Germany's nationalistic government was anxious to put an end to centuries of economic stagnation and to assert the country's primacy in Europe.

In this favorable climate, Philipp Muehsam, a young German entrepreneur, founded a small business dealing in the transportation and sale of raw materials on the river Spree, the chief artery of Germany's new capital, Berlin. Named after its founder, the Philipp Muehsam company did a flourishing business. As the capital city of the largest European country, Berlin was rapidly becoming the showplace of everything modern in the late nineteenth century, and also the center of the country's new chemical industry. In fact, the modern German chemical industry was by the turn of the century the most advanced in the world and the first to employ academically trained researchers.

Contributing to Germany's emerging chemical industry became the chief role of the Philipp Muehsam company. By the turn of the century, its core businesses focused on petroleum as well as on the purchase and distribution of industrial chemicals. Such activities necessitated an international transportation network, which would be upset temporarily during the upheavals of World War I and subsequent civil unrest. Back on its feet during the 1920s, the company expanded its network under the leadership of Philipp Muehsam's successors, and despite the worldwide economic depression of the 1930s, the firm remained the largest distributor of petroleum and industrial chemicals in Germany.

During this time, one of Germany's largest industrial concerns, the Hugo Stinnes corporation, had been eyeing the Philipp Muehsam company. In 1938, it made a bid for the company and acquired it. The name of the firm was changed to Brennstoff-Chemikalien-Transport AG, and while its traditional operations in petroleum and industrial chemical distribution remained, a new and important branch was added—the allocation of mineral oil byproducts of petroleum—which would be indispensable to the manufacture of cosmetics during the postwar era.

Wartime, however, generated other needs. While raw materials such as petroleum could still be obtained in the vast Nazi-held territories of eastern Europe during the second world war, daily allied bombing took its toll on Brennstoff's business, which during this time consisted wholly of distribution and transportation. By the end of the war, Brennstoff-Chemikalien-Transport AG lay in utter ruin. The parent company, the vast Hugo Stinnes corporation, was confiscated by the occupation authorities, with only a small branch of the company left in the hands of the Stinnes family. Brennstoff, renamed Brenntag AG after the war, in order to disassociate itself with its prewar past, belonged to this branch. Meanwhile that part of the Stinnes firm that had been confiscated by the allies was reconstituted by the able Dr. Heinz P. Kemper, who was chosen by the American occupation authority in West Berlin because of his non-party affiliations. In 1964, the Hugo Stinnes firm bought the Brenntag company for what was considered the immense sum of 13 million DM.

Brenntag had been slowly recovering from the turmoil of the war years. Headquarters were moved in 1948 from Berlin in Germany's eastern zone to the more secure town of Muelheim on the Ruhr, in western Germany. With only 20 employees, the company slowly recaptured its former lead in the chemical transportation industry.

Recovery would not have been possible without major currency reform in the western zones in 1948, the unification of the three occupation zones into the Federal Republic of Germany in 1949, and the onset of the Marshall Plan for European economic recovery which followed unification. Chastened by its wartime alliance with the government, Brenntag became decidedly more attuned to the market, especially in the international arena. Management divested the company of its former shares in various manufacturing enterprises as well as of its shipping business, and concentrated instead on broadening its product lines and increasing its focus on chemical distribution and transportation.

Of great urgency in the postwar years was expansion into international markets. Aggressive inroads, most particularly in the biggest and richest market of all—the United States—were made in the 1950s, in the company's first venture on the North American continent. During this time, thousands of tons of industrial chemicals landed in the ports of the low countries for transshipment throughout Europe by Brenntag AG. Inroads were also made into communist eastern Europe, an area to which Brenntag had had commercial ties for decades. In the following three decades, eastern Europe would constitute a stable but limited market for Brenntag's chemical products. This market would explode in significance and range with the fall of communism in the late 1980s.

New product lines were developed in the prosperous 1950s, including aromatic petrochemicals for the cosmetics industry, synthetic materials and resins, and chemical solvents, all of which would be purchased and distributed to the major European chemical manufacturers from sources in Europe and overseas.

The largest transportation and distribution company in West Germany, Hugo Stinnes AG, purchased Brenntag from the Bank fuer Gemeinwirtschaft in 1964 for what was considered an extremely high price. With one stroke, Stinnes had plunged into the lucrative industrial chemical distribution market, which complemented its other businesses in the distribution and transportation of raw materials and petroleum, as well as overseas shipping. The transaction represented a major step towards diversifying Stinnes (which altered its name in 1976 to Stinnes AG) as well as towards greatly broadening Brenntag's customer base. By then Brenntag's sales revenues were in the hundreds of millions of dollars; 20 years later, they would exceed a billion. Another advantage of Brenntag's acquisition by Stinnes was the greater financial resources of the parent company, which continues to endow Brenntag with a secure economic base. In 1965, Stinnes AG and Brenntag were acquired by Germany's largest firm, the energy company VEBA A.G. Stinnes remains a wholly owned subsidiary of VEBA.

After becoming a member of the Stinnes Group of companies Brenntag's growth was dramatic. Branch offices were established throughout Germany and the rest of Europe. Out of necessity the company became involved in more than just the buying and selling of a wide array of products, including industrial chemicals, agricultural chemicals or made-to-order specialty chemicals. Large investments were also made in fleets of trucks, storage facilities, and tanks that remain indispensable in the distribution of Brenntag's products. Sales offices expanding in key geographical areas rapidly transmitted and facilitated customer orders.

In the late 1980s, Brenntag underwent tremendous expansion. The fall of communism in eastern Europe and the demise of the Soviet Union enabled Brenntag to expand its bases in eastern Europe and open new branches in Warsaw, Prague, and even Moscow. With the fall of the Berlin Wall, Brenntag was one of the first west German companies to expand into eastern Germany, opening up fifteen branches in a year, and establishing Brenntag affiliates in Erfurt, Chemnitz, and former east Berlin.

Under chairperson and CEO Dr. Erhard Meyer-Galow, the core businesses of Brenntag still lie in providing chemicals to major processors and manufacturers throughout Europe and the United States. Just as Stinnes AG consists of many companies, Brenntag also came to represent a group of companies, specializing in different chemicals and services. For instance, in the same city on the Ruhr, Brenntag Eurochem GmbH provides made-to-order specialty chemicals, while a host of other Brenntag companies in Germany provide recycling services, packaging materials, drying and cleaning assistance, waste hauling, consulting and marketing, and, generally, an increasingly sophisticated and detailed list of chemical products and services to today's chemical processors.

Outside of Europe, Brenntag is most heavily represented in the United States, where a Brenntag affiliate, SOCO Chemical Inc. in Pennsylvania, coordinates all U.S. activities, involving seven American distribution firms with branches in 48 locations throughout the country. Even during the recession of the 1990s, Brenntag's U.S. business fared well, although cost cutting and streamlining accounted for much of the gain in profitability.

Beginning in the late 1980s and early 1990s many Europeans and Americans have publicly criticized chemical firms and their suppliers for their roles in polluting and diminishing the world's natural resouces. In addition, stringent new environmental laws have forced many of these companies out of business and burdened the remaining with enormous cleanup and safety costs. As the largest chemical provider and transporter in Europe, Brenntag has survived the onslaught of environmental legislation and public criticism and has managed to adapt to and even profit from these challenges: recycling and waste disposal loom as strategic business segments in the future.

With its widespread global distribution and transportation network in an era of increasingly free trade, Brenntag's future seems promising. Even if the world market for chemical raw materials contracts, the possibilities for recycling and efficient waste disposal are numerous. Furthermore, the company continually researches new service functions to offer potential and long term customers, assuring its global leadership in the chemical service industry well into the next century.

Further Reading:

Brenntag, Your Partner in the Market, Duesseldorf: Econ Verlag, 1974.
Making Sure the Chemistry Is Right, Muelheim an der Ruhr, Germany: Brenntag AG, 1991.
Stinnes AG Annual Reports, Muelheim an der Ruhr, Germany: Stinnes AG, 1991–92.
Young, Ian, "Stinnes Agrarchemie Builds Five Centers," *Chemical Week,* February 3, 1993, p. 13.
——, "On the Road to Quality in Europe's Competitive Market," *Chemical Week,* July 22, 1992, pp. 30–32.

—Sina Dubovoj

Briggs & Stratton Corporation

12301 West Wirth Street
Wauwatosa, Wisconsin 53222
U.S.A.
(414) 259-5333
Fax: (414) 259-5313

Public Company
Incorporated: 1909 as Briggs & Stratton Corp.
Employees: 8,295
Sales: $1.04 billion
Stock Exchanges: New York
SICs: 3519 Industrial Combustion Engines; 7699 Repair
 Services; 3429 Hardware

Briggs & Stratton Corporation, headquartered in Milwaukee, Wisconsin, is the world's largest producer of air-cooled gasoline engines for outdoor power equipment as well as locks for automobiles and trucks. The company designs, manufactures, markets, and services these products for various manufacturers worldwide.

In 1909, Stephen Foster Briggs was a young college graduate and inventor when he and Harold M. Stratton, a successful grain merchant, founded Briggs & Stratton Corp. The partners incorporated their company in the state of Wisconsin, and with $25,000 began to produce a six-cylinder, two-cycle engine that Briggs had made while a student at North Dakota State College. They experienced tough times at first as their six-cylinder engine proved too costly for mass production. A brief foray into the automobile assembly business also failed, nearly driving the partners into bankruptcy.

Nevertheless Briggs had a knack for inventions and in 1910 he received a patent for a new gas engine igniter, which included a novel mechanism that could start an automobile engine with a single spark. Although it was not an overwhelming success, the company had found its niche as a producer of electrical specialties for the booming automobile industry. The business soon took off, becoming by 1920 the largest producer of specialty lights, ignitions, regulators, and starting switches in the United States. Sales also shot up, approaching $4 million. Briggs & Stratton customers included all the major automobile makers, including Chevrolet, Dodge, Ford, Hudson, Hupp, Kissell, Maxwell, Nash, Studebaker, and Willys-Overland. The market for electrical specialties proved so profitable that it accounted

for two-thirds of Briggs & Stratton's total business through the mid-1930s. In 1920, the company expanded operations into the East Plant, a five-story concrete and steel building at 13th and Center Streets in Milwaukee. The plant employed 1,400 workers with an annual payroll of $1.5 million.

In the early years, Briggs & Stratton ventured into various new markets, often with little success. The production of refrigerators, crystal radios, headsets, radio tuners, and a device called the battery eliminator all were shortlived. The company also tried making oil filters, air cleaners, and a series of stamped metal items, including key storage cabinets, soap containers, calendar banks, candy display stands, and coin operated paper towel dispensing cabinets.

In 1924, Briggs & Stratton reincorporated in the state of Delaware. That year, with profits soaring, the company discovered another profitable market, the automotive lock business. A new die cast automobile lock cylinder outsold competing brass models, and within five years, Briggs & Stratton had become the largest producer of automotive locks with more than 75 percent of the total market. Briggs & Stratton's new BASCO autobody hardware, including door handles, inside knobs and levers, compartment locks, door locks, hinges, and keys also became standard features on many of the leading models of motor cars. For the ever expanding automobile market, the company introduced in 1938 the Cushion Action Starter Drive, a new automobile self-starting mechanism that became standard on the Ford V8, Mercury, and Lincoln Zephyr. Its automotive division also provided supplies to airline, marine, and cabinet manufacturers.

In 1919, the company acquired the A. O. Smith Motor Wheel and the Flyer, a two-passenger buckboard-like vehicle. The Motor Wheel was a gasoline-engine driven wheel, designed for attachment to the rear of a bicycle, thus converting it into a kind of motor cycle. The wheel sold for about $90 and could get approximately 100 miles per gallon. Briggs & Stratton had high hopes for sales worldwide and tried to market the Motor Wheel in Spanish-speaking countries and in Asia where it could also be used on rickshas. When sales proved disappointing, Briggs & Stratton re-engineered the Motor Wheel to produce the first American motor scooter. Despite being one of the least expensive automobiles on the road, the Flyer could not compete with the Ford Model T and other popular models. Only 2,000 Flyers sold between 1920 and 1923. In 1924, the Motor Wheel and related items were sold off.

The company, however, soon became successful in the engine manufacturing business by producing a stationary version of the Motor Wheel, which could power various kinds of equipment. In 1923, the Model PB engine was introduced, providing a popular and compact power source for washing machines, garden tractors, and lawn mowers. Production in 1925 of the overhead valve, ¾ horsepower, Model F series engine proved useful for a wide variety of industrial and agricultural equipment, including compressors, generators, and pumps. In 1931, Briggs & Stratton introduced a best–seller for washing machine producers, a small low-profile engine that could fit under washing machine tubs. This engine remained popular until 1936 when the Model WM (Washing Machine) engine rolled off the assembly line. The washing machine business was the company's major market for engines until the Second World War.

In 1928, Briggs & Stratton acquired the Evinrude Outboard Motor Company, which it sold less than a year later. Founders Stephen Briggs and Harold Stratton had differing views on the market potential for outboard motors. Stratton was against diversifying the company's products. Briggs, on the other hand, was enthusiastic, and he formed a new company, Outboard Motors Corp., with Ole Evinrude, a maker of outboard motors since 1909. The new partners merged Evinrude's company, Evinrude Light Twin Outboard, with Lockwood-Ash Motor Co. and purchased the Evinrude Outboard Motor Co. from Briggs & Stratton. Briggs served as chair and Evinrude as president.

Success as a producer of electrical specialties and small engines proved a boon for the company's fortunes during World War II. Briggs & Stratton quickly became one of the nation's 200 largest military suppliers, producing everything from detonating fuses and artillery ammunition, to ignition switches for airplanes and airplane guns. The company also profited as a supplier of engines for electric and radio generators, pumps, compressors, ventilating fans, saw rigs, mobile kitchens, repair shops, emergency hospitals, and water purification equipment. The war effort proved so lucrative that between 1938 and 1944 net income increased six-fold, from $785,000 to more than $6,000,000.

Following the war years, Briggs & Stratton, already the biggest producer of small gasoline engines, pursued a greater share of the market for lawn and garden equipment caused by the postwar boom. With the rapid suburbanization of America, the Briggs & Stratton name became virtually synonymous with the lawn mower. The rapidly growing market for powered home use equipment also stemmed from the appearance of inexpensive rotary lawn mowers, powered by relatively lightweight two-cycle engines. Briggs & Stratton's original four-cycle engine, weighing about 40 pounds, was too cumbersome for lawn mowers and garden equipment. As a result, the company introduced in 1953 aluminum die cast engines with chrome plated pistons. These were not only lighter than competing models but also could withstand greater engine pressure and temperatures. In 1954, Briggs & Stratton patented its new die cast technique for the production of four-cycle engines, which rapidly became the industry standard. The company subsequently filed a patent infringement suit against the Clinton Machine Company, one of its major competitors. Briggs & Stratton eventually lost the case, allowing the industry to freely use the newly developed die cast process. In 1955, Briggs & Stratton opened a new plant in Wauwatosa, Wisconsin, to keep pace with rising demand for the aluminum engines. The plant was expanded in 1967 and again seven years later to increase production.

In 1948, Briggs resigned to join Outboard Motors Corp., the company he helped found. Briggs had been president of Briggs & Stratton from 1909 until 1935 when he became chairperson. While with the company, Briggs had received about 60 patents for various inventions, mostly for lighting switches and locks and their mechanisms produced for the automobile industry. Later, at Outboard Motors Corp. he would receive patents for engine components, including a starting circuit, valve lifters,

and a valve actuating mechanism that could be mechanically self-adjusted.

Briggs was succeeded by Charles Lyons Coughlin, a fellow electrical engineering student who had known Briggs at South Dakota State College. Coughlin had joined the company in 1910, but left in 1918 for the Ladish Drop Forge Company. In 1923, he rejoined Briggs & Stratton as vice president and general manager. He became company president in 1935, and later chief executive officer and chairperson in 1970.

Coughlin's leadership brought Briggs & Stratton rising profitability. Net sales more than doubled from $40 to $90 million between 1953 and 1959. By 1965, sales volume had risen to a record $105.1 million. Briggs & Stratton's profitability stemmed from a conservative approach in sticking with its two principal lines of manufacturing, the production of small air-cooled gasoline engines and the production of automobile parts. The company also benefitted enormously from a market that was not big enough to attract major competition. In 1966, *Forbes* magazine estimated that 90 percent of its sales were in "small engines, used mostly in power lawn mowers but also in air compressors, pumps, generators, etc." The remaining ten percent were in auto locks and switches.

In 1970, Vincent R. Shiely was named president of Briggs & Stratton. Shiely had joined the company in 1959 as administrative vice president, later becoming executive vice president in 1963. Shiely stayed with Briggs & Stratton's conservative approach, which continued to pay impressive dividends. In the 1970s, net sales shot up from about $212 million to almost $591 million from 1973 to 1979. The company's purchase of a manufacturing plant in Milwaukee from the Square D Co. expanded its production capacity for various components, and brought new facilities for research and development, engineering, and sales. The Burleigh plant, built in Wauwatosa in 1955, was also expanded to keep pace with demand for Briggs & Stratton engines. In 1976, Shiely became the company's chairperson and, by the time of his death in 1976, was also chief executive officer.

Following Shiely's death, Lawrence G. Regner was elected to the chair, and Frederick P. Stratton, Jr. became president and chief operating officer. By 1980, Briggs & Stratton remained unrivaled as the world's lowest-cost producer of small engines. The company enjoyed rising profits while selling motors to power-equipment makers at prices they could never match if they tried to produce their own. Among Fortune 500 companies, Briggs & Stratton ranked 405th in sales but 94th in profit margin (8.2 percent) and 44th in stockholders' return on equity (23.5 percent).

For all its success, however, the company was soon on the run from Japanese competitors. "In many ways," said a reporter in *Forbes,* in 1986, "Briggs & Stratton was a sitting duck." Big Japanese producers, Honda in particular, began targeting the small engine market after sales for motorcycles peaked in the early 1980s. In 1984, Honda reportedly spent $12.5 million advertising its lawn and garden equipment, fully 20 percent of the industry's total advertising budget. Honda's move into the small engine market came at a bad time for Briggs & Stratton. In the 1970s, a weak dollar had boosted the company's market share worldwide. But a recession and a strong dollar in the early 1980s allowed such competitors as Honda, Kawasaki, Suzuki, and Mitsubishi to make inroads by supplying U.S. equipment makers with engines at lower cost.

For the most part, due to its overwhelming market dominance and low production costs, Briggs & Stratton fended off the competition. Despite a strengthening dollar, the company retained its markets in Europe but lost considerable ground in Asia as its cost advantage disappeared. Its exports precipitously dropped from 25 percent of sales or $179 million in 1980, to 14 percent of sales or $99 million in 1985. In the United States, Briggs & Stratton relied on low manufacturing costs to beat out Japanese producers in the engine market itself. But the Japanese were quick to provide more sophisticated engines aimed at the higher-priced segment of the market where Briggs & Stratton's cost advantage was less overwhelming. In response, the company produced a slew of new products, including an improved line of its basic 3.5 and four horsepower engines introduced in 1985, as well as a wholly redesigned line of other engines. The company also doubled spending on engineering and research and launched a $2 million consumer advertising campaign to bolster its brand name.

In addition to trying to maintain market share, Briggs & Stratton concentrated on cost reduction to ensure its position as the industry's low cost producer. Labor costs, which accounted for 50 percent of total expenses, also were 50 percent higher than those for the Japanese. Briggs & Stratton's ability to remain competitive with this considerable cost disadvantage reflected its remarkable efficiency. In 1983, the company experienced a three-month strike to win additional flexibility to remain competitive. Also during this time, Briggs & Stratton opened a highly automated nonunion engine plant in Murray, Kentucky, which required far fewer employees than at the main engine facility in Wauwatosa, Wisconsin. The new plant provided not only a significant savings in labor costs, but greater flexibility with which to experiment with new manufacturing techniques.

None of these efforts, however, produced an immediate payoff. In 1985, earnings dropped 31 percent from their $49 million 1980 high, operating margins fell from 13.8 percent to 10.8 percent, and return on equity from 22.3 percent to 12.1 percent. The big difference occurred in sales volume, which declined a precipitous 30 percent since 1980.

In 1986, George A. Senn was elected as Briggs & Stratton's fifth president. Senn had joined the company the year before as an executive vice president. When he resigned in 1988, Richard E. Marceau was elected president and chief executive officer. Marceau had risen through the company, first as human resource director and then as vice president for administration. In 1991, Marceau retired and Frederick Stratton Jr., grandson of co-founder Harold M. Stratton, assumed the office as president. During this five-year transitional period, the company's fortunes continued to slip. In 1989, Briggs & Stratton suffered its first major loss in more than 50 years, incurring a $20 million net drop in income. The company, however, continued aggressive efforts to improve its position in the industry. Capital expenditures in 1989 totaled a record $79.5 million, including

spending on new equipment and tooling for its new nonunion assembly plant in Poplar Bluff, Missouri.

What looked like a company in decline in the 1980s made a strong comeback in the early 1990s as it began recovering market share from such formidable competitors as Kawasaki and Suzuki. A boost in productivity stemmed partly from lower raw material costs and lower operating expenses. Moreover, Briggs & Stratton benefitted from a weakening dollar relative to the yen as well from substantial increases in product development spending from 1.5 percent of sales in the early 1980s to 2.5 percent of sales in 1992. Its two nonunion plants also were manufacturing engines more cheaply and efficiently.

Briggs & Stratton has continued to strengthen its market position, which is impressive given the stiff competition that now characterizes the small engine industry. The company faces tough domestic competition from Tecumseh Products Company, Kohler Co., Kawasaki Heavy Industries, Ltd., and Onan Corporation. Two domestic lawnmower makers, Lawn Boy Inc. and Honda Motor Co., also produce their own engines. Eight Japanese small engine manufacturers are worldwide competitors, the largest being Honda and Kawasaki. Italy's Tecnamotor S.p.A., owned by Tecumseh, is a major competitor in Europe.

In 1992, Briggs & Stratton reincorporated in the state of Wisconsin. In the same year, engines, parts, and related products accounted for 93 percent of Briggs & Stratton's total sales, a percentage that has changed little since 1983. The company's chief market continues to be air–cooled four-cycle gasoline engines in the two to 18 horsepower range. The lawn and garden equipment industry accounts for 86 percent of its engine sales, a market which had held remarkably steady since the early 1980s. Manufacturers install Briggs & Stratton engines mostly on walk-behind mowers, riding mowers, garden tillers, and shredders. Briggs & Stratton engines also power snow throwers, garden tractors, lawn edgers, vacuums, generating pumps, pressure washers, and various other equipment. The majority of its engines are still produced at the main engine facility in Wauwatosa, Wisconsin.

The engines are sold in the United States and Canada by Briggs & Stratton's own sales force. In overseas markets, the company relies primarily on independent representatives, assisted by a network of regional offices in Norway, Switzerland, the United Arab Emirates, Singapore, and Milwaukee. Exports accounted for 21 percent of all engines and parts sales in 1992, up from 14 percent of sales in 1984. One reason for Briggs & Stratton's success has been its emphasis on customer service, which includes a worldwide service network of over 35,000 authorized service dealers through which it sells replacement engines and service parts.

Approximately seven percent of Briggs & Stratton's sales are currently in automotive locks. Unlike its early die cast models produced in the 1920s, the company now makes, sells, and services mechanical and electromagnetic locks for North American auto companies. Briggs & Stratton mostly produces locks for steering column ignitions, glove boxes, car doors, gas caps, and other items.

Briggs & Stratton appears well positioned to continue as a leading producer of small engines and automotive locks. The company, however, faces uncertainty over the development of national emission standards for lawn, garden, and other equipment powered by small air–cooled engines. The company is concerned that if the Environmental Protection Agency fails to develop emission standards by 1994, some states may adopt existing California provisions. Briggs & Stratton has noted that it could "tolerate a different standard for California, which accounts for about 5 percent of the U.S. market, but we would face difficulties if California and other states were on one standard and the rest of the country were on another.''

Further Reading:

Briggs & Stratton Corporation Annual Report, Wauwatosa: Briggs & Stratton Corporation, 1984.
Forbes, April 1, 1986, pp. 56, 86.
Forbes, April 7, 1986, p. 56.
Forbes, February 5, 1990, p. 204.
Forbes, June 22, 1992, p. 12.
Fortune, July 28, 1980, p. 55.
The History of Briggs & Stratton Corporation, Wauwatosa: Briggs & Stratton Corporation.

—Bruce P. Montgomery

The Budd Company

3155 W. Big Beaver Road
P.O. Box 2601
Troy, Michigan 48007-2601
U.S.A.
(313) 643-3500
Fax: (313) 643-3593

Wholly Owned Subsidiary of Thyssen Aktiengesellschaft (AG)
Incorporated: 1912
Employees: 9,100
Sales: $1.5 billion
SICs: 3079 Plastics Products; 3321 Gray and Ductile Iron
   Castings; 3465 Automotive Stampings; 3549 Metalworking
   Machinery; 3714 Wheel & Brake Products; 3949 Sporting
   Goods; 3711 Chassis Frames for Passenger Cars & Light
   Trucks

The Budd Company is the leading automotive stamping manufacturer and one of the top automotive suppliers in the United States. With over 20 manufacturing and assembly facilities, Budd produces components for approximately half of the passenger cars and trucks made in North America. Widely acknowledged as a pioneer in the field of transportation, Budd has contributed many industry advancements, particularly in materials technology for automobile and rail car design. For over eight decades, the company has successfully weathered the numerous fluctuations of the transportation industry by alternately diversifying and consolidating its operations to capitalize on market trends. Budd's tenacity and innovative spirit are reflected in the company's slogan "Budd On the Move."

Budd was founded in Philadelphia in 1912 by Edward Budd as The Edward G. Budd Manufacturing Company. Budd established his business with a single press and thirteen former coworkers from Hale & Kilburn Company, a metal stamping and die-making manufacturer, seeking to realize his dream of building an all-steel automobile body. Auto and truck bodies of the early 1900s were comprised primarily of wood. The process of varnishing the wood to make it resilient enough to be used in automobiles was costly and time consuming. Budd's all-steel design resulted in car bodies that were less expensive to manufacture, required considerably less production time, and were stronger than wood-steel composites. Budd presented his idea to the Hupp Motor Company in 1912 and earned his first contract

for steel body panels from Hupp prior to leaving Hale & Kilburn. News of Budd's innovation spread quickly and within a year, the company had truck body orders for Packard and Peerless and auto body contracts with Garford Motors and Oakland Motor Company.

Budd's first big break came in 1914, when the Dodge brothers ordered 5,000 steel bodies for their new touring model. The sedan was so successful that Dodge placed a second order for 50,000 additional auto bodies and was thereafter Budd's largest customer until its acquisition in 1925 by Chrysler Corporation. Encouraged by this early success, Budd founded the Budd Wheel Company in 1916 to manufacture wire wheels, another move to eliminate wood from cars and trucks. During that time, Budd also entered into a joint effort with Michelin Company of France to market steel disc wheels in the United States. Budd's customer base increased steadily and by 1917, the company could boast such additional clients as Ford, Buick, Willys-Overland, and Studebaker.

In 1923, Budd registered another industry first by building an all-steel enclosed car body. Budd's design rejected the standard box-like appearance of current models in favor of a more rounded style, which was adopted by Dodge in 1925 and later by other automakers as well. That year, Budd expanded its business to the auto capital of North America by purchasing a manufacturing plant in Detroit from Liberty Motor Car Company. To further broaden its potential client base, Budd entered the European market.

The 1930s were years of experimentation, expansion, and hardship for Budd as the company struggled during the Great Depression. In 1930, Budd International Corporation was created to handle the company's limited European ventures. Budd's overseas endeavors were less than successful, however, and Budd International posted financial losses between 1930 and 1935. Faced with declining sales of its auto components as the auto industry suffered as a whole during the Depression, Budd diversified its interests and began to develop products for other transportation markets. Company engineers explored the potential large-scale uses for stainless steel, a lightweight, rust resistant metal used predominantly in hand-held tools. In 1931, the company manufactured the first stainless steel airplane, which was successfully test-piloted for 1,000 hours of flight time. Although the company gained recognition for its latest design, Budd did not pursue business in the airline industry until World War II.

While working at Hale & Kilburn, Edward Budd had also gained experience in rail car construction. During the early 1930s, Budd utilized that knowledge to design and manufacture passenger rail cars. In 1934, Budd produced the first streamlined stainless steel passenger rail car. Called the Pioneer Zephyr, the car was touted for its high speed and light weight; three Zephyrs weighed approximately the same as a single Pullman-Standard passenger car. The Zephyr was also the first rail car to be diesel powered. Although the company lost money on the initial venture, Budd later relied on its growing rail car sales to supplement company revenues when its auto components business slowed. For over two decades, Budd designed and built various passenger car lines, including Rockets, Silver Meteors, and Champions, among others. In conjunction with the new rail cars, Budd also pioneered the railway disc brake, which appeared on the market just prior to World War II. Budd railway disc brakes offered superior braking capabilities to the standard wheel tread system and were soon widely accepted by the railroad industry.

In 1940, Budd added to its list of industry breakthroughs by unitizing auto bodies, a manufacturing process in which the multi-part chassis frame was replaced with a one-piece component comprising the roof, sides, and underbody. The Nash Motors Company was the first to contract Budd to build the new auto bodies, and Budd's 1940 sales reached $69 million, a substantial return on the $100,000 in capital Edward Budd used to found his company in 1912.

With the advent of World War II, Budd became a supplier for the U.S. government. In 1942, Budd turned out a stainless steel cargo plane called the Conestoga RB-1, which was aptly nicknamed a "flying box-car." The navy purchased the contract for the planes and 17 Conestogas were manufactured to transport heavy military cargo. For decades after the war, Budd's Conestogas were among the fleet of one of the world's largest cargo companies. Edward Budd died shortly after the war, and his son, Edward G. Budd, Jr., assumed control of the company.

The Second World War enabled Budd to recoup its losses from the Depression and by 1950, company sales reached $290 million with record net earnings of $18.3 million. However, in 1951 and 1952 strikes by the oil industry and steel worker labor unions forced Budd to lay off 4,500 production workers. These strikes also adversely affected Budd's largest customer, Chrysler Corporation, which was forced to idle as many as 25,000 workers at different times. In response to these events as well as internal problems at Budd that slowed delivery of its components, Chrysler moved a large portion of its auto parts production in-house. Other auto makers soon followed suit, and Budd's net profits for 1954 were only one-third those of 1950. With the auto stamping and components division at the company losing ground, Budd again diversified, acquiring an airplane parts manufacturer and creating divisions in nuclear energy, aerospace, defense, and electronics. In 1954, the company introduced the first all-plastic bodied automobile for Studebaker. The following year, Ford contracted Budd to build the bodies for its new Thunderbird. The Thunderbird was a huge success, and Budd's auto stamping sales began to rebound.

During the 1960s, Budd again expanded and reorganized. Returning to the international market, the company acquired interests in industrial and transportation businesses in several European countries, extending into South America, Australia, and Mexico as well. At home, Budd concentrated its efforts on strengthening its auto industry sales. Toward the end of the decade, the company invested $125 million to upgrade its auto components and plastics operations. In addition, Budd acquired Gindy Manufacturing, a truck trailer producer, and Duralastic Products Company, a polyester and fiberglass manufacturer. Budd also established Budd Automotive Company of Canada Limited in Kitchener, Ontario. In 1972, the company further cemented its ties to the auto industry by moving its headquarters from Philadelphia to Troy, Michigan, a suburb of Detroit. At that time, auto products sales accounted for over 90 percent of company profits. Budd's move to Detroit and renewed commitment to the industry paid off.

While Budd's auto sales rebounded, the railroad industry began fading in the late 1950s as consumers displayed an increasing preference for automobile and air travel. Budd's rail car sales had almost ground to a halt until the early 1960s when Budd was awarded contracts by the Pennsylvania and Long Island railroads for its newest high-speed, Metroliner rail cars. In addition, Budd penetrated the subway commuter market in 1963, underbidding competitors for a contract with the New York City Transit Authority for 600 stainless steel subway cars—a $68 million project. While Budd continued to compete in the market and maintained a position as a leading rail and subway car producer, the Railway Division posted losses of over $27 million between 1967 and 1970. Aside from the general decline in rail travel, Budd's Metroliner cars were plagued with problems, many of which were the result of faulty supplier components. The company's reputation suffered, and Budd considered selling its rail car operations in 1970. Budd decided to hold on to the division, however, restructuring it in 1974 in hopes of capturing the market for replacement cars, as many railroads were looking to retire aging models. Budd reentered the market in the late 1970s with the SPV-2000, a new line of self-propelled cars. The cars were costly, however, and the company was repeatedly underbid by competitors including Nissho-Iwai American Corporation, a Japanese-American firm that beat out Budd for two sizable contracts. Although Budd was able to generate some business, including a $150 million contract from Amtrak in 1980, the Railway Division was not consistently profitable and was eventually eliminated.

Budd's auto group sales reached new heights in 1976 and 1977, and sales in the Plastics Division more than doubled between 1972 and 1976. By 1977, the company employed approximately 19,000 workers and had sales of $1.3 billion. Budd's success did not last, however, as two major oil crises and a national recession resulted in a substantial decline in automobile sales. The company was bought in 1978 by Thyssen AG, a German steelmaker and auto components manufacturer. The terms of the acquisition stipulated that Budd would remain fairly autonomous, though rumors abounded that the new parent company would step in to control day-to-day operations. Thyssen did not, however, and instead provided extensive financial resources for Budd.

Soon after the acquisition, Budd decided to concentrate solely on the auto industry, a decision that led to major changes throughout the company during the 1980s. New standards were established in quality and cost control, and production and administrative activities were reviewed. Most of the non-automotive subsidiaries were eliminated, and the company focused on streamlining its primary divisions: Stamping and Frame, Wheel and Brake, Foundry Products, and Plastics. Although Budd was now operating with only half the employee base, the company achieved the same level of sales in 1987 as it had in 1979.

The large cash flow provided by Thyssen enabled Budd to upgrade its manufacturing and technical facilities. The Plastics Division, which had steadily expanded during the 1970s, received particular attention as the amount of plastics used in cars increased drastically. The Budd Plastics Research Development Center, opened in the 1970s, afforded state-of-the-art equipment that enabled company engineers to develop advanced technical processes in producing plastic compounds and sheet moldings for use in several products including cars and trucks, textiles, appliances, farming equipment, typewriters, and computers. In the late 1970s, the Plastics Division began research on developing a sheet molding compound (SMC) that could be formed as quickly as steel is stamped. The company's first effort resulted in Flex 2000, a strong plastic SMC that was used in auto components. The Plastics Division continued its research into SMCs in the 1980s. Eight years of research culminated in 1986 with the introduction of the Budd System 59, a process through which plastic materials could be molded into parts at the "assembly line speed" of only 59 seconds per part. Budd System 59 more than doubled plastic components output at the company and was a viable alternative to the galvanized sheet metal traditionally used by automakers.

Budd's long-term relations with parent Thyssen have proven advantageous for both companies during the 1980s and 1990s. Chair and CEO, Siegfried Buschmann, commented in *Automotive Industries* on Budd's successful interactions with Thyssen: "Thyssen gives Budd technological assistance on some of our North American programs, and we give Thyssen the benefit of Budd's knowledge on some of theirs in Europe." Budd's commitment to industry advancement is reflected in its intensive employee training programs, teamwork philosophy, and quality control incentives. Deemed a top-quality components supplier by the automotive industry, the company seems well positioned for continued success.

Principal Subsidiaries: Budd Canada Limited; Connelly Skis, Inc.; Greening Donald Company Ltd.; Milford Fabricating Company; Philips-Temro Group; Waupaca Foundry, Inc.

Further Reading:

Barks, Joseph V., and George A. Weimer, "Budd's Latest Chapter Is Another Moving Story," *Iron Age,* March 5, 1979, pp. 28–30.
Campanella, Frank W., "Budd to Chalk Up Profits Gains This Year and Next," *Barron's,* November 29, 1976, pp. 27–9.
Coffman, Cathy, "Zeroing in on Automotive," *Automotive Industries,* July, 1989, pp. 41–2.
Fleming, Al, "Budd Looks to Future After Weathering Bad Times," *Automotive News,* February 2, 1987, p. 218.
"Goodbye Philadelphia, Hello Detroit," *Forbes,* October 1, 1973, pp. 26–7.
"A High-Speed Bid for Business," *Business Week,* February 4, 1967, pp. 126–28.
Information Guide, Troy, Michigan: The Budd Company, 1992.
Richards, Gilbert F., *"Budd on the Move" Innovation for a Nation on Wheels,* New York: The Newcomen Society in North America, 1975.

—Shannon Young

Cabot Corporation

75 State Street
Boston, Massachusetts 02109-1806
U.S.A.
(617) 345-0100
Fax: (617) 342-6103

Public Company
Incorporated: 1922 as Godfrey L. Cabot, Inc.
Employees: 5,400
Sales: $1.5 billion
Stock Exchanges: New York Boston Pacific Coast
SICs: 2895 Carbon Black; 2819 Industrial Inorganic
   Chemicals Nec; 1311 Crude Petroleum & Natural Gas;
   1321 Natural Gas Liquids

Cabot Corporation is a diversified, global chemical and plastics manufacturer with industry leadership in such areas as carbon black, fumed silica, tantalum powder production, and plastics compounds. It is also involved in liquified natural gas importation and distribution and the manufacture of industrial safety products.

Godfrey Lowell Cabot, the founder of Cabot Corporation, lived to be 101, and the choices he made early in his career set much of the company's course to the present day. Born in 1861, he was both a Cabot and a Lowell, a son of two of the most powerful and prestigious old Boston Brahmin merchant families. After graduating from Harvard in 1882, he went to the oil and gas fields of western Pennsylvania to start a business. There he found that the industry produced huge amounts of carbon debris, waste products of gas blow-offs and refining.

Godfrey's older brother Samuel had founded a paint and stain business, using coal tars to make black pigment. Godfrey decided to build his business around carbon black, the very substance that was fouling the oil fields. Distinct from soot, this substance, a form of carbon sometimes called lamp black, had been around for a long time. Prehistoric cave dwellers used it to draw animals on cave walls, and the Egyptian pharaohs used it as a pigment. The Cabots saw similar applications for it.

The Cabots built a plant in Buffalo Mills, Pennsylvania, that used natural gas to produce carbon black in 1882, and in 1884 Godfrey patented a carbon black production process that used stationary plates and rotating burners. In 1887 Godfrey bought out Samuel's interest in the business.

At about this time, a glut developed in the carbon black market; at the same time, new uses were being found for natural gas, which was the raw material for carbon black. Cabot's response was to purchase gas leases and drill on the sites, drilling his first successful gas well in Saxonburg, Pennsylvania, in 1888. He continued, despite the glut, to buy up small carbon black factories as well, and by 1897 he was probably the largest producer in the industry.

In 1898, with the exhaustion of the Pennsylvania gas fields, Cabot moved his operation to West Virginia, where he acquired oil and gas leases, which he drilled successfully. He continued to add gas sites in West Virginia, consolidating his holdings, and building a natural gasoline extraction plant near Elizabeth, West Virginia, in 1914. These holdings were the forerunners of Cabot's natural gas processing plants in the Southwest.

While the advent and spread of high-speed presses and similar applications greatly expanded Cabot's business, World War I demonstrated the potential for carbon black in the modern economy. It had been known for a while that carbon black could inhibit damage to materials caused by the sun; a few years before the war, the India Rubber Gutta-Percha and Telegraph Works Co. of Silvertown, England, began to manufacture automobile tires using carbon black as a stabilizing or reinforcing agent. During World War I the United States began using carbon black, and its superior properties became evident in improved tread wear and lower rates of tire failure. After the war, its use spread throughout the tire industry, providing a tremendous burst of growth to Cabot and other suppliers. The company came to excel in producing different grades and types of carbon black for different applications.

In 1922 Cabot's company was incorporated as Godfrey L. Cabot, Inc. At about this time, the locus of carbon black production was shifted out of West Virginia, first, unsuccessfully, to Louisiana, and then to Texas. Carbon black plants in the East were sold; gas production and distribution continued, though it was cut back. Thomas Cabot, Godfrey's son, opened Cabot's Southwestern Division, headquartered in Breckenridge, Texas, in 1925. Two years later, headquarters were moved to Pampa, Texas.

By 1930 Cabot had built eight carbon black plants in Texas and one in Oklahoma. In the early 1930s Cabot used a new technique to develop a pelletized, dustless carbon black, which was tradenamed SPHERON. Bulk sales of this easily transportable product fueled Cabot's growth in the mid-1930s, in spite of the Depression. This in turn led to the construction of other carbon black plants in 1937 and 1938.

As was the case from the very beginning of Godfrey Cabot's enterprise, carbon black production and energy were developed in tandem. Cabot formed Cabot Shops, Inc., in 1930 to construct the carbon black plants. It also made oil well pumping units. In 1935 Cabot began drilling for oil and gas in Texas and built two natural gas processing plants in West Texas near two of its carbon black plants. Residue from the gas process was delivered to the carbon black plants and used as raw material.

Although Godfrey L. Cabot, Inc. was able to stay afloat, the period from 1925 to 1939 was not a boom period for the company. The Depression greatly cut back demand for gas as well as carbon black. In fact, the carbon black facilities in the Southwest experienced losses that were barely balanced by gas and gas distribution profits from West Virginia, Pennsylvania, and New York.

By 1939 Cabot had sales of nearly $7 million. Natural gas accounted for more than 50 percent of sales, while carbon black yielded about 35 percent. In that year, too, war changed the nature of the business. As Japan spread its control over the rubber plantations in Malaya and the East Indies, the United States was faced with a cutoff of shipments of natural rubber. The government responded by imposing restrictions on the use of natural rubber and by constructing synthetic rubber plants. Cabot stockpiled 100 million pounds of carbon black at its own expense when it anticipated shortages for 1943 to 1945. The substance was considered so important to the war effort that a governmental interagency carbon black committee was set up when production lagged in 1942, and funds were made available to producers. Among the facilities built or added to by Cabot during this period, with government support, included plants in McCoy, Louisiana; Borger, Texas; Guymon, Oklahoma; and Wickett, Texas.

After the war, Cabot converted several of its carbon black plants from gas process to oil process. This move helped set the stage for Cabot to become an international company later, as oil did not need to be piped and plants could be built closer to their markets.

By 1950 the company had become the largest producer of carbon black and reaped the benefits of a general upsurge in worldwide demand. Also, as GIs returned home, automobiles were sold in increasing numbers, and those automobiles needed tires. In 1950 Cabot built its first carbon black plant in Europe, near Liverpool, England. Plants followed in Canada (1953), France (1958), and Italy (1960). In addition, plants partially owned by Cabot were opened in Australia (1959) and in the Netherlands (1960); both of these facilities relied heavily on Cabot technology.

During this period Cabot continued to do research that improved carbon black processes and products, opening a research facility in Cambridge, Massachusetts. The company also began to branch out. In 1952 Cabot began importing fumed silica, and in 1957 began production of the substance in the United States under the name Cab-O-Sil. Fumed silica is an ultra-fine high purity silica that is used to provide reinforcement, viscosity control, and free flow properties to a variety of products, including silicones, adhesives and sealants, reinforced plastics, and coatings. It is used extensively in the automotive, cosmetics, paint and ink, construction, and pharmaceutical industries. Cab-O-Sil is the leading producer of fumed silica in North America.

At this time, Cabot also became involved in a study group on liquified natural gas (LNG). This involvement led to the opening in 1971 of Distrigas in Everett, Massachusetts, the only LNG terminal and distribution center in New England. Cabot LNG Corporation supplies between 5 percent and 25 percent of New England's liquified natural gas needs, including those of power companies.

In 1960 all of the various Cabot businesses and subsidiaries were united into Cabot Corporation. The company went public in 1963 with the sale of 12 percent of its common stock. In 1962 founder Godfrey Cabot died.

Expansion continued throughout the 1960s, particularly overseas. Subsidiaries and plants were opened in Argentina, Colombia, Germany, and Spain. In 1963 Cabot entered into two completely new arenas. The company began experiments on plastic polymers and compounds and in 1963 began producing titanium, a high-performance metal, at its facility in Ashtabula, Ohio. The company also launched considerable research in the area of experimental plastic polymers and compounds. It eventually became a world leader in the production of thermoplastics used in films as well as in injection-molded and extruded plastic products. By the end of the 1960s, it was clear to Cabot that production of high-performance materials was a high-growth area.

To this end, the company, under CEO Robert A. Charpie, acquired the Stellite Division from Union Carbide in 1970. According to the 1970 annual report, ''Stellite has profoundly changed the nature of the Company by launching Cabot in a new direction, that of high performance materials, by providing major diversification strength, and by broadening our technological base in a way that is complementary to the technical skills we have in the performance chemical field.''

The main business of this new division consisted of nickel- and cobalt-based alloys that were designed to withstand extreme heat, corrosion, and wear. Such materials were used in gas turbine engines, electrical power generating stations, chemical processes equipment, and other like applications. In 1978 Cabot acquired Kawecki Berylco Industries, which enabled the company to produce beryllium-copper, tantalum, and columbium products as well as aluminum alloys. Tantalum in particular is used extensively by computer and electronics manufacturers, as well as in aerospace, ballistic munitions, and various chemical processes.

Apart from gains made by entry into the high performance metals business, Cabot's energy component experienced major growth in the 1970s as a result of the energy crisis of 1973–1974. The value of Cabot's oil and gas reserves shot up, and this provided a major impetus to step up exploration, particularly in the Gulf of Mexico and mid-continent. The company withdrew from exploration outside the United States. In addition, the company undertook further development in West Virginia, and the pipeline and distribution systems there were upgraded.

The company also expanded its gas processing and pipeline business in the 1970s. It acquired further industrial gas pipelines in West Virginia and completed another gas processing plant in Texas. Most significantly, it acquired TUCO, Inc. in 1979, which added about 500 miles of pipeline and two gas processing plants to its holdings in the Southwest.

Although Cabot's energy holdings increased in value, the energy crisis was not without a downside. The cost of the type of oil needed for carbon black production tripled, putting a severe squeeze on profits. Cabot invested heavily in new, more efficient technology and instituted programs to reduce raw material costs.

However, in the 1970s, Cabot, on the advice of the Boston Consulting Group, came to see its chemical businesses, including carbon black, as "cash cows." In essence, cash was extracted from this vital area of the business and put into diversification into metals manufacturing, ceramics, semiconductors, and other businesses in which Cabot had little expertise. Chemical plants were ignored and allowed to deteriorate. This destabilized the entire company. On top of this, gas prices collapsed in the 1980s, leaving Cabot with vast liabilities from acquisitions and plant investment, but much reduced income.

In 1987 the Cabot family, which owns 30 percent of the company, replaced Charpie and tapped Samuel Bodman as CEO in hopes of turning the company around. Among other things, he stopped the slide of the chemicals component of the company by investing $500 million to upgrade the plants. Bodman also divested the metals and ceramics businesses and got out of energy exploration and production in order to concentrate the company on its strong suits in organic industrial chemicals such as carbon black, fumed silica, high performance materials, and plastics.

The result was that through the early 1990s, the company consistently had operating revenues around $1.5 billion, and in 1992 earned 12.5 percent on equity. By concentrating on its core businesses, Cabot Corporation seems to be well positioned for growth, particularly in the Far East, where the company is projecting that as much as one-third of its revenues will come by 1998.

Principal Subsidiaries: North American Carbon Black; Latin American Carbon Black; European Carbon Black Division; Pacific Asia Carbon Black; Cab-O-Sil; Cabot Plastics International; Cabot Performance Materials; Cabot Safety Corporation; Cabot LNG Corporation; TUCO, Inc.

Further Reading:

Berlin, Rosalind Klein, "The Smutty Story of Cabot Corp.," *Fortune*, December 5, 1988, p. 133.

Bodman, Samuel W., "Cabot Corporation 1992 Annual Meeting of Stockholders," Cabot Corporation, February 14, 1992.

Chakavarty, Subrata N., "White Slacks and Carbon Black," *Forbes*, October 26, 1992, p. 122.

"Cabot CEO Looks To Future Growth," *Chemical Marketing Reporter*, March 8, 1993, p. 9.

Plishner, Emily S., "Cabot Concentrates on Microparticulate Growth," *Chemical Week*, March 10, 1993, p. 14.

—Kenneth F. Kronenberg

Carlisle Companies Incorporated

101 South Salina Street
Syracuse, New York 13202
U.S.A
(315) 474-2500
Fax: (315) 474-2008

Public Company
Incorporated: 1986 as holding company for Carlisle Corp.
Employees: 4,290
Revenue: $528 million
Stock Exchanges: New York
SICs: 3069 Fabricated Rubber, Not Elsewhere Classified;
3089 Plastics Products, Not Elsewhere Classified

Carlisle Companies Incorporated is a diversified corporation that manufactures rubber and plastics products in three areas: construction materials, transportation products, and general industry, including food service plastics. Carlisle Companies is a highly decentralized company with most functional decisions for each division made by the division management. The headquarters, which was moved from Cincinnati, Ohio, to Syracuse, New York, in 1989 comprised only about 21 of Carlisle's over 4,000 employees.

The present day Carlisle Companies Inc. was incorporated in 1986 as a holding company for the original company, Carlisle Corporation, founded in 1917 as a manufacturer of inner tubes. Later it became a major manufacturer of bicycle tires, brake linings, and rubber roofing. In the 1970s the company also diversified into the manufacture of electronics components.

For years, Carlisle had tried to compete with the big rubber companies for the automobile tire market, but in 1980, a new strategy began to pay off for the company. Carlisle simply decided not to compete with the big tire companies for the automobile original equipment market. Instead, the company sold half its products to the replacement market and also concentrated on specialty products such as snowblower, tractor, motorcycle, and dirt-bike tires. Carlisle chairperson George Dixon told *Forbes* that the company's new resolution was "not to get trampled by the elephants." So while the economic recession hurt such big tiremakers as Firestone and B. F. Goodrich, Carlisle's net earnings were $26 million, representing a 38 percent improvement over the year before, and its stocks were soaring.

During this time, Carlisle was also very successful in the rubber roof market, which accounted for most of the company's earnings and brought in 43 percent of its profits for 1980. The rubber roofing market was strong, having become a popular and effective alternative to the traditional felt and asphalt coverings of flat roofs, and Carlisle led the market with 40 percent of its sales. Furthermore, Carlisle's best-selling Sure-Seal and other construction materials helped make up for any losses in other divisions of the company. Although growth in the rubber roof industry was attracting competition from larger rubber companies, Carlisle was confident in its ability to compete with "the elephants" in this market, because of its years of experience in production of the single-ply rubber sheeting. Its president, Malcolm Myers told *Forbes,* "When it comes to single-ply roofing, we're the giants." He also commented that it would probably take some time before the other companies could even begin to produce a product as good as Carlisle's. To further secure its lead, Carlisle opened a new plant in Greenville, Illinois, to manufacture single-ply rubber roof sheeting. The Greenville plant, as well as a plant in Carlisle, Pennsylvania, were equipped with special machines to automate the manufacture of the huge rubber sheets, measuring 40 feet by 100 feet or larger.

Another market in which Carlisle held a unique niche was in providing contractors with complete roofing systems, including the rubber sheeting, all pipe seals, flashing, metal fasteners, edging, and adhesives. Contractors installing Carlisle roofs were required to learn proper installation from Carlisle representatives, who then inspected installations before guarantees could be issued.

Other areas in which Carlisle dabbled included the manufacture of specialty wire and cable for data communications, magnetic computer tapes, and magnetically coated plastics for floppy disks.

Carlisle's strength in its market niches earned it a place among the Fortune 500 companies in 1985 with sales of $527 million. The following year, a holding corporation, Carlisle Companies Inc., was incorporated to oversee operations at Carlisle and the other companies that were being added to the group, such as Data Electronics, purchased in 1986 for $33.4 million in cash and Hardcast, Inc., acquired the following year. In 1988, Carlisle bought Ivan software, a developer of utility software, while selling its International Wire Products Company. Shortly thereafter, Carlisle decided to sell its interest in Graham Japan Limited, a joint venture in Japan that sold computer tapes made by Carlisle.

Carlisle's corporate headquarters, which had been based in Cincinnati since 1971, were moved to Syracuse, New York, in 1989. President and chief executive officer Stephen Munn maintained that its new location would provide more convenient access to the country's major financial institutions. Munn, a former executive of Carrier Corporation, an air conditioning manufacturer based in Syracuse, welcomed E. Douglas Kenna, former president of Carrier, as Carlisle's new chairperson.

In 1990, Carlisle became one of only 170 U.S. companies to form joint ventures with the Soviet Union. Carlisle's subsidiary, SynTec Systems, had a 49 percent share, and the Soviet Union retained a 51 percent share of the Moscow-based Krovtex, which sold and installed rubber roofs in the Soviet Union. The roofing materials were manufactured in the United States by Carlisle SynTec Systems, the largest company in the corporation's construction materials division. The Soviet Union was a complicated place to conduct business and became even more complicated when the country broke apart into separate republics in 1992. Krovtex continued to operate as a joint venture following the breakup, despite chaotic conditions, and the company foresaw strong long-term potential in Russia and other Eastern European markets.

As part of its plan to grow 15 to 20 percent yearly, in 1990 Carlisle purchased Brookpark Plastics Inc. of Lake City, Pennsylvania, and Off-Highway Braking Systems, a division of B.F. Goodrich Aerospace based in Bloomington, Indiana. Brookpark, a compression molder of diversified plastics products, became part of Continental Carlisle, Inc., while Off-Highway, a maker of braking systems for off-highway vehicles, with manufacturing facilities in The Netherlands and Brazil, became part of Carlisle's Motion Control Industries Inc. With the addition of the former Goodrich division, Carlisle was for the first time capable of manufacturing a complete brake system, as it already manufactured brake linings, pads, and other brake system components.

In September, 1991, Carlisle purchased SiLite Corporation, a maker of reusable mugs, cups, and dishes for restaurants and cafeterias, with manufacturing facilities in California, Illinois, and Wisconsin. Carlisle already had plastic foodware production facilities in Oklahoma and Pennsylvania, and SiLite, with sales of $37 million in 1990, was a welcome addition.

Due to the effects of recession on the automobile and truck industries, Carlisle's profits fell substantially in 1991, as sales of its plastic parts for interior and exterior trim, as well as brake components for the heavy trucking industry declined. The company also suffered losses in the one-half inch computer tape market.

Consequently, the company began a restructuring strategy designed to consolidate or sell parts of its slumping data communications and electronics businesses. Carlisle had entered the electronics industry in the 1970s, seeing a need to diversify into these potentially profitable and growing new product lines since its current product lines and markets had already reached maturity. By the 1990s, however, the electronics competition was stiff, the market and prices were slumping, and Carlisle was losing money.

Carlisle Memory Products group, which manufactured and marketed cartridges for backing up main memory tapes of small and mid-sized computer systems, was sold to Verbatim Corporation in 1992. The company also sold the rest of its magnetic tape business. Having divested itself of its unprofitable, peripheral divisions, Carlisle began to strengthen its core businesses, acquiring ECI Building Components Inc., a manufacturer of components for metal roofing and siding. ECI had sales of $32 million in 1991, and its acquisition strengthened Carlisle's marketing position, particularly in the Southwest and West, as metal became an accepted roofing material for many nonresidential buildings.

Carlisle also consolidated some plants. Carlisle Tire and Rubber, which mainly manufactured tires for use on lawn and garden equipment, relocated its Indianapolis wheel plant to Aiken, South Carolina. Two Continental/SiLite factories were closed and their operations were moved to other plants.

Internationally, Carlisle acquired a brake shoe factory in Canada in order to increase its share of the heavy-duty after market. Because shipping of these heavy assemblies was very expensive, the market for these brake shoes was regional. Carlisle continued to expand its foreign sales with more than 40 percent of its off-highway braking systems for heavy machinery and other vehicles being sold outside the United States. Furthermore, the company entered a joint venture with Rutgerswerke, a large German manufacturer, in Mexico, producing brake pads and truck brake linings for the small but growing Mexican truck market.

During this time, the company's Tensolite division began moving away from the commodity wire market and into the aerospace and electronics markets. Its line of precision-coated wires and cables was selected for use in Boeing's 737s and 757, representing the first time Boeing, the leading airframe maker, used a single wiring system in its planes.

In 1993, Goodyear sold its roofing products business to Carlisle Companies Inc., strengthening Carlisle's position as the number one supplier of nonresidential roofs. Carlisle also became the leading supplier of pneumatic tires and specialty wheels to makers of riding mowers, garden tillers, and other lawn care equipment such as utility carts. With plans to expand its market for wheels and tires to include the golfing industry, the company also began manufacturing and marketing Softpave, shock-absorbing, bonded rubber crumb tiles for use on golf practice ranges and walkways. A related product, Playguard tiles, provided a soft, shock-reducing surface for use on playgrounds. These products were manufactured from recycled scrap from Carlisle's tire-making plants, as well as from used tires and rubber bought from other suppliers who first removed the steel belts. The use of recycled material helped reduce the company's costs and was good for the environment.

Despite its success with roofing materials and other rubber products, however, Carlisle's food service market represented the largest segment of its business in the early 1990s. Carlisle's Continental/SiLite International division manufactured more than 6,000 different plastic products and was a leader in the market for plastic permanentware, having captured a large share of the market in cafeterias of schools, colleges, and correctional institutions. The division dominated the growing market for display food containers in deli departments and salad bars of supermarkets, which were upgrading their counters. Although fast-food restaurants had represented a growing market for Carlisle in the 1980s, that market stabilized in the 1990s while mid-priced family-type restaurants became a growing market for the company's kitchen products as well as dinnerware, beverage dispensers, and salad bar containers. Also a manufacturer of acrylic gift and table accessories sold in major department stores, Continental/SiLite expanded its lines, adding high quality pewter items.

Carlisle intended to continue its focus on its core industries as it approached the twenty-first century, emphasizing its strategy in its mission statement: "to serve customers worldwide by building on our strengths in rubber, plastics, friction and precision coating products, and other technologies in which we can develop a competitive advantage.

Principal Subsidiaries: Geauga; Carlisle Syntec Systems; Carlisle Tire and Rubber; Motion Control Industries; Tensolite; Continental/Silite International; Netstor; Braemar; DSI; Vistatech.

Further Reading:

Annual Reports, Syracuse, New York: Carlisle Companies Incorporated.

"Carlisle Makes It the Hard Way," *Fortune,* April 29, 1985, pp. 320–7.

Flax, Steven, "Where the Rubber Meets the Roof," *Forbes,* April 13, 1981, pp. 58–61.

—Wendy J. Stein

Carter-Wallace, Inc.

1345 Avenue of the Americas
New York, New York 10105
U.S.A.
(212) 339-5000
Fax: (212) 339-5100

Public Company
Incorporated: 1880 as Carter Medicine Company
Employees: 4,170
Sales: $673,390 million
Stock Exchanges: New York
SICs: 2834 Pharmaceutical Preparations; 2844 Toilet
  Preparations; 2879 Agricultural Chemicals Nec

A diversified health care company that has exhibited a consistent knack for anticipating business trends, Carter-Wallace, Inc. is more than 110 years old. The company markets and makes toiletries, proprietary drugs, diagnostic specialties, pharmaceuticals, and pet products. Best known for such products as Arrid deodorant and Trojan condoms, Carter-Wallace has more recently emphasized its laboratories division, where work on various medications points the way to future profits.

Carter-Wallace's roots can be traced back to the 1800s and a modest pill compounded by an Erie, Pennsylvania, doctor for folks suffering from digestive distress. "Carter's Little Liver Pills" were first advertised by a sign placed in Dr. John Samuel Carter's pharmacy window, but the pills' popularity soon spread beyond the capacity of the pharmacy's back room. By 1859 a four-floor plant had been built to produce the liver pills. Dr. Carter had also created other products, but it was the sales of the liver pills that led New York businessman Brent Good to suggest a merger to make a nationwide business. In 1880 Carter Medicine Company was born.

In its first year of business, the company spent a third of its revenues on advertising. Coupled with all the other start-up expenses, plus the move to New York, the first year ended in the red, but belief in the product remained strong. By its second year Carter was exporting to Canada and England and enjoying vigorous sales in the United States. By 1890 the company had already outgrown its new quarters and moved to larger ones. Soon imitators were popping up everywhere and an attorney was retained to battle the counterfeiters. With the loss in 1884 of

Samuel Carter—the company's president and the son of the pill's inventor—Carter Medicine Company entered a new era.

The 1890s was a time of uncertainty and financial panic in the United States and Carter Medicine Company suffered along with nearly every other business. It was just recovering when another economic crash rattled the country in 1907. Companies stabilized again just in time for World War I to alter the global economy. What sustained the Carter Medicine Company through these times was the fact that Carter's Little Liver Pills had become such a staple household item. Meanwhile, the company continued to operate like many family-owned corporations. Brent Good passed the presidency on to his son Harry Good; Harry's brother-in-law, Charles Orcutt, later succeeded him. Another new era for the company was ushered in when Harry Hoyt, Sr., who was Orcutt's son-in-law, became managing director in 1929. Hoyt bought controlling interest in the company and instilled Carter-Wallace with his axiom that "a business cannot stand still." His energy and aims mark the company today.

Hoyt's first order of business was to expand beyond the company's one profitable product, the liver pills. Creating new products meant risk and investment. It was difficult at first to convince trustees of his vision. Hoyt wanted to cut dividend payments and spend the money on the development of new products. While this struggle for change was taking place, the government dropped a blow: the Department of Agriculture contested the use of the word "liver" on the pills' labels, since the pills were not really targeted for liver ailments. This was catastrophic for a product whose brand name had been familiar to households for more than half a century. In light of all the money it had invested in advertising and brand recognition, the company decided to fight to retain its brand name and eventually won.

The Federal Trade Commission brought similar charges against the company in 1943. For 17 years the company battled in the courts to retain its name. The decision came back in 1959: "liver" had to be dropped from all advertising. The product, whose name was known in every home and painted on the sides of barns across America, was renamed Carter's Little Pills.

Meanwhile, Hoyt was pioneering research for new products even through the hardships of the 1930s. With so many Americans living hand-to-mouth during the Depression, few could afford liver pills, and sales sank. This only fueled Hoyt's determination to diversify. Research pointed to deodorants and antiperspirants. At the time there were two dominant brands in the United States, and each had a weakness: one was a stainless dry cream that was a deodorant only; the other a liquid antiperspirant that often stained clothes and irritated skin. The challenge became how to find a dry, stainless cream that could stop perspiration while deodorizing, yet not irritate the skin. A research chemist from Princeton, John H. Wallace, was tapped for the task. In 1935 the company launched the product that would soon outstrip its liver pills in sales and brand-name recognition: Arrid.

Between an ad campaign that saturated the public and a product that really did meet consumer needs, Arrid became the largest selling deodorant in the United States. These two characteristics of the Arrid product became Carter-Wallace trademarks: the effective use of advertising, combined with a product that was developed instead of copied. In order to keep ahead of its many imitators and competitors, Arrid was constantly improved. The success of the deodorant soon led to the construction of a new plant in New Brunswick. Carter's sales topped the $1 million mark for the first time in 1935. To reflect its new direction, the company's name was changed to Carter Products, Inc., in 1937. For ten years, the original formula of Arrid was a top-seller. After that, various improvements were used to further boost sales.

Another innovation was a new depilatory product introduced in 1940. Designed primarily as a hair remover for women, Nair became another company success. During World War II Carter Products also produced foot powders for the armed forces. Indeed, through 1945, war work absorbed much of the company's attention.

In 1949 another product innovation was unveiled: an aerosol shaving product named Rise that was the first pressurized shaving cream. The product's explosive popularity prompted many imitations, including a Colgate product so similar that Carter sued for infringement of patent rights. This case was won by Carter more than ten years later.

Attention turned to ethical drugs as the newest market. The company began to look at the development of prescription drugs. This led to another Carter-Wallace cornerstone, Miltown, a tranquilizer that was the first of its kind. It relaxed muscles and also relieved mental stress. Following its introduction in 1955, Miltown's sales doubled and tripled each of the subsequent five months. By 1958 Carter was again constructing a new plant to handle production demands.

Celebrating its 75th anniversary in 1955, Carter Products looked back on a remarkable record of growth. Its products were selling in 54 countries. Two years later, the company listed stock on the New York Stock Exchange. The company served as a sponsor of such radio programs as "Amos 'n Andy" and "Fibber McGee and Mollie," and was a pioneer among television advertisers, thus making Carter products familiar to millions.

When sales and profits took a plunge in the 1960–1961 fiscal year, Carter claimed that one contributor was the fact that the company's patented meprobamate tablets—commercially known as Miltown—were being purchased abroad in violation of patent laws. When the United States brought antitrust charges against Carter Products, accusing it of creating a monopoly on meprobamate, the company contested the charge. After a year of hearings, the case was concluded and Carter won the patented right to be sole manufacturer of meprobamate. This victory is significant as it secured one of Carter's steady sources of income. Sales rebounded in the following year.

In 1961 Harry Hoyt, Sr., was named chairman of the board. A new product was released that same year, a muscle relaxant with the generic name carisoprodol and the brand name Soma. While a success, Soma was no rival for Miltown. It did, however, signal further diversification. Carter soon purchased a majority interest in Frank W. Horner, Ltd., a Canadian drug company with sales of more than $5 million. Horner would become one of Carter's most profitable outlets. As a leader in drugs that dealt with diabetes, nausea, and antibiotics, Horner brought new strengths aboard. About the same time, Carter acquired 50 percent interest in Millmaster Chemical Corporation, a company with more than $10 million in sales.

The Wallace Laboratory division of Carter Products had compiled more than 13 product innovations by the mid-1960s. In 1965 the company name was changed to Carter-Wallace, Inc., a reflection of this division's importance to the firm. Arrid Extra Dry Anti-Perspirant Spray Deodorant was introduced in 1968. It was the only aerosol spray of its kind, another product revolution, and it quickly shot to the head of its market in sales. It remains a blockbuster Carter product today.

Having outgrown its executive offices, Carter-Wallace moved in 1968. Lambert Kay Company, a manufacturer of pharmaceutical and nutritional products for pets, was acquired around that time. By 1970 company sales topped $125 million. While toiletries and proprietary drugs represented the largest percentage of sales, prescription drugs were becoming an increasingly substantial portion of sales. At this juncture, the company was marketing 32 products at home and abroad and Wallace Laboratories was concentrating on three major groups of therapeutic agents: anti-inflammatory compounds, anti-arteriosclerotic compounds and antihistamines. The company had obviously come a long way from the days when its staple product was Carter's Little Liver Pills. To keep ahead in the competitive pharmaceutical industry, Carter acquired majority interest in two research organizations: Industrial Biological Laboratories and the Laboratory for Analytical Blood Studies.

With the patent on meprobamate set to expire in 1972, Carter-Wallace concentrated on new income sources. As a result of a licensing agreement with Cameo, Inc. of Ohio, Carter-Wallace received the rights to manufacture and sell Pearl Drops. This liquid tooth polish was another one-of-a-kind product at the time. Sales were solid enough to prompt the company to purchase the product outright within three years.

Still, the many economic uncertainties of the 1970s had an impact on Carter-Wallace. A record profit drop came in 1974. Inflation, high energy and labor costs, and wary consumers all contributed to the downturn. Carter-Wallace bought Princeton Laboratories Products Company, a manufacturer of diagnostic kits, for $10 million around this time. This seemed a promising new field at the time. It proved to be even more lucrative than expected. One of Princeton's primary customers was the Wampole Division of Denver Chemical Company. Wampole led the country in sales of pregnancy tests, as well as diagnostic tests for rheumatoid arthritis, streptococcal infections, and mononucleosis. Adding Wampole to the Carter-Wallace roster required that Denver Chemical be acquired. Carter-Wallace made the purchase for $25 million.

While Hoyt, Sr., was chairman of the executive committee, his son, Harry Hoyt, Jr., became chairman of the board and CEO. Hoyt, Jr., had by that time been with the company for 25 years; his brother Charles had worked alongside him for 22 of those years.

In 1976 earnings again fell dramatically. The plunge was largely the result of publicity regarding the dangers of aerosol emissions. Carter-Wallace fought back with aggressive advertising and promotional expenditures. Closing in on its 100th birthday, the company began to feel an improvement in its financial health. In 1979 it purchased the Pharmaceutical Products Division of Mallinckrodt, Inc., which specialized in cough and cold medications, antihypertensives, and diuretics.

The 1980s were another era of explosive growth for the company. In 1985 Carter-Wallace acquired Youngs Drug Products Corporation, the privately held maker of Trojan-brand condoms. It was Carter-Wallace's first foray into that industry. With the advent of the contraceptive pill and IUDs in the 1960s, condoms had become a relic of a method of pregnancy prevention. During the 1970s the pill and penicillin were the preferred guardians against pregnancy and venereal disease. When Carter-Wallace began manufacturing Trojans, condom sales had dropped to half of what they had been in the previous ten years. But within less than a year of the acquisition, condoms were being cited as the only known protection against the sexual transmission of AIDS. Condoms quickly became an omnipresent topic in the media. Sales soared and Trojans—a longtime brand on the market—accounted for about 55 percent of the sales.

It was a revolution both in the country and for the company. Condoms had long been associated with illicit sex and prostitution, relegated to vending machines or beneath-the-counter sales in pharmacies. By 1986, however, condoms were widely available, displayed openly in retail stores and even supermarkets. First-time buyers accounted for a great amount of the increase; in fact, women were buying about 50 percent of condoms sold in 1986. With the AIDS epidemic dominating the public's attention, condom sales were assured even without advertising, but Carter-Wallace took an early lead in magazine advertising anyway, committing itself to a multimillion-dollar ad campaign early in the AIDS information explosion. In an industry where brand loyalty is high, the Trojan brand led the way in sales, followed by Ramses and Sheik brands, both made by the same company, Schmid. In 1988 Carter-Wallace bought Mentor's condom business, which, combined with Trojans, gave it about 62 percent of the market. Carter-Wallace states that its condom products accounted for about ten percent of its sales and 15 percent of its earnings in 1987.

The bulk of the company's revenue at that time was derived from the sale of deodorants and prescription drugs. Drug sales were growing at four percent a year, increasing from $152 million in 1983 to $209 million in 1987. This division accounted for nearly half of company sales in 1987. While the lucrative patent protection of Miltown had expired, Carter-Wallace had established an effective strategy of licensing foreign drugs and bringing them into U.S. markets. Dwarfed in size by some of its competitors in this field, Carter-Wallace focused more on solid products with steady sales than on the discovery of cutting-edge drugs.

Anti-perspirants were still the company's largest consumer division in 1987. While sales of Rise and Pearl Drops fell in the face of increased competition from rivals, sales of Sea & Ski suntan lotion and Answer pregnancy tests bloomed. Sea & Ski was another example of the company's ability to spot growth industries before they become unaffordable. Pregnancy testing

kits also became a boom product in the late 1980s. By 1990 home pregnancy test manufacturing had become a $100 million industry. The year prior, Carter-Wallace had acquired Hygeia Sciences, Inc., a subsidiary of Tambrands Inc. and the producer of First Response, the number one selling brand of home pregnancy tests. Carter-Wallace's own Answer product was at that time the fourth ranked kit in terms of market share; coupled with First Response, Carter-Wallace was able to secure a 31 percent share of the market. In 1989 drugstore sales of tests rose nearly 30 percent, and supermarket sales were on the rise as well. Sales were attributed to the increased interest in self-health-care, plus the increased reliability of the tests. With First Response, Carter-Wallace shifted the product's pitch for the first time to young women who might not want to be pregnant, especially college students, while also maintaining traditional ads aimed at the 50 percent of test users who, according to market research, wanted to be pregnant. With a new market niche within an expanding market, Carter-Wallace was again just ahead of the trends.

By the end of 1990, the company had shifted its strategy slightly and increased its research and development spending by 20 percent over the previous year; the company further claimed that it would increase spending in this area by another 20 percent in 1991. Carter-Wallace tested drugs for the treatment of such ailments as epilepsy, asthma, and angina. Consumer goods and drugs are fairly recession-proof industries. The company seemed on solid footing. Carter-Wallace purchased Dramamine, a motion-sickness product, from Procter & Gamble Company in 1991. Sales of the well-established brand were then about $13 million.

Earnings declined despite a rise in sales in early 1992, due to R&D outlays. Meanwhile, Trojan condoms increased its stranglehold on the condom industry; it gained 60 percent of market share, with sales still on the increase. In July 1991 the FDA seized 1.2 million Trojan brand natural-membrane condoms, contending that the lambskin condoms were not effective protection against sexually transmitted diseases and that the condom labels did not note this. Carter-Wallace argued, however, that it was in the process of complying with relabeling the condoms in the wake of the discovery that only latex condoms had pores small enough to prevent transmission of diseases.

In November 1991 Fox Broadcasting Company broadcast an advertisement for the Trojan brand, thus becoming the first national broadcast television network to run a condom commercial. Condom spots had run on some local and cable stations, but this national ad was a ground-breaker. It came on the heels of basketball great Magic Johnson's announcement that he would retire after testing positive for the virus associated with AIDS. Just when ad and sales plateaus had seemed to be reached in this area, the news of Johnson's test results triggered another jump in condom sales. Between 1985 and 1991, condom sales worldwide more than doubled.

In late 1991 there was much speculation about Carter-Wallace's soon-to-be released drug, felbamate, a drug that controls epileptic seizures. Sales were projected to be $100 to $200 million annually. The drug, known by the brand name Felbatol, was still awaiting FDA approval in the spring of 1993. In 1992 Schering-

Plough Corporation signed an agreement with Carter-Wallace for marketing rights for felbamate outside of North America.

Principal Subsidiaries: Laboratoires Fumouze S.A. (France); Carter Products, Canada; Frank W. Horner, Inc. (Canada); Carter-Wallace, Limited (United Kingdom); Carter-Wallace (Australia) Pty. Limited; S.p.A. Italiana Laboratori Bouty (Italy); Carter-Wallace, S.A. (Mexico)

Further Reading:

Appelbaum, Cara, "Carter-Wallace Buys A New Strategy for Pregnancy Tests," *Adweek's Marketing Week,* May 28, 1990, p. 10.

"Barriers to Entry," *The Economist,* November 30, 1991, p. 71.

"Carter-Wallace Ends Bid to Buy P&G's Dramamine," *Wall Street Journal,* May 28, 1987, p. B3.

"Carter-Wallace Net Fell in Fourth Period; Stock Drops Sharply," *Wall Street Journal,* May 7, 1991, p. C21.

"Carter-Wallace Inc.," *New York Times,* May 18, 1991, p. 37.

"Carter-Wallace Intends to Buy Line from P&G," *Wall Street Journal,* May 20, 1991, p. A12B.

Cutler, Blayne, "Condom Mania," *American Demographics,* June 1989, p. 17.

Elliott, Stuart, "The Sponsor Is the Surprise in Fox's First Condom Ad," *New York Times,* November 19, 1991, p. D19.

"FDA Panel Supports Approval of 2 Drugs for Treating Epilepsy," *Wall Street Journal,* December 16, 1992, p. B8.

Hamilton, Patricia, "Corporate Dynasties," *D&B Reports,* March-April 1992, p. 16.

Hawng, Suein, "Carter-Wallace Discontinues Sales of Diabetes Device," *Wall Street Journal,* October 7, 1991, p. A7D.

Horowitz, Bruce, "Trojan Gets A Condom Ad on Network TV," *Los Angeles Times,* November 19, 1991, P. D1.

Katz, Donald, "The Investor: Counting on a Cure," *Esquire,* November 1987, p. 71.

Lazo, Shirley, "Speaking of Dividends," *Barron's,* July 27, 1987, p. 45.

Leinster, Colin, "The Rubber Barons," *Fortune,* November 24, 1986, pp. 105–118.

Marcial, Gene, "Be Cautious With Carter-Wallace," *Business Week,* February 23, 1987, p. 116.

McFadden, Michael, "AIDS Stock Worth the Gamble," *Fortune,* April 13, 1987, pp. 113–114.

Palmer, Jay, "Who Needs Hype?" *Barron's,* February 29, 1988, pp. 13, 60.

"Protection Money," *Forbes,* February 23, 1987, p. 8.

Sullivan, Joseph, "Condoms Seized by U.S. Agents In a Label Case," *New York Times,* July 27, 1991, p. 26.

Teitelbaum, Richard, "Prescription: More R&D," *Fortune,* December 17, 1990, p. 128.

"Too Far, Too Soon?" *Forbes,* September 16, 1992, p. 209.

Valeriano, Lourdes Lee, "Carter-Wallace Inc. Agrees to Relabel Lambskin Condoms," *Wall Street Journal,* October 14, 1991, p. B6.

—Carol Keeley

Centex Corporation

3333 Lee Parkway
P.O. Box 19000
Dallas, Texas 75219
U.S.A.
(214) 559-6500

Public Company
Incorporated: 1950 as Centex Construction Company
Employees: 5,500
Sales: $2.16 billion
Stock Exchanges: New York London
SICs: 1521 General Contractors—Single-Family Houses;
  1522 General Contractors—Residential Buildings, Other
  Than Single-Family; 1531 Operative Builders; 1541
  General Contractors—Industrial Buildings and
  Warehouses; 1542 General Contractors—Nonresidential
  Buildings, Other Than Industrial Buildings and
  Warehouses; 3241 Cement, Hydraulic

Throughout the decades, housing starts have been one of America's leading "economic indicators"—the number of new units reflects consumer confidence and buying power. One company that has made the most of housing starts is Centex, one of America's most successful diversified building companies—in fact, in 1992 Centex Real Estate Corporation (aka Centex Homes) ranked number one among single-family home builders in the United States.

This is no small achievement considering that the home construction business overall "is the most fragmented in the country," according to Richard D. Hylton in a *New York Times* article. "By some analysts' estimates, at any one time about 60,000 builders are operating nationwide. Most build fewer than 25 homes a year; only a few are big enough to raise money in the public markets." Centex has proved itself one of the big players, with a history that mirrors America's residential habits and growth since World War II.

The company got its start just after the war, a time characterized by a new affluence and interest in expansion. In 1945 Texas native Tom Lively "scraped together $500 and drew up his 5 feet 6 inches to talk business with Ira Rupley, a successful Dallas land developer," as a 1956 *Newsweek* article related. A young entrepreneur, Lively had "left his home town of Whitewrite, Texas, in 1937, [and] for years had scraped along selling clothing and hardware and 'a little of this and that' before settling on real estate."

Rupley, who had made his name in home construction, entered into partnership with Lively on a still-unnamed building company. They began "modestly enough with a scattering of single and double houses around Dallas," notes *Newsweek*. "Not until 1949 did they undertake their first big subdivision, a project of 300 houses selling for $6,500 each." The success of the subdivision led to the 1950 formation of the Centex Construction Company.

For its first few years, the company concentrated its building efforts exclusively in Texas; but by the mid-1950s Centex was ready to expand. One of its early projects was also an historic one. It was Centex that built Elk Grove Village near Chicago, America's first master-planned community. It was the forerunner of modern master-planned areas, and to this day boasts some 7,000 homes, all built by Centex.

By 1960 Centex Construction Company had produced some 25,000 residences in several states. The company began expanding its operations to include the production of housing materials. Centex opened a cement manufacturing business with facilities in Texas and Nevada, then bought out a Dallas contractor, J. W. Bateson, which had specialized in commercial buildings. Reflecting its new diversification, the company changed its name during the 1960s to Centex Corporation.

In 1969 Centex went public, selling 500,000 shares of common stock. By this time the builder's net worth stood at about $10 million, with gross revenues of almost $100 million. Today company stock is traded both nationally and internationally.

As Centex moved into the 1970s, it increased its scope of operations. The company acquired two leading builders, one in Chicago, the other Dallas-based Fox & Jacobs, then the largest builder of single-family homes in the Southwest. Of that company, a *Fortune* article noted in 1976 that Fox & Jacobs' strategy for producing affordable housing seemed to be working. The article noted that the Centex subsidiary was able to "turn over its $1 million inventory of building materials fifteen times a year. The extraordinarily fast turnover is the key to the company's ability to hold down prices and still keep profit margins healthy on houses in a wide variety of sizes." Expansion continued when Centex bought Frank J. Rooney, Inc., Florida's largest general contractor.

The 1970s became a peak time for building—and as need dictated, Centex expanded its cement business in Texas and became a partner in another cement plant in Illinois. Centex also opened an oil-and-gas plant that would come to be named Cenergy. But for all its diversification efforts, Centex was still primarily associated with one region of the United States. Explains William Barrett in a 1990 *Forbes* article, "In fiscal 1979, 72% of the company's . . . homes were built in Texas, a dangerously high concentration. Centex executives started cutting back there and expanding elsewhere before the economic bust set in, but not nearly fast enough." As Barrett continues, per-share profits fell 59%, "from $3.44 in the year ending March 1981 to $1.41 for the following period."

A rebound of sorts began in the 1980s, with Centex's homes numbering more than 100,000. That decade saw the company increase its market from eight cities to 35 (by 1992 the number would rise to 39) through a combination of new business launches and acquisitions. One particularly key acquisition was that of the John Crosland Company, a major name in the Carolinas.

At the same time, Centex was also trimming and consolidating its forces to build a stronger organization. The oil-and-gas business Cenergy, for example, was sold as a separate company in 1984; this divestment more firmly planted Centex in the construction business.

Today, Centex operates several subsidiaries, all aimed at supporting the building business. For instance, one offshoot is Centex Mortgage Banking, which by 1985 had changed its name to CTX Mortgage Company and had expanded into all of the builder's major markets. Its purpose was to establish home prices and facilitate mortgages for Centex customers. According to company history, CTX initiated title and insurance operations, thus clearing the way to develop real estate as well as build on it. That development subsidiary made its debut in 1987 as Centex Development Company. By fiscal 1992, CTX Mortgage Co. had cleared $2.5 billion in home loans.

Centex banking interests don't end there, however. The corporation runs its own savings and loan institution, Texas Trust Savings Bank, FSB. The smaller interest provided just one percent of Centex's total 1992 revenues, with the bulk of incoming money (53 percent) coming from the building and mortgage banking subsidiaries. Contracting and construction services are also a big part of Centex's subsidiary interests. With Centex Cement Enterprises, another subsidiary, the company has the ability to produce and deliver not only cement, but also ready-mix concrete and gypsum boarding.

But it is the homes themselves that bring Centex into the public eye. A typical Centex home is far from "typical"; a staff of three in-house architects trek to different building sites around the United States to determine just the kind of residence that will fit the development best. With the architects designing upwards of 300 home concepts each year, there are plenty of options from which to choose. Thus, a "typical" Centex home can span from 900 to over 5000 square feet, and cost from as little as $50,000 to as much as $1.1 million (the higher-end projects are sold under the name Centex Custom Homes).

Centex has also involved itself with "Homes Across America," a building initiative of Habitat for Humanity. Habitat was formed to provide volunteer-constructed, low-cost homes for those who otherwise couldn't afford housing. Centex participation has resulted in activity in all of its markets; the company announced in 1992 that 23 Habitat homes would be built in the following year.

Though its primary focus is on residential homes, Centex has had a hand in the development of some public buildings. Contracts for 1992 included Veterans Administration medical centers in Detroit and Indianapolis; hospital expansions in San Diego and Miami; a wastewater treatment plant in Hot Springs, Arkansas; and even a Wal-Mart in Paducah, Kentucky. Other high-profile Centex projects include Cinderella's Castle, EPCOT Center's Land Pavilion, and the Grand Floridian Beach Resort, all built for Disney World in Orlando, Florida.

The company's success can be attributed in part to the team-building attitude demonstrated by its top managers. Indeed, "in an industry famous for its flamboyant, ego-driven characters, [CEO Larry] Hirsch and his crew are quiet, low-key types who keep pretty much to themselves," reports Barrett. When CEO successor William J. Gillilan was introduced, a New York Times article quoted a securities analyst as remarking: "One of the beauties of Centex is that they are decentralized. The company has demonstrated its ability to grow and to build its markets without running into the control problems that have plagued others." Centex describes its business plan as based on a "3-D" strategy: diversify, decentralize, and differentiate.

Whatever the strategy, it has resulted in top scores for Centex. A Builder survey of America's top 100 building manufacturers ranked by closings rated Centex number one. Its unit output in 1992 (9,184) easily outdistanced second-place, Michigan-based Pulte Homes (6,493). As Builder goes on to report, Centex also posted a 29 percent increase in closings over 1991, as well as a ten percent increase in gross revenues covering the same period.

While the early 1990s was not a banner period for the home building industry, conditions have begun to improve. While hardly recession-proof, Centex took advantage of the times. Then-CEO Larry Hirsch even remarked to Forbes, "I think a national recession would be a tremendous opportunity for Centex." As Forbes' Barrett explains, Hirsch meant that a recession would "drive down the cost of land and interest rates—the bread of life for home builders—and would almost certainly weed out some smaller, highly leveraged competitors."

These predictions proved correct. By late 1992, with a slow recovery in the works, housing interest rates dropped to new lows and sales began to take flight. "Wall Street has started to appreciate home builders as manufacturers of a basic consumer product," a securities analyst told Builder. Centex benefited, posting 1992 revenues of $2.3 billion, with the high margins attributed to improvements in both the home-building and mortgage banking areas. (The company claims the distinction of never having reported either a quarterly or an annual loss since becoming a public company.)

For all Centex's success in Texas, Florida, and other densely populated areas, one important region has proven difficult for the company to penetrate. The company entered highly competitive southern California several years ago, but the area proved "a tough market to crack," as Centex president Tim Eller told Builder. Eller noted, however, that the shaky economy "has given us an opening we needed. We expect to increase our volumes there significantly." Eller's words reflect the confidence of Centex founder Tom Lively, who told Newsweek in 1956: "We're only beginning. We will build in every market that justifies it. And with the growing American population, [we] face a limitless future."

Principal Subsidiaries: Fox & Jacobs; CTX Mortgage Company; J.W. Bateson Co.; M.H. Golden Co.; Illinois Cement Co.

Further Reading:

Barrett, William P., "A Tremendous Opportunity," *Forbes,* May 28, 1990, pp. 72–76.
"Builder 100," *Builder,* May 1993, p. 172.
"How a Texas Outfit Builds a Good Cheap House," *Fortune,* April 1976, p. 164.
Hylton, Richard D., "Home Building Is Good for Some," *New York Times,* April 27, 1990.
"Lively's the Name," *Newsweek,* March 26, 1956.
"New Operating Chief Is Selected at Centex," *New York Times,* January 8, 1990.

—Susan Salter

Cessna
A Textron Company

Cessna Aircraft Company

One Cessna Blvd.
Wichita, Kansas 67277
U.S.A.
(316) 941-6000
Fax: (316) 941-7812

Wholly Owned Subsidiary of Textron Inc.
Incorporated: 1927 as Cessna-Roos Company
Employees: 5,800
Sales: $818.0 million
SICs: 3721 Aircraft; 3728 Aircraft Equipment

Based in Wichita, Kansas, the aviation capitol of the United States, Cessna Aircraft Company is the world's largest manufacturer of private aircraft. Cessna began its operations building small propeller-driven aircraft for the private pilot market, eventually expanding into the manufacture of corporate jets. The company has since become the leading private jet manufacturer in the industry.

In 1911 the company's founder, Clyde V. Cessna, a farmer who was also employed as a mechanic and auto salesman for Overland Automobiles, attended an air show in nearby Oklahoma City at the Moisant International Aviation Air Circus. Cessna was immediately taken with the urge to fly. Aware of the large sums paid to exhibition barnstormers, Cessna sensed an opportunity and travelled to New York, where he purchased a French Bleriot aircraft from the Queens Airplane Company in the Bronx. He assembled the plane from a kit, using one of his own water-cooled engines. Having never before flown, Cessna wheeled the craft out onto a salt plain near Jet, Oklahoma, to begin practice runs. As his brother Roy watched, Cessna bounced his craft on a takeoff run, eventually ending up ditching its nose into the ground.

The pilot emerged without serious injury but, determined to fly, he repaired the Bleriot for another try. Cessna smashed the airplane eleven more times before he got the hang of it. On the thirteenth try he managed to get enough altitude to avoid crashing. But because he had not yet learned to turn, he was forced to immediately set the craft down. And because he had never landed, the flight ended with yet another crash. In June of 1911, after several modifications, Cessna made his first completely successful flight, and with practice he became a fairly good pilot. He was paid $300 to perform at an air show in Jet, and before the end of the season, he flew three more exhibitions.

Through the spring and summer of 1912, and for several years after, Cessna made small changes to his airplane, customizing it by incorporating new controls and changing the balance and surfaces of the craft. Each year he gave flying demonstrations throughout Kansas and Oklahoma. In the fall of 1916 Cessna was offered a rent-free space at the Jones Motor Car factory in Wichita, Kansas, in order to manufacture a new model. In return he was asked to paint the words "Jones-Six," the name of a car model, on the bottom of the wings of his new airplane. This craft, built over the winter of 1916–1917, was the first airplane manufactured in Wichita.

Cessna's next model, the Comet, emerged in 1917. With a partially enclosed cockpit, the Comet became the manufacturer's most successful model. Cessna planned to promote the design at one of the 60 air shows in which he was booked to perform during 1917, but American involvement in World War I forced him to abandon his sales efforts. Engines, propellers, and other important supplies were earmarked for larger manufacturers. Cessna was effectively put out of business. He returned to his home near Rago, Kansas, and resumed farming.

In 1925 Cessna was lured back to Wichita by two business partners, Walter Beech and Lloyd Stearman, who persuaded him to begin making airplanes again. The three men established the Travel Air Manufacturing Company, with Cessna as president. While the company built a line of biplanes, a conflict began to emerge between Beech and Cessna. Beech favored the two-wing designs while Cessna wanted to build a monoplane. In 1926 Cessna rented his own shop, where he designed and built his single-wing aircraft. He later flew this plane in a demonstration for Beech, who was forced to concede that Cessna's design was an excellent one, resulting in the manufacture of monoplanes by Travel Air. Two later models, the City of Oakland and the Woolaroc, were the first civilian planes to be flown to Hawaii.

Further differences with Beech and Stearman, however, led Cessna to leave the partnership in 1927. He established his own shop in Wichita, and began work on a radical design that eliminated the need for wing struts, the bars that supported the plane's wings. After successfully building his strutless "A" series monoplane, Cessna organized another firm and sold shares in his new company. Victor Roos, a major shareholder, was made a partner, and the company was incorporated as the Cessna-Roos Company on September 8, 1927. Roos helped Cessna to acquire an 11-acre site at First Street and Glenn Avenue, where they established a 5,000-square foot factory and an adjacent paint shop. Roos, however, received a lucrative offer to become general manager of the Swallow Airplane Company, and left the business in December.

Cessna reorganized his enterprise as the Cessna Aircraft Company, and began offering five variations on the "A" series, each with a different type of engine. While these were called AWs—the "W" stood for Wright, the engine manufacturer—Cessna began work on a heavier BW series. However, the Commerce Department, which then certified aircraft designs, would not approve the use of a more powerful Wright engine without a lengthy stress analysis. To maintain sales, Cessna was forced to substitute a smaller engine in the BW. But he soon began work on an even more powerful third series, the CW-6, which featured a 225-horsepower engine.

In 1929, on the success of these models, Cessna financed development of an improved "D" series. Members of this series, the Chief and the Scout, were to be built at another new facility, an 80-acre site southeast of Wichita. Here, Cessna was building a 55,000-square foot plant, although it was during construction that the stock market crashed, plunging the country into the Great Depression.

By 1930 the demand for private aircraft all but disappeared. In an attempt to bolster sales Cessna designed a glider, the CG-2, which he sold for only $398. He attempted several other experimental designs, but by 1931 was forced to close down his plant and rent out his buildings. While the Cessna Aircraft Company did not go bankrupt, no airplanes were built for three years. In fact, Clyde Cessna and his son Eldon were prevented by the company's board of directors from even attempting to restart operations at the plant. Instead, the pair opened another small shop and founded the C.V. Cessna Aircraft Company. At this site Cessna and his son built the CR-1, CR-2, and CR-3 racing models and the C-3 cabin cruiser.

Meanwhile, in June of 1933, Cessna's nephew Dwane L. Wallace graduated from Wichita University with a degree in aeronautical engineering. He went to work for the Beech Aircraft Company, which occupied a section of the closed Cessna factory. When Beech later moved to another plant, Dwane and his brother Dwight persuaded Cessna's board to allow their uncle to reopen the plant. Production was resumed on January 10, 1934, and the Wallace brothers joined the company as officers. The new team designed another cantilevered—sans wing struts—craft, the C-34 Airmaster, which test pilots George Hart and Dwane Wallace flew on nationwide demonstrations. The new model put the company back on its feet, particularly after it garnered numerous prestigious awards.

In 1935 Clyde Cessna, now age 55, sold his shares in the company to the Wallace brothers. He remained president of Cessna Aircraft until October 8, 1936, when he retired. He returned to his 640-acre farm in Rago and invented new farm implements until his death in 1954. Under the Wallaces, the Cessna Aircraft Company built its first twin-engine aircraft in 1938. The T-50 Bobcat was designed and built in nine months—production had barely started in March of 1939 when priority military orders for the new plane began to come in. The U.S. Army used the T-50 as a trainer, designated AT-8. Meanwhile, the Royal Canadian Air Force weighed in with similar orders, calling theirs the Crane I.

With a growing backlog of military orders, Cessna was forced to expand. The company, which employed 200 people in July of 1940, had more than 1,500 workers just seven months later. As hostilities in Europe began, with Germany's invasion of France, the army increased its orders from Cessna. The company delivered several new variations on the T-50, including AT-17 trainers and UC-78 utility cargo aircraft. The basic T-50 design, however, was the mainstay at that time. In April of 1942, during the darkest days of the war, the army ordered Cessna to manu-

facture 1,500 CG-4A troop/cargo gliders. These craft, which were designed by the Waco Aircraft Company, were intended for use in an allied invasion of Europe.

Cessna built a new plant for the gliders at Hutchinson, Kansas, 60 miles northwest of Wichita. While half the order was later cancelled, Cessna and other builders were kept busy subcontracting for other manufacturers. In addition, Cessna designed a large twin-engine cargo airplane, called the C-106, that was made from freely available non-strategic materials. The company received an order for 500 of these planes, but this was later cancelled when the army decided to use planes from Douglas and Curtiss. Had Cessna been able to build its C-106s for the army, the company may have graduated into another class, with such manufacturers as North American, Boeing, Consolidated Vultee, Douglas, and Lockheed.

In 1944 Cessna occupied 468,000 feet of factory space—nearly ten times the amount it had in 1939—and employed 6,074 workers. With the end of the war imminent, however, the company was forced to turn its attention to the inevitable evaporation of military orders. Futurists had long predicted the emergence of family flight, describing sedan aircraft suitable for jaunts to grandma's house, a picnic spot, and even the grocery store. These planes were to be simple, light designs that were affordable and rugged. Before the end of the war, Cessna began work on a fabric-skin model, the 190/195 series P-780. But pilots of these air sedans would first need to learn how to fly, so the company briefly shelved the P-780 to rush two small trainers, the 120 and 140, into production.

The revolution in flight materialized shortly after the war, and although it never reached the proportions—an airplane in every garage—that futurists had envisioned, it seemed everyone was learning to fly. Cessna built nearly 8,000 trainers by the early 1950s, but the boom was short lived. Output of 120/140s fell from 30 per day to only five. Demand for the 190/195—now with metal skins—and a new model, the 170, remained strong, however.

After the war, Cessna had established a fluid power division that manufactured hydraulic components. With limited applications in aircraft, the hydraulic products were sold mainly to manufacturers of farm equipment, though the fluid power group later became one of Cessna's most profitable divisions. In 1952 Cessna purchased the Seibel Helicopter Company. This small concern flew its first helicopter in 1954, celebrating the event a year later with a demonstration landing on the summit of Pike's Peak. The company built a YH-41 helicopter for the U.S. Army in 1957, and by 1961 was building CH-1 Skyhook models. With declining sales, however, the business of Cessna Helicopters was wound up in 1963.

Meanwhile, the company had begun to cultivate a new market for its winged aircraft: corporations. As executives found a greater need to travel long distances in less time, a market for business aircraft emerged. Cessna was one of the first to exploit this opening by producing the 310, an airplane designed specifically for executives in 1954. That same year Cessna entered the jet age when it began production of T-37s. These small jets were used as trainers by the air force, which purchased more than 1,000 T-37s. In 1959 Cessna brought out an all-metal, 100-

horsepower plane, the Model 150. This aircraft was extremely popular with flight schools and flying clubs, and was singularly responsible for Cessna's strong growth during the 1960s.

Output reached 3,000 per year by 1966. The following year, production of the popular 150 was relocated to a facility at Strother Field in Winfield, Kansas. The 150s were again manufactured in Wichita for a brief time during 1969 when a recession dried up the market, but production resumed at Winfield in 1973. With strong growth from the 150 program, Cessna began acquiring numerous companies in related fields. The company purchased the Aircraft Radio Corporation in 1959, and the following year took over the McCauley company, which manufactured propellers and other aircraft components.

In 1960 Cessna became affiliated with SNA Max Holste, a French manufacturer located in Reims. Cessna later purchased 49 percent of the company, which changed its name to Reims Aviation. As Cessna's agent in the European market, Reims Aviation assembled a variety of Cessna designs, principally the Model 150. Cessna upgraded its position in the business market in 1965, when it introduced the 411, a cabin class airplane. The company also turned out its first general purpose agricultural airplane, the Ag Wagon. In 1968, Cessna began production of the A-37B twin-jet attack aircraft for the U.S. Air Force.

Lear, also located in Wichita, entered the business market in the mid-1960s with a line of business jets. As a result, Lear nearly cornered the corporate market, forcing such companies as Cessna—with the broadest product line in the industry—to respond in kind. Cessna began work on its first business jet, the Citation 500, in 1969, although the first of this series wasn't delivered until 1972. Nevertheless, the Citation became an important source of strength for Cessna, whose private plane business had begun to fall flat. Amid financial reverses, Cessna launched a productivity campaign and its executives—including chairman Dwane Wallace—took salary cuts. In addition, the number of employees, which was 16,200 in 1974, was cut to 13,000 by 1976.

The outlook for Cessna began to improve as it delivered its 100,000th single-engine airplane in 1975 and introduced the large Titan cargo plane a year later. In 1978 the company redesigned the successful 150, redesignating it the 152. However, questions had begun to arise about the integrity of Cessna's construction. Several highly publicized plane crashes seemed to indicate some propwash—the force stemming from the propellors wake—problems with Cessna tail sections. According to a *Wall Street Journal* article, the Federal Aviation Administration (FAA) grounded one model—the Conquest—in 1977 after the National Transportation Safety Board concluded that a particular crash was the result of ''poor-inadequate design.'' The FAA allowed the planes to return to the sky, however, after Cessna made some significant changes to the tail section.

Eager to make up for lost profits on the redesign, Cessna's chairman Russell Meyer, who had succeeded Wallace in 1975, stepped up production of Conquests and Citations, which were in demand as business planes after the energy crisis caused airline prices to skyrocket. Before long, inventories of crucial parts became so low that Cessna was forced to store $40 million

worth of half-completed jets. In addition, the company found itself competing for an appropriate number of skilled workers with such formidable rivals as Boeing, Lear, Beech, and Piper, all located in the same area. As these problems began to take their toll, the short-term debt needed to cover Cessna's faltering operations began to mount, and before long the company was also facing a $92 million debt crisis.

Meyer's response was to close the jet production line for several weeks while parts inventories were replenished. Stocked aircraft were completed and sold, and production was resumed at lower levels. By 1979 Cessna was outselling Lear, and in 1980, the year Cessna's sales topped the billion dollar mark, Cessna achieved a record high market share of 54 percent. In an attempt to get more airplanes out of the factory, Cessna inaugurated a clever marketing scheme in 1982. Rather than try to sell its planes in a recessionary economy, Cessna offered leases with maintenance contracts. Companies could now finance the new Citation I, II, and III business jets with money from their operating budgets, rather than purchasing them with capital funds. While customers could cancel the leases on short notice, Cessna was allowed to depreciate the aircraft, an important tax shelter.

In 1983 Cessna sold its ARC Avionics division to the Sperry Corporation, predecessor to Unisys. In the meantime Cessna identified an important new market: fleet sales. That year Federal Express placed the first of several bulk orders for Cessna's new Caravan turboprop utility aircraft, suitable for serving smaller metropolitan markets. With Cessna's business increasingly dominated by corporate and fleet jet sales, the private plane business became an ever smaller part of the company's operations. Still, the flight schools Cessna had established in 1970 continued to train private pilots in great numbers.

As the company's product liability insurance costs began to mount—annual premiums were in excess of $35 million—Cessna solicited bids from companies that were interested in acquiring the aircraft manufacturer. In October of 1985 General Dynamics, a large defense contractor, purchased Cessna for $663.7 million. Both companies stood to benefit from the transaction. Cessna would be able to take advantage of General Dynamics's stable cash position, technology, and experience in contracting, while providing its parent company with expertise in lightweight structures that could prove useful in cruise missile projects.

That same year, in response to increasingly stronger competition from the used aircraft market, Cessna began a campaign to refit and upgrade older Citation jets. In 1988 Cessna sold its fluid power division to the Eaton Corporation, and the following year the company's 40 percent interest in Reims Aviation, which had been manufacturing the Caravan, was purchased by Paris-based Compagnie Française Chaufour Investissement. Cessna continued its production of the successful Caravan, however.

Although a part of General Dynamics, Cessna was allowed to maintain managerial autonomy. Self-insured against lawsuits, it was now also self-funded and producing a profit for its parent company, but by 1991 General Dynamics, seeking to concentrate on its core defense businesses, announced its intention to sell Cessna. Textron, parent of Bell Helicopter, offered $600 million for Cessna. The deal was completed in January of 1992 with Cessna's autonomy intact, while Meyer continued as chairman.

Cessna remains the largest private aircraft manufacturer in the United States. With its line of cargo craft and advanced private jets, including the new Citation X, Cessna still offers the broadest product range in the industry. Whether or not the synergy between Cessna and Textron endures, the airplane manufacturer is likely to remain America's leading small aircraft manufacturer.

Principal Subsidiaries: Cessna Finance Corporation; McCauley Accessory Division.

Further Reading:

Campanella, Frank W., "Single-Engine Aircraft Hiking Cessna's Profits," *Barron's,* January 26, 1976, pp. 60–65.
"Cessna: 50 Years and 139,000 Aircraft," *Interavia,* September 1977, pp. 860–861.
"Cessna Milestones," Company Document; *An Eye to the Sky,* Company History; Textron Incorporated Annual Report, 1993.
"Cessna: Relying on Its Big Planes, New Sales Tactics and Austerity," *Business Week,* October 11, 1982, pp. 95–96.
"Cessna Sells Reims Interest," *Flight International,* March 4, 1989, p. 8.
Frasier, Steve, "Cessna Aircraft Company Struggles to Overcome Design, Factory Woes," *Wall Street Journal,* December 26, 1980, pp. 1–5.
"A History of the Cessna Aircraft Company," *Cessna Guidebook,* Flying Enterprise Publications, Dallas, 1973.
"New Parent to Benefit Cessna" (and related article), *Flight International,* October 12, 1985, p. 27.
Phillips, Edward H. and Anthony L. Velocci, Jr., "Cessna Officials Expect No Changes After Acquisition by Textron Corp.," *Aviation Week & Space Technology,* January 27, 1992, p. 36.
"Sales Zoom for the Light-Plane Makers," *Business Week,* March 10, 1973, pp. 157–160.
"Snafu Unsnarled," *Fortune,* June 1, 1982, p. 11.
Warwick, Graham, "General Dynamics to Sell Off Cessna," *Flight International,* October 23, 1991, p. 5.

—John Simley

Charles Schwab
Helping Investors Help Themselves™

Charles Schwab Corp.

101 Montgomery St.
San Francisco, California 94104-4122
U.S.A.
(415) 627-7000
Fax: (415) 627-8538

Public Company
Incorporated: 1971
Employees: 4,600
Sales: $909 million
Stock Exchanges: New York Midwest Philadelphia Pacific
SICs: 6211 Security Brokers and Dealers; 6282 Investment
  Advice; 6719 Holding Companies, Nec

The Charles Schwab Corp., through its operating subsidiary Charles Schwab & Company, Inc., is the largest discount stock broker in the United States. It also deals in securities, investments, and other low-cost financial services.

Charles Schwab, the company's founder, had received an M.B.A. degree from Stanford University and had been working for a small California investment advisor when, in 1971, he founded his own company. He and two partners created a stock mutual fund that soon had $20 million in assets. However, they ran into trouble with securities regulators, when it was learned that they had failed to register the fund. This error temporarily forced Schwab out of business, but he soon reopened a small money-management firm in San Francisco.

On May 1, 1975, the U.S. Congress deregulated the stock brokerage industry by taking away the power of the New York Stock Exchange to determine the commission rates charged by its members. This opened the door to discount brokers, who took orders to buy and sell securities, but did not offer advice or do research the way larger, established brokers like Merrill Lynch did. This presented an opportunity to win individual investors well enough versed in the stock market not to need the advice offered by established brokers. Schwab quickly took advantage of deregulation, opening a small San Francisco brokerage, financed primarily with borrowed money, and buying a seat on the New York Stock Exchange.

The new discount brokers, whose commissions might be only 30 percent of the rates before deregulation, were scorned by the old-line brokerages. During his first few years as a discount broker, Schwab had to contend with bad publicity generated by the older firms, some of whom threatened to break their leases if landlords allowed Schwab to rent offices in the same building.

Schwab fought back by buying newspaper ads featuring his photograph and asking customers to contact him personally, helping to build the firm's credibility. Possibly the most important early decision made by Schwab was to open branch offices around the United States. He reasoned that even investors not needing advice would prefer doing business through a local office instead of a toll-free telephone number. The move won customers and helped differentiate Schwab from the large number of discount firms appearing after deregulation.

Over the next few years Schwab did several things to pull away from the pack. The company offered innovative new services including the ability to place orders 24-hours a day. It bought advanced computer systems to quickly deal with huge volumes of orders. And it continued its heavy advertising, seeking to project an upscale image. Top executives were given expensive foreign cars, and an interior design staff was commissioned to help showcase certain new branches. Some industry analysts maintain that with these measures Schwab helped bring discount brokering into the mainstream of financial institutions.

However, the firm's rapid expansion was costly. Partly as a result of this, and partly because sales were dependent on the sentiments of small investors, profits were erratic. To raise money Schwab sometimes turned to employees and larger customers. By 1980 Schwab was by far the largest discounter. That year, in part to fund further expansion, Schwab decided to take the company public. The offering was called off, however, when some problems caused by the attempted conversion to a new computer system proved an embarrassment to the company. Raising sufficient capital in private became more difficult, partly because of the erratic earnings. Finally, in 1983, Schwab arranged for San Francisco's Bank of America to acquire the company for $55 million in Bank of America stock. Bank of America also agreed to supply Schwab with capital. It loaned Schwab $50 million over the next three years, but Schwab remained one of the most highly leveraged brokerages.

The sale to Bank of America may have provided needed capital, but it fettered the company with banking regulations. Schwab wanted to offer new, proprietary lines of investments including Charles Schwab mutual funds. However, federal law at the time forbid banks and their subsidiaries from underwriting such securities. Although Schwab initially sought to challenge the law, as its wording contained some ambiguities, Bank of America did not want to irritate banking regulators. Tensions between Schwab and its parent were further exacerbated because Bank of America was experiencing difficulties, and the price of its stock was falling, making Schwab's stake in it worth less.

Schwab introduced the Mutual Fund Marketplace in 1984 with an initial investment of $5 million. The Marketplace allowed customers to invest in 250 separate mutual funds and switch between them using Schwab as the bookkeeper. All of a customer's mutual fund accounts were put on a single monthly statement. The company's profile was further raised in 1984 when Schwab's book *How to be Your Own Stockbroker* was published. In it Schwab presented himself as a populist fighting against Wall Street stockbrokers in the name of the average investor. He contended that there is an inherent conflict of interest when a firm owns stock in inventory, writes favorable research recommendations on those stocks, and has commissioned salespeople sell those stocks to the public. At the same time, the company was moving into an elegant new headquarters building in downtown San Francisco.

In 1985 Schwab had 90 branches and 1.2 million customers, generating $202 million in revenue. Though it was far larger than its leading discount competitors, it was small compared with the largest retail brokerages, which had over 300 branches. The firm was growing in other ways, however. It offered personal computer software called the Equalizer, which allowed investors to place orders via computer as well as call up stock information and obtain research reports.

In 1987, Charles Schwab and a group of investors bought the company back from Bank of America for $238 million. Seven weeks later, he announced plans to take the company public. The buyback had resulted in $200 million of debt, and the public offering was partly designed to eliminate some of this debt. It was also intended to raise money for further expansion. Schwab wanted to increase the number of branches to 120, including offices in Europe.

The discount brokerage business had grown intensely competitive. Discounters handled a significant amount of retail equity trades by 1987, but hundreds of firms had entered the field, including banks, savings and loans, and mutual fund companies. Since Schwab was clearly the player to beat in discounting, competitors' advertisements specifically offered rates lower than Schwab's. Nevertheless, at this time Schwab had 1.6 million customers, about five times as many as its nearest competitor, Quick & Reilly Group. In 1987 the firm had sales of $465 million and profits of $26 million, twice the industry's average profit margin. To achieve this success, Schwab was spending about $15 million a year on advertising.

Schwab was already doing well in its expanded product line. Mutual Fund Marketplace had attracted $1.07 billion in client assets by year-end 1986. The company was also offering Individual Retirement Accounts, certificates of deposit, money-market accounts, and Schwab One cash-management accounts. Despite these successes, Schwab was badly hurt by the stock market crash of October 1987. By mid-1988, trading volume had fallen to about 10,400 trades a day, a 40 percent drop from the months before the crash. Schwab cut costs to maintain profitability, cutting managerial pay anywhere from five to 20 percent and laying off employees. Charles Schwab cut his own pay 20 percent for six months, and put branch expansion plans on hold. The firm also raised its trading commission ten percent, so that it needed only 8,000 trades a day to break even, down from 12,000 trades. Even with the cost-cutting, the firm's 1988 earnings plummeted 70 percent to $7.4 million on sales of $392 million.

However, by 1989 Schwab was expanding again. It bought Chicago-based Rose & Co. for $34 million from Chase Manhattan, and as the fifth-largest discount broker in the United States,

Rose & Co. brought Schwab 200,000 new customers at a cost of about $70 each. With the purchase, Schwab controlled about 40 percent of the discount market, though discounters made only eight percent of all retail commissions. Over the long run, Schwab realized its best strategy was to win customers from the full-service brokers. To help create more independent stock investors, it pioneered a service called Telebroker that let customers place stock orders and get price quotes from any touch-tone telephone 24 hours a day. It also released a new version of the Equalizer. The software had already sold 30,000 copies at $169 each since its introduction.

Individual investors returned to the stock market in 1989, and the firm's income surged to $553 million, with profits of $18.9 million. Income was further helped by an increase in client assets, from $16.8 billion in 1987 to $25 billion in early 1990. Commissions accounted for 70 percent of revenue, down from 85 percent in 1987.

Throughout the 1980s, Schwab updated its Mutual Fund Marketplace to allow customers to switch among funds in different families by a telephone. Customers paid a commission ranging from .6 percent to .08 percent, with a minimum of $29. Analysts were generally positive, pointing out that the amount of interest lost from having a check in the mail would pay for most of the service's commission fees. In 1991 Schwab also acquired Mayer & Schweitzer, an over-the-counter stock market maker, getting itself into a new and lucrative market.

Meanwhile Schwab was opening branch offices at a furious pace—17 in 1992 alone—and doubling the amount of money it spent on advertising. Schwab's aggressive stance helped raise its share of the discount market to 46 percent as it attracted more than 40,000 new accounts a month. In 1992 Schwab acquired its first corporate jet, spending $12 million on a model with enough fuel capacity to reach London, where it was opening its first European branch. These additional costs helped drag down third-quarter earnings in 1992 when stock trading temporarily tapered off. The dip was a reminder that the company was still highly dependent on commissions, and caused its stock to drop 20 percent.

Schwab cut advertising by 20 percent and took other steps to slow the growth of its costs. It made a greater share of new branch offices into "bare bones" operations with only one broker. Schwab already paid its 2,500 brokers less than other discounters, an average of $31,000 a year, compared with $50,000 at Fidelity Brokerage Services and $36,000 at Quick & Reilly. The firm also continued searching for ways to become less dependent on commissions. The introduction in July of 1992 of a way to trade mutual funds by eight outside fund companies, resulting in no sales fee, attracted more than $500 million in assets within two months and over $4 billion by July of 1993; it was thus the most successful first-year pilot of any new service in Schwab's history.

During 1992 Schwab customers opened 560,000 new accounts at its 175 branch offices, while assets in customer accounts grew 38 percent to $65.6 billion. Revenue soared to $909 million, with record profits of $81 million. As a result of these successes, Schwab announced plans to open 20 more branch offices in 1993 and several proprietary mutual funds. Schwab remained dependent on commissions, but was working steadily to ease its dependency even as it rapidly increased its customer base, largely at the expense of full-service brokerages.

Further Reading:

Bianco, Anthony, ''Charles Schwab vs. Les Quick,'' *Business Week,* May 12, 1986.

Heins, John, ''How Now, Chuck Schwab?'' *Forbes,* June 15, 1987.

——, ''After Cost Cuts, What?'' *Forbes,* May 1, 1989.

Oliver, Suzanne L., ''One-Stop Shopping,'' *Forbes,* November 11, 1991.

Shao, Maria, ''Suddenly the Envy of the Street is Schwab?'' *Business Week,* March 19, 1990.

Siconolfi, Michael, ''Schwab's Profit Stumbles Amid Rise in Expenses Coupled with Less Trading,'' *Wall Street Journal,* September 29, 1992.

—Scott M. Lewis

Charming Shoppes

Charming Shoppes, Inc.

450 Winks Lane
Bensalem, Pennsylvania 19020
U.S.A.
(215) 245-9100
Fax: (215) 638-6914

Public Company
Incorporated: 1969 as Fashion Bug, Inc.
Employees: 14,000
Sales: $1.02 billion
Stock Exchanges: NASDAQ
SICs: 5621 Women's Clothing Stores; 5641 Children's &
Infants' Wear Stores; 5611 Men's & Boys' Clothing
Stores

Charming Shoppes, Inc., is a leading retailer, specializing in women's apparel. Founded in 1940 with a single store in Philadelphia, Charming now operates over 1200 stores in more than 40 states; all of its store operations are under the names Fashion Bug and Fashion Bug Plus. The stores are large by apparel industry standards (averaging 8,000 square feet) and are usually located in strip malls as opposed to larger (indoor) shopping centers. The stores target middle income people and specialize in junior, misses' and large-size women's apparel, including sportswear, outerwear, intimate apparel, and accessories. The company is also moving into other markets such as shoes and casual men's apparel in some of its stores. A public company since 1971, Charming Shoppes, Inc., is a Fortune 500 company.

Charming Shoppes was opened on September 13, 1940, under the name "Charm Shoppes," by Morris and Arthur Sidewater in Philadelphia. In the 1930s, Morris (Moe) had been a buyer for Associated Merchandising in New York and Arthur (Artie) performed as a dancer on tour with Red Skelton. Apparently, Moe and Artie had long talked about opening up a women's clothing store and, with borrowed money, opened up Charm Shoppes. The two ambitious businessmen had rough going in the beginning, bringing in only $480 in sales in the first week of business. In addition, they received legal notice that very same week that they had to change their store's name because the name "Charm" was already registered. Rather than give up the business completely, the Sidewaters agreed to add "ing" to

their name and were paid $235 to buy a new sign. The $235 put their accounts in the black for the first time.

It wasn't long before the new store became a thriving business. By the end of the decade the Sidewater brothers were discussing expansion. In order to open up and manage the new stores, Moe and Artie took on additional partners, with each partner managing his/her own store. In these early days, the two Sidewater brothers did their own advertising, a task at which they proved quite effective; with his previous experience as a buyer, Moe Sidewater displayed a keen understanding of fashion trends.

In 1950 the Sidewaters began a life-long business relationship with Artie's good friend, David Wachs, and David's brother, Ellis. The four formed the Sidewater/Wachs alliance and opened stores in Norristown, Pennsylvania, and Woodbury, New Jersey. Both stores were promoted with grand openings that featured local celebrities. The Woodbury store was the largest retail establishment in the town at that time.

By 1960 the four partners were ready to open the first Charming Shoppes store in a large suburban shopping center. Sensing that suburban shopping would be the wave of the future, Sidewater/Wachs felt the new stores should operate under a new name. The first "Fashion Bug" was introduced into the Black Horse Pike Shopping Center in Audubon, New Jersey, that year. This sparked a period of tremendous growth for the company as they added "Fashion Bug" stores to an additional eight shopping centers throughout Pennsylvania, New Jersey, and New York.

In 1971 the four primary partners decided to take Charming Shoppes public, offering stock issues for public sale. By this time the company had 21 stores, 18 partners, and accelerated growth rates in sales, with further potential yet untapped. Moe had taken over the primary tasks of management and systems control and, in looking toward cost cutting, began to computerize the operations; all credit charges and payments were consolidated onto a computer system installed in the company headquarters. In addition, the company centralized its bookkeeping and credit operations on computer and centralized the Fashion Bug charge accounts, thus making it possible to charge merchandise in any store. The company became a pioneer in the use of computerized cash register (point-of-sale) terminals that offered direct control over inventory.

After the computerization of much of the company's operations the company experienced its highest growth rates in its history. By the late 1970s, Charming Shoppes had 60 stores. To accommodate this accelerated growth, the company opened an additional buying office in Bensalem, Pennsylvania, that housed offices and a distribution center. The distribution center, innovative for its time, gave Charming greater control over its inventory and was soon imitated by Charming's competitors.

The centralization of operations also included a reorganization of the buying operations. Up until this time, each store manager acted as the buyer for that store. But due to the more complicated and diverse clothing markets, buyers now had to become specialists, individuals trained to select a particular type of clothing. To accommodate this trend, Charming centralized buyers into one buying division, with each buyer reporting to a specific clothing department and helping the distribution center ship out new merchandise to the stores. The larger stores also led the company to expand its display and interior design staff.

The company continued to expand during this period of reorganization. By the end of the 1970s the number of stores increased from 60 to 100 and the company again moved its headquarters to a larger location, its present Bensalem offices, a 400,000-square-foot facility. Growth continued unabated into the 1980s, as the number of stores increased six-fold in comparison with the previous decade. The company streamlined its distribution process in order to improve the flow of merchandise.

The increasing complexity associated with managing the Charming Shoppes network of stores has led to a management overhaul in recent years. For its first 30 years of existence, the entire 900-store network was essentially managed by the partnership of the four brothers from two families, the Wach and the Sidewaters. By 1987, however, the company leadership saw the need to re-evaluate their management and decision-making strategy for the future. This involved a reorganization of the managerial hierarchy.

Wachs, according to the *Wall Street Journal*, "took over at the opportune time for change. Like other women's apparel retailers, Charming Shoppes . . . saw demand plunge for its once-popular sportswear, leaving it laden with costly inventories. Accompanying this consumer turnoff to tired fashions and miniskirts were other pesky problems: price rises from overseas suppliers hurt by the falling U.S. dollar, and uncertainty of supplies from abroad." The *Journal* went on to laud the company's efforts at reorganization, charging that the Charming Shoppes "merchandising prowess faltered as too many chefs played with its marketing recipe."

In an attempt to remedy the perceived stagnation of management, in 1987 David Wachs took over as chairman and CEO and implemented a management restructuring geared toward attracting professional managerial expertise in an attempt to recapture its core market constituency: middle income women, aged 25 to 45, seeking a range of apparel, from dress wear to sports wear.

The management "revolution" was also viewed as necessary since management expertise was crucial to keep the company growing. This shake-up, referred to by the *Wall Street Journal* as a "blood transfusion," broke up the family control that had previously determined long-term marketing strategy.

Charming Shoppes remains in a solid competitive position, whatever its recent difficulties. The company's fiscal 1993 sales were up by more than 15 percent. Charming's sales and profitability throughout the years have been consistently solid. As *Women's Wear Daily* reports, the company ended fiscal year 1993 with net income of $81.1 million on sales of more than $1.1 billion, a marked improvement from just ten years before, when net income was just $12.1 million on sales of $174.3 million.

According to some industry analysts, Charming's success has been largely a function of its strip mall locations, its direct control over its distribution and sourcing, and its private label credit card program. These factors remain crucial: Developers are projected to build more strip malls; the company sources 75 percent of its own goods, eliminating the need for middlemen; and its credit card program promotes customer loyalty and multiple purchases.

Most importantly, in the words of Charming's chairman, David Wachs, in the women's retail market, "we are the low-cost operator." In the end, for a given quality level, the lowest cost producer will always have the competitive advantage. The low cost strategy depends heavily on the strip mall sites; rents are historically about 40 percent lower at strip malls than large shopping centers, and the strip mall sites offer greater growth potential, according to some analysts. Further, the company's reliance on strips, which often includes exclusive rental contracts, excludes much of the competition in the women's apparel industry.

Another way in which Charming Shoppes is able to maintain its competitive cost structure is via its vertically integrated structure. The company, which already sources a high percentage of its own goods, plans on increasing this figure to 75 to 80 percent in the next couple of years. In pursuit of this increased efficiency, which has further contributed to the low cost strategy, Charming has capitalized its operations, investing in the latest electronics technology for clothing pattern design, computerized inventory control, and design.

Investors' analysis of the expected future earnings is optimistic and Charming plans to expand to 2000 stores, according to CEO David Wachs. This expansion will include new merchandising efforts into the sportswear and ready-to-wear departments, with special emphasis on men's wear.

Principal Subsidiaries: C.S.A.C., Inc.; C.S.F. Corp.; C.S.I.C., Inc.; Charming F.S. Co.; Diversified Fashions, Inc.; Fashion Service Corp.; J.M. Balter, Co.; J.P.A. Service Co.; Kirkstone Ltd.; Winks Lane, Inc.; International Apparel, Inc.; CSI Industries, Inc.; Executive Flights, Inc.; Specialty Fixtures, Inc.; Ericool Co. Ltd.; Evatone Trading Co.; FB Clothing, Inc.; Fashion Acceptance Corp.; Sentani Trading Ltd.; Yardarm Trading Ltd.; W.L. Distributors, Inc.; FSHC, Inc.; Charming Shoppes of Delaware, Inc.

Further Reading:

Charming Shoppes, Inc. Annual Reports, Bensalem, PA: Charming Shoppes, Inc., 1979–1992.
"The History of Charming Shoppes," *In Touch*, Charming Shoppes, Vol. 8, no. 8, August, 1986.
Hymowitz, Carol, "At Charming Shoppes, A Blood Transfusion," *Wall Street Journal*, October 10, 1988.
Macintosh, Jeane, "Charming Shoppes' Fashion Bug Flies High," *Women's Wear Daily*, November 25, 1992.

—John A. Sarich

Chemcentral Corporation

P.O. Box 730
Bedford Park, Illinois 60499
U.S.A.
(708) 594-7000
Fax: (708) 594-6328

Private Company
Incorporated: 1926 as the William J. Hough Co.
Employees: 800
Sales: $620 million
SICs: 5169 Chemicals and Allied Products, Not Elsewhere
Classified

Chemcentral Corporation, one of North America's "big three" chemical distribution companies, retains a broad clientele through a network of local and regional sales offices. Unlike market leader Van Waters & Rogers (VW&R) of Univar, which trades broad commodities of organics and inorganics, and second place Ashland Chemical, which also manufactures chemicals and focuses on hydrocarbons, Chemcentral focuses solely on distribution, offering a wide variety of chemical commodities and specialties. In the early 1990s, Chemcentral followed a relatively conservative strategy, avoiding major risks and relying on traditional localized sales to increase the volume but not the scope of its operations. This followed a formative period of bolder acquisitions; the combined result is an organization with a solid position across the United States and a healthy, albeit small, presence in Canada. Furthermore, with 18 branches across Mexico, Chemcentral ranks as one of the larger chemical distributors in that market.

William J. Hough and Halbert G. Sampson founded the forerunner of Chemcentral, the William J. Hough Co., in Chicago in June 1926 after the closing of the Chicago branch of Columbia Naval Stores, a naval store supplier. Hough had been a manager at Columbia for ten years, and Sampson had worked as a bookkeeper at the branch since 1919. While Columbia had focused solely on the business of naval stores, Hough and Sampson had become interested in supplying other commodity lines as well and had started a partnership of their own while continuing on in their capacity as Columbia employees. The vice-president of Columbia, C. W. Dill, gave the two employees his approval on their side venture, and the friendly arrangement continued through the mid-1920s when the Columbia branch closed in order to free up capital for its parent company. Eager to take advantage of the opportunity, Hough and Sampson pooled their resources and borrowed $80,000, acquiring the assets of Columbia's Chicago branch. They then liquidated their partnership and incorporated the William J. Hough Co.

The Hough Company first assumed the business of Columbia in Chicago. The company was successful and eagerly awaited an opportunity to expand. Three years later, in 1929, such an opportunity arose. The Thoerner Manufacturing Company of St. Louis was in a line of business similar to that of Hough, when Columbia's C. W. Dill and several of the Hough stockholders bought it and incorporated as the Dill-Hough Company. Dill's son, Orville Dill, was transferred from sales in the Chicago office to manage the new St. Lewis concern. Hough would continue its policy of acquisition and expansion throughout the following two decades.

Companies in Detroit, Toledo, Cleveland, and Milwaukee followed shortly after the St. Louis expansion. In a mutually beneficial arrangement Hough and Sampson teamed up with Spencer Thomas, the president of Western Rosin Company in Detroit, to form the Paint Thinner Co. of Detroit. Through the new company Hough would be able to break into the distribution market in Detroit, while Thomas was offered the chance to expand his chemical storage and filling service to include distribution as well.

During this time the Great Depression was driving many small distributorships into fast bankruptcy. In 1931, a turpentine, linseed oil, and naphtha distributorship in Grand Rapids, Michigan, was put up for sale. Hough and Western Rosin recognized this opportunity to broaden the scope of their collaborations, and, acting swiftly, they bought the Grand Rapids operation, renaming it the Western Oil & Turpentine Co.

Also among the faltering companies was The American Mineral Spirits Company, which had sold its chemicals through separate small distributors in Detroit, Milwaukee, and Cleveland. These small distributors, however, had each amassed great debts and were eventually acquired by American Mineral. When American Mineral needed capital, it invited Hough to buy an interest in each of the distributors. Although Hough's existing Detroit distribution company, Paint Thinner, had been competing with American Mineral's Detroit distributor, Hough now would own large shares in both. Also during this time, however, Western Rosin experienced severe financial losses, and in 1935 all of these Detroit companies were consolidated as the Western Rosin & Turpentine Corporation in 1935, owned largely by the Hough Company.

Some four years after the Detroit consolidation, the Hough Company again set its sights on growth, this time in Cincinnati, Indianapolis, Buffalo, and Houston. Joining with American Mineral once again, the two companies formed the Amsco Products Company of Cincinnati in 1939. Also that year, Hough started a branch of the Chicago office in Fort Wayne, Indiana. The expansions into Indianapolis, Buffalo, and Houston were delayed until after World War II. Then in 1946, Hough and American Mineral cooperated once again and opened companies in these three cities: the Buffalo Solvents & Chemicals Co., the Hoosier Solvents & Chemicals Co., and the Texas Solvents & Chemicals Company.

By 1946, the Hough group of companies numbered ten distinct entities, including Hough and American Mineral themselves. The product lines of all the companies were similar, including naphtha, turpentine, rosin, linseed oil, alcohol, and antifreeze. Buyers included paint manufacturers, users of paint, paint stores, "automotive jobbers," and gasoline stations. And suppliers included Columbia Naval Stores and to a lesser extent Hercules, which provided turpentine, gum rosin, rosin size, and rosin oil; American Mineral and several other companies supplied petroleum solvents, Publicker Industries provided denatured alcohol, and Exxon (then Stanco of the Standard Oil Co. of New Jersey) provided "new era" products such as Toluene, Xylene, and other hydrocarbon solvents.

However, operations of the smaller companies in the group remained decentralized and inconsistent. Border skirmishes resulting from overlapping territories flared often between members. Company-wide agreements with suppliers were impossible to reach because of individual manager preferences, and personnel transfers were difficult across companies. Furthermore, as R. T. Hough wrote in *Your Company . . . CHEMCENTRAL,* "attainment of a financial capitalization balanced in proportion to each company's requirement was needlessly hard to achieve."

The solution was the implementation of a centralized management for policies and objectives of the entire group combined with decentralized branch management for all buyers except those preferring national accounts. The reorganization was formalized on June 1, 1948, when the Central Solvents & Chemicals Company replaced the William J. Hough Company and acquired all outstanding shares of Hough and the other nine in exchange for shares of its own stock. All member companies changed their names to include the phrase Solvents & Chemicals Company, prefixed by their regional location, and a central staff and a system of regional managers, supervising three or four branches each, evolved over the next decade at Central Solvents. American Mineral retained its name and character as primarily a supplier, not a distributor, and after some years became disassociated from Central Solvents & Chemicals, abstaining from nominating its two members to the board. (Several years later, American Mineral was bought by Unocal and became Unocal's Chemical Division.)

In the mid-1950s, expansion resumed. More Midwest offices arrived first with extensions into Canada, followed by the Southwest and Mexico, the Southeast, the Middle Atlantic States, and New England. Market share in California and the Pacific Northwest accrued more recently and by the early 1990s was contributing significantly to the company's overall profile. The company growth over these succeeding decades was driven by an expanding market. In both 1974 and 1976, for example, the overall chemical distributing market achieved record sales.

By 1980, the size of the organization once again demanded greater centralization and overall coordination. As a result, all companies of Central Solvents dropped their prefixes and as-

sumed the across-the-board name of Chemcentral Corporation. Smaller distributors who added "Solvents & Chemicals" to their own names were now clearly differentiated from those companies in the national Central Solvents organization. In addition, suppliers and buyers appreciated the mitigation of identity confusion that the prefixes and imitators had created.

After a period of continued growth, the 1980s brought about a substantially different business environment. Calls for greater environmental regulations had been increasing through the 1970s, and by 1980, Chemcentral felt the implications. That year, the Environmental Protection Agency (EPA) sued three chemical companies for alleged toxic waste leaks; Chemcentral-Detroit was one of these three. The EPA asserted that a variety of toxic chemicals, primarily organic solvents, had leaked and spilled at the company's Romulus, Michigan, facility during a transfer from tank trucks to underground storage tanks. Alleging that the chemicals ended up in a stream that feeds a tributary of the Detroit River, the EPA asked the court to bar Chemcentral from allowing further leaks and to require that it clean up its existing contaminations. By the early 1990s, general industrial pollution and improperly treated human waste had rendered the Detroit River one of the most polluted in the nation, so as a company that had sought to dispose of its chemical waste in a proper fashion, Chemcentral was incensed by the allegations, finding them misguided. The company expressed its opinion of the situation in its 1993 in-house company history, calling for "a system that *rewards* success instead of *threatening* it with regulation and litigation." Nevertheless, the company complied with tighter regulations and more stringent operating practices.

While the mid- to late-1980s witnessed overcrowded markets and slower growth, prompting the sale of Chemcentral's Canadian operations in 1983 to a Toronto distributor, the company still looked ahead to taking conservative risks for substantive growth. In Canada, for instance, Chemcentral looked forward to further business opportunities depending on the passage of the North American Free Trade Agreement (NAFTA). In 1992, in anticipation of a growing market, Chemcentral commenced the installment of an entirely new computer system. And after a relatively poor 1991 sales growth, Chemcentral experienced a resurgence in early 1992 in Detroit and the Midwest, as well as in the Southeast and the Northeast.

Chemcentral finished the completion of a $1-million branch expansion in Minneapolis in 1991 and planned additional expansions in 1992 in Tulsa and Philadelphia. The company also planned to broaden its product line, although only where it perceived an already-existing demand, refusing the risk of adding a product for which it must create demand. The organization focused in 1992 on products for five key chemical markets, including coatings, adhesives, printing and graphics, rubber and plastics compounding, and consumer specialties, with additional attention to the markets for oil-field chemicals, urethanes, and electronics. The organization then encompassed 51 territories comprised of 32 branch operations complete with offices and warehouses as well as 19 "resident sales territories," consisting of one sales representative serving customers and developing the market, and relying on third-party warehouses and nearby Chemcentral terminals for storage and delivery. In

1992, Chemcentral established new resident sales territories in Mobile, Alabama, and Greenville/Spartanburg, South Carolina. In May 1993 Chemcentral reported sales in 1992 of $620 million, representing 9 percent growth over 1991 levels. While Chemcentral then shied away from major acquisitions and ventures into wholly new markets overseas, still the company planned to build on its local roots across the North American market; with that more reliable strategy, Chemcentral anticipated significant growth in the years to come.

Further Reading:

Hough, R. T., *Your Company . . . CHEMCENTRAL,* Bedford Park, Illinois: Chemcentral Corp., 1993.

Morris, Gregory, ''Chemcentral's Local Focus Adds Up to National Breadth,'' *Chemical Week,* October 14, 1992, p. 59.

——, ''North American Operations Weather the Storm,'' *Chemical Week,* August 5, 1992, p. 28–29.

''Toxic Waste Leaks Alleged in U.S. Suits Against 3 Firms,'' *Wall Street Journal,* October 8, 1980, p. 21.

—Nicholas Patti

Chesapeake Corporation

1021 East Cary Street
P.O. Box 2350
Richmond, Virginia 23218
U.S.A.
(804) 697-1000
Fax: (804) 697-1199

Public Company
Incorporated: 1918
Employees: 5,062
Sales: $888.4 million
Stock Exchanges: New York
SICs: 2631 Paperboard Mills; 2621 Paper Mills; 3554 Paper
Industries Machinery; 2611 Pulp Mills

A paper and packaging company, Chesapeake Corporation recently celebrated its 75th anniversary. Chesapeake's primary businesses are tissue and kraft paper products and packaging. Tissue products, such as napkins, account for more than half of the company's sales, and converted products, such as corrugated containers and displays, account for about a third. Chesapeake continues to pioneer innovations in the napkin industry and to profit from its popular line of white linerboard.

Elis Olsson, a Swedish-born papermaker, was already a recognized pioneer in the industry when he moved his family from Quebec to Virginia in 1918. Olsson had become director of a corporation he organized with the help of a Norwegian shipping financier, Christoffer Hannevig. Olsson had helped to develop the first kraft process mill in Canada. Kraft paper is the heavy brown paper produced from unbleached pulp that is used for such items as grocery bags. Another of Olsson's technical innovations was the first commercial paper mill boiler to use wastewood and bark for fuel. He also engineered the first modern chemical recovery boiler. When Olsson first moved to West Point, the paper industry was in its infancy.

Chesapeake Corporation began via an agreement to lease the assets of Chesapeake Pulp & Paper Company, a subsidiary of Fox Paper Company, based in Ohio. Included with the leased assets was a sulphate mill in West Point that dated to 1914. The company had not proven profitable and the assets were leased with an option to buy, as the original owners wished to withdraw from the operation. Upon his arrival, Olsson quickly invested in plant improvements; pulp and board mills had dete-

riorated throughout the United States during World War I. Olsson also put his technical skills to use, revamping the tricky sulphate process that produced paper from pine.

Chesapeake was profitable by 1921, but president Hannevig's shipping empire went under and he resigned from the company. Olsson thus sought both financial backing and a new company president. It was hard to find supportive investors in the shaky post-war climate, but H. Watkins Ellerson, president of one of Chesapeake's pulp customer companies, agreed to back the enterprise and serve as president of a reorganized Chesapeake. Olsson became vice president, but for all practical purposes he ran the company. One of the first decisions of the restructured corporation was to buy the West Point mill instead of leasing. In 1922 bonds were issued to cover the purchase price, as well as the cost of needed plant improvements.

By 1926 Chesapeake was producing kraft paper, market pulp, crude turpentine, and box board on an average of 85 tons a day. It paid its first dividends the same year, a tradition uninterrupted except by the Depression. In 1929 Olsson was named president; he remained a leader in the company for the next 30 years, 14 of them as chairman of the board.

The 1930s were a time of growth for Chesapeake, despite the Depression. In 1932 Chesapeake became the second company in Virginia to hire a professional forester and begin a program of reforestation. Reforestation had been a company undertaking since 1922. As orders dropped off during the Depression, salaries and wages were cut. Nonetheless, Chesapeake's earnings reached the million-dollar mark for the first time in 1934. Chesapeake worked with Camp Manufacturing Company to erect and operate a pulp and paper mill in Franklin, Virginia, in 1936. The new mill was named Chesapeake-Camp Corporation at the time; its name later changed to Union Camp Corporation. Chesapeake eventually sold its interest in the mill.

In 1941 the company name was changed to The Chesapeake Corporation of Virginia. Its stock was offered on the New York Stock Exchange for the first time in 1944. During the labor shortage of World War II, Chesapeake maintained its production levels with the help of women—who worked at office jobs, as well as at cutting pulp wood in the forests—and German and Italian prisoners. In 1945 Olsson became company chairman. His son, Sture Olsson, assumed the position of president of the company in 1951.

Chesapeake acquired two box and container companies in 1961: Baltimore Paper Box Company and Miller Container Corporation. Miller went on to become the Roanoke division of Chesapeake Packaging Company. Between 1962 and 1964, Chesapeake invested $21 million into an expansion program that included its second paper machine and a new power plant. In 1967 Scranton Corrugated Box Company, Inc., was acquired. It became the Scranton division of Chesapeake Packaging Company.

In 1968 Sture Olsson resigned as president to serve as chairman of the board. That same year, Chesapeake acquired the Binghamton Container Company, now a division of the Chesapeake Packaging Company. The company's next major acquisition came in 1977 when it purchased a packaging company that eventually became the Louisville and St. Anthony divisions of Chesapeake Packaging Company.

The 1980s were a time of great growth and change for Chesapeake. During this decade it vaulted to a position as a Fortune 500 company and instituted a policy of decentralization. Changes commenced with the election of J. Carter Fox as president and CEO of Chesapeake. Only 41 years old at the time, he was the youngest CEO in the industry. Fox had moved up the ranks at Chesapeake. He first worked as a summer maintenance helper while still in school, then joined the company full-time in 1963 as a project accountant. As president and CEO, Fox reorganized the company's management structure. By putting managers in charge of operating units, the company was better able to focus on niche markets. The company was also restructured to reflect its four core business segments—treated wood, point-of-sale displays, table napkins, and brown and white linerboard boxes. Fox also oversaw trimming of the company, unloading unprofitable units such as plywood and sawmill plants.

In 1981 Chesapeake opened its first wood treating plant in Pocomoke City, and a new wastewood-fueled boiler went on-line at West Point. The new boiler helped to cut oil consumption by about five percent of total energy consumed. Chesapeake's energy program was often ahead of the industry in its utilization of residual and self-generated sources of energy. About this time, Chesapeake wrapped up a $51 million capital improvement program at West Point that was designed—among other advances—to allow the company to bear a greater wood inventory at the mill, thus minimizing its reliance on outside woodyards. In order to meet production demands, the company's sawmill and plywood plants were supplied primarily by contract loggers who harvested wood off private and company-controlled timberlands. These timberlands were in the Blue Ridge Mountains of Virginia and North Carolina, as well as in parts of Maryland and Delaware. In 1982 about 75 percent of the raw material used to produce needed pulpwood and chips came from southern pine. As the company had experienced four serious wood shortages between 1968 and 1982, management of the woodlands was critical. Decentralization helped to minimize the shortages, as an area manager was designated to oversee and coordinate land management, acquisition, and wood procurement.

Decentralization began in earnest in 1983, when the company was divided into three investment centers. Chesapeake was one of the few pulp and paper companies in the United States to make expansion plans in 1983. The industry was still recovering from the recession and prices for key pulp and paper products were just beginning to bounce back.

In order to utilize the valuable company-owned land in Delaware, Maryland, and Virginia, Delmarva Properties, Inc. was established. Delmarva concentrated on developing various residential, recreational, commercial, and industrial lots on some of the properties too valuable to manage as timberlands. Chesapeake also modernized its West Point via a $73 million expansion project; this included a major revamp of the mill's roll handling system to reduce paperwork and order error and make inventory more accurate. The improved system was in place by 1984. Chesapeake acquired its tenth container plant, Color-Box,

Inc. of Indiana, that same year. It also purchased a wood-treating plant near Fredericksburg, Virginia. The company's name was shortened during this period to Chesapeake Corporation from The Chesapeake Corporation of Virginia.

In an interview in *Pulp & Paper* magazine in 1984, Chesapeake president and CEO Fox said that the company's small size worked to its advantage. The company could manufacture different special market products to suit individual customer needs. "Only in this way can we hope to successfully compete with some of our competitors who in many cases are much larger firms with far greater financial reserves than Chesapeake," said Fox. Another of the company's advantages, he said, was that "Chesapeake has the closest linerboard mill to the northeastern U.S. market, and we can offer overnight service to the New York City area."

It was during this time that Chesapeake began plumping up its capacity to produce linerboard through expansions and upgrades. It also expanded its production of market pulp. Both these product lines were hard-hit in 1982 and 1983. To counterbalance the dip in sales, Chesapeake negotiated a multi-year labor agreement that lowered wages and reduced staff by five percent. The amount spent on capital improvements was justified by the fact that the company had only one mill and had to keep it running efficiently. In 1985 the company acquired Wisconsin Tissue Mills Inc., of Wisconsin and Plainwell Paper Co., Inc., of Michigan. Prices for pulp and linerboard, however, continued to be depressed.

In 1986 Chesapeake completed the conversion of its paper machine at West Point and began production of a new product—corrugating medium. This enabled the company to offer its customers a uniform, high-quality linerboard. The company's new high-speed Tri-Kraft linerboard machine was the first of its kind in North America, using multi-ply technology to produce linerboard and thus producing a sheet with superior strength and uniformity. Start-up costs affected the company's earnings for that year, but ultimately the gamble paid off. When Chesapeake began offering white linerboard instead of the common brown, sales dramatically increased. Companies preferred the white because logos and advertising could be clearly read from them.

In 1987 the company moved its corporate headquarters from West Point to Richmond. According to Fox, this was done so that paper-mill staff there could operate as independently as the other decentralized operations. A $160 million expansion was approved to add a fourth paper machine to the Wisconsin Tissue facilities. This project, completed in 1990, boosted that mill's production capacity by more than 70 percent. Chesapeake also acquired Distinctive Printing and Packaging Co., thus expanding its point-of-sale display business.

In 1988 Chesapeake's earnings rose 71 percent, in large part because of the boom in sales of white corrugated boxes. Chesapeake Packaging Company was reorganized to better handle the national sales of point-of-sale display. The company also continued its acquisition of other properties with the purchase in 1988 of a wood-treating plant in Holly Hill, South Carolina, followed shortly by the acquisition of Displayco Midwest Inc.

In 1991 Chesapeake combined with Toronto-based StakeTech to form a $2.5 million venture called Recoupe Recycling Technologies to market a "steam explosion" system of paper recycling. Using basic pressure cooker technology, the system saves water and energy and produces more uniform pulp than other processes. Sales for that year declined a bit; the recession, low demand, and continued pricing pressures were cited. Chesapeake underwent another management restructuring that year, with Paul Dresser becoming chief operating officer.

Pulp market prices dipped in 1992, costing the company some $2 million in the fourth quarter alone. The year was a disappointing one, although the company held a 20 percent share of the mottled white linerboard market that year, a business that was still growing at a rate of seven percent a year. Chesapeake was also doing well in the areas of commercial tissue and point-of-sale corrugated displays.

The industry as a whole seemed to be gradually recovering in 1993, with prices stabilizing and a stronger economy improving demand. With most of its intensive capital spending improvements behind it, Chesapeake hopes that it is poised for a period of growth as it heads into the twenty-first century.

Principal Subsidiaries: Wisconsin Tissue Mills Inc.; Chesapeake Paper Products Company; Woodlands Division; Chesapeake Packaging Co.; Chesapeake Consumer Products Company; Wood Products Division of Chesapeake Forest Products Company; Delmarva Properties, Inc.; Stonehouse Inc.

Further Reading:

Betts, Dickey, "Air-Assisted Separation, New Skim Tank Ups to Yield at Chesapeake," *Pulp & Paper,* August 1982, pp. 86–89.

"Big Recovery in the Making," *Industry Surveys,* May 14, 1992, pp. B75–B79.

"Chesapeake Corporation," *New York Times,* February 20, 1990, p. D4.

"Chesapeake Corporation," *Wall Street Journal,* April 19, 1991, p. A7B.

"Chesapeake Corporation," *New York Times,* June 14, 1991, p. D4.

"Chesapeake Corporation," *Wall Street Journal,* January 13, 1993, p. 4.

Clark, Barry, "Chesapeake Modernizes Mill With Computerized Roll Handling System," *Pulp & Paper,* March 1984, pp. 62–65.

Jereski, Laura, "Recovering," *Forbes,* February 15, 1993, pp. 240–241.

Koncel, Jerome, "First Quarter Results Disguise a Bright Future," *Paper Trade Journal,* June 1986, p. 52.

"Long-log, Tree-length Requirements Increase," *Forest Industries,* August 1982, pp. 22–23.

Smith, Kenneth, "Chesapeake Producing Multi-Ply Liner on New Management at West Point," *Pulp & Paper,* April 1986, p. 108.

——, "P&P Interview: Chesapeake Looking for Recovery, Record Sales in 1984," *Pulp & Paper,* April 1984, pp. 130–134.

Stipp, David, "Recycling Waste Paper with a Pressure Cooker," *Wall Street Journal,* January 7, 1991, p. B1.

Taylor, Robert, "Redesigned Waste Oil Reclamation System Cuts Chesapeake Fuel Costs," *Pulp & Paper,* December 1983, p. 94.

Wagner, Barbara Hetzer, "Companies with Star Potential," *Business Month,* December 1989, p. 45.

Wuerl, Peter, "Chesapeake Starts Up $73 Million Tri-Kraft Machine at West Point Mill," *Paper Trade Journal,* April 1986, pp. 44–45.

—Carol I. Keeley

Chesebrough-Pond's USA, Inc.

33 Benedict Place
P.O. Box 6000
Greenwich, Connecticut 06836
U.S.A.
(203) 661-2000
Fax: (203) 625-1968

Public Company
Incorporated: 1955 as Chesebrough-Pond's Inc.
Employees: 3,200
Sales: $880 million
SICs: 2844 Toilet Preparations

Chesebrough-Pond's USA, Inc. represents such cornerstone household items as Vaseline Petroleum Jelly, Pond's beauty creams, Q-Tips swabs, and Ragú spaghetti sauce. With roots dating back to the turn of the century, the company had experienced constant growth and profitability, until it was destabilized by its acquisition of the Stauffer Chemical Company, which in turn led to its takeover by Unilever N.V. in 1986.

Chesebrough-Pond's officially came into existence in 1955 when Pond's Extract Company merged with Chesebrough Manufacturing Company, Consolidated. Both of these companies had remarkably long and rich histories. Chesebrough Manufacturing dated back to 1880 and Pond's had been in operation since the 1870s. The companies had remarkably similar origins: both were launched by chemists who hoped to create household remedies for various ailments.

Theron Pond had begun working with witch hazel in the 1840s in his laboratory in Utica, New York. Pond's Extract was the witch hazel formula he developed and began marketing in 1846. International operations began as early as the 1870s, when Pond's opened an office in London. The company had manufacturing plants in Canada and Great Britain by 1933, producing its internationally known skin creams as well as other toiletries and cosmetics that had been added to the company's product line. By 1955, Pond's products were selling in more than one hundred countries.

At the same time that Pond's was growing, a chemist named Robert Chesebrough was experimenting with a residue of petroleum that formed on the rods of oil pumps during the petroleum boom of the mid-1900s. Stories had been circulating among oil field workers about the healing powers of this residue. Chesebrough worked for years to duplicate this substance. In 1870, satisfied with his research, Chesebrough began selling Vaseline Petroleum Jelly. Sales were good enough for the fledgling company to open an office in London in the 1870s, with subsidiaries in France and Spain. Demand was strong enough for Chesebrough to make distribution arrangements with Colgate & Company in 1873. Chesebrough Manufacturing Company began operating under Standard Oil in 1881, and moved from Brooklyn to Perth Amboy, New Jersey. Chesebrough resumed independent operations in 1911. It had plants in Canada and Great Britain by 1923, and by the mid-1950s, Chesebrough had 25 products for sale in nearly 120 countries. Most of the products were petroleum jelly-based toiletries.

During this time, Chesebrough and Pond were not unacquainted. Pond's chairperson, Clifford Baker, was also a member of Chesebrough's board of directors. The two companies merged in June of 1955, becoming Chesebrough-Pond's Inc. After absorbing the costs of its expansion and merger, Chesebrough-Pond's jumped ahead in profits and sales, going from about $47 million in sales in 1954 to about $117 million in 1963. The company maintained its popular product lines, while developing and introducing new products and acquiring other companies. In 1956, Chesebrough-Pond's acquired Seeck & Kade, the makers of Pertussin Cough Syrup, which had been a widely known product since its introduction in Germany in 1896. Chesebrough-Pond's soon introduced variations of the popular Pertussin brand, such as Pertussin Medicated Vaporizer—the first medicated spray of its kind—introduced in 1959.

Chesebrough-Pond's acquired Prince Matchabelli, Inc. in 1958, moving into a new product field. Matchabelli was the fragrances and toiletries division of the Vick Chemical Company. By 1960, two other companies had been added to the Chesebrough-Pond's fold: Aziza Eye Cosmetics, a division of Mauvel, Ltd., and Northam Warren, maker of Cutex nail care products. Aziza was blended into the Matchabelli operations. Cutex soon became the worldwide sales leader in its field. Two years later the company acquired Q-Tips, a popular cotton swab and baby product since its appearance in the United States in the 1920s. Under Chesebrough-Pond's, Q-Tips became even more successful. Within two years of the Q-tip acquisition, its profits more than doubled.

Chesebrough-Pond's was careful to keep its growth streamlined and controlled. Plant facilities were combined and purchasing was done centrally at the company headquarters. Product lines were constantly revised, unprofitable products discontinued, and new ones improved.

Among the company's innovations of this period were the first flavored lipsticks—introduced in 1964 through Cutex and instant hits—and a line of cosmetics for sale in food chains. Marketing modestly priced cosmetics in a new display format and in "blister" packaging in busy food store chains was a huge success. In the meantime, Chesebrough-Pond's international operations were also thriving. Despite the currency fluctuations of the early 1960s, Chesebrough-Pond's boasted its eighth consecutive year of sales increases in 1963. The company also had subsidiaries in Argentina, Australia, Brazil, India, and elsewhere.

During this time, a young man who had come to Chesebrough as a trainee in 1946 was working hard to build a Chesebrough presence in Australia. Ralph E. Ward had gone to Lafayette College on a GI Bill after flying as a fighter pilot in World War II. Ward worked from 1946 to 1957 as head of Chesebrough's Australian division—building a business from scratch. His success there led Ward to become the vice president of the company's Far Eastern business in 1957. By 1960, Ward was piloting all international activities for Chesebrough. His unbroken timeline of successes lead to Ward's being tapped for the top job in 1968. Chesebrough then had a reputation for steady growth based on its mature, high-margin brand name products—just the sort of profile that attracts takeovers.

One of Ward's first acts as president and CEO of Chesebrough was to purchase Ragú Packing Company. Ragú was then a small spaghetti sauce company based in Rochester, New York, and Chesebrough paid $44 million for it in 1969. Wall Street reportedly guffawed at the act: a nearly 90-year-old personal products company suddenly entering the food business was considered absurd. However, while Ragú enjoyed hearty regional sales, Chesebrough launched an aggressive marketing campaign to make Ragú a national brand. Three years after the move, Ragú was the top-selling spaghetti sauce in the country, in a market that was expanding. Two out of every three purchases of spaghetti sauce was Ragú by 1972. By 1982, Ragú held 58 percent of that $350 million-a-year market.

Another sharp diversification came in 1973 when Chesebrough acquired Health-tex for $194 million. Health-tex was then a manufacturer of children's apparel that enjoyed success in the New York City area where the company was based. Distribution was expanded from regional to national, and another age-range of apparel was added to the line. However, the industry proved complex. High labor costs, competition from imports, delivery problems, and the delicacy of manufacturing seasonal clothes lines before understanding the current line sales trends, were all factors that combined to keep Chesebrough from immediately profiting from its Health-tex acquisition.

The next large–scale success was the $27 million acquisition of the Maine-based G.H. Bass & Company in 1978. Here again, Chesebrough found a company with strong regional recognition. Bass was a New England shoe company with strong sales, particularly of its Weejuns loafers and Sunjuns sandals. Just as the company readied its nationwide marketing push, the "preppie" look flooded fashion, and Bass sales rocketed. The traditional, conservative shoes Bass produced were perfect for the conservative fashion boom. By 1981, two plants had been added to meet demand. For a time, the yearly sales gain in this division was 71 percent. Even after the squarely traditional fashion trend tapered off, Bass shoes had a significant position in the market.

In addition to its acquisitions, Chesebrough also focused on internal growth. The company had a knack for new products and promotions. In 1978, a home permanent product, called Rave, featuring no ammonia and no odor was released. Rave soon became the top-selling product in a revitalized market. Chesebrough also helped to rejuvenate the hand lotion business in the 1970s. Jergens was the top performer in that niche at the time, and hand lotion was generally considered a product for senior citizens. However, Chesebrough launched Vaseline Intensive Care lotion as a "therapeutic skin care" product for all ages, and the lotion overtook Jergens within a year. Sales surged, inspiring competition from Procter & Gamble. Chesebrough countered with another new product, Pond's Cream & Cocoa Butter lotion. This was followed by an update of Vaseline Intensive Care lotion, and by 1980, Chesebrough was rewarded with more than a quarter of the lotion market. By 1981, hand lotion was a $200 million a year industry.

In 1979, Chesebrough sales were more than $1 billion. This was on the eve of the company's centennial and marked 21 consecutive years of increased dividends. Even during the recession of 1974 and 1975—the country's worst downturn since the 1930s—Chesebrough posted around ten percent profit increases. By 1980, the company still enjoyed about 15 percent annual earnings growth, with some divisions performing better than others. At that time, health and beauty aids were tied with packaged foods as the company's best performers domestically.

In 1982, Chesebrough acquired Prince Manufacturing, Inc., maker of more than 40 percent of the tennis racquets then sold in the United States, paying $62 million in stock for the company. The following year, Chesebrough's record began to falter. Prince Manufacturing's earnings were unusually stagnant for 1983. Bass hadn't been performing well because of high wage costs, so the company moved parts of its production to Brazil and Taiwan. Still, demand for casual shoes had fallen sharply, adverse foreign currency translations hurt the international division, and the overall economic environment dug into Chesebrough's nondurable sales. By 1984, with profits still flat, the company again sought to defend itself against possible takeover by buying back $70 million worth of shares from investor-corporate raider Carl Icahn, and spending $95 million for the industrial plastics division of Icahn's privately held company—which was valued at half the price tag.

Chesebrough made a surprising $1.25 billion bid for Stauffer Chemical Company in 1985. Makers of weed killers, pesticides, and flame retardants, Stauffer had been suffering from a lackluster performance at the time. And while Stauffer did have a food ingredients business with fair sales, speculation was that it was a self-protective, antitakeover move on Chesebrough's part. The company was already having difficulties with its Ragú, Bass shoes, Prince tennis racquets, and Health-tex clothing sales. Even the flagship product, Vaseline, had dropped in sales. In 1984, for the first time in 29 years, Chesebrough's earnings declined. Its heavy debt load and depressed earnings made the company again ripe for takeover.

Showing an interest in Chesebrough was Unilever N.V., the world's largest consumer products company in 1986, with sales of more than $24 billion. In December of 1986, Chesebrough agreed to a $3.1 billion takeover bid by Unilever. An Anglo-Dutch conglomerate, Unilever stood to gain from Chesebrough's overseas sales, then accounting for almost a quarter of its overall annual sales. It also broadened Unilever's U.S. earnings base—tripling its personal care products there—and brought solid brand names into the giant's portfolio. Immediate speculation was that Unilever would unload Chesebrough's faltering units. Meanwhile, Chesebrough had introduced new products into its successful cornerstone Ragú line, already benefitting that segment's profits. Ward was replaced by Richard G. Finn as president and CEO.

Unloading the losing portions of the Stauffer Chemical unit, the Prince tennis racket business, and the ailing Bass shoe operation helped reduce the purchase price. The Faberge Salon division of Chesebrough was sold to Conair Corporation in 1990. That same year, the company signed an agreement with Elizabeth Taylor to launch her own fragrance. The resultant Passion line met with immediate success.

Chesebrough returned to concentrating on the strength of its marketing innovations and internal product development. In 1991, Vaseline Intensive Care products developed a innovative ad campaign, featuring a simulated television newscast called "Skin Science Updates." Also that year, however, Chesebrough was hit with a bill for $21.5 million in damages, awarded to a five-year-old child regarding an eardrum damaged by a Q-Tip. The following year, the company unveiled a major renovation of its Pond's product lines. Pond's was then the number one facial cleanser in a $500 million segment.

During this time, Unilever, while a top seller of personal products worldwide, was second in the United States to the Procter & Gamble Company. By 1993, the company was aggressively positioned to build its presence in the American skincare, haircare, cosmetics, and fragrance businesses, largely with the help of Chesebrough-Pond's.

Further Reading:

Behar, Richard, "The Too-Scorched Earth?," *Forbes*, December 16, 1985, p. 54.
"The Case for Betting on Chesebrough-Pond's," *Fortune*, December 1983, pp. 178–179.
"The Case for Chesebrough," *Forbes*, August 27, 1984, p. 150.
"CEO: The Silver Medal Winners," *Financial World*, March 15, 1982, p. 22.
"Chesebrough-Pond's Inc.," *Forbes*, April 28, 1980, p. 136.
"Chesebrough-Pond's the Experts in Skin Care," *Discount Store News*, May 18, 1992, p. 61.
"Chesebrough's Finn Feels an Upturn," *Women's Wear Daily*, October 30, 1992, p. 6.
"A Company for All Seasons," *Financial World*, June 15, 1980, pp. 51–52.
"Conair Buys Faberge," *New York Times*, July 26, 1990, p. D4(L).
"Entrepreneurship Is the Only Way," *Financial World*, March 15, 1982, pp. 24–25.
Failla, Kathleen, "Piloting Stauffer Back to Profitability," *Chemical Week*, March 26, 1986, p. 19.
Foster, Geoffrey, "Core Concerns at Unilever," *Management Today*, May 1988, p. 62.
Govoni, Stephen, "Two Cheers for a Rather Odd Match," *Financial World*, March 20, 1985, pp. 35–37.
"Head Scores an Ace of a Sale," *Newsweek*, July 5, 1982, p. 55.
Kagan, Cara, "Pond's Dips Into Moisturizers," *Women's Wear Daily*, November 6, 1992, p. 6.
King, Resa, "Unilever-Chesebrough: Why $3 Billion Looked Like a Song," *Business Week*, December 15, 1986, pp. 32–33.
"Knock, Knock," *Forbes*, December 29, 1986, p. 126.
McCarthy, Michael, "In Counterattack, Unilever Looks to Leverage P&G's Lowballing," *ADWEEK Eastern Edition*, March 23, 1992, p. 3.
McGraw, Carol, "Liz Taylor Stars in Battle Over 'Passion' Fragrance," *Los Angeles Times*, December 3, 1990, pp. A1, A21.
Miller, William, "Chesebrough-Pond's," *Industry Week*, October 19, 1992, p. 43.
Millstein, Marc, "A Simple Skin Care Solution," *Supermarket News*, September 28, 1992, p. 32.
Orr, Andrea, "Unilever Deal Called Good for Chesebrough," *Women's Wear Daily*, December 3, 1986, p. 4.
Rudnitsky, Howard, "Vanity, Thy Name Is Profit," *Forbes*, May 25, 1981, pp. 47–48.
——, "Chesebrough-Pond's: The Unsung Miracle," *Forbes*, September 28, 1981, pp. 105–109.
"Serendipity," *Forbes*, January 17, 1983, p. 16.
Sloan, Pat, "Chesebrough Shakeup," *Advertising Age*, February 16, 1987, p. 1.
——, "Chesebrough Puts New Face on Its Brands," *Advertising Age*, January 27, 1992, p. 3.
Stevens, Amy, "Chesebrough-Ponds hit with 421.5 million in damages over Q-Tips," *Wall Street Journal*, May 14, 1991, p. B5(E).
Stovall, Robert, "Less Glamour, More Value," *Financial World*, December 15, 1983.
——, "The Power of the Consumer," *Financial World*, October 16, 1985, p. 62.
"Unilever's U.S. Invasion," *Fortune*, January 5, 1987, p. 12.
"The Urge to Go Home," *Economist*, December 6, 1986, p. 87.
"A Vaseline Commercial That Looks Like News," *New York Times*, November 29, 1991, p. D5(L).
Warner, Liz, "Night of Long Knives at Chesebrough," *Marketing*, October 22, 1987, p. 1.

—Carol I. Keeley

ciba

Ciba-Geigy Ltd.

P.O. Box CH-4002
Klybecstrasse 141
Basle, Baslestadt 4002
Switzerland
(061) 697-7507
Fax: (061) 697-2539

Public Company
Incorporated: 1884
Employees: 90,554
Sales: SFr 22.20 billion (US$14.87 billion)
Stock Exchanges: Geneva Zurich Basle
SICs: 5161 Chemicals and Allied Products; 2865 Cyclic
   Organic Crudes and Intermediates and Organic Dyes and
   Pigments; 2834 Pharmaceutical Preparations

Ciba-Geigy is the largest chemical company in Switzerland. But since the country offers only a limited market and lacks many essential raw materials, Swiss chemical companies have been forced to enter foreign markets; and in order to compete successfully, they have had to lead the world in certain technologies.

In the early years of the twentieth century, the world's strongest chemical industries were in Germany, the United States, and Switzerland. German companies, fearful of losing their leading position to rapidly advancing American firms, openly colluded and coordinated business strategies. After World War I the German companies formed a cartel, the notorious IG Farben. In order to remain competitive with the Germans, the three largest Swiss chemical companies, Ciba Ltd., J.R. Geigy S.A., and Sandoz Ltd., formed a similar cartel called Basle AG. This trust lasted from 1918 to 1951. By 1970, however, market conditions led Ciba and Geigy to merge, forming one of the world's leading pharmaceutical and specialty chemical companies.

Geigy is the older of the two companies—one family member was in the drug business as early as 1758. Through several generations, the Geigy family had married into the prosperous silk manufacturing establishment in Basle and then became established in the dye trade in 1883. Only a few years later, the Geigy family set itself apart from other dyers in Basle by embracing newly discovered synthetic dying processes.

A few years earlier, in 1859, a French silk weaver named Alexander Clavel moved to Basle, where he established a dyeworks called the Gesellschaft für Chemische Industrie im Basle, or Ciba. In 1884 Clavel abandoned silk dying for a more lucrative trade in dyestuff manufacturing. Ciba gained a reputation for Fuchsine, a reddish purple dye, and Martius yellow.

By 1900 Ciba was the largest chemical company in Switzerland. With a major alkali works located at Monthey, it was one of the only Swiss manufacturers of inorganic dyes. Ciba, however, started a limited diversification into the pharmaceutical business with the introduction of an antiseptic called Vioform. Between 1900 and 1913 net assets quadrupled while profits nearly tripled. Geigy, during this period, remained steadfastly, committed to organic dye production; some of the dyes were still derived from coal tar.

Early in the century both Ciba and Geigy established factories in Germany, due in part to a labor shortage in Switzerland, but also to avoid enforcement of environmental laws designed to reduce pollution in the River Rhine.

Until World War I, German chemical companies dominated the world dye trade with a 90 percent market share. Those companies, including BASF, Hoechst, and Bayer, could easily have run Swiss competitors out of business through price competition; they had proven their ability to hold back the American chemical industry in its infancy. Instead, Ciba and Geigy developed practices that would permit international expansion while not provoking the Germans. Central to this strategy was the abandonment of bulk dye production (a German specialty) in favor of more expensive specialty dyes.

In time, the German companies developed a vested interest in the survival of their Swiss counterparts. Eighty percent of the raw materials used by the Swiss companies came from Germany. In eliminating Swiss competitors, the German companies would eliminate customers whose capacity they could not economically absorb. Furthermore, competition among German companies to fill a sudden void left by the Swiss could have destabilized the careful balance maintained by the cartel. As Swiss companies became acclimated to the German system, they were granted certain privileges, such as an exclusive right to export to Germany. Cooperation between Swiss and German companies also took the form of an occasional profit-sharing pool, as the one that existed between Geigy, Bayer, and BASF for black dye.

The onset of World War I in Europe in 1914 severely upset the equilibrium that had existed between Ciba, Geigy, and their German counterparts. Unable to secure raw materials and chemical intermediaries from German suppliers, factories in Basle were forced to suspend dye production. The Swiss later negotiated an agreement with the British, who had been dependent on German dyes and were unprepared for their trade embargo. The British agreed to supply the Swiss with raw materials on the condition that Swiss dyes would be sold preferentially to Britain. While Swiss factories in Baden were seized by the German government, the Swiss were free to export to the lucrative (and formerly German) markets in Britain and the United States and to establish factories in France and Russia.

Ciba's profits increased dramatically, from SFr 3 million in 1913 to SFr 15 million in 1917. The end of the war, however, reopened world markets, but left the industry in a severe state of overcapacity. By 1921 Ciba's profits had fallen to SFr 1 million. At this time the German companies decided to reform their cartel, this time under the aegis of a large holding company called IG Farben. Ciba, Sandoz, and Geigy were invited to join IG Farben but, true to Swiss neutrality, elected instead to form their own cartel, Basle AG.

Basle AG, founded in 1918, was fashioned after IG Farben. The group consisted of Ciba, Geigy, and Sandoz—virtually the entire Swiss chemical industry. The agreement mandated that all competition between the three companies would cease, technical knowledge would be freely shared, and all profits would be pooled. Ciba would receive 52 percent of the group's profits, while Geigy and Sandoz would each be entitled to 24 percent. Any sales between the companies were to be invoiced at cost, raw materials would be purchased jointly, and the manufacture of any product would be assigned to whichever company could produce it at the lowest cost.

From the cartel's inception, Geigy's weak market position was a source of tension for its partners. Geigy still produced vegetable dyes, which were gradually losing market share to organic dyestuffs. Despite Sandoz's contention that it was being forced to subsidize Geigy, Basle AG remained stable. In fact, it was considered more successful than the larger and more powerful IG Farben. All three firms invested their profits into a broader range of chemical interests, including chemicals and pharmaceuticals. By 1930 these divisions contributed more than one quarter of the group's profits. A joint venture between Sandoz and Geigy led to the establishment of the Cincinnati Chemical Works, a subsidiary that gave Basle AG a tariff-free foothold in the American market.

In 1929, placing profit before independence, Basle AG joined with IG Farben to create the Dual Cartel. French dyemakers joined the group shortly afterwards, forming the Tripartite Cartel. In 1932, with the addition of the British cartel Imperial Chemical Industries, the group was again renamed the Quadrapartite Cartel. This pan-European cartel existed until 1939, when World War II forced its dissolution.

Due to the secrecy characteristic of Swiss firms, little is known about Basle AG's activities during the war; the company had subsidiaries in both Allied and Axis nations. At one point, Ciba angered its partners by placing its shares in Cincinnati Chemical Works under the custody of an American trust. Apparently fearing the eventual seizure of those shares by the alien property custodian, Geigy and Sandoz protested in American courts but were unable to retrieve Ciba's shares.

In 1940 Dr. Paul Mueller, a researcher with Geigy, discovered the insecticidal properties of DDT. Originally thought safe enough to be sprayed directly on refugees to eradicate lice, DDT was considered a "wonder chemical." Research during the war led to the development of several ethical drugs, including Privine, a treatment for hay fever, and Nupercaine, a spinal anesthetic used in childbirth. The companies also developed drugs for treatment of high blood pressure and heart disease.

After the war Ciba notified Geigy and Sandoz that as a result of U.S. antitrust laws, the 1918 agreement could not be respected among subsidiaries in the United States. Geigy made a similar declaration regarding American assets in 1947. Two years later Sandoz again raised the issue of cross-subsidization and proposed that the cartel be dissolved. Geigy opposed the motion, but Ciba, unwilling to abandon its lucrative markets in the United States, eventually sided with Sandoz; the postwar environment no longer justified cartelization for self-protection. Basle AG was finally dissolved in 1951.

Geigy's poor financial performance called into question its survivability outside the cartel. During the 1950s, however, the full market potential of DDT was realized. Suddenly profitable, Geigy expanded its market in agri-chemicals by introducing a corn herbicide called triazine.

Both Ciba and Geigy grew steadily during the 1950s. Between 1950 and 1959, Ciba's sales grew from SFr 531 million to SFr 1026 million, and Geigy's grew from SFr 260 million to SFr 738 million. By 1960 both Ciba and Geigy were diversified manufacturers, competing directly in pharmaceuticals, dyes, plastics, textile auxiliaries, and agricultural and specialty chemicals. Each year Geigy's sales grew stronger, until in 1967 the company overtook Ciba.

Although older than Ciba by 25 years, Geigy maintained a more youthful image. While Ciba sold itself as the company "where research is the tradition," Geigy recruited engineers with the slogan, "future with Geigy." But in 1970, while Ciba and Geigy personnel were quibbling over their respective talents, the leaders of both companies were discussing a possible merger.

The idea to merge was first raised when the two companies jointly established a factory at Toms River, New Jersey. With increasingly difficult conditions in export markets—particularly the United States—officials of the two companies began to explore the benefits of combining their textile and pharmaceutical research; Geigy's strength in agricultural chemicals complemented Ciba's leading position in synthetic resins and petrochemicals.

Ciba and Geigy were both in excellent financial condition. However, some of the same market conditions that had led them to form Basle AG in 1918 were once again prevalent. Competition against German companies in export markets had intensified. But it was as a defense against emerging petrochemical industries in oil-rich Persian Gulf states that the merger was most attractive.

The largest obstacle to a merger between Ciba and Geigy was U.S. antitrust legislation. Antitrust sentiment in the United States was so strong that federal prosecutors vowed to block the merger in Switzerland if it threatened to restrain American trade in any way. In order to win approval in the United States, Ciba agreed to sell its American dyeworks to Crompton and Knowles, and Geigy consented to turn over its American pharmaceutical holdings to Revlon. Despite further challenges, including one from consumer advocate Ralph Nader, the merger was approved.

Mechanically, the merger consisted of a takeover of Ciba by Geigy. This was done to minimize tax penalties amounting to SFr 55 million. Geigy's chairman, Dr. van Planta, assumed the chairmanship of the new company, with Ciba's chairman, Dr. Kappeli, serving as honorary chairman.

As promised, the Ciba-Geigy merger has proven "synergistic." The more profitable but less diversified Geigy has benefited from Ciba's research capabilities. Ciba, on the other hand, has profited from Geigy's more modern approach to marketing and management. In the United States, the company's American subsidiary passed the one billion dollar sales mark in 1978, and doubled that figure only six years later. The company's worldwide sales that year were SFr 17.5 billion, 30 percent of which came from U.S. operations. Despite a 14 percent drop in profits between 1978 and 1980, Ciba-Geigy has maintained strong annual sales growth since 1981; profits as a percentage of sales was 8.1 percent in 1985.

In contrast to its impressive performance on the balance sheet, Ciba-Geigy has suffered a few problems with its public image. In the mid-1970s a Ciba-Geigy product marketed in Africa as an ordinary analgesic produced a horrifying side-effect: the loss of large pieces of flesh. In addition, its plant at Toms River discontinued production of Posgene in response to a Greenpeace campaign that warned the community of a possible accident similar in magnitude to the tragedy in Bhopal, India.

Troubles at Toms River continued: in 1982 the plant was added to the U. S. Environmental Protection Agency's (EPA) list of "Superfund" cleanup sites when more than 120 chemicals were discovered in local groundwater. Then, in 1984, investigators found a leak in the ten-mile conduit leading from Ciba's facility. The company discontinued dye, resin, and additive production at Toms River in 1986 and pleaded guilty to one charge of illegal waste disposal in March of 1992. The corporation paid more than $60 million in fines and landfill and groundwater cleanup costs and agreed to make donations to New Jersey state conservation projects. The Toms River experience, combined with tightening European Community pollution regulations, helped convince Ciba-Geigy to cite the environment as one of its focuses.

Environmentalism became one of the cornerstones of Ciba's "Vision 2000" strategy, a long-term plan to balance the economic, social, and environmental objectives of the company. The company logo was shortened to just "ciba," but the formal name remained unchanged. The corporation was reorganized from functional/geographical units into 14 separate businesses with autonomous research and development, production, and marketing divisions. Ciba's businesses could be grouped into three basic areas: healthcare, agriculture, and industry.

The company considered its Pharma, Plant Protection, and Additives divisions primary businesses. Pharma, the single largest operating unit, ranked among the world's top five pharmaceutical concerns. The corporation's leading product was Voltaren, an anti-rheumatic. Ciba's Pharma unit also claimed the second most popular smoking cessation patch, Habitrol (known as Nicotinell outside the United States). Habitrol encountered stiff competition in the 1990s, but was launched in France and Canada in 1992 and received over-the-counter status

in the United Kingdom and Italy that year. One problem with transdermal nicotine patch sales was that the product created a self-defeating market: if the treatment worked, patients would eventually end the therapy; if the patches were ineffective, smokers would not buy them. Ciba-Geigy purchased the Dr. R. Maag plant protection business from Hoffman-La Roche in 1990 and achieved majority ownership of Bunting Group's plant protection business in 1992.

Ciba-Geigy's Self Medication, Diagnostics, and Ciba Vision units were recognized by the corporation as growth enterprises. Self Medication was expanded with the 1992 acquisition of Fisons' North American business, and the purchase of Triton Diagnostics buttressed the Diagnostics group. Ciba Vision's contact lenses, lens care products, and ophthalmic medicines ranked number two worldwide.

Ciba-Geigy's Seeds and Composites units were considered long-term investments. In 1990, the company announced that it had successfully inserted marker genes into corn cells that produced fertile plants and passed the new traits on to viable seeds. The company thereby entered the race to genetically engineer plants with the most attractive traits.

The core industrial businesses of Ciba-Geigy in the early 1990s included Textile Dyes, Chemicals, Pigments, Polymers, and Mettler Toledo scales. The leading market positions of these businesses allowed them to function as "cash cows" for research and development in other areas. For example, Ciba's textile dyes, additives, and Mettler Toledo units ranked number one worldwide in their respective categories.

Ciba's reorganization included the divestment of its Flame Retardants and Water Treatments Chemicals businesses, valued at approximately $100 million. The units were sold to FMC Corp. in 1992. Ciba-Geigy's sales and profits increased steadily in the late 1980s and early 1990s to reach 1992 figures of more than SFr 22 billion in revenue and SFr 1.52 billion in profits. The majority of Ciba's sales, 36 percent, were made in European Community countries. Overall European sales comprised 43 percent of the total, while North America contributed 32 percent, Asia constituted 13 percent, and Latin America made up 7 percent.

Ciba-Geigy is one of the five largest chemical companies in the world. And, while it is widely diversified within the industry, it has maintained a steady emphasis on sophisticated chemicals—whether they are pharmaceuticals, plastics, pigments, or pesticides. (Until it was sold, Airwick, which made air fresheners and other consumer products, was one of Ciba-Geigy's very few low-tech ventures.) The company had plans to strengthen existing product lines and limit diversification to compatible high-technology operations in biotechnology, laser applications, and diagnostics.

Principal Subsidiaries: Ciba-Geigy International AG, Ciba-Geigy SA, Centre de recherches agricoles; Ciba-Geigy Munchwilen AG, Ciba-Geigy Verkaufs-und Vertriebsgesellschaft AG; Ciba-Geigy Services AG, Ciba-Geigy Handels-und Marktberatungs AG; Compagnie des Forces Motrices d'Orsieres; Mettler Toledo AG, Zyma SA, Dispersa AG; Ciba Vision Management AG; Dr R. Maag AG; Ciba-Geigy PLC (United Kingdom);

Ciba-Geigy PLC (United Kingdom); Societe Anonyme Ciba-Geigy (France); Laboratoires Ciba-Geigy SA (France); La Quinoleine SA (France); Ciba-Geigy GmbH (Germany); Pfersee Chemie GmbH (Germany); Ciba-Geigy Marienberg GmbH (Germany); Ciba-Geigy Holding Deutschland GmbH (Germany); Ciba-Geigy S.p.A. (Italy); Chemical Insurance Company Limited (Bermuda); Befico Ltd. (Bermuda); Ciba-Geigy Finance and Investment Limited (Bermuda); Ciba-Geigy Canada Limited; Ciba-Geigy Corporation (U.S.A.); Ciba Corning Diagnostics Corp. (U.S.A.); Geneva Generics Inc. (U.S.A.); Ohaus Scale Corp. (U.S.A.); OCG Microelectronic Materials, Inc. (U.S.A.); Sociedade Agricola Germinal Ltda. (Brazil); Ciba-Geigy Mexicana, SA de CV.; Ciba-Geigy (Japan) Limited; Ciba-Geigy (Malaysia) Sendirian Berhad; Ciba-Geigy (Pty.) Limited (South Africa), Ciba-Geigy Australia Limited (Australia).

Further Reading:

Ciba-Geigy Ltd. Annual Report, 1992.

Enri, Paul, *The Basle Marriage: History of the Ciba-Geigy Merger,* Zurich, Switzerland: Neue Zurcher Zeitung, 1979.

Gebhart, Fred, "Skin Patch Makers Fight to Be No. 1 in War on Nicotine," *Drug Topics,* January 20, 1992, p. 26.

Hunter, David, "Ciba-Geigy: Back to the Roots for Renewed Growth," *Chemical Week,* June 21, 1989, p. 21.

Kirschner, Elisabeth, "Ciba-Geigy and New Jersey Settle Toms River Battle," *Chemical Week,* March 11, 1992, p. 14.

Lichtenstein, William, "The Toms River Experience," *Chemical Engineering,* April 1991, p. 45.

McCarthy, Joseph L., "Alex Kraurer: Ciba-Geigy," *Chief Executive,* July/August 1992, p. 20.

Morris, Gregory D., "Ciba-Geigy Enters the $1.5 Billion/Year Corn Biotech Race," *Chemical Week,* September 12, 1990, p. 12.

Shon, Melissa, "Nicotine Patch Market Takes a Fall, But Why?," *Chemical Marketing Reporter,* September 14, 1992, p. 5.

Wilsher, Peter, "The Feeling Grows That Going Green Is Good for Business," *Management Today,* October 1991, p. 27.

—update by April S. Dougal

The Clark Construction Group, Inc.

7500 Old Georgetown Rd.
Bethesda, Maryland 20814-6195
U.S.A.
(301) 657-7100
Fax: (301) 657-7263

Private Company
Incorporated: 1906 as The George Hyman Construction
  Company
Sales: $1.3 billion
Employees: 5,000
SICs: 1542 General Contractors—Nonresidential Buildings

The Clark Construction Group, Inc. (CCG), is a billion-dollar, general building contractor of commercial buildings located in the Washington, D.C., area. Its twin pillars are its two principal subsidiaries, The George Hyman Construction Company, the oldest and largest component of CCG, and Omni Construction, Inc., established in 1977. CCG is an industry leader, the largest in the state of Maryland and one of the largest construction companies in the nation. The company has built or renovated many of the most important buildings in the nation's capital (including 17 of the city's subway stations). CCG also is constructing the country's largest waste water recycling facility, located in Los Angeles county. The firm has constructed more than 400 projects throughout the United States, and has won over 350 major awards for building excellence.

The present day Clark Construction Group evolved out of its biggest subsidiary, The George Hyman Construction Company. A. James Clark, current CEO of The Clark Construction Group, Inc., which he established in 1982, had become an employee of Hyman in 1950. The founder of the company, George Hyman, was at that time still president of the firm, which he had founded single-handedly in 1906.

George Hyman was a Lithuanian immigrant, arriving in the United States in 1899 at the age of 16, as much to escape anti-Semitism in his homeland as to make his own fortune. His was the typical rags to riches American immigrant story. Hyman started as a peddler hawking his wares from a cart. From there he established his first modest business as a grocer. Desiring a quicker route to riches, he headed West, to the "Indian territory," or Oklahoma. Newly opened to pioneers and land grabbers, the demand for construction materials and knowledge in Oklahoma was insatiable. There Hyman entered the construction business, building up a fortune, which he invested in turn in the exploration of the new oil fields of Texas, where he moved in 1901. Several years later he headed back east.

In 1906 Hyman launched the construction company bearing his name, headquartered in a back alley storage shed in Washington, D.C. There was much government construction work to be had, as the District of Columbia experienced a sudden spurt of growth under the dynamic leadership of worldly, cosmopolitan President Theodore Roosevelt. Hyman's "specialty" was excavation. This was an exceedingly cumbersome and slow process that utilized horses and mules as a central component of the work. Moreover, competition in the construction business was becoming increasingly fierce. Hyman got wind of an advanced new method for demolition and excavation work: the steam shovel. No one in the capital had one, and despite his friends' warnings about this untried, untested implement, Hyman staked a considerable investment in the steam shovel. It was an instant success, and positioned him well ahead of his competitors.

Until his marriage in 1914, Hyman was willing to re-locate to wherever his work demanded; dams were being built all over the country, and excavation was in high demand. But Hyman's bride refused to part with her husband for long or go trekking about the country with him, which persuaded him to stay in the Washington, D.C., area. The decision to remain in one place turned out to suit him, and from then on his company became identified closely with the nation's capital.

Business boomed during the prosperous years of the First World War. While recession hit afterwards, the capital was better off than elsewhere; victory in war and the peace settlement afterwards added to Washington's importance and prestige. The building boom never really stopped in the city until the Great Depression.

For four years, until 1926, Hyman was in a partnership with the head of a local building firm, James Parson, Jr., to establish the Parson and Hyman Co., Inc., of which Hyman became president. Hyman took this step to qualify to do general contracting work (Hyman was previously regarded as a subcontractor only). The combined forces worked well, and by 1923, the firm was handling over one million dollars in construction work. The 1920s coincided with an upsurge in the building of schools, and Hyman's company built many of the educational facilities still in use in the District of Columbia. In 1926, when Parson ended his business partnership with Hyman and the company was renamed The George Hyman Construction Company, the firm had just completed its first commercial office building. Hyman hired his nephew Benjamin T. Rome as his right hand man, and together they expanded the company's options, negotiating contracts with clients and bidding on government construction, the federal government's preferred way of doing business.

All construction ground to a halt with the onset of the Great Depression. Hyman no longer could afford to pay his office staff nor the rent on his office, located in a luxury commercial building that his firm had built. He and Benjamin Rome relocated into the back alley shed that had served as original company headquarters. There was not enough work to justify even an assistant, so Rome returned to graduate school. In 1933, however, construction work in the capital increased, in large part because of new government contracts. New federal buildings soon were popping up all over the Washington, D.C., area. Hyman quickly secured two major government building contracts, which led to others. By 1938 the worst was over and The George Hyman Construction Co. once again was housed in the luxury commercial building it had vacated years earlier, with Benjamin Rome and others back on the job.

There was a frenzy of government building projects during the World War II years, many of them couched in secrecy. Hyman's firm secured 20 major building contracts in this time, including the construction of the Naval torpedo factory in nearby Alexandria, Virginia, that manufactured every torpedo used by the United States during the Second World War.

Following the war, Hyman's firm was heavily involved in the expansion of the University of Maryland campus in College Park, receiving over the years a total of 17 building contracts. By 1950, when construction of the new chemistry building proceeded, there was a need for another engineer. The daughter of a friend of Rome's was engaged to an energetic young engineer, A. James Clark, who applied for the vacancy and got the job. The future founder of the Clark Construction Group worked as a field engineer during the day in College Park, Maryland, while also engaged in night courses in accounting at American University in order to qualify for more lucrative and responsible managerial positions in Hyman's firm. By the time of Hyman's death in 1959, Jim Clark had risen in rank to number two man in The George Hyman Construction Company: in 1960 he became general manager of the firm as well as vice president, while Benjamin Rome took the helm as the company's new president.

By then, the firm had prospered not only from the many University of Maryland building contracts, but from lucrative government building contracts as well. The World War II years had transformed the District of Columbia into the capital not only of the wealthy, powerful United States, but of the entire ''free world.'' One monumental building after another went up in the 1950s, most of them engaging Hyman and others as contractors. The huge Senate office building, the District of Columbia's General Hospital, the six-story east wing of the Museum of Natural History, and many private commercial building contracts were executed by The George Hyman Construction Company. By the end of the 1960s, Jim Clark had succeeded Benjamin Rome as president of the firm, with Rome remaining as treasurer and chairman.

Jim Clark's business perspective reflected that of a younger generation, impatient with the traditional ways of doing things. At the Hyman firm, the way of doing business for over 60 years had been to keep the firm small, a philosophy that the founder felt ensured efficiency, and to limit its project area to the Washington, D.C., area. The nation's demographics, however, were changing rapidly, and the Sun Belt was becoming the up and coming growth area. Clark counseled expansion.

As president of Hyman, the youthful Clark set about realizing his new strategy. In 1970 the firm expanded into the Atlanta,

Georgia, area. Later, branches were opened in Virginia, Florida, and California. By the late 1970s, Hyman was the largest construction company in the state of Maryland, and a national pacesetter in the construction industry. In 1969, the year Clark became president of Hyman, annual sales revenues were $57 million. A decade later, sales were ten times greater.

In 1977 Clark established the Omni Construction Company, Inc. Omni was established as a non-union or open shop, and almost immediately secured the lucrative contract to build the luxury Four Seasons Hotel in the capital. By Omni's first anniversary of operation, it had contracts totalling a hefty $43 million. Omni's incorporation as a subsidiary was followed in 1982 by the creation of a new parent company of both Omni and Hyman, The Clark Construction Group, Inc. (CCG).

The 1980s and 1990s saw Omni and Hyman involved in projects as diverse as the new addition to the Lincoln Center in New York, the vast LA Convention Center, the expansion of McCormick Place in Chicago, the Ronald Reagan office building in Los Angeles, and the Miami Beach convention center. Meanwhile, more projects were awarded to the Clark Construction Group in the Washington, D.C., area, including the new Canadian Chancery, the renovation of the building currently housing the National Museum of Women in the Arts, the restoration of the famous Willard Hotel, and the widely praised Orioles Park at Camden Yards, home of the Baltimore Orioles baseball team.

CCG has weathered the recession extremely well thanks to a strategic plan that called for more geographic and product diversity. Prisons, hospitals, and waste water treatment plants joined with corporate build-to-suit projects to generate $1 billion in new contracts in 1991 and 1992.

CCG is expected to continue this strategy under the present generation of senior management that Clark has put in place over the past five or six years. These younger leaders include Hyman President Peter C. Forster and Omni President Dan T. Montgomery. They are joined by a number of key executives who are directing operations in a variety of markets and product areas.

Principal Subsidiaries: The George Hyman Construction Company; Omni Construction, Inc.

Further Reading:

Crenshaw, Albert B., ''Hyman Gets Big Chicago Contract,'' *Washington Post,* September 28, 1991, p. C1.
The George Hyman Construction Company, Seventy Five Years of Building, 1906–1981, Bethesda, MD: G. Hyman Construction Co., 1982.
''Hyman Low Bidder on Courthouse: Greenbelt Project Was Hotly Pursued by Builders,'' *Daily Record,* May 22, 1992, p. 3.
Powers, Nan, ''The Big Build Up (the Washington Development Scene, Jim Clark),'' *Warfield's,* October 1989, pp. 69–73.
Samuel, Paul D., ''OMNI Joint Venture Wins Contract for $14 Million Towson Jail Annex,'' *Daily Record,* May 29, 1992, p. A7.

—Sina Dubovoj

Clark Equipment Company

100 North Michigan St.
P.O. Box 7008
South Bend, Indiana 46634
U.S.A.
(219) 239-0100
Fax: (219) 239-0237

Public Company
Incorporated: 1903 as George R. Rich Manufacturing
     Company; 1906 as Celfor Tool Company; 1916 as Clark
     Equipment Company.
Employees: 6,316
Sales: $802.72 million
Stock Exchanges: New York
SICs: 3537 Industrial Trucks & Tractors; 3531 Construction
     Machinery & Equipment; 3714 Motor Vehicle Parts &
     Accessories

Clark Equipment Company designs, manufactures, and sells
industrial trucks, tractors, and motor vehicle parts as well as
construction machinery and equipment. The company's products, including skid-steer loaders, construction machinery,
transmissions for on-highway trucks and axles, and transmissions for off-highway equipment, are sold throughout North
America, South America, and Europe.

Clark began in 1903 as the George R. Rich Manufacturing
Company, a small company in Chicago owned by executives of
the Illinois Steel Company. This side business was named after
the mechanic who designed and manufactured a new, more
durable drill that Illinois Steel used for drilling holes in steel
railroad rails. Despite meeting the needs of the larger company,
Rich Manufacturing did not prosper because production volume
was insufficient. To increase production, the company needed
both a larger facility and a larger client base. In 1904 Rich
Manufacturing moved to Buchanan, Michigan where the city's
chamber of commerce was offering free rent and cheap power
to attract industry.

Even with a new, larger facility, the company did not perform
well. Rich Manufacturing was delinquent on $30,000 worth of
bills and only had $3,000 in receivables. The owners believed it
was the result of the drill's metallurgy. They hired Eugene
Clark, a 33–year-old Illinois Steel employee and mechanical
engineer, as a consultant to determine the product's shortcom-

ings. Clark conceded that the metallurgy of the drill was poor,
but also found fault with both the management and basic operations. Clark agreed to manage Rich Manufacturing if the owners
would make him an equal partner.

Clark moved to Buchanan and reorganized the company's operations. After a year under his management, Rich Manufacturing
was paying its bills on time and reported profits of more than 16
percent on sales of its Celfor Drill. In 1906 the company received $25,000 from the partners, which was used to design
new drills of tungsten steel. The high-speed tungsten drill bits
had three times the work life of their carbon steel bit predecessors and improved workers' productivity. That same year, Clark
changed the name of the company to Celfor Tool Company to
tie the product's name more directly with the company. Over
the next few years, Celfor Tool experienced the ups and downs
of a company's first years in business. The company had lost a
large supply of drills in the San Francisco earthquake in 1906
and had its plant burned down in 1907. By 1909, however, year-
end results were strong enough that the company paid its first
dividends to investors.

Also in 1909 Clark traveled to Europe and discovered that
superior steel castings were being manufactured by using electric furnaces. Believing there were opportunities in the United
States for such a process, Clark and the other investors of Celfor
Tool built a second plant called the Buchanan Electric Steel
Company. With Clark as president, Buchanan's objective was
to produce high-quality, high-grade castings and new technologies. Buchanan supplied outside customers as well as Celfor,
and in 1912 the company recorded its first two consecutive
months of profits. Shortly thereafter, the company diversified
into other products that utilized its ability to produce steel alloy
castings. This diversification enabled Buchanan to become only
the second company in the nation to produce steel disc wheels
for the automobile industry.

Under Clark's direction, both Celfor Tool and Buchanan continued to grow. Clark focused his companies' efforts in the truck
industry rather than the automobile industry because he felt that
cars were luxury items and that the market was near saturation.
In contrast, he perceived the truck as an industrial tool, and
predicted that truck use would increase as the country's economy grew. As a result, Buchanan began producing strong,
durable steel truck wheels that replaced the wooden-spoke truck
wheels that were fragile and broke down regularly. He also
hired R. J. Burrows, a former chief engineer at a local automobile axle supplier, to design a truck axle that would be stronger
and more durable than the unreliable chain drives. Burrows
designed an internal gear drive axle that became smaller, or had
a "final reduction" at the wheel. The new design replaced a
majority of chain drives and became the industry standard for
truck axles.

In 1916 Clark merged Celfor Tool and Buchanan and formed
Clark Equipment Company. With the merger came new ideas
for products. Foundry workers built a gas-powered shop buggy
with a box fixed on three wheels to assist them in carting sand,
supplies, and rough castings around the shop. The design was
primitive; the buggy had no brakes (so it stopped only when it
ran into something), and required that the driver steer right to
turn left. Plant visitors, however, recognized the buggy's value

and asked to purchase the new product. The first redesign included improved steering and the addition of brakes. Introduced during World War I, five of the first ten buggies went to the U.S. arsenal. They replaced the battery-powered towing tractors that tended to stall when hauling trailer train loads of explosives to storage facilities. At the time of the redesign, the product was named Trucktractor. Over the next ten years, the Trucktractor evolved so that the box was made to dump first by gravity then mechanically. A subsequent model consisted of a platform truck with the ability to pick up materials and move them to other areas. Later an innovation allowed the platform truck to lift. In 1927 all of the features were combined to create the lift truck. This vehicle was able to pick up material, move it to another area, and elevate it for stacking or placement.

Throughout the 1920s, the company continued to grow. Clark had four plants that produced drills, reamers, electric steel castings, axles, wheels, and the Trucktractor. In 1927 Clark began producing transmissions for one of its axle customers. While the transmissions were not a natural progression from one of the company's existing products, Clark adapted by manufacturing the cases itself and purchasing the gears from the Frost Gear Company, a supplier that Clark later acquired. The first contract was for 15,000 transmissions, a daunting order even for more experienced suppliers. Still, Clark was able to complete the order and turn a profit. In 1928 Clark achieved sales of nearly $12 million and net revenue of ten percent. That same year, Clark became a public company, and the initial stock offering yielded $3.5 million in new capital. The following year, the company achieved record sales of $15.5 million.

These successes and the accompanying strong financial results were largely the reason why Clark was able to survive the Great Depression. Company sales declined 42 percent in 1930, 33 percent in 1931, and another 50 percent in 1932. Clark reported its first operating losses in more than 20 years in 1931. By the end of 1932, sales had dipped to $2.3 million, or 14.8 percent of 1929 sales. However, Clark's capital reserve allowed the company to continue to develop new products and emerge from the 1930s financially viable. Clark developed the Auto-Tram prototype, a fast, aluminum rail car, for the 1934 World's Fair. While the prototype did not sell, Clark was selected by the president's commission to develop the undercarriage for trolley street cars and subway systems. Clark supplied these industries with undercarriages for the next 20 years. By 1939 Clark had developed a new line of heavy duty lift trucks and towing tractors that were especially useful to the military during World War II. In the early 1940s, monthly production at the Trucktractor division shot as high as 2,500, up from the 1939 average of about 60. By 1943 sales were $77 million, up from $12.5 million four years earlier. The widespread use of the company's lift trucks by production workers and the military during the war made the Clark name nearly synonymous with lift trucks by the 1940s.

Eugene Clark died in 1942 and was succeeded by executive vice-president Albert Bonner. George Spatta, the vice-president of manufacturing, became president in 1945 after Bonner's sudden death. Following the end of the war, Clark focused on improving current product development. By the 1950s, Clark was heavily dependent on the automotive industry for its sales, earning nearly three quarters of its total revenues from axles and transmissions production for six major U.S. automotive compa-

nies. In an effort to reduce Clark's single industry business risk, management actively pursued a strategy of product diversification through development and acquisition. In 1953 Clark acquired Ross Carrier Company, a local manufacturer of large lift trucks, straddle carriers, and cable cranes. Ross Carrier sold its products under the "Michigan" trademark and had a well established distribution network. Using the manufacturing capabilities of Ross Carrier, Clark developed a new line of rubber-tired front end loaders, and marketed the construction machinery under the Michigan brand name. By 1958, Michigan brand sales were $50 million. In 1959 Clark acquired Brown Truck Trailer, through which it entered the highway trailer business.

During the 1960s, Clark acquired several companies to provide more balance among its product lines. In 1961 Tyler Refrigeration was acquired, while Hancock Scraper was added in 1966 to expand the product line in Clark's construction machinery division. Three years later, Clark acquired Delfield Food Service Equipment Company; this acquisition complemented the Tyler purchase and expanded the company's commercial food industry product line. Also in 1969 Clark acquired the Melroe line of skid-steer loaders and agricultural products. By the early 1990s, Melroe Company was a wholly owned subsidiary of Clark, selling skid-steel loaders under the Bobcat trademark and its agricultural sprayers under Spra-Coupe.

During 1960s Clark became an international company, first through distribution and licensing agreements in Europe then through direct investments in overseas plants. By the end of the decade, Clark, now under the direction of Walter Schirmer, established a worldwide dealer network through which it marketed its diverse product lines. Clark's expansions of the 1960s exceeded the company's ability to fund additional growth. As a result, the company refocused its resources on core businesses and divested product lines without strong long-term potential. Clark sold its commercial refrigeration business, closed its highway trailer division, and ceased operations at several overseas facilities. Following this retrenchment, the company's efforts were directed to product innovations and product line development. New products such as electric and gas-powered forklifts, advanced loaders and scrapers, and new series of transmissions as well as new models of the Bobcat product line again positioned Clark well in its core industries. By the end of the decade, Clark boasted sales of more than $1.4 billion and operated 15 major manufacturing plants in the United States and ten throughout Canada, Europe, Australia, and South America.

The recession of the 1980s again forced Clark to retrench and cease some operations such as the crane and scraper business. Other consolidation efforts included selling the credit company and service businesses that had previously provided Clark with a more vertically integrated business system. Despite these changes, Clark continued to focus on product development, and product improvements were made in each of the company's primary business units.

In 1990 Clark sold its finance subsidiary in France, liquidated its finance operations in the Netherlands, and divested all other non-operating finance holding and insurance companies. These actions resulted from management's strategic plan to focus efforts on manufacturing and expanding the company's presence in the on-highway and off-highway markets. Also in 1990, management purchased a controlling interest in Hurth Axle S.p.A., an Italian manufacturer and distributor of off-highway axles. The company was made a subsidiary of Clark and was renamed Clark-Hurth Components. The terms of the sale included an immediate purchase of 83 percent of Hurth's outstanding stock and an agreement to purchase the remaining 17 percent of outstanding stock in four equal installments at the pre-determined price of $27 million. At the end of 1992, Clark owned 91.6 percent of Hurth's stock.

Despite management's efforts to strengthen its core products, Clark's fork lift business was not performing up to expectation. Fork lift sales provided 44 percent of Clark's revenues but only 12 percent of its profits in 1990. Management dropped its prices to maintain its 20 percent U.S. market share in an industry that had overcapacity and faced increasing competition from other U.S. and Japanese companies. As sales and margins continued to fall, Clark sold its material handling subsidiary to Terex Corporation in 1992. The agreement reduced the company's overall annual sales but improved its profit margins. Terms of the sale provided Clark with an increase of cash and eliminated $30 million in liability claims against the subsidiary that Terex assumed.

In 1991, after restating for the sale of the fork lift business and excluding a $244.9 million non-cash charge for post-retirement benefits, Clark reported a nearly $93 million loss from its four remaining business segments: Melroe, Clark-Hurth Components, Clark Automotive, and VME, the company's 50 percent joint venture with AB Volvo. By the 1990s, Clark had internationally integrated each of the business segments. Clark Automotive's on-highway products were manufactured in Brazil and sold to the nation's automobile industry and the medium-duty truck industries in South and North America. Melroe's off-highway products were manufactured in the United States and through licensees in Australia and Japan and sold worldwide under the Melroe and Bobcat names. Clark Hurth products were manufactured in the United States, Europe, and through a li-censee in South Africa and sold to construction, mining, and material handling equipment industries throughout the world.

Despite the continued soft world economies, Clark reported a net profit in 1992, due in large part from its $20.2 million profit from its non-joint venture concerns. VME improved its performance, but still reported a net loss due to continued restructuring costs and acquisitions. Melroe was responsible for 51 percent of Clark's total sales. Its market position remained strong, and its share of world skid-steer loaders was over 50 percent. Sales from Clark-Hurth accounted for 30 percent, and Clark Automotive accounted for 18 percent of Clark's total sales.

As Clark moves toward the 21st century, it will continue to focus on product development, product improvement, and cost containment. Management will combine business acquisitions with product development to build a product base that is less sensitive to business cycles and consistent with Clark's core businesses. Clark will pursue maintaining and improving the company's market position in its core industries at margins that are consistent with capital and investors' needs and expectations.

Principal Subsidiaries: Melroe Company; Clark Automotive Products Company (Brazil); Clark-Hurth Components Company (91.6%); VME Group N.V. (50%—joint venture with AB Volvo, Sweden).

Further Reading:

Berss, Martha, ''Crying Uncle,'' *Forbes,* December 9, 1991, p. 186.
Clark Equipment Company Annual Reports, South Bend: Clark Equipment Company, 1990–92.
Jaffe, Thomas, ''Clark's Cash: Clark Equipment Co. Sells Forklift Truck Division to Terex Corp.,'' *Forbes,* July 6, 1992, p. 128.
McKernan, Leo J., ''Remarks at the 1992 Clark Equipment Company Annual Meeting of Stockholders, Part II'' May 11, 1993.
Phillips, B. E., *Plus Faith Unlimited: The Story of Clark Equipment Company,* New York: The Newcomen Society in North America, 1979.

—Allyson S. Farquhar-Boyle

Commercial Credit Company

300 St. Paul Place
Baltimore, Maryland 21202-2120
U.S.A.
(410) 332-3000
Fax: (410) 332-3734

Subsidiary of Primerica Inc.
Employees: 4,600
Sales: $1.523 billion
SICs: 6351 Surety Insurance; 6141 Personal Credit
   Institutions; 6719 Holding Companies Nec

Primarily a consumer finance company, Commercial Credit Company also offers insurance, credit cards, and mortgage financing. The company focuses on market segments that are often underserved by banks and other financial service companies due to demographics or credit ratings. Its branches are located in malls and other areas with a heavy volume of consumer traffic.

CCC was founded in Baltimore in 1912 by Alexander E. Duncan and a group of eight businessmen. The company initially lent money to companies using their accounts receivable as security. However, in 1916 the firm branched out of commercial financing, entering the growing field of auto finance, which represented the firm's greatest growth area until the 1930s, when the Great Depression caused auto sales to plunge. During this time, the firm bought several factoring companies, service providers that buy accounts receivable at a discount from banks and then collect the outstanding monies. CCC later consolidated these factoring companies under the name Textile Banking Co., Inc.

CCC then bought the American Credit Indemnity Co. of New York, which insured accounts receivable against customer default or bankruptcy. It continued its move into insurance by buying Calvert Fire Insurance, a casualty company that covered physical damage to autos and appliances it was financing. This helped CCC win financing business with auto dealers, since the dealers hoped to gain business repairing Calvert-insured cars.

The credit controls and decline in auto manufacturing during World War II badly pinched CCC's business. To help generate income, CCC bought several companies that were making money from war-related demands, manufacturing products ranging from pork sausages to printing presses. Competitors like CIT Financial Corp. also diversified into manufacturing during the war. But unlike CIT, CCC held onto its manufacturing operations when the war ended and its finance business became stable again.

By the late 1950s CCC was the largest commercial finance company in the United States, with annual volume at nearly $1 billion at ten to 15 percent interest. But despite the rising volume of the consumer credit business, CCC was becoming less profitable. Competition had become cutthroat, and that, combined with the rising cost of capital, was hurting profits. Auto financing remained the core of the firm's business, at over 50 percent of its receivables. However, the automotive industry was notoriously cyclical, and CCC was up such against giants as General Motors Acceptance Corp. To broaden its appeal, the firm began moving into the leasing of equipment and autos, as well as personal loans and farm equipment and boat financing.

With commercial finance being hurt, CCC decided to diversify again, this time staying closer to its primary businesses. In 1956 it bought Dearborn Motors Credit Corp.—a financier of Ford tractors—from a group of Ford executives. CCC renamed the corporation Commercial Credit Equipment Corp. and began financing a full range of farm equipment. In 1958 it started a national drive to get financing business from boat dealers and manufacturers, and the following year it bought the long-term auto leases of Greyhound Rent-A-Car.

In the mid-1960s CCC's fortunes took a turn for the worse. Textile Banking lost $25 million in 1965 due to weak businesses it had bought earlier. The firm was vulnerable to fluctuations in interest rates because it acquired a large proportion of its funds through short-term borrowing. Interest rates were higher than they had been in decades, so CCC had to pay $14 million more for its money in 1966 than the year before. Nevertheless, the firm earned $25.4 million in 1965 on sales of $307.4 million. In 1966 Bertold Muecke was named CCC chairperson. Muecke revamped Textile Banking's management and sold off its unprofitable businesses. Its ten manufacturing companies had $170.7 million in sales, but profits of only $215,000.

By 1967 CCC had about 1,000 offices throughout the United States, and almost $500 million in outstanding personal loans. It had become the third–largest personal loan firm, behind Household Finance and Beneficial Finance, with over $3 billion in total assets and more than $2 billion in life insurance in force. Although the firm had plenty of cash, its stock was doing poorly, making it a tempting takeover target. Loews Theatres Inc. quietly began buying CCC stock, announcing a takeover attempt in April 1968 when it had acquired ten percent of the company. The board of CCC rejected the offer and began looking for a desirable merger candidate. After talks with several companies, CCC agreed to merge with Minneapolis-based Control Data Corp. Loews initially vowed to fight the merger, and a public fight ensued, which Control Data eventually won. CCC received Control Data shares worth $582 million.

Control Data was much smaller than CCC, earning $8.4 million in 1966 with only $350 million in assets. However, CCC was already financing and leasing computers, and Control Data had big plans to open a worldwide network of computer data centers, as well as sell and lease its computers. Control Data lacked the capital for this plan, and the two companies hoped they could be of mutual benefit to one another. CCC was to contribute capital and assist in the leasing of computers and in time-sharing operations.

CCC generally had a low profile during its years under the ownership of Control Data. The firm consolidated its leasing units in 1970 and formed a real estate finance unit the following year. In 1974 CCC formed an insurance division. It also bought 70 percent of France's Credit Français and formed a joint venture with Japan's Nippon Shinpan, a major consumer finance company. Beginning in the late 1970s the firm made a number of acquisitions including Gulf Insurance in 1976 and Great Western Loan & Trust in Texas in 1977. In 1981 CCC bought the Electronic Realty Association, a real estate franchising network.

Meanwhile the relationship between CCC and Control Data was eroding. Computers became rapidly less expensive and more powerful in the 1970s, and many corporations that had leased mainframes from Control Data began to buy their own computers. As this trend intensified, Control Data no longer needed CCC to help it with leasing. CCC also expanded into a wide area of financial services—too many, in the eyes of some critics. CCC opened a national bank based in Delaware, two state-chartered banks, and two savings and loans that offered mortgages, credit cards, and a variety of other services. It owned 21 percent of midsize brokerage Inter-Regional Financial Group Inc. Its business financing expanded to include vehicle and airplane leasing as well as life and casualty insurance. It lent a total of $577 million to foreign countries, about half of them in Latin America. Because of Control Data's large losses in the computer business, CCC lost its investment-grade credit rating, forcing it to pay more for its money.

Meanwhile Control Data used CCC resources to help it open a network of over 100 business centers, which offered data processing, consulting, and commercial loans to small businesses. The centers were expensive to run, consuming more than $100 million between 1983 and 1985. CCC began closing the centers by late 1984. It also transferred its ERA real estate brokerage to Control Data and began phasing out withdrawals at some of its savings and loans. This move caused a run at several Rhode Island offices. As a result of these problems, CCC had a 6.7 percent return on equity in 1984, half the industry average. CCC had become a drag on Control Data's earnings. In late 1984 Control Data tried to sell CCC but found no takers.

CCC was forced to sell more of its peripheral businesses and pay down its debt. Thereafter, the company began regaining its health, earning about $80 million in 1985 on revenue of about $1.1 billion. The firm had $5 billion in assets. However, CCC found a buyer in September 1986, when Sanford I. Weill became chair and chief executive and took the company public. Weill was a well-known Wall Street figure who had built securities giant Shearson Lehman Brothers and been president of American Express Co. Control Data reduced its stake in CCC to about 20 percent while Weill and other CCC executives bought ten percent. The remaining 70 percent was sold to investors in a public stock offering.

Weill brought a group of experienced finance executives with him to CCC, paying them less than they had earned elsewhere but rewarding them with CCC stock. The new management took CCC out of life insurance, vehicle leasing, and overseas lending, and tripled operating profits within a year. In September 1987 CCC bought back Control Data's remaining stake for $22 per share.

In 1988 Weill used the rejuvenated CCC as a springboard to buy Primerica Corp. Primerica's stockholders were given CCC shares on a one-for-one trade. Because of a difference in dividends, Primerica holders were also given $7 per share in cash. The total price was $1.54 billion. Primerica owned 54 percent of the new company but only four of 15 seats on the board of directors. Although CCC was the buying company, the Primerica name was kept as the name of the new company. CCC became a Primerica subsidiary, the leading component of Primerica's consumer services division. CCC's 1988 profits were $161.8 million on sales of $943.7 million.

By 1989 CCC had 490 offices in 29 states and $3.4 billion in receivables. Weill continued to make changes to strengthen its financial performance, tightening underwriting criteria and monitoring loans through more sophisticated systems. Greater emphasis was placed on collecting loans and resolving problems. In April 1989 the firm acquired Action Data Services, a data processing supplier, partly to do in-house data processing. In late 1989 CCC acquired the branch offices and loan portfolio of Barclays American Financial for $1.35 billion. Barclays, based in Charlotte, North Carolina, was a branch of Barclays Bank PLC that specialized in consumer loans and home equity lending. The acquisition, which brought 220 offices in 29 states and $1.3 billion of receivables, was seen as increasing CCC's loan portfolio by 40 percent at a reasonable price. While Barclays offices that overlapped with CCC's were closed, the purchase brought CCC back into the western United States, which it had left during the consolidation of 1985. The firm had about $190 million in profits for the year.

In 1991 CCC bought Landmark Financial Services Inc., the consumer finance branch of MNC Financial, for about $370 million. By the end of 1992 CCC had 695 branch offices in 39 states and was planning to open 50 more offices during the next year. Newer offices were being opened with staffs of only two or three, verses four or five for older offices, and used one-third less space. These and other cost control efforts had brought operating expenses down to 4.28 percent of average receivables. The branch office network used a goal system that encouraged mangers to treat their office like their own business, giving them control over revenues and expenses. Because they were more aware of the conditions of a local economy, they were given flexibility in determining if customers met CCC's credit requirements. Top performing managers were given large bonuses.

In 1993 CCC introduced a new computer-based branch information system called Maestro. The system automated point-of-sale marketing and credit evaluations, allowing branches to quickly determine which products a given customer was qualified for. Prior to that time, customer data was written on forms and credit checks were done by telephone and mail.

Further Reading:

Bartlett, Sarah, ''Sandy Weill Is Doing Just Fine on Main Street, Thank You,'' *Business Week,* September 21, 1987.

Bianco, Anthony, ''Commercial Credit Has a Hot New Asset: Sandy Weill,'' *Business Week,* September 29, 1986.

''Commercial Credit Goes Afield,'' *Business Week,* March 5, 1960.

Houston, Patrick, ''An Ugly Duckling Becomes Control Data's Swan,'' *Business Week,* July 8, 1985.

Keller, John J., ''Primerica's Commercial Credit to Buy Barclays Unit's Branches,'' *Wall Street Journal,* November 27, 1989.

Levy, Robert, ''Journey For Muecke,'' *Dun's Review,* December 1967.

''Marrying For Money,'' *Business Week,* June 22, 1968.

—Scott Lewis

U·S·A·/WORLDWIDE

Cone Mills Corporation

1201 Maple Street
Greensboro, North Carolina 27405
U.S.A.
(919) 379-6220
Fax: (919) 379-6832

Public Company
Incorporated: 1891 as the Cone Export and Commission
    Company
Employees: 7,800
Sales: $705.4 million
Stock Exchanges: New York
SICs: 2211 Broadwoven Fabric Mills—Cotton

The Cone Mills Corporation is the world's largest manufacturer
of denim fabric, and the United States' largest printer of home
furnishings fabrics. With a broad range of offerings, the company operates 12 plants, most of which are located in North
Carolina. Started by two brothers with a background in wholesale groceries, Cone grew steadily throughout its early years,
concentrating on the manufacture of denim for work clothes.
The competitive world textile industry caused the company to
begin making cutbacks in the late 1970s, and it moved to
diversify its product mix in order to maintain profitability.

Cone Mills was founded by Moses and Caesar Cone. They were
the two eldest sons of a Baltimore wholesale grocery merchant,
Herman Cone, who had immigrated to the United States from
Bavaria in the 1840s, changing his name from Kahn to what he
considered a more American spelling. In their teens, Cone's
sons worked with him in his store. By 1876, the business had
expanded to include tobacco and leather goods, and Moses and
Caesar had begun to travel the American southeast, taking
orders from merchants for their father's goods.

In their travels, the brothers had an opportunity to observe the
textile industry of the south. Beginning in the late 1880s, the
Cones made investments in three Southern cotton mills: the C.
E. Graham Manufacturing Company of Asheville, North Carolina, the Salisbury Cotton Mills, and the Minneola Manufacturing Company. All three of these factories used outmoded equipment to produce coarse, low quality plaids and sheeting. The
fabrics enjoyed a vogue as a result of their low cost, yet in
competition with the products of more modern Northern mills,
they sold slowly.

Convinced that there was a glut of coarse plaids on the market,
the Cone brothers convinced their own business partners, as
well as other Southern mill owners, to diversify their offerings.
The Cones assigned brand names to key products, and published guarantees of quality. With these steps, sales began to
rise. By 1890, the Cones had convinced 38 of the roughly 50
southern mill owners that they could benefit from hiring a
selling agency to market their products. Faced with declining
profits in their grocery business, Moses and Caesar, along with
their father and another brother, Julius, liquidated H. Cone &
Sons, in order to form the Cone Export & Commission Company in 1890. The enterprise was known facetiously by its
competitors as the "plaid trust." The brothers signed five-year
contracts with the mill owners to market their goods, at a five
percent commission.

With fundraising for the new business complete, Moses Cone
went to New York in 1891 to set up an office. Although as a
southerner he met with some hostility, he soon was able to
establish his place in the business community, and the company
was able to move to Worth Street, in the heart of the textile
industry. Soon, the Cones were able to sell more fabric than
they could provide, as mill owners left their selling syndicate.

The Cone brothers vowed to go into the fabric production
business themselves. Their plans to build two mills, one for
denim and one for flannel, were delayed by a financial panic in
1893, but within two years, the Cones had moved ahead,
constructing a denim mill on land they owned in Greensboro,
North Carolina. Since the plant was near its supply of raw
materials, the cotton fields of the South, the Cones named their
new factory the Proximity Cotton Mill, and set up a holding
company for this plant and the others in which they held an
interest called the Proximity Manufacturing Company. In 1896,
the first lengths of fabric rolled off the big looms at Proximity.
Caesar Cone felt that denim, a sturdy fabric for use in work
clothes, would be in constant demand as the United States
expanded and industrialized.

Just three years later, the Cones opened Revolution Mills, a
modern facility to weave soft cotton flannel. In 1902, a second
denim plant was under construction. Called White Oak, it was
named for the enormous tree that grew on its site. With ten
different warehouses for cotton and its own power plant, the
mill began turning out indigo blue denim by 1905. Moses Cone
died at age 51 in 1908, and his brother carried on the company,
opening a fourth mill, the Proximity Print Works, in 1912. This
facility was designed to "finish" or print cotton with multiple
colors, creating a type of cotton product new to the South.

More than just a workplace, the Cone mills became an entire
world for their employees, who were cared for in a paternalistic,
and some would say totalitarian, system by the mill owners. The
Cones built housing near their mills, both boarding houses and
single family homes, which made up segregated Cone villages.
Stores sold dairy products and meat produced on company
farms. For each village, the company built a school and donated
land for churches. Two mill YMCAs were built to provide
outlets for recreation, and the company also instituted a Welfare
Office, with social workers and nurses to look after its employees.

By 1913, the Proximity Manufacturing Company owned all or half interests in seven cotton production facilities. During the following year, the company paid both its first dividend, and its first income taxes. In 1915, the company began to produce denim fabric for Levi's jeans, opening up an important new market. With the coming of World War I in 1914, Cone products continued to be in demand, both by the allies overseas, and then, after 1917, by the American armed forces. In March of that year, Caesar Cone, the company's only living founder, died after a brief illness, and leadership of the company was turned over to his younger brothers, Julius and Bernard.

During the 1920s, as the American economy boomed in the "Jazz Age," the Cones undertook cautious expansion, as they converted from wartime practices back to civilian production. In 1920, the company bought the Salisbury Cotton Mills, which produced chambrays, coverts, ticking, and upholstery cloth. Further diversification came in 1925, when the Cone's New York distribution arm began marketing cotton blankets and felts produced by the Houston Textile Company of Texas. Over the next six years, the company gradually took over the Eno Cotton Mills of Hillsborough, North Carolina, which manufactured fine combed broadcloth for shirts.

In the late 1920s, the company also bought two gingham mills, the Cliffside Mill and Haynes Mill, which also had their own railroad to bring their products to the nearest main rail line. The Cones scrapped the mills' old box looms and installed terry-cloth manufacturing equipment, enabling the Cones to enter the towel market. In addition, the company bought a mill built on solid granite called the Granite Cotton Factory from a Greensboro bank. On the same property, Cone also established the Tabardrey Manufacturing Company.

With the stock market crash of 1929 and the ensuing Great Depression, the Cones refrained from any further expansion throughout most of the 1930s. The company did introduce two new cotton fabrics, a light-weight flannel called "flannelette," and a crepe called "Proximity Plisse." Despite the popularity these products enjoyed, the company was forced to curtail production at its plants as the Depression wore on. In a move that would bode well for the future, however, Cone introduced "deeptone" denim in 1936, a smoother, darker indigo fabric that was designed to appeal to wearers more than the earlier, rougher fabrics.

By 1941, Cone was on more secure financial footing, and the company acquired the Florence Mills and its subsidiary, the American Spinning Company. Further expansion was halted with the American entry into World War II, when wartime production goals were implemented. In addition to an accelerated output of denim, Cone found itself producing such unfamiliar items as camouflage cloth, tent cloth, and osnaburg, for use in sandbags.

Seventy percent of the output of the fabric mills of North Carolina was diverted to the defense effort during the war, and at its end, it was clear that the Cones' operations needed to undergo a reorganization to thrive in the newly competitive civilian market. Accordingly, in 1945, the company merged all its separate mill properties into the Proximity Manufacturing Company, and also dissolved the old Cone Export and Commis-sion Company, replacing it with a similar entity under the control of Proximity.

This move was followed in 1946 by the purchase of two more cotton mills, bringing to 16 the number of textile manufacturing facilities owned by Cone. In the next year, Cone branched out for the first time into synthetic fibers, purchasing a rayon plant next to one of its old cotton mills, and later adding a rayon spinning plant to up its production.

On the first day of 1948, Proximity's president announced that the company would change its name to Cone Mills Corporation. Further expansion followed this switch. In 1950, Cone merged with the Dwight Manufacturing Company, a producer of twills and drills located in Alabama, and in the following year, the company was purchased outright. Also in that year, Cone formed the Guilford Products Company, manufacturing cloth diapers to serve the growing market produced by the postwar baby boom.

In November, 1951, Cone made its largest organizational shift to date, selling stock to the public for the first time. In trading on the New York Stock Exchange, the company's shares were valued at $28.58. In the wake of the company's debut as a publicly traded enterprise, Cone moved to further consolidate its similar operations, and to diversify its activities to protect itself against weakness in demand for any one product. In 1952, the company purchased the Union Bleachery in Greenville, South Carolina. In doing so, Cone gained the first license for the "Sanforizing" process granted in the United States.

Despite the fact that denim pants were beginning to be worn by teenagers as fashion statements, as opposed to being worn exclusively by manual laborers, as a necessity, the demand for denim began to drop in the mid-1950s, causing Cone to look to development in its other areas of business for growth. The company began to emphasize its dyeing, printing, and finishing operations. Its flagship Proximity Cotton Mills was converted from the manufacture of denim, which was no longer in high demand, to the production of poplins, twills, and corduroy.

In 1957, Cone purchased three converting companies, and also moved further into the synthetics field, forming Spinco fabrics for blended and synthetic goods. Increasingly, the company found its market share threatened by products from other nations, where labor costs were lower. In response to this threat, in the following year, Cone stepped up its marketing efforts, and streamlined its manufacturing operations further, forming a finishing division to coordinate its various activities in that field. In addition, Cone inaugurated a Research and Development Department, to facilitate innovation in textile production. Overall, despite these efforts, the company's financial results throughout the 1950s were somewhat uneven.

In the 1960s, Cone began to diversify its operations further. In the first year of the decade, the company branched out into the decorative fabrics field, purchasing a controlling interest in John Wolf Textiles, which marketed fabrics for use in home furnishings. In the following year, Cone strengthened its presence in the furniture industry by organizing Olympic Products, which made polyurethane foam cushions and other foam products. This marked the company's first step outside the textile industry. In addition to this expansion in its activities, Cone broadened its geographical scope in 1961, buying an 11 percent interest in Fabrica Argentina de Alpargatas, which manufactured fabric, shoes, and other consumer goods in Brazil, Argentina, and Uruguay.

As a result of cotton pricing structures imposed by the federal government, Cone found itself losing its competitive edge in pricing for all-cotton fabrics to foreign producers. To combat this trend, the company began to increase the amount of synthetic fibers that it used in the fabrics it wove. These synthetic blends resulted in the introduction of stretch fabrics in 1962, and permanent press fabrics in 1964. In the following year, the company made a major shift in emphasis from all-cotton products to those made from a mix of cotton and synthetic fibers. These fabrics, which were used for newly fashionable casual and leisure-wear clothes, brought a higher price than simple cotton. Cone eventually offered more than 170 different blended cotton and synthetic products.

By the end of the decade, however, Cone had also seen a resurgence in the demand for its first product, denim, as jeans became a staple among the baby boom generation, evolving from functional work clothes to a fashion item. The extent of denim's domination of the youth fashion market was demonstrated in 1969, when Cone's denim warehouse at its White Oak plant was flooded after a torrential downpour fell on Greensboro. Faced with the task of washing and dying vast amounts of fabric, the company decided, at the suggestion of one of its marketing employees, to run the damaged fabric through a bleach solution while restoring it, to randomly remove its indigo dye. The resulting product, dubbed "pinto wash" denim, touched off a fashion fad. As further evidence of denim's popularity, Cone's Proximity Cotton Mills were converted back to their original function, the manufacture of denim, in 1970, to meet the growing demand. In addition, the company was producing a growing quantity of corduroy, as this fabric became a popular fashion item.

Cone continued to purchase companies that fit into its existing operations, adding a cushion manufacturer, the Prelude Company, in 1970. By the following year, however, it had become clear that some divisions of the company were not profitable, and Cone shut down two weak operations, a blanket plant in Houston, and the John Wolf Apparel Fabrics Division.

In 1972, Cone expanded its program to sell off unused real estate that the company had acquired over the years, buying the Cornwallis Development Company, a real estate developer, which became a separate Cone division. This company would eventually profitably develop over 1,000 acres of land in the Greensboro area.

Throughout the 1970s, Cone struggled against an industry-wide tide of cheap imported fabrics, which worked to keep profits down. The company relied heavily on its two main products, denim and corduroy, which enjoyed continuing fashion popularity. In 1974, Cone opened a new denim factory at its Cliffside plant. In 1975, the company embarked upon a nine-year program of plant modernization that was designed to make operations as efficient as possible, so that costs could be kept low.

Early in the 1980s, Cone entered another new market when it purchased the Chemical Chair House company, which manufactured molded urethane foam for use in the furniture and transportation industries. After changing its acquisition's name to Conitron, Cone built a new urethane plant for this company in Trinity, North Carolina. In the following year, Cone added to its polyurethane plant holdings when it purchased Ragan Hardware to add to its Olympic Division.

In 1983, Cone became a victim of the rage for corporate stock speculation when it became the object of a hostile takeover attempt by Western Pacific Industries. In response, the company engineered a leveraged buyout of all its outstanding stock, going private once again.

In further efforts to combat the impact of imported fabrics on its market, Cone joined with other American textile manufacturers to promote increased consumption of domestic products. "Crafted with Pride in the U.S.A." became the rallying cry for a public relations campaign designed to offset the impact of lower prices for imported products. Nevertheless, this factor, in combination with a loss in popularity for corduroy, caused Cone to close, convert, or sell ten of its mills in the years between 1977 and 1990. Such founding pillars of the company as the Proximity Cotton Mills and Print Works, the Revolution Mill, and the Minneola Mill shut their doors forever during this time.

In addition to these measures, Cone streamlined its operations, and turned its attention to quality improvement programs and customer service. And, in 1990, the company decided to move its Marketing Division to Greensboro. In the following year, Cone returned to the stock market, offering shares in the company in June, 1992. At the same time that it strengthened its financial standing through this move, Cone—continuing a strategy begun in late 1991—moved to shrink its operations, withdrawing from the corduroy manufacturing business, as well as other areas. This, along with increased sales and lower prices for cotton, resulted in a return to profitability for Cone as it moved into the mid-1990s. With its lengthy history and diversified operations, Cone appeared well suited to prosper in the competitive textiles market in the years ahead.

Further Reading:

A Century of Excellence: The History of Cone Mills, 1891 to 1991, Greensboro, NC: Cone Mills Corporation, 1991.

—Elizabeth Rourke

CONSOLIDATED PAPERS, INC.

Consolidated Papers, Inc.

P.O. Box 8050
Wisconsin Rapids, Wisconsin 54495
U.S.A.
(715) 422-3111
Fax: (715) 422-3469

Public Company
Incorporated: 1894 as Consolidated Water Power Company
Employees: 4,937
Sales: $904.23 million
Stock Exchanges: OTC
SICs: 2671 Paper Coated & Laminated—Packaging; 2621
   Paper Mills

Consolidated Papers, Inc., is a leading producer of coated printing papers for the printed communications industry that operates more than 60,000 printing and publishing establishments in the United States and Canada. Coated printing papers, also called enamel papers, are specially finished, glazed papers used for such things as magazines, brochures, and corporate annual reports, as well as catalogs, newspaper inserts, and direct mailings. Focusing on this specialty paper has insulated Consolidated from some of the factors that have impacted the paper industry in the past decade. However, the company did fall prey to the advertising recession of the late 1980s and early 1990s, which affected magazine publishing in particular. Consolidated is also a leading manufacturer of lightweight coated and specialty papers used in food packaging and labeling. Other products include custom-designed corrugated displays and containers and paperboard products.

In 1894, several small water power concerns on the Wisconsin River organized to form the Consolidated Water Power Company. Eight years later, the company expanded its operations to include the manufacturing of paper, changing its name to Consolidated Water Power & Paper Company. Consolidated started up the world's first electrically powered paper machines in 1904. Over the next decade, the company manufactured newsprint and wallpaper, as well as power. Expansions included the acquisition of Biron Division in 1911 and Interlake Division in Appleton, Wisconsin, in 1916. By 1919, the company had constructed a hydroelectric plant and paper mill in order to manufacture tissue, waxing, and specialty papers.

With the acquisition of Newaygo Timber Company, Limited in 1920, Consolidated grew to include timberlands acreage in Ontario, Canada. The previously acquired Biron division was converted in 1929—along with the Wisconsin Rapids division—to produce book and writing papers.

Emmett Hurst launched the company's forestry program in 1930. Five years later, Consolidated developed and introduced the Consolidated Massey coater. This revolutionized the industry by producing the first coated paper manufactured by a single high-speed operation. Over the next seven years, Consolidated converted five paper machines to the high-speed coating process and began to focus on the production of coated papers.

In addition to the coating technology, Consolidated developed an exceptionally strong plastics material in 1943. During World War II, in order to produce aircraft materials, the company formed a Plastic Division, which later became Consoweld Corporation. In 1945, the company acquired Wisconsin River Division, converting it to produce coated printing papers. The merger with Ahdawagam Paper Products Company in 1948 expanded Consolidated's product line to include paperboard containers and cartons.

Throughout the 1950s, Consolidated concentrated on the sale and production of its coated papers, introducing a new line of coated papers and launching a major national advertising program. In 1959, a new research & development center was completed. Another groundbreaking invention in paper-coating technology came in 1961, with the Dip Roll Blade coater. At this point, the company was undergoing conversion from roll to blade coating. This same year marked the one millionth ton of enamel papers sold by Consolidated's merchants. In 1962, the company named was changed to the one it holds today: Consolidated Papers, Inc.

Toward the end of the 1960s, construction began on a $37 million kraft pulp mill and power complex. Kraft paper is a stronger grade of pulp that replaced sulfate. Consolidated purchased Castle Rock Container Company, a corrugated container plant, in 1970. The next decade reflected increased environmental as well as market considerations as the company began pouring its capital into modifications and expansions. In 1970 and 1971, the company put more than $1 million into primary wastewater treatment plants, and in 1972 announced plans for an $8.6 million treatment plant to serve the Wisconsin Rapids, Biron, and Kraft divisions. A pollution abatement program was completed that same year. In 1973 ground was broken for a $2.7 million sheet converting plant in Wisconsin and a $5.6 million lumber/chip complex in Ontario, Canada, which closed in 1984. The following year, Consolidated began a $12.8 million modification program at its Kraft Division to increase pulp capacity by 26,000 tons a year. In 1975, the company launched a $6 million boiler plant to burn coal and bark. Consolidated then broke ground for a $4 million secondary treatment plant.

Two years later, a $64.6 million papermaking expansion project was underway to increase enamel paper capacity by 95,000 tons per year and a new thermomechanical pulp system was begun at the Biron Division. Also in 1977, Consolidated introduced another frontrunner in paper-coating technology: the short-dwell-time applicator. This applicator is considered the progenitor of the current state-of-the-art in lightweight coating. Greater automation was introduced into various production aspects in 1978, such as high-speed computerized presses and an automatic splicer.

The 1980s were volatile years in the paper industry. The explosion in the use of computers and copying machines created a boom in the paper industry early in the decade. Consolidated's earnings benefited particularly with the increase in direct-mail advertising and color inserts in newspapers, which made use of the company's specialized lightweight coated papers. The company at this point had enjoyed steady, above-average profit margins and had become a solid leader in specialized papers. Consolidated started the 1980s with the construction of a new office building in Wisconsin Rapids and the celebration of its forestry program's 50th year. The company also acquired sole ownership of Consoweld Corporation that year and began a $1.5 million expansion program for that company. Consoweld was sold to LOF Plastics, Inc. in 1985.

In order to catch up with demand, Consolidated began a multimillion dollar expansion program in 1981, seeking to increase capacity of specialty coated papers by 24 percent. The following year, it began a $17 million Wisconsin Rapids Division expansion. In 1985, Consolidated celebrated its 50th year of manufacturing coated printing and specialty papers. At this point, the Wisconsin-based company was considered the world's largest producer of enamel papers. The company was also producing lightweight, coated specialty papers for packaging and labeling, in addition to more conventional corrugated containers—used for shipping large items such as refrigerators and televisions—and paperboard products.

While the company's manufacturing base was centralized in Wisconsin, Consolidated's timberland base spread across 670,00 acres of Wisconsin, Michigan, Minnesota, and Ontario. By 1985, the company was generating about 23 percent of its raw material requirements, a goal it had set for itself some six years prior, when management analyzed long-term fiber requirements against softwood availability. At that point, a softwood shortage was forecast for the upper Midwest by the year 2030—about the same time demand was expected to have doubled. To circumvent this shortage, Consolidated's timberlands division intensified all aspects of reforestation, including harvesting, site preparation, planting, seedling research, and production. A program was laid out which included the replanting of 2,000 acres annually for the first five years. By 1983, 3,500 acres were planted. The following year, 3,300 acres were planted. Most of the acreage was being converted from low-quality hardwoods to red pine—chosen for its preferred fiber and rapid growth—and the goal was to plant 50,000 acres by the year 2000. In 1985, however, some 7,000 acres were being harvested annually and that was still not meeting the growth rate.

In addition to these incentives to the timberlands division, the company was instituting a program to recycle sludge material from its Water Quality Center. Made up of natural materials used in the papermaking process, sludge was spread on commercial farmland as a combination fertilizer/soil amendment. This saved on landfill costs while improving soil fertility. The sludge—called ConsoGro—and its application was the result of a six-year research program conducted by Consolidated. Another environmentally sound breakthrough about this time was the addition of peroxide to the high-density storage stage of production in order to increase pulp brightness and output. This proved an innovative solution with the added benefit that hydrogen peroxide is environmentally safe.

In 1986, Consolidated's Biron mill won *Newsweek*'s "Mill of the Year" award for the second time in four years. The Biron Division was the focal point of Consolidated's largest capital project, an expansion investment of $215 million of internal cash flow. The result was a state-of-the-art coating plant. Company chairperson and CEO George Mead told *Pulp & Paper* magazine in 1987, "When I joined this industry, the general feeling was that companies our size did not have the muscle to keep up. They were thought to be inadequate in financing and in depth of skilled personnel. Many companies felt they had to become part of larger, more powerful organizations in order to survive. We have shown that this is not necessarily true."

The following year, Consolidated announced a $96.7 million capital expense program. This included a further $46 million expansion of pulp production at the Kraft Division. To be completed in 1989, the project was intended to increase chemical pulp production. Another $22 million was slated for improvements of the production of heavier coated free-sheet papers. Some of this money was also earmarked for further computerization of inventory.

Further expansion plans were announced in 1989 to produce top quality coated paper for annual reports and high-grade brochures. That same year the Paperboard Products Division added a seven-color press to its equipment, allowing it to produce high-quality, multicolor folding cartons. Diversifications such as these helped protect Consolidated from the rumblings in the industry caused by the recession as well as the fact that papermills everywhere had been running near capacity and fear of a shortage was setting in. Coated paper had proven to be a more profitable and steady business than commodity paper. The company's operating margin remained more than 20 percent in eight out of ten years between 1979 and 1989.

Being a largely family-run company had kept Consolidated small and disciplined. In 1992, nearly 30 percent of Consolidated's employees had been with the company for more than 20 years—a remarkable record of loyalty. In 1989, 41 percent of company stock was in the hands of one of its founder's descendants, including then chairperson George Mead. In the manner of a conservative, family-run company, Consolidated had generally avoided accumulating debt, opting instead to finance capital spending out of its own cash flow. And its growth was always on par with industry demands and internal manageability. However, all of the intensive expansion projects around this time resulted in a considerable long-term debt for the first time in Consolidated's history. As of 1992, Consolidated was generating sufficient cash to subtract from its debts, while still spending enough to keep its plants current and competitive.

Consolidated was also ahead of the landfill problems that plagued many industries in the late 1980s. The company's solid waste management program worked closely with consultants, regulatory agencies, and the community to develop a plan that included landfills on company-owned land as near to treatment plants as possible. Water quality and water renewal center landfills are also located on land near the treatment plants, which allows Consolidated to keep a close watch on the operations. Such environmental requirements have significantly affected Consolidated's profits in recent years. Between 1991 and 1993, the company spent $34.4 million in its Kraft Division alone for environmental improvements that brought it up to regulatory codes. Also, the increased demand for recycled fiber content in Consolidated's papers has introduced costly variables, as contamination of recycled fiber is a problem, and producing specialty papers of different weights with recycled pulp is a technological challenge.

In 1990, the development and expansion of wetland mitigation sites around these water quality and water renewal centers began. Consolidated also joined with the Wisconsin Department of Natural Resources to enhance wildlife management and habitat development on company-owned land adjacent to the Mead Wildlife Area. Company forestlands are managed as a source of pulpwood for papermaking, as well as a source of enjoyment to the public through hiking, hunting, and other recreation.

In 1991, Consolidated filed a patent infringement complaint against two companies that sold technology based on the short-dwell coater technology, which Consolidated had developed in 1977. Also named in the suit were several companies that licensed the paper-coating technology from the firms by which Consolidated claimed to be violated. This was a rough time for the entire coated paper industry as advertising in magazines—among the largest consumers of lightweight coated papers—plunged with the sustained economic downturn. Consolidated's sales were punished. The economy also affected the company's heavyweight coated paper profits.

In 1992, Mead announced he would step down from the position of CEO in October of 1993 while remaining chairperson.

President Patrick Brennan is to succeed Mead as CEO. Although *Business Week* declared 1992 paper industry earnings ''a nightmare,'' Consolidated appeared to be outlasting the soft economy and maintaining its spot in the Fortune 500 list.

Principal Subsidiaries: Consolidated Water Power Company; Newaygo Forest Products Limited.

Further Reading:

Bartocci, Stephen, ''Consolidated Mill Adds Peroxide to Boost Brightness, Maintain Stability,'' *Pulp & Paper,* November 1985, pp.147–149.

Coleman, Matthew, ''Primary/Secondary Sludge Recycled,'' *Pulp & Paper,* April 1985, pp. 130–131.

''Consolidated Papers,'' *Wall Street Journal,* November 3, 1992, p. B11.

''Consolidated Papers Claims Patent Violation on Coater,'' *Pulp & Paper,* October 1991, p. 31.

''Consolidated Papers Expands Pulp Capacity,'' *Pulp & Paper,* January 1988, p. 23.

Flanders, Lou, ''Screening Processes Introduced at MOTG-North Winter Meeting,'' *Pulp & Paper,* March 1991, pp. 114–115.

Griffin, Griff, ''Mechanized Site Prep Crews Lead Intensified Program,'' *Forest Industries,* April 1985, pp. 38–40.

Harrison, Andy, ''New Technology Solves Permitting Problems for Landfill Expansion,'' *Pulp & Paper,* September 1989, pp. 213–218.

Koncel, Jerome, ''Quality Emphasized in All Aspects of Pulping Operations,'' *Paper Trade Journal,* January 1986, p. 28.

Lurie, Sidney, ''It's the Time to Think Big,'' *Financial World,* March 7–20, 1984, p. 6.

McGough, Robert, ''Consolidated Papers: Family Knows Best,'' *Financial World,* May 16, 1989, p. 15.

Smith, Kenneth, ''Consolidated Paper's Biron 26 LWC Paper Machine Starts Up Smoothly,'' *Pulp & Paper,* July 1987, pp. 113–115.

Stowall, Robert, ''A World Turned Upside Down,'' *Financial World,* February 7, 1989, p. 99.

—Carol I. Keeley

Cooper Tire & Rubber Company

Lima & Western Avenues
Findlay, Ohio 45840
U.S.A.
(419) 423-1321
Fax: (419) 424-4108

Public Company
Incorporated: 1960
Employees: 7,207
Sales: $1.17 billion
Stock Exchanges: Chicago New York Pittsburgh
SICs: 3011 Tires & Inner Tubes; 3069 Fabricated Rubber
    Products Nec; 3052 Rubber Plastics Hose & Belting; 3714
    Motor Vehicle Parts and Accessories; 3061 Mechanical
    Rubber Goods

Cooper Tire & Rubber Company ranks among the top ten tiremakers in the world and is one of only two independent tire manufacturers in the United States. The company has developed a niche market within a huge commodity by concentrating on the manufacture of replacement tires. Its products are marketed through independent dealers and distributors under two brands, Cooper and Falls Mastercraft. The company also makes tires for several private label marketers. Cooper surpassed $1 billion annual sales for the first time in 1991, and although it is one of the smaller major tire companies, its earnings have lead the industry: the company has paid dividends every year since 1950, and has increased the dividend annually since 1980. While passenger car and truck tires constitute the majority of Cooper's production, the company is also involved in the manufacture of such engineered automotive products as vibration control devices, window and door sealing systems, hoses, and adjustable seating devices that provide lumbar support for passenger cars. Cooper is also one of the world's largest inner tube producers. Manufacturing is accomplished at ten plants in Ohio, Mississippi, Arkansas, Georgia, Indiana, and Mexico.

In 1914, brothers-in-law John F. Schaefer and Claude E. Hart bought the M and M Manufacturing Company in Akron, Ohio. Schaefer and Hart entered the industry in the midst of a period of vigorous growth; between 1910 and 1916, tire production doubled every two years. And as real incomes increased over the decade, and the Ford Motor Company introduced its more affordable Model T, the demand for tires increased. Tire manu-

facturers increased capacity, designed new machinery, and promoted their new products.

At that time, Ohio was a hub of tire manufacturing: one-third of the United States' 134 tire companies were located in the state, and in the early decades of the twentieth century, Akron alone supplied one-third of the country's rubber goods. In this "rubber capital of the world," M and M Manufacturing produced tire patches, cement, and repair kits. These products were in demand during the early years of the automotive tire industry because the first pneumatic tires were easily punctured. Poor tire quality also prompted consumers to seek rebuilt tires, and in 1915, Schaefer and Hart purchased a tire rebuilding business, The Giant Tire & Rubber Company, also in Akron.

In 1917, the Giant Tire & Rubber operations, including its staff of 29, were moved to Findlay, Ohio, into buildings abandoned by the failed Toledo Findlay Tire Company. Also that year Ira J. Cooper, whose name would later come to represent the company, joined Giant's board of directors. Fire destroyed the main building of the Giant plant in 1919, but reconstruction of a new, single story plant began immediately. As Giant rebuilt and continued to grow, Cooper became involved in forming his own company to manufacture new tires, The Cooper Corporation, which began operations in 1920. As founder, Cooper emphasized dedication to three principles: good merchandise, fair play, and a square deal. This "Cooper Creed" would serve as a corporate doctrine for many years to come.

The tire industry underwent several changes during the 1920s. New tire and rim designs made it easier for consumers to replace worn or punctured tires, and improved durability meant they would have to do so less often. Lower pressure tires developed during the decade improved comfort and road handling. Technological advances in the manufacturing process helped larger companies gain economies of scale that made them more competitive and promoted a consolidation of the industry in the 1920s and 1930s.

In 1930, The Giant Tire Company and The Cooper Corporation merged with the Falls Rubber Company of Cuyahoga Falls, Ohio, to form the Master Tire & Rubber Company. Falls had been a minor tire manufacturer established in the 1910s. Within one year, production at the three plants totaled 2,850 tires per day. At that time, the company marketed tires under several brand names, including Falls, Giant, Sterchi, Hoover, Savage, Linco, Williams, Swinehart, Tigerfoot, and Englert. Downsizing in the 1930s brought all tire operations to Findlay by 1936.

Ira J. Cooper died in 1941, the first year the Cooper oval trademark was registered and used. In those early years of the brand's identification, the logo also included a banner proclaiming the tires' "armored-cord" construction. The present red, white, and blue logo is one of the most easily recognized emblems in the tire industry.

During World War II company manufactured pontoons, landing boats, waterproof bags and camouflage items, inflatable barges, life jackets and tank decoys, and, of course, tires, to benefit the Allied effort. The company's contribution to the war effort was acknowledged in 1945 by the armed forces in a special ceremony bestowing the Army-Navy "E" Award. Soon after the war, the company name was officially changed to Cooper Tire & Rubber Company, in recognition of Cooper's contribution to Master Tire & Rubber.

The postwar era heralded expansion at Cooper and in the industry as a whole. Many factors contributed to the growth of the business. Increasing disposable income facilitated extensive car ownership. The expansion of the interstate highway system and suburbanization in the postwar era meant more wear and tear on tires, which in turn increased demand for replacement tires. Furthermore, rail transportation was replaced by buses, taxis, and trucks for local and long-distance needs. In 1956 Cooper purchased a plant from the Dismuke Tire and Rubber Company in Clarksdale, Mississippi. The refurbished plant helped Cooper meet demand for tubes and tread rubber.

Between 1947 and 1964, Cooper Tire developed its own national wholesaling system. The company strengthened its ability to supply private brand customers and earned retailer loyalty by pledging not to open its own sales outlets. This marketing scheme simultaneously enabled Cooper to avoid the vagaries of the retail market.

Cooper went public in 1960. The distribution of shares facilitated another decade of growth for the company. Also that year a plant at Auburn, Indiana, where all automotive and custom engineered rubber parts were produced, was acquired. In 1964 an industrial rubber products division was established as a separate corporation known as Cooper Industrial Products, Inc. A second industrial products plant near El Dorado, Arkansas, was acquired to expand those operations.

Capital improvements at the corporate headquarters during the 1960s included a new warehouse, which made operations at the Findlay plant more efficient. A research and engineering building was added to the location in 1964 to accommodate testing, laboratories, tire design, engineering, and sales training operations. Also that year, the company completed the first phase of construction on its new tire plant in Texarkana, Arkansas.

One year later, production facilities at the Texarkana, El Dorado, Auburn, and Clarksdale plants were expanded. Original outlets in Los Angeles and Atlanta were replaced with new and enlarged Cooper factory branches. Before the decade was ended, the Texarkana plant was expanded and a modernization plan was completed. The modernization included installation of one of the first cold feed tread tire tubers in the industry and inauguration of one of the largest 27 Banburys in the tire business.

In the 1970s, Cooper strove to convert from bias-ply to radial tire manufacture. Bias tires had been produced by placing cords in rubberized fabric at an angle of 25 to 40 degrees to the direction traveled. Radial tires were first conceived in 1913, but the first practical application of the idea was not achieved until 1948. Radial assembly called for cords or belts that were arranged at a 90 degree angle to the direction traveled. Advantages of radial construction included: improved wear (from an average of 23,000 to 40,000 miles), improved handling, and lower fuel consumption. The disadvantages, however, prohibited many companies from making the conversion until the 1970s. They included more complex and time-consuming production requirements, incompatibility with bias tires on the

same vehicle, and diminished cushioning. For a brief period, many manufacturers in the industry compromised by introducing a bias-belted tire, but steel-belted radials became the norm in the late 1970s. Once the core of the tire industry, the bias-ply market had shrunk almost 75 percent by 1977.

Cooper completed research and development of its own radial tire manufacturing equipment and in-house product testing in 1973, and began full-scale production of steel-belted radial passenger tires at the Findlay and Texarkana plants the following year. During this time, Cooper purchased a plant in Bowling Green, Ohio, for the manufacture of reinforced hose and extruded rubber products. Within three years, the plant was upgraded to produce rubber trunk, car door, window, and sunroof seals.

Near the end of the decade, the United States government imposed the Uniform Tire Quality Grading System (UTQGS) to regulate the manufacture and labeling of bias and belted tires to help consumers in comparative shopping for tires. A voluntary system of tire grading had been proposed by the National Highway Traffic Safety Administration and accepted by the Rubber Manufacturers Association in 1966, but the guidelines were expensive and hard to enforce. The federal government advanced regulations several times during the 1970s, but grading did not begin until 1979 for bias-belted tires and 1980 for radial tires.

The 1980s were years of significant change for Cooper Tire and the tire industry overall. Many American manufacturers scrambled to lower production capacity as the domestic market became saturated. From 1979 to 1987, a total of 23 U.S. plants were closed in the rush to downsize. Ironically, some of the industry's contraction could be attributed to successful technological advances that produced radial tires that withstood three times more mileage than previous models.

But while many of the world's original equipment tire manufacturers strove to consolidate in the face of steadily falling automobile sales, Cooper executives calmly delineated strategies for continued growth and even expansion of production. Cooper based its plans on several consistent factors that president and chief operating officer Ivan Gorr described in a 1987 study. First, Cooper executives observed that there was as yet no other form of personal transportation that could provide the speed and convenience of the automobile, and therefore, no alternatives for the pneumatic tire. Planners at Cooper also noticed that, as auto manufacturing in the United States improved in the 1970s, consumers kept their cars longer. Demand for replacement tires grew in proportion to the average age of cars.

So as its competitors deserted plants, Cooper bought them and upgraded them. By overhauling older facilities, Cooper added capacity for one-third the cost of building new ones. In 1981, the Texarkana plant reached a production record of over five million tires. The following year, a three-phase expansion project at Texarkana was undertaken, and three building additions at the Findlay plant were completed. Production capacity continued to increase with the purchase of a radial tire plant at Tupelo, Mississippi, and even more expansion at the Findlay plant.

By 1983, Cooper was ranked among the "Fortune 500" register of America's largest industrial companies, and a year later net sales exceeded $500 million. Over the next two years, Cooper made its first foreign acquisition, Rio Grande Servaas, S.A. de C.V., in Piedras Negras, Mexico, a manufacturer of inner tubes. The Cooper sales force was honored in the 1980s with the designation "best in the rubber industry" by *Sales & Marketing Management Magazine's* annual survey of industry executives. And in 1985, Cooper Tire & Rubber Company was enumerated among *The 101 Best Performing Companies in America.*

Research and development at Cooper were enhanced by several capital investments during the decade. A technical center for design, research and development, and testing was completed in 1984 at the Auburn, Indiana, engineered products plant. The following year saw the completion of an addition to Findlay's Research and Engineering complex. The expansion facilitated increased in-house tire testing. A third addition enhanced the Findlay facility in 1988.

Distribution was also improved during the 1980s, with centers opening or expanding in Moraine, Ohio; Atlanta, Georgia; and Tacoma, Washington. Cooper warehousing capacity totaled 3.2 million tires by mid-decade. By the end of the 1980s, distribution centers at Findlay and Moraine were granted foreign trade subzone status from the United States Department of Commerce. The designation diminished and suspended Cooper's payment of duty on imported raw materials.

As the company celebrated its 75th anniversary, Cooper's emphasis on the replacement tire market was rewarded. Statistics showed that the replacement tire market was three times larger than the original equipment market, and had grown much faster over the decade. Investors appreciated the company's performance as well, and Cooper's stock rose 6,800 percent during the 1980s. And with a per share price that amounted to fourteen times earnings, Cooper was insulated from takeover threats.

During the 1980s, foreign competitors took over six of the United States' largest tiremakers. By early 1990, six companies controlled 80 percent of the free world's capacity for tire production after the scramble for market share. The acquiring corporations reasoned that their size would provide bargaining power with American automakers as well as economies of scale. However, domestic tire prices remained stuck at 1985 levels.

Cooper's capital investments paid off in the 1990s. The company's efficient means of production propelled the highest gross profit margins in the industry at 33 percent. When larger competitors turned to the replacement market and tried to undercut Cooper's prices, those high margins gave the company leeway to join in the price wars.

Despite a lingering U.S. recession, Cooper's net sales topped the $1 billion mark in 1991, and the company added almost a quarter of a billion more the following year. Capital investments continued to grow in the 1990s: the company purchased a 1.8 million square foot tire manufacturing plant in Albany, Georgia, in 1990, expanded its Findlay location by a total of 299,000 square feet, and expanded the Bowling Green facility. Cooper reached a record level of $110.2 million in capital investments in 1992.

Despite these large cash outlays, the company maintains an enviable debt-to-equity ratio of one to ten. As one of the most efficient and profitable tire manufacturers in the world, Cooper Tire & Rubber Company hopes to capture more of the market for engineered products and maintain its reputation for high-quality production.

Further Reading:

Abelson, Reed, "Companies to Watch: Cooper Tire & Rubber," *Fortune,* October 9, 1989, p. 82.

Blado, Anthony, "Cooper Tire: Under Some Pressure," *Financial World,* July 10, 1990, p. 18.

Bremner, Brian, and Zachary Schiller, "Three Who Bucked the Urge to Merge—and Prospered," *Business Week,* October 14, 1991, p. 94.

Byrne, Harlan S., "Cooper Tire & Rubber: Ohio Company Sets the Pace in the Replacement Market," *Barron's,* November 26, 1990, p. 39.

Gorr, Ivan, "Cooper Tire: Successful Adaptation in a Changing Industry," *Journal of Business Strategy,* Winter 1987, pp. 83–86.

"Our History," Cooper Tire & Rubber Company, 1993.

Schiller, Zachary, "Why Tiremakers Are Still Spinning Their Wheels," *Business Week,* February 26, 1990, pp. 62–3.

"The Tire Industry's Costly Obsession with Size," *Economist,* June 8, 1991, pp. 65–66.

—April S. Dougal

COSMAIR, INC.

Cosmair, Inc.

575 Fifth Avenue
New York, New York 10017
U.S.A.
(212) 818-1500
Fax: (212) 984-4056

Private Company
Incorporated: 1953
Employees: Over 3,800
Sales: $1.2 billion
SICs: 2844 Toilet Preparations

Cosmair, Inc. manufactures and markets a wide range of cosmetics, hair preparations, and perfumes as the sole United States licensee of France's cosmetic mogul, L'Oréal S.A. It has grown to become a power in the beauty products industry through marketing expertise, research and development, and a vast distribution network. The company's products are widely accepted and can be found in beauty salons, department stores, specialty stores, drug stores, and mass merchandising outlets across the United States.

Cosmair was founded in 1953 as a distributor of L'Oréal hair styling preparations to American beauty salons. It was formed as a U.S. licensee between Jacques Corrèze, who was Cosmair's chairman for 38 years, and L'Oréal. Cosmair's 20 employees produced and distributed hair care preparations to U.S. beauty parlors, allowing American women to use the same hair coloring formulas that their French counterparts had utilized since 1907. By the end of the 1960s, Cosmair had firmly established a position in the American market. It began marketing French designer Guy Laroche's perfume line in 1966, and in 1967 it became the U.S. licensee for Lancôme, a respected line of color cosmetics, fragrances, sun products, and skin treatments.

Lancôme was initially developed in 1935 by French fragrance merchant Armand Petitjean, who coined the name and the product's rose logo after an excursion to ancient Le Chateau de Lancôme in France. The line, known for its quality and elegent packaging, has remained one of Cosmair's strongest divisions. Lancôme's product names, printed in both English and French, created a French mystique popular with upscale buyers. In addition, Cosmair rigorously trained its counter salespeople to maintain Lancôme's reputation as a competitive, prestigious brand. The salespeople built a broad base of loyal clientele by recommending Lancôme products for specific cosmetic problems and conducting in-store "mini-facials" to demonstrate the Lancôme product line. Customers were also given samples of skin care and cosmetics as "promotional gifts-with-purchase." Lancôme's reputation was also enhanced by the opening of the Institut de Beauté in 1977. Based on L'Oréal's original Parisian Institut founded in 1936, the premier "salon" provided expert skin applications and treatments. Although Lancôme was unprofitable in America from 1971 to 1978, the division experienced meteoric growth in the following years "growing in volume at the rate of 40%-50% a year" as reported in *Barron's* by Gigi Mahon.

In the 1970s Cosmair successfully expanded into a broader segment of the American hair care market, turning to consumers who wanted hair care and hair color mixtures that could be applied at home. The L'Oréal Hair Care Division debuted a major new product line called Préférence with the now famous slogan, "Because you're worth it." Préférence was heavily advertised and marketed towards potential buyers in food, drug, and large discount stores. Later the brands Excellence and Colorations—hair care, permanent wave, and hair colorant supplies—were added and marketed under the Professional Salon group.

L'Oréal Chairman and CEO Francois Dalle, the well-known French entrepreneur, appointed Lindsay Owen-Jones as President and CEO of Cosmair in 1981. Owen-Jones developed a new vision of growth for Cosmair based on his marketing and strategic acumen, and proved a primary force in shaping the company into the successful organization it is today. Cosmair experienced unprecedented changes in the 1980s, and sales tripled over the course of four years to $600 million by 1984.

The L'Oréal Cosmetics Division was based on a group of existing products: nail polishes and lipsticks. These soon grew to include a wide range of color cosmetic products, each priced to sell at $6. Anaïs Anaïs was formulated in 1981 by another Frenchman, Jean Cacharel, who was attempting to duplicate the fragrance of the scarce Madonna Lily. Another brand, Drakkar Noir, by Guy Laroche, became a top seller in men's fragrances by 1984 with a marketing campaign that targeted younger male consumers via the advertising slogan, "Feel the power." Italian stylist Georgio Armani's fragrances were enlisted in 1984, as well as those of chic designer Paloma Picasso, daughter of the famous painter Pablo Picasso.

In 1983 Cosmair staged a coup that dramatically boosted its standing within the industry. As it planned the introduction of a pioneering hair styling foam called "mousse," the company bought up the entire supply of customized aerosol cans available in Europe. This move left Cosmair in a very advantageous position six months later when it debuted its Free Hold Styling Mousse, which was eventually named "Product of the Year" by *Fortune* magazine. Challengers were prevented from competing in the styling mousse market for several months until the inventories of aerosol cans could be fortified. As a result, by 1985 Cosmair dominated the profitable $150 million U.S. mousse market with 40 percent of the market share.

Cosmair also gained notoriety in 1984 with its purchase of Warner Cosmetics, a subsidiary of Warner Communications, for $146 million. Warner Cosmetics produced cosmetics and fragrances under the brand names of designers Ralph Lauren (Lauren, Chaps, and Polo), Gloria Vanderbilt (Vanderbilt) and Paloma Picasso (Paloma Picasso). The management of both Cosmair and Warner Cosmetics foresaw advantages in the merger. As reported by Catherine Ellis Hunter in *Drug & Cosmetics Industry,* the gains included "international distribution and expert research facilities for Warner, marketing creativity and domestic know-how in fragrance marketing for Cosmair." By 1985 Vanderbilt was the top selling women's fragrance in America.

In 1985 Cosmair brought France's most successful skin care line, Biotherm, to the United States. International in flair, Biotherm's forte was in reputable body, face, and sun commodities displayed in prestigious department and specialty stores. Biotherm products have included Symbiose Naturel, a daily treatment that features a "natural mineral enzyme" as an anti-aging protectant; Contour Total, a cream or gel to fight cellulite; Bioperfection, a liposome formulated treatment makeup with natural colors; Aqualogic, an emollient designed to aid skin in finding its correct moisture level; and Actif Nuit, an overnight facial skin cream.

Biotherm focused its advertising efforts on women between the ages of 30 and 45 through advertisements in traditional beauty magazines such as *Elle, Harper's Bazaar, Glamour,* and *Vogue.* Later on in the decade Cosmair began distributing the brands Biologics 30, 40, and 50, targeted to women of those specific ages. Biotherm also created a club for purchasers, Centre Biotherm. With no purchase required, consumers could sign up at the department store counter to receive newsletters and obtain discounts. Another service, Biotherm's "Skin Fitness Program," gave consumers private skin consultations, pinpointing skin care problems. In 1992 Cosmair vigorously cut its Biotherm distribution in an attempt to make it more price competitive and, as stated by Biotherm's general manager in *Women's Wear Daily,* to make Biotherm pricing "more affordable" and appealing to a broader range of clientele.

In 1985 L'Oréal had a 24 percent market share (in dollars) compared to competitor Clairol's 58 percent in the realm of hair coloring. The following year Cosmair debuted the Stu-Stu-Studio product line that allowed purchasers young and old to style their hair "anyway they liked it." The product line of spritzes, sprays, styling gels, and mousses was chicly packaged into "a virtual styling tool box," as reported in a company brochure. The company also expanded its upscale L'Oréal cosmetic line into mass-merchandising outlets such as drugstore chains, and set the price 20 to 30 percent higher than the prices of the products of competitors.

To create and promote its numerous new products Cosmair far outspent the industry average; this had a negative impact on profits. According to William Meyers in *The New York Times,* "Cosmair's strong performance notwithstanding, its heavy spending on research, advertising and promotion has kept it from turning in blockbuster profits.... Cosmair's advertising and promotion budgets, analysts say, total about $230 million, or 35 percent of sales, higher than the industry norm of about 25 percent." In 1987 the L'Oréal Cosmetics Division made the decision to cut product distribution by almost 3,500 stores to

concentrate on major stores and to acquire the significant shelf space needed to install their new modern display system. Sales from 1985 to 1987 fell significantly. The move reduced the importance of promotional activities and "refocused on basic business, holding off new-product launches," noted Pat Sloan in *Advertising Age.*

Cosmair was also troubled by so called "knockoff fragrances," as reported in *Advertising Age,* where "the practice of linking a product with an established product marketed by another company" became very commonplace in the industry. In 1986 Cosmair had won a temporary restraining order against S.C. Johnson Co. that prohibited the distribution of its new L'Envie shampoos and conditioners. L'Envie, produced by the Agree shampoo and conditioner line, printed Cosmair's Vanderbilt fragrance title on the containers. Cosmair declared trademark infringement and unfair competition as reasons for the court order. Although Johnson claimed to be solely in the shampoo and conditioner selling business, Cosmair charged that its marketing strategies copied those of "knockoff-fragrance marketers" by printing misleading material on the wrapping. Cosmair also accused Johnson of being intentionally aware of and cashing in on "the reputation and goodwill of Cosmair's Vanderbilt brand." The lawsuit was later dropped when both companies agreed on new labeling and ad disclaimers. Rather than "inspired by," Johnson was forced to use the phrase, "A fragrance similar to Vanderbilt perfume."

Product innovation rebounded from the late 1980s into the early 1990s. The L'Oréal Cosmetics Division again became profitable in 1988, largely due to the introduction of Lash-Out Lash Extending Mascara. Lash-Out became the number one mascara seller in the United States that year. Other new cosmetic products included such brands as Mattique Illuminating Matte Foundation, Colour Supreme LongWearable Lipstick, Splash Out (a waterproof version of Lash-Out mascara) and Hydra Perfecte Protective Hydrating Makeup.

In fragrances, Glorious was introduced as an offshoot of Vanderbilt in 1987. Paloma Picasso's sophisticated bath-fragrance line and designer cosmetics continued to expand with Mousse Hydratante Parfumée, introduced in 1989 as a non-greasy body moisturizing foam scented with the classic "Paloma Picasso" perfume.

Collaboration between Cosmair and Ralph Lauren also increased in the early 1990s. Ralph Lauren and Cosmair debuted a woman's fragrance called Safari in 1990 and a separate division was established in the following year composed entirely of Lauren designer fragrances. In 1991 Polo Crest, a citrus-scented perfume, was introduced for men with a logo patterned after the traditional Lauren crest. Safari for men was debuted in 1992. In hair care, Colorvive Technicare was introduced as Cosmair's premier line for the daily care of color-treated hair. Other innovative hair coloring brands, such as Crescendo, Majirel, and Majiblond, were created under the L'Oréal Keralogie group. Diacolor, another invention, combined "the soft and gentle properties of semi-permanent color with the long-lasting results of permanent hair color," as reported in a company brochure.

The Lancôme Division continued to capitalize on its French mystique, but adapted its message to an American way of life. For instance, the moisturizer TransHydrix was not only to be marketed as an emollient, but also as a guard against skin dehydration. Lancôme's leadership in the industry was further strengthened by the introduction of Niosôme Daytime Skin treatment. Poudre, Teint, and Blush Majeur makeup products were also part of the line-up, and in 1991 Lancôme debuted Tresor, a floral-oriental fragrance, which soon became popular in Europe and America.

One of the fastest growing segments in the cosmetic business by 1990 was the so-called "anti-aging" skin treatment market. In 1987 Cosmair and two other cosmetics firms—Shiseido Cosmetics Ltd. and Christian Dior Perfumes Inc.—were warned by the Food and Drug Administration (FDA) about their "anti-aging skin treatment" claims, as reported by a staff reporter for *The Wall Street Journal.* Cosmair's Lancôme Niosome Systeme Anti-Age Daytime Skin Treatment was pointed out as a violator. The FDA stated that the companies "must seek new-drug status for the treatments if they want to keep making certain claims in labelling."

Undaunted by this event, Cosmair introduced an upscale, anti-aging facial treatment and France's most popular skin care line to America in 1989 under the brand name Plénitude. Plénitude was launched with a $35 million Euro-style ad campaign, designed by Publicis, Paris. As reported in *Advertising Age*, the brand was released under the slogan, "Reduces signs of aging." Plénitude products were primarily distributed through drug stores, mass volume retailers, and combination stores. In 1990 another product was added, Plénitude Action Liposomes, touted as "skin care of the future," according to Pat Sloan in *Advertising Age*. Sales of Plénitude skin care were estimated at $75 million by 1991. As George Klarsfeld, general manager of Cosmair's L'Oréal cosmetics and fragrance division, said in *Advertising Age*, Plénitude's success has been attributable to demographic growth of baby-booming women and a "very good quality-for-value concept." Oil of Olay, produced by Procter & Gamble Company's Richardson-Vicks subsidiary, is Cosmair's main competitor in this market.

In 1990 Cosmair held 5.6 percent of the U.S. women's fragrance market behind industry leaders Estée Lauder (12.5 percent) and Revlon (11.6 percent). In the men's fragrance category, Cosmair has been listed as the second ranked company with 23.5 percent of market share, trailing only Unilever's 25 percent share of the market. In 1991 Cosmair was the sixth largest marketer of cosmetics in the United States, with $1.1 billion in sales and more than 3,600 personnel employed throughout the United States and Puerto Rico. Sales ending 1992 were estimated at around $1.2 billion. 1992 divisions included 1) the Professional Salon Division, made up of L'Oréal Technique Professionale and L'Oréal Professional Salon Products, 2) the L'Oréal Hair Care Division, 3) the L'Oréal Cosmetic & Fragrance Division, 4) Lancôme, 5) Biotherm, 6) the European Designer Fragrance Division, 7) the Ralph Lauren Fragrance Division, and 8) Cosmair Caribe, which serves Puerto Rico. The company's laboratories are located in Clark, New Jersey. As reported in 1991 by Steven Greenhouse in *The New York Times*, the three major stockholders of the privately held company are the Nestlé company, with about 70 percent;

L'Oréal, with four percent; and Liliane Bettencourt, daughter of L'Oréal's founder, with 26 percent.

Cosmair, Inc. further solidified its position in the industry on June 21, 1993, with the purchase of Redken Laboratories, one of the world's largest beauty products companies, with a presence in 36 countries.

As Cosmair faces the future, it has been focusing most of its marketing efforts on cosmetics and fragrances. For instance, as reported by Pat Sloan in *Advertising Age*, another Ralph Lauren men's fragrance is slated for introduction in spring 1994. With its broad line of profitable perfumes, cosmetics, and hair care products, Cosmair is expected to remain one of America's most powerful beauty companies well into the 1990s.

Principal Subsidiaries: Gloria Vanderbilt Fragrances; Redken Laboratories.

Further Reading:

Born, Pete, "Ride 'em Ralph: Lauren Hits TV Trail for Men's Safari," *Women's Wear Daily,* August 21, 1992, pp. 1, 5.
"Cosmair Inc.," *Advertising Age,* September 28, 1988, p. 62.
"Cosmair, Inc.," New York: Cosmair Inc., April 1991.
"Cosmair Plans to Cut Biotherm Doors, Prizes," *Women's Wear Daily,* November 16, 1992, p. 32.
Fine, Phyllis, and Vogel, Margaret, "Vanitie$," *Marketing & Media Decisions,* December 1987, pp. 109, 124, 126.
Greenhouse, Steven, "L'Oreal Official Dies After Quitting in Controversy," *The New York Times,* June 27, 1991, sec. D, p. 9.
"Hue & Cry: A Marketing Newsletter," *Drug & Cosmetics Industry,* July 1985, p. 7.
Hunter, Catherine Ellis, "Warner Cosmetics: The Bride Looks Better," *Drug & Cosmetics Industry,* March 1985, pp. 26–29.
Mahon, Gigi, "Sweet Smell of Success: Meet Cosmetics Executive Lindsay Owen-Jones," *Barron's,* December 5, 1983, pp. 30, 32, 34.
"Making up ground in the mass market: Klarsfeld details how Plenitude broke through," *Advertising Age,* March 1, 1991, p. 32.
Meyers, William, "Cosmair Makes a Name for Itself," *The New York Times,* May 12, 1985, sec. 3, pp. 1, F25.
Moskowitz, Milton, Robert Levering, and Michael Katz, eds. *Everybody's Business,* New York: Doubleday, 1990, p. 157.
"New President For Cosmair," *The New York Times*, January 19, 1984, sec. D, p. 2.
"The Order Changeth!" *Drug & Cosmetics Industry,* July 1991, p. 14.
"Other people moving," *Advertising Age,* July 15, 1991, p. 28.
"Package reduction," *Advertising Age,* May 13, 1991, p. 50.
Schnorbus, Paula, "Vial Strategies," *Marketing & Media Decisions,* June 1987, pp. 125, 130, 136, 138.
Sloan, Pat, "Cosmair eyes new L'Oreal lines," *Advertising Age,* September 24, 1984, p. 10.
——, "Cosmair knocks off suit," *Advertising Age,* March 31, 1986, p. 6.
——, "Cosmair suit tries to knock off knockoffs," *Advertising Age,* March 24, 1986, p. 6.
——, "Hair-coloring battle to flare: L'Oreal new products hides roots; bad news for Clairol," *Advertising Age,* September 21, 1992, p. 4.
——, "L'Oreal puts on a new face for skincare launch," *Advertising Age,* May 15, 1989, pp. 1, 70.
——, "L'Oreal banks on rising star," *Advertising Age,* April 2, 1990, p. 47.
——, "L'Oreal cosmetics get big ad push," *Advertising Age,* April 23, 1990, p. 12.
——, "Maturing scents: Polo, Aramis prepare to fight young rivals," *Advertising Age,* October 14, 1991, p. 21.

——, " 'Remade' Cosmair makes run at Revlon," *Advertising Age,* February 6, 1984, pp. 4, 56.

——, "Skincare faces new products," *Advertising Age,* January 23, 1989, pp. 1, 52.

"Three More Concerns Are Warned by FDA On Skin-Care Claims," *The Wall Street Journal,* April 30, 1987, p. 15.

—Kim Tudahl

CRANE ®

Crane Co.

100 First Stamford Place
Stamford, CT 06902
U.S.A.
(203) 363-7300
Fax: (203) 363-7295

Public Company
Incorporated: 1865 as Northwestern Manufacturing
   Company
Employees: 8,500
Sales: $1.31 billion
Stock Exchanges: New York
SICs: 3492 Fluid Power Valves & Hose Fittings; 3052
   Rubber & Plastics Hose & Belting; 3431 Metal Sanitary
   Ware; 3432 Plumbing Fixtures, Fittings & Trim; 3561
   Pumps & Pumping Equipment; 3581 Automatic Vending
   Machines; 3589 Service Industry Machinery Nec; 3625
   Relays & Industrial Controls; 3724 Aircraft Engines &
   Engine Parts; 3728 Aircraft Parts & Equipment Nec; 3769
   Space Vehicle Equipment Nec; 5031 Lumber, Plywood &
   Millwork; 5074 Plumbing & Hydronic Heating Supplies

Crane Co. is a diversified manufacturer of engineered industrial products, serving niche markets in aerospace, fluid handling, automatic merchandising, and the construction industry. Crane's wholesale distribution business provides the building products markets and industrial customers with millwork, windows, doors and related products, plumbing supplies, valves and piping, actuated valves, and flow control systems.

From its inception in 1855 as a crude bell and brass foundry run single-handedly by its founder, Richard Teller Crane, the company grew into an S&P 500 Company with international subsidiaries that generate more than a billion dollars of sales in fields ranging from heating to waste water treatment to aerospace to vending machines. From 1984 onward, the company began a general plan of growth and decentralized management that it hoped would enable it to survive recessionary patterns of the 1990s by spreading out gains and losses between its diverse businesses.

Crane Co. roots extend back to Richard Teller Crane's first effort to cast lightning rod tips and couplings in a foundry that he established in Chicago. Born in Patterson, New Jersey, on May 15, 1832, Richard Crane moved into the work force at an

early age. By the age of nine, he worked as a cotton mill operator; by age 15 he learned brass and bell foundry and brass finishing trades as an apprentice in a Brooklyn foundry; by the age of 21, he had gained further experience in a locomotive plant and several printing press machine shops. He migrated westward in 1855 to join his uncle, Martin Ryerson, who ran a successful lumber business in Chicago. Ryerson lent his young nephew a corner of the Ryerson lumber yard to launch the makeshift foundry that would become a multinational company over the ensuing century.

Richard Crane built a 14-by-24 foot wooden shed and secured patterns and brass for couplings and copper for lightning rod tips. The sand that he had turned up excavating the furnace served as raw material for molding. After nearly a year as the sole employee—molder, furnace tender, metal pourer, casting cleaner, and salesman—Crane hired two experts from Brooklyn and started a partnership with his brother, Charles, changing the shop name to R.T. Crane and Brother. Markets quickly expanded beyond Chicago to Wisconsin, Kentucky, and Iowa.

The first substantial order came from P.W. Gates & Co., a Chicago manufacturer of mill equipment and freight cars. Gates' supplier had run out of copper and could not fill an urgent order for journal boxes, the metal containers installed on railroad cars to lubricate axles. After delivering the castings on schedule, Crane won the confidence of Gates & Co. and eventually received all future orders for brass castings.

Following their first big order, the Crane brothers moved to rapidly expand operations and diversify product lines. After building a three-story structure and upgrading production facilities, they began production of engine parts for the emerging railroad business, as well as plumbing and fixtures for new developments in steam power, called "steam warming" at the time. In order to fill a $6,000 contract to supply the new Cook Country Court House in Chicago with steam heating, Crane designed and manufactured a wide variety of globe and check valves, pipe fittings, steam cocks, branch tees, and hook plates. Their success won the company a similar contract for the newly constructed Illinois State Penitentiary in Joliet, Illinois, which, in turn, won them further credibility and sustained business in the provision of steam heating supplies. With the onset of the Civil War, the company also became a major government supplier of fittings for saddlery, brass fittings, plates, knobs, spurs, and wagon equipment.

By 1865 the Crane brothers completed construction of an industrial-size factory on Jefferson Street, which enabled them to expand all facets of business operations and manufacture a full line of valves in materials ranging from cast iron to malleable iron and brass. That same year, the company was incorporated and renamed the Northwestern Manufacturing Company, reflecting its broadening interests.

In 1866 the company printed its first catalogue, which contained products as diverse as fire hydrants, ventilating fans, machine tools, water pumps, bung bushings for beer barrels, and steam engines. The advent of the Bessemer smelting process for iron brought low-cost steel to the United States, further assisting Crane in his development of diverse and durable products.

Crane's entry into the elevator business began in 1867, when the company designed an engine with a safety valve to control elevator speed with heavy loads. From the 1870s until the mid-1890s, Crane provided 95 percent of the hoists used in American blast furnaces. In addition, the company established a presence in passenger elevator manufacturing in 1872, spinning off a separate subsidiary called the Crane Elevator Company that remained a major competitor in the field for over three decades. With increased focus on industrial manufacturing, it sold its elevator division in 1895 to a joint venture that eventually became the Otis Elevator Company.

1871 literally brought a blaze of change, as the company survived the Chicago fire and helped save the city by providing large steam pumps to displace river water to city mains. That same year, Charles Crane retired from the business and sold his share to Richard, making the original founder sole proprietor once again. To emphasize the family heritage after his brother's departure, Richard changed the name to Crane Brothers Manufacturing Company in 1872.

In the late 1880s Richard T. Crane contributed to the rise of industrial automation. He pioneered line production in foundries and invented numerous mechanized systems to increase industrial efficiency in its plants. The company developed a steam-powered conveyor system for moving molds and pouring metal. It also fine-tuned the use of multiple-purpose machines, such as a machine that simultaneously bored cylinders, crosshead guides, and crank shaft bearings for steam elevator engines. Other innovations included oil pumps for the lubrication of engine-driven cylinders, an alarm to signal low water levels in steam boilers, a pipe lap joint that set new standards in the industry, and state-of-the art ceiling plates and pipe hangers.

With increased innovation and business volume, the company expanded rapidly. In 1884 a branch operation was opened in Omaha that proved so successful that another was established in Los Angeles, California, in 1886. Within a few years, branch operations became standard company practice, sprouting up wherever Crane products were in demand. In 1870 a four-story extension was added to the Jefferson Street plant, and in 1881, a second large pipe mill was constructed. By 1880 Crane operated four production facilities employing more than 1,500 workers.

In 1890 the company officially adopted the name Crane Co. Though its name was shortened, Crane's business continued to grow rapidly. A new age of increasingly taller buildings demanded greater numbers of pipes, valves, and fittings for water and steam systems with higher performance standards. In addition, commercial electricity depended on massive steam engines, which in turn required stronger and cheaper fluid control equipment. Anticipating the need for new materials and innovative solutions to remain competitive, Richard T. Crane established a chemical laboratory in 1888. The company developed iron castings of uniform tensile strength, a notable achievement for the period. Before long, the rise of large steam power plants outdated even uniform fittings in cast iron, forcing the company to innovate in steel production. In 1907 Crane negotiated for a German steel innovator, Zenzes, to join its staff and supply his coveted patents. By 1910 Crane was producing valves and fittings with minimum tensile strength of 60,000 psi.

During the first decades of the twentieth century, Crane invested in metallurgical research that paid off for the company and the industry at large. Experiments designed to test the effects of high temperatures on various metals culminated in a series of papers published in 1912 that became engineering classics. In addition, a number of Crane quality control procedures became industry standards. Crane inspection of pipe threads using gauges was adopted by the American Society for Testing Materials, and Crane's practice of tapping and gauging steel flanges eventually served the whole industry as the Pipe Thread Standard.

Crane expanded to East Coast markets with the 1903 acquisition of the Eaton, Cole & Burnham Company in Bridgeport, Connecticut. The company continued to expand its production line, introducing a complete line of air brake equipment, pop safety valves, and drainage fittings, among other products. A 160-acre, electrically powered plant was constructed in Chicago in 1909. After Richard Crane's death in January of 1912, his role as president was briefly passed on to the eldest son, Charles R. Crane, and then more permanently transferred to Richard T. Crane, Jr., in 1914.

Among the ventures introduced by the new president was an extensive line of practical, decorative bathroom ensembles supported by acquisitions of sizable pottery and enamelware operations and by unprecedented marketing efforts. The copy for a 1925 advertisement in *National Geographic Magazine* began, "Your personal taste and appreciation of beauty in form and color can be reflected in the appointments of your bathroom. . . ." Among other initiatives to corner the rising bathroom market, Crane retained an imminent industrial designer, Henry Dreyfuss, to conceive an entire fixture line.

In the years following World War I, Crane established its first operations outside the United States. In 1918 Canadian operations were incorporated as a separate company, Crane Limited, which grew to include Canadian Potteries Ltd., Warden King Ltd., and Crane Steelware Ltd. over the ensuing 20 years. Distribution also expanded to Europe, with the first branch houses established in France in 1918 and in England in 1919. Manufacturing operations were established in those countries in 1925 and 1929, respectively.

While losses during the depression years strained operations, they also prompted replanning and increased efficiency, and served to usher the company into World War II as a reliable and flexible supplier. While Crane reported its first operating loss in 1931, it rebounded within two years to offer shares on the New York Stock Exchange in 1934. After sustained growth during the next decade, the company was ready to supply the United States Navy with valves and fittings for the war effort. From a pre-war steel valve production capacity of 6,000 tons per year, Crane increased its capacity to an annual rate of 25,000 tons by mid-1942. By supplying the Navy, the Atomic Energy Commission, and new manufacturers of high-octane fuel using catalytic cracking techniques, Crane gained ample experience in designing and manufacturing a wide range of metal-alloy valves and fittings resistant to corrosion, high temperatures, and extreme strain.

Following the war, Crane was able to transfer its war efforts to the peace dividend, meeting increased demands in the petrochemical, chemical, and atomic power industries. With the 1951 acquisition of Hydro-Aire Incorporated, Crane entered the business of precision aircraft products and flow control equipment, supplying filters and valves to all manufacturers of turbine type aircraft engines. In 1953 Crane developed a household hydronic heating system; it ranked as one of the country's largest manufacturers of residential heating by 1956. In the late 1950s the company shareholders elected a new chairman and chief executive officer, Thomas Mellon Evans, whose strategy was to streamline the distribution network and broaden the industrial product base. A major consolidation of distribution houses and the reorganization of a separate "profit center" resulted in the creation of Crane Supply Company. The October 1959 acquisition of the Chapman Valve Manufacturing Company of Indian Orchard, Massachusetts, significantly expanded domestic valve operations, especially on the East Coast. The following year, acquisition of the 97-year-old Cochrane Corporation in Philadelphia, Pennsylvania, extended Crane's fluid control line to include steam boilers, water, steam and waste water treatment equipment. The Cochrane Division became the nucleus of Crane's growing involvement in the business of pollution control.

By the 1960s, Hydro-Aire catered to the space program with production of life-support and coolant pumps. It also expanded its role in the realm of aerospace by taking the lead in anti-skid braking systems, fuel and hydraulic pumps, valves and regulators, actuators, and solid state components.

Expansion continued through the 1960s. In 1961 the Deming Company, a manufacturer of residential and industrial pumps and water systems, was acquired. Four years later, Crane acquired a highly specialized fluid control company, the Chempump Division of Fostoria Corporation, which specialized in leak-proof, trouble-free pump systems for exotic or dangerous fluids.

By the mid-1960s Crane had extended its international operations to Italy, with Crane-Orion, Italy; the Netherlands, with Crane Nederland, N.V.; Spain, with the acquisition of that country's largest valve manufacturer, Fundiciones Ituarte, S.A. and the formation of Crane-FISA, S.A.; Australia, with the new valve plant, Crane Australia Pty., Ltd.; and Mexico. Crane Canada Ltd. and Crane U.K. also made significant acquisitions in 1964 and 1966. Through rising space-age technology, Crane expanded beyond terrestrial boundaries, collaborating with the U.S. Space Team and the Brookhaven National Laboratory's test studies of solar energy, among other projects.

In an effort to improve its position in the area of building products, Crane acquired Huttig Sash & Door Company in 1968, adding milled wood products, windows, and doors to its line. The 1969 acquisition of CF&I Steel Corporation, a vertically integrated steel company, marked an unprecedented diversification into a major industry beyond its existing areas. CF&I provided everything from iron ore, coal, and limestone to carbon and alloy steel. It represented the largest acquisition in Crane's history and, by 1975, represented the company's single largest business interest. The 1979 acquisition of Medusa Cor-

poration, a cement and aggregates company, added yet another basic materials industry to Crane's list.

In 1980 Crane began a shift in business strategy away from cyclical basic materials businesses toward a diversified mix that would earn higher returns for shareholders. In February 1984, T.M. Evans resigned as chairman and director of the company, leaving his post to the newly elected R.S. Evans, who ushered in a major restructuring effort. On July 13 of that year, the company sold its U.S. Plumbing Division for approximately $9.5 million. One year later, Crane spun off CF&I Steel to its shareholders, and in 1988 shares in Medusa Corporation were made available to its shareholders as well.

While Crane's restructuring involved substantial paring down, it also called for new acquisitions in light-to-medium manufacturing. In 1985 the company acquired UniDynamics Corporation, expanding diversification in numerous areas: defense and aerospace/defense contracting, fluid controls, vending machines and coin validators, automation equipment, fiberglass-reinforced polyester and laminated panels, and electronic components.

The late 1980s and early 1990s were marked by management efforts to fine-tune the UniDynamics acquisition; several divisions deemed incompatible with the restructuring plan were sold and appropriate acquisitions were made. In February 1987, 12 Crane Supply plumbing, heating, and air conditioning wholesale distribution branches in southern regions of the United States were sold. Substantial additions were made to the company's U.S. valve line, including valve maintenance and value-added services. In April 1992 Crane's Canadian subsidiary, Crane Canada, Inc., acquired certain assets of Jenkins Canada, Inc., a manufacturer of bronze and iron valves, for approximately $4 million.

The Ferguson Machine Co., the largest supplier of intermittent motion control systems in the world, was established as a division of the Defense and Specialty Systems Group of Crane, and in August 1986 Ferguson acquired PickOmatic Systems of Detroit, a leader in cam-activated mechanical parts handling equipment. Crane's Cochrane Environment Systems division acquired Chicago Heater Company, Inc., a designer, manufacturer, and servicer of deaerators and surface condensers, reinforcing Cochrane's market leadership. Additionally, Huttig Sash & Door Company expanded to become the third largest distributor of wood building products in the industry. Pozzi-Renati Millwork Products, Inc. was acquired in February 1988, providing Crane with a strong initial entry into the East Coast market; Palmer G. Lewis Co., a distributor of building material, was acquired in June 1988; and Rondel's, Inc., a distributor of doors, windows, and molding, was acquired in April 1993.

The Crane Co.'s Hydro-Aire Division was augmented in 1990 by the $40-million acquisition of Lear Romec Corp., a manufacturer of pumps for the aerospace industry. In September of that year the diaphragm pump line of the Crown Pump Company was added to Crane's Deming pump line, increasing Crane's share of the industrial pump market. That same year, a Crane attempt to acquire Milton Roy Co., a manufacturer of metering pumps, was halted by an antitrust suit in which Milton accused Crane of a "greenmail" scheme to manipulate the market in order to acquire Milton stock. Milton repurchased all shares held by Crane for $8.2 million.

Downturns in residential construction, in defense spending, and in the aerospace industry, paired with weak economies worldwide, strained key Crane divisions in the early 1990s. Hydro-Aire, the leader in electronically controlled anti-skid brakes for the aerospace industry, saw declines in profitability of 13 percent and 18 percent in 1991 and 1992, respectively. The April 1993 sale of the precision ordnance business of Unidynamics/Phoenix to Pacific Scientific Company reflected further reduction in Crane's declining defense business. These losses, however, were offset in part by strong increases in revenues at National Vendors for automated merchandising equipment; at Huttig, which serves the residential construction industry; and at Kemlite and Cor Tec, Crane's suppliers of fiberglass-reinforced panels to the transportation industry. R.S. Evans, Crane's Chairman and CEO, noted in the 1992 annual report that ''one benefit of a diversified business mix is that a recession rarely cuts across all units with equal impact.''

Despite the recessionary trends of the early 1990s, Crane was able to increase total operating profit for the year by seven percent and improve productivity, on a sales-per-employee basis, by six percent. During 1992 Moody's upgraded the company's senior debt rating from Baa2 to Baa1, while Standard & Poor's reconfirmed the company's A- credit rating on the $100 million senior notes.

Principal Subsidiaries: UniDynamics Corp.; Ferguson Machine Co., S.A.; Crane GmbH; National Rejectors, Inc., GmbH; Dyrotech Industries, Inc.; UniDynamics/St. Louis, Inc.; UniDynamics/Phoenix, Inc.; Huttig Sash & Door Co.; Crane Australia Pty., Ltd.; Crane Ltd.; Crane Canada Inc.

Further Reading:

''Crane Announces Stock Incentive Plan Vesting,'' *PR Newswire*, June 11, 1990.
''Crane Co. Acquires Jenkins Canada,'' Crane Co., April 1, 1992.
''Crane Co. Announces Acquisition and Divestiture,'' *Business Wire*, April 2, 1993.
Crane Co. Annual Reports, Stamford, CT: Crane Co., 1975, 1992.
Crane Co. Corporate History, Stamford, CT: Crane Co., 1993.
''Crane Co. Purchases PickOmatic Systems,'' *PR Newswire*, August 11, 1986.
''Crane Co. Subsidiary Expands Distribution Network,'' *PR Newswire*, February 16, 1988.
''Crane Purchases Chicago Heater,'' *PR Newswire*, June 18, 1987.
''Crane Sells Its U.S. Crane Supply Operation,'' *PR Newswire*, February 27, 1987.
Goldstein, Alan, ''Dateline: Milton Roy Co. Repurchases Crane Co. Shares,'' *St. Petersburg Times*, February 13, 1990.

—Kerstan Cohen

Data General

Data General Corporation

4400 Computer Drive
Westboro, Massachusetts 01580
U.S.A.
(508) 366-8911
Fax: (508) 898-4003

Public Company
Incorporated: 1968
Employees: 6,900
Sales: $1.12 billion
Stock Exchanges: New York London
SICs: 3571 Electronic Computers; 3577 Computer Peripheral
    Equipment, not elsewhere classified; 5045 Computers,
    Peripherals, and Software; 7372 Prepackaged Software;
    7378 Computer Maintenance and Repair

Data General Corporation is a manufacturer of multi-user computer systems: minicomputers, workstations, and servers. During the minicomputer boom in the 1970s, Data General was one of the fastest growing U.S. companies and was considered one of the leaders in minicomputers. Since minicomputers began losing sales to personal computers in the 1980s, however, Data General had difficulties adjusting its market focus. In the early 1990s the company began to establish itself in the area of workstations, servers, and data storage systems. With 33 subsidiaries and more than 250 sales and service offices in 60 countries, Data General is a significant international company, earning about half its revenue from foreign sales.

The minicomputer, a medium-scale, cabinet-sized computer that functions either as a single workstation or as a multi-user system with numerous terminals, was first introduced in 1959 by Digital Equipment Corporation. In 1968 Esdon de Castro and two other young engineers, quit their jobs at Digital to start their own company, Data General. At Digital they had been working together on a project for a new 16-bit computer, faster than the existing model that functioned at a rate of only 12-bit units. It is unclear whether they had planned ahead to start their own business with technology they were developing at Digital, or whether they quit because management had turned down a proposal of de Castro's to build a whole new series of computers that would have made much of Digital's line obsolete. The end result was that Data General's first product, the 16-bit

NOVA minicomputer sold very well by filling a gap in Digital's product line. Ten years later Digital's president told *Fortune* magazine, ''What they did was so bad we're still upset about it.'' But Digital never sued the new company for any theft of intellectual property.

De Castro and his two colleagues, joined by salesperson Herb Richman of Fairchild Semiconductor, obtained financial backing from lawyer Frederick Adler. To start the company Adler put up $50,000 of his own money and raised much of the rest of the founding capital, which totaled $800,000. With that Data General was incorporated on April 15, 1968, and set up operations in what had been a beauty parlor in Hudson, Massachusetts. A year later the company moved to Southboro. De Castro was president and CEO, Richman became vice-president of marketing and sales, and Adler served as secretary and a board member in addition to managing the finances for the first few years.

Data General's first machine, the NOVA, unveiled at the annual national Computer Conference in 1969, was a great success. Besides having several features that Digital's comparable computers lacked, the Data General multi-purpose minicomputer was produced very cheaply and thus could be sold at a relatively low price, averaging $26,000. The NOVA had the advantage of specially designed large circuit boards, which reduced the amount of hardware in the computer. The company shipped more than 200 of these minicomputers in its first year.

At the time, the minicomputer market, unlike that for mainframes, primarily consisted of engineers, scientists, and purchasing agents of original equipment manufacturers (OEMs). Therefore, it was relatively easy for a new company such as Data General to break in with inexpensive advertisements in key trade journals. These clients were more interested in a bargain than a famous brand name, and Data General offered volume discounts as high as 40 percent. Furthermore, the company did not have to provide a service organization as the big computer manufacturers did, since its clients were technically capable of taking care of the computers themselves. Soon 70 percent of Data General's clients were OEMs, which packaged custom software and peripherals with core computers and resold them to the final customer.

Shrewd business management from the beginning also aided Data General's successful growth. It went public after only a year of business, in 1969, and, raising money by offering stockholder equity shares, did not have to go into debt. The owners used the stock as a means of growth rather than hoarding a majority for themselves. When they made a second public offering several years later, the founders followed the advice of Adler and each sold some of their own stock in the process. Data General stock was listed on the New York stock exchange on December 28, 1973.

The company was also known for keeping down its overhead costs. It had low receivables and inventories as a percentage of sales. A relatively large proportion of the sales crew's pay was from commissions. With all its computer lines simple and compatible with each other, Data General did not have to develop new systems software. Its R&D expenditures were not put into risky new technology areas, but rather spent on ways to improve and cut costs on existing products. Finally, its offices, even after moving its headquarters a second time in 1977 to the present location in Westboro, have been kept simple, and there have been almost no executive perks.

Data General's early advertising style was aggressive, compatible with the business behavior of its OEMs and in sharp contrast to the polite customer support offered by the mainframe companies such as IBM. Data General thus sought to differentiate itself from its chief competitor, Digital, precisely by the aggressiveness of its sales staff. Although it may have seemed that Data General had a long way to go the take on Digital, which held 85 percent of the minicomputer market, there was no company in firm second place. In a similarly aggressive style, Data General was quick to take copiers of its designs to court.

Data General quickly followed the new trends in technology, learning from the leader's mistakes, and providing cheaper machines. The company kept its prices down by such techniques as using plug-in printed circuit boards in its computers, instead of hand-wired ones, the first minicomputer manufacturer to do so. In 1973, Data General was the first major company to introduce a minicomputer with a new core memory design permitting twice as much memory on a single circuit board as was then standard. Thus, the NOVA 2, at the same price as its predecessors, could support more complex software. This enabled them to run programming languages such as FORTRAN, which previously had been used only on mainframe computers. In the mid-1970s Data General introduced its second product line, the more powerful ECLIPSE scientific and commercial computers. These new minicomputers did not differ greatly in their architecture from the NOVA and were compatible with the NOVA in their system software.

In 1978, just ten years after its founding, Data General, as the fastest growing computer company to date, was listed 500th in the Fortune 500 rankings with sales at $380 million. Yet it ranked much higher than that in profits. With a goal of providing stockholders a high short-term rate of return on their investments, Data General was able to maintain its 30–40 percent growth rate. Expansion was manifested in the hiring of 7,000 new employees between 1974 and 1978. Managerial complications associated with such rapid growth caused the company to fail only once in fulfilling customer orders, in 1973. However, it was unable to substantially increase its 8–11 percent share in the minicomputer market, because the market was growing even faster at the incredible rate of 40–45 percent annually.

Meanwhile, Data General had grown in other directions, as well. It established its Canadian, European, and Asian operations, and created a technical service organization. It also began manufacturing its own computer components, setting up a semiconductor operation in Sunnyvale, California, to produce its own microprocessors and other chips. Around 1976 de Castro decided to fully integrate the company by also producing peripherals.

Eventually the company's physical growth became too complex to be run in the same manner it had been. For too long de Castro had tried to manage the whole company himself. Lack of coordination led to a costly proliferation of research projects. In one case two competing research groups were funded to develop a 32-bit "supermini," a minicomputer powerful enough to compete with a mainframe. Internal disagreements in 1976–77 among engineers, concerning whose project team would design the new computer, postponed execution of the project, while Digital's 32-bit VAX, introduced in 1977, was becoming very popular. After a frantic year and a half of work, chronicled in Tracy Kidder's best-selling book *The Soul of a New Machine*, Data General finally announced its 32-bit MV/8000 in April 1980. This was the upgraded version of the ECLIPSE line. But the company's delay resulted eventually in a smaller share of the new supermini market. Meanwhile, during the fourth quarter of 1979, the hiring and training of many employees for its new service department resulted in a decline in earning for the first time.

In response to managerial deficiencies, in 1980 the founders decided to reorganize the company into a divisional structure. Already in 1979 the company had started a transition away from a strictly functional organization, by establishing product-oriented groups. Now new executives were brought in from outside, and decision making was decentralized among three divisions, each oriented to a different target market. In addition to new middle level managers, a new senior vice-president, Robert C. Miller, a veteran of IBM, was appointed in 1982 to head the company's three business divisions, relieving de Castro from day-to-day operations.

However, these changes were not enough to put Data General back on the fast track. The real problem the company faced in the 1980s was that the minicomputer boom had slowed and so had Data General's sales. Earnings in fiscal 1981 fell from $55 million to $41 million. In fiscal 1982 profits dropped an additional 51 percent to $24.6 million, while revenues grew that year by only 9.3 percent to $806 million. Since then, Data General had not been able to regain for long the rate of growth it had seen in the 1970s. Basically, it was unable to adjust itself quickly enough to serve the new growth segment of the market: personal computers and workstations.

In 1981, the year Data General shipped its 100,000th computer, it made its first entry into the lower-end personal computer market with its "Enterprise." Unfortunately, this product failed due to its high price and limited software ability, reflecting the company's lack of familiarity with the new mass market for personal computers. Data General's next personal computer, released in 1983, had the ability to run both standard PC software and some of the software that ran on the company's minicomputers. But by then the competition from Apple, IBM, and others was overwhelming, and sales tended to be only to existing minicomputer clients. A laptop computer released the following year was also unsuccessful, because its display was not satisfactorily legible, and demand was overestimated.

Meanwhile, under new management, Data General began selling direct, in IBM fashion, to end-user clients, rather than to OEMs. It went after these new, commercial markets with its superminis by incorporating more software, peripherals, and support. The company developed an office automation system, combining functions such as word processing, electronic mail, and filing, which it named CEO (Comprehensive Electronic Office), and which ran on the new MV/series of superminis. Its customers tended to be large corporations that had previously been served by IBM or Wang Laboratories.

However, this change of client required a different kind of sales force focusing on the computer's abilities to solve office problems rather than its abilities to process data and support programming languages. "Its hard selling tactics were increasingly out of step with a changed marketplace," observed a 1982 *Forbes* article. Many of Data General's most successfully aggressive salespeople left the company at this time. Another obstacle that faced the company in this new market was a preference by customers who already had computer systems to stick with their previous supplier. It was one thing for Data General to try to take on Digital in the minicomputer wholesale market of the 1970s, but, as later became clear, it was a wasted effort to try to take established end-user clients away from IBM.

Sales temporarily rebounded in early 1984, up 40 percent, bringing revenues over the $1 billion mark. The organizational restructuring of 1980 was finally paying off, and retrained sales crews brought in a few big accounts with the company's office automation system, including the U.S. Forest Service and E.F. Hutton. Data General's latest high-end supermini, the MV/10000, in 1983 was indeed superior to the competition.

The spurt was short-lived, however. Expecting continued high growth, de Castro had added nearly 3,000 new employees and increased capital spending by 78 percent to meet the expected new demand. But it did not materialize. With its only successful products in the slowing minicomputer market and with the computer industry as a whole in a slump by the mid-1980s, high growth could not be sustained. Profits plummeted 70 percent in 1985. The following year, Data General suffered its first losses, which accelerated to $127 million in fiscal 1987.

The company reacted by downsizing. Already in 1986 it had closed its semiconductor plant in Sunnyvale, laying off 75 employees. It also closed two plants that made computer terminals and printers and merged two internal computing operations, eliminating 400 more jobs. The following year 1,000 were laid off and three more facilities were shut down. In cutting back on marketing and service, de Castro, once again fully in charge following Miller's resignation in 1987, decided to focus sales for the time being on its traditional, more familiar market of OEMs.

A major reason minicomputers were becoming less popular than personal computers and workstations was that the latter were built with standard "off-the-shelf" microprocessors for use with common systems software, a concept referred to as "open systems." Minicomputers, on the other hand, were built with the manufacturer's own unique hardware and software. Open systems gave the user the ability to exchange software and data between various brands of computers. Realizing this, de Castro decided to base Data General's next generation of computers on the simpler, yet faster RISC (reduced instruction set computing) microprocessors made by Motorola and run them

on a UNIX-based operating system. This was the AViiON line, introduced in April, 1989. With the experience and technology to produce at low cost, Data General had a potential advantage in a market of standard computer systems. Furthermore, purchasing existing microprocessor chips and operating systems software licenses would save the company the engineering costs in these areas. In 1988 Data General was continuing to close plants and lay off workers and was losing what share it had in the declining minicomputer market. Market share had fallen to 0.9 percent of worldwide revenues for 1989, according to market researcher Info Corp.

In December 1990, before the AViiON could prove itself, the board of directors, apparently fed up with mounting losses for five straight years, removed de Castro from the chair and replaced him with Ronald Skates, who had already been CEO for two years. Skates proceeded to pare costs and plan Data General's future around the AViiON line. Skates cut research and developed expenditures to eight percent of annual sales from de Castro's 12 percent. He withdrew funding from major joint development projects with other companies, and he accelerated the layoffs, reducing the work force by 50 percent between 1986 and 1991. To help pay off debts, in March 1991 he sold off the Japanese subsidiary Nippon Data General for about $46 million.

The AViiON was relatively successful, grossing $200 million in revenue in fiscal 1991 to help make that year profitable. Most AViiON sales were of its high-end server, a computer designed to store data used by other computers linked with it in a network. However, the market for such server computers was still relatively small. AViiON sales were unable to offset declining sales of minicomputers, and Data General fell back into the red in 1992.

The company's latest product strategy introduced in late 1992 was data storage systems. It formed a new division dedicated to producing storage products based on the high-reliability technology of redundant arrays of inexpensive disks (RAID). The system, called CLARiiON, was to be used especially in conjunction with the UNIX-based computers of other manufacturers, such as IBM, Sun, and Hewlett-Packard. With CLARiiON, Data General was the first large company to provide RAID for UNIX. With a maximum capacity of 24 G (billion) bytes, the desk-side CLARiiON was able to store more data than most companies needed, but it was hoped that it would be used to provide the support for new memory-intensive applications, such as imaging and voice recognition. For clients who missed the high storage capacity of mainframes, but wanted open systems, RAID was the answer.

By early 1993 the company had completed two straight quarters of profits, and sales of its AViiON and CLARiiON systems were steadily growing. While other large computer companies, such as Digital and IBM, were beginning to cut back, Data General had already completed its downsizing. From its high of 18,000 employees in 1985 it had reduced itself to a lean 6,900. Data General looked like it was ready to move ahead.

Principal Subsidiaries: Data General Europe, Inc. (France); Data General, Ltd. (United Kingdom); Data General GmbH

(Germany); Data General Australia Pty, Ltd.; Data General (Canada) Ltd.; Data General de Mexico, S.A. de C.V.

Further Reading:

"Advantage, Adler!," *Forbes,* January 15, 1977, pp. 66–67.

Ballou, Melinda-Carol, "Revamped DG on the Revenue Rebound," *Computerworld,* February 8, 1993, p. 85.

Beam, Alex, "Data General: The Ax Keeps Falling," *Business Week,* June 23, 1986, pp. 49–50.

——, "Who's Breathing Down Whose Neck Now?," *Business Week,* November 25, 1985, pp. 132–136.

Churbuck, David, "The Soul of Another Machine," *Forbes,* November 11, 1991, pp. 336–337.

"Data General Corp.," *Datamation,* June 15, 1988, p. 90.

"Data General's High-Stakes Bet on Desktop Computers," *Business Week,* August 1, 1983, pp. 76–77.

"Data General Tries for Its Second Wind," *Business Week,* March 7, 1983, pp. 75–83.

"The Fourth Wave," *Forbes,* September 19, 1988, pp. 179–180.

Helm, Leslie, "The New Data General Is Leaner—But Is it Meaner?," *Business Week,* August 17, 1987, pp. 86–88.

"How Data General Started Humming Again," *Business Week,* January 30, 1984, pp. 53–57.

Kidder, Tracy, *The Soul of a New Machine,* Boston: Little, Brown, 1981, pp. 16–27.

Kindel, Stephen, "Data General," *Financial World,* July 26, 1988, pp. 28–32.

Lewis, Geoff, "These Minis Could be Out of Fashion for Good," *Business Week,* November 21, 1988, p. 106.

Lindholm, Elizabeth, "Data General Corp.," *Datamation,* June 15, 1992, p. 80.

"The Long Hairs vs. the Stuffed Shirts," *Forbes,* January 15, 1976, pp. 30–31.

McWilliams, Gary, "Data General: RISC-ing Most of its Chips," *Business Week,* November 27, 1989, p. 195.

——, "Will Fast and Cheap be Data General's Salvation?," *Business Week,,* March 25, 1991, pp. 104–105.

Nash, Kim S., "DG Makes Waves in RAID Storage Market," *Computerworld,* September 21, 1992, p. 109.

"New Memories Boost Minicomputer Capacity," *Business Week,* July 7, 1973, pp. 72–73.

Seneker, Harold, "Data General—Life in the Fast Lane," *Forbes,* March 3, 1980, pp. 72–74.

Uttal, Bro, "The Gentlemen and The Upstarts Meet in a Great Mini Battle," *Fortune,* April 23, 1979, pp. 98–108.

Wiegner, Kathleen K., "Better Late?," *Forbes,* October 11, 1982, pp. 118–123.

—Heather Behn Hedden

Delta Woodside Industries, Inc.

233 N. Main Street, Suite 200
Greenville, South Carolina 29601
U.S.A.
(803) 232-8301
Fax: (803) 232-6164

Public Company
Incorporated: 1983 as Alchem Capital Corp.
Employees: 8,400
Sales: $705 million
Stock Exchanges: New York
SICs: 2261 Finishers of Broad Woven Cotton Fabric; 2211
   Broad Woven Fabric Mills, Cotton

Delta Woodside Industries, Inc. is a holding company engaged, through its six operating subsidiaries, in the manufacture and sale of textile fabrics and apparel. The company operates 34 textile and apparel plants and 27 garment outlet stores. Its 8,400 employees work in seven different states, plus Costa Rica. Sixty-seven percent of Delta Woodside's 1992 sales were generated by the company's textile fabrics division. Two of Delta Woodside's subsidiaries, Delta Mills Marketing Company and Stevcoknit Fabrics Company, operate mainly in this division. Delta Mills manufactures fabrics for several markets, including apparel, home furnishings (drapery linings, bedspreads, lamp shades), institutional (surgical tapes), and industrial (sail cloth and rip stop nylon). Stevcoknit primarily serves the apparel market, producing terrycloth and rib fabrics primarily for athletic wear. In addition to a textile fabrics division, Delta Woodside operates an apparel division which includes the Duck Head Apparel Company, Inc. and Delta Apparel, Inc. Apparel contributed about 29 percent of the company's net sales in 1992. Duck Head Apparel produces goods that are sold by department stores and specialty outlets, including Delta Woodside's 22 Duck Head retail outlets operated by Duck Head Retail Operations, another operating subsidiary. Delta Apparel produces knit items, many of which are sold to screen printers and sporting goods stores, under both the Delta Apparel label and under private brand labels. Delta Woodside also owns Harper Brothers, a small office supply company. Office products and other nontextile operations account for about four percent of Delta Woodside's sales. Harper Brothers runs an office products distribution center with six branches.

Delta Woodside was founded by Bettis Rainsford and Erwin Maddrey in 1983. The idea of starting a textile company first occurred to Rainsford when he heard that a mill in his home town of Edgefield, South Carolina, was closing. The shutdown of Edgefield Cotton Yarns, Inc. meant the loss of about 200 local jobs, and the idea of buying the plant appealed to Rainsford, who had returned to Edgefield after law school and dabbled in the nursing home, newspaper, and geothermal energy businesses. Lacking any knowledge of the textile industry, Rainsford hooked up with Maddrey, the former president of Riegel Textile Corp., also in South Carolina. The two men purchased Edgefield Cotton for $4 million, most of which they borrowed.

Following their acquisition of Edgefield Cotton, Rainsford and Maddrey joined forces with Buck Mickel, another local business operator and former vice chairperson at Fluor Corp. A company called Alchem Capital Corp. was formed, 50 percent of which was owned by RSI Corp., an outdoor equipment and office supply company controlled by Mickel. Over the next few years, Alchem grew at a steady rate, mostly by taking over mills cast off by larger companies in the struggling textile industry. Alchem's first important acquisition of this period was Woodside Mills, Inc., formerly a division of Dan River, Inc., in 1984. Four South Carolina plants were included with the $31 million purchase of Woodside Mills, whose products included textile fabrics used in the apparel, home furnishings, industrial, and medical markets. These facilities were the Easley Plant in Easley; the Haynsworth Plant in Anderson; and the Furman and Beattie Plants in Fountain Inn.

Alchem completed two important acquisitions in 1985. The company paid Cannon Mills about $4 million for its Maiden Knitting Mills, a circular knitter of finished apparel fabrics. Alchem also purchased Royal Manufacturing Co. that year. Royal, a manufacturer of men's underwear and sportswear with annual sales of about $30 million, was bought from the family of Morris H. Senderowitz, which had founded the company in Allentown, Pennsylvania, in 1910. The acquisition of Royal added four more plants to Alchem's growing collection. In 1986, Alchem made its largest purchase yet, acquiring the Stevcoknit and Delta Fabrics divisions of J.P. Stevens & Co. Stevcoknit, which produced singleknit and doubleknit fabrics, was purchased for $94 million. Delta Fabrics's products included lightweight cottons and polyester blends for sportswear and government orders, as well as bottomweight fabrics of synthetic fibers for men's wear. The acquisition of these two J.P. Stevens divisions more than doubled Alchem's size, adding 11 plants to Alchem's ten existing facilities, and increasing the company's work force from 2,500 to 6,000.

Late in 1986, Alchem's name was changed to Delta Woodside Industries, Inc. The company's yearly sales had grown to over $380 million by this time, with earnings of close to $18 million. The following year, Delta Woodside went public, offering two million shares of common stock over-the-counter at $14 a share. At that time, about 25 percent of Delta Woodside's revenue was generated by the sale of unfinished woven fabrics, over 40 percent by finished woven fabrics, another 25 percent by knit fabrics, and the remainder by completed apparel. For fiscal 1987, net sales reached $417 million.

In 1988, Delta Woodside acquired Stanwood Corporation for about $14 million. Stanwood, a manufacturer of knits, underwear, and sportswear, had yearly sales of about $110 million and employed about 3,000 workers. The deal for Stanwood was structured as an exchange of one million shares of Delta Woodside stock for all of Stanwood's assets, which included 1.5 million square feet of factory space at 11 plants in Georgia, Tennessee, and Costa Rica. For the fiscal year ending in July of 1988, Delta Woodside's earnings were $27.6 million, up from $21.3 million the previous year, on net sales of $489 million. In October of 1988, the company's stock was listed on the New York Stock Exchange for the first time. Toward the end of that year, plans were made to consolidate Stanwood's headquarters into the Royal Manufacturing division headquarters in Greenville, as well as to consolidate Stanwood's dyeing, knitting, and finishing operations into the Maiden facilities. The company also earmarked $20 million for the completion of its new yarn plant in Spartanburg.

The steady flow of new acquisitions continued into 1989. In February of that year, the company paid about $14 million for O'Bryan Bros., Inc. By the middle of 1989, Delta Woodside's vertical integration was generally complete, with company products ranging from commodity yarns to finished apparel. By that time, the company employed about 9,500 workers in its 37 plants. For the year ending July 1, 1989, Delta earned $9.9 million on sales of $569 million. In November of 1989, Delta Woodside merged with its long-time affiliate RSI Corp., Buck Mickel's company. This followed the spin-off of much of RSI's business to stockholders. The remaining incarnation of RSI consisted only of the Harper Brothers office supply operation. The last step of the merger was the amendment of RSI's articles of incorporation, changing the combined company's name to Delta Woodside Industries, Inc. Although the merger was structured in such a way that Delta Woodside was technically merged into RSI, the actual effect of the merger was the purchase of RSI by Delta Woodside at a cost of $1.1 million.

Delta's sales and earnings slumped badly in 1990. Including the new office supply operation, the company's sales dropped to $500 million, while earnings sank to $4.4 million. These setbacks were blamed primarily on weak demand in the retail sector, creating pressure throughout the chain of production. In January of 1990, the company's 89-year-old Easley Plant was closed as part of a modernization program. The plant's print-cloth production was moved to Woodside Mills' Beattie Plant in Fountain Inn, South Carolina. A few months later, Delta purchased the assets of the Shirt Knitting division of Durham Hosiery Mills, Inc. The division, with sales of about $48 million, was added to the company's Duck Head Apparel operation. Its plants (three in Tennessee and one in Georgia) employed about 1,200 people.

As the company entered the 1990s, increasing emphasis was placed on its Duck Head brand apparel line. The clothing was advertised in such publications as *Playboy* and *Sports Illustrated,* and televised ads were featured during college football games. Four retail outlets for "factory second" Duck Head merchandise were added, bringing the total of such stores in South Carolina, Georgia, and Tennessee to seven. In 1991, Delta Woodside benefited from a huge rush of sales attributable to the Persian Gulf War. During the nine-month period ending in March of 1991, the company's sales of camouflage and other fabrics to the Defense Department leaped to $49.2 million, well over twice the total for that period the previous year. For the same period, sales in Delta's woven fabrics division grew by 38 percent. These gains were not company-wide, however, as both Stevcoknit and Duck Head Apparel showed sales declines for that nine-month stretch.

For the fiscal year ending in June of 1991, sales rebounded to $590 million. The biggest gains were made by the Duck Head product line, whose sales reached $61.7 million. The Duck Head line also diversified its products, adding woven and knit shirts, shorts, and women's wear to its original array of casual cotton men's pants. Three-fourths of Delta's net sales for the year were generated by the fabrics division, as was 86 percent of the company's operating profit. In this division, about $313 million in sales came from woven fabrics, while about $128 million worth of knitted fabrics were sold.

Duck Head clothing continued as one of Delta's more important product lines in 1992. Gross sales of Duck Head apparel more than doubled over the course of the year, totaling over $130 million in fiscal 1992, despite the overall sluggishness of the national retail market. Spurred by the Duck Head line, the company's apparel division showed a 69 percent increase in sales and an impressive 267 percent growth in operating profit for the year. As a result of the apparel division's success, a rearrangement in management took place that split the division into two separate management teams, one responsible for Duck Head operations, the other for Delta Apparel. The fabrics division held steady for fiscal 1992. Sales and profit figures for both woven and knit products, as well as the balance between them, were comparable to those for the previous year. The company continued to supply woven fabrics for casual and tailored pants made by such well-known brands as Levi Strauss, Lee, Haggar, and Farah. While the sale of government products declined by 20 percent for the year (largely due to the war's end), a 25 percent increase in commercial finished cotton business picked up the slack.

As a whole, Delta Woodside's net sales set a company record of $705 million for fiscal 1992. Apparel operations accounted for about 29 percent of sales, closing in on the company's stated goal of 33 percent in the product mix. Net income, at just over $40 million, was also the highest in company history. In mid-1992, Delta's original yarn plant in Edgefield, South Carolina, the company's birthplace, was closed. Shortly thereafter, a new ultramodern plant, also located in Edgefield, went into production. The new plant was named after company co-founder Bettis Rainsford. The Rainsford Plant produces combed cotton and cotton-polyester yarns used in the manufacture of knit fabrics for men's and women's apparel. Much of the yarn is used internally in the company's Stevcoknit operations.

In January of 1993, Delta Woodside announced that it had acquired a 100 percent interest in Nautilus International, Inc., the Virginia-based manufacturer of fitness equipment. Nautilus had sales estimated at $18 million in 1992 and employed about 256 people. Delta also purchased 70 percent of the shares of Apparel Marketing Corporation, a New York-based company that held the license to manufacture apparel under the Nautilus brand name. This acquisition gave Delta another recognizable trade name, in addition to Duck Head, under which to market apparel. It also gave the company a solid inroad into the lucrative fitness wear business. Around the same time, Delta announced that it had completed the purchase of a new facility called the Harmony plant at Grecia in Costa Rica, which was set up to employ 210 people. The Harmony plant was acquired for the purpose of manufacturing men's pants under the Duck Head brand name.

Founded in 1983, Delta Woodside has attained a position of prominence in its industry in a remarkably short period of time. Part of the company's success can be credited to the philosophical consistency of its management, which has shown an extraordinary knack for locating unwanted plants and divisions that are ripe for resurrecting. If this knack continues to serve the company well, and if lingering woes in the world of retail fabrics do not become chronic, then Delta Woodside's brisk rise toward the top of the fabric industry could very well continue.

Principal Subsidiaries: Delta Mills Marketing Company; Duck Head Apparel Company, Inc.; Delta Apparel, Inc.; Duck Head Retail Operations; Harper Brothers; Stevcoknit Fabrics Company.

Further Reading:

Addis, Ronit, "Iconoclasts," *Forbes,* April 17, 1989, pp. 49–56.

Burritt, Chris, "Say Alchem to Buy Delta, Steveco From Stevens," *Daily News Record,* February 28, 1986, p. 2.

Clune, Ray, "Delta Woodside Sees Turnaround," *Daily News Record,* November 8, 1990, p. 9.

"Corporate Critics Confidential: Textile Industry," *Wall Street Transcript,* June 19, 1989, p. 93967.

Delta Woodside Industries, Inc. 1992 Annual Report, Greenville, South Carolina: Delta Woodside Industries, Inc., 1992.

"Delta Woodside Industries, Inc.," *Wall Street Transcript,* September 26, 1988, pp. 50–51.

"Delta Woodside Net Down 56%," *Daily News Record,* August 23, 1990, p.11.

"Delta Woodside's Sales to Military Skyrockets," *Daily News Record,* June 13, 1991. p. 7.

Isaacs, McAllister, "Delta Woodside's Rainsford: the Man, the Plant: Quality," *Textile World,* December 1992, pp. 32–38.

MacIntosh, Jeane, "Delta Sees Apparel Unit Sales Soaring to $400M," *Daily News Record,* March 20, 1992, p. 2.

Meagher, James P., "Delta Woodside Industries Inc.," *Barron's,* August 8, 1988, pp. 93–94.

"Renegades," *Success,* February 1990, pp. 30–31.

Robertshaw, Nicky, "Delta Woodside Industries Going Public," *Daily News Record,* December 4, 1986, p. 2.

Stilwell, Wesley, "Alchem to Acquire Royal Mfg.'s Assets," *Daily News Record,* February 11, 1985, p. 34.

—Robert R. Jacobson

The Dial Corp

The Dial Corp.

Dial Tower
1850 North Central Avenue
Phoenix, Arizona 85077
U.S.A.
(602) 207-4000
Fax: (602) 207-5455

Public Company
Incorporated: 1926
Employees: 29,300
Sales: $3.4 billion
Stock Exchanges: New York Pacific Tokyo
SICs: 2841 Soap & Other Detergents; 3711 Motor Vehicles
   & Car Bodies; 4581 Airports, Flying Fields & Services;
   5947 Gift, Novelty & Souvenir Shops

The Dial Corp. is a Fortune 500 company comprised of three business segments: consumer products, service companies, and transportation manufacturing and service parts. Dial soap is perhaps the most recognizable item the company produces, but Dial Corp. is involved in myriad areas of business. Products varying from Armour Star canned meats to Purex laundry detergent, the services of Premier Cruise Lines, and the manufacturing segment Motor Coach Industries, all attest to The Dial Corp.'s diverse portfolio of companies. Since the 1970s, the corporation has undergone several episodes of restructuring and name changes, and in 1993 management was considering the private sale of the transportation manufacturing and service parts segment in order to concentrate its resources on consumer products and services.

The Dial brand name was first given to a unique deodorant soap developed by researchers at the Chicago-based meat processing business of Armour & Company. Introduced in 1948, Dial featured a newly developed germicide, known as AT-7, that was believed to reduce up to 80 percent more of the bacteria found on the skin than other soaps. Said to provide "Round the Clock Protection," Dial was first advertised in the *Chicago Tribune*, on paper printed with scented ink. The innovative advertisement attracted a great deal of attention, and the soap achieved high sales from the onset. One Chicago store reportedly sold more than 4,000 bars in one day.

Dial soon became the leading deodorant soap in the country. In 1953 the company adopted a slogan—"Aren't you glad you use Dial? Don't you wish everybody did?"—that would continue to be used into the 1990s. In 1966 Armour announced that it would begin marketing aerosol can and roll-on deodorant products as well as shaving creams under the Dial brand name. Over the next five years, the new Dial products achieved record sales, and a shampoo was added to the Dial line.

In 1970 Armour was acquired by the Greyhound Corporation. The country's leader in the motorcoach industry since 1930, Greyhound, under chairperson and CEO Gerald H. Trautman, had begun to diversify its operations in the 1960s in response to declining bus ticket sales. As automobiles and airline tickets became less expensive and bus line profits dwindled, Greyhound acquired small companies in the fields of automobile leasing, money orders, insurance, and catering. Greyhound board members were approached by Armour in the late 1960s when General Host threatened Armour with a hostile takeover, and Greyhound was persuaded to add Armour-Dial to its subsidiaries. The 1970 $400 million purchase was Greyhound's first major acquisition. To reduce its investment, Greyhound immediately sold $225 million of Armour assets, retaining only the meat-packing and consumer products subsidiaries. The meat-packing operation was renamed Armour Foods, while the consumer products operation was renamed Armour-Dial.

In 1971 construction was completed on a new plant for manufacturing Dial soap in Aurora, Illinois. However, while Armour-Dial was now better equipped to meet consumer demands for the soap, the company was also faced with the possibility of having to alter the soap's ingredients. Although Dial had an excellent record of consumer satisfaction and the company had neither received any complaints during the soap's 23-year history nor been given any reason to consider the product unsafe, the U.S. Food and Drug Administration found during this time that one of the soap's germicidal ingredients, hexachlorophene, was dangerous if misused or ingested. When the FDA banned the use of the chemical in cosmetics and restricted its use in soaps, Armour management planned, in conjunction with the FDA, to continue to market Dial with a label on the packaging warning users that the soap was for external use only and should be thoroughly rinsed off the skin after each use. Eventually, however, researchers at the company were able to develop an alternative ingredient that proved to be as successful as hexachlorophene had been as a germicide. Although the formula of Dial changed, it continued to rank as one of the nation's most popular soaps.

In 1971 Armour-Dial's headquarters were moved to Phoenix, Arizona, where operations were reorganized under two primary headings: the Toiletries & Household Products Division and the Administrative Division.

Although Trautman had taken Greyhound from bus line to successful conglomerate, the company was still known on Wall Street as "the dog," due to the unpredictable swings in profits and losses it incurred from year to year. Problems were attributed to the rapid expansion of Greyhound's holdings to include such a vast and unrelated an array of products and services. Furthermore, while Armour Foods and Armour-Dial accounted for over 50 percent of the company's revenues, their earnings proved extremely erratic, ranging from nine percent growth one year to 21 percent the next. The Armour Foods subsidiary in particular had also been troubled by frequent restructuring and changes in management. In general, analysts found that Greyhound was suffering from a lack of focus.

An overhaul of the company began in 1982 when John W. Teets was named chairperson and CEO. Teets began working for Greyhound in 1964 when he took a job managing the company's restaurants at the New York World's Fair. Recently devastated by a series of personal tragedies, including the deaths of both his wife and his brother as well as a fire that destroyed a restaurant of which he had been part owner, Teets threw himself into his new job at Greyhound, working long hours and exhibiting a determination and enthusiastic management style that was soon noticed by Greyhound executives. He was promoted to president of Post Houses, a Greyhound subsidiary that ran bus terminal restaurants, where he remained until 1968, when he accepted an offer from a Chicago-based restaurant chain. Teets returned to Greyhound in 1976 to head the company's Food Service Group subsidiary. By this time he had become known for his ability to help struggling companies return to profitability, and he was soon credited with turning around the entire food service division. By 1980 Teets held the executive office of vice chairperson and was a contender for the presidency when Trautman retired.

Upon his appointment as president and CEO, Teets acted quickly to restructure the company, quickly establishing his reputation as a tough and demanding leader through his implementation of a new standard of 15 percent return on equity, a level of performance that he expected of each subsidiary. Reexamining Greyhound's holdings, he was quoted in *Forbes* as concluding that the company needed to ''lean down, be tougher in the marketplace,'' through a long term agenda that included selling off several subsidiaries and cutting costs. In 1983, in one of his first major decisions, Teets cut the wages of union food and commercial workers at Armour Foods. When the workers refused to accept the cut, Teets shut down the 29 plants and sold the operations to Conagra Inc., which offered Greyhound a 15-percent stake in its company, a deal equalling around $150 million.

Also that year the company was faced with a widely publicized Greyhound bus drivers strike. The bus line had experienced dramatic losses in ridership and nearly $35 million in operating losses in 1981 and 1982. Finding that Greyhound drivers were earning as much as 50 percent more than drivers at competing companies, Teets threatened to replace them with nonunion employees if they did not accept a cut in wages. A violent 47-day strike ensued, during which buses were kept running by nonunion labor. Eventually Teets prevailed, and union drivers returned to work at a lower wage. Although Teets was able to cut its operating costs, Greyhound never recovered financially, and early in 1987, he sold the Greyhound bus company to a group of investors from Dallas.

Having restructured the company's interests, Teets began a plan of selective acquisitions that would better fit the company's portfolio. Relying on the unmitigated success of the Armour-

Dial division to provide expert management in the field, Greyhound acquired Purex Industries Inc., makers of laundry soap, for $264 million in 1985. The purchase doubled Greyhound's consumer product sales, and after a brief period of losses, the company recaptured its market share. Two years later, the company restructured the consumer products subsidiary along product lines, creating a personal care division that handled the marketing of bath and deodorant soaps, as well as the new and profitable Liquid Dial soap; a household and laundry division responsible for such items as detergents, air fresheners, and cleansers; and a food division that during this time introduced Lunch Bucket single-serving microwaveable meals.

By the late 1980s Greyhound had completed its plans for restructuring. With profits high from the sales of the popular Dial, Purex, and newly acquired Brillo steel wool soap pads, and stock prices low at around $27 per share, the streamlined company was ripe for a takeover, and rumors spread on Wall Street. In order to discourage raiders, Teets was faced with the challenge of raising the stock prices. By 1991, however, the company's debts had shrunk, its earnings improved dramatically, and stock prices had risen to $44 per share.

To minimize confusion for its investors and consumers by distinguishing the company from the Greyhound bus line it had sold off three years before, the company changed its name to Greyhound Dial in March 1990. At the time Teets decided to retain ''Greyhound'' as part of the company's new name in order to reflect the ten subsidiaries the company still owned that carried the Greyhound name, such as Greyhound Exhibitgroup. Within the year, however, when Greyhound Dial switchboard operators were still receiving numerous calls regarding bus routes and fares, management decided to make the message clearer still by renaming the company The Dial Corp.

In 1991 The Dial Corp. reported a loss of $57.6 million due to its restructuring and the costs involved in spinning off some of its subsidiaries. Revenues were up from $3.5 to $3.6 billion, however, and management estimated that without the one-time charges against earnings in 1991, The Dial Corp. would have reported a net income of $122.4 million.

Principal Subsidiaries: Aircraft Service International Group; Dial Consumer Products Group; Dobbs International Services, Inc.; Exhibitgroup Inc.; GES Exposition Services, Inc.; Greyhound Leisure Services, Inc.; Greyhound Lines of Canada Ltd.; Jetsave Inc.; Motor Coach Industries, Inc.; Premier Cruise Lines, Ltd.; Restaura, Inc.; Transportation Manufacturing Corporation; Travelers Express Company, Inc.; Universal Coach Parts, Inc.

Further Reading:

Byrne, Harlan S., ''Investment News & Views: Dial Corp.,'' *Barron's,* August 26, 1991, pp. 37–8.
The Dial Corp. Annual Reports, Phoenix: The Dial Corp., 1990–92.
''Dial Corp. Restructures Along Product Lines,'' *Arizona Business Gazette,* January 5, 1987.
''Dial Enjoys Its Liquid Assets,'' *Packaging Digest,* July 1989, pp. 74, 79.
Gillespie, Phyllis, ''Turning the Dial,'' *Arizona Republic,* December 22, 1991.

The Greyhound Corporation Annual Reports, Phoenix: The Greyhound
   Corporation, 1975–88.
Kiley, David, "Greyhound Dials Up a Name Change—More or Less,"
   Adweek's Marketing Week, March 5, 1990, p. 5.

Stuart, Alexander, "Greyhound Gets Ready for a New Leader," *Fortune,* December 15, 1980, pp. 58–64.
"Will More Soap Help Greyhound Shine?" *Business Week,* March 11, 1985.

—Tina Grant

Dow Chemical Company

2030 Willard H. Dow Center
Midland, Michigan 48674
U.S.A.
(517) 636-1000
Fax: (517) 832-1465

Public Company
Incorporated: June 11, 1947
Employees: 61,000
Sales: $18.97 billion
Stock Exchanges: New York Midwest Pacific Amsterdam
   Antwerp Basel Bern Brussels Dusseldorf
SICs: 2819 Industrial Inorganic Chemicals Nec; 2821
   Plastics Materials & Resins; 2812 Alkalies & Chlorine;
   2869 Industrial Organic Chemicals Nec

To say that Dow is a very large chemical company is an understatement. Its annual sales are roughly equal to the Gross National Products of Kenya and Uganda combined. At last count the company offered more than two thousand different products. Approximately half of Dow's income comes from basic chemicals, but plastics, specialty chemicals, consumer products, and pharmaceuticals are also important to the company.

Herbert Dow began his career around 1890, when he convinced three Cleveland businessmen to back his latest project, which involved the extraction of bromide from brine. Dow's idea was to extract the huge underground reservoirs of brine, souvenirs of prehistoric times when Lake Michigan had been a sea. This brine was being used for salt, but Dow was determined to distill bromides and other chemicals from it. His first venture, called Canton Chemical, failed and was superceded by Dow Chemical.

Dow's use of an electric current to separate bromides from the brine was revolutionary. He was experimenting with electrolysis at a time when the electric lightbulb was still viewed with suspicion. (At the time, President Harrison refused to touch the newly installed light switches in the White House for fear of electrocution.) However, Dow constructed primitive cells from wood and tar paper, and began producing bromides, as well as bleaching agents, for another fledgling company by the name of Kodak.

In the first years of this century Dow began to sell his bromides abroad, but the Deutsche Bromkonvention, a powerful group of German bromide producers, declared an all-out price war against Dow Chemical. German and British bleachmakers (bromide is used in bleach) reduced the price of their product from $1.65 to 88 cents a pound in the United States, which was less than cost. Dow's plants depended on a price of $1.65 in order to make a profit. While other American bleachmakers closed for the duration of the price war, Dow went deeper into debt and fought for his share of the domestic and foreign markets. One of his successful tactics was to purchase the imported bromide that the Germans were selling in New York at a price below cost, and then resell it in Europe where the price of bromide was still $1.65 per pound.

After the bromide war came World War I, which, among other things, ended German domination of the world chemical industry. The German naval blockade forced American industry to turn to American chemical makers for essential supplies. Dow was pressed into the manufacture of phenol, used in explosives, and magnesium. At the time these two substances had limited use outside of munitions, but they were later to play an important role in the development of Dow Chemical and chemical technology in general. Phenol would later be required for the manufacture of plastics, and magnesium, a metal that would make aviation history.

After the war Congress protected the fledgling American chemical industry by imposing tariffs, so that the country would not become dependent on foreign chemical manufacturers again. By 1920 Dow Chemical was selling four million dollars worth of bulk chemicals like chlorine, calcium chloride, salt, and aspirin every year. By 1930 sales had climbed to $15 million and the company stock had split four times. Before the stock market crashed in 1929 the price per share had climbed to $500.

Dow's success drew the attention of Du Pont, which wished to acquire the midwestern bromide manufacturer until Herbert Dow threatened to leave the company and take his engineers with him. Without Herbert Dow's leadership and ingenuity the company was not regarded as worth the price of purchase and Du Pont subsequently withdrew its offer.

Herbert Dow died just as the Great Depression began and was replaced by his son Willard. Willard Dow, like his father, considered research, as opposed to production or sales, the key to the company's future. Despite the state of the economy, Willard Dow approved expenditures for research into petrochemicals and plastics. The company's product line expanded to include iodine, ethylene, and materials to flush out oil from the ground. A new plant was constructed that would extract bromine from sea water. There was also a rumor on Wall Street that Dow's new method could also extract gold from the seawater, which turned out to be true. However, for every $300 worth of gold, $6,000 worth of bromine could be recovered.

During World War II Dow Chemical's new research resulted in handsome rewards. Even before America's entrance into the war, Dow had started to expand in preparation for future hostilities. One of its first wartime contracts was with the British, who desperately needed magnesium. Dow produced some of the mineral at its new plant in Freeport, Texas, which derived magnesium from seawater. Dow later supplied the metal to the United States and even shared its patented process with other companies.

Before World War II the potential value of magnesium in the manufacture of airplanes had gone unnoticed, and during this time Dow Chemical was the only U.S. magnesium producer. Yet even with a monopoly on the metal, the company lost money on its production. This was typical of Dow Chemical at that time; it often invented a product and then patiently waited for a market. During the war Dow produced over 80 percent of the magnesium used by the United States, which later led to federal investigations into whether or not Dow had conspired to monopolize magnesium production in the country. The U.S. press, however, sided with Dow and eventually the charges, which had included accusations of a conspiracy with German magnesium manufacturers, were dropped.

Besides manufacturing magnesium the company also made styrene and butadiene for synthetic rubber. After the bombing of Pearl Harbor the Japanese had conquered the rubber plantations of the Far East and soon the commodity was in short supply. Due to the fact that Dow had persisted in plastics research during the Depression, it was at the forefront of manufacturing synthetic products. Besides making styrene and butadiene, it molded Saran plastic, now known as a food wrap, into pipes, or had it woven into insect screens to protect soldiers fighting in the tropics.

After the war the company had to adapt to the postwar economy. One of management's concerns was that Dow Chemical had placed such a strong emphasis on research and development in the past that it sometimes ignored the fact that it was supposed to be making profits. The marketing and sales departments were reluctantly increased. Said one man employed at the time, "You got the feeling that Willard looked on sales as a necessary evil."

Despite the fact that Dow had to share trade secrets with its competitors during the war, it ranked as the sixth-largest chemical company in the country and was well positioned to take advantage of the increasing peacetime demand for chemicals. Its product line was extensive and included chemicals used in almost every conceivable industry. Bulk chemicals accounted for 50 percent of sales and plastics accounted for 20 percent of sales, while magnesium, pharmaceuticals, and agricultural chemicals each accounted for 10 percent of sales.

Dow expanded significantly during the postwar period, going heavily into debt in order to finance its growth. The man who presided over this expansion was Willard Dow's brother-in-law, Lee Doan (Willard Dow had been killed in a plane crash). One of Doan's first tasks was to reorganize the company and make it more customer-oriented. Willard and Herbert Dow's tenures had been previously described by insiders as "capricious." The emphasis now was on long-range planning.

In the year of Willard's death, 1949, sales were $200 million, but ten years later they had nearly quadrupled. Products such as Saran Wrap began to make Dow a high profile company. Dow's growth surpassed that of its competitors, and the company was soon ranked fourth in the industry. The company's plants had previously been located in Texas and Michigan, but during the

1950s important production centers were built elsewhere. Foreign partnerships like Ashai Dow in Japan were formed, and the company expanded its presence in the European market.

Dow began the 1960s with a change of leadership. Ted Doan succeeded his father and, with Ben Branch and Carl Gerstacker, reorganized the company. Communication had become a problem because of Dow's vast size, so the company was broken into more manageable units which could be run like small businesses. Marketing, however, became more centralized. The management liked to think of their company as democratic, with overlapping lines of responsibility. The structure of the company was deliberately arranged so that employees would use their own initiative to invent new products and to manufacture existing products at a lower cost. The strategy worked.

Throughout the 1960s Dow's earnings increased approximately ten percent each year. Among the company's hundreds of products, however, one began to receive an inordinate amount of publicity—napalm. Beginning in 1966 the company became the target of anti-Vietnam War protests. Company recruiters were overrun on college campuses by large numbers of placard-waving students. Dow defended its manufacture of the searing chemical by saying that it was not responsible for U.S. policy in Indo-china and that it should not deprive American fighting men of a weapon that the Pentagon thought was necessary. Critics charged that the gruesomeness of the weapon made it imperative for the company not to cooperate with the government. Right or wrong, the public outcry against Dow demoralized a company that wanted to be associated with Handy Wrap rather than with civilian Vietnamese casualties.

At the beginning of the 1970s *Forbes* magazine predicted that Dow would have trouble growing because of its indebtedness. In 1974, however, the same *Forbes* reporter was subjected to criticism by chief executive officer Carl Gerstacker because Dow had a record year. The oil embargo was beneficial for Dow since it had its own petroleum feedstocks with which to manufacture its various specialty chemicals, while its competitors could not find the necessary petroleum. Noted Gerstacker: "Price wasn't the problem in '74; it was availability." Dow increased the price of many of its chemicals and its earnings increased, despite a strike in its hometown of Midland, Michigan. After the six-month strike, Dow gave the strikers a ten percent bonus and gave each pensioner two thousand dollars worth of bonds. Company stockholders did not mind management's sudden display of generosity; that year they received a 30 percent return on equity.

The year 1975 was followed by an oversupply of petrochemicals and a business slowdown, and the company's earnings began to slide. Since the company was doing almost half of its business overseas, an unfavorable rate of exchange added to the above problems with the result that earnings also decreased.

By 1978 a change of leadership was deemed necessary; Gerstacker's retirement from the board of directors was the end of an era. Gerstacker's management strategy was that, "you should have as much debt as you can carry." During recessions and slowdowns, borrowed money was used for research and development as well as for plant expansion. He was an administrator in the tradition of Herbert Dow, but the moves that had catapulted Dow to a position of leadership in the chemical industry seemed unwise in the business climate of the late 1970s. P.F. Oreffice, who Gerstacker had referred to as "a little old lady in tennis shoes" because of his conservative fiscal policy, became president and chief executive officer.

Soon after his promotion, Oreffice reorganized Dow as most of his predecessors had done after their appointment. These frequent reorganizations were less a testimony to the inadequacy of the previous organization than an admission that the company was outgrowing previously successful arrangements. This time management was reorganized on a geographical basis, since Dow had plants all over the world. In 1980, the year of the reorganization, sales exceeded $10 billion for the first time.

In the early 1980s a pattern of write-offs that depressed earnings began to emerge. In 1983 the write-off of two ethylene plants and a caustic soda plant caused earnings to drop 16 percent. Ethylene, a lead additive which prevents knocking in automobile engines, had been an important product for Dow at one time. In 1985 earnings fell 90 percent from the previous year as additional ethylene plants were closed.

Another factor that depressed 1985 products was the decrease in price and demand for basic chemicals. Dow derived 50 percent of its income from commodity chemicals that are sold by the ton. Foreign competitors, Arab chemical companies in particular, invaded the American market in the same way that Dow once invaded the European bromide market. To make matters worse, the market for commodity chemicals is sensitive to world economic conditions. Dow's position as an American company complicated matters further. When the dollar is strong, as it was in 1984 and part of 1985, the company's exports are harder to sell and its foreign earnings, when converted to dollars, are smaller.

In 1981 Dow purchased Merrell Drug, thus expanding its pharmaceutical division. In 1984 Dow purchased Texize, which boasted a strong line of detergent products, from Morton Thiokol. Research spending remained at almost 90 percent of cash flow. Extra-strong ceramics and plastics for the electronics industry are among the numerous specialty chemicals that Dow hoped would account for two-thirds of its sales in the 1990s. The company still placed a premium on innovation, however, and stated that it anticipated placing 15 to 25 new products on the market each year. The expansion into pharmaceuticals, specialty chemicals, and household products, however, some felt, required a new approach to management. According to an analyst with Kidder and Peabody, "If you're running a monolithic chemical business, management is the same across all products. Now they're going to have hundreds of small businesses to manage."

The company appointed a new chairman of the board, Robert Lundeen, and launched a new ad campaign, in which working for Dow was equated with "doing something for the world." Eager to rid itself of the adverse publicity surrounding topics such as Vietnam and alleged environmental abuse, Dow actually supported an increase in the Environmental Protection Agency's budget and a strengthening of rules regarding hazardous waste. This marked a significant philosophical turnaround for a company that had argued against a ban on dioxin in the 1970s.

Despite its changes in management, however, Dow was hurting in 1985, as it failed to recapture market share lost during the 1980–1982 recession. Profits tumbled from $805 million in 1980 to $58 million in 1985. Frank Popoff was appointed president and CEO from his position as head of Dow Chemical/Europe. Largely on the strength of Popoff's decisions, the firm improved marketing and sales of value-added products, which commanded higher prices. Dow began to win market share in this higher-margin area as it increasingly concentrated on finding new applications for existing products.

The company's efforts found a ready-made market in the auto industry, which was in the midst of a campaign to increase efficiency and cut costs. Dow concentrated on other durable sectors like appliances, housewares, and electronics as well. It also looked into packaging and the recreation and health-care industries. Since Dow already made so many plastics, chemicals, and hydrocarbons cheaply, increased sales of them at higher margins offered an immediate hike in profits. This strategy was immediately successful, and the company received a further boost when the U.S. dollar began to fall, making it easier for Dow to sell against German companies and other competitors.

Oil prices fell in 1986, further feeding Dow's recovery. With the dollar continuing to fall and the world economy humming, the spread between raw material costs and final prices expanded until the firm's plastics business was making a record 25 to 30 percent on sales during mid-1987.

Dow continued to diversify through acquisition, but tried to concentrate on firms with a base in chemicals, paying special heed to firms with technologies or distribution systems deemed not practical for Dow to develop internally. A joint venture in agricultural chemicals, called Dow Elanco, was begun with Eli Lilly. Dow acquired 39 percent of Marion Laboratories, a pharmaceuticals firm, for $2.2 billion, then joined it with Dow Merrell, making it a public company with a 67 percent Dow stake.

By 1988 commodity chemicals accounted for just 53 percent of the firm's $13.3 billion in sales. Its move into pharmaceuticals was proving to be a success, with $1.1 billion in sales a year. Its star drug was Seldane, an antihistamine with sales that were reaching hundreds of millions of dollars. Total Dow sales for 1989 reached $17.6 billion, an increase of $7 billion over five years earlier, with profits up to $2.5 billion.

In 1990, however, the world economy headed into recession. As in past recessions, the chemical industry, plagued by overcapacity, began a price war and began cutting output. Dow was the leading low-cost producer of commodity chemicals, hydrocarbons, and plastics. Rather than cut capacity, Dow continued to produce chemicals at a lower profit margin in the hopes of keeping its market share and driving out weaker competitors. Profits fell, but the company maintained its position in the marketplace; even DuPont was forced to cut production of polymers.

The Persian Gulf War temporarily caused the price of oil to rise, further hurting Dow. When the war ended, the slowdown in the chemical industry continued. Many in the industry believed that it was just another cycle in a cyclical industry. Popoff, however, maintained that the slowdown represented a more fundamental shift in the industry, one that was eroding the advantages of bigger firms. The strategy, Popoff felt, was now to be as lean and fast as small firms while maintaining an R&D advantage.

Despite these beliefs, Dow was forced to build new plants for commodity chemicals when a Canadian supplier decided to become a competitor. Dow began building ethylene plants in Alberta, Canada, and Freeport, Texas. Even after 40 years in Asia, sales there still acounted for less than 10 percent, while European sales accounted for 31 percent of total sales. But with Europe mired in recession and sales there slowing, Dow began pushing into Asia again, building a petrochemicals plant in China, where it enjoyed an expanding polyurethane business.

Though its growth had been slowed by the downturn in chemicals, Dow had nevertheless reduced its dependence on commodity chemicals from 80 percent of sales in 1980 to 45 percent in 1992, making it one of the world's most diversified chemical firms. It has also vastly improved its environmental reputation over the past decade via both advertising efforts and tangible results in elevating its environmental record. Dow Chemical remains, as the *Wall Street Journal* noted in 1991, "the industry's bellwether petrochemical stock."

Principal Subsidiaries: Admiral Equipment Co.; Boride Products, Inc.; Cayuse Pipeline, Inc.; Dofinco, Inc.; Domoclean International Inc.; Dorinco Reinsurance Co.; Dow Chemical Delaware Corp.; Dow Chemical Inter-American Ltd.; Dow Chemical International Energy Co.; Dow Chemical International Inc.; Dow Chemical International Ltd.; Dow Consumer Products, Inc.; Dow Corning Corp. (50%); Dowell Schlumberger Inc.; Dow Engineering Co.; Dow Financial Services Corp.; Dow Interstate Gas Co.; Dow Pipeline Co.; Great Western Pipeline Co., Inc.; Louisiana Gasification Technology Inc.; Merrell Dow Pharmaceuticals, Inc.; Metal Mark Inc. (50%); Midland Pipeline Corp.; The Cynasa Co. (90%). The company also lists subsidiaries in the following countries: Argentina, Australia, Belgium, Brazil, Canada, Chile, China, Colombia, Ecuador, Finland, Greece, Indonesia, Italy, Japan, Kenya, Malaysia, The Netherlands, Netherlands Antilles, New Zealand, Norway, Panama, Philippines, Saudi Arabia, Singapore, South Africa, Spain, Sweden, Switzerland, Thailand, United Kingdom, and Venezeula.

Further Reading:

Duerksen, Christopher J., *Dow vs California: A Turning Point in the Envirobusiness Struggle*, Washington, DC: Conservation Foundation, 1982.

Harman, Adrienne, "Metamorphosis," *Financial World,* February 2, 1993.

Meyer, Richard, "Avoiding the Fifth," *Financial World*, November 15, 1988.

Poland, Alan Blair, *A History of the Dow Chemical Company*, Ann Arbor: University Microfilms, 1980.

Quickel, Stephen, "Uncle!," *Financial World,* May 15, 1990.

—updated by Scott M. Lewis

E. I. du Pont de Nemours & Company

1007 Market Street
Wilmington, Delaware 19898
U.S.A.
(302) 774-1000

Public Company
Incorporated: 1915
Employees: 125,000
Sales: $37.8 billion
Stock Exchanges: New York
SICs: 2911 Petroleum Refining; 2221 Broadwoven Fabric
   Mills—Manmade; 2819 Industrial Inorganic Chemicals
   Nec; 2869 Industrial Organic Chemicals Nec

Du Pont is the oldest family name in American pre-industrial wealth. Its reputation is synonymous with organic chemistry. Founded in 1802, the company began as a partnership in gunpowder and explosives. Du Pont grew from a family business to a multinational conglomerate through the acquisition of its competing companies, and through the diversification of product lines.

Founder Éleuthère Irenée duPont de Nemours was born to French nobility. He studied with the chemist in charge of manufacturing the French government's gunpowder, Antionne LaVoisier. The years of turmoil preceding the French Revolution caused him to immigrate to the United States in 1797. He chose to build his production facilities on a site on the Delaware's Brandywine River, which was central to all of the states at the time and provided sufficient water power to run the mills. DuPont rapidly established a reputation for superior gunpowder. He died in 1834, leaving his sons Alfred and Henry to buy out French financiers and continue the business. His sons expanded the company's product line into the manufacture of smokeless powder, dynamite, and nitroglycerine.

One century after its founding, the gunpowder and explosives combine faced dissolution when senior partner Eugene duPont died at the age of 62, after having served 42 years. With no new leadership the surviving partners decided to sell the company to the highest bidder. Alfred I. duPont, a distant relative of the founder, purchased the firm with the aid of his cousins. Alfred was intent on saving the family business. Although he had

grown up working in gunpowder yards, he lacked the organizational skills needed to run the firm. His cousins Pierre S. duPont and Thomas Coleman possessed the financial acumen and led the family company to unprecedented success. The purchase price was set at $12 million, but secret investigations by the cousins unveiled company assets conservatively valued at $24 million. The old partnership also held a great deal of undervalued shares in other companies, among them their direct competitors in the gunpowder business, Hazard and Laflin & Rand. Not having the initial capital for the purchase, the young cousins negotiated a leveraged buy-out giving them a 25 percent interest in the new corporation and 4 percent paid on $12 million over the next 30 years. Coleman was president, Pierre treasurer, and Alfred vice president of E. I. du Pont de Nemours & Company. The only cash involved in the takeover was $8500 in incorporation fees.

Sound management, luck, and hidden wealth resulted in the acquisition of 54 companies within three years. Pierre set out to dominate the industry through pay-offs and by purchasing minority shareholders and vulnerable competitors. When the cousins first incorporated in 1902, the company controlled 36 percent of the U.S. powder market. By 1905 it held a 75 percent share of the market. Du Pont alone supplied 56 percent of the national production of explosives, with $60 million in estimated assets; it had become one of the nation's largest corporations.

A new method of operation was required to keep track of the rapidly growing organization. The cousins solicited the aid of Amory Haskell and Hamilton Barksdale, managers who had reorganized their dynamite business into an efficient organization. They remodeled the unwieldy company using elaborate family tree charts composed of levels of managers. The new structure revolutionized American business and gave birth to the modern corporation. The system of organization worked so well that Pierre bailed out the then struggling General Motors Corporation, buying 23 percent of the shares and applying the skills Du Pont had perfected. (The Department of Justice later ordered Du Pont to divest its General Motors holdings in 1951.)

Du Pont grew to command the entire explosives market. So dominant were they by 1907 that the U.S. government initiated antitrust proceedings against them. Du Pont was deemed a gunpowder monopoly in 1912 and ordered to divest itself of a substantial portion of its business. In addition, early years of incorporation were fraught with tension between Alfred and his more practical cousins. Arguments ensued over the modernization of the Brandywine yards. Coleman and Pierre saw modernization as the only way to fully utilize the plant. The quarrel, along with other incidents, prompted Coleman and Pierre to take away Alfred's responsibilities in 1911. In effect, this left Alfred a vice president in name only.

Modernization, diversification, good management, and a command of the market characterized Du Pont's industrial era phase. The experiments of Du Pont chemists with a product known as guncotton, an early form of nitroglycerine, led to the company's involvement in the textile business. The end of World War I proved the peacetime use of artificial fibers to be more profitable than explosives. In the 1920s Du Pont acquired French rights for producing cellophane. Du Pont made it moistureproof, transforming cellophane from a decorative wrap to a packaging material for food and other products. Du Pont also produced the clothing fiber Rayon in the 1920s, and used a stronger version of the fiber for auto tire cord.

Du Pont gradually moved away from explosives and into synthetics. Their most important discovery, Nylon, was created in 1930 by a polymer research group headed by Wallace H. Carothers. The synthesis of nylon came from the hypothesis that polymeric substances were practically endless chains held together by ordinary chemical bonds. Long chain molecules could be built one step at a time by carrying out well-understood reactions between standard types of organic chemicals. Carothers chose one of nature's simplest reactions—alcohols reacting with acids to form esters. By reacting compounds with alcohol groups on each end with analogous acids, polyesters were produced. Super polymers were later formed when a molecular still was used to extract the water that was formed in the reaction. The excess water had created a chemical equilibrium that stopped reaction and limited chain growth. Experimentation with diamine-dibasic pairs produced a molten polyamide that could be drawn into filaments, cooled, and stretched to form very strong fibers. Du Pont later marketed a 6-6 polymer, which was made from the inexpensive starting compound Benzene. The new fiber proved remarkably successful. It was employed as a material for undergarments, stockings, tire cord, auto parts, and brushes.

A large number of plastics and fibers followed. Products such as Neoprene (synthetic rubber), Lucite (a clear, tough plastic resin), and Teflon (a resin used in non-stick cookware) became commonplace. Fibers like Orlon (a bulky acrylic fiber), Dacron polyester, and Mylar became household names. Du Pont quickly became known as the world's most proficient synthesizer. The range of textiles that they supplied reoriented the whole synthetic field.

Not every Du Pont invention was a success, however. Corfam, a synthetic leather product, proved to be a disaster. Lammont duPont Copeland, the last duPont to head the company, invested millions of dollars into promoting Corfam in the 1960s. The product was not successful due to the fact that, although the material lasted practically forever, it lacked the flexibility and breathability usually found in leather products. Lammont relinquished the chief executive post in 1967 and was succeeded by Charles B. McCoy, son of a Du Pont executive. Irving Shapiro took the post in 1974. Shapiro had served Du Pont well, acting as the principal lawyer negotiating the antitrust suit brought against Du Pont and General Motors Corporation.

Shapiro lead Du Pont for six years during a period when the fibers industry stagnated from overcapacity. Du Pont's stream of synthetic fiber discoveries had led it into a trap, for it left them content to exploit the fiber market without looking elsewhere for new products. The demand for fibers collapsed in the mid-1970s, causing a halt in the company's main business. Climbing raw material costs and declining demand combined to depress the market in 1979. The innovator of a new technology had been the last to recognize that the market it created was losing momentum. The collapse compelled Du Pont to concentrate exclusively on repairing its old business, delaying actions to create a new base. Du Pont's rebuilding efforts were also hindered by reducing its commitment to research and development. Continued reliance on fibers caused Du Pont to be one of the worst hit chemical companies in the 1980 recession.

Du Pont's continued attention to the fibers business, however, resulted in an important discovery in 1980. Kevlar was added to the company's assemblage of synthetic textiles. Du Pont scientist Stephanie Kwolek discovered the solvent that unclumped the hard chains of molecules comprising an intractable polymer. The resultant revolutionary material proved to be light yet strong, possessing a tensile strength five times that of steel. Fabrics made of Kevlar were heat and puncture resistant. When laminated, Kevlar outstripped fiberglass. Du Pont made the largest financial gamble in its history, investing $250 million in a Kevlar plant expansion. Applications for Kevlar ranged from heat resistant gloves, fire resistant clothing, and bullet resistant vests to cables and reinforcement belting in tires. Kevlar also proved successful in the fabrics industry: one half of the police force in the United States soon wore Kevlar vests. Kevlar's true success, however, depended on the price of its raw material—oil. Kevlar showed no threat of becoming a steel replacement, since the price of its production was considerably higher.

Du Pont reacted to the depressed market in textiles by arranging mergers and acquisitions of other companies in other industries. Du Pont's takeover of the Conoco Oil company (the United States's number two petroleum firm) was the largest merger in history. Issues of anti-trust were prevalent in negotiation for the merger, but in the end Du Pont bought Conoco for $7.8 billion. Du Pont merged with Conoco to protect itself from the rise in crude oil prices. As oil supplies dwindled, a supply of Conoco oil and coal as raw material for Du Pont's chemicals provided a competitive advantage. Conoco's sites in Alberta, Canada, and off the north slope of Alaska provided large amounts of these resources. Du Pont's only disadvantage in the Conoco takeover was the introduction of Edgar Bronfman, chairman of the Seagram Company, the world's largest liquor distiller, into a minority position in Du Pont-Conoco. Conoco had been a major acquisition target for Seagram. The merger left Seagram with 20 percent of Du Pont. Bronfman saw himself as a long-term investor in Du Pont and desired an important voice in the company's direction. However, Seagram and Du Pont arrived at an agreement whereby Seagram could not purchase more than 25 percent of Du Pont stock until 1991.

Growth and greater financial security came to Du Pont in 1980 when they bought Remington Arms, a manufacturer of sporting firearms and ammunition. The Remington Arms unit of Du Pont made a number of multi-million dollar contracts with the army to operate government-owned plants. Du Pont also expanded its scope in the early 1980s with other major purchases. New England Nuclear Corporation, a leading manufacturer of radioactive chemicals for medical research and diagnosis, was acquired in April of 1981, and Solid State Dielectrics, a supplier of dielectric materials used in the manufacture of multilayer capacitors, was acquired in April of 1982.

Du Pont management was determined to reduce the company's dependence on petrochemicals. It decided to take some risks in becoming a leader in the life sciences by delving into development and production of biomedical products and agricultural chemicals. In April of 1982 Du Pont purchased the agrichemicals division of SEPIC. In November they acquired the production equipment and technology for the manufacture of spiral wound reverse osmosis desalting products. In March of 1986 Du Pont acquired Elit Circuits Inc., a producer of molded circuit interconnects.

In addition to mergers and acquisitions, Du Pont became heavily involved in joint ventures. Du Pont had agreements with P. D. Magnetics to develop, manufacture, and sell magnetic tape. It also became involved with PPG Industries to manufacture ethylene glycol. Aided by Olin Corporation, it planned to construct a chlor/alkali production facility. Du Pont also forged extensive connections with Japanese industry. The 1980s united them with Sankyo Company (to develop, manufacture, and market pharmaceuticals), Idemitso Petrochemicals (to produce and market butanediol), Mitsubishi Gas Chemical Company, and Mitsubishi Rayon Company. Furthermore, Du Pont established connections in Europe. They became partners with N.V. Phillips (to produce optical discs), EKA AB (to produce and market the Compozil chemical system for papermaking processes), and British Telecom (to develop and manufacture optoelectronic components).

In addition to stock chemicals and petrochemically based synthetic fibers, Du Pont looked to the life sciences and other specialty businesses to produce earnings. Edward G. Jefferson, a chemist by training, succeeded Shapiro and directed the company into the biosciences and other specialty lines. Du Pont supported these businesses with large amounts of capital investment and research and development expenditures. The fields of interest were genetic engineering, drugs and agricultural chemicals, electronics, and fibers and plastics.

Du Pont had the kind of multi-national marketing capability and the resources to become a major influence in the life sciences. The company sought ways to restructure living cells to mass produce specific micro-organisms in an attempt to produce commercial quantities of interferon, a human protein that is potentially useful in fighting viruses and cancer. Du Pont claimed to be the first company to have purified fibroblast interferon, one of the three types of human interferon in the mid-1970s. Du Pont developed a blood profile system, artificial blood, and a test for acquired immune deficiency syndrome (AIDS). They created drugs that control irregular heartbeats, aid rheumatoid arthritis pain, and were anti-narcotic agents. In addition to new drugs, Du Pont worked to develop new pesticides and herbicides. Du Pont built a $450 million business as a major supplier to the electronics industry, providing sophisticated connectors and the dry film used in making printed circuits. Du Pont also developed new high performance plastics. The company's scientists developed a process called group transfer polymerization for solvent based polymer acrylics. This was the first major polymerization process developed since the early 1950s.

In the early to mid-1980s Du Pont had approximately 90 major businesses selling a wide range of products to different industries, including petroleum, textile, transportation, chemical construction, utility, health care, and agricultural industries. Business operations existed in more than 50 nations. Du Pont had eight principle business segments: biomedical products; industrial and consumer products; fibers; polymer products; agricultural and industrial chemicals; petroleum exploration and pro-

duction; petroleum refining, marketing and transportation; and coal. Total expenditure for research and development amounted to more than $1 billion in 1985, and over 6000 scientist and engineers were engaged in research activities.

But by this time Du Pont was bloated with the numerous businesses it had acquired over the years. Management decided to return to its former policy of focusing on areas of maximum profit. It began moving away from commodity production, instead concentrating on oil, health care, electronics, and specialty chemicals.

By 1987 the changes were paying off in some areas, as discretionary cash flow reached $4.5 billion. Biomedical products represented only 4 percent of sales, but the firm was moving into the large markets for cancer and AIDS testing and research. Breaking into its new markets was expensive, however. Earnings soared at rivals like Rhone-Poulenc and Dow Chemical, which were less diversified. Meanwhile Du Pont's pretax income climbed only 4.5 percent, to 3.8 billion in 1988, although sales climbed by 8 percent. Du Pont still had problems with quality control. In 1988 Ford Motor Co. gave Du Pont's contract for mirror housings to General Electric because paint kept flaking off of Du Pont's plastic, according to an April, 1989, *Business Week* article.

Edgar Smith Woolard, Jr., became president in 1989, backed by the Bronfman family. As part of his mission to raise the price of Du Pont's stock and prevent a takeover, the firm bought back about 8 percent of its outstanding stock. The electronics division had $1.8 billion in annual sales and had won business in films and imaging, though it was losing money in the highly competitive areas of fiber optics and optical disks. In addition, the pharmaceuticals business was still losing money. Investment in research and equipment had reached $1.8 billion since 1982, yet most of the drugs under development were years from the market. One area of clear success was Du Pont's textile business. The $5.8 billion division was the firm's most profitable.

Seeking to raise public awareness of its fibers, Du Pont started a consumer products catalogue featuring household items made from its products. The catalogue mentioned copyrighted fiber names like Lycra, Zytel, and Supplex as it advertised the clothes, sporting goods, and housewares. Du Pont had reason to be interested in maintaining brand-name recognition in fibers. Lucre, a stretch polymer invented in 1959 and originally used for girdles, became a huge hit after being adopted for biking clothes and other exercise outfits during the early 1980s. By the end of the decade, Lucre clothing had become fashionable. Big name designers incorporated it into their wardrobes, and by 1990, Lucre profits topped $200 million a year. Du Pont's patent on Lucre, the generic name of which is spandex, had long since expired, but Du Pont had continued to improve the fabric and was its only major manufacturer. To make certain things stayed that way, the firm announced in 1990 that it would spend $500 million over three years to build or expand Lucre plants.

Another important area for Du Pont was pollution control and cleanup. According to *Forbes* magazine, the firm was one of the country's biggest air polluters, and was in the process of spending well over $1 billion on pollution control and clean up. The firm's chlorofluorocarbon business was being replaced by chemicals less harmful to the ozone layer, at a cost of another $1 billion. Du Pont also stood to make money, however, by creating safer herbicides and expanding into the growing recycling market. Partly because of these trends, Du Pont's sales of agricultural chemicals tripled between 1985 and 1990, to $1.7 billion.

Du Pont continued to cut costs and sell off unprofitable operations. The firm closed its declining Orlon division and laid off two layers of vice presidents. In 1991 it sold half of Consolidation Coal Co. for over $1 billion to Germany's Rheinbraun A.G. Although the coal unit was profitable, Du Pont decided it would rather invest in fibers and chemicals than in the coal business.

The Gulf War temporarily drove up oil prices and refinery margins, leading to profits of over $1 billion for Conoco in 1990. But a worldwide recession was hurting most of the rest of the company. Profits for 1991 fell to $1.4 billion on sales of $38.7 billion, down from sales of $40 billion in 1990. The firm's electronics products had garnered little prestige within the industry, and had fallen well behind earlier projections. So Du Pont began pulling back, beginning by selling an electronic connectors business with $400 million in annual sales. Du Pont also took a step back from pharmaceuticals, putting that division into a joint venture with Merck & Co.

As it approached the mid-1990s, Du Pont was back to concentrating on its core businesses of chemicals and fibers. It was cutting employment to reduce costs, and trying to put fewer layers between sales staff and top management.

Principal Subsidiaries: Conoco Coal Development Co.; Conoco Inc.; Conoco Shale Oil Inc.; Consolidated Coal Co.; Continental Pipe Line Co.; Continental Overseas Oil Co.; Douglas Oil Co.; Du Pont International Sales Corp.; Fairmont Supply Co.; Kayo Oil Co.; Louisiana Gas System, Inc.; Remington Arms Co. Inc. The company also lists subsidiaries in the following countries: Argentina, Australia, Belgium, Brazil, Canada, Colombia, Dubai, Finland, France, Guatemala, Indonesia, Italy, Japan, Liberia, Libya, Luxembourg, Mexico, The Netherlands, New Zealand, Norway, Peru, Philippines, Puerto Rico, Singapore, Spain, Sweden, Switzerland, Taiwan, Thailand, United Kingdom, and Venezuela.

Further Reading:

Chandler, Alfred D., Jr., and Stephen Salsbury, *Pierre S. duPont and the Making of the Modern Corporation,* New York: Harper & Row, 1971.
Colby, Gerald, *duPont Dynasty,* Secaucus, NJ: Lyle Stuart, 1984.
Mosley, Leonard, *Blood Relations: The Rise and Fall of the duPonts of Delaware,* New York: Atheneum, 1980.
Norman, James R., ''Turning Up the Heat at Du Pont,'' *Forbes,* August 5, 1991.
Taylor, Graham D. and Patricia E. Sudnik, *Du Pont and the International Chemical Industry,* Boston: Twayne, 1984.
Weber, Joseph, ''Du Pont's Version of a Maverick,'' *Business Week,* April 3, 1989.
Weber, ''Du Pont's Trailblazer Wants to Get Out of the Woods,'' *Business Week,* August 31, 1992.
Weiner, Steve, ''But Will They Ever Know Zytel from Lycra?,'' *Forbes,* June 26, 1989.

—updated by Scott M. Lewis

EAGLE EP PICHER

Eagle-Picher Industries, Inc.

580 Walnut Street
Cincinnati, Ohio 45202
U.S.A.
(513) 721-7010
Fax: (513) 721-2341

Public Company
Incorporated: 1916 as the Eagle-Picher Lead Company
Employees: 6,402
Sales: $611.5 million
Stock Exchanges: New York
SICs: 3295 Minerals—Ground or Treated; 3625 Relays &
   Industrial Controls; 3613 Switchgear & Switchboard
   Apparatus; 3812 Search & Navigation Equipment

Eagle-Picher Industries, Inc. is a Cincinnati-based diversified industrial concern which primarily supplies machinery and parts to other companies. The company provides an excellent example of how a once small enterprise survived the demise of several of the industries it operated in, managing to diversify without courting disaster as one of America's many ill-fated conglomerates.

The earliest predecessor of Eagle-Picher was established as a partnership in Cincinnati in 1842. Two brothers, Edgar and Stephen Conkling, set up a small operation to produce white lead, a by-product of corrosion that was especially useful as a durable paint when mixed with linseed oil. In 1847, the Conkling brothers went into partnership with William Wood, who later took over the company when Edgar Conkling joined the Texas West Railroad Company. With new partners, Wood moved the company to a new location in 1858 and changed the name of the firm to the Eagle White Lead Works.

Great instability came to the metals market after the Civil War. Overcapacity, a lack of commodity price controls, and strong competition from the ready-mix paint industry pushed Eagle and several other white lead manufacturers to the brink of bankruptcy. By 1887, a consortium of eastern lead companies formed a powerful association called the Lead Trust. The Trust tried and failed on numerous occasions to include Eagle in its collaborations. William Christie Wood, who succeeded his father as president of Eagle in 1883, led the fight to keep Eagle independent. He initiated strong financial controls and attempted to branch the company into related businesses. Wood

left in 1887, and was replaced by G. W. Boyce, who stayed for six months, and was then succeeded by Benjamin H. Cox.

Unable to sustain the company in light of the actions of the powerful 31 Lead Trust firms (which merged to form the National Lead Company in 1891), Cox hired three managers away from his Cincinnati rival, the Eckstein White Lead Company. These managers, led by John B. Swift, reorganized Eagle in an effort to fend off National Lead. The company had a strong customer base and a solid reputation for quality.

Certain that he could not succeed indefinitely, Swift attempted to vertically integrate the company like Standard Oil had done. Several years passed when, finally, in 1903, Eagle and several other independents secured a stake in the American Metal Company, a mining and smelting house. Meanwhile, Eagle diversified the product line to include lead pipe and plumbing supplies.

In December of 1905, after receiving an invitation to join National Lead, Eagle received an inquiry from the Picher Lead Company, a mining outfit in Joplin, Missouri, proposing a buyout. With a steady supply of lead from Picher, Eagle would be free of National Lead's ability to influence market prices. The transaction was completed on April 5, 1906.

Eagle, which had expanded its operations, provided Picher with capital to expand its facilities and fund further exploration in the mineral-rich tri-state region of Missouri, Oklahoma, and Kansas. Picher tried unsuccessfully for several years to locate new mineral deposits on the Quapaw Indian lands of the tri-state area. Fearing that the region had been depleted, Picher began wildcat drilling, again without success.

Late in 1913 a Picher drill rig became stuck in five feet of mud while being shipped during a thunderstorm. Picher suggested drilling in place before ordering the rig dismantled. To everyone's surprise, the chance drilling yielded an extremely rich lead-zinc ore concentrate that led to twenty more strikes by 1915, and the establishment of a huge zinc smelter at Henryetta, Oklahoma. The following year, Eagle and Picher formally merged into a single company.

However, the merger failed to address the problem of separate cultures, a facet that caused considerable division for many years. Many Picher employees held a strong grudge against Eagle, which they felt didn't fully appreciate the work they did in the tri-state. Oliver S. Picher, who became president of the new company, chose Chicago as the neutral site on which to establish a new headquarters. In 1919 he ordered the decentralization enterprise, forming an organization like General Electric, General Motors, and DuPont, in which specific divisions enjoyed operating autonomy.

Under Oliver Picher, Eagle-Picher became the nation's leading zinc manufacturer, as well as one of its largest lead producers. Growth in the zinc market was augmented by World War I, in which demand for zinc in brass artillery and other weapons increased dramatically. Seeking to enter the finished zinc products markets, Picher acquired a zinc oxide plant at Hillsboro, Illinois.

Clearly set on a strong path, Eagle-Picher lost considerable momentum the following year when Oliver Picher died suddenly. The board appointed Swift to succeed Picher as president. Swift continued Picher's diversification strategy by purchasing the Midland Chemical Company's lithopone plant at Argo, Illinois. From its origins in lead, Eagle-Picher had become one of the nation's only integrated mine-to-market zinc companies.

Swift ordered the company's research department, established in 1915 by Picher, to develop new uses for zinc. This led to several partnerships with battery companies in 1922, and the development of highly efficient lead batteries. Thus, with the advent of automobiles, a promising new market was created as demand for white lead pigment had begun to trail off.

Buoyed by the newfound productivity of the tri-state deposits, Eagle-Picher began buying large tracts of land in the region adjacent to its existing mines, organizing them under a new subsidiary, the Consolidated Lead and Zinc Company. Eagle-Picher expanded its production capacity in 1925 by taking control of the Ontario Smelting Company of Hockerville, Oklahoma. This enabled the company to squeeze additional ores out of mines that were thought to have been depleted.

Now listed on the Cincinnati Stock Exchange, Eagle-Picher entered a difficult period in 1927 when yields from the tri-state mines began to decline. Arthur Bendelari succeeded Swift as president of the company in February of 1928, and later moved the company's headquarters back to Cincinnati.

Serious declines occurred in the months following the stock market crash in 1929. To improve managerial efficiency, Bendelari reorganized all the company's production interests into a new subsidiary, Eagle-Picher Mining and Smelting. The subsidiary also shielded the parent company from potential liabilities in its field operations. As the Great Depression set in, lead and zinc prices continued to plummet. Eagle-Picher remained solvent mainly from the use of cash reserves accumulated during the boom years of the 1920s.

George Washington Potter, a veteran of the tri-state mines and a rival to Bendelari, recommended the establishment of a central smelting facility to replace the more than 200 smaller smelters located in the area. Potter won government permission to centralize production, and the right to operate Eagle-Picher locomotives on railroads in the region. The Central mill opened in October, 1932. During this time, the company also began producing slag wool, an insulation product made from smelter wastes. This stable, fire-proof material proved highly successful, bolstering the company's product line.

In 1933, Eagle-Picher faced a serious threat from the International Union of Mine, Mill and Smelter Workers, which had begun to organize workers in the tri-state region. Eagle-Picher and the Ore Producers Association to which it belonged refused to recognize the union, which called a strike for representation in May of 1935. Subsequently, Eagle-Picher helped to establish a rival company-sponsored union called the Blue Card Union. Using gangs of thugs, the local sheriff, and even the National Guard, the Blue Card succeeded in breaking the strike and seriously disrupting the union's activity in the area.

The union filed suits against Eagle-Picher and other companies with the National Labor Relations Board, charging interference in the administration of a labor union. The union prevailed, and Eagle-Picher gained a proven reputation for opposing union activity and being uncompromising and difficult in negotiations. Despite its legal victory, however, the union had little success in the tri-state.

Fearing that Eagle-Picher was losing control of its operations, the company's board asked Joel M. Bowlby, a Chicago accountant, to perform an analysis of the company. In January, 1937, Bowlby recommended further decentralization of the enterprise, creating fully autonomous divisions. Bendelari resigned shortly thereafter due to ill-health and was replaced by Joseph Hummel, Jr.. During this time, Potter approached management with a plan to acquire the Commerce Mining and Royalty Company, which held extensive ore reserves and several mills in the tri-state area, in addition to the Northeast Oklahoma Railroad. The $10 million deal was finalized in 1938, and Commerce was added to Eagle-Picher as a separate division, following Bowlby's recommendations.

The Commerce acquisition did little more than extend the life of a dying industry in the tri-state region. However, during this time, the Germans invaded Poland and war began in Europe, creating a huge demand for war industry minerals, including Eagle-Picher's lead and zinc. Production capacity was expanded to meet the new demand, and in late 1941 the company even took over a zinc operation in Taxco, Mexico. To cope with the new demand, Eagle-Picher enlisted the Robert Heller consulting firm to present its own set of recommendations. Heller advised elevating Bowlby to the presidency and shuffling Hummel off to head the board.

Bowlby's ascension to the presidency was well timed. As a bookish accountant who possessed tremendous knowledge of the company, he was perfectly suited for the job. A fact that became evident after Pearl Harbor, when the company came under the direction of the War Production Board.

Eagle-Picher held several advantages over other wartime industries. Unlike Singer, which converted from sewing machines to machine guns, and Ford, which went from automobiles to bombers, Eagle-Picher already produced what it needed to: slab zinc, paint pigments, lead and zinc oxides, bearing metals, antomonial leads, solders, and insulation products.

The war brought a production boom back to the tri-state area. But even so, Eagle-Picher had difficulty operating its mines at capacity with a workforce depleted by conscription, despite increased mechanization and the addition of another mine near Tucson. Furthermore, the company's profits from war production were strictly controlled by the government. Meanwhile, Potter, who had given so much to the company, became seriously disillusioned with Eagle-Picher under Bowlby, who used wartime profits to move Eagle-Picher out of mining and into manufacturing. Potter resigned in protest in 1944.

The war brought Eagle-Picher into several new markets, particularly production of germanium, the first semiconducting material, essential to the invention of the transistor in 1947 as well as to the development of solid state electronics. The company also emerged from the war with highly-advanced battery systems which held tremendous commercial potential. Commercialization of these products required no conversion back to the civilian economy.

Having dropped the name "Lead" from its name in 1945, Eagle-Picher purchased smelters and fabricating plants in Dallas and East Chicago in 1946, and the Alston-Lucas paint company two years later. Hoping to build on the postwar housing boom, the company also purchased the Orange Screen Company, a manufacturer of screen doors and windows.

In the attempt to diversify, Eagle-Picher purchased a diatomaceous earth plant, which produced filtration products, in Clark, Nevada. Abandoning an effort to exit the metallic products business, Eagle-Picher later purchased the Kansas City Smelting and Refining Company, the Cleveland Lead Works, and parts of the Southern Lead Company.

The International Union tried to assert its influence again in 1946, when it called 600 workers out on strike. While the company compromised here, a second strike in 1948 gave Eagle-Picher an incentive to stand up to the union, and its offer was eventually accepted by the union.

Bowlby resigned in 1948 due to a family illness, and was replaced by T. Spencer Shore, a company director and partner with Goldman-Sachs. Shore set new, more meaningful corporate performance goals based on earnings per share. He also limited Eagle-Picher's acquisitions to closely held companies serving specialized industrial markets. Shore understood that Eagle-Picher could not run these companies as well as their original management. He added the condition that acquisitions require the management of these companies to remain after being taken over by Eagle-Picher. Other emerging conglomerates of the day, including Textron, Ling Electronics (later LTV), and ITT, did not understand this and succeeded in destroying many of the companies they took over.

Eagle-Picher saw a second defense-related increase in demand during the Korean War, when American forces again became engaged in combat and the military began massive stockpiling efforts in the event of a wider war with communist countries.

Still, with the decline of the tri-state area, the need for the Mining and Smelting subsidiary disappeared. These operations were converted back into an operating division of Eagle-Picher. Back on the acquisition trail in 1952, Eagle-Picher took over the Ohio Rubber Company of Willoughby, Ohio, making it a division of the company.

In 1954, Shore liquidated Eagle-Picher's Paint and Varnish and Metallic Product divisions, which were only marginally profitable, and used the proceeds to acquire the Fabricon Products division of Fisher Body for $9.9 million. Fabricon manufactured plastic products for the automotive, food, and packaging industries. Eagle-Picher later acquired another plastics company, Wilson and Hoppe, which it merged with Fabricon.

After divesting its Mexican operations for $1.4 million in 1956, Eagle-Picher purchased the Chicago Vitreous Corporation, a porcelain enameling company, and the Gora-Lee Corporation, a Connecticut-based rubber molds manufacturer. The company's

divisional structure made these acquisitions all the easier to metabolize.

During the early 1950s, Bell Labs, RCA, Texas Instruments Incorporated, Raytheon, Sylvania, and General Electric provided strong markets for Eagle-Picher germanium, which was used to develop even more advanced transistor products. By 1955, Eagle-Picher held 95 percent of the market. This market dried up quickly, however, after Texas Instruments developed a silicon transistor made, essentially, from sand. Eagle-Picher failed to develop its own silicon business winding up that operation in 1960.

Nevertheless, Eagle-Picher continued to benefit from its leading research in silver-zinc battery technologies, which gained new importance with the development of rocket and missile programs during the 1950s. The "couples" battery, named for its dual chamber construction, led Eagle-Picher's product line in a zero defects quality program. The battery program ultimately drew Eagle-Picher into the prestigious and profitable aerospace and defense business, as well as into space exploration. Eventually, Shore combined the germanium and battery operations into a new electronics division.

During the early 1960s, Eagle-Picher continued to diversify by taking over several other companies, including the Akron-based Standard Mold tire products company, Davis Wire, a steel fence and net manufacturer in Los Angeles, and the Premier Rubber Manufacturing Company in Dayton. In 1966, to emphasize its increasingly diverse nature, the company changed its name from the Eagle-Picher Company to Eagle-Picher Industries. Shore maintained his strict acquisition policy and, because Eagle-Picher remained in closely related markets, came to hate the description of the company as a "conglomerate."

Under Shore, who retired in favor of William D. Atterbury, in 1967, Eagle-Picher fell short of establishing dominant horizontal or vertical monopolies, but remained too closely tied to specific industrial markets to be considered typically diversified. Acquisitions continued that year, with the Detroit-based gasket maker, Wolverine Fabricating and Manufacturing, and the Markey Bronze Corporation. The following year Eagle-Picher took over Cincinnati Cleaning and Finishing, a manufacturer of cleaning solvents, and Union Steel, which produced welded wire and sheet metal. In 1969, Eagle-Picher acquired the Ross Pattern and Foundry company, a manufacturer of aluminum castings for the automotive, electronics, and aerospace industries.

With lowered growth from divestitures and operating profit, Atterbury attempted to raise investment capital by emphasizing the synergy of Eagle-Picher's various divisions. The profit-center approach to these divisions served the cause well. The company raised sufficient capital to purchase the A. D. Weiss Lithograph Company and the Hillsdale Tool company. Meanwhile, in March, 1972, Eagle-Picher spun off Davis Wire to a group led by the division's management for $23.5 million.

In 1973, Eagle-Picher acquired the Johnson Manufacturing Company, Faulkner Concrete Pipe, and Plas Chem, an anti-corrosion chemical company. These were followed in 1976 with the purchase of Elmac, a mining supply company, and Pritchett

Engineering, a precision machining company serving the petroleum industry.

Many of Eagle-Picher's industrial markets were adversely affected by a serious recession in 1979 that bottomed out in 1982. This caused numerous operational reverses at Eagle-Picher and placed the company on shaky ground for its next challenge, a spate of lawsuits related to the use of asbestos in Eagle-Picher's insulation products.

Thomas Petry, appointed president in March 1981 to ensure an orderly transition as Atterbury approached retirement age, was forced to take action in 1984 when more than 19,000 asbestos injury claims had been filed. The wave of litigation meant easy money for lawyers, whose actions led several other manufacturers, including Johns-Manville, into bankruptcy.

Petry, however, elected to ride out the litigation by funding settlements with money from a special reserve that was replenished with operating income. To lessen the effect of the suits, Eagle-Picher concentrated on expansion from its other operations. This strategy succeeded in keeping the company out of bankruptcy, but still seriously damaged earnings. Petry succeeded Atterbury as chairperson in 1989, and was replaced as president by John W. Painter.

As the volume of settlements increased, Eagle-Picher was forced to divest several operations, including the Akron Standard and flight operations divisions, to maintain the fund. By 1991, however, the company could not keep up and was forced to file for reorganization under bankruptcy laws. This had the positive effect of halting all injury settlements.

In March of 1992, Painter retired, and his duties were assumed again by Thomas Petry. The company remained under court protection, as the number of property damage claims reached 1,000, and personal injury claims ballooned to more than 160,000. While operations remained strong, the asbestos litigation continued to loom. When cleared of the courts, Eagle-Picher will again be exposed to an expensive and potentially ruinous onslaught from personal injury lawyers.

Although it remains diversified within related industrial markets, Eagle-Picher has begun to move toward greater centralized control, made necessary by asbestos litigation. The company remains organized in three main divisions, an industrial group, a machinery group, and an automotive group.

Principal Subsidiaries: (Organized as divisions) Cincinnati Industrial Machinery; Construction Equipment; Electronics; Fabricon Products; Hillsdale Tool and Manufacturing Company; Eagle-Picher Minerals, Inc.; Michigan Automotive Research Corporation; Orthane; Plastics; Ross Aluminum Foundries; Rubber Molding; Specialty Materials; Transcoil, Inc.; Trim; Wolverine Gasket; Eagle-Picher Europe (Germany); Eagle-Picher Far East (Japan).

Further Reading:

Eagle-Picher Industries, Inc. Annual Reports, Cincinnati: Eagle-Picher Industries, Inc., 1989–92.

Knerr, Douglas, *Eagle-Picher Industries, Strategies for Survival in the Industrial Marketplace, 1840–1980,* Columbus: Ohio State University Press, 1992.

—John Simley

DeBartolo

The Edward J. DeBartolo Corporation

7620 Market St.
Youngstown, Ohio 44513
U.S.A.
(216) 758-7292
Fax: (216) 758-3598

Private Company
Founded: 1944
Employees: 15,000
Sales: $700 million
SICs: 6552 Subdividers & Developers Nec; 6531 Real Estate
Agents & Managers; 1542 General Contractors—
Nonresidential Buildings, Other Than Industrial Buildings
and Warehouses; 1522 General Contractors—Residential
Buildings, Other Than Single Family; 6512 Operators of
Nonresidential Buildings

The Edward J. DeBartolo Corporation has been a leader in
American retail development for almost half a century. The
company owned and/or operated over 78 million square feet of
retail space by the early 1990s, and its commercial assets
surpassed 95 million square feet. Headquartered in
Youngstown, Ohio, the company holdings included over 100
retail malls and community shopping centers, nine office projects in operation or under development, and three hotels. Aside
from its real estate and commercial holdings, the company has
also dabbled in horse racing facilities and owned professional
sports teams.

The company was founded by Edward J. DeBartolo, regarded as
a pioneer of the suburban shopping center. DeBartolo was born
in a small suburb of Youngstown. His stepfather, Michael
DeBartolo, was an Italian immigrant and master stone mason.
Edward entered the world of work after graduating from Notre
Dame University with a degree in civil engineering in 1934. He
helped his step father with the family paving and general
contracting company and operated a strip mine in East Pales-
tine, near Youngstown. During World War II, DeBartolo served
in the Pacific theater with the Army Corps of Engineers, saving
his pay in hopes of beginning his own business.

After his service during the war DeBartolo founded his own
company in 1944 constructing gas stations, supermarkets, and

other single-purpose buildings. In 1948, he started building
subsidized housing for World War II veterans in Boardman,
Ohio, just south of Youngstown. Witnessing the wave of people
moving out of Youngstown into less urban communities, De-
Bartolo had a hunch that the new residents of his housing
development would appreciate local shopping facilities. He had
also discerned one of the primary events that led to the birth of
the modern shopping center: postwar suburbanization.

The many factors that contributed to the development of regional shopping centers came together after World War II. First
came the "baby boom," which generated more consumers than
most existing retail facilities could handle. Then, the country's
mass transit system, on which many consumers relied to transport them into town for shopping, failed to accommodate the
growing populous. An increased disposable income allowed
many of these shoppers to purchase automobiles, which permitted consumers to travel farther on the newly-improved roads
of the postwar era. More stringent labor laws shortened the
work week to five days, which facilitated more leisure time than
ever before. All of these factors combined in the late 1940s and
early 1950s to create an environment that encouraged the development of the shopping mall.

In 1948 DeBartolo built Belmont Plaza, his first "strip style"
shopping center (so named because the stores were arranged
side by side in a long strip) as an alternative to shopping in
downtown Youngstown. As a developer, DeBartolo made
money by renting out space in the shopping center for a percentage of retailer's proceeds. Shopping centers in general offered a
large selection of products and services in an attractive atmosphere that provided a feeling of security as well as free, abundant parking. Developers soon found that the variety of retailers
encouraged consumers to shop longer and, usually, spend more
money.

DeBartolo incurred heavy debt to construct his first major shopping center, Boardman Plaza, in 1951. Many local businessmen
speculated that the plaza would fail. But the endeavor was a
huge success, prompting the young developer to purchase an
airplane and begin selecting Midwestern corn fields near the
intersection of major highways for his shopping centers. He
built an average of five strip malls (or community centers, as
they are known in the industry) per year over the next fifteen
years, earning the nickname "Plaza King" by the late 1950s.

In those early years, the DeBartolo Corp. instituted its "concept
to completion" method of development. Everything from land
acquisition to leasing, construction, marketing, and renovation
was accomplished internally, employing market analysts, site
planners, financiers, architects, designers, construction supervi-
sors, leasing professionals, lawyers, mall managers, and marketing specialists.

The company purchased its first horse racing track, Thistledown
Racing Club, in 1960 for $5.1 million. The suburban Cleveland
site featured a large, $4.2 million parcel of real estate on which
DeBartolo hoped to eventually build a large-scale mall. Although the developer expected racing to be nothing more than
an interesting sideline, by 1976 he owned a total of four race-
tracks, including Balmoral Trot Park, outside Chicago, for

which he paid $10 million, and Louisiana Downs, outside Shreveport, which cost $27 million.

DeBartolo had built more than 100 strip malls by 1965. Noting a population surge in Florida, DeBartolo banked on the success of Walt Disney Co.'s planned Disney World theme park near Orlando. He sold most of the strip malls and parlayed the proceeds into enormous investments in Florida real estate during the 1960s.

In 1966 DeBartolo opened Summit Mall in Akron. The project put the development company at the forefront of large-scale retail trends; at the time, Summit was the only fully enclosed regional mall in Ohio. Over the next ten years, DeBartolo built 31 regional shopping malls, leading an industry trend toward larger shopping centers with a wider array of merchandising approaches. He also operated four Holiday Inns, held a controlling interest in three Florida banks, and operated Ohio's only duty-free storage zone, at the Port of Toledo.

However, like many American entrepreneurs, DeBartolo hit hard times during the deep recession of the early 1970s. The 1973 oil crisis precipitated increased consumer outlays for housing and energy related expenses, which depleted disposable income and paralyzed retail sales volume. Faced with a substantial debt load, the corporation's cash flow was scarcely sufficient to service debt, and some locations even had trouble meeting payroll. The crisis proved serious enough that DeBartolo was forced to close Louisiana Downs, a race track near Shreveport, Louisiana, just 50 days after its opening in 1975.

The crisis passed with the economic rebound of the late 1970s, and DeBartolo was positioned to take advantage of the improved economy. In 1976, he opened what was then the world's largest regional shopping center, Randall Park Mall. He had waited 16 years to utilize the site adjacent to the Thistledown racetrack. At 2.2 million square feet, the ''superregional center'' featured a ten-story Holiday Inn and cost $180 million to develop. DeBartolo expected the mall alone to attract 80,000 to 85,000 customers daily. The completion of Randall Park Mall helped the Edward J. DeBartolo Corp. achieve assets estimated at nearly $1 billion at the end of 1976. Other investments during this time included DeBartolo's purchase of the San Francisco 49ers football team for his then 30-year-old son, Edward Jr., as well as the Pittsburgh Penguins hockey team for daughter Denise York DeBartolo.

DeBartolo's Florida land investments of the 1960s paid off in the 1980s, when even the state's most depressed areas began to rebound. By the end of the decade, DeBartolo operated 26 malls in Florida. According to one jealous rival quoted in a June, 1989 *Barron's* article, DeBartolo ''owned'' Florida; over one third of his property was concentrated in that state.

The developer expanded his sporting properties with the 1981 purchase of the Pittsburgh Civic Arena. The following year, the corporation purchased a New Orleans race track, and in 1985, DeBartolo built another, Remington Park, in Oklahoma City. DeBartolo later sold the Balmoral Track to former Clevelander and New York Yankees owner George Steinbrenner III. Over the years, DeBartolo had tried to purchase several other professional sports franchises, including baseball's Cleveland Indians and Chicago White Sox, but was prevented from doing so,

presumably because ownership of sports teams and racecourses would represent a conflict of interests.

In the 1980s, DeBartolo and many others in the development industry became interested in the retail side of the shopping center business. These larger developers reasoned that ownership of a major retail chain would provide ready-made anchors for future developments, which would ease some of the stress of opening new malls.

DeBartolo made one of his first bids for a retail chain in 1986. He became closely associated with Canadian businessman Robert Campeau when the two became competitors in a takeover war for Allied Stores Corp. that year. One of America's major retailers, Allied operated 684 stores, including Brooks Bros. and Bonwit Teller. While DeBartolo eventually let Campeau purchase Allied, he acquired a 50 percent interest in the corporation's five regional shopping malls in the bargain. His association with Campeau also facilitated a joint venture for the development of between 50 and 100 retail malls. The two moguls agreed that future DeBartolo malls would be anchored by Campeau's top-of-the-line stores, which included Federated's Bloomingdale's, Burdines, and Abraham & Straus, and Allied's Jordan Marsh, Stern's, and The Bon.

Just after the Allied deal, DeBartolo joined clothing store company The Limited in an effort to purchase Carter Hawley Hale Stores (CHH). The Carter Hawley Hale group then owned such stores as The Broadway, Neiman-Marcus, Bergdorf Goodman, and Contempo Casuals. CHH repulsed the hostile takeover with the help of General Cinema, but that didn't halt DeBartolo's quest for an influential retail partner. In 1988 he teamed up once again with Campeau in the latter's $6.6 billion takeover of Federated Department Stores. DeBartolo's $480 million equity loan earned him a seat on the Campeau Corp. board as well as 7.5 percent of Federated. Later that year DeBartolo became a partner with Dillard Department Stores in their purchase of Cleveland's Higbee Company. The partnership, Ho Holding Associates, acquired Higbee's department stores for $165 million.

In 1987, DeBartolo's wife of 44 years died, driving the already hard-working billionaire to work even more zealously. It has been estimated that he works from 5:30 or 6:00 a.m. until 7:00 p.m. each day, including weekends and holidays, and rarely, if ever, takes vacations. In addition to his long days, DeBartolo is known for his keen attention to detail; he has been so closely involved with the company's projects that he chose the color scheme for the seats at one racing facility.

The retail development industry of the 1980s was characterized by diversity. With many traditional markets saturated, developers no longer followed traditional formulas. As large suburban regional markets were built out, leading developers began to shift their focus to the middle-markets that had been passed over by the first wave of development. Although these generally small town areas offered fewer consumers, developers hoped that their newer, more comprehensive shopping centers would provide the most attractive retail opportunity in the area. DeBartolo's Crystal River Mall, opened in 1989, was an example of the format.

DeBartolo opened two malls and seven community centers in 1988. The community centers put the corporation at the forefront of a new trend that saw developers building strip malls alongside previously built regional malls. These adjacent developments had several advantages. They enabled the company to glean profit from land that was previously sold to others, and also made the property as a whole more attractive and cohesive. Tax benefits also influenced DeBartolo's actions: if the land was sold, the company would be required to pay taxes on the proceeds.

Another development category that emerged in the 1980s was that of in-fill or "twilight-zone" development. These shopping centers were constructed in urban in-lying, or "trolley-car," suburbs that had previously been inadequately serviced by major shopping facilities. Rivercenter, in San Antonio, and New Orleans Centre were examples of this trend. DeBartolo's urban mall experiment was short-lived, however, because of the many obstacles to downtown building. The projects required cooperation with local and federal government for subsidies, and extra planning for deck parking and high-rise buildings. These barriers prevented DeBartolo from building additional urban shopping centers.

Many developers focused on simply remodeling older shopping centers, which had taken on a "cookie-cutter" appearance in the 1970s. The refurbishing trend combined with a change in the basic function of shopping centers, from strictly merchandising outlets to sources of entertainment that featured cinemas, hobby shows, live entertainment, and food.

The corporation's existing properties grew by almost 300,000 square feet in 1988, and DeBartolo had plans to augment or renovate five locations in 1989. That year, a DeBartolo executive told *Chain Store Age Executive* magazine that the company's portfolio of shopping centers was so large that it could begin a "never-ending cycle of rehabs."

By the end of the decade, the DeBartolo Corp. was the exclusive or joint owner of 59 regional shopping malls around the United States, reportedly owning or managing ten percent of the country's total mall retail space. Company representatives estimated that 40 million customers visited DeBartolo's malls and shopping centers weekly.

However, saturation and diversification of the shopping center industry and a late 1980s and early 1990s recession caused DeBartolo to move more cautiously in the early 1990s. Whereas in the past, the company might have gone ahead on a mall project that would have only one or two anchor stores, by the 1990s, DeBartolo required commitments from four or five anchors before proceeding. Although many developers, including DeBartolo, continued to open millions of square feet in retail space, much of the expansion was accomplished using previously purchased parcels. In May 1991, Richard S. Sokolov, senior vice president-development, told *Chain Store Age Executive* magazine that the DeBartolo Corp. had not initiated new projects for 1991, and that the company was building projects with financing commitments made before the end of the 1980s. He also noted that several projects were postponed due to a lack of traditional financing.

The early years of the decade also saw DeBartolo entering joint ventures with former competitors to build major shopping centers. In 1990, the company joined Chattanooga-based CBL and Associates to develop the Mall of the Avenues, Jacksonville, Florida's first "galleria," a glass-enclosed mall with several promenades or tiers. That same year, DeBartolo teamed up with Faison Associates of Charlotte, North Carolina, to build the Virginia Center Commons in the growing Richmond, Virginia, market. The Brandon Town Center, a 1.1 million square foot cooperative venture of DeBartolo and JMB Retail Properties of Chicago, was planned for a 1994 opening in Florida. A limited partnership arranged with Homart Development put DeBartolo in charge of some of the financing, while Homart was responsible for development, management, and leasing for a Fort Lauderdale project. These creative arrangements will undoubtedly continue, considering the overall development climate.

In 1991 the corporation came out on top of *Chain Store Age Executive's* list of "Fastest Growing Developers" with 3.89 million square feet opening. However, financial problems began to surface as the recession lingered on. The problems started the year before when Campeau Corp. defaulted on DeBartolo's $480 million loan. When Campeau's Federated Department Stores Inc. filed for bankruptcy court protection in January, it became the largest Chapter 11 case ever filed by a retailer, and DeBartolo became just another creditor hoping to collect.

In 1991, the real estate downturn forced layoffs of about ten percent of DeBartolo's workforce, and in 1992, company executives bandied about asset sales. By the end of the year, the corporation had divested the Pittsburgh Penguins hockey team, one corporate jet, one Florida mall, and two office buildings.

It appeared that the company's fortunes were changing when DeBartolo joined Dillard Department Stores in the purchase of four Higbee Co. stores, but by mid-year DeBartolo sold a second mall in Florida and its Higbee's interest to Dillard. DeBartolo's financial difficulties came to a head in the fall of 1992, when the corporation agreed to refinance over $4 billion in debt. The financing agreement with four banks deferred principal payments on the debt for five years and advanced $300 million in new loans.

As patriarch DeBartolo entered his 80s, the question of corporate succession has also cropped up. Whether the company is to be run by son Edward J. DeBartolo, Jr. or will be taken public remained to be seen in the early 1990s. The DeBartolo Corporation has endured the vagaries of the development and retail businesses for over 40 years. In the early 1990s, industry analysts speculated that retail development was in the midst of a dramatic, fundamental change from past decades of rapid growth. As one of the top retail development firms, the DeBartolo Corp. continued to anticipate and adjust to the changing times.

Further Reading:

Angle, Terry, *Shopping Malls: A Place to Go,* Kent, Ohio: Kent State University (thesis), 1974.

"Big Numbers Don't Tell the Story: The Pipeline is Drying Up for Many of the Fastest Growing Developers," *Chain Store Age Executive,* May 1992, pp. 56–68.

Bredin, Alice, "Shopping Center Regional Focus: Creative Deal-making in Florida," *Stores,* August 1992, pp. 64–65.

"Campeau Defaults on Loans From Major Lenders," *Plain Dealer (Cleveland),* March 9, 1990, p. B12.

Clark, Sandra. "DeBartolo to sell its share in Higbee chain to Dillard," *Plain Dealer (Cleveland),* July 18, 1992, p. D1.

"DeBartolo Amassed Vast Fortune by Building Shopping Centers," *Plain Dealer (Cleveland),* October 8, 1986, p. A12.

"DeBartolo Ends Pact on Assets of Campeau," *Plain Dealer (Cleveland),* October 17, 1990, p. G1.

"DeBartolo seeks to enter Campeau case," *Plain Dealer (Cleveland),* January 20, 1990, p. F2.

"DeBartolo Selling a Second Florida Mall," *Plain Dealer (Cleveland),* June 26, 1992, p. G3.

"Developers Get the Retail Bug," *Business Month,* October 1988, p. 43.

"Developers Keep on Building," *Chain Store Age Executive,* May 1990, pp. 52–59.

Dolgan, Bob. "DeBartolos Add Cup to Four Super Bowls," *Plain Dealer (Cleveland),* May 29, 1991, p. E5.

Ellers, Richard, and Thomas W. Gerdel, "DeBartolo Offers Allied Stores $4 billion," *Plain Dealer (Cleveland),* October 8, 1986, pp. A1, 12.

Evans, Michael. "Development Activity Defies Odds; Top Developer Survey," *National Real Estate Investor,* January 1992, pp. 81–92.

Feinberg, Samuel. *What Makes Shopping Centers Tick,* New York: Fairchild Publications, 1960.

"The Final Days of Big Development?" *Chain Store Age Executive,* May 1991, pp. 62–74.

Gilbert, Nick, "Outflanked," *Financial World,* March 10, 1987, pp. 38–40.

Hazel, Debra, "DeBartolo: At the Forefront of Trends," *Chain Store Age Executive,* May 1989, pp. 56, 62.

"Horne's Sells 5 Stores," *Plain Dealer (Cleveland),* February 27, 1992, pp. A1, 8.

"Joint Venture Opens on Harmonious Note," *Chain Store Age Executive,* November 1990, p. 96.

Kelly, Michael. "DeBartolo's Empire: Randall Park Mall Its Super Jewel," *Plain Dealer (Cleveland),* August 8, 1976, sec. 2, pp. 1, 4.

King, Ralph, Jr., "How Long? How Deep?" *Forbes,* October 29, 1990, pp. 113–120.

Kowiniski, William Severini. *The Malling of America,* New York: William Morrow and Company, Inc, 1985.

Laing, Jonathon R., "King of Malls: Despite His Billions, Edward DeBartolo Remains a Shadowy Figure," *Barron's,* June 12, 1989, pp. 8–9, 18–30.

Lebovitz, Hal, "What Makes Eddie Run?" *Plain Dealer (Cleveland),* June 20, 1976, sec.3, p. 2.

Lubove, Seth, "The Disney Touch," *Forbes,* April 16, 1990, pp. 90–91.

"Meeting of Minds in Jacksonville," *Chain Store Age Executive,* May 1990, pp. 72, 74.

"Never Look Back, Never Give Up: After 45 Years, Edward J. DeBartolo Continues to Look for Challenges," *Chain Store Age Executive,* November 1989, pp. 70–72.

"New Financing to Aid DeBartolo Corp.," *Plain Dealer (Cleveland),* October 14, 1992, p. C2.

"Real Estate Slump Forces DeBartolo to Lay Off 53," *Plain Dealer (Cleveland),* February 6, 1991, p. F6.

"Report Says DeBartolo Corp. Is Planning to Sell Assets," *Plain Dealer (Cleveland),* February 12, 1992, p. H2.

Sternlieb, George, and James W. Hughes, eds., *Shopping Centers: U.S.A.,* Piscataway, New Jersey: Center for Urban Policy Research, 1981, pp. 1–18.

"Virginia Center an Un-'Commons' Mall," *Chain Store Age Executive,* May 1991, pp. 114, 116.

—April S. Dougal

EG&G Incorporated

45 William Street
Wellesley, Massachusetts 02181
U.S.A.
(617) 237-5100
Fax: (617) 431-4255

Public Company
Incorporated: 1947 as Edgerton, Germehausen & Grier, Inc.
Employees: 37,000
Sales: $2.69 billion
Stock Exchanges: New York
SICs: 3823 Process Control Instruments; 8742 Management
    Consulting Services

EG&G Incorporated is an organization of scientists, engineers, and management specialists that has assumed the difficult responsibility of ensuring that nuclear weapons are maintained precisely as they are intended. Its job is to prevent accidents, see that detonations are carried out correctly, and monitor the performance of nuclear weapons and other governments' compliance with test ban treaties. While nuclear weapons projects comprise a major portion of EG&G's business, the company is also a world leader in environmental, oceanographic, and electronics disciplines. EG&G engineers major water and land reclamation projects, studies atmospheric changes, and builds devices as varied as amplifiers, artificial limbs, and pollution testing equipment.

EG&G was established by three nuclear engineers from the Massachusetts Institute of Technology shortly after the end of World War II. These engineers, Harold E. Edgerton, Kenneth J. Germehausen, and Herbert E. Grier, had been involved in the American effort to construct an atomic bomb during the war. So valued were their contributions that after the war the government asked them to establish a company to manage further development of the country's nuclear weapons. The three established a small partnership called Edgerton, Germehausen & Grier on November 13, 1947, and quickly began collecting contracts to advise the government on nuclear tests in Nevada and on South Pacific islands.

One of the first employees of the new company was Bernard J. O'Keefe, another MIT graduate who had worked for Dr. Grier during the war. O'Keefe served with the 21st Bomber Command in the Mariana Islands during the war, and is said to have personally wired the bomb that later destroyed the Japanese city of Nagasaki. O'Keefe was sent to Japan after its surrender to investigate that country's progress with nuclear technology and recruit promising Japanese scientists for other atomic projects. A specialist in the design and development of electronic instrumentation and controls, O'Keefe quickly gained an important position in the growing firm.

Inconvenienced by the length of the company's name, employees soon began to rely on the simple acronym EG&G, which later became its official name. In order to maintain close contact with MIT and its excellent nuclear and electronic engineering programs, EG&G set up its headquarters in Bedford, Massachusetts, in Northwest suburban Boston.

EG&G was involved in America's effort to build a more powerful nuclear weapon, the hydrogen bomb. That year, Grier and O'Keefe were present at a Nevada test site to personally witness an H-bomb detonation. After the weapon failed to explode, Grier and O'Keefe flipped a coin to determine who should scale the 300-foot test tower and disarm the bomb. Although O'Keefe lost, he won the special distinction of being the first man to disarm a live H-bomb.

O'Keefe had a second brush with disaster in 1958 when he witnessed an H-bomb detonation at Bikini Atoll in the South Pacific. There, shifting winds in the upper atmosphere caused a radioactive cloud of fallout to shower his bunker.

These experiences taught O'Keefe the awesome destructive power of nuclear weaponry and the dangers of radioactive fallout. As an engineer and manager he was bound to perform his company's contracts, but grew personally opposed to the use of nuclear weapons. This sharpened his sense of responsibility toward the emerging form of warfare, a quality that was not lost upon the government's Atomic Energy Commission.

As a result of EG&G's experience with detonations, and O'Keefe's concern for nuclear non-proliferation, the company became increasingly involved in distant monitoring projects, particularly as they related to Soviet nuclear tests. By observing changes in the atmosphere, EG&G was able to determine the incidence and strength of Soviet tests and provide important data on the progress of Moscow's weapons program. In the process, EG&G gained highly specialized knowledge in environmental sciences. These skills had numerous applications outside the weapons industry, in such areas as pollution control and environmental management.

As early as 1960, O'Keefe and the company's three founders had considered establishing a new environmental analysis business, which would lessen EG&G's dependence on low-margin government contracts and permit the company to enter new commercial markets. But at the time, neither public concern nor legislation placed a high value on such endeavors.

Three years later, the United States, the Soviet Union, and the United Kingdom signed a protocol that banned nuclear tests in the atmosphere, above ground, in the water, or in outer space. With this document, EG&G appeared to lose a major portion of its business. However, the protocol did not prevent underground tests, which were far more complicated. EG&G remained the only company with the proper supervisory credentials to manage this type of nuclear testing. The company was forced to develop geologic analytical capabilities and become a tunneling and mining operation as well.

Furthermore, the government had also laid plans to establish a kind of oceanographic equivalent to NASA. Eager to take a place in this organization, EG&G invested heavily in oceanographic research. While the underwater NASA never materialized, the efforts enabled O'Keefe to further cultivate new commercial markets for EG&G, including excavation and water transmission.

During this time the company's three founders moved further into retirement, taking ceremonial "executive chairman emeritus" positions. As a result, O'Keefe became the de facto head of the company. EG&G also pursued a strong acquisition campaign, taking over 13 companies between 1964 and 1967.

By 1967 a strong environmental movement began to form in the United States. With legislation still years away, EG&G began laying plans to play an important role in the environmental projects it was sure would result.

EG&G was divided into four main operating divisions. The smallest of these was EG&G International, which was primarily concerned with oceanography. The standard products and equipment division, which grew fastest during the 1960s, produced a variety of machines and electronic devices. EG&G's largest segment remained its nuclear detonation and monitoring business. But perhaps the most innovative and interesting division was the nuclear technology group, which was involved in the design of nuclear rocket engines for interplanetary propulsion.

Other noncombat nuclear projects included "nuclear landscaping" projects, in which controlled nuclear explosions could carve out harbors, canals, and other types of passages. EG&G's CER Geonuclear unit participated in tests wherein nuclear explosions were used to fracture layers of rock so that otherwise inaccessible gas and oil reserves could be exploited. These public works projects, while feasible, failed to gain public support. In fact, opposition to nuclear technology in general increased as people grew wary of the safety of nuclear energy. In addition, nuclear excavation would have required an unlikely waiver of the 1963 Nuclear Test Ban Treaty.

With the evaporation of good commercial prospects for its nuclear engineering expertise, EG&G was forced to rely again on military projects. Despite efforts to step up mechanical and electrical engineering work (partly by acquiring a spate of small research companies), EG&G mustered only four percent annual growth during the late 1960s.

Interest in nuclear power increased dramatically during the 1973–1974 Arab oil embargo, in which Americans sought to reduce their costly dependence on imported oil. Realizing that the world's oil exporting nations stood to permanently lose their largest customer, the United States, King Faisal of Saudi Arabia promptly called for an end to the embargo. But while Americans regained access to Arab oil, the end of the embargo was disastrous for the American nuclear energy industry—and for EG&G. The end of the embargo removed one of the great

justifications for nuclear power, and gave anti-nuclear activists time to properly organize legislative battles.

While EG&G was being locked out of yet another promising commercial application of its technologies, it attempted projects in other fields. Some years earlier, in an effort to develop a new process for purifying nuclear isotopes, EG&G developed a flash tube that was ideal for photocopiers. However, by the time an application could be developed, Xerox had already saturated the market with conventional designs. In another ill-timed move, the company bet that environmental laws would cause demand for the unconventional Wankel engine to rise. EG&G purchased a Texas automobile testing agency in hopes of winning large emission monitoring contracts. However, the oil embargo destroyed the market for the clean, but gas-eating Wankel, and automobile environmental legislation was abandoned.

During this time, with the encouragement of the government, EG&G established a minority-dominated subsidiary, EG&G Roxbury, in a neighborhood of Boston, hoping to help strengthen the economic structure of the community. The project failed, however, when bureaucrats failed to properly support the program, causing only a few sales to be made from the subsidiary. After a few years of disastrous results, the entire program was wound up.

EG&G's environmental division, which languished after the oil embargo, finally began to take off in 1976. Rather than concentrating on environmental compliance, the group evolved into a comprehensive resource efficiency operation that could provide complete oceanographic, atmospheric, and geophysical analysis. By conserving resources, operations could more easily achieve pollution and waste reduction targets.

Another area of success was in port development. Although unable to blast out custom designed harbors with nuclear devices, EG&G was a world leader in oceanographic studies and channel engineering. The company designed numerous tanker ports in the Persian Gulf and bauxite harbors in South America.

In 1979, President Jimmy Carter asked Bernard O'Keefe to serve as chairperson of the government's synthetic fuels corporation. Having already been asked to serve on a transition team for then-presidential candidate Ronald Reagan, however, O'Keefe refused Carter's offer.

With the election of Reagan in 1980, the United States took a sudden turn toward military armament programs. EG&G found a sudden resurgence in its flagging nuclear testing business and was tapped to develop a number of new nuclear weapons systems, including the MX missile and the Strategic Defense Initiative.

A self-described "card carrying member of the military-industrial complex," Bernard O'Keefe wrote in his book *Nuclear Hostages* that the United States and the Soviet Union were locked in an arms race that neither of them could control. Ironically, EG&G remained deeply involved in a number of Reagan administration projects O'Keefe opposed, including the MX, the neutron bomb, and stationing of nuclear missiles in Europe. Nevertheless, EG&G's pretax operating profit doubled from the new business.

EG&G also became involved in the space shuttle program, checking the spacecraft's electrical components, loading its fuel, and managing the Cape Canaveral space center during shuttle missions. EG&G's site management abilities won it a position with the Department of Energy's elite Nuclear Emergency Search Team which investigates nuclear extortion threats. The company also won a contract to manage the government's troubled Rocky Flats installation outside Denver. This facility, which manufactures nuclear weapon triggers, was widely criticized for mismanagement under Rockwell International.

O'Keefe retired from EG&G during this period of strong growth, and was succeeded by John M. Kucharski. Under President George Bush, and with the subsequent collapse of the Soviet military threat, the number of EG&G nuclear test projects decreased significantly. Pressure increased for EG&G to quickly cultivate profitable new commercial ventures to offset the loss of revenue from military contracts.

Because this process had been an ongoing concern of EG&G for nearly 30 years, the company had considerably greater success than other companies that faced similar circumstances. The conversion to commercial projects went smoothly, though much of the urgency was tempered by the growth of site management contracts and rising demand for nuclear non-proliferation monitoring.

Principal Subsidiaries: EG&G Alutech, Inc.; EG&G Astrophysics Research Corp.; EG&G (Australia) Pty. Ltd.; EG&G Automotive Research, Inc.; EG&G Birtcher, Inc.; EG&G Benelux B.V. (Netherlands); EG&G Canada Ltd.; EG&G Chandler Engineering Company; EG&G Defense Materials, Inc.; EG&G Dynatrend, Inc.; EG&G E.C. (UK); EG&G Energy Measurements, Inc.; EG&G Exporters Ltd. (U.S. Virgin Islands); EG&G Florida, Inc.; EG&G Flow Technology, Inc.; EG&G Frequency Products, Inc.; EG&G Gamma Scientific, Inc.; EG&G GmbH. (Germany); EG&G Holdings, Inc.; EG&G Hydro, Inc.; EG&G Idaho, Inc.; EG&G Instruments GmbH. (Germany); EG&G Instruments, Inc.; EG&G International Marine Services, Ltd. (Hong Kong); EG&G InterTech, Inc.; EG&G Investments, Inc.; EG&G Ireland, Ltd. (Cayman Islands); EG&G Japan, Inc. (U.S.A.); EG&G Judson Infared, Inc.; EG&G KT Aerofab, Inc.; EG&G Ltd. (UK); EG&G Management Systems, Inc.; EG&G Missouri Metals Shaping Company, Inc.; EG&G Mound Applied Technologies, Inc.; EG&G Power Systems, Inc.; EG&G Pressure Science, Inc.; EG&G Rocky Flats, Inc.; EG&G S.A. (France); EG&G Scanray International, Inc.; EG&G Sealol, Inc.; EG&G Sealol Eagle, Inc. (51%); EG&G Sealol (Sealol Egypt); EG&G SpA (Italy); EG&G Special Projects, Inc.; EG&G Structural Kinmatics, Inc.; EG&G Ventures, Inc.; EG&G Washington Analytical Services Center, Inc.; Antarctic Support Associates (Columbia); Asmuss-Sealol (NZ) Limited (New Zealand; 25%); B.A.I. VmbH. (Austria); B.A.I. SARL (France; 71%); Benelux Analytical Instruments S.A. (Belgium; 92.3%); Berthold A.G. (Switzerland); Berthold Analytical Instruments, Inc.; Berthold France S.A. (99.2%); Berthold GmbH. (Germany); Berthold Instruments U.K. Ltd. (55.3%); Berthold Munchen GmbH. (Germany; 60%); Berthold Systems, Inc. (30%); Berthold U.K. Ltd. (80%); Betron Scientific B.V. (Netherlands; 25%); Crosby Drive Investments, Inc.; Dextra Medical, Inc. (19.5%); Dilor S.A. (France; 20%); Eagle EG&G Aerospace Co., Ltd. (Japan; 49%); EC III,Inc. (Mexico; 49%); Frank Hill Assoc., Inc.; Geometrics, Inc.; NOK EG&G Optoelectronics Corp. (Japan; 49%); Labserco Nuclear, Inc. (15%); Laboratorium Prof. Dr. Rudolf Berthold oHG. (Germany; 96.2%); Reticon Corp.; Reynolds Electrical & Engineering, Inc.; Rotron, Inc.; Safex Control B.V. (Netherlands; 10%); Sealol Hindustan Ltd. (India; 20%); Sealol Kuwait KSC (49%); Sealol S.A. (Venezuela); Seiko EG&G Co., Ltd. (Japan; 49%); Societe Civile Immobiliere (France; 82.5%); Vactec, Inc.; Wakefield Engineering, Inc.; Wellesley B.V. (Netherlands); Westpark, Inc.; Wickford N.V. (Netherlands Antilles); Winchester, Inc.; Worster Ltd. (Cayman Islands); Wright Components, Inc.

Further Reading:

"Bombs for Peace," *Forbes,* September 15, 1969, pp. 71–72.

"EG&G," *Moody's Industrial Manual 1992,* pp. 215–219.

"EG&G Plays Big Role in Nuclear Weaponry, Other Defense Work," *Wall Street Journal,* May 21, 1984, p. 1–21.

"Hope for the Wild Ones—But Don't Count Them," *Forbes,* May 15, 1975, pp. 110–114.

"One-Stop Environmental Aid," *Business Week,* July 19, 1976, pp. 44–47.

"Personality: A Pioneer of the Nuclear Age," *New York Times,* January 15, 1967, p. F3.

"Pounds of Plutonium in the Ventilation Ducts," *New York Times,* December 12, 1989, p. 12.

"Spread Eagle Champ," *Forbes,* April 17, 1978, pp. 83–85.

—John Simley

ELIZABETH ARDEN

Elizabeth Arden Co.

1345 Avenue of the Americas
New York, New York 10105
U.S.A.
(212) 261-1000
Fax: (212) 261-1315

Wholly Owned Subsidiary of Unilever PLC
Incorporated: 1911
Employees: 7,000
Sales: $2.25 billion
SICs: 2844 Toilet Preparations; 2841 Soap & Other
    Detergent

For decades Elizabeth Arden Co. cosmetics and perfumes have been synonymous with luxury and prestige. A world leader in the cosmetics industry since the 1920s, Elizabeth Arden was acquired by Unilever PLC, a conglomerate of consumer product companies. Despite intense competition and a severe recession, Elizabeth Arden's "White Diamonds" perfume was the number one selling fragrance in the country in 1991, and the company's fine line of cosmetics and perfumes continues to earn numerous quality awards. Elizabeth Arden, who founded the company in 1911, can be credited with single-handedly laying the foundations of the modern American cosmetics industry.

Elizabeth Arden was born Florence Nightingale Graham in Canada during the late 1870s. Named for the renowned nurse who served during the Crimean War, Florence grew up in a large, poverty stricken family. When she was unable to finish high school because her family lacked the finances, she persuaded herself that nursing was her true vocation and began training for that profession. Florence quickly realized her mistake. It was sales, not suffering humanity, that finally lured her and tapped her real talents.

While a student nurse, Florence had met a chemist experimenting with a facial cream that could help acne sufferers. The concept intrigued her, leading to her conviction that most women would give anything for beauty. An unsuccessful early attempt to start a mail-order business marketing her own version of face cream failed largely because of her father's impatience with his madcap daughter's strange concoctions. Instead Florence toiled at a series of jobs in Toronto that afforded her a chance to display her salesmanship. At one point employed as a dental assistant, she doubled the dentist's sales in a short time

when she hit upon the idea of persuasively writing each patient to explain the necessity of regular dental check-ups.

Nearly 30 years old and unwilling to marry for fear of losing her independence, Florence set off for New York City in 1908. Landing a job as a bookkeeper for the prominent Squibb Pharmaceutical Company, she was impressed by the state-of-the-art laboratories and the constant attention to research and development. This inspired her to fashion a small lab of her own, where she might "scientifically" test out her own beauty ideas. Before venturing into this unknown arena, however, Florence quit her job at Squibb to become an assistant in a newly established beauty culture salon. Catering to a wealthy clientele, these early beauty parlors came to be the nucleus of the future cosmetics industry. They emphasized skin care rather than hair care, and the methods for achieving glowing skin did not rest with makeup as much as with skin massage and the applications of creams and lotions.

Unfamiliar with the concept of beauty salons before coming to New York, what she learned there helped Florence lay the foundations for the cosmetics industry she was to eventually build. Florence was hired as a "treatment girl" to deliver facial massages, mix the facial concoctions of the owner, Mrs. Eleanor Adair, and give manicures. Florence displayed unusual talent and sales ability, and quickly learned all the aspects of the beauty culture field.

Until then, Florence Nightingale Graham had never worn cosmetics. Even in the early twentieth century, a proper woman simply hoped for a healthy complexion—facial "paint," usually applied without skill or finesse, was considered disreputable. However, higher levels of female education coupled with the women's suffrage movement provided the stimuli for change. By the time Florence arrived in New York, shorter hair and cosmetics were becoming increasingly associated with emancipation.

Soon Florence felt confident enough to go into business for herself. Without funds to finance the endeavor on her own, however, she formed a partnership with Elizabeth Hubbard in 1910. While the nameplate bore the partner's name—Florence Nightingale was rejected as suggestive of a hospital ward—the cosmetic mixtures and other ideas were clearly Florence's. She dubbed her pricey lotions and powders "Grecian," endowing them with a romantic allure and prestige that would become her trademark.

Instead of a parlor, the establishment was referred to as a salon, since Florence thought it would appeal to higher class society women. Although the partners could barely afford the rent, Florence had insisted on lavish quarters in a brownstone on New York's Fifth Avenue, which was rapidly turning into a major business district. The partners quarreled soon after their salon opened its doors, however, and Elizabeth Hubbard abruptly departed, leaving Florence to pay the huge rent. Borrowing $6,000 from her brother to keep her salon open, Florence worked as a manicurist after hours to supplement her income.

In addition to the problems of trying to pay the rent, it was necessary for Florence to decide on a name for her salon. While the suffragettes were taking steps towards women's rights, their emancipation had not reached the point where "Miss" connoted respectability, and Florence decided to use "Mrs." Her former partner's name, Elizabeth, appealed to her, although a new last name was harder to come by. She finally chose Arden after reading the name in a poem by Alfred, Lord Tennyson. The new name seemed to evoke the prestige and understated glamour that Florence not only craved for her business, but for herself as well. Thus Florence Nightingale Graham became Elizabeth Arden.

After hours, when she was not manicuring nails for extra income, Elizabeth experimented with cosmetics. One of her distinctive contributions was the addition of fragrance to the lotions and powders of the day, which had been lacking scent. The facial creams sold at the time were greasy and heavy, but Elizabeth hired a chemist to formulate a light, fluffy cream that became an instant success. It was at this point that she developed her "total beauty" idea. The concept initially involved sharing her salon quarters with a "prestige" hairdresser and a milliner; later a clothing shop was included. Eventually the idea was further expanded to include beauty spas.

Elizabeth Arden's hard work and imagination paid off, making her salons enormously profitable. Without serious competitors for the first several years after establishing her business, her success was also aided by changing attitudes toward equality of the sexes. Emancipation had progressed so far as to soften the prejudices against women who wore short hair and cosmetics. Times were changing so rapidly that by 1914, Elizabeth Arden removed the "Mrs." from her nameplate and substituted "Miss." It was good for business.

A steady stream of products was marketed in the initial years of Elizabeth Arden's business, including rouges and fragrant, tinted powders that she taught her "girls" to apply with subtlety and finesse. In 1914, on the eve of the outbreak of World War I, Elizabeth traveled to Paris, her first trip abroad. During her summer-long sojourn, Elizabeth became acquainted with the more sophisticated Parisian techniques of beauty culture and makeup application. She brought these techniques back with her, in addition to the cosmetic products, including the eye makeup worn by wealthy dames of Paris society. Though chemists improved on the products, Elizabeth found it difficult to convince her clients to apply it—eye makeup for many was going too far. It was America's entry into the First World War, however, that provided the necessary catalyst. While the men were away at war, women found themselves employed in many lines of work formerly closed to them, and as they gained even greater independence, many of the restrictive taboos became outdated. Women began experimenting with Elizabeth Arden's eye makeup, the first to be introduced in the United States.

Elizabeth Arden's Venetian line of cosmetics along with her velvety Cream Amoretta—in her signature chic bottling—were being sold in department stores all over the east coast, and her salon with the famous red door was duplicated in Washington, DC, in 1914, proving an instant success. A year later Arden perfumes were introduced, further expanding the line of products offered in the salons. However, her reign as undisputed queen of cosmetics was not due to last. After the war, competition came to the fore, marking the beginning of the lifelong personal animosity between Elizabeth Arden and her chief rival,

Helena Rubenstein. The cosmetics industry began growing at a rapid pace and became steadily more lucrative, especially to women, for whom it was one of the few lines of business in which they could rise to the top and be leaders.

However, Elizabeth Arden was, more often than not, the industry standard bearer. By the start of World War II in Europe, there were dozens of Elizabeth Arden salons all over the world, and hundreds of products being marketed, including soaps, bath salts, even toothpaste, as well as perfumes to go with either morning, afternoon or evening dress. No one advertised cosmetics as frequently nor as lavishly as Elizabeth Arden. This was in accord with her philosophy, held throughout her life, that in order to make money, one had to spend it. Meanwhile American women were in fact spending six million dollars annually on cosmetics by 1925, barely fifteen years after Elizabeth Arden had hung up her shingle. That year her company reaped over two million dollars in sales, a figure that doubled only four years later.

During the Depression, Elizabeth Arden predicted—and advertised accordingly—that the American woman would not stint on beauty. Unlike most American businesses, Elizabeth Arden's company earned handsome profits during those years, even making strides with innovative lipsticks which, until 1932, had come in only a few basic shades. Elizabeth Arden believed that just as perfume should go with the costume, so too should lipstick. Her "lipstick kit" containing several different shades was a big hit at the height of the Depression, creating a sensation in the industry as competitors scrambled to imitate the concept. Then in 1934 she established her extremely successful "beauty spa" in Maine—another was opened in Arizona in 1946—where women shed excess pounds and immersed themselves in Elizabeth Arden bath salts and after bath lotions for $500 per week. By the mid-1930s there were 29 Elizabeth Arden salons around the world, while her company manufactured and marketed 108 different products.

The outbreak of the Second World War, which spelled a loss of overseas markets and raw materials, did not catch Elizabeth Arden by surprise. Just as she had done before World War I, Elizabeth Arden stocked up on raw materials early, and offset the loss of income from her overseas salons by concentrating on expanding her domestic market. Her products were not only carried in department stores coast to coast, but the war years saw Elizabeth expanding into all of the major drugstore chains of the day. Consequently in 1944, at the height of the war, business at Elizabeth Arden's was booming, and the company remained a pacesetter. A line of clothing was added in the 1950s, and Elizabeth Arden became the first in the industry to target male customers by marketing men's fragrances and opening a "men's boutique."

Elizabeth Arden continued her reign as grande dame of the cosmetics industry until her death in 1966. By then the cosmetics industry in the United States had grown into a multi-billion dollar business, and large corporations were mass producing personal care products that, while lacking in prestige, could be sold at much lower prices. Friends and relatives had urged Elizabeth to sell her profitable business as early as 1929, when a $15 million offer was made. She refused, and no further mention was ever made of selling or merging. However, negotiations for the sale of the company began shortly after her death. Elizabeth Arden Co. was finally acquired in late 1970 by the pharmaceutical company, Eli Lilly & Co., which cut costs and instituted streamlined procedures before putting it up for sale again in 1987. The company changed hands twice more until 1990 when it was purchased by the Anglo-Dutch conglomerate Unilever PLC. Two years later Unilever established the Prestige Personal Products Group, which included Elizabeth Arden Co. and Calvin Klein.

A constant during these changeovers was Elizabeth Arden's president and CEO, Joseph F. Ronchetti, who had joined the company after Elizabeth's death. In 1986, when the company was still a subsidiary of Eli Lilly, Ronchetti devised a five-year plan to revitalize Elizabeth Arden Co. and make it more competitive. While the budget for advertising—especially targeted at baby boomers—was doubled, more modern packaging and innovative bottling was instituted. Ronchetti stuck with the plan throughout the changes in ownership. By the end of the five years, advertising was conducting an average of 200–300 promotions a month, and research and development had created many pace-setting products, including a line of ultraviolet (UV) sun protection creams and lotions that was distinguished by awards from the Skin Cancer Foundation. In addition, Elizabeth Taylor's White Diamonds became the number one selling fragrance in 1991 after the famous actress personally introduced the scent in ten U.S. cities. Elizabeth Arden had also become more responsive to its social environment—animal-testing of cosmetics is virtually never done, and considerable donations were made to such causes as AIDS research and child welfare. When Ronchetti was succeeded as president and CEO in 1992 by Robert M. Phillips, Elizabeth Arden Co. had not only profited during the recession, but was one of the fastest growing cosmetics companies in the industry, increasing its sales in one year by 24 percent—three times higher than the industry average.

Unilever's purchase of Elizabeth Arden, coupled with that of Fabergé, Inc. in 1990, made the conglomerate the second-largest cosmetics company in the world. With a distribution network in virtually every country on earth, in addition to state-of-the-art research facilities, Elizabeth Arden Co. stands to benefit from its acquisition by the corporation. Under the helm of Phillips, Elizabeth Arden Co. plans to branch out into new international markets in Asia, the Pacific Rim, as well as eastern Europe, bringing long-deprived consumers there a special blend of beauty.

Further Reading:

"Arden's Colorbox Blockbuster to Assist Children's Charity," *Women's Wear Daily,* September 25, 1992, section 1, p. 6.

"Elizabeth Arden Company Creates In-House Media Department," *New York Times,* February 4, 1991, p. C9(N), D9(L).

"Elizabeth Arden Losing Its Chief in a Merger," *New York Times,* June 13, 1992, p. 19(N), 37(L).

Elizabeth Arden: The Woman, the Company, the Legacy, New York: Elizabeth Arden Co., 1993.

Lewis, Alfred Allan and Constance Woodworth, *Miss Elizabeth Arden,* New York: Coward, McCann & Geoghegan, 1972.

Raj, D. D., "Global Cosmetics & Household Product Industry—Industry Report," *Merrill Lynch Capital Markets,* December 1, 1992.

Rice, Faye, "Elizabeth Arden: Profiting by Perseverance," *Fortune,* January 27, 1992, p. 84.

Stern, Aimee L., "How Elizabeth Arden Gave Itself a Makeover," *AdWeek's Marketing Week,* September 9, 1991, pp. 18–19.

Unilever United States, Inc. 1991 Report to Employees, New York: Unilever United States, Inc., 1991.

Zinn, Laura, "Beauty and the Beastliness," *Business Week,* June 29, 1992, p. 39.

—Sina Dubovoj

Esprit de Corp.

900 Minnesota Ave.
San Francisco, California 94107
U.S.A.
(415) 648-6900
Fax: (415) 641-5964

Private Company
Incorporated: 1968
Sales: $900 million
Employees: 1,200
SICs: 2331 Women's/Misses' Blouses & Shirts; 2335
   Women's/Misses Dresses; 2339 Women's/Misses
   Outerwear Nec; 3144 Women's Footwear, Except Athletic;
   3171 Women's Handbags and Purses

One of the most successful companies in the fashion industry, Esprit de Corp. designs, manufactures, and distributes sportswear for women and children in over 35 countries. More than two-thirds of the company's total sales volume is generated by international sales. In addition to marketing clothing, footwear, and accessories, Esprit seeks to foster social responsibility among its customers. Through advertising and corporate programs, the company shows its commitment to such causes as AIDS awareness, feminism, and environmental conservation.

Esprit was built primarily by Doug Tompkins and Susie Tompkins, a husband-and-wife team whose personal and political values informed the company's business strategy. The couple met outside Lake Tahoe in 1963, when Susie Russell offered the hitchhiking Doug Tompkins a ride in her Volkswagen. Both Susie and Doug were from wealthy backgrounds and had dropped out of high school to explore more Bohemian lifestyles. After several months of travel together in Mexico and the western United States, they married and settled in San Francisco. There they embraced the social causes and fashions of the city's active counterculture.

In 1964 Doug, an enthusiastic skier and rock climber, invested $5,000 to start a retail business devoted to mountaineering equipment. Called North Face, the store was established in a prime location across from San Francisco's popular City Lights Book Store, and it soon became very successful. Because of his capable staff who oversaw daily operations, Doug was able to spend much of the year on international rock climbing and skiing expeditions. Susie remained in San Francisco, raising the

couple's two children and occasionally assisting at the North Face store.

During this time, Susie Tompkins became interested in a business venture proposed by her friend Jane Tise. Together they formed the Plain Jane Dress Company, which offered puffed-sleeve, acrylic minidresses that Tise designed and Susie distributed. After the Plain Jane dress line became successful locally, it was marketed to New York department stores by Allan Schwartz, a salesperson who became a partner in the company. Late in the 1960s, having sold the North Face operations for approximately $50,000, Doug Tompkins joined Plain Jane as a partner. While Tise and Susie designed the product and added new designs and labels to their popular line, Doug and Schwartz handled the marketing and sales responsibilities, targeting affluent California households with colorful, oversized catalogs.

By 1970 Plain Jane had sales exceeding more than $1 million a year. Doug and Susie Tompkins owned roughly 45 percent of the company, while Tise and Schwartz held the other 55 percent. At this time, some observers allege, Doug Tompkins stepped up his interest in the company, making bold decisions concerning the company's direction and professing an interest in taking charge. He was instrumental in steering the company's focus to more contemporary designs as the American hippie look subsided. In 1972, after he and Susie visited several countries in Asia, Doug decided to move manufacturing operations to Hong Kong, where clothing could be produced less expensively.

Schwartz and Tise sold their shares to the Tompkinses in 1976. Although Schwartz left the company immediately thereafter, Tise remained as chief fashion designer until 1979, when she reportedly became dissatisfied—as Schwartz had—with the lack of input allowed her by the Tompkinses. That year Susie took charge of the design department. By this time the company had expanded its product line under several different labels to include pants, blouses, and skirts. These different divisions of the company were soon reorganized and consolidated, and Plain Jane was renamed Esprit de Corp. The company's trademark loose-fitting casual designs in bold colors caught on, and Esprit rapidly evolved into one of the most popular clothing companies among 18- to 24-year-old women.

During the early 1980s Esprit swiftly expanded and distinguished itself in the business community through both its sales and the way in which it reflected the eclectic tastes of Susie and Doug Tompkins. An art and architecture enthusiast, Doug Tompkins spent a great deal of time and money to renovate the San Francisco winery that would become the company's new headquarters. Featuring skylights, wood floors, and Amish quilts on the walls, the brick building gained national recognition among architects and interior designers. The facility offered Esprit employees access to tennis courts, a running track, and a trendy cafe. Seeking to create an enjoyable work atmosphere to match the spirit of Esprit clothing, the Tompkinses encouraged employees to dress fashionably yet casually; high heels were not permitted on the easily scuffed wood floors of the headquarters building. Furthermore, the Tompkinses offered a unique benefits package. In addition to a 52 percent discount on Esprit clothing, employees received subsidized tickets to the theater, ballet, and opera, as well as free vacations in the mountains and foreign language lessons. Employees came to refer to the workplace as "Camp Esprit" and "Little Utopia."

From 1979 to 1985 the company's sales increased from $120 million to $700 million. As design director, Susie approved all drawings and fabrics, while Doug held the titles of president and "image director." During this time, Esprit became the first clothing company to require department stores to relegate a part of their sportswear section specifically for use as a "shop within a shop." While the concept called for a relatively large amount of floor space, expensive track lighting, and signs, many department stores complied because of the Esprit line's high sales volume. Catalogs also served as an important marketing strategy in the early 1980s, and oversized, glossy booklets featured pictures of employees and other "real people" modeling Esprit clothes alongside quotes of their personal philosophies. In an interview Doug Tompkins asserted that the Esprit customer is of "above-average intelligence and knows the difference between 'substance and superficiality.' Women who wear Esprit," he concluded, "are the new feminists."

Between 1984 and 1986 the company borrowed nearly $75 million to open several retail stores, the first of which was a superstore in Los Angeles that showcased Doug Tompkins's taste and cost about $15 million to build. Subsequent stores were established in New Orleans, San Francisco, and Aspen, Colorado, and by 1987 there were 14 Esprit retail stores nationwide. Department store owners carrying Esprit clothing regarded these retail outlets as unfair competition, but the company disagreed.

As Esprit grew, however, some critics charged that the company was overextending itself. In late 1986 and 1987, Esprit experienced losses for the first time in its history. Earnings fell from $62 million to $10 million, representing an 83 percent downturn. Several reasons were given for the abrupt reversal. The *San Francisco Examiner* suggested that competitors were copying Esprit designs and offering them at lower prices and reported that some retailers complained about the inferior quality and design of new lines. The Tompkinses maintained that while the company may have tried to expand too rapidly, its spring lines were selling well. They pointed to the decline of the U.S. dollar as the primary reason for the company's losses. Furthermore, they maintained, while international sales were escalating, Esprit's foreign operations were jointly owned with local investors so that profits were reinvested in the foreign market.

In 1986 Doug Tompkins turned Esprit over to Corrado Federico, who became the company's president, while Doug remained as Esprit's CEO and chairperson. Exploring ways to cut the company's costs and consolidate its operations, Federico implemented a freeze on hiring and bonuses that year. Although employees were soon required to pay for coffee and phone calls made in the office, the Tompkinses ensured that some of the unique benefits that made up Esprit's image as a fun, creative workplace remained. The following year the Esprit work force was cut by 30 percent, and Doug Tompkins brought in experts from rival fashion companies to manage the newly consolidated divisions.

It became apparent, however, that Esprit was experiencing personal conflicts that were leading to the company's decline. Critics cited both Esprit's failure to stay abreast of fashion trends as well as irreconcilable differences that had developed between Susie and Doug Tompkins as reasons for the company's troubles. The Tompkinses had begun to argue about what direction the company should take. Susie regarded the company's image as too young, maintaining that customers were seeking a more sophisticated look. She realized Esprit's original customers had grown up and wanted to introduce a line of corporate wear for the loyal Esprit buyer. Doug, on the other hand, argued that the company's youthful image was too important to change and that corporate women would not purchase Esprit. The couple subsequently became estranged.

In March of 1988 the *Wall Street Journal* reported on the rift between the Tompkinses. While the column focused on the couple's relationship and Doug's alleged extramarital affairs with women in the company, it also reported that weak financial management and the design department's failure to note the fashion world's shift to a more traditional look were hurting business. In addition, interviews with former Esprit employees revealed that tension in the workplace was being fostered by two factions—those who sided with Doug and those in Susie's camp. The article also revealed that Doug was seeking minority equity partners to help maintain the struggling Esprit retail stores.

When Susie Tompkins petitioned a San Francisco court to appoint a third director to help run Esprit in March 1988, a judge advised that she and her husband resolve the situation without legal intervention. The following month, hoping to the reverse the stalemate, the Tompkinses appointed three new directors, Peter Buckley, Isaac Stein, and Robert Bartlett, to turn Esprit around. By May of that year the new board recommended that Susie and Doug each remain 50 percent owners of Esprit but that they give up their operating control of the company. Under the plan Esprit president Federico became chief executive officer. Doug was given the title of chief executive officer of Esprit International operations and was required to abandon the idea of expanding Esprit's retail establishments through outside financiers. While many of Doug's duties at Esprit remained the same, Susie's role at the company changed dramatically. No longer the chief fashion designer, she was effectively out of the business. As a "fashion consultant" to Esprit she kept in close contact with the management team, but announced that she would spend time away from Esprit, concentrating on her volunteer work for such social causes as AIDS awareness. Early in 1989, Susie and Doug Tompkins filed for divorce.

That year Doug pursued his growing interest in environmental conservation within the parameters of the fashion industry by instituting a new marketing strategy in which the company actually advised the customer not to buy Esprit clothing if she did not need it. Doug argued that consumerism in general, and especially in the fashion industry, was leading to the destruction of natural resources and that Esprit should thus introduce clothing that would outlast the seasonal fads. Doug's "buy only what you need" campaign included hang tags with the warning on each article of clothing, as well as a new line of fashions in more traditional, muted colors. Initially the line was profitable, but it eventually declined, and, during this time, critics noted that Doug seemed to be more interested in ecology than fashion.

While Esprit had recovered from the previous two year's losses, the company was still regarded as unsteady and lacking a corporate vision. In July of 1989 Esprit announced a new plan to refocus Esprit under one Tompkins. Doug was given the option to buy out Susie's 50 percent within 120 days of the agreement. If he did not, both halves of the company would go up for sale at an auction. Clothing and footwear manufacturing giants Benetton and Reebok became interested in acquiring Esprit, when, after the requisite 120 days, Doug had not exercised his option.

Analysts speculate that by forcing the auction of the company Doug had initially hoped to acquire Esprit for a lower price than he would have paid to buy out Susie's share. However, as Reebok and Benetton became interested in purchasing Esprit, the price would have escalated. Furthermore, during this time, Susie was recruiting financial backing from the venture capitalist Bruce Katz, Esprit head of Far East operations Michael Ying, and Isaac Stein. One day before the bidding on Esprit was to close, Doug and Susie worked out a deal and Esprit never went to auction. Industry observers believed that Doug had been concerned that both he and Susie would lose the company to higher bidders, and, in order to keep Esprit in the family, he accepted Susie's offer in return for some interest in the company's international division.

Susie Tompkins returned to head Esprit amid much publicity. Trade journals, newspapers, and magazines depicted her as the victor in the war to control Esprit. Some observed, however, that the recession of the early 1990s could prove particularly challenging for the company and her leadership. Under Susie's ownership, Stein was named Esprit's chairperson. Federico remained president until his resignation in April of the following year; Stein subsequently assumed the presidency. Appointing herself creative director, Susie brought back the design team with which she had worked before leaving Esprit in 1988. Expressing the desire to produce casual fashions that exuded social awareness, she stated that her mission was to ensure "that Esprit inspire good values."

In 1991 the recently appointed "image director," Neil Kraft, produced the "What would you do?" advertising campaign that surveyed young people about how they would like to change the world. The $8 million campaign featured quotes from America's young people on such global concerns as racism, abortion, and environmentalism. Although the advertisements won several awards and generated a great deal of media attention, sales figures were nevertheless disappointing. The following year Kraft left Esprit, and his duties were taken over by Fritz Ammann, who was named chief executive officer while Stein remained chairperson.

Pursuing her goal of promoting a socially responsible work force, Susie Tompkins replaced the employees' free vacation program with a lunchtime lecture series featuring controversial figures speaking on current issues. She also established a volunteer program that paid Esprit employees for working ten hours per month at a nonprofit organization, providing that the employee matched that amount of time on his own. Furthermore, the ecological soundness of Esprit's manufacturing practices was monitored by a new environmental and community affairs department in the company called the "Eco Desk."

The Ecollection line of Esprit clothing and accessories, touted as both ecologically sound and fashionable, was introduced early in 1992. The line featured buttons made from reconstituted glass or carved from nuts, organically grown or vegetable dyed cloth, and purses handwoven in a Mexican cooperative. Also that year Susie introduced the adult clothing line she had conceived years before. Tompkins referred to the designs as "creative career" wear for the Esprit customer who had matured. The tailored trousers, sophisticated, pleated skirts, jackets, and vests were manufactured in earth tones such as plum, green, brown, and burgundy. Tompkins maintained that these clothes were functional as well as fun and appropriate for the business world. The unconventional fashion show at which the Susie Tompkins collection debuted received mixed reviews. Rather than provide a runway and models, Susie commissioned Reverend Cecil Williams of San Francisco's popular Glide Memorial Church to give a sermon on the troubled lives and deplorable living conditions of youth in America's inner cities. The show, featuring videotape and choral accompaniment, cost more than $5 million to create. While some reviewers were entertained, others reportedly were offended by Esprit's tactics. Nevertheless, the company claimed that the line generated $13 million in sales.

During the year, however, Susie decided to step down as creative director of Esprit. In formal statements both she and the company contended that she was leaving—as her ex-husband Doug had—to focus on her outside interests. Despite her lack of title at Esprit, Susie remain involved as an advisor and consultant.

Having focused on downsizing its operations and containing costs, Esprit continues to achieve profits, and its sales in department stores as well as in more than 30 Esprit retail and franchise stores have recovered since the late 1980s. Furthermore, good relations between management and employees at Esprit have been restored. Analysts now speculate that the future success of the company will depend on its ability both to follow and influence the quickly changing fashions in women's sportswear.

Further Reading:

Benson, Heidi, "Reinventing Esprit," *San Francisco Focus,* February 1991.

"Catching the Spirit at Esprit: The Tompkinses Go to Riches with Rags," *Money,* July 1986, pp. 56–57.

Dorrans Saeks, Diane, "Always True in Her Fashion," *Metropolitan Home,* September 1992.

Dobbin, Muriel, "Fashion by Esprit," *Baltimore Sun,* May 30, 1985.

Ginsberg, Steve, "Getting Serious," *Los Angeles Times,* March 6, 1992.

Greenberg, Freddi, "The Greening of Esprit," *Working Woman,* October 1985, p. 110.

Itow, Laurie, "The New Color at Esprit: Red," *San Francisco Examiner,* March 1, 1987.

"Joi d'Esprit?" *California Business,* May 1, 1987.

King, Ralph Jr., "How Esprit de Corp. Lost Its Esprit," *Forbes,* March 21, 1988, pp. 91, 94.

Klensch, Elsa, "Making It Work! Susie Tompkins, the Spirit in Esprit: An Interview," *Vogue,* August 1987, pp. 344, 376.

Marlow, Michael, "Susie's Esprit: New Looks, New Outlook," *Women's Wear Daily,* September 10, 1990, pp. 1, 6–7.

McGrath, Ellie, "Esprit: The Sequel," *Working Woman,* September 1991, pp. 67–69.

Rapp, Ellen, "The War of the Bosses," *Working Woman,* June 1990, pp. 57–59.

Rapaport, Richard, "Goodbye Susie: The Rise, Fall and Repositioning of Esprit and Its Founders," *California Business,* September 1, 1992.

Waldman, Peter, "Flagging Spirit: Esprit's Fortunes Sag as Couple at the Helm Battle Over Its Image," *Wall Street Journal,* March 16, 1988, pp. 1, 17.

White, Constance C. R., "Susie Tompkins: Crossing a New Bridge," *Women's Wear Daily,* March 10, 1993.

White, Constance C. R., "Tompkins Gets Her Line," *Women's Wear Daily,* March 2, 1992.

—Tina Grant

Federal Paper Board Company, Inc.

75 Chestnut Ridge Road
Montvale, New Jersey 07645
U.S.A.
(201) 391-1776
Fax: (201) 573-4426

Public Company
Incorporated: 1916
Employees: 6,900
Sales: 1.46 billion
Stock Exchanges: New York
SICs: 2611 Pulp Mills; 2631 Paperboard Mills; 2657 Folding
   Paperboard Boxes

Federal Paper Board Company, Inc., is a leading producer of recycled and bleached paperboard, which is used to make packaging, brochure covers, sports cards, and paper cups. It also produces market pulp, uncoated free sheet paper, lumber, folding cartons, and paper and plastic cups. The market for its products is primarily domestic, although its presence abroad has been expanding, and it has facilities in the United Kingdom. Federal Paper Board celebrated its 75th birthday in 1991 and has a history of strong leadership and daring acquisitions. During its 75 years, it had only three presidents: founder William Shortess, J. R. Kennedy, and John R. Kennedy, Jr.

William Shortess founded Federal Paper Board Company in 1916. During his tenure as president, from 1916 to 1941, he acquired mills throughout the Northeast. According to Richard Blodgett's book *Federal Paper Board at Seventy-Five,* written for the company's 75th anniversary, "The joke about Will Shortess was that he couldn't drive by a paperboard mill without buying it."

Shortess's first mill, which he called Federal Paper Board Company, was just across the tracks from his former employer's Bogota, New Jersey, mill, which Shortess had quit in 1916 over a dispute with the owner. Only a few months later, he bought his second mill, in Versailles, Connecticut. By the end of the 1920s, he had purchased eight mills, and when he died in 1942, he owned nearly a dozen. Shortess's practice was to buy them and modernize their equipment in order to boost production and streamline their operations, and he sold only one mill during his years as president. All of the mills Shortess acquired produced recycled paperboard.

Shortess was something of a gambler in business. The company grew quickly but was often on shaky ground. His purchases usually added debt to the company, which was often on the verge of bankruptcy because of such large debts. His decade of purchases left the company in trouble in 1929, as Shortess and Federal fell behind on loan payments. Creditors took control, but allowed Shortess to continue to manage the company. He rallied to the situation—he cut costs, stopped buying mills, and attended to basic operations. Despite the Great Depression, he was able to pay the creditors and regain control of his company. The creditors, however, advised him to hire a financial executive, J.R. Kennedy.

In 1935, Shortess acquired an 80 percent interest in S-C-S Box Company in Palmer, Massachusetts, when that company was unable to pay $100,000 that it owed for paperboard purchases. S-C-S specialized in production of egg cartons, clothing boxes, and bakery boxes, and when business was down, it made jigsaw puzzles to sell at local five-and-dimes for ten cents each. Purchase of this company gave Shortess a built-in customer for paperboard from his other factories. In the 1940s and 1950s, S-C-S Box was a leading producer of paperboard boxes for tomatoes. By the late 1970s, this company was the last of Shortess's acquisitions to be operated by Federal, and in 1990, it too was sold.

Shortess died in 1942. *Federal Paperboard at Seventy-five* sums up the Shortess era as "a time of risk-taking, growth, consolidation and narrow escapes from financial disaster." Joanna Shortess, Shortess's widow, inherited the business and was determined to become president and manage the company, even though she had taken no interest in company matters while Shortess was alive. Three Federal employees offered to buy the company: Federal's financial officer, J.R. Kennedy, and Federal mill managers Guy Freas and Howard Brown. While Joanna Shortess was reluctant to sell to them, she did offer to give them each ten percent ownership and the remaining 70 percent when she died—as long as she became president and a full and active partner, participating in management of the company.

However, the three men turned her down and continued with their plans to try to buy the company. Almost a year after her husband's death, Joanna Shortess sold the company to Kennedy, Freas, and Brown for $1.5 million with no money down. She had agreed to a non-interest-bearing, 90-day promissory note secured by shares of the company, and within those 90 days they arranged alternate, long-term financing from the Metropolitan Life Insurance Company. The sale actually included four companies, Federal Paper Board with five mills, Acme Paper Board with four mills, Liberty Paper Board with one mill, and S-C-S Box Company.

Kennedy became the company president, Brown was chairperson, and Freas served as executive vice president. Under Kennedy's management, Federal's sales went from $7 million in 1942 to almost $250 million in the early 1970s. The early years, however, were a struggle. During World War II, raw materials became scarce, and mills had to scramble to get the wastepaper they needed to produce paperboard. For Federal the challenge was simply to survive until the war ended.

However, the years following the war were boom years for American businesses, including Federal Paper Board Company. Demand for paperboard soared—only to drop off again from its record high sales in 1947 when the economy settled down again. Choosing to be optimistic about the future and believing that the economic boom would continue, the three partners agreed to a major capital spending program to modernize its existing plants and acquire new plants.

Federal had continued to produce folding cartons at its S-C-S plant and decided after the war to go into this business more seriously. As paperboard boxes in which hundreds of products are packaged—including cereal, crackers, and macaroni—folding cartons are so named because they are shipped flat to the consumer products company. For 15 years, if a folding box company was close enough to one of Federal's paperboard mills, Federal bought the company. By 1957, carton sales accounted for 72 percent of Federal's sales. Federal replaced aging facilities with new ones.

In 1952, Federal offered shares of stock to some of its employees and in 1953 went public. In 1955, it was listed on the New York Stock Exchange. By going public, Federal raised money to finance several acquisitions. In 1953, it bought National Folding Box Company, surprising other members of the industry who knew National to be a top company while Federal was new to the business. Federal also bought seven other carton companies over the next ten years. By the end of the decade, products marketed in Federal's folding cartons included Colgate toothpaste, G.E. light bulbs, Bayer aspirin, Camel cigarettes, Coca-Cola, Pepsi-Cola, and Fab laundry detergent. Federal had quickly become the second largest folding carton manufacturer in the country.

However, Federal was also beginning to face a new problem—most of its paperboard mills were more than 50 years old and rapidly becoming inadequate to fill Federal's needs. Federal acquired several paperboard companies, and in 1961, it built the largest paperboard mill in the world in Sprague, Connecticut. Production at the Sprague Mill experienced several glitches before the mill was up and running efficiently. However, its design allowed for periodic updates and by the early 1990s it had doubled its capacity and was still considered a "state-of-the-art" mill. In fact, in 1991, the Sprague mill was still the "newest" paperboard mill in the country, and as such, was at the center of the recycling business and the only mill in the United States to use a recycled paperboard making method called the Inverform process.

One of the ventures that had given Kennedy the time and money to survive Sprague's early years, even when it was losing money because of early production problems, was the acquisition of Federal Glass Company in Columbus, Ohio, in 1958. This acquisition was Federal Paper Board's only diversification outside of its core business of paperboard and related products. (Although both were named Federal, there was no relationship between the two companies before the 1958 purchase.) Federal Paper Board had been interested in diversifying into the corrugated box industry, and Federal Glass owned Hercules Box, a small corrugated box company. Kennedy saw Hercules as an opportunity to get a corrugated box division up and running. While Hercules and the division failed to grow as large as

Kennedy had hoped, Federal Glass proved to be an important investment.

Federal Glass produced quality glass tableware and was the industry leader in machine-blown glass. It sold its products to decorator companies to embellish and resell to department stores. Federal also began to sell glassware to restaurants and hotels, started making direct sales to department stores and other retail outlets, and also entered the "promotion" market, manufacturing the inexpensive glasses given as premiums by gas stations, grocery stores, and other retailers. Federal Glass's sales increased from $11 million in 1958 to $39 million in 1972. It made money while Federal Paper Board was updating or replacing old facilities and trying to bring the Sprague plant up to an efficient operational level.

However, the 1973 OPEC oil embargo lowered demand for the glass company's wares and increased its costs. With gasoline shortages, oil companies no longer sought to attract customers with premiums. At the same time, production costs skyrocketed because the glassmaking process required so much energy. In 1973, sales and profits fell sharply. When the company became profitable again in 1976, Kennedy tried to sell it to another glassmaking company. However, the Federal Trade Commission blocked the sale, charging antitrust violations. After trying in vain for two years to either find another buyer or convince the FTC to reverse its ruling, Federal Paper Board reluctantly closed Federal Glass.

Federal Glass, however, had also provided the financial leverage Federal Paper Board had needed to buy a Riegelwood, North Carolina, mill a few years earlier. Riegelwood was a huge paperboard mill for which Federal Paper Board paid $115.6 million in 1972. At the time, Federal had annual sales of about $160 million, and Riegelwood sales were nearly $80 million, so purchase of the operation represented immense growth. Federal wanted this mill so that it could get into the bleached board business, a goal of the company's for 20 years. At that time, demand for the all-white bleached paperboard was increasing, while the market for recycled paperboard, with its grey color, was slipping.

The purchase of the Riegelwood operation may have been the key to Federal's success, decades later, for by the 1990s, Federal's business was predominantly bleached paperboard. Federal was fortunate enough to buy the facility at the lowest point of a recession in the paperboard industry, and following the purchase, paperboard prices began to climb again. Purchase of Riegelwood also included Federal's first timberlands and a market pulp operation for producing processed wood fiber to market to other paper companies. During the next decade, Federal Paper put nearly $300 million into Riegelwood to increase its paperboard-making capacity and update machinery.

The purchase of Riegelwood had been the first major acquisition by the new president John R. (Jack) Kennedy, J.R. Kennedy's son. But it was not the first major deal that he pulled off. Early in his presidency, he faced a serious threat to Federal Paper Board when Simkins Industries, Inc., a paperboard company in New Haven, Connecticut, announced plans to take over Federal. Although Simkins was a $28-million-a-year company, and Federal had sales of $108 million, the threat was real.

Simkins' president, Leon J. Simkins, informed Kennedy that he was going to make a cash tender offer of $35 per share for up to 43 percent of Federal's stock. At the time, its price on the New York Stock Exchange was about $27 per share. Jack then phoned his father and his brother, Quentin—Federal's vice-president—the company's lawyers, and other key people, and they went into action. Their strategy was to buy as much stock as they could and to ask friends to purchase it as well in order to keep it out of Simkins' hands. Among Federal's "friends" who agreed to purchase stocks were Lever Brothers, Hess Oil, Colgate-Palmolive Company, and Topps Chewing Gum. Employees bought shares, even if they could afford to buy only one or two. This activity drove the price per share above Simkins' offered $35, and shareholders found it more profitable to sell through the stock exchange. These defensive tactics have since become illegal, but they were legal and effective for Federal in 1967. To further ensure that it would remain autonomous, Federal made Simkins' offer less and less attractive to shareholders by raising dividends and splitting the stock three-for-two so that shareholders would keep their stock instead of selling it. Federal also sued Simkins, claiming purchase by Simkins would constitute an antitrust violation by creating a paperboard monopoly in the Northeast. Simkins countered by charging Federal with manipulating its own stock prices with its defensive tactics. Eventually Simkins gave up its bid to take over Federal, and both suits were dropped. In subsequent years, Federal fought off several other takeover bids as well.

Following the purchase of Riegelwood, Jack Kennedy looked for another bleached paperboard operation in the South. In 1982, he made an offer on Continental Group, Inc.'s mill in Augusta, Georgia, as well as its 150,000 acres of nearby timberland. Continental, a can company, had diversified into paperboard in the late 1950s. Although the paperboard division was marginally profitable, Continental turned down Federal's bid of $300 million. A few years later, the entire Continental Group was taken over and some of its assets, including the Augusta mill, were put up for sale to finance the purchase. Kennedy then bought the operation and surrounding land for $317 million in 1985. This purchase doubled the size of Federal's bleached paperboard business, and the company jumped from fifth place to second place in the domestic bleached paperboard business. Within a few years, Federal launched a five-year expansion and modernization project which was completed in 1992.

In 1989, Federal purchased Thomas Tait & Sons Ltd., a mill in Scotland that produced uncoated freesheet, the white paper for copiers and printers. With this purchase Federal began competing head-to-head with Scandinavia for the freesheet market in the United Kingdom. It also gave Federal a presence in the European Community and a guaranteed customer for market pulp from its Riegelwood facility.

Federal became a major competitor in the paper cup industry by acquiring two paper cup plants, one in 1989, the second a year later. With the merger of these two operations, Federal almost instantly held 14 percent of the paper cup market. Kennedy anticipated this would be a growth industry because of the environmental move away from styrofoam and back to paperboard disposables. However, during the early 1990s, this remained a highly competitive market, and demand was down because of a poor economy.

Although decades earlier, the core of Federal's business had been the folding carton business, in 1991, the company made the decision to pull back from that market because it was no longer a growth industry. It sold four of its carton plants in 1992, retaining four carton plants that provided packaging for specific products, including cigarettes.

Federal was also in a good position to benefit from the movement towards recycling of all types of paper. Its Sprague, Connecticut, plant was central to Federal profits because of its high capacity to process recycled paper products into paperboard for packaging. Towns desperate to dispose of newsprint and other wastepaper without having to pay exorbitant "tipping" fees to the dumps, were giving away material that had cost Sprague $100 per ton.

Federal's five lumber plants produced almost 582 million board feet of lumber in 1992. It owned 566,000 acres of timberland, and it leased another 127,000 acres. That year, it cut 15,400 acres and replanted 18,000 acres with more than 12 million seedlings.

Although the economy was in a recession in the first half of the 1990s, Federal was optimistic about its future. Most of its facilities had modern, efficient equipment to allow the company to benefit from an economic recovery, and its recycled paper operations were likely to grow as more and more companies shopped for recycled paperboard.

Principal Subsidiaries: Thomas Tait & Sons, Ltd (Scotland); Imperial Bondware Corp.

Further Reading:

Annual Report, Montvale, New Jersey: Federal Paper Board Company, Inc., 1992.

Blodgett, Richard, *Federal Paper Board at Seventy-Five,* Essex, Connecticut: Greenwich Publishing Group, Inc., 1991.

—Wendy J. Stein

Ferro Corporation

1000 Lakeside Avenue
Cleveland, Ohio 44114-1183
U.S.A.
(216) 641-8580
Fax: (216) 696-6958

Public Company
Incorporated: 1919 as Ferro Enameling Company
Employees: 6,000
Sales: $1.10 billion
Stock Exchanges: Midwest Boston New York
SICs: 2816 Inorganic Pigments; 3299 Nonmetallic Mineral
    Products Nec; 3089 Plastics Products Nec; 2819 Industrial
    Inorganic Chemicals Nec; 2899 Chemicals and Chemical
    Preparations Nec; 2851 Paints, Varnishes, Lacquers,
    Enamels, and Allied Products; 3264 Porcelain Electrical
    Supplies; 2893 Printing Ink; 2865 Cyclic Organic Crudes
    and Intermediates and Organic Dyes and Pigments

Ferro Corporation is a leading worldwide producer of specialty
coatings, colors, ceramics, plastics, and chemicals for a wide
variety of markets, including: building and renovation, home
appliances, household furnishings, leisure products, transportation, industrial products, and packaging. The company has
manufacturing plants in 23 countries and marketing operations
in more than 100 nations worldwide.

Ferro was founded in 1919 by Harry D. Cushman as the Ferro
Enameling Company. Cushman had worked for the American
Rolling Mill Co. (Armco) of Cleveland since the early 1900s
when he and fellow employee Raymond L. Williams decided to
strike out on their own with a porcelain enamel shop, making
themselves president and vice president, respectively.

In the early 1920s enameling was based on the manufacture of
frit, a glass compound. The business commenced in 1920 with
an investment of $1,000. As a subcontractor, Ferro Enameling
Company applied porcelain enamel finishes to component parts,
then returned the parts to the client for assembly. In its first year
of operation, Ferro produced 59,000 pounds of porcelain
enamel.

During that first year, salesman Robert A. Weaver approached
Harry Cushman with an unusual proposal. Weaver offered to
provide marketing and other services through a separate com-

pany, and leave the technical aspects of the business to the
original enterprise. He had been involved in sales and advertising with several porcelain enameling companies in the 1910s
and, like his prospective clients, hoped to go into business for
himself.

Cushman and Williams agreed to Weaver's proposition, and in
1920 Weaver founded the Ferro Enamel & Supply Co. to sell
and service Ferro Enameling Co. products. The two companies
endured early financial problems but soon grew in the favorable
economic climate of the 1920s.

By passing marketing responsibilities on to Weaver, Cushman
was given more time to concentrate on the technical aspect of
the enameling business. His early emphasis on technical research and development started a tradition of scientific inquiry
at Ferro that would continue throughout the company's history
and drive its growth and expansion. Cushman's emphasis on
quality control gave birth to the company's logo in 1921. The
"Check-Mark-Within-a-Circle" has evolved over the decades,
but remained the trademark into the 1990s.

While Cushman concentrated on the technical aspects of the
business, Robert Weaver formulated a new marketing plan that
later would be known as "systems marketing." He proposed
that the company not limit its products to porcelain enamel frit,
but also produce the tools customers needed to complete the
enameling process.

Soon Ferro Enamel & Supply Co. was in the business of designing and manufacturing complete equipment for enameling,
from furnaces to finishing. In 1926 the company formed an
engineering division to handle this burgeoning business that
grew with the expanding appliance industry. The division's first
technical achievement came in 1928 when Ferro patented the
"U-type" continuous furnace, which soon became an industry
standard.

In 1923 Weaver came up with another innovative marketing
tool. He founded the industry's first trade journal, *The Enamelist,* to foster use of enamel coatings. The periodical featured
advertising, news, and semi-technical pieces. It was emulated
by competitors, and eventually evolved into *The International
Enamelist,* reflecting Ferro's global scope.

The company's first international expansion came in 1927 after
a Ferro executive from Canada suggested that the company
build a plant in his adopted homeland. In its first three years of
operation, Ferro Enamels (Canada) Limited, Canada's first porcelain enamel supplier, imported the product from the United
States. But by the end of the decade, the company opened a
modest plant in Ottawa.

Ferro ventured across the Atlantic Ocean before the decade's
end, but the company took many factors into account before
deciding on its overseas locations. At the time, long-distance
communications still posed a problem. Political and currency
stability and the initial investment were also considered before
Ferro settled on England and Holland as subsidiary locations.

Despite the relatively high shipping costs associated with exporting, The Ferro Enameling Company (England) Limited was
undertaken as strictly a marketing business in 1929. The com-

pany was established in a Wombourne warehouse about 120 miles from London. Ferro chose Rotterdam as its Holland site for production and distribution because of its access to fuel and raw materials, and for its situation on the largest port in continental Europe.

This first decade of growth ended with three events that shaped Ferro's future: the decision to sell shares in Ferro Enameling Company on the American Stock Exchange and the October 1929 stock market crash that precipitated worldwide depression. The onslaught of the Great Depression motivated Ferro Enamel & Supply to merge with Ferro Enameling to form the Ferro Enameling Corporation in the spring of 1930. The company was struck another blow when Harry Cushman, recently named chairman of the new entity, died in May. Co-founder Raymond Williams replaced Cushman as chairman, and Robert Weaver was elected president.

In Weaver's continuing quest to promote Ferro's porcelain enameled products, he advanced the idea of an all-porcelain house in 1932. The company's first attempt at the concept featured porcelain enameled steel shingles on the outside and porcelain amenities inside. A second model, opened that same year, was subjected to various strength tests to illustrate the durability of Ferro's products. Although the company would make forays into the residential building materials market in the 1940s and 1970s, the products did not catch on.

Despite the deepening recession, Ferro continued to expand in the 1930s. In 1933 the company acquired Allied Engineering Co. of Columbus, Ohio, and made it a second engineering division. Allied was a recognized leader in the design and manufacture of china, pottery, and tile kilns, having created the industry's first circular kiln.

Ferro dramatically expanded its international influence in the 1930s, establishing businesses in four countries within just two years. Ferro France, founded in 1934 about 150 miles from Paris, imported porcelain enamel frit from Ferro Holland for its first year in operation, then inaugurated a smelting facility the following year. Ferro Enamels (Australia) Ltd. in Victoria, Ferro Brazil in Sao Paulo, and Ferro Enamel S.A. (Argentina) were created in 1935 with the cooperation of American Rolling Mills Co., former employer of Ferro's two founders.

As the world emerged from the Great Depression, Ferro expanded its operations in Britain and Holland with manufacturing facilities in England and enlargement of the Holland business. Ferro achieved 100 percent ownership of both the Holland and Canada enterprises in 1937, making the operations full-fledged subsidiaries.

Ferro augmented its product line and improved its original products near the end of the 1930s. The corporation purchased the Ceramic Supply Company (Cesco) in 1936 to supply kiln furniture and compliment its Allied Engineering Division's kiln business. Ferro's sales more than doubled over the course of this difficult decade, but net income grew by only 15 percent, from $390,000 to $457,500.

Ferro penetrated the paint industry in 1940 with the purchase of the Chase Drier & Chemical Co. in Bedford, just outside Cleveland. Later renamed Bedford Chemical, the company made metallic soaps that promoted the paint drying process. This timely acquisition initiated Ferro's Chemical Division and provided inroads for wartime contracts.

As the United States' entry into World War II grew imminent, the federal War Production Board prohibited all industrial production except "war work." The ban included a Ferro mainstay, appliance manufacture, thereby threatening the company's future. Sales manager Dud Clawson earned the gratitude of his co-workers (and the presidency of Ferro in 1947) when he negotiated U.S. government contracts to manufacture incendiary products like thermit, an iron oxide-aluminum metal powder, and the newly-developed napalm, a liquid explosive. Over the course of the "Great War," Ferro produced more than 61 million pounds of thermit and more than eight million pounds of napalm. The government even asked Ferro to take over a munitions plant in Marion, Ohio. Ferro's unanticipated involvement in the war effort earned it five Army-Navy "E" awards.

The company's overseas outposts were more directly affected by the war. In Holland, Rotterdam was unmercifully shelled for four days in 1940. The city was occupied by Germany throughout most of the war, and inhabitants concerned themselves more with day-to-day survival than with frit. Similar conditions prevailed in occupied France. Ferro England supplied hospital ware and military canteens for the government.

After the war Ferro concentrated on reconstruction of war-damaged plants in Europe and expansion of other international interests. Canadian facilities were moved to Oakville, Ontario, and expanded by 1947. A new South African subsidiary, Ferro Enamels (Pty.) Ltd., imported ceramic products from Ferro's England subsidiary.

Ferro also focused on meeting postwar demand for appliances in the United States. The company built two new frit manufacturing facilities in Nashville, Tennessee, and Los Angeles, California, to meet market requirements. In 1946 Ferro research perfected a new frit composition that soon became an industry standard.

Ferro's Color Division grew rapidly in the postwar era. It had been established in 1939, but the work had been suspended during the war. The company's line of porcelain enamel was soon complemented with a series of ceramics pigments that catapulted Ferro to international leadership in the field. And recognizing the ascendancy of plastics, the company developed a third line of coloring agents engineered for that market. By 1947 the Color Division produced almost 5,000 different colors for the enamel, clayware and plastics fields.

Ferro focused on expanding its product base through technological research and acquisitions in the 1950s, and changed its name to Ferro Corporation in 1951 to reflect these new aspirations. When the U.S. Supreme Court eliminated the Owens-Corning Fiberglas Company's monopoly on the fiber glass industry that year, Ferro invested heavily in five domestic fiber glass plants. But the company's profit margins never met industry standards, and the operations were eventually divested in the late 1970s.

Ferro's gel coat business fared much better than its fiber glass enterprise. This durable plastic coating developed at Ferro's Los

Angeles plant in 1953 was used to coat fiber glass boats, and soon became an important product line for the company.

Ferro applied two criteria to new acquisitions: each must have the potential for growth and competent management in place. During the 1950s two specialty ceramics companies were purchased that contributed to Ferro's diversification goals: the Louthan Manufacturing Company in East Liverpool, Ohio (1954); and the American Clay Forming Company of Tyler, Texas (1957). In 1957 these two companies were organized with the Cesco Company as members of the Refractories Division.

Technological developments in the 1950s revolutionized Ferro's primary business, porcelain enameling. After observing a customer's experimental frit cooling process, Ferro engineers spent several years developing a procedure that used water-cooled steel rolls to cool molten frit. The new process was cheaper and cleaner than the centuries-old water cooling technique, and gave Ferro an advantage in the industry.

The Korean War precipitated another major development for Ferro when the company was asked to develop camouflage colors for the U.S. Army Engineer Corps. The Color Division maintained sole rights to produce camouflage colors for many years, and continued to hold more than three-fourths of the market through the 1980s.

Ferro expanded its international presence in the 1950s with the launch of international businesses in Mexico (1951), West Germany (1951), Italy (1958), Japan (1950), and Hong Kong (1953). After postwar reconstruction, Ferro Holland grew quickly, subsuming many competitors and launching many foreign subsidiaries. Ferro Holland also developed a technical advance in ceramic tile glaze that cut production costs in half. Ferro England and Ferro France expanded research facilities, entered the plastics field, and brought modern equipment on line.

The end of the decade was marked by the untimely death of president Dud Clawson. Over the course of the 1950s, Clawson had managed dramatic growth and expansion at Ferro: sales rose from $17 million to almost $64 million during that time. He was succeeded by Harry Marks, a 25-year Ferro veteran who would serve 17 more years as president, chairman, and CEO.

The company continued its acquisitions spree in the 1960s, adding nine domestic companies in the chemical and ceramics fields and making the largest purchase in its then-48-year history. Although some of the purchases were short-lived, others further expanded Ferro's product line. The addition of Pittsburgh's Vitro Company at the beginning of the decade eventually propelled Ferro to leadership in the glass color industry. Other acquisitions added coated fabrics, porous ceramic components, and specialty organic and inorganic chemicals to the conglomerate's list of products.

In 1967 Ferro purchased the Electro Refractories and Abrasives Company and thereby entered the high-temperature ceramics industry. The massive acquisition took several months to negotiate, and brought such specialty products as cements, diffusing plates, and silicon carbide under Ferro's growing product umbrella.

Technological developments in the 1960s were encouraged and consolidated with the construction of a Central Research Division where research on porcelain enamel, glaze, and pigments was undertaken. One of the center's innovations was the development of "self-cleaning" coating for household ovens, which was instantly popular.

Ferro's international businesses in Japan, Holland, Canada, and Australia grew during the 1960s, and new extensions in Spain and India spread the company's global influence. The Holland subsidiary's reorganization of Ferro's French business raised that operating unit to full ownership.

Ferro's dramatic growth in the 1960s required a move into larger headquarters, and in 1969 the company moved to Cleveland's new trade center at Erieview Plaza. Driven by acquisitions, the conglomerate's sales more than doubled over the decade from $64 million to $148 million; net income kept up with that pace.

Despite economic fluctuations, a worldwide oil crisis, new environmental regulations, and shifts in top management, Ferro managed to record several accomplishments in the 1970s. Cliff Andrews was elected president and chief operating officer in 1972; he added CEO and chairman to his list of titles in 1975 and 1976. But within just six months of those promotions, Andrews was obliged to leave his post because of poor health. Ad Posnick ascended to the presidency and chief executive officership in 1976 and led the company throughout the 1980s and into the 1990s.

Ferro established manufacturing facilities in Portugal and Venezuela and expanded operations in Spain, West Germany, Japan, and Brazil. Ferro Canada reached $10 million in sales in 1973, and Ferro Holland grew so large and complex that a holding company, Ferro (Holland) B.V., was organized to manage those businesses. Political instability and anti-American terrorism plagued Ferro's Argentinian subsidiary in the 1970s and forced the company to take extraordinary measures to protect its employees.

Technological developments were facilitated by a new corporate Technical Center that replaced the Central Research Division in 1970. Ferro's Frit Division developed forehearth colors, enabling the company to produce small runs of colored glass by the early 1970s. VEDOC organic powder coatings developed in the 1970s helped Ferro capture a vital share of the paint and enamel market. VEDOC stood for "versatile, everlasting, durable organic coating": the product line was used to finish appliances, automotive parts, and outdoor furniture.

Ferro's Refractories Division grew in the 1970s with the acquisition of the Gem Manufacturing Company, and Ferro began manufacturing vacuum-formed products like catalytic converters, insulation, and refractories for the steel industry following the purchase of the Gemcolite and Therm-X companies. The acquisition of the Keil Chemical Company in 1974 expanded Ferro's Chemical Group. At the end of the decade, Ferro purchased Transelco, Inc., a manufacturer of extremely specialized ceramic materials for the optical and electronics fields.

Having entered the plastics field just after World War II, Ferro expanded those operations into a full-fledged division in 1979 with the purchase of five plastic color businesses. The new Thermoplastic Colors and Compounds Division manufactured and marketed a comprehensive line of thermoplastic colorants.

By the end of the decade Ferro had evolved into a highly diversified worldwide conglomerate with sales of almost $600 million. But a deep recession in the early 1980s forced divestments and a mid-decade reorganization. The company identified thermoplastics as its new core business early in the decade and worked to bring those new operations to profitability. The new kid on the block, Ferro had competition in the industry that included established companies like General Electric, Imperial Chemical, Hercules, and Rhone-Poulenc. Occupied by the competition, Ferro was threatened with takeover by Crane Company, which acquired 22.4 percent of Ferro's stock between 1980 and 1982. Ferro blocked the hostile action by repurchasing 1.73 million shares from Crane in late 1982.

In the latter half of the decade, plastics became Ferro's fastest-growing business, providing up to a third of revenues. The company acquired plastics manufacturers in France, Portugal, and Great Britain, and established or expanded plastics operations in Holland, Canada, Spain, South Africa, and Brazil. Ferro added a plastics lab to its corporate Technical Center, and focused on the food packaging industry as a growth vehicle.

Ferro's reorganization started with the development of a new mission statement to establish general goals for the corporation, but soon progressed to more concrete changes. Over the course of the decade, the corporation pared down its specialty ceramics division to concentrate on high-margin niche markets and sold its Allied Division and coated fabric business. In an effort to streamline operations, Ferro Europe was reorganized to include three core product lines: frit, pigments, and plastics.

Ferro Corporation moved into a new headquarters in time for its 70th anniversary in 1989. The renovated building featured Ferro architectural products, including ceramic tiles, engineered plastic materials, and powder coatings. The company entered the 1990s with a strong earnings growth of 24 percent annually from 1985 to 1989, surpassing $1 billion in worldwide sales by 1988.

But Ferro was not without problems. As the corporation's share price plummeted from over $40 in 1989 to under $20 in 1990, takeover threats came from four directions. Scarce raw materials and low profit margins kept the plastics division hamstrung, and both sales and earnings dropped from 1990 to 1991.

That year, Albert C. Bersticker succeeded Ad Posnick as president and CEO. Even before advancing to Ferro leadership, Bersticker set out to enhance the company's positives and eliminate the negatives. His plan to restructure the company featured three primary parts: an emphasis on income over sales growth, concentration on core businesses, and reliance on Ferro's long history of global, technological, and customer service advantages. The strategy equated into $60 million in capi-

tal investments, the elimination of 12 percent of the company's U.S., European, and Latin American salaried workforce, and increased corporate debt from about 20 percent up to 40 percent.

A number of changes occurred in the early 1990s. In March of 1992 Ferro sold its steel mill products business in Tyler, Texas, to Vesuvius USA Corporation; two months later, though, Ferro's Plastic Colorants and Dispersions Division acquired ICI Americas, Inc.'s PDI business unit, which produces polyester, epoxy, and urethane dispersions. A year later Ferro purchased Bayer S.p.A.'s ceramic frit and color operations in Milan, Italy.

As the 1990s progressed, Ferro Corporation continued to find strength in its core businesses and international companies. The company continued to hold about 40 percent of the world's steel and porcelain enamel markets. Foreign sales brought in more than half of the company's revenues and 75 percent of net earnings, and had profit margins of 5 percent of sales.

Principal Subsidiaries: Ferro France S.A.R.L; Eurostar S.A. (France); Ferro Chemicals S.A. (France); Ferro (Deutschland) G.m.b.H.; Ruhr-Pulverlack G.m.b.H. (Germany); Ferro (Great Britain) Ltd.; Ferro (Holland) B.V.; Ferro (Italia) S.R.L.; Metal Portuguesa S.A. (51%); Ferro Enamel Espanola, S.A.; Ege-Ferro Kimya A.S. (Turkey; 49.9%); Ferro Enamel Argentina, S.A.; Termoplasticos de Ingenieria S.A.; Ferro Enamel do Brasil I.C.L.; Ferro Enamel do Sul I.C.L.; Nutriplant I.C.L. (50%); Ferro Ecuatoriana S.A. (49%); Ferro Mexicana S.A. de C.V.; Ferro de Venezuela, C.A. (49%); Ferro Corporation (Australia) Pty. Ltd.; Ferro Industrial Products Ltd. (Canada); Ferro Far East, Ltd. (Hong Kong); Excel Frits and Colours Limited (India; 40%); P.T. Ferro Mas Dinamika (Indonesia; 55%); Ferro Enamels (Japan) Ltd. (10%); Nissan-Ferro Organic Chemical Co. Ltd. (Japan; 51%); NFE Co. Ltd. (Japan; 50%); Ferro Plastics (N.Z.) Ltd. (New Zealand); Ferro Industrial Products Limited (Taiwan, Republic of China); Ferro Toyo Co., Ltd. (Taiwan, R.O.C.; 60%); Ferro-TPI (Thailand) Co.Ltd. (44%); Ecotech Italia S.P.A. (Italy).

Further Reading:

Bozsin, Michael A., Harold P. Connare, and Catherine N. Scott, *Ferro: The First Seventy Years, 1919–1989,* Cleveland: Ferro Corporation, 1990.

Kiesche, Elizabeth S. and Debbie Jackson, ''JV Talks Falter,'' *Chemicalweek,* January 29, 1992.

Lappen, Alyssa A., ''Someone Else's Turn?,'' *Forbes,* February 4, 1991, p. 94.

Marcial, Gene G., ''At Ferro, It's 'Move Over, Mario,' '' *Business Week,* October 29, 1990, p. 92.

McConville, Daniel J., ''Despite a Trying Year, Ferro Keeps a Confident Outlook,'' *Chemical Week,* November 21, 1990, pp. 36–37.

Moskal, Brian S., ''The Buck Doesn't Stop Here,'' *Industry Week,* July 15, 1991, pp. 29–30.

—April S. Dougal

First Brands Corporation

P.O. Box 1911
Danbury, Connecticut 06813-1911
U.S.A.
(203) 731-2300
Fax: (203) 731-2518

Public Company
Incorporated: 1986
Employees: 3,000
Sales: $989 million
Stock Exchanges: New York Philadelphia, Midwest, Pacific
SICs: 2673 Plastics Foil & Coated Paper Bags; 2899
    Chemicals & Chemical Preparations; 2869 Industrial
    Organic Chemicals NEC

First Brands is a leading consumer products company with operations based on a number of major brands: STP oil, Glad and Glad-Lock plastic wrap and bags, Prestone antifreeze, Simoniz car waxes, polishes, and cleaners, and Scoop Away and Ever Clean cat litter products. A product of a leveraged buy-out, the company was organized in 1986. Unlike many other products of the leveraged-buy-out mania that existed during the 1980s, the company's brands were not collected from hostile raids.

First Brands may trace its ultimate origin to an accidental gas leak at a Union Carbide plant in Bhopal, India, on December 3, 1984. The disaster produced a cloud of poison gas that claimed 2,000 lives and injured 200,000 people. Union Carbide, one of the world's largest chemical products companies, was at the time a hugely successful firm. Through a decades-long process of careful acquisitions and mergers, it had branched into many different types of operations. In fact, it was so diversified that various divisions had lost their focus and had begun to stumble in the market.

The company reached this bloated state during the 1970s and early 1980s, when chairmen F. Perry Wilson and William Sneath blindly pursued industrial expansion. With every new line of business, Carbide grew larger, but proportionally less profitable. By 1984, the company was ready for a restructuring.

The disaster in Bhopal was the critical event that caused Union Carbide to make painful decisions about its future. Several divisions were particularly weak and non-strategic, including plastics, metals, and carbon products. By shedding these peripheral operations, Union Carbide would realize an immediate and badly needed financial windfall. The company would emerge a smaller, but more profitable enterprise that could more easily concentrate on its core operations.

The Bhopal incident caused a flood of lawsuits charging negligence and wrongful death. The government of India, eager for retribution, pressed its claims with great vigor; it even temporarily jailed Union Carbide's chairman when he arrived at Bhopal to personally inspect the damage. The mounting liabilities forced Union Carbide to commence its reorganization immediately and liquidate underperforming assets to raise cash for legal settlements. Within a year the company took more than $1 billion in write-offs and dumped 4,000 salaried jobs. Analysts predicted the demise of Union Carbide, either by liquidation or hostile takeover.

In 1986, amidst this chaos, Union Carbide did become a target of a hostile takeover. Samuel Heyman and Harold Simmons, who had earlier battled each other for control of G.A.F., shared control of that company, and now, in a rare instance of agreement, decided to use G.A.F. to launch a bid for Union Carbide.

Weakened by Bhopal, Carbide was forced into defensive action. The company had two consumer products divisions—Eveready Batteries and Home and Automotive Products; while Eveready was sold to Ralston Purina, the Home and Automotive Products division was bought by Alfred E. Dudley and 23 other managers in Carbide's consumer products area. They raised $9.52 million (enough to purchase an 11.9 percent share), and collected an additional $70.5 million from First Boston, Manufacturers Hanover, and Metropolitan Life. For the balance, $760 of debt was raised from banks, shareholders, and a public high-yield bond issue.

The group, organized as the First Brands Corporation, took control of Union Carbide's STP business, its Glad and Glad-Lock line of plastic bags, Prestone antifreeze, and Simoniz waxes. The deal, concluded in mid-1986, also included product lines and factories in Asia, Canada, and Europe. First Brands entered 1987 as a new corporation with $76.6 million in capital and an astonishing $674 million of debt. With debt at 8.8 times equity, even the slightest mishap could plunge the company into bankruptcy and liquidation.

The company's first action was to cut the work force by 9.4 percent. Second, First Brands established its headquarters at a more conservative office building near the airport in Danbury, Connecticut—a far cry from the posh suites once occupied across town at Union Carbide. To first reduce its expansive acquisition financing, First Brands had sold its Glad Bag manufacturing equipment for $168 million, and leased it back under a less costly arrangement.

In a move that required considerably more creativity, the company set out to improve the value of its brands. With the help of an excellent research and development department, First Brands began shoring up its STP and Glad products. More than 30 product variations were introduced, including Glad bags with handles, Son of a Gun protectant, STP fuel additives, a new Prestone formula, and recyclable garbage bags; by far, their most successful new product was Glad-Lock Zipper Bags with its "Yellow and Blue Make Green" interlocking closure system.

First Brands began a massive effort to increase sales because greater cash flow would enable it to more quickly pay down its debt. With the acquisition of its brands, the company inherited a highly efficient distribution system. This network was well suited for expansion and was targeted for supplying new retail outlets.

First Brands' automotive products had been available primarily in automotive and discount stores. The largest outlet for Glad wrap and bags was grocery stores. But a new, more powerful retail phenomenon came into being during the late 1980s: warehouse outlets. Retailers such as Pace, Sam's Wholesale Club, and Price Club had established huge numbers of large stores that carried a limited number of products in great quantities. Consumers who were willing to purchase products in large containers or by the case were afforded impressive savings. Most of the discount over retail prices was absorbed by the retailer, who was selling in great volume with very little overhead.

First Brands cultivated important new supply arrangements with these warehouse stores. Its distribution network was required only to ship the product in great quantities with little or no responsibility for point-of-purchase displays, promotional material, or other marketing devices. Prestone, Glad bags, STP products, and others were sold, literally, by the truckload at these stores. In addition, small investments in advertising provided a highly significant stimulus to sales because warehouse store customers were often purchasing First Brands products in large quantities.

A large chemical plant explosion and increasing demand for ethylene glycol from non-antifreeze manufacturers resulted in spiraling prices. As a result, antifreeze prices—and profit margins—skyrocketed. Under normal circumstances, Prestone accounted for less than 20 percent of First Brands' sales. Now, however, the brand was up to 27 percent of sales and 30 percent of total earnings.

The danger was that sudden oversupply or the cooling of the economy could produce an antifreeze glut that would slash earnings. Still holding a large debt load, First Brands was hopeful that the tight market would continue. By early 1990, supplies of ethylene glycol gently began to stabilize, and antifreeze prices took a safe, measured decline.

Looking to continue lowering its costs and also expand its fast-growing Glad-Lock product, First Brands took a major step in early 1992. The company announced plans to expand Glad bag manufacturing capacity and relocate certain product operations from a Connecticut plant to Virginia, where costs and taxes were lower. In the process, the company trimmed a further 325 jobs, bringing its total work force down to about 3,350. The company still maintained Glad plants in Georgia and Arkansas.

In February of 1989, to raise additional cash and rid itself of an unprofitable operation, First Brands sold its European operations (including operations in France and Germany and a distributor in Spain) to Dow Brands for a gain of $27 million. A year earlier, First brands had made its first acquisition, Himo-

lene, Inc., a commercial can liner manufacturer and marketer. These efforts enabled First Brands to post an impressive turnaround: in 1987 the company lost $7 million on sales of $837 million, but only two years later, it registered a profit of $61 million on sales of $1.2 billion.

With the company having passed its crisis, First Brands' institutional investors who controlled ownership felt the time was right to realize a profit on the leveraged buy-out, and sold a 30 percent share of the company to the public. Metropolitan Life and First Boston proposed selling their then 48 percent interest in First Brands in late 1990. On this news, the company's share price climbed from $19 to $28, implying that First Brands was worth $600 million. But, unable to locate an interested acquirer at that price, Met Life and First Boston later cancelled the offer.

First Brands suffered a small setback in 1991 when the Federal Trade Commission charged that the company made false claims about the degradability of Glad bags. In fact, the bags, when exposed to the elements, did break down and were suitable for composting. However, the government charged that the bags did not decompose properly when buried in landfills. Under a consent decree, First Brands agreed to end broad claims that Glad bags were degradable. The incident had no impact on First Brands' growth.

The company's astonishing success with reviving its brands produced the higher cash flows it wanted. In the case of Prestone, the brand had achieved its maximum share in the market, and very high unit sales expenditures could not be recouped with declining margins. But with the economy slowing down and glycol prices dropping, the antifreeze market took a precipitous drop.

In an effort to use its antifreeze production capacity in light of a soft multi-year market condition, First Brands sought out a completely different type of customer. In addition to marketing Prestone antifreeze to consumers, the company pursued large retailers with an offer to manufacture their private label antifreeze. First Brands now manufactures antifreeze for almost all major antifreeze retailers, including Wal-Mart and K Mart. However, this places the discount store brands in direct competition with Prestone, a premium brand.

Economically, this has no negative effect on profits from antifreeze production. Because the store brands are in a different category from Prestone, they do not dilute its well-established quality equity. As long as Prestone maintains an optimal market share, it is rational for First Brands to manufacture—and realize a profit from—competing brands. In the process, it also keeps First Brands' antifreeze operation working at capacity.

First Brands also has expanded its private label business in the plastic wraps and bags division. Like Prestone, the company's flagship Glad brand achieved market leadership, but a small amount of excess production capacity remained. These plastic products are labeled with the names of regional store chains and sold in a variety of outlets.

Having made substantial progress in eliminating its long term debt—from 90 percent of capital in 1986 to 53 percent in 1993—First Brands began a new type of effort to expand its portfolio of products. In addition to creating further extensions of existing brands, the company made its second acquisition. First Brands purchased A&M Pet Products for $50 million in 1992. A&M, a manufacturer of premium clumpable cat litter products, received the same treatment as First Brands' other products. The new brand was put into additional distribution, again using warehouse stores and other major channels, and backed with good promotion.

It is possible that First Brands could repeat this "brand growing" strategy for an even wider variety of products. As long as it can maintain its focus on established consumer products—and avoid non-strategic operations it doesn't understand as well—First Brands may be poised for strong growth. The elimination of non-core businesses has become the new trend in American business. While diversification affords insulation from erratic business cycles, it also diverts a company's focus from the mission of its core businesses. For the same reasons that Union Carbide was forced to dispense of its consumer products businesses to concentrate on chemical operations, First Brands has avoided moving into areas outside its core business. This is the company's greatest strength; it does only what it can do very well.

First Brands is well respected for its marketing capabilities. Perhaps not yet on a par with giants such as Procter & Gamble, the company is clearly in the same league. In order to graduate to Procter & Gamble status, First Brands will likely have to boost its research and development organization, or make more acquisitions.

In its first six years of operation, First Brands has actually *invented* few completely new products. This is a result of low expenditures on R&D, which amount to about one percent of the company's sales. But while its future growth may depend on research and acquisitions, First Brands is not exceptionally well prepared to act; the brands it owns were developed under ownership of Union Carbide or acquired, and it still is heavily leveraged. There have been bright spots, though, with the company's invention of an antifreeze recycling process that eliminates the need for disposal, and its highly publicized blue bag recycling program that reduces costs for municipalities.

Nonetheless, it is possible that bold efforts to invent products or make acquisitions are not yet advisable for First Brands. The company continues to carry a substantial, but decreasing debt burden and is owned in large part by a few large financial institutions. For the time being, the company must remain focused on maintaining high cash flow. But for its efforts, First Brands has been cited as a model leveraged-buy-out and a company to watch.

Principal Subsidiaries: A&M Pet Products; First Brands Asia Ltd. (Hong Kong); First Brands (Canada) Corporation; First Brands Philippines, Inc.; First Brands Puerto Rico, Inc.; STP (Europe) Limited; Himolene, Inc.; Prestone Technology Systems, Inc.; STP Consumer Services, Inc.

Further Reading:

Byrnes, Nanette, "All Grown Up with Someplace to Go," *Financial World,* March 2, 1993.
"Dow Chemical Agrees to Buy First Brands' European Business," *Wall Street Journal,* February 8, 1989, p. C17.
Frank, Allan Dodds, "Shark Bait?," *Forbes,* November 18, 1985, pp. 114–19.
Meier, Barry, "Carbide Stock Is Rising to Pre-Disaster Levels on Hopes for Quick Pact on Bhopal Claims," *Wall Street Journal,* July 1, 1985, p 35.
Roberts, Johnnie L., "First Brands Pulled from Sales Block by Major Investors," *Wall Street Journal,* October 31, 1990, p. A6.
Saddler, Jeanne, "First Brands Settles FTC Case on Claims about Trash Bags," *Wall Street Journal,* October 10, 1991, p. B6.
Vogel, Todd, and Leah J. Nathans, "First Brands: Anatomy of an LBO that Worked," *Business Week,* December 4, 1989, p. 104.

—John Simley

First Mississippi Corporation

P.O. Box 1249
Jackson, Mississippi 39215-1249
U.S.A.
(601) 948-7550
Fax: (601) 949-0228

Public Company
Incorporated: March 19, 1957
Employees: 1,347
Sales: $524.7 million
Stock Exchanges: New York
SICs: 2865 Industrial Organic Crude Dyes & Pigments; 2869
  Industrial Organic Chemicals Nec

First Mississippi Corporation is the largest company chartered in Mississippi and the only company from that state to be listed on the New York Stock Exchange. Operating in one of the more economically underdeveloped regions of the United States, First Mississippi is a crucial local enterprise. In addition to providing employment and tax revenue, it is one of the country's most important niche market chemical manufacturers, producing a line of primary products for the agricultural industry.

First Mississippi originated through a small agricultural cooperative venture that was created specifically for the benefit of cotton farmers in the Mississippi River Delta. In the years following World War II, the nation's return to a peacetime economy left several industries in disarray. Chemical commodities, particularly nitrogen fertilizer, were in short supply. Without this important factor of production, Mississippi farmers stood to lose as much as 30 percent of their annual yields.

The farmers organized and, working through the Mississippi Farm Bureau, proposed the establishment of a new fertilizer manufacturing cooperative located in Mississippi. Eager to gauge the feasibility of such a project, the Bureau's director, Owen Cooper, traversed the state to test the idea with farmers. The concept was enthusiastically supported because, as owners of their own plant, farmers would enjoy greater control over production. And because the plant would be located in Mississippi, it would stem the loss of agricultural dollars to businesses in other states. In addition, the state government was ready to support any venture that would develop industry in Mississippi while improving agricultural yields.

On December 13, 1947, the Farm Bureau organized a stock sale to Mississippi's farmers. The proceeds would be used to build and operate an anhydrous ammonia fertilizer plant located at Yazoo City, about 40 miles north of Jackson, in east-central Mississippi. Eighteen months later, the farmer's cooperative, called the Mississippi Chemical Corporation, had amassed $3 million in capital. The facility was built shortly afterward and put into production. Demand for the cooperative's fertilizer was so great that it had to be expanded to double its original capacity.

By operating within the market, Mississippi Chemical "exported" excess fertilizer to patrons in other states. Because profits from the operation were distributed to the owners as a rebate—called a patronage refund—the farmers collected a direct benefit from their investment. As Mississippi Chemical grew in both scale and profitability, the cooperative spawned proposals for further expansion. The primary motivation was the cyclical nature of the fertilizer industry; many had grown to expect a large patronage refund, but in bad times were left disappointed.

Transformed into savvy businessmen, the farmers developed a plan to diversify Mississippi Chemical's operations into non-related industries to dampen the effects of the occasional down market. This idea quickly gained the backing of the Mississippi business community and the governor's office. On March 19, 1957, Governor J. P. Coleman approved the charter of a new enterprise built around Mississippi Chemical and backed by 21 businessmen, including Fred Anderson, who served as the company's president. As this was the first industrial experiment of its kind, the new company was given the name First Mississippi Corporation. Again, Owen Cooper was placed in charge of raising capital for the new parent company. Hoping to maintain the company's independence from New York financiers and bankers, he developed a plan to transfer the farmers' equity from Mississippi Chemical to First Mississippi. The owners were mailed penny postcards and asked to choose between a patronage refund check or an equivalent value in First Mississippi shares.

Under its charter, First Mississippi was established to develop the state's industries. First Mississippi's directors, whose aims were philanthropic, served without compensation during the first years of the company's existence. Many farmers and an increasing number of non-farming investors supported the idea. Over a period of years, First Mississippi gradually built up enough capital to acquire a variety of companies within the state. Much of this growth was poorly managed, however. Among the businesses taken on by First Mississippi—all of which were failing—were a swimming pool contractor, an egg carton manufacturer, a pipe maker, an animal food company, a metal extruder, and real estate and insurance agencies.

As losses mounted, First Mississippi's board selected a new project development manager named Jack Babbitt. Babbitt's mission was to regain control over First Mississippi's sprawling empire by identifying nonstrategic or noncore operations and selling them. In 1964, just as Babbitt's efforts began to show results, Fred Anderson died suddenly, leaving the company without a president. Babbitt and Cooper, who helped to establish First Mississippi, persuaded another of the company's founders, LeRoy Percy to succeed Anderson.

Having sold off its problem operations, Babbitt and Cooper decided to refocus the company on what it did best—chemical manufacturing. With demand rising, First Mississippi began construction on a duplicate plant at Yazoo City. Separately, the two proposed a joint venture with CF Industries, a farmers' cooperative based in Chicago. Under the terms of the agreement, First Mississippi and CF Industries would build a second anhydrous ammonia plant, with a daily capacity of 1000 tons, and sell the production to CF members through its network. The joint subsidiary was called First Nitrogen, Inc. First Mississippi and CF had difficulty finding a suitable location for First Nitrogen. The joint subsidiary had to be located on the Mississippi River to facilitate transportation of the product north to CF. However, there were no suppliers of natural gas—a primary ingredient in manufacturing fertilizers—existed in the available locations.

In 1965 Babbitt gained the attention of Texaco, which at the time was interested in extending a pipeline up the western bank of the Mississippi River, in Louisiana. First Mississippi offered to locate the First Nitrogen plant at Donaldsonville, Louisiana, giving Texaco a reason to build the extension, and then offered to purchase gas from Texaco on a 20-year contract. First Nitrogen's Donaldsonville plant began operation a little more than a year later, in October of 1966. It proved to be so profitable that after only nine months in operation, CF exercised its option to buy out First Mississippi's 50-percent share of the subsidiary for $4.4 million (nearly double what First Mississippi had originally invested). First Mississippi immediately returned to Donaldsonville because of its access to gas. Working with its Mississippi Chemical and Coastal Chemical subsidiaries, the company set up a third subsidiary called Triad Chemical.

Triad was created to operate an ammonia plant capable of producing 1000 tons per day and a second facility to manufacture 1200 tons of urea—powdery nitrogen fertilizer—daily. The urea plant, one of the largest of its type in the world, was fashioned after a design from a Dutch company. In its first year of operation, the ammonia plant turned out 368,000 tons, then a world record. This helped First Mississippi recover from a dismal year in 1969, when it lost $1.1 million, to a $500,000 profit in 1970.

A year later, however, a routine inspection of the facilities revealed a serious problem with corrosion that could have rendered the facility inoperable and worthless, but a design fix was developed by the company's engineers. Able to count once again upon the long-term health of Triad's output, Babbitt began searching for new customers for the company's urea. He later sealed an agreement with the Ashland Oil Company to jointly build and operate a melamine plant using Triad urea. Melamine is a plastic used in making resins, adhesives, surface coatings and molded products. The new company, Melamine Chemicals, Inc., was jointly owned by First Mississippi and Ashland Oil, but was hindered by delays caused by design modifications. Fortunately for First Mississippi, its other operations were doing well enough to support the costs of these modifications and maintain profitability.

While Melamine was under construction, First Mississippi announced plans to build another chemical facility within the state. The company created a subsidiary named the First Chemical Corporation to run a $7 million complex at Pascagoula for manufacturing aniline and related nitrated aromatic chemicals. The target markets for this production were automotive, pharmaceutical, plastics and photographic companies. The First Chemical plant was developed specifically to reduce First Mississippi's exposure to the volatile fertilizer markets. The basic design was licensed from the Swiss company Lonza, but was substantially improved upon by First Mississippi chemical engineers. The modifications raised utilization of the catalyst from ten percent to about 50 percent and later won First Mississippi a share of future licensing revenues on subsequent designs sold by Lonza.

The construction of these two new plants deeply concerned board members, who feared that the company had overextended itself. Jack Babbitt held discussions with the Williams Companies, based in Tulsa, Oklahoma, about the possibility of being acquired. Williams wanted to enter the fertilizer business to complement its other operations. However, the board considered the dangers in setting up Triad and First Chemical to be only temporary; once in operation, they were likely to run profitably. In addition, the members opposed selling Mississippi's largest indigenous industrial enterprise to a company in Oklahoma.

While Williams failed to get control of First Mississippi, it successfully persuaded Jack Babbitt to switch companies. Babbitt, one of the primary architects of First Mississippi's growth, left in September of 1971. Before he left, he designated a successor, Kelley Williams. Williams, not related to Babbitt's new employer, joined First Mississippi in 1967 as a chemical engineer and manager of corporate planning and development. Only 37 years old in 1971, Williams had demonstrated strong leadership capabilities during his brief tenure. LeRoy Percy and Owen Cooper were reluctant to make Williams' appointment permanent, however, and began a search for a new chief executive.

After eight months, Percy and Cooper were sufficiently impressed with Williams and made his appointment permanent. Williams established a detailed expansion strategy for First Mississippi during this period. As part of that plan, the company acquired a large fertilizer manufacturing facility at Fort Madison, Iowa from the Atlantic Richfield Company on August 31, 1973. In what *Forbes* described as "Jonah swallowing a big whale," First Mississippi, with only $31 million in assets, took over Arco's $75 million manufacturing complex and the $25 million retail office that came with it.

To carry out the Arco deal, First Mississippi asked the Chase Manhattan Bank, which helped finance the Triad plants, to provide a $31 million loan and float an additional $46 million in industrial revenue bonds. While the acquisition was a huge gamble for First Mississippi, Williams believed that the company could manage Fort Madison better than Arco had and that the fertilizer market was poised for significant demand growth. A month after the deal was completed, federal price controls on fertilizers were lifted, and market prices began to climb. Production was increased to meet the rising demand, and the resulting operating profit and sale of 58 of 121 retail outlets was used to help repay the loan.

The Fort Madison plant, renamed FirstMiss, Inc., quadrupled First Mississippi's volume and helped the company to turn in a $20 million profit in 1974. The following year this figure climbed to $41 million. The successful Fort Madison acquisition won First Mississippi recognition from Wall Street. In January of 1975, First Mississippi became the first Mississippi-chartered company to be listed on the New York Stock Exchange.

Able to resume its diversification campaign, First Mississippi began studying possible acquisitions of businesses involved in oil, gas, and mineral exploration. In 1974 the company established its own natural gas exploration business. Meanwhile, First Mississippi and six oil companies began to look at expansion at Donaldsonville. The consortium decided to build another 1,150 ton per day fertilizer complex adjacent to the Triad facility. The venture, called AMPRO, allowed First Mississippi to market the plant's products, while the six oil companies would provide natural gas for the facility from offshore gas fields in Louisiana.

When the plant was completed in the fall of 1977, however, the Federal Energy Regulatory Commission, a government agency created after the 1973–74 energy crisis, refused to allow the oil companies to exploit the Louisiana gas reserves. Borrowing profits from the booming fertilizer business, First Mississippi stepped up its natural gas exploration efforts. By 1976 the company had 96,000 gas-producing under lease. While this was not enough to supply the AMPRO facility, First Mississippi and its partners managed to secure contracts that allowed the plant to open in 1980.

During this time, AMPRO took the Federal Energy Regulatory Commission to court, hoping to reverse the agency's order. But the federal court could only ask the commission to reconsider its decision. By the time alternate sources of natural gas were located, AMPRO had spent $3 million and the plant opening was delayed by three years. The supply bottleneck caused First Mississippi to step up its work in the oil, gas, and minerals exploration businesses. In 1978 these businesses were grouped under a subsidiary called First Energy Corporation. A year later, after formally including oil and gas into its list of primary businesses, a second energy crisis occurred, resulting from the overthrow of the Shah of Iran.

During this time, First Energy Corporation made a huge strike at the Irene Field in Louisiana's Tuscaloosa Trend. The company set up a series of wells on the site that proved to be extremely productive. Once again, First Mississippi had a highly profitable resource that it could use to help build other operations. The strike could not have come at a better time. The FirstMiss plant at Fort Madison had gradually become obsolete during the 1970s. In addition, export markets for American fertilizer manufacturers dried up and modern, more efficient competitors emerged. Unable to compete without massive and costly upgrades, FirstMiss was forced to close its Fort Madison plant in October of 1981.

While the bulk of First Mississippi's company-building profits were now coming from the Irene Field, the search went on for other promising ventures. Dedicated to expansion in the oil and gas business, First Energy looked for more unexplored fields. Southeastern leases, where the company hoped to look first, had been thoroughly picked over. Instead, First Energy turned to the vast unexplored tracts in the Rocky Mountains and leased 700,000 acres from the Emerald Oil Company. The exploration effort was later increased to cover more than 1.5 million acres of land. As a result, oil and gas revenues climbed from $7 million in 1976 to $50 million in 1981.

Mineral exploration also continued to grow. A massive armament program, launched during the final year of the Carter Administration and amplified by President Reagan, created a high demand for precious metals and "strategic minerals." First Mississippi bought mineral leases in 1980, beginning with a 9,000-acre claim in New Mexico called the "Silver Bar," which it acquired in a surprise move over the Christmas holidays when other bidders were on vacation. The exploration of coal, a bridge between the mineral and energy businesses, was a high priority for First Mississippi, particularly as the past energy crisis—and the virtual moratorium on nuclear power plants—served to increase the demand for coal.

In late 1981, after considering more than 100 claims, First Mississippi decided to purchase the Pyramid Mining company based in Owensboro, Kentucky. In addition to providing greater diversification, Pyramid's coal reserves were estimated at about 100 million tons. While revenues in the 1980s tripled over those of the previous decade, net income was erratic. Attributing this to mere overcapacity in fertilizer and other markets, First Mississippi pressed ahead with further acquisitions. The company purchased interests several high-technology enterprises, including the International Genetic Sciences Partnership, the Technology Applications Services Corp. (now Plasma Energy), Imperial Technology Kellwyn, Inc. and the Opti-Rad partnership. In addition, the company moved into insulation products, and the mineral extraction group brought First Mississippi into the gold mining business.

In 1989 First Mississippi recorded its best performance to date. But by this time it had become apparent that much of this success was due to temporary conditions and could not be sustained. Convinced that the strategy of growth through diversification could not provide stable growth, Kelley Williams decided to gradually spin off every venture that was not compatible with First Mississippi's core businesses. First Mississippi wound down its coal mining and industrial insulation operations and most of its high-technology ventures. (The Pyramid mine, which lost $3.8 million in its last two years, was closed because of low demand arising from industry preparations for federal Clean Air Act compliance.) With the businesses it retained, First Mississippi consolidated its Plasma Energy unit with Callidus Technologies to achieve better economies. Continuing its shift toward core chemical operations, First Mississippi purchased a Dayton, Ohio chemical plant from Monsanto, and reached a long-term contract to supply American Cyanamid with a key herbicide ingredient.

In many respects, First Mississippi's move back to related chemical operations mirrors the reorganization that occurred 30 years earlier. Having discovered that its nonrelated businesses actually declined in tandem, First Mississippi decided now, as it had then, that it would stick to those businesses it knows best.

Principal Subsidiaries: First Chemical Corporation; Quality Chemicals, Inc.; EKC Technology, Inc.; FirstMiss Fertilizer, Inc.; AMPRO Fertilizer, Inc.; Triad Chemical, Inc. (50%); Pyramid Mining, Inc.; First Energy Corporation; FEC Marketing, Inc.; FRM, Inc.; FirstMiss Gold, Inc. (81.9%); Callidus Technologies, Inc.; FirstMiss Steel, Inc.; Industrial Insulations of Texas, Inc.; Plasma Energy Corporation; Plasma Processing Corporation; SCE Technologies, Inc.; Star Corrosion & Refractory, Inc.; Power Sources, Inc. (50%).

Further Reading:

"Eye-Opening Results Attained By First Mississippi," *Jackson Daily News,* August 27, 1980, p. 2.

"First Miss Adapting," *Mississippi Business Journal,* June 8, 1992.

"First Mississippi: At the Crossroads," *Jackson Daily News,* April 21, 1985.

"First Mississippi Corporation, The First Twenty-Five Years," address by J. Kelley Williams, Newcomen Society in North America, 1982.

"First Mississippi Says Good Times Not Too Far Away," *Mississippi Business Journal,* January 18, 1993, p. 5.

"The First Mississippi Story," *Farm Chemicals,* April 1975.

—John Simley

FIRST OF AMERICA.

First of America Bank Corporation

108 East Michigan Avenue
Kalamazoo, Michigan 49007
U.S.A.
(616) 376-9000
Fax: (616) 376-7273

Public Company
Incorporated: 1971
Employees: 10,387
Sales: $20 billion
Stock Exchanges: New York
SICs: 6021 National Commercial Banks; 6022 State
   Commercial Banks; 6035 Savings Institutions; 6712 Bank
   Holding Companies

First of America Bank Corporation is one of the Midwest's largest bank holding companies and is ranked among the top 35 banking companies in the country based on net income, profitability, and size. Its 566 branch banks in Michigan, Illinois, and Indiana offer conventional checking and savings programs as well as numerous other financial services including mortgage loans, retail credit, and investment opportunities.

First of America traces its origins to 1863 when the first National Bank Act was passed by Congress and signed into law by President Abraham Lincoln. The law allowed for the chartering of national banks, which, for the first time in the country's history, would issue standardized national bank notes as legal tender. At the time, chartering a national bank required capital ranging from $200,000 for larger cities to $50,000 for small towns. The new national banks were required to deposit one-third of their capital in bonds with the U.S. government, and in exchange they could circulate up to 90 percent of the deposited amount in standard bank notes. The new system, with its government-backed currency, restored national confidence in paper money and eventually helped the country sustain the economic hardships of the Civil War.

At the beginning of 1863, the city of Kalamazoo, Michigan, had two private banks and a population of around 6,000. By the end of the year a third bank, a national bank, was established. Latham Hull, a well-known and respected businessman in the community, was elected president of the First National Bank of Kalamazoo, which was established with a capital investment of $50,000. The bank's first cashier was Thomas S. Cobb.

Throughout the 19th century, Kalamazoo's First National Bank served a largely rural community by receiving deposits as well as making business loans and investments. By the turn of the century, First National had capital stock of $100,000 and estimated assets of $84,000. In a review of Kalamazoo's banks, published in a June 1902 edition of the *Kalamazoo Telegraph,* First National's facilities were praised as among the area's most efficient and handsome, featuring marble partitions, mahogany woodwork, and "the most modern conveniences known to the banking world."

In 1912 the First National Bank was merged with the Michigan National Bank, one of the two originally privately held banks in Kalamazoo that had later received national charters. Charles Campbell, Michigan National's president, became president of the newly formed bank, which took the abbreviated name of First National Bank. Eight years later the bank's name was again changed to First National Bank and Trust Company of Kalamazoo to reflect the fact that a trust department had been added to its business.

On February 14, 1933, at one of the lowest points of the country's Great Depression, Michigan's Governor Comstock ordered a statewide bank holiday in order to avoid the possibility of a nationwide banking collapse. Like the other three banks in Kalamazoo, the First National Bank and Trust was forced to close for about one week, during which time patrons relied on credit from merchants. One week later, the banks were allowed to reopen on a limited basis, accepting deposits and permitting their customers to withdraw no more than 5 percent of their deposits on Thursdays only. A national bank holiday was declared by President Franklin Roosevelt a few weeks later, but by April 1933 the First National Bank and Trust withstood examination, was declared solvent, and was reopened permanently.

In 1936 and 1939 First National expanded its market area by opening offices in the neighboring communities of Vicksburg and Galesburg, respectively, and as First National's physical presence expanded so did its services. In 1940 bank loans previously extended only to area businesses were offered to individuals, and a personal loan department was established. During World War II First National and most other Michigan banks were kept busy with war bond sales, handling industrial payrolls, and maintaining ration banking accounts. With much of the nation's male work force serving in the war, large numbers of women went to work outside the home, and in Michigan over 3,500 women were employed as bank tellers.

In the years immediately following the war, First National opened several more branches in nearby towns. During this time the bank also began to experiment with new systems and conveniences for its customers. In 1952 First National became the first bank in the country to offer a charge account plan to customers. The service became a model for other Michigan banks, and First National frequently hosted banking representatives sent to study the details of the plan and its record keeping procedures.

Furthermore, in 1959 the bank began making available in-plant financial services for the area's larger industries and businesses, providing assistance with payroll and record keeping. Four years later, as it prepared to celebrate its 100th anniversary in 1963, First National maintained 18 offices in and around Kalamazoo. Computerization of banking transactions was established during this time, and in 1967 First National and American National Bank became equal partners in a venture to establish the Great Lakes Computer Center.

Although First National Bank had by 1970 grown into a successful business worth about $300 million, it had, in accordance with Michigan state law, been unable to make acquisitions beyond a 25-mile radius of Kalamazoo. When that law was repealed in 1971, and Michigan banks were allowed to develop into holding companies, First National was poised to take its business statewide. Acquiring banks in the Michigan towns of Calumet and Deerfield, First National became a holding company on March 20, 1972, and was renamed First National Financial Corporation. As the first statewide bank holding company in Michigan, First National had approximately $348,300,000 in assets.

Thereafter First National began rapidly acquiring banks throughout the state. Over the next five years, the corporation owned 12 banks and was ranked the seventh largest bank holding company in Michigan. In 1977, it became the state's largest holding company when it joined forces with American Bankcorp, Inc. of Lansing, Michigan, in a merger that also represented the state's largest. That year, in his report to shareholders, Chairperson James H. Duncan claimed he and newly retired American Bankcorp chair Joseph Foster had "accomplished much of what we set out to when our respective holding companies were formed. . . . We can now present to you a truly diversified investment in a $1.5 billion bank holding company that spans Michigan and serves most of the major cities and economic areas of our State." The newly merged organization, renamed the First American Bank Corporation, reportedly had acquired a total of 18 commercial banks that ranged in size from $7 million to over $460 million in assets.

Until 1981, First American had expanded as far north as Michigan's Upper Peninsula, but had limited its acquisitions to smaller community banks. It entered the larger Detroit market in 1981, when it acquired the Wayne Oakland Bank, reportedly worth $458 million in assets. By the end of that year four more Detroit banks were added to First American's list, all part of the acquisition of Detroit's struggling Northern States Bancorporation. Although the corporation reported an increase in assets to $3.6 billion that year, up from $2.5 billion in 1980, analysts observed that its earnings dropped 21 percent. Chairperson James H. Duncan held responsible the country's economic recession, which hit Michigan's auto and agricultural industries particularly hard during the early 1980s and therefore affected First American, the state's largest agricultural lender.

The corporation took the name First of America Bank Corporation on January 14, 1983. At that time it had 28 affiliate banks and about $3 billion in assets, ranking as the fifth largest banking company in Michigan. During the early 1980s automatic teller machines were introduced at First of America's banks, providing customers with banking services at all hours and convenient locations. In *Kalamazoo: The Place Behind the Products,* Massie and Schmitt observed that although in the bank's early years President Latham Hull signed each bank note

personally, and that such procedures had been replaced by plastic cards and computerized machines, the bank, through its commitment to improving services through technology, continued to give personalized attention to customers and communities. In 1985, when First of America's chairperson James H. Duncan stepped down and Daniel R. Smith took over, First of America boasted nearly $5 billion in assets.

Although Executive Vice President Richard D. Klein told *Barron's* at that time that First of America had "not felt it necessary or prudent to go out of our territory to seek loans or deposits," expansion into Indiana and Illinois began in 1986. Perhaps the most important of its out of state acquisitions was completed on November 1, 1989, when First of America reportedly paid about $250 million, or 5.6 million shares of First of America common stock, for the Midwest Financial Group, Inc., based in Peoria, Illinois. Fending off a hostile takeover attempt from the Kansas City, Missouri-based Commerce Bancshares, management at the struggling Midwest considered First of America's philosophies and practices compatible with their own and welcomed its offer. Midwest provided the holding company with 38 more offices and $2.3 billion in assets. As a result of the merger, First of America became the fifth largest bank in Illinois, and the largest in that state operating outside of Chicago.

From the period 1972 to 1987 First of America had acquired 58 banks. During this time the corporation attracted attention for its successful implementation of a "community banking" strategy, in which it preferred to acquire banks in slow, rural economies and turn them into smoothly operating First of America bank branches that would flourish when the economy turned around. Rather than attempting to gain the banking business of large companies and industries, such branches focused primarily on collecting deposits locally and lending conservative amounts of money to local businesses and residents. This strategy fostered a sense of community pride and involvement, which helped to maintain customer satisfaction while also making it possible for the corporation to avoid losses from risky foreign and commercial lending. In accordance with its conservative policies, the corporation would extend no more than $20 million in credit to any one party, an amount significantly lower than most banks. However, most decisions, including pricing for loans and deposit products, were left up to individual bank management, so that under its community banking strategy, First of America's banks retained a significant degree of independence and autonomy.

While the decision-making process remained flexible for each First of America branch bank, the corporation began centralizing the record keeping of all its banks in response to inconsistencies and inefficiencies resulting from its many mergers and acquisitions. Consequently, a new Operations and Data Processing Center in Oshtemo, Michigan, featuring a network of 7,900 data terminals, was opened in 1991.

One of the reasons cited for First of America's rapid growth and financial success in the late 1980s and early 1990s was the knowledge and experience of its management team. Dubbed "the savvy crew from Kalamazoo" by *Bankers Monthly* magazine in 1990, the group consisted of Smith, Klein, who had been promoted to vice chairperson, President and Chief Operating

Officer Richard Chormann, and executive vice presidents John Rapp and Thomas Lambert. Most of the men had strong ties to Kalamazoo, having attended college there and having begun work for the First National Bank in the late 1950s and early 1960s. Firmly dedicated to the corporation's community banking strategy, a program that had seen successful in both favorable and unfavorable financial conditions, they chose to ignore the trends toward riskier investments popular among many large financial institutions. Robert Bruce Slater noted in *Bankers Monthly*, that "by sticking to what they know best, community banking, the top management team at First of America is way out in front."

Although the corporation's net income and earnings per share dropped slightly in 1992, management contended that such losses reflected several one-time only acquisition costs incurred during the 1992 fiscal year rather than the overall performance of the corporation. As First of America approached the twenty-first century, its management regarded its foundation as strong for continued financial growth and a possible expansion of its geographic range.

Further Reading:

Dubashi, Jagannath, "Prophet Without Honor," *Financial World,* August 22, 1989, pp. 59–61.

Dunbar, Willis F., *Kalamazoo and How It Grew . . . and Grew,* Kalamazoo: Western Michigan University, 1969.

F. W. C. "Growing at Home," *Barron's,* February 4, 1985, pp. 48–49.

Gatton, T. Harry, *A History of Michigan Banking,* Lansing: Michigan Bankers Association, 1987.

Massie, Larry B., and Peter J. Schmitt, *Kalamazoo: The Place Behind the Products,* Windsor Publications, 1981, pp. 56, 254.

Slater, Robert Bruce, "The Savvy Crew from Kalamazoo," *Bunkers Monthly,* September 1990, pp. 21–28.

"Who Says Banks Are Dull?," *Financial World,* March 15, 1982, pp. 51–52.

Willoughby, Jack, "Think Small, Grow Big," *Forbes,* August 22, 1988, p. 96.

—Tina Grant

Fluor Corporation

3333 Michelson Drive
Irvine, California 92730
U.S.A.
(714) 975-2000
Fax: (714) 975-5981

Public Company
Incorporated: 1924 as Fluor Construction Company
Employees: 43,605
Sales: $6.60 billion
Stock Exchanges: New York Chicago Pacific Amsterdam
   London Swiss
SICs: 1629 Heavy Construction Nec; 1542 Nonresidential
   Construction Nec; 1541 Industrial Buildings &
   Warehouses; 8711 Engineering Services; 1799 Special
   Trade Contractors Nec; 1521 Single-Family Housing
   Construction

Fluor Corporation is one of the world's largest engineering, construction, maintenance, and related technical service companies. Fluor Daniel, the company's largest unit, provides engineering and construction services ranging from site selection and design to construction and plant maintenance for a broad range of industries. The company also has considerable investments in the coal industry, producing steam coal for the electric generating industry and metallurgical coal for the steel industry.

Fluor's story begins with a Swiss emigré who, upon arriving in the United States knew only one English word—"hello." Born in 1867, John Simon Fluor was a carpenter who had gained engineering experience while serving in the Swiss army. Fluor emigrated in 1888 at the age of 21, joining his two older brothers who had settled in Oshkosh, Wisconsin. The three pooled their money in 1890 to start a saw and paper mill called Rudolph Fluor & Brother. J. Simon Fluor's contribution was $100; he served as manager at the mill.

In 1903 the company name changed to Fluor Brothers Construction Company, with J. Simon Fluor as president. Nine years later he traveled on his own to California and started a general construction business under his own name. With innovative methods and precise work, Fluor built his venture's reputation quickly. The Southern California Gas Company asked him to build an office and numerous meter shops in 1915, and afterward Fluor received a contract for a compressor station

from Industrial Fuel Supply Company. Fluor recognized that the emerging California petroleum industry held enormous potential, so in 1921 he began to tailor his engineering and construction work to meet the demands of the field.

Fluor received a contract to erect a cooling tower in 1921. Believing that those in use at the time were inefficient and wasteful, he designed the "Buddha tower," a radical advancement which not only cooled water more efficiently but reduced water loss. The name came from the tower's resemblance to Buddhist shrines. Fluor soon began manufacturing the towers. The oil and gas companies quickly recognized the Buddha towers' merit, and used them at many installations.

Fluor incorporated his business as Fluor Construction Company in 1924 with a capital investment of $100,000. He began manufacturing large engine mufflers, expanding the company from strictly engineering to engineering and construction. After outgrowing two different facilities, Fluor built new quarters in Los Angeles and consolidated all general offices in one building in 1927.

In the mid-1920s, Fluor started involving his sons in the family business. He retained the presidency until 1943, although his sons ran the company. Fluor's eldest son, Peter Earl, became executive vice president and general manager. Peter Fluor seemed to be a born salesman, and associates called him "the company engine." He led Fluor's development through the Depression and World War II.

Fluor's business continued increasing until the stock market crashed in October 1929. Between 1924 and 1929 annual sales grew from $100,000 to $1.5 million. In need of additional capital in 1929, the company reincorporated and changed its name to Fluor Corporation, Ltd. to reflect its involvement in fields outside construction. At the time of the reincorporation, Peter Fluor and his brother J. Simon Fluor, Jr. encouraged company employees to take advantage of the company's success by offering them Fluor stock at one dollar per month per share. The brothers initiated many employee benefit programs and were considered enlightened employers.

Until 1930 Fluor operated primarily within California. That year, Peter Fluor pushed for expansion, contrary to his father's wishes, and sold Fluor's services to the Panhandle Eastern Pipeline Company. The contract was for construction of compressor stations on an oil pipeline from Texas to Indiana. The company also opened a Kansas City office. Fluor's expansion got another boost later that year when the Shell Oil Company hired the firm to build a $100,000 refining unit in Illinois. It was the company's largest refining contract to date and helped establish Fluor as a major competitor in the refining construction field.

Fluor's business decreased sharply during the Depression years, but the company's leadership wanted to keep its skilled personnel on the payroll. Thus many Fluor employees with sophisticated expertise worked as laborers until business improved. Also during the Depression, Fluor registered patents on two of the company founder's inventions. They were the Fluor aerator tower, patented in 1932; and the Fluor air-cooler muffler, patented in 1938.

The pressures and energy needs of World War II led Fluor into more new work areas. Early in the war years, Fluor had only a few months to develop facilities and personnel capable of producing high-octane gasoline and synthetic rubber. Later, Sinclair Oil Company selected Fluor to design and build a sulfuric alkylation plant at its California refinery. Between 1940 and 1943, Fluor facilities produced more than a third of all 100 percent octane gasoline in the United States, and the Fluor staff developed three patented procedures to improve oil and gas processing.

In 1944 J. Simon Fluor died. Peter Fluor succeeded him as president, and J. Simon Fluor, Jr. became executive vice president. Peter Fluor died unexpectedly in 1947 at age 52. An interim officer followed him in the presidency, and in 1949 the permanent successor, Donald Darnell, took over. After a few years of declines in business, Fluor turned to the U.S. government for contracts in the early 1950s, and thus entered another new area of work. The company participated in construction of a large materials testing reactor for the Atomic Energy Commission in Arco, Idaho. Many more assignments in the nuclear field followed.

The immediate postwar years were a time of significant international expansion for the company; the firm secured contracts for refineries and natural gas plants in Canada and Venezuela. In 1946 a contract for a grassroots refinery in Montana solidified Fluor's reputation as a refinery engineering firm and helped lead to an assignment to expand the Aramco facilities in Saudi Arabia. The company formed its Gas-Gasoline Division in Houston in 1948.

By the time the Korean War created massive petroleum product needs in 1950, Fluor's reputation was so widespread that it was a natural choice for many energy-producing projects. In the first half of the decade, Fluor actively diversified its operations, contracting work for the U.S. Air Force at Dhahran Air Base and for refineries in Puerto Rico. In the early 1950s Fluor introduced a new technique that has since become standard in the industry: using scale models in the design of process facilities. The models helped Fluor staff become specialists in lifting large vessels at job sites. More projects followed, including designing and building plants for the petrochemical industry in Canada, Scotland, Australia and South Africa. A London office opened in 1957. In the late 1950s Fluor's expertise in building helium plants gained the company contracts with Britain's Bureau of Mines and Office of Saline Water.

During this period of rapid expansion and large international contracts, Darnell became chairman of the company, J. Simon Fluor, Jr. became president and chief executive officer, and J. Robert Fluor, grandson of the founder, became executive vice president.

As the company grew, Fluor's leadership recognized the critical value of recruiting a staff trained in the most current, sophisticated construction methods. Because the marketplace during the 1950s was short of workers with the skills Fluor demanded, the company established in-house training and college tuition reimbursement programs, both of which are still in use.

In 1962 J. Robert Fluor, an engineer and former U.S. Air Force pilot who bred thoroughbred horses, became president and chief executive officer of the company. His tenure was significant for Fluor Corporation in four major ways: internationalization, computerization, acquisitions in the offshore oil drilling industry, and mining acquisitions. In the first case, Fluor built refineries in Korea and Iran, extending its operations into two more nations. In the computerization area, the company began using computers throughout its offices for both engineering projects and management needs during the 1960s.

Fluor's extensive diversification into offshore drilling began in 1967 with the merger of five companies into Fluor under the divisional name Coral Drilling. Around the same time Fluor established a new subsidiary called Deep Oil Technology for deep-ocean recovery of oil. In 1968 the company created Fluor Ocean Services, an umbrella management company headquartered in Houston. Ocean Services quickly became a worldwide company. Fluor's largest offshore drilling acquisition occurred in 1969, when the company took over the Pike Corporation of America. Pike's operations had been consolidated under three separate companies—Western Offshore Drilling and Exploration Company, Republic Supply Company of California, an equipment distributor, and the specialty tubing and pipe distributor Kilsby Tubesupply.

Fluor's involvement with the mining and metals industry also began in 1969. The company purchased Utah Construction and Mining Company, forming the subsidiary Fluor Mining & Metals, Inc. Fluor Australia, another mining interest, was set up soon afterward. In later years mining would become a significant interest for Fluor.

The company's activities in the 1970s focused heavily on the international natural resources industries: oil, gas and nuclear power. Fluor also set up subsidiaries and management organizations in Europe, Indonesia, South Africa, Alaska and Saudi Arabia, the last being a $5 billion gas program. In 1973 Fluor consolidated its oil and gas activities to form Fluor Oil and Gas Corporation. It completed the world's largest offshore facility for natural gas in Java in 1976.

The financial figures for three consecutive years demonstrate the rate of the company's expansion: 1973, $1.3 billion; 1974, $4.4 billion; 1975, $9 billion. New corporate offices opened in Houston and Irvine to accommodate the company's rapidly growing staff. Fluor executives attributed a large part of the company's success to its task force management concept, under which every Fluor project received all the tools, personnel and resources to get the job done, and the project director had full authority and responsibility for the entire project.

In the late 1970s the Saudi Arabian minister of industry asked company president J. Robert Fluor to help improve Saudi Arabia's poor image in the United States. At that time Fluor chaired the board of trustees at the University of Southern California. He asked executives of 40 major companies that dealt with the Saudis to fund a $22 million Middle East Studies Center at the university. The center was to be run by a former oil company employee and controlled by the donors. The university faculty and the Los Angeles Jewish community blocked the project because of the irregularity of its intended relationship with its fund sources. Fluor Corporation's public relations department claimed the affair had been distorted by the ''Jewish Press.''

Along with Fluor's extensive and sometimes controversial international involvement, the company also made a significant domestic expansion by acquiring the Daniel International Corporation in 1977. Daniel was an industrial contractor with revenues over $1 billion a year that in many ways complemented the Fluor portfolio. Daniel's operations were primarily based in the U.S., whereas Fluor worked largely overseas. The two had different client lists and were involved in different kinds of projects. Most Fluor employees were members of labor unions, but most of Daniel's employees were not. Despite, and in some cases because of, their differences, the two companies integrated efficiently.

This was not the case, however, with the purchase of St. Joe Minerals in 1981. The acquisition happened at a time when Fluor had a healthy cash flow from its growing engineering and construction sectors. Management knew about the mining industry from its experience building facilities for mines. Fluor executives determined that metals prices ran counter-cyclically to the market variations in the construction industry, making mining the perfect complement to building. Thus the company successfully bid $2.2 billion for St. Joe.

In the next several years Fluor posted significant losses. The company was not prepared for the crash in metals prices of the early 1980s. The fall was compounded by a deep recession, a reduced inflation rate, and a collapse in petrochemical plant building because of the oversupply of oil. From a high of $71 in 1981, Fluor stock fell to lower than $20 by 1985, and the company accumulated $724 million in debt.

After J. Robert Fluor's death in 1984, David S. Tappan, Jr. moved up from the Fluor presidency to become chief executive officer. Tappan brought a great deal of international experience to the position and looked for ways to ease the company's dependence on oil contracts. As the company continued to lose money from 1983 through 1986, it earnestly sought a return to profitability, finally deciding it must divest some of its holdings and restructure the entire enterprise. Fluor sold all the oil properties and some of the gold affiliated with its St. Joe Minerals operation, all its offshore drilling facilities, and some of the corporate offices it had built during the 1970s.

The company also divested its South African operations in 1986. Fluor's stated political position on the issue was that the company "still believes sanctions and withdrawal of U.S. firms from South Africa are counterproductive to achieving a peaceful solution to the problems of racial inequality. But as uncertainties of continued operation in South Africa escalate, we felt that an orderly transfer of ownership at this time would be in the best interests of all concerned." Fluor retained a repurchase option on the divested South African assets.

Concurrent with Fluor's divestiture of its South African operations in 1986, the company underwent extensive restructuring. The dramatic losses incurred throughout the early 1980s had convinced Tappan that Fluor's survival would not be assured if the company remained almost entirely dependent upon the cyclical oil industry for its business. The collapse of oil prices in the beginning of the decade marked the end of Fluor's $1 billion-plus contracts to construct oil refineries and petrochemical facilities, and the company began to suffer disastrous losses,

recording its largest at $633 million in 1985. In order to lessen its dependence on the oil market and to develop a more diversified clientele, Tappan decided in 1986 to merge Daniel International with Fluor to create Fluor Daniel Inc. Operating as the major subsidiary of Fluor Corp., the creation of Fluor Daniel enabled the company to capitalize on the industrial business that had been Daniel's strength. Instead of almost exclusively constructing facilities for the petroleum industry, Fluor now began to contract for plant modernizations, chemical plant constructions, factory retro-fits, and high-tech plant construction. To further strengthen its move toward diversification, Tappan reorganized Fluor into five market sectors: process, power, industrial, hydrocarbon, and government.

The transformation proved successful. After losing $60 million in 1986, Fluor posted a profit the following year of $26 million and by the end of the decade had bolstered its earnings to $147 million, on over $7 billion in sales. Although Fluor continued to construct petroleum refineries for $1 billion and upwards— most notably in Saudi Arabia—the company's recovery was due to the diversity of its clientele. Fluor now designed, constructed, and maintained buildings and equipment in more than 30 industries.

This diverse customer base served Fluor well in the early 1990s when a recession crippled many construction companies. The company increased its operating profit throughout the downturn, benefiting from a $5 billion contract to manage and construct the production facilities of Saudi Aramco and other work in the Middle East resulting from the destruction of petroleum facilities during the war in the Persian Gulf.

In 1992, under the stewardship of Leslie G. McCraw, a former vice-president of Fluor who replaced Tappan a year earlier, Fluor continued to increase its profits in the engineering and construction business and augment its investment in the coal industry. For the fifth consecutive year Fluor Daniel recorded an operating profit, increasing 15 percent from 1991 to $191 million. Revenues for the year were buoyed by a $2.2 billion Department of Energy contract to manage the clean-up and dismantling of a plutonium plant in Ferndale, Ohio. The company's coal mining concern, A.T. Massey Coal Company, increased its reserves of high-quality, low-sulfur coal to nearly one billion tons, ranking it among the five largest U.S. coal companies. While Fluor's coal business thrived, generating an operating profit of $80 million, the company's lead concern, The Doe Run Company, suffered from a considerable drop in the price of lead. By the end of the year, McCraw decided to end Fluor's presence in the lead industry, discontinuing the Doe Run operation.

Clearly, the decision to diversify in 1986 was instrumental in Fluor's recovery from the drastic decline in petroleum-related construction during the early 1980s. The company's performance since diversifying bodes well for its future prospects, especially considering its consistent increase in earnings throughout the recession in the early 1990s. As the need for environmental waste management begins to build, Fluor appears poised to reap the rewards. If Fluor continues to expand its customer base and develop new niches of business, the company should experience a rate of growth comparable to the steady rise it has enjoyed since 1987.

Principal Subsidiaries: Fluor Constructors International Inc.; Fluor Daniel Inc; A.T. Massey Coal Company

Further Reading:

Byrne, Harlan S., ''Fluor Corp.,'' *Barron's,* October 21, 1991, pp. 51–52.

''Doe Run: How To Clean Up On The Cheap,'' *Fortune,* December 16, 1991, p. 102.

Fluor, J. Robert, *Fluor Corporation: A 65-Year History,* New York: Newcomen Society, 1978.

McCraw, Leslie G., ''Developing Global Strategies at Fluor Corp.,'' *Site Selection,* April 1990, pp. 391–392.

Perry, Nancy J., ''Flush Times For Fluor,'' *Fortune,* November 6, 1989, p. 113.

Poole, Claire, ''Construction,'' *Forbes,* January 7, 1991, pp. 126–128.

Wrubel, Robert, ''Transforming Fluor,'' *Financial World,* May 30, 1989, pp. 28–29.

—updated by Jeffrey L. Covell

FMR Corp.

82 Devonshire St.
Boston, Massachusetts 02109
U.S.A.
(617) 570-7000
Fax: (617) 439-0043

Private Company
Incorporated: 1946
Employees: 7,000
Operating Revenues: $1.47 billion
SICs: 6282 Investment Advice

Boston-based FMR Corp. is the holding company for, among other businesses, the largest mutual fund group in the world, Fidelity Investments, with over $170 billion under management. Since the late 1970s the privately held FMR Corp. has branched out into a wide range of financial services, from credit cards to discount brokerage—Fidelity Brokerage Services, Inc. is the second largest discount brokerage house in the country—to insurance. In addition, a chain of art galleries, a transportation service, real estate, and publishing concerns make up the balance in the ''portfolio'' of this financial giant, whose extraordinary growth is closely tied to the powerful influence of one family, the Johnsons, namely Edward II and his son, Edward ''Ned'' III.

FMR traces its history to 1930, when the Boston money management firm of Anderson & Cromwell—later Cromwell & Cabot—organized Fidelity Shares. Designed to serve smaller investment accounts, the firm's steady $3 million in assets were invested in Treasury notes rather than stocks. Efforts to boost the shareholder base using various distribution arrangements proved unsuccessful, although the firm did become a pioneer in shareholder communications by regularly updating shareholders through letters and reports on portfolio holdings. In 1938 Fidelity Fund opened its own offices, and Cromwell & Cabot began receiving a fee for its investment advice. Later that year, as the fund evolved and became more of an independent entity, Fidelity's president and treasurer began to draw salaries from the fund itself. Two years later a regulatory statute, the Investment Company Act of 1940, went into effect and enabled the accelerated growth of such mutual fund houses as Fidelity.

When Fidelity Fund's president resigned in 1943, the fund's directors recruited Edward C. Johnson II to take over, while he retained his position as treasurer and counsel to the large Boston investment trust Incorporated Investors. Johnson, a graduate of Harvard Law School, came from a wealthy Boston family—his father was last in the line of Johnson family partners in Boston's premier retail dry goods store, C.F. Hovey & Company. Serving his father as trustee on family trust funds, Johnson's position with Fidelity Fund provided him with an opportunity to consolidate his family's investments and give free rein to his fascination with picking stocks.

Johnson had found his calling, and his uncanny gift for choosing moneymaking stocks provided the fuel for the company's remarkable expansion—by 1945 the fund's assets had risen to $10 million, and Johnson gave up his position with Incorporated Investors to devote his time to Fidelity. The following year Fidelity's contract with Cromwell & Cabot expired, and rather than renew it, Johnson chose to manage the fund himself and create a new firm, Fidelity Management & Research Company, to act as advisor. Also in 1946 Johnson began developing a group of Fidelity funds, beginning with the launch of the Puritan Fund. In the ensuing decade a variety of different investment groups were started, all under the umbrella of the Fidelity Group of Funds. Johnson continued to supervise Fidelity's portfolio until the mid-1950s, when the company's rapid growth necessitated shifting his attention to executive and administrative tasks. In the decade from 1947 to 1957, under his guidance, assets under management at Fidelity soared from $16 to $262 million.

A well-established leader of the Boston financial community and a Wall Street legend, Johnson was a strong-willed chief executive who took an almost paternalistic interest in the company and in nurturing talent at the fund. Throughout his life, he never wavered in his fascination with the vagaries of the stock market, keeping a daily stock market diary for over 50 years, in order to sharpen his understanding of market fluctuations.

One of the talented young men who came under Johnson's tutelage was his son, Edward C. ''Ned'' Johnson III, who joined Fidelity in 1957 after working at State Street Bank. In that year two ''growth'' funds were added to the Fidelity Group. Ned was put in charge of the Trend Fund, while Gerry Tsai, another protégé of the senior Johnson, became manager of the Capital Fund. The 1960s were a golden period for Fidelity, with the Trend and Capital Funds the high-performance heroes of that decade. From 1960 to 1965 assets under management swelled from $518 million to $2.3 billion. However, Tsai, who was considered the prodigy of the investment world, eventually left Fidelity in 1965 after recognizing that it was Ned who was destined to succeed the elder Johnson as CEO.

The first hint of FMR's later growth came in 1969, when Fidelity International was organized in order to serve overseas investors. Based in Bermuda, the firm became independent from the U.S. holding company in 1980, at which time its mutual fund and pension assets had risen to $10 billion. By the end of the decade, however, the foreign operation had reunited with the U.S. operation.

By 1972, when Ned Johnson took over executive control from his father, the seemingly boundless growth of the 1960s had dissipated, and Fidelity was experiencing an uncharacteristic downturn in business—during the two years from 1972 to 1974, assets had shrunk 30 percent. Under Ned's control, the company began an ambitious expansion program, diversifying from its mutual fund base into a broad range of financial services. The new strategy seemed to work and by the late 1970s, Fidelity regained the momentum it had lost. Among the new services made available by the company was the Fidelity Daily Income Trust (FDIT), the first money market fund to offer check writing, which was launched in 1974. Bypassing traditional brokerage distribution channels, Fidelity offered the new fund directly to the public, using print advertising and direct mail. Two years later, Fidelity launched the first open-end, no-load municipal bond fund, and in 1979 Fidelity became the first major financial institution to offer discount brokerage services. That year Fidelity also organized an arm of the company to serve institutional investors.

During the late 1970s and much of the 1980s, Fidelity became the envy of the investment industry with the remarkable success of its Magellan equity fund. Under the management of investment wizard Peter Lynch, Magellan became America's best-performing mutual fund. Beginning in 1977, when Lynch became manager, the mutual fund seemed to take off through a run of inspired stock-picking. Leading America's ten-year fund performance rankings for most of the 1980s, Magellan consistently posted higher percentage gains than Standard & Poor's 500-stock index, the standard of the industry. Typical of its performance, the fund scored an average annual gain of 21.1 percent in the five year period ending March 31, 1989, which compared favorably to the 17.4 percent annual gain posted by S & P's top 500 stocks.

Magellan had more than 1,000 companies in its portfolio—many more than the 200 or so that most big equity funds hold. Industry observers traced Magellan's success to the combination of Lynch's remarkable knowledge, his gift for picking stocks, a willingness to take risks, and the heavy promotion undertaken for the fund by Fidelity. During the 13 years that Lynch was in charge, Magellan grew at a breakneck pace—from $20 million in 1977 to $12 billion by 1990, the year that Lynch left the company.

By the early 1990s Magellan had lost its star status, although it still ranked among the top ten best-performing funds in the industry. In the meantime another Fidelity fund, Fidelity Select Health, a biotech fund, had taken over the number one spot, as Magellan moved to number three. The top five was rounded out by yet another one of Fidelity's funds, Fidelity Destiny 1. Most of Fidelity's top performers were now coming from its 36 "select" funds based on narrow industry segments.

Magellan was not the only fund to reap the rewards of Fidelity's advertising campaign. Beginning with Ned Johnson's leadership, the company began to more aggressively promote its services, keeping a high profile in the industry and before the general public through its big-budget marketing efforts. By the early 1990s the company's advertising budget was $28 million per year, making it the biggest advertiser in the mutual fund industry. Meanwhile, Fidelity was also reaching the public through a nationwide network of branch offices, launched in 1980.

Like his father, Ned Johnson was also fascinated by Japanese culture, inspiring him to adopt Japanese-style management. The company was vertically integrated in order to make it more self-sufficient. One of the functions brought in-house was the back-office account processing that banks usually handle for mutual funds. Fidelity was then able to capitalize on these operations by selling its services to other investment firms. Johnson was also prompted to create a closer relationship with employees and management. Ideas for improving business were solicited, while promoting an atmosphere of team loyalty.

In the late 1960s Fidelity began—before many other banking and investment firms—to invest a large share of their budget in technology, with an eye toward becoming technologically self-reliant. As a result Fidelity was able to stay on top of the data-processing and telecommunications revolution that was beginning to transform the financial industry. This strategy continued, and as the company entered the 1990s Fidelity was spending more than $150 million a year in the technology realm. The company was at the forefront of the group of financial firms making the transition from traditional roles to one of technology-based customer service, offering a kind of one-stop financial services shopping convenience.

An example of these advances was the interactive, automated-service telephone system that Fidelity was one of the first to install in 1983. The following year the firm began offering computerized trading through Fidelity Investors Express. This service allowed customers to do their own stock trades through home personal computers—what had become known as desktop investing. Fidelity also had custom-designed software to help representatives tap more information, including margin calculations and options analysis, while responding swiftly to customer requests. By the early 1990s Fidelity had upgraded its phone answering system to the point where it could handle 672 calls simultaneously on its automated toll-free lines, while a master console in Boston routed calls to the first available operator around the country. Fidelity also has its own electronic stock trading system, called the Investor Liquidity Network, that matched buy and sell orders from its brokerage and fund operators with those of outside institutional investors.

With the advent of the 1990s Fidelity had embarked on a new strategy to maintain its competitive advantage. Increasingly, it was aiming to be a low-cost personal financial advisor, moving in on territory traditionally associated with banks and brokers. Fidelity first crossed the line into banking's territory in 1983, by offering its USA checking service to customers with a minimum balance of $25,000. At the same time, Fidelity's enormous research and technology capabilities were being mobilized to provide customers with guidance in a wide range of areas, from retirement savings to planning for a college education.

Previously, Fidelity's custom services had been targeted at its richest clients, but by the early 1990s the firm was offering a wide range of services to all of its six million customers. After a slow start, the discount brokerage operation, which lost money in its first nine years, was expanded in the late 1980s with the addition of three new offices. This service eventually became the second largest in the country. In 1987 Fidelity also moved into the insurance and annuity business by offering its customers in certain states such products as single-premium policies, deferred annuities, and variable life policies. In 1989 Fidelity offered the new Spartan Fund, which offers a low expense charge for larger, less active investors. Throughout the 1980s the company's institutional business grew, and by the end of the decade, Fidelity had become the largest manager of 401(k)s. From 1984 to the end of the decade, institutional assets under Fidelity management grew from $9.9 billion to $40 billion.

The stock market crash of October 19, 1987, had its repercussions for Fidelity. The company's assets fell by almost $5 billion in the wake of that event, and Fidelity was forced to reduce the number of its employees to about 5,300 from 8,100. Eventually, Fidelity slowly began to regain its work force, now numbering over 7,000. Fidelity was also affected by the insider trading scandals that brought the curtain down on the hedonistic 1980s. In 1992 a federal district court jury in Manhattan convicted former Fidelity Investment portfolio manager Patricia Ostrander of accepting an illegal gift from Michael Milken, which she hid from Fidelity. Ostrander had invested her fund's money in a particularly risky Drexel Burnham deal that in just two years turned $13,200 into $755,300.

By the end of the first 20 years of Ned Johnson's reign, assets under Fidelity Investment's management had grown 21 percent annually, and with the close of 1991 FMR Corp. had posted record revenues of $1.5 billion—up 16 percent from the previous year. Profits that year were also at record-breaking levels, reaching $90 billion. During those two decades FMR became a highly diversified corporation with some 41 companies under its umbrella—among the financial companies were such firms as an art gallery, a limousine service, an employment agency, and a publishing concern. In addition, in April of 1992 Fidelity Investments purchased 7.5 percent of banking giant Citicorp's common stock. Worth $480 million, this stake made Fidelity the largest single shareholder of common stock in the nation's largest banking company.

Over the course of the company's history, Fidelity has proven itself time and again by taking risks and seizing opportunities, and despite a recently skittish investor market and a sluggish economy, the company has maintained its competitive edge. In the meantime the Johnson family, with 47 percent of the stock—worth approximately a billion dollars—and most of the voting shares, do not give any indication that the company will go public. The other 53 percent of the stock is owned by employees, principally senior managers, who must sell their shares back to the company when they leave.

Principal Subsidiaries: FMR Texas; Advanced MobileComm Inc.; Advanced Mobile Communications International, Inc. (The London Pager); Boston Coach Corp.; Capital Publishing, Inc.; Charitable Gift Fund; COLT (City of London Telecommunications); Community Newspaper Company, Inc.; Fidelity Consumer Financial Services, Inc.; Fidelity Investments Life Insurance Company; Fidelity Publishing; Fidelity Trust Company; J. Robert Scott, Inc.; Proxy Edge; Teleport Communications Boston; Wentworth Gallery Ltd., Inc.; World Trade Center Boston; Fidelity Investments Canada Limited; Strategic Advisors, Inc.; Fidelity Investments Southwest Company; Fidelity Properties Inc.; Fidelity Security Services, Inc.; Fidelity Systems Company; FMR Kentucky, Inc.

Further Reading:

Churbuck, David, ''Watch Out, Citicorp,'' *Forbes,* September 16, 1991.

Eaton, Leslie, ''Junk Ethics: Michael Milken's Powers of Persuasion Included Bribery,'' *Barron's,* August 3, 1992, pp. 8–9, 20–26.

''Fidelity Fights Back,'' *The Economist,* August 8, 1992, pp. 67–68.

Fierman, Jaclyn, ''Fidelity's Secret: Faithful Service,'' *Fortune,* May 7, 1990, pp. 86–92.

Helm, Leslie, et al, ''Fidelity Fights Back: Can CEO Johnson Revive the Behemoth of the Mutual Fund Industry?'' *Business Week,* April 17, 1989, pp. 68–73.

McCartney, Robert J., ''Mutual Fund Firm Fidelity Buys Big Stake in Citicorp,'' *Washington Post,* April 28, 1992, pp. D1, D4.

Schwartzman, Sharon, ''Fidelity's Formula: Technology Keeps Customers Happy,'' *Wall Street Computer Review,* July, 1991, pp. 27–32.

Smith, Geoffrey, ''Fidelity Jumps Feet First into the Fray,'' *Business Week,* May 25, 1992, pp. 104–106.

Stern, Richard L., ''Henry Ford Meet Ned Johnson,'' *Forbes,* September 3, 1990, pg. 42.

—Timothy Bay

Fort Howard Corporation

P.O. Box 19130
1919 South Broadway
Green Bay, Wisconsin 54307
U.S.A.
(414) 435-8821
Fax: (414) 435-3703

Private Company
Incorporated: 1919
Employees: 6,200
Sales: $1.185 billion
SICs: 2676 Sanitary Paper Products

One of the largest tissue manufacturers in the United States, Fort Howard Corporation accounts for about a quarter of the domestic bathroom and facial tissue market, and features a product line that also includes towels, napkins, and related products. Fort Howard has a reputation for privacy and self-sufficiency, having operated as a private company from its founding in 1919 until 1971, and then again after a management-led leveraged buyout in 1988. Today, Fort Howard is a billion-dollar company.

During World War I, Austin Edward Cofrin left New Hampshire to become a superintendent of the Northern Paper Company in Green Bay, Wisconsin, but he lost his job when a new management team took over that paper company. Just 35 years old at the time, Cofrin turned to other investors and workers to raise $350,000, with which he started his own paper company. In 1920 Cofrin oversaw 43 employees, while also covering the positions of secretary and treasurer in his new company. The 30,000-square-foot building that housed his plant was old and so was the machinery. Cofrin could not afford to buy a mill to turn timber into pulp; instead, he made paper from recycled items, such as rags.

Soon the young man from a modest New Hampshire farm family was running one of the top paper mills in Green Bay. Cofrin became president of the Association of Commerce in 1927 and was a well-known figure in Green Bay. Despite his public standing, however, by the late 1920s Fort Howard was already earning its nickname, The Fort, by carefully guarding its production techniques and balance sheets, and revealing its strong distaste for the press. Behind the walls surrounding the plant, Fort Howard was grooming a team of technicians and managers and perfecting its production and marketing methods.

In 1946, A. E. Cofrin's son, John Cofrin, joined the firm. Though it would be some time before John Cofrin would take over the reins, he learned by his father's example to keep the company as self-sufficient as possible. Fort Howard generates its own power, runs its own truck fleet, and makes many of its own chemicals. Its proprietary de-inking technology has been a primary factor in its high operating income margins. This technology allowed Fort Howard to buy low-grade waste paper, de-ink it, cook it to pulp, and make new paper that could then be converted into tissue and paper towel products.

John Cofrin became president of the company in 1960, after his father suffered a stroke. During this time, the company was forced by securities regulations to open its books to the public. In 1969, Fort Howard moved the bulk of its property, then located in Ashwaubenon, to Green Bay. Common stock for Fort Howard was offered for the first time in 1971. The following year, Fort Howard joined the New York Stock Exchange and saw its sales top the $100 million mark. It was a decade of dizzying growth and change for the company.

Four years after John Cofrin became president, Paul J. Schierl joined the company. Schierl, a magna cum laude Notre Dame law graduate, took over as president in 1974 as John Cofrin became chair of the board. Just a few months after that move, Cofrin had surgery for throat cancer and died of a brain hemorrhage afterward. John Cofrin's death marked the end of an era in many ways. He had continued his father's legacy of close-to-the-chest operations while honing internal efficiency, and had seen many men made rich by the stock of his father's company. The Cofrin holdings were estimated to be about 40 percent of the corporation by the 1960s. Schierl was considered the company's bridge into modernity in some ways, though he too honored the company's traditions of tight-lipped self-sufficiency and a balance sheet that was in the black.

In 1975, Schierl's first year as president of the company, sales topped $200 million. By 1978, Schierl had expanded beyond The Fort's boundaries, opening a paper mill in Muskogee, Oklahoma. Two years later, the company's founder, A. E. Cofrin, died at age 96. Had he lived another year, he would have seen Fort Howard hit the Fortune 500 List. In 1982, sales reached $537 million.

At this point, Fort Howard was selling its paper products, such as tissues, toilet paper, paper towels, and napkins, primarily to a variety of institutions that included airports, schools, hospitals, plants, and restaurants. Consumer brands accounted for only about 13 percent of Fort Howard's sales in 1983. The company's profit margin was aided by the fact that more than 90 percent of its pulp came from recycled paper—much cheaper than virgin pulp—and its entire U.S. work force was nonunion. While business was booming, David acquired Goliath: Fort Howard purchased Maryland Cup Company, a company with larger sales, though less profits, than Fort Howard. Maryland Cup's strength was in the flourishing fast-food market, for which it made plastic products, such as disposable tableware, plates, and cups. Sales for Maryland were $656 million when Fort Howard gobbled it up. The price tag was about $536 million. With this acquisition Fort Howard became a billion-dollar company with a work force of more than 14,000.

In 1984, Schierl became chair of the board, with Donald H. DeMeuse taking the president's desk. A new $500 million paper mill was begun on a Georgia site in 1985. That same year, sales rose to $1.36 billion. Also in 1985, Fort Howard acquired Lily-Tulip Inc., a buy that would prove costlier than expected. The cash price was $332 million, which exceeded the fair market value of Lily-Tulip's assets by more than $260 million. That and the cost of closing and reconsolidating the Maryland Cup facilities—and merging the results with Lily-Tulip to form Fort Howard Cup—led to the company's first flat earnings since going public in 1971. In addition to the new plant in Georgia, Fort Howard was investing a third of a billion dollars to upgrade its facilities in Green Bay and Oklahoma.

At this point, the company's success was largely attributed to its credo of self-sufficiency. It reinvested its earnings in the business—a business that was, to some extent, cushioned from competition due to the high cost of machinery. Fort Howard's de-inking technology allowed the company to use a broad range of wastepaper grades and to process wastepaper more efficiently, recovering the fibers that were the principle raw material in paper-making. But the company's strength was also a weakness: the de-inking process and Fort Howard's energy sources generated odors, effluents, and emissions that caused considerable friction between the company and environmentalists.

In the summer of 1985, there was a dramatic showdown between Fort Howard and a Greenpeace sailboat on the Fox River. The Fox River is one of the most heavily industrialized rivers in the United States, with 15 pulp and paper mills along its 40-mile lower stretch. Fort Howard is only one of these, but Marc Hudson, writing in *Audubon* magazine, called it one of the largest single contributors of PCB (polychlorinated biphenyls) pollution to the Great Lakes, via the Fox River. PCB is only one of many potential contaminants that began impacting the birds and fish along the Fox River. After aggressive attention to the problem in the late 1970s resulted in decreased PCB readings, the levels steadied again around 1982, but several community action groups were formed in an effort to rescue the river. Fort Howard was by no means the only company targeted for complaints. However, when a Greenpeace boat made a symbolic visit to the river, Fort Howard built a security fence, stationed guards, and greased the plant's chimney, a move for privacy that seemed extreme to some observers. A diver for Greenpeace climbed the security fence and was arrested, but not before he had discovered three discharge pipes instead of the one pipe Fort Howard had reported to the Department of Natural Resources (DNR). Greenpeace tried to play this item up, while the company and the DNR played it down.

Schierl himself publicly voiced his regret at the escalated drama of the Greenpeace confrontation. No one would dispute that relations remained tenuous between the company and environmentalists, but Fort Howard's reputation was not formed along those lines alone. As the largest employer in Brown County, Fort Howard had a certain rapport with government officials and citizens. Countering its image as a polluter of area waters, the company was cited for its recycling efforts, including the

recycling of old telephone books and programs for collecting and recycling office wastepaper. And the Fort Howard Paper Foundation, which originated in 1953, has dispensed hundreds of thousands of dollars annually, shifting in focus over the years from gifts of medical equipment to support for youth-related activities and education issues.

In 1988, Fort Howard Corporation and Morgan Stanley Leveraged Equity Fund formed FH Acquisition Corporation and took the company private. The buyout group was headed by CEO and chair Schierl, as well as other top executives of the company. The leveraged buyout left the company struggling with its roughly $3.7 billion debt. It was originally reported that Fort Howard's cash flow would service the debt. Morgan ended up with about 75 percent equity ownership.

In the meantime, the company was still struggling to right itself from the 1987 economic crash and the assimilation of its Maryland Cup and Lily-Tulip acquisitions. Cup sales had been suffering along with the stock market, and with these acquisitions, Fort Howard's focus had shifted from manufacturing, which had been its expertise, to marketing. But the company still had not regained its equilibrium. Fort Howard Cup had cut back on its sales organizations, not realizing that price alone wouldn't sell the cups. The unit began losing market share almost immediately. The company sold its cup unit in 1989 for $620 million, taking a loss on the $864 million it had spent building it. The unit was spun off through Morgan as Sweetheart Holdings Inc., with the acknowledgement that it could become profitable once its marketing errors were corrected. In 1989, the company also sold its Pacific Basin cup business and, the following year, its European disposable food service operation.

The overleveraged Fort Howard was still left groaning beneath cash interest payments. Basic business was solid, but cash flow slowed. In 1990, the company secured a $250 million cash infusion from shareholders, including Morgan Stanley. A portion of the proceeds were to be used to retire many high-yield junk bonds as part of major refinancing. In the meantime, although the company had been reporting strong operating profits, it experienced net losses because of its debt load. Schierl quit in 1990, and Donald DeMeuse became CEO and president.

Also in 1990, Fort Howard launched a 100 percent recycled toilet tissue and paper towels line under the Green Forest label. A similar line had already been introduced with success in the United Kingdom. Fort Howard considered it a niche opportunity, convinced that Americans were becoming more and more concerned about recycling. The company also kept its $180 million expansion program on schedule, including a new tissue machine, a new boiler, and a natural gas-fired steam and electric cogeneration facility.

In 1992, Fort Howard was prepaying a portion of its bank debt with a loan led by Bankers Trust Company. The company remained very highly leveraged at the close of 1992, and was suffering as well from a competitive market as more companies were being called upon to invest in recycling facilities. The company saw some margin deterioration after decades of steadiness. Still, in the early 1990s Fort Howard, with its management team primed and determined to steady the company's course, had the advantage of being a low-cost producer with a leading market share in the commercial segment of the tissue market.

Principal Subsidiaries: Harmon Associates; Ecosource.

Further Reading:

Anders, George, "Fort Howard Corp. Said It Is Lining Up $250 Million Equity Infusion by Holders," *Wall Street Journal,* November 16, 1990, p. A4.
Berman, Phyllis, "A Sweetheart of a Deal," *Forbes,* September 3, 1990, pp. 39–40.
Berss, Marcia, "Real Testing Time," *Forbes,* January 21, 1991, pp. 61–62.
Brown, Ann, "After Iran and Ivan," *Forbes,* December 15, 1986, p. 211.
Bulkeley, William, "Today's Mystery: Who Buys All Those Souvenir Spoons?" *Wall Street Journal,* June 6, 1991, p. A1.
Darby, Elizabeth, "Strictly Personal," *BUZZWORM: The Environmental Journal,* November-December, 1990, p. 20.
"Destec Builds Cogeneration Plant at Fort Howard Mill," *Pulp & Paper,* October 1991, p. 29.
"Destec to Build, Co-Own Plant," *Wall Street Journal,* August 26, 1991, B2.
Foran, Pat, "Key to Winning Battle of Fort Howard Remains Beating Down Debt," *Business Journal-Milwaukee,* May 27, 1991, pp. 61–64.
Forsyth, Randall, "Dabbling in Junk," *Barron's,* December 11, 1989, p. 55.

"Fort Howard Capital Infusion," *Wall Street Journal,* December 10, 1990, p. A3.
"Fort Howard Chief Quits," *New York Times,* August 2, 1990, p. D3.
Goel, Vindu, "Fort Howard Corp. Introduces 100% Recycled Toilet Tissue, Paper Towels," *Wall Street Journal,* March 2, 1990, p. B4.
Goodwin, William, "Bankers Trust Leads Loan to Fort Howard," *American Banker,* September 15, 1992, p. 16.
Hudson, Marc, "Dispatches," *Audubon,* July 1987, pp. 24–41.
Lopez, Julie Amparano, "If They Skipped the Recycling, There Would be Plenty to Read," *Wall Street Journal,* January 19, 1990, p. B1.
"Management Launches Bid for Fort Howard," *Pulp & Paper,* August 1988, p. 21.
Mendes, Joseua, "As Junk Bond Prices Fall, Some Glittering Jewels Emerge," *Fortune,* February 26, 1990, p. 33.
Mitchell, Constance, "Junk Bonds See Sharp Price Increases on News of Possible Recapitalization by Fort Howard," *Wall Street Journal,* November 16, 1990, C15.
Schultz, Abby, "Corporations Float $2.2 Billion of New Issues in Tepid Market; News America Cuts Offering," *Wall Street Journal,* October 16, 1992, p. C15.
Stovall, Robert, "Five Losers That Need Dumping," *Financial World,* April 21, 1987, p. 112.
"Tinkering with Success," *Forbes,* October 10, 1983, pp. 179–180.
"The Strengthening Case for Paper Stocks," *Fortune,* March 5, 1984, p. 151.
Woessner, Robert, "Inside The Fort," *Green Bay Press-Gazette,* March 3, 1986.

—Carol I. Keeley

Fruit of the Loom, Inc.

5000 Sears Tower
233 South Wacker Drive
Chicago, Illinois 60606
U.S.A.
(312) 876-1724
Fax: (312) 993-1749

Wholly Owned Subsidiary of Farley Inc.
Incorporated: 1955
Employees: 32,000
Sales: $1.8 billion
Stock Exchanges: American Chicago Pittsburgh Pacific
SICs: 2322 Men's/Boys' Underwear & Nightwear; 2341
    Women's/Children's Underwear; 2329 Men's/
    Boys'Clothing Nec; 2252 Hosiery Nec; 2211 Broadwoven
    Fabric Mills, Cotton; 2321 Men's and Boy's Shirts; 2253
    Knit Outerwear Mills; 2254 Knit Underwear and
    Nightwear Mills

Fruit of the Loom, Inc., a global manufacturer and marketer of family apparel, is America's biggest seller of men's briefs. The company's brands, which include BVD, Munsingwear, and the namesake Fruit of the Loom, are among the best known in the world. With more than 50 manufacturing facilities, the company has operations in eleven states, Canada, Northern Ireland, and the Republic of Ireland, and produces almost one billion garments per year.

The history of the company involves two separate entities: the B. B. & R. Knight Brothers textile company and The Union Underwear Company. The Knight Brothers established a textile company in Pontiac, Rhode Island, in the mid-nineteenth century. Their high quality broadcloth was recognized as some of the best fabric for the homemade clothing and linens that were common at the time. In 1851, when trademarking was still in its infancy, the brothers gave their cloth the imaginative name "Fruit of the Loom."

Rufus Skeel, one of the merchants who sold the Knight brothers' cloth commercially, operated a dry goods store in New York's Hudson Valley, and his daughter, an artist, painted pictures of local apple varieties. Over time, her paintings became associated with the "Fruit of the Loom" name. Soon the apple accompanied the name on printed labels that identified the Knight brothers' increasingly popular cloth. The serendipitous

combination of the two components helped make Fruit of the Loom the first branded textile product in America. When the federal patent and trademark office opened in 1871, the trademark (which had grown to include a cluster of fruits) received the United States' 418th patent.

As long as women made their own clothing and linens, Fruit of the Loom textiles remained in demand. But the development of the manufactured apparel industry in the early twentieth century considerably diminished the fabric market. The market for piecegoods declined as homemakers did less sewing and began to favor readymade clothing and linens. Although the original product's market dwindled, the trademark still enjoyed popularity, so in 1928, the Fruit of the Loom Company began to license the brand to manufacturers of finished garments.

At about the same time that Fruit of the Loom lost its direct consumer market, a young immigrant named Jacob (Jack) Goldfarb decided to start his own clothing business. Goldfarb learned about the apparel industry through his work with the Ferguson Manufacturing Company. There he noticed that Ferguson only made low-priced "sale items" available to those retailers who also purchased the company's higher priced goods. Goldfarb reasoned that if he could provide retailers with strictly lower-priced, quality undergarments, he could establish a popular business.

He decided to concentrate on the most popular style of men's underwear of the nineteenth century, the unionsuit, and named his endeavor The Union Underwear Company. Like the term "unionsuit" itself, there is some controversy about the origin of the company name. Some historians assert that the term unionsuit referred to the "union" of a top and bottom, while others maintain that the name grew out of the fact that members of the Civil War-era Union Army wore the garment. Whether the name for The Union Underwear Company alluded to the United States or the construction of its clothing remains a mystery as well.

Oddly enough, Goldfarb started his manufacturing business without a factory. He purchased cloth from one supplier, had it delivered to a cutter, then sent the parts to a sewing shop for finishing and shipping. Union Underwear's first garments were sewn by nuns in and around Indianapolis, Indiana, the site of the company's first finishing plant.

Goldfarb continued to work under this complex system even through the onset of the Great Depression. Then, in 1930, he was approached by some promoters from Frankfort, Kentucky, who were looking for an industry that would provide employment and increase the city's tax base during the lengthy depression. The municipality offered to build a plant for the business, which would bring all of Union's operations to a single location. Goldfarb agreed to the lucrative offer, and within five years employed 650 people.

Union Underwear and Fruit of the Loom's fortunes converged near the end of the decade. In his quest to become a national marketer, Golfarb purchased a 25-year license for the Fruit of the Loom trademark in 1938. He was certain that the well-known brand would propel his products to national prominence.

Union Underwear built a second plant—which produced broadcloth "boxer" shorts—in Bowling Green, Kentucky, on the eve of World War II. When America joined the Allied effort in 1941, the company was enlisted to manufacture millions of pairs of G.I. shorts. Union Underwear received numerous commendations from the government for its contribution on the homefront.

Goldfarb made several promotional innovations in the postwar era that set Union Underwear and the Fruit of the Loom label apart from other undergarment manufacturers. Before World War II, underwear was usually sold separately, but in the late 1940s, Goldfarb introduced a printed cellophane bag with three pair of shorts inside. The new packages were displayed separately to call attention to Union's branded undergarments. The move established a trend that has become an industry standard for most basic underwear. And even though Goldfarb was only a licensee of the trademark, he became the only licensee to invest his own funds in consumer advertising.

The company expanded its product line from unionsuits and boxer shorts to include knit underwear in 1948, and opened its third plant in Campbellsville, Kentucky, in 1952. The plant provided internal knitting and bleaching facilities for Union manufacturing for the first time, helping the company to gain more vertical control of production and facilitating the production of a wider variety of men's and boy's undergarments.

Goldfarb continued his promotional innovations when Union became the first underwear company to advertise on network television in 1955. The company purchased spots during Dave Garroway's "Today Show." Union also utilized banners, posters, signs, price tickets, newspaper slicks, and a cooperative advertising program to support Fruit of the Loom sales. Consumer advertising campaigns were coordinated with such seasonal events as Father's Day, Back-to-School, and Christmas to maximize the company's advertising dollar.

Around the same time, Union allied itself to the mass merchandisers that were beginning to spring up in the mid-1950s. The company's growth was soon tied to these new retailer's success: by the early 1990s, 45 percent of men's basic underwear was sold by discount stores.

The mid-1950s saw the start of a string of acquisitions that would place Union Underwear in several different hands over the next three decades. In 1955, Union Underwear was taken over by the Philadelphia & Reading Corporation, a newly-formed conglomerate. The new corporate structure provided Union with additional resources, enabling it to extend its manufacturing operations.

By this time, Union Underwear had grown to become Fruit of the Loom's dominant licensee, and to most people, the name had come to mean underwear more than fabric. The licensee, in fact, had grown larger than Fruit of the Loom. In order to assure the availability of its well-known trademark, Philadelphia & Reading acquired the Fruit of the Loom Licensing Company in 1961.

In 1968, Union Underwear's parent was purchased by Northwest Industries. The consolidation furnished new capital which further facilitated the company's growth. That same year, Gold-

farb stepped down from the chair to be replaced by Everett Moore, who had joined the company in 1932 at the Frankfort plant.

Union Underwear strove to energize advertising for men's underwear in the late 1960s and early 1970s. In 1969 the company contracted sportscaster Howard Cosell to appear in five television commercials over three years. Next, British comedian Terry Thomas was named spokesperson, as advertisers hoped that an English representative would lend an air of quality and endurance to their commercials. The use of celebrity spokespersons brought more public attention to Fruit of the Loom underwear, but the company continued to seek more brand recognition and market share.

In 1975, Union made advertising history with the first "Fruit of the Loom Guys" campaign. The commercials featured three men in costume as a bunch of grapes, an Autumn leaf, and an apple, all elements of the brand's trademark. The characters helped propel the Fruit of the Loom brand to 98 percent recognition and doubled Union's share of the market for men's and boy's underwear.

Also that year Moore retired and was succeeded by John Holland. In 1976 Union acquired the century-old BVD trademark. The company began to merchandise BVD as a completely separate line of underwear aimed at the more upscale department store market. Union also began to expand its product line to include "Underoos" decorated underwear for boys and girls in 1978, and began to supply blank T-shirts for the screen print market during the 1970s. The expansion into plain T-shirts soon evolved into a huge business known as Screen Stars, which sold unbranded T-shirts, sweatshirts, and sweatpants to wholesalers who imprinted them for promotional uses.

Union did not escape the trend toward leveraged buyouts of the 1980s. In 1984, William F. Farley acquired Union Underwear when he bought Northwest Industries for $1.4 billion. Farley privatized the parent company and renamed it Farley Industries. Just two years earlier, Farley had made his first major acquisition, defense contractor Condec Corp. In the 1980s tradition of leveraged buyouts and junk bonds, Farley parlayed his acquisitions into larger and larger conquests until, by the end of the decade, he had fashioned a textile and apparel conglomerate with $4 billion in annual sales and 65,000 employees worldwide.

In 1985, the conglomerate was restructured, $260 million in shares were sold, and Union Underwear was renamed Fruit of the Loom, Inc. to relate the business more closely to its famous trademark. Farley, a former encyclopedia salesperson, worked to improve Fruit of the Loom's operational efficiency and squeeze more profits out of the company's number-one status as the holder of a 35 percent share of the undergarment market. Farley proceeded to sell the bulk of Northwest Industries' other businesses and cut costs at Fruit of the Loom. The proceeds of the asset sales were combined with revenues from bond issues to finance domestic modernization and expansion into Europe.

Over the course of the 1980s, those manufacturing changes facilitated Fruit of the Loom's evolution from an underwear manufacturer into an apparel company. Farley and Chief Executive Holland decided to expand into men's fashion underwear, women's underwear, and socks over the course of the decade, putting the Fruit of the Loom label on sportswear in 1987. Women's panties became one of the brand's most popular extensions. The company launched that division in 1984 and led the category with a ten percent share within four years. Fruit of the Loom also made apparel history with its popular pocket T-shirt. Produced in a rainbow of colors, the wardrobe staple's flexibility made it a consumer favorite for decades.

In 1982, sales of men's and boy's white underwear made up 80 percent of the company's revenues, but by 1988, brand extensions comprised more than 40 percent of revenues. The activewear market also grew much more rapidly than the underwear category: activewear sales tripled in the 1980s, while the underwear market grew only about six percent annually.

Capital improvements had enabled Fruit of the Loom to expand into newer, faster-growing markets, but they also left the company saddled with debt. Fruit's debt-to-equity ratio of 3.5-to-1 contributed to three out of four years of losses before the decade was over. Interest expenses also consumed ten percent of annual sales revenues in 1989. At the same time, Fruit of the Loom was threatened on two fronts: low priced imports began to eat into Fruit of the Loom's 38 percent market share of basic men's undergarments, and the company's largest competitor, Sara Lee Corp.'s Hanes Knit Products, was raising the ante in the "underwars."

In an effort to promote its move from department stores to discount merchandisers, Hanes introduced "Inspector 12" into its advertising campaigns in 1982. The curmudgeonly quality-control character claimed that her brand fit better and shrank less than Fruit of the Loom's. Fruit of the Loom fired back with promotions that featured the tagline, "Sorry, Hanes, you lose!" The war escalated into a legal battle that ended with an out-of-court settlement wherein the two competitors agreed to pull the offending ads.

The Fruit of the Loom Guys were phased out when the company launched its more modern "We fit America like we never did before" campaign. Introduced in 1988, the television spots featured family scenes, including a mother dropping her daughter off at the school bus, and also included the first views of a woman in a pair of panties on network television. The $25 million campaign, created by Grey Advertising, Inc., emphasized Fruit of the Loom's move into basic apparel for both sexes and all ages.

The brand extensions, expanded capacity, advertising blitz and years of debt paid off in 1988 when Fruit of the Loom made its first profit since its acquisition by Farley. The mid-1980s capital investments had pumped up domestic operating margins to 20–25 percent, and European plants began earning profits in the early 1990s. Sales had actually grown 13 percent annually since 1976 to $1 billion in 1988, but debt had consumed all of the income.

In 1990, Fruit of the Loom unveiled the underwear industry's first network advertisements that featured a male model sporting the flagship white briefs. The commercials asked the musical question, "Whose underwear is under there?" The answer was provided by hunky celebrities Ed Marinaro, Patrick Duffy, and James DePavia. Lawyers for Grey Advertising spent two weeks battling one of the big three networks to air the commercials that would have been banned just three years earlier. Over the next two years, Fruit of the Loom's celebrity underwearers would include soap-opera star Don Diamont, action-adventure hero David Hasselhoff, and sitcom dad Alan Thicke.

In 1991, Fruit of the Loom introduced the "It's your time," campaign for its growing line of casualwear, which was extended to include garments for infants and toddlers. The company enlarged its array of brands that year through a licensing agreement with the upscale Munsingwear brand in the hopes of expanding Fruit of the Loom's retail distribution.

The company's financial restabilization continued. Debt was reduced by more than $332 million with the help of sales totaling $1.4 billion, a stock offering of $100 million, a decline in capital expenditures, and the conversion of $60 million of debt into equity. Fruit of the Loom's European sales surged 43 percent over 1990 as these divisions hit stride.

And despite a lingering recession in the United States, the company once again found its capacity constrained. Farley and Holland predicted that Fruit of the Loom would invest $125 million in new equipment and increase the workforce by 3,000 at plants in the United States, Canada, and Europe in 1992. With strong ties to mass merchandisers, major product launches, and line extensions, Fruit of the Loom hoped to increase sales 15 percent each year, decrease debt load, and grow per share earnings by one third annually in the 1990s.

Further Reading:

Applebaum, Cara, "Fruit of the Loom Sticks with Stars," *Adweek's Marketing Week,* February 4, 1991, p. 8.

"Fruit of the Loom, Hanes Stretch from Skivvies into Active Wear," *Adweek's Marketing Week,* December 2, 1991, p. 7.

Corwin, Pat, "More Options in Men's Underwear," *Discount Merchandiser,* September 1990, pp. 36–39.

"Boyswear Brightens the Apparel Picture," *Discount Merchandiser,* December 1991, pp. 52–54, 69–70.

"Commanding Lead in Men's Underwear," *Discount Merchandiser,* August 1992, pp. 38–45, 61.

Esquivel, Josephine R., "The Pains and Gains of '91," *Bobbin,* June 1992, pp. 50–60.

Fannin, Rebecca, "Underwear: Inspector 12 Takes on the Fruits," *Marketing & Media Decisions,* April 1988, pp. 55–6.

Greising, David. "Bill Farley in on Pins and Needles," *Business Week,* September 18, 1989, pp. 58, 61.

"Bill Farley Could Lose His Shirt—and His Underwear," *Business Week,* March 11, 1991, p. 86.

Laing, Jonathan R., "Love that Leverage!" *Barron's,* May 1, 1989, pp. 6–7, 31–33.

Levine, Joshua, "Marketing: Fantasy, Not Flesh," *Forbes,* January 22, 1990, pp. 118–120.

Oneal, Michael, "Fruit of the Loom Escalates the Underwars," *Business Week,* February 22, 1988, pp. 114, 118.

Zipser, Andy, "Cherry-picking Fruit of the Loom," *Barron's,* May 20, 1991, pp. 30–31.

—April S. Dougal

Gaylord Container Corporation

500 Lake Cook Rd.
Suite 400
Deerfield, Illinois 60015-5269
U.S.A.
(708) 405-5500
Fax: (708) 405-5505

Public Company
Incorporated: 1986
Employees: 4,150
Sales: $722.8 million
Stock Exchanges: American
SICs: 2653 Corrugated & Solid Fiber Boxes; 2631
   Paperboard Mills; 2621 Paper Mills; 2674 Uncoated Paper
   & Multiwall Bags; 2819 Industrial Inorganic Chemicals,
   Nec; 2869 Industrial Organic Chemicals, Nec

Gaylord Container Corporation is a major national manufacturer and distributor of corrugated containers, containerboard, unbleached kraft paper, multiwall bags, grocery bags and sacks, and specialty chemicals. By the 1990s the company served more than 3,000 customers through a network of three paper mills, 24 converting plants, one graphics plant, and marketing operations throughout the United States. An aggressive strategy of expansion in the late 1980s was followed by an unexpectedly long cyclical low in the early 1990s, reducing profits and mandating financial reorganization. After completing a prepackaged bankruptcy agreement with bondholders in November of 1992, Gaylord refinanced debts and emerged from bankruptcy in a stronger position. With a new capital structure, it entered the 1990s shaken but hopeful.

Gaylord dates back to the aggressive buying strategies of a group headed by Marvin Pomerantz and Warren Hayford in the mid-1980s. The two partners were best known as Chicago veterans of International Harvester Co. (later named Navistar International Corp.), where Hayford served as president and Pomerantz as executive vice-president during the tumultuous late 1970s and 1980s. From 1983 to 1985, the paper industry was in a slump, with a key product, 42-pound linerboard, priced as low as $260 a ton (down from $350) and mills operating at 90 percent of capacity, a depressed rate for an industry run on extremely narrow margins. Pomerantz and Hayford took advantage of paper facilities available at bargain prices.

In December of 1985, the team of Pomerantz and Hayford started Mid-America Packaging, Inc., by acquiring an unbleached kraft paper mill and a multiwall bag manufacturing facility owned by Weyerhaeuser Company for $28 million, 20 percent of which was their own money. The rest was financed through a consortium of banks. Gaylord Container Corporation, in turn, acquired its business on November 17, 1986, from Crown Zellerbach Corporation for approximately $260 million. The transaction included three containerboard and unbleached kraft paper mills, 14 corrugated container plants, three corrugated sheet plants, a specialty chemicals facility and a cogeneration facility. While Gaylord and Mid-America were affiliated by common ownership after November 17, 1986, they merged on June 1, 1988, with Gaylord as the surviving corporation.

The merger marked yet another collaboration between Pomerantz and Hayford, whose careers had crossed before in the bag industry. Pomerantz had been virtually born into the business. As the son of Polish immigrants in Des Moines, he helped his father generate income during the depression by collecting used cotton and burlap bags for recycling. After World War II, the family business turned to paper bags. In 1961 Pomerantz founded Great Plains Bag Co., which was acquired by Continental Can Co. (renamed Continental Group, Inc.) in the early 1970s to become the largest brown bag company in the world.

During a stint at Continental, Pomerantz met Hayford, a senior executive who had been instrumental in the Great Plains acquisition. In 1979 Hayford left to become president of Harvester, where Pomerantz joined a year later as top lieutenant. But heavy equipment manufacturing proved less than permanent for the pair, who left by 1982. Pomerantz served on the board of directors for the Stone Container Corporation, still the industry leader in paper and paperboard production. Hayford served a short term as president of GenCorp Inc., formerly General Tire Corp. By the mid-1980s, however, the two realigned their interests to establish Gaylord Container Corporation.

After Gaylord was incorporated in 1986, its management pushed for rapid growth and new capital investment in an otherwise lagging industry. "Since we acquired Gaylord in 1986," Pomerantz was quoted as saying in a 1988 *Chicago Tribune* article, "we have made substantial investments in our plants to increase productive capacity and improve both quality and cost effectiveness." Gaylord already ranked as the number nine containerboard company, with 4 percent of the U.S. market. An August 29, 1988, article in *Crain's Chicago Business* projected that the newly public company would approach sales of $800 million by 1989, making it an immediate entry on the Fortune 500.

A sustained positive outlook depended in large part on the U.S. economy. Since many products were shipped in corrugated boxes, their demand rose and fell with industrial production. The packaging industry was also affected by the value of the dollar, influencing import competition by its relative strength. For company optimists, prospects in late 1988 looked good, barring a recession in the following year or a rapid run-up in the value of the dollar.

Pomerantz and Hayford proved to be such optimists, emphasizing capital investment at a rate that reflected hope for the future.

"Pomerantz is a high-stakes roller," commented Gary Palmero, an analyst at Oppenheimer & Co. "He'll look like a genius if the market stays strong. Our company isn't forecasting a recession for next year, so it seems to me that Gaylord is taking a good gamble at this point." The gamble consisted, in part, of $300 million in spending over the three-year period beginning in September of 1988. The capital investment program included a layout of approximately $175 million to construct a new linerboard machine at the Bogalusa, Louisiana, plant, boosting capacity by 50 percent; approximately $65 million to rebuild and modernize the linerboard machine at the West mill in Antioch, California; and nearly $60 million to expand and enhance manufacturing capabilities at existing converting facilities. The company also invested roughly $120 million to maintain and upgrade existing equipment during the same three-year period. In addition, Gaylord acquired four plants and related inventories of the container products division of Fibreboard Corporation for approximately $156 million in March of 1988. One exception to the overall pattern of acquisitions was the November 1988 sale of its Baltimore, Ohio, paper mill to the principals of Somerset Capital Corp. of Boston for about $16.7 million.

Despite Gaylord's active investment in its future, Wall Street showed signs of uncertainty. Having planned its initial public offering for the spring of 1988 at a price of $28, the company faced a soft market and finally offered 4.4 million shares of common stock at $20.50 a share on July 7th. By August of that year, the shares had fallen below $17, reflecting anxiety over the company's debt—amounting to 75 percent of capital—and the cyclical nature of the paper industry, according to H. Lee Murphy in *Crain's Chicago Business*.

Nevertheless, capital investment and growth continued well into 1989. In March of that year, Gaylord agreed in principle to form a joint venture with Central National Gottesman Inc. to market Gaylord's containerboard and other paper products in overseas markets. By May, Gaylord and Gottesman each assumed a 50 percent interest in Gaylord Central National, Inc. (GNC), the primary agent for export sales, which amounted to 4 percent of net sales by 1992. In September of 1989 Gaylord's Mid-America Packaging Division acquired U.S. Gypsum's multi-wall bag manufacturing facility in Oakmont, Pennsylvania.

In May of 1989 the company entered the grocery bag business by buying a New York-based grocery bag and sack converting facility from Stone Container Corp. The facility was operated as a joint venture, Gaylord Bag Partnership (GBP), controlled by a Gaylord subsidiary and a corporation led by two bag businessmen, Joel Buser and Sam Posner. Gaylord—which produced approximately 200,000 tons of grocery bag and sack paper at its mills in Pine Bluff, Arkansas, and Bogalusa, Louisiana— supplied the paper needs of the converting venture. In June of 1992, Gaylord acquired all remaining interest in GBP, the partnership was dissolved, and GBP operations were integrated with those of the corporation. In December of 1989, the company acquired from Boise Cascade Corporation corrugated container plants in Marion, Ohio, and Torrance, California, for approximately $17 million. And in February of 1991, Gaylord acquired a 50 percent interest in Bay Sheets, Inc., a producer of corrugated sheets.

Responding to concerns of customers and to newly enforced government regulations, Gaylord focused increasing attention on environmental matters as it entered the 1990s. According to its 1992 annual report, the company made capital expenditures of approximately $2.5 million, $1.2 million, and $4.0 million in fiscal 1992, 1991, and 1990 respectively for environmental purposes. The $65 million paper machine rebuild at the Antioch mill, enabled it to use recycled fibers in new ways. "We can use more of a blend of fibers, such as base sheet and top sheet of 100 percent virgin fibers, and a 100 percent recycled sheet in the middle; or we can use a mix of 65 percent recycled and 35 percent virgin; or almost any other combination," explained Pomerantz in a 1990 *American Papermaker* article. The company introduced ENCORliner and ENCORpack linerboard and packaging trademarks featuring 100 percent recycled fiber content, high quality and superior strength.

By 1992 Gaylord had the capacity to recycle nearly 1,750 tons per day of old corrugated containers and corrugated container plant clippings. Additionally, in order to curtail excess packaging, Gaylord developed a high-performance linerboard called Performance Specified Liner (PSL). PSL possessed essentially the same performance characteristics as standard linerboard, but with appreciably lower basis weight and, therefore, less material to end up as potential solid waste. The company's efforts in developing PSL marked important steps toward environmental awareness that would characterize the 1990s and beyond.

By 1991 worsening losses and increased debt forced Gaylord to assess its options for survival. Beginning in the fall of 1989, operations were adversely affected by such factors as a substantial decline in the selling prices for Gaylord products and an increase in the cost of raw materials, particularly wood chips on the West Coast. Wood chip costs at the East mill increased by 65 percent from the fourth quarter of 1988 to the first quarter of 1991, when the mill was idled. Gaylord's earnings before interest, taxes, depreciation, and amortization declined from approximately $166 million in fiscal 1989 to approximately $92 million and $81 million in 1992 and 1991, respectively. In addition to reduced earnings, the company was seeking to get out from under a crushing 1991 debt of $807 million, of which $181 million was bank debt.

Debt-rating agencies were quick to target the faltering corporation. Standard & Poor's downgraded its rating on Gaylord's subordinated debt to triple-C from B-, affecting approximately $400 million in notes. Similarly, Moody's Investors Service Inc. lowered Gaylord's rating on two junk bond issues and projected that Gaylord's fiscal loss in 1991 would exceed the loss of $23.2 million on sales of $718.3 million in 1990. Over the course of the year, Gaylord reduced operating expenses and capital expenditures by cutting work force levels, reducing selling and administrative expenses, deferring nonessential maintenance expenditures, and postponing select capital expenditures.

Many analysts attributed Gaylord's problems to the East mill acquisition. Sherman Chao, a senior forest product and paper industry analyst for Salomon Bros. Inc., claimed in *Crain's Chicago Business,* "Gaylord probably tackled more than they should have." Gaylord officials defended their strategy by emphasizing the cyclical nature of the paper product business and the tendency of companies to invest at the bottom of the cycle. This cycle was particularly long, however, and was aggravated by unusually low product prices and rising costs of raw material.

Whatever the causes, Gaylord faced an untenable debt that initiated a series of refinancing plans. Beginning on May 15, 1991, the corporation suspended payment of interest on its subordinated debt, pending development of a comprehensive plan to reduce debt and debt service requirements while ongoing business operations continued. By September 11, 1992, $134.5 million of accrued but unpaid interest on subordinated debt had accumulated. Beginning in June of 1991, the corporation also suspended payment of principal under its bank credit agreement. Certain holders of subordinated notes formed an unofficial bondholder committee that negotiated with Gaylord to arrive at viable debt restructuring plans. In August of 1991, the Corporation offered bondholders three choices in what the *Junk Bond Reporter* called "a Chinese menu" approach to the company's $570 million debt. Bondholders could choose between a new bond worth 44.5 cents on the dollar and a 14 percent coupon and 22 shares of common stock for each bond; a bond worth par and a 4.25 percent coupon and 18 shares of stock; or 53.3 cents in cash. The final solution, however, turned out somewhat differently.

A financial restructuring plan was developed wherein the Gaylord's subordinated debt securities were exchanged for new senior subordinated debt securities featuring lower principal payment requirements and lower annual interest expense. Namely, holders of $528.8 million of subordinated debt received almost $367.8 million in new senior subordinated securities, six million shares of Gaylord Class A common stock, and 31.8 million redeemable exchangeable warrants for Class A shares. The six million shares of stock and warrants totaled 72 percent of the company's equity.

In July of 1992 the U.S. Securities and Exchange Commission declared effective the terms of the proposed exchange, and the company began soliciting the approval of its bondholders, banks, and equity holders to complete the restructuring through the filing of a pre-approved plan with the U.S. Bankruptcy Court. After majority approval, the prepackaged plan was filed on September 11th and confirmed by the court on October 16th. On November 2, 1992, Gaylord consummated its restructuring and emerged from bankruptcy. "They've done a nice job restructuring and their long term prospects look good," noted Oren Cohen of Salomon Brothers in the October 26, 1992, volume of *Investment Dealers' Digest*. "As bankruptcies go, Gaylord's went relatively smoothly," according to Brian Bogart of Duff & Phelps Corp. in *Crain's Chicago Business*.

The complicated restructuring package reduced total debt to about $621 million from $827 million and reduced annual interest expenses by $38 million. Nevertheless, Gaylord was not fully at ease by 1993. Its debt-to-capital ratio stood at approximately 83 percent. After its first quarter, ending December 31,

1992, the company recorded an operating loss of $1.6 million, compared with operating earnings of $4.8 million for the same period of the previous year. Nor had paperboard and other paper product prices rebounded, as the industry remained stuck in the fifth year of a down cycle.

Yet the 1993 Standard & Poor's industry survey projected a much stronger economy in 1993, with rising prices and earnings for paper companies. The survey also emphasized the high efficiency, high yield potential of new mills and machines developed during the down cycle. Even without large price increases, Standard & Poor's forecasted impressive gains in earnings as capital investments would begin to pay off. In Gaylord's 1992 annual report, Pomerantz remarked that 1993 would be marked by "uncertainty around the timing of an economic recovery and pricing for our products. . . . Our return to profitability is directly tied to our ability to realize higher prices for our products."

In June of 1993, Gaylord used proceeds from a successful $525 million offering mainly to redeem other debt and prepay $70 million of its bank borrowings, according to company spokesperson Kathryn Chieger, cited in *The Bond Buyer*. Chieger explained that the company was "taking advantage of what we believe are favorable market conditions to do a refinancing." Waiting for those favorable conditions to yield higher prices for its products, Gaylord was poised to exchange the financial box into which it had fallen for the corrugated boxes that were its specialty.

Principal Subsidiaries: Gaylord Container Corporation Mid-America Packaging Division.

Further Reading:

"Gaylord Container Acquires Multi-Wall Bag Plant from United Sates Gypsum," *PR Newswire,* September 6, 1989.

Gaylord Container Corporation annual reports, Deerfield, IL: Gaylord Container Corp., 1988–92.

"Gaylord Container Enters Grocery Bag and Sack Business," *PR Newswire,* May 17, 1989.

"Gaylord Container Extends Recycling Abilities at Antioch," *American Papermaker,* vol. 53, no. 8, p. 23.

"Gaylord Reports First Quarter Fiscal 1993 Results," *PR Newswire,* January 27, 1993.

"Gaylord's Three Choices Regarded as Creative," *Junk Bond Reporter,* vol. 1, no. 28, p. 1.

Klein, Elizabeth, "Beleaguered Gaylord Eyeing Refinancing," *Crain's Chicago Business,* February 25, 1991, p. 36.

Murphy, H. Lee, "How Gaylord Found Growth in Big Packages," *Crain's Chicago Business,* August 29, 1988, p. 3; "Price Hike May Hold Key to Gaylord Uptick," *Crain's Chicago Business,* March 1, 1993, p. 34.

O'Donnell, Kathie, "Gaylord's Plans for $525 Million Deal to Redeem Debt Sends Its Junk Higher," *The Bond Buyer,* March 26, 1993, p. 3.

Zuckerman, Gregory, "Upbeat Future Predicted for Gaylord," *Investment Dealer's Digest,* vol 5., no. 43, p. 3.

—Kerstan Cohen

GENCORP

GenCorp Inc.

175 Ghent Road
Fairlawn, Ohio 44333-3330
U.S.A.
(216) 869-4200
Fax: (216) 869-4211

Public Company
Incorporated: 1915 as General Tire & Rubber Company
Employees: 13,500
Sales: $1.94 billion
Stock Exchanges: Boston Cincinnati Midwest New York
   Philadelphia Pacific
SICs: 3764 Space Propulsion Units & Parts; 3489 Ordnance
   & Accessories Nec; 3089 Plastics Products Nec; 3714
   Motor Vehicle Parts & Accessories; 3764 Space
   Propulsion Units & Parts; 3949 Sporting & Athletic Goods
   Nec; 2821 Plastics Materials & Resins; 2822 Synthetic
   Rubber; 3069 Fabricated Rubber Products Nec; 3083
   Laminated Plastics Plate & Sheet; 3499 Fabricated Metal
   Products Nec

As the parent corporation for three principal segments—
Aerojet, GenCorp Automotive and GenCorp Polymer Products—GenCorp, Inc., headquartered in Fairlawn, Ohio, operates 28 manufacturing facilities throughout the United States, Canada, and Ireland, as well as one of the most sophisticated research centers in the world. This center, GenCorp Research, provides support for new technology development within the company's segments. GenCorp's investment in technology also extends to a world-class design center for its polymer segment in Salem, New Hampshire, and two design and engineering centers for its automotive segment in Indiana and Michigan.

A. William Reynolds heads GenCorp's management team as chairman of the 11-member board of directors and serves as chief executive officer. Since electing Reynolds in 1985, GenCorp has taken a significant shift in management approach and business strategy; businesses unrelated to core technologies have been divested, and key positions in aerospace, automotive, and related polymer products have been strengthened through reorganization and selected, carefully targeted acquisitions, joint ventures, and technology exchange agreements.

Focused efforts in GenCorp's three principal areas, in order to broaden customer bases and to expand the company's global

position, and an on-going commitment to quality in all facets of the business serve as a foundation for progress in the future. GenCorp's vision, as it moved toward the 21st century, was to emerge as one of the most respected diversified companies in the world.

GenCorp was founded as the General Tire & Rubber Company in 1915 in Akron, Ohio, by William O'Neil, a former Firestone dealer. In order to create more dealerships, Firestone had gradually reduced O'Neil's service area until the dissatisfied O'Neil formed his own company, Western Tire and Rubber, in 1911 to make repair materials. In 1915 O'Neil moved from Kansas City to Akron, where his father, Michael O'Neil, owned a department store. The O'Neils established General Tire & Rubber with $200,000 in capital, mostly provided by Michael, who became company president, while William became general manager. The two hired a number of Firestone managers to help manage the new business.

General Tire initially manufactured repair materials but began producing tires in 1916, aiming its wares at the high end of the market. Its first manufactured product was a premium replacement automobile tire, "General Jumbo," for Model T Ford trucks. By 1917 the company was expanding its factory and dealership network, embarking on its first advertising campaign, and growing despite a difficult economic environment made worse by World War I.

General Tire became a medium-sized company during the 1920s, holding 1.8 percent of U.S. tire sales by 1929, when it had 14 retail stores. In 1931, with the Great Depression weakening many smaller rubber firms, General Tire bought Yale Tire and Rubber of New Haven, Connecticut, and by 1936 added India Tire and Rubber Company in Mogadore, Ohio. General Tire was now a leader in the tire industry, with 2.7 percent of U.S. tire sales in 1933. Although its sales were minuscule compared with Goodyear's 30 percent of the market, General Tire was considered an important player because of its concentration in the market for higher-priced tires. In addition, the Depression pushed General Tire to diversify. During the 1930s the firm began investing in local radio stations, and in 1942 purchased the Yankee Network, a Boston-based chain of radio stations.

During World War II General Tire, like other tire companies, switched part of its production to defense needs. The firm produced defense items in Akron, Ohio, as well as in California and West Virginia and by 1945 acquired a controlling interest in the Aerojet Engineering Corporation, an Azusa, California-based rocket manufacturer. A plant General Tire had built in Indiana to make mechanical goods was converted to the production of aviation and other military supplies. The war also boosted synthetic rubber production, which later expanded into civilian sectors.

General Tire was among a number of medium-sized tire firms that expanded immediately after the war, fueled by a boom in car sales. It began the process with the purchase of the Pennsylvania Rubber Company and 45 percent of Mansfield, a medium-sized rubber concern. When television got off the ground, the company's media division moved into it, going on the air from WNAC-TV Boston in 1948.

The start of the Korean War in 1950 disrupted supplies of natural rubber, leading to U.S. Government quotas on rubber consumption until 1952. Synthetic rubber became the primary raw material in U.S. rubber production, and General Tire opened a synthetic rubber plant in Odessa, Texas, in 1956. Tire production was changing in other ways; tubeless tires were accepted by 1960, as were synthetic fibers like nylon and rayon, which held tires together more firmly.

General Tire continued to expand its line of retail stores, growing from 72 stores in 1955 to 107 in 1957 to 164 in 1961. The firm also continued to diversify. Aerojet growth continued after World War II, and an industrial products division that manufactured plastic and metal parts for aircraft and electric appliances was started; the Aerojet General Corporation was formed in 1953. Subsequent programs like Aerobee, Titan, Polaris, and Minuteman required expansion of operations at its facilities in Sacramento, California.

In 1956 General Tire bought a majority interest in A.M. Byers, a manufacturer of steel pipe and wrought iron. General Tire moved further into the media with the purchase of television stations in New York, Los Angeles, and Memphis. In 1955 it bought RKO Radio Pictures from Howard Hughes for $25 million. General Tire sold RKO's motion picture properties to Desilu in 1958, and broadcasting operations were consolidated as RKO-General, Inc., a radio and television subsidiary headquartered in New York City. Trouble later began for RKO in 1965, when a series of license challenges were filed with the Federal Communications Commission (FCC). Hearings and license reviews would continue over the next 25 years.

In 1960 company founder William O'Neil died, and his sons assumed control of General Tire. Jerry O'Neil ran the tire business in Akron, Thomas O'Neil ran RKO in New York, and John O'Neil, General Tire's chief financial officer, lived in Washington, D.C.

A decline in the tire business, following the oil embargo of 1974 added to the firm's woes. General Tire made one-third of its tire sales directly to U.S. auto companies, and when those companies were hurt later in the decade by Japanese competitors, General Tire's profits declined. RKO had always been a minority contributor to the firm's bottom line, but when General Tire's profits fell 29 percent in 1979 to $82 million, RKO's contribution was a record 43 percent.

In 1981 General Tire was the fifth-largest U.S. tire maker, but tire making operations were so troubled that it considered selling off its other operations. A cable television operation named Cablecom General Inc. was the first to go, selling for $105.8 million. Tire production at the Akron, Ohio, plant of the General Tire & Rubber Company was closed in 1982, after 66 years of operation. In addition, Jerry O'Neil took on General Tire's rubber unions to win concessions necessary to make tires more competitive. Aerojet sold some of its industrial companies, but continued to negotiate major new defense programs, including the Peacekeeper ICBM Missile, and follow-on contracts for various tactical missile and ordnance products.

General Tire struggled to improve its tires, signing technical agreements with Germany's Continental Gummi-Werke in 1982 and Japan's Toyo Tire & Rubber Company in 1983.

General Tire had 17 percent of the truck market in 1976, but only around 12 percent in 1981.

In 1982, RKO's license for its Boston television station was denied, but the challenge against its New York station was dropped. The FCC approved the relocation of the New York station to Secaucus, New Jersey, and issued a five-year license renewal. RKO also began spending more to buy the rights of popular TV reruns, including the popular series *Colombo.*

In early 1980 Jerry O'Neil took steps to bring in a non-family member to succeed him as chief executive officer and initiated restructuring efforts to form a holding company called GenCorp Inc. In 1985 A. William Reynolds, a former TRW Inc. executive, was named chief executive officer of GenCorp and later, in 1987, was elected chairman of GenCorp's board of directors. The restructuring plan went forward; General Tire and its industrial products, and chemicals, and plastics divisions, along with Aerojet General and RKO, became subsidiaries of the holding company.

With a bachelor's degree with honors from Harvard University, and a masters in business administration from Stanford University, Reynolds immediately introduced formal strategic planning and other professional management techniques. He also began solving GenCorp's problems, including the continuing litigation over its RKO broadcasting properties; a settlement with the government over groundwater contamination in Sacramento—an Algerian breach-of-contract suit—and the sale of GenCorp's interest in Frontier Airlines.

Reynolds announced a restructuring that involved selling the Los Angeles and New York television stations as well as the RKO radio stations. By 1989 GenCorp had sold all of its RKO broadcasting companies and exited the broadcasting business.

In 1987 GenCorp faced a hostile takeover attempt and responded by accelerating its restructuring plans. With the sale of General Tire and RKO Bottling, a beverage bottling operation, as well as a plan to repurchase shares of common stock, GenCorp successfully prevented the takeover. While addressing these divestitures, GenCorp also took measures to ensure the effectiveness of its on-going businesses. The company then made the decision to focus on high technology and high growth in aerospace, automotive (other than tires), and related polymer products.

GenCorp's DiversiTech subsidiary was reorganized into two new units, GenCorp Polymer Products and GenCorp Automotive. No longer a tire producer, GenCorp Automotive has grown to be a leading supplier of vehicle sealing systems, reinforced plastic components for vehicle bodies, and vibration control products. Two technology joint ventures with Japanese suppliers were finalized in 1990, and a significant number of new programs were launched, including passenger car and light truck components for Mazda, Toyota, Chrysler, General Motors, and Kia, a Korean company. New technology, facility revitalization, and new launch programs continued in 1991 and 1992. GenCorp formed a valuable strategic alliance and technology agreement with Henniges, a major German auto supplier. By 1993 GenCorp Automotive was supplying components to 98 percent of North American car platforms and a growing number of Japanese, Korean, and European platforms.

GenCorp Polymer Products continued to provide steady results in the early 1990s, and with the opening of a state-of-the-art production facility in Green Bay, Wisconsin, and the acquisition of Reneer Films, in Auburn, Pennsylvania, it was well positioned to maintain its high level of profitability. GenCorp Polymer Products has a major position in the design, styling, and manufacture of residential wall coverings and is the world's premier source for commercial wall coverings for new construction and refurbishment. The segment is the world's largest styrene butadiene latex producer, manufacturing coatings for publication-grade and lightweight packaging papers, carpet textile, and tire cord adhesives, and primary binders for high performance and general-purpose tapes. Its research capability provides innovative new lattices for paper towels, disposable wipes, and high performance lattices. The Penn Racquet Sports unit of GenCorp Polymer Products is the leading manufacturer of tennis balls and racquetballs in the world, with major market positions in the United States and Europe.

Four divisions are organized under Aerojet, GenCorp's aerospace and defense segment. The Aerojet Propulsion Division has the only facility in the world with the unique capability to design, develop, test, and produce both liquid and solid propellant motors. The Aerojet Electronics Systems Division is an acknowledged leader in the design, development, testing, and manufacture of airborne, space-borne, and ground-based electro-optical, microwave, and millimeter wave sensors, as well as in sophisticated warhead design and manufacture. Aerojet's Ordnance Division plays a major role in the production of air dispensed munition systems, medium caliber ammunition, advanced conventional ordnance, and heavy metal products for defense. The Aerojet ASRM Division is designing, developing and producing NASA's (National Aeronautics and Space Administration) new-generation Advanced Solid Rocket Motor for the space shuttle. GenCorp's Aerojet segment has taken steps to ensure it can compete effectively in the declining defense industry environment of the 1990s and beyond.

Principal Subsidiaries: Aerojet; GenCorp Automotive; GenCorp Polymer Products.

Further Reading:

Dworkin, Peter, ''The O'Neil Brothers' $350 Million Hassle With the FCC,'' *Fortune,* April 21, 1980.
French, Michael J., *The U.S. Tire Industry,* Boston, MA; Twayne Publishers, 1991.
''General Tire: Pondering Spinoffs to Make the Most of Its Assets,'' *Business Week,* September 7, 1981.
''General Tire Changes More Than Its Name,'' *Business Week,* January 30, 1984.
''General Tire: Searching Again for a Driver to Map the Road to Growth,'' *Business Week,* February 13, 1984.
Schiller, Zachary, ''GenCorp Isn't All in the Family Anymore,'' *Business Week,* June 24, 1985; ''Is It Just Beginner's Luck at GenCorp?,'' *Business Week,* November 25, 1985.

—Scott M. Lewis

Genentech, Inc.
Genentech, Inc.
Genentech, Inc.
Genentech, Inc.
Genentech, Inc.

Genentech, Inc.

460 Point San Bruno Blvd.
San Francisco, California 94080
U.S.A.
(415) 266-1000
Fax: (415) 266-2501

Subsidiary of Roche Holdings, Ltd.
Incorporated: 1976
Employees: 2,200
Sales: $515.9 million
Stock Exchanges: NASDAQ New York
SICs: 2834 Pharmaceutical Preparations; 6794 Patent Owners
   and lessors; 8731 Commercial Physical Research.

Genentech, Inc. became a pioneer of biotechnology when it was founded in the late 1970s. The 60 percent-owned subsidiary of Roche Holdings Ltd. discovers, develops, manufactures, and markets human pharmaceuticals for significant medical needs. The company fabricates organisms from gene cells, organisms that are not ordinarily produced by the cells. Conceivably this process, referred to as gene splicing or recombinant DNA, may lead to cures for cancer or AIDS. The potential success of this young science causes it to flourish, attracting entrepreneurs and investors. After being swept up in a wave of takeovers and mergers that shook the industry in the late 1980s, Genentech has emerged as one of the most solid biotechnological companies in the world. Founded in 1976, Genentech was financed by Kleinman, Perkins, Caufield and Byers, a San Francisco high-tech venture capital firm, and by its co-founders, Robert Swanson and Herbert Boyer. Swanson, a graduate of the Sloan School of Management at MIT, was employed by Kleinman, Perkins, where he learned of the achievements of Cetus, a biotechnology firm founded in 1971; he decided to investigate the prospect of marketing DNA products. Initially, the concept was met with little enthusiasm, but in Herbert Boyer, a distinguished academic scientist, Swanson found someone who enthusiastically supported his plan. One of the first scientists to synthesize life (he had created gene cells with Stanley Cohen), Boyer wanted to take his research further and to create new cells.

Boyer and Swanson decided to leave their respective jobs and to found Genentech (genetic engineering technology). Thomas J. Perkins, a partner with Kleinman Perkins, who became Genentech's chairman, suggested that the new company contract out its early research. Swanson followed Perkins's advice, and contracted the City of Hope National Medical Center to conduct the company's initial research project.

Boyer and Swanson wanted to exhibit their grasp of the relevant technology before they attempted to market products—to achieve credibility for Genentech. To accomplish this goal, Boyer intentionally selected an easily replicated cell with a simple composition, Somatostatin. The first experiment with Somatostatin required seven months of research. Scientists on the project placed the hormone inside a bacteria E. coli, found in the human intestine. The anticipated result was that the bacteria would produce useful proteins that duplicated Somatostatin, but that did not happen. Then a scientist working on the project hypothesized that proteins in the bacteria were attacking the hormone. Somatostatin was protected, and the cell was successfully produced. Although it established credibility for the company, the experiment brought no real financial returns. Boyer and Swanson intended to produce human insulin as Genentech's first product.

Early in the summer of 1978 Genentech experienced its first breakthrough in recreating the insulin gene. This development required an expenditure of approximately $100 million and 1,000 human years of labor. By 1982 the company had won approval from the Food and Drug Administration. Eli Lilly & Co., the world's largest and oldest manufacturer of synthetic insulin, commanded 75 percent of the American insulin market, and Swanson knew that Genentech stood little chance of competing with them. He informed Lilly's directors of Genentech's accomplishments, hoping to attract their attention: he believed that the mere threat of a potentially better product would entice Lilly to purchase licensing rights to the product, and he was correct. Lilly bought the rights. This maneuver provided ample capital for Genentech to continue its work. By 1987 the company was earning $5 million in licensing fees from Lilly.

Swanson pursued a similar strategy with the company's next product, Alpha Interferon. Hoffmann-La Roche purchased the rights to Interferon and paid approximately $5 million dollars in royalties to Genentech in 1987. Revenues from these agreements helped to underwrite the costs of new product development, which can run from $25 to $50 million per product prior to FDA approval.

The first product independently marketed by Genentech, human growth hormone (HGH) or Protropin, generated $43.6 million dollars in sales in 1986. Demand for HGH increased as the medical profession learned more about the drug's capabilities and diagnosed hormone inadequacy more frequently. Protropin enjoyed record-setting sales over the next six years, topping $155 million by 1991. Approved by the FDA in 1985, HGH helps to prevent dwarfism in abnormal children. Genentech's entry into the market was facilitated by an FDA decision to ban the drug's predecessor because it was contaminated with a virus. By the end of the 1980s a ''new and improved'' version of HGH patented by Eli Lilly had also received approval from the FDA. Lilly's drug, unlike Genentech's version, actually replicated the growth hormone found in the human body. To counter this potential threat to their market, Genentech sued the FDA to force the agency to determine which company holds exclusive rights to the product. At the end of 1991, Genentech's

Protropin maintained an impressive 75 percent share of the HGH market.

Such legal disputes are not unusual for biotechnology firms still in their infancy. Because the products of the industry duplicate substances found in nature, they challenge long-established patent laws. Traditionally, products and discoveries determined as not evident in nature receive patent awards. Biotechnology firms contest these standards in the courtroom, attempting to force alterations in the law, to make it conform to the needs of the industry. Companies apply for broad patents to secure against technological innovations that could undermine their niche in the marketplace. For start-up firms such as Genentech, patent battles consume large sums of money in both domestic and foreign disputes.

Genentech introduced tissue plasmogen activator (t-PA), in 1987 as Activase, a fast-acting drug that helped to break down fibris, a clotting agent in the blood. At $2,200 per dose, t-PA was marketed as a revolutionary drug for the prevention and treatment of heart attacks. When Genentech failed to provide the FDA with evidence that Activase prolonged the lives of heart attack victims, the federal agency delayed approval until 1988. The drug brought in almost half of the company's $400 million 1989 revenues.

But Activase was soon battered with legal and clinical setbacks. Genentech's claim to exclusive ownership of natural t-PA and all synthetic variations on it was struck down in Britain when the British firm Wellcome Foundation Ltd. challenged Genentech's patent in the British courts, claiming it was overly broad. This decision against the company, viewed more as an annoyance than a serious blow, may be reversed on appeal. Future patent decisions may hinge on Genentech's contention that the source of a biotechnology product—purification versus production by recombinant techniques—should determine its uniqueness.

Clinical data showed that the drug caused serious side effects, including severe internal bleeding. A European study indicated that the drug was faster, but no more effective, than some competitors costing just $200 per dose. The troubles continued when a controversial study comparing Activase, SmithKline Beecham PLC's Eminase, and another firm's streptokinase was released in March 1991. The International Study of Infarct Survival (ISIS-3) found all three drugs to be equally effective at keeping people alive, which again reflected badly on Activase's high cost. Genentech discounted several of the research methods used, then commissioned its own 40,000-patient comparative trials to be completed in 1993.

The regulatory, legal, and clinical roadblocks that stymied Genentech's introduction of Activase, combined with competition from large pharmaceutical and chemical companies that bought into biotechnology in the late 1980s, culminated in Genentech's 60 percent acquisition by Switzerland's Roche Holdings Ltd. The merger was one of many in 1989 and 1990, which resulted in such pharmaceutical giants as SmithKline Beecham PLC and Bristol-Myers Squibb Company. Genentech used the $2.1 billion influx of capital to fund research, finance patent disputes, and invest in cooperative ventures to develop synthetic drugs using biotechnological discoveries.

In 1989, Genentech increased advertising support for Activase and other products by 360 percent. The marketing support and an intensive sales campaign helped Activase capture about 50 percent of the t-PA market. In 1990, Genentech launched the first commercial life sciences experiment in space when it sponsored research aboard the space shuttle Discovery.

Activase faced stiff competition when it entered the market. Delays in approval gave competitors such as Biogen and Integrated Genetics the opportunity to catch up with the industry leader. A dozen or so companies filed patents for similar drugs. Genentech could not expect to easily secure foreign markets for its new drug either. Competition was stiff; this relatively new industry has had little time to carve out established markets, and there are important competitors, particularly in Western Europe. In 1991, however, Genentech won an exclusive patent for recombinant t-PA in Japan. Genentech also had several new products in Federal Drug Administration trials in 1991. An insulin-like growth factor for the treatment of full-blown AIDS patients and relaxin, an obstetric drug, were in development that year. Genentech's DNase, for use in the management of cystic fibrosis and chronic bronchitis, entered Phase III FDA trials. The firm's HER2 antibody entered clinical trials in 1991 as well. This treatment for breast and ovarian cancer was first developed from mouse cells. Genentech was also able to begin marketing of interferon gamma, or Actimmune, in 1991. The product's relatively meager sales of $1.7 million were connected to the small number of patients suffering from chronic granulomatous disease, an inherited immunodeficiency.

Genentech's relationship with Roche led to the establishment of a European subsidiary of Genentech that would develop, register, and market DNase in 17 primary European countries. Genentech also allotted Roche an exclusive license to sell DNase anywhere but Europe, the United States, Canada, and Japan.

Although Genentech's revenues only rose one percent during the first half of 1992, it was one of only five biotech firms to show a profit for the period. Many biotechnology firms, including Genentech, were nonplussed by the lagging earnings figures, as concerns (and funds) were focused on research and marketing.

The applications of biotechnology extend beyond health care; they also affect the agricultural and chemical industries. Agriculture still remains a dominant industry in the United States, and experiments in cell replication could transform that industry. Technological innovations affect not only farmers but also food processors, plant-oil manufacturers, the forestry industry and the ornamental and floral industries. Over the next 30 years the discoveries of biotechnology will alter human existence. At the forefront, Genentech helps to establish new precedents for the field, yet it suffers the consequences of its position. The company has shown it has the capability to regroup, plan effective strategies and move on to find revolutionary solutions to both medical and social problems.

Principle Subsidiaries: Genentech Development Corp.; Genentech Venture

Further Reading:

Baum, Rudy, ''Knotty Biotech Issues Receive Attention,'' *Chemical & Engineering News,* April 27, 1992, pp. 30–31.

Hamilton, Joan, ''How Long Can Biotech Stay in the Stratosphere?'' *Business Week,* November 25, 1991, p. 224.

''Heart Attack Drugs: Trials and Tribulations,'' *Economist,* March 19, 1991, pp. 86–87.

''Mergers and Acquisitions: Strategic is the Word,'' *Institutional Investor,* January 1991, pp. 74–81.

''A Natural Selection,'' *Chief Executive,* May 1992, pp. 34–39.

Slutsker, Gary, ''Patenting Mother Nature,'' *Forbes,* January 7, 1991, p. 290.

Thayer, Ann, ''Biotech Firms' Revenues up But Earnings Win First Half,'' *Chemical & Engineering News,* August 31, 1992, pp. 15–16.

Westphal, Christoph, and Sherry Glied, ''AZT and t-PA: The Disparate Fates of Two Biotechnological Innovations and Their Producers,'' *Columbia Journal of World Business,* spring/summer 1990, pp. 83–100.

—updated by April S. Dougal

GENERAL TIRE ⒼⒼ®

General Tire, Inc.

One General Street
Akron, Ohio 44329-0012
U.S.A.
(216) 798-3000
Fax: (216) 798-3170

Wholly Owned Subsidiary of Continental Aktiengesellschaft
Incorporated: 1915 as The General Tire & Rubber Company
Employees: 8,500
Sales: $1.4 billion
SICs: 3011 Tires & Inner Tubes

General Tire, Inc., is a world leader in the manufacture and marketing of tires of all kinds and is a major exporter of tires around the world. A subsidiary of Continental Aktiengesellschaft (A.G.), Europe's second-largest tire and rubber manufacturer—and the fourth-largest in the world—as of 1987, General Tire constitutes the biggest and most important component of this German tire holding company.

On the eve of the twenty-first century, the worldwide tire and rubber industry was in the hands of five major producers. In the nineteenth century, long before the invention of synthetic rubber and only a few decades after the discovery of vulcanization, hundreds of rubber and tire companies vied with one another. A very unlikely city, Akron, Ohio, was dubbed the "rubber capital of the world" in the late nineteenth century, and it was in Akron that the General Tire and Rubber Company was established in 1915. It is one of the few original American tire companies to have survived to the present day.

The founder of the company, William F. O'Neil, was a native of the city, although he and his partner, Winfred E. Fouse, had first entered the rubber tire business in Kansas City, Missouri. In early 1909 O'Neil and Fouse pooled their capital and established the Western Rubber & Supply Company (renamed the Western Tire & Rubber Company in 1911), which only sold already made tires. Both partners, however, had bigger dreams; they were natives of Akron, where O'Neil's father, a wealthy merchant, agreed to give the two young entrepreneurs a loan in order to open a tire manufacturing business. In 1915 The General Tire & Rubber Company was launched. While O'Neil's father was president of the new company, William

O'Neil, in the role of general manager, wielded most of the authority, and delegated little of it until his death in 1960.

Although there were hundreds of tire companies in the United States at the time, it was a propitious era for tires; in 1915 the number of passenger cars in the United States had surpassed two million, with one million produced in 1915 alone. In addition, World War I boosted the U.S. economy in almost all respects. Even the lower middle class by then could afford Model Ts. Because of more frequent blowouts, the vast majority of cars in those days came equipped with two spare tires, and the more expensive models even came with four spares. Hence business was more than ample for tire companies, and The General Tire & Rubber Company even turned out a profit in its first year of operation.

One year later, the company manufactured its first tire bearing the General name. It was the first oversize tire on the market, especially fitted for passenger cars. No stranger to advertising, O'Neil paid $5,000 in 1917 to the prestigious *Saturday Evening Post* for a full page ad introducing his new tire. While large scale national advertising was common, it was highly uncommon—for a tire company at least—to appeal to individual car owners rather than to the car manufacturers in Detroit. O'Neil's was an innovative marketing approach, and it worked. Franchised tire dealerships became crucial to the success of the General Tire & Rubber Company. The company also initiated the concept of trading in used tires for a complete set of "Generals," as the tires were dubbed.

The growing importance of trucks and their particular tire needs did not escape the company's notice. Almost from the outset of its existence, truck tires became a specialty. The General Tire & Rubber Company pioneered the recapping of truck tires and came out in the 1930s with a series of low-pressure truck tires. By 1934 the company's research and development specialists had experimented with a revolutionary new "drum method" for producing truck tires that dramatically slashed the cost of manufacturing them and at the same time accelerated the speed at which they were manufactured by 50 percent. Without the "drum method" of truck tire production, the tremendous wartime demand for tires would not have been met. In 1940 The General Tire & Rubber Company produced the largest truck tire in the world.

In 1923, only eight years after General Tire's establishment, it had earned its first million dollars in sales after taxes (forty years later, the company would achieve its first billion dollars in sales). Its product innovations continued apace. The company had already come out in 1920 with its "General Jumbo" low pressure tire, which became a great success with car owners because of its superior mileage and maneuverability. In the late 1920s and throughout the financially difficult years of the Great Depression, General Tire not only pioneered in the development of truck tires, but entered the airplane tire business and continued to churn out new automobile tires, such as the Dual 8, the Dual 10, and the Squeegee. The company had acquired its first subsidiary in Mexico, and was exporting its tires throughout the world. Despite these signs of vigor and the fact that the 1930s witnessed the biggest vehicle registration in history—surpassing the 100 million mark by the mid-1930s—the company made no profit throughout most of the decade. Its survival alone had to stand as testimony to its vitality.

The survival years of the Depression gave way to prosperity during World War II. The dearth of natural rubber and the initial poor quality of synthetic rubber, however, hindered General Tire's profit potential. There was virtually a halt to all civilian automobile tire production, and many smaller tire companies were closed by the government or turned into munitions plants. While The General Tire & Rubber Company continued to function, the company built a munitions plant in Mississippi and operated it for the duration of the war. It also fulfilled other wartime requests, including building intricate pontoon bridges and improved gas masks.

At the beginning of the war, with founder O'Neil still at the helm, the company had ventured outside the tire business by purchasing a 50 percent interest in the Pasadena, California-based Aerojet Engineering Corporation, which would become Aerojet General in the near future. This purchase marked the onset of an explosion of growth and diversification at the end of the war, which, among other distinctions, would make General Tire the country's biggest private radio and television owner by 1960.

The postwar years heralded great prosperity for General Tire. As for the tire business, the company began to supply General Motors, hence entering the new car or ''original equipment'' market in a significant way (it had already entered the original equipment market for trucks in the 1930s, as a supplier for International Harvester). Plant expansion was initiated: in 1959 the world's largest tire test track was completed in Uvalde, Texas; in 1967 the company's fourth tire plant in Bryan, Ohio, was completed, followed in 1973 by the construction of a radial tire manufacturing facility in Mt. Vernon, Illinois. William O'Neil did not live to see the company reap its first billion dollar sales in 1963. By then, however, he had witnessed radical changes in his company.

In the postwar years, The General Tire & Rubber Company gradually ceased to be exclusively a tire manufacturer and marketer. It entered the entertainment business, followed by tennis ball, wrought iron, and soft drink production, as well as chemicals and plastics manufacturing; in the early 1980s General Tire even began motion picture and video production. The identity of the company had altered so drastically that by 1984, the shareholders agreed to change the name and transform the company into a holding company consisting of four major subsidiaries. General Tire, Inc., emerged as the tire manufacturing entity, a separate corporation operated independently. GenCorp, Inc., would be the name of the new parent company.

The formation of General Tire, Inc., in a sense signaled a return to the original identity and purpose of The General Tire and Rubber Company. With subsidiaries in Canada (closed in 1991) and Mexico (sold in 1993), it was the fifth major tire company in North America, consisting of six manufacturing facilities, a tire fabric processing plant, and the giant Uvalde, Texas, tire test center, the largest in the world.

In 1987 GenCorp underwent large-scale restructuring, in part to ward off a hostile takeover attempt by General Acquisition, Inc.

When one of Europe's largest tire manufacturers, Continental Aktiengesellschaft of Hanover, Germany, became interested in the possibility of purchasing General Tire, the shareholders of GenCorp were more than willing to sell.

Continental is one of Europe's oldest tire manufacturing companies, and the first tire company in the world to develop—in 1904—tires with treads. Flush with capital from one of its most successful years, Continental was determined to broaden its market base, which was largely domestic. The acquisition of General Tire, Inc., would give Continental a firm foothold in North America. In June of 1987 General Tire was sold to the German tire group for $628 million, thereby transforming Continental into the fourth-largest tire company in the world. Gone, possibly forever, were the days when hundreds of tire companies could profit by serving the same domestic market. In the 1990s more than 80 percent of the tires sold worldwide are produced by five major tire companies, only one of which, Goodyear, is American.

The result of General Tire's purchase was an overall revitalization. The company was downsized—its Canadian plant was closed, a retail chain was sold, and the number of employees decreased by 20 percent—and restructured into three major business units. Unfortunately, the huge cost of restructuring was barely recouped when the recession of the early 1990s took its severe toll on the company. Under Chief Executive Officer Alan L. Ockene, the company weathered the recession as it had, decades earlier, the even severer Great Depression. By 1993, the company had broken even and introduced such innovative new tire products as the Hydro 2000, a premium, all-weather tire designed to provide optimum performance on wet roads and the Genseal tire, which repairs itself of minor punctures. Both new products are ultra-premium tires that cater to the more affluent customer, to whom General Tire's new products will increasingly be marketed. In 1991, at the height of the recession, Ford Motor Company distinguished General Tire with its TQE (or top quality) Award, which only twelve of Ford's 4,000 tire suppliers received that year.

Even with the dominance of the world tire market by a handful of companies, the future of the tire and rubber industry is precarious. Competition is extremely intense, the cost of labor keeps escalating, and environmental demands are increasing. Recycling of the mountains of used tires generated by tire manufacturers in an environmentally acceptable manner, installing expensive emission controls in factories, and developing ''energy saving'' tires were some of the concerns of General Tire in the early 1990s.

There is, however, great potential in specialized tires, including the self-sealing automobile tire, bicycle tires, wet-weather driving tires, or the ''energy saving'' automobile tire. Manufacturing specialized tires has always been General Tire's strength. The truck tire, which the company pioneered from the outset, is another specialized product that performs well on the market.

Successful restructuring and downsizing, coupled with General Tire's traditional strengths in specialized tires, held the possibility of making the company a formidable competitor in international markets. In the early 1990s it was already the largest component of the giant and highly successful German tire and rubber manufacturer Continental A.G. More so than any other tire company in the world, including the world's largest, Michelin, Continental has made inroads into the newly opened Eastern European and Russian markets, which promised to be extremely lucrative in the twenty-first century.

Further Reading:

Birkland, Carol, "Tires: The Evolution Continues," *Fleet Equipment,* May 1991, pp. 18–25.

Bowman, Robert, "Warehousing: General Tire," *Distribution,* March 1989, p. 119.

Continental Aktiengesellschaft Annual Report, Hanover, Germany: Continental Aktiengesellschaft, 1991.

Crovitz, L. Gordon, "Continental Divide: Blowout of Tire Merger Bid Underscores Europe's Unfinished Business," *Barron's,* December 16, 1991, p. 12.

Kalail, Edward G., "General Tire Reorganizes Company Into Three Major Business Units," *Business Wire,* April 3, 1992, sec. 1, p. 1; "General Tire Announces Price Increase on All Private Brand Products Sold to Replacement Customers in U.S.," *Business Wire,* April 10, 1992, sec. 1, p. 1.

O'Neill, Dennis John, *A Whale of a Story, the Story of Bill O'Neil,* New York, NY: McGraw-Hill, 1966.

Soffen, S. L., "Global Tire Review—Industry Report," *Shearson Lehman Brothers, Inc.,* November 16, 1992.

—Sina Dubovoj

Genetics Institute, Inc.

87 Cambridge Park Drive
Cambridge, Massachusetts 02140
U.S.A.
(617) 876-01170
Fax: (617) 868-1024

Public Company
Incorporated: 1980
Employees: 870
Sales: $88 million
Stock Exchanges: NASDAQ
SICs: 8731 Commercial Physical Research

Genetics Institute, Inc., (GI) is a biotechnology firm engaged in the research, development, and commercialization of pharmaceuticals through recombinant DNA and other genetic technologies. The company has developed drugs to make the blood of hemophiliacs clot, as well as substances that stimulate the production of red and white blood cells, and proteins that enhance bone growth. Despite its successes in the laboratory, GI has been hampered by the lengthy regulatory requirements for testing new drugs, and by patent disputes, in its quest for profitability in the hotly competitive biotechnology industry.

GI was founded in December of 1980. The company grew out of the desire of the then-president of Harvard University to exploit the commercial possibilities of work being done in the university's biological laboratories. Under the sponsorship of the Harvard Management Group, a number of scientists met at the Chicago airport Hilton in the summer of 1980 to discuss a venture. Although the meeting was not a roaring success, the group nonetheless decided to continue its attempts to found a ''Bell Labs'' of biotechnology, where cutting-edge science would yield products with commercial uses. Through genetic engineering, the scientists hoped to create protein-based substances for use in medical therapies. These products would then be licensed to other companies, so that GI could concentrate its efforts on investigation in the lab, rather than marketing and sales.

In September of 1980, Harvard's faculty voted against the university's involvement in a commercial venture, but the two principal scientists involved, Dr. Mark Ptashne and Dr. Thomas Maniatis, decided to forge ahead on their own, and set out to raise the necessary funds. By the end of the year, the two had

convinced a consortium of four venture capitalists to chip in a total of $6 million to start the new firm. With the money in place, Ptashne and Maniatis invited half a dozen other scientists to come aboard, and began the search for a chief executive officer. This role was filled by drug company executive Gabriel Schmergel, who signed on in April, 1981.

GI's first order of business was to fill out its staff and obtain suitable lab space. The company recruited five additional scientists, including three MIT postdoctoral students Ptashe met at a party. On June 1, 1981, GI ceased operating out of Ptashe's home, as employees moved into laboratory facilities in a building that had formerly been Boston's Women's Lying-In Hospital. GI's space, spread over five floors, included delivery and recovery rooms, as well as the old morgue, in addition to rooms designed as laboratories and offices.

In these temporary quarters, GI sought to research and develop new biological products for use in health care, agriculture, and industry. Among the company's first efforts was a very ambitious and arduous program to develop a recombinant form of factor VIII, the blood component that enables clotting, for people with hemophilia A, or classic hemophilia. GI set out to find and clone the gene that produced factor VIII, in order to use the gene to engineer a rapidly growing cell line in Chinese hamster ovary cells, then to produce human factor VIII, and to use this cell line to produce factor VIII in 2,500-liter cell culture tanks. The factor VIII project was undertaken with funding from the Baxter Travenol Laboratories, Inc., which marketed blood clotting factors made from donated human blood, which carries with it the associated risks of transmitting blood borne viruses such as hepatitis and AIDS.

Using substances derived from the blood of pigs, GI researchers began to search for a factor VIII gene. By the summer of 1982, the scientists' efforts had stalled as they ran out of the precious porcine factor VIII used in their experiments. Contacting its supplier, GI ''negotiated with them to scale up to ten hogs from two,'' in producing the substance, as company scientists later told the *Wall Street Journal*. By the end of the year, GI learned that a team at another biotechnology firm was also working to develop recombinant factor VIII, and the company intensified its efforts in a race to conclude its work first. At this time, GI also strengthened its partnership with Baxter Travenol, when the company purchased $4.9 million of GI's stock, to acquire a minority interest in the company.

GI also began to seek funds and physical space for projects other than the factor VIII effort. In addition to its agreements with Baxter Travenol, GI received funding from a Japanese firm, Chugai Pharmaceutical Company, and a Swiss company, Sandoz, Ltd. GI eventually licensed Sandoz to conduct human tests and to file for FDA approval for a new protein that speeded white blood cell production, called GM-CSF.

In October, 1983, the company entered into collaboration with the Allied Health and Scientific Products Company. In return for $5 million to $15 million of funding over three years, Allied earned exclusive rights to any recombinant-DNA based diagnostic products for medical uses that GI developed in its labs. In addition, Allied purchased $10 million of GI stock. The companies planned to focus their joint venture on tests for sexually transmitted diseases, cancers, and certain viruses. Allied assumed responsibility for conducting clinical trials of any substances produced, along with manufacturing and marketing them.

By the end of 1983, GI had started to see progress in its efforts to develop human blood clotting factor VIII. The company announced that it had isolated and cloned part of the gene for factor VIII, an important step towards producing the substance for testing, and eventually, clinical use. GI's competitors in San Francisco, however, were in hot pursuit, as the two groups rushed to be the first into print with their final results. At the end of August, 1984, GI submitted a comprehensive write-up of its efforts to the prestigious British biology journal, *Nature,* and in late November, the journal published its results as well as those of its competitor.

In July, 1984 the company announced an agreement with a Japanese company, Chugai Pharmaceuticals, to develop recombinant erythropoietin (EPO). This product is a protein that acts to regulate production of red blood cells in the body and can be used to treat severe anemia, such as that found in kidney dialysis patients. Another biotechnology firm, Amgen, was producing the drug in commercial quantities in conjunction with its Japanese partner on this project.

In October, 1984, the first GI employees moved into new company facilities, constructed specifically for GI in Cambridge, Massachusetts. The entire company had made the move out of Boston by summer of the following year. At that time, GI embarked on its first overseas venture, forming a branch office in Japan. In addition to this geographic expansion, the company also turned its attention to fields outside the medical arena. In November, 1984, GI purchased one-third of a company called United Agriseed, and four months later it announced that it would form a joint venture to develop biological insecticides.

In the following year, GI sold stock to the public for the first time, offering 2.875 million shares of common stock in May, 1986. Proceeds from this sale yielded $79 million. With the capital produced by this move, the company announced that it would build a $25 million plant in Andover, Massachusetts, to manufacture products made through recombinant DNA technology.

In September, 1986, GI entered into an agreement with another drug company, Burroughs Wellcome. With the biotechnology arm of this company, GI set up WelGen manufacturing. This company was slated to manufacture pharmaceuticals derived from advances in biological sciences. WelGen, of which GI owned half, planned to build its $40 million plant in Rhode Island.

In early October, 1986, GI unveiled interleukin-3, which it hoped would help speed up blood cell production in patients who had undergone radiation and chemotherapy. Tests in humans were slated to begin in the following year. Despite these advances, GI failed to turn a profit by the end of the year. The company notched losses of $4.5 million in 1986, following a loss of $1.7 million in the previous year, and it was predicted that GI would remain in the red until 1990.

In July, 1987 GI's efforts in the field of EPO seemed to pay off when the company received a U.S. patent on purified EPO, based on material derived from human urine. In October of that year, Amgen was awarded a patent on the DNA sequence encoding EPO, and then sued GI for infringement of this patent. GI, in turn, filed a countersuit.

In addition to the developments involving EPO, GI also announced that it had created a new form of tissue plasminogen activator, or TPA, which it believed would help to dissolve blood clots that cause heart attacks. In a joint venture with a company called NeoRx, GI also sought to develop a new class of cancer drugs.

At the end of 1987, GI announced that it would withdraw from the plant biotechnology business by selling its 27 percent stake in United AgriSeeds, Inc. to the Dow Chemical company for about $12 million. In addition, GI sold its proprietary technology for the production of a bacterial parasite pesticide to the Ecogen company. With these moves, the company refocused its energies exclusively on the development of therapeutic substances for use in humans. Despite this solidification, GI continued to suffer financial losses, even though its revenues increased. At the end of 1987, company losses had reached $10.4 million.

By 1988, GI's fate had begun to rest as much on the activities of lawyers as on the efforts of scientists. The company found itself hampered by legal complications in moving forward with almost all of its most promising development products. In February, 1988, GI won a summary judgement that EPO produced by competitor Amgen infringed on GI's homogenous EPO patent. More than six months closer to putting its product on the market, Amgen persisted in its legal quest to exclude the GI-licensed EPO from the marketplace. Because GI had licensed its patents for the drug to its Japanese collaborator, Chugai Pharmaceuticals, Inc., the company stood to earn royalties on only 5 to 10 percent of its sale. Seeking to end the legal strife, GI and Chugai strove unsuccessfully to settle the dispute with Amgen out of court.

In July, 1988, GI won another victory when it was granted a broad-based patent for its work on genetically engineered factor VIII, which promoted blood clotting in hemophiliacs. In the next month, however, GI found itself back in court, when Genentech sued the company for infringement of its patent for TPA, or tissue plasminogen activator. GI responded to this move by filing a countersuit against Genentech, alleging unfair competition.

In January, 1989, GI announced that it had formed a partnership with the Syntex Corporation, a drug company, to develop substances to fight rheumatoid arthritis, cancer, and other diseases. In the same month, the company won a further battle in its patent wrangle with rival Amgen, when a judge from the International Trade Commission refused to block imports of EPO from Japan. Three months later, in March, 1989, GI agreed to cross-license its factor VIII clotting factor with Genentech, thereby avoiding yet another suit over patent infringement. Both companies, and their partners, agreed to bring their own products to market independently, and not to challenge each others' rights in court.

The legal struggle over EPO continued throughout 1989, taking another twist in December, when a federal judge ruled that both GI and Amgen had valid patents related to EPO. This decision was seen as a victory for GI, since it left open the possibility that the company could file an injunction to stop its competitor from producing the drug. Nevertheless, both sides appealed the court's ruling. In November, GI had been awarded a patent for genetically engineered interleukin-3, which helped in the formation of human blood cells. Several other of the company's therapeutic substances were moving through clinical trials toward the market.

GI suffered a legal reversal in April, 1990, when a jury ruled that the company had infringed on three patents held by Genentech for TPA, its anti-heart attack drug. Just nine days later, GI was set back in its attempts to win FDA approval for its form of EPO so that it could bring the product to market with its partners. Although a lower court had ordered Amgen, GI's competitor, to temporarily cross-license its product with GI's, a higher court suspended this order, allowing Amgen to further delay the arrival of GI's EPO to the market.

Legal tangles notwithstanding, GI continued to move ahead with the development of new products. One of the most promising of these was bone morphogenetic protein 2 (BMP-2), a genetically engineered human protein which appeared to activate the natural process of bone growth. Using this substance, GI scientists were able to stimulate bone growth in laboratory animals, and hoped to transfer this process to humans.

In March, 1991, GI lost a crucial battle in its legal dispute over EPO, when a Federal appeals court upheld the Amgen patent but invalidated GI's patent as not enabled. This came as a serious blow to the company, which had hoped to capture a significant portion of the American market for the drug. In addition, GI had completed building a factory in Andover, Massachusetts, to manufacture other products. GI, which had lost $29 million in 1990, had hoped to begin turning a profit on the basis of its licensees' U.S. sales of EPO, and those expectations were dashed by the court's decision. GI asked the U.S. Supreme Court to overturn the decision. But in August, 1991, the company took a special charge against its earnings, and set aside $11 million to cover any damages that might be awarded to Amgen. At this time, Amgen also gained a $25 million attachment of GI's real estate holdings, pending future damage awards in the case.

One month later, GI announced that the American Home Products Corporation would purchase 60 percent of the company, for $666 million. With this move, GI acquired a significant fresh new source of income to support its research activities. In October, 1991, GI's appeal to the Supreme Court in its dispute with Amgen over EPO came up empty when the justices refused to review the lower court's decision. Two months later, in December, 1991, the U.S. Patent Office put the final seal on the matter when it followed the legal precedent and ruled in favor of Amgen's right to three U.S. patents for EPO.

Despite this decisive setback on the question of American sales of EPO, GI's drugs based on this technology, named Recormon and Epogin, are being sold in Europe and Japan. GI's efforts in other areas had also begun to show fruit by 1992. The com-

pany's genetically engineered anti-hemophiliac factor, named "Recombinate AHF" was approved for sale in the United States, Canada, and Sweden. In mid-1993, Recombinate AHF received the Committee for Proprietary Medicinal Products (CPMP) recommendation for approval, placing it in the home-stretch for market introduction in the European Committee. This was the second time that GI's factor VIII product received approval ahead of its San Francisco rival's product. Since GI made the drug concentrate from which Recombinate was manufactured, the company stood to share significantly in its success.

Also in mid-1993, Baxter settled a patent infringement lawsuit concerning Recombinate AHF that was brought against it in 1987. This settlement, along with GI's settlement with Amgen of all outstanding EPO patent matters in May of 1993, removed much of GI's patent litigation uncertainties. Along with the introduction of GI's recombinant factor VIII product in several countries, this marked a turning point in the company's fortunes.

In addition to the revenues it gained from Recombinate AHF, GI earned royalties on the sale in several European countries of another substance, GM-CSF, trade-named Leucomax AM-CSF, which enhances blood cell growth in cancer patients. In addition to these three products, from which GI received royalties on sales, three other proteins had been developed and licensed to other drug companies for development and marketing. Worldwide sales of these products in 1993 are anticipated to be $450 million.

Three additional drugs to which GI maintained U.S. marketing rights, including BMP-2 (bone growth), a macrophage colony stimulating factor designed to fight cancer and lower cholesterol, and interleukin-11, reached the stage of clinical trials by the early 1990s. The latter substance was licensed to the Genetic Institute/Yamanouchi joint venture in November, 1992, for testing and marketing in Japan.

Late in 1992, GI withdrew from a previous partnership when it sold its share in WelGen, its Rhode Island manufacturing venture, to its partner, Burroughs Wellcome, for $24 million. GI invested these funds in the expansion of its own manufacturing facilities in Andover, Massachusetts. In addition to this upgrading, GI acquired a building in Cambridge to house its Small Molecule Drug Discovery program, an effort that emerged from the Syntex collaboration but was expanded with Wyeth-Ayerst, a subsidiary of American Home Products.

In early 1993, GI expanded its geographical reach when it opened a small European office in Paris. In addition, the company moved ahead in its clinical trials of its BMP-2, which promised to help speed bone growth and healing. In March, 1993, GI received its eighth U.S. patent in this field. With a potential market value of hundreds of millions of dollars, observers warned that rights to a bone growth factor could touch off another bitter legal dispute.

As it moved into the mid-1990s, GI strove to become a fully integrated discoverer, developer, manufacturer, and marketer of biopharmaceuticals. Although its efforts kept it on the cutting edge of genetic engineering, more than 10 years after its inception the company had yet to achieve a position of steady profitability, as large investments in research remained potential, but not yet actual. With promising products nearing marketability, and a steady stream of new discoveries in the pipeline, GI hoped to see its scientific efforts reap financial rewards in the coming years.

Principal Subsidiaries: SciGenics, Inc.

Further Reading:

Andrews, Edmund L., "Amgen Wins Fight Over Drug," *New York Times,* March 7, 1991, p. D1.

"Baxter Acquires Interest in Genetics Institute," *Journal of Commerce,* December 2, 1982.

Bishop, Jerry E., "Blood Pressure: Biotech Firms Race to Market a Protein Hemophiliacs Need," *Wall Street Journal,* July 25, 1985, pp. 1, 10.

"Genetics Institute, Allied Complete Pact," *Journal of Commerce,* October 3, 1983.

Genetics Institute, Inc. Annual Report, Cambridge: Genetics Institute, Inc., 1992.

"Genetics Institute Inc. Assets Are Attached Pending Amgen Suit," *Wall Street Journal,* August 19, 1991.

"Genetics Institute Is Set Back in Bid for Approval of Drug," *Wall Street Journal,* January 15, 1991, p. B7.

Gupta, Udayan, "Four Closely Held Technology Firms Are Seen Making Public Offerings Soon," *Wall Street Journal,* March 13, 1986.

"Patent a Vindication for Genetics Chief," *New York Times,* July 6, 1987.

Phillips, Carolyn, and Jerry E. Bishop, "Baxter Travenol Says Boston Firm Seeks to Make Protein Needed in Blood Clotting," *Wall Street Journal,* December 2, 1983.

Riordan, Teresa, "A Fight Looms as 2 Companies Race to Develop Proteins That Can Speed Bone Repairs," *New York Times,* March 22, 1993.

Stipp, David, "Genetics Institute and Genentech Agree to Cross-License Drug for Hemophiliacs," *Wall Street Journal,* March 22, 1989.

Stipp, David, "Genetics Institute Gets Patent for Use of Experimental Drug to Cut Cholesterol," *Wall Street Journal,* June 5, 1991.

"10 Years Ago—A Look Back," *Genevents: Employee News from Genetics Institute,* July 1991, p. 1.

Waldholz, Michael, and David Stipp, "American Home Products to Buy 60% of Genetics Institute for $666 Million," *Wall Street Journal,* September 20, 1991, p. A4.

—Elizabeth Rourke

GITANO≡

The Gitano Group, Inc.

1411 N. Broadway
New York, New York 10018
U.S.A.
(212) 819-0707
Fax: (212) 730-0319

Public Company
Incorporated: 1987 as Gitano, Inc.
Employees: 3,200
Sales: $826.5 million
Stock Exchanges: New York
SICs: 2331 Women's/Misses' Blouses & Shirts; 2321 Men's/
   Boys' Shirts; 2325 Men's/Boys' Trousers & Slacks; 5621
   Women's Clothing Stores

The Gitano Group, Inc., is one of the United States' largest apparel merchandisers. Its ability to give its discount-priced clothing a high-fashion image brought the young company tremendous growth and widespread name recognition during the 1980s. Gitano's roots lay in Orit Corp., a wholesale general merchandiser founded in 1971 by Morris Dabah, an Israeli immigrant. The business struggled, and three years later the elder Dabah was joined by his oldest son, Haim, who gave up his own career to help his father.

By 1976 the focus of Orit Corp. had become apparel, and Haim Dabah, along with brothers Ezra and Isaac, had introduced the Gitano brand of jeanswear, which would prove to be the basis of the family's fortune. Haim Dabah gave the Gitano label an image of youthful sexiness that upscale brands like Calvin Klein and Ralph Lauren were successfully merchandising. Spending millions on advertising using high-fashion imagery and styling while distributing to such mass merchandisers as Wal-Mart and K-Mart, the Dabahs saw Gitano brand sales grow steadily. By 1980 revenue had reached $30 million annually. Using South American and Asian manufacturers that were guaranteed minimum production levels, the Dabahs were able to keep prices low and provide discounters with fashionable yet budget-priced apparel. Haim was in control of Gitano's high-profile marketing strategy, while Isaac oversaw production decisions.

Throughout the 1980s Gitano was able to ride the wave of designer-brand popularity by dominating the niche of bargain-priced jeanswear. Distribution was focused on the mass mer-

chandisers, but the Gitano brand proved so popular that department stores such as Macy's carried the line. The company was feeling confident enough to step boldly into the menswear arena in 1987 with lofty sales goals. Gitano sought to use the same tactics that had brought it such stunning success in women's wear: namely, by heavily promoting an affordably priced brand name while seeking to distribute at all retail levels.

In September of 1988 Gitano went public under its new name, The Gitano Group, Inc. (it had been incorporated in 1987 as Gitano, Inc., to serve as a holding company for Orit Corp.), with an offering of two million shares and raised $38.3 million. The Dabah family remained in control with a 70 percent stake. A second offering was held in June of 1990 and amassed $56.6 million. The funds were used to pay off debt and to fuel an ambitious expansion program. A big step was Gitano's decision to move into the retail side of the business by opening its own series of stores. Originally seen as an outlet for selling off excess inventory, the Gitano stores soon became full-fledged retailers with their own cadre of designers and buyers.

In December of 1988 Gitano bought the rights to the Gloria Vanderbilt trademarks from Murjani Worldwide B.V. for $15 million in cash. The struggling Gloria Vanderbilt brand, which had hit hard times early in the 1980s, was given an image make over as Gitano sought to expand the line's appeal to younger women. Although another company held onto certain license rights for the Gloria Vanderbilt name, thus restricting Gitano's control over the brand's image, the line proved to be a success in such mid-priced retail stores as Macy's and Nordstrom.

In October of 1989 Gitano acquired 50 percent of the common stock of Regatta Sport, Ltd., and a year later it acquired the remaining 50 percent. Another acquisition in 1990 was its licensee the Accessory Network Group, Inc. Gitano took these bold steps to expand just as the apparel market began to slow in 1989. As the economy stalled, Gitano saw its profits shrink even as sales grew. Haim Dabah, who had created Gitano's public image and overseen its highly effective marketing strategy, struggled in his role as president with financial planning and budgetary controls. Analysts pointed toward a loose management structure, which often seemed to foster internal competition.

Ill-conceived expansion saw the Gitano stores grow to more than 100 by 1991, even as the country suffered the effects of recession. The costs associated with these stores contributed to the growth of administrative expenses by 20 percent in 1990. As a result, the stores did not turn a profit. The company's manufacturing facilities—in Mississippi, Jamaica, and Guatemala—suffered from the same lax management and poor oversight, and they produced waste rates much higher than the industry average.

The recession only highlighted and compounded Gitano's problems. Many small retailers that had been Gitano customers went out of business, and more people were shopping at mass merchandisers, where the margins are razor thin. In 1990 earnings plummeted 73.8 percent, even though sales climbed 29 percent over the previous year to $806 million. Late in the year Haim Dabah undertook a major reorganization program; Gitano wanted to return its focus to jeanswear while improving quality and streamlining the production process. To do this, the company made an effort to customize service to its retailers, focusing particularly on the mass merchandisers that accounted for the bulk of Gitano sales—fully 90 percent—and paring down its customer list. To cut its inventory and thus avoid costly markdowns, Gitano shifted away from a system of producing apparel and then waiting for orders to a process whereby only goods that had been presold would be produced. Finally, Gitano started to exit from its retail business.

In 1991 Gitano felt the initial painful steps of downsizing—cutting its customer base from 3,600 to 1,200 and dumping $57 million worth of unwanted inventory—brought it reduced sales for the first time in its history. Gitano lost $62.5 million in 1991, and restructuring costs contributed $12.2 million. Sales dropped to $780.4 million. In June of 1992 Peter C. Kells, formerly an executive at Coca-Cola and Revlon, was brought in as chief financial officer. Gitano's lenders responded positively and in July of that year the company was able to extend its credit line. Despite efforts to continue downsizing—the company's manufacturing plant in Ruleville, Mississippi, was closed—Gitano's finances continued to be precarious, and a $78 million restructuring charge against second quarter earnings triggered a default on its bank agreements. An announced $237.9 million loss for 1992 stunned Wall Street, especially as sales had topped the previous year's by $46 million. Restructuring costs for the year came to $101.5 million.

The Dabah family's financial plight was exacerbated by problems associated with the Children's Place, a children's apparel chain that the family bought in 1989. It was put under the control of Ezra Dabah, who also continued to steer the Gitano children's wear division until 1991. Although separate from Gitano, the Children's Place was a major Gitano customer and by July 1992 owed the company $27 million. The Dabah family was forced to funnel its own funds into the money-losing retailer as well as pledge Gitano stock as collateral to the chain's lenders. As a result, the family's stake in Gitano was reduced from 70 percent to 43 percent.

In August of 1992 Gitano announced that senior management was being reorganized. Haim Dabah became chief executive officer and Peter Kells was named chief operating officer; Morris Dabah, formerly chief executive officer and chairman, remained chairman. It was also announced that Gitano had received an extension of its credit and that certain debt covenants on which the company was in default were waived. Gitano hoped that these moves would emphasize its commitment to financial discipline. The company reported a loss of $97.8 million in the first nine months of the year.

In November of 1992 the Dabah family—Morris, Haim, Isaac, and Ezra—filed for bankruptcy; also named in the filing was the holding company that held the stock for the Children's Place. The surprise move was prompted by one of its lenders selling off a block of Gitano stock that it had been holding as collateral. The family feared that sell-offs by other creditors would further depress Gitano stock and destabilize the restructuring process.

In February of 1993 Gitano sold its Accessory Network division to companies owned by the division's president and vice-president; it was to continue on as a licensee of Gitano. Gitano hoped

to realize $10.5 million in licensing proceeds; the nearly $15 million the sale raised was used to pay bank debt and as working capital. Also early in 1993, the company shuttered its Regatta Division but planned to continue to use or license the trademark.

Late in February of 1993 Haim Dabah was replaced as chairman and chief executive officer by Robert Gregory, Jr., an apparel executive who had previously served as president and chief operating officer of VF Corporation—maker of Lee and Wrangler jeans. Haim Dabah was to continue on as president and focus exclusively on Gitano's marketing efforts, with which he had helped spur impressive early growth. Isaac Dabah was seen as being steered away from senior management, and Morris Dabah moved on to become chairman emeritus. It was simultaneously announced that Gitano had received a two-year extension on its credit lines. The company indicated that it was seeking to pare down to all but its essential operations, namely anything other than its Gitano or Gloria Vanderbilt clothing lines, both of which continued to be profitable. By mid-1993 all the Gitano stores had been closed, and its remaining plant in Mississippi was also shut down. Results for 1992 showed that dramatic steps would need to be taken; the net loss for the year was about $236 million, although sales were $46 million above those of 1991.

In a retail environment where attractive prices and timely fashions are just as important as a strong image, Gitano has sought to recreate itself so as to step firmly into the future. Analysts pointed to the company's ever-increasing sales and the continued consumer appeal of Gitano jeanswear and the popularity of the Gloria Vanderbilt line as indicators of the strength and promise of The Gitano Group, Inc.'s core businesses; they saw a profitable future for the company as long as there was strict fiscal management. Robert Gregory, as quoted in *Women's Wear Daily*, summed up Gitano's situation as he stepped in to manage, "They had no operating systems in the company for things like forecasting, product planning, inventory control, quality control, and distribution. It's impossible to manage a business without these controls." He added, "They became overdiversified, uncoordinated, and eventually unprofitable. We're trying to reduce the diversification and get down to a more manageable business ... to bring some focus back to Gitano."

Principal Subsidiaries: Gitano Licensing, Inc.; G.V. Licensing, Corp.; G.V. Products Corp.; Noel Industries, Inc.; Orit Corp.

Further Reading:

Auerbach, Jonathan, "Robert Gregory, ex-VF Prexy, to Head Gitano," *Women's Wear Daily,* February 24, 1993, p. 1.
Furman, Phyllis, "Gitano's Redesign Takes a Harsh Toll," *Crain's New York Business,* September 2, 1991, p. 1; "Investments Pressing Dabahs," *Crain's New York Business,* July 13–20, 1992, p. 1.
The Gitano Group, Inc., annual reports, New York: The Gitano Group, Inc., 1992–93.
Gordon, Maryellen, "Gitano's New CEO Sets Goal: Reestablish Name," *Daily News Report,* March 3, 1993, p. 10.; "Gregory's Plan for Revitalizing Gitano," *Women's Wear Daily,* March 3, 1993, p. 11.
Lettich, Jill, "Gitano Makes All the Right Moves," *Discount Store News,* September 17, 1990, p. 107.

Morgenson, Gretchen, "Greener Pastures?" *Forbes,* July 6, 1992, p. 48.

Oliver, Suzanne, "Your Best Loss Is Your First Loss," *Forbes,* May 27, 1991, pp. 356–58.

Orgel, David, "A Giant Step for Gitano," *Daily News Record,* February 8, 1988, p. 9.

Pomice, Eva, "Chic for the Masses," *Forbes,* February 23, 1987, p. 27.

Stodghill, Ron, "Is This Any Way to Run the Family Business?" *Business Week,* August 24, 1992, pp. 48–49.

—Cheryl Collins

The Glidden Company

925 Euclid Avenue
Cleveland, Ohio 44115
U.S.A.
(216) 344-8000
Fax: (216) 344-8900

Wholly Owned Subsidiary of ICI Americas Inc.
Incorporated: 1917 as The Glidden Company
Employees: 4,600
Sales: $900 million
SICs: 2851 Paints and Allied Products; 5198 Paints,
    Varnishes & Supplies

America's third largest paint company, after Sherwin-Williams Co. and PPG Industries, Inc., Glidden Co. produces branded paints that dominate the American household consumer market. Glidden is a subsidiary of ICI Americas, Inc. and a member of the world's leading paint manufacturer, ICI Paints.

The company still bears the name of one of its founders, Francis Harrington Glidden. In 1875 Glidden, along with Levi Brackett and Thomas Bolles, founded a Cleveland varnish-making business, which they called Glidden, Brackett & Co. The business produced 1,000 gallons of varnish each week and made deliveries via horse and wagon. As partners retired over the years, the company's name went through several changes until 1894, when it became The Glidden Varnish Company. By that time, Glidden employed 18 workers in a new factory and was turning out a variety of industrial finishes for furniture, pianos, carriages, and wagons.

Although it had always concentrated on industrial finishes, in 1895 the company introduced Jap-A-Lac, a color varnish for the consumer market. Gradually gaining marketshare, Jap-A-Lac became one of the better-known varnish brands in 1903, when Glidden established a remarkable $60,000 advertising account for the product.

At the age of 85, Francis Glidden retired from the business, turning the company over to Adrian D. Joyce and his associates after a public sale. Joyce became president of The Glidden Company when it was incorporated in 1917, a position in which he would remain until 1950, when his son, Dwight P. Joyce, succeeded him. Within the first two years of his career at the helm of Glidden Adrian Joyce oversaw the acquisition of ten

paint and varnish companies across the country. The companies, some of which had been established as early as the 1850s, included the Adams & Elting Co., American Paint Works, T.L. Blood & Co., Campbell Paint & Varnish Co., Forest City Paint & Varnish Co., Heath & Milligan Manufacturing Co., Heath & Milligan Manufacturing Co. of California, Nubian Paint & Varnish Co., Twin City Varnish Co., and A. Wilhelm Co.

Glidden spent the 1920s integrating vertically through the acquisition of chemical and pigment companies. In 1921, Glidden formed the Chemical & Pigment Co., a subsidiary that was supplanted with the 1924 purchase of Euston Lead Co. in Scranton, Pennsylvania. Two years later, the National Barium Co. and St. Louis Lithophone Co. were added to the roster of companies, and in 1927 Glidden formed the California Zinc Co. and Afterthought Zinc Mining Co. The Metals Refining Co. in Hammond, Indiana, rounded out Glidden's chemicals and pigments purchases for the decade.

This nine-year buildup brought Glidden into the ranks of the leading producers of lithophone, a white pigment produced through the combination of barium and zinc ore derivatives. Lithophone was widely used in the paint, rubber, and linoleum industries. The company's Chemical & Pigment operations also produced pigments for ceramics, printing ink, and automotive industries. These operations allowed Glidden to supply the paint manufacturing business as well as several other industries.

Acquisitions in the coatings field continued throughout the 1920s with the purchase of The Chemical & Pigment Co., Inc., The Diamond Paint Co., Euston Lead Co., Metals Refining Co., and the Mamolith Carbon Paint Co. Inc. Glidden spent the years before the Great Depression developing lacquers and coatings of all types for decoration and preservation of wood and metal surfaces. Although the company was an influence in the consumer market, most of its business centered on original equipment manufacturers in the automotive and industrial fields as well as contractors, dealers, and 30 retail stores.

The Glidden Food Products Co. was created in 1920. This subsidiary refined vegetable oils and produced "oleomargarine." By the onset of the Great Depression, Glidden had formed a sturdy conglomerate that was able to purchase smaller companies disadvantaged by the economic turmoil. In 1929, Glidden acquired the assets of Voco Nut Oil Products, Inc., Wisconsin Food Products Co., Troco Co. of Illinois, Colgate-Palmolive-Peet Co.'s vegetable oil refinery, and E.R. Dunham Manufacturing Co. The purchase of Durkee & Co., a leading manufacturer of salad dressings, meat sauces, pickles, spices, and condiments, for $1.8 million in mid-1929 precipitated a name change for Glidden's food subsidiary to Durkee Famous Foods, Inc. Durkee was widely known as the maker of Durkee Famous Sauce, reportedly a favorite of President Abraham Lincoln. Glidden and Durkee would enjoy a half-century of cooperation.

Late in 1929, the operations of the Portland Vegetable Oil Mills Co. were incorporated into Durkee's business, and in 1933 Van Camp Oil Co. was rescued from bankruptcy and added to Durkee's long list of operating companies. All of Durkee's assets were later acquired by Glidden in 1936, when the subsidiary became a division. In the meantime, Glidden's Chemical &

Pigment business continued to grow, via the 1932 acquisition of Nelio-Resin Corp., manufacturer of a patented combination of turpentine and resin. A joint venture with Metal & Thermit Corp. of New York to form American Zirconium Corp. in 1933 further enhanced these operations. Nelio-Resin was brought into Glidden as a division in 1935, and in 1936 the Chemical & Pigment Co. was reorganized as a division. Glidden's pre-World War II chemicals acquisitions were rounded out in 1938 with the purchase of pine tar and turpentine producer Southern Pine Chemical Co.

Glidden also branched out into the soybean business, building a soybean oil extraction plant in Chicago in 1934. The operations were incorporated as Glidden's Holland Mills, Inc. subsidiary three years later. The versatile soybean business complemented both the paint and foods operations: soybean oil was used in the production of paint and linoleum as well as in margarine. Furthermore, Glidden was one of only two American companies licensed to use a German process for producing lecithin, a soybean oil byproduct used by paint and rubber as well as candy and margarine makers. Soybean flour and proteins were used in the production of plastics, paper coatings and sizings, and synthetic resins. By the mid-1940s, Glidden had developed a full line of soy-protein and water-based paints. In 1938 Glidden was able to reorganize Holland Mills as a division, but just one year later, the plant was destroyed by fire.

The company emerged from the Great Depression with $50.17 million in sales and $1.73 million in net income in 1940. During that decade, Glidden expanded the operations of its three divisions through the acquisition of the Yadkin Valley Ilmenite Co., a mining concern that supplemented the Chemicals & Pigments Division, and the remaining interest in the American Zirconium Corp. joint venture. The soybean business was eventually rebuilt through the acquisition of Standard Cereal Co.'s Indianapolis plant, and the construction of a hydrogen plant in New Jersey enhanced Durkee's vertical integration for the production of hydrogenated oils.

By the end of World War II, Glidden ranked as one of the leading manufacturers of margarine. Its spreads were sold under the Durkee, Troco, and Dinner Bell tradenames. Margarine sales made up a substantial portion of the Durkee division's total revenue. The acquisitions of the 1930s and 1940s helped triple Glidden's sales from $50.17 million in 1940 to over $170 million in 1945.

In 1948 Glidden revolutionized the consumer paint industry with the introduction of its first water-borne latex paint, Spred Satin. The invention of latex paint reduced the use of petroleum-based solvent in paints by about 90 percent, and Spred Satin would remain a leading brand for over 40 years.

After a year of limited distribution, Spred Satin was introduced nationally with ads in the September issue of *Life* magazine. Consumers bought 100,000 gallons of the product in 1948, and within three years that figure had skyrocketed to 3.5 million gallons. Paint sales drove Glidden's sales to $188.61 million in 1950.

The company shored up its retail distribution network in the 1950s with the purchase of several sales outlets and paint plants. In 1950, the company acquired general sales agent E. W.

Colledge G.S.A., Inc., of Jacksonville, Florida. Mound City Paint & Color Co., the Zapon industrial finishes business of Atlas Powder Co., and the domestic paint business of General Paint Corp., followed in close order. The General Paint acquisition included plants at Tulsa, Portland, and 21 retail branches.

Glidden organized a new subsidiary, Glidden International C.A., in Venezuela in 1955 to license, manufacture, and distribute the company's products outside the United States and Canada. By the mid-1960s, the international group encompassed operations in over 25 countries around the world.

In 1958, Glidden sold its soybean processing and grain merchandising operations to Central Soya Co., Inc., for $3.76 million, and acquired R.C. Pauli & Sons, a bulk spice processor based in San Francisco. By the end of the decade, paint accounted for 46 percent of Glidden's sales, while the Durkee and chemicals operations contributed 40 percent and 14 percent, respectively.

The early 1960s saw expansion of Glidden's chemical division with the acquisition of three powdered metals businesses, a fiber glass manufacturer, and a chemicals company. The Durkee foods group also grew dramatically in the 1960s, with the acquisition of seven foods companies. In 1962 the company purchased specialty grocery products manufacturer Olney & Carpenter, Inc., and acquired Gretchen Grant Kitchens Inc., a frozen pastry maker, in 1964. A flurry of additions in 1965 brought Dailey Pickle Co., Allied Foods, Zippy, Inc., Chris & Pitts Bar B-Q Sauce, Inc., and B.M. Reeves Co. Polarized Meat Co. (Moosic, Pennsylvania), a frozen meats company.

In 1967, Glidden merged with SCM Corp. (formerly Smith-Corona Company) after being threatened with a takeover by Dallas' Greatamerica Corp. and General Anniline & Film of New York. SCM had broached the subject with Glidden in the past, but was forced into the role of "white knight" by Greatamerica's 40 percent tender offer.

At the time of the merger, Glidden's annual sales eclipsed SCM's by almost $100 million, at $364.2 million. And although Glidden's food division was hard to rationalize with SCM's office machine and typewriter business, the two companies hoped that Glidden's paper coatings research and its many manufacturing facilities would complement SCM's office copier business. SCM also acknowledged that the foods and coatings businesses were growing and would contribute to overall finances. Glidden was reorganized as the Glidden-Durkee division of SCM.

The $251 million merger swapped .46 shares of SCM common stock for each Glidden common share. But before the deal was completed, SCM also had to swap debt for new stock offered in the fall of 1967 in order to buy back Greatamerica's 2.1 million Glidden shares. Glidden raised SCM's annual sales to $640 million and profits to $23.6 million. But two other factors pushed the merger: Glidden enhanced SCM's technological capabilities with a comparatively small investment of time and money, and the acquisition put SCM itself out of the reach of the 1960s takeover artists.

By the late 1970s, the Glidden-Durkee operations accounted for two-thirds of SCM's $1.3 billion revenues, but the company's diverse operations had spawned a bloated bureaucracy. In 1976, SCM directed the reorganization of Glidden-Durkee along product lines. The Coatings & Resins and Foods units were headquartered in Cleveland, the Chemical-Metallurgical group was centered in Baltimore, and Organic Chemicals operations were based in Jacksonville, Florida.

Each of the four divisions had its own financial, engineering, marketing, and legal staff, and was headed by an experienced Glidden-Durkee or SCM executive who reported to former Glidden vice president of Coatings & Resins and director Paul W. Neidhardt. From 1972 to 1977, earnings for Glidden-Durkee's food, chemicals and paper products increased by at least one-third. Coatings and consumer products grew as well, but not as dramatically.

Beginning in the mid-1970s, Glidden's Coatings & Resins Division jettisoned many industrial and chemical coatings lines to concentrate on "specific high-growth-potential markets." The division left the automotive and appliance finishes markets but maintained its position in the container industry (with interior coatings for food, beer, and soft-drink containers), custom-top grain finishes for wood products, coil coatings, gel coats, and nonautomotive applications of powdered coatings.

Furthermore, Coatings & Resins was forced to pull out of Europe in the mid-1970s. Its French subsidiary was liquidated in 1975, the German affiliate was disposed of in 1976, and the Italian company was sold in 1977. Although fluctuations in currency rates and restrictions on imports adversely affected European markets, the division's Central and South American businesses enjoyed increased sales and income and even invested $14 million in a three-million-gallon per year paint plant in Sao Paulo, Brazil, in the late 1970s.

By that time, Glidden had captured ten percent of the consumer paint market despite competition from 600 rivals. The company's paints stood fourth among leading manufacturers, behind Sears, Roebuck & Co., Sherwin-Williams, and Pittsburgh Paint & Glass. The company was number three in trade sales to contractors. From 1982 to 1986, Glidden's paint shipments grew seven percent annually, or twice the U.S. industry average. The company expanded its powder coatings operations during the first half of the decade, and saw its operating income rise 40 percent, to $51.4 million in 1984, an increase of almost $20 million from 1983.

Such success drew the attention of powerful international acquirers. During the mid-1980s, Glidden became enmeshed in a series of large-scale transactions involving two of the world's largest conglomerates, Hanson Trust plc and Imperial Chemical Industries plc. Hanson acquired SCM, then sold Glidden's American and Canadian operations to rival Imperial Chemical Industries (ICI) for $580 million. The shift in ownership made ICI the world's leading paint manufacturer, and gave ICI the leader in the do-it-yourself paint market.

The addition of Glidden to ICI's American operations more than doubled that subsidiary's annual sales to $3 billion and increased ICI's corporate presence in the United States dramatically. In 1987, Glidden continued its paint innovations with the release of its Rustmaster Pro corrosion-resistant paint. This revolutionary water-soluble vinyl resin protected metal by first creating a barrier impervious to water and oxygen, then by promoting a chemical reaction at the surface of the metal inhibiting oxidation. The coating, which was made available only to industrial contractors, stood up to 10,000 hours of exposure in a salt-spray chamber at 100 degrees Fahrenheit. Glidden's ten years of research had resulted in a coating that one technician called "Saran Wrap for steel" in a June 1988 Chemical Week article.

While this advance was remarkable, some industry analysts observed that the paint's resilience would diminish the second-purchase market. Reduced paint and solvent consumption slowed the paint industry to average growth of about two percent annually. Rauch Associates predicted near-term growth to slow even further to 1.2 percent. These dismal figures urged increased advertising spending in the early 1990s.

In 1991, Glidden doubled its media budget to $12 million in the hopes of increasing its number-one share of the consumer market from 13.6 percent. Television ads by Cleveland's Meldrum & Fewsmith agency featured witty musical renditions of such popular songs as "Whole Lotta Shakin' Goin' On" and "Stormy Weather," as well as National Football League tie-ins, and won the agency an award in 1993.

Glidden hoped to spur sagging paint sales using an environmental pitch as well in the early 1990s. Spred 2000—and its professional counterpart, Lifemaster 2000—a virtually odorless paint with no petroleum-based solvents or volatile organic compounds, was the first paint of its kind to be offered in the United States. The move marked a trend in the paint industry toward more environmentally safe paints, but was not hailed as a rescue from the paint business's doldrums.

Further Reading:

Alper, Joseph, "Glidden's Antirust Secret is Out," *Chemical Week,* June 15, 1988, p. 10.
Cooke, Stephanie, "ICI Wants to be a Household Name in the U.S.," *Business Week,* September 1, 1986, p. 40.
Dunn, Don, "Color This Paint Green," *Business Week,* June 29, 1992, p. 130.
"Everybody Wants Glidden," *Chemical Week,* May 27, 1967, p. 22.
"Expand or Die," *Forbes,* November 15, 1967, p. 23.
Gibson, W. David, "ICI Americas: Sales up 100% in Three Years, with More Acquisitions to Come," *Chemical Week,* November 5, 1986, pp. 22–25.
"The Glidden Company," Cleveland, Ohio: Public Relations, ICI Paints—North America, 1993.
"Glidden-Durkee's Faber," *Chemical Week,* July 9, 1975, p. 40.
"Glidden's William D. Kinsell, Jr.," *Chemical Week,* April 20, 1977, p. 76.
Kemizis, Paul, "Wait-and-see Stance Taken on Zero-VOC Architectural Paints," *Chemical Week,* October 14, 1992, pp. 52–53.
"Strange Bedfellows?" *Financial World,* October 11, 1967, pp. 5, 22–23.
"Streamlining the Management at SCM," *Business Week,* February 21, 1977, pp. 96, 98.
"U.S. Paint Industry Faces Reduced Growth," *Modern Paint & Coatings,* May 1991, pp. 10–16.
Wical, Noel, "Exec Recalls Humble Start of Latex Revolution," *Advertising Age,* May 8, 1978, p. 62.

—April S. Dougal

Gordon Food Service Inc.

333 50th St. S.W.
P.O. Box 1787
Grand Rapids, Michigan 49501
U.S.A.
(616) 530-7000
Fax: (616) 249-4165

Private company
Incorporated: 1946
Employees: 2,000
Sales: $830 million
SICs: 5141 Groceries—General Line; 5142 Packaged Frozen
   Foods; 5147 Meats & Meat Products; 5146 Fish &
   Seafoods; 5144 Poultry & Poultry Products; 5143 Dairy
   Products, Except Dried or Canned; 5148 Fresh Fruits &
   Vegetables; 5046 Commercial Equipment Nec

Gordon Food Service Inc. (GFS) is the largest family-owned
food service distributor in the United States and provides hospitals, restaurants, college dormitories, hotels, and other institutions with a wide variety of foods, beverages, and paper products. Marketed primarily in a territory that extends from
Michigan's Upper Peninsula to southern Ohio and Indiana, and
from Chicago to Cleveland, GFS's product line includes national brand names as well as products carrying its own GFS
label. Having introduced new operations, technologies, and
training methods that have since been adapted in other
organizations, GFS is regarded as an innovator in the food-
service industry.

GFS traces its origins to the turn of the century when Isaac Van
Westenbrugge, a 23-year-old Dutch immigrant living in Grand
Rapids, Michigan, borrowed $300 from his brother to start up a
business providing dairy products to local grocers. Van
Westenbrugge and his wife maintained a barn in back of their
house for storing their merchandise, which they inspected by
hand for freshness. Delivering cheese, butter, and eggs in a
horse-drawn wagon to Grand Rapids stores, Van Westenbrugge
became a successful businessman known for his commitment to
high quality products and dependable service. Eventually he
was able to rent business space in the wholesale food district of
Grand Rapids.

Within a few years, Van Westenbrugge sought to expand, and,
quitting his delivery business, he entered a partnership in gen-

eral grocery wholesaling. This venture ultimately dissolved in
1913, however, when he and his partner could not agree on
product lines and expansion policies. Van Westenbrugge then
began a new business in his original field of dairy product
distribution, carrying the standard eggs, cheese, and butter,
while adding new products on occasion, such as "renovated"
butter—made in the summer and re-churned for freshness in the
winter—and Blue Ribbon brand margarine. Van Westenbrugge
was able to provide quicker service this time, having replaced
his horse and wagon with two rebuilt delivery trucks.

In 1916 an industrious young man named Ben Gordon, a classmate of Van Westenbrugge's daughter Ruth, began working
part-time for Van Westenbrugge after school and on Saturdays
loading and unloading the trucks. Gordon soon left to serve in
the army during World War I, and when he returned in 1918, he
moved to Indiana to pursue an opportunity with the Nucoa Nut
Butter Company. Nucoa manufactured an inexpensive butter
substitute made with coconut oil, a popular alternative during
the war years when the price of butter rose to more than a dollar
a pound. Gordon invested $1,500 to establish a sales and distri-
bution office for Nucoa in Terre Haute, but after less than a year,
as the war ended and butter prices plummeted, the venture
failed, and Gordon returned to Grand Rapids. He began working for Van Westenbrugge again, this time as first assistant.
Later that year Gordon married Ruth Van Westenbrugge.

Over the next ten years, the company began to deliver a wider
variety of food products, introducing Philadelphia Cream
Cheese, Rival Dog Food, Best Foods Mayonnaise, and several
other items on its routes. The business grew rapidly, and in 1932
Kraft cheeses were added to the product line. In 1935 Gordon
bought into Van Westenbrugge's business, and the name was
subsequently changed to Gordon-Van Cheese Company. Two
years later Gordon's brother Frank, having left his position as
the manager of an A&P grocery store in order to work at
Gordon-Van, was put in charge of opening and managing a new
branch in Traverse City, Michigan.

The Gordon-Van Cheese Company went out of business in
1941 when it was purchased by Kraft. As part of the deal, Ben
and Frank Gordon were employed by Kraft as general managers, but within a year they sought to return to their roles as
independent food distributors. At this time, however, Ben was
unable to participate in a competitive business venture, due to
an injunction from Kraft. Therefore, Frank saw to the daily
operations of their newly formed company, Gordon Food Service, while Ben went to work for the Office of Price Administration as a food price specialist. When Ben was able to rejoin
Frank in the business in 1946, GFS was in full operation,
servicing retail outlets in Grand Rapids, Kalamazoo, and Traverse City with a fleet of seven trucks. That year Gordon Food
Service was incorporated, with Ben Gordon as president and
Frank Gordon as treasurer.

In 1947 Ben's oldest son, Paul, a college graduate and World
War II veteran, joined GFS as a salesperson. That year, the
company opened a fourth sales center and warehouse in Lansing. The following year, the company's headquarters and main
warehouse in Grand Rapids moved into a new facility that
featured refrigerated storage space for frozen food products.
Frozen foods became the focus of GFS's sales push in the

1950s. Among the first frozen foods the Gordons distributed was a new item becoming popular in restaurants at the time, french fries. By the end of the decade, GFS had employed two salespeople, and the company's concerns began to shift from merely selling to providing "food service," a new concept that came to denote broader and more thorough service to larger, institutional markets. Rather than arriving at a retail establishment with a supply of products for the merchant to choose from, as had been the norm at GFS, the new GFS sales staff began spending certain days taking advance orders and other days delivering.

By 1960 GFS was redefining its business as a food-service distributor with a product line consisting mainly of frozen foods. The company had profited from the need for a local frozen food distributor in southwestern Michigan. With limited freezer space, Grand Rapids operators were forced to place small frozen food orders frequently. Because orders had to be brought in from Detroit or Chicago, many stores had difficulty stocking enough frozen food to meet customer demands. GFS was positioned to step in to fill this need and others. Throughout the 1960s the company expanded its sales staff as well as its product line, which came to feature grocery and disposable items.

In 1962 GFS built a new 54,000 square foot headquarters and warehouse in Grand Rapids. This building would be added on to several times over the next ten years, eventually becoming the largest distribution facility of its kind in the country at 400,000 square feet. In its first year of operation the warehouse was also the site of the first annual trade show—featuring informational seminars and booths highlighting new food products—held by GFS. During this time, Ben and Frank began preparing to turn the company over to the next generation of Gordons. In 1965 Paul Gordon was made president of GFS, while Ben became the company's chairperson and Frank stepped in as vice-president. John Gordon, Ben's younger son, who had joined the company in 1953 as the manager of the Traverse City operation, was appointed secretary-treasurer.

GFS became fully committed to the food-service industry in the mid-1970s when it discontinued the last of its accounts with retail establishments. Marketing mainly to restaurants, hotels, and schools in western Michigan, the company had around 4,000 steady customers by 1974 and achieved $36 million in annual food-service sales that year. Realizing that GFS drivers had a great deal of contact with customers, the company changed the title of driver to "sales serviceman" and provided this staff with special training in customer relations and sales. In recognition of this commitment to customer service as well as its continued growth and success, GFS received the first annual "Great Distribution Organization" award by the trade magazine *Institutional Distribution* in 1974.

Years of technical innovation and expansion followed for GFS. Committed to exploring newer and more efficient means of keeping records and filling orders, the company transferred much of this information onto microfiche in 1977. The microfiche price books and customer records, along with handheld viewers, allowed sales representatives to carry much of the information they needed with them in a briefcase or pocket when calling on customers. In 1980 the company's Grand Rapids warehouse was among the first of its kind to become automated when a computerized order selection and sorting system was installed for its warehouse products.

Given its rapidly expanding territory, GFS soon needed more distribution space than its Grand Rapids facility could provide. In 1985 the company broke ground for a second distribution center in Brighton, Michigan, intended to service the eastern half of its territory. The 40 foot high, $15 million facility was slated for completion in August of the following year, but was delayed due to an accident in which several 400-foot-long racks of processed food crashed to the floor. No one was injured, but the building suffered water damage. Nevertheless, the Brighton Distribution Center opened only a few months later than expected. Run by the same mainframe computer that controlled the Grand Rapids warehouse, the highly mechanized Brighton center featured automatic inventory selection machinery and nearly 20,000 feet of conveyor belts that carried products directly into GFS delivery trucks.

The GFS product line also expanded during the 1970s. Noting that increasingly health conscious Americans were selecting more meals from restaurant salad bars and purchasing more raw vegetables from grocery stores, GFS began marketing fresh, pre-cut vegetables to customers interested in saving preparation time. By 1989 the company offered more than 100 different vegetable items. Also added to the GFS menu were ethnic foods, as the popularity of Chinese, Mexican, Cajun, and other cuisines increased in the Midwest. Furthermore, in addition to its already wide variety of canned goods, meats, dairy products, frozen foods, and main dish items, the company expanded its line of disposables, including paper napkins and silverware, as well as other nonfood food items, such as coffee machines and soap dispensers.

By 1991 nonfood products accounted for nearly 20 percent of the company's sales. Another ten percent of GFS sales was attributed to its Marketplace stores located in Michigan, Indiana, and Ohio. GFS began opening the cash and carry retail outlets in the mid-1980s to serve individuals and groups planning to host large gatherings or events. The 26 Marketplace stores offer complete lines of meats, seafoods, desserts, vegetables, and other items, such as coffee cups and stir sticks, economically priced in bulk quantities. Sales staff are available to help the customer plan an event, offering advice on how much food should be purchased or how to most successfully meet an already planned budget. Nonetheless, the bulk of GFS's business remains in commercial markets. In addition to its traditional customers—hotels, restaurants, country clubs, nursing homes—the company also gained large sales from supermarkets wishing to use a food-service distributor to stock their delis and salad bars. In 1987 GFS reported $530 million in sales from an estimated 10,000 active accounts. The following year it was given the Great Distributor Award for a second time.

GFS credits its success to the high quality of its products, the innovations it has effected in food-service industry, and the dedication of its employees. Besides providing its staff with state of the art equipment and facilities, GFS educates its sales force through ongoing and comprehensive training programs. Furthermore, the company offers several incentive plans, including profit sharing and individual performance awards. *Insti-*

tutional Distribution reported in 1988 that the average GFS sales representative handled 55 accounts translating into a yearly sales figure of $2.9 million. Hoping to achieve an increase in sales of 15 percent every year, GFS equipped its sales force with laptop computers. This allowed sales associates to access information about product availability, food preparation instructions, and menu suggestions.

By 1991 GFS sales reached $800 million and the company had become the eighth largest food-service distributor in the country, offering more than 10,000 products to its 10,000 customers. At the beginning of the year Paul Gordon's son Dan (who had joined GFS in 1972), took over the presidency while Paul became the company's chairperson. Under Dan Gordon, the company saw more expansion. Purchasing a 20-acre lot on Clay Avenue around the corner from its corporate headquarters, the company erected a $35 million, 16 million cubic-foot warehouse and distribution center that featured 32 receiving docks, a five mile long system of conveyor belts, and computer controlled machinery to stack cases of food and track them as they were shipped. The Clay Avenue Distribution Center was completed in 1992.

Analysts predict that GFS will strive to remain an independent, family-owned business. While the company will perhaps seek to explore markets outside of the Midwest, it will remain committed to advancing the food-service industry through technology and providing dependable service in its current sales territory—strategies that have brought the company a large measure of success and profit.

Further Reading:

Bologna, Michael J., ''GFS Credits Its Customers, Employees for Inspiring High-Tech Center,'' *Grand Rapids Press,* May 19, 1991.
''The Great Distributor Organization Award: Gordon Food Service,'' *Institutional Distribution,* July 1988, pp. 74–280.
Hulm, Trevor, ''Major Collapse Delays Opening of Warehouse,'' *Ann Arbor News,* August 7, 1986.

—Tina Grant

Great American Management and Investment, Inc.

2 North Riverside Plaza
Chicago, Illinois 60606
U.S.A.
(312) 648-5656
Fax: (312) 454-1819

Public Company
Incorporated: 1979
Employees: 12,200
Sales: $1,280.7 million
Stock Exchanges: NASDAQ
SICs: 3496 Fabricated Wire Products; 3264 Porcelain
    Electrical Supplies; 2873 Nitrogenous Fertilizers; 3563 Air
    & Gas Compressors; 6512 Nonresidential Building
    Operators; 6719 Holding Companies Nec

A cursory look at Great American Management and Investment, Inc. (GAMI), may indicate that the company's primary function is as a manufacturer of electrical equipment. In fact, GAMI is a holding company, a type of investment trust, that buys underperforming companies, shores them up, and either pulls in revenue from the firms or sells them at a profit. The driving force behind GAMI is Samuel Zell, a celebrated Chicago financier. Zell, who also controls companies such as Itel and Nucorp, is responsible for transforming GAMI from a bankrupt real estate company into a small conglomerate.

Great American Management and Investment's origin ultimately stems from a piece of tax legislation enacted in 1960. This law exempted certain types of real estate trusts from taxation and created an entirely new market for so-called corporate "shelter brokers." One of the financial instruments that got its start from this legislation was the REIT, or real estate investment trust. Many banks established subsidiaries and joint ventures with real estate experts during this period, offering financing in exchange for the management expertise needed to administer a real estate investment.

As the industry built around this type of investment trust began to take off in the late 1960s, an Atlanta-based financial holding company called UniCorp began laying the foundation of a REIT business through its consulting subsidiary, the Great American

Management Corp. The subsidiary staffed a separate unit, called Great American Mortgage and Investment, and began to build a portfolio of lending operations throughout the southern United States.

Great American Mortgage and Investment opened for business in August 1969, concentrating its business in the economically vibrant states of Georgia, Florida, and Texas. The group's primary trustee, James P. Furniss, was well-connected in the regional lending industry, having previously served with the Citizens & Southern National Bank in Atlanta.

GAMI restricted its lending primarily to short term construction projects and development loans, secured by first mortgages. It distinguished itself immediately through its approaches to loan origination and asset and liability management. The company pioneered real estate profit participation agreements with banks. These agreements gave GAMI access to real estate development in hundreds of small markets, while local banks gained access to funding and the talent to administer a tax-exempt real estate investment. The benefits of the loan, as well as its risks, were shared by GAMI and its partner banks. The proximity of the participating banks to the developments also enabled them to keep a close eye on the loans for GAMI.

GAMI also conducted equity participation agreements directly with developers. GAMI provided all the funding necessary for a project, while the builder contributed construction know-how and services. Because they invested jointly, the risks were distributed evenly between the builder and GAMI.

At the end of GAMI's first year in operation, the company had amassed more than $43 million in net invested assets. A year later, this number grew to nearly $240 million. Earnings remained stable, generating a healthy income for GAMI and its investors. By 1973 GAMI was the sixth-largest REIT enterprise in the country. About 80 percent of its lending was concentrated in construction lending, 13 percent in land loans, and six percent in junior mortgage loans.

Hoping to expand on this impressive record of growth, GAMI floated $25 million in senior subordinated debentures. This enabled the company to build a tiered debt structure similar to those maintained by major industrial corporations. The flotation expanded GAMI's borrowing base from $80 million to about $105 million, and ballooned its total leveraged debt reserve from $238 million to more than $313 million.

GAMI had the funds and reputation necessary to maintain its exponential growth rates, and a vibrant economic environment in which to operate. Only a crisis of the greatest magnitude could threaten the complex web of investments GAMI had constructed. The crisis of great magnitude erupted only months later, when Arab forces launched an attack on Israel. In retribution for American support for Israel during the war, Arabian oil exporters arranged to withhold shipments of crude oil to the United States and its allies.

The effect was immediate and devastating. Virtually every domestic economic indicator plunged. Oil prices surged and the American economy fell into a deep recession. This caused interest rates to rise dramatically, drying up whatever investment capital had existed. GAMI, with tremendous debt obligations and a rising number of defaults on its hands, was destroyed. The company became the target of numerous lawsuits—including one from the Teachers Retirement System of Georgia—that sought the return of investors' principal and immediate redemption of accrued interest.

During 1975, GAMI changed its name to resemble that of the UniCorp unit that created it: Great American Management and Investment. The company continued to be known as GAMI. The oil embargo ended in 1974, but left intact an emboldened oil cartel and an enduring cycle of inflationary pressures. GAMI had hoped to wait out the storm and return to profitability when the economy settled down. Unfortunately, the company proved unable to regain stable financial footing. GAMI's directors scrambled to refinance debt and delay debenture payments to avoid default. The directors settled with groups when necessary and continued their furious efforts to get the company back on its feet. The claims caught up with GAMI in March 1977, when the company finally filed for chapter 11 bankruptcy protection.

The following September, GAMI's management was attacked by the Securities and Exchange Commission, which petitioned the bankruptcy court to convert the proceedings to chapter 10. This would have allowed the court to dismiss the company's management and appoint its own trustee. In January, ten days before the court could exercise such authority, GAMI's directors presented the court with another plan of reorganization. This alternative would have paid down senior creditors, mostly banks, at 90 cents on the dollar and given them 50 percent ownership of GAMI.

A major shareholder of GAMI was Samuel Zell, whose interest in the company resided in a paper company called SZRL Investments. Zell was distinguished by his penchant for conducting high finance in blue jeans and riding a motorcycle to work. Zell entered the real estate trade while a law student at the University of Michigan during the mid-1960s. There, he and a classmate named Robert Lurie began taking contracts to manage student housing, earning $50,000 a year as graduate students. After graduation, Zell and Lurie established Equity Financial & Management to buy run-down properties, repair them, and sell at a profit. During the 1980s, changes in the tax code made it more difficult to locate and profit from undervalued properties.

They turned instead to making small corporate investments, beginning in 1980 with a 3.5 percent stake in GAMI. Specifically alluring to Zell and Lurie was GAMI's $110 million tax loss carry forwards. With profitability restored, the pair stood to shelter profits from taxes for several years. In 1980, SZRL and another creditor, Morgens, Waterfall & Company, began negotiations with GAMI's chairman, Carl W. Knobloch, and his board to substantially reduce the company's blistering $142 million bank debt. The two companies, which controlled 46 percent of GAMI, offered to provide capital liquidity in return for three board seats, including one for Sam Zell. With no other alternatives available, Knobloch embraced the offer.

Zell quickly became deeply involved in GAMI's affairs, regularly eclipsing the chairman's authority and preparing his own directives. Zell proved highly effective in winning new debt covenants and resolving claims against the company. After winning additional financing, Zell began an acquisition campaign. Zell failed in his first acquisition attempt, a bid for the Angeles Corporation, a Los Angeles-based real estate syndication firm. As a major—but still minority—shareholder, Zell lacked the unquestioned authority he wanted to close other types of deals. This changed in December 1982 when Zell bought out Morgens-Waterfall's 27-percent share of GAMI for $24 million. With small additions that both companies had made over the years, this left Sam Zell personally in control of 51 percent of GAMI.

As Zell was based in Chicago, he decided to move GAMI's headquarters to his existing office at Riverside Plaza. Most of the company's existing staff in Atlanta, however, was allowed to stay in that city. The next large opportunity that presented itself to Sam Zell was First Capital Financial, a real estate and property concern based in Coral Gables, Florida. GAMI acquired this company in September 1983 for $60 million. Some years later, First Capital headquarters also was relocated to Chicago, while property management functions were centralized in Atlanta.

In 1984, Zell privately—that is, with no involvement from GAMI—gained control of another failing firm called Itel. Over the next four years, Zell transformed Itel from a bankrupt equipment lessor into a large transportation company, operating seven small railroads, leasing rail cars and containers, dredging harbors, and manufacturing wiring products. In February 1985, Zell began building what would later become a major line of business for GAMI when he engineered the company's purchase of the Lapp Insulator division of the Clevepak Corporation. Lapp was acquired through a GAMI subsidiary called Jefferson Management for $31.5 million.

Lapp was a leading producer of porcelain-based insulating devices, such as those that hold power lines to utility poles. Established in LeRoy, New York, in 1917, Lapp had grown up with the electric power industry in the United States, and was a major supplier of insulators and other products primarily designed to power utilities. Another of the many acquisitions carried out by GAMI occurred only days later, when the company bought the Commodore Corporation for $5 million. This company, based in Syracuse, Indiana, built mobile homes.

Days after that, another GAMI subsidiary called S&P Investments negotiated the acquisition of the domestic agricultural business of Kayser Aluminum & Chemicals for $105 million, including $98 million in debt. S&P held 80 percent of the venture, while a partnership of managers retained the balance. S&P subsequently changed its name to Kayser Agricultural Chemicals. Unlike the other companies, Kayser, with 450 employees, remained at its headquarters in Savannah, Georgia.

In December 1985, Robert Lurie joined GAMI's management as a director. Lurie, president of Zell's Equity Financial Management Company, was subsequently appointed president of GAMI, succeeding Zell in the day-to-day management of the company.

On April 2, 1986, GAMI acquired the remaining operations of the Clevepak Corporation. Based in Purchase, New York,

Clevepak was a leading manufacturer of building products, process equipment, specialty packaging, and technical ceramic products. The acquisition also ended a legal battle brought by Clevepak shareowners over compensation for preferred shares in the company. GAMI's rapid expansion in the industrial building products business, largely through the takeover of Clevepak, necessitated the creation of a new business unit within GAMI. This new subsidiary, called Eagle Industries, was created with a $125 million line of credit from Heller Financial, Inc. Eagle thus became the parent company of eight GAMI operating units, including Lapp Insulator; electrical products manufacturer Hart & Cooley; Mansfield Plumbing Products; Chemineer, a manufacturer of waste products devices; a pumping products company called Pulsafeeder; the ceramic seal company Ceramx; Equality Specialties, a maker of ribbons and specialty packaging; and Clevaflex, a manufacturer of flexible carburetor air ducts.

Zell was closely tied to numerous financial analysis groups in Chicago. In addition, he served as head of numerous other venture capital concerns, including Itel and Equity. It was through these contacts that he assembled GAMI's complex hodgepodge of businesses. And as a result of these contacts and Zell's acquisitions, GAMI became almost completely divorced from its origin as a real estate investment trust. As a small scale industrial combine, GAMI succeeded in centralizing many of the administrative functions of the companies it acquired. Having reduced or eliminated the administrative costs involved in running these companies, GAMI was able to greatly improve its operating efficiency and profitability.

A number of companies were regarded as beyond salvaging, and these were sold off or written down. By and large, however, it was not GAMI's style to impose a rigid system of management on its subsidiaries. Particularly under Lurie, GAMI treated each of its divisions as autonomous business units whose managements were individually responsible for performance. This acquisition and management philosophy was extended to the DeVilbiss Company, which GAMI acquired from the Champion Spark Plug Company in March 1988 for $95 million. DeVilbiss manufactured coatings, consumer compressors, and mechanical health care products, and was added to the Eagle division.

A month later, Zell fought a small battle with the Allen Group, a venture capital firm not unlike GAMI. Zell was unhappy with a change in management at Allen and fought, successfully, to gain recognition on the board. During 1988 Zell's Itel company purchased a 17 percent stake in Santa Fe Southern Pacific, a large railroad holding company. While investigating ways to boost share value, Zell was suspected by other shareholders of Santa Fe Southern Pacific of trying to take over the railroad and marry its operations with those of Itel. Such a scheme, if true, never materialized.

In 1989 GAMI completed a takeover of the Jepson Corporation, a conglomerate of ten manufacturing companies, for $222 million. Through Eagle, GAMI also took over Amerace, a manufacturer of electrical cable connectors and components and highway safety devices, for $134.5 million. The two deals left GAMI highly leveraged. GAMI's percentage of capital funded by debt climbed from 24 percent in 1983 to 92 percent after the Jepson and Amerace deals. This placed GAMI in a fragile position, particularly in light of a mild but prolonged recession. Zell and Lurie, however, remained convinced that they could extract new operating economies and synergies from their new companies. As long as cash flow remained at current levels, they were safe.

Only 48 years old, Lurie died of cancer in June 1990. His death was not unexpected, but it deeply shook Zell, who had depended greatly on his partner. Zell assumed Lurie's position as president of GAMI, and led the board's decision to elevate several other managers from the company's operating units onto the board of GAMI.

In need of a new partner to oversee the daily operations of GAMI's sprawling empire, Zell told *Forbes* "I only made one phone call." He offered an associate in the investment banking community, Warren Hellman, an 18 percent share of GAMI for $50 million. Hellman refused to bite unless Zell spun off GAMI's Firstate Saving & Loan, a healthy Orlando-based S&L that Hellman considered a political liability. Zell balked, but later sold Firstate to himself.

Hoping to pare down GAMI's high debt, Zell began spinning off units he considered to be at the top of the recovery cycle. First to go was Eagle's pump maker, Pulsafeeder, which he sold to the Idex Corporation for $50 million. Next, Zell proposed spinning off Eagle Industries itself, but only to GAMI shareholders. He planned to distribute one share of Eagle Industries for each share of GAMI as a special dividend. This would allow Eagle to be publicly traded on the NASDAQ. The distribution, planned for November 1992, was halted only a week before it was to be carried out. Citing deteriorating capital markets, Zell postponed the distribution until better access to debt funding could be established.

Great American Management and Investment remains essentially what Zell made it: a diversified holding company. Controlled in large part by Zell and Equity Financial, its association with operating units such as Eagle is likely to remain close even if the unit is sold to GAMI investors. GAMI seems certain, however, to remain the primary investment and venture capital instrument of Zell and his partners for the foreseeable future.

Principal Subsidiaries: Eagle Industries, Inc.; First Capital Financial Corporation; Equality Specialties Division; Vigoro Corporation (46%).

Further Reading:

"Trendsetter: Great American Mortgage," *Financial World*, January 10, 1973, pp. 10–11.

"Debt Restructuring is Sought by Great American Mortgage," *Wall Street Journal*, July 7, 1975, p. 15.

"First Capital Financial Sold," *Wall Street Journal*, September 8, 1983, p. 23.

"Great American Management Backed on Debt Revision Plan," *Wall Street Journal*, November 19, 1981, p. 24.

"Great American Trust to Postpone Payment of Debenture Interest," *Wall Street Journal*, March 15, 1976, p. 18.

"Highly Leveraged Zell Firm Walks Tightrope," *Crain's Chicago Business*, January 22, 1990.

"Holder Groups of Great American Management Seek to Alter Accords," *Wall Street Journal*, November 26, 1980, p. 7.

"Less Debt, More Equity," *Forbes*, October 1, 1990, p. 260.

"Plan of Great American Management to End Chapter 11 Status Filed," *Wall Street Journal*, January 17, 1978, p. 12.

"Plan to Acquire Angeles is Terminated by Great American Management," *Wall Street Journal*, July 7, 1982, p. 32.

"Sam Zell, the Perpetual Dealmaking Machine," *Business Week*, June 26, 1989, pp. 88–89.

"Stake in Great American Management is Raised to 51% by Zell Group," *Wall Street Journal*, December 17, 1982, p. 7.

—John Simley

Great Lakes Bancorp

401 East Liberty Street
Ann Arbor, Michigan 48104
U.S.A.
(313) 769-8300
Fax: (313) 930-6740

Public Company
Incorporated: 1890
Employees: 950
Assets: $2.7 billion
Stock Exchanges: NASDAQ
SICs: 6035 Federal Savings Institutions

Great Lakes Bancorp is the second largest savings bank in Michigan, operating 46 branches statewide and in northern Ohio. Specializing in residential mortgages, Great Lakes also offers its customers loans for construction and commercial business as well as checking services and savings plans.

Great Lakes Bancorp began late in the nineteenth century as a savings and loan association. The concept of a savings and loan had originated in 1831 when a ''building club'' was formed in Philadelphia for the purpose of helping its members purchase homes through loans made from membership dues. The idea eventually gained popularity nationwide, and the savings and loan, or thrift industry, was founded. By the late 1890s, nearly 5,000 associations were operating in the United States with assets of around $500 million.

Great Lakes traces its origins to the establishment of the Huron Valley Building and Savings Association. The association received its charter from the State of Michigan after generating start-up capital of $50,000, and opened for business in January 1891. Located in two rented rooms in Ann Arbor's municipal courthouse, Huron Valley Building and Savings initially consisted of one employee, John Miner, who for a salary of $11 per month acted as secretary and teller. The association was supervised and managed by H. H. Herbst.

The association experienced steady growth throughout its first 30 years. During World War I, the economy boomed and resulted in dramatic increases in the average American standard of living and income. As the housing industry experienced gains, so did the thrift industry. By 1920 Huron Valley's assets had reached $200,000, and five years later the association was able to move from the courthouse into a brand new office building in downtown Ann Arbor. Assets increased to over $1 million in 1926, and by the end of the decade, just before the stock market crash in October 1929, Huron Valley's assets exceeded $2 million. Also that year, H. H. Herbst died and was succeeded by William L. Walz, Ann Arbor's mayor since 1909 and the first person to hold the title of president at Huron Valley. During his 12-year term, Walz rose to become one of the most respected bankers in Michigan, serving as a top elected official in the Michigan Banking Association and representing the state at conferences in Washington, D.C.

Like Michigan's banks, Huron Valley posted losses during the Great Depression. Unlike the banks, however, it was not forced to close during the bank holidays declared in 1932 by Michigan's Governor Comstock, and early the following year by President Franklin D. Roosevelt. Customers of the building and savings during this time were neither limited as to the amount of money they could withdraw nor forced to do their banking business on certain days. Thus, despite the unstable economic outlook, the association remained solvent, and, in fact, acquired a local competitor, the Ann Arbor Building and Loan Association, in what may have been the first merger in the thrift industry.

After the Depression, legislation was enacted to help the country recover economically and protect financial institutions. In 1935 the Banking Act was passed, creating, among other things, the Federal Savings and Loan Insurance Corporation (FSLIC), which would allow thrifts to insure their depositor's moneys. As a provision of the Banking Act, savings and loans were able to apply for federal charters, and federal insurance was available to them as long as the majority of the loans they extended to customers were used for mortgages.

In 1939, after receiving its federal charter, the Ann Arbor Building and Loan Association was renamed Ann Arbor Federal Savings, a name that management felt would better represent its services and the community, as well as capitalize on the increasing national recognition of the University of Michigan. Over the next few years, Ann Arbor Federal Savings underwent a period of rapid growth. The country's housing industry boomed again during and shortly after World War II, and, holding strictly to its business of accepting deposits and extending long-term mortgage loans, the company thrived. In 1940 its assets were around $4 million and a major renovation and expansion of the bank's building was undertaken. The following year Walz died, and his son, William C. Walz, who had been an employee and member of the board at Ann Arbor Federal Savings, assumed the presidency. He remained in that position for 28 years, as the company continued to prosper.

On April 1, 1978, the company merged with First Federal Savings of Battle Creek to form Great Lakes Federal Savings. The bank regards this merger as one of the most significant, and profitable, in its history, as the combined assets of the two savings institutions amounted to over $678 million.

The company's corporate activity over the next ten years consisted primarily of acquisitions and mergers. In 1981 it acquired East Lansing's First State Savings and Loan Association, and its assets rose to $900 million. The following year, after a merger with United Federal Savings of Saginaw, Great Lakes Federal became Michigan's third largest savings and loan association, with assets totaling $1.5 billion. It had now expanded its business to include most of Michigan, excepting only the state's Upper Peninsula and the Detroit area.

The company was restructured in 1983, changing its status from that of a mutual association owned by its depositors to a corporation whose stock was traded publicly. After decades of national regulation, at this time interest rate requirements were lifted by the U. S. Congress, encouraging competition between savings and loans and banks. While banks generally benefitted from the deregulation, the thrift industry was forced to lower interest drastically to compete. In addition to home mortgages and deposits then, Great Lakes Federal, like most other savings and loans, began offering a broader range of products and services to its customers. These included automobile and commercial loans as well as stock and bond mutual funds, annuities, tax-advantaged municipal funds, and three-month certificates of deposit. In 1987, Great Lakes Federal received permission from its shareholders to again rename the company, this time to Great Lakes Bancorp, which was, as *Detroit News* reporter Eric Starkman observed, "a name [that] sounds decidedly more like a bank." A subsidiary, Great Lakes Mortgage Company, was also formed in 1987.

The following year Great Lakes Bancorp made several more acquisitions. In addition to the deposits of Regency Savings Bank, it acquired Security Savings of Indianapolis, which added six Indiana branches to Great Lakes Bancorp's holdings and represented the company's first venture outside of Michigan. In March of 1989 Dollar Federal Savings of Hamilton, Ohio, was acquired, and Great Lakes Bancorp became Michigan's second largest savings bank with assets exceeding $3 billion from its 57 branches.

As the company became larger, Great Lakes management focused on maintaining the quality of service it had offered as a smaller, community financial institution. In an attempt to create more personalized service, five regional presidents were appointed and many of management's decisions were decentralized. Helping to foster good relations with the bank's customers, the new presidents were assigned to oversee all aspects of their regions' retail lending, retail banking, and new business development. In a statement quoted in the *Ann Arbor News,* Chairperson Roy E. Weber noted that while other banks consolidated, becoming large impersonal institutions, Great Lakes strove to become more "flexible to pursue a successful community banking strategy in [a] competitive environment."

In 1991 the company purchased First Federal of Michigan's Ann Arbor branch. Acquisitions slowed, however, when a three-year analysis of its branch system revealed that the company ought to refocus on its primary market areas: Ann Arbor, Saginaw, and Battle Creek. After selling off four of its branches, by the end of the year Great Lakes maintained 53 branches. Its assets for 1991 were recorded at $3.3 billion. Further refining of the bank's portfolio resulted in 44 branches in four main market areas: Saginaw, Battle Creek, Ann Arbor, and the northern Cincinnati region of Butler County.

Strengthening its links to the communities it served, broadening its product lines, and improving the returns on shareholders' investments became priorities for the firm. Maintaining high quality service through a personal approach should eventually draw more customers than larger more impersonal banking corporations. Great Lakes Bancorp seemed well positioned to maintain its competitive status in future years.

Principal Subsidiaries: Great Lakes Mortgage Company; Security First Corporation; GLB Service Corporation II; 401 Service Corporation.

Further Reading:

"Great Lakes Bancorp Adds Personal Touch," *Saginaw News* (Michigan), October 12, 1988.
"The Great Lakes Centennial Story," *Channels: A Newsletter for the Employees of Great Lakes Bancorp,* Vol. 5, No. 1.
Judge, Paul, "Great Lakes Bancorp Moves to Decentralize," *Ann Arbor News* (Michigan), October 6, 1988.
Starkman, Eric, "Bank Ability," *Detroit News,* March 15, 1987.

—Tina Grant

GUILFORD FABRIC

GUILFORD MILLS, INC. • GREENSBORO, NC

Guilford Mills Inc.

4925 W. Market St.
Greensboro, North Carolina 27407
U.S.A.
(919) 316-4000
Fax: (919) 316-4357

Public Company
Incorporated: 1946
Employees: 4,364
Sales: $614 million
Stock Exchanges: New York Philadelphia Midwest
SICs: 2258 Lace & Warp Knit Fabric Mills

Guilford Mills Inc. is the leading producer in the United States of warp, or flat, knit fabric. The company knits, dyes, and finishes nylon, acetate, and polyester yarn and sells finished fabrics to the apparel, automotive, and home furnishings industries. Guilford fabrics are used in lingerie, sportswear, lounge-wear, swimwear, children's sleepwear, bedsheets, mattress ticking, bedspreads, upholstery, and draperies. In the automotive industry, Guilford fabrics are used for automobile roof interiors and seat covers. Guilford is the only U.S. automotive textile company with manufacturing facilities abroad—the company has production plants in the United Kingdom and shares owner-ship of Mexico's largest warp knitting company.

Guilford Mills was founded in 1946 in Greensboro, North Carolina. James Hornaday set up shop in a garage with half a dozen employees and six warp-knit machines to produce synthetic fabrics for ladies' lingerie. The company's first perma-nent knitting plant was built four years later in Greensboro, and in 1961, Guilford started its first dyeing and finishing plant, which Hornaday hoped would enable Guilford to charge more for its material. Charles (Chuck) Hayes, who later became Guilford's chairman and CEO, was hired that same year to oversee the new operation. At that point, Guilford had 60 machines and was a medium-sized operation.

Guilford quickly introduced innovative dyeing and finishing techniques that included laminating, napping, embossing, and coating. From its beginnings in lingerie, Guilford branched out and supplied warp knit fabric to manufacturers of sleepwear, dresses, swimsuits, and other apparel. The company also sup-plied fabric for window treatments, automotive interiors, shoes, and luggage.

Twenty-one years after its founding, Guilford had a second dyeing and finishing plant up and running. By 1968, Hayes, 33, was president of the company, which had turned increasingly to the production of warp knit fabrics. Warp knit is a specialized fabric made by a machine knit process. The nylon, acetate, and polyester yarns run in a lengthwise direction in the fabric, forming interlocking loops. With progressive production strate-gies, the company quickly grew to $3 million in sales.

Hayes is credited with building the company from a small knitter of synthetics into the world's largest and most efficient producer of warp knit fabric. Under Hayes's direction, the com-pany won business away from larger competitors and made shrewd acquisitions and partnerships. And Guilford produced low-priced synthetic knockoffs of more expensive, natural-fiber fabrics.

The company went public in 1971. Hayes became the chairman and CEO one year later, and the company listed its stock on the American Stock Exchange. In the early 1970s, Guilford ac-quired Astrotex, Ltd., of New York and launched the Guilford-National joint venture in Kenansville, North Carolina. When velour, a velvety cotton fabric priced at a steep $8 a yard, became popular in the 1970s, Hayes and his team of fellow executives decided to develop a cheaper, synthetic substitute. Although the company had to invent a new way to dye the velour-like material, Guilford perfected a synthetic velour in 1978 that generated six to eight years of profitability. During the late 1970s, Guilford acquired the Chadalon Nylon Extruding Plant in Georgia and started a major bonding and laminating division at the Greensboro, North Carolina site.

In 1981 Guilford organized a joint venture in the United King-dom with Carrington-Viyella plc. The new company was called Guilford-Kapwood Ltd., and Bryan Lodder, a Briton, was appointed to oversee it. Two years later, Guilford bought out the British company, which was renamed Guilford Europe. Lodder was in charge of European operations.

Guilford's executives refer to 1984 as the company's "golden year." Stock was listed on the New York Stock Exchange. During the previous five years, Guilford's sales had increased 70 percent. In 1984 the company earned $24.3 million on sales of $456.9 million—a 5 percent margin that was the envy of the industry. Giants like Burlington and J. P. Stevens had margins of 2 and 1.1 percent, respectively.

"Commodity, the volume, our low cost, our low overhead—everything was just in place, and we were it," Guilford CEO Hayes was quoted as saying in the May 1992 issue of *Busi-ness—North Carolina.* "It all came together because at that time we had the most advanced line of warp-knit products in the world and had replaced a lot of woven fabrics at lower selling prices, but at better margins to us. It all clicked at the same time."

Guilford took advantage of the "click" and used profits to embark on an aggressive acquisitions campaign. The market in synthetics was beginning to fade by the mid-1980s, and to survive, Guilford realized it needed to increase market share. The company acquired two competitors in 1985—TRT Corp., of Augusta, Georgia (a fabric printing operation), and Lumber-ton Dyeing & Finishing Co. of North Carolina. The following year, 1986, Guilford bought up Gold Mills Inc. of Pennsylvania and FEF Industries of North Carolina. The company bought into Grupo Ambar, S.A. de CV, a warp knitter in Mexico City in 1987. These acquisitions doubled sales between 1984 and 1988 and gave Guilford a 60 percent share in warp knitting, its primary business.

In addition to acquisitions in the warp knit business, Hayes pushed Guilford to learn new technologies. The company branched into the circular-knit business. Circular knits are twice the size of the standard 60-inch fabric width and are produced on special knitting machines. Wide-width circular knit fabric is popular with apparel makers because more garments can be cut from less fabric.

Guilford began producing circular knit fabric in 1989, using prototype equipment. Because the fabric was double the standard width, Guilford needed new machinery to dye it. The company converted its Augusta, Georgia, printing plant into a state-of-the-art, circular-knit finishing facility. The conversion eventually cost Guilford more than $30 million in equipment and resulted in millions of dollars of losses.

By the mid-1980s, Guilford was one of Greensboro's major employers. In 1987 the company had sales of $539.1 million, and in 1988, Guilford was Number 461 on the Fortune 500 list. In 1988 the company combined Guilford/U.K. and Guilford/U.S. manufacturing facilities to form the International Marketing Division. The company also set up a partnership with Suminoe Textile Co of Japan, a leading supplier of textiles to the automotive industry. The two companies planned to share marketing resources and technical knowledge and supply American and Japanese car manufacturers with fabric for head and door liners. Guilford had pioneered the automobile headliner market in 1986 and was eager to expand into car upholstery and other auto interior fabrics.

In 1988 industrial fabrics, including automotive, made up 24 percent of Guilford's business. Apparel fabrics constituted 62 percent of the company's sales, and home furnishings were 14 percent. The company's headliner fabrics could be found in more than half of all American cars, and its seat cover business was booming. Also in 1988, Guilford acquired Krislex Knits, Inc., which had been one of Guilford's major suppliers of circular knit fabric.

By the end of the 1980s, the Guilford had more than 4,500 employees at 14 plants. But the company was having trouble making the transition from warp knits to the realm of circular knits, which required a fashion and consumer-oriented approach and in which raw materials were costlier and quality control crucial. In making warp knits, running 100,000 yards of seconds was of little consequence—it was prohibitively expensive with circular knits.

According to CEO Hayes, speaking in the May 1992 *Business—North Carolina* article, Guilford was ill-prepared for the transition. "The mentality was warp knit," he said. "There was a tremendous difference in culture that did not mesh together."

On top of the circular knit problems, Guilford suffered growing pains in the latter half of the decade and had difficulty integrating the six companies it had acquired since 1984. Growth slowed in 1989, the same year that a Miami Beach financier began building a stake in Guilford. Industry analysts wondered if the financier Victor Posner, owner of the Graniteville Co. corduroy plant, planned a takeover.

Guilford's CEO, Chuck Hayes, appointed Bryan Lodder as president of the company. Hayes retained the titles of chairman and CEO, but assured Lodder that he would have total autonomy. Lodder was president until 1991, when Hayes assumed that position.

By the end of the decade, a number of factors had converged to cut into Guilford's profits. A slump in clothing sales and a growing flood of cheap imports, along with a decrease in automotive production, slowed growth considerably. By 1990, Guilford stock had fallen to $21 from its high of $39.50 in 1987. That year, the company lost $22.6 million when it closed the Augusta, Georgia, circular-knit dyeing and finishing plant. The operation was moved to facilities in Lumberton and Greensboro. Sales for 1990 were $544.1 million.

Guilford marked 1990 with innovation, becoming the first U.S. mill to introduce microdenier specialty fabrics, which have a high-filament count that gives a silk-like feel to stretchy fabrics. The company also began a market launch into sports and fashionwear made with cotton Lycra spandex. In 1991, Guilford launched the Feminine Mystique Foundations Lines and the Infiknits wide-width circular knits line of natural fibers and Lycra blends. The production of fine denier specialty yarns allowed Guilford to create unique, exclusive fabrics. That year, Guilford's sales were $528.8 million and income was $15.9 million, and the company had slipped to the last slot on the Fortune 500 list. Guilford was not alone in its struggles—the *Wall Street Journal* of April 2, 1992, reported that profits for the Fortune 500 companies were "an unparalleled disaster" in 1991. Profits for the group fell 41 percent that year.

Guilford continued its program of restructuring and redirecting itself in 1992. CEO Hayes took on the additional roles of president and chief operating officer. The company planned to invest $100 million in new machinery and equipment and set a goal to become a global contender in the automotive market, building on its sales to Toyota, Nissan, and Honda in addition to General Motors and Ford Motor Co.

1992 also saw Guilford's continued development of its wide-width circular knits business. The company showed strong growth for Infiknits, its naturally finished, 100 percent cotton and cotton/Lycra spandex fabric line. Against the backdrop of a slow rebound in the textile industry, Guilford's share of the women's domestic swimwear market continued to rise, driven by innovations in fabrication. Guilford formed a partnership with Hunter-Douglas, a major player in the home fashions industry, to produce the Silhouette line of vertical blinds and pleated shades.

Guilford's automotive business unit also showed recovery, with worldwide growth in automotive and van interiors and residential upholstery. The unit emerged as a technological and design innovator, selling its bodycloth and headliner fabrics to automakers in the United States, Europe, and Japan.

Always driven to research and innovation, Guilford began developing a technical center in Greensboro to combine its engineering, technology, research, and product divisions under one roof. The company focused in 1992 on the further development of microdenier fabrics. Improvements in process technology and modifications of equipment were also high priorities. At the International Fabric Association International's 81st convention/industrial fabric and equipment show, Guilford introduced Tacfast, a new hook-and-loop fastener system for applying carpet tiles.

For the 1992 fiscal year, Guilford had $614.9 million in sales—an increase of 16.3 percent over 1991—and an income of $24.9 million. The company expected to continue technological upgrading of equipment and planned strategic expansion in its fibers and automotive units. Capital expenditures of $80 million were planned for fiscal 1993.

Principal Subsidiaries: Guilford FSC, Inc.; Guilford Mills (U.K.) Ltd.; Guilford Europe Ltd.; Gold Mills Inc.; Guilford Airmont, Inc.; Guilford Mills (Michigan), Inc.

Further Reading:

Avery, Sarah, "Salesman Orients Textile Firm to Japan," *Greensboro News & Record,* February 13, 1989, 99:44, p. C-4.

Bailey, David,"Look Back in Anger: For Guilford Mills to Face the Future, Chuck Hayes Had to Come to Grips with Where He'd Been," *Business—North Carolina:* May 1992, 12:5, p. 28.

"Fiber Selection: Wet Processing Implications," *Textile Industries,* August, 1970, pp. 144–169.

"For Guilford Mills, Added Value Multiplies Profits," *Textile World,* December 1983.

"Fortune 500 Group Had 41 Percent Plunge in '91 Profits," *Wall Street Journal,* April 2, 1992, sec. C, p. 21.

Geremski, Terence E., "Guilford Mills Reports Record Second Quarter Earnings," *PR Newswire,* January 18, 1993.

Guilford Mills Annual Report, Greensboro, N.C.: Guilford Mills Inc., 1992.

Heerwagen, Peter, "North Valley Home to Fortune 500," *North Valley Business Journal,* June 1992, 3:8, p. 1.

Hopper, Kathyrn, "Guilford Mills Eyes Deal with Financier," *Greensboro News & Record,* May 22, 1990, 100:142, p. A-6.

——, "First Quarter Loss Pressures Guilford Mills," *Greensboro News & Record,* February 19, 1990, 100:50, p. C-1.

Kunz, Mary, "What Makes a Survivor?" *Forbes,* January 26, 1987.

Luber, Diane, "Guilford Mills: Digesting New Ventures," *Greensboro News & Record,* January 23, 1989, 99:23, p. C-8.

——, "Guilford Mills to Sell One Plant in Lumberton, Expand Another," *Greensboro News & Record,* September 29, 1988, 98:273, p. C-5.

Mildenberg, David, "Posner Raises Guilford Mills Stake: Company to Phase out Georgia Plant," *Greensboro News & Record,* January 27, 1990, 100:27, p. A-7.

O'Hanlon, James, "Knitting Up a Storm," *Forbes,* January 21, 1980, p. 81.

Patterson, Ramona, "Guilford's Krislex Purchase Creates Room to Grow," *Business Journal—Charlotte,* January 11, 1988, 2:40, p. 11

Robinson, Russ, "Textiles, Tobacco, Furniture Continue to Reign in Triad," *Business—North Carolina,* May 1986, 6:5, p. 31.

Seidel, Leon, "Everything's Coming Up Tricot," *Textile Industries,* January, 1970, pp. 94–95, 154.

Smith, William C., "Industrial Textiles Mood: Upbeat Despite Economy," *Textile World,* December 1992, 142:12, pp. 70–72.

Snow, Katherine, "Textiles' Recovery Needs Consumers to Catch Up," *Business Journal—Charlotte,* December 30, 1991, 6:37, p. 12.

—Marinell Landa

H.B. Fuller Company

H.B. Fuller Company

2400 Energy Park Drive
St. Paul, Minnesota 55108
U.S.A.
(612) 645-3401
Fax: (612) 645-6936

Public Company
Incorporated: 1887 as Fuller Manufacturing Company
Employees: 5,800
Sales: $933.72 million
Stock Exchanges: NASDAQ
SICs: 2842 Polishes and Sanitation Goods; 2851 Paints and
Allied Products; 2891 Adhesives and Sealants; 2899
Chemical Preparations, nec

A top performer among specialty chemicals firms, H.B. Fuller Company markets adhesives, sealants, coatings, paints, formulated cleaners, waxes, and several other products in over 100 countries. Fuller's international markets, which have been aggressively pursued since the 1970s, account for more than half of the company's overall revenue. The company originated during the late nineteenth century as the first paste and glue manufacturer in Minnesota. Despite a long list of successes, Fuller ranked as the second smallest adhesive firm in the country up until World War II, at which time majority ownership and management of the company was passed from one of the founder's sons, H. B. Fuller, Jr., to Elmer Andersen, a highly successful sales manager. Andersen inaugurated a "double it in five" strategy, a systematic campaign for decentralized growth that would ensure 14 percent annual sales increases, or the doubling of sales every five years. By 1950, the company had become the fourth largest adhesives manufacturer in the country. When Andersen's son, Tony, assumed leadership of the company in 1971, further rapid paced growth came through overseas expansion. Since the early 1980s, Fuller's growth has generally slowed; in addition, net earnings have decreased in four of the last 12 years. Nonetheless, the company's reorientation to a market-driven strategy, its willingness to take regular risks on the international front, and its longstanding commitment to "place the customer first" have all earned the company esteem as a competitive, long term player in an industry where a service edge can make all the difference.

The company was launched in 1887 when Harvey Benjamin Fuller, Sr., traveled from Chicago to St. Paul, Minnesota, with the sole intention of inventing and selling glue. In Chicago Fuller had experimented with glue mixing, while successfully buying, repackaging, and marketing an existing adhesive that was guaranteed to "cement everything." His marketing took the form of various promotional rhymes, including clever Mother Goose spoofs: "Maid was in the garden, hanging out her clothes/Along came a blackbird, and nipped off her nose/When she found her nose was off, what was she to do/But go and stick it on again with FULLER'S 'PREMIUM' GLUE." Fuller regarded St. Paul, together with its "twin city" Minneapolis, as the ideal urban center to establish his business, for general industry was thriving there and competition was scarce. In addition, flour, then a key ingredient in gluemaking, was in abundant supply due to a strong agricultural base and such rising concerns as Pillsbury and General Mills's precursor, Washburn-Crosby Company.

Fuller's business plan was simple. "What the world needed," according to *A Fuller Life* and H. B. Fuller, Sr., "was a convenient, economical, strong adhesive—an adhesive so versatile that homemakers and manufacturers could both use it." His equipment was also simple: an iron kettle and the family's wood-burning stove. Soon Fuller concocted a wet, flour-based paste with which he was satisfied. He then began selling the mixture in small batches to local paperhangers, who were generally glad not to have to make their own glue. As the Fuller brand name gained recognition, Fuller realized his business required outside capital to sustain growth. The company was incorporated when three Minneapolis lawyers agreed to invest a total of $600. Thereafter, Fuller Manufacturing Company marketed its glue to a wide variety of customers, including flour mills, shoe companies, box manufacturers, bookbinders, printers, and households. The company also made and sold laundry blueing and did a brisk business in ink for the city schools. By 1888, the company, which was really just Fuller serving as jack-of-all-trades, added its first employee, Fuller's oldest son, Albert. Two years later the company moved into its own manufacturing facility, where Albert assumed primary responsibility for filling orders and discovering new formulas while Harvey generated more revenues by expanding his sales areas.

In 1892 the company acquired a Minneapolis competitor, The Minnesota Paste Company, for $200. Although several decades later such acquisitions would become regular occurrences, Fuller meanwhile was destined to grow by internal development, particularly through a succession of inventions by the founder that greatly expanded both its product line and its manufacturing capabilities. In late 1893 Harvey successfully produced Fuller's Cold Water Dry Wall Cleaner, intended for use on wallpaper (at that time it was customary to clean walls twice yearly, but existing cleaners tended to decompose under warm conditions), and applied for a patent. The item was in wide production by the following spring and became enormously popular. The elder Fuller's next invention was Fuller's Cold Water Dry Paste, which became even more successful than Fuller's Cleaner. Because it was packaged dry, without the added weight of water, the product could be shipped at lower cost, saving both the manufacturer and the customer money. In addition, Fuller's Paste was remarkably easy to work with, and advertisements boasted that "a child can mix and use it." By 1898, Fuller Manufacturing was posting annual sales of $10,000. By 1905, the company was not only shipping its paste and cleaner to both coasts, it had also entered markets in England, Germany, and Australia.

One setback for the firm, however, was the lack of an obvious successor to the post of president, for Albert and Roger, Fuller's middle son, both left the business. Furthermore, Fuller's youngest son, Harvey Jr., was more inclined to a career in art than manufacturing. However, upon his graduation from the University of Chicago in 1909, Harvey Jr. joined the company full time and made an immediate impact by bolstering advertising and creating the first comprehensive catalog of Fuller products.

Increasing its work force to include an experienced bookkeeper, a stenographer, and a sales manager, Fuller Manufacturing entered the 1910s prepared for heightened growth. In 1915 the firm reincorporated as H.B. Fuller Company and issued stock valued at $75,000. World War I, already underway, was to be the primary impetus for Fuller's short-term growth. With the engagement of American troops came the need for shipping mass quantities of food overseas. U.S. canneries were ready to comply but had a need for a quality adhesive that would speed the labeling process. Fuller filled that need and prospered. After the war, however, Fuller's sales dropped off and Harvey Sr. fell ill, dying late in 1921.

During this difficult period, when the company faced the possibility of bankruptcy, Harvey Jr. made what was undoubtedly his greatest decision: hiring a full-time chemist named Ray Burgess. By the time Harvey inherited the presidency from his father, the company had regained its momentum, due in large part to Burgess's self-taught genius and his ability to develop customized adhesives and formulas for the industrial market. The list of Fuller products expanded to several dozen by the mid-1920s and record-setting sales of $157,000 capped the end of the decade.

In 1930, following the stock market crash, Fuller acquired The Selvasize Company of St. Paul, the maker of a combination plaster and wallpaper adhesive, for $2,000. Fuller, with steady customers in 38 states and a near monopoly on glue production in the Twin Cities, remained relatively healthy throughout the Great Depression. A number of events highlighted the 1930s. The company hired its first degreed chemist, who became responsible for several new patents, such as Ice Proof, a glue resistant to cold water. In addition, a research team was formed, Fuller began a full-scale entry into international markets, and Elmer Andersen, a business administration graduate and budding salesman, joined the company, which celebrated its fiftieth anniversary in 1937.

Also during this time, Burgess developed an important new product known as Nu-Type Hot Pick-Up. Until Burgess's invention, the company, like its competitors, had marketed several hot pick-up glues for use in automated labeling; however, all such glues were notoriously difficult to work with, either too hard or too sticky in bulk form, and always cumbersome to apply in measured amounts. Nu-Type Hot Pick-Up was the first

glue that solved each of these problems. Consequently, Fuller cornered the hot glue market nationwide.

Not all the corporate news was as favorable, however. The company, with just half of one percent of industry sales, was still conspicuously overshadowed by such giants as National Adhesives Corporation, which controlled approximately 65 percent of the market. Every new sale, therefore, mattered greatly, which made all the more devastating the revelation in late 1937 that three of Fuller's regional salesmen had been undercutting the company's orders through the creation of a bogus firm, which they now claimed to represent. Sales, depressed already by the still struggling economy, dropped from $212,000 that year to $165,000 the following year. Even more devastating to the company's long-term prospects was the debilitating stroke Harvey Fuller suffered in 1939.

In March 1941 a large Chicago competitor named Paisley Products approached the ailing St. Paul firm with an acquisition offer. Both Fuller, then in his mid-50s, and Andersen, 32, attended a meeting with Paisley's representatives, who formally proposed to purchase H.B. Fuller Company for $50,000. Fuller was prepared to retire but was also discouraged by the low offer he had received. Andersen provided an alternative solution. His plan involved assuming leadership of and a majority position in the company himself, while still allowing Fuller to retain at least a 25 percent stake. The deal was completed in July after Andersen borrowed heavily to finance a $10,000 down payment on the stock he was required to purchase. Mere months later, Pearl Harbor was attacked.

Far more so than the previous war, World War II afforded the company a chance to develop a broad line of adhesives that the government demanded for an equally broad array of uses. Fuller became one of the nation's first companies to specialize, among other areas, in waterproof adhesives. It thus earned a place on the government's recommended suppliers list which, in turn, brought it enhanced recognition nationally. The company scored another victory when it was able, during the midst of rationing, to supply Nabisco with raw glucose from its inventory, which had been dramatically enlarged by Andersen as a cost-saving measure. Nabisco subsequently became a major user of Fuller's adhesives for its boxed foods and other products. Both during and following the war, the company focused on decentralizing operations—bringing the product closer to the customer—by establishing a number of branch plants, beginning with Kansas City in 1943. At the close of the decade, Fuller ranked fourth among U.S. adhesives companies, behind National Starch (now owned by Unilever), Paisley Products (acquired by Fuller in 1975), and Swift.

In 1949, Andersen was elected to the state senate and became a part-time company president. Al Vigard assumed control of day-to-day operations in Andersen's absence; he later became president when Andersen extended his political career by receiving the governorship of Minnesota in 1960. A steady introduction of new products, a systematic development of a strong nationwide sales force, and a greater attention to international expansion typified this transitional era. In 1958, the company launched H.B. Fuller Company (Canada) Ltd. in Winnipeg. Shortly thereafter, Fuller Adhesives International of Panama was established. Numerous other international subsidiaries followed, each of which conformed to the Fuller blueprint for growth. A three-stage process, this blueprint called for: 1) building export volume to a high level; 2) forming or acquiring a subsidiary, or sometimes establishing a co-venture with a non-competitor, in a clearly defined market; and 3) sustaining the business by hiring and training a local work force to produce customized products.

One of Fuller's most significant ventures outside the United States was Kativo Chemical Industries Ltd. A promising but nearly bankrupt paint, inks, plastics, and chemicals business based in Costa Rica, Kativo was begun by a Kansas inventor named Dr. Frank Jirik. During the early 1960s, Fuller acquired a minority interest in the company, but by early 1967 Jirik approached Elmer Andersen with a proposal that Fuller assume a majority interest to fuel the company's plans for expansion. In *A Fuller Life,* Andersen recounted the visit that clinched his decision: "It was Kativo's people who made all the difference to us. . . . We trusted them. We had confidence in them and we cut them loose. We decided to send no U.S. Fuller employees to work in the Kativo operation." In addition, Andersen awarded the 13 Kativo executives the right to own stock in the company they had helped build. Soon Kativo became the heart of Fuller's Latin American operations, from Mexico to Argentina. Surviving plant and monetary losses from both the June 1979 revolution in Nicaragua and General Noriega's rampages during the U.S. invasion of Panama ten years later, Kativo and its related businesses still rank among the fastest-growing in the Fuller fold (1992 sales for Latin America increased by 16.3 percent, to $140 million). One of Kativo's original executives, Costa Rican native Walter Kissling, eventually served as president and chief operating officer of Fuller.

In 1971, three years after Fuller went public, Tony Andersen became company president. International sales accounted for around 15 percent of total revenues, and Andersen was given the primary responsibility of boosting this figure, while increasing overall volume. Consequently, he became a president routinely in transit, flying from one country to the next. Not until 1980 did he return to head U.S. operations full-time. During the interim, he oversaw some two dozen acquisitions—half in foreign countries—and, significantly, the first of these provided important new market entries into Japan and Europe. From 1971 to 1980, sales grew from $60 million to $296 million. Andersen's greatest contribution to the company, however, came shortly after his return to the St. Paul headquarters. In what was then an unpopular maneuver, he decided to revamp the company's entire infrastructure, which because of rapid geographic-oriented expansion had become both inefficient and inconsistent. A market-driven organization stressing product and price uniformity was Andersen's answer. Due to an economic downturn, the payoff was slow to come. However, by 1985 earnings had improved dramatically, and three years later, Andersen was named executive of the year by *Corporate Report Minnesota.*

Fuller inaugurated the 1990s by broadening its Asia/Pacific operations with a hot-melt production plant in Guangzhou, China. Plant expansions around the globe, as well as continuing investment in research and development, have typified the company through 1992. In April of that year, Elmer Andersen officially stepped down as company chairperson. In a speech to shareholders, he optimistically stated, "the past is prologue: you ain't seen nothing yet." During this time, however, Andersen's statement was somewhat eclipsed by publicity surrounding Fuller's Resistol glue and its use as an inhalant by children in Latin America. Widely respected for its sponsorship of charitable and educational causes, Fuller pulled the product from markets in Honduras and Guatemala in the fall of 1992 and continues to fund social programs that help minimize such abuse. Furthermore, first and second quarter earnings for 1993 declined by 51 percent and 12.5 percent, respectively. Much of the first quarter decline, though, was attributed to a one-time retroactive sales adjustment caused by inadvertent overbilling. A sluggish European economy accounted for much of the remaining decline in both quarters. Notwithstanding such news, Andersen was undoubtedly right. The billion-dollar threshold is easily within reach of the company. If Fuller, as it has long pledged, sticks "to its responsibilities, in order of priority, to its customers, employees, stockholders and communities," it should continue "to be a leading and profitable worldwide formulator, manufacturer and marketer of quality specialty chemicals," year after year.

Principal Subsidiaries: H.B. Fuller Peru, S.A.; H.B. Fuller Ecuador, S.A.; Fiber-Resin Corporation; Foster Products Corp.; H.B. Fuller Argentina S.A.; H.B. Fuller Chile, S.A.; H.B. Fuller Co. Australia PTY, Ltd.; H.B. Fuller Austria GmbH; H.B. Fuller Automotive Products Inc.; H.B. Fuller Belgium N.V./S.A.; H.B. Fuller Canada Inc.; H.B. Fuller Co. (N.Z.) Ltd. (New Zealand; 99%); H.B. Fuller France S.A. (99%); H.B. Fuller Gmbh (Germany); H.B. Fuller Intl., Inc. (Australia, Hong Kong, Singapore); H.B. Fuller Japan Co., Ltd.; H.B. Fuller Mexico, S.A.; H.B. Fuller Netherlands B.V.; H.B. Fuller Sverige AB (Sweden); H.B. Fuller Taiwan Co., Ltd.; H.B. Fuller U.K., Ltd.; H.B. Fuller Dominicana, S.A.; Kativo Chemical Industries (Costa Rica; 85%); Kativo Commercial S.A. (Costa Rica); Kativo Commercial S.A. (Honduras); Kativo de Guatemala, S.A.; Kativo de Honduras, S.A.; Kativo de Panama S.A.; Kativo El Salvador, S.A.; Kativo Nicaragua, S.A.; Prakoll, S.A. (Spain); TEC Incorporated; H.B. Fuller (China) Adhesives, Ltd.

Further Reading:

A Fuller Life: The Story of H.B. Fuller Company, 1887–1987, St. Paul: H.B. Fuller Company, 1986.
"Fuller's Brush with Fame," *Corporate Report Minnesota,* June 1984, p. 23.
Fuller World, January/February 1992 (full issue).
Gelbach, Deborah L., "H.B. Fuller Company," *From This Land: A History of Minnesota's Empires, Enterprises, and Entrepreneurs,* Northridge, CA: Windsor Publications, 1988, pp. 358–61.
"H.B. Fuller Co.," *City Business,* March 26, 1993, p. 18.
"H.B. Fuller Net Falls 51% in Quarter; Nonrecurring Sales Adjustment Cited," *Star Tribune,* March 23, 1993, p. 5D.
Kunz, Virginia Brainard, *A Modern Renaissance St. Paul,* Northridge, CA: Windsor Publications, Inc., 1986, pp. 142–45.
Levering, Robert, Michael Katz, and Milton Moskowitz, *The 100 Best Companies to Work for in America,* Reading, MA: Addison-Wesley, 1984, pp. 112–14; new edition, New York, NY: Doubleday, 1993, pp.136–40.
Mundale, Charles I., "H.B. Fuller's Caribbean Initiative," *Corporate Report Minnesota,* July 1983, pp. 55–60.

Papa, Mary Bader, "Executive of the Year (Anthony L. Andersen): Building for the Future by Sticking to the Basic Values of the Past," *Corporate Report Minnesota,* January 1988, pp. 31–39.

Peterson, Susan E., "H.B. Fuller Honors Outgoing Chairman Andersen, Celebrates Company's Continuing Good Health," *Star Tribune,* April 17, 1992, p. 1D; "Glue Issue Dominates Fuller Meeting," *Star Tribune,* April 16, 1993, p. 3D; "H.B. Fuller Reports Lower Second-Quarter Earnings," *Star Tribune,* June 23, 1993, p. 5D.

Pitzer, Mary J., "Fuller's Worldwide Strategy: Think Local," *Business Week,* November 16, 1987, p. 169.

Schafer, Lee, "H.B. Fuller and the Indignities of War," *Corporate Report Minnesota,* March 1990, p. 14.

Teresko, John, "Too Fast a Pace? Andersen Has a Strategy for the Next Leg of the Race," *Industry Week,* September 15, 1986, pp. 59–60.

Zemke, Ron, and Dick Schaaf, "H.B. Fuller," *The Service Edge: 101 Companies That Profit from Customer Care,* New York: Penguin Books, 1989, pp. 458–61.

—Jay P. Pederson

Harnischfeger Industries, Inc.

Harnischfeger Industries, Inc.

Harnischfeger Industries, Inc.

P.O. Box 554
Milwaukee, Wisconsin 53201
U.S.A.
(414) 671-4400
Fax: (414) 797-6717

Public Company
Incorporated: 1884 as Pawling & Harnischfeger
Employees: 11,600
Sales: $1.4 billion
Stock Exchanges: New York
SICs: 3554 Paper Industries Machinery; 3532 Mining
    Machinery; 7373 Computer Integrated Systems Design

In many ways, the history of Harnischfeger Industries, Inc., parallels the history of the United States: built on an immigrant's dream at the turn of the century, it weathered the Great Depression and two World Wars, then fell victim to the problems afflicting many Rust Belt companies. Excess capacity, depressed markets, high production costs, and inefficient production methods brought Harnischfeger a crushing debt load that pushed it to the brink of bankruptcy in the early 1980s. Harnischfeger trimmed down, diversified, and made some brilliant acquisitions in the late 1980s to make a stunning comeback.

Like many century-old American enterprises, Harnischfeger traces its origins to an industrious immigrant with a dream. In 1884 Henry Harnischfeger was working at a sewing machine company in Milwaukee. Born in Germany, Harnischfeger had worked previously as a locksmith, a machinist, and a machine maker. He was a foreman in the sewing plant when the company appeared about to go under. Forming a partnership with Alonzo Pawling, a pattern maker in the same plant, Harnischfeger launched a small machine and pattern shop in Milwaukee.

It was a modest beginning. The company had one milling machine, one drill press, one planer, and two lathes. After each snowstorm, someone had to shovel the flat roof so it wouldn't collapse. Wind whistled in through the building's cracks. Milwaukee was bustling at the time, however, and before long Pawling and Harnischfeger's reputations as craftsmen brought business to their door. Located in the midst of many booming manufacturing companies on Walker's Point, Pawling and Harnischfeger were soon building machines for knitting, grain-

drying, stamping, brick-making, and milking, as well as conducting their regular repair work. The company was called Pawling & Harnischfeger and was commonly known as P&H. Soon, the small shop was expanding.

Harnischfeger's dream was to build a line of machinery that the company could produce and market itself. His chance came in 1887 after a tragedy occurred at a nearby plant, when another manufacturer's overhead crane fell, killing a workman. An engineer at that plant, H. A. Shaw, designed a more durable, safer crane powered by three electric motors. P&H soon hired Shaw, and their first electric overhead crane was shipped in 1888. It was a risky investment for the small company, which had built a three-story brick plant and large foundry and hired more workers.

In 1892 Shaw left with his patent to form his own company, and 1893 saw the onset of a severe economic downturn. Struggling beneath debt and with little work, the foundry was kept in operation by an order from the Pabst Brewery for six grain-dryers. A few years later Shaw lost exclusive rights to manufacture the electric crane, and Pawling & Harnischfeger immediately jumped back into production. Adding a line of electric hoists—essentially smaller versions of the crane—as well as electric motors and controls, the company was prospering by the turn of the century, with nearly 100 employees.

In 1903 a fire destroyed Harnischfeger's main shop; the following year the company built a new plant in West Milwaukee on land that had been purchased for expansion. Covering twenty acres, the plant was state-of-the-art at the time; it eventually became the world's leading manufacturer of overhead cranes. Soon after moving to the new facility, Harnischfeger began streamlining its operations and making the parts it had previously purchased from suppliers. Eventually the company designed, manufactured, and repaired every component of every product it sold, demonstrating self-reliance and accountability that brought repeat business from its customers.

Throughout the company's growth, Harnischfeger oversaw the business affairs while Pawling handled the engineering. Pawling's health declined in 1911, and he asked Harnischfeger to buy out his share of the business. Three years later, Pawling died and the company became Harnischfeger Corporation, retaining P&H as its trademark out of respect for its co-founder.

The heavy equipment industry is notoriously cyclical, alternating boom with bust. The year Pawling's health began to fail was a bust year. During those times, the company was saved by an order from J. I. Case Company for 1,000 gasoline tractor engines. The demand for cranes resumed in 1913, then skyrocketed with the start of World War I a year later.

In the meantime, Henry Harnischfeger was looking for other products to help even out the cycles of the heavy equipment market, and he eventually settled on excavating and mining equipment. After the war, the company's engineers designed the world's first gasoline-powered dragline, a truck-mounted machine that could lift, pile-drive, clam, and drag. They also created a backhoe and a shovel-type excavator mounted on crawlers. With ample applications in both mining and construction, the products were instantly successful, and Harnischfeger became well known in those industries throughout the world.

The main plant was expanded to handle this manufacturing; by 1930 the number of employees had grown to 1,500.

This modest diversification, however, did not offset the effects of the Great Depression. There was no market for Harnischfeger products, and the company lost money every year from 1931 to 1939. Harnischfeger was forced to offer used equipment— returned because customers couldn't afford to keep it—at fire-sale prices just to raise cash. In 1937 and 1938 the company suffered strikes and became a union plant.

Founder Henry Harnischfeger had died in 1930, and his son Walter became president. Despite the weak market demand, Walter Harnischfeger continued to innovate and improve the company's products. Harnischfeger replaced the rivets in its cranes with all-welded design and fabrication in the 1930s, creating cranes and excavators that were stronger, lighter, and less costly. Harnischfeger also sought more ways to diversify in the 1930s and 1940s, making welding machines, welding elec-trodes, diesel engines, and even pre-fabricated houses. Other Harnischfeger innovations changed the industry, while not ex-actly becoming household words. These included the electro-magnetic brake and control system, Magnetorque, designed by Harnischfeger's engineers in 1946.

World War II rocked the world, but revived the American econ-omy. By 1940 Harnischfeger's plant was operating at full capacity again, and it had spent millions on plant additions. The company's cranes lifted tanks and heavy artillery in defense plants, its hoists positioned planes on aircraft carriers, and its excavators dug foundations for new buildings. Despite the burgeoning demand, chronic material shortages, a lack of skilled workers, and increased government regulation made it a difficult time for the company.

Harnischfeger hit its stride during the postwar industrial boom. From $29 million in sales in 1946, Harnischfeger grew steadily to $86 million by 1957, despite periodic economic downturns. New plants were built in Michigan, Illinois, and California, and plants were added and expanded in Milwaukee. Harnischfeger had also developed a market overseas, and companies were licensed abroad to build Harnischfeger cranes and excavators. Agreements were signed with Rheinstahl Union Brueckenbau of West Germany in 1952 and Kobe Steel, Ltd., of Japan in 1955.

Growth begets growth. In 1951 Harnischfeger borrowed $5 million in order to develop better products. In 1956 it joined the American Exchange, opening itself up to more shareholders. Previously, the company had been largely a family-owned company, though listed on the Midwest Stock Exchange.

In 1959 Walter Harnischfeger became chairman of the company and his son, Henry, became president. During this period indus-tries were becoming more complex, and Henry Harnischfeger felt challenged to choose between being an average competitor in several tough fields or the leader in two or three. Between 1964 and 1968, Harnischfeger streamlined its operations. The prefabricated home and diesel engine lines were dropped, and road-building equipment and welding product divisions were all dropped or sold. By the late 1960s Harnischfeger had two divisions. The Construction and Mining Division produced dig-ging and lifting machines, such as electric and hydraulic exca-

vators, and truck- and crawler-mounted cranes, while the Indus-trial and Electrical Division manufactured overhead cranes and hoists, as well as the electrical motors and controls needed to power them. The two divisions were essentially run as separate companies, with individuated engineering and marketing re-sponsibilities.

From there, product lines were broadened and improved, espe-cially for the larger products. Between 1969 and 1979 the average capacity of Harnischfeger's mining equipment dou-bled. In 1964 the company introduced stacker cranes to serve material handling markets. In 1967 it offered a new line of hydraulic backhoes and cranes for the booming hydraulic con-struction equipment market. Easier to operate and more mobile, these machines were very successful in the industry.

Harnischfeger's global presence also grew, with 25 percent of its production being exported in 1965 and 40 percent of Ameri-can output being exported a decade later. The company's li-censed overseas partners and subsidiaries continued to grow, the largest being Harnischfeger GmbH, based in Germany, with distribution in Europe, the Middle East, and North Africa.

The restructuring of the 1960s left the company well poised for growth in the 1970s. After the oil embargo of 1973, new coal reserves were opened and oil pipelines and mass transit systems were built, increasing sales of Harnischfeger machinery. An-nual sales grew from $150 million in 1970 to $646 million in 1981, excluding nearly $200 million sourced from overseas licensees. The company's stock was listed on the New York Stock Exchange for the first time in 1971. The company contin-ued to borrow funds to fuel growth, pouring nearly $200 million into upgrading its plants and equipment, as well as into research and development, between 1975 and 1980. In the late 1970s, however, economic recession and high interest rates hit the company hard. Unhappy with its balance sheet, Harnischfeger sought to bring its debt-equity ratio into better focus by lowering capital requirements and cutting production costs. In 1979 Harnischfeger's interest bills alone came to about $28 million, and debt was roughly 40 percent of total capital in 1980.

The heavy equipment industry was hit hard by the recession, and Harnischfeger lost money for the first time since the end of the Depression in 1938. Harnischfeger also fell victim to politi-cal change abroad: the company had been about to ship a $20 million order to Iran when the Ayatollah Ruhollah Khomeini came to power, halting all trade between Iran and other coun-tries. At the same time, the inflated deutsche mark was dulling the competitive edge of Harnischfeger's German subsidiary.

The recession spread across the globe and by 1981 had de-pressed many of Harnischfeger's primary markets. In 1982 sales dropped by a third, and the company reported a $77 million loss; staving off bankruptcy, the company went into technical default on some of its loan agreements. In 1983 sales fell to less than half of 1981 sales and the company lost another $35 million, some of the losses due to plant closings and discontinued product lines. The company's work force plunged from 8,000 in 1979 to 3,800 in 1982. Harnischfeger was no longer concerned about growth; it was concerned about sur-vival.

In 1982 Henry Harnischfeger became chairman and CEO, and the position of president was assumed by William Goessel, formerly of Beloit Corporation, a manufacturer of papermaking machinery headquartered in Beloit, Wisconsin. For the first time in its nearly 100 years, Harnischfeger's president wasn't a Harnischfeger. The year Goessel became president was one of the company's darkest, with some plants operating at less than 20 percent of capacity. In his first week on the job, Goessel was told the company would run out of cash in six weeks; then he learned that the company was in technical default on $175 million of debt. Goessel closed some operations, slashed the work force, sold off excess inventory, and set about restructuring Harnischfeger's finances. He shifted the focus of operations from old technologies to computerized systems. The ailing construction equipment business, which had accounted for about half of Harnischfeger sales at one point, was sold.

The heavy equipment industry was going through vital changes at the same time, with the crane market shrinking while competition was increasing both at home and abroad. Leveraged buyouts and closings threatened several of the major construction crane manufacturers. In 1984 Harnischfeger announced that it would be buying virtually all of its construction cranes from Kobe Steel, which then owned about 10 percent of Harnischfeger's stock. Family interest in Harnischfeger had been reduced to 5 percent. Between debt restructuring, public stock offerings, and cash from liquidations, Harnischfeger was able to pay its debts to private lenders by 1984 and report a profit that year. With the wolves gone from the door, at least until the ten-year notes came due in 1994, the company was again free to shift its focus back to growth.

The new focus was material handling. In 1983 sales of mining, construction, and material handling equipment and systems were about equal, but the automated factory systems market seemed to be booming. Many factories were modernizing and retooling, using computerized systems to upgrade efficiency in production lines. In 1984 Harnischfeger formed a new subsidiary—Harnischfeger Engineers—to tap this market; by year's end General Motors and Nabisco Brands were customers.

Automated material handling systems are computer controlled complexes of machinery that unload raw materials at the receiving dock, steer work through the factory, and send finished goods out for shipping. The systems include stacking cranes that retrieve parts in inventory and vehicles that are automatically guided by electric wires embedded in a factory floor. Harnischfeger seemed an unlikely competitor in the industry, but by the end of 1984 Harnischfeger Engineers was building a $5 million automated warehouse at a General Electric jet engine plant in Massachusetts.

One of the company's most notable milestones was the 1986 acquisition of Beloit Corporation. A manufacturer of pulp and papermaking machinery, Beloit was founded in 1858 and was also family run. The purchase was made for $175 million during a down cycle in the paper industry. About seven months later, at the onset of a boom in papermaking equipment and pulp and paper systems, the newly formed holding company, Harnischfeger Industries, sold a 20 percent stake in Beloit to Mitsubishi for $60 million. By 1988 Beloit was Harnischfeger's largest and most profitable unit, and by 1990 Beloit's sales were nearly $1.1

billion. It was a brilliant acquisition for Harnischfeger Industries and gave the parent company cash to reinvest in all its units.

Also purchased that same year was Syscon Corporation, for $92 million. This company provided software to the defense industry and was a leader in information systems integration. Harnischfeger's Systems Group—which included Syscon and Harnischfeger Engineers—was conceived as a counterbalance to the cyclical nature of mining equipment and papermaking machinery sales. Much of Syscon's work was with the U.S. Department of Defense, making it vulnerable to military cutbacks, but the company's work increasingly involved computer-based information systems designed to reduce paperwork, and therefore could be of use in all federal departments as well as large companies. By 1990 Syscon was developing systems for the U.S. Departments of Labor and Education.

Harnischfeger was prospering in 1988, thanks to these acquisitions, the paper boom, and the improving climate in the mining industry. It was a record year, ending with doubled earnings. Two more common stock offerings were made in 1987 and 1988 to help bolster the balance sheet. In 1989 income from operations was up 65 percent over 1988. By 1990 roughly 60 percent of Harnischfeger's sales and earnings stemmed from papermaking machinery. Beloit equipment was used in producing 70 percent of the world's newsprint and writing and printing grade papers, as well as half of the world's tissues, towels, and napkins. Replacement parts for these machines was a thriving business as well.

Harnischfeger had clearly weathered its storms. The company announced in 1990 that it was shopping for new acquisitions. That same year, the paper cycle began a cyclical downturn. While orders for papermaking machines dropped, a quarter of Beloit's paper-machine manufacturing had been sub-contracted in order to avoid the expense of expanding, so even with business decreasing, Beloit maintained presentable margins. Meanwhile, the Mining Equipment Division was still expanding, with sales of its massive electric-powered shovels growing nearly 20 percent in the first half of 1990. The poorest performing unit was still the material handling business, which supplied overhead cranes and hoists. Harnischfeger announced plans to buy a stake in Measurex Corporation in 1990, but not more than 20 percent due to a seven-year "standstill" agreement between the companies. A Cupertino, California company, Measurex makes industrial process-control systems, primarily for the paper industry. Beloit and Measurex entered a joint agreement on marketing, sales, and development.

William Goessel passed the reins to Jeffery T. Grade in 1991. Grade, then president, became CEO, and Goessel stayed on as chairman of the board. The paper slump continued and Beloit's paper machine orders suffered in 1992, hurt by industry overcapacity and a lingering global recession. Mining equipment sales were strong that year, while the material handling division had an increase in sales but a dip in operating profits. Stalled defense contracts hurt Syscon in 1992, but caused the company to broaden its commercial and federal agency business bases. Goessel retired as chairman in early 1993, and Grade became chairman and CEO.

Principal Subsidiaries: Beloit Corporation; Harnischfeger Corporation; Harnischfeger Engineers, Inc.; Syscon Corporation.

Further Reading:

"A Centennial History of the Harnischfeger Corporation," Milwaukee: Harnischfeger Industries, Inc., 1984.

"Back from the Brink," *Industry Week,* July 9, 1984, pp. 16–17.

Bettner, Jill, "Digging Out," *Forbes,* June 18, 1984, pp. 110–111.

Briggs, Jean, "Those Deadly Words—Too Soon," *Forbes,* October 27, 1980, p. 149.

Byrne, Harlan, "Harnischfeger Industries, Inc.," *Barron's* March 5, 1990, p. 53.

"Firm Plans to Buy Stake, Possibly 20%, of Measurex," *Wall Street Journal,* May 31, 1990, p. A4.

"From Old Tech to High-Tech," *Financial World,* November 14, 1984, p. 107.

Goodman, Jordan, "Scaling the Wall of Adversity," *Money,* May 1985, pp. 103–104.

"Harnischfeger Expects Lower Fiscal '93 Profit Than Analysts Predict," *Wall Street Journal,* January 14, 1993, p. B4.

"Harnischfeger Industries, Inc.," *New York Times,* May 24, 1991, p. C4.

"Harnischfeger Industries, Inc.," *Business Journal-Milwaukee,* February 13, 1993, p. 14.

"Harnischfeger Industries, Inc.," *Business Journal-Milwaukee,* March 9, 1992, p. 11.

"Harnischfeger Industries, Inc.," *Business Journal-Milwaukee,* March 5, 1990, p. 30.

Huber, Robert, "Do You Want to Cook Hamburgers?" *Production,* December 1988, pp. 34–39.

Jerenski, Laura, "The Naked Truth," *Forbes,* May 18, 1987, pp. 86–87.

Kirchen, Rich, "Goessel Continues to Turn on the Juice at Harnischfeger," *Business Journal-Milwaukee,* March 19, 1990, p. 13.

Lazo, Shirley, "Speaking of Dividends," *Barron's,* March 14, 1988, p. 79.

Lazo, Shirley, "Speaking of Dividends," *Barron's,* December 10, 1990, p. 64.

McFadden, Michael, "Prospering Merchants of Productivity," *Fortune,* December 10, 1984, p. 50.

"Measurex Corp.," *Insider's Chronicle,* July 30, 1990, p. 3.

"Measurex Corp.," *Wall Street Journal,* August 15, 1990, p. B2.

"Measurex Corp.," *Wall Street Journal,* October 15, 1990, p. A5.

"Stake in Measurex Increased to 14%," *New York Times,* August 28, 1990, p. D4.

Rose, Robert, "Laden with Cash, Harnischfeger Seeks Acquisition," *Wall Street Journal,* March 19, 1990, p. B3.

Rottenberg, Dan, "Adrenaline in the Rust Belt," *Business Month,* May 1990, p. 43.

Rudolph, Barbara, "Construction, Mining, Rail Equipment," *Forbes,* January 2, 1984, pp. 190–193.

"Supplier Companies," *Pulp & Paper,* December 1991, p. 129.

"13D Highlights," *Insider's Chronicle,* April 24, 1989, p. 2.

Wrubel, Robert, "Harnischfeger: Paper Profits," *Financial World,* June 26, 1990, p. 16.

—Carol I. Keeley

Harsco Corporation

P.O. Box 8888
Camp Hill, Pennsylvania 17011-8888
U.S.A.
(717) 763-7064
Fax: (717) 763-6424

Public Company
Incorporated: 1956
Employees: 10,500
Sales: $1.94 billion
Stock Exchanges: New York Boston Philadelphia Pacific
SICs: 3795 Tanks and Tank Components; 3711 Motor
    Vehicles & Car Bodies; 3443 Fabricated Plate Work,
    Boiler Shop; 3491 Industrial Valves; 3446 Architectural
    Metalwork; 3494 Valves and Pipe Fittings, Nec

Harsco Corporation was formed in 1956 as the result of a merger between Harrisburg Steel Corporation, Heckett Engineering Inc., and Precision Castings Co. Within the next three decades, through a series of acquisitions—which were integrated as company divisions and subsidiaries—as well as divestitures of unprofitable divisions and profitable joint ventures, Harsco grew into a multinational *Fortune* 500 company.

By the early 1990s Harsco was a diversified international company marketing 17 different types of products and services for defense, industrial, commercial, and construction applications. The company boasted nearly 270 manufacturing, reclamation, distribution, and service facilities located in 36 states in the United States and in 13 foreign nations.

The diversity of the markets served has enabled Harsco to withstand economic and political pressures that can affect revenues and profits. Recessions and slow economic times can alter demand for some of its products and services, and governmental budgets can affect demand for defense-related products. In general, any upturn in the domestic industrial and commercial sectors has a positive effect on most of the company's product lines. Additional revenue growth comes from international sales and acquisitions.

Harsco Corporation is structured into three main business groups, which are managed through more than 20 operating companies formed into 11 divisions. The groups are Industrial Services and Building Products, Engineered Products Group,

and Defense Group. Many of the divisions within these groups are domestic or international leaders in their specific markets.

The Industrial Services and Building Products Group includes three market-leading divisions, Heckett Engineering, Patent Scaffolding, and Reed Minerals. The group serves the worldwide steel industry through metal reclamation and specialized steel mill services; supplies scaffolding equipment to electric utilities; serves the construction industry with scaffolding, shoring, and concrete forming equipment and industrial plant maintenance; and serves the roofing shingle industry through the reclamation of coal slag and the manufacture of roofing granules and slag abrasives for construction and general industrial uses.

In the early 1990s the Industrial Services and Building Products Group accounted for 18 percent of the company's total revenues. The group is especially affected by ups and downs in the commercial construction industry, because it depends on the demand for infrastructure repair and rebuild projects, metal reclamation, and roofing granules. A weak construction market hit the Patent Scaffolding division during the recession of the late 1980s and early 1990s. As a result, three domestic branch offices were closed, two domestic offices were consolidated, and some foreign offices were shut down. At the same time, increased demand can come unexpectedly. The devastating Hurricane Andrew in Florida and harsh weather conditions in the South in 1992 spurred demand for roofing granules, as many homes needed to be rebuilt.

Harsco Corporation's Engineered Products Group consists of 18 operating units that provide domestic and international markets with various commercial, energy-related, and general industrial applications. Serving the transportation market are Fairmont Tamper, IKG Industries, and Structural Composite Industries. Providing for the gas containment and regulation segment of the energy industry are Taylor-Wharton Cylinders, Taylor-Wharton Cryogenics, Plant City Steel, and American Tank and Welding Co. Plant City Steel is an international leader in the production and distribution of containment products such as propane tanks, cryogenic vessels, and steel high pressure cylinders. American Welding and Tank Company is at the top of its market in the production and sale of domestic propane tanks.

Other divisions of the Engineered Products Group include the Patterson-Kelley division, which supplies heat transfer equipment for industrial applications. Astralloy provides steel for use in the mining, steel, pulp, and paper industries. Nutter Engineering makes equipment for the gas processing, refining, and chemical industries. Combat Engineering Ltd. supplies warmair heating systems. Pocono Fabricators makes special cement used for such purposes as lining steel tanks. Also part of the Engineered Products Group are Capitol Manufacturing, which serves the industrial, hardware, and oil industries, and Sherwood, which makes couplings and precision valves for industrial and commercial markets.

Like the Industrial Products Group, the Engineered Products Group is subject to slowdowns and upturns in the general industrial sector. Increased revenues come from higher appropriations for infrastructure repair and rebuild programs and any recovery in the natural gas industry. In the early 1990s this group accounted for 24 percent of the company's total sales.

The third and final group comprising Harsco Corporation is the Defense Group, which includes BMY Combat Systems and BMY-Wheeled Vehicles. BMY Combat Systems is a world leader in the design, manufacture, and support of such military products as howitzers, earthmovers, and recovery vehicles. BMY-Wheeled Vehicles is one of three armored tracked vehicle makers in the United States and a major supplier of wheeled vehicles for the U.S. military and its NATO (North Atlantic Treaty Organization) allies. The Defense Group contributes 48 percent of Harsco Corporation's total revenues. In fact, sales for 1992 set a record, but they came after sizeable lulls in 1988 and 1989, when the U.S. Pentagon slashed budgets as the cold war ended. In addition to sales to the U.S. Government, several foreign governments bought trucks, tank recovery vehicles, howitzers, ammunition carriers, and other defense equipment from Harsco.

Harsco's history dates back to between 1953 and 1955, when the Harrisburg Steel Company acquired Heckett Engineering—which became a division of Harsco's Industrial Products and Building Services Group—Taylor-Wharton, and Precision Castings Co., Harris's first three major acquisitions. Heckett Engineering Co. had been founded in 1939 by a Dutch immigrant, Eric Heckett, who installed the first successful large-scale metallic recovery plant in the United States at Republic Steel's South Chicago plant. The Heckett of the 1990s, a division of Harsco's, is a leader in slag processing and uses specialized equipment and technology to retrieve the greatest quantity of recoverable metallics from slag. The scrap is then refined and returned to make steel at large mills and mini-mill steel producers. Heckett also provides environmental services such as dust suppression, material handling activities, and total scrap handling and preparation.

Heckett's operations are divided into a North American business unit that operates at 40 locations in the U.S., Canada and Mexico and an International business unit that has operations in more than 20 locations in Europe, Asia, Africa, and the Far East. By the early 1990s Heckett was the Harsco's largest and most profitable non-defense business.

The original Harrisburg Steel Company also acquired Taylor-Wharton, which became the Harsco division and consisted of Taylor-Wharton Cryogenics and Taylor-Wharton Cylinders. Taylor-Wharton Cryogenics has facilities on three continents and manufactures cryogenic storage vessels. Taylor-Wharton Cylinders was originally founded in 1742 and is the oldest metalworking company in continuous operation in the nation. This division is the international market leader in high pressure cylinder production.

About a decade after the 1956 merger that created the Harsco Corporation, the company embarked on a high level of acquisition activity. In 1966 Harsco acquired the Irving Subway Grating Co., the first commercial steel grating company, founded in 1912. In the same year, Harsco acquired two other grating makers and formed them as the IKG Industries Division. In 1974 Patterson-Kelley Co. Inc. was merged with Harsco. Patterson-Kelley had begun operating in 1880 as a producer of

water heaters for commercial and industrial sites. The company was the first to develop fully packaged water heaters that could be easily installed with just a few connections.

Originally, Patterson-Kelley operations were part of the Taylor-Wharton Co. division, but in 1976 the Patterson-Kelley division was established. The division consists of six operating units that make water heaters and other equipment for the chemical processing industry. One of its units, Air-x-changers is a leading international supplier of air-cooled heat exchangers. This division is especially sensitive to conditions in the natural gas processing and petrochemical industries. Slowdowns in these industries can depress demand for Patterson-Kelley's products.

Continuing its acquisitions, in 1982 Harsco bought Astralloy-Vulcan Corp., a world leader in the supply and fabrication of high-strength and wear-resistant steels used in the mining, steel, and pulp and paper industries. The following year the company acquired Structural Composites Industries, Inc., the world's largest manufacturer of compressed gas composite cylinders and Super Tanks. Structural Composites Industries makes compressed gas composite cylinders used in self-contained breathing apparatus used by firefighters, coal miners, and rescue workers; manufactures gas storage equipment used for the inflation of aircraft escape slides, life rafts, and helicopter flotation bags; makes oxygen storage equipment for aircraft, home therapy, and hospitals as well as energy storage equipment for military systems.

In 1983 Harsco acquired Reed Materials Inc., which was the first company in the United States to convert utility coal slag into granules for asphalt roofing shingles. Reed Materials, operating at 15 facilities in 12 states, is also one of the major sources for slag blasting abrasives for industrial surface preparation. In addition, it is the first U.S. granule supplier to provide artificially colored slag granules for manufactuers' use on the exposed surface area of an asphalt shingle. Reed Minerals' blasting abrasives made from utility slag provide a lower health risk to workers because they have a lower free silica content than sand.

In 1986 Harsco acquired Easco Corp. and merged Easco's operations with IKG Industries Division. In the same year, Borden Metal Products Co. was bought and also folded into the IKG Industries Division. The division is the world's largest producer of bar grating for various commercial, industrial, building, and transportation-related applications. IKG Industries markets its products under three trade names, IKG Borden, manufacturing steel, aluminum, and fiberglass gratings; IKG Greulich, which makes bridge flooring systems; and IKG Deck Span, a producer of safety grating.

The IKG division is affected by economic conditions in the industrial, construction, and energy markets at home and abroad. Poor economic conditions lowered demand for the division's products. As a result of slow sales in the late 1980s and early 1990s, one plant was shut down in 1993.

Other activity in the 1980s and early 1990s included the 1986 sale of the Broderick Division to Broderick Co. In 1989 Harsco acquired certain assets of Railway Maintenance Product Division and created Heckett Technology Services Inc. as a wholly owned subsidiary.

From 1989 to 1990 the Harsco's Defense Group was able to stem some of its losses due to Pentagon cutbacks by supplying equipment to the U.S. Army and foreign nations. In 1989 the U.S. Army chose to purchase the M88A1E1 made by BMY-Combat Systems. The vehicle is a 139,000-pound updated version of the company's M88 recovery vehicle that aids disabled tanks on the battlefield. With new tanks weighing 70 tons, a strong recovery vehicle is needed to tow the tanks to safety, when they are rendered inoperable in the midst of battle. In 1990 BMY-Combat Systems was awarded a contract to supply howitzers to South Korea. The Persian Gulf War of 1990 also helped to spur sales for "Big Foot," a five-ton truck whose tires partially deflate for sand travel.

Acquisition and divestiture activity also continued. In 1990 Harsco acquired Universal Granule Inc. and formed another wholly owned subsidiary, Heckett Yugoslavia Ltd. The following year, Harsco sold its unprofitable CanTex division to a subsidiary of Sumitomo Corp. and in 1992 sold its hydraulic tools product line to a subsidiary of Textron, Inc.

Also that year, Harsco acquired the Tamper business of Canron Inc. of Toronto for its Engineered Products Group. This company was a wholly owned subsidiary of Ivaco, Inc., of Montreal, but its U.S. headquarters was in South Carolina, where railway maintenance-of-way equipment for the domestic and international railroad industry is made. Tamper's other facilities were located in Australia and the United Kingdom, where it is known as Permaquip, and in India. Harsco integrated Tamper's operations into its Fairmont Railway Motor Division and renamed it Fairmont Tamper. Tamper, the company's third most profitable unit in the early 1990s, was expected to bring to Harsco its expertise in handling concrete ties, which are the standard in Europe as well as in U.S. passenger rail lines.

In 1992 Harsco announced that it was combining its defense business with FMC Corporation. The BMY-Combat Systems Division and FMC's Defense Systems Group would be jointly owned with FMC holding a controlling interest of 60 percent. According to Malcolm W. Gambill, chairman and chief executive officer of Harsco, "In an era of shrinking defense budgets, this combination will remove unneeded higher cost capacity, while combining lower cost capacity with advanced integrated systems technology and logistical capabilities for our customers in stronger, consolidated organization. We see this partnership as a very positive way to address the changes that are occurring in the defense industry and are highly optimistic about its prospects."

The joint venture was part of the defense industry trend toward consolidation as a result of lower spending on defense on the part of the Pentagon. The new company would hold strong positions both in the United States and internationally in the sales of tracked combat vehicles, artillery systems, recovery vehicles, armored gun systems, and combat earthmovers. The joint venture was contracted to build the U.S. Army's Multiple Launch Rocket System carrier and the Navy's Vertical Launch Systems in addition to a range of naval guns, artillery systems, and tracked vehicles such as the Bradley Fighting Vehicle.

Harsco's acquisition activity continued in the early 1990s. In 1993 the company acquired a majority equity position in INFLEX, S.A., a manufacturer of steel cylinders for permanent and liquefied gases. INFLEX, based in Buenos Aires, Argentina, has a production facility in San Luis. Gambill commented, "The acquisition of INFLEX, S.A. strengthens Harsco's Gas Containment division by extending our global reach into South America. Our goal is to become the world leader in the near-term in the gas containment market, and INFLEX strategically positions us for further domestic and international growth."

Also in 1993 Harsco bought the assets of Wayne Corp., a manufacturer of school buses. Production was transferred to the BMY-WVD facility in Marysville, Ohio. This was a defense conversion effort so that the skills and capabilities of the work force as well as plant facilities could be used if defense work lessened.

Throughout its history, Harsco Corporation has been able to adjust to varying economic and political conditions. In addition to exploring new markets globally, adding to its assets with acquisitions, and divesting itself of units with disappointing sales, the Harsco of the early 1990s had the goal of developing new proprietary products and services.

Principal Subsidiaries: Heckett Technology Services Inc.; Heckett Yugoslavia Ltd.

Further Reading:

"Briefs," *New York Times,* September 27, 1991, D3; September 25, 1992, p. D3.
"Business Brief," *Wall Street Journal,* January 7, 1993, p. B4.
Colodny, Mark M., "Frank Carlucci Goes Hunting," *Fortune,* February 25, 1991, p. 155.
"Company Briefs," *New York Times,* July 11, 1990, p. D3.
"FMC and Harsco Are Planning to Merge Most Operations in the Defense Sector," *Wall Street Journal,* December 3, 1992, p. A5.
Harsco Corporation Annual Report, Camp Hill, PA: Harsco Corporation, 1992.
Johnston, Phil W., "Clunk, Clang, Clatter," *Popular Science,* May 1989, p. 56.
"News Briefs," *Aviation Week & Space Technology,* December 7, 1992, p. 19.
"A Profile of Harsco Corporation," Camp Hill, PA: Harsco Corporation.
"A Sleeping Beauty With a Suitor," *Business Week,* November 19, 1990, p. 128.

—Dorothy Kroll

Hartmarx Corporation

101 North Wacker Drive
Chicago, Illinois 60606
U.S.A.
(312) 372-6300
Fax: (312) 444-2695

Public Company
Incorporated: May 10, 1911, as Hart, Schaffner & Marx
Employees: 20,000
Sales: $1.05 billion
Stock Exchanges: New York, Chicago
SICs: 2311 Men's/Boys' Suits & Coats; 2337 Women's/
    Misses' Suits & Coats; 2325 Men's/Boys' Trousers &
    Slacks; 6719 Holding Companies Nec

Hartmarx is the parent company of Hart, Schaffner & Marx, a well-known apparel manufacturer, and several other clothing companies. The company's primary line of business is designing, assembling, and marketing premium quality suits for men and women. The company also manufactures and sells sportswear and has begun licensing its products for manufacture in new growth markets in Asia. Until recently, Hartmarx was also a major retail company, maintaining a massive network of clothing shops located mostly in shopping malls. The operation was growing considerably burdensome in recent years, serving only to sap the company's profits from manufacturing. In 1992 Hartmarx divested all of its retail operations, with the exception of those belonging to its Kuppenheimer discount division.

The history of Hartmarx was largely noneventful until the 1960s, when wise merchandising decisions brought the venerable Hart, Schaffner & Marx name to a broader market. This was followed by strong internal growth in the 1970s, and an initially successful acquisition campaign in the 1980s. But by 1990 the once profitable company was deeply in debt and losing money. In response, Hartmarx's management began a massive restructuring of the business that may take years to turn the company around. The success of the campaign is likely to determine whether Hartmarx survives.

Hartmarx traces its history to 1872 when, immediately after the great Chicago Fire, brothers Harry and Max Hart pooled their life savings of $2,700 and opened a small men's clothing store on Chicago's State Street. "Harry Hart and Brother" opened a second store a few blocks south in 1875. Max Hart became

fascinated with labelling after working as a delivery boy for his father's butcher shop. His job, applying labels to delivery packages, taught him the importance of branded products. At the clothing store, he pursued this interest by asking tailors to affix Hart brand labels to the clothes they sold. A short time later, a downstate Illinois merchant expressed an interest in the label and asked to sell Hart suits.

In 1879 the Harts' brothers-in-law, Levi Abt and Marcus Marx, joined the partnership, which was renamed "Hart, Abt and Marx." The small shop continued to prosper on sales to businessmen in Chicago's Loop financial district.

At the same time, however, the wholesale business began to grow, overtaking the retail operations. On the strength of wholesale production, Hart Abt and Marx won contracts to produce clothing for the United States military. This introduced the partners to prefabricated off-the-rack clothing, and marked their entry into the ready-made suit trade.

Marx and Abt left the business in 1887. However, a cousin named Joseph Schaffner took their place. Schaffner was an excellent businessman who oversaw much of the early growth of the small firm, which had been renamed Hart, Schaffner & Marx.

The industrial revolution added newer, more efficient tailoring methods that reduced the time to make a suit. With such favorable economics, many suit manufacturers entered the catalog business, introducing their own brands. Hart, Schaffner & Marx responded in 1897 by running national advertisements for its products and began selling off-the-rack suits through a variety of distributors. Hart, Schaffner & Marx commissioned well-known illustrators to paint pictures for style books and retail posters. These ads portrayed the company's latest fashions in rich surroundings, establishing Hart, Schaffner & Marx as a premium brand.

By 1906 the company had branched into unusual sizes for men who were unusually tall, short, or overweight. Hart, Schaffner & Marx thus became a mass-market brand, enabling virtually any man to have a fine quality suit at a lower price than a custom tailored suit. On May 10, 1911, after years of steady growth, the partnership was incorporated.

In 1917 the company introduced the first tropical worsted suits. Hart, Schaffner & Marx's production facilities were also pressed into service during World War I making uniforms.

While it operated a number of small retail outlets of its own in 1926, the company expanded its retail presence considerably with the acquisition of Wallach's, a large clothing chain. Hart, Schaffner & Marx continued its expansion over the next 30 years by taking over the operations of numerous other smaller retailers, opening new stores, and placing a strong emphasis on advertising.

After producing a large quantity of uniforms for the government again during World War II, Hart, Schaffner & Marx began making bolder acquisitions. In 1954 the company took over Society Brand, a major manufacturing house. Ten years later Hart, Schaffner & Marx added Hickey-Freeman, a premium brand. The company acquired Jaymar-Ruby in 1967 and, in

1969, added M. Wile. In fact, Hart, Schaffner & Marx made so many acquisitions between 1966 and 1969, that the U.S. Justice Department became involved. The government filed suit against the company on anti-trust grounds, complaining that Hart, Schaffner & Marx had established an anti-competitive domination of the clothing market. The company settled with Justice Department lawyers by signing a consent decree in which Hart, Schaffner & Marx was obliged to sell off several recent acquisitions and promised to purchase no more companies for a period of 10 years. This agreement took effect in June of 1970.

The consent decree was not a serious setback for Hart, Schaffner & Marx. Instead of external growth, the company merely changed its emphasis to internal growth. This was actually a better strategy because the company had launched several successful lines during the 1960s that required attention.

One night in 1966, television host Johnny Carson walked on stage to deliver his nightly *Tonight Show* monologue wearing a turtle neck sweater and a collarless Nehru jacket. Within a week the nation's stores had been depleted of both items, and Carson had unwittingly established himself as a fashion trend setter. Celebrity endorsements were not new, but the episode demonstrated to many the value of using stars to introduce new styles. The idea was not lost upon Hart, Schaffner & Marx, which got an agreement to market a new casual line of suits under the Johnny Carson name and, later, Jack Nicklaus's name.

Hart, Schaffner & Marx introduced the Austin Reed brand name during the 1960s. In 1974 the company rolled out a line of tailored clothing under the Christian Dior name, followed by Nino Cerruti, Allyn St. George, and Playboy. These new lines were created under contract to their designer namesakes and proved highly successful as fashion leaders.

Also in 1974, as part of its divestiture, Hart, Schaffner & Marx sold 20 stores to Hughes & Hatcher, a rival chain of shopping mall clothing stores. In September of 1979, nearly a year before the expiration of the consent decree, Hart, Schaffner & Marx acquired Intercontinental Apparel under special agreement for $2.9 million. Intercontinental was the U.S. licensee of the Pierre Cardin line and brand name. With strong brand names and a wide variety of styles available, Hart, Schaffner & Marx had built a very solid position in the market.

When the terms of the consent decree expired in June of 1980, Hart, Schaffner & Marx, with 275 retail outlets, immediately embarked on an acquisition binge. The company took over Bishop's men shops in September of 1980 and branched into women's clothing by taking over the Country Miss chain for $12.5 million in January, 1981.

While Hart, Schaffner & Marx had registered strong gains of six percent annually, the market was growing at twice that rate. Despite the strength of its Hickey-Freeman and Christian Dior lines, the company was being ravaged by discount brands, which had become especially popular during the recessions of the 1970s. The company's own Playboy line flopped because "men didn't want bunnies on their buttons," and may have regarded the logo as tired and pretentious.

Thus, on December 1, 1982, after losing out significantly to discount brands, Hart, Schaffner & Marx acquired the Kuppenheimer Manufacturing Company for $25.8 million. Kuppenheimer, a major factory retail operation with 41 outlets, dominated the market of inexpensive suits, defined as those costing $200 or less, and had been a strong competitor of Hart, Schaffner & Marx. The acquisition gave Hart, Schaffner & Marx a greater piece of the $4 billion suit market, 80 percent of which is controlled by discount brands such as Kuppenheimer. It also enabled the company to avoid diluting its premium brands with the lower scale Kuppenheimer line.

The company acquired Briar Neckwear in July, 1985 and, in December of 1986, acquired the casual suit jacket manufacturer H. Ortisky. The following year Hart, Schaffner & Marx took over the nine-store Detroit retail chain Anton's, and in 1988 purchased Boyd's, a small retail chain in St. Louis, and the Washington, D.C.-based upscale retailer Raleigh's. In February of 1989 the company also added the Biltwell Company, a clothing manufacturer.

Along with the strong external expansion carried out during the 1980s, Hart, Schaffner & Marx carried out a large modernization campaign aimed at updating equipment and processes. The company also underwent a profound restructuring. The business of Hart, Schaffner & Marx had grown so large that the flagship company in the organization was unable to run it efficiently. In effect, Hart, Schaffner & Marx had become an enterprise consisting of more than a dozen separate little companies, each with its own administrative structure. In order to better coordinate the activities of these independent little operations, the company decided to create a new parent organization.

In keeping with voguish corporate names such as Navistar, Unisys, Ameritech, and Primerica, a team of senior executives led by John R. Meinert settled upon the truncated name Hartmarx, which allowed the company to preserve the exclusivity of its Hart, Schaffner & Marx name. When the name change was made official on April 13, 1983, the new holding company took possession of Hart, Schaffner & Marx and its numerous subsidiary companies. Along with the creation of Hartmarx came a reorganization plan aimed at eliminating 23 redundant administrative functions within the company (eliminating 800 jobs) and a campaign to redecorate the Kuppenheimer outlets. These efforts, which ate up more than $41 million in earnings by 1987, went $10 million over budget and yielded far less than the projected $12 million annual savings.

Amid this crisis, on October 27, 1986, Hartmarx's chair and chief executive officer Richard P. Hamilton resigned suddenly and without official explanation. The company was stunned by Hamilton's immediate departure and, while it offered no explanations of its own, analysts speculated that Hamilton's disagreements over the company's strategy compelled him to leave.

He was replaced by a troika consisting of Meinert, Harvey Weinberg, a former head of the retailing group, and Elbert Hand, who headed the company's manufacturing group. The new leadership team pressed ahead with the consolidation effort, centralizing purchasing, payroll, credit, and distribution at offices in Chicago, Dallas, and Columbus, Ohio. Having increased operating efficiency, the company now had only to increase its sales volume.

Meanwhile, Hartmarx struggled to expand Kuppenheimer and began advertising promotions with a fictional "Mr. Kuppenheimer" character. The timing could not have been worse. As the nation emerged from the 1982–85 recession, consumers' tastes went back to more expensive name brands. Despite Kuppenheimer's facelift, men avoided the stores.

Generally, however, sales from all 440 of the company's retail outlets were up, largely due to the success of the conservatively tailored Hickey-Freeman and Hart, Schaffner & Marx lines, as well as new brands such as Racquet Club and Henry Grethel, which Hartmarx purchased from Manhattan Industries. This enabled the company to obtain and service financing necessary to acquire the companies it had. But, while the balance sheet remained strong, debt remained high. When sales began to lag, profits fell quickly. By 1990 impatient investors had begun to abandon Hartmarx, beating its share price to 18, about half of what it had been only three years earlier.

Weinberg attempted to stem losses by bringing on John Eyler, a former CEO of Kohl's Main Street chain. Eyler recommended price decreases on several high-end suit lines and pressed for greater utilization of the computer network. In 1991 Hartmarx borrowed the superstore ploy from The Limited, opening as many as three retail stores in a single, larger space. This brought down rent fees and allowed the company to run a single back office. Still, Hartmarx proved unable to take advantage of the economies it had set up. The manufacturing and licensing operations remained strong, but the retail business incurred heavy losses. In January 1992 the company suspended dividends for the first time in 53 years.

Faced with a fifth consecutive year of lowered returns, Hartmarx finally took action on September 18, 1992. On that day, the company announced that it had sold its HSSI retail stores subsidiary for $43 million, basically exiting the retail store business. However, the Kuppenheimer operation, with its 120 retail operations, remained intact. Then, on September 21, the company announced the issue of $30 million in new shares to raise cash, and on October 10 announced the closure of its Old Mill/Country Miss outlet stores. Hartmarx also began negotiations with its creditors to gain more favorable terms on its outstanding obligations.

The $30 million capital infusion came from a single company called Traco International N.V., controlled by Saudi businessman Abdullah Taha Bakhsh. Traco (the name is a conglomeration of "trading and construction") thus emerged with a 22 percent stake in Hartmarx. While little is known about Bakhsh or his company, Hartmarx directors voiced concern over his motives but were content that he had helped the company avoid bankruptcy. An additional 21.4 percent of Hartmarx shares were controlled by Taiba Corporation, owned by Abdel Mohsen Y Abu Shukhaiden, another Middle Eastern businessman about whom little is known. Taiba authorized Traco to vote its shares, giving that company nearly 44 percent voting rights.

Now just a marketing and manufacturing company, Hartmarx counted on high cash flow from these profitable businesses to offset investor concern with its high debt. Strategically, the company also refocused its business on apparel other than suits, and made bold plans to expand its promising sportswear (mainly golfwear) lines. The decision to exit the retail business was necessary and long overdue. As long as Hartmarx was in the retail business, it could not sell its products to hundreds of other retailers. In effect, it was in competition with potential customers.

Several more operations were sold off, including the company's 14 Sansabelt outlets and its 37.5 percent interest in Robert's, a retail chain in Mexico City. The remaining task was to protect and ensure viable identities for each of its brands; venerable Hartmarx brands could not be sold at thrift department stores.

Hartmarx thus emerged from a very difficult period properly structured, but not yet out of the woods. Its ability to recover from its debt crisis will most likely depend on a wider economic upswing that will return consumers to stores and an aggressive advertising campaign that will boost sales of Hartmarx brands.

Principal Subsidiaries: Hart Schaffner & Marx, Inc.; Intercontinental Branded Apparel, Inc.; Universal Design Group, Inc.; Henry Grethel Apparel, Inc.; Hickey-Freeman Clothes, Inc.; Bobby Jones International, Inc.; Trans-Apparel Group, Inc.; Biltwell Company; Karl Lagerfeld Company; The Kuppenheimer Company; Barrie Pace Catalog; International Women's Apparel, Inc.

Further Reading:

Hartmarx Annual Reports, Chicago: Hartmarx Corporation, 1986, 1992.
"Hartmarx: Cashing in on Discount Suits Without Losing Its Upscale Image," *Business Week,* May 14, 1984, p. 200.
"Hartmarx Corp.," *Moody's Industrial Manual,* 1992.
"Hartmarx Is Suddenly Looking Threadbare," *Business Week,* January 29, 1990, p. 40.
"Hartmarx: Restoring the Specialty Group," *Daily News Record,* February 11, 1991, pp. 10–11.
"Hartmarx Unveils Its Game Plan," *Daily News Record,* October 15, 1992, pp. 1–5.
"Hart, Schaffner & Marx: Suiting up for the Eighties," *Duns' Business Review,* September 1, 1980, pp. 20–21.
"Hart, Schaffner & Marx: Expanding Boldly from Class to Mass Markets," *Business Week,* October 20, 1980, pp.74–75.
"Has Anyone Seen this Man?" *Chicago Tribune,* April 16, 1993, sec. 3, p. 3.
"How Hartmarx Plans to Recapture its Youth," *Adweek's Marketing Week,* May 1, 1989, pp. 34–38.
"A New Cut for the Gray Flannel," *Forbes,* December 28, 1987, pp. 61–64.
"A Retailored Hartmarx Still Needs Some Altering," *Business Week,* March 9, 1987, p. 109.
"Tailored Growth," *Barron's,* December 4, 1984, pp. 55–56.
"Whole Cloth," *Barron's,* April 4, 1983, p. 59.

—John Simley

HAWORTH

Haworth Inc.

1 Haworth Ctr.
Holland, Michigan 49423
U.S.A.
(616) 393-3000
Fax: (616) 393-1570

Private Company
Founded: 1948
Employees: 5,000
Sales: $650 million
SICs: 2541 Wood Partitions & Fixtures; 2542 Partitions &
    Fixtures Except Wood; 2522 Office Furniture Except
    Wood

Haworth Inc. is the third largest manufacturer of office furniture in the United States, after Steelcase Inc. and Herman Miller, Inc. Named as one of the 100 Best Companies to Work For in 1992, the western Michigan-based company considers itself quality conscious and, above all, dedicated to its customers. Haworth is privately held by members of the Haworth family, and, competing in the $7 billion a year office furniture industry, the company has distinguished itself as a strong presence in the international market.

Haworth began as a hobby for its founder, Gerrard W. Haworth, a graduate of Western Michigan University and the University of Michigan, who began teaching industrial arts in a Holland, Michigan, high school in 1938. Hoping to eventually help finance college educations for his children, Haworth sought to supplement his income by beginning a part-time woodworking business out of his garage. Over the next ten years, his craftsmanship was recognized, and the number of orders he received for wood products grew.

Hoping to turn his passion for woodworking into a full-time profession, Haworth approached a local bank for a loan in 1948. However, having had no prior business experience, he was rejected as too great a risk. Undaunted, Haworth mortgaged his home and accepted a $10,000 loan from his father, and, once obtaining the money he needed to begin business, he quit his teaching position, purchased secondhand shop equipment, and founded Modern Products. During its first two years, the company employed six woodworkers at a small plant in Holland and received orders for a wide variety of products, but in 1951

Modern Products won a contract that would determine the course of its business.

That year Haworth was approached by an architect who had designed an office partition to be used at the new United Auto Workers union headquarters in Detroit. Haworth accepted the job of producing the partitions, and set about planning the prototype. Referred to as a "bank partition," the product measured 66 inches high, consisting of 43 inches of wood and 12 inches at the top made of glass. The pre-built partitions were well received at the UAW headquarters, and, speculating that other companies might also be interested in them, Haworth decided to focus his business on their production.

Business boomed over the next ten years, growing 30 to 40 percent annually, sometimes more, and in 1959 Modern Products became a national manufacturing concern. In 1961 the company moved to larger facilities, and during this time, Haworth's teenage son Richard began working at Modern Products, sweeping floors and operating some of the machinery. In 1964, having graduated from Western Michigan University with a Bachelor's degree in business, Richard became an assistant sales manager at Modern Products, working at a plant in his hometown of Holland. Within two years he was promoted to vice president for research and development, but was soon obliged to leave the company for service in the U.S. Army. When Richard returned to Modern Products in 1969, his father relied on him to help develop a new type of office furniture product.

During the 1960s, competitor Herman Miller, Inc. of Zeeland, Michigan, had introduces the innovative Action Office System, consisting of movable panels, shelves, cabinets, and desktops that could be rearranged to create workstations and open spaces to accommodate a variety of floorplans. Richard countered with the development of a unique moveable panel insulated with carpeting in order to reduce noise and help ensure privacy. Modern Products began manufacturing these new panels in 1971, and the following year the company's sales were estimated at $6 million.

Over the next few years Richard Haworth became increasingly interested in panel design. Christopher Palmeri, in an article in *Forbes,* stated that Richard's colleagues remembered him "anonymously visiting competitors' showrooms and taking their furniture apart" in order to learn more about panel construction. During this time he devised a method of installing electrical wiring inside panels that would exert a tremendous influence on the industry. Modern Products's prewired panels, introduced and patented by Richard Haworth in 1975, could be easily snapped together and eliminated the client's need to pay extra for electricians to wire office spaces. The new line of these panels, called Uni-Group, was a huge success, and that year sales increased sharply to around $10 million, while the number of people employed at Modern Products grew to 136.

Also that year the name of the company was changed to Haworth, Inc., and a new corporate headquarters was established in Holland. In 1976 G. W. Haworth stepped aside, becoming chairperson and naming his son president. Richard Haworth oversaw years of phenomenal growth at Haworth Inc. Not only did the office systems and furniture industry as a whole become more profitable in the 1980s, but Haworth consistently grew at a rate more than two times the industry average. In 1980 Haworth set up a European division after reportedly spending nearly $30 million to acquire West German chair manufacturing company Comforto GmbH. By 1986 Haworth had become the country's third largest office furniture manufacturer; its sales exceeded $300 million, and its staff of 2,600 was producing office chairs, filing cabinets, and fabrics, in addition to the popular panels. Three years later, the company opened a showroom in London and estimated that nearly ten percent of its sales were generated in foreign countries.

During its expansion, Haworth became involved in a legal dispute with industry giant Steelcase Inc., which would last nearly five years. Steelcase had begun marketing a panel similar to Haworth's pre-wired panel in the late 1970s. Claiming that Steelcase had infringed on his patent, Richard Haworth sought compensation from the company in the early 1980s. Steelcase argued, however, that their pre-wired systems were developed by their own staff and brought into question Haworth's right to the patent. So in November 1985 Haworth filed a civil lawsuit against Steelcase. The case was tried in a Michigan court, and in May 1988 a U.S. District Court judge ruled in favor of Steelcase. However, in January 1989, the decision was overturned by the U.S. Court of Appeals, which found several errors in the Michigan court's interpretation of the case and ruled that Haworth's rights as patent holder had been infringed upon. Steelcase was subsequently refused an appeal to the U.S. Supreme Court, and analysts have speculated that Haworth may have won over $100 million from the company. Richard Haworth filed a similar suit against Herman Miller Inc. in 1992, declaring in *Forbes* that although litigation leads to bad will between the companies, "we believe we have to protect what we invest in."

The late 1980s were a difficult time for the office systems industry. Aggressive discounting and the increased sale of used office equipment led to a "shakeout" of the industry's smaller companies and to decreased earnings for Steelcase, Herman Miller, and Haworth. Nevertheless, Haworth continued to gain market share, and in 1990 it purchased the Mueller Furniture Company, a Holland-based manufacturer of wooden tables and chairs. In December of that year *Industry Week* magazine compared Haworth to an "overachieving younger sibling, who's content not just to catch up, but to overtake big brother's lead."

During this time, Haworth's unique corporate philosophy attracted attention in the business community. Referring to employees as "members," Haworth espoused a participative management style, in which all members were required to spend one hour per week brainstorming ways in which Haworth could better serve the customer. During busy periods, the company paid members overtime for this one-hour commitment. Characterizing its approach as "customer-driven," Haworth produced a creed for its members that, in the words of Richard Haworth,

"put profit last on purpose because we believe profits are a result of doing the right thing, focusing on quality, our customers, and giving our employees freedom to do what's right."

In response to customer needs for a more open, interactive workspace than the panelled workstations provided, Haworth introduced new products in the 1990s. Conference tables were developed that could be easily rearranged to form circles, U-shapes, or individual tables, as were panels of lower heights made of transparent materials. Furthermore, Haworth made available adjustable-height work surfaces. The Trakker adjustable table, for example, contained a computer memory that could be programmed to adjust the table to as many as 19 different heights. The computer could be set to periodically remind users to adjust the table in order to lessen their chances of stress injuries.

Haworth's vision for the 1990s included ambitious plans to increase its presence in the international market. In 1992 the company estimated that 22 percent of its revenues were generated in foreign countries, and, through a series of acquisitions and investments, it hoped to increase that figure to 50 percent by the year 2000. Haworth's overseas companies remained locally managed, a practice that American management believes will help Haworth establish better relations globally. In 1993 Haworth became the first American company in its field to achieve ISO certification, having met the rigorous standards set by International Organization for Standards, in Geneva, Switzerland, established as a world-class business quality system.

Principal Subsidiaries: Comforto GmbH (Germany); Mueller Furniture Company; Lunstead, Inc.; Kinetics, Inc.; Ordo S.A. (France).

Further Reading:

Benson, Tracy E., "America's Unsung Heroes," *Industry Week,* December 3, 1990, pp. 12–22.
Crawley, Nancy, "Haworth, No. 3, 'Tries Harder'," *Grand Rapids Press,* October 12, 1986.
——, "Reuther Order Gave Haworth His Start," *Grand Rapids Press,* October 12, 1986.
Geran, Monica, "Haworth in Chicago," *Interior Design,* January 1988, pp. 223–24.
"Haworth's International Initiative," *Industry Week,* February 15, 1993, p. 26.
McClenahen, John S., "Global Citizen: Commitment to People and Community," *Industry Week,* January 4, 1993, pp. 31, 34.
Palmeri, Christopher, "Smart Boy," *Forbes,* May 11, 1992, p. 146.
Radigan, Mary, "Haworth Recalls Years of Growth for WMU Club," *Grand Rapids Press,* February 24, 1993.
Schrodt, Anita, "Material Handling Innovations Showcased: Mich. Furniture Manufacturer is Customer-Driven Company," *Journal of Commerce,* February 23, 1989.
Sullivan, Elizabeth, "G. W. Haworth: Inside Track," *Grand Rapids Business Journal,* March 29, 1993.

—Tina Grant

Helene Curtis Industries, Inc.

325 N. Wells Street
Chicago, Illinois 60610-4791
U.S.A.
(312) 661-0222
Fax: (312) 661-2250

Public Company
Incorporated: 1927 as the National Mineral Company
Employees: 3,200
Sales: $1.17 billion
Stock Exchanges: New York
SICs: 2844 Toilet Preparations

Helene Curtis Industries, Inc. manufactures and markets personal care products, primarily shampoo, hand and body lotions, and deodorants and anti-perspirants. Shampoo constitutes Helene Curtis' primary strength—the company is the second leading shampoo producer after Procter & Gamble. Helene Curtis continues to be run by the original founding family, and, while remaining a moderately sized company, still commands major shares of its markets, making it one of the fastest growing companies in the multi-billion dollar personal care industry.

Helene Curtis was founded in Chicago in 1927 as the National Mineral Company by Gerald Gidwitz and Louis Stein. The company started out manufacturing just one product, the Peach Bloom Facial Mask. Made of special clay mined in the hills of Arkansas, the facial mud packs were packaged and sold to beauty salons nationwide. At a time when personal care products were becoming increasingly more sophisticated, Gidwitz and Stein recognized that their sole product could not sustain the company with its limited market. The partners soon shifted the company's emphasis to hair care products, beginning a long history of producing successful, innovative personal care products.

The Depression years, ironically, turned out to be among the company's most successful. As the straight hairstyles of the 1920s gave way to a rage for waves, Gidwitz sensed opportunity in hair care. At the time cumbersome electric waving machines took hours to wave hair and were extremely expensive for beauticians to purchase. Thus, such hair care was usually only available to the well-off. This changed when researchers at the National Mineral Company developed ''machineless'' waving pads and designed a machine that could mass produce them. The pads created a revolution in the hair

care industry, drastically simplifying the permanent wave process, and consequently allowing people to have professional beauty care at an affordable price.

Gidwitz determined that there was another aspect of hair care that could provide an opportunity for the company. Until that time most people washed their hair with laundry or plain soap, since the products available specifically for use on hair were harsh and overpriced. The company developed Lanolin Creme Shampoo, one of the nation's first detergent-based shampoos, introduced in the mid-1930s. The popularity of the shampoo, available only in beauty salons, prompted National Mineral Company to follow it up with Suave Hairdressing in 1937. The demand for the hair tonic became so great, the company began manufacturing small retail sizes for salon resale.

Turning its attention to wartime production during World War II, the company's name changed to National Industries, Inc., and factories were converted to manufacture aircraft gun turrets, electric motors, radar equipment, and motion picture sound projectors for the military. The company also maintained its presence in the hair care industry with the introduction of Empress, a further innovation for permanent waves. A revolutionary non-toxic chemical perm, Empress utilized a cream oil solution wrapped on wooden rods. National Industries also branched off into the manufacture of hairdryers and other professional beauty supplies. Gerald Gidwitz, in the meantime, became president and CEO during the war years.

After the war National Industries shifted its focus back to the manufacture of personal care products. The renewed emphasis on this industry prompted a name change, and the company became Helene Curtis after Louis Stein's wife and son. It was at this time that Suave Hairdressing and Lanolin Creme Shampoo were introduced for retail sale in department and drugstores, and quickly began outselling the competition. In 1948, reflecting the company's growth, Helene Curtis moved to a new corporate headquarters and manufacturing facility.

In 1950 Helene Curtis developed the generic term hair spray for its new aerosol product, Spray Net. Other successful, and effective, products introduced during the 1950s included the spray-on deodorant Stopette and a non-prescription dandruff shampoo called Enden. These two products were advertised on television during such shows as *What's My Line?* and *Oh! Susanna,* helping to make Stopette the best selling deodorant on the market, a position it maintained for a number of years.

In addition, the company expanded its product line with several acquisitions, including Kings Men male toiletries, Lentheric fragrances, and Studio Girl cosmetics. By the mid-1950s Helene Curtis products were being manufactured and sold in 25 countries. Another milestone occurred in 1956 when Helene Curtis went public after 32 years of private ownership, selling 375,000 shares of Class A stock for ten dollars a share.

Helene Curtis further broadened its line of personal care products in 1960, when Tender Touch, the first popularly-priced bath oil, was marketed. In addition the company began to build on the success of its Suave brand, introducing shampoos, creme rinses, and wave sets. Other innovative products launched during the 1960s were Quik-Care hair conditioner, the synthetic hair oil First Time, and Secure, a pressed, powder-dry deodorant with a patented formula.

In 1961 Helene Curtis's stock was accepted on the New York Stock Exchange, and by the middle of the decade the company had licensed its products in 81 countries. Capitalizing on a consumer hair trend, the Professional Division of Helene Curtis launched the Wigette line of small hairpieces made of human hair, as well synthetic versions under the Nature Blend brand name.

The 1970s saw Helene Curtis making further advances in permanents. UniPerm became the first compact machine to give perfect permanent waves, while the Professional Division introduced Moisture Quotient and the One Better permanent—the first perm to combine the advantages of alkaline waving and conditioning. In addition, a shampoo called Everynight, designed for frequent use and targeted at teens, was exclusively advertised by tennis star Chris Evert. In the meantime the Suave brand, which had sold its billionth bottle, expanded its selection of fragrances and formulas, and in 1977 Suave became the highest selling shampoo in the United States. A Suave brand roll-on antiperspirant/deodorant was launched, marking the company's first entry in that category. By the end of the decade Helene Curtis was represented in more than 110 countries.

Helene Curtis joined the *Fortune* 500 group of companies in the 1980s, and established itself as the growth leader in the personal care industry. During a time when many of the company's competitors were growing through acquisition, Helene Curtis instead kept to its long-standing strategy of fueling growth through continued innovation and further brand extensions. Also, the company was making significant strides in its international markets, especially Japan, one of the first international markets in which Helene Curtis established a presence during the 1950s. By the mid-1990s the Japanese market accounted for more than 20 percent of the company's annual sales.

Building on Suave's name and reputation—the brand held fast to its position as the top daily hair care brand in the United States—Helene Curtis entered the skin care lotion with several different formulas. In addition, a new line of Suave antiperspirant/deodorants strengthened the company's presence in that category. A new brand was launched in 1982, however, with a $35 million investment and the introduction of Finesse conditioner. The product, with its patented, time-activated formula designed to give both light and deep conditioning as necessary, proved so popular that the premium-priced brand was expanded to include shampoo and hair spray, as well as the Finesse Nutricare line of hair care items.

Helene Curtis followed up on the success of Finesse with the $40 million launch of the Salon Selectives brand of shampoos, conditioners, and hair sprays. By offering customized products that combined the company's salon heritage with a mid-range price, first-year sales reached $40 million, recouping Helene Curtis's initial investment. By 1988 both Salon Selectives and Finesse had joined Suave as leaders in their market segments, and the brands' success in the United States was matched by their popularity in international markets. Meanwhile the Professional Division strengthened its lead position in the salon category with the introduction of such products as Post Impressions, a waving system that eliminated post-perm odor and dryness, and the Attractions line of hair care products with collagen. The Quantum brand was also launched with the Quantum Acid

Perm that quickly became, as it continues to be, the bestselling permanent wave brand.

The company's product lines were not alone in their expansion during the 1980s—as business had boomed, so had the need for additional manufacturing capacity. In 1982 Helene Curtis completed construction of a plant in City of Industry, California. This was followed in 1989 by a $32 million, state-of-the-art distribution center that, at 376,000 square feet, had double the capacity of the former facilities. In addition, the company's corporate headquarters had been relocated in 1984.

In 1990 Helene Curtis introduced Degree antiperspirant/deodorant—at that time the company's most successful new product launch. With a formula that is activated as body heat rises—and aided by a $50 million advertising campaign—Degree quickly garnered a large share of the market, achieving the company's market share goal for the brand's first year in only eight months. This success was followed by yet another entry into the hair care market with the introduction of the Vibrance brand. By the end of fiscal 1992 Helene Curtis had attained the billion dollar mark with total sales of $1.02 billion.

Although moderate in size compared to its competitors, Helene Curtis is one of the fastest growing personal care companies in the United States. While the company maintains its leading U.S. position, Helene Curtis's success continues to span the globe—nearly one third of the company's sales are derived from overseas markets, twice that of the 1980s. In an era of falling trade barriers and economic unions, further expansion into international markets will likely be the key to the company's continued success.

Principal Subsidiaries: Helene Curtis, Ltd. (Canada); Helene Curtis B.V. (Netherlands); Helene Curtis Australia PTY Ltd.; Helene Curtis New Zealand; Helene Curtis Japan, Inc.; Helene Curtis Enterprises, Inc. (Tokyo); Helene Curtis Scandinavia AB; Loma Holdings, Inc.; Economy Beauty Supply Co.

Further Reading:

Crown, Judith, ''Selling Brands Abroad,'' *Crain's Chicago Business,* Feb. 24, 1992, p. 13.
Freeman, Laurie, ''Using Finesse: Helene Curtis Looks Overseas,'' *Advertising Age,* March 6, 1989, p. 36.
Helene Curtis: Beauty Innovations Around the World Since 1927, Chicago: Helene Curtis Industries, Inc., 1978.
''Helene Curtis Industries, Inc.,'' *The Market for Toiletries and Cosmetics,* New York: Business Trends Analysts, Inc., 1989, pp. 515–19.
Helene Curtis Industries, Inc. Annual Report, Chicago: Helene Curtis Industries, Inc., 1992.
Kalish, David, ''Personal Care: Salon Selectives—Cheap Chic,'' *Marketing and Media Decisions,* March 1989, pp. 95–98.
Raj, D. D., ''Global Cosmetics and Household Product Industry,'' *Merrill Lynch Capital Markets,* December 1, 1992.
——, ''Helene Curtis—Company Report,'' *Merrill Lynch Capital Markets,* October 20, 1992.
''Skin Care Market Shows New Signs of Vitality,'' *Drug & Cosmetic Industry,* August 1992, pp. 28–29.
Sloan, Pat, ''Degree Makes Leaders Sweat,'' *Advertising Age,* December 10, 1990, p. 16.

—Sina Dubovoj

⊔ herman miller

Herman Miller, Inc.

8500 Byron Road
Zeeland, Michigan 49464
U.S.A.
(616) 772-3300
Fax: (616) 654-3418

Public Company
Incorporated: 1959
Employees: 6,001
Sales: $805 million
Stock Exchanges: NASDAQ
SICs: 2521 Wood Office Furniture; 2522 Office Furniture
Except Wood; 2541 Wood Partitions & Fixtures; 2542
Partitions & Fixtures Except Wood

Herman Miller, Inc., is one of the leading manufacturers of
office furniture and furniture systems, second only to Steelcase
in sales. Ranked since 1986 among the top ten in *Fortune*
magazine's annual list of the 500 most admired companies,
Herman Miller is esteemed as an innovator in furniture design,
as well as for its unique commitment to employee relations and
the environment. The company maintains operations in 35
countries.

Herman Miller was founded by D. J. De Pree, who bought the
Michigan Star Furniture Company in 1923 with his father-in-
law, Herman Miller, and a small group of local businessmen.
The company was located in Zeeland, a town in western Michigan near the city of Grand Rapids. Settled primarily by Dutch
immigrants, many of whom handed down a legacy of skill in
crafting fine furniture, Grand Rapids and its surrounding areas
had by the turn of the century become a hub for American
furniture production. Nevertheless, the industry suffered from a
lack of innovations, and despite the abilities of its employees,
Michigan Star Furniture Company, like most furniture companies in the area, had developed as a manufacturer of high-end
traditional style home furnishings, which were modifications of
European designs.

De Pree renamed the company after his father-in-law, a major
shareholder well known in the community, and set about trying
to turn the struggling company around. However, both profits
and employee morale during this time were low, and this trend
continued through the Great Depression. In 1931 Herman Miller was primarily producing traditional furniture for the home,
such as bedroom suites, which it marketed to such retailers as

Sears Roebuck. De Pree's company was near bankruptcy.

That year De Pree was approached by the industrial designer
Gilbert Rohde, who reportedly entered the Herman Miller
showroom unannounced with a plan for a new look in furniture
design. De Pree listened to Rohde's ideas and, attracted to the
designer's straightforward approach, employed Rohde to design
a new line of furniture for Herman Miller.

Rohde speculated that the decreasing size of modern homes
would inspire a demand for a smaller, simpler, and lighter
furniture style that De Pree referred to as more "more honest"
than that of traditional pieces. Rohde's first designs, completed
in 1933, were exhibited at the Chicago World's Fair, where they
met with approval from retail buyers and enthusiasm from the
general public. In less than five years, most furniture makers
had adopted more functional styles similar to those of Rohde.

During this time De Pree, a profoundly religious man, had
begun to regard furniture design as a moral issue, and he
admired the simplicity, high quality, and utilitarianism of the
modern designs. This sense of moral responsibility also per-
vaded De Pree's management style. In an often-repeated anec-
dote regarding the origins of the company's commitment to its
employees, De Pree visited the home of a millwright who had
died on the job at Herman Miller in 1927. At the request of the
widow, De Pree remained to hear some poetry that she read
aloud. Profoundly moved by the poems, he inquired as to the
author's identity and was told that the millwright had written
them. De Pree became intrigued by the question of whether he
had employed a millwright who happened to write poetry, or a
poet who worked as a millwright, and after that he sought to
realize and encourage the hidden strengths and talents of all of
his employees.

After Rohde's first efforts for Herman Miller met with success,
he turned his attention to designing office furniture. Seeking to
design an office more functional than decorative, he produced
several different desktops, pedestals, and drawers, all of which
could be interchanged to form a desk that would suit the user's
individual needs. The Executive Office Group, the designs for
which Rohde completed in 1939, was introduced in 1942. It
included a creative L-shaped desk. Rohde also produced a
design for a sectional sofa, manufactured by Herman Miller,
that would exert a substantial influence on sofa designs in the
years to come. With its revolutionary product line, Herman
Miller's sales continued to climb and the company experienced
considerable growth in the 1940s.

Rohde died in 1944, and one year later George Nelson, a young
architect and the editor of the periodical *Architectural Forum,*
was contracted as design director. By this time the company had
abandoned all of its traditional furniture lines in order to focus
solely on the contemporary. Nelson produced several creative
and profitable office furniture designs as well as the classic
Storagewall shelving and storage system, the "slat bench," the
"pretzel armchair," and other residential pieces while also
helping the company develop graphic design and advertising
departments. Among his most important accomplishments at
Herman Miller, however, was bringing the company together
with such important design artists as Isamu Noguchi, Alexander
Girard, and Charles and Ray Eames, which broadened the company's reputation for quality and innovation.

Charles Eames is widely regarded as a genius in contemporary furniture design. Working in collaboration with his wife, Ray, Eames experimented with new materials, such as molded plywood, fiberglass, aluminum, and wire, producing several distinctive pieces, primarily chairs, for Herman Miller. In 1946 he produced an influential design for a molded plywood side chair, and in 1956 he produced perhaps his most famous piece, known as the 670 swivel lounge chair. Consisting of a molded plywood back shell and seat shell with rosewood veneer padded with down, covered in leather, and supported by a five-prong stand, the 670 chair is known for its support and comfort as well as its light weight and casual form. The chair, one of Herman Miller's most successful products, was widely copied by other furniture companies.

By 1950 Herman Miller's sales had increased to $1.7 million. That year the company initiated the Scanlon management plan. Named after its inventor, a lecturer at the Massachusetts Institute of Technology, the plan was based on the idea that employees could serve as a valuable source of ideas for operations and cost effectiveness and should therefore be called on to participate in management decisions. The plan called for team organization and provided employees with various incentives, including financial rewards for productivity gains. Revolutionary at the time, the plan proved successful for Herman Miller and has since been adopted by several other major companies.

During the 1960s D. J. De Pree's son Hugh took over operations, and Herman Miller began changing the configuration of the American office floorplan. The Action Office System, introduced in 1964, included freestanding desks, files, etc., that could be configured a variety of ways to form work arenas, specific to individual work needs. Then in 1968 Action Office products replaced the traditional construct of individual offices or large rooms with partitions and panels supporting desk components that could be easily moved or added on to, allowing for efficient use of floor space. The concept was created by a newly formed research team, headquartered in Ann Arbor, Michigan, and headed by inventor and sculptor Robert Propst. The team spent four years researching the needs of office workers, finding that the open plan system broke up the monotony of previous plans and provided an illusion of privacy for each employee while also allowing proximity for easy communication with coworkers. Furthermore, the Herman Miller Action Office system had the advantage of being cheaper to manufacture than the heavy wood furniture previously favored. It was the first open plan panel system in the world and subsequently fostered a multi-billion-dollar industry.

Herman Miller became a public corporation in 1970, and its stock rose steadily. In 1976 the company made a hit with its Ergon chair, designed by Bill Stumpf and based on the science of ergonomics, in which the worker's physical relationship to his or her environment and duties is given special consideration. The chair, featuring a five-pronged aluminum pedestal on casters and comfortably padded with an adjustable back support and seat, became widely used in American offices.

Although sales of the Action Office components continued to increase during this time, research during the 1970s indicated some drawbacks to the product. Some customers complained that the cubicles lacked privacy while simultaneously engen-

dering a feeling of isolation among employees, who could hear but not see one another. In 1975 Herman Miller contracted Stumpf and designer Don Chadwick to come up with a solution. Chadwick and Stumpf worked for nearly three years on the project, traveling to Europe to study contemporary office buildings in an effort to capture a more humane spirit in their new office designs. In December 1978 they presented their design, entitled Buroplan, to Herman Miller. However, the plan's combination of futuristic windows, archways, balustrades, and windows with traditional freestanding desks was considered too eclectic, and the company rejected it, subsequently offering the two a chance to design a new office chair which was based on the design elements of the project.

Due to special challenges in finding the right materials, the chair took Chadwick and Stumpf five years to design, but the result met with enormous approval. Manufactured in 1984, the Equa chair was designed to provide ''seating equity,'' or equal comfort for both the employee who spends a long period of time in the chair and the employee who sits only between frequent periods of motion. Offering support and comfort, without complicated mechanical adjustment knobs and levers, the Equa chair was offered in two models, a standard model selling for $320 and a high backed, leather model that retailed for $1,100. *Time* magazine later named the Equa chair one of three best products of the decade. The following year elements of Chadwick and Stumpf's Buroplan resurfaced in Ethospace interiors, an alternative to the Action Office system designed by Stumpf and Jack Kelley, which offered the worker a greater sense of control and more natural light.

Company sales saw unprecedented growth during the 1970s and early 1980s, increasing from $49 million in 1975 to $492 million in 1985. During this time Hugh De Pree stepped down and was replaced by his brother Max. Max De Pree developed a plan in which employees were allowed to become shareholders in the company, a practice that contributed to the company's inclusion in 1984 in *The 100 Best Companies to Work for in America*, by Robert Levering and Milton Moskowitz. However, earnings and stock prices fell late in 1985, and industry analysts speculated that the decline in orders from the computer and electronics industries and the large number of companies copying and marketing Herman Miller designs were to blame. Some maintained that Herman Miller had focused too long on improving its internal operations and had ignored the increase in competition. Others, including Herman Miller representatives, attributed the decline in earnings to the disappointing sales of the Ethospace system. Nevertheless, the company surprised investors, overcoming the slump by implementing an aggressive program to sway large corporate customers away from their competitors. They reported sales of $714 million in 1988, up 20 percent from the previous year.

The following year Max De Pree published a book on the Herman Miller management style, entitled *Leadership Is an Art*. Writing that ''everyone has the right and duty to influence decision-making and to understand the results,'' De Pree emphasized the need to treat all employees as important contributors. He also stressed that in order to promote competence in a staff, a leader needs to form a ''covenant'' with the employees, attending carefully to their need for ''spirit, excellence, beauty, and joy.'' Finally, De Pree maintained, the signs of a failing company included a ''dark tension'' among employees, an increase in the distribution of memos and manuals, and a lack of interest in company anecdotes and extracurricular functions. De Pree's book was well received, providing managers in other companies with insights to Herman Miller's success.

By 1990 Herman Miller's sales had reached $865 million, and the company began to expand its scope, acquiring other companies as subsidiaries and addressing new issues in the industry. The preceding year Meridian, a manufacturer of metal file cabinets, storage cases, and desks, was acquired. Other acquisitions included Miltech and Integrated Metal Technology, which fabricated sheet metal parts. Milcare, spun off from Herman Miller in 1985, sought to fill the needs of the healthcare profession, adapting the Action Office equipment for use in nursing stations, medical libraries, and hospital rooms. Also during this time Herman Miller sought to become a leader in conservation. Extensive recycling programs were implemented and the use of endangered tropical hardwoods, including the rosewood in the Eames 670 swivel lounge, was discontinued in favor of walnut, cherry, and other more plentiful hardwoods. The company has won several awards for its efforts to protect the natural environment.

Herman Miller furniture, particularly from the 1940s and 1950s, has become valuable among collectors. Several pieces are on exhibition in such major museums as the New York Museum of Modern Art, the Whitney Museum, and the Smithsonian Institution, and a large collection of Herman Miller furniture is featured at the Edsel Ford Design History Center in Dearborn, Michigan. Herman Miller's reputation for quality and integrity is widely recognized, and the company remains confident of continued success well into the 21st century.

Principal Subsidiaries: Meridian, Inc.; Phoenix Designs, Inc.; Integrated Metal Technology Inc.; Milcare Inc.; Powder Coat Technology, Inc.; Herman Miller Japan, Ltd.; Herman Miller Canada, Inc.; Herman Miller Ltd., England; Herman Miller Et Cie, France; Herman Miller (Australia) Pty, Ltd.; Herman Miller Deutschland, Inc. (Germany).

Further Reading:

Ager, Susan, ''Philosopher of Capitalism,'' *Nation's Business,* March 1986, pp. 77–78.

Berman, Ann E., ''Herman Miller—Influential Designs of the 1940s and 1950s,'' *Architectural Digest,* September 1991, pp. 34–40.

Berry, John, *Herman Miller Is Built on Its People, Research, and Designs,* Zeeland, Michigan: Herman Miller, Inc., 1992.

Brammer, Rhonda, ''Not Miller Time? A Furniture Company Loses Some of Its Gloss,'' *Barron's,* October 7, 1985, p. 18.

De Pree, Max, *Leadership Is an Art,* Doubleday, 1989.

Geber, Beverly, ''Herman Miller: Where Profits and Participation Meet,'' *Training: The Magazine of Human Resources Development,* November 1987, pp. 62–66.

Greenwald, John, ''Advice to Bosses: Try a Little Kindness,'' *Time,* September 11, 1989, p. 56.

Herman Miller, Inc. Annual Reports, Zeeland, Michigan: Herman Miller, Inc., 1986–1990.

Labich, Kenneth, ''Hot Company, Warm Culture,'' *Fortune,* February 27, 1989, pp. 74–78.

McClory, Robert J., ''The Creative Process at Herman Miller,'' *Across the Board,* May 1985, pp. 8–22.

Morrison, Ann M., ''Action Is What Makes Herman Miller Climb,'' *Fortune,* June 15, 1981, pp. 161–77.

Nelson-Horchler, Joani, ''The Magic of Herman Miller,'' *Industry Week,* February 18, 1991, pp. 11–17.

Skolnik, Rayna, ''Battling for the Power of the Seats,'' *Sales & Marketing Management,* April 1987, pp. 46–48.

''Three Furniture Giants Acquire Competitors,'' *Michigan Business,* March 1990, pp. 12–13.

Wechsler, Dana, ''A Comeback in Cubicles,'' *Forbes,* March 21, 1988, pp. 54, 56.

—Tina Grant

HOLNAM

Holnam Inc.

6211 N. Ann Arbor Road
P.O. Box 122
Dundee, Michigan 48131
U.S.A.
(313) 529-2411
Fax: (313) 529-5512

Public Subsidiary of Holdernam Inc.
Incorporated: 1981
Employees: 5,785
Sales: $1.0 billion
Stock Exchanges: New York
SICs: 3241 Cement—Hydraulic; 1442 Construction Sand & Gravel; 3273 Ready-Mixed Concrete

Manufacturing and marketing over 320 types of cements and other construction related products, Holnam Inc. also mines limestone, maintains a natural gas pipeline, operates a cement trucking company, engages in the development of real estate, and processes sand and gravel. Holnam was originally formed in 1981 as a subsidiary of Holdernam Inc., a wholly owned subsidiary of the publicly traded Swiss corporation Holderbank Financière Glaris Ltd. Beginning in March 1990 a succession of mergers and acquisitions made Holnam the largest cement company in North America.

Holnam produces and delivers nearly ten million tons of cement, the primary ingredient in concrete, each year. To produce cement, varying amounts of limestone, shale, clay, iron ore, and sand, are ground and mixed and then burned in a kiln where temperatures range from 350 to 3,400 degrees Fahrenheit. The resulting substance, known as clinker, is then mixed with gypsum and ground into the fine, gray powder that is cement, which may be mixed with sand, gravel, and water to produce concrete. The basic Portland cement, said to have the qualities of a particular building stone quarried on the British Isle of Portland, is available in several strengths suited for various applications in sidewalks, highways, building foundations, dams, and retaining walls. Holnam's masonry cements, including Rainbow brand custom color masonry cement, are used in both stone and stucco constructions, including walls, chimneys, manholes, and catch basins. Other construction needs are filled with Portland Pozzolan cement, which contains volcanic ash. Finally, Holnam also produces concrete mixtures for mass pourings as well as fly ash admixtures that serve to strengthen concrete by incorporating fly ash, a man-made byproduct resulting from the combustion of coal.

Holnam Inc. was first developed as a holding company for the U.S. interests of Holderbank, the world's largest producer of cement products and related services. Holderbank originated with a Swiss cement company called the Aargauische Portlandcement-Fabrik Holderbank-Wildeggbegan, founded in 1912 by Ernst Schmidheiny. The company was a success, and increased production capacity and earnings enabled it to acquire its rival, the Rheintalische Zementfabrik of Ruthi, in 1914. Beginning in the 1920s, the founder and his son expanded the company beyond Swiss borders, acquiring the Nederlandse Cement Industrie and the Ciments d'Obourg in Belgium, as well as constructing plants in Egypt and in Greece. To control its growing international empire, the company regrouped its interests in 1930 under an umbrella company known as Holderbank Financière Glaris Ltd.

The companies that would eventually comprise Holnam originated as early as 1953, when Holderbank founded its first North American enterprise, St. Lawrence Cement Inc., in Canada. Within two years, the first of St. Lawrence's cement plants was completed in Beauport, Quebec. The company's second plant, in Mississauga, Ontario, was established in 1956 and has since become Canada's largest cement plant. St. Lawrence eventually gained a third plant in Canada and two more in the northeastern United States.

Holderbank's first U.S. venture, the Dundee Cement Company in Dundee, Michigan, was formed in 1958, becoming fully operational two years later. Like St. Lawrence, Dundee continued to expand under Holderbank's supervision. Its second plant in Clarksville, Missouri, on the Mississippi River, was completed in 1967 and featured the world's largest cement kiln, which measured 760 feet long and 25 feet in diameter and could accommodate 1.4 million tons of clinker a year. In 1978, Dundee acquired the Santee Portland Cement Corporation of Holly Hill, South Carolina, which marketed cement and mortar exclusively in the southeastern states. Dundee's final acquisition, the January 1990 purchase of Northwestern States Portland Cement Co., located in Mason City, Iowa, provided the company with another large facility.

In 1986 Holderbank reportedly paid nearly $110 million for a 66 percent interest in the struggling Denver-based Ideal Basic Industries. Ideal maintained nine plants in the mid-central, western, and southwestern regions of the United States, allowing Holderbank to explore new markets. Soon after the purchase, renovations were begun on Ideal's obsolete production facilities. Holderbank reportedly absorbed an extra $5.7 million increase in interest charges to renovate the Fort Collins, Colorado, plant alone. Ideal continued to struggle, however, posting a $24.1 million loss on sales of $245 million in 1989.

With the acquisition of Ideal, Holderbank gained a commanding 14 percent market share in the United States, ahead of its foreign competitors Blue Circle Industries of the United Kingdom and Lafarge Coppée of France. Furthermore, employing superior, highly cost-effective production techniques to gain a market advantage over rival U.S. cement makers, Holderbank had established a significant presence in North America during the building boom of the 1980s. However, recognizing the dependence of the cement industry on both business cycles and the construction industry, and becoming aware of the threat of a worldwide economic downturn, Holderbank began to consolidate its global activities for greater profitability toward the end of the 1980s. In 1988, preparing to consolidate and reorganize its U.S. companies, Holderbank contributed its interests in St. Lawrence, Dundee, and Ideal to Holnam Inc., a holding company Holderbank established nine years earlier as a subsidiary of Holdernam Inc.

Two years later Holnam had been recreated, through mergers and acquisitions, as the country's largest cement manufacturer. First, in March of 1990, Dundee and Ideal merged under the name Holnam Inc., which was then listed on the New York Stock Exchange. In the transaction, Holderbank acquired the remaining 34 percent interest in Ideal and retained 89.3 percent of Holnam's outstanding common stock, with minority shareholders owning the remainder. Holnam remained a direct subsidiary of Holdernam.

In its new form Holnam was comprised of Ideal Basic Industries, Dundee Cement Company with its subsidiaries Santee Cement Company and Northwestern States Portland Cement Co., and a 60 percent interest in St. Lawrence Cement, whose stock is traded separately on the Montreal and Toronto exchanges. The company established headquarters in Michigan, and Mark von Wyss, who had served as president at Dundee since 1971, became Holnam's president and chief executive officer. Peter Byland was named chairperson, a position in which he also served at St. Lawrence.

In the months immediately following the merger Holnam continued to expand. In August 1990, the company purchased the United Cement Company, whose facility represented the only cement plant in Mississippi, for approximately $60 million. Two months later the company paid approximately $2 million for Diversified Manufacturers, Inc. (DMI), an Alabama-based producer of masonry cement and stucco. C-Cure of Florida, a business similar in scope to DMI, was purchased by Holnam in March of the following year. During this time Holnam reorganized, providing a central management structure for manufacturing, transportation, distribution, and marketing.

Financially, Holnam experienced difficulties during the first two years after the merger. Although revenues in 1990 reached one billion dollars, and the company was ranked in the *Fortune* 500 list, Holnam sustained an overall loss of $28 million. A downturn in the construction industry as well as higher costs for fuel and pollution control equipment were cited as principal reasons for the heavy losses. The following year sales fell to $979 million as the company posted a net loss of $95 million. Furthermore, for the first time ever, St. Lawrence also reported losses. Analysts noted, however, that the economic recession during this time caused similar losses to be realized by Holnam's competitors throughout the industry.

Environmental issues also played a major role in Holnam's operations in the early 1990s. Public concern over Holnam's cement kilns arose in several areas of the country, when the company applied for permits to burn chemical wastes to fuel their kilns. Referring to the proposal as a "win-win situation," Holnam maintained that besides providing the company with an economical alternative to burning coal or oil, it offered the country a safe and practical means to dispose of municipal and industrial waste, thereby reducing the need for landfills and conserving the natural resource of coal. Objections were raised both by local residents and environmentalists, who feared that the chemicals released into the air during the burning would be hazardous to plant and animal life in the area. Although protestors in Colorado convinced Holnam to abandon plans to burn wastes at the LaPorte and Fremont County kilns, subsequent research did not conclusively find the burning to be dangerous. Holnam did receive permission from other state regulatory agencies, however, and by the end of 1991 kilns in California, Alabama, Michigan, Missouri, and other locations began burning paint thinners and dry cleaning solvents for fuel. Others, including the Seattle operation, burned shredded tire scraps. Yet Holnam was unable to resolve other environmental problems so economically. The Dundee plant reportedly spent $17 million on controlling the emissions from its smokestacks, while another $2 million was spent to clean up the plant in Mason City, Iowa.

In 1991, forming a committee to work in cooperation with a consulting firm, Holnam studied the market, seeking ways to make the company profitable. Deciding to streamline its operations, the company closed its Denver offices as well as some of its bulk distribution terminals, maintaining its shipping fleet of five tugs, 75 barges, and 397 railroad cars. Renewing its commitment to its core products, Holnam introduced bagged cement and mortars into its Wisconsin, Missouri, Michigan, and Ohio markets, setting up new warehouses in the Midwest and promoting the products through new packaging and advertising.

During this time, the company terminated its relationship with BoxCrow Cement Company, a Texas-based company whose business and assets Holnam had acquired with an option to purchase before the merger in 1989. As part of the original agreement, the company had extended working capital loans to BoxCrow. By 1991 these loans totaled over $30 million, and BoxCrow was still experiencing cash flow problems and weak sales. Believing it unlikely that BoxCrow would be able to repay the loans, Holnam cut its losses by terminating the agreement.

In its relatively new role as the country's leader in cement production, Holnam continued to seek out ways of making operations more efficient and cost-effective, while exploring new, related product lines. Encouraged by forecasts of an upswing in the construction industry, Holnam expected its cement companies to return to profitability in the mid-1990s.

Principal Subsidiaries: St. Lawrence Cement Inc. (Canada; 59.7%); Braswell Sand & Gravel Co., Inc.; Braswell Concrete Products, Inc.; Braswell Industries; Graysonia, Nashville & Ashdown RR. Co.; Lousiana-Nevada Transit Co.; Thorstenberg Materials Co., Inc.; Kevaland Texas Corp; Ideal Dominicana, S.A.; Southern Cement Transport, Inc.; Belmont Bay Investing Corp.; Ideal Coal Co.; Ideal Development Corp.; Kevaland Corp.; Delta Cement Corp.; Dundee Investment Co.; Holnam Texas Inc.; Holchem Inc.; Holnam Resources, Inc.; Holnam West Materials, Ltd.; United Cement Co.; Northwestern States

Portland Cement Co.; Pacific Portland Cement Co.; Three Forks Portland Cement Co.; Westbay Community Associates, Inc.

Further Reading:

Holnam Inc. Annual Report, Dundee, MI: Holnam Inc., 1991.

Mitchell, Jerry, "Chem Waste, Holnam Linked: Joint Venture to Supply Kiln Fuel," *Mississippi Business Journal,* January 11, 1993, p. 1.

Seebacher, Noreen, "Cementing a Spot on the Fortune 500," *Detroit News,* April 15, 1991.

Wernle, Bradford, "Dundee is Home to New $1 Billion Company," *Crain's Detroit Business,* March 26–April 1, 1990, pp. 1, 47.

—Tina Grant

Huntsman Chemical Corporation

2000 Eagle Gate Tower
Salt Lake City, Utah 84111
U.S.A.
(801) 532-5200
Fax: (801) 536-1581

Private Company
Incorporated: April 1983
Employees: 1,500
Sales: $900 million
SICs: 2821 Plastics Materials Synthetic Resins

The Huntsman Chemical Corporation is the largest manufacturer of polystyrene in the United States. Although it also produces a number of other types of plastic, the company remains virtually unknown to the general public. Its customers are large corporations that have used Huntsman plastics to make such familiar objects as McDonald's Corporation clamshell burger containers and L'eggs pantyhose egg shells. Huntsman is privately owned and operated. But where other family-owned corporations generally maintain a family member as a titular senior executive, Huntsman employs most of its founder's family in important positions.

Huntsman was established in 1982 when Jon Meade Huntsman, a devout Mormon businessman with a declining fortune from a previous business, engineered a series of leveraged takeovers of other companies' polystyrene operations. At the time, the polystyrene market was in a deep recession. Huntsman, however, had extensive experience with the industry and was convinced that its downward cycle had bottomed out. He learned that the Shell Oil Company was eager to sell its $67 million polystyrene plant at Belpre, Ohio. Shell wanted to abandon this and other noncore industries and was ready to sell the facility at loss. The company offered the plant to Huntsman for $42 million, but warned that he would never be able to make the deal as an individual. Having taken the advice as a challenge, Huntsman became determined to make the deal work. He pledged $500,000 in collateral against his home, and added $1.3 million from his existing businesses. He approached ARCO Oil and Gas with an offer to purchase $1.8 million worth of styrene monomer, the raw material for polystyrene, over 13 years. In return, he wanted ARCO's support in securing his deal.

ARCO was interested in securing a long-term supply contract and offered Huntsman a $10 million loan. With his supplier on board as a partner, he later won a $29 million loan from the Union Bank of California. Huntsman then negotiated the balance, $3 million, as a deferred loan from Shell and convinced that company to secure $12 million of his loan from the Union Bank. Convinced that Huntsman was crazy, Shell executives sent the entrepreneur a bronze sculpture called *The Riverboat Gambler* inscribed with the words, ''From your friends at Shell.'' The oil company regarded its Belpre plant as a money-losing facility operating at only 60 percent of its capacity. Huntsman, however, saw a plant that could nearly double its output with no additional investment. Despite Shell's lack of confidence in Jon Huntsman, the transaction was completed in late March of 1983. The oil company sold its Belpre plant to the Huntsman Chemical Corporation, a company formed specifically for the deal.

Huntsman, described as a deeply religious Mormon and father of nine, had a long history with polystyrene. While in high school, Huntsman struck up an acquaintance with Harold Zellerbach, president of Crown Zellerbach Corp. Zellerbach arranged a scholarship for Huntsman at his alma mater, Wharton. Upon graduation, Zellerbach refused to give Huntsman a job at his company. ''You are the most natural entrepreneur we have ever met,'' noted Zellerbach. He advised Huntsman to avoid the stifling bureaucracy of a corporation and strike out on his own. Dejected, Huntsman turned to his in-laws for work. They ran Olson Farm, a simple egg business in Los Angeles, and put Huntsman to work as a manager. Here he gained crucial experience with farmers and also noted the substantial losses incurred from inadequate packaging.

Hoping to design a better egg carton, Huntsman established contact with the polystyrene operations of the Dow Chemical Co. in 1965. Dow later purchased Olson Farm and several egg carton manufacturers, grouping them into a new company called Dolco Packaging. Huntsman was appointed Dolco's president, and the company soon began turning out durable plastic egg cartons. The arrangement immersed Huntsman in Dow's corporate structure, and after three years of mounting frustration with bureaucracy, Huntsman resigned his post in 1970.

With his brother Blaine, Jon Huntsman raised $300,000 and secured a $1 million loan from San Francisco-based Hambrecht & Quist. The brothers then established Huntsman Container and purchased a polystyrene plant from Monsanto. The new firm turned out polystyrene egg cartons, meat trays, eating utensils, and fast-food containers. In 1970, with the business still in its infancy, Jon Huntsman was recruited into government service. An active Republican, Huntsman took a position with the Department of Health, Education & Welfare. He was later promoted to a staff secretary for President Nixon. But in his absence, the business of Huntsman Container floundered. The small company desperately needed its founder's energy, direction, and salesmanship.

Returning to Salt Lake City in 1973, Huntsman began a policy of personally visiting all his clients, using a small airplane. He succeeded in reviving accounts, but soon faced a more ominous problem. The oil crisis of 1973–1974 threw his suppliers into a quandary. With plenty of demand, Huntsman now found it difficult to secure supplies of styrene monomer from oil companies. He resorted to brokering petroleum compounds, often in eight-way transactions, just to ensure that the company had the necessary materials to stay in business. At one point, business became so poor that Huntsman had to skim profits from a small religious record album business he had established some years before in his garage.

Finally, in 1976, Huntsman sold his container business to Keyes Fiber. After nearly ten years of excruciating work, Huntsman was left with a tiny fortune which he considered completely out of proportion with his effort. Huntsman later told *Forbes,* ''I determined that when I moved into business again, I would not have partners or shareholders.'' But before he had that opportunity, Huntsman was dispatched by his church to Washington, D.C., where he was instructed to perform missionary work. He remained there for three years and returned to Utah in 1982. It was at this point that Huntsman negotiated his deal with Shell.

Revitalized and confident from his stint as a missionary, Huntsman was ready to get back into business. Having learned the brutal cyclicality of the chemical business, and the importance of good customer relations, he began to assemble a long list of customers. Once again, Huntsman was on the road meeting with customers and pressing them for suggestions. He learned that some needed faster delivery and others wanted altered formulations. This dedicated footwork raised demand for polystyrene so significantly that within only a few months the Belpre plant was operating at 100 percent of capacity. With profitability restored, Huntsman paid down his company's debt.

But by 1985, as Shell had warned, the industry was racked with oversupply as other producers stepped in. Rather than ride it out, Huntsman convinced his backers to waive certain loan covenants that restricted him from making additional acquisitions. Huntsman's strategy was to take advantage of an emerging buyer's market for polystyrene plants. In 1986 the German chemical company Hoechst A.G. announced its intention to shut its three polystyrene plants at Chesapeake, Virginia, and Peru, Illinois. Huntsman learned that Hoechst was desperate to close the plants, so he offered to pay Hoechst $45 million for the three facilities at the end of five years. With a chance to simply wash its hands of the troubled plants, Hoechst agreed. With this latest acquisition, Huntsman had become America's largest styrene manufacturer, using the world's most advanced styrene technologies.

Tired of the vicious cycles in styrene, Jon Huntsman saw a need to diversify into closely related but separate markets, such as polypropylene. Having just exhausted his goodwill with bankers to make the Hoechst deal, Huntsman decided to sell a share in his company to raise the necessary cash for more acquisitions. He agreed to sell 40 percent of Huntsman Chemical to Great Lakes Chemical Corp. for $52 million, a portion of which was used to acquire a polypropylene plant at Woodbury, New Jersey from Shell.

Meanwhile, due to the terrible state of the polystyrene market, other producers exited the business, cutting production or shifting to other more profitable compounds. Within a month of the Hoechst deal, demand began to strengthen. A year later the glut had disappeared and Huntsman, with four plants in operation, was back in the black. By 1988 the company was at last out of debt. As a sign of family involvement in the company, Huntsman's wife Karen personally vetoed her husband's proposal to take the company public in 1988.

In 1989 Huntsman purchased the European packaging business Skelmersdale that had once been a part of the old Huntsman Container concern. Still on the hunt for a larger polypropylene operation, and with cash left over from Great Lakes Chemical, Huntsman set his sights on Aristech, a major polypropylene manufacturer that was weakened by a lawsuit for hazardous waste contamination. After a friendly bid for the company was rejected, Huntsman launched a hostile takeover of Aristech. Determined to resist this effort, Aristech's management made its own successful bid for control, enlisting the help of Japan's Mitsubishi Corporation.

Spurned from diversification, Huntsman's most important product remained polystyrene. The plastic was used to make toothbrushes, packing material, television and computer casings, and, most visibly, billions of thermal clamshell containers for McDonald's larger sandwiches. During 1990, Huntsman increased operating capacity at each of its plants. In 1991 the company established a joint venture with General Electric Company to manufacture styrene acrylonitrile at Bay St. Louis, Missouri. The company successfully managed to expand internationally; its first overseas facility was a small polystyrene plant at Stanslow, England that it acquired from Shell in May of 1984. This was followed by a second plant in Carrington, England. By 1986 Huntsman had a minority stake in Dynopor, a Singapore-based styrene venture and a plant in Mansonville, Quebec, Canada.

Huntsman also made successful inroads into the former Soviet Union, a direct result of his friendship with Occidental Petroleum founder Armand Hammer. Huntsman, a great philanthropist, also contributed substantial sums to relieve suffering after a killer earthquake devastated Soviet Armenia. For these activities, Huntsman was permitted to establish a number of joint venture plants, including a styrene plant at Gorlovka, Ukraine and another at Sheremetyevo Airport in Moscow (to make catering trays). These plants remain in operation, despite the collapse of the Soviet Union and the interruption of supplies.

In 1991 Huntsman was dealt a small but significant blow when McDonald's abruptly curtailed use of Huntsman's polystyrene clamshell containers. Without so much as a phone call, McDonald's cancelled about ten percent of Huntsman's business. Shortly afterward, the Sara Lee Corporation stopped using Huntsman polystyrene for its L'eggs containers. The changes were prompted by the Environmental Defense Fund, which portrayed polystyrene manufacturers as environmental monsters. In fact, the substitute packaging the Fund endorsed was allegedly more harmful than polystyrene.

In response, Huntsman donated several million dollars to an environmental research facility at Utah State University to study the issue. Huntsman also banded together with other polystyrene manufacturers, Dow, Mobil and Amoco, to form the National Polystyrene Recycling Corporation. The group has not yet succeeded in reopening styrene demand, and it is not likely to do so until new technologies can be developed that make the plastic biodegradable. Still, wider uses for styrene are continually being developed. These have, for the most part, compensated for the loss of a few packaging applications.

Such shocks are common in the chemicals markets and Huntsman is well-equipped to handle them. While family run, the company still depends heavily on the talents of its founder who, despite a bout with prostate cancer, remains a vital part of the organization. Continuing his company's effort to diversify, Huntsman engineered the acquisition of the food and industrial film business of the Goodyear Tire and Rubber Company in 1992. The following year, Huntsman purchased Mobil Chemical's polyethylene bakery bag manufacturing business. These operations blunt Huntsman's exposure to the volatile polystyrene market and permit it to concentrate its energies on more profitable lines of business.

Further Reading:

"Entrepreneur on the Fast Track," *Chemical Week,* May 21, 1986, p. 27.

"Huntsman Chemical: A Centralized Approach," *Chemical Week,* December 9, 1992, pp. 56–59.

"Huntsman Quits Race to Acquire Aristech Chemical," *Chemical Week,* February 28, 1990, p. 6.

"Huntsman: Seeking a Broader Base," *Chemical Week,* August 14, 1991, pp. 22–23.

"Jon Meade Huntsman," *Forbes 400,* October 19, 1992, p. 156.

"Re-inventing Polystyrene," *Adweek's Marketing Week,* October 14, 1991, pp. 16–17.

"Shell Oil Polystyrene Business Bought by Salt Lake City Firm," *Wall Street Journal,* March 21, 1983, p. 30.

"This Guy is Going to Lose Everything," *Forbes,* November 27, 1989, pp. 169–176.

—John Simley

IMC Fertilizer Group, Inc.

2100 Sanders Road
Northbrook, Illinois 60062
U.S.A.
(708) 272-9200
Fax: (708) 205-4804

Public Company
Incorporated: 1988
Employees: 5,000
Sales: $1.06 billion
Stock Exchanges: New York Midwest
SICs: 2819 Industrial Inorganic Chemicals, Nec

IMC Fertilizer Group, Inc. (IMCF) was created in 1988 when the onetime International Minerals & Chemicals Corporation divested its fertilizer assets in the form of a new, publicly traded company. As the fertilizer market was then in the midst of a long and disastrous slump, the spin-off proved to be most beneficial for the parent company, which promptly changed its name to Imcera Group, Inc., and entered the market of high-tech health and animal care products. IMCF, meanwhile, the largest private-sector producer of phosphate and potash fertilizers in the world, was left to contend with the continuing collapse of its domestic and international markets, which never recovered from the price shocks caused by the 1973–74 oil crisis. IMCF's strategy was a proposed joint venture with its nearest domestic competitor, Freeport-McMoRan Resource Partners, itself the result of a divestment move similar to that which created IMCF. If the joint venture was approved by antitrust regulators, it would control nearly half of all United States phosphate production—an enviable position to occupy, if and when the fertilizer market regained its former health.

The ancestor of IMCF was formed at the end of the nineteenth century, a time when farmers in the United States and western Europe were switching from traditional fertilizers to the use of commercial chemical fertilizers. Scientific experiments in the first half of the nineteenth century had identified precisely the nutrients needed for plant growth and continued soil fertility. Chief among these were nitrogen, phosphorus, and potassium, known by their chemical symbols as the basic N-P-K triad of nutrients. During the preceding centuries of farming, trial and error experiments had discovered sources for each of these nutrients in such traditional fertilizers as animal manure, bones,

guano, and fish scrap; but with the progress of chemical knowledge came the search for methods by which N-P-K could be produced in their most concentrated and inexpensive forms. In the United States commercial fertilizer was especially desired in the eastern and southern states, where older, over-farmed land responded well to their application. By the last quarter of the nineteenth century a strong business had grown up around the phosphate mines of Florida and Tennessee.

The earliest predecessor of IMCF was founded in 1897 in Tennessee by Thomas C. Meadows and his brother-in-law Oscar L. Dortch. Meadows was an engineering graduate of Vanderbilt University who understood the potential market for Tennessee's phosphate rock, which when treated with sulphuric acid yielded a product rich in the form of phosphorus most readily absorbed by growing plants. With Oscar Dortch, Meadows formed T.C. Meadows & Co. to mine, process, and sell this "superphosphate" both by itself and in ready-mixed fertilizer containing suitable proportions of the other two basic nutrients, nitrogen and potash. These would have to be purchased on the market from sources originating as far away as Germany and Chile, making the business of fertilizers capital intensive and encouraging the development of large combines capable of supplying all three ingredients.

With that in mind, Meadows & Co. changed its name in 1899 to United States Agricultural Corporation and began acquiring the assets it would need to survive in the rapidly consolidating fertilizer industry. In 1900 it gained control of two companies engaged in the Florida phosphate mines, Florida Mining Company and Peoria Pebble Phosphate Company. Because Florida's phosphate fields, located in the central and northern parts of the state, were richer and easier to mine than those of Tennessee, they soon became the backbone of the U.S. phosphate industry. In most cases the mines were laid in remote, inhospitable, and sparsely settled areas where employers such as United States Agricultural could find few workers to perform the manual labor then required to extract phosphate. The mining companies turned this to their advantage, however, by building primitive "company towns" and importing convicts from the state of Florida and others from neighboring Georgia and Alabama. The combination of high-grade phosphate and cheap labor enabled United States Agricultural to make an excellent return on its Florida operation and attracted the attention of outside investors eager to get into the growing fertilizer industry.

Among the financial backers rounded up by Meadows and Dortch, the most important was Waldemar Schmidtmann, member of an Austrian family that controlled one of the largest potash mines in Germany—Kaliwerke Sollstedt. Potash is the most abundant mineral source of potassium and for many years virtually all of the world's known potash was found in Germany, giving that nation a powerful bargaining chip in its trade with the United States. An industrial cartel set prices and controlled production of German potash; only intermittently effective, the cartel was nevertheless sufficiently troublesome for United States importers to make the possibility of ownership in a German potash mine extremely appealing. Thus Meadows and Dortch were happy to listen when Schmidtmann proposed a union of their respective holdings, and in 1901 the Austrian became a partner in the newly renamed International Agricultural Corporation (IAC). Along with an investment of cash,

Schmidtmann also brought to IAC a part interest in Kaliwerke Sollstedt, guaranteeing the U.S. company access to two of the three basic fertilizer nutrients.

IAC moved swiftly into the finished product end of the fertilizer business as well, buying up mixed fertilizer plants from Maine to Alabama in an effort to complete the vertical integration of the company. IAC was also heavily involved in the growing export market for high-grade Florida phosphate, whose value as a plant nutrient was gradually being recognized around the world. It would not be long before the peasants of China and villagers of remote Bulgaria were introduced to the wonders of commercial fertilizer, and, especially as population pressure increased in Asia and Africa toward the middle of the twentieth century, the export of phosphate and mixed fertilizer became increasingly important to the U.S. fertilizer industry.

By 1910 IAC was firmly established as one of the handful of consolidated companies dominating the U.S. fertilizer business. Controlling between 30 and 40 subsidiary companies engaged in every aspect of fertilizer production, IAC generated revenues of approximately $8.5 million, on which it earned a net income of about $1 million. The industry as a whole had enjoyed a tremendous upsurge over the preceding 20 years; U.S. commercial fertilizer consumption more than quadrupled, while the traditional methods of organic fertilization all but disappeared from the landscape.

Problems arose with the approach of the World War I, however. Not only was IAC and the entire U.S. fertilizer industry dependent on German potash mines, German scientists had also developed the first reliable method of fixing atmospheric nitrogen in the form of ammonia, which could then be used in the production of two radically different but equally crucial materials—fertilizer and explosives. The war forced the U.S. government into a frenzied development of its own nitrogen-fixing process and the fertilizer industry into a long search for domestic sources of potash. IAC temporarily lost access to its Sollstedt mine in Germany, but upon the war's conclusion in 1918 resumed its imports of potash, leaving to other companies the 20-year search for North American deposits.

It was not until the late 1930s, when war again threatened to cut off German supplies, that IAC joined other fertilizer concerns in exploring the American Southwest for potash. Oil drilling had established the presence of potash near Carlsbad, New Mexico, as early as the mid-1920s, and in 1937 IAC invested $100,000 in the Union Potash Company in exchange for a portion of its findings. When these proved sizable, IAC effectively bought out Union Potash and built itself a state-of-the-art potash facility in time to meet its own needs before the onset of World War II in 1939. IAC has remained one of the largest American producers of potash, pioneering several new techniques at the Carlsbad mine and in 1962 opening a second major deposit at Esterhazy, Saskatchewan. The latter required five years of engineering effort to complete its 3,000-foot shaft but yielded an enormous find of unusually high quality potash.

Phosphate, however, remained the strength of IAC. The company continued to buy or lease acreage in the central Florida area, where in 1929 it pioneered the flotation method for separating phosphate pebbles from surrounding sludge, thereby greatly increasing the yield potential of any given mine. Shortly before that, IAC had opened its first major phosphate processing plant in Wales, Tennessee, where raw phosphorus was converted into a variety of products, including such fertilizers as superphosphate and diammonium phosphate and also cleaning agents like tri-sodium phosphate. By 1939 IAC was the largest producer of phosphate rock in the world. Population pressure in Asia and Latin America, combined with the needs of larger, state-owned farms in Eastern Europe and Russia, gave to the business of fertilizers an importance that ensured that the decades of the 1950s and 1960s would be highly profitable for manufacturers such as IAC.

As if anticipating the postwar explosion in its foreign trade, IAC in 1941 changed its name to International Mineral & Chemical, Inc. (IMC) and also shifted its headquarters from Atlanta to downtown Chicago. With the war's end in 1945, American agricultural methods were studied and adopted by nations first awakening to the problems of overpopulation and land exhaustion, and America's agriculture depended above all else on large quantities of fertilizer. Soon Japan was importing potash for its burdened rice fields, followed by India and a host of lesser Asian countries, while in the impoverished lands of Africa chemical fertilizers were adopted with the hope of averting wholesale famine. As long as the world's leading suppliers of commercial fertilizer were located in the United States and western Europe, fertilizer prices only strengthened as developing and communist countries upped their usage. Producers such as IMC responded by increasing capacity and enjoyed a 20-year period of solid profits and continued expansion.

In 1963 IMC made its belated entry into the nitrogen business, forming a joint venture with Northern Natural Gas of Omaha, Nebraska, to build an ammonia plant on the Mississippi River in Cordova, Illinois. A year later IMC underscored its faith in the export business by building its own ocean shipping terminal near Tampa, Florida, with storage facilities for phosphate rock and chemicals and a mechanized loading system capable of handling 2,500 tons per hour. At the same time, to solidify its land transportation IMC began assembling its own fleet of rail cars, ensuring itself of adequate rolling stock for the highly seasonal business of mixed fertilizers. The company also took a few tentative steps toward diversifying its holdings with the 1967 purchase of two industrial mineral firms and the acquisition a few years later of several container companies.

By that time, however, the world fertilizer market was in the midst of a radical change. Third World and Communist-bloc nations had placed great emphasis on developing indigenous supplies of the basic fertilizer nutrients, seeking to free themselves of dependence on the Western multinationals, and as a result total world production was up sharply by the early 1970s. Many of the new producers were under government control or enjoyed state subsidies, making it impossible for Western suppliers to offer competitive pricing. This shift was dramatized by the oil crisis of 1973–74, when skyrocketing energy prices pushed fertilizers up by as much as 300 percent, providing further impetus for the development of Third World and Communist-bloc supplies. (The production of nitrogen in the form of ammonia is extremely energy-intensive, and as nitrogen is the most widely used fertilizer in the world, fertilizer prices tend to follow the cost of energy.)

Fertilizer prices quickly returned to pre-1973 prices, but the turmoil only confirmed the resolve of IMC president Richard A. Lenon to pursue a program of diversification. In 1975 IMC paid $207 million for Commercial Solvents Corporation, a major producer of industrial chemicals, hydrocarbons—including explosives—and pharmaceuticals, including various growth hormones for livestock. Commercial Solvents also brought with it a sizable ammonia plant in Sterlington, Louisiana, to which IMC soon added a second facility in an effort to protect itself against any further price panics in the nitrogen market. 1975 was also the year in which IMC's new state-of-the-art processing plant began operations near Mulberry, Florida, increasing the company's production of phosphate and other chemicals in anticipation of energy-driven cost and price surges.

Unfortunately for IMC, however, the fertilizer market has drifted continually downward ever since the mid-1970s. What the business periodicals referred to as "the notoriously cyclical fertilizer industry" was in fact entering a depression that has proven to be all but permanent. Worldwide use of fertilizers continued to climb, but an ever greater percentage of fertilizer was produced in developing and centrally planned economies. According to the World Bank, in 1950 the capitalist West produced about 70 percent of the world's fertilizer; by the 1980s that figure was down to around 30 percent, with the bulk of the new producers located in Communist-bloc countries that could sell their excess fertilizer below Western market prices. Exacerbating this general decline was the recession suffered by U.S. agriculture throughout the 1980s, when grain surpluses drove down the commodity markets and idled many farms in the United States and Canada. Further, the use of phosphates in detergent was banned by the Environmental Protection Agency in the 1970s, while a growing proportion of the U.S. public expressed concern about the presence of nonorganic fertilizers in their food.

In the meantime, IMC management made a number of poor business decisions in the early 1980s. The company embarked on a vast expansion of its Florida phosphate rock holdings, doubled the capacity of its processing plant at Mulberry, and pursued a technique for uranium oxide recovery at a time when the nuclear energy industry had been brought to a standstill by opposition from environmentalists. When the fertilizer market hit a ten-year low in 1986, new IMC Chairman George Kennedy succeeded at last in diversifying the company's holdings with the purchase of Mallinckrodt Corporation from Avon, Inc., for $675 million. Mallinckrodt, a 115-year-old St. Louis firm, was powerful in medical imaging technology and pharmaceuticals. IMC soon added Pitman-Moore, an Illinois-based manufacturer of animal health products.

IMC's Kennedy then made the kind of brilliant strategic decision that will doubtless be the subject of a business school case study. Recognizing the fundamental weakness of the fertilizer business, which then supplied about half of corporate revenue, he made IMC into a holding company with three separate subsidiaries—IMC Fertilizer, Mallinckrodt, and Pitman-Moore. When fertilizer prices rose briefly in early 1988, he sold off 62 percent of IMC's stock in a public offering, then gradually sold the remainder of IMC's holdings back to IMC itself. By means of this adroit maneuver, IMC freed itself of the troubled fertilizer business while picking up the cash to make another major purchase in 1989, when it added Cooper Animal Health Group. Kennedy changed IMC's name to Imcera Group, Inc., and has fared splendidly ever since.

IMCF has not prospered to nearly such a degree. U.S. agriculture remained weak, while the demise of communism brought an enormous amount of fertilizer into the open market at bargain prices; the formerly state-controlled economies were desperate to obtain cash from the West. The severe recession that began in 1989 was a further blow to IMCF's fortunes, as were a 1992 special charge of $166 million for accounting charges and a 1993 settlement of a lawsuit for $169 million. The suit was brought by various parties following an explosion at a nitroparaffin plant in Sterlington, Louisiana, in May of 1991; eight employees were killed and many injured by the explosion, which occurred in a plant operated by IMCF although owned by Angus Chemical Company.

With fertilizer prices dropping to their lowest levels since the mid-1970s, IMCF formed a joint venture in 1993 with Freeport-McMoRan Resource Partners to pool their phosphate holdings. While it is hard not to see this move as the rather desperate attempt of a staggering giant to salvage what it can from a hopeless situation, it may yet prove to be a winning combination once the world fertilizer market returns to some semblance of order. With one half of all U.S. phosphate production, the new joint venture would obviously dominate a healthy phosphate market, but as of 1993, it remained only the largest player in a losing game.

Further Reading:

Chemical Week, January 27, 1993, p. 9.

"Growing With Agriculture to Feed a Hungry World," Northbrook, Illinois: IMC Fertilizer corporate publication, c. 1991.

"IMC Group Charts Chemical Course," *Chemical Week,* September 17, 1975, p. 18.

"IMC: Slimmer Profits for a Fertilizer Giant," *Chemical Week,* March 17, 1982, pp. 44–50.

Improving the Supply of Fertilizers to Developing Countries, Washington, DC: The World Bank, 1989.

Kemezis, Paul, "Imcera's Quick-Change Act," *Chemical Week,* July 18, 1990, pp. 22–24.

Nelson, Lewis B., *History of the United States Fertilizer Industry,* Muscle Shoals, AL: Tennessee Valley Authority, 1990.

"Prairie Province Goes Wild Over Potash," *Business Week,* July 21, 1982, pp. 110–114.

—Jonathan Martin

Inland Container Corporation

4030 Vincennes Road
Indianapolis, Indiana 46268
U.S.A.
(317) 879-4222
Fax: (317) 879-4234

Private Subsidiary of Temple-Inland Inc.
Incorporated: 1925 as Inland Box Company
Employees: 7,500
Sales: $1.25 billion
Stock Exchanges: New York Pacific
SICs: 2653 Corrugated & Solid Fiber Boxes (Primary); 2631
    Paperboard Mills; 2679 Converted Paper & Paperboard
    Products Nec

Inland Container Corporation, based in Indianapolis, Indiana, is one of the United States' largest producers of containerboard and corrugated shipping containers. In 1992 the company ranked among the top four producers of containerboard, with about 8 percent of U.S. production. In 1984 Inland Container and Temple-Eastex Inc., those subsidiaries of Time Inc. conducting its forest products business, were spun off and merged as Temple-Inland Inc., a holding company with interests in paper, packaging, building products, and financial services. By the 1990s, Temple-Inland's operations were divided between Inland Container and two other major subsidiaries: Temple-Inland Forest Products Corporation, responsible for the Bleached Paperboard and Building Products groups; and Temple-Inland Financial Services, conducting financial activities ranging from mortgage and consumer banking to land development and insurance. Of the three subsidiaries, Inland Container represented the largest manufacturing unit, accounting for approximately 46 percent of revenues in 1992.

Inland Container Corporation dates back to 1918, when Herman C. Krannert founded Anderson Box Company in Anderson, Indiana. Though this original business would eventually become a subsidiary of its larger successor, company records officially trace Inland's origins to Krannert's founding in 1925 of Inland Box Company in Indianapolis. After nearly a year of production in rented space, the fledgling company moved into a newly constructed plant. By 1929, Inland Box Company had grown sufficiently to warrant purchase of a second plant, the Gardner & Harvey Container Corporation in Middletown, Ohio.

In 1930 the company name was changed to Inland Container Corporation. By the end of the 1930s, the company had expanded operations to Chicago, Milwaukee, and Evansville.

The 1940s marked a period of ambitious planning cut short by World War II. With no paper supply of its own, Inland moved toward a joint venture to build a kraft mill with Agar Manufacturing Company, which already ran four operations in the Northeast. But plans were deferred, first by the war, and then by Agar's acquisition by International Paper Company.

Following the war, however, renewed efforts in mill development culminated in a joint venture, Georgia Kraft Company, of which Inland owned 40 percent and the Mead Corporation owned the other 60 percent. With the 1948 completion of its first mill in Macon, Georgia, the joint venture began production of linerboard. To accommodate expanding business, Georgia Kraft began construction of a second mill at Rome, Georgia, in 1952. Two years later construction was completed, and the Rome linerboard mill began production. In 1955 Inland acquired an additional 10 percent of the joint venture, granting Inland and Mead equal shares in a lasting partnership.

The 1960s marked a period of continued growth and new business ventures. By 1960, the company boasted 19 box plants, including several sheet plants, and sales of $93 million, up from $77 million five years earlier. In April of that year, 175,000 shares of Class A common stock were put on the market, representing Inland's first public trading. Inland entered the glass container business with its purchase of Fairmount Glass Company in 1961 (this attempt at diversification was relatively short-lived, and Fairmount was sold in 1969). Also in 1961, Georgia Kraft met higher demand with an additional paper machine at Rome and construction of a new mill in Mahrt, Alabama, which started production in 1966. Anticipating continued growth in the 1970s, Inland broke ground for its first wholly owned paper mill, at New Johnsonville, Tennessee, in 1969.

The 1970s marked a period of internal change for Inland, with changing duties of key officers and important changes in asset management. On January 1, 1970, Henry Goodrich, who had joined the company in 1968, was elected both president and chief executive officer. As CEO, Goodrich replaced Herman Krannert, the company founder and CEO since 1925. As president, he filled a post that had been filled first by George Elliott, from 1952 to 1963, and Philip Holton, president from 1963 to 1970. The 1972 death of Herman Krannert further changed the company's profile. The founder's wife and the Krannert Charitable Trust made a secondary offering of the company's stock in the fall of 1972, setting the ground for company stock listings on the New York Stock Exchange. Inland stock was first traded on the exchange on December 12, 1972.

The 1970s were also characterized by continued growth resulting in new plants and geographic expansion. In 1970, with sales at $197 million, the company moved to the West Coast with the acquisition of a Bell, California, plant. Western potential was further developed in 1973, when Inland acquired the Newark and Santa Fe Springs box plants and the Newark mill. Growth continued closer to the home front as well, as the construction of the Newport, Indiana, recycle mill was completed in 1975, beginning production of containerboard using recycled material as its furnish. The success of this mill, paired with growing emphasis on recycling, would foster unprecedented recycling innovation into the 1990s.

In May of 1978 it was announced that Inland would become part of Time Inc., a move that many analysts, such as Robert J. Cole of the *New York Times,* expected would reduce Time's dependence on publishing as its primary business. Inland had become an attractive target for acquisition, with 1978 sales of $397 million, over twice the figure at the start of that decade. The merger, finalized in November of that year, provided extra impetus to the already established pattern of growth. By 1980, Inland sales had jumped to $597 million.

In addition to the merger with Time, the late 1970s brought yet another shift in upper management. In October of 1979 Henry Goodrich returned to Alabama to become chief executive officer of Sonat, Inc., and was replaced by Jack Ames as third CEO of Inland.

In the early 1980s changing market conditions together with continually increasing costs, prompted new strategies to supplement Inland's core container business. Georgia Kraft Company entered the lumber and plywood business with sawmills in Greenville and Rome, Georgia, and Cottonton, Alabama, and a sizable plywood and lumber mill at Madison, Georgia. In 1981 the corrugated box plant in Indianapolis was closed. Because it was the original plant built by the Krannert family in 1926, the decision was a difficult one, according to company officials. But new market conditions under the relatively new ownership of Time called for new business strategies.

Trying new strategies of its own, Time Inc. in 1983 formed Temple-Inland Inc. to hold all the stock of Temple-Eastex Inc. and Inland Container Corp. for purposes of stock distribution. Time's board of directors authorized the distribution of 90 percent of the outstanding common stock of Temple-Inland Inc. to holders of Time common stock of record on January 11, 1984, at the rate of 0.36 of a share of Temple-Inland common stock for each share of Time stock.

On January 26, 1984, Temple-Inland was spun off from Time Inc. Standard & Poor's reported that although the spinoff eliminated a significant source of earnings and cash flow for Time, these businesses generated lower returns on capital than Time's magazine publishing and video operations. A January 4, 1984, article in *PR Newswire* anticipated that Time's earnings base would be less cyclical and operating margins and returns would improve measurably. Standard & Poor's raised the ratings of Time's outstanding senior debt to "AA" from "AA−" and maintained its "A-1+" commercial paper rating. Publicly rated industrial development revenue bonds and pollution control bonds issued by Temple Eastex Inc. and Inland Container—which were still guaranteed by Time, despite the spinoff—were also raised to "AA" from "AA−."

After the spinoff, Temple-Inland was poised for conservative but constant growth. Despite a severe recession in the forest products industry in the early 1980s, the company fared comparatively well in large part because of its high operating efficiencies. Furthermore, Temple-Inland inherited a conservative capital structure from Time Inc., with total debt to total capitalization at 23 percent and debt leverage checked by moderate capital spending plans.

Despite moderate capital spending plans after the spinoff, Inland measured substantial growth. Construction of a recycled linerboard mill in Ontario, California, began in 1984, and production started in 1985. In October of 1985 Inland completed the sale of its Eastex Packaging Inc. unit to Manville Forest Products Corp., a subsidiary of Manville Corp., to generate an after-tax gain of about $7 million. That same year Georgia Kraft Company was dissolved, with Inland becoming the sole owner of the Rome, Georgia, linerboard mill. Inland undertook a five-year, $190-million improvement program to increase the production capacity of Inland-Rome by approximately 25 percent. In 1986 Inland acquired a linerboard mill in Orange, Texas, along with three box plants from Owens-Illinois. These and other investments reinforced the company after a recessionary debut to the 1980s.

On July 24, 1987, Jack Ames retired as chief executive officer of Inland, and Ben Lancashire became chairman, president, and chief executive officer of the company. Lancashire oversaw unprecedented growth early in his tenure. In 1988 Inland sales exceeded $1 billion for the first time. In November of 1989 Temple-Inland's board of directors approved capital expenditures for Inland of $200 million, to be distributed between a $160-million recycle mill, a $25-million white top production line at its Orange, Texas, mill, and a new, $15-million box plant in the Richmond, Virginia, area.

These and other investments marked the late 1980s. In 1989 Inland moved to a new corporate headquarters building in northwest Indianapolis. In 1990 the company purchased Indianapolis-based Pakway Container Corporation, operating three box plants, and California-based Crockett Container Corporation, operating four box plants; this brought Inland's box plant total to 40.

Construction of the Maysville, Kentucky, 100 percent recycled linerboard mill began in 1991, continuing recycling concerns that began in the 1970s and became a socially and economically mandated process by the 1990s. Among other groups promoting recycled goods, the "Buy Recycled Business Alliance," comprised of major American corporations, began pressuring suppliers to provide higher volumes of recycled packaging materials and greater recycled content in finished goods. Temple-Inland's 1992 annual report projected that over 40 percent of the company's containerboard would be recycled by 1993. On October 8, 1992, just 18 months after groundbreaking, the Maysville mill began production. Located on a 250-acre site on the Ohio River, about 60 miles east of Cincinnati, the mill was capable of producing 600 tons per day—210,000 tons per year—of 100 percent recycled linerboard. The Maysville mill was the first in North America to use a proprietary ultra-efficient lightweight contaminant removal process that Inland called "advanced recycling." Overall yield from the process on incoming OCC (old corrugated containers) was about 90 percent, with the remaining 10 percent flushed through the system and sent to landfills. Anticipating growing markets in recyclables, the mill was designed to expand capacity to as much as 300,000 tons per year. With the Maysville mill, Inland maintained its position as the largest U.S. producer of 100 percent recycled containerboard and linerboard.

In addition to its dependence on 100 percent recycled furnish, a particularly unique aspect of the Maysville mill was its energy provision negotiated with the nearby East Kentucky Power Cooperative's Spurlock generating station. The utility signed an agreement to sell Inland 250,000 pounds of steam per hour and between 20 and 25 MW to heat process water and dry paper. Low-pressure steam was supplied directly to the mill, eliminating the need for smokestacks at the mill and totally eliminating air emissions.

While most capital projects of the 1980s and 1990s focused on expanding capacity and increasing quality of containerboard mills, Inland also emphasized increasingly complex graphics needs in packaging. In 1992 the company's $17-million Graphics Resource Center began operations in Indianapolis, representing one of the largest preprint linerboard presses in the world. The press is capable of running at 1,200 feet per minute, with an eight-color central impression cylinder with two additional downstream print stations and full robotics capability. The main product is preprinted linerboard printed according to client specifications and then shipped to Inland plants and converted into boxes.

Even with a weak national economy and high costs of raw material paired with low selling prices, Inland entered the 1990s with considerable promise. In 1992, record production of both containerboard and corrugated boxes helped post earnings of $112.3 million, up 49 percent from $75.4 million in 1991. And even though the average selling price of boxes in 1992 remained six percent below the historical highs of 1989, it rose two percent above 1991 levels. Further price recovery depended on overall economic prosperity, both domestic and international, as Clifford J. Grum, chairman and CEO explained in Temple-Inland's 1992 annual report: "The growth momentum of the U.S. economy this year and the pace of recovery of other world economies will determine the ability of our company to restore profit margins in our paper businesses."

While Inland's price recovery depended on uncertain, international economic recovery, its overall stability was insured, in part, by the stability of its parent company. In a December 20, 1992, article for the *Dallas Morning News,* David LaGesse noted that Temple-Inland's financial services group helped feed the company's bottom line during lean years for its wood-based products—boxes, paper, and lumber—in the early 1990s. As a

result, the company was able to continue capital investment in its paper, box, and saw mills, while many competitors cut corners to survive the recession. Many analysts predicted a strong recovery in the event of economic turnaround. "Temple-Inland is among the best-positioned companies," said Evadna Lynn, an analyst with Dean Witter Reynolds Inc. in New York, in the same article. With its seven paper mills, 39 corrugated box manufacturing plants, and the support of its Inland-Temple holding company, Inland Container was poised for uncontained prosperity.

Principal Subsidiaries: Rexford Paper Company; Crockett Container Corporation; Pakway Container Corporation; Glass Container Plant, Owens-Illinois de Puerto Rico (20%); Chemical Company, Harima M.I.D. Inc. (Japan; 25%).

Further Reading:

"Ben J. Lancashire Elected Chairman," *PR Newswire,* July 14, 1987.

"East Kentucky Co-Op Begins First-Ever Steam Sales to Inland Container Mill," *Industrial Energy Bulletin,* April 9, 1993, p. 2.

Ferguson, Kelly H., "Inland Starts up Greenfield Recycled Containerboard Mill at Maysville, KY," *Pulp & Paper,* December 1992, p. 40.

Holtzapfel, Mike, "Inland-Rome Rebuilds Machines for Major Boost in Production," *American Papermaker,* December 1990, p. 45.

Inland Container Corporation: A Brief History, Diboll: Temple-Inland Inc., 1993.

"Inland to Close Original Box Plant," *Reuters,* August 28, 1981, AM Cycle.

Jones, Alex S., "Time Inc. Profit Widens," *New York Times,* January 31, 1984, p. D5.

LaGesse, David, "S&L Purchase Keeps Firm out of the Woods; Temple-Inland Profits by Branching Out," *Dallas Morning News,* December 20, 1992, p. 1H.

"S&P Lowers Inland Container Rating," *PR Newswire,* February 3, 1984.

"Standard & Poor's Raises Time Ratings," *PR Newswire,* January 4, 1984.

Temple-Inland Annual Report, Diboll: Temple-Inland Inc., 1992.

"Temple-Inland Approves Unit Expenditures," *Reuters,* November 3, 1989, BC Cycle.

"Temple-Inland Completes Sale of Eastex Packaging," *PR Newswire,* October 28, 1985.

"Temple-Inland Inc.; Planned Capital Expenditures for Subsidiary," *S&P Daily News,* November 6, 1989.

"Time Distributes Temple-Inland Shares," *PR Newswire,* November 17, 1983.

—Kerstan Cohen

INTERFACE.

Interface, Inc.

P.O. Box 1503
Orchard Hill Road
LaGrange, Georgia 30241
U.S.A.
(404) 882-1891
Fax: (404) 882-0500

Public Company
Incorporated: 1973 as Carpets International of Georgia, Inc.
Employees: 3,735
Sales: $594 million
Stock Exchanges: NASDAQ
SICs: 2273 Carpets and Rugs; 2221 Broad Woven Fabric,
    Man-made; 2819 Industrial Inorganic Chemicals, Not
    Elsewhere Classified

Interface, Inc., is the world's leading manufacturer and marketer of carpet tiles. Carpet tiles are uniformly custom-sized squares of floor covering that cling to floors without the aid of adhesives. They are popular in office design because of their flexibility in redecoration and easy removal and replacement for rewiring and other repair work. These modular carpet systems, marketed under the brand names Interface and Heuga, are used throughout the world, primarily in commercial and institutional settings. Interface is also the leading producer of interior fabrics for open plan office furniture systems in the United States. The fabrics for these systems, which are usually enclosed, customized work stations, are produced by the company's Guilford of Maine, Inc., subsidiary. Interface is also involved in specialty chemical production. The company's most important chemical is Intersept, an antimicrobial chemical agent used in some carpet manufacturing. Intersept is produced by another subsidiary, Rockland React-Rite, Inc.

Foreign sales account for just over half of Interface's revenue, and the company has 25 production and distribution facilities worldwide, as well as more than 150 sales and marketing outposts in 90 different countries. Interface currently controls about 40 percent of the international carpet tile market.

Interface, Inc., was founded in 1973 by Ray C. Anderson, the company's only chairman and chief executive officer to date. Prior to that time, Anderson had been working as a research manager for Milliken & Co., a privately owned textile firm. On behalf of Milliken, Anderson was sent abroad to research the technology for manufacturing carpet tiles in preparation for Milliken's prospective entry into that field. While visiting Carpets International Plc. (CI), a large British company specializing in carpet, Anderson was introduced to a process called "fusion bonding." Anderson immediately recognized the potential of this process for producing carpet tiles, as well as the huge market for carpet tile in the United States that had not yet been tapped. In 1973 he carried out the dream of millions of would-be entrepreneurs, quitting his secure job with Milliken & Co. in order to start his own business.

Interface first appeared as a joint venture with Carpets International Plc., called Carpets International of Georgia, Inc. (CI-Georgia). Of the initial seed money for the company, $750,000 (half of the total) came from CI, the rest from Anderson and various backers mostly from his home town of West Point, Georgia. The new company produced its first piece of carpet on New Year's Eve, 1973. On its first day of operation, Carpets International of Georgia had only 15 employees, including Anderson. The company's first year of operation was a financial disaster. It lost $400,000 on sales of just over $800,000. Skyrocketing prices for petrochemicals, an important raw material in the carpet industry, were a large part of the problem. These price increases were the result of the 1973 oil embargo, and the recession that ensued.

On the other hand, the company's association with an established firm like Carpets International gave it several advantages. The most important of these was access to advanced technology. CI was able to provide cutting technology superior to that of companies like Milliken, saving the company 10 percent on the cost of yarn. Other technology was made available that enabled CI-Georgia to develop special bonding equipment. This equipment made it possible to install carpet tiles without glue, bonding the four-ply carpet fibers to a fiberglass backing. These contributions, along with the beginning of the office building boom, helped CI-Georgia triple its sales to $2.4 million by the end of 1975. The company also turned its first profit that year.

During the second half of the 1970s there was tremendous growth in the white-collar segment of the U.S. economy. About 800,000 office jobs per year were created between 1975 and 1980, causing huge demand for office furnishing. It was during this period that modular carpet systems became extremely popular among office managers and interior designers. Carpet tiles allowed designers to install floor coverings that were pleasing to the eye, while at the same time were easy to remove and replace, whether for cleaning, redecorating, or accessing wiring beneath the floor. By 1978, Interface's sales had reached $11 million. In 1979 the company introduced a special carpet product for use in hospitals. Hospital administrators had been seeking ways to soften the cold, institutional feel of their interiors. Carpet in hospitals had long been considered impractical because of the difficulty in cleaning spilled blood and other medical messes. Using its fusion bonding technology, Interface developed extremely dense carpet tiles that were more resistant to the burdens of hospital use, as well as easy to remove for cleaning. It took a few more years, however, to overcome the medical community's resistance to carpet based on hygiene. To solve this problem, Interface eventually developed Intersept, a chemical adhesive that killed germs while it held carpet tiles in place.

In the early 1980s Carpets International Plc. began to face fierce competition from a flood of broadloom carpet being imported into the United Kingdom. Meanwhile, the American joint venture continued to grow, with sales swelling to $57 million in 1982. As CI continued to flounder, the American firm took over 10 percent of CI's equity in the company, and changed its name to Interface Flooring Systems, Inc. The two companies continued to move in opposite directions. While Interface's sales leaped again in 1983, to $80 million, CI teetered on the edge of bankruptcy. Since CI was still Interface's largest shareholder, Anderson was understandably concerned about who might end up controlling 40 percent of his company. In order to avert receivership for CI, Interface concocted a plan to provide a $4 million loan convertible to 41.3 percent future equity in CI. The agreement also gave Interface the option to purchase another 8.8 percent of CI shares for about $2.3 million through 1987, the year the loan was due. Interface also went public for the first time in 1983, selling its shares over-the-counter. The company raised $14.4 million in its initial offering.

Interface purchased CI's carpet tile division for $8.4 million in 1984, giving Interface entry into the European market for the first time. This transaction gave Interface ownership of CI's Illingworth and Debron brands of carpet. Around the same time, Interface acquired Carintusa Inc. from CI, for $440,000. Carintusa, the sole U.S. distributor of woven English-broadloom carpet manufactured by CI, was based in Los Angeles, California. In the same period, Interface also acquired Chemmar Associates, Inc., merging it with its Interface Research Corp. subsidiary. Chemmar was the licensor of Intersept, the antimicrobial agent developed for hospital carpets. Aided by these acquisitions, Interface's sales climbed to $107 million for 1984. By that time, after only 11 years of existence, Interface already controlled about 30 percent of the growing U.S. carpet tile market. This figure put the company in a virtual tie for the lead in market share with Milliken & Co., Anderson's former employers.

In 1985 Interface exercised its option to convert its CI promissory note, acquiring 41.3 percent of Carpets International Plc. By this time, CI's interest in Interface had been reduced to 25.6 percent. The company's overseas business began to pick up around this time as well, particularly in oil-rich Middle Eastern countries. As the 1980s progressed, Interface began to diversify beyond carpets into related industries. The company purchased Guilford Industries for $97 million in 1986. Guilford was a textile company that specialized in fabrics for office furniture systems, including cubicle dividers, walls, and ceilings. This acquisition gave Interface the ability to market complete office furnishing packages, an idea that proved to be appealing to designers both domestically and abroad. Interface also began to expand its specialty chemical operations that year. Two Georgia-based companies, Rockland Corp. and React-Rite, Inc., were acquired on the last day of 1986, for a combined total of about $4 million. With the addition of these two companies, Interface improved its ability in polymer chemistry, essential to the further development of its Intersept program.

Interface swallowed up what was left of Carpets International in 1987. CI's remaining debt was then paid off, and its broadloom carpet business sold. By this time, CI's name had been changed to Debron Investments Plc. For 1987, Interface reported sales of

$267 million, nearly double the previous year's figure. During that year, the company's name was changed to Interface, Inc., and Interface Flooring Systems, Inc., was retained as the name of the company's North American carpet tile subsidiary. Interface became the undisputed world leader in carpet tiles in 1988, with the acquisition of Heuga Holdings B.V., a Dutch company with sales of more than $200 million. Heuga was one of the world's oldest manufacturers of carpet tiles. Interface had been trying to acquire the company since about 1983, when it was first put up for sale by the 13 children of Heuga's founder. At that time, Interface was not able to complete a deal. The company that did buy Heuga was subsequently acquired by Ausimont N.V., a firm that was not interested in the carpet tile business. From Ausimont, Interface purchased not only Heuga but Pandel, Inc., another wholly owned subsidiary. Heuga contributed manufacturing facilities in the Netherlands, the United Kingdom, Canada, and Australia. Pandel's U.S. plant produced carpet tile backing and mats. That company recorded sales of $10 million in 1987. The acquisition of Heuga expanded Interface's international business enormously, gaining the company contracts with a number of major British firms, as well as such prominent Japanese companies as Hitachi, Tokyo Marine, and Nomura Securities. It also helped Interface further diversify into residential carpet tile sales, which had accounted for about a quarter of Heuga's European business. With the addition of Heuga, the company's revenue jumped dramatically once again, reaching $582 million.

In early 1990 Interface acquired the assets of Steil, Inc., based in Grand Rapids, Michigan. Steil had for several years been the exclusive U.S. distributor of Guilford's open line panel and upholstery fabrics. Later that year, the company invested in Prince Street Technologies, Ltd., a producer of upper-end broadloom carpet. Prince Street, based in Georgia, received a loan from Interface in exchange for the right to acquire an equity interest. Interface generated an all-time high of $623 million in revenue in 1990.

Sales shrank for the first time in the company's history in 1991, largely due to the recession in the global economy. In that year, Interface generated net income of $8.9 million on sales of $582 million. During 1991, Interface Service Management, Inc. (ISM), was formed in conjunction with ISS International Service System, Inc., a Danish firm specializing in facility maintenance. The creation of ISM enabled Interface to provide its customers with a more integrated interior system in which all of its furnishing needs could be supplied by one source. In Europe the company launched a similar project, in which independent service contractors were licensed to provide maintenance services. These contractors operated under the name IMAGE (Interface Maintenance Advisory Group of Europe). Interface also reorganized its corporate structure in late 1991. The company's operations in Asia and the Pacific Islands were unified under a new holding company, Interface Asia-Pacific, Inc. Interface Europe, Inc., was also formed, merging Interface International, Inc., which had controlled operations in the United Kingdom, with the holding company that owned Heuga and its various European subsidiaries.

By 1992, Interface's antimicrobial chemical Intersept was being used in over a dozen product categories. These categories included paints, wall coverings, ceiling tiles, carpet, fabrics, and coating materials. The marketing of Intersept was assisted by the formation of The Envirosense Consortium, a group of companies that use Intersept in the manufacture of a variety of products. The Envirosense program was initiated as a response to increasing cases of and concern regarding building-related illnesses and other health concerns associated with indoor work atmospheres. Interface's sales rebounded somewhat in 1992. Sales for the year were $594 million. Net income increased by over 37 percent, to $12.3 million.

In January of 1993 Interface announced that it had acquired the low-profile access flooring system of Servoplan, S.A., of France. The acquisition, through the company's U.S. and French subsidiaries, included all patents, know-how, and production equipment relating to this flooring system. Interface had previously marketed the Servoplan system in North America alone, and the positive response of its customers led the company to seek worldwide control of the system's manufacture and distribution. At the time of the acquisition, Anderson indicated that the system would be sold under the name Intercell.

The following month, Interface announced another acquisition. The company's Guilford of Maine subsidiary had acquired the fabric division assets of Stevens Linen Associates, Inc., a leading producer of panel and upholstery fabric for office furniture systems. This acquisition, related to Stevens Linen's Chapter 11 reorganization proceedings, was made in order to ease Guilford's expansion into decorative fabric markets. Stevens' Dudley facility was attractive partly because of its close proximity to Guilford's fabric operation in East Douglas, Massachusetts, from which activities at Dudley could be supported. Another acquisition occurred in June of 1993, when Interface bought Bentley Mills, Inc., a manufacturer of designer-oriented broadloom carpet used for commercial and institutional settings.

Interface, Inc., is a company that has managed to become the world leader in its core industry in less than 20 years of operation. With the exception of the recession year of 1991, the company has been able to increase its sales every year it has existed. Through the remainder of the 1990s, Interface will very likely be able to continue this pattern of expansion, primarily by introducing its products to a wider range of commercial customers in Asia and continental Europe. In addition, Interface's specialty chemical operations seem poised for continued growth, as public attention to occupational health increases, and the potential hazards of higher technology in the office environment come under closer scrutiny.

Principal Subsidiaries: Interface Flooring Systems, Inc.; Interface Europe, Inc.; Interface Asia-Pacific, Inc.; Guilford of Maine, Inc.; Rockland React-Rite, Inc.; Interface Research Corporation.

Further Reading:

Interface, Inc., Annual Report and Form 10-K 1991, LaGrange, Georgia: Interface, Inc., 1992.
"Interface's Premium: The Tiles That Bind," *Financial World,* August 7, 1984, pp. 81–82.
Lappen, Alyssa A., "Carpet Tile King," *Forbes,* April 17, 1989, pp. 60–64.
Lee, Shelley A., "Magic Carpet Ride," *Business Atlanta,* October 1992, pp. 111–19.

—Robert R. Jacobson

The Interlake Corporation

550 Warrenville Road
Lisle, Illinois 60532-4387
U.S.A.
(708) 852-8800
Fax: (708) 719-7277

Public Company
Incorporated: June 23, 1905, as By-Products Coke
    Corporation
Employees: 4,800
Sales: $708.2 million
Stock Exchanges: New York, Chicago
SICs: 3535 Conveyors & Conveying Equipment; 3728
    Aircraft Parts & Equipment Nec; 3399 Primary Metal
    Products Nec

The Interlake Corporation, once a company within the steel industry, is currently engaged in the design, manufacture, and sale or distribution of a variety of engineered metal products, although it no longer manufactures steel. The company's primary customers are in the automotive, aerospace, materials handling, and packaging industries. Interlake has 11 manufacturing plants in the United States, in addition to operations in Canada, the United Kingdom, Germany, Belgium, and Australia. Interlake exemplifies some of the conditions operating within the American steel industry in the 20th century, providing an interesting example of how changes in that industry caused companies to re-evaluate their core businesses and adapt to new market conditions.

The earliest predecessor of Interlake was a small furniture shop in Shelbyville, Missouri. There, in 1880, a furniture maker named M. E. McMasters developed a barbed steel staple that he used to join wooden bed rails. The staple was a rigid metal form with teeth cut into it. When hammered into place, it held two pieces of wood securely at a specific angle. In 1882 the business relocated to Quincy, Illinois where the operation was reincorporated as the Quincy Plate and Staple Manufacturing Company. After several years making metal plates and staples of the type invented by M. E. McMasters, the company added a line of new implements to the product line, prompting yet another name change, this time to the Quincy Hardware Manufacturing Company.

In 1889, however, the enterprise was acquired by the Acme Flexible Clasp Company under undocumented circumstances.

Acme Flexible Clasp, basically a manufacturer of hinges and other small metal products, was based in Chicago. Business was very strong in that city during the late 1890s and early 1900s. Much of the damage from Chicago's great fire had been repaired, and the city was by now a growing metropolis and railway and shipping terminus.

Demand for building materials was so strong that by 1904 Acme was forced to build a new production facility on Chicago's Archer Avenue. The company's headquarters were moved to this site from Clark Street, as were other small production shops. After changing its name again to Acme Steel Goods Company, the firm purchased a 133-acre site on the Little Calumet River at Riverdale, Illinois in 1917. A year later the company built a hoop mill on the site.

In 1926 Acme Steel built a second rolling mill, and three years later added the number three hot mill, both of which were used to produce formed and sheet steel, as opposed to block ingots. The new plants were built at the Riverdale site, which had become the company's center of production.

The company endured several years of hardship during the Great Depression, but was among the first to recover as a result of President Roosevelt's heavy industry-oriented New Deal Programs. Some years later, during World War II, Acme Steel became deeply involved in war production, turning out a variety of steel products for artillery and mechanized armament manufacturers. Steel products and production quotas were strictly enforced by the government's War Production board. So, while Acme was unable to profit greatly from its war production, it was provided a valuable opportunity to establish relationships with new customers.

In 1947, after the close of the war, Acme acquired the Hoffert Machine Company in Racine, Wisconsin. This brought Acme into a new line of finished products, manufacturing stitching machines for the boxboard and graphic arts industries. Acme made its first international expansion in 1952 when it established a steel strap slitting and painting facility at Scarborough, Ontario.

In 1954 the company added a new building at Riverdale for the production of stitching and strapping tools and machines and other accessories. The company continued its expansion in 1956 by acquiring the Newport Steel Company in Newport, Kentucky. With the acquisition of Newport, Acme became a producer of steel ingots made from scrap steel and pig iron, freeing it from increasingly unstable supply prices. Newport also manufactured hot and cold rolled steel products, silicon and alloy sheets and bars, and electric weld line and conductor pipe, in addition to other steel products.

A year later Acme closed its Archer Avenue plant and transferred all production from that facility to Riverdale. In 1959 Acme opened a new steel line at Riverdale using the more efficient, higher quality oxygen converter system. The expansion caused Acme's debt to grow from $5.2 million in 1955 to $35 million in 1961. To make matters worse, six top officials retired simultaneously, leaving Acme with scant managerial expertise at the highest level. By 1964, however, the worst was over. Acme chair G. Findley Griffiths retired half the company's preferred shares and reduced debt by $20 million.

Despite its measured growth and expansion into new product lines, Acme was not a fully integrated steel manufacturer, although it began making its own raw steel in 1956 for downstream use and thus could be considered semi-integrated. It was mainly involved in the final stage of steel production, manufacturing finished products, and had no control over the price or availability of scrap, coal, or iron ore. Larger companies that were most successful at this time had control over these various factors and were thus able to exercise greater control over the market, to the detriment of companies such as Acme. This concentration of power was later illustrated by President Kennedy's showdown with United States Steel.

Another small company limited to one primary production process was Interlake Iron Corporation. Interlake, headquartered in Cleveland, produced pig iron, coke, and ferroalloys. Interlake sold its pig iron primarily to foundries and steel companies. Interlake was slowly being squeezed out of its limited market by new materials, changing technologies, and growing pig iron imports.

Interlake had considered diversification as early as 1949 but had dismissed all proposals as too risky or not yet urgent. By 1964, however, the pig iron market had collapsed and the situation had become urgent. Now, however, the company was not financially sound enough to pull off a diversification.

Interlake president Thaddeus F. Bell met with Griffiths to discuss a merger. Interlake's ore mining companies, Erie Mining in Minnesota and Wabush Mines in Canada, would provide an adequate source of iron ore for Acme's finishing plants. In addition, Interlake operated a blast furnace only 15 miles from Acme's Riverdale facility. This would enable molten iron to be transported by special rail cars directly from Interlake's furnaces to Acme's steel plant, eliminating the need for secondary melting facilities.

Acme Steel, with $138 million in assets, and Interlake, with $136 million in assets, formally merged in 1964. The new company, called Interlake Steel Corporation, instantly became a much stronger organization. The combined operations included steel plants in Riverdale and Wilder, Kentucky, and pig iron and coke plants in South Chicago, Erie, Pennsylvania, and Toledo, Ohio.

Griffiths was named chair of the new company, Bell was named president. George Enos, who had become chair of Interlake after merging his coal mining company with Interlake some years earlier, became a director.

In 1967 Interlake's management scrapped a proposed $200 million expansion program and decided instead to begin a diversification strategy aimed at reducing the company's dependence on its core steel business. The first move in this direction came in 1968 when Interlake purchased a two-thirds interest in the American subsidiary of the Swedish company Hoganas A.B. The subsidiary, Hoeganaes Corporation, was a ferrous metal powder manufacturer based in Riverton, New Jersey. The company also acquired Redirack Industries, Ltd., a Canadian firm that specialized in the manufacture of warehouse storage products. The company later introduced a new line of manual and automated stacker-retrievers that could neatly stack boxes or pallets of stock in warehouses.

In 1969 Interlake opened a technical research facility at Riverdale and later that year acquired the Gary Steel Supply Company, a warehousing and pickling operation at Blue Island, Illinois.

Also in 1969, Interlake took over Lodi Fab Industries of Lodi, California. This company manufactured storage rack systems, adding new products to the mix and providing Interlake with a presence in the Western United States. In 1970, after dropping "Steel" from its name to emphasize the growing diversification, Interlake purchased the Burmac Corporation, a steel strapping equipment and storage system manufacturer based in Ottawa, Illinois.

By 1972 Interlake had reduced the volume of its steel sales to 68 percent of total sales. In addition, 30 percent of the company's steel output was consumed by Interlake's nonsteel operations. While this showed rapid diversification away from steel, Interlake's new chair Reynold C. MacDonald continued to press on.

In the steel operations that remained, MacDonald encouraged the growth of specialty steel operations, producing smaller quantities of unusual steel that larger producers would charge a premium for. The company's profitability was held back by prohibitions on imports of Rhodesian chromium, and sales at Hoeganaes had dropped in 1970 and 1971, but rebounded in 1972. The production of steel had another drawback. In 1972 MacDonald stated that Interlake had already invested $1.5 billion in pollution controls and anticipated being forced to spend another $3.5 billion. "You look at those numbers," McDonald noted, "and ask how do you get the job done and keep your steelmaking facilities up to date?" Some environmentalists accused the company of poor pollution control practices, but an Interlake spokesperson pointed out that Interlake had taken a leadership role in pollution control efforts beginning in the early 1960s, and in fact was recognized by the Chicago City Council in 1965 for its contributions toward combatting air pollution.

Continuing its campaign of expansion, in April of 1973 Interlake acquired the Selma, Alabama-based silicon metal and ferroalloy manufacturer Alamet (Alabama Metallurgical Corporation). In 1974, Interlake formed a joint venture with Kawasaki Steel. The company, Kawatetsu/Interlake, Ltd., was created to market storage rack systems in Japan. In October of that year, Interlake acquired Dexion Comino International, a British material handling firm.

In December, Interlake established a joint venture with the Ford Motor Company, Wheeling Pittsburgh Steel, and Pickands Mather & Company to build and operate a huge coal mine near Pikeville, Kentucky. Each company was ensured a share of the mine's production, which exceeded 1.25 million tons per year. The company also took over the A. J. Bayer Company in December of 1974. Bayer, located in Shepherdsville, Kentucky, was a manufacturer of conveyor systems, which became a part of Interlake's material handling business.

Hoeganaes had record sales in 1972, 1973, 1974, and 1976, and introduced a new powdered welding alloy called Atomweld 525. Hoeganaes produced more than 50 percent of the metal powders in the Western Hemisphere. Despite the success of some of its products, the company faced a lagging demand for metal powders. In anticipation of future growth, Interlake increased its control of the company to 80 percent, and expanded its production capacity.

In April of 1976, Interlake acquired the Arwood Corporation. Based in Rockleigh, New Jersey, Arwood was principally engaged in the die casting and investment casting business.

By 1978 some of Interlake's larger steel production assets began to exhaust their useful lives. That year the company took a $15.7 million write-off for closing its merchant pig iron complex at Toledo. Interlake sold the adjacent coke battery to Koppers.

In December, 1978, Interlake President Frank Burgert was elevated to assistant to Reynold MacDonald. He was replaced by Frederick C. Langenberg, who reportedly had great plans to restructure the company's steel business. His initial emphasis was on moving Interlake away from its aging steel and strapping businesses and into newer lines such as castings, specialty metals and the material handling operations.

In 1980, after steel workers at Interlake's Wilder and Newport, Kentucky locations refused the company's request for a one-year wage freeze, MacDonald authorized shuttering the plants in those locations. While this involved a $37 million write-off, the plants were only marginally profitable. Also in 1980, Interlake closed Burmac and sold off the Gary Supply company. The company closed or sold several other smaller operations during the 1980s, including the die casting, silicon, and ferro-alloy business, and in 1982 repurchased $20 million worth of shares that had been controlled by the Madison Fund.

Sales at Hoeganaes, meanwhile, grew slowly, especially after a second plant was opened at Gallatin, Tennessee. Also experiencing better sales was the Globe silicon metal and ferroalloy division.

In 1986 Interlake reorganized along holding company lines. The iron, steel, and strapping business were transferred to a new company called the Acme Steel Company, and all other assets were transferred to the newly formed Interlake Companies, Inc. Both companies were, in turn, controlled by a new parent company called The Interlake Corporation.

The directors subsequently voted to spin off shares of the Acme Steel Company to Interlake shareholders, absolving Interlake of the steel operations. Acme Steel was back but, with all the company's steel operations, it was no longer part of Interlake.

The company's improved prospects as a result of the reorganization produced an unintended result: a raider. In July of 1989, Mark IV Industries, a corporate takeover group, announced plans to purchase as much as 15 percent of Interlake. As with other similar acquisitions, the plan may have been to carve up Interlake and sell its pieces to other companies at a premium.

Interlake immediately took drastic action. The company declared a huge one-time $45 dividend, created an employee stock ownership plan that snapped up $20 million worth of shares, and dove $550 million into debt. Even if Mark IV could gobble up Interlake, it was likely to spit it out. It was a classic poison pill defense, in which the suitor would be faced with a radically altered and much less attractive balance sheet if the takeover bid went through.

This defense was costly, but it succeeded. It enabled Interlake to concentrate its energy on what were now its core businesses: Hoeganaes, Dexion, Material Handling and Packaging, and Chem-tronics, a components manufacturer that Interlake had purchased in 1984 for $52 million.

By 1991, Interlake was operating under recessionary conditions, which hurt sales growth but did not deter the company from enhancing its long–term competitive position. Interlake continued to emphasize cost reduction and productivity increases while investing heavily in new product development. While the company's sales volume has decreased in recent years, operating income has risen and losses have been reduced. The company's transformation to solid financial performance is in progress, but far from complete.

Interlake is today a diversified metal products company that no longer manufactures steel. Its business is divided among five main divisions. Among them, Hoeganaes remains one of the world's largest manufacturers of ferrous metal powders, which are used to manufacture precision parts for automobiles, light trucks, farm and garden equipment, and other products. Chemtronics is involved mainly in the production of precision aerospace components and jet engine repair. Dexion, headquartered in Great Britain, is one of the leading storage systems manufacturers, with the bulk of its sales growth in Eastern Europe and the Middle East. Interlake's domestic material handling unit has recently concentrated on providing complete storage solutions for warehouses and distribution centers. The Interlake packaging group manufactures a variety of strapping and packaging systems for the graphic arts, steel, lumber, brick, newspaper, textile, corrugated, can, and bottle industries.

Principal Subsidiaries: The Interlake Companies, Inc.; Chemtronics, Inc.; Interlake Packaging Corp.; Dexion Group PLC; Hoeganaes Corp. (80%).

Further Reading:

"From the Frying Pan," *Forbes*, June 1, 1964, pp. 42–43.
"Good Match," *Forbes*, February 15, 1965, p. 30.
"Stockholders OK Merger of Acme Steel, Interlake Iron," *Steel*, December 21, 1964, p. 32.
"Steel Takes a Back Seat as Interlake Diversifies," *American Metal Market*, May 30, 1972, pp. 1–7.
"Interlake May Act to Expand Hoeganaes Metal Powder Unit," *American Metal Market*, April 16, 1974, pp. 1–25.
"Langenberg to be Interlake President, Chief Operating Officer," *American Metal Market*, December 20, 1978, p. 1.
"Changing the Mix," *Barron's*, April 27, 1981, pp. 39–46.
"Reorganization Is Completed at Interlake," *American Metal Market*, June 6, 1986, p. 4.
"Interlake's Plan Is Viewed as Ploy to Thwart Suitor," *Wall Street Journal*, p. B2.
"The History of Interlake, Inc.," Company Document, April 4, 1978.
"Interlake Corp.," *Moody's Industrial Manual 1992*, p. 3186.
The Interlake Corporation Annual Report, 1991.

—John Simley

Jackson National Life Insurance Companies

Jackson National Life Insurance Company

5901 Executive Dr.
Lansing, Michigan 48911
U.S.A.
(517) 394-3400
Fax: (517) 394-7107

Wholly owned subsidiary of Prudential Corporation plc
Founded: 1961
Sales: $16.6 billion
Employees: 1,300
SICs: 6311 Life Insurance

Jackson National Life Insurance Company is one of the top life insurance companies in the United States, with 17 regional offices, 80,000 agents, and customers in 45 states and the District of Columbia. Jackson National began as a small, regional life insurance carrier in 1961. The company was founded by A. J. (Tony) Pasant, a Lansing, Michigan, insurance salesman and field manager with 16 years of experience. Pasant had a firm belief in keeping customers happy and overhead low. Named after his hero, President Andrew Jackson, the agency Pasant founded initially retained 12 employees and reported assets of $650,000 in its first year of business.

Pasant's insurance team originally consisted of conventional and independent agents. By 1971, however, Pasant had fired most of his sales force and had adopted the "piggybacking" system of selling insurance: he recruited independent agents to act as brokers, selling Jackson National insurance while maintaining positions at other major insurance companies. Pasant attracted agents through direct mailings and advertisements in trade journals. According to *Forbes,* for the relatively low cost of an ad, he was able to hire workers while avoiding training and recruiting expenses. Furthermore, Pasant was able to sell policies at competitive prices, pay his agents favorable commissions, and entice customers with high annuity rates.

Over the next decade Jackson National established a presence in several U.S. states outside of Michigan. In 1982 it created the subsidiary Jackson National Life Insurance Company of Texas. The following year it sold policies worth $7.6 billion. Although earnings grew only 25 percent in 1984 (down from 85 percent the year before), the decrease was attributed to slightly low annuity sales and expenses incurred from the construction of the company's new Lansing headquarters that year. By 1986 Jackson National was one of the country's fastest growing insurance companies with assets of $2.2 billion and 550 employees. Of the approximately 2,000 insurance companies in the United States at the time, Jackson National ranked 18th in new policies sold, 91st in assets, and 60th in premium income. Its success made it an attractive prospect for investors.

In one of the most significant events of the company's history, Jackson National was acquired by Prudential Corporation plc of London in 1986. Prudential—unrelated to the American insurance company of the same name—was founded in London in 1848. The United Kingdom's largest provider of individual and industrial life insurance policies, Prudential experienced steady growth and became known for its determination to meet the needs of its customers. The company's collection system, established in the 1920s, required each representative to be responsible for a specific territory and to personally visit policyholders at their homes. The "man from the Pru" became a national institution. Prudential rigidly adhered to the product and philosophies on which their strength was built until the 1970s when management observed that the company would have to change to respond to a changing market. In 1978 Prudential began to decentralize, reorganizing and becoming a holding company. The resulting success of this move prompted Prudential to establish a presence in the United States, and it began with the purchase of Jackson National for $608 million.

Prudential was provided with an opportunity to learn from Jackson National's technological advancements; the U.S. company's computerized records and efficient office procedures served as a model for its new parent. Prudential provided Jackson National with financial resources, experience in a wider variety of insurance products, and opportunities for growth for both the individual employee and the company. According to the agreement, Prudential purchased approximately 11.9 million shares of Jackson National stock for about $51 per share and retained an option to buy 2.5 million more shares. The company was merged with its wholly owned subsidiary, Jackson National Life Insurance Company of Texas, and its business was thereafter controlled by Prudential. Jackson National was allowed to keep its name and its management team. Tony Pasant, who remained in his position as president, commented at the 1986 annual meeting that "this merger is a compliment of the highest order to everyone who is or has been involved with Jackson National Life."

Seeking to expand its product line, in February of 1988 Jackson National became one of the first insurance companies in the United States to offer accelerated death benefits, or living benefits. For about an eight percent increase in annual fees, holders of these benefits were allowed to draw 25 percent of their benefits before their death to help cover costs related to heart attacks, cancer, strokes, heart bypass surgery, or kidney failure. A deduction of 25 percent was applied to the death benefit. The plan also allowed holders to use the money for equipment necessitated by any of the five conditions, such as wheelchair ramps. The option, marketed as Lifeline Ultimate, drew a mixed response. While many commented that the plan allowed people to collect money at a time when it was really needed, some found the benefits not worth the plan's cost.

Jackson National's premium income consisted of term life insurance, ultimate life insurance, life single premiums, and annuities. Term insurance, available in a variety of plans, provided basic and limited coverage subject to rate increases and convertible, upon request, to other Jackson National plans. Ultimate insurance and interest-sensitive whole life insurance were fixed premium policies that guaranteed the premium paid, a death benefit, and a minimum cash accumulation value. The company regarded ultimate and interest-sensitive plans as its most comprehensive coverage. Annuities provided a guaranteed monthly tax deferred income for the retired policyholder. Life single premiums, available as an individual policy or as a rider to an already existing policy, represented a combination life insurance policy and annuity program. Nearly all of Jackson National's assets were invested in investment-grade, publicly traded bonds, an option the company regarded as safe, yet productive. The company regarded real estate and mortgage investments as too risky.

Tony Pasant died in 1990, and his son, David A. Pasant, who had worked at Jackson National for 20 years, became president and chief executive officer. Since its acquisition by Prudential, Jackson National has annually received superior ratings by the industry's premier analysts, A. M. Best Co. Despite the difficult economic climate of the early 1990s, Jackson National continued to produce record revenues, assets, and profits, a fact the company attributes to its conservative investment policy and its philosophy of "doin' it right." According to David Pasant in the company's 1991 annual report, the catchphrase emphasizes the company's commitment to "providing the best service in the shortest possible time."

During 1992, the company formed Jackson National Life of Michigan as a wholly owned subsidiary, transferring all of its Michigan business to the new company. Also incorporated in 1992 was Jackson National Financial Services, Inc., a broker-dealer formed to distribute mutual funds and variable products.

In 1992 the company was ranked by *Fortune* magazine as the 23rd largest life insurance company, and assets were reported at $16.6 billion on earnings of $212 million. Furthermore, the company's individual life insurance and individual annuities statistics qualified it as the country's fifth largest insurance writer. Having received a $300 million surplus contribution from Prudential in 1991, the company's capital and surplus exceeded $1 billion in 1993, doubling from 1990 levels. As a representative of 50 percent of Prudential's foreign investments, Jackson National has helped its parent achieve assets in excess of $90 billion. Jackson National is regarded as well positioned for continued expansion and financial growth.

Principal Subsidiaries: Jackson National Life of Michigan.

Further Reading:

Donahue, Christine, "Piggyback," *Forbes,* April 9, 1984, pp. 168–169.
Jackson, Luther, "Jackson National Life Takeover is Approved," *Detroit Free Press,* November 26, 1986.
Jackson National Life Insurance Company Annual Report, Jackson, Michigan: Jackson National Life Insurance Company, 1991.
Joyner, Tammy, "Insurance Policies Benefit the Living," *Detroit News,* February 19, 1990.
McCaughan, Pat, "Jackson National Life to Join London Insurance Company," *Lansing State Journal,* September 19, 1986.
"When it Pays to Have a Heart Attack," *Money,* April 1988, pp. 25–26.

—Tina Grant

Japan Leasing Corporation

Japan Leasing Corporation

12-1 Yurakucho 1-chome
Chiyoda-ku
Tokyo 100
Japan
(3) 3214-2341
Fax: (3) 3214-4530

Private Company
Incorporated: August 1, 1963 as Japan Lease International
   Corporation
Employees: 1,154
Sales: ¥692.37 billion (US$6.80 billion)
SICs: 6159 Miscellaneous Business Credit; 6141 Personal
   Credit Institutions; 7359 Equipment Rental and Leasing
   Nec; 7377 Computer Rental and Leasing

The Japan Leasing Corporation is one of the largest commercial leasing companies in Japan. The company is owned by a diverse combination of Japan's largest companies. This owners' club, which consists of about 80 corporations, includes Ricoh, NEC, Hitachi, Komatsu, Toshiba, Mitsubishi, Marubeni, and the Long Term Credit Bank of Japan, with whom it has especially strong ties.

The company was established by Kiyoshi Ichimura, then head of the Ricoh Company, a manufacturer of automated office equipment and electronic consumer goods. Ichimura founded the company because he saw a potential in Japan for leasing operations similar to those in the United States. He noted that American leasing firms provided small- and medium-sized companies with greater flexibility by allowing them to conserve capital while outfitting offices and factories. Rather than spending millions of dollars at a time purchasing equipment, these companies could merely rent the equipment from a leasing company. In the 1960s Japan was entering a period of very strong export-led economic growth. Even small companies with very little capital, but with the right product and proper marketing, were capable of tremendous growth. The demand for leased property was clearly increasing.

Thus, Ichimura founded the Japan Lease International Corporation on August 1, 1963. Backed by numerous banks, general trading companies (*sogoshosya*), insurance companies, and manufacturers, the company, was initially capitalized at ¥1 billion ($4.7 million). The company secured financing from

banks to purchase equipment; later the door was opened to such direct financing measures as CP issue and lease receivables securitization. In 1964 the company began leasing office machines, and the following year, Japan Lease International started offering maintenance leases of motor vehicle fleets. By 1966 medical equipment leases had become heavily in demand. The company created a Japan Flying Service subsidiary in 1965 to deal in leases of small aircraft. The following year Japan Lease International established the Japan LP Gas Meter Lease Company, a subsidiary dedicated to the lease of household liquid gas fuel meters to consumers.

This period of strong growth in the Japanese economy was characterized by intensive utilization of available capital and feverish acceleration of technological innovation. A given model of equipment was often run into the ground or became obsolete after little more than a year. The demand for leased equipment contributed greatly to Japan Lease International's volume, which by 1966 had exceeded ¥10 billion ($47 million) annually.

The success of the company inspired many imitators, mostly as leasing subsidiaries of banks. Between 1967 and 1969 several companies entered the market as competitors to Japan Lease International. Concerned more with the profitability of their growing industry than individual market share, these companies banded together in 1969 to form the Japan Leasing Association, an organization dedicated to the preservation of favorable regulations for the leasing industry. Ichimura was elected the first chairman of the new group. Partly due to good lobbying efforts, the group won new regulations for an institutional cross-border lease system from the Ministry of International Trade and Industry, Japan's government industry board. This enabled Japan Lease International to engage in larger scale projects, including leasing of aircraft. The expansion of business required several increases in the company's capitalization. Three increases were completed by 1971, raising the company's capitalization to ¥2.5 billion ($11.8 million).

Japan Lease Services, another subsidiary, was created in 1969 to handle maintenance services for the company's fleet of leased automobiles. In 1970 the company established Nippon International Container Services to handle institutional leasing of shipping containers. Japan Lease International carried its expansion to foreign markets in 1971, opening a subsidiary office in the United States. Additional offices were established in Hong Kong in 1972, Singapore in 1973, and Brazil in 1975. The company's clients in these cities were often off-shore affiliates of Japanese companies that were located in these countries. Japan Lease International therefore followed some its most profitable clients to promising new foreign markets.

The energy crisis of 1973 caused serious hardship in oil-dependent Japan. Because of rising uncertainty in industrial markets, few businesses were willing to make further investments in new plant and equipment. As a result, demand even for short-term equipment leases declined sharply. But even under these circumstances, Japan Lease International registered only small declines in its rate of growth. The lapse in demand was only temporary, and did not prevent the company from expanding into a wider variety of equipment leases.

In order to better handle the increasingly diverse nature of its leasing business, the company formed a separate subsidiary, the Japan Machinery Leasing and Sales Company, in 1974. This new unit specialized in large capital leases and supervised the sale of equipment after it had been fully depreciated or was no longer marketable for lease. To avoid disputes with tax authorities about the economic substance of the lease, buy-out options, common on American and many European leasing contracts, are rarely found on Japanese lease contracts. Instead of offering leased capital on an up-front rent-to-own basis, the company provides re-lease options to lessees at reduced rental fees at the conclusion of a lease. In that way, Japan Lease International's mainstay business has been the "finance" lease.

In 1976 the company branched into money lending. Although it was not a bank, it now was functioning in many of the same capital markets. By 1977 the volume of Japan Lease International's contracts exceeded ¥100 billion ($474 million), ten times its volume only ten years earlier.

Japan Lease International changed its English name in 1978 to Japan Leasing Corporation, corresponding to the change of the Japanese name in 1967. Also that year, the company began leasing a larger range of aircraft, including wide body DC-9s and B-747s. Japan Leasing also began to branch into grocery and fast food store leases, providing land and completely outfitted facilities for a franchisee or owner. The company also provided lease arrangements for a number of hotels. By 1980 Japan Leasing's volume exceeded ¥200 billion ($948 million), representing a doubling rate of only three years. That year Japan Leasing established an agency agreement with the China National Machinery Import and Export Corporation, opening the door for equipment leases to firms operating in the People's Republic of China.

A second oil shock in 1979 and 1980 caused further slowdowns in capital spending. Like the 1973 oil shock, this crisis depressed Japan Leasing's sales growth only temporarily, producing a pent-up demand for leases when the crisis had passed. Still, by 1982, competition had grown substantially. That year company President Tetsuo Nishio was forced to rein in costs by initiating a company-wide consolidation program. This effort continued for several years as Japan Leasing continued to lose new business to competitors.

Japan Leasing began making yen-denominated cross-border leasing agreements in 1981. Yen-based cross-border contracts offered lessees lower, more stable interest provisions than other currencies. The first yen leases went for aircraft to China Airlines, Japan Air Lines, Air France, and Air New Zealand. In 1982 Japan Leasing concluded another yen lease agreement with a ¥57 billion contract to supply 555 rail cars to the Belgian National Railways Company. Treated as a product, yen leases contributed greatly to the company's growth. In a further effort to win new sales, Nishio ordered a strengthening of Japan Leasing's investigation procedures. This was intended to improve the company's reaction time and ensure that customers' needs were being met.

Japan Leasing branched into home loans in February of 1982, broadening its competition with banks. By this time, auto leasing became an especially important business to Japan Leasing. As late as 1983 the company maintained leases for only 25,000 automobiles, many of which came with maintenance contracts. By 1989 that number had doubled, causing a need for the creation of another subsidiary dedicated to auto leases. This company, Japan Leasing Auto Corporation, was established in April of 1988.

Japan Leasing established several other subsidiaries during the 1980s, including a United Kingdom office in 1983, a Shanghai-based joint venture called Pacific Leasing, and JLA Credit in the United States in 1985. In 1987 opened JL Tourist, a travel agency. The rapid expansion of business helped to bring sales up to ¥400 billion in 1990. The company's rate of growth, still in double digits, had begun to fall.

Japan Leasing launched several commodities investment funds in 1991 and established new financing arms in the United States and United Kingdom in 1990. In August of that year Japan Leasing helped set up the Fieldstone Private Capital Group, a company specializing in complex structured leasing transactions—mostly consisting of aircraft—and privatizations in the public utilities sector. The company had become increasingly nervous about the aircraft leasing business, particularly as recession-weary markets in Europe and North America threatened to result in overcapacity, a jet glut, and potentially millions of dollars of non-performing assets.

Tetsuo Nishio, now chairman of Japan Leasing, called 1990 a "difficult" year, as the company was only able to register 19.1 percent sales growth. The following year, growth had fallen into single digits, prompting Nishio to start up his consolidation program again. The primary features of this program were concentrated on better utilization of computer systems to improve sales performance. The company announced no lay-offs. Much of the slower sales growth could be attributed to a worldwide recession that began late in 1989. The company mused about its lowered rates of growth by citing the common 30-year cycle of modern corporations. In an executive speech, a director of Japan Leasing suggested that few corporations are able to maintain sales growth indefinitely and are bound mainly by the size of the world market. Under the best conditions, companies exhaust their capacity for double-digit sales growth after 30 years.

This theory may not apply to Japan Leasing. The company's market, which now is international in scope, is populated with many competitors. Japan Leasing has substantial experience in providing machinery and financing for numerous fields, including petroleum and chemical production, mining, forestry, and tourism. As a supplier and possible business partner, Japan Leasing serves an important role in Japan's export-oriented economy. The company facilitates export sales by offering easy terms to foreign customers. Without the assistance of Japan Leasing, manufacturers such as Hino Motors, Komatsu, and Mitsubishi might have had some difficulty making their products affordable in many developing countries.

Principal Subsidiaries: Japan Leasing Auto Corporation; Japan LP Gas Meter Lease Co., Ltd.; Japan Machinery Leasing and Sales Co., Ltd.; Ginza International Hotel Co., Ltd.; Choshu Kanko Kaihatsu Co., Ltd.; Communication Science Corporation; CJK Co., Ltd.; J.L. Rec Corporation; Nippon Mitek Co.,

Ltd.; J.L. Tourist Corporation; Singapore Leasing International (Pte) Ltd.; Japan Leasing (Hong Kong) Limited; Japan Leasing (USA), Inc.; Japan Leasing do Brasil S.A.; P.T. Central Sari Metropolitan Leasing Corp. (Indonesia); Japan Leasing (UK) Limited; Aviation Capital Enterprises Ltd (UK); Nova Northwest Capital, Inc. (USA); JLA Credit Corporation (USA); Fieldstone Private Capital Group, L.P. (USA); Fieldstone Private Capital Group Ltd. (UK); Fieldstone Private Capital Group (Asia) Ltd. (Hong Kong); Pacific Leasing Corporation (China); ILC Group Ltd. (UK); ILC Finance Ltd. (UK); ILC France S.A.; UNIMET Computer Marketing GmbH. (Germany); ILC Finanziaria SpA./ILC Italia SpA. (Italy).

Further Reading:

"The Leasing Profession: On the Way to a New Structure" and "Leasing Market Reaching Saturation," speeches by Osamu Nagano, Managing Director, Company Documents.

"Who is Saying What in the U.S. Arranger Market?" *Asset Finance & Leasing Digest*, August 1992, pp. 7–11.

"Fieldstone Private Capital Group, Ltd.," Prospectus.

"Japan's Expanding Cross-Border Leasing Market," *Aircraft Leasing*, November 1989, pp. 25–30.

Annual Reports, Tokyo: Japan Leasing Corporation, 1981 1983, 1986, 1990, 1991, 1992.

—John Simley

tion began and the dressings were shipped in large quantities throughout the United States. By 1890 J&J was using dry heat to sterilize the bandages.

The establishment of a bacteriological laboratory in 1891 gave research a boost, and by the following year the company had met accepted requirements for a sterile product. By introducing dry heat, steam, and pressure throughout the manufacturing process, Johnson & Johnson was able to guarantee the sterility of its bandages. The adhesive bandage was further improved in 1899 when, with the cooperation of surgeons, Johnson & Johnson introduced a zinc oxide–based adhesive plaster that was stronger and overcame much of the problem of the skin irritation that plagued many patients. J&J's fourth original design was an improved method for sterilizing catgut sutures.

From the beginning, J&J was an advocate of antiseptic surgical procedures. In 1888 the company published *Modern Methods of Antiseptic Wound Treatment*, a text used by physicians for many years. That same year, Fred B. Kilmer began his 45-year stint as scientific director at J&J. A well-known science and medicine writer, and father of poet Joyce Kilmer, Fred Kilmer wrote influential articles for J&J's publications, including *Red Cross Notes* and *The Red Cross Messenger*. Physicians, pharmacists, and the general public were encouraged to use antiseptic methods, and Johnson & Johnson products were promoted.

R. W. Johnson died in 1910 and was succeeded as chairman by his brother James. It was then that the company began to grow quickly. To guarantee a source for the company's increasing need for textile materials, J&J purchased Chicopee Manufacturing Corporation in 1916. The first international affiliate was founded in Canada in 1919. Several years later, Robert W. Johnson's sons, Robert Johnson and J. Seward Johnson, took an around-the-world tour that convinced them that Johnson & Johnson should expand overseas, and Johnson & Johnson Limited was established in Great Britain a year later. Diversification continued with the invention of Band-Aid brand adhesive bandages and Johnson's Baby Cream in the early 1920s.

The younger Robert Johnson, who came to be known as "the General," had joined the company as a mill hand while still in his teens. By the age of 25 he had become a vice-president, and he was elected president in 1932. Described as dynamic and restless with a keen sense of duty, Johnson had attained the rank of brigadier general in World War II and served as vice-chairman of the War Production Board.

The General firmly believed in decentralization in business; he was the driving force behind Johnson & Johnson's organizational structure, in which divisions and affiliates were given autonomy to direct their own operations. This policy coincided with a move into pharmaceuticals, hygiene products, and textiles. During Robert Johnson's tenure, the division for the manufacture of surgical packs and gowns became Surgikos, Inc.; the department for sanitary napkin production was initially called the Modess division and then became the Personal Products Company; birth control products were under the supervision of the Ortho Pharmaceutical Corporation; and the separate division for suture business became Ethicon, Inc. Under the General's leadership, annual sales grew from $11 million to $700 million at the time of his death in 1968.

Johnson & Johnson

One Johnson & Johnson Plaza
New Brunswick, New Jersey 08933
U.S.A.
(908) 524-0400
Fax: (201) 214-0332

Public Company
Incorporated: 1887
Employees: 84,900
Sales: $13.75 billion
Stock Exchanges: New York
SICs: 2844 Toilet Preparations; 2834 Pharmaceutical Preparations; 3842 Surgical Appliances and Supplies; 3941 Surgical and Medical Instruments; 3851 Ophthalmic Goods; 2835 Diagnostic Substances; 2676 Sanitary Paper Products

One of America's most admired companies, Johnson & Johnson (J&J) ranks as the third-largest biotechnological company in the world and the fifth-largest pharmaceutical concern in the United States, and claims to the largest over-the-counter (OTC) drug company in the world. J&J has manufacturing facilities at 194 locations in 48 countries, and markets its products in 158 countries worldwide.

The 168-unit conglomerate traces its beginnings to the late 1800s, when Joseph Lister's discovery that airborne germs were a source of infection in operating rooms sparked the imagination of Robert Wood Johnson, a New England druggist. Johnson joined forces with his brothers, James Wood Johnson and Edward Mead Johnson, and the three began producing dressings in 1886 in New Brunswick, New Jersey, with 14 employees in a former wallpaper factory.

Because Lister's recommended method for sterilization—spraying the operating room with carbolic acid—was found to be impractical and cumbersome, Johnson & Johnson (J&J) found a ready market for its product. The percentage of deaths due to infections following surgery was quite high and hospitals were eager to find a solution.

J&J's first product was an improved medicinal plaster that used medical compounds mixed in an adhesive. Soon afterward, the company designed a soft, absorbent cotton-and-gauze dressing, and Robert Wood Johnson's dream was realized. Mass produc-

Following his father's lead as a champion of social issues, Johnson spoke out in favor of raising the minimum wage, improving conditions in factories, and emphasizing business's responsibility to society. Johnson called for management to treat workers with respect and to create programs that would improve workers' skills and better prepare them for success in a modern industrial society. Johnson wrote a credo outlining the company's four areas of social responsibility: first to its customers; second to its employees; third to the community and environment; and fourth to the stockholders.

In 1959 McNeil Pharmaceutical Company was purchased by Johnson & Johnson. In that same year Cilag-Chemie, a Swiss pharmaceutical firm was purchased, followed in two years by the purchase of Janssen Pharmaceutica.

In 1963 Johnson retired. Although he remained active in the business, chairmanship of the company went outside the family for the first time. Johnson's immediate successor was Philip Hofmann, who, much like the General, had started as a shipping clerk and worked his way up the ladder. During Hofmann's ten-year term as chairman, Johnson & Johnson's domestic and overseas affiliates flourished. Hofmann was another firm believer in decentralization and encouraged the training of local experts to supervise operations in their respective countries. Foreign management was organized along product lines rather than geographically, with plant managers reporting to a person with expertise in the field.

In the early 1960s federal regulation of the health-care industry was increasing. When James Burke—who had come to Johnson & Johnson from the marketing department of Procter & Gamble—became president of J&J's Domestic Operating Company in 1966, the company was looking for ways to increase profits from its consumer products to offset possible slowdowns in the professional-products divisions. By luring top marketing people from Procter & Gamble, Burke was able to put together several highly successful advertising campaigns. The first introduced Carefree and Stayfree sanitary napkins into a market that was dominated by the acknowledged feminine-products leader, Kimberly-Clark. Usually limited to women's magazines, advertisements for feminine hygiene products were low-key and discreet. Under Burke's direction, Johnson & Johnson took a more open approach and advertised Carefree and Stayfree on television. By 1978 J&J had captured half of the market.

One of Burke's biggest challenges was Tylenol, a non-aspirin (acetaminophen) pain reliever. Ever since J&J had acquired McNeil Laboratories, maker of Tylenol, the drug had been marketed as a high-priced product. Burke saw other possibilities, and in 1975 he got the chance he was waiting for. Bristol-Myers Company introduced Datril and advertised that it had the same ingredients as Tylenol but was available at a significantly lower price. Burke convinced J&J Chairman Richard Sellars that they should meet this competition head on by dropping Tylenol's price to meet Datril's. With Sellar's approval, Burke took Tylenol into the mass-marketing arena, slashed its price, and ended up beating not only Datril, but number-one Anacin as well. This signaled the beginning of an ongoing battle between American Home Products, maker of Anacin, and McNeil Laboratories.

Sellars, Hofmann's protege, had become chairman in 1973, and served in that position for three years. Burke succeeded Sellars in 1976 as CEO and chairman of the board, and David R. Clare was appointed president.

Johnson & Johnson had always maintained a balance between the many divisions in its operations, particularly between mass consumer products and specialized professional products. No single J&J product accounted for as much as 5 percent of the company's total sales. With Burke at the helm, consumer products began to be promoted aggressively, and Tylenol pain reliever became Johnson & Johnson's number-one seller.

At the same time, Burke did not turn his back on the company's position as a leader in professional health-care products. In May 1977 Extracorporeal Medical Specialties, a manufacturer of kidney dialysis and intravenous treatment products, became part of the corporation. Three years later, J&J acquired Iolab Corporation, maker of ocular lenses for cataract surgery, and effectively entered the field of eye care and ophthalmic pharmaceuticals. The increased in-house development of critical-care products resulted in the creation of Critikon, Inc., in 1979, and in 1983 Johnson & Johnson Hospital Services was created to develop and implement corporate marketing programs.

In September 1982 tragedy struck Johnson & Johnson when seven people died from ingesting Tylenol capsules that had been laced with cyanide. Advertising was canceled immediately, and Johnson & Johnson recalled all Tylenol products from store shelves. After the Food and Drug Administration (FDA) found that the tampering had been done at the retail level rather than during manufacturing, Johnson & Johnson was left with the problem of how to save its number-one product and its reputation. In the week after the deaths, Johnson & Johnson's stock dropped 18 percent and its prime competitors' products, Datril and Anacin-3, were in such demand that supplies were back-ordered.

Johnson & Johnson was able to recoup its losses through several marketing strategies. The company ran a one-time ad that explained how to exchange Tylenol capsules for tablets or refunds and worked closely with the press, responding directly to reporters' questions as a means of keeping the public up to date. The company also placed a coupon for $2.50 off any Tylenol product in newspapers across the country to reimburse consumers for Tylenol capsules they may have discarded during the tampering incident and offer an incentive to purchase Tylenol in other forms.

Within weeks of the poisoning incidents, the FDA issued guidelines for tamper-resistant packaging for the entire food and drug industry. To bolster public confidence in its product, J&J used three layers of protection, two more than recommended, when Tylenol was put back on store shelves. Within months of the cyanide poisoning, Johnson & Johnson was gaining back its share of the pain-reliever market, and soon regained more than 90 percent of its former customers. By 1989 Tylenol sales were $500 million annually, and in 1990 the line was expanded into the burgeoning cold remedy market with several Tylenol Cold products; the following year saw the launch of Tylenol P.M., a sleep aid. James Burke's savvy, yet honest handling of the Tylenol tampering incident earned him a spot in the National

Business Hall of Fame, an honor awarded in 1990. Litigation over the incident was finally resolved in 1991, almost a decade after the initial tampering. McNeilab Inc. settled with over 30 survivors of the poisonings for more than $35 million.

In 1989 Bristol Myers Co. launched an aggressive advertising campaign that positioned its Nuprin brand ibuprofen pain reliever in direct competition with Tylenol. The move compounded market share erosion from American Home Products' Advil ibuprofen. Both products claimed to work better than Tylenol's acetaminophen formulation.

Burke and Clare retired in 1989 and were succeeded by three men: CEO and Chairman Ralph S. Larsen, who came from the consumer sector; Vice Chairman Robert E. Campbell, who had headed the professional sector; and President Robert N. Wilson, who had headed the pharmaceutical sector. The three men were responsible for overseeing the network of 168 companies in 53 countries.

Larsen moved quickly to reduce some of the inefficiencies that a history of decentralization had caused. In 1989 the infant products division was joined with the health and dental units to form a broader consumer products segment, eliminating approximately 300 jobs in the process. Over the next two years, the reorganization was extended to overseas units. The number of professional operating departments in Europe was reduced from 28 to 18 through consolidation under three primary companies: Ethicon, Johnson & Johnson Medical, and Johnson & Johnson Professional Products. A European Professional Sector office was also set up in Brussels in preparation for the emerging European Common Market.

J&J was able to counter increasing criticisms of rising health care costs in the United States and around the world in the 1990s due in part to the company's long-standing history of social responsibility. The company pioneered several progressive programs including child care, family leave, and "corporate wellness" that were beginning to be recognized as health care cost reducers and productivity enhancers. In addition, weighted average compound prices of J&J's health care products, including prescription and OTC drugs and hospital and professional products, grew more slowly than the U.S. consumer Price Index from 1980 through 1992. These practices supported the company's claim that it was part of the solution to the health care crisis. In 1992 J&J instituted its "Signature of Quality" program, which urged the corporation's operating companies to focus on three general goals: "Continuously improving cus-

tomer satisfaction, cost efficiency and the speed of bringing new products to market."

Principal Subsidiaries: Advanced Care Products; Chicopee; Codman & Shurtleff, Inc.; Critikon, Inc.; Ethicon, Inc.; Iolab Corporation; Janssen Pharmaceutica Inc.; Critikon Canada Inc.; Johnson & Johnson Consumer Products, Inc.; Johnson & Johnson Development Corporation; Johnson & Johnson Finance Corporation; Johnson & Johnson Health Management, Inc.; Johnson & Johnson Hospital Services, Inc.; Johnson & Johnson Interventional Systems; Johnson & Johnson Medical Inc.; Johnson & Johnson Othopaedics, Inc.; Johnson & Johnson Professional Diagnostics, Inc.; LifeScan, Inc.; McNeil Consumer Products Company; McNeil Pharmaceutical; Noramco, Inc.; Ortho Diagnostic Systems Inc.; Ortho Pharmaceutical Corporation; Personal Products Company; Therakos, Inc.; Vistakon, Inc.

Further Reading:

Ballen, Kate, "America's Most Admired Corporations," *Fortune,* v. 125, February 10, 1992, 40–72.

Dumaine, Brian, "Is Big Still Good?" *Fortune,* v. 125, April 20, 1992, 50–60.

Fannin, Rebecca, "The Pain Game," *Marketing & Media Decisions,* v. 24, February 1989, 34–39.

Guzzardi, Walter, "The National Business Hall of Fame," *Fortune,* v. 121, March 12, 1990, 118–126.

Jacobs, Richard M., "Products Liability: A Technical and Ethical Challenge," *Quality Progress,* v. 21, December 1988, 27–29.

Kardon, Brian E., "Consumer Schizophrenia: Extremism in the Marketplace," *Planning Review,* v. 20, July/August 1992, 18–22.

Keaton, Paul N., and Michael J. Semb, "Shaping up That Bottom Line," *HRMagazine,* v. 35, September 1990, 81–86.

Matthes, Karen, "Companies Can Make It Their Business to Care," *HR Focus,* v. 69, February 1992, 4–5.

McLeod, Douglas, and Stacy Adler, "Tylenol Death Payout May Top $35 Million," *Business Insurance,* v. 25, May 20, 1991, 1, 29.

Murray, Eileen and Saundra Shohen, "Lessons from the Tylenol Tragedy on Surviving a Corporate Crisis," *Medical Marketing & Media,* v. 27, February 1992, 14–19.

Weber, Joseph, "No Band-Aids for Ralph Larsen," *Business Week,* May 28, 1990, 86–87.

——, "A Big Company That Works," *Business Week,* May 4, 1992, 124–32.

Winters, Patricia, "Tylenol Expands with Cold Remedies," *Advertising Age,* v. 61, August 27, 1990, 3, 36.

——, "J&J Sets Nighttime Tylenol," *Advertising Age,* v. 62, February 18, 1991, 1, 46.

—Mary F. Sworsky
updated by April S. Dougal

Kaufman △ Broad

Kaufman and Broad Home Corporation

10877 Wilshire Blvd.
Los Angeles, CA 90024
U.S.A.
(310) 443-8000
Fax: (310) 443-8098

Public Company
Incorporated: 1957 as Kaufman and Broad Building
   Company in Michigan; 1972 as Kaufman and Broad
   Development Group; 1986 as Kaufman and Broad Home
   Corporation in Delaware
Employees: 960
Sales: $1.09 billion
Stock Exchanges: New York
SICs: 1521: General Contractors—Single-Family Houses;
   1522 Residential Construction; 6162 Mortgage Banking;
   6552 Subdivider/Developer

Kaufman and Broad Home Corporation is a residential real
estate development company whose primary business is building single-family homes in the western United States and Paris,
France, for the entry level and first-time trade up markets. The
company also provides mortgage banking services to its home
buyers in the United States through its wholly owned subsidiary, Kaufman and Broad Mortgage Company, and offers commercial development, condominium and apartment complex
development, and renovation services through its four divisions
in France. Kaufman and Broad is the largest home builder in
California and among the largest residential and commercial
builders in the metropolitan Paris area. In addition, the company
builds some residential housing in Toronto, Ontario through its
Victoria Wood Development Corporation division.

Kaufman and Broad began in 1957 in Detroit, Michigan,
as Kaufman and Broad Building Company. The cofounders,
Don Kaufman and Eli Broad, took their initial investment of
$25,000 and developed two model homes in the Detroit suburb
of Madison Heights. They targeted the entry-level housing market and positioned the company as one that provided well-
designed and affordable first homes. The styling and price were
well matched for the market; in its first year in business, the
company posted sales of $1.7 million, or about 136 homes with
the average sale price of $12,500 for a new three-bedroom

house. First year net income of almost $33,000 was nearly 2
percent of sales and exceeded the cofounders' initial investment.

In 1959, Kaufman and Broad expanded into the contract housing business and developed elderly housing and college dormitories as well as new homes for the armed forces and public
housing agencies. Sales tripled from their first year in business
to $5.1 million, and net income improved to 7 percent of sales.
The following year, the company began building homes in
Arizona. In 1961, the company went public and raised about
$1.8 million in its initial public offering. Total revenue more
than doubled from two years prior to $11.7 million, and net
income was more than 5 percent of sales.

By the end of 1962, Broad and Kaufman had delivered more
than 300 entry-level priced homes in Phoenix and Tempe, Arizona. That same year, the company introduced a new product in
Detroit, "Townehouses," which were attached single family
homes. Again, the company understood the needs of the market
well; 400 town house units were sold in 30 days. That same
year, Kaufman and Broad was listed as one of the country's 200
fastest growing companies by *Standard and Poor*'s and became
the first home builder to be listed on the American Stock
Exchange. Another first for the company in 1962 was becoming
the first builder to successfully obtain financing commitments to
provide qualified buyers with mortgage loans.

Kaufman and Broad continued to expand into other markets. In
1963, the company entered southern California and developed
an attached town house community in Orange County. Sales
continued to be strong, and year end net revenue again more
than doubled from the two years previous to $31.8 million.
Acquisitions of smaller local and regional builders enabled the
company to enter other markets such as San Francisco, Chicago, New York, and other cities in the northeast portion of the
United States.

In 1964, the company moved its corporate headquarters to Los
Angeles from Phoenix, where it had moved earlier in the 1960s.
That same year, Kaufman and Broad opened a division in
Chicago to handle sales and development in that metropolitan
area. The home designs remained value-conscious as the company expanded its market focus to include the first-time trade up
buyers as well as the entry level market. Having been successful
with the financing commitments it was able to obtain and develop over a three-year period, Kaufman and Broad founded the
International Mortgage Company in 1965. The creation of this
wholly owned subsidiary allowed the company to provide financing directly to its customers without involving banks or
other financial institutions. In the same year that Kaufman and
Broad vertically integrated into mortgage services, it consolidated production activities by ceasing operations of its contract
division. The division completed homes, schools, and public
buildings for an Indian reservation in Fort Wingate, New Mexico, as its final project.

Diversification into other businesses continued throughout the
rest of the 1960s. In 1966, the company entered into the relatively new business of cable TV franchising with the formation
of its second wholly owned subsidiary, Nation Wide Cable-
vision. Within five years, the subsidiary was operating fran-

chises in 51 communities on the west coast of the United States. In 1969, the company founded Kaufman and Broad Home Systems, Inc., through which the company entered into the manufactured housing business. By 1971, Home Systems operated eight plants throughout the country and had sales of 9,000 units.

Also in the late 1960s, Kaufman and Broad's residential housing business was growing as well. Through its acquisition of the local building company Kay Homes in 1967, the company became the largest home producer in the San Francisco Bay area. Kaufman and Broad model homes were introduced in Paris, France in 1969, two years after the company's first overseas office was opened there. The company's growth during these years was due in part to customer service programs and good public relations. Kaufman and Broad was recognized by President Johnson in 1967 for its commitment to participate in low-income housing programs. In that same year, the company began offering a five-year limited home warranty, the first in the industry to do so. The following year, FHA, VA, and Fannie Mae approved International Mortgage for home mortgages, making it one of only a few builder mortgage subsidiaries with that approval.

In 1968, in an effort to better define itself as a diversified corporation, the company changed its name to Kaufman and Broad, Inc. A year earlier, the company had become the largest publicly held housing corporation, its growth attributable, in large part, to happy customers. Forty percent of its sales were secured through referrals from satisfied customers. In 1969, it became the first housing builder to be listed on the New York Stock Exchange.

Additional acquisitions in 1970 of Victoria Wood Development Corporation in Toronto, Canada and in 1971 of Sun Life Insurance Company further expanded and diversified Kaufman and Broad. Following the purchase of Sun Life, the company reorganized its on-site housing activities as a new entity, Kaufman and Broad Development Group. By 1972, Kaufman and Broad was America's largest multinational housing producer and the largest single-family home builder in Paris. The company operated on-site divisions in more than five states, as well as Canada, France, and West Germany. In 1973, the company entered the pre-cut Custom Home market with plants in Denver, Colorado and Minneapolis, Minnesota and the high-rise condominium business with its construction project in New Jersey. Net housing revenues for 1973 had increased to $264.4 million with net income more than 9 percent of sales.

As a result of high interest rates and a national recession—and the concomitant soft new home sales in 1974—the company experienced its first end of the year net loss. Despite the loss, Kaufman and Broad maintained its new market growth and customer service efforts strategy to assure long term profitability. In 1975, it expanded into new markets such as Brussels, Belgium, introduced new products, and offered new services such as the industry's first 10-year homeowner warranty. By 1977, the recession had subsided and the housing market had rebounded; the company celebrated the sale of its 100,000th home, which was an industry first. Sales in Europe were growing as well. By 1977, under the direction of Bruce Karatz, president of the French division, the company celebrated the sale of its 4,000th home overseas. Under Karatz, the division

staged one of what industry analysts said was the most creative advertising campaigns in home building: construction of a model home on the roof of an eight-story department store in downtown Paris. More than a half million people toured the home, which featured, among other things, a car inside the attached garage.

As the company entered the 1980s, its growth was again threatened by high interest rates and an industry recession. In an effort to better align its diverse business interests and to improve operations, the firm was reorganized into four operating groups: Kaufman and Broad Development Group for home building; International Mortgage Company for mortgage services; Home Systems for manufactured housing; and Sun Life for life insurance. A change in executive management also occurred in 1980. Bruce Karatz, president of the French division for the past four years, returned to the states and became the president of the Kaufman and Broad Development Group. His strategy for continued growth in home building was to concentrate on select regional markets that offered strong economic fundamentals. His long-term strategy to become the top producer in those areas that had solid growth potential and exit those markets that did not resulted in Kaufman and Broad phasing out its divisions in Illinois, New Jersey, Germany, and Belgium by 1989. The recession of the early 1980s and the new management's corporate strategy resulted in the company exiting other markets over the next several months, and by the following year Kaufman and Broad had reduced its on-site activities to California, France, and Canada. Market consolidation also was evident in the French division, where management focused its efforts within a 25-mile radius of Paris and exited areas outside the metropolitan area.

While the company was revising its operating strategies, management improved the quality control and customer service programs to increase referrals and maximize customers' perception of improved value. Following the recovery of the national economy, Kaufman and Broad concentrated its building efforts in key markets, including the manufactured homes business segment, improving housing revenues by 55 percent in 1985. Additionally, the corporation set company records for year-end financials in both revenue and net income. With the improved sales, the company had become the largest single-family home builder in California. The following year, Kaufman and Broad Land Company was formed to manage property purchasing. Home building in California continued to be strong, with communities such as East Hills in Anaheim, which sold 52 of the 54 homes available in the first weekend.

In 1985, the company acquired Bati-Service, an entry level home builder in France. This purchase made Kaufman and Broad's French division the third largest builder in the country. That same year in California, the two regional offices each divided into two new divisions. The four divisions allowed the company to address the specific needs of the local community. Corporate management efforts decentralized the divisions, so each division was held responsible for its own construction, planning, and local operations. Marketing and purchasing, however, remained a corporate focus. For the entire California market, the company introduced "The California Series," a marketing strategy that allowed all divisions to achieve cost efficiency in advertising and promotional programs. The concept was developed to improve economies of scale, to achieve a consistent single corporate image, and to increase brand awareness of Kaufman and Broad homes throughout the state.

In 1986, the corporation again reorganized. Kaufman and Broad Development spun off from Kaufman and Broad Inc., and formed Kaufman and Broad Home Corporation. All on-site housing activities, with the exception of manufactured housing, transferred to the new organization to focus on real estate development. That same year, a new commercial development division in Paris was formed, Kaufman and Broad Developpement. Within two years, this new division had completed a senior citizen apartment complex and 12 office buildings in Paris.

In 1989, the French division approved plans to build Washington Plaza, a new Paris office complex, securing $600 million from pre-sales to groups of institutional investors, a transaction that represented the largest single real estate deal in that country's history. Two new divisions were formed in Paris in 1989: Maisons Individuelles and Kaufman and Broad Renovation. The Renovation division was established to refurbish older office buildings in the downtown area. Management expanded into this new business because it felt that it provided a new growth opportunity given the scarcity of land in that area. By 1989, due in large part to the division's commercial development activities, French revenues more than quadrupled from four years prior.

Despite a slowing U.S. economy and uncertainty over the country's involvement in the Persian Gulf crisis, 1990 was a record year for Kaufman and Broad. End of year revenues of $1.37 billion were the highest in company history. Lower sales in California were more than offset by strong French division operating results, which was led by a 57 percent increase in commercial revenues.

The following year, the French division, along with several banks, announced the $1.7 billion, four-year redevelopment project for the Esso Corporation headquarters' property in Paris. For 1991, Kaufman and Broad's net orders worldwide for new construction increased from the previous year, and included California, where the nation's recession continued. Sales in California were positively impacted by the company's expansion into the Sacramento market.

In 1992, Kaufman and Broad had record deliveries in California, up 27 percent from the previous year. The company also increased its overall percentage of the new home sales market statewide to 6 percent, the highest of any builder in the state and up from 4 percent in 1991. Market penetration in the state was solid, with the company marketing homes in 72 communities. Also in 1992, the company continued its market expansion and established a new division in California and one in Las Vegas, Nevada, bringing the total number of divisions in the region to 11. Management attributed the company's success in 1992 to its extensive use of television advertising targeting renters, an audience that was not being reached in the real estate sections of newspapers. This was a marketing technique that few home builders had used, and it was coupled with an ''off-site'' telemarketing program designed to reach potential buyers who did not visit sales offices. According to company executives, the advertising spots generated more than 75,000 sales leads and resulted in approximately 700 incremental sales.

As Kaufman and Broad entered the middle of the 1990s, sales continued strong in the California region, supported by the company's commitment to value and affordability; the average price for a Kaufman and Broad new home is typically thousands of dollars below the statewide average. Moreover, its mortgage subsidiary supported the majority of its sales by offering competitive mortgage programs designed for first-time buyers and financed more than three-quarters of the company's California home purchases. The state's population is expected to increase by six million by the end of the century, bringing in additional first-home buyers. In Paris, the company's commercial development activities were expected to continue to sustain the division's growth. Kaufman and Broad's position in Paris is expected to grow along with the increasing demand for office locations by foreign companies wishing to do business in Paris, one of the economic centers of the new European Community.

Principal Subsidiaries: Kaufman and Broad Mortgage Company.

Further Reading:

The Kaufman and Broad Home Corporation Annual Reports, Los Angeles, CA.
''Posth, Mark A., ''Home Alone,'' California Builder, February/March, 1993.
''Professional Achievement Awards,'' Professional Builder & Remodeler, January, 1993.
Sylvester, David, ''A Hot Homebuilder,'' Fortune Magazine, February 13, 1989.

—Allyson S. Farquhar-Boyle

Kellwood Company

600 Kellwood Pkwy.
Chesterfield, Missouri 63017
U.S.A.
(314) 576-3100
Fax: (314) 576-3180

Public Company
Incorporated: 1961 as Kellwood Company
Employees: 14,000
Sales: $914 million
Stock Exchanges: Boston Chicago New York
SICs: 2311 Men's & Boys' Shirts, Coats & Overcoats; 2321
Men's & Boys' Shirts, Except Work Shirts; 2325 Men's &
Boys' Separate Trousers & Slacks; 2331 Women's,
Misses' & Juniors' Blouses & Shirts; 2335 Women's,
Misses' & Juniors' Dresses; 2337 Women's, Misses' &
Juniors' Suits, Skirts & Coats

Kellwood Company is a leading international private label and
brand label manufacturer, marketer, and merchandiser of apparel, home furnishings, and recreational products. Sold
through distribution channels from mail order to department
stores, Kellwood's apparel products are the core of its business.
The company's line of women's apparel accounts for 73 percent
of its apparel sales, followed by men's and children's apparel,
representing 24 percent and 3 percent, respectively. With 34
plants in Canada, the United States, the Caribbean Basin, and
the Far East, Kellwood has experienced substantial periods of
growth through prudent international and domestic acquisitions
that have given the company a diverse line of soft goods.

In 1961, 15 independent suppliers of soft goods to Sears, Roebuck & Co. merged to form Kellwood. The name was derived
from the surnames of Sears executives Charles H. Kellstadt and
Robert E. Wood. The merger brought together disparate managements and a diverse line of products, as well as 7,000
employees, 22 plants, and combined sales of more than $86
million. This made the newly formed company the third largest
apparel manufacturer in the United States. The union was
sought in order to centralize and streamline the management of
the individual companies. With 90 percent of its products sold
to Sears and with Sears holding a 22 percent interest in the
company, the consolidated management of Kellwood provided
financial, engineering, and design services for the plants of the

original companies that, initially, operated as 15 autonomous
divisions. From these separate divisions, the company's leadership was drawn, with Maurice Perlstein, president of McComb
Manufacturing Co., elected as Kellwood's first president. In its
first year, the Chicago headquartered Kellwood offered a variety of apparel, bedspreads, tents, sleeping bags, and tarpaulins.

Two years later, the company had surpassed sales objectives set
out in its five-year plan adopted the year before. Still almost
entirely dependent on Sears for its sales, Kellwood added all-
weather coats and other outerwear, plus children's shirts, shorts,
and pants, to its product lines. Sales grew to $100 million, and
the company expanded to 29 locations in 11 states. Kellwood
also expanded beyond the United States' borders for the first
time, establishing a plant in Kingston, Jamaica. This initial
foray into production outside the United States marked the
beginning of Kellwood's international involvement that, years
later, would define the company's success.

In 1964 Fred W. Wenzel, the former president of Hawthorn
Company (one of the original 15 companies), was elected chief
executive officer and chairman of the board, holding the latter
position for 27 years. Also in 1964 Kellwood's corporate logo, a
stylized ''K'' representing a thread through the eye of a needle,
was created. By Kellwood's fifth anniversary, sales had increased 75 percent since its formation. The company invested
its initial success toward expansion and also began enlarging
the breadth of its concerns. By 1966 it possessed 36 plants in 13
states and employed over 11,000 people. Also in 1966, the
company's headquarters were moved from Chicago to St. Louis. The previous year construction had been completed on its
first data processing center, located in Tennessee, giving Kellwood the capability to effectively track inventory and lower
administrative costs. In this signal year, Kellwood also displayed its future penchant for assimilating apparel companies
by acquiring the Stahl-Urban Company, a manufacturer of
men's and boys' outerwear and pants, as a subsidiary.

After ten years of business, Kellwood still outpaced the goals
established by the company's original founders and had become
the largest supplier of soft goods to Sears. Sales objectives for
its ten-year plan had been surpassed in 1968, three years ahead
of schedule, as each year of operation engendered record sales
figures. Expansion during the decade caused earnings to fluctu-
ate, but by 1971 the company stood on solid ground. As the
company focused on acquiring companies that complemented
its line of products, the organization of the manufacturing
facilities was realigned to create a more homogenous structure
than the original configuration. Instead of each division operating more or less independently, the manufacturing facilities
were organized into eight consumer oriented groups.

Soon after the 1961 merger, Kellwood began opening factory
outlet stores within its manufacturing facilities. Created to sell
the company's irregular and surplus merchandise, these outlet
stores had proliferated through Kellwood's brief history. Starting with three in 1965 and increasing to 17 five years later, the
number of outlet stores had grown to 29 by 1973. In that year, a
new operating group, Ashley's Outlet Stores, was formed to
effect a shift in the marketing focus of the factory outlets from
surplus stores toward genuine retailing concerns.

As 1974 drew to a close, Kellwood had experienced 14 years of robust growth in both plant expansion and diversification of its product lines. The number of employees had grown to 18,000 and 62 plants operated in 17 states. Having posted record sales each year since its formation and having increased its earnings to $8.5 million from less than $2 million in its first year, the company thrived under the beneficent marketing umbrella of Sears. By supplying Sears with apparel and other soft goods to market and sell according to specifications made by Sears (a segment of the apparel industry called private label business), Kellwood enjoyed the security and tremendous volume base the retail and mail-order catalog giant provided. Sears accounted for 80 percent of Kellwood's sales, so the success of Sears largely translated into success for Kellwood—a relationship mutually beneficial during Kellwood's nascent years. By cornering the market as Sears's largest supplier of apparel, Kellwood had ascended into the upper echelon of the apparel industry at an enviable pace.

Kellwood's success ceased, however, in 1975. A decline in sales by Sears, coupled with a recessive economy, caused earnings to plunge to just over $400,000 from the previous year's $8.5 million. This disappointing year quickly demonstrated the inherent dangers of bonding one company's future too closely with another's. Although drastic changes were not made overnight, the failure of 1975 convinced Kellwood's management to reconsider its relationship with Sears and re-examine the company's future direction.

By the following year, Kellwood rebounded and earnings jumped back up to more than $7 million. The Stahl-Urban subsidiary expanded its profitable product lines of apparel and outerwear under a licensing agreement with the National Football League that had been initiated in 1971. Kellwood also tapped into the accelerating demand for Western style clothing by manufacturing Tough-Skin jeans and corduroys for Sears.

Not forgetting the lesson of 1975, Kellwood made its first move toward developing a company more reliant on brand label business than private label business with its acquisition of the U.S. rights to the Van Raalte brand of women's hosiery and bodywear in 1977. As the popularity of disco dancing and physical fitness swept the country, the demand for the tight, lightweight dance tops, originated by Danskin, boomed, and Kellwood hoped to gain a foothold in the market share under the Van Raalte label. With Danskin possessing an almost unassailable advantage in the bodywear market, Kellwood aimed for usurping the number two bodywear manufacturer—Sears. This objective, however, did not indicate an assault on Sears by Kellwood. Sears still purchased 80 percent of Kellwood's volume and owned 22 percent of its soft goods supplier.

Indeed, most of Kellwood's production energies were spent fulfilling Sears's soft goods orders. The American consumer's desire for denim products continued to rise, and by 1977 the sales of jeans and pants to Sears exceeded all of Kellwood's other product lines. Men's casual slacks, sport coats, and warmup suits were added to its list of apparel products, as were down coats and vests. As consumers headed outdoors more frequently in the late 1970s for exercise and recreation, Kellwood added backpacks—sold under the Hillary label after famed mountain climber Sir Edmund Hillary—to its existing line of tents and sleeping bags.

Kellwood continued to enlarge its brand label business in 1978, a year in which sales exceeded $500 million and earnings reached nearly $13.5 million, by purchasing the rights to the Fruit of the Loom name for hosiery. With this move, Kellwood hoped to garner a portion of the $1.39 billion sheer hosiery market from its two largest manufacturers, Hanes Corp. and Kayser-Roth, producers of the L'eggs and No-Nonsense lines. Kellwood had experience in this area; the company had manufactured hosiery for Sears since 1965 under Sears's Cling-Alon label.

In 1980 Kellwood significantly increased its offshore involvement by acquiring nearly a half interest in Smart Shirts Ltd. of Hong Kong. In 1972 Kellwood formed a subsidiary named Kellwood International Ltd. in Hong Kong to facilitate its import and export activities. A producer of high quality shirts and blouses under labels such as Gant, Arrow, and Eagle, Smart Shirts held the largest import quotas for shirts entering the United States, with sales of $86 million and earnings of more than $9 million. With a laudable clientele list that included Macy's of New York, Inc., Federated Department Stores, The May Company, and J.C. Penney Company, Inc., the acquisition of Smart Shirts would eventually enable Kellwood to lessen its dependence on Sears.

By the following year, Kellwood had completely redefined its corporate strategy. The small steps taken since 1975's downturn toward more parity between private and brand label business and less dependence upon Sears had not been enough to satisfy Kellwood's management. Although Sears would continue as a significant customer for Kellwood's products, more balance was desired. Chairman Wenzel commented in *Barron's,* "Our philosophy is not to do less business with Sears, but to reduce that percentage by selling more to other customers."

To accomplish this task, Kellwood's management decided to significantly increase its involvement in offshore manufacturing and sourcing, the practice of shipping U.S.-cut fabric overseas to be sewn and then returning the finished product back to the United States—at a more favorable tariff rate than a pure import as allowed by the 807 Tariff regulations. (To remain competitive, U.S. apparel companies needed to source because of the high cost of domestic production.) The company concentrated its focus on Central America, the Caribbean, and the Far East. Kellwood also re-examined the diverse businesses and products with which it was involved. Kellwood's marketing and production efforts under the Van Raalte and Fruit of the Loom labels were discontinued because of inconsistent profits.

As a result of its sharpened focus, Kellwood entered its third decade of business as a company still largely involved in private label business, seeking to diminish its reliance on Sears by developing a broader customer base. By 1982 earnings had rebounded from a disappointing $216,000 two years earlier to over $8 million. The decisions made a year earlier began to take shape with the introduction of a new line of women's apparel manufactured under the private label of 14 large department stores. The shift away from Sears—albeit a modest one at this point—affected Kellwood's sales volume, but earnings had climbed due to sharp reductions in inventory and by cutbacks in some of its product lines and manufacturing facilities. A move toward securing a greater international presence was also made in 1982 when Kellwood increased its holdings of Smart Shirts to 82 percent. With two large manufacturing facilities in Taiwan and Hong Kong, Kellwood increased its profits by manufacturing certain products in the more cost-efficient Far East.

In July of 1984, Kellwood purchased the remaining shares of its stock held by Sears, thereby ending the investment relationship between the two companies that had spanned nearly a quarter of a century. By the following year, Kellwood's sales to Sears were equal to the amount of sales made to its other customers. This significant drop in sales to Sears once again affected Kellwood's sales volume, but the 1985 acquisition of Cape Cod-Cricket Lane, Inc., a maker of women's coordinated sportswear, helped lift its sales figures and enlarged its domestic operations. Kellwood's presence in the Far East was fortified in 1983 by purchasing the remaining percentage of Smart Shirts and by the acquisition of a company slated to operate under Smart Shirts' management in the free-trade area of Sri Lanka. Created in 1984 to aid Kellwood's search for and acquisition of companies in the Far East, Kellwood Asia Ltd. enabled the company to expand its international operations. Kellwood worked with local manufacturers in the Caribbean and Central America on a contract basis to source its products under 807 regulations.

In the latter half of the 1980s, Kellwood augmented its acquisitions of both domestic and offshore apparel companies by purchasing companies featuring fashion-oriented, branded merchandise. As opposed to the lower-priced products it had supplied to Sears in the previous two decades, the higher-priced products required less inventory and typically offered greater profit potential. In 1986 Parsons Place Apparel Company became the second domestic marketing oriented company to be purchased after Cape Cod-Cricket Lane. This increase in Kellwood's domestic, branded segment was followed by the purchase of E Z Sportswear and its subsidiary, En Chanté, Inc., as well as Robert Scott Ltd, Inc., David Brooks Ltd, Inc, and Andrew Harvey Ltd. in 1987, and Crowntuft Manufacturing Corp. in 1989. These acquisitions helped to counterbalance the continued drop in sales to Sears. By the end of the decade, Sears's portion of Kellwood's sales had fallen to roughly one quarter.

Kellwood's decision in 1981 to discontinue products and close facilities it deemed unprofitable or inconsistent with its new corporate thrust affected two long-standing entities of the company. In 1985 the recreation division was sold and, a year later, Ashley's Outlet Stores, which operated approximately 100 stores at the time, was also sold. The sale of the recreation division, however, did not signal the end of Kellwood's involvement with recreational goods. In 1989 Kellwood purchased American Recreation Products, Inc. as a subsidiary.

Kellwood's Far East operations also grew with the 1989 acquisition of Saipan Manufacturers, Inc. located in the Northern Mariana Islands. A manufacturer of men's shirts and sport shirts for export into the United States, the company fell under Smart Shirts management. By the end of the decade, Smart Shirts accounted for more than 40 percent of Kellwood's operating profits and provided another economic boost to supplant the losses from Sears.

As Kellwood entered the 1990s, its growth over the previous 30 years positioned it as one of the leading apparel manufacturers in the United States. With over 250 major retail accounts that involved approximately 25,000 individual stores, the company's customer base had evolved from almost complete dependence on Sears to a large and diverse clientele. The addition of California Ivy Inc. in 1992 and A. J. Brandon in 1993 increased the number of divisions and subsidiaries to 14. It remains to be seen if the Kellwood's aggressive pursuit of domestic and foreign companies continues to fuel its success in the 1990s and beyond. However, with its broad line of both brand and private label apparel and its line of recreation and home furnishing products, Kellwood's products will most likely be staples in American homes.

Principal Subsidiaries: Smart Shirts Limited (Hong Kong); A.J. Brandon Inc.; American Recreation Products, Inc.; California Ivy Inc.

Further Reading:

Byrne, Harlan S., "Ailing Market Fails to Faze Apparel Producer," *Barron's,* January 8, 1990, pp. 42–43.
Cochran, Thomas N., "A Product of Logical Growth," *Barron's,* September 12, 1988, p. 47.
Kellwood: A History, St. Louis, Missouri, Kellwood Company, 1982.
Kellwood Company Annual Reports, St. Louis: Kellwood Company, 1983-1992.
Maturi, Richard J., "On Its Own . . . and Thriving," *Barron's,* March 10, 1986, p. 57.
Millman, Nancy F., "High-Stepping Bodywear Market Meets New Rival," *Advertising Age,* August 28, 1978, p. 236.
Millman, Nancy F., "Kellwood Firming Plans to Snag Hosiery Share," *Advertising Age,* October 23, 1978, pp. 2, 112.
"Seventeen Suppliers of Sears to be Merged into Single Operation," *Wall Street Journal,* September 12, 1961, p. 10.
"Soft-Goods Profits," *Barron's,* February 14, 1983, pp. 48–50.
"World Enough?" *Forbes,* April 1, 1972, p. 49.

—Jeffrey L. Covell

The Kelly-Springfield Tire Company

12501 Willow Brook Rd.
Cumberland, MD 21502-2599
(301) 777-6000
Fax: (301) 777-6290

*Wholly Owned Subsidiary of The Goodyear Tire & Rubber
   Company*
Incorporated: 1894 as the Consolidated Rubber Tire Co.
Employees: 7,000
Sales: $850.50 million
SICs: 3011 Tires

The Kelly-Springfield Tire Company, which became a wholly
owned subsidiary of The Goodyear Tire and Rubber Company
in 1935, is one of the oldest continuously operating tire companies in the nation. The company has the distinction of being the
first to develop and manufacture solid rubber tires for carriages
and the early automobile. Currently a manufacturer of at least
54 brands of tires for cars, trucks, and farm vehicles, Kelly-
Springfield distributes to private dealers and store chains
throughout the country. Kelly-Springfield is the country's most
important manufacturer of custom brand tires and the world's
top producer of farm tires. The company owns and operates the
world's largest tire manufacturing plant in Fayetteville, North
Carolina.

As with countless American firms, Kelly-Springfield was
founded by a young, dynamic entrepreneur, Edwin S. Kelly. A
native of Springfield, Ohio, he established The Rubber Tire
Wheel Company in 1894. Rubber (named by British scientist
Joseph Priestly in the early 19th century because it "rubbed
out" pencil marks) was relatively new, especially vulcanized
rubber, which was a treated rubber that was processed to stay
firm under heat. Charles Goodyear was the first to develop
vulcanization, a process he patented in 1844. Thereafter, the
demand for rubber was insatiable.

At the time Edwin S. Kelly was growing up, carriages had gone
unpadded for centuries. Carriage rides were uncomfortable,
slow, and often unsafe. One of the first applications of vulcanized rubber was to cushion wheels. Only the wealthy could
afford rubber padding, which took years to perfect and often fell
off the wheel when a carriage turned. American entrepreneurs
began tinkering with solutions to this problem. One of these was
Arthur W. Grant of Springfield, Ohio, a superintendent in the

Tricycle Manufacturing Company. In 1893, Grant approached
Edwin Kelly with a blueprint of his new and superior solid
rubber carriage tire, with two internal wires and a specially
designed rim. The two entrepreneurs had not yet gone into
business together to form The Rubber Tire Wheel Company.
Hence Kelly took the blueprint to the B. F. Goodrich Company,
where the product was manufactured and tested.

The test passed with flying colors. Grant (who would receive a
patent for his invention in 1896) and Kelly pooled their resources and in 1894, established their new tire company in
Springfield, Ohio. Considering the tremendous consumer demand for rubber—heightened by the bicycle craze that had
erupted in the late 1880s—the new firm flourished. It did not
manufacture the newfangled rubber tires, however. Rubber tires
were procured from the Goodrich company in rolls; Grant
himself would cut and fit the tires according to his blueprint.
Soon the Rubber Tire Wheel Company was making tires for a
world market.

Perhaps it is surprising that only five years after Grant and Kelly
had opened their company for business, they decided to put it up
for sale. Though the new solid rubber carriage tire was selling
well, the owners had financed start-up costs with loans. Selling
the firm to the McMillin Company in 1899 for one million
dollars cleared them both of debt. While Grant decided to leave
the tire business, Kelly stayed on as general manager and vice
president of the renamed firm, the Consolidated Rubber Tire
Company (which changed its name for the last time in 1914 to
the Kelly-Springfield Tire Company). It continued to sell the
"Kelly" tire, which would be the company's sole brand name
tire until the 1930s.

Hence the Rubber Tire Wheel Company was not disbanded, but
remained under new ownership and with a new name. Edwin
Kelly remained manager and vice president of the Consolidated
Rubber Tire Company until 1905. He had proved receptive to
Grant's new and superior solid rubber tire in 1893, and likewise
was ahead of his time when it came to recognizing the potential
of the new horseless carriage.

As vice president, Kelly set about to provide a manufacturing
base for Kelly tires, and purchased the Buckeye Rubber Company in New Jersey for this purpose. More importantly, he
became the driving force behind the acquisition of the Columbia Pneumatic Wagon Wheel Company, thus establishing a
foothold in a revolutionary and still new invention: the compressed air, or pneumatic, tire.

The advent of bicycles in the 1880s had given further stimulus
to the evolution of rubber tires. Solid rubber tires did not work
well on bicycles. Air compressed (pneumatic) tires were first
developed for the bicycle in the late 1880s, giving the biker a
smooth, gentle ride, fast speeds, and maneuverability. These
innovative tires would serve as the prototype for horse-drawn
carriages and the future horseless carriage. The Consolidated
Rubber Tire Company took a conservative approach to the
revolutionary new tire, however. The company continued to
manufacture the solid rubber tire for cars, in which it had the
largest world market share, well into the 1920s. In 1909 it also
came out with the solid rubber tire specifically designed for

trucks, called the Caterpillar. It quickly became the number one brand of truck tire in the world.

The company did not begin manufacturing pneumatic auto tires until 1908. While other companies had entered the pneumatic tire business earlier, cars were not yet being mass produced and were a luxury that only the rich could afford. The market for pneumatic car tires therefore remained small until Henry Ford's mass assembly lines churned out Model-Ts at more affordable prices. The First World War tremendously escalated the demand for tires of all types, creating a world market for pneumatic auto tires by 1918.

By then, the Consolidated Rubber Tire Company had changed its name to the Kelly-Springfield Tire Company, whose corporate headquarters were located in New York City. Wartime profits enabled company managers to plan the construction of the biggest and most modern tire manufacturing facility in the world in Cumberland, Maryland, which was in close proximity to the company's distribution centers. Begun in 1917, the facility was not completed until 1921, during a severe postwar recession. While hard times would give way to boom years, Kelly-Springfield rarely made a profit throughout the prosperous 1920s. The succeeding Depression had a devastating effect on the firm, which soon went bankrupt. Had it not been for the emergence of a dynamic new company leader, Kelly-Springfield might have closed its doors forever.

A born salesman, Edmund S. Burke became president of Kelly-Springfield in 1935, and remained at the helm until 1959. Under his management, streamlining and consolidation took place, all sales offices were moved to Cumberland, and Goodyear Tire and Rubber Company was persuaded to purchase Kelly-Springfield as a wholly owned subsidiary. Having barely survived the Depression, Goodyear was skeptical at first and cash was tight. Nevertheless an agreement was signed that year, and The Kelly-Springfield Company ("The" officially was affixed to the company name in 1932) became part of the Goodyear family of business enterprises. By then, the worst of the Depression was over and the turnaround in Kelly-Springfield's fortunes had begun.

Burke's philosophy was modern, but still highly conservative. Only one new tire brand (the "Vogue,") emerged and no expansion followed, his belief being that small was best. One innovation that he tolerated was the growing trend of selling products in gasoline stations. Burke approved the sale of Kelly tires in the proliferating gas stations of the 1930s, which considerably boosted company sales and profitability for the first time since the end of the First World War.

Advertising was the one area in which no expense was too great. Since its earliest days, Kelly-Springfield's predecessors had advertised heavily and imaginatively, in all major glossy magazines of the day. From 1915 to 1930, Kelly-Springfield sponsored Broadway shows, entitling the company to be advertised during intermissions. If a prominent person bought Kelly tires, the company felt free to advertise that fact, while famous names in sports and theater were actively recruited to promote tires. Burke kept up the barrage of advertising, including the most spectacular and expensive, like the huge electric sign displays in New York's Times Square and other major cities. Even during

World War II, when Kelly-Springfield was not producing tires, tire advertising continued unabated.

The onset of the Second World War brought the first major crisis in the rubber industry: a dearth of natural rubber. The U.S. government began strictly rationing rubber, even ordering the shutdown of small rubber companies. The Kelly-Springfield Tire Company, under Burke's helm, sensed that it was on the list, and acted quickly. In November, 1941, the company switched from producing tires to munitions, although no one in the company had experience in this "product." Nevertheless the conversion turned out to be a success; in the last month of munitions production, July, 1943, The Kelly-Springfield Company churned out over 23 million eight-inch explosive shells. By then, synthetic rubber had been invented, and the government ordered the company to return to tires, of which there was a dire shortage.

The company prospered during and after the war, but no new brand of tire came on the market, nor did Burke revise his philosophy that "small was best." When he retired in 1959, the company was 60 years old and had changed little over the years. In 1959 there was only one custom brand tire, the "Vogue," while 25 years later there would be thousands of different custom brands and sizes of tires. Over the same period the company expanded from only one plant in Cumberland, Maryland, to plants throughout the nation, including the largest in the world. While quality was at an all time high in 1959, attention to consumer preferences was just beginning.

Although Kelly-Springfield continued as a subsidiary of Goodyear Tire and Rubber Company, it operated with wide latitude, even acquiring its own subsidiaries in the course of its relationship with Goodyear. In 1962, Kelly-Springfield acquired the Star Rubber Company (a company that originally devised the first radial tires), along with three other corporations connected to Star: the Hicks Rubber Company, Richmond Rubber Company, and Richmond Tire & Rubber Company. At the time of their acquisition, Star and the Richmond companies had long ceased manufacturing tires, preferring to distribute tires and inner tubes wholesale. In 1975, these subsidiaries merged as divisions within Kelly-Springfield. Likewise, in 1987, The Lee Tire & Rubber Company was acquired by Kelly-Springfield as a subsidiary, also merging with Kelly-Springfield several years later (the company has no subsidiaries in the early 1990s). Goodyear relies on Kelly-Springfield's wide distribution network and sets its targets; research and development, manufacturing and sales are up to Kelly-Springfield.

Since Burke's retirement, expansion and growth and an explosion of new custom brand tires have become the pattern at Kelly-Springfield, as well as growing profits (its first $1 billion in sales was achieved in the late 1980s). Still exclusively a tire manufacturer, Kelly-Springfield also branched into farm equipment tires and distributes its products through every major store chain—including Sears, WalMart, and K-Mart—as well as through thousands of private dealers. Production of its tires has soared with the construction of additional facilities under Burke's successor, President and CEO George B. Newman. In 1961, the Tyler, Texas plant was built, followed quickly by new facilities in Freeport, Illinois and finally, the largest tire manufacturing plant in the world, in Fayetteville, North Carolina, constructed in 1969. The overseas market has not been neglected. Approximately 70 countries currently market Kelly-Springfield tires, thanks in part to Goodyear's international distribution network.

On the eve of the 21st century, Kelly-Springfield has become a large, modern, profitable tire company that manufactures over 50 Kelly-Springfield brands of tires and thousands of custom brand tires. Competition is intense, and Kelly-Springfield's parent company, Goodyear, is the only major American tire company that has survived takeover bids from foreign concerns.

Mr. Lee N. Fiedler, president and CEO of Kelly-Springfield in the early 1990s, is faced with an array of challenges, probably the greatest of which is environmental. As a subsidiary of Goodyear, Kelly-Springfield complies with Goodyear's environmental guidelines, such as converting used tires, which in the past ended up in huge scrap heaps, into reusable energy, primarily for use by electric utility companies. In the 1980s, Kelly-Springfield made the switch from imported oil to coal in its manufacturing facilities, installing expensive effluent emissions controls in all factories to reduce emissions 50 percent by 1995.

While high performance and private brand tires sold well even during the 1990s recession, stricter environmental laws mean that the tire of the future will have to be more energy efficient, lending itself not to greater but to lower (55 mph) speed limits. The 1992 Invicta GFE auto tire that saves fuel by reducing the rate of friction and thus reducing gas use by 4 percent, is an example of "the tire of the future." In order to remain a major player in the $40 billion dollar worldwide tire industry, Goodyear and its subsidiary, Kelly-Springfield, will have to develop many more environmentally friendly tires.

Further Reading:

"The Bounce Is Back at Goodyear," *Fortune,* September 7, 1992, pp. 70–72.
The Goodyear Tire & Rubber Company Annual Reports, Akron, OH: The Goodyear Tire & Rubber Company, 1991–92.
Jackson, Kenneth A., *The Kelly-Springfield Story,* Cumberland, MD: The Kelly-Springfield Tire Company, 1988.
"Kelly-Springfield Tire (Lee/Star division renamed Associate Brand)," *Rubber World,* May 1992, p. 18.
"Marketer of the Month: You'll Find Lee Fiedler Where the Rubber Meets the Road," *Sales & Marketing Management,* December 1992, pp. 36–37.
"Why Tiremakers Are Still Spinning Their Wheels," *Business Week (Industrial/Technology Edition),* February 26, 1990.

—Sina Dubovoj

Kesko Ltd (Kesko Oy)

Satamakatu 3, P.O.B. 135–136
SF-00161
Helsinki, Finland
(358) 0 1981
Fax: (358) 0 655 473

Public Company
Incorporated: 1940
Employees: 6,816
Sales: FIM $26.64 billion (US $5.08 billion)
Stock Exchanges: Helsinki
SICs: 2095 Roasted Coffee; 5064 Electrical Appliances, TV,
    & Radios; 5083 Farm & Garden Machinery; 5091
    Sporting & Recreational Goods; 5112 Stationery & Office
    Supplies; 5136 Men's and Boys' Clothing; 5137 Women's
    and Children's Clothing; 5139 Footwear; 5141 Groceries;
    5142 Packaged Frozen Goods; 5143 Dairy Products; 5148
    Fresh Fruits & Vegetables; 5191 Farm Supplies; 5411
    Grocery Stores; 5311 Variety Stores; 5511 New & Used
    Car Dealers; 5551 Boat Dealers; 5561 Recreational
    Vehicle Dealers

The largest trading company in Finland, Kesko Ltd is the parent corporation of the K-Group, comprising some 2,400 independent retailer-shareholders who operate nearly 2,700 stores specializing in groceries, leisure goods, and consumer durables. Total sales for the K-stores in 1992—FIM $32.2 billion, or US $6.14 billion—exceeded that of the corporation itself. Kesko's largest division by far is Foodstuffs, which represents 71 percent of the K-Group outlets and 59 percent of corporate sales. The Agricultural and Builders' Supplies and Non Food Divisions form the remainder of the company. The Non Food Division, reorganized on January 1, 1992, consists of departments devoted to clothing, household goods, leisure goods, home electronics, and shoes. Kesko also serves as one of Finland's major importing firms, handling such international brands as Audi, Brooks, Browning, Daewoo, Fuji, Volkswagen, and Yamaha. Through its subsidiaries, many of which fall within the domain of the Agricultural and Builders' Supplies Division, Kesko enjoys additional diversity as a major participant in the construction and agribusiness industries, despite troubling economic trends that caused a nearly 20 percent decline in division sales from 1990 to 1991.

Kesko was formed following mergers and dissolutions of nearly a dozen retailer-owned wholesale companies active in Finland prior to World War I. By the beginning of World War II, only four such companies, called the group of rural retailer companies, were left to vie for market share against other competitors in the rural foodstuffs industry. These four were Maakauppiaitten Oy, founded in 1906 and headquartered in Helsinki; Kauppiaitten Oy, founded in 1907 and located in Vaasa; Oy Savo-Karjalan Tukkuliike, founded in 1915 and centered in Vyborg; and Keski-Suomen Tukkukauppa Oy, founded in 1917 and located in Jyväkylä. The early association of these four main companies represented a transition in Finland's goods distribution system from traditional wholesale trade to owner-operated wholesale companies, a transition upon which Finland's entire cooperative movement was ultimately modeled. Two large central companies already in existence, the Finnish Co-operative Wholesale Society SOK and the Central Cooperative Society OTK, would eventually be surpassed by this group that joined to form Kesko. Even during their infancy, three of the core four—Maakauppiaitten, Kauppiaitten, and Savo-Karjalan Tukkuliike—represented sizeable businesses with extensive office networks and net sales second only to the two central co-ops.

According to the corporate publication *50 Years of Kesko*: "Attempts were made to merge the retailer-owned wholesale companies almost from the very beginning, as the first negotiations on the matter took place as early as in 1908." Although prior to the formation of Savo-Karjalan Tukkuliike or Keski-Suomen Tukkukauppa, these original negotiations led to a series of meetings throughout the 1910s and 1920s, during which time several small mergers took place. A large merger of the core four almost succeeded in 1928, prevented only by "the 'strong men' of the two biggest companies," who had "firm opinions about the principles of the new company, and the other companies could not accept them." The firm opinions, of course, pertained to how the new company would be managed and what degree of administrative clout each of the original managers would retain following the merger.

One positive outcome of the 1928 negotiations was the formation of two organizational bodies, Vähittäiskauppiaiden Tukkuliikkeiden Yhdistys (VTY) and Kauppiaitten Keskuskunta. The purpose of the former was to serve as a consortium for more uniform purchasing by the four; the latter was to serve as a joint-service cooperative for the importation of wholesale goods as well as domestic industrial production, as the Kauppiaitten company already operated a Lahti shirt factory and a Helsinki coffee roastery. According to *50 Years of Kesko*, "Kauppiaitten Keskuskunta did not become a very significant company during the 1930s but, in the end, it became the seed of Kesko" because of its registration of the K-emblem and the Kesko logo. In late March 1940, following another decade of ongoing but disappointing negotiations as well as the conclusion of the Winter War with Russia, new talks among the four companies resumed. Despite one potentially considerable stumbling block—Savo-Karjalan Tukkuliike's loss of most of its eastern Finland operations to Russian control during peace negotiations—Kesko Oy became a reality by October. Combined sales at the time totaled FIM $1.25 billion; retailer-shareholders for the group numbered some 5,800.

Fittingly, the chair of the largest merged company, Maakauppiatten's Oskari Heikkilä, was elected Kesko's first chairperson. The company's original supervisory board consisted of 21 other members, with seats apportioned according to the net sales of the predecessor companies. The name Kesko, which had no historical ties to any of the founding companies, was adopted. Interestingly, the formation of Kesko did not *legally* constitute a merger because all four companies dissolved themselves and distributed their net assets to shareholders, who in turn subscribed to new shares of capital in Kesko, a wholly new limited liability company.

From the end of World War II to 1950, Kesko's district network grew from 19 to 22 regional offices while K-emblems spread to the stores of some 3,700 shareholders. Through the formation of Consultative Committees, introduction of purchase discounts, and implementation of support services, Kesko began to transform itself from a strictly wholesale concern to a central company devoted to its members. Beginning in 1950, the emphasis on district expansion and internal restructuring was exchanged for diversification beyond foodstuffs, into the related areas of animal feed, fertilizer, and agricultural machinery, as well as the construction industry.

During the late 1950s, as Finland altered from a primarily agrarian and rural to a primarily industrial and urban economy, Kesko adapted itself as well. Large numbers of K-stores located in outlying regions had to be closed, while nearly as many new K-stores had to be erected closer to urban centers. Coincident with this dramatic upheaval for Kesko retailers, the central company faced shortages in capital, spiralling growth in personnel, and mounting transportation and distribution expenses.

The most significant action taken by the company during this period of growth and transformation was the decision to take Kesko public, through a division of the company's stock into exclusive and ordinary shares. Thus, in 1960, Kesko was listed on the Helsinki Stock Exchange, and new capital was available to solve its problems while governance of the company remained in the hands of the exclusive shareholders, the retailers themselves. Enormous advancements during the 1960s, including the completion of a central warehouse in 1965 and the implementation of long-term retail development programs, paved the way for significant growth during the 1970s. During this decade, Kesko came into its own and saw its combined market share rise from 23 percent to almost 30 percent. Confident, after weathering the rationing policies and manufacturing shortages of the 1950s and 1960s, that foodstuffs could steadily generate at least half of corporate sales, Kesko poised itself for more rapid growth in its Agricultural and Builders' Supplies Division.

During the 1980s, Kesko fulfilled its longtime plan of divesting itself of most of its manufacturing operations, which over the years had come to include a margarine factory, flour mill and bakery, match factory, ryecrisp company, meat processing company, bicycle factory, clothing factory, and coffee roasting plant. The process had been a slow one, for at the beginning of the decade the last three still remained within the company's holdings. Management decided to retain only the roastery, the strongest performer in net sales of all Kesko's manufacturing units. "The necessity of having a coffee roastery of our own has been generally approved," according to *50 Years of Kesko,* "because coffee has been the most important campaign product ever since the Second World War." Kesko's establishment in 1991 of Viking Coffee Ltd., a roastery jointly owned with a Swedish central company, affirms the company's continuing commitment to this important "micro-market."

Having become the largest central trading company in Finland, Kesko entered the 1990s streamlined (its district offices progressively pared down to just nine) and prepared for strong continuing growth. However, due to a depressed national and global economy, the company saw net sales decline by 6.5 percent from 1991 to 1992. Chair and Chief Executive Eero Utter nonetheless found cause for optimism in the increased market share for most of Kesko's product groups: "Although the Kesko Corporation's profit for 1991 decreased from the previous year, the Corporation and the whole K-Group has coped and will continue to cope with the recession very well in comparison with other companies." Despite relative anonymity in the United States, Kesko has emerged as a singularly important Finnish company, controlling some 40 percent of the overall grocery market. Its ranking by *Fortune* in August 1992 as the 56th largest global service company further demonstrates that the critical decision to go public back in 1960 has repaid the cooperative handsomely.

Principal Subsidiaries: K-Cash & Garry Ltd.; Auto-Span Oy; Keskometalli Oy; K-Motts Oy; K-maatalousyhtiöt Oy; K-yhtiöt Oy; MK-mainos Oy; Interrent Oy; Suomen Väri Oy; VV-Auto Oy Viking Coffee Ltd. (50%).

Further Reading:

A Capital K Is the Key to the Finnish Market, Helsinki: Kesko Corporation, 1991.
Fifty Years of Kesko, Helsinki: Kesko Oy, 1990.
"The 500 Largest Foreign Companies (table)," *Forbes,* July 28, 1986, p. 192.
"The Global Service 500 (table)," *Fortune,* August 24, 1992, p. 212.
Kesko Annual Report, Helsinki: Kesko Corporation, 1991.

—Jay P. Pederson

KeyCorp

One KeyCorp Plaza
Albany, New York 12201-0088
U.S.A.
(518) 486-8000
Fax: (518) 487-4057

Public Company
Incorporated: 1970 as First Commercial Banks Inc.
Employees: 17,000
Assets: $30.11 billion
Stock Exchanges: New York
SICs: 6712 Bank Holding Companies; 6022 State
    Commercial Banks; 6021 National Commercial Banks

KeyCorp is one of the nation's 30 largest banks with banking
and other financial services subsidiaries in the Northeast, the
Northwest, including Alaska, and the Rocky Mountain states.
On Wall Street, KeyCorp is often called the "Wal-Mart of
banking" because it serves many small towns and has cultivated a folksy image—similar to that of the mass merchandiser
Wal-Mart—by lending mostly to consumers and small businesses. KeyCorp refers to itself as "America's neighborhood
bank."

While other banks, such as First Interstate Bancorp and Bank-
America Corp., operate in several states, they do not, according
to the *Wall Street Journal,* have the regional diversity of Key-
Corp. These banks with interstate holdings are more confined to
specific parts of the country, while KeyCorp's holdings span
many regions. Unlike other banking leaders whose headquarters
are located in Manhattan, KeyCorp is headquartered in Albany,
New York. The makeup of KeyCorp's banking network is also
very unusual. While KeyCorp is a coast-to-coast bank, its
empire of more than 800 banking offices is concentrated in the
nation's northern tier, skipping over the Midwest entirely.

KeyCorp's history dates back to 1825 when New York Governor Dewitt Clinton signed a bill chartering the Commercial
Bank of Albany, KeyCorp's direct ancestor. In 1865, Commercial Bank was reorganized under the National Banking Act of
1864, and its name was changed to National Commercial Bank
of Albany. Also during this time, another bank that would
eventually become part of KeyCorp opened—the Trust and
Deposit Company of Onondaga in Syracuse, established in
1869.

In 1919, the Trust and Deposit Company of Onondaga merged
with First National Bank of Syracuse to become First Trust and
Deposit. Around the same time, the National Commercial Bank
of Albany went through another reorganization, consolidating
with Union Trust Company to become National Commercial
Bank and Trust Company. These two new banking concerns
operated independently until 1971 when First Trust and Deposit
was merged into National Commercial Bank and Trust Co.
(now incorporated as First Commercial Banks Inc.) With that
transaction, First Commercial had 89 offices in New York State.
The name was changed to Key Bank Inc. in 1979, and the
institution adopted its present name six years later.

Victor J. Riley, Jr., became president and chief executive officer
(CEO) of the bank in 1973; he would continue to serve in this
capacity for over 20 years, making him the longest tenured CEO
of any of the top fifty banks in the country. Riley led the bank
from its days as a strictly upstate New York bank to its position
as the country's twenty-ninth largest financial institution in
1991 with $23 billion in assets, up from $2.4 billion ten years
before. Between 1981 and 1991, the bank's stock produced an
impressive 810 percent total return including dividends, third
among the 50 largest banks, according to the company's annual
report.

During the 1970s and early 1980s, KeyCorp bought banks
throughout the upstate area as well as 25 offices from the Bank
of New York. Initially, Riley's plan was for KeyCorp to become
a regional concern by acquiring banks in New England as well,
starting with its purchase of a bank in Maine. However, at the
same time, to keep the large New York banking establishments
from dominating the New England banking system, a move was
made to exclude New York banks from purchasing banks in
Massachusetts and Connecticut.

Riley looked to the west when his New England strategy was
thwarted. He anticipated that when U.S. trade with Asia increased, the economies of western states would also improve.
KeyCorp bought a string of banks, and in the four years between
1985 and 1990 quintupled its assets from $3 billion to $15
billion. While other banks were focusing on large cities, especially in the Northeast, KeyCorp was focusing on areas of low
population in which banking services were scarce. Furthermore,
KeyCorp avoided the pricing wars that often occurred in highly
competitive markets.

While eastern banks were buying up other eastern banks at
premium prices, KeyCorp continued its westward expansion,
acquiring inexpensive and promising banks in Wyoming, Idaho,
and Utah. In 1985, Riley bought two banks in Alaska and
Alaska Pacific Bancorporation; he used Alaska's interstate
banking laws to purchase a bank in Oregon, which became
known as Key Bank of Oregon. The next year, KeyCorp acquired Northwest Bancorp of Albany, Oregon, and Pacwest
Bancorp of Portland, Oregon, which also became part of Key
Bank of Oregon.

Many leaders in the banking industry thought Riley was making
a mistake when he started buying banks in Alaska and the
Northwest in 1984. Critics doubted his ability to manage such
banks from a home office in Albany, New York. The purchase
certainly seemed like a mistake when oil prices dropped dramat-

ically, and Alaska plunged into a recession. KeyCorp moved quickly to restructure loans for borrowers hit by recession and foreclosed on loans when necessary.

KeyCorp also continued to buy banks in small towns and cities in New York State. In 1986, it acquired four savings banks in the mid-Hudson Valley. In the same year, it increased its western holdings by purchasing Beaver State Bank in Beaver, Oregon.

Although KeyCorp had been shut out of acquisitions in much of New England a few years before, in 1987 Riley bought eight branch offices in Maine from Fleet/Norstar Financial for $14 million. They became part of Key Bank of Maine. KeyCorp also opened a unique subsidiary based in Albany—Key Bank USA N.A., which provides banking services by mail to customers nationwide who were not within a Key Bank region.

Regional diversity has advantages and disadvantages for KeyCorp. On the positive side, KeyCorp is not so vulnerable to economic slumps in one region. Director H. Douglas Barclay told the *Wall Street Journal,* "Problems in one or two states can be contained. Over time it all balances out." While the Northwest was in a slump, the Northeast was booming. Then, the tables were turned and the Northwest picked up while the Northeast was in recession. However, geographic diversity also made KeyCorp expensive to run, with operating costs as a percentage of assets high. Top executives also spent a lot of time on the road, visiting branches far from the Albany headquarters.

Consistent with the small town approach, Riley rarely replaced personnel in the banks KeyCorp purchased, choosing instead to stay with management familiar to the local population. He told *Business Week,* "You cannot go into a new state and start shuffling people around and maintain yourself as a retail bank."

The small town philosophy also helped the bank avoid costly bad loans. KeyCorp's policy was to lend to people and businesses in the areas it served. It avoided the pitfall of many other banks—lending outside the states in which it had branches. In 1990, bad loans made up only four percent of its $9.9 billion loan portfolio; most of those bad debts were at its Alaska banks, hard hit by a decline in oil exploration. Furthermore KeyCorp's lending practices were financially conservative. The company did not make any loans greater than $20 million and its average commercial loan was only about $2 million. Furthermore, no single industry group represented more than 24 percent of KeyCorp's commercial loans.

After more than ten years of acquisitions that had brought KeyCorp into the top 50 list, KeyCorp shifted its focus to reducing its high overhead costs. In 1990, its efficiency ratio was about 66 percent, meaning that about sixty-six cents worth of every dollar in revenue was spent on overhead. By the end of 1992, its efficiency ratio had improved to 61.9 percent and was more in line with the efficiency ratios of comparable banks. KeyCorp merged its operations into two computer centers and brought its four mortgage companies together as one. The banking company also sold a car-leasing business and a finance company that were unprofitable.

Still KeyCorp lacked a standardized reporting system for its hundreds of branches. This became a priority for William Dougherty, the company's chief financial officer, who set to work linking KeyCorp's branches by computer and consolidating its back-office operations. By the end of 1992, all of KeyCorp's banks were linked electronically, with primary processing centers in Albany and in Tigard, Oregon. Six secondary sites handled business more suited to regional processing.

In line with the current trend in banking toward consolidation of holdings, KeyCorp consolidated several New York State operations into one financial institution. Key Bank of Eastern New York, Key Bank of Central New York, and Key Bank of Western New York became a single nationally chartered bank, Key Bank of New York State, N.A., with its offices in Albany.

KeyCorp benefitted from the country's thrift crisis in the early 1990s by buying from the government assets of two large failed New York thrifts—Empire Federal Savings and Loan and Goldome Savings Bank. With the Goldome purchase, KeyCorp moved from its status as an unknown in the mortgage industry to become the nineteenth largest mortgage banker in the nation. Furthermore, the Goldome purchase turned out to be profitable as the market for new and refinanced mortgage loans boomed, with interest rates the lowest they had been in decades.

In 1992, KeyCorp acquired Valley Bancorporation of Valley Falls, Idaho, which became part of Key Bank of Idaho. KeyCorp also bought the 48 branches of Security Pacific Bank in Washington, which became part of Key Bank of Washington. The company negotiated several other deals as well that were completed in early 1993: Puget Sound Bancorp, with assets of $4.7 billion merged with Key Bank of Washington; 40 branches of New York's First American Bankshares and nine branch offices of National Savings Bank of Albany were acquired; and KeyCorp also bought its first holding in Colorado—Home Federal Savings of Fort Collins.

By the end of 1992, KeyCorp had its operations and its expenses under control, using a computer system to keep track of its coast-to-coast snowbelt holdings. Its earnings were also looking better. For a long time earnings stood at 90 cents for every $100 in assets, but in 1992, they pulled past the industry standard of one dollar per $100 in assets.

While other banks in the Northeast had been saddled with bad real estate loans, KeyCorp's net earnings were increasing because its Northwest holdings, which in 1990 made up more than 39 percent of its holdings, were booming. Although it owned banks in some larger western cities, the majority of its banks were located in small towns such as Troy, Idaho, with a population of 820 and Gig Harbor, Washington, with a population of 2,429.

Victor Riley and William Dougherty have been credited with taking KeyCorp into the ranks of the top 50 financial institutions. According to *The Economist,* KeyCorp's "loan book and profitability are the envy of other banks." That article explained that KeyCorp avoided the "easy money" made from big development loans for commercial property and corporate loans for highly-leveraged transactions. This kept KeyCorp out of some of the deep troubles that other banks encountered. KeyCorp also refrained from making loans to third world nations. In 1990, the bank's largest loans added up to only $560 million of a $10.4 billion loan portfolio. *The Economist* also credited KeyCorp's success to "rigorous financial and credit controls" over the banks it bought as well as its effective cost controls. In 1992, the bank held only 25 loans that were worth more than $12.5 million and only one worth more than $30-million, a loan to the owner of the bank's headquarters in Albany.

KeyCorp began testing a Vision 2001 computer system and planned to have it fully installed by the end of 1993. At a cost of $15 million to $20 million, the system would help branch bankers market a wide range of credit services by allowing users to input new loan information, forward loan applications to managers, and access credit scoring data. The system could also aid in loan servicing and collection.

As it approached the twenty-first century, KeyCorp anticipated growth in the area of trust products, as the "baby boomers" entered middle age and started to think about retirement. KeyCorp planned to expand its trust services and products. In early 1993, KeyCorp's assets were more than $30 billion. Riley and Dougherty planned to increase KeyCorp's net assets to $40 billion by the mid-1990s, while still earning at least a 15 percent return on equity in order to keep attracting investors.

Since KeyCorp's reputation is not that of a "high tech bank," but rather a personal, neighborhood bank, Riley and Dougherty admit that attaining assets of $40 billion may be difficult. Riley told *The Economist* that the key would be to keep tight controls on the finances and operations but at the same time maintain management power at the local banks where the person-to-person banking takes place. KeyCorp's annual report explained that services that are "visible to the customer are managed locally," including loan approval and product pricing. Data processing, loan reviews, and audits, "invisible services," were handled by KeyCorp, the parent company.

While it was important to maintain that small town flavor and person-to-person service, to Riley, investors were the key to growth. He told *Financial World* "We've worried an awful lot about the depositor [in this country], but we've given no concern to the investor. And today, we *need* the investor if we're going to continue to raise capital, which is an absolute necessity." Nevertheless, banks have not proved to be attractive investments in recent years, and Riley maintained that KeyCorp would not buy banks just to meet their goal of $40 billion. His first priority would be to protect earnings.

Principal Subsidiaries: Key Bank of Alaska; Key Bank of Idaho; Key Bank of Maine; Key Bank of New York; Key Bank of Oregon; Key Bank of Washington; Key Bank of Utah; Key Bank of Wyoming; Key Bank USA N.A.; Key Bank Life Insurance, Ltd.; Key Brokerage Company Inc.; KeyCorp Mortgage Inc.; Key Pacific Mortgage, Inc.; Key Services Corporation; Trust & Investment Management Group; Key Trust Company; Key Trust Company of Alaska; Key Trust Company of Florida, N.A.; Key Trust Company of Maine; Key Trust Company of the Northwest; Key Trust Company of the West; KeyCorp Leasing Ltd.; NCB Properties Inc.; Niagara Asset Corporation; Niagara Portfolio Management Corp.

Further Reading:

Benoit, Ellen, "The Hunger," *Financial World,* December 11, 1990.
——, "KeyCorp's Northern Lights," *Financial World,* October 31, 1989.
Jereski, Laura, "Small Towns Add Up to Big Banking for KeyCorp," *Business Week,* April 30, 1990.
"A Small Success," *The Economist,* November 10, 1990.
Wilke, John R., "The Inter-Regional: Nationwide Banking Is Getting a Preview at Growing KeyCorp Offices from Alaska to Maine," *Wall Street Journal,* May 31, 1991.
Wiseman, Paul, "Life of Riley—A Wild and Woolly Banker," *USA Today,* September 14, 1992.
——, " 'Wal-Mart of Banking' Built on Discipline," *USA Today,* September 14, 1992.

—Wendy J. Stein

KitchenAid®
For the way it's made.™

KitchenAid

2000 M-63 North
MD-4302
Benton Harbor, Michigan 49022
U.S.A.
(616) 923-5000
Fax: (616) 923-3214

Wholly owned subsidiary of Whirlpool Corporation
Incorporated: 1924 as KitchenAid Manufacturing Company
Employees: 3,500
Sales: $600,000
SICs: 3634 Electric Housewares & Fans; 3639 Household
   Appliances Nec

KitchenAid manufactures and markets a full line of premium-price home appliances, including microwave and conventional ovens, cooktops, refrigerators, dishwashers, in-sink garbage disposal units, and automatic clothes washers and dryers. The company also continues to manufacture the product on which its name was built, the popular KitchenAid electric stand mixer. Acquired in 1986 by the Whirlpool Corporation, the largest appliance maker in the world, KitchenAid has increased its market share through the expansion of its product line.

The name KitchenAid was first introduced as a brand name for an electric stand mixer developed by The Hobart Manufacturing Company in 1919. In the early 1900s Hobart had begun producing the first electrically driven machines for grinding food items, including coffee beans, peanuts, and hamburger. In 1915 the company's subsidiary, Troy Metal Products, introduced the first model of an electric mixer. Designed to mix large quantities quickly, the appliance featured "planetary action," in which an individually rotating beater traveled in one direction around the inside of a mixing bowl. Allegedly, when Hobart executives brought the first mixers home for testing, one executive's wife remarked, "I don't care what you call it, but I know it's the best kitchen aid I ever had." KitchenAid was subsequently adopted as the mixer's trademark.

The KitchenAid mixer became widely popular during the 1920s and 1930s. Like most housewares at the time, the mixers were sold either door to door or through a KitchenAid party at which a salesperson demonstrated the appliance's functions by using it to prepare a meal for the guests, who were then encouraged to order a KitchenAid mixer. During this time several attachments

were developed for use in mixing a variety of foods, and the KitchenAid name was also given to an electric coffee mill introduced by Hobart. In 1924 Hobart's Troy Metals subsidiary was renamed the KitchenAid Manufacturing Company, and its headquarters were set up in Dayton, Ohio.

In 1926 Hobart acquired another appliance manufacturer that would figure prominently in KitchenAid's future. The Crescent Washing Machine Company was founded by Josephine Cochran, who had built a dishwashing machine—initially for her own use in the home—that was named the top invention at the 1893 World's Fair. Quickly realizing the marketing potential for such machines in restaurants and other institutions, she founded the Crescent company in 1880, which built both hand and power operated dishwashers. More than forty years later, Hobart, already recognized as a leader in the commercial dishwasher market, purchased the highly successful Crescent company and began to explore further the feasibility of producing a dishwashing machine for use in the home. Research and development were curtailed during World War II, but finally, in 1949, Hobart introduced a new home dishwasher, the KD-10, featuring a patented washing mechanism and the KitchenAid brand name. The KitchenAid home dishwasher soon established a reputation for reliability.

KitchenAid gradually came to be known for other products as well. In 1966 Hobart acquired the Plumbing Equipment Division of the National Rubber Machinery Corporation. Benefiting from the expertise of this division, the company developed a KitchenAid food waste disposer, which it began to market in 1968. An instant hot water dispenser was brought out in 1971, and the following year the KitchenAid trash compactor was introduced.

During the 1980s the company underwent several changes. In an effort to broaden its product line, it acquired a major manufacturer of built-in cooking equipment, the Chambers Corporation of Oxford, Mississippi. KitchenAid subsequently introduced a line of ovens and stovetops. By 1985 the company was one of the most successful manufacturers of home appliances, while Hobart had become one of the foremost producers of appliances for use in commercial kitchens.

That year the company was approached by the Whirlpool Corporation, a leading manufacturer of home appliances interested in acquiring KitchenAid, and a deal was soon negotiated whereby Whirlpool would pay $150 million for KitchenAid while Emerson Electric Company would purchase KitchenAid's dishwasher and trash compactor operations. However, an antitrust suit filed by appliance manufacturers White Consolidated Industries and Magic Chef delayed the acquisitions for a year. The two companies alleged that Whirlpool's arrangement with Emerson would give them an unfair amount of power in the market, allowing them to take away a substantial amount of business from White and Magic Chef. After an investigation by the Federal Trade Commission, the suit proved unsuccessful, and in February 1986 KitchenAid was acquired by the Whirlpool Corporation.

Whirlpool had several immediate plans for its new acquisition. In August of that year, KitchenAid's Ohio staff was relocated to St. Joseph, Michigan, to be nearer Whirlpool's Benton Harbor headquarters. St. Joseph native and Whirlpool chairman, president, and chief executive officer Jack D. Sparks had arranged for Whirlpool to purchase a historic brick school building to serve as the KitchenAid division's new administrative, marketing, and sales headquarters. Whirlpool reportedly spent over $3 million to purchase and renovate the building through an "adapative reuse" renovation plan that aimed to preserve the structural integrity of the building while modernizing it for office use. Beginning in October, the Jack D. Sparks Administrative Center was opened to the public for tours, amid much celebration and local press coverage.

Also during this time, the company began developing plans to market a full line of major home appliances under the KitchenAid name, to be introduced through an aggressive marketing strategy targeted at, according to KitchenAid president Glen S. Olinger, affluent and "quality conscious" consumers. KitchenAid first exhibited the entire line at the National Association of Home Builders Show in Dallas in early January 1987. Making the appliances available to the general public that spring, the company offered high profit margins to selected dealers who carried the entire KitchenAid major appliance line. They also assisted in the construction of elaborate store displays, some of which featured full-sized kitchen units entirely equipped with KitchenAid appliances.

The marketing strategy was twofold. First, KitchenAid hoped to emphasize the quality of their products by selling only to "quality oriented" dealers, rather than those whose focus was on sales volume and low prices. Second, the company hoped to discourage customers from "cherry-picking" their appliances from a variety of brand names in favor of, in the words of former KitchenAid president Ken Kaminski, "selecting a single full line brand of high-end appliances." Kaminski noted that customers could then benefit from having "a full kitchen's worth of appliances with coordinated colors and styling, and one point of contact for sales, delivery, use and care and after-the-sale services."

KitchenAid considers the marketing strategy a success, noting rapid and impressive growth in all product categories since the Whirlpool acquisition. The traditional KitchenAid stand mixer sold in record numbers in the late 1980s and early 1990s, and the major appliance line reportedly has experienced double digit annual growth since its debut.

In 1987 Sparks retired as president and CEO of Whirlpool. Taking his place was David R. Whitwam, whose strategy included a reorganization of Whirlpool's subsidiaries. The once centralized appliance group, which included KitchenAid, Whirlpool, Roper, and Estate brands, was subsequently divided into separate independent business units: Roper and Estate marketed budget appliances; Whirlpool represented the mid-range brand; and KitchenAid remained the premium line of appliances. By 1988 KitchenAid had achieved a total of $308 million in sales, and three years later KitchenAid appliances were being sold in nearly 4,000 retail outlets, roughly 30 percent of all

outlets in the country. At this time the brand divisions were again reorganized, this time into a North American Appliance Group (NAAG), set up to distinguish the American brands from Whirlpool's growing international concerns.

Boosting its advertising budget by ten percent in 1990, KitchenAid also developed a television adverstising campaign that proved profitable. The following year the company began airing a series of ads featuring a reunion of three generations of one family congregating in the kitchen, which is full of KitchenAid appliances that have also endured over the years. Advertising experts noted that the sentimental depiction of a traditional family reunion was particularly effective during a time in which America was engaged in a war in the Persian Gulf and consumers were sympathetic to the homecomings that received much publicity. Furthermore, the KitchenAid ads received a tremendous amount of exposure since the company had purchased the majority of its ad space during major network news programs popular during the war.

Despite the economic recessions during 1990 and 1991, which hit the appliance manufacturing industry particularly hard, KitchenAid remained a profitable component of Whirlpool, steadily gaining market share.

KitchenAid products are manufactured in Ohio, South Carolina, Mississippi, Indiana, Arkansas, Ontario, and Quebec, and its appliances are distributed throughout North America. Regarding the 1990s consumer as more sophisticated and concerned about quality, KitchenAid also opened a design center in St. Joseph, Michigan, which was committed to the improvement of product design through market research. As global marketing became increasingly important to parent Whirlpool, KitchenAid also hoped to explore designs and technology used by appliance manufacturers worldwide, after having established itself as the premier marketer of premium home appliances.

Further Reading:

Berg, Eric N., "The Appliance Brand-Name Game," *New York Times,* August 23, 1990, p. D1.
Berry, Jon, "KitchenAid and Norman Rockwell," *Adweek's Marketing Strategy,* February 11, 1991, p. 4.
Mumford, Louis, "A New Career for Old School," *South Bend Tribune,* October 2, 1986.
Pepple, Steve, "Whirlpool Aiming at Affluent Buyers," *St. Joseph Herald Palladium,* October 2, 1986.
Schiller, Zachary, "Is the Latest Appliance Merger One Too Many?" *Business Week,* March 25, 1985, pp. 31, 34.
Stuart, Don, "KitchenAid Grows Through Emphasis on Quality," St. Joseph, Michigan: KitchenAid, 1991.
Verespej, Michael A., "Whirlpool's New Kitchen Recipe," *Industry Week,* September 21, 1987, p. 56–57.
Whirlpool Annual Reports, Benton Harbor, Michigan: Whirlpool Corporation, 1986, 1989, 1990.
Zellner, Wendy, and Zachary Schiller, "A Tough Market Has Whirlpool in a Spin," *Business Week,* May 2, 1988, pp. 121–22.

—Tina Grant

The Koll Company

4343 Von Karman Avenue
Newport Beach, California 92660-2083
U.S.A.
(714) 833-3030
Fax: (714) 833-3755

Public Company
Incorporated: 1962
Employees: 1,200
Sales: $725 million
Stock Exchanges: NASDAQ
SICs: 1531 Operating Builders; 1542 Nonresidential
   Construction Nec.; 6531 Real Estate Agents & Managers;
   6552 Real Property Subdividers and Developers

Founded in 1962 by visionary developer Donald M. Koll as a general construction firm, The Koll Company has grown to become one of the nation's largest real estate investment, development, construction, and management firms, having developed in excess of $6 billion worth of office buildings, manufacturing facilities, business and industrial parks, research and development facilities, retail centers and residential communities throughout the West and Southwest United States.

Donald Koll's timing was perfect. The Koll Company, headquartered in Newport Beach, California began as a real estate developer in Southern California at a time when there was little development in the area. Orange County, California, was primarily an agricultural area that would later become a bustling metropolis, with hundreds of thousands of homes, businesses, ancillary shopping centers, business parks, and recreational facilities. Riding the wave of the California real estate boom of the 1970s and 1980s, The Koll Company became a major force in real estate development in the West.

The Koll Company is operated through several subsidiaries with regional offices throughout the nation. Koll Construction, a wholly owned subsidiary of The Koll Company, is one of the largest construction firms on the West Coast with annual revenues in excess of $275 million. Koll International Commercial and Koll Resorts International, both wholly owned by The Koll Company, are involved in developing real estate in Mexico. Koll Management Services, Inc., 64 percent owned by The Koll Company, provides property management services to property owners throughout the nation. Formed in 1988, Koll Manage-

ment Services quickly grew to be one of the largest property management firms in the field, went public in 1991, and was the first publicly traded firm of its kind.

Through Koll Real Estate Group (KREG), a wholly owned subsidiary, The Koll Company has developed in excess of $6 billion worth of commercial, retail, and residential real estate. KREG has 10 offices in major cities in California, Washington, Oregon, Arizona, Colorado, and Texas.

Until the recent recession, most of the Real Estate Group's work involved the development of office buildings, industrial parks, and mixed-use commercial centers in joint ventures with financial partners, typically large insurance companies. Since the downturn in the office and industrial real estate markets, KREG has become more heavily involved in developing public projects in partnership with government entities, build-to-suit projects for corporate clients, and the development of retail and health care facilities.

KREG also has an active real estate consulting service, providing environmental, permitting, financial, and work-out consultation to owners of land and property. Its most prominent client in this arena is The Bolsa Chica Company, which owns a large environmentally sensitive ocean-front property in Orange County. KREG has developed a site plan for the parcel in consultation with local government and environmental groups, and is pursuing government approvals.

Donald Koll has been doing business in Mexico for decades and has owned property there since the late 1970s. But in the early 1980s he began to acquire resort property in the Los Cabos area of Mexico, at a time when the political and economic climate in Mexico were precarious at best. This investment gave Koll a strong presence in Mexico and positioned The Koll Company for development in Mexico when the time was right. Previous U.S. administrations discouraged foreign investment. Then a major building destruction in Mexico caused by an earthquake created shortages of industrial, commercial, and residential property throughout Mexico.

It was likely these events that spurred Koll to seize the opportunity to make additional acquisitions in Mexico and led to the 900-acre Palmilla project and the 1,800-acre Cabo del Sol project. Already, Koll has invested more than $75 million in these two prime resorts. The two master-planned resorts in the Los Cabos area will feature 4,700 homes, five hotels, four golf courses, two tennis clubs, a health spa, water sports center, medical center, and shopping center. The Palmilla golf course is the first Jack Nicklaus-designed course in Latin America and is a private course open only to members and guests of Hotel Palmilla. The first of two 18-hole golf courses at Cabo del Sol is now open to the public.

To help finance this development in Mexico, Koll secured a $55 million construction loan in 1991 for infrastructure development from Banco Nacional de Comercio Exterior. Thereafter, Koll Resorts International entered into a joint venture with Empresas ICA, Sociedad Controladora S.A. de C.V. (ICA), for the development and management of the Cabo del Sol resort. ICA is one of Mexico's largest holding companies, with assets in excess of $2.4 billion, and the largest construction company in Mexico. The estimated value of Cabo del Sol after buildout is

$750 million. Over the long run, Koll Resorts International hopes to develop resort and commercial properties in Mexico totalling more than $1 billion.

The international division has also been seeking U.S. capital for investment in Mexico and is actively developing build-to-suit projects for U.S. firms in Mexico City, Guadalajara, and Monterrey. Koll International Commercial has focused its attention on developing industrial properties in Monterrey, speculative high-rise development in Mexico City, and retail centers throughout Mexico. In addition, Koll expects the passage of the North American Free Trade Agreement (NAFTA) to create a trading block with a combined economy of $6.3 trillion to emerge as a major force in the world economy. With more and more American companies doing business in Mexico, their need for real estate facilities in Mexico should expand as well. Koll International Commercial hopes to be available to accommodate expansion of U.S. and Mexican operations throughout Mexico. Koll International Commercial has also assisted Koll Management Services in its analysis of Mexico as a growth market.

Koll Construction was hit hard during the recession and the resulting building slump of the early 1990s, with annual revenues slipping from $540 million in 1989 to under $300 million in 1993. Although Koll Construction had been a strong participant in the speculative development activity in the 1980s, its focus in the 1990s has been on corporate build-to-suits and public agency and tenant build-out projects to take up some of the slack. These assignments include a $40 million construction contract at the 560,000 square foot federal building and courthouse in Los Angeles; a $37 million construction contract to build a 418,000 square foot complex for NCR Corp. in San Diego; a $28 million contract to erect a General Services Administration building in downtown Los Angeles; a $27 million tenant improvement project for several government agencies slated to occupy a 780,000 square foot building in San Francisco; a $25 million contract at St. Joseph's Medical Center in Orange County, California; a $25 million renovation on the 250,000 square foot facility of a Dallas credit card processor; construction of a 61,165 square foot library and a 21,160 square foot theater for Portland Community College; renovation and tenant improvements for the 200,000 square foot headquarters of San Diego Gas & Electric; a 67,000 square foot library for the City of Newport Beach; and a $23 million contract to construct the Oregon Museum of Science & Industry in Portland.

Koll Construction was forced to downsize its operations in the early 1990s because of the prolonged slump in the real estate market. Some of the projects it was working on at that time included an 830-acre project near Sky Harbor Airport in Phoenix; a contract to develop Sierra Health Services' 175,000 square foot corporate headquarters in Las Vegas; and the 220,000 square foot First Nationwide Bank complex in Sacramento, developed with Ford Motor Land Company.

One of the bright spots for Koll Construction was its joint effort with the City of Anaheim to develop a new city hall structure as part of the redevelopment agency's master plan for the area. The city saved $1.3 million on the construction, and the construction was completed two months ahead of schedule in 1992. The 11-story city hall was just a small piece of the Koll Anaheim Center project. Because of the slowdown in the construction industry, contracts were obtained at prices lower than original estimates.

Koll Management Services has become the star performer of The Koll Company, employing more than 600 people among 107 field offices. Begun in 1988, by 1993 it was managing a property portfolio of 100 million square feet, serving nearly 11,000 clients around the country. And with a client list including some of the country's largest players in real estate, such as Aetna, Ford Motor Land Company, and The Irvine Company, the company was poised for a bright future.

Koll Management Services went public in 1991, trading on NASDAQ, and became the first property management firm to do so. It was ranked two years in a row among *Forbes* magazine's 200 best-managed small companies in the U.S. In 1991, Koll Management Services achieved profits of $2.7 million on sales of $29.1 million. Lawrence Horan, a real estate analyst at Prudential Securities, said in 1992 that he expected Koll Management Services to sustain 20 percent earnings growth for several years.

The public offering raised $11.9 million. Following the public offering, Koll Management Services had added nearly $6 million in operating capital to its war chest (after underwriting and other costs) and provided more than $5 million to The Koll Company. Flush with cash from the offering, Koll Management Services could now pursue its strategy of acquisitions and expansion. The company began acquiring regional property management firms, expanding into new markets and seizing on what it perceived to be an increasing demand for professional managers by large, institutional property owners, and by corporations with large owned or leased real estate portfolios.

Shortly after the public offering, Koll Management Services acquired Newport Beach-based Sunwest Asset Management, adding 7.3 million square feet to its portfolio and entering new markets in Nevada and Arizona. At about the same time, the company inked a joint venture arrangement with Boston-based CC&F Asset Management to manage 15 million square feet in Boston, Washington D.C., Baltimore, and Chicago. Other deals that came in quick succession include acquisition of Swearingen Management Company's Texas and Oklahoma-based portfolio of 4.2 million square feet; Tishman West's portfolio of 3.8 million square feet in New York, Chicago, Georgia, California, and Virginia; and the recent 30-million-square-foot Rubloff portfolio in several major East Coast and Midwest markets. And prior to the public offering, the company had already acquired four other property management firms, adding 5 million square feet to its portfolio.

The company also invested in sophisticated computer systems, enabling it to provide better reporting to its clients and to branch out into asset management, advising property owners about buying and selling properties, receivership services, and various consulting capabilities.

Competition can be expected to increase in the property management field as a whole, and particularly for Koll Management Services, as many developers who have curtailed activities as a result of the real estate slump will be looking to use their skills as real estate experts and enter the field of property management. But William Rothe, president of Koll Management Services, said in 1992 that the real estate slump would be a boon to large and efficient managers like Koll. An industry shakeout seemed likely whereby only the most efficient managers would survive. In the event of such a shakeout large corporations would be motivated to seek out good property managers as a way of cutting their own costs.

Although The Koll Company has generally been focused on real estate development in the western and southwestern parts of the country, Koll Management Services is likely to help globally expand the company's empire. Koll Management Services already stretches across the nation and is likely to begin managing properties in Mexico as well. It has already begun actively pursuing property management opportunities in Mexico City and has considered establishing operations there.

Koll Management Services also boasts several wholly owned subsidiaries of its own: Koll Carlsbad Management Company, Koll Asset Management Company and Koll Management of Oregon, Inc. Koll/Tipton Management Services, L.P. and Koll/CC&F Management Services are 51 percent and 50 percent owned, respectively, by Koll Management Services.

Even though Koll Management Services seems to be on a fast track to success, it remains well behind industry leader Trammell Crow, which has 230 million square feet under management. Although Koll Management Services can lean on The Koll Company, which naturally gives all its property management business to its subsidiary, the percentage of its portfolio gained through its parent company has continued to steadily decline.

Koll Management Services has made up for this decline in the years following the public offering, by winning some notable contracts: four separate contracts from California Federal Bank to manage more than 325,000 square feet; a management and leasing contract for WestPark, a 604,000 square foot business park in Redmond, Washington; a 75,000 square foot management and leasing contract in Seattle for Aetna Realty Investors; and the management contract for One Colorado, a 275,000 square foot retail and entertainment center in Pasadena, California.

Facilities management is a growth business for Koll Management Services, which is benefitting from many corporations' desire to outsource functions previously carried out by in-house corporate real estate offices. The company's facilities management portfolio has grown from one million to 11 million square feet in less than two years, and clients include Bank of America, NationsBank, McDonnell Douglas, Hughes, and Sun Microsystems.

One of the major undertakings of Koll Management Services in its campaign to leap to the forefront of the industry is to train its employees through the funding and operation of Koll College, which offers company employees and its service providers over 20 different courses related to property and asset management and customer service. Koll College has been funded by Koll Management Services to the tune of $500,000 annually and includes courses on tenant relations, marketing, lease terminology, and facilities management, among others.

The Koll Company has shown that it can roll with the ever-changing tides of the U.S. real estate market, shifting its focus to remain strong throughout the decades to come. With its entry into real estate investment, development, and management in Mexico, it is possible that it will become a company of worldwide dimensions in the next century.

Principal Subsidiaries: Koll Construction; Koll International Commercial, Koll Resorts International; Koll Management Services, Inc.

Further Reading:

''Bolsa Chica Names Koll as Chairman, Plans California Move,'' *The Wall Street Journal*, March 17, 1993, p.A5.
''Koll Management: A New Way to Profit from Property,'' *Barron's*, October 19, 1992, pp. 40–41.
Koll Management Services, 1992 Annual Report, Newport Beach: 1992.
''Koll's KMS Sees Opportunities in Slow RE market,'' *Orange County Business Journal*, May 4–10, 1992.
The Koll Company: Company History, Management Organization, Major Market Areas, Portfolio Statistics, Clients, Biographies, Newport Beach: The Koll Company, April, 1993.
The Koll Company: Update 1993, Issue No. 1.
Reprints, *Commercial Property News*.
Smith, Carter, *America's Fastest Growing Employers*, Holbrook, MA, 1992, pp. 178–179.

—Kathie Levine

L.A. Gear, Inc.

2850 Ocean Park Boulevard
Santa Monica, California 90405
U.S.A.
(310) 822-1995
Fax: (310) 581-7709

Public Company
Incorporated: 1979 as Good Times, Inc.
Employees: 749
Sales: $430.19 million
Stock Exchanges: New York
SICs: 3149 Athletic Shoes; 3143 Men's Footwear, Except
   Athletic; 3144 Women's Footwear, Except Athletic; 3149
   Children's Footwear

L.A. Gear, Inc. revolutionized the world athletic shoe market in
1985 by developing shoes that incorporated the comfort of
sneakers with the frills of fashion shoes. Company founder
Robert Greenberg's ability to design shoes that appealed to
young women fueled L.A. Gear's rapid rise to third place in
athletic shoe sales behind Nike and Reebok by 1990. The
success of the shoe sales led to L.A. Gear's diversification into
men's and children's shoe markets and casual apparel markets.
L.A. Gear's product appeal was not universal, however. As L.A.
Gear tried to expand into the men's market, its shoes were not
well received. Through a series of marketing mishaps, the company lost vital market share. In the early 1990s, however, the
company relied on the support of a financial investor, recruited
new management, concentrated on footwear quality and distribution, and began to pull out of its slump.

L.A. Gear evolved out of the long-time entrepreneurial adven-
tures of Robert Greenberg. Greenberg attributed his entrepreneurial bent to his father, who sold fresh produce in Boston, and
to his father's subscription to *Forbes* magazine. "I always
wanted to be the president of a company on the New York Stock
Exchange," Greenberg told *Los Angeles Magazine*, adding that
had his father subscribed to *Sports Illustrated* he would probably have been a baseball player. As an entrepreneur, Greenberg
has a legacy of picking and riding trends. The one-time hairdresser incorporated a roller skating rental shop in 1979 under
the name Good Times, Inc., and that company eventually grew
into a skate-manufacturing business called United Skates of
America. But when skate sales waned, he spotted the profitabil-

ity of novelty shoelaces and sold $3 million worth in three
months. In 1982 Greenberg opened a Los Angeles apparel store
that sold major brand name clothes, shoes, and accessories. In
this store Greenberg launched the L.A. Gear clothing label.

The L.A. Gear brand name actually came from a T-shirt sales-
woman's comment in the company warehouse. After the sales-
woman declared her shirts were "real L.A. gear," a clerk jotted
down the name and submitted it for the contest Greenberg had
introduced to find the right name for the retail store. "Of course,
I looked at the piece of paper and threw it away," Greenberg
told *Los Angeles Magazine*. "But at four in the morning, I woke
up and thought, 'My God, L.A. Gear!' " Initially, the L.A. Gear
label signified casual clothes, shoes, and sandals. By 1984,
however, Greenberg decided to concentrate the company's
efforts on wholesale shoe sales, and closed the unprofitable
retail store. Business partner Ernest Williams, however, "felt
there was no room for another athletic-footwear company,"
Greenberg told *Los Angeles Magazine*, and Williams broke
their partnership.

It did not take Greenberg long to establish a presence in the
athletic shoe market. Greenberg tapped his lengthy experience
with companies in the Orient to find independent companies
who would produce and distribute his shoes. L.A. Gear entered
the athletic shoe market with the Canvas Workout shoe in 1985,
and the company soon met with great success. Greenberg's shoe
designs were targeted at fashion-conscious females between the
ages of 12 and 35 who wanted stylish, comfortable shoes,
according to *Forbes*. The overwhelming reception in the marketplace pushed sales from $200,000 at the beginning of the
year to $1.8 million at the end of 1985.

In 1986 L.A. Gear became a public company, and the money
raised from the stock offering allowed the company to diversify.
L.A. Gear's main business was footwear, but in the late 1980s it
began producing sport and casual wear for men, women, and
children. The apparel division featured knit tops and sweat
clothes with bold L.A. Gear graphics and basic five pocket jeans
decorated with frills. The company also continued to develop its
shoe lines. Building on the enormous success of the Canvas
Workout shoe for women, L.A. Gear began to spruce up its line
of basic women's shoes with gold lame, fringe, pastel colors,
and spangles. For men, the company produced bold, jazzy
hightops for basketball. L.A. Gear's children's shoes stimulated
young eyes with black and white checkerboard and cow spot
designs. The company also marketed street shoes called Street
Hikers that combined an urban appearance with the comfort of
sneakers. Even though L.A. Gear continued to market its original styles into the early 1990s, it unveiled new styles every year.

Business Week contributor Kathleen Kerwin attributed L.A.
Gear's almost instant success in footwear sales to their ability to
appeal to the 80 percent of customers who "rarely set foot on a
tennis or basketball court." L.A. Gear's growth in sales and
product recognition surpassed that of the entire footwear market. Sales increased 200 percent in 1986 and doubled the next
year. In 1988 and 1989, *Business Week* selected L.A. Gear as
one of the best small American companies. *Business Week*,
Wall Street Journal, *Los Angeles Times*, and *Fortune* highlighted L.A. Gear's stock as the best performer on the New

York Stock Exchange in 1989. In 1990 company sales peaked at $818.8 million.

Despite L.A. Gear's phenomenal performance, skeptics questioned the endurance of the brand. In 1990 L.A. Gear was thought to be a "flash in the pan," Montgomery Securities' apparel analyst Alice Ruth told *Institutional Investor*. Skeptics based their fad theory on L.A. Gear's relatively weak sales in sporting-goods stores, the conventional athletic shoe outlets. But Ruth touted the staying power of L.A. Gear because it was inundating department stores and mass merchandisers. Noting the narrow focus and clientele of sporting-goods stores, *Los Angeles Magazine* contributor David Jefferson called Greenberg's decision to capture a larger clientele in department stores such as Nordstrom, May Co., and Bullock's a "brilliant marketing strategy."

By 1990 Greenberg felt the company was secure in its niche. "We've taken the number three position now. Our brand is growing and consumer confidence is gaining everyday," he told the *Wall Street Transcript*, adding that he expected the company "should only fuel itself now." The majority of L.A. Gear's success, however, laid in the hands of the two men responsible for the L.A. Gear image: Greenberg and Sandy Saemann. Greenberg designed the shoes. His friend and former colleague in the skate business, Sandy Saemann, masterminded the marketing. Greenberg's and Saemann's appeal to fashion-conscious females was unique. "L.A. Gear has really hit on a formula no one else has," John Horan, publisher of *Sports Management News*, told *Advertising Age* in 1989. "They take a shoe that's not a real technical shoe, so not expensive to produce, put some spangles and some colored trim on it," and "put their money into marketing and advertising." Saemann designed ads that were not as "slick" as ads for Reebok or Nike but were "effective," according to Marcy Magiera in *Advertising Age*. "They sold sex and sizzle," noted *Business Week*.

L.A. Gear's ads focused on the sunny glamour of the Los Angeles lifestyle, featuring beautiful young blondes wearing little else besides their L.A. Gear shoes. In 1990 Horan told *Advertising Age* that "of all the ads out there, [L.A. Gear's] seem to turn the sales on and off."

Encouraged by its success in the women's market, L.A. Gear decided to expand its sales in the men's market in 1989. L.A. Gear employed the same fashionable design and glamorous marketing techniques that had proved successful in the women's market to enter the men's market. Relying on jazzy designs and what industry analysts considered unusual endorsers, L.A. Gear marketed shoes in what they called the "fashionable" basketball market, featuring boldly designed hightops called Street Slammers, Hot Shots, and Brats. The men's market, however, was highly competitive; men's athletic shoes accounted for 70 percent of L.A. Gear's competitors' total sales but only 20 percent of L.A. Gear's total sales. Yet L.A. Gear's strategy of emphasizing fashion in the men's market seemed an odd strategy for growth because "men typically pay less attention to style," wrote Kerwin in *Business Week*. Avia marketing chief Bruce W. MacGregor added in *Business Week* that "technology has been the fashion" in the men's market.

Rather than hiring a young sports superstar like Bo Jackson, Nike's endorser, L.A. Gear hired retiring Los Angeles Laker Kareem Abdul-Jabbar to endorse a line of basketball shoes called Jabbars. One analyst predicted in *Business Week* that this move would appeal to the "geriatric crowd," rather than foster the category growth the company wanted. The company's main endorser was an even more unlikely athletic shoe sponsor. Pop singer Michael Jackson was paid close to ten million dollars to be the company spokesperson and to design a line of shoes and T-shirts. The company's use of Michael Jackson was "more than a growth opportunity, they're trying to maintain their fashion image," Paine Webber analyst Frank Podbelsek told *Advertising Age*. Under the umbrella theme "Unstoppable," L.A. Gear prepared to tap Michael Jackson's worldwide popularity by coordinating the Jackson line rollout with the release of a collection of his greatest hits called "A Decade." Michael Jackson's album was never released and his black, heavily buckled shoes did not sell well. His endorsement and the line were both quickly discontinued. This series of events cost the company several million dollars.

L.A. Gear paid the price for these misadventures in increased inventories and diminished profits. Inventory stockpiling due to unrealistically high sales projections caused the company to discount almost all their shoe styles to liquidate the inventories. Yet selling the shoes at discounts angered retailers because it made their prices seem exorbitantly high and degraded the L.A. Gear brand image, according to the *Los Angeles Times*. Bad marketing decisions, coupled with rebellious retailers who began to refuse L.A. Gear shelf space contributed to a net loss for the company in 1991. The company's market share continued to expand in 1991, but at the expense of profits.

Aware that fashionable men's athletic shoes would not generate profits, the company decided to branch into the men's technical shoe market with the introduction of the Catapult basketball shoe in 1991. The one-hundred-dollar Catapult, which featured a fiberglass and graphite heel supporting an air cushion, was marketed without the L.A. Gear brand name to "distance Catapult from L.A. Gear's young, low-price image," creative director Michael Albright told *Advertising Age*. As part of their new strategy, the company choose a more typical endorser: Karl Malone, a Utah Jazz basketball star. Unfortunately, problems with product quality interfered with initial sales. After the company outfitted a Marquette University basketball team in Catapult shoes, one player tripped on his shoe sole as it peeled off during a televised game. The company reported that it was working to improve the shoes' quality and the university team continued to wear the shoes.

L.A. Gear's entrance into the technological shoe market was not without other problems. Initially, L.A. Gear failed to differentiate its technology enough to please competitors. Nike filed a suit against L.A. Gear in 1991 alleging the Catapult infringed on Nike's patented 'spring moderator' technology. By 1993 the suit was still pending, and the company continued to market the Catapult. In a similar case, L.A. Gear paid Reebok one million dollars and licensing fees in an out-of-court settlement in 1992. L.A. Gear's Regulator series infringed on the patented technology of the Reebok Pump. Under the licensing agreement, L.A. Gear continued to develop its line of inflatable shoes under the Regulator and the Gauge brand names. Moreover, they built on

Catapult technology with the Twist-a-pult shoe, which allows the wearer to adjust the amount of cushion offered by the Catapult mechanism.

L.A. Gear's efforts to establish a significant presence in the men's market left them facing financial troubles. In 1991 the company went into technical default on its bank loan, and to free itself from the confines of the bank's regulations, it looked for an investor to support the company through its slump. Trefoil Capital Investors, L.P., an investment fund managed by Shamrock Advisors, Inc., invested $100 million in L.A. Gear, giving Trefoil a 34 percent stake in the company. In accordance with its investment agreement, Trefoil assumed control of the board after L.A. Gear was unable to pay Trefoil dividends for three consecutive quarters, and they began to make a number of changes. Mark Goldston, a one-time Reebok marketing executive, was given responsibility for L.A. Gear's business dealings as President and Chief Operating Officer; several new managers were hired to bring the company back to profitability; and Greenberg was encouraged to concentrate on what he did best—designing shoes and picking trends. Greenberg announced he would work without pay until the company made money. By the end of the year, however, *Advertising Age* reported that L.A. Gear's market share had dropped to eight percent from its high of 11.8 percent in 1990.

As Trefoil increased its control of the company's operations and added new senior managers, Greenberg decided to resign. He told the *Los Angeles Times* that "after eight years of constant involvement with L.A. Gear, I can now devote more time to my family." And as a one-time L.A. Gear employee told the *Los Angeles Magazine*, "People who build a billion-dollar company aren't always the people who can run a billion-dollar company." Upon Greenberg's resignation, Stanley Gold, a man known for his ability to return companies to profitability, was positioned as Chairman and CEO by Trefoil. The Trefoil-picked management had a record of success in the footwear industry, as well as a reputation for saving floundering companies.

The new management began to pare down the business as the company's drop in market share moved it from third to fourth place among footwear companies. Scattered corporate offices were consolidated in a new Santa Monica, California, headquarters, which reduced costs and brought all senior management together. To further reduce costs, the company closed its apparel production and marketing facilities, opting to license its name to a few garment-making companies instead. Goldston stressed in *PR Newswire* that the licensing agreements increased "the range and quality of non-footwear products that will be offered both domestically and internationally under the L.A. Gear brand name." In 1992 the cost-cutting measures included a 45 percent staff reduction.

To lend consistency to the company's image, Goldston announced in a 1992 article in *Advertising Age* that the company would separate the fashion and fitness products into distinct lifestyle and athletic shoe divisions that "will run as stand-alone companies in the marketplace." The divisions would be distinguishable by the diamond-shaped L.A. Gear logo for the lifestyle shoes and the square L.A. Tech logo for the high-tech athletic line. The children's shoes would also be marketed separately using the Bendables logo that featured a drawing of a baby. Such demarcations would allow the divisions to market their products to suit the needs of very different markets. Shoe quality and distribution were also enhanced after the company reevaluated the independent manufacturers and distributors with which it was doing business. In 1992 L.A. Gear signed a sourcing agreement with LASCO, an affiliate of Pentland Group plc, the world's largest sourcing agent, respected throughout the footwear industry. LASCO would be responsible for inspecting the quality of the finished products as well as supervision of production, scheduling, and all foreign shipping. The company's shoes continued to be manufactured mainly in The People's Republic of China, Indonesia, South Korea, and Taiwan.

Trefoil also updated the "dated blondes-at-the-beach" advertising strategy, noted *Advertising Age* contributor Marcy Magiera. The company decided to break with the industry marketing trend of using a media buyer and search for a full-service outside advertising agency that would handle both creative work and media planning. Ogilivy and Mather was chosen to create ads and buy media space in late 1991. "Get in Gear," the new umbrella theme, was unveiled at the 1991 Sporting Goods Manufacturer's Association Super Show in Atlanta, Georgia. Goldston, concerned about contemporizing L.A. Gear's image, said of the new theme that "our strategy is athletic lifestyle and the theme line is one that can be used for years and years," according to *Advertising Age*.

Along with the new advertising theme came a new advertising strategy. The company would no longer spend mammoth amounts on superstar sponsors; a three-year endorsement budget was set at eight million dollars, according to the *Los Angeles Magazine*. The long list of celebrity endorsers was pared to three: Hakeem Olajuwon, Joe Montana, and Karl Malone, who would continue to represent the men's line of technical sport shoes.

L.A. Gear products continued to be sold in more than 75 countries into the 1990s. California-based advertising agency Saatchi & Saatchi DFS retained responsibility for L.A. Gear's $34 million international advertising account.

Despite L.A. Gear's marketing mishaps and difficulty penetrating the men's athletic shoe market, L.A. Gear's future still seems bright. The Trefoil-picked management team has demonstrated its ability to reduce costs, improve quality, streamline distribution, and woo retailers into giving their products more shelf space. The company reached licensing agreements with several different companies, including Cradle Togs, Inc., and York Luggage. Its new products, including the L.A. Lights series of lighted athletic shoes for adults and children, have been well received in the market. L.A. Gear seemed poised in the mid-1990s to regain its position as a healthy footwear company.

Further Reading:

Burchfield, Stephanie, "L.A. Gear Announces Licensing Agreements Signed With Sweatshirt Apparel, U.S.A.; Steinwurtzel Acquisition and Coordinated Apparel," *PR Newswire*, August 25, 1992, sec. 1, p. 1.

Cullinane, Kevin, "L.A. Gear's 3rd Quarter Shows $11-million Loss," *Los Angeles Times*, October 5, 1991, sec. D, p. 3.

Jefferson, David J., ''Don't Walk a Mile in His Shoes: Can Disney Magic—and Money—Put Former L.A. Gear Shoe King Robert Greenberg Back on the Fast Track?,'' *Los Angeles Magazine*, December 18, 1991, sec. 1, p. 114.

Kerwin, Kathleen, ''L.A. Gear Is Going Where The Boys Are,'' *Business Week*, June 19, 1989, p. 54.

''L.A. Gear +184.6% (No. 2),'' *Institutional Investor*, March, 1990, pp. 52–53.

''L.A. Gear, Inc. (L.A.),'' *Wall Street Transcript*, August 6, 1990, p. 98, 110.

Lazzareschi, Carla, ''L.A. Gear CEO Greenberg Says He'll Step Down,'' *Los Angeles Times*, January 27, 1992, sec. D, p. 1.

Magiera, Marcy, ''L.A. Gear's Comeback Plan: Fashion, Fitness Shoes to Get Separate Identities,'' *Advertising Age*, June 29, 1992, p. 12.

——, ''L.A. Gear Creative Review Ahead?,'' *Advertising Age*, June 17, 1991, p. 48.

——, ''L.A. Gear Looks for New Image,'' *Advertising Age*, November 4, 1991, p. 2.

——, ''L.A. Gear Shifts Ahead,'' *Advertising Age*, December 23, 1991, p. 26.

——, ''L.A. Gear Toughens Up . . . ,'' *Advertising Age*, January 30, 1989, p. 76.

——, ''Rebound Team: L.A. Gear Relies on Montana, Jackson,'' *Advertising Age*, July 2, 1990, pp. 3, 30.

——, ''Small Rivals Leap as L.A. Gear Stumbles: But No. 3 Shoe Marketer Is Planning Comeback,'' *Advertising Age*, June 8, 1992, p. 12.

Paris, Ellen, ''Rhinestone Hightops, Anyone?,'' *Forbes*, March 7, 1988, pp. 78, 80, 84.

—Sara Pendergast

Lancaster Colony Corporation

37 W. Broad Street
Columbus, Ohio 43215
(614) 224-7141
Fax: (614) 469-8219

Public Company
Incorporated: 1961
Employees: 4,700
Sales: $500.5 million
Stock Exchanges: NASDAQ
SICs: 3069 Fabricated Rubber Products; 2035 Pickles,
   Sauces and Salad Dressings; 2051 Bread, Cake, and
   Related Products; 2098 Macaroni and Spaghetti; 3229
   Pressed & Blown Glass; 3714 Motor Vehicle Parts and
   Accessories; 3999 Manufacturing Industries

Lancaster Colony Corporation's 16 subsidiaries manufacture a wide variety of products, including beach balls, automotive products, crystal stemware, and salad dressings. These products are sold to such steady retail and food industry customers as Kmart Corporation, Ford Motor Company, and the fast food chains Arby's and Long John Silver's. The corporation comprises three largely autonomous divisions: Housewares and Candles, Automotive Accessories, and Food Products.

The corporation was founded in 1961, when Ohio entrepreneur John B. Gerlach decided to organize the companies in which he was a major stockholder. He chose to incorporate them in Delaware, as subsidiaries under a central holding company he called Lancaster Colony Corporation.

Individually well-established, profitable companies, the new subsidiaries together represented a hodgepodge of manufactured items. Indiana Glass in Dunkirk, Indiana, specialized in decorative gifts and stemware, and Jackson Corporation was an Ohio-based producer of injection-molded plastic housewares. Lancaster Glass Corporation, an industrial supplier concentrating on components for televisions and scientific instruments, was also part of the lineup, as were National Glove, a source of work gloves, and Pretty Products, which turned out ''Rubber Queen'' kitchen and bath accessories and industrial components.

Although Lancaster Colony had no readily apparent focus, Gerlach, an experienced investor, had deliberately assembled

this collection of manufacturers according to a personal maxim: all of his companies operated with common production techniques and distribution channels. This pragmatic principle also brought Pitman-Dreitzer & Company into the fold in the early 1960s. A manufacturer and importer of gift items and decorative glassware, Pitman-Dreitzer fitted the Gerlach strategy perfectly and offered merchandise suitable for giftware departments of retail outlets and boutiques.

Variations on Gerlach's corporate theme came in 1966, when the string of Lancaster Colony subsidiaries was expanded by two. The newcomers, both targeting retail chain outlets, were Enterprise Aluminum, a manufacturer of cookware, and Barr, Inc., which produced balls and other sporting equipment. Both settled comfortably into their designated market slots, as did August Barr, acquired in 1969.

Finely honed market and production strategy was only half of the 1960s success story for Lancaster Colony's consumer products. Just as important were cutting-edge production techniques, state-of-the-art facilities, and creative design, all of which kept the company's glassware and bath accessories competitive in a market whose products rapidly became obsolete due to the trendy tastes of home decorators.

Other segments of the company inventory were constantly updated to keep pace with scientific advances. Glass envelopes for small television sets, cathode ray tubes, and parts for oceanographic equipment, lighting systems and other industrial components with secure market niches made up a healthy 30 percent of company inventory by the end of the decade. Net sales figures for all these, plus housewares (contributing 60 percent of company inventory) and recreational equipment (about seven percent) rose steadily through the 1960s, soaring from $24.2 million in fiscal 1963 to $63.5 million by 1969. This success prompted the Lancaster Colony to go public on May 7, 1969, and, by the end of the fiscal year, the corporation boasted about 1,250 shareholders.

In 1970 the company finalized a $4.6 million purchase of the T. Marzetti Company, a Columbus-based salad dressings manufacturer. Encouraged by the increase in public demand for salad bars, the new Marzetti owners soon broadened their range with seven new flavors and spent $1 million on a line called Frenchette, previously the property of the Carter-Wallace company. The two moves added 26 percent to sales by 1972.

In other new marketing ventures, Tiara Exclusives, launched in 1970, began selling Lancaster Colony glassware through a party-plan marketing strategy that provided part-time jobs for homemakers. Along with several other similar businesses, such as Avon and Tupperware, Tiara enjoyed an undisputed success, employing 750 active party-plan counselors by 1972.

Candles were also added to the growing string of Lancaster Colony products during this period. Candle-Lite Inc., costing 87,550 adjusted shares, was added to Lancaster Colony's holdings in 1972, while Christian & Company came aboard the following year. Between them, the two companies were equipped to supply a full range of tapers as well as scented and hand-decorated candles, all of which were eagerly snapped up by longtime wholesale customers such as florists' supply houses and retail outlets.

Loma Housewares, a company based in Fort Worth, Texas and a division of Vistron Corporation, was purchased for $6.2 million, a price Lancaster Colony gladly paid in order to open up the lucrative new Texas market area to established Lancaster Colony houseware lines.

Automotive products also hit the spotlight during the early 1970s. Splash guards and heavy-duty bumpers for trucks now came from newly acquired Koneta Rubber, a leading manufacturer in the industry. Also in the automotive line, management chose to enhance their aftermarket accessories sales at the same time, by offering Pretty Products' "Rubber Queen" line of auto mats on new hanging racks that made selection easier for shoppers.

All new products received the in-house support of a huge new warehousing facility in Georgia, from which merchandise was issued nationwide. Slowed only slightly by a 9-week strike at Barr, Inc. in addition to higher prices for raw materials at the Marzetti subsidiary, the net earnings for 1973 reached $130.7 million.

As the decade progressed, Lancaster Colony began to pay close attention to its food-producing subsidiaries. In 1977, in accordance with its custom of acquisitions offering products saleable in existing markets, the corporation bought Quality Bakery Company, whose annual turnover of $5.5 million made its price of 210,000 common shares worthwhile. The following year the addition of New York Frozen Foods fleshed out the food division along with Frozen Specialty Bakers and Bakery Equipment Leasing Company.

Not all of Lancaster Colony's acquisitions were successful. One effort doomed to failure was a 1977 attempt to buttress glass-manufacturing operations through the $45 million purchase of the Columbus-based Federal Glass Division of the Federal Paper Board Company. The deal fell under the scrutiny of the Federal Trade Commission, which regarded the purchase as providing Lancaster Colony with an unfair competitive advantage. The FTC eventually allowed the purchase to proceed on the grounds that it would provide hundreds of needed jobs for the community. Still, the company faced further difficulties. The subject of wages for unskilled workers brought an impasse, as the American Flint Glass Workers Union insisted on the wages equal to those paid by the previous owners. Lancaster Colony concluded that it could not pay the same wage and still make a profit, and, on this sour note, the deal was finally scrapped in 1979.

Although sales figures for many of Lancaster Colony's products dipped due to an economic recession in the early 1980s, its automotive products division actually benefited during this period. Nearly thirty percent of the division's 1982 inventory was shipped to Ford, General Motors, and Chrysler, even though the market for new automobile equipment was declining. On the other hand, the automotive "aftermarket" grew, as many drivers passed up new cars, choosing instead to refurbish their older vehicles with relatively inexpensive accessories, of which car mats were a prime example. Both channels were an important earning force for the company, bringing in $105 million in sales for 1982 alone.

The specialty foods division also maintained profitability. By the end of fiscal 1982 11.5 percent of company profits came from frozen pies, partially baked frozen breads, noodles (courtesy of Inn Maid Products, acquired in 1981) and salad dressings. Lancaster Colony continued to look for ways to expand in the food market. Just as they had opened new vistas in Texas by buying Loma Housewares, they now chose to enter the Atlantic seaboard area by acquiring a local manufacturer. In 1983 New York-based Pfeiffer salad dressing operations, previously a subsidiary of Hunt-Wesson Foods, joined the Lancaster Colony lineup.

While most products were finding ready markets, cookware, which had comprised 12 percent of houseware sales and ten percent of profits in 1982, began to lose steam in the mid-1980s. In 1985, the housewares division lost $3.05 million on sales of $160.4 million. These losses prompted a major restructuring in 1986, to allow for the closing of several facilities, and the consolidation of Housewares and Candles into a single unit under a single team.

Furthermore, due to overseas competition, the company closed the Fostoria Glass plant in West Virginia, but kept the name to be used on products from other facilities. By the end of March, production had ceased at National Glove Inc. in Mount Sterling, Ohio. The Loma Housewares plant in Texas was the next to go, along with the Barr, Inc. unit at Sandusky Ohio, where inflatable plastic balls, rubber bumper parts, and automobile components had been produced. Such products remained lucrative, however, and their production was moved to other manufacturing facilities, the automotive parts now coming from the plant in Coshocton, Ohio, where rubber housewares had originally been made. The Nelson McCoy Pottery Company, a 1974 acquisition, was sold to a Columbus-based group headed by Intercoastal Investments Corporation.

Lancaster Colony now focused attention on the profitable automotive and food specialty divisions. By the end of 1986 the company had purchased LRV Corporation of Elkhart Indiana, in exchange for 700,000 shares of stock. With affiliates in Utah and Canada, LRV broadened the Lancaster Colony line of truck accessories with bed liners sold under the Protecta and Line-A-Bed names, and tool boxes, also for trucks. The same year Lancaster Colony bought a second auto accessories company called A-Mar, Inc. changing the subsidiary's name to Dee Zee. It proved to be a profitable acquisition, adding aluminum running boards, side rails, kick plates, and tailgate protectors, all of which were soon on display in custom auto stores.

These two acquisitions enhanced sales considerably. Reflecting the plant closings and sales, 1987 net sales were $429.6 million, sinking slightly from the 1986 total of $456.8 million, but by 1988 the figures had begun to rise again, reaching $453.4 million.

By the late 1980s, corporation president John Gerlach, Jr. had become concerned over the possibility of a hostile takeover attempt by the Newell Company, an Illinois-based home furnishings company to which Lancaster Colony had sold its aluminum cookware division in 1986. Newell, with a 5.6 percent share of the company, wanted more, and in 1990 they challenged Federal anti-trust legislation to seek as much as a 15 percent stake in Lancaster Colony, by combining their own consumer glassware operations with Lancaster Colony's $100 million operations.

Although at least one quarter of Lancaster Colony stock was controlled by management, who would not part with it easily, caution was exercised since Newell had recently been successful in acquiring the Anchor Hocking glass company after a hostile takeover bid.

As a precautionary measure the company's Employee Stock Ownership Trust borrowed $10 million to increase its ownership. Newell was undeterred, but Gerlach did not lost heart.

Gerlach speculated that the solution might lie in shifting incorporation from Delaware to Ohio. The State of Ohio had passed anti-takeover laws in the wake of British financier Sir James Goldsmith's attempted hostile takeover of Goodyear Tire and Rubber and had given their anti-takeover law protective shields, in the form of two tough statutes. The first of these required that a hostile acquirer wait three years before an actual merger could be documented. The second allowed for backup support for any threatened company, demanding board or stockholder approval before 20 percent of company stock could be acquired. The 10,000 or more Lancaster Colony stockholders could certainly provide such a bulwark of support, in the unlikely event of a problem.

Although Newell had evidently lost hope for a takeover by March 1991, reducing its stake to less than five percent, Gerlach did not drop the idea of shifting incorporation. At the stockholders' meeting in November 1991, he requested approval for this move, pointing out that it would bring the company an annual tax savings of between $30,000 and $40,000. The move was approved, and Lancaster Colony was incorporated in Ohio on January 2, 1992.

Principal Subsidiaries: Colony Printing & Labeling Inc.; Dee Zee Inc.; Fostoria Glass Company; Indiana Glass Company; LRV Acquisition Corporation; Lagrande Molded Products Inc.; Lancaster Colony Canada Inc.; Lancaster Colony Commercial Products Inc.; Lancaster Glass Corporation; New York Frozen Foods Inc.; Pretty Products Inc.; T. Marzetti Company; T. Marzetti Company West; Quality Bakery Company Inc.; Reames Foods Inc.; Waycross Molded Products Inc.

Further Reading:

"Barr Inc. Plant Shut," *Columbus Dispatch,* June 4, 1986, p. 1H.
Bowden, William D., "Lancaster Colony Gains Markets and Profits through Acquisitions," *Investment Dealer's Digest,* February 15, 1972, p. 25.
——, "Lancaster Colony Expects to Show Continued Operating Improvements," *Investment Dealers' Digest,* Nov. 10, 1981, p. 21.
"Business Section," *Columbus Dispatch,* April 15, 1986, p. 1E.
"Glass Firm Attracted to Ohio Laws," *Columbus Dispatch,* November 18, 1991, p. Q1E.
"Lancaster Colony Bid for Glass Firm Ends, Apparently for Good," *Wall Street Journal,* April 3, 1979, p.14.
"Lancaster Colony Buys Pickup Truck Accessory Company," *Columbus Dispatch,* Dec. 24, 1986, p. 12D.
Lancaster Colony Corporation Annual Reports, Columbus, Ohio: Lancaster Colony Corporation, 1963–1992.
"Lancaster Colony Corporation," *Wall Street Journal Transcripts,* December 13, 1982, p. 68032.
"Lancaster Colony Drops Plan to Buy Federal Paper Unit," *Wall Street Journal,* July 22, 1977, p. 5.
"Lancaster Colony Products Aimed at Home, Industry, Leisure Time," *Investment Dealer's Digest,* January 20, 1970, p. 30.
"Lancaster Colony Purchase Plan," *Wall Street Journal,* Feb. 1, 1977.
"Lancaster Colony Sets Closing of Glove Factory," *Columbus Dispatch,* March 6, 1986, p. 2G.
"Lancaster Colony to Sell Gift, Art Pottery Subsidiary," *Columbus Dispatch,* May 3, 1986, p. 10C.
"Lancaster Colony Wants Ohio Incorporation," Business First of Columbus (Ohio), November 4, 1991.
"Lancaster Colony Will Close Fostoria Glass Plant in West Virginia," *Columbus Dispatch,* Feb. 26, 1986, p. 2H.
"Lancaster Sells Unit to Newell," *Wall Street Journal,* November 3, 1986, p. 41.
"Newell is Seeking More of Lancaster," *Wall Street Journal,* September 15, 1990, p. 33.

—Gillian Wolf

LDDS-Metro Communications, Inc.

Lefleur's Bluff Tower
4780 I-55 North, Suite 500
Jackson, MS 39211
U.S.A.
(601) 364-7000
Fax: (601) 360-8533

Public Company
Incorporated: 1989 as LDDS Communications, Inc.
Employees: 1,000
Sales: $801 million
Stock Exchanges: NASDAQ
SICs: 4813 Telephone Communications, except Radio

LDDS-Metro Communications is America's fourth-largest telephone company, behind AT&T, MCI Communications Corp., and United Telecommunications Inc.'s Sprint. The long-distance provider emerged from a massive pack of third-tier telephone companies through a strategy of acquisitions in the late 1980s and early 1990s.

LDDS provides long-distance service to small- to medium-sized business and commercial customers. The company's profitability depends on its ability to realize line costs per minute that are less than revenues per minute. Line costs per minute include two elements, access charges and transport charges. Access charges are the costs that local exchange carriers (LECs), commonly known as "Baby Bells," impose for the privilege of originating and terminating calls. They constitute the bulk of LDDS's line costs. The remainder, in the form of transport charges, include the cost of transmitting calls between or within local access transport areas (LATAs).

Long Distance Discount Services, Inc. was formed in 1983 in Hattiesburg, Mississippi, when the breakup of AT&T enabled thousands of competitors to start reselling long-distance telephone service to individual and business customers. Bill Fields convinced several investors to lease a local Bell system Wide-Area Telecommunications Service (WATS) line and resell time on the line to businesses. Long-distance resellers like LDDS bought time from regional Bell companies in volume and sold it, often at a discount, to business customers. LDDS owned the switches, or nodes, of its network, and leased the lines from local providers. The sophisticated long-distance technology was designed to handle a high volume of calls. Some observers compared the long-distance telephone industry to the airline industry: there was a fixed cost for getting calls or seats from one place to another, and the more customers a telecommunications company or airline had, the lower its costs would be. Price competition among these companies was ruthless. Assuming that the "Baby Bells" would continue to lease the lines at a fixed rate, Fields signed up 200 customers. But when Bell started raising the charges for the use of the lines, LDDS began to lose money.

By the early months of 1985, the fledgling business was losing $25,000 each month. It became clear to Fields that he was failing at the day-to-day management of LDDS, and he first tried to sell the company. Later in 1985, several owners signed LDDS over to Bernard Ebbers, one of the initial investors. By the time Ebbers became president and chief executive officer, LDDS was $1.5 million in debt.

Ebbers was a Canadian who came to the United States on a basketball scholarship to Mississippi College. After graduation he became a high school baseball coach. He later worked in the garment trade as a distributor, but lost interest in the low-margin industry. Ebbers seized the chance to buy a 40-room motel in Columbia, Mississippi, in the 1970s, borrowing the necessary money to establish himself in the business. In the real estate market of the late 1970s, the value of prime properties could double over the course of five years. Ebbers parlayed his one hotel into 12 by the early 1980s, garnering healthy operating and asset gains.

As head of LDDS, Ebbers worked to control costs. He kept overhead low with lean operations and unpretentious offices. The streamlined LDDS brought on new clients with a claim of customer service that larger long-distance companies could not offer. LDDS did not use telemarketing to solicit new business, but mobilized a direct sales force to make personal contacts. After the initial face-to-face solicitation, LDDS made monthly, and sometimes weekly, office calls to ensure that the customers' service was satisfactory. The company provided an alternative to the major long-distance carriers' across-the-board packages by tailoring service to each customer's calling patterns, which simultaneously maximized routing efficiency and cut costs. The major long-distance carriers at this time were also exerting a great deal of effort to secure big-ticket clients; LDDS was able to take advantage of this by concentrating on small business customers who were falling through the cracks.

Within six months of Ebbers' move into the driver's seat, the company had moved into the black. In 1986 revenue rose to $8.6 million, and a year later, sales had grown to $18 million. By 1988 annual revenues had skyrocketed to $95 million. Consolidation and acquisitions were the principal factors that enabled LDDS to accomplish this rapid growth during the last five years of the 1980s. The company leveraged its assets in order to buy other third-tier long-distance companies, including: Telesphere Network, Inc. (1987); Com-Link 21, Inc. (1988); Com-Link 21, Inc. of Tennessee (1988); Telephone Management Corporation (1988); and Inter-Comm Telephone, Inc. (1989). The acquisitions cost the company a total of $34.87 million, but expanded LDDS's geographic network to include

Missouri, Tennessee, Arkansas, Indiana, Kansas, Kentucky, Texas, and Alabama.

Each company LDDS assumed control of performed better after acquisition. Part of the success was attributed to the LDDS standards of customer service, but the economies of scale gained when more companies came on line also brought higher profitability. LDDS applied its customer service ideals to new acquisitions through a decentralized system wherein each state office set its own sales goals. Companies in the system formulated their own marketing strategies in response to local market conditions.

LDDS's annual earnings grew from $641,000 in 1986 to more than $4.5 million in 1989. That same year the company merged with 17-year-old, Nashville-based, Advantage Company, a public company that was losing money when the two consolidated. The merger benefited both companies—it enabled LDDS to reduce its debt and finance future purchases through stock offers, and it brought Advantage into profitability. By the end of that year, LDDS' revenue-per-employee stood at $360,000, more than double the industry average, and triple that of some of LDDS's higher-priced competitors. LDDS also pursued other avenues to spur growth. Its 14 percent annual internal growth rate was fueled by thorough infiltration of its growing markets.

Despite the economic downturn of the early 1990s, LDDS continued its upward climb. The long-distance telephone business was not adversely affected by the economic climate, as the telephone had long since established itself as an indispensable part of the business world. In fact, LDDS made two acquisitions that year, purchasing Mercury, Inc., for $10.3 million and Tele-Marketing Corporation of Louisiana for $15.5 million. Despite the recession, LDDS' 1990 profit was $9.8 million, ten times its 1986 total. Sales had grown sixteenfold in that same time span.

LDDS made three acquisitions in 1991, using cash, stock, and bank debt to finance purchases that totaled $90 million. National Telecommunications of Austin was purchased with a combination of $27 million in cash and stock. The acquisition of Phone America of Carolina established an LDDS presence in North and South Carolina and eastern Tennessee. These two companies had combined annual revenues of $51 million. LDDS also made its largest acquisition up to that time with the purchase of MidAmerican Communications Corporation. Mid-American provided long-distance service to Nebraska, Missouri, Kansas, Illinois, Wisconsin, North Dakota, Minnesota, Colorado, New Mexico, and Arizona. The acquisitions enabled LDDS to increase its sales by 71 percent over 1990 to $263.41 million.

Between 1983 and 1991, LDDS spent more than $200 million to purchase about 24 smaller companies. The additions brought the LDDS network to 27 states, a system that excluded only the Northeast and Northwest. The downside of all this growth was that it left the company with $165 million in long-term debt, and a negative net worth.

At about the same time, AT&T started trying aggressively to win back customers of all sizes. Despite its dramatic success, LDDS and other third-tier long-distance companies had only captured about one percent of the total long-distance market at this point. In the 1990s the big three telecommunications companies aimed for the small- and medium-sized businesses they had previously neglected.

LDDS did not stand idly by, however, In 1992 LDDS acquired Shared Use Network systems, Inc.; Automated Communications, Inc.; Prime Telecommunications Corporation; TFN Group Communications, Inc.; and Telemarketing Investments, Ltd. These companies, combined, expanded LDDS service in Arizona, Florida, Iowa, Nebraska, Nevada, New Mexico, New York, Ohio, Utah, Virginia, and West Virginia. The new affiliates filled in LDDS's service network and brought a total of $66 million in annual revenues. But a much more important development for the company in 1992 was its merger with Advanced Telecommunications Corporation. The Atlanta-based company had $350 million in annual sales spread over a network of 26 southern states. The merger increased LDDS's annual revenues by 30 percent to $801 million in 1992. Although merger-related expenses caused LDDS to take a loss of $8 million for the year, the company expected to realize significant cost savings, increased opportunities for acquisitions, and a wider variety of products with the consolidation. Cost savings were achieved through LDDS's ever-enlarging networks, which produced a situation where a larger percentage of the company's calls originated and terminated within its service area. Therefore, more calls stayed on the network of low-cost transmission facilities that were owned or leased by LDDS. And, of course, increased volume lowered the per-minute costs.

LDDS has dodged rumors and predictions of imminent takeover almost since its inception; in an effort to put to rest such speculation, in 1993 the company announced an agreement to merge with Metromedia Communications Corporation (MCC) of East Rutherford, New Jersey, and Resurgens Communications Group, Inc. of Atlanta. The agreement stipulated that LDDS shareholders would collect about 68.5 percent of the fully diluted equity of the combined company, while MCC and Resurgens shareholders secured the remainder. LDDS issued 19 million new common shares in conjunction with the merger and made a private placement of $50 million in convertible preferred stock.

The merger extended LDDS's network to include all 48 mainland states, and company executives projected that the new entity, renamed LDDS-Metro Communications, Inc., would achieve annual revenues of $1.5 million in 1993. LDDS moved into a new headquarters in Jackson, Mississippi, in May 1993. The company planned to continue its growth strategy of strong internal progress and selective acquisition and consolidation of other third-tier telecommunications companies.

Principal Subsidiaries: Long Distance Discount Services, Inc.; Com-Link-21 Inc.; Com-Link 21 Inc. of Tennessee; Telephone Management Corp.; Inter-Com Telephone, Inc.; Advantage Companies, Inc.; National Telecommunications of Austin; TeleMarketing Corporation of Louisiana; Prime Telecommunications Corp.

Further Reading:

"Bernie Ebbers saved the company," *Mississippi Business Journal*, November 1989, p. 316.

Gianturco, Michael. "Telephone numbers," *Forbes*, June 22, 1992, p. 108.

Jones, Kevin D. "LDDS: from zero to $150 million in six years, but analysts say it's a takeover target," *Mississippi Business Journal*, November 1989, pp. 26–30.

Selz, Michael. "LDDS Communications wins big by thinking small," *The Wall Street Journal*, July 26, 1991.

—April S. Dougal

Learjet

Nothing else comes close.™

Learjet Inc.

One Learjet Way
P.O. Box 7707
Wichita, Kansas 66277-7707
U.S.A.
(316) 946-2450
Fax: (316) 946-3235

Subsidiary of Bombardier, Inc.
Incorporated: 1964 as Lear Jet Corporation
Employees: 3,500
SICs: 3721 Aircraft

An innovator in aircraft technology, the Learjet company is one of many legacies of the twentieth century inventor and industrialist William Powell Lear. Although best known for his bold effort to build the world's first private jet, Lear has a distinguished history of other inventions that are seldom acknowledged. But it was the fortune from these earlier ventures that provided Lear with the capital to establish the Learjet company.

Lear was born in 1902 into a poor family in Hannibal, Missouri. When he was six, after his parents divorced, Lear moved to a Chicago tenement with his mother. Completing his education through the eighth grade, Lear befriended a young junk dealer and began spending much of his time tinkering with discarded electronic devices. At age 16, Lear began work as a mechanic at Chicago's Grant Park Airport. There he gained technical knowledge and skills relating to aircraft, while he acquired exposure to the business world and proper social comportment during his brief tenure as an assistant in the office of a prominent businessman.

By the age of 20, Lear was an experienced self-taught radio technician. He established a small shop in Quincy, Illinois, and set out to improve home radio sets. He succeeded in miniaturizing radio coils, eliminated the need for storage batteries, and made other modifications that are still in use today. His business became profitable, and his work soon brought him to the attention of such major manufacturers as Majestic and Motorola.

Still fascinated with flying, Lear bought a small airplane, learned to fly, and began work on an aircraft navigation radio. In 1931 he began a sales tour, demonstrating his Lear Radioaire. However, few pilots had the money to purchase such a radio

during the economic hardships of the Great Depression, and fewer still saw the need for such a communication device since it was common at that time for pilots to navigate simply by following railroad lines between cities.

By 1934, Lear had exhausted his small radio fortune and was bankrupt. Depressed, but determined, he returned to his workshop and began mapping out yet another invention. This next product was the "Magic Brain," a common electronic chassis that could be used in a variety of radio set models. Lear assembled, demonstrated, and sold the idea in only two weeks, receiving a contract for $250,000 from RCA.

Next Lear returned his attention to aircraft navigation, using his second fortune to develop the Learscope Direction Finder, a radio triangulation device. These advances earned Lear an honored place in the development of aviation and won him the friendship of such prominent aviation pioneers as Amelia Earhart. More importantly, with access to the nation's leading manufacturers, Lear was able to easily market other advances, including an improved omnidirectional navigation device that could home in on any ground station, regardless of frequency.

During World War II, Lear concentrated the efforts of his company on electromechanical devices for military aircraft, including cowl controllers and auto pilot devices. After the war, Lear Incorporated pioneered all-weather flying instruments that won Lear a commendation from President Truman and an honorary degree from the University of Michigan.

By 1959 several airplane manufacturers began to exploit the new market for business aircraft. During this time, however, these predominantly piston-powered business airplanes were relatively slow, and Lear began to envision a smaller, quicker jet-powered craft with superior flying characteristics. He was especially impressed with a jet-powered Swiss fighter-bomber called the P-16 and began laying plans to model a passenger jet after the Swiss airplane. But with no outright demand for such a craft, Lear encountered adamant opposition from his own board of directors. If a market existed, they reasoned, some other major manufacturer would be working on it.

Determined to build the jet, Lear sold his controlling interest in his $100 million company to the Siegler Corporation (this company remains in existence as Lear-Siegler). He then moved to St. Gallen, Switzerland, where he began to design a factory using Swiss machine tools, which he considered the finest in the world. During this time, Lear also worked with the French aircraft manufacturer Sud-Aviation (now Aerospatiale), Air France, and Lear-Siegler to develop a "blind landing" device for the French Caravelle jetliner.

Returning to the United States, Lear decided to locate his new company in Wichita, Kansas, home of competitors Cessna, Beech, and a major Boeing facility. There, he reasoned, he could draw upon an experienced work force and deal with banks that were familiar with aircraft manufacturing. With $10 million of his own money, plus an additional $8 million borrowed from Wichita banks, he set up a factory at Wichita Municipal Airport in January, 1963, employing a workforce of 75 people.

In a bold move, Lear decided to skip the normal step of hand-building a prototype for flight testing, instead moving directly into production. Without a prototype, he risked the possibility that his designs might fail, forcing him into a costly redesign and retooling process that would surely sink his company. However, Lear reasoned that in the two years it might take to perfect a prototype, competitors would have ample time to develop similar models, and he was unwilling to invite competition. As a result, Lear had to be absolutely sure of every aspect of the Learjet's design. He considered the aircraft's P-16 heritage to be a good basis for refining the design and handling characteristics.

Exactly nine months later, on October 7, 1963, the first Learjet Model 23 rolled out of the 96,000-square foot facility for its maiden flight. Despite a later nonfatal crash of the first model, others flew exactly as Lear envisioned they would, and sailed through FAA certification in a near record nine months. When the first Learjet was delivered on October 14, 1964, Lear had collected 72 firm orders for the new jet. This sent other companies scrambling into the market. However, it was five years before Cessna produced a jet, and even longer before companies such as Dassault could make a dent in the market. Thus, Lear's bold gamble paid off. He had, for the time being, a monopoly on the business jet market. ''In a situation like this,'' he remarked, ''you're either very right or very wrong.''

Because of its jet-fighter progenitor and a good marriage of air frame and General Electric engines, the rugged Learjet exhibited astonishing climb performance and high cruise speeds. It could transport up to six passengers in spacious comfort at up to 540 miles per hour and climb to 40,000 feet in only seven minutes. The Learjet-23 also was highly economical to operate, costing an average of only 50 cents per mile to fly.

Despite an impressive backlog of orders for the jet, the Lear Jet Corporation lacked the capital necessary to proceed with production. Having exhausted his investment—and that of the banks—Lear decided to take his company public. On November 30, 1964, Lear sold a 38 percent interest in his company to the public for $5 million. During the following year Learjet shares fluctuated between a low of $8 and a high of $89.

Meanwhile, Lear continued work on several other projects, including the briefly popular 8-track audio tape system, which offered listeners the convenience of being able to play an entire tape of music without interruptions for rewinding or turning the tape over. With this invention he founded a stereo division of Learjet, based in Detroit, in 1965. Later that year he established an avionics division at Grand Rapids, where Learjet engineers designed and built aircraft electronics systems. In September of 1966, to reflect its diversification, the company changed its name to Lear Jet Industries.

In the meantime, Bill Lear grew bored with his administrative duties. He pursued a variety of personal projects, including the development of a costly steam-powered bus and several profitable real estate transactions. He could, at any time, be found on the production line, in the drafting rooms, out flying or, by one account, cooking himself a hamburger in the company cafeteria.

Lear's diversity of interests and disinclination to be tied down to a desk sometimes caused him to make hasty or ill-conceived decisions. He purchased a small helicopter manufacturer that produced little more than losses, and his stereo division continued to lose millions of dollars as the 8-track tape declined in popularity.

However, the greatest weakness in Learjet Industries was the sales network. Eager to get orders for the jets, Lear hastily assembled a list of dealerships throughout the country. Many of these dealers ignored their sales boundaries and few had ever sold an airplane in the Learjet's price range. As a result, the front line sales force was fragmented, disorganized, and unprofessional. Without an effective marketing program, even the profitable Learjet could no longer stem the wider losses. That year, the company lost $12 million on sales of only $27.5 million.

Once again starved for capital, Lear sought an able, deep-pocketed partner. Early in 1967 he began negotiations with Charles C. Gates, president of the Denver-based Gates Rubber Company. At the time, Gates was attempting to diversify into aircraft properties. He had just acquired two large retail aircraft service companies, Combs Aircraft in Denver and the Roscoe Turner Aeronautical Corporation in Indianapolis, renaming them the Gates Aviation Corporation.

Meanwhile, Lear had upgraded the Model 23 to include a stronger windshield and engine fire suppression and a new pressurization system. The Model 24, as it was called, also allowed 500 additional pounds of takeoff weight. However, the cost of developing and certifying these improvements were costly, and Learjet continued to experience financial difficulties. Fortunately, Gates agreed to purchase Lear's 62 percent share of the company on April 10, 1967, only a few weeks before a potentially disastrous annual meeting.

Lear remained as chairperson of the newly formed Gates Learjet company until April 2, 1969. During that time, Gates Rubber pumped $16 million into the failing subsidiary, helping to launch a new eight-passenger Model 25. Gates Learjet lost $4.6 million on $34.6 million in sales in 1968, but a year later turned a $2 million profit on $58 million in sales. Gates's vision of a synergistic manufacturing and service organization began to take shape. In 1969 Gates merged his Gates Aviation Corporation services companies with Learjet to form a single operation that included manufacturing, sales, and maintenance. With the addition of another service facility in Palm Springs, California, and four more sales offices, Gates established an effective sales organization to replace the earlier hodgepodge dealer network.

In October of 1970, unable to properly manage both Gates Rubber and Learjet, Gates asked G.H.B. Gould, head of Learjet's marketing department, to lead the aircraft company. Gould was killed in a car crash only six months later and was succeeded by Harry Combs, who had joined Gates Rubber after his own company, Combs Aircraft, was acquired by Gates.

In May of 1971, Combs oversaw the reorganization earlier proposed by Gould of the Learjet properties. The troubled stereo division was absorbed by Gates Rubber, leaving three aircraft properties: Learjet manufacturing, Combs-Gates sales and service, and the Jet Electronics and Technology (JET) avionics operation. In addition, the Lear helicopter business was closed, and a training agreement was established with Flight Safety International—the pioneer simulator-training firm—to help pilots avoid errors that had resulted in a number of crashes in early-model Learjets.

Under Combs's leadership, Gates Learjet became even more viable, marking a $6.9 million profit on $115.4 million in sales in 1975. Profit nearly doubled the following year, but fell to $9.3 million in 1977. This dip was mainly attributable to development costs for a new "Longhorn" series of Learjets featuring a new wing design and construction of a $3 million, 75,000-square foot manufacturing facility at Tucson.

Like Wichita, Tucson had become an aircraft mecca during World War II, when manufacturing operations were expanded to meet the demand of local air force bases. The location offered its own pool of experienced aerospace workers, and provided Gates Learjet with a specialized facility. The Wichita factory produced a number of unpainted Learjets that were flown to Tucson where they were painted and their interiors were finished. This eliminated a troublesome bottleneck in Wichita that slowed output.

During those years, Gates Learjet developed several new aircraft, including the fanjet-powered Models 35 and 36, and Century III series, which featured improved "Softflite" wing leading edges. In April, 1977 the Models 24 and 25 were certified to fly at 51,000 feet, well above weather and all but military air traffic. The Longhorn Models 28 and 29 featured longer wings and vertical wingtip fences known as winglets that improved lift and maneuverability. These new models were the first Learjets without wing tanks.

Bill Lear, who founded two large companies, received 150 patents, and was instrumental in the development of modern avionics and business jets, died of leukemia in a Reno hospital on May 14, 1978. Although no longer associated with Lear Siegler or Gates Learjet, his name remained with both companies, and his innovations continued to be in wide use in the aviation industry. Bill Lear's last business aircraft venture continued after his death. The all-composite Lear Fan, which he had conceived several years earlier, flew in 1980.

After Harry Combs was promoted into Learjet's parent company, Gates appointed Bermar "Bib" Stillwell to head the aircraft company. In the months that followed, Gates Learjet added five new service facilities overseas and purchased the Connecticut-based Air-Kaman service company.

Stillwell retired in 1985 and was succeeded by James B. Taylor, who took the helm of Gates Learjet at a time when "bizjet" sales had fallen so much that Learjet had to temporarily halt production. To reduce costs, Taylor laid off employees, and to raise cash, he sold the company's Jet Electronics & Technology division to BF Goodrich.

In August of 1987 Gates received an offer for its 64.8 percent share of Learjet from Integrated Acquisition, a New York-based financial group. Eager to cut its losses, Gates agreed to part with its Learjet shares for nearly $57 million.

Integrated Acquisition initially retained Taylor as head of the company. But in January of 1988, after buying up all outstanding shares in Learjet, the partners fired Taylor in favor of Beverly (Bev) Lancaster, head of the company's growing aero-

space division. The company subsequently dropped Gates from its name and sold its Combs Gates service operations to AMR, the parent of American Airlines.

During the 1980s, Learjet had been named as a major subcontractor to numerous defense, aerospace, and commercial aviation projects headed by Boeing, Martin Marietta, LTV, Textron, General Dynamics, and McDonnell Douglas. These projects included work on F-5, F-111, F-15 and F-16 fighter jets, B-1B bombers, KC-135 tankers, and later the Space Shuttle. All of this work was conducted in Wichita, which was a significant factor in much of the Learjet production being transferred to Tucson.

The company also discovered an important new market in military sales. Special versions of the Learjet 35 and 36 were built for the Brazilian, Thai, Japanese, Finnish, and Mexican military forces.

The largest military order for Learjets came from the United States Air Force, which ordered more than 80 Model 35s, designated C-21As. Learjet also won a contract to service this fleet and created the Gates Learjet Aircraft Services Corporation (Glasco) for that purpose.

Despite a recovery in jet sales, Integrated Resources was saddled with repayment obligations on $2 billion in debt that it could no longer meet. Learjet was profitable but unable to secure loans because of its parent company's poor condition.

Nevertheless, in 1989 Learjet succeeded in acquiring the thrust reverser business of the Aeronca company, which it transferred from Middletown, Ohio, to Wichita. The addition of these devices to Learjet aircraft substantially reduced landing distances, enabling it the use of shorter runways.

By 1990 Integrated had fallen under Chapter 11 bankruptcy protection. Several new acquisitors expressed interest in purchasing Learjet, including Chrysler's Gulfstream Aerospace unit, British Aerospace, and Toyota Motor Sales. During this crisis, Brian Barents, a former marketing VP at Cessna and Toyota, was appointed president of Learjet. Within months he negotiated Learjet's rescue by the Canadian manufacturing conglomerate Bombardier.

Bombardier gained fame during the 1960s as the manufacturer of Ski-Doo snowmobiles. With the passing of the snowmobile fad, the company expanded into the mass-transit railcar industry, buying out troubled manufacturers such as Pullman-Peabody, Budd, and UTDC. In 1986 Bombardier took over the loss-ridden aircraft company Canadair (at the time owned by the Canadian government) and expanded its presence in the aerospace market in 1989 by acquiring Belfast-based Short Brothers Aviation. The company bid for Learjet only a year later, and in early 1992 purchased DeHavilland Canada from Boeing.

Bombardier took control of Learjet on April 9, 1990, paying $75 million and assuming $38 million of debt. The acquisition was favorably received. Learjet, with great manufacturing capacity and a strong customer base, could benefit from the stability provided by a financially strong parent company and manufacturing and marketing synergies with other Bombardier aerospace companies. Bombardier had assembled a product line ranging from light business jets to large commuter aircraft.

Like all other Bombardier subsidiaries, Learjet remains an autonomous, independently managed unit. It maintains an important position in the company's product line, manufacturing jets for markets independent of those its sister companies occupy. The entire line of Learjet aircraft, including the models 31A, 35A, 45, and 60, provide a strong complement to the larger Canadair Challenger—which Bill Lear helped to develop some years before his death.

Principal Subsidiaries: Gates Learjet Aircraft Service Corporation (GLASCO).

Further Reading:

Christy, Joe, *The Learjet,* Tab Books, 1979.

"Development of the Learjet Model 23," *American Aviation Historical Society,* Fall 1989.

"Gates Agrees to Sell its Learjet Stake For a Third Time," *Wall Street Journal,* March 11, 1987, p. 30.

"Gates Learjet Halts Civilian Production Line," *Aviation Week & Space Technology,* September 24, 1984, p. 26.

"Gates Learjet Postpones Consolidation," *American Metal Market,* December 31, 1984, p. 32.

"Lear Jet Again Seeking Potential Suitors," *New York Times,* December 2, 1989, p. 35.

"Learjet Launch to Bridge the Gap," *Flight International,* September 18, 1990, p. 20.

"Learjet Milestones" (company document), Wichita, Kansas: Learjet, Inc.

"Lear 60 Deliveries to Begin in January," *Flight International,* May 19, 1992, p. 16.

"Let's Make a Deal," *Forbes,* April 27, 1992, pp. 62–64.

"New Life for Learjet," *Business & Commercial Aviation,* July 1990, pp. 41–44.

Serling, Robert J., "One Grand Story" (company advertising supplement), Wichita, Kansas: Learjet Inc.

"William Powell Lear, Sr." (biography), Wichita, Kansas: Learjet Inc.

—John Simley

Lee Apparel Company, Inc.

P.O. Box 2940
Shawnee Mission, Kansas 66201
U.S.A.
(913) 384-4000
Fax: (913) 384-2360

Wholly Owned Subsidiary of the VF Corporation
Incorporated: 1889 as the H. D. Lee Mercantile Company
Employees: 10,350
Sales: $510 million
SICs: 2325 Men's/Boy's Trousers & Slacks; 2339 Women's/
    Misses Outerwear; 2329 Men's/Boy's Clothing

Lee Apparel Company, Inc. is the second largest manufacturer of jeans in the United States. The company, which got its start in the dry goods business before moving into the production of denim clothing, leads in sales of women's jeans and holds a significant share of other clothing markets as well. After focusing its production on work clothes throughout the first half of the twentieth century, Lee took advantage of the sales boom in fashion jeans throughout the 1960s and 1970s. Although its market decreased considerably during the 1980s, the company has been rejuvenated through its introduction of innovative new denim processing and finishing techniques.

Lee was founded in 1889 by Henry David Lee and several business associates in Salina, Kansas. As a teenage hotel clerk in a small Ohio town, Lee saved his earnings and, investing them skillfully, was eventually able to take over the Central Oil Company, which distributed kerosene oil for lighting. Stricken with tuberculosis and advised by doctors to relocate to a more hospitable climate, Lee sold his business to John D. Rockefeller's Standard Oil Company in the late 1880s and moved to Kansas, bringing several associates from his oil company with him. In Kansas, Lee and his associates sought out a five-year charter from the state to run a wholesale grocery business that would sell fine food products under several different brand names, including "Mother's Style," "Cadet," and "Summer Girl." The company's start-up financing totaled $100,000, with one quarter of it reportedly contributed by the town of Salina.

Lee's business rapidly prospered, benefiting from its position as the largest food supplier between Denver and Kansas City. The market it served was enjoying a period of rapid growth, as it developed from frontier to a more settled, prosperous area.

Within its first ten years, the company had branched out into three additional businesses, the H. D. Lee Flour Mills Company, the Lee Hardware Company, and Kansas Ice and Storage. Soon, the Lee company was also selling sewing materials, furnishings, paper goods, and school supplies. By the turn of the century, Lee's enterprise represented the largest wholesale grocery and dry goods business in the Midwest.

The company experienced a setback on December 4, 1903, when its headquarters in Salina, and all its inventory, burned to the ground. Although losses totaled $575,000, the company recovered quickly, building two new, fireproof buildings on its property.

The most important addition to the Lee company's product line came in 1911, when Lee became frustrated by infrequent deliveries of work clothes, such as overalls and dungarees, from a manufacturer in the east. Recognizing the benefits of being able to produce the needed items himself, and encouraged by the continuing growth of the American population and economy, Lee decided to open a garment factory in Salina to produce overalls, jackets, and dungarees.

Two years later, Lee began manufacturing the item that would make the company famous. Legend has it that the idea originated with H. D. Lee himself, who noticed that his chauffeur needed a sturdy one-piece outfit that could easily be pulled over his uniform when he needed to service Lee's car. The Lee Union-All basically consisted of a jacket and a pair of work pants sewn together at the waist, and it proved practical for farm and factory workers who wanted to shield themselves from the dirt of their work, which got between their clothes and skin.

By 1915, the charter of the Lee company had been expanded to account for its new interest in clothing manufacturing, and the company had opened a second factory, designated for the exclusive manufacture of Union-Alls, in Kansas City, Kansas. In 1916, two more factories were opened, in Kansas City, Missouri, and South Bend, Indiana.

The following year, Lee became the first company in the apparel industry to introduce a nationwide advertising campaign, placing a full-page ad in the *Saturday Evening Post*. The company's business received a further boost during this time as the United States entered World War I, and Lee was asked to manufacture as many Union-Alls as possible for the U.S. Army. The Lee garment became the official fatigue uniform for American soldiers fighting in Europe.

After the war's end, Lee continued to expand, moving into a new nine-story building in Kansas City, Missouri, in 1919, which replaced its smaller Kansas City, Kansas, facility. The following year, Lee launched its first consumer promotion campaign, introducing a ceramic doll, named "Buddy Lee," that wore miniature Lee clothes manufactured in the company's factories.

Over the next two years, Lee continued to move away from a broader background in groceries and dry goods and toward its new identity as a clothing manufacturer. As the company narrowed its product line, it also simultaneously embarked upon a dramatic geographic expansion, opening a new plant and warehouse in Minneapolis as well as storage facilities in San Francisco and Los Angeles. Also during this time a factory in Trenton, New Jersey, was closed, so that a larger one could be opened.

Throughout the 1920s, Lee continued to develop its line of apparel, introducing new fabrics and new designs for special purposes. In 1924, the company produced pants made for seamen and loggers, and also began to manufacture cowboy pants made of heavyweight 13-ounce denim, which would come to be known as "jeans." The following year, the company introduced Lee Jelt Denim, an 11½-ounce cloth that featured twisted threads that provided strength and durability. In 1926, there was a flurry of innovation, as jeans with zippers and U-shaped saddle crotches as well as work clothes with sliding fasteners were brought to market. Furthermore, Lee began to offer tailored sizes, which corresponded to waist and inseam measurements. The following year, color-fast dyed herringbone twills and hickory striped denim were incorporated into the company's product line. In addition, Union-Alls fastened with newly-invented zippers were renamed "Lee Whizits" after a consumer contest to choose a new name.

In 1928, H. D. Lee died of a heart attack at the age of 66, and control of the company was left to Leonard C. Staples, the husband of Lee's niece. Under the guidance of Staples, Lee continued to post strong gains in sales until the end of the decade.

With the coming of the Great Depression in the wake of the stock market crash in 1929, however, Lee's fortunes suffered. A sharp slump in sales caused declines in profits, and the company was forced to reduce wages. Nevertheless, within five years Lee was again profitable and, predicting its best performance since the start of the decade, the company was able to declare a special dividend to stockholders.

In 1936, Lee moved to identify itself more fully with the Western world of cowboys and rodeos by forming the Rodeo Cowboys Association. The company also opened a plant in San Francisco to produce its trademark denim cowboy pants, now known as Lee "Rider" pants. For the first time, the company's logo was rendered in a "hair-on-hide" leather label that featured the letters of its name connected in a way that resembled the mark of a cattle brand. By 1939, Lee had become the largest producer of work clothes in America, as sales reached $6.4 million. With six plants in operation, the company was able to fully restore its pay rates to their pre-Depression levels.

Soon after Lee had fully returned to profitability, the United States entered World War II, and the country's economy was once again thrown into turmoil as it concentrated its efforts on wartime production. With fabric scarce under a government rationing plan, Lee was forced to curtail its manufacture of products for the civilian marketplace, causing shortages of its goods for consumers. However, the company did convert its factories to manufacture clothing for the war effort. In 1943, Lee changed its official name to "H.D. Lee Company, Inc.," dropping the word "Mercantile" to better reflect its primary emphasis on garment manufacturing.

With the war's end in 1945, the U.S. economy entered a period of rapid growth, and Lee expanded along with it. The company began to market its products not just to working people, who needed the rugged garments for practical reasons, but to upper middle-class Americans, who were caught up in the romance of the West, eager to visit dude ranches, and beginning to regard denim pants as fashionable rather than merely functional. During this time, Lee began to purchase other clothing manufacturers to increase its production capacity. Eloesser-Heynemann Company, a workwear maker based in San Francisco, was bought in 1946. Three years later, the Bruce Company, a Kansas clothing maker, was also purchased. Also in 1949, Lee introduced Lady Lee Riders for women, specifically designed to fit women better than standard men's jeans.

At this time, Lee shed a remnant of its past as a foods wholesaler when it sold its former grocery warehouse in Salina, Kansas. The company left the food business altogether in 1950 when it turned over its grocery division to Consolidated Grocers of Chicago for about $3 million. With the money earned from this sale, Lee sought to further expand its garment business.

Throughout the 1950s, Lee struggled to keep up with the increasing demand for its products. The company continued to acquire factories, including Sun Garment of St. Joseph, Missouri, and began building new facilities as well as adding on to those it maintained. One new factory, built in the town of Chetopa, Kansas, gave its name to a new heavy-duty twill fabric that Lee began to market in 1952 under the name Chetopa Twill.

From 1952 to 1956, Lee also moved to strengthen its identity as a purveyor of Western wear by bringing in the founder of the Cowboy Hall of Fame and the Western Heritage Center to serve as corporate chairperson. With the company's new image, production and sales of Lee products continued to grow.

In 1954, the company introduced "Leesures," its entrant in the new and rapidly growing leisure sportswear market. Three years later, the company began to market clothes for boys under the brand name "Double Knees." Lee ended the decade with its introduction of the Lee Westerner line of products, which featured dressy white jeans and jackets. In 1961, the style of this line was further refined with the addition of center creases and narrower pants legs. Lee promoted this line of clothing with the slogan, "the clothes you need for the life you lead," hoping to appeal particularly to high school and college students.

By the 1960s, as postwar baby boom had begun to wind down, denim jeans were more and more becoming the uniform of the younger generation. The company worked to meet the demand for its product as jeans exploded in popularity. Additional plants were opened in Virginia, Georgia, Louisiana, Missouri, Kansas, and Texas. In 1964, five years after its establishment of an international division, Lee opened its first overseas factory, in Sint Niklaas, Belgium.

Also that year, Lee introduced stretch denim, to appeal to young women, and "no iron" permanent press slacks for men, under the "Lee Prest" brand name. These innovations contributed to a continuing record of profitability, which began to attract the attention of investors interested in either acquiring the company or merging it with their own operations. Lee's directors turned down an offer from the Work Wear Corporation in 1967, as well as a proposal from U.S. Industries the following year. In 1969, however, the shareholders of the company agreed to sell their assets to the VF Corporation of Pennsylvania, which manufactured Vanity Fair lingerie.

With the infusion of capital from the company's sale, Lee was able to invest in expanded production capabilities. The company modernized its manufacturing facilities in the United States and also became involved in joint ventures overseas, entering into agreements with factories in Scotland, Belgium, Spain, Australia, Brazil, and Hong Kong.

As Lee moved into the 1970s, the company continued to vary its offerings to meet current fashion trends. Flared leg bottoms on jeans and leisure pants were introduced. In 1972, the company began to sell a polyester double-knit leisure suit, which it marketed in a wide variety of colors as a sporty alternative to the business suit. In 1973, Lee introduced jeans designed especially for women under the "Ms. Lee" brand name. The company's long term commitment to jeans tailored specifically for women gave it a strong leading spot in this market. Six years later, the company formed a Youthwear division to market products for children.

With the end of the 1970s, however, came the end of the rapid expansion of the jeans market. Industry-wide, sales for denim pants peaked in 1981, and then went into a steady decline. Lee was forced to close several plants in response to the slump. In an effort to offset declines in profits from dropping sales, Lee invested further in modern equipment, to make its manufacturing process as efficient as possible. The company installed automatic cutters to produce pieces for 32 pairs of jeans at once, as well as automatic belt loopers and pocket setters.

In addition to updating its equipment, Lee also began to experiment with the very essence of the garments it manufactured, its denim. Traditional jeans had been sprayed with corn starch as a fixing agent, resulting in a garment that shrunk and faded dramatically when the customer washed it. In an effort to provide jeans that fit more accurately, Lee began to pre-wash its own denim, a step known as "wet processing." In 1982, "stone washed" jeans were introduced. This was followed by "acid-washed" denim, which produced an even more faded look.

In addition to innovation in its basic product line, in 1983 Lee expanded its offerings to include products for infants and toddlers, in an effort to appeal to faithful customers of the 1960s and 1970s who had by this time become parents. The company also began to sell "Dress Blues" made of denim that did not fade, stretch jeans, corduroy jeans, and denim with cable stripes. In 1986, Lee began marketing looser pants and pleated pants under the label "Relaxed Riders," for girls and women, and "Easy Riders" for men.

Continued consumer demand for denim with novel finishes led Lee to further experimentation with its wet processing. A wide variety of objects, including bottle caps, golf balls, shredded tires, ropes, and wood, were thrown into washing machines with denim pants, producing a look referred to as "distressed" in the fashion industry. In 1986, the company introduced "Frosted Riders," for which Turkish pumice stones were used to soften the fabric. Anticipating continued demand for washed denims, Lee made a large investment in washing machines and laundries. Furthermore, the company engaged experts in chemical and mineral washes, and acquired sources of raw materials (such as rocks) in Mexico, Greece, and the western United States for use in their processes. By the end of the 1980s, the company was preparing its fabrics in over 70 different ways, marketing such products as "Glacier," "Pepper," and "Bubble" denim.

Innovation in processing was complemented by development in equipment, as Lee put in place computer technology to speed up its manufacturing processes. The company opened a new distribution facility in Mocksville, North Carolina, in January, 1990, to warehouse and ship its products. By 1992, an industry-wide return to basics had pushed up sales of jeans once again, and Lee introduced "Lee Basics," designed to appeal to younger consumers. Anticipating higher sales, the company announced that it would add 570 jobs to its payroll.

As the Lee company moved into the mid-1990s, it had a long history and a venerable brand name to its credit. As a significant player in the American jeans industry, it should look forward to years of continued growth and prosperity.

Further Reading:

Madison, Cathy, "Lee Changes Into Something More Comfortable," *Adweek,* August 6, 1990, p. 4.

Magiera, Marcy, and Pat Sloan, "Levi's, Lee Loosen Up for Baby Boomers," *Advertising Age,* August 3, 1992, p. 9.

One Hundred Years of Excellence, Shawnee Mission, Kansas: The Lee Apparel Company, 1989.

Stafford, Diane, "Lee Maps New Line of Jeans," *Advertising Age,* March 10, 1986, p. 28.

—Elizabeth Rourke

LENNOX *International Inc.*

Lennox International Inc.

P.O. Box 799900
Dallas, Texas 75379-9900
U.S.A.
(214) 497-5000
Fax: (214) 497-5299

Private Company
Incorporated: 1904 as Lennox Furnace Co.
Employees: 7,000
Sales: $1.05 billion
SICs: 3585 Refrigeration and Heating Equipment; 3567
  Industrial Furnaces and Ovens

Lennox International Inc. is one of the largest privately owned companies in the world. Through its three manufacturing subsidiaries, Lennox produces a broad range of residential and commercial heating, air conditioning, and refrigeration equipment and components. These three subsidiaries are Lennox Industries Inc., Heatcraft Inc., and Armstrong Air Conditioning Inc. Lennox International is owned almost entirely by members of the Norris family, which has controlled the company since 1904; John W. Norris, Jr., is chairman of the board and chief executive officer. About 100 descendants of founder D. W. Norris own shares of Lennox.

Lennox Industries Inc. is the core business of Lennox International. This subsidiary is an international manufacturer of residential and commercial heating and air conditioning equipment. Lennox products are marketed directly to its network of 6,000 independent dealers in 70 countries throughout the world, a unique set-up in the heating, ventilating, and air conditioning (HVAC) industry. Lennox Industries' facilities include four factories in North America and one in England, as well as numerous sales and distribution centers, dealer service centers, and a large research and development laboratory. Over half of the parent company's revenue is generated by Lennox Industries. Heatcraft Inc. has been part of Lennox International since 1973. Heatcraft, with headquarters in Grenada, Mississippi, has two divisions: the Heat Transfer Division, which produces heat transfer surfaces, including coils and copper tubing, as well as other components; and the Refrigeration Products Division, which manufacturers unit coolers, air-cooled condensers, cooling towers, and custom refrigeration products. The other Lennox subsidiary, Armstrong Air Conditioning Inc., is based in

Bellevue, Ohio, and manufactures a broad range of residential furnaces and air conditioners.

Lennox got its start in Marshalltown, Iowa, in the last years of the 19th century. Two inventors, Ernest Bryant and Ezra Smith, patented a design for a riveted-steel sheet metal coal furnace, a significant improvement over the cast iron furnaces of that time. Bryant and Smith hired Dave Lennox, who operated a machine shop in Marshalltown, to build the equipment necessary to manufacture their furnace. Bryant and Smith did not have adequate financial backing for the project, however, and when they could not pay Lennox for his work, Lennox took over the furnace patents, altered the design, and set out to market the furnace himself. Shortly thereafter, Lennox decided to sell the furnace business. It was purchased in 1904 by D. W. Norris, editor and publisher of the local newspaper. He incorporated the operation as Lennox Furnace Company, and proceeded to sell 600 furnaces in the company's first year. The Lennox method of distribution, selling, and delivering products directly to authorized dealers was established in the company's first years of operation. Company president Norris established a direct link to dealers using newspaper advertising, his area of expertise.

The superiority of the Lennox sheet metal furnace over the cast iron models commonly in use quickly became apparent. Cast iron furnaces were prone to warping after years of continual heating and cooling. This often caused the shell to crack, and smoke and coal gas could leak into a living space. The Lennox model solved this problem, since no warping occurred. By 1923, the company had expanded enough to open a warehouse in Syracuse, New York. Two years later, a factory was built in that city. In 1927 Lennox acquired the Armstrong Furnace plant in London, Ohio. The Armstrong facility, which produced steel coal furnaces, was moved to Columbus, Ohio, the following year.

John W. Norris, son of company president D. W. Norris, went to work for Lennox in 1927 following his graduation from Massachusetts Institute of Technology. By the early 1930s, the younger Norris had set up a research department in the back part of a warehouse. Several important industry developments came about as a result of Norris' research. Among these developments was the addition of blowers to furnaces in the mid-1930s. Around the same time, oil and gas burning furnaces were introduced as well. The appearance of oil and gas forced-air furnaces completely changed the face of the residential heating market. During this period Norris developed a line of smooth, porcelain-enameled cabinets in which to house the furnaces, revolutionizing furnace design for years to come. This marked the first time aesthetics were taken into account in the design of heating equipment, in recognition of the increasing use of the American basement as a living area. A gas forced-air furnace specifically designed for attic or crawlspace installation went into production in 1939.

As the demand for Lennox equipment increased, new facilities were added. In 1940 a new and larger factory was built in Columbus. This plant was also a center for sales, distribution, and product service support for parts of the country that the Marshalltown and Syracuse facilities could not support. By the onset of World War II, Lennox held an important place in the heating industry. During the war the company's production included not only heating equipment for military use, but also parts for aircraft and bombs. A precision machine shop in Lima, Ohio, was purchased for that purpose in 1942. Demand for Lennox products soared when the war was over. By the end of the 1940s, several new divisions were added, including a factory in Fort Worth, Texas, and sales centers in Atlanta, Los Angeles, and Salt Lake City. In 1949 D. W. Norris died, and John W. Norris, Sr., became president of Lennox.

Lennox continued to expand quickly in both its product line and geographical scope in the 1950s. In 1952 Lennox began manufacturing air conditioning systems. Its first model was a three-ton water-cooled air conditioner, produced at the newly expanded Fort Worth plant. Within the next couple of years, compressors and air conditioning systems for industrial and commercial use went into production as well. Lennox went international in 1952, with the creation of Lennox Industries (Canada) Ltd.

In 1955 the Lennox Furnace Co. changed its name to Lennox Industries Inc. in order to better reflect the broader range of products being manufactured. Further innovations created by Lennox during that decade included commercial air conditioning systems that saved energy by using outside air whenever possible; and modular systems for high-rise buildings, in which each floor was heated and cooled separately from the others.

Lennox expanded the scope of its operations in 1962 with the creation of an International Division. A full-production facility was established in Basingstoke, England (outside of London), and sales offices and warehouses serving most of Western Europe were opened in the Netherlands and in West Germany. By this time, the Canadian operation included a manufacturing plant in Toronto, Ontario, as well as a sales and distribution facility in Calgary, Alberta. Among the products introduced by Lennox during the 1960s were the Duracurve heat exchanger, which eliminated noise and cracking in gas furnaces, and multizone rooftop units for heating and cooling.

In 1971 Norris was succeeded as president by Ray C. Robbins. Under Robbins, Lennox continued to expand at a rapid pace during the 1970s. In 1973 Lennox acquired the Tennessee-based Heatcraft Inc. from PEP Industries. Heatcraft, a manufacturer of electric heating and cooling components such as coils, condensing units, and copper tubing became a wholly owned subsidiary of Lennox. The following year Lennox began construction of a new factory for the production of commercial heating and air conditioning equipment in Stuttgart, Arkansas. Later in the decade, Lennox began to outgrow some of its facilities, and a migration to the Dallas area began. The company's Marshalltown Research and Development Laboratory and the heat pump research facility in Fort Worth were consolidated into a larger, more modern location in Carrollton, Texas, in 1977.

The following year the company's corporate headquarters were relocated from Marshalltown to Dallas. The Midwest Division sales headquarters and manufacturing plant located in Marshalltown remained intact. 1978 also marked the debut of the LOGIC (Lennox Objective Guide to Installation Comparisons) computer program for the analysis of HVAC designs, and the opening of a computerized corporate data center. In 1979 testing was completed on a home-sized solar-powered air conditioning system, produced by Lennox in cooperation with Honeywell under government contract.

John W. Norris, Jr., became president and CEO of Lennox in 1980. Robbins stayed on as chairman of the board. By 1981, the company's unique distribution system boasted a total of 6,000 dealers throughout the United States and Canada, supplied by a network of 31 warehouses. That year, Lennox controlled 17 percent of the residential market for gas forced-air furnaces. The company did nearly as well in the central electric heating and unitary air conditioner markets, with 14 percent and 15 percent shares respectively. In 1982 Lennox made a major gain in the home heating industry with the appearance of the first pulse combustion gas furnace, a high efficiency forced-air unit that marked the first major improvement in home heating in 20 years. The G14 Pulse furnace operated with no open flame, igniting tiny bursts of gas and air at a rate of about 60 bursts a second. It operated at over 90 percent fuel efficiency, a significant improvement over the 55 percent energy efficiency of most furnaces in use at that time. With the introduction of the Pulse, sales at Lennox reached an estimated $600 million for 1982.

In 1983 Lennox built a copper tube plant in Bossier City, Louisiana. The following year, the company introduced the Power Saver air conditioner, the first two-speed air conditioner to achieve a 15.0 Seasonal Energy Efficiency Ratio (SEER). The expansion and consolidation of company facilities continued in the mid-1980s. In 1985 Lennox began an expansion program at its National Parts Distribution Center in Urbandale, Iowa, just outside of Des Moines. The compressor research lab in Fort Worth was integrated into the Carrollton research and development complex that year as well. A year later Lennox International Inc. was formed as the parent company for Lennox Industries and Heatcraft. Around the same time, Heatcraft acquired the Grenada, Mississippi, coil manufacturing and copper mill facility of SnyderGeneral Corp. This facility was expanded in 1987 to include the production of precision tools and dies for making heat transfer products. Lennox began offering limited lifetime warranties on its Pulse furnaces in 1987, prompting its competitors to come up with similar warranty programs of their own. In 1988 Heatcraft acquired another of SnyderGeneral's facilities, a refrigeration products manufacturing plant in Wilmington, North Carolina.

Two important technological developments occurred at Lennox in 1988: the introduction of the first heat pump to use a scroll-compressor; and a licensing agreement with Powell Energy Products to develop and market thermal energy storage systems using Powell technology. 1988 also marked the reacquisition of Armstrong Air Conditioning. Lennox had owned Armstrong from the mid-1920s into the 1950s, when it was sold off. Armstrong was purchased by Johnson Corp. in 1962, which was in turn acquired by Magic Chef in 1971. Magic Chef became a division of Maytag in 1986, and its name was lengthened to Magic Chef Air Conditioning. It was this division that Lennox International purchased from Maytag in 1988. It was then renamed Armstrong Air Conditioning Inc., a wholly owned subsidiary of Lennox International.

Early in 1989, Lennox announced a reorganization of its corporate structure, in which each of its three operating subsidiaries would have its own president and chief operating officer. Donald W. Munson was named to head Lennox Industries; Robert L. Jenkins became president of Heatcraft; and Robert E. Johnson was named to lead Armstrong. Other developments that year included the opening of a new Lennox Industries sales and distribution center in Wilmington, Massachusetts, to serve dealers in New England and eastern New York. Also, the Research and Development Laboratory in Carrollton, Texas, was approved by the American Gas Association as an accredited lab for certification testing.

In 1990 work was completed on a new corporate headquarters for Lennox International and Lennox Industries in Richardson, Texas, a suburb of Dallas. The following year the company launched another reorganization plan, in which its sales management, marketing, and product ordering teams were united in the new headquarters, a change from the previous arrangement of five semi-autonomous regional divisions. At the same time, production was consolidated into four locations, meaning the closing of the Fort Worth facility. Also in 1991, Norris was voted in as chairman of the board. Robbins' title was elevated to chairman emeritus. Donald Munson retired in July of 1992, and Thomas J. Keefe, a member of the Lennox International board, took over as president and chief operating officer of Lennox Industries. Later that year, a ten-year anniversary celebration for the Pulse furnace took place in Marshalltown, Iowa, the company's birthplace and furnace manufacturing location, during which the one millionth Pulse furnace was dedicated. Meanwhile in Europe, the company's Basingstoke, England, facility, operated by Lennox for over 30 years, was closed. Its operations were moved to a new, 100,000-square-foot plant in Northampton.

Lennox introduced its new "Diplomat" line of central air conditioners, heat pumps, and gas furnaces in early 1993. The Diplomat line was developed as a means of gaining a stronger foothold in the residential new construction market, an area that Lennox had often been priced out of in previous years. Garnering a significant share of this market will help ensure Lennox International's ongoing importance in the HVAC industry through the remainder of the 1990s.

Principal Subsidiaries: Lennox Industries Inc.; Heatcraft Inc.; Armstrong Air Conditioning Inc.

Further Reading:

Consdorf, Arnold P., and Behrens, Charles W., "A Combination of Change and Stability," *Appliance Manufacturer,* November 1977, pp. 40–47.

Duffy, Gordon, "Lennox Gears Up for Expansion in New Home and World Markets," *Air Conditioning, Heating, and Refrigeration News,* January 25, 1993, pp. 102–04.

"Gas Furnaces: Lennox Is Hot in Ownership Now and in the Future," *Appliance Manufacturer,* July 1983, p. 38.

The History of Lennox, Dallas: Lennox International Inc., 1992.

Lennox International Inc. Profile, Dallas: Lennox International Inc., 1993.

"Lennox Link to Dealers Thrives on Direct Communication," *Appliance Manufacturer,* October 1981, p. 54.

"Lennox Moving Corporate HQ to Dallas Area," *Air Conditioning, Heating, and Refrigeration News,* March 20, 1978. p. 1.

"Lennox Reorganizes," *Air Conditioning, Heating, and Refrigeration News,* April 8, 1991, pp. 1–2.

"The Lennox Story," *Appliance,* February 1982, special section.

"Lighting a Fire under Furnace Sales," *Business Week,* October 25, 1982, p.82.

"Special Section: Lennox International," *Appliance Manufacturer,* August 1990.

"Sun-Powered Home Air Conditioner," *Machine Design,* June 21, 1979, p. 8.

—Robert R. Jacobson

The Leslie Fay Companies, Inc.

1400 Broadway
New York, New York 10018
U.S.A.
(212) 221-4000
Fax: (212) 221-4045

Public Company
Incorporated: 1984
Employees: 4,500
Sales: $836.6 million
Stock Exchanges: New York
SICs: 2335 Women's/Misses' Dresses; 1337 Women's
  Misses' Suits and Coats; 2339 Women's/Misses'
  Outerwear; 2341 Women's/Children's Underwear

The Leslie Fay Companies, Inc.—the second-largest maker of women's clothing sold to department stores—designs, manufactures, and markets moderately priced and better priced women's dresses, suits, blouses, coats, and sportswear. Its clothes are marketed under several labels, including Albert Nipon, Kasper for A.S.L, Evelyn Pearson, and Castleberry Knits.

Leslie Fay was founded in 1947 by Fred Pomerantz, who had produced dresses for the Women's Army Corps during World War II. The company was named for his daughter and offered department stores substantial profit margins for carrying the company's line of stylishly conservative women's wear. Pomerantz was a colorful figure in the New York garment district; he reportedly had a liking for gambling, and people on the street knew when he was at work because his distinctive Rolls-Royce was parked outside the company's Broadway offices.

Leslie Fay went public in 1952. From 1959 until April of 1982, the business was called Leslie Fay Inc. Pomerantz's son John became president of the company in 1972. He had joined the company in 1960, right after he graduated from the Wharton School with a bachelor's degree. John continued to run the company much as his father had run it. When other companies were turning to computers in the early 1980s to help keep track of daily sales at stores around the nation and were using market testing to determine whether its styles would sell, Leslie Fay continued to make deals with a handshake and telephone stores weekly for sales figures, unlikely business practices for a public company of its size. Practices such as these may have worked

for a smaller company, and it may have worked before the 1980s, a decade of takeovers and business opportunism. In 1982 Leslie Fay was taken over through a leveraged buyout for $58 million and became a private company operating under the name The Leslie Fay Company.

In 1984, in another leveraged buyout, the company became known as The Leslie Fay Companies, Inc. This time, management and outside investors paid $158 million to buy out the investors from the 1982 takeover. The leveraged buyout by managers and investors brought John and his wife, Laura (also a company official), 1.7 million shares of stock, or a 8.7 percent share, for which they paid $162,000; that worked out to a bargain at only nine cents a share. In 1986 the company went public again, however, with management and institutional investors still controlling 55 percent of the outstanding shares.

The fashion industry in general was enjoying a period of prosperity in the mid-1980s, and Leslie Fay was growing fast. Leslie Fay and other garment industry companies, though, were subject to the ups and downs of fashion, and Leslie Fay watched its stocks rise and dip, from $18 per share in 1986, down to $9 in 1989, and then up to the upper teens again by the early 1990s.

Leslie Fay acquired several companies during the end of the 1980s, buying the assets and trademarks of Albert Nipon, Inc., for $8.3 million and Mary Ann Restivo, Inc., for $5.3 million in 1988. It also assumed Mary Ann Restivo's $3.9 million in liabilities. In 1989 Leslie Fay acquired Non-Stop Fashions, Inc., and NS Petites Inc.

All of these changes signalled a new era for Leslie Fay, which had awakened to the need to transform its image. It had received feedback from upscale stores, which were longtime customers, that Leslie Fay apparel was too drab and matronly. Leslie Fay responded to the criticism by bringing in new designers. It also adopted a new marketing approach, following the lead of Calvin Klein and Liz Claiborne by opening boutiques within department stores. Pomerantz convinced 500 retailers to install the boutiques, even though there were doubts that Leslie Fay's $100 dresses could generate enough sales to justify the expense.

Leslie Fay also updated its marketing by talking directly to consumers through fashion shows and videotapes and by inviting consumers to talk directly to the company through a toll-free phone number. It also launched a $8.5 million ad campaign. The new approach paid off, and Leslie Fay left behind its production-oriented approach to become a sophisticated, consumer-driven dress manufacturer. In 1990 sales revenues were $859 million, triple what they had been only ten years earlier.

Because Leslie Fay had a strong brand name, it phased out some labels and replaced them with a Leslie Fay label. It also sought to broaden its base by licensing the use of its name for coats, shoes, lingerie, and children's clothing, so that the company would become known as a manufacturer of a broad assortment of moderately priced clothing.

In 1991 Leslie Fay sold its Head Sports Wear division to Odyssey International Group in order to focus on women's apparel. Leslie Fay received $47.5 million in cash and non-interest-bearing notes for the division that carried ski, tennis, and golf apparel for men and women. Pomerantz used the proceeds from the sale to reduce the company's bank debts.

In June of 1992 Leslie Fay announced it would acquire Hue International, a hosiery firm with 1991 sales of $35 million. Hue sold colorful legwear for women, including tights, socks, knee-socks, bodywear, and leggings. Leslie Fay anticipated that the purchase of this company would give Leslie Fay entry into a segment of the apparel market that it had not previously reached.

Despite positive changes through acquisition, Leslie Fay needed to stimulate lagging sales, and reduced prices on its dresses by at least ten percent in the fall of 1992. Management announced that this was part of a long-term marketing strategy. Its dresses and pantsuits, which had sold for $89 to $139 each, were lowered $10 to $20. Leslie Fay felt the price reduction would not hurt the company because now it would sell more dresses before marking them down. It announced that it would reduce the number of styles it made and also planned to discontinue its Mary Restivo label. The Mary Restivo division had losses of $2.9 million on sales of $5.5 million.

Despite the recession that had hit the national economy and the garment industry, 1992 appeared to be a favorable one for Leslie Fay until October of that year. Instead, 1992 turned out to be one of the worst years of the company's existence, although the extent of the problem was not known until early 1993. Until then, despite several warning signs, Pomerantz, industry analysts, and Wall Street investors had no idea that Leslie Fay was not as healthy as profit statements seemed to indicate.

In late January of 1993, Pomerantz learned that the company's books had been doctored to show 1992 profits that did not exist. Although there did not seem to be any funds missing, outside auditors determined that the company had not had profits of $23.9 million as reported, but instead had actually lost $13.7 million. The last quarter of 1991 had also been misreported— by as much as 42 percent. News of the discrepancies sent Leslie Fay stock plunging from 12⅜ in January to 5¼ by the beginning of March. Several stockholders initiated lawsuits against the company. According to reports, Pomerantz did not pay close attention to the financial operations of the company, which were not even housed in the New York headquarters but were instead located in Wilkes-Barre, Pennsylvania.

The company had a reputation for creating pressure to meet profit goals, but 1992's profit goals were particularly ambitious because of an unhealthy economy and a 20-year decline in dress sales, a disquieting trend for Leslie Fay because they depended on dress sales for one-third of its total sales. The company also faced serious problems with retailers' and consumers' negative responses to its apparel lines.

Leslie Fay fashion styles had been criticized as over-priced and old-fashioned. Department stores had been cutting back on orders, in part because they were having a hard time selling Leslie Fay fashions specifically, but maybe even more significantly because many department stores were in trouble due to serious competition from discount and outlet stores. Leslie Fay's marketing strategy, however, still centered around department stores, some of which were filing for bankruptcy, including key Leslie Fay customer, Macy's.

According to the *Wall Street Journal,* while the company was reporting profits and keeping its stock prices up, Pomerantz had been calling department stores to try to persuade them to order more Leslie Fay merchandise. Many retailers said they had cut their Leslie Fay orders by as much as 15 percent in the previous two years. It was reported that Pomerantz was offering the retailers rebates or markdown money of millions of dollars if they had to slash prices on Leslie Fay apparel to move their inventory. Markdown money—payment that the manufacturer gives stores in cash or discounts on future orders as a guarantee of profits even if the store has to mark down the merchandise— was a common practice, but Leslie Fay's markdown money allegedly was extremely high by industry standards.

Analysts had heard rumors of declining sales in July of 1992. The company noted that orders for the fall season were down, but shortly after that the company forecasted that earnings for 1992 would be higher than those for 1991. Pomerantz had also offered to buy back up to a million shares of Leslie Fay stock, a move that showed his own optimism about the company and reassured Wall Street.

Pomerantz said he had expected fall 1992 orders to pick up, but in September, when they had not, he ordered the price cuts across the board on all future orders. Retailers and other businesses in the industry were surprised because the expected response to slow sales would have been to cut production. Instead, the company would have to sell more merchandise, albeit at more attractive prices, to make money.

In October Pomerantz announced a substantial decline in net income because of the difficult retail market. Company officials, however, still did not question the profits recorded at year-end. Pomerantz and others received substantial bonuses based on the company's reported $23.9 million profit. Pomerantz alone received $2.2 million.

Pomerantz said he knew nothing about the doctored books and that it appeared to be the work of the company controller and his staff. According to the *Wall Street Journal,* the misleading figures were chiefly an overstatement of the number of garments manufactured, coupled with an understatement of the manufacturing cost of each item. Leslie Fay's strategy of cutting prices instead of production could ''inflate phantom profits.''

The *Wall Street Journal* noted that such accounting practices were not uncommon among small, private companies in the industry. But Leslie Fay had grown into a large public company, and for a business its size to play the small company game, the results were disastrous. According to ex-employees, in order to meet profit goals invoices were backdated and recorded as revenue even though the money had not been received. The financial department might have survived this practice if the market had remained strong, but the recession hurt performance, as did a poor response to the company's merchandise. It became impossible to cover a shortfall with revenue from the next quarter as sales dropped. The *Wall Street Journal* noted that the company had fostered such deep reservoirs of good will since its founding by Fred Pomerantz that the company's serious problems were ignored for too long by the rest of the industry and department stores.

Pomerantz and the other company officials returned their bonuses shortly after the 1992 losses were reported and placed responsibility on the shoulders of the controller—who had confessed to the misstatements of profit. Industry analysts, company officials, and others wondered what his motive could have been. The compensation package of the controller was not tied to profits, and no money was missing. According to Pomerantz, senior level management had known nothing about the overstated profits.

Leslie Fay was still picking up the pieces of its accounting mess long after the discrepancies were revealed. But business had to go on. Pomerantz claimed that the incident did not threaten the company's viability. Just before the profit misstatements were discovered, Leslie Fay had announced big plans that the company expected would boost sales. It planned to replace its Breckenridge, Joan Leslie Evening, and Outlander labels with one new label, Theo Miles. The Theo Miles brand was intended to compete in the $2-billion better-price market against the leader Liz Claiborne. Leslie Fay predicted that the new line would bring in wholesale earnings of $130 to $140 million in its first year and $500 million by 1998. Laura Pomerantz, who had been a senior vice president, was named to a newly created post as executive vice president over the company's better brands, including the new Theo Miles label. She already headed the Albert Nipon and Leslie Fay Evening lines.

Although trying to look forward, The Leslie Fay Companies, Inc., in 1993 still faced several lawsuits by shareholders who contended that they had been misled about the company's financial health. In addition, the company was faced with some serious and potentially long-term problems: declining department store sales and the perception that Leslie Fay styles are old-fashioned.

Principal Subsidiaries: Non-Stop Fashions, Inc.; NS Petites Inc.

Further Reading:

Agins, Teri, "Leslie Fay Says Irregularities in Books Could Wipe Out '92 Profit; Stock Skids," *Wall Street Journal,* February 2, 1993, section A, p. 4.

Agins, Teri, "Loose Threads: Dressmaker Leslie Fay Is an Old-Style Firm That's in a Modern Fix," *Wall Street Journal,* February 23, 1993, section A, p. 1.

Berton, Lee, and Teri Agins, "Shareholders Sue Leslie Fay Following Disclosure of Accounting Investigation," *Wall Street Journal,* February 3, 1993, section B, p. 2.

Lesly, Elizabeth, "Who Played Dress-Up with the Books?," *Business Week,* March 15, 1993, p. 34.

—Wendy J. Stein

Lincoln Property Company

3300 Lincoln Plaza
500 N. Akard
P.O. Box 1920
Dallas, TX 75201
U.S.A.
(214) 740-3300
Fax: (214) 740-3313

Private Company
Incorporated: 1965
Employees: 4,000
Sales: $800 million (estimated)
SICs: 1542 General Building Contractors—Nonresidential
   Buildings, Other Than Industrial Buildings and
   Warehouses; 1522 General Building Contractors—
   Apartment Buildings; 1541 General Building
   Contractors—Industrial Buildings and Warehouses; 1542
   Nonresidential Construction, Nec; 6552 Land Subdividers
   & Developers, NEC; 6512 Operators of Nonresidential
   buildings; 6513 Operators of Apartment Buildings; 6531
   Real Estate Agents and Managers

Lincoln Property Company is one of the top five developers in the country of both office buildings and residential apartment complexes, with projects in every major U.S. city and some in Europe. It specializes in high-rise office towers and market rate and luxury apartments, although it also has built warehouse, retail, and hotel space. In addition, it has become increasingly involved in rental management.

Lincoln Property was founded in Dallas on Lincoln's birthday in 1965 as a partnership between Trammell Crow and Mack Pogue. Crow, at age 50, was already the successful owner and president of a Dallas-based warehouse building company, Trammell Crow Co., which had pioneered the concept of building before tenants are obtained. Pogue, who was named president of the new company at age 30, had recently become a commercial real estate broker following a career as a high school football coach. The original aim of Lincoln Property was to build garden apartment houses in Dallas.

The company soon became known for its suburban landscaped apartment communities with luxuries such as private clubs, swimming pools, and equipped gymnasiums. Such amenities added, for example, $1000 to the cost of each unit, as was the case at the community Willow Creek in Dallas. Projects at that time were typically worth around $5 million, from which Lincoln could make a profit of about $400,000. Very quickly the company was building apartment projects through partnerships in other cities throughout the country, such as St. Louis, San Francisco, and Denver. Eventually it even expanded overseas with projects in Madrid, Brussels, London, and Paris.

Then, in the mid-1970s, the sudden rise in interest rates and the halt in construction loans from banks nearly put Lincoln out of business. Lincoln had acquired several hundred million dollars in land for future development, and was locked into paying 14 percent interest for the property on which it was unable to build. Pogue quickly restructured loans and sold off $600 million in land, some of it at a loss, and managed to stay solvent. When real estate later picked up, Lincoln began expanding once again, although from time to time it sold off some of its property in order to have cash on hand, even when it was no longer necessary.

Having successfully learned from his mentor Crow how to master the real estate business by making deals, Pogue decided to move out on his own. In 1977 he bought out Crow's share in the company for $150 million, and Lincoln proceeded to grow independently, eventually to become Trammell Crow's closest competitor. Pogue began to diversify Lincoln's activities into developing office parks and towers, research-and-development warehouses, hotels, and shopping centers.

To carry out these plans, in 1979 Pogue took on a new, permanent partner, William Duvall, to manage development projects in other regions of the country. Duvall's responsibility was to form operating partnerships in various cities typically with real estate brokers, compensating them primarily according to the equity of the building project while paying them relatively small salaries. The local operating partner was the best-positioned person to market the new building to tenants, and sometimes also proved helpful in winning Lincoln the permit or bid to build. For example, with the connections to municipal government through a local partner in Boston, Lincoln succeeded in 1985 in gaining the city planning board's approval to erect an office building on the site of an historic store.

Having learned his lessons from the real estate crash of the 1970s, Pogue thereafter pursued a more conservative strategy of financing. Since the late 1960s financiers had been demanding larger shares of the profit, and now Lincoln was quite willing to oblige, giving up equity for less debt and thus passing most of the risk on to the equity investor. "Our policy is real simple," Pogue told the *Wall Street Journal* in 1986. "We put no cash into our deals. None. The only way you can lose money is if you spend it." Since funding Lincoln's first high-rise office building in north Dallas in the late 1970s, the Metropolitan Life Insurance Co. was Lincoln's chief financial partner until 1985. Lincoln also developed other sources of its own for capital: a real-estate investment trust, a junk-bond fund, and a European capital-raising unit in Geneva, Switzerland.

Typically Lincoln paid only for the architects, land options, and miscellaneous fees up front, at around $2 million, while its investing partners, such as Metropolitan Life, paid for the land purchase, short-term bank loans, and construction costs. It also paid a 2 to 3 percent development fee to Lincoln that would cover the latter's operation costs, and could amount to $30 million on the largest, billion-dollar projects. The deal gave Metropolitan Life half ownership of the building, whereby Lincoln repaid Metropolitan Life for half the construction costs in monthly installments over 15 years. Income from the rents would be split between the two partners. Lincoln had the advantage, though, that if rents were not sufficient to cover its monthly payments to the investor, it did not have to make up the difference. Also, if at any time Lincoln wanted to abandon a project, it lost only its own share.

Thus, Lincoln's high-rise office building projects rapidly spread across the country, encouraged by the building boom of the early 1980s. Some of its larger office building projects included the Lincoln Plaza in Dallas, the Lincoln Centre high-rise in Minneapolis, the Allegheny International Tower in Pittsburgh, the Sun Bank Center in Orlando, the Lincoln Tower in Miami, and major office buildings in Austin, San Francisco, Los Angeles, Washington, D.C., and Boston. Between 1979 and 1986 Lincoln built 20 million square feet of office space, equivalent to five Pentagons, according to *Fortune* magazine. During this period Metropolitan Life put in a total of about $2 billion and 10 percent of all of its real estate investments into Lincoln's projects. By 1985 Lincoln was starting projects worth $1.6 billion, 22 times that of its projects a decade earlier, and had $4 billion in assets and $1.4 billion in annual construction put in place, with major projects in 14 cities. It had become the third-largest diversified developer in the country, after Trammell Crow and Toronto-based Olympia & York, and was regarded as the most aggressive developer of them all. In 1986 it was ranked the 25th-largest private company in all industries in the United States. The following year it had revenues of $2.1 billion and staffed 5000 employees.

For its office buildings Lincoln emphasized top quality, such as numerous quick elevators, and employed renowned architects. Although its rents tended to be 10 percent higher than average for the area, its newer buildings also rented faster than the average for a given locality. To provide the office buildings with centralized telecommunications services, Lincoln took advantage of AT&T's breakup and created its own telephone company subsidiary, LinCom Corp.

Meanwhile, Lincoln did not abandon development in apartment projects. By 1980 it was already ranked among the top 10 housing builders. For example, it was the top-ranked builder in fast-growing Denver in 1984, with 14,000 units completed there that year. In 1986 income from apartment rentals was $43 million per year, with $8 million generated from one apartment project alone, the 7,100-unit Villages community in Dallas. As office construction slowed down in the mid-1980s, apartment construction expanded. Zoning restrictions in the Midwest, California, and Northeast restricted housing supply on one hand, but led to increased rental rates on the other. Thus, once it overcame the obstacle of obtaining a building permit, Lincoln could build more profitable apartments than before.

Lincoln's building practices, in which it assumed minimum financial risk, have been blamed for leading to overbuilding, particularly of office buildings and hotels. Lincoln, though, was not the only developer to build ahead of demand during the 1980s' real estate boom. Office towers were built because the capital existed, not because of any demand for office space. Deregulation of savings and loan institutions had allowed these firms to make excessive investments in real estate, and other developers also took advantage of this. Tax breaks offered to investors beginning in 1982 further encouraged development. Thus, investors were eager to put their funds to work, and developers such as Lincoln were just as eager to take development fees from the investors. The inevitable consequence of overbuilding was an inability to find tenants. For example, when the Lincoln Centre in downtown Minneapolis opened in 1987, it had a single tenant occupying just one of its 31 floors. This compared with Lincoln's average occupancy rate of 91 percent for office space that had been built in the early 1980s.

Although Metropolitan Life stopped investing in Lincoln's high-rise building projects in 1985, other eager investors stepped in to fill the gap. Most prominent was the securities firm Drexel Burnham Lambert with mortgage-backed bonds. Also, beginning in December of 1985, a group of insurance companies took advantage of a new type of "asset-backed" security, a type of 15-year bond, and invested $146 million of these in Lincoln's development projects.

Then, in the late 1980s, the real estate industry's boom turned into a bust, and so did Lincoln's fortunes. The collapse of the market was due mostly to oversupply, especially of office buildings, and the consequent fall in rents, but other factors contributed. A 1986 federal tax law eliminated previous tax loopholes for real estate losses and thus discouraged investment. New federal regulations restricted the amount that lending institutions could invest in real estate. At the same time, banks on their own stopped financing real estate once the collapse in the market had become evident. They began requiring the developers to put up more equity than the latter were able or willing to do. Furthermore, the credit crunch came just at the time when many of the developers' five- and seven-year mortgages of the early 1980's development boom were coming due. To make matters worse, the economy entered a recession by 1990, and demand for new commercial space further waned.

Lincoln suffered, although its policy of low risk investment saved it from total financial ruin. While the national occupancy rate for office buildings fell to 86 percent in 1986, Lincoln's joint-venture practices allowed it to break even with occupancy rates as low as 65 percent. One 39-story, $100-million building in New Orleans, however, had an occupancy rate as low as 40 percent one year and a half after its completion in 1984. This extremely low occupancy rate was due to the downturn in the local oil and gas industry. Although Lincoln had to cut back on building, the amount of office space it had built ensured that it would have continuing income from rents. By 1987 it had developed 61 million square feet nationwide and had approximately $5 billion in assets. But rents dropped on average 41 percent from 1981 to 1986 as a result of the glut in high-class office space, and Lincoln as the landlord lost out.

Lincoln kept itself afloat by selling off property, often back to the insurance companies that were its investment partners in the projects. In 1987 Lincoln sold its 50 percent share in the $300-million Lincoln Centre in Dallas to its partner, Metropolitan Life (although the company kept the Lincoln Plaza, where its offices are headquartered). This was followed by the sale of its half-interest in the $100-million Lincoln Centre in Minneapolis, for which it received a mere $6.5 million, and the $100-million Energy Center in New Orleans, both sold back to Metropolitan Life. It sold its share in the $22-million Lincoln Pointe in Tampa back to Aetna and sold other buildings in Austin and Miami considerably below their potential value. Lincoln still had more serious financial problems with its smaller projects of shopping malls and warehouses, in which it had a greater stake.

As the real estate crisis worsened, Lincoln was forced to default on some loans. It had a negative annual cash flow of as much as $75 million in 1989. Since Lincoln was essentially a series of partnerships, financial problems could be handled one by one in isolation. Five of Lincoln's partnerships however, ended up having to file for protection from creditors under Chapter 11 of the U.S. Bankruptcy Code. In 1990 Lincoln sold $200 million in Texas properties including industrial buildings, shopping centers, and land to the NCNB Texas National Bank in order to settle its defaulted loans with that bank. It still had $1.4 billion in property in Dallas, although this was down from $4.5 billion in 1985. That year Lincoln also sold off its stake in the telecommunications business. Its LinCom subsidiary, which in the meantime had been renamed Amerisystems and later merged with a Westinghouse subsidiary, was sold to Fairchild Communications Service. Lincoln also scaled back by reducing its staff by about 40 percent between 1988 and 1990.

Although Lincoln recovered, emerging from financial restructuring in 1990, the big building days were not to return soon, since many real estate markets then had a three to five year oversupply of buildings. Instead Lincoln sought contracts as building managers, often for the very buildings it was selling back. Its managed properties increased by 10 percent between 1988 and 1990.

Lincoln also refocused on the rental apartment business. Although the apartment market was also hit by the credit crunch and recession, a steady increase in demand in certain parts of the country, such as California, enabled the value of rental property to rise. Lincoln even purchased apartment projects of other developers to increase its property management portfolio. It acquired 1,100 units in Phoenix and 800 in Denver in 1990 in the belief that the market had bottomed out. By 1991 Lincoln had become the nation's largest management company, overseeing 84,008 apartments, with Trammell Crow as the second largest. Although its construction was down 30 percent from the previous year to 2,580 constructed units, Lincoln was ranked the 12th-largest home builder in the country. In 1992 it ranked

as the third-largest rental apartment builder, based on its 1,866 units started.

As Lincoln entered the 1990s it continued to be active in commercial development as well. It was still ranked the seventh most active developer in 1989. The following year it had several new development projects in progress totaling over half a billion, although this was down from its previous annual peak of activity of $1.5 billion in projects. Its lenders included some of the same institutions as before: Metropolitan Life, Prudential Life, and the Teachers Insurance & Annuity Association. Projects that Lincoln completed in 1992 included the largest tower in the southeastern United States, the 60-story NCNB National Bank building in Charlotte, North Carolina; the Orlando City Hall, in Orlando, Florida; the GSA Warehouse in Chicago; and apartment communities in New Jersey, Virginia, and California. In 1992 Lincoln, which was still under Pogue's management, ranked as the fifth-largest developer based on total number of square feet under development, finally putting the company ahead of its erstwhile competitor, Trammell Crow.

Further Reading:

Carlton, Jim, ''Apartment Developers Face Adversity: Starts in 1990 Are Down from Peak Set in 1985,'' *Wall Street Journal,* January 17, 1991, p. 4.

Dorris, Virginia Kent, ''NCNB Center Lifts Charlotte's Skyline,'' *Engineering News Record,* January 20, 1992, pp. 46–50.

Fisher, Daniel, ''Dallas Still Landlord for Housing Industry,'' *Dallas Times Herald,* March 19, 1991, p. B1.

Huey, John, ''The Giant Developers of Dallas Began Small, Took Enormous Risks,'' *Wall Street Journal,* March 24, 1986, p. 1, 14.

Huntley, Patrick, ''Lincoln Property Sells Stake in Telecommunications Firm,'' *Dallas Business Journal,* October 26, 1990, p. 4.

Marsh, Steven, ''Local Builders Ranked Among Nation's Top 100,'' *Rocky Mountain Business Journal,* May 20, 1985, p. 21.

McKenzie, Linda, ''Top Developer Survey,'' *National Real Estate Investor,* January 1993, pp. 80–87.

''Much More Than Garden-Type Apartments,'' *Business Week,* March 14, 1970, pp. 146–47.

Musilek, Joe, ''Lincoln Centre Opens with 30 of 31 Floors Empty,'' *Minneapolis-St. Paul CityBusiness,* August 12, 1987, p. 1.

O'Reilly, Brian, ''This Builder Wants It All—Without Risk,'' *Fortune,* May 12, 1986, pp. 50–57.

Pacelle, Mitchell, ''Real Estate: Big Investors Maker Room for Apartments,'' *Wall Street Journal,* p. B1.

Staton, Tracy, ''Stepping away from the Precipice,'' *Dallas Business Journal,* p. 1.

Taylor, John H., ''The Dinosaurs Are Dying,'' *Forbes,* May 1, 1989, pp. 92–100.

—Heather Behn Hedden

Liz Claiborne, Inc.

1441 Broadway
New York, New York 10018
U.S.A.
(212) 354-4900
Fax: (212) 719-9049

Public Company
Incorporated: January 19, 1976
Employees: 8,000
Sales: $2.19 billion
Stock Exchanges: New York
SICs: 2339 Women's & Misses' Outerwear, Nec; 2335
    Women's & Misses' Dresses; 2389 Apparel &
    Accessories, Nec; 2329 Men's & Boys' Clothing, Nec;
    2331 Women's & Misses' Blouses and Shirts; 2337
    Women's & Misses' Suits and Coats; 2253 Knit
    Outerwear Mills; 5632 Women's Accessory and Specialty
    Stores

Since its inception in 1976, Liz Claiborne, Inc. has grown to be the largest women's apparel manufacturer in the world. The company designs and markets a complete line of sportswear, professional clothing, costume jewelry, accessories, and cosmetics under the labels Liz Claiborne, Elisabeth, Liz & Co., and Dana Buchman. It also designs sportswear and accessories and markets fragrances for men under the Claiborne label. Products are manufactured through contracts with independent factories in 50 nations and are marketed through prominent department and specialty stores worldwide. The company is expanding rapidly overseas, pushing its clothes into such elegant European retailers as Harrod's and Selfridge's.

Elisabeth "Liz" Claiborne was born in Brussels and raised in Europe and New Orleans. Her natural artistic flair led toward her goal of becoming a fashion designer. At age 20 she got her first break when she won a design contest sponsored by *Harper's Bazaar* magazine. Soon after that, she was employed as a sketcher and model in New York's garment district and worked her way through the ranks at several design firms. After working for 16 years as the chief designer in Jonathan Logan's Youth Guild division, she realized that the working woman needed more wardrobe options. Unable to sell the concept of stylish, sporty, and affordable clothes for America's working woman to her employer, Claiborne left the company and joined her husband, Arthur Ortenberg, and another partner, Leonard Boxer, to found Liz Claiborne, Inc. in 1976. The three pooled $50,000 in savings and borrowed an additional $200,000 from friends and family to launch the company specializing in fashionable, functional, and affordable women's apparel. Shortly thereafter, Jerome Chazen joined the trio. The company showed a profit its first year and became the fastest growing, most profitable U.S. apparel company in the 1980s.

Claiborne's timing was perfect; she began providing career clothes to women just as they started entering the work force in record numbers. As Jerome Chazen stated in *Fortune,* "We knew we wanted to clothe women in the work force. We saw a niche where no pure player existed. What we didn't know was how many customers were out there." Clothes designers had not fully exploited one of the largest growing groups in America—women baby-boomers penetrating the labor market. Liz Claiborne ignored the traditional industry seasons of spring and fall, opting instead for six selling periods, including pre-spring, spring I, spring II, summer, fall, and holiday, to provide consumers with new styles every two months. These short cycles allowed more frequent updates of new styles and put clothes on the racks in the appropriate season. By adding cycles, stores cut their inventory costs and overseas suppliers were able to operate more efficiently with the two extra cycles filling their slack periods. Liz Claiborne also made the decision not to field a traveling sales force. This determination, although disregarding conventional industry wisdom, stimulated the company's rapid growth. With virtually no overhead, Liz Claiborne was set for swift growth as sales skyrocketed.

Liz Claiborne is greatly concerned with listening to its customers. At the company's back-office operation in North Bergen, New Jersey, $10 million worth of IBM computers spit out information on sales trends throughout the country. This automated inventory network allows quick response to market demand. In addition to this network, Liz Claiborne employs about 150 specialists to solicit feedback from customers at stores around the country and 21 consultants who make sure that clothes and displays are arranged in stores according to company diagrams. Ninety-five customer service telephone operators field questions from retailers.

During the 1980s Liz Claiborne evolved from a basic sportswear business to a multifaceted fashion house. By the early 1990s, it boasted 19 divisions and three licensees, whereas in 1980 it had just one division. The company went public in 1981 at $19 per share, raising $6.1 million. A petite sportswear division was introduced in 1981, and a dress division was added in 1982. A 1984 foray into girls' clothes failed by 1987. Four new divisions were launched in 1985, including Claiborne, the company's expansion into men's clothing. Liz Claiborne discovered that 70 percent of its women customers were also purchasing clothing for their husbands. Also created in 1985 was the accessories division, which was formerly a licensee. Some components of this line include leather handbags, small leather goods, and bodywear.

The company further expanded and introduced its signature scent in September of 1986. The cosmetics division began as a joint venture with Avon Cosmetics Ltd., and in 1988 the company regained full rights to the line. This division has since marketed a new fragrance, Realities, and the Claiborne fragrance for men. In the fall 1993, the group introduced Vivid, its third women's fragrance. The year 1988 also marked an important milestone for Liz Claiborne, Inc. After only ten years, the company was on *Fortune*'s list of the top 500 industrial companies. It was one of only two companies started by a woman to achieve that distinction. Also, as an 11-year old enterprise, it was one of the youngest companies ever to make the cut.

In 1989 the Dana Buchman division was launched. This division specializes in a line of higher-priced women's career clothes created for the bridge market. Its prices span the difference between moderately priced ready-to-wear sportswear and designer creations. In mid-1987, however, a slump hit the apparel business. Retail sales stalled in early 1988, inventories increased, and operating margins narrowed. In 1988, for the first time ever, Liz Claiborne's net earnings fell—by an estimated 11 percent, to $102 million. After years of 20 percent increases, sportswear sales increased only about three percent in 1988. Sales gains were getting hard to come by.

Searching for new avenues, Liz Claiborne focused on a long-overlooked group of consumers and introduced its Elisabeth division specializing in apparel for larger women. The line offered everything from career clothing and activewear to social occasion dressing. The line has been very well received and is a market leader. Sales rose 23.4 percent to $161 million in 1992. More important, in 1988 the company moved into the retail apparel business when it opened its first retail stores, offering the First Issue brand of casual women's sportswear. This break into apparel retailing was an expensive and highly risky proposition. Thirteen stores were launched that year and the company showed that it could be successful in this type of diversification. It currently operates 40 First Issue specialty stores throughout the United States and planned to add 16 more stores, mostly in 1993.

The company opened its first Liz Claiborne stores in 1989. These 18 stand-alone stores are placed in affluent suburban malls and serve as laboratories for the company to test new designs and product presentations. They provide the company with immediate information regarding market trends through state-of-the-art bar coding and other electronic data interchange systems. Three Elisabeth stores were also opened serving the larger-sized consumer. Overall, sales of the retail division rose 20 percent to $92.9 million in 1992. In addition, the company operates 55 factory-outlet stores that market unsold inventory from past seasons. Sales achieved record levels in this area also, up 34.5 percent to $113.9 million. Liz Claiborne positions these outlets at a distance from the stores where its products are customarily sold.

In addition to the company stores, Liz Claiborne dominates the selling floors of major department stores—sometimes more than half the allotment for women's apparel. Because profits and volume have increased for Liz Claiborne, so has its influence at the manufacturing and retail ends of the business. The company does not own any factories; all of its merchandise is made through contracts with independent factories in 50 nations. The company has reduced its reliance on Hong Kong, South Korea, and Taiwan in favor of countries like Malaysia, China, and Sri Lanka, where labor is less expensive. Less than

ten percent of Liz Claiborne's products are made in the United States. There are drawbacks, though, to not owning the factories. To ensure that goods are produced to the high standards consumers expect, Liz Claiborne employs an overseas staff of almost 700 who regularly visit the factories.

At the retail end, Liz Claiborne commands extensive clout. The company has a rigid noncancellation policy, meaning that if spring merchandise does not sell well in stores, retailers are still unable to cut summer orders. But Liz Claiborne does generate what is known as strong "sell through." Its clothes are rarely marked down—only about five percent of its merchandise versus the industry norm of 15 percent. To reduce the risk of markdowns the company produces fewer goods than the level of demand forecast. Therefore, retailers get better profit margins and allow Liz Claiborne more space on the floor. But because of limited space in department store floors, the company is expanding abroad. In 1988 sales and marketing efforts began in Canada. In January of 1991 Liz Claiborne, Inc. entered Great Britain, and later in the year it was introduced into Spain. Merchandise is also sold to stores in the United Kingdom, Ireland, and the Netherlands. Liz Claiborne has tailored its strategies when marketing its products outside the United States. In some United Kingdom stores, the company leases space and sells the product itself. In Japan, it markets through a mail-order catalog, and in Singapore Liz Claiborne has granted a retail license for the operation of Liz Claiborne stores. This strategy seems to be working well as international sales totaled $108.1 million in 1992, while only six years ago $1.4 million of sales came from outside the United States.

The greatest challenge to the company came in 1989, when Liz Claiborne and Arthur Ortenberg announced they would resign from active management in order to pursue philanthropic interests. They established the Liz Claiborne and Art Ortenberg Foundation, a private organization dedicated to protecting wildlife and the environment. This foundation also serves the needs of the public through programs in the fields of human services, the environment, health care, the arts, and education.

The company was not damaged by the founders' departure. A broad array of new products has been introduced, including jewelry and sport shoes. Liz Claiborne further expanded its business to women's and men's optical frames, eyewear (fashion sunglasses and readers), and women's hosiery through licensing, and these revenues continue to climb. Tailored suits for the working woman debuted in 1991. This division is expected to generate sales of $100 million within five years. In May of 1992 Liz Claiborne acquired three new labels from the bankrupt Russ Togs. Crazy Horse is casual wear marketed in department and specialty stores. Russ offers updated career and casual apparel and is sold in moderate areas of department stores. The Villager is offered in national and regional chain department stores. This line focuses on career clothing and some casual wear. These and future acquisitions will broaden the company's distribution and will allow opportunities for expanding clothing lines and creating new products.

Although sales for 1992 increased 9.3 percent to a record $2.2 billion and the company's ten percent return on net sales remains one of the highest in the apparel industry, Liz Claiborne is not satisfied with past accomplishments. While the number of working women between the ages of 25 and 54 grew 43 percent in the 1980s, this demographic group will increase only about 25 percent during the 1990s. The company needed to become more visible in order to maintain market share. The combination of recession, increased competition in moderately priced sportswear, and the push into new markets have led Liz Claiborne to seek a higher profile. In October of 1991, the company launched its first print advertising campaign for apparel and accessories.

Liz Claiborne realized that cooperative advertising with retailers and its domination of department store floors was not enough anymore. Instead, the company needed to solidify its fashion image and create a global corporate image. Advertising is critical if the company is to preserve strong relationships with consumers and retailers. Also, Liz Claiborne cannot expect to gain a foothold in Europe with an unadvertised fashion brand. Since floor space in Europe is much more limited, a company needs to advertise its image to get into the stores. Liz Claiborne does have an advantage in that the company stands for quality, value, and fit—exactly the standards of the Europeans and Japanese.

Liz Claiborne's $6 million advertising campaign broke in the November 1991 issues of 15 consumer publications, including *HG, Vanity Fair* and *Elle.* The ad campaign is just part of Liz Claiborne's objective to increase visibility. In the fall of 1991, the company originated Women's Work, a philanthropic enterprise pairing women artists and writers with community groups in projects addressing domestic violence and work/family conflicts. For example, in Chicago, children's author Leah Komaiko collaborated with a group of city kids to write a book on working mothers. It is distributed through Reading Is Fundamental (RIF), schools, libraries, and reading programs.

The company that Liz built is noted for its well-organized management, distribution, and sales teams. In an industry where turmoil is a tradition, Liz Claiborne has cultivated a strong team to run every aspect of the business. The company has continued to meet industry challenges by following four guidelines it has instilled from its beginning: listen to consumers; create first-class products addressing their needs; price products with the consumer in mind; and always try to do more, and do it better. In 1992 *Fortune* once again named Liz Claiborne, Inc. as one of the ten most admired corporations in America, further reinforcing that the company has indeed achieved success and will continue to thrive into the 1990s.

Principal Subsidiaries: Claiborne Limited (Hong Kong); Liz Claiborne Cosmetics, Inc.; Liz Claiborne Accessories, Inc.; Liz Claiborne Accessories-Sales, Inc.; Liz Claiborne Export, Inc.; Liz Claiborne Foreign Holdings, Inc.; Liz Claiborne International, Ltd. (Hong Kong); Liz Claiborne (Israel) Ltd.; Liz Claiborne (Italy) Inc.; L.C. Licensing, Inc.; Liz Claiborne Sales, Inc.; Liz Claiborne-Texas, Inc.; LCI Investment, Inc.; LCI Holding, Inc.; Liz Claiborne (Canada) Limited; Liz Claiborne, S.A. (Costa Rica); L.C. Caribbean Holdings, Inc.

Further Reading:

Appelbaum, Cara, ''Stepping Out,'' *Adweek's Marketing Week,* November 18, 1991, pp. 20–21.
Deveny, Kathleen, ''Can Ms. Fashion Bounce Back,'' *Business Week,* January 16, 1989, pp. 64–70.
Gannes, Stuart, ''America's Fastest-Growing Companies,'' *Fortune,* May 23, 1988, pp. 28–40.
Hass, Nancy, ''Like A Rock,'' *Financial World,* February 4, 1992, pp. 22–24.
Liz Claiborne, Inc. Annual Reports, New York: Liz Claiborne, Inc., 1991–92.
Sellers, Patricia, ''The Rag Trade's Reluctant Revolutionary,'' *Fortune,* January 5, 1987, pp. 36–38.
Zinn, Laura, ''Liz Claiborne Without Liz: Steady As She Goes,'' *Business Week,* September 17, 1990, pp. 70–74.

—Carol Kieltyka

Loctite Corporation

10 Columbus Blvd.
Hartford Square
Hartford, Connecticut 06106
U.S.A.
(203) 520-5000
Fax: (203) 520-5073

Public Company
Incorporated: 1953 as the American Sealants Company
Employees: 3,587
Sales: $561.2 million
Stock Exchanges: New York
SICs: 2891 Adhesives & Sealants

The Loctite Corporation is a major transnational corporation that specializes in chemical products, particularly adhesives, glues, and sealants. The name "Loctite" is a trade name that caught on after the discovery of the company's flagship product. The liquid chemical substance revolutionized the machine tool industry because it replaced mechanical locking devices, such as lock washers. When applied to locks and bolts, the new liquid would harden and lock them together, leading some to refer to the new product as the "liquid washer." The applications of the innovation were widespread throughout industry and, in its 40 years, Loctite has become the leading producer of sealants and adhesives in the world; the majority of Loctite's revenues come from its overseas operations. Most of the company's products are used for industrial applications, but consumer products, notably Super Glue, also make up a solid portion of the Loctite's sales revenues.

The story of the Loctite Corporation began at Dr. Vernon Krieble's chemistry laboratory at Trinity College in Hartford, Connecticut, in 1953. Krieble's son Robert Krieble, who was also a chemist, worked for General Electric Company's chemical business in Pittsfield, Massachusetts. Bob had been working on the development of a synthetic sealant that was labeled "anaerobic permafil." Being anaerobic, the substance would cure only when deprived of oxygen. The problems associated with handling the product puzzled him, and he consulted his father about the chemical's strange behavior. Vernon Krieble discovered that the liquid, when applied to nuts, bolts, and fasteners would flow into the crevices and harden and lock them together. The major problem that remained was how to package the product while keeping it aerated; if it was packaged in a sealed container it would harden. The problem was solved after the Plax Company, a division of Emhart Corp., introduced a polyethylene substance that was permeable to oxygen.

Although the original technology was sold by General Electric Company, the Kriebles patented their product as an entire system—anaerobic sealants stored in Plax bottles. The Plax bottles eliminated the need for separate storage devices and aerating devices, such as air compressors, to keep the liquid from hardening. This product became the pilot product of the American Sealants Company which Professor Krieble formed in 1953.

The Kriebles's began cautiously, selling the sealant system to a few companies in the Hartford area. By 1955, however, Professor Krieble retired from Trinity College and was eager to devote time to the commercial development of the product. Krieble convinced a group of Trinity alumni to put up $100,000 to start production. This liquid locknut became known as "Loctite" and made its public debut at a press conference in New York City. Despite the initial publicity and sales of $7,000 in 1956, the company remained in the red until 1960 when it reached a profitable sales figure of $1 million. Anticipating growth, the company moved to a production facility in Newington, Connecticut, and established a distribution facility in Australia. A plant in Puerto Rico opened in 1962.

Loctite would prove invaluable for mechanical engineers searching for ways to enhance friction. Despite precise machining, there are generally some inner spaces that are sources of leakage, looseness, and wear in machinery and motors. Kenneth Butterworth described in *The Loctite Story* that "Loctite liquids flow into all of that surface roughness, then harden because there's no oxygen available. The hardened Loctite keys the two surfaces together." Initially engineers were skeptical about this technique for bonding surfaces and worried that its widespread adoption could reduce the need for precise engineering. Business people were also wary, but they were intrigued by the potential for cost reductions.

The fact that Loctite was extremely cheap to produce and eliminated the need for mechanical locking devices, such as lockwashers, helped the company overcome such skepticism. Because Loctite competed directly with mechanical locking devices, Krieble priced its product in the same range—although the actual manufacturing cost was much less. The company educated customers about Loctite's usage and potential. The Loctite system also included customer equipment and products required for assembly line applications. As Butterworth noted in *The Loctite Story,* "We don't just sell a bottle of glue, we sell a system and the system can cost one million dollars." The strategy was a huge success in the 1960s, and the Loctite method was used in threadlocking, pipe-sealing and the development of different strengths and viscosities; sealing machine tool parts (which obviated the need for machines to be built to close finishes, a costly process); and developing a completely bonded assembly for motors used in hand-held power tools for the Black & Decker Corporation.

As its liquid washer grew in popularity, American Sealants changed its name to the Loctite Corporation in 1963. President Vernon Krieble died in 1964 and his son Robert succeeded him, presiding over a line of cyanoacrylate adhesives—better known as Super Glue—and a new anaerobic structural adhesive. By 1965, the company's tenth year, Loctite sales reached $2.8 million with a net income of $260,000.

By 1968 the company was poised to enter into the booming automobile market. Foreign automakers embraced Loctite to help stop vibrations in their smaller, higher revving engines. Detroit-based automakers, however, waited seven years to adopt the product and initially used it for threaded and fitted parts, thereby replacing a wide class of locking fasteners prone to loosening. By the mid 1970s, as U.S. automakers began to produce smaller lightweight vehicles, Loctite developed new product lines. Notable among these was 1973's Dri-Loc line of eight products designed for various locking and sealing strengths and for sealing equipment at different temperatures. Other new products followed into the early 1980s, including a new generation microanaerobic adhesive that does not activate until the parts are assembled. This reduced the cost of producing small motors, which could now be built as self-contained units.

Despite being founded on the basic technology of the Loctite product, the company has sought to expand its product range and scope throughout its history. Most of these products were developed by Loctite's engineers. The most significant addition to the Loctite product stable was Super Glue, developed in the company's labs in Ireland and Connecticut. Basic research and development produced new acrylics, silicones, and urethanes, but Loctite also expanded its industrial product base through several key corporate acquisitions. Most notable among these acquisitions was Permatex, an automotive line acquired in 1972 and Woodhill Chemical Sales Company purchased in 1974. Permatex's gasket dressings made it a leader in the automotive repair market; Woodhill's product line of adhesives opened up new markets for car and home repairs. It was Woodhill that introduced Super Glue to hardware stores across the country. The two companies were combined into the automotive and consumer division of Loctite in 1974.

The growth of various Loctite product lines as well as corporate acquisitions helped the company expand into international markets. In many cases, successful companies were established separately by Loctite agents; these companies were eventually purchased by Loctite. The company went public in 1970, merging with the International Sealants Corporation. At that time International's sales were $5 million compared to Loctite's $18 million. CEO Kenneth W. Butterworth stated in *The Loctite Story* that the merger of International into Loctite was the most significant in Loctite's history, giving Loctite foreign revenues (accounting for 60 percent of total revenues) and making Loctite a solid transnational corporation.

Although the Krieble family still maintains a controlling interest in Loctite, it no longer runs the company. In 1986, 26 percent of the company's stock was purchased by Henkel Corporation, a German chemical conglomerate, with whom Loctite had several joint ventures. In 1991 the Krieble family sold 9.8

percent of its 12.5 percent stock holdings in the company. Some experts interpreted this move as an indication of a crisis at Loctite, and the Krieble's announcement of their intention to sell sent Loctite stock prices plummeting. They stabilized shortly thereafter, however.

Although Loctite's sales were hard hit during recessions in the 1980s and 1990s, the company's product diversity and expansion into new markets helped keep its bottom line growing. In addition, as a transnational corporation, Loctite was insulated somewhat from the instability in demand markets that often occurs during a recession; the declining profitability from operations in a recession in one country was buffered by growing markets in other economies. The consumer market remains strong, but because most of Loctite's industrial sales are to overseas firms, the company is particularly vulnerable to fluctuations in the foreign exchange markets. The strong dollar of the early to mid-1980s was particularly devastating because the company lost sales to cheaper imports. Of course, with substantial foreign operations, a stronger dollar meant that foreign profits would translate into larger dollar denominated profits, but this not enough to offset the domestic decline in sales. Nonetheless, by the late 1980s growth in Loctite's mass of profits was still quite strong.

Loctite's Butterworth looks forward to continued product diversification to fuel future growth. Product diversification led to revenues of $400 million in 1988, only 25 percent of which derive from the original anaerobic "Loctite" product line. Loctite's diversification also extends geographically. Reliance on foreign sales has also grown substantially; in 1960 foreign sales accounted for 20 percent the company's sales, while in the early-1990s they represented 60 percent of sales and 80 percent of profits.

Loctite remains solidly profitable worldwide, and its sales in the past five years have grown by double digits. Loctite has been extremely successful at assessing future markets and may be eyeing Eastern Europe. Robert Krieble has organized the Krieble Institute and has made speeches across eastern Europe about his company's formation—a brilliant discovery coupled with small start-up costs was all it took to begin a major company. Loctite's production facilities are flexible to allow quick adaption to new markets. The company's products are, for the most part, standardized and only require labelling in different languages, which is no problem for Loctite's electronic labelling system. If the markets for industrial goods in Eastern Europe and China ripen, Loctite is in a position to move quickly to meet demand.

Principle Subsidiaries: DL-Loctite, Inc.; Loctite Corporation Automotive and Consumer Group; Loctite Luminescent Systems, Inc.; Loctite Vsi, Inc.

Further Reading:

Butterworth, Kenneth W., *The Loctite Story,* New York: The Newcomen Society of the United States, 1988.
Cowan, Alison Leigh, "A Family's Odd Bid to Cash Out," *New York Times,* May 26, 1991.
Giragosian, Newman H., *Successful Product & Business Development,* New York, Marcel Dekker, Inc., 1978.

Grant, Ellsworth S., *Drop by Drop: The Loctite Story,* Hartford, Connecticut, Loctite Corporation, 1983.

Hulstein, Calvin, "Assembling with Anaerobics," *Chemtech,* October, 1980. "Loctite Corporation: Diversification Distances It from Cyclical Woes," *Barron's,* October 3, 1988.

"Loctite Corporation Reports 8 Percent Earnings Gains for December Quarter and for 1992," *Barron's,* February 1, 1993.

"Loctite Heirs Plan to Sell a Stake," *New York Times,* March 21, 1991.

McClenahen, John S., "Robert Krieble's Capitalist Crusade," *Industry Week,* April 6, 1992.

"Why Ignore 95% of the World's Market: Loctite Thinks Globally, Profits Locally," *Business Week,* October 23, 1992.

—John A. Sarich

Longview Fibre Company

P.O. Box 639
Longview, Washington 98632
U.S.A.
(206) 425-1550
Fax: (206) 425-3116

Public Company
Incorporated: 1927
Employees: 3,450
Sales: $6.9 billion
Stock Exchanges: New York
SICs: 0811 Timber Tracts; 2411 Logging; 2421 Lumber
    Mills; 2611 Pulp Mills; 2621 Paper Mills; 2631
    Paperboard Mills; 2653 Corrugated & Solid Fiber Boxes;
    2674 Merchandise and Grocery Bags

An owner and operator of tree farms in Oregon and Washington, Longview Fibre Company produces logs for sale as well as for a range of paper and containerboard products. Because of its size and versatility, Longview has accessed many niche markets. The company's Longview, Washington, pulp and paper mill encompasses a 350-acre site producing 2,600 tons of paper products daily, making Longview one of the largest manufacturers of packaging. The company also operates one sawmill and holds 14 converting plants throughout the United States that produce corrugated and solid fiber containers, merchandise and grocery bags.

Longview Fibre Company was first conceived in the mind of Monroe Wertheimer of Thilmany Pulp and Paper Company, based in Wisconsin. Wertheimer had noted the waste wood being produced by a new sawmill overseen by the now defunct Long-Bell Lumber Company. The idea was to utilize that waste wood at a paper mill in Longview, Washington. The first concern was whether or not the wood produced by the Northwestern sawmill—which came from Douglas fir trees—would make suitable paper. After experimenting in Wisconsin with wood shipped from Longview, Wertheimer collected a group of investors and launched the new paper mill. Elected as president was H. L. Wollenberg, formerly an oil company executive. Wertheimer's son, R. S. Wertheimer, became Longview Fibre's vice-president and resident manager. Wertheimers and Wollenbergs remain among the company's directors and corporate officers.

Longview's beginning sparked the company's tradition for utilizing waste wood fiber. Wood from the douglas fir tree, a dominant species in the Northwest, was formerly wasted; it had been burned before Longview decided to utilize its wood chips in the production of kraft paper. The method was a cornerstone on which Longview Fibre was built, and it continued into the 1990s. Longview was also the first to utilize sawdust in the manufacture of paper.

Once arrangements were made with Long-Bell to provide a plant site, waste wood, steam, and electricity, all the newly formed Longview Fibre Company needed was a pulp mill and a containerboard machine, which were constructed within a year. When Longview Fibre first opened its doors in 1927, there was one containerboard machine and 300 committed employees. The company's goal was to produce high-quality paper products. The total output at that time was 100 tons per day.

A second paper machine was up and running by 1928. The following year, Longview acquired General Fibre Box Company, which had a large container plant in Springfield, Massachusetts. Despite the financial difficulties of the Great Depression, earnings throughout the 1930s were good enough for Longview to expand considerably. In 1933 a third paper machine was installed at the Longview mill. Also during the 1930s, the first electrostatic precipitators were installed in Longview's recovery furnaces to enhance air emission control. Longview's box plants were enlarged in 1934. Then a fourth paper machine was purchased, followed by the fifth machine in 1941. By 1948 a newly constructed container plant in Los Angeles began operations. Another newly built plant was opened in Oakland in 1950 and has been in operation since.

At the same time that the company was expanding its production capacities, it was acquiring timberlands. Its first purchase was in 1941, and through the years a number of acquisitions of small parcels of timberlands in Oregon and Washington grew into the 525,000 acres Longview owned by the early 1990s. The lands were purchased because the company recognized the importance of having its own timber supply. Timberlands provide the company with a wood supply for its own use in making paper should there ever be an extreme wood fiber shortage, a condition that began to appear alongside of environmental pressures that surfaced in the late 1980s. The majority of Longview's timberlands are in Oregon. They are managed for timber harvest and the logs are sold to independent solid-wood products manufacturers. Since 1951 the company has engaged in a full-scale, sustained-yield forest management program. They grow the trees, practice forestry, harvest the trees, and market the logs. Longview has a professional forest management staff that manages tree farms and hires contractors to do harvesting, road construction and other forestry work.

A sixth paper machine was installed at the Longview mill in 1951. Business was profitable enough for the Los Angeles and Oakland, California, plants to double their capacity in 1955, in an effort to keep pace with growth on the Pacific coast. Longview took a leading role around that time of converting wooden boxes—used for such things as transporting fruits and vegetables—to fiber or paperboard boxes. This conversion brought so much business to Longview that they built a new container plant in Seattle, Washington, in 1955. The following year a seventh paper machine was helping the Longview mill meet demands. Whenever a paper machine was added to the equipment fold, it required other additions as well, such as pulp machines and recovery equipment. These were all signs of growth.

Longview Fibre acquired Downing Box Company in 1960. Downing produced both corrugated and solid-fiber boxes and added four plants to the Longview fold. The plants were in Milwaukee, Wisconsin; Minneapolis, Minnesota; and Cedar Rapids, Iowa. That same year, the company started running its eighth paper machine. In 1961, the ninth was added. A new container plant near Minneapolis was constructed from scratch in 1963, in order to serve the Twin Cities area. In 1966 Longview Fiber acquired Waltham Bag Company, a producer of grocery bags out of a Massachusetts-based factory and owner of warehouses in other locations in the East. A tenth paper machine was put into operation that year, and another newly constructed container plant was completed in Amsterdam, New York, in 1967.

The industry was in flux during the 1970s. Whiles sales dipped and energy costs soared, many companies concentrated on investing in updating existent equipment. Longview pursued the development of its profitable converted products business and continued its capital investment programs. During this time, two more container operations were built, one in Yakima, Washington, and another in Twin Falls, Idaho. And another paper machine was added to the Longview mill in 1974. The economic slump of the late 1970s impacted Longview in much the same way that the economic downturn of the late 1980s would: depressed purchases—such as fewer appliance sales—meant fewer boxes sold. In addition, the housing slump hurt lumber sales.

In 1980 Longview suffered its worst earnings drop—a staggering 97 percent plunge after 53 years in business. Not only was the company suffering from the housing slump that was pummeling the entire lumber industry, but Longview was hit doubly hard because it was then buying wood chips from independent lumber mills in order to make paper. The independent mills were down because of the collapsed housing market; the price of wood chips more than doubled in a few months time, from $60 per ton to $130. Fluctuations in the lumber business had always been balanced for Longview by its paper business, especially since most of its paper business was in grocery bags and containers, a fairly recession-proof market. With the severe crunch in the late 1970s and early 1980s, Longview was in a bind: it had to meet its paper commitments despite the pounding it would take on wood chip prices.

Another contributor to that year's dip in earnings was the Mt. St. Helens eruption; the resultant pollution obliged Longview to purchase a water clarifier it had not previously needed. This was added to $6 million worth of other unanticipated repair bills that year. Financially conservative like his father, Longview President Dick Wollenberg invested approximately $35 million back into the company's paper business. This included $5 million for two new chipping plants so Longview could reduce its dependency on outsiders. This would prevent a repeat of the painful month of April Longview had in 1980, when the company was forced to shut down its paper mill for two weeks because of a shortage of chips. The overall strategy was to focus more on

high-margin items such as bleached papers and lighter-weight papers. Despite paper-making being a highly capital-intensive business, it had long been a profitable one for Longview Fibre.

Over the next two years, many modifications were made in Longview Fibre's paper machine, pulping, power, and recovery areas in order to save on energy costs and increase efficiency. This was part of the company's overall upgrading. Energy costs are substantial in an operation the size of Longview's. Still, the continuing recession rocked the industry. The price of 1,000 board-feet of logs dropped nearly 28 percent in 1982 from its high in 1979. By 1984 Longview's margins on logs was only 23 percent.

Longview continued its capital improvements agenda, investing close to $100 million in its pulp and paper mill and converting plants by 1987. This translated into gains in output and quality; reduction in energy costs; and improved product mix and mill utilization. Fourteen converting plants were at work making corrugated and solid-fiber shipping containers and paper bags in Washington, California, Idaho, Minnesota, Wisconsin, Illinois, Iowa, and Massachusetts, while Longview's primary paper grew to maximum capacity. Longview also acquired a site for a box plant in Spanish Fork, Utah, and closed down an unprofitable bag plant in Kansas City.

Prices rose on all four of Longview Fibre's product lines in 1987, as domestic and export markets revived. In 1986 about 40 percent of the company's timber production was sold in Japan, China, and Hong Kong. The company-owned 487,000 acres of tree farms looked well poised to profit from a decline in competition from Canada and the South, as well as from government-owned timber in the Northwest.

More expansion projects were announced in 1988, including a twelfth paper machine to produce lightweight bag and specialty kraft paper grades and a new recycling plant to process old corrugated containers and new kraft clippings. Between 1983 and 1988, improvements had been made on every paper machine at the Longview mill, greatly increasing production rates. Other changes alongside the mill modernization program was Longview's handling of raw material. Whereas previously close to 90 percent of the company's materials arrived by rail, by 1989 truck dumps had been rebuilt to accommodate larger rigs, and 274 trucks, 4 barges and 60 railcars were handled daily. Also in 1989, the company built a new used-box recycling plant. It has since been expanded twice and reuses boxes from the Midwest and the Pacific Northwest. The used-box recycling plant, recognized as state-of-the-art in its field, reflected the growing public demand for recycled fibers, but was also built, according to Longview, because of reduced wood supply brought about by environmental pressures—particularly the issue of the northern spotted owl—in the timberlands.

The northern spotted owl, threatened with extinction, has a native habitat in the Pacific Northwest. To protect the bird, restrictions were placed on harvesting and foresting within its habitat circles. That habitat encompassed private as well as public lands, and restrictions impacted the industry. A wood shortage due to reduced harvesting drove up the price of wood chips—they more than doubled between 1990 and 1993—in the Pacific Northwest, and owl protection restricted Longview's managing of its timberlands. Longview was still buying nearly half of its wood chip supply from independent saw mills in 1993, and as the major wood source for independent mills was federal forests, costs soared. The best use for timber is not to grind up entire trees for making paper, but to use the residual from trees cut for lumber.

The Pacific Northwest had been in the center of the spotted owl/ ancient tree controversy and also the worldwide dioxin/water quality controversy, which came to a full boil in the early 1990s. While the world was overcutting forests from Scandinavia and Canada to Africa and South America, demand for tree products kept growing, particularly in foreign markets. The forest-rich Pacific Northwest became a prime base for export, which intensified the struggle for its preservation. Longview was considered the most conservative of loggers in the region; in fact, it was said to be the only lumber company in the region that could accelerate its timber harvesting. Profits in all product lines inched upward as the battles raged on. The spotted owl issue became a point of war between the lumber industry and environmentalists, and with the change of administration in 1993, the shift of focus in Washington, D.C., went from industry to environment.

Meanwhile, Longview Fibre's healthy cash flow brought about talk of leveraged takeovers and, by the spring of 1990, the Robert Bass Group owned 8 percent of Longview. Just over a quarter of the company was owned by officers, directors, descendants of the company's founding families, and employees. While log prices improved somewhat, prices for wood chips remained high and earnings low. Takeover rumors peaked, then calmed when the Bass Group lowered its stake in the company to less than 5 percent. In the summer of 1990, a strike was averted when pulp mill workers approved a new four-year contract that had been in dispute. That same year, the company's twelfth paper machine started producing lightweight paper.

Fire weather caused some concern in 1992, when a long west coast drought threatened to limit log production. Nonetheless, Longview Fibre officials said demand and prices were strong in the log market. Prices for paper and paperboard products declined during that same time. While earnings improved by 93 percent in 1992, the mill production was still down due to lagging paper markets and industry over-capacity. In 1992 Longview Fibre started the first ever solid wood products mill; the central Washington mill utilizes very small logs and includes special equipment from Finland. The mill produces dimension lumber and timbers in both standard and metric sizes for markets at home and abroad. Meanwhile, Longview Fibre Company's main pulp and paper mill maintained a daily production capacity of 3,000 tons, in addition to three container divisions and bag plants. Its size and longevity in a changing industry have attested to the company's adaptability.

Principal Subsidiaries: Longfibre Limited; Longtimber Company of Oregon.

Further Reading:

"Bass Group Cuts Stake in Longview," *New York Times,* November 2, 1990, p. D4.
"Box Plants Learn Ink is the Key Link," *Paperboard Packaging,* November 1986, p. 32.
Denne, Lorianne, "Longview Fibre Gears Up For a Fight," *Puget Sound Business,* January 29, 1990, p. 14.
Drapeau, Jacques, "Longview Fibre Lowers Steam Use by Reducing PV Air Temperatures," *Pulp & Paper,* September 1983, pp. 167–169.
Ducey, Michael, "Longview Fibre Modernization Plan Shifts to Pulp Mill, Recovery Block," *Pulp & Paper,* July 1989, pp. 96–97.
Guide, Robert, "Mill-Wide Process Changes Reduce Energy Use at Longview Fibre," *Pulp & Paper,* March 1982, pp. 114–116.
Harris, William, "Catch-22," *Forbes,* September 14, 1981, p. 214.
"Long Longview," *Barron's,* December 10, 1990, p. 44.
"The Long View on Longview," *Forbes,* March 5, 1990, p. 176.
"Longview Fibre Co.," *Business Journal-Portland,* July 30, 1990, p. S33.
"Longview Fibre Co.," *Insiders' Chronicle,* August 20, 1990, p. S37.
"Longview Fibre Co.," *Wall Street Journal,* August 20, 1992, p. B4.
Maturi, Richard, "Logging Profits," *Barron's,* June 22, 1987, p. 56.
Shortt, Lee, "Condensate Treatment Program at Longview Fibre Reduces Corrosion," *Pulp & Paper,* September 1986, p. 166.
Wilma, D. D., "Press Rebuild Improves Mullen, Output of Linerboard Machines," *Pulp & Paper,* February 1982, pp. 57–58.
"Woodsman's Song," *Forbes,* April 6, 1987, p. 194.

—Carol I. Keeley

Loral Corporation

600 3rd Ave.
New York NY 10016-2485
U.S.A.
(212) 697-1105
Fax: (212) 661-8988

Public Company
Incorporated: 1948 as Loral Electronics Corp.
Employees: 22,000
Sales: $2.88 billion
Stock Exchanges: Boston Midwest New York Pacific
   Philadelphia
SICs: 3812 Search & Navigation Equipment; 3699 Electrical
   Equipment & Supplies not elsewhere classified; Computer
   Peripheral Equipment not elsewhere classified; 3571
   Electronic Computers; 7372 Prepackaged Software; 3663
   Radio & Television Communications Equipment

Loral is one of the largest electronic warfare companies in the
world. It specializes in radar and infrared detection equipment,
and is also involved in satellite communications. Loral Electronics Corp. was founded in 1948 in New York by William
Lorenz and Leon Alpert, who combined the first syllables of
their last names to create the name of their company. Radar and
sonar detection methods played an important role during World
War II, and the young firm concentrated its efforts in this area,
winning contracts for advanced airborne radar systems and
U.S. Navy navigation computing. In 1959, with a series of U.S.
military contracts under its belt, Loral went public, offering
250,000 shares at $12 each. It used the proceeds to build and
equip a new building at its Bronx, New York, headquarters. It
also bought Willor Manufacturing Corp., which made stamped
metal parts, and the electronic equipment-leasing arm of Allor
Leasing Corp.

In 1961 Loral formed a division for developing communications, telemetry, and space navigation systems for satellites. It
also bought American Beryllium Co. Inc. of Sarasota, Florida,
for 95,840 shares of stock. American Beryllium was one of the
largest precision machiners of beryllium, a lightweight, toxic
material that could withstand harsh environments. Under Loral
it became a contract manufacturer of components for aerospace
guidance systems and nuclear reactors. Loral also bought Arco
Electronics in 1961, through a stock trade, and in 1963 acquired

A&M Instrument Co., Circle Plastics, and Lerner Plastics, a
manufacturer of packaging for prescription medicines and other
products. To help pay for this expansion, Loral took a $15
million loan from Massachusetts Mutual Life Insurance Co. in
1965.

Loral won a $3.9 million Navy contract for doppler navigation
radar in 1965, and in 1969, a $14 million contract from General
Dynamics for advanced electronics for the Air Force F-111 and
a $3.9 million contract for airborne countermeasures for the
RF4C plane. By the late 1960s, Loral specialized in radar
receivers, which identified the signatures of enemy radar systems on missiles and anti-aircraft guns, separating them from
the numerous nonthreatening signals also present.

Despite its contract successes, Loral's buying spree was hurting
the company by the late 1960s. Most of its acquisitions were
unprofitable and unrelated to Loral's primary business. It gained
the reputation of being a company with good engineers and bad
management. Loral lost $3 million in 1971. It could not make its
loan payments and was on the ropes. Lorenz and Alpert were
ready to sell half their interest, when Robert Hodes, a Loral
director, helped bring in troubleshooter Bernard Schwartz to
turn the company around.

Alpert and Lorenz resigned from Loral's board and management in 1972, and Schwartz became president and chief executive officer with a $2 million investment that brought him about
11 percent of the company. Schwartz was a former accountant
who had helped turn around a packaging materials business run
by his brother during the mid-1960s. In 1968 he became the
chief strategist in the diversification of Leasco, a computer
leasing company.

Schwartz reduced Loral's costs through measures like reducing
security at the firm's South Bronx plant. To make certain he
understood what his engineers were doing, Schwartz secretly
hired a Columbia University Ph.D. candidate to give him lessons in advanced electronics, realizing that in order to grow, the
firm needed to move from simply building components to building entire electronic-warfare systems. To help win and keep
talented engineers, he began offering stock options. This move
helped bring Frank Lanza, a vice president of the Dalmo Victor
division of Textron, to Loral, where he became executive vice
president and engineering chief.

Schwartz renegotiated the firm's loans and quickly sold many
of Loral's money-losing acquisitions, concentrating on getting
the firm's government contracts back on schedule and within
cost. An important project to design a computerized display
system for a Lockheed-built U.S. Navy plane was running badly
behind schedule, so Schwartz flew to California to meet with
Lockheed officials. He convinced them that Loral could finish
the job and got their backing for the firm's bid to produce the
components.

By late 1973, with the firm's work back on schedule, Loral
began looking for ways to expand its markets. An important
early victory was the contract to develop the radar-warning
receiver for the U.S. Air Force's F-15 fighter plane. To counter
NATO warning receivers, the Soviet Union constantly shifted
its radar signals, meaning that NATO planes had to have their
receivers taken out and rewired to detect the new signals. Loral

proposed a system that used computer tape to reprogram the microcomputers in the warning receivers. This could be done in 20 minutes rather than the days or weeks required for rewiring. Actually putting this system into practice took Loral over four years and required an investment of $2 million beyond the $20 million invested by the U.S. government. Loral's system proved successful, and by 1980 had resulted in $400 million in orders.

Electronic warfare gear had been low on lists of defense priorities, but the 1973 Yom Kippur war changed that. Egypt used Soviet radar-guided weapons to shoot down 100 Israeli planes in one week. Israel's American-made fighters did not have the equipment to detect and jam the radar frequencies used by the missiles, which caused NATO countries to increase electronic warfare spending 600 percent over the next seven years. In 1974, Loral began buying again, and, for $4.5 million, purchased Conic, a maker of missile-tracking systems and microwave communications equipment. Conic, which had profits of $1.1 million in 1973, provided Loral the means to lessen its dependence on government contracts.

Another success was a $4.8 million, 1975 deal with the Belgian air force for an integrated radar system. Loral had no international experience and had never built the tracking and jamming equipment required for an integrated system. However, no single company built all these components, so Loral decided to go after the contract, though it faced competition from bigger firms like ITT and Sanders Associates. To increase Loral's chances of winning the contract, Schwartz signed an agreement with MBLE, one of Belgium's biggest electronics houses, that arranged for MBLE to produce part of the system if Loral won the contract. It did. The victory simultaneously made Loral a full supplier of electronic warfare gear and put it on the map of NATO weapons suppliers.

The radar system's deadlines were so tight that Loral was only able to meet them by investing so much effort that it lost money on the deal. However, Loral executives believed that Belgium would later expand the contract. It did so in 1979, bringing Loral a further $75 million. Other countries soon expressed interest in buying the system. In the late 1970s Loral sold electronic surveillance systems worth about $200 million to Canada, Britain, and West Germany. In each case Loral agreed to share the production with companies of the purchasing countries to help seal the contract.

In 1979 Loral acquired Frequency Sources Inc. through a stock trade. Frequency, which made smaller components for electronic warfare and telecommunications systems, had about $27 million in sales. By the end of the decade, Loral was the largest electronic warfare company in the United States.

Loral's successes led to a significant rise in the price of its stock. As a result, the firm was able to raise $58 million in a January 1980 stock offering. The money was used to make acquisitions and pay for a new $25 million electronics headquarters in Yonkers, New York, intended to help the firm attract talented engineers.

The electronic warfare market continued to grow during the 1980s, the result, in large measure, of a defense buildup fueled by the Reagan administration's Cold War policies, and by the Falklands War, during which a $200,000 missile severely damaged a $50 million battle cruiser. Loral made equipment for virtually every electronic warfare system in the U.S. military, including new airborne warning systems. Even so, Loral became the number two electronic warfare company (though by far the most profitable) when Dallas-based E-Systems surpassed its $197 million in electronic warfare sales. In 1981 Loral had total sales of $255 million, with profits of $24 million and an order backlog of $346 million. The reprogrammable radar receiver for the F-15 had become a top-selling product, with 750 sets delivered by 1982 and the likelihood of at least 250 more. The integrated system originally designed for Belgium had been bought by Israel as well. The U.S. government had passed over it, however, in favor of a nonintegrated system developed by ITT, Westinghouse, and Itek.

Loral did well partly because it put much of its resources into improving products before customers were even ready for the improvements. This led to it meeting or exceeding reliability requirements. Identifying problems early—before they had a chance to mushroom—also brought projects in on schedule and without cost overruns. Because many problems came from subcontractors, Loral frequently sent its own personnel out to review the subcontractors' operations in progress.

Loral's nondefense businesses were also doing well. Its $15 million plastic packaging business was as profitable as its electronic warfare unit, and its $30 million telecommunications business was growing again by 1982 after two slow years. Nevertheless, defense was the firm's major priority, and in 1986 it sold the packaging division to its president while trying to purchase Sanders Associates, which was for sale. Lockheed's bid of $1.18 billion beat out Loral's $980 million offer, but Loral made a major acquisition the following year when it bought Goodyear Aerospace Corp. from Goodyear Tire & Rubber for $588 million. Loral and Goodyear Aerospace already supplied electronics for some of the same military hardware, so integration was expected to be fairly easy.

In 1989 Loral bought the electro-optic division of Honeywell for $58 million. The division, which specialized in guidance systems, had been for sale for a number of years, and many industry analysts felt that Loral had gotten a good price, given the division's annual sales of $130 million. The same year Loral sold the aircraft braking and engineered fabrics divisions of Goodyear Aerospace for $455 million. The buyer was a group headed by Schwartz and included Manufacturers Hanover and Shearson Lehman. The deal raised a few eyebrows and led to a number of lawsuits, though few felt the price was unfair.

Loral's experience with guidance systems helped it become a leader in flight simulation and training, and in 1989, it won a Special Operations Force training and rehearsal contract worth up to $2 billion over the next 15 years.

Loral won a major contract to supply U.S. Air Force F-16 fighters with radar warning systems in 1989. However, after a complaint from competitor Litton Industries, the U.S. General Accounting Office found that Loral had improperly acquired information on Litton's system. Loral pleaded guilty to three charges and the government awarded a bigger share of the contract to Litton. As a result, Loral took a $10.5 million charge against earnings. Still, profits reached $87.6 million in 1989 on sales of $1.187 billion.

With the Cold War over and analysts predicting that defense expenditures would decrease dramatically, many defense companies began downsizing and selling defense-related divisions. Loral, however, felt that regional and tribal conflicts would replace the superpower standoff. It therefore maintained its commitment to defense and looked for bargains offered by other corporations.

In July 1990, Loral bought 51.5 percent of Ford Aerospace for $715 million, a purchase that virtually doubled the size of Loral. Ford Aerospace had $1.8 billion in sales and $120 million in profits in 1989. Its primary focus was the building of commercial and military satellites, an area in which Loral had previously been involved only as a supplier of components and subsystems. The purchase strained Loral's finances, and it quickly sold off parts of the company, recouping about 40 percent of the purchase price.

Some industry observers considered Loral's move risky. However, when the showdown leading to the Persian Gulf war began a few months later, electronic warfare played an important role during the hostilities. The Tomahawk missiles used in the initial attack on Iraq used Loral computer guidance systems and received much praise for their accuracy during the war. (Postwar analysis, however, muddied the picture somewhat.)

In 1991 Loral sold 49 percent of Space Systems/Loral to three European aeronautics firms for $182 million. In 1992 the firm bought 90 percent of LTV's aerospace and missile division for $261 million. Loral won a $202 million contract to supply the

U.S. Army with a new anti-tank missile, a $71 million Air Force contract for REACT missile launch control centers and a $141 million contract to maintain tethered aerostar radar systems for the Air Force. Loral also worked on its civilian businesses, notably becoming a partner in a mobile phone services company called Loral Qualcomm Satellite Services.

As the mid-1990s approached, Loral was an increasingly strong defense company, though it was trying to diversify into civilian telecommunications markets through its work on medical diagnostic imaging and computer-related information management. The company was nevertheless in the process of completing a three-year layoff of 5,800 employees. Although the layoff cut costs, it resulted in $49 million in severance payment expenses.

Principal Subsidiaries: Loral Electro-Optical Systems; Loral American Beryllium; Loral Conic; Loral International; Loral Randtron Systems; Loral Rolm Mil-Spec Computers; Loral Space Information Systems; Loral Systems Company; Loral Systems Manufacturing Company; Space Systems/Loral.

Further Reading:

Alster, Norm, "Thank You, Saddam," *Forbes,* October 15, 1990, pp. 81–85.
Annual Report, 1992, New York: Loral, 1992.
Chakravarty, Subrata, "Concept Reborn," *Forbes*, June 21, 1982, pp. 84–86.
Kraar, Louis, "The Brooklyn Boy Who Debugged Loral," *Fortune,* June 16, 1980, pp. 102–111.
"Loral Corp., Defense Supplier, Aims for Advance in Sales, Net," *Barron's,* March 17, 1975.

—Scott M. Lewis

L'Oréal

41, rue Martre
92117 Clichy
France
(1) 47 56 83 68
Fax: (1) 47 56 86 42

Public Company
Incorporated: 1939
Employees: 27,600
Sales: FFr 4.23 billion (US$7.17 billion)
Stock Exchange: Paris
SICs: 2844 Toilet Preparations; 3353 Aluminum Sheet, Plate
& Foil; 2657 Folding Paperboard Boxes; 2099 Food
Products Nec

L'Oréal, one of the largest companies in France, is the world's largest manufacturer of high-quality cosmetics and perfumes, producing such well-known brands as Lancôme, Ambre Solaire, and Cacharel. Its total sales are $2.4 billion ahead of those of its closest competitor, Unilever, and more than double those of Revlon and Shiseido. It boasts a world-wide distribution network as well as the industry's highest research-and-development budget and the largest cosmetological laboratories in the world.

L'Oréal's story begins in turn-of-the-century Paris, at a time when women of the demi-monde dyed their hair, their choice restricted to fiery red or coal black. In 1907, Eugène Schueller, a young chemist, began to concoct the first synthetic hair dyes by night in his kitchen and sell them to hair salons in the morning under the brand name of Auréole. His strategy was successful; within two years he established the Société Française des Teintures Inoffensives pour Cheveux, which soon afterward became L'Oréal.

In 1912, the company extended its sales to Austria, Holland and Italy and by 1920 its products were available in a total of 17 countries, including the United States, Brazil, Chile, Peru, Equador, Bolivia, and the Soviet Union, and in the Far East. At this stage, L'Oréal consisted of three research chemists and ten sales representatives.

Schueller's timing had been singularly fortunate. The end of World War I was celebrated by the Jazz Age, when short hairstyles became fashionable, with a new emphasis on shape and color. By the end of the 1920s, there were 40,000 hair salons in France alone and L'Oréal's new products O'Cap, Imédia Liquide, and Coloral captured the growing market. In 1928 the company made its first move toward diversification, purchasing the soap company Monsavon.

In the 1930s and 1940s, platinum-haired screen idols such as Jean Harlow and Mae West made blond hair especially popular and bleaches such as L'Oréal Blanc sold well. L'Oréal was quick to make use of both old and new media to promote its products. In 1933, Schueller commissioned famous artists of the time to design posters and also launched his own women's magazine, *Votre Beauté*. Dop, the first mass-market shampoo, was promoted through children's hair-lathering competitions at the highly popular French circuses and by 1938 L'Oréal was advertising its hair products with radio jingles.

During this period L'Oréal demonstrated its ability to meet new consumer demands. When the Front Populaire won the 1936 elections and introduced the first paid holidays for French workers, L'Oréal's Ambre Solaire was ready to capture the new market for suntan lotions. Meanwhile the company's sales network was expanding on both a national and an international scale. Products began to be sold through pharmacies and perfumers and new Italian, Belgian, and Danish subsidiaries were established between 1936 and 1937.

Even the outbreak of World War II in 1939 failed to curb the company's growth. At a time of strict rationing, women permed their hair and bought cosmetics to boost their morale. L'Oréal launched the first cold permanent wave product, Oréol, in 1945. At the same time the company continued to expand; by the end of the war there were 25 research chemists and distribution had been extended to the United Kingdom, Argentina, and Algeria.

During this period, François Dalle and Charles Zviak joined the group, both recruited by Monsavon at a time when the cosmetics industry held far less attraction for graduate chemical engineers than the atomic-energy or oil industries. Both men would play an important role in the company's future; by 1948, Dalle had already been appointed joint general manager of L'Oréal.

The consumer boom of the 1950s and the arrival of new blond screen idols Marilyn Monroe and Brigitte Bardot (originally a brunette) meant further expansion for L'Oréal. By 1950, a research-and-development team of 100 chemists had created further innovative products, including the first lightening tint, Imédia D, introduced in 1951, and the first coloring shampoo, Colorelle, introduced in 1955, which answered an increasing demand for subtlety. The company advanced further into the field of skin care, entering into technological agreements with the company Vichy, in 1954. Vichy was to become part of the L'Oréal group in 1980.

Eugène Schueller's promotional talents were recognized in 1953 when he was awarded an advertizing Oscar. Schueller died in 1957 and François Dalle took over as chairman and CEO at 39 years of age.

The 1960s were years of revolution, both cultural and commercial. As music and fashion became increasingly teen-oriented, there was a growing interest in conserving—or simulating—youthful looks. At the same time hundreds of new boutiques, supermarkets, and chain stores sprang up to supply this rapidly growing market. L'Oréal made a growing commitment to capital investment. In 1960 a new research-and-production center was established in Aulnay-sous-Bois, bringing the number of research staff up to 300. In 1963 and 1964 the company opened new cosmetological and bacteriological facilities, evidence of a highly scientific approach to skin care. Another production unit, Soprocos, opened in St. Quentin in 1965, and over the decade new distribution outlets were established in Uruguay, Algeria, Canada, Mexico, and Peru. L'Oréal was listed on the French stock exchange in 1963, during a period of restructuring within the group. In 1962, owing to the boom in hair-product sales, L'Oréal sold Monsavon in order to concentrate on its core business. At the same time it bought the hair-hygiene specialist Cadoricin. In 1964 L'Oréal bought Jacques Fath perfumes and a year later Lancôme, thereby gaining a significant entry into the high-quality skin-care, make-up, and perfume market and gaining increased access to perfumery outlets. Garnier, a hair-product company, and Laboratoires d'Anglas were also added to the group. In 1968 the company took major stakes in Golden in the United Kingdom and in Ruby, a personal hygiene and household products manufacturer. In the same year, L'Oréal bought the fashion and perfumes house, André Courrèges.

With increased resources and expertise, L'Oréal launched a number of successful products, many of which are market leaders to this day. These included the hair spray Elnett, Récital hair dyes, and the perfume Fidji. Fidji was launched under the Guy Laroche brand name.

In 1969, L'Oréal recruited a young Welshman, Lindsay Owen-Jones, from the prestigious Fontainebleau business school INSEAD. An Oxford languages graduate, he would go on to become the fourth chairman and managing director of L'Oréal. At the age of 25 he became general manager of L'Oréal's public-products division in Belgium and turned around unprofitable subsidiaries in France and Italy, before going to the United States to take charge of L'Oréal's distributor, Cosmair Inc., in 1980.

L'Oréal benefited from the emphasis on health and fitness in the 1970s. From this time onwards, L'Oréal's earnings outstripped those of any other French blue chip and grew twice as fast as the cosmetics-industry average. L'Oréal's success permitted further commitment to research and development; the number of research staff rose from 500 in 1970 to 750 in 1974. New production facilities were opened in France and in 1979 the International Centre for Dermatological Research was established at Sofia-Antipolis, in the South of France, for the treatment of skin disorders and aging.

Over the decade, structural and tactical changes were made within the group, based on the findings of the 1969 management study done by McKinsey & Co. The year 1970 saw the establishment of new operational divisions and management structure. A few years later, the company began to speed up the process of internationalization, with particular emphasis on New Zealand, Australia, Japan, and Hong Kong. In 1976 L'Oréal signed a technical-assistance contract with the Soviet Union.

Expansion into overseas markets—particularly Japan—was aided greatly by the company's new alliance with the Swiss foods giant Nestlé, to whom Eugène Schueller's daughter, Madame Liliane Bettencourt, sold nearly half of her L'Oréal stock in 1974. The two allies established a French holding company, Gesparal, which is 51 percent-owned by Bettencourt and 49 percent-owned by Nestlé. Gesparal controls 72 percent of L'Oréal's voting rights. Bettencourt is the largest individual shareholder of Nestlé, holding roughly five percent.

Throughout the 1970s, L'Oréal continued to make purchases within the cosmetics and hair-care industry: Biotherm in 1970; Gemey, Ricils, and Jeanne Piaubert in 1973; and Roja in 1975. The latter merged with Garnier in 1978. This was also a time for diversification for L'Oréal. In 1973 it took a controlling stake of 53.4 percent in the pharmaceutical company Synthélabo, a specialist in the production of cardiovascular drugs and hospital materials, followed in 1979 by the purchase of Metabio-Joullie, manufacturer of aspirins, over-the-counter drugs, veterinary, cosmetic, and dietary items. Metabio-Joullie and Synthélabo were merged in 1980 under the latter's name. In 1977 L'Oréal ventured into another complementary field, magazine publishing, taking stakes in Marie-Claire Album and Interedi-Cosmopolitan.

Meanwhile in the new division Parfums et Beauté International, several of L'Oréal's most successful products were launched—Vichy's moisturizer Equalia and the Cacharel perfume Anaïs Anaïs, now reckoned to be the world's best-selling perfume. In addition, the well-known Kérastase hair products were redesigned.

The 1980s were particularly favorable for L'Oréal. François Dalle won the post of first vice president on Nestlé's administrative council, the title of Man of the Year in the chemicals and cosmetics sector from the Fragrance Foundation of the United States, and title of Manager of the Year from the *Nouvel Economiste*. In 1984, he gave up the leadership of L'Oréal, although he continued to act as chairman of the group's strategic committee. The position of chairman and CEO went to Charles Zviak. Lindsay Owen-Jones became vice president and Marc Ladreit de Lacharrière, joint vice president, soon to take control of the company's financial policy.

This event was followed by some restructuring within the group; in 1985 the Parfums et Beauté division was split into three departments—Lancôme/Piaubert, perfumes, and active cosmetics—and five geographical areas. At the same time the new management clearly felt it necessary to centralize control of the company's finances, and in 1987 a financial bulletin was issued announcing the creation of L'Oréal Finances, which would implement the financial strategy established approximately ten years before.

In 1986, L'Oréal's shares were distributed to investors outside France for the first time when the company raised FFr 1.4 billion through a one-for-ten rights issue, offering new shares to stockholders. This was followed, in 1987, by a one-for-five stock split.

At this time L'Oréal began to play an increasingly active role in the management of Synthélabo, which, after merging with Metabio-Joullie, had become France's third-largest pharmaceutical company. Synthélabo's research-and-development budget was increased considerably, allowing the company in 1982 to become the first private laboratory to participate in the World Health Organization's project for research and education in neuroscience.

During the 1980s Synthélabo enhanced its international status, setting up joint marketing affiliates in the United States and Britain with the U.S. company G. D. Searle, and establishing joint ventures in Japan with Fujisawa and Mitsubishi Kasei. The company also took controlling stakes in Kramer of Switzerland, in 1982, and LIRCA of Italy in 1983. Nevertheless Synthélabo continued to report poor sales figures, owing to difficulty in updating its product line and unfavorable market conditions in France. L'Oréal subsequently reiterated its commitment to Synthélabo, keeping restructuring to a minimum and increasing its holding from 63 percent to 65 percent after October 1987's Black Monday when the shares fell considerably. L'Oréal saw that the solution to Synthélabo's problems lay in extending its overseas sales, thereby offsetting unfavorable domestic pricing and reimbursement policies. By the end of the decade, profitability had improved and some promising new drugs were ready to be approved for marketing in the 1990s.

Meanwhile, L'Oréal's research-and-development facilities continued their steady growth, with research staff reaching 1,000 by 1984. L'Oréal's enormous commitment to research resulted in the success of products such as Lancôme's Niosôme, launched in 1986, one of the few anti-aging creams found to be effective by independent dermatologists.

If this was the age of high-tech skin care, it was also the era of designer brands; in 1980 a new distribution company, Prestige et Collections, was created for Cacharel, whose perfume Loulou, launched in 1987, went on to become a best seller. In 1984, Nestlé took over Warner Cosmetics of the United States on behalf of L'Oréal's U.S. agent Cosmair, thereby acquiring for the group the prestigious names of Ralph Lauren, Paloma Picasso, and Gloria Vanderbilt. At this stage, however, L'Oréal was interested only in the perfumes and cosmetics divisions of the designer brands. In 1983, the company sold its 49.9 percent stake in the couture house Courrèges to Itokin of Japan, although it retained 100 percent of Courrèges Parfums.

A further addition to the L'Oréal group was the Helena Rubenstein skin-care and cosmetics range. In 1983, L'Oréal began by taking major stakes in Helena Rubenstein's Japanese and South American subsidiaries, the former integrated with Lancôme in the new Japanese affiliate, Parfums et Beauté, in 1984. In 1988, L'Oréal bought Helena Rubenstein Inc., a U.S. company that was in financial difficulties as a result of the sharp drop in sales following the founder's death. It would not be an easy matter to bring the company back into profit. Bought in the same year, Laboratoires Goupil, a dental-care-products manufacturer whose toothpastes held over 90 percent of the French market, was also unprofitable, but it was felt that L'Oréal's skillful marketing could remedy the situation. L'Oréal's last acquisition of the 1980s was the skin-care specialist Laboratoires Roche Posay.

While making acquisitions, L'Oréal also took the opportunity to sell off unwanted components of the group. These included the personal hygiene and comfort products of Laboratoires Ruby d'Anglas and Chiminter, which were felt to be too far outside the group's main area of interest and not in accord with L'Oréal's policy of internationalization.

L'Oréal was keen to diversify into communications. In 1984 the company took a 10 percent stake in the French pay-TV company, Canal Plus, with the stake raised to 10.4 percent in 1986. In 1988, L'Oréal took a 75 percent stake in Paravision International, an organization charged with the creation, production, and distribution of audiovisual products for an international audience. The following year, L'Oréal entered by way of Paravision into a joint venture with the U.S. company Carolco Pictures Inc., to handle foreign television-distribution and programming rights.

In 1988, Lindsay Owen-Jones became the new chairman and chief executive of L'Oréal at the age of 42. Marc Ladreit de Lacharrière became director and executive vice president while Charles Zviak moved on to the chairmanship of Synthélabo. Zviak died the following year, having been one of the few chemists to attain leadership of a major French company. The end of the decade was marked further by rumors of L'Oréal's involvement in a proposed joint takeover bid for the French luxury-goods company Louis Vuitton Moët Hennessy, together with Vuitton's head, Monsieur Racamier, and Paribas/Parfinance. Although the existence of such a plan was denied by L'Oréal, the company joined with Orcofi, a Vuitton-controlled holding company, to buy 95 percent of the perfume and couture house Lanvin.

L'Oréal explained that although Vuitton owned Dior and Givenchy, competitors in the perfume and cosmetics market, L'Oréal had no Vuitton shares and no intention of attacking the company. On the contrary, the Vuitton alliance would give L'Oréal an entrée into the field of luxury goods. Although Lanvin lost money since L'Oréal's acquisition, company officials remained optimistic, declaring that the experience gained from running a luxury boutique is valuable in itself.

In 1991 L'Oréal found itself embroiled in a bitter dispute with Jean Frydman, a former director of Paravision. Frydman—who holds dual Israeli-French citizenship—had filed suit against the company, charging it with "fraudulent behavior and racial discrimination," stemming from the 1989 sale of the Frydman family's 25 percent share of Paravision—L'Oréal's film distribution division—after being pressured by François Dalle. Frydman alleged that L'Oréal violated a 1977 French law prohibiting companies from participating in an Arab boycott against Israel when the company forced his resignation and the sale of the family's stake at an unfair price because of his business ties to Israel. The ensuing investigation created a minor scandal in France by digging up unsavory facts about founder Eugène Schueller's anti-Semitic, fascist politics during World War II. Later that year, however, Frydman dropped the suit in exchange for a letter of apology from Dalle.

The cosmetics industry is still growing, but there is increasing rivalry. While L'Oréal's alliance with Nestlé should protect it from corporate marauders, it is still vulnerable to competition in Western markets from Japanese competitors Shiseido and Kao—although 90 percent of the turnover of both companies come from their home market—and from Unilever, following the latter's takeover of Elizabeth Arden and Fabergé.

In the years following his appointment as chairman and CEO, Owen-Jones set about making L'Oréal a genuinely international company. He began cultivating an integrated international team of top managers, enabling the company to quickly respond to and capitalize on consumer trends worldwide. Owens-Jones also supported greater cooperation between L'Oréal's numerous brand names and divisions. After Lancôme Niosôme was developed in 1986, L'Oréal then translated the new technology into a mass market L'Oréal skin care line sold under the name Plentitude. Plentitude was launched in Europe and Australia in the late 1980s, and within two years of its U.S. launch in 1989, it had captured a 10 percent share of the market.

It was precisely this kind of synergy between subsidiaries, analysts say, that led to L'Oréal's 15 percent overall profit growth in the 1980s. In the boom years of the 1980s, high-end lines such as Lancôme, and Helena Rubenstein performed extremely well. When the prestige market slumped in the early 1990s, such mass market lines as L'Oréal were poised to pick up the slack.

L'Oréal has said that it sees opportunities for further profit growth in the United States, which represents one-third of the world market. Currently, despite having full control of strategy, management, and marketing in this region, L'Oréal reaps only 5.5 percent from the profits of its sole U.S. agent Cosmair Inc. One advantage of this system for L'Oréal has been protection from the weakness of the U.S. dollar and from high marketing costs—Cosmair handles a sales volume of over $1 billion that provides the company with the flexibility to launch new products which can then be transferred to L'Oréal affiliates worldwide. Other markets targeted for expansion include Japan.

L'Oréal was one of the first western companies to set up shop in the former Soviet Union, forming Soreal, a joint-venture with the Russian chemical company Mosbytchim. L'Oréal invested $50 million in the venture to produce approximately 40 million units of deodorant, perfume, shampoos, and hair sprays annually. Soreal products were sold in 1992 at a mere 100 outlets in Moscow and at an additional 10 throughout Russia. Hard currency was difficult to come by as banks either collapsed or were unaccustomed to dealing with Western businesses. In order to obtain the equipment necessary to upgrade production, Soreal created Maroussia, a women's fragrance that was imported to Western Europe in exchange for machinery and materials.

L'Oréal's structure remains unchanged, with the group consisting of a federation of competitive companies, including 147 production and distribution facilities worldwide, divided into five divisions. Only research and development facilities and overall management control are centralized.

There has been speculation as to the fate of L'Oréal when Bettencourt, in her mid-60s in 1990, relinquishes her corporate

involvement. The French government is taking a strong interest in the issue. French government agreements restrict foreigners from taking over French companies before 1994. Should she decide to sell, Nestlé will have first option to purchase.

As consumers became more environmentally aware, L'Oréal fell under increasing pressure to conform to new standards of product safety. The company has been forced to phase out the use of chlorofluorocarbons which are said to be harmful to the ozone layer. L'Oréal has also come under attack from the animal-rights lobby, which accuses the company of subjecting laboratory animals to inhumane tests, although L'Oréal claims that animal testing of new products is down to 5 percent from 50 percent in 1985.

As L'Oréal entered the mid-1990s, the company found itself engaged in a battle with rivals Proctor & Gamble and Unilever for worldwide domination of the mass cosmetic and fragrance markets. L'Oréal seemed determined to remain the leader, hiking its advertising budget by as much as 50 percent for some products, and creating a whole new image for most of its color cosmetics. The company was also reaching out to customers by repackaging its merchandise and making display cases more accessible and user-friendly. L'Oréal also planned to expand into the mass-market fragrance business, introducing at least two new fragrances by 1995. Owen-Jones seemed to have laid the groundwork necessary to support such an expansion, and L'Oréal appeared well prepared to defend its number one position, fortified by a strong research and development base, sharpened marketing skills and a sound balance sheet.

Principal Subsidiaries: Lancôme Parfums et Beauté; Helena Rubenstein Inc.; Parfums et Beauté International et Cie; Cie et Artoisienne de Gestion; Diparco; H.U.P (Germany, 98.6%); Laboratoire Garnier Paris; L'Oréal UK; Soreal (Russia).

Further Reading:

Benjamin, Patricia, "Sitting Pretty," *Business,* January 1987.
Deeny, Godfrey, "L'Oréal Execs Probed by Magistrate for Joining Arab Boycott of Israel," *Women's Wear Daily,* May 15, 1991, p. 27.
Dorn, Pete, "Lindsay Owen-Jones: A World Vision for L'Oréal," *Women's Wear Daily,* October 12, 1990, pp. 10–11.
Echikson, William, "L'Oréal: Aiming at High and Low Markets," *Fortune,* March 22, 1993, p. 89.
Fearnley, Helen, "L'Oréal—Not Just A Pretty Face," *Financial Weekly,* May 5, 1988.
L'Oréal, Paris, France: L'Oréal.
"L'Oréal's Dark Roots," *Time,* July 1, 1991, p. 56.
Raper, Sarah, "Ex-L'Oréal Head Settles Race Bias Case," *Women's Wear Daily,* December 23, 1991, p. 3.
——, "Taking Russia: Tough Times at the Factory," *Women's Wear Daily,* August 7, 1992, p. 4.
Tosh, Mark, "L'Oréal's 1990 Net Rises 15.2%; Sales Gain 11.7%" *Women's Wear Daily,* April 17, 1991, p. 21.

—Jessica Griffin
updated by Maura Troester

M. A. Hanna Company

1301 E. 9th Street
Suite 3600
Cleveland, Ohio 44114-1860
U.S.A.
(216) 589-4000
Fax: (216) 589-4109

Public Company
Incorporated: 1923
Employees: 6,400
Sales: $1.33 billion
Stock Exchanges: New York Midwest
SICs: 2821 Plastics Materials & Resins; 2891 Adhesives &
Sealants; 3087 Custom Compounding of Purchased
Plastics Resins; 2952 Asphalt Felts and Coatings; 3069
Fabricated Rubber Products, Nec; 2865 Cyclic Organic
Crudes and Intermediates and Organic Dyes and Pigments;
5162 Plastic Materials and Basic Forms and Shapes; 1011
Iron Ores

The M. A. Hanna Company is one of the world's top 20
specialty chemicals companies. In the mid-1980s the company
transformed itself from a world-class mining company to an
influential specialty chemicals conglomerate. Hanna manufactures, augments, and markets plastic and rubber compounds,
color and additive concentrates for the plastics industry, and
plastic resins and engineered plastic shapes. Hanna also produces specialty polymer products for the printing, textile, construction, and automotive industries. The company ranks among
Fortune magazine's list of America's 500 largest companies,
with 36 manufacturing facilities and 169 distribution outlets
throughout the world. Throughout the 1990s Hanna hoped to
"build a focused specialty chemicals company capable of delivering superior growth and a premium stock valuation," according to a revised mission statement.

Company namesake Marcus Alonzo Hanna was born in 1837
on his parents' Lisbon, Ohio, farm. His father, Dr. Leonard
Hanna, moved to Cleveland in 1852 after competition from
railroads undermined the family investment in a canal project.
After trying a grocery business, Dr. Hanna joined with his
brother Robert and another investor in a copper and iron trading
venture in the late 1850s. The partners soon expanded operations to include coal mining.

When young "Mark" was expelled from Western Reserve
College for distributing a risque flyer at a student event, he went
to work for his father as a warehouse clerk. Mark worked as a
deckhand and purser on his father's Great Lakes ships, then
joined the Union Army in the Civil War. Dr. Hanna died in 1862
after a long illness, and his minerals trading firm dissolved. At
war's end, Hanna began a courtship with Charlotte Rhodes that
launched the company that would keep his name long after it
passed from his family's hands.

Hanna's future father-in-law, Daniel P. Rhodes, was a rigid
Democrat who initially opposed his daughter's involvement
with Hanna, an active Republican. But when Rhodes' son left
Rhodes & Co. and Hanna made some ill-fated investments,
Hanna joined his father-in-law's pig iron and iron ore business.
Hanna aggressively acquired more mines and diversified Rhodes & Co. into lake steamers, docks, warehouses, and shipbuilding. His entry into Rhodes & Co. coincided with a dramatic expansion of the Midwest's commercial and industrial
influence. The company stimulated this growth at its very
source: it brought coal from Ohio and Pennsylvania to the
shores of Lake Erie to fuel midwestern industries, and shipped
iron ore and pig iron to regional steel factories.

Daniel P. Rhodes died in the 1880s, and Hanna inherited the
conglomerate that by that time included mining, shipping, street
and freight railways, hotels, and a bank. Hanna's brothers,
Howard Melville and Leonard Colton, and a partner, Arnold C.
Saunders, renamed the business M. A. Hanna & Company in
1885.

The new company purchased interests in iron ore, coal mines,
and blast furnaces. Mark Hanna was soon known for his compelling personality, sharp business sense, and energetic bearing.
He became a prominent industrial executive, builder of a shipping line, and owner of Cleveland's opera house. As his business influence grew, he aspired to political power as well.
Hanna purchased the *Cleveland Herald* newspaper to boost
Republican support, and financed the gubernatorial and presidential campaigns of William McKinley. His massive $3.5 mil-
lion campaign contributions earned him the nickname "Red
Boss" ("red" for iron dust and "boss" for his political activities), a U.S. Senate seat, and the rancor of some of the nation's
largest newspapers. Hanna turned the company over to his
brothers in 1896 so that he could chair the National Republican
Committee full time. He was elected U.S. senator in 1897, and
served until his death in 1904.

Howard M. and Leonard C. Hanna continued on with the family
business. Howard would become known as the businessman of
the family, and his son would lead the company in the early 20th
century. Leonard was remembered more for his civic and philanthropic contributions to the city of Cleveland. Marcus
Hanna's corporate legacy would end with son Daniel R., whose
involvement precipitated a leadership crisis at Hanna.

Howard Melville Hanna, Jr., Daniel's cousin, was groomed for
leadership of the family company. When, in 1915, he grew
disgusted with Daniel's playboy lifestyle and apparent lack of
commitment to the business, Howard bought Daniel out of
the Hanna company. Within the next six years, Leonard C.,
Howard, Sr., and cousin Daniel all died, leaving Howard,
Jr., to steer the Hanna ship virtually alone. The abrupt change

in leadership had coincided with lagging earnings, tax hikes, a decline in the coal industry, and lessened demand for iron ore.

George M. Humphrey became Hanna Company's last partner when he invested in the firm in 1922. He had joined the company in 1917 as a legal advisor, and quickly built a promising business and personal relationship with Howard Hanna, Jr. A. C. Saunders continued as a partner until 1922, when the M. A. Hanna Company was incorporated with Matthew Andrews as chairman of the board and Howard M. Hanna, Jr., as president. Humphrey and Hanna used the influx of capital from that first stock offer to encourage growth at the company's profitable divisions, and sold off Hanna's losing divisions. Their work to promote efficiency during the 1920s helped carry M. A. Hanna through the Great Depression profitably.

When chairman Matthew Andrews died in 1929, Howard M. Hanna, Jr., was elected chairman and George M. Humphrey was made president. Humphrey was instrumental in the creation of the National Steel Co. that year. In conjunction with the national trend toward vertical integration, National Steel combined the Great Lakes Steel Co., a sheet steel business in Detroit, with Pittsburgh's Weirton Steel and Hanna's Lake Superior iron ore properties, ships, and lakefront blast furnaces.

The consolidation enabled National Steel to integrate all aspects of the steel business, from raw materials to finished product, in one company. Ernest Weir, of Weirton, served as chairman of the new company, George Fink of Great Lakes Steel was president, and George Humphrey chaired the executive committee. In exchange for its iron ore operations, Hanna received more than one-fourth of National Steel's capital stock, making Hanna the conglomerate's biggest shareholder. Having the most modern plants in the United States on the eve of the Great Depression made National Steel one of the country's most efficient and profitable steel works.

Although the company's primary activities were still concentrated in coal, iron ore, blast furnaces, and lake shipping, they were set off into separate companies with Hanna exchanging its assets for common stock of large affiliates like National Steel Corp., Consolidation Coal Co., and eventually, Hanna Mining Co.

The Hanna company had three primary spheres of operation in the 1930s. The oldest was the ore and lake coal group, which incorporated Hanna's 20 Lake Superior ore mines, a mine in Missouri, and one in New York. National Steel became a "cash cow" for this division of Hanna—it could count on the associated company as a customer in bad times, like the Depression, yet continue to sell to National's competitors as well. The ore and lake division also included the Franklin Steamship Corp., a subsidiary that provided shipping on commission for other companies. In 1945 Franklin Steamship was consolidated with the rest of Hanna's iron ore businesses as Hanna Coal & Ore Corp. Later named Hanna Mining Co., Franklin Steamship would evolve into Hanna's primary business in the 1960s.

Hanna's Susquehanna Colleries division, the company's second sphere of operation, handled the company's anthracite coal assets, which included three Pennsylvania mines with combined capacity of 12,000 tons daily by 1946. And the company's third division concentrated on investments in a wide variety of indus-

tries, including rayon, oil, plastics, copper, tobacco, and banking. The division grew increasingly important in the 1930s and 1940s. Hanna purchased significant interests in: Standard Oil (.3 percent); Seaboard Oil of Delaware (.8 percent); Cleveland's National City Bank (5.1 percent) in 1933; Industrial Rayon Co. (17.2 percent) in 1935; Union Bank of Commerce (8.4 percent) in 1941; Consolidated Natural Gas (.3 percent) in 1943; Durez Plastics & Chemicals (11.6 percent) in 1945; and Pittsburgh Consolidation Coal (37.8 percent), which was formed in 1945.

In 1946 Hanna transferred its stock holdings in Northwestern-Hanna Fuel Co., which operated six coal docks in upper lake ports, and all of its coal mine operations in Ohio, to the Pittsburgh Consolidation Coal Co. for $2.43 million and 325,000 common shares. Hanna retained management of the shipping and mining interests as part of its lake coal business.

The company's sizeable investments entitled it to a voice in the management of many of the companies it financed, and, by the end of World War II, Hanna decided "to concentrate our holdings in a few companies in which we have confidence and then help in every way we can to build those companies into the strongest possible position in their respective fields." M. A. Hanna closed 1946 with $77 million in assets and holdings in some of North America's most important companies. Its own operations were conducting research to make lower grades of Lake Superior ore available, and exploring manganese deposits in Arizona and minerals deposits in South America.

During the 1950s M. A. Hanna evolved through exchanges of stock and property into an investment company, while the Hanna Mining subsidiary concentrated on production and shipping. In 1951 M. A Hanna acquired Canada's Empire Hanna Coal Co., Ltd., and made it into a division. Hanna Mining Co. went public in 1958 and purchased 84,300 class B shares in M. A. Hanna. M. A. Hanna, in turn, owned 46 percent of Hanna Mining. The two companies also shared several board members.

The 1950s also saw Hanna Mining Co. in a controversy over government nickel contracts. As the only nickel miner in America, Hanna Mining produced emergency military stockpiles of the metal between 1953 and 1960. The United States Senate accused Hanna Mining of excessive profit-taking during hearings in the early 1960s, charging that the company made $10 million profit after taxes on an investment of $3.6 million.

In 1961, after Gilbert W. Humphrey (son of George M. Humphrey) had advanced to president and CEO of M. A. Hanna, the company announced plans to dispose of direct business activities. By doing so, M. A. Hanna became the United States' largest closed-end investment company, with assets of about $500 million. As part of the plan, mining, shipping, and dock operations of companies affiliated with M. A. Hanna and the company's substantial investment in Iron Ore Co. of Canada were sold to Hanna Mining Co. M. A. Hanna's anthracite coal properties were sold to a new independent group, Empire Hanna Coal was purchased by outside interests, and Hanna's Great Lakes coal and vessel fueling business was sold to Consolidation Coal Co.

Within just three years, the market value of M. A. Hanna's three principal holdings—National Steel Corp., Consolidation Coal

Co., and Hanna Mining Co.—had grown to $422.9 million. In 1964 Hanna Mining's directors were so confident in the new organization of their company that they proposed a three-for-one stock split and a dividend increase. But in less than a year, the company's fortunes changed, and M. A. Hanna proposed that it be liquidated, leaving Hanna Mining as an autonomous corporation. Hanna Mining purchased one million shares of National Steel from M. A. Hanna and became the operating agent for National Steel iron ore mines and ships. M. A. Hanna sold its bituminous coal properties to Consolidation Coal Co. for $5.5 million.

After the liquidation, Hanna Mining became the focus of the management's worldwide operations. Hanna Mining reported six consecutive years of record high profits. The increases came from flourishing investments in Iron Ore Co. of Canada and National Steel. Overseas mining activities in Australia, Guatemala, and Brazil also contributed to Hanna's prosperity. Hanna enjoyed steadily increasing earnings in the 1970s, when the company entered into joint mining ventures in Liberia, Colombia, Australia, and Brazil, and established a copper mining project in Arizona. Within just one year at the end of the decade, earnings tripled.

The company reached record sales in 1981 of $400 million with $44 million in net income. But Hanna plummeted from that summit in the 1980s, when foreign competitors initiated their devastating assault on the U.S. steel industry. The situation was exacerbated when, in 1981, Canadian financier Conrad Black of Norcen Energy Resources, Ltd., initiated a year-long takeover battle. Black's purchase of a large block of Hanna stock in October 1981 quickly captured the attention of Hanna chairman Robert F. Anderson and other members of the board. After a relatively brief, but heated federal hearing, Black and Hanna made a standstill agreement that gave Black 20 percent of Hanna in exchange for $90 million. Black became a director, and the last descendant of an M. A. Hanna & Company partner, George M. Humphrey II, resigned from his position as senior vice president by 1984.

In 1982 Hanna lost $80 million on $300 million in sales, and was forced to shut down all of its operations (except one Brazilian iron ore mine) for three weeks in December of that year. During that break, the company essentially abandoned its long-held position in mining and began a massive restructuring. Between 1982 and 1986 Hanna racked up more than $320 million in losses, and its roster of employees plunged from 8,000 to 3,500. When Martin Walker became CEO and chairman in 1986, he led the switch from mining to plastics. Between 1980 and 1985 Hanna Mining sold 60 percent of its coal and iron businesses and a batch of preferred stock to finance an acquisition binge that concentrated on distribution and compounding in two fields: construction aggregates and polymers. Soon after, Hanna closed its last U.S. iron mine.

Within less than a year, the company spent half a billion dollars to convert itself from a major mining company to an influential polymer compounder, plastics distributor, and colorants producer. In 1986 the company purchased Burton Rubber Processing; colorants processors Allied Color Industries and Avecor; and Day International, a major processor, distributor, and manufacturer of polymer printing blankets. Hanna also purchased PMS Consolidated, the world's leading plastic colorants pro-

cessor; Colonial Rubber Works, a big compounder; and Cadillac Plastic, the number one distributor of plastic shapes in 1987. The purchases revived Hanna's sales from $130 million in 1986 with a $104 million loss, to $460 million in 1987, and a $37 million net. Hanna surpassed $1 billion in worldwide sales before the decade was out.

In 1990 Hanna acquired leading French plastics colorant producer Synthecolor S.A., a company with an estimated $25 million in annual sales. In 1991 Hanna purchased Seattle plastics distributor FibreChem for $70 million, and hiked its formulated colorants capacity with the opening of a new PMS Consolidated plant. The addition of DH Compounding, a joint venture with Dow Chemical, that same year gave Hanna a total of four compounding units. Another Canadian takeover threat was thwarted that year, when Brascan, a Canadian natural resources conglomerate, gobbled up 30 percent of Hanna, which repurchased the stock at a premium to avoid the takeover.

CEO Walker told *Chemicalweek* in 1991 that Hanna hoped to become "less a subcontractor and more a proprietary company" in the last decade of the 20th century. The decision to refocus came on the heels of an early 1990s recession that highlighted Hanna's dependence on contract work that distanced the company from the end users of its products and services. The company sold its share of Iron Ore Company of Canada to Mitsubishi Corp. in 1992, and divested the oil interests of Midland Southwest Corp. early in 1993. It planned to jettison its remaining natural resources businesses during the first half of the decade to focus on the polymers industry.

Principal Subsidiaries: Burton Rubber Processing, Inc.; Colonial Rubber Works, Inc.; DHCompounding Company; MACH-1 Compounding; Southwest Chemical Services; Plastic Distributing Corporation; Allied Color Industries, Inc.; Avecor, Inc.; PMS Consolidated; Wilson Color; Synthecolor S.A. (France); Wilson Color (Belgium); Bruck Plastics Co.; FibreChem, Inc.; Plastic Distribution Corporation; Cadillac Plastic Group; Day International Printing Products; Day International Textile Products; Hanna Insurance Services; BenePlan Strategies.

Further Reading:

Gerdel, Thomas W., "Hanna's Last Iron Mine in U.S. to Shut," *Cleveland Plain Dealer,* May 14, 1985, p. 1E.

Gleisser, Marcus, " '60s Caught Hanna in Debate about U.S. Nickel Contracts," *Cleveland Plain Dealer,* October 8, 1984, p. 14E.

Gleisser, "Hanna Family in High and Low Society," *Cleveland Plain Dealer,* October 9, 1984, p. 14E.

Gleisser, "Hanna Has Come Long Way, Marcus," *Cleveland Plain Dealer,* October 8, 1984, p. 14E.

Gleisser, "Hanna Mining Seeks Revival of Old Name," *Cleveland Plain Dealer,* March 21, 1985, pp. 1C, 2C.

Gleisser, "Last Humphrey Leaves Hanna," *Cleveland Plain Dealer,* September 22, 1984, p. 3B.

Gleisser, "Takeover Attempt Tangled Affair," *Cleveland Plain Dealer,* October 10, 1984, p. 5B.

McConville, Daniel J., "M. A. Hanna Prepares for Better Days," *Chemical Week,* June 19, 1991, pp. 25–26.

McGough, Robert, "High Iron," *Financial World,* April 11, 1992, pp. 26–27.

Rose, William Ganson, *Cleveland: The Making of a City,* Kent, Ohio: Kent State University Press, 1990.

—April S. Dougal

MAXXAM Inc.

5847 San Felipe
Suite 2600
Houston, Texas 77257-2887
U.S.A.
(713) 975-7600
Fax: (713) 267-3710

Public Company
Incorporated: 1955 as Cuban American Oil Company
Employees: 12,000
Sales: $2.2 billion
Stock Exchanges: American Pacific Philadelphia
SICs: 3354 Aluminum Extruded Products; 3355 Aluminum
  Rolling and Drawing, Nec

MAXXAM Inc. is a multi-faceted corporation that operates in three separate industries: aluminum, forest products, and real estate. Aluminum accounts for about 86 percent of MAXXAM's sales. The company's aluminum business is conducted through its 68 percent-owned subsidiary Kaiser Aluminum Corporation. Kaiser is a fully integrated producer of alumina, primary aluminum, and fabricated aluminum, with facilities in nine states and five foreign countries. The next largest share of MAXXAM's revenue is generated by its forest products operations. These operations are conducted through two wholly owned subsidiaries: Pacific Lumber Company and Britt Lumber Co., Inc. MAXXAM sold about $223 million in forest products in 1992. Through the 123-year-old Pacific Lumber Company, MAXXAM owns about 196,000 acres of timberland in Humboldt County, California, where over 300 million board feet of redwood and Douglas fir lumber are produced yearly at the company's five saw mills and other related facilities. MAXXAM's real estate business is conducted through MAXXAM Property Company, MCO Properties Inc., and Horizon Corporation. The company's real estate holdings, concentrated mainly in the Southwest, include large land holdings, residential communities, and commercial rental operations. Real estate generated about $70 million in revenue in 1992.

The company that would eventually evolve into MAXXAM was formed in 1955 as Cuban American Oil Company. In 1960 the company's name was changed to McCulloch Oil Corporation of California. The company was founded and guided through its early years by Robert McCulloch, an independent oil explorer. The method by which McCulloch built his company was to organize syndicates of investors annually to cover the costs of oil exploration. For a minimum investment of $10,000, participants in the program would receive all of the benefits from a productive exploratory well until their investments were repaid, and two-thirds interest in any further oil field development that took place as a result of the exploration. For organizing the syndicate and operating the program, McCulloch would retain the remaining one-third share. From 1956 to 1965, the company drilled 167 exploratory wells. 39 of these wells actually produced oil. 179 of the 247 development wells drilled during this period were producers, although none of these finds represented what could be called a major oil strike. In 1966, McCulloch Oil had gross revenues from oil and gas sales of approximately $2.7 million. About $24 million was raised that year through the outside investor program.

In 1965 McCulloch-Hancock Oil & Gas Properties, Inc., was merged into McCulloch Oil Corp. of California. McCulloch-Hancock was created by members of a McCulloch exploration syndicate to operate oil and gas properties that had been completed. According to the terms of the deal McCulloch-Hancock shareholders received two-thirds of a share of McCulloch Oil common stock for each share of McCulloch-Hancock. The merger gave McCulloch Oil total possession of McCulloch Gas Transmission Co., the firm that operated a 100-mile natural gas pipeline system located in northeastern Wyoming.

In the second half of the 1960s, under president C. V. Wood, Jr. McCulloch Oil's biggest gains came in real estate rather than oil, where a major strike continued to elude the company. In 1965 the company unveiled Lake Havasu City, a planned community in Arizona. By the end of 1968, Lake Havasu had about 4,000 permanent residents, 140 businesses, a handful of industrial facilities, and a full range of public services. The city was also fully outfitted for major tourism, including hotels, golf courses, camp grounds, trailer parks, and a marina. During this period of rapid development, 50 salesmen were stationed at Lake Havasu City, and prospective buyers were flown in at no cost on the company's six airplanes to see the property. Lake Havasu received global attention in 1968 when McCulloch Oil purchased the London Bridge for $2.4 million and had it shipped in pieces to the development, where it was reassembled as a tourist attraction. By the end of 1968, McCulloch Oil's sales had grown to $39 million, largely thanks to the expansion of its real estate endeavors. In fact, land sales accounted for around three-fourths of that year's net income. The company was not idle in its other areas, however. In 1969 McCulloch Oil drilled its first test well on the North Slope of Alaska, not far from Prudhoe Bay, where other companies had found gigantic oil reserves. The company also acquired several thousand acres of potential silver mining property in Colorado. In addition, operations at the Wyoming gas pipeline were expanded. Output from the pipeline in 1969 was about five times what it had been only three years earlier.

In 1969 the company's name was shortened to McCulloch Oil Corporation. That year, a partnership was developed with Investors Diversified Services, Inc. (IDS) of Minneapolis, in which IDS would take responsibility for the efforts to coordinate the sale of units in the participant investor programs, while McCulloch Oil would focus on the actual field operation of the programs. Numerous acquisitions, including coal, gas, oil, and real estate operations, aided the company's expansion in the early 1970s. Among these were the 1970 purchases of Omega Gas Company and Richland Gas Company. Two small airlines, Vance International Airways, based in Seattle, and Oklahoma Airmotive, were also acquired that year, as were four Kentucky coal companies, each located in Letcher County. The success of Lake Havasu led Wood to launch further "new cities" around this time. Towns were developed at Fountain Hills, Arizona, and Pueblo West, Colorado. In 1971 McCulloch Oil bought 22,500 acres of property near Elko, Nevada, for the development of Spring Creek, a new city designed to contain 5,500 home sites, as well as an array of recreational facilities, including a golf course, an equestrian center, a shooting range, trout ponds, and an Old West town center.

The following year, however, a change in accounting rules dampened McCulloch Oil's real estate gains. Beginning in 1972, the company could record as revenue only payments actually received on land purchased, rather than count the entire sale price upon completion of the deal. The company reported a net loss of $731,000 in 1972, largely due to this accounting change. Two profitable years followed, but in 1975, the land division lost over $5 million. Plagued by defaults resulting from that year's recession, as well as inflation and increased government regulation, the expenses of developing and maintaining the new cities became overwhelming. By late 1976, Wood announced that the company would take a $60 million write-off to exit the land development business entirely. During that year, the price of McCulloch Oil stock sank to $3 a share, after peaking at $36 back in 1972. Nevertheless, the company managed to earn over $7 million in profit in 1975 on sales of $124 million, thanks mostly to solid years in its oil, gas, and coal mining operations.

IDS, McCulloch's partner in oil and gas exploration programs, was bought out in 1976 for a little over $8 million. In 1977 McCulloch Properties Inc., the land-development subsidiary run by Robert McCulloch, Jr., son of the company's founder, pleaded guilty to 19 counts of fraud concerning sales at the Pueblo West development. The charges involved promises of improvements on the property made by salesmen to prospective buyers that could not be kept. Similar accusations in connection with other properties followed. To facilitate the company's retreat from the land development business in the wake of these legal and financial setbacks, a new company was formed with a former company executive. All of McCulloch Properties' assets were sold to the newly created Pratt Properties Inc., 49 percent of which was to be owned by Lorne Pratt, a former executive vice-president of McCulloch Properties. Two years later, however, Pratt sold all of his shares back to McCulloch Oil so that he could pursue his own personal real estate ventures.

Merlin Witte became company president in 1977, and Wood stayed on as chairman of the board. That year, Robert McCulloch, the company's founder, died from a combination of drugs and alcohol. In 1978 Charles Hurwitz, a Houston entrepreneur, began to take an interest in McCulloch Oil, and his involvement would have a dramatic influence on the company's future. Hurwitz had begun his career as a stockbroker with Bache & Company. He was running his own investment firm by the time he was 24 years-old. After a couple of failed insurance and investment ventures, not to mention brushes with the Securities and Exchange Commission, Hurwitz purchased a New York real estate company called Federated Development Company in 1973. He began to acquire stock through Federated Development and its wholly owned subsidiary Federated Reinsurance Company. In 1978, Hurwitz acquired 13 percent of McCulloch Oil stock from Black & Decker Manufacturing Company, which had inherited that share by virtue of its 1973 purchase of McCulloch Corporation, a manufacturer of chain saws. Although he was initially opposed by most of the company's management, Hurwitz managed to get two representatives elected to the McCulloch Oil board at the 1978 annual meeting, and he himself became a director shortly after that. Wood resigned his chairmanship in July 1979. McCulloch, Jr. resigned from the board as well. The leadership vacuum was eventually filled in March 1980, when Hurwitz became both chairman and chief executive. Hurwitz then named William Leone to replace Witte as president. When this change in the company's power structure was completed, with Hurwitz and his associates firmly in charge, the company's name was changed to MCO Holdings Inc. Witte emerged from the scrap as a Hurwitz ally, and became president of MCO Resources Inc., one of the company's principal subsidiaries.

By 1981 MCO's sales had grown to $173 million. Hurwitz led MCO through a period of diversification through acquisitions over the next few years. At the same time, the company shed many of its energy holdings. In 1982 MCO gained controlling interest in Simplicity Pattern Company, the well-known maker of sewing patterns, with annual sales of about $82 million. Hurwitz also became chairman and chief executive of Simplicity. The same year, MCO sold its interests in the Midway Sunset oil field in California for about $155 million. The company's Manley-McGinn oil properties were also disposed of for another $115 million. Another move made in 1982 was the purchase of about 37 percent interest in Maxxam Group Inc., an investment partnership also controlled by Hurwitz. Maxxam essentially consisted of the remnants of Simplicity, retained for use as an instrument for real estate purchases, after that company's core pattern business had been sold off. In 1982 and 1983 MCO purchased shares that eventually amounted to a 23 percent holding in United Financial Group, Inc., the parent company to United Savings of Texas.

In 1986 MCO, through the Maxxam Group, completed a takeover attempt launched the previous year on Pacific Lumber Company. The $863 million purchase of Pacific Lumber was made through junk bond king Michael Milken of Drexel Burnham Lambert, and was one of the earliest instances of a hostile takeover financed by the sale of junk bonds. The takeover was spurred in part by Hurwitz's discovery during an aerial survey that Pacific actually owned about 30 percent more standing timber than was believed, a fact that kept the company's stock price artificially low. Shortly after the buyout, the cutting rate on Pacific Lumber properties was doubled. This infuriated environmentalists, many of whom have continued to hold a grudge against Hurwitz because of this practice.

MCO purchased the remaining portion of the Maxxam Group it did not already own and merged it into the company as a wholly owned subsidiary in May 1988. Two months later, MCO Resources, Inc., the company's energy subsidiary, was sold to

United Meridian Corporation. In October of that year, the company's name was changed to MAXXAM Inc. Before that month was over, MAXXAM had made its most important acquisition yet, the $930 million purchase of Kaiser Aluminum Corporation. Once again, Drexel Burnham Lambert junk bonds covered a sizeable portion of Kaiser's purchase price.

With Kaiser Aluminum in the fold, MAXXAM's sales reached $2.4 billion in 1989, with net income of $117 million. In 1990 Kaiser's chairman and chief executive John Seidl replaced the retiring William Leone as president of MAXXAM. The following year, 13 percent of Kaiser was sold to the public, with MAXXAM retaining control of the rest. The company's sales began to shrink gradually as the 1990s began. MAXXAM'S 1990 figures were net income of $162 million on sales of $2.36 billion. The following year, the company reported net income of $57 million on sales of $2.25 billion. 1992 was a particularly bleak year for MAXXAM, due primarily to a deeply depressed global aluminum market. As sales dipped to $2.2 billion, the company posted a $7.3 million net loss for the year. Contributing to MAXXAM'S difficulties were increased aluminum production capacities among countries in the Western world, combined with much higher levels of aluminum exports from the former Soviet Union. In spite of these problems, several of the company's facilities set production records in 1992. In addition, a major expansion project at the company's Jamaican alumina operation was completed, and a new extrusions facility was launched in London, Ontario.

In contrast to the aluminum operations, MAXXAM's forest products operations made gains in 1992. Operating income from this industry reached $65 million, an increase of nearly 16 percent from the previous year. Late in 1992 and into 1993, MAXXAM began an effort to refinance the bulging debt it had built up in acquiring Pacific Lumber and Kaiser Aluminum. $400 million in new 10-year bonds was issued to replace existing debt that was due in 1995. Though this move increased the actual size of the debt, it took advantage of favorable interest rates at the same time. In June 1993, MAXXAM raised $120 million through a public offering of several million depositary shares of Kaiser aluminum stock. This sale reduced MAXXAM's holding in Kaiser to about 68 percent of the common stock.

Because of the cyclical nature of the aluminum industry, combined with the lingering sluggishness of the global economy in the early 1990s, MAXXAM's unimpressive performance during this period was not unexpected by company management. Like many industrial corporations, MAXXAM has concentrated on reducing costs and increasing efficiency during this downturn.

Principal Subsidiaries: Kaiser Aluminum Corporation (68%); Pacific Lumber Company; Britt Lumber Co., Inc.; MAXXAM Property Company; MCO Properties Inc.; Horizon Corporation.

Further Reading:

Barrett, William P., ''Sucker Play?'' *Forbes,* August 5, 1991, pp. 39–40.
Hayes, Thomas C., ''Hurwitz Group Buying 33% of Simplicity Stock,'' *New York Times,* May 11, 1982, p. D6.
Hollie, Pamela G., ''The Man Who Won McCulloch Oil,'' *New York Times,* July 13, 1980, p. 10.
''J. M. Seidl Will Head Maxxam,'' *American Metal Market,* September 28, 1990, p. 2.
Lichtenstein, Grace, ''Land Concern Pleads Guilty to 19 Counts of Criminal Fraud,'' *New York Times,* February 23, 1977, p. D1.
MAXXAM Annual Report 1992, Houston, Texas: MAXXAM Inc., 1993.
''McCulloch Oil Corp. and McCulloch-Hancock Propose to Consolidate,'' *Wall Street Journal,* March 17, 1965, p. 5.
''McCulloch Oil Forms New Firm to Direct Its Land Operations,'' *Wall Street Journal,* July 20, 1977, p. 4.
''McCulloch Oil Hits Gusher With Big Arizona Land Holdings,'' *Barron's,* March 31, 1969, pp. 38–42.
''McCulloch Oil Says Net Increased 30% in 1969,'' *Wall Street Journal,* February 17, 1970, p. 11.
Parrish, Michael, ''Western Environmentalists' Enemy No. 1,'' *Los Angeles Times,* August 19, 1990, p. D1.
Sansweet, Stephen J., ''Once Unwelcome as a Holder, Hurwitz Has Become McCulloch Oil Chairman,'' *Wall Street Journal,* March 27, 1980, p. 16.
''What Drove McCulloch Out of New Towns,'' *Business Week,* November 22, 1976, pp. 62–64.
Wright, Robert A., ''$10,000 Will Buy Stake in Oil Hunt,'' *New York Times,* February 19, 1967, p. F1.

—Robert R. Jacobson

Medtronic, Inc.

7000 Central Avenue, N.E.
Minneapolis, Minnesota 55432-3576
U.S.A.
(612) 574-4000
Fax: (612) 574-4879

Public Company
Incorporated: 1957
Employees: 9,200
Sales: $1.33 billion
Stock Exchanges: New York
SICs: 3845 Electromedical Equipment; 3841 Surgical and
   Medical Instruments; 8099 Health and Allied Services,
   nec.

Medtronic, Inc. is the world's leading therapeutic medical device company, with about 47 percent of the $1.3 billion global pacemaker market. The company's product lines include cardiac pacemaker systems, implantable neurological pain management systems, tachyarrhythmia management systems, prosthetic and bioprosthetic heart valves, angioplasty catheters, implantable drug administration systems, and disposable devices for handling and monitoring blood during surgery. Established in 1949, Medtronic has since grown to become a Fortune 500 business.

Medtronic, Inc. was founded as an outgrowth of Earl Bakken's part-time work at Minneapolis's Northwestern Hospital. Although much of his time was consumed with graduate studies in electrical engineering, Bakken found time to repair the centrifuges, electrocardiograph machines, and other intricate electronic equipment at the hospital where his wife served as a medical technologist. Bakken and his brother-in-law, Palmer Hermundslie, surmised that they could make a living at repairing medical equipment. In 1949 Bakken quit school, and Hermundslie left his job at a local lumber company so the pair could form the medical equipment repair service they dubbed "Medtronic."

Bakken and Hermundslie worked out of a small garage in Northeast Minneapolis in the early years of the company. During Medtronic's difficult first year, there was one month the business grossed a meager eight dollars. In 1950, however, the partners contracted as sales representatives for the Sanborn Company, the Gilford Instrument Company, and Advanced Instruments, Inc. In the early part of the decade, over half of their sales in the five-state region around Minneapolis came from selling the merchandise of the other companies.

As Bakken gained experience with medical professionals and their instruments, he was also called upon to advise them in their experiments. Over the course of Medtronic's first decade Bakken built almost 100 custom-made—often single-use—devices for medical research. Soon Medtronic was manufacturing several medical research products, including two types of defibrillators, forceps, an animal respirator, a cardiac rate monitor (or "squawk box"), and a physiologic stimulator. Manufacturing of these early instruments was primitive by today's standards—parts were handmade or surplus, quality control was accomplished by visual examination, and products were packed in newspaper and shipped in recycled boxes.

During the late 1950s Medtronic's history became inextricably connected to the history of open heart surgery. Bakken's reputation for service had earned him a part-time job repairing medical electronics at the University of Minnesota Medical School. At that time, Dr. C. Walton Lillehei was researching a battery-powered device that would conduct a mild electric shock to the surface of a patient's heart in order to combat the heart block that caused fatalities in about 10 percent of open-heart surgeries.

Electrically stimulated pacemaking had taken off in the 1950s when several physicians developed external machines that extended the lives of patients who otherwise would have died. These early external pacemakers had several disadvantages, however. The high-voltage electrodes used often burned patients' skin, the devices were large and unmanageable, and they had to be plugged into the wall, thus restricting patients' mobility and making power failures life-threatening events.

Dr. Lillehei, a pioneer of open-heart surgery at the University of Minnesota Medical School, had asked a doctoral student in the electrical division of the physics department to develop a portable, battery-powered device that could stimulate the heart directly with a low voltage current at an adjustable rate of 50 to 110 pulses per minute. After six months, Dr. Lillehei became frustrated with the student's lack of progress. In desperation, he asked Bakken, the lab's part-time repairman, to design an appropriate device. Bakken observed an open-heart experiment on a dog, and within six weeks returned to Dr. Lillehei with the world's first transistorized, battery-powered, wearable pacemaker. The instrument was a little larger than a bar of soap, and incorporated wire leads that were attached directly to the heart, eliminating the severe irritation caused by electrodes attached to the skin. Bakken's invention was honored by the National Society of Professional Engineers as one of ten outstanding engineering products for the period from 1954 to 1984.

Medtronic earned a reputation as a front-running producer of biomedical engineering devices in the late 1950s. Bakken's external pacemakers were used at the Mayo Clinic in Rochester; the University of Minnesota; the National Institutes of Health in Bethesda, Maryland; Walter Reed Medical Center in Boston; and Mount Zion Hospital in San Francisco. By the end of the decade the devices had also been used outside the United States, in Canada, Australia, Cuba, Europe, Africa, and South America.

The partnership between electronics and cardiac research continued to advance open-heart surgery—and Medtronic—throughout the 1950s. Dr. Samuel Hunter of St. Joseph's Hospital research laboratory in St. Paul, Minnesota, worked with Norman Roth, an electrical engineer at Medtronic, to create a silicone rubber patch with two stainless steel electrodes imbedded in it. This "bipolar" electrode could be sutured to the heart and required about 70 percent less current than Bakken's pacemaker system. After animal experiments, an external pacemaker using the patented "Hunter-Roth" electrode was implanted in a human patient in 1958.

Even these advances, however, left room for improvement. Although small, the external pacemaker was still cumbersome. The device's wires could also be accidentally extricated from the heart, and the wounds caused by wires passing through the skin from the pacemaker to the heart required vigilance against infection. In 1958 Dr. William Chardack and electrical engineer Wilson Greatbatch overcame these difficulties when they built the first implantable pacemaker in America. The device, which incorporated the Hunter-Roth bipolar wire lead, was first successfully implanted in a human in 1960. By October of that year, Medtronic had purchased the exclusive rights to produce and market the "Chardack-Greatbatch implantable pulse generator." The company received 50 orders for the device within the last two months of 1960.

The growing company organized its distribution outside the United States and Canada through the employment of the Picker International Corporation of White Plains, New York. Picker specialized in electrical medical equipment sales, and had an international network of 72 foreign sales offices. Fourteen Medtronic sales representatives covered the United States and Canada, beginning in 1960. The company introduced several ingeniously named products that year, including the Telecor heart monitor; the Cardiac Sentinel, an alarm that automatically summoned aid when a patient's heart rate became critical and stimulated the heart with an electronically regulated pulse; and a Coagulation Generator that stanched bleeding during surgery without damage to nearby tissue.

The growing product line and increasing demand both enabled and required the company to move to a new, larger facility in 1961. The building was financed with $215,000 of convertible debentures and accommodated accounting, sales, engineering, production, medical services, a prototype lab, cafeteria, library, and an auditorium designed for sales training and technical seminars. Despite Medtronic's dramatic sales increases—from $180,000 to over $500,000 from 1960 to 1962—the company incurred losses during the same time period. Expenses, like the appointment of Picker International, the cost of building a new headquarters, new product research, and attendance at major medical and engineering conventions, increased faster than sales. Early in 1962 the company eased its financial tensions through a bond-offering of $200,000 and a $100,000 bank loan. The credit helped Medtronic turn a profit of $17,000 for the first three months of fiscal 1962.

Medtronic introduced several new products during the 1960s. Its electrocardiogram (EKG) transmitter sent a representation of a patient's heart rate up to 500 feet, enabling physicians to diagnose a patient's maximum exertion. The company's "vein eraser" used a high-frequency electric current to eliminate varicose veins. Gastrointestinal and pediatric pacemakers were also released during this time.

Research continued throughout the 1960s on Medtronic's most important product, the implantable pacemaker. The company developed an endocardial catheter, a wire lead inserted through the jugular vein to the heart. When pacemakers with this "transvenous" lead were introduced to the market in 1965, they seized a substantial portion of pacemaker sales. Medtronic also introduced a pacemaker that compensated for irregular heart beats. In the past, pacemakers induced a heartbeat through electric shock whether the heart beat naturally or not. Medtronic released external and implantable pacemakers with this feature in 1966 and 1967, respectively.

New product introductions and pacemaker improvements helped sales surge to over $12 million by the end of the 1967–1968 fiscal year. Profits increased dramatically as well, exceeding $1 million that year. A two-for-one stock split distributed some of the profits to shareholders. Medtronic also invested in its future with three additions to the company's original facility. A clean room facility for the assembly of implantable products was equipped with both a filtration system that purified the air and an environmental control system to regulate temperature and humidity. By this time, Medtronic products were inspected through x-ray technology, rather than visually. The improvements raised the company's quality control standards significantly, preparing Medtronic for impending U.S. Food and Drug Administration regulations.

Medtronic established a European Service Center in 1967 to provide technical support for that continent, which generated 80 percent of overseas sales. A major manufacturing facility in Kerkrade, Holland, was completed in 1969 to supply the region. The local production site helped keep Medtronic's prices competitive and was a first step toward the reclamation of overseas sales from Picker International. Later that year, Medtronic formed its own international division to accommodate direct European sales. In 1970, the company was able to drop its contract with Picker International and control international sales, which accounted for 30 percent of total sales by that time.

The international operations were divided geographically into four regions: Europe/Africa/Middle East, Canada, Latin America, and Asia/Pacific. Direct sales offices were established in 19 countries, and technical centers and manufacturing plants were erected in primary markets. Technical Development Centers in Paris, Toronto, Minneapolis, and Miami encouraged cooperative research projects with local medical researchers. Service Centers in Tokyo and Lebanon helped distributors in the Asia/Pacific and Middle East regions provide customers with technical information.

Medtronic also gained control of its primary North American distributors during the late 1960s and early 1970s. In 1968 the company purchased John Hay & Company, Ltd., a medical sales organization headquartered in Vancouver, British Columbia. The A.F. Morrison Company was acquired the following year, and by 1973 Medtronic accomplished complete jurisdiction over its North American sales with the purchase of the Medical Specialty Company and Corvek Medical Equipment.

The 1970s also saw the development of new products in two primary areas: cardiovascular and neuro-rehabilitation. Cardiovascular products developed for the diagnosis and treatment of heart disease included a nuclear-powered pacemaker. Medtronic's pacemakers were also made smaller, more resilient, and more reliable during the decade. The use of hybrid circuitry enabled the company to offer smaller, less obtrusive pacemakers, and the development of lithium iodide batteries provided a more reliable, longer-lasting power source. These improvements enabled patients to wear the devices up to ten years without fear of failure. Medtronic worked with Dr. Samuel Hunter in the early 1970s to develop a sutureless myocardial lead that was screwed directly into the surface of the heart. The improvement permitted attachment under local anesthesia through a small incision, and thereby reduced the trauma involved with the normally invasive procedure. The company consolidated pacemaker production vertically through the creation of Micro-Rel, Inc., a manufacturer of hybrid circuits, and the acquisition of Energy Technology—later renamed Promeon—a producer of lithium batteries. Other cardiovascular equipment developed in the 1970s helped physicians diagnose patients instantaneously and monitor them by telephone. Cardiovascular products contributed the bulk of Medtronic's sales.

Medtronic's neuro-rehabilitation area, which also experienced heightened development in the 1970s, manufactured products that helped relieve chronic and acute pain. The Neuromod Transcutaneous Electrical Nerve Stimulator (TENS) alleviated pain through electrical stimulation applied externally. A similar device, called the PISCES system, was surgically implanted on the spinal cord to treat otherwise unmanageable pain of the trunk, arms and legs. These pain-relieving electrical systems could be used instead of destructive surgery and heavy drugs.

Like many other American companies, Medtronic was affected by high inflation during the late 1970s. The company reacted with tighter inventory controls and close monitoring of general and administrative expenses. Tougher regulatory policies instituted by the Nuclear Regulatory Commission and the Food and Drug Administration also increased research costs through requirements for tougher clinical and follow-up testing. Despite economic barriers, however, Medtronic surpassed $100 million in annual sales in fiscal 1976. That year, the company was ranked as one of *Fortune* magazine's 1,000 largest U.S. corporations. Medtronic's workforce multiplied as well, from less than 500 to over 3,400. By 1977, the company's international sales had increased dramatically—up to $60 million, from just $1 million ten years earlier. The company used the income to initiate a heart valve subsidiary in 1977. Kastec Corporation was named for its director, Robert L. Kaster, who held five U.S. heart valve patents.

Medtronic experienced several leadership changes during the 1970s. In 1974, Earl Bakken gave up the day-to-day responsibilities of the presidency to become chairman of the board. Thomas E. Holloran replaced him for just two years, followed by Dale R. Olseth, who was elected president and chief executive officer. By the end of the decade, Medtronic had made its first major acquisition, Medical Data Systems, an Ann Arbor, Michigan, nuclear imaging company. Annual sales topped $200 million by 1980.

In the 1980s, Medtronic sought to further diversify its product line, while keeping its strong emphasis on pacemakers. Routine reinvestment of more than eight percent of annual revenues during the decade fueled research and development of new and improved medical devices, and by 1981 annual sales had reached another milestone, the $300 million mark. William R. Wallin was named president and CEO in 1985.

Computer technology helped Medtronic develop pacemakers that catered to a patient's particular requirements. The Spectrax SXT, a programmable pacemaker that could be reprogrammed after the initial implantation without performing surgery, led the market soon after its release in 1981. In 1985 the Activitrax pacemaker was the first such device to automatically adjust the rate of heart stimulation in accordance with the rate of activity. The pacemaker passed U.S. Food & Drug Administration trials in 1986. That same year Medtronic solidified its position in this "rate-responsive pacing" with the purchase of Biotech of Bologna, Italy, and Vitatron of Dieren, the Netherlands. Biotech's pacemakers adjusted the heart rate according to the rate of respiration, and Vitatron's devices responded to variations in the heart's electrical timing to achieve the same basic results as Medtronic's Activitrax. Medtronic made other technological adjustments in pacemakers in the 1980s. Improved leads reduced the number of times that they dislodged from 20 percent to less than 2 percent, and the use of platinum and steroids improved the leads' conductivity, reducing inflammation of heart tissue.

The company's developments in the late 1980s and early 1990s included cardiovascular and cardiopulmonary products, and neurological and drug delivery devices. Angioplasty utilized a balloon catheter that could be inflated to clear clogged veins and arteries. Medtronic entered the field overseas in 1987, and in the United States the following year, with the introduction of its Prime angioplasty catheter. The company complemented its activities in the field with the acquisition of Versaflex Delivery Systems, Inc., of San Diego, another manufacturer of angioplasty catheters.

Medtronic became involved in cardiovascular surgery in 1987 with the acquisition of Johnson & Johnson Cardiovascular. The company produced the industry-leading Maxima membrane oxygenator, a device used during open heart surgery to reoxygenate blood. Neurological devices introduced in the late 1980s included the Selectra and ComfortWave electrical nerve stimulators, used to treat sprains and back pain. Medtronic's nerve stimulators were also indicated for the treatment of scoliosis and angina. La Jolla Technology, Inc., another producer of electrical nerve stimulators, was acquired in 1987 to strengthen Medtronic's position in this industry. The company also expanded its product line to include programmable, electronic drug delivery systems that could be either implanted or charged by electric current, and projected drugs through the skin.

With many acquisitions and new product introductions in the late 1980s and early 1990s, Medtronic was able to increase its annual sales from $300 million in 1981 to more than $1 billion in 1991. That year, William W. George was made president and CEO, succeeding Winston R. Wallin, who became chairman of the board.

However, with all the successes in the 1980s came some setbacks. A government review of pacemaker implants culminated in hearings by the U.S. Senate Special Committee on Aging that revealed a study showing overuse of pacemakers in Maryland. In 1983 Medtronic voluntarily recalled a new pacemaker lead when it recorded relatively high failure rates in clinical tests. These disadvantages resulted in slowed pacemaker sales—in 1985, Medtronic reported its first year without an increase in sales and earnings. Medtronic was also involved in expensive patent litigation with such large medical manufacturers as Eli Lilly & Co. and Siemens AG during the decade.

The outlook improved in the late 1980s, when Medtronic developed a pacemaker-cardioverter-defibrillator (PCD) that was designed to combat tachyarrhythmia, a life-threatening condition involving a heart that beats too fast. Although the condition could be diagnosed before problems arose, the quick onset of tachyarrhythmia often claimed lives before medical help could arrive. The PCD was created to slow the heart rate and condition the organ to beat at a normal rate. In cases where the heart would not slow, the PCD was programmed to apply higher-voltage shocks, and in case of emergency, even defibrillate the heart. The PCD passed FDA tests in 1993, and promised to further raise Medtronic's position in the medical device business, as well as save lives.

By the early 1990s, Medtronic had developed six primary areas of expertise: bradycardia pacing, tachyarrhythmia management, cardiopulmonary, heart valves, intreventional vascular, and neurological. In 1992, the company's international sales contributed 40 percent of total revenues, justifying new facilities and expanded operations in Japan, China, and Eastern Europe. Sales and earnings continued to grow in the 1990s, to $1.18 billion and $161 million, respectively, in 1992.

Principal Subsidiaries: Medtronic Europe (Belgium); Medtronic of Canada Ltd.; Medtronic Asia-Pacific (Japan).

Further Reading:

Dubashi, Jagannath ''Change of Pace,'' *Financial World,* March 17, 1992, pp. 26–27.
Medtronic Beginnings, Minneapolis: Medtronic, Inc., 1993.
Moore, Michael P., ''The Genesis of Minnesota's Medical Alley,'' *University of Minnesota Medical Bulletin*, Winter 1992, pp. 7–13.
Nelson, Glen D., M.D., ''A Brief History of Cardiac Pacing,'' *Texas Heart Institute Journal*, v. 20, 1993, pp. 12–18.
Toward Man's Full Life, Minneapolis: Medtronic, Inc., 1990.

—April S. Dougal

SIMON

MELVIN SIMON & ASSOCIATES, INC.

Melvin Simon and Associates, Inc.

P.O. Box 7033
Indianapolis, Indiana 46207
U.S.A.
(317) 636-1600
Fax: (317) 263-7924

Private Company
Incorporated: 1960
Employees: 3,200
SICs: 6552 Subdividers and Developers Nec

Melvin Simon and Associates Inc. (MSA) is one of the top three developers of shopping centers and mixed-use real estate projects in the United States. Owned entirely by brothers Melvin and Herb Simon, Indianapolis-based MSA built upwards of 170 shopping centers in the three decades beginning in 1960, playing a major role in the retailing revolution that replaced "Mom and Pop" stores of every description with the massive shopping malls that now dot the American landscape. MSA hurtled into the 1989 real estate recession with a huge load of projects in tow, including the Mall of America in Minneapolis, which at 4.2 million square feet is the largest indoor shopping center in the country; after asset sales and work force reductions, MSA came through the recession in tolerable shape but now faces questions about the permanent appeal of mega-malls such as the Mall of America.

MSA was founded in 1959 by Melvin Simon, a Bronx native, with his younger brothers Herb and Fred. After military service in the mid-1950s at Fort Harrison near Indianapolis, Mel Simon elected to stay in the Midwest, accepting a $100-a-week job as the leasing agent for property manager Albert J. Frankel. His first assignment was to find tenants for the Eastgate Shopping Center in Indianapolis, an experience that gave Simon a taste of the shopping center business and its unlimited future prospects. Postwar prosperity encouraged Americans to consume goods at an unprecedented rate while at the same time spawning a mass migration from cities and farms to the new suburban communities, where land was cheap and population density low. The combination of available land, high consumer demand, and a populace dependent on the automobile inspired the birth of the shopping center, where a dozen or more stores with space for parking could be built cheaply and quickly at the intersection of major roads. The "strip centers," as they were called, lacked both the homey appeal of the neighborhood shops they drove out of business and the cachet of the big city retailers such as Marshall Field's and Macy's; in fact, strip centers lacked every virtue except the two most important in retailing—convenience and price. Their convenience was obvious to anyone who used a car to do his or her shopping, and the price benefits were derived from the economies of scale made possible by the shopping centers' larger stores, most of which had franchise affiliations with national retailers.

A man of ambition such as Mel Simon could hardly ignore the potential for investment. After a few years with the Frankel company, Mel and his youngest brother Herb Simon founded MSA in 1959 to begin developing shopping centers of their own. The brothers' first project was Southgate Plaza in Bloomington, Indiana, a typical strip center anchored by a grocery store and filled out with a half dozen smaller tenants. The brothers had little cash and were often forced to ask friends for investment equity (those who declined to participate would have years to regret their decision) but for the most part developers in the 1960s and 1970s could borrow 100 percent of the construction costs of a shopping center once they had secured its anchor tenant—either a grocery chain or, later, department stores. The revenues generated by tenant leases would be sufficient to repay debt and provide seed money for the brothers' next project. Once established, the pattern was easily continued; as vice-president Thomas Domagala later described to *Forbes,* "You would go out, find a cornfield, and build a product that was cookie-cutter-type stuff." The Simons made a point of retaining equity whenever possible, thus building the tremendous asset base that later allowed them to borrow funds for larger and larger projects.

In the meantime, the nature of the shopping center was continually evolving. The strip center concept gave way to much larger entities that came to be known as "malls," where two rows of stores faced each other across a common walkway. The first of these was built in 1954 in Seattle; two years later, the first enclosed mall went up outside Minneapolis, where severe weather has always encouraged the growth of indoor malls. MSA was not slow to adopt this innovation, building their first indoor center in Fort Collins, Colorado, in the mid-1960s and following it up with a long line of bigger and more elegant examples culminating in the Mall of America mentioned above. Indoor malls offer obvious advantages in regions of extreme climate, but they also enable more subtle and effective marketing than is possible outdoors, where the customer's attention is easily distracted by weather conditions and where the quality and intensity of light changes continually. By the late 1960s MSA, along with other major developers, had shifted heavily to indoor projects, particularly for centers of any size.

Along the way, the Simon brothers acquired a reputation as honest and cordial negotiators, in sharp contrast to many of their fellow developers. Their modesty and good-humored approach to business won them important support among the bankers and merchants of Indianapolis, a town that does not cotton to big-city egos and publicity hounds. As one retail executive told *Institutional Investor,* "When Mel and Herb discuss a project with you, it's a joy. They never squeeze or play hardball." On the other hand, the brothers were famous for quarrelling with each other during negotiations in a manner that drew comparisons to the Marx brothers; in the midst of one particularly heated argument Mel Simon is said to have taken off a shoe and thrown it at his brother. Of the two, Mel Simon is considered to be far more volatile and eccentric than Herb, and for a time early in their careers Mel earned the sobriquet "Meshugganer [Crazy] Mel" for his bright red suits and outlandish manner. Yet the Simons have never shown any interest in becoming public personalities along the lines of Donald Trump, preferring to let their projects grab the publicity while they move quietly on to their next deal.

By the early 1970s the brothers were wealthy men and their ambitions had grown accordingly. The crude strip centers of 1960 were now vast enclosed malls such as the giants built by MSA in Baltimore (Golden Ring) and El Paso, Texas (Cielo Vista), each of them offering shoppers three or four "anchor" tenants like Saks or Montgomery Wards plus scores of smaller retailers, restaurants, game rooms, and in some cases play lots for children. Malls were getting bigger and more lavishly decorated, gradually taking on the appearance and even the function of small cities. For suburbs too diffuse to have a "downtown," the mall became a kind of de facto city center, with clusters of adjoining apartment complexes and office buildings, while inside the mall suburbanites found an ersatz Main Street to replace the long abandoned or demolished real one. Critics of this evolution (and there were many) pointed out that the rise of large malls and shopping centers doomed entire generations of independent drug, department, shoe, and toy store owners, grocers, bakers, butchers, florists, hair stylists, auto mechanics, stationers, dressmakers, barkeeps, cafe and restaurant proprietors, and in general anyone whose business could not be absorbed into the larger matrices of mall and franchise corporate planning—a mass extinction to rival that of the dinosaurs, and equally permanent.

In the mid-1970s Melvin Simon set himself up as a Hollywood producer. He made an impressive number of pictures over the next five years, some of them *(The Stuntman, Zorro, the Gay Blade)* well-received by critics and others *(Love at First Bite, Porky's)* better left unmentioned, but as a business venture Simon's Hollywood career was a decided failure, costing the mall mogul as much as $30 million. Simon returned to the retailing business in time to participate in its most significant development since the shopping center itself: urban mixed-use projects. Just as the suburbs had made possible the creation of the shopping center and later the mall, a resurgent interest in city living made the 1980s the decade of urban redevelopment. Many members of the "Baby Boom" generation could not afford or did not wish to live in the suburbs where they grew up, choosing instead to settle in gentrified areas of major cities, often the older and more congested parts of the city near downtown. This population of ex-suburbanites kept their suburban tastes, however, demanding the convenience of shopping centers in the middle of crowded and expensive cities. Since land was prohibitively expensive, developers such as MSA had only two sources of space, building up or reusing abandoned structures.

MSA became involved in many projects of this kind in the 1980s, several of them large enough to give the Simon name national publicity. The first of the mixed-use developments was Two West Washington in downtown Indianapolis, a city in which the Simon brothers are heavily invested both financially and as citizens. In 1987, for example, they intervened when the city's professional basketball team was about to relocate elsewhere, eventually buying the Pacers franchise in order to ensure its future in Indianapolis. As Melvin Simon later explained to *Institutional Investor,* "Sometimes you gotta do certain things . . . Indianapolis has been very, very good to us over the years." The development at Two West Washington was another instance of the Simons' civic pride, but it was only the precursor of a much larger project begun in 1982 and more than ten years in the making, Circle Centre. The latter is an enormous effort on the part of the Indianapolis business and government to revivify the city's downtown area by converting three-and-a-half city blocks of aging brick buildings into an enclosed mall featuring two anchors, eighty shops, a multiscreen movie theater, and an entertainment complex. MSA served as managing partner of the project from its inception, after years of frustrating setbacks finally getting it off the ground in the early 1980s with the help of fourteen leading corporations who joined the venture as limited partners.

MSA entered the big leagues of United States real estate development with the completion in 1985 of St. Louis Centre, an elegant two-block-long arcade connecting a pair of department stores with a twenty-one story office building near downtown St. Louis. The $200 million project had been stalled for several years when the Simons were asked to take over its management. "Once they entered the picture in St. Louis," an MSA vice-president later commented to *Institutional Investor,* "people suddenly felt great about the project. Everyone just rallied around." Indeed, bolstered by the 1980s' bullish economy, the Simons were able to rally support for an amazing number of projects of every kind in the succeeding years. Fashion Mall, a Plantation, Florida, joint venture that opened in 1988, saw MSA go from elegance to opulence in its 660,000 square feet of retail space trimmed with marble tiling and dotted with full-grown palm trees; attached to the shopping mall was a seven-story office building and Sheraton Hotel. Similar projects were undertaken in Arlington, Virginia, and Orlando, Florida, where the Seminole Properties development grew to be several times the size of Fashion Mall in all three categories of retail, office, and hotel. The stage was set in 1989 for MSA to embark on some of the most ambitious real estate projects in United States history—unfortunately, just as the country headed into its worst real estate depression since World War II.

The real estate slump beginning in 1989 hit hardest the office market, crippling even such stalwarts as Olympia & York; but it also brought MSA's retail business to a near standstill after the frenzy of the 1980s. It was not possible to gauge the extent of damage suffered by the privately held MSA, but the depression certainly left the Simon brothers trying to fill an enormous number of leases around the country. In New York, MSA had undertaken the renovation of the former Gimbels' department store on 33rd Street into A & S Plaza, a $400 million, 150-store mall in the heart of Manhattan. A joint venture with New York developers Larry Silverstein and William Zeckendorf, Jr., A & S featured a seven-story glass atrium over which hangs an ornate, animated clock. Across the Hudson River in Jersey City, MSA was involved in Newport Centre, a 200-acre community whose plans included a regional mall, the tallest office building in the state of New Jersey, as many as 9,000 housing units, and the Jacques Cousteau Ocean Center. MSA's partner in the project was The Lefrak Organization, also a New York development firm.

Finally, last but hardly least of MSA's pre-slump ventures was the Mall of America outside Minneapolis. The largest mall ever built in the United States, Mall of America makes use of the entire site once occupied by the Minneapolis Twins baseball stadium, its 600–800 specialty stores and four anchor tenants form a vast rectangle around the interior entertainment section which includes a theme park (complete with roller coaster and dancing dolphins), two-story miniature golf course, fourteen movie theaters, scores of restaurants and bars, and a walk-through aquarium. Circling the enclosed mall are 13,000 parking spaces—''more parking on decks,'' Melvin Simon told *Indoor Business Magazine,* ''than in the whole city of Indianapolis.'' MSA is the developer and manager of the $625 million development and owns about 23 percent; its partners are Teachers Insurance and Canada's Triple Five Corporation, builders of the even larger West Edmonton Mall in Edmonton, Alberta.

With such huge exposure in a down market, the Simons have had to unload assets and refinance as many properties as possible to take advantage of low interest rates. According to *Business Week,* David Simon, thirty-year-old son of Melvin, was assigned to help stabilize his father's strained finances, and the company subsequently cut about 20 percent of its Indianapolis work force and sold or refinanced an estimated $1 billion in property. The cash was needed to pay debt on its various overgrown projects, of which Newport Centre, A & S Plaza, and Mall of America were all still suffering low occupancy rates in the early 1990s. Some critics feel that the age of the mall is over, while others single out behemoths like Mall of America as especially vulnerable. ''Customers often end up confused and exhausted,'' noted *Forbes* writer Steve Weiner about West Edmonton Mall. If Mall of America were to prove a failure MSA, would surely survive the blow, but a mistake the size of a baseball stadium is hard to explain the next time one goes shopping for a loan.

Further Reading:

Greising, David, and William C. Symonds, ''Guys and Malls: The Simons' Crapshoot,'' *Business Week,* August 17, 1992, pp. 52–53.
''The Mall Moguls,'' *Indiana Business Magazine,* April 1991, pp. 10–13.
''Melvin Simon: Growth Through Diversification,'' *Chain Store Age Executive,* May 1989, pp. 46–54.
Meyers, William, ''The Brother Act from Indianapolis,'' *Institutional Investor,* September 1986, pp. 179–185.
Osborn, Thomas, ''Revolutionizing the Retail Landscape,'' *Marketing Communications,* October 1988, pp. 17–25.
Weiner, Steve, ''No More Plastic Plants,'' *Forbes,* March 20, 1989, pp. 107–108.

—Jonathan Martin

▲▼▲ MENASHA CORPORATION

Menasha Corporation

P.O. Box 367
Neenah, Wisconsin 54957-0367
U.S.A.
(414) 751-1000
Fax: (414) 751-1236

Private Company
Incorporated: 1875 as Menasha Wooden Ware Company
Employees: 4,100
Sales: $581 million
SICs: 2653 Corrugated & Solid Fiber Boxes (Primary); 2421
  Sawmills & Planing Mills; 2631 Paperboard Mills; 2759
  Commercial Printing, Nec; 3081 Unsupported Plastics
  Film & Sheet; 3089 Plastic Products, Nec; 3999
  Manufacturing Industries, Nec; 4213 Trucking, Except
  Local

Menasha Corporation is a rapidly growing, diverse family business serving six major markets: forest products, packaging, promotional graphics, information graphics, plastics, and material handling. From its 19th-century origins in woodenware production, Menasha shifted to paper-based packaging and material handling products in the 1930s, earning its reputation as a "box maker," even though packaging accounted for only one-third of total sales by the early 1990s. From the 1980s onward, active acquisitions resulted in rapid growth and diversification, carrying Menasha well beyond its original scope of interests in packaging and woodenware. By the early 1990s, the company employed over 4,000 workers in over 40 operations in the United States, Europe, and Japan.

Menasha's origins date back to entrepreneurial efforts of woodenware manufacturers in the mid-19th century midwest. In 1849 a pail factory was founded in Menasha, Wisconsin. The undercapitalized venture was then sold to Elisha D. Smith for $1,200 in 1852 and named Menasha Wooden Ware Company. By 1871, 250 employees manufactured products ranging from pails to tubs, churns, measures, butter tubs, fish kits, kannikins, keelers, and clothes pins. After further growth, the operation was incorporated on May 24, 1875. Expanded size involved expanded risk, and in 1875 the original pail factory was destroyed by fire. Twelve years later, in 1890, the entire company was devastated by yet another fire, with only the Cooperage Shop escaping destruction. But quick reconstruction was followed by further expansion. In 1895 the founder's son, Charles R. Smith, merged a broom handle and barrel factory with the Menasha Wooden Ware Company, creating the world's largest manufacturer of turned woodenware.

During the first decade of the 20th century, timberlands and related operations were acquired throughout Wisconsin and the Pacific Northwest, providing vital raw materials as the company grew over time. By 1915, Menasha supplied 27 million feet of timber annually and was the United States' foremost producer of wooden food packaging in bulk. In 1929 the company began production of wood flour with its plant in Tacoma, Washington. In 1969 lumber products were further expanded as Menasha merged with the John Strange Paper Company, creating the Appleton Manufacturing Division and a majority interest in the Wisconsin Container Corporation, later to become Menasha's Solid Fibre Division. By 1980, wood fibre production—used primarily as industrial fillers and extenders in products such as plywood and molded plastics—had increased enough to warrant an additional wood fibre plant in Centralia, Washington, and the 1987 purchase of yet another plant in Marysville, Washington.

Over time, Menasha would form its Forest Products Group specifically to develop its timber interests. By the early 1990s, its Land & Timber Division managed the corporation's 100,000 acres of timberlands in the Pacific Northwest alone, meeting worldwide timber needs. In addition, the Wood Fibre Division produced organic based wood flours. In 1990 the Menasha's Forest Products Group broke new ground by entering the export market for hardwood chips from Alaska's interior. The move was regarded as unique on several accounts: first, Alaska's interior had been traditionally neglected in favor of other forests, such as the Tongass National Forest in the state's southeastern region; secondly, Menasha focused on the hardwood chip industry instead of round-log White Spruce, the conventional choice for export; and finally, the new, untapped industry lacked developed transportation systems. Despite potential for substantial growth in the new operation, Menasha showed reservations, as voiced by Chris Maisch, forester for Menasha's Fairbanks operations, in a November 16, 1990, article in the *Alaska Journal of Commerce:* "We don't want to create false expectations. At the end of 12 months we're going to take a look at the numbers and make another decision."

While timber development provided raw materials for woodenware and wood packaging, its uses changed toward paper production as Menasha moved into production of corrugated containers. In 1926 Menasha Wooden Ware was split into two separate but affiliated companies, the Menasha Wooden Ware Company and the Menasha Wooden Ware Corporation. Accommodating changes in packaging technology, the latter organization produced Menasha's first corrugated containers in 1927. By 1935, corrugated containers had supplanted their wooden predecessors, and Menasha discontinued its line of barrels, converting woodworking plants to the manufacture of toys and juvenile furniture. To supply its growing corrugated business with necessary raw materials, the corporation acquired an interest in the Otsego Falls Paper Company in Michigan, which would eventually be fully acquired to head off Menasha's Paperboard Division. Its paper machines would produce corrugating medium for several markets: the production of corrugated containers at Menasha's own container plants, outside sales, and trading in exchange for additional types of paperboard used but not manufactured by Menasha.

From the post-war era into the early 1960s, Menasha focused on expansion of its core business in corrugated containers and timber, acquiring and developing new facilities for corrugated medium, containers, plywood, wood fiber, and lumber. Major investments in the G. B. Lewis Company of Watertown, Wisconsin, led to Menasha's funding of that company's reorganization and Menasha's subsequent entry into plastic handling containers and other plastic products. With diminishing emphasis on woodenware products and increased diversity in the field of plastics, Menasha Wooden Ware Corporation changed its name to Menasha Corporation in 1962.

Corporate growth occasioned new emphasis on community services. In 1953 the Menasha Corporation Foundation was formed as an independent philanthropic organization funded by one percent of Menasha's pretax earnings. By the 1990s, the Foundation provided substantial support for charitable, educational, health and welfare, cultural, and environmental projects and programs. In education, the foundation contributed to a wide variety of colleges and universities, in addition to sponsoring scholarship programs for its employees and other qualified students. At the University of Wisconsin-Stout and Oregon State University, the foundation also sponsored fellowships for select students studying packaging or forestry. Beneficiaries of health and welfare allocations included the United Way campaigns in communities where Menasha had plants, and various chapters of Special Olympics, hospitals, retarded children's workshops, mental health centers, medical research appeals, and other concerns. The foundation also contributed to various cultural organizations, including the New Dramatists in New York City, Wisconsin Public Broadcasting, the Bergstrom-Mahler Museum in Neenah, Wisconsin, and the Oregon Coast Music Festival in Coos Bay, Oregon. Starting in the 1980s, the foundation increased contributions to environmental groups, including the Nature Conservancy, the Sigurd Olson Environmental Institute, the Ruffed Grouse Society, and the International Crane Foundation.

In the 1960s Menasha began a move toward packaging innovation and diversification that would position it as a main industry player by the 1990s. As part of a strategy to increase its share of the Midwest's corrugated market, the company purchased a plant in Coloma, Michigan, from Twin Cities Container Company. In addition to expansion of existing container plants and paperboard operations, Menasha began production of multicolor corrugated containers, foreshadowing future advances in graphics that would figure strongly a decade later. In 1967 new corporate offices were established in the town of Neenah, Wisconsin, replacing the former headquarters that had been destroyed by fire in 1964. Then, in 1968, the company purchased Vanant Packaging Corporation and developed its Sus-Rap Packaging operation, custom engineering and manufacturing interior protective packaging items to meet specific end-use requirements. Primary products of that line included Sus-Rap, Menasha Pads, and SuperFlute protective packaging. In 1969 a new container plant was opened in Grants Pass, Oregon, and in 1972 the Hartford Container Company, of Hartford, Wisconsin, was acquired. Further expansion in packaging brought the 1977

purchase of a plant in Mt. Pleasant, Tennessee, and then the 1989 purchase of Colonial Container of Green Lake, Wisconsin.

In 1991 Menasha and other packers benefited from a new common carrier rule, Alternate Rule 41/Item 222, that permitted savings on freight costs and increased productivity. The rule emphasized packaging stacking strength, as opposed to weight specifications of older rules. Consequently, packagers could use lighter but stronger combinations of liner and medium in their corrugated containers, reducing shipping costs and clearing the way for high-performance containers that offered not only better printability and runnability, but promoted reduction in solid waste, according to Bill Whitsitt, materials and testing consultant for Menasha, in a March 29, 1991, article for *PR Newswire*.

Just as changing packaging technologies had introduced corrugated containers to the woodenware arena in the 1930s, so the rise of plastics in the 1950s pushed Menasha to innovate and diversify in various areas of plastic manufacturing. In the postwar period, Menasha made initial investments in the G. B. Lewis Company of Watertown, Wisconsin. It's funding of the Lewis Company's reorganization introduced Menasha to the field of plastic material handling containers for the first time. The Lewis Company and plastics in general would become keys to long-term growth and diversification. In 1973 Menasha Corporation assisted in the construction of two new G. B. Lewis company plants in Monticello and Manchester, Iowa. The following year Menasha continued to strengthen its profile in plastics by acquiring the Poly-Hi Corporation of Fort Wayne, Indiana, a leading manufacturer of ultra high density polyethylene extruded products. By 1975, G. B Lewis had been fully acquired, and Menasha formed the LEWISystems and Molded Products Divisions of its Plastics Group. Success of LEWISystems prompted the 1980 purchase of Dare Pafco Products Company of Urbana, Ohio, to increase that division's capacity. Similar growth patterns of Poly-Hi also called for increased manufacturing capabilities, prompting the 1981 acquisition of Scranton Plastics Laminating Corporation of Scranton, Pennsylvania. Menasha's plastics operations expanded into reusable plastic and metal products with the 1984 acquisition of Traex Corporation of Dane, Wisconsin, specializing in such items as serving trays, dispensers for straws and condiments, tumblers, bus boxes, and ware-washing racks used in the food service industry worldwide.

Menasha's Plastics Group went international in 1985, when the corporation launched its first foreign joint venture with the Japanese firm of Tsutsunaka Plastic for the production of ultra high density polyethylene products. The joint venture's capital was set at Y15 million, with projected sales of Y1 billion for 1988. In 1987 Poly-Hi operations extended operations to Europe, with construction of a plant in Scunsthorpe, England. And in 1988 a precision injection molder of thermoplastics and engineered resins, Thermotech, was added to the Plastics Group. That division produced high performance plastic components for various applications including automotive, electrical/electronic appliances, and medical equipment.

Menasha's developments in packaging and plastics were paralleled, and often supplemented, by innovations in graphics and promotional labeling. In 1977 the corporation acquired a graphics container plant in Roselle, New Jersey, which it then moved to South Brunswick, New Jersey. In 1982 Vinland Web-Print, a producer of web-printed paper and plastic film products, was also acquired. Construction of an additional graphics container plant was completed two years later, in Olive Branch, Mississippi. Expanding into identification and merchandising tags and labels, the corporation acquired Mid America Tag & Label in 1985, followed by its 1986 acquisition of Murfin Inc., a Columbus, Ohio, web fed screen printer of label and identity products. With the 1987 acquisition of Neenah Printing, the corporation extended its graphics operations to a full range of printing services in commercial, business forms, and packaging applications, ranging from sample booklets to high image lithographic brochures. In 1989 the corporation added Labelcraft, Inc., of Farmingdale, New Jersey, to its Mid America division, specializing in custom designed tags and pressure-sensitive labels. Production capacity for those items was further augmented by the 1990 purchase of Denney-Reyburn of West Chester, Pennsylvania, and Tempe, Arizona.

The investments quickly paid off, winning valuable accounts in the early 1990s. In 1992 Mid America collaborated with the Pillsbury Corporation to design a pressure-sensitive label for the newly introduced Hungry Jack Syrup. Intended to create a "family" message for the complete Hungry Jack breakfast line and differentiate between regular and light versions of the syrup, the labels were given an honorable mention in the 1991 Tag and Label Manufacturers Institute annual awards. That same year, Mid America's label for DowBrands' Perma Soft shampoos and conditioners was designed to deliver an upscale feeling by its "no-label" look. The labels won first-place honors in the 1991 TLMI competition.

Over the course of its business expansion, Menasha also developed a Material Handling Division to manufacture reusable plastic container systems including recycling containers, food handling products, small parts bins, work-in-process containers, Stack-N-Nest containers, distribution containers, and transport trays, among other products. In 1986 the corporation's Molded Products Division introduced plastic pallets designed to maximize warehouse inventory stacking and reduce work-in-progress inventories by virtue of their uniform weight. Their wooden predecessors had not only been costly to maintain, but could vary by several pounds in weight, resulting in inventory error of up to thousands of parts in lightweight merchandise. In 1991 similar plastic pallets, marketed as Convoy Opte-packs, were combined with reusable corrugated sidewalls to maximize carrying volume and strength.

In response to heightened environmental concerns of the 1980s and 1990s, Menasha took initiatives to literally clean up its act, along with its surroundings. In its "Environmental Mission Statement," the corporation noted that "environmental and industrial hygiene goals can and should be consistent with economic health." And in 1989 negotiations were made with several discounters, including Wal-Mart, to provide products like unbleached cellulose packing material that could replace bubble wrap; other products included recyclable shipping boxes, video cases, and other ecological alternatives. "This isn't a gimmick," stated Larry Jenkins, sales and marketing manager of consumer products for Menasha, in a December 18,

1989, *Discount Store News* article. "There is a great deal of concern over this issue, and because we provide these products at the same price as competing ones, interest among retailers had been high," he continued.

In 1991 Menasha Corporation consolidated its developed industries into six primary business groups: Forest Products, Packaging, Promotional Graphics, Information Graphics, Plastics, and Material Handling. The Forest Products Group consisted of the Land and Timber division, Menasha Development, and Wood Fibre; Promotional Information Graphics Group consisted of Mid America, Murfin, Neenah Printing, and Printed Systems; the Packaging Group was made up of Menasha Packaging, Paperboard, and Color divisions; the Material Handling Group included Convoy, LEWISystems, and Special Products; and the Plastics Group combined Appleton Manufacturing, Molded Products, Thermotech, Traex, and Poly Hi Solidur. Such an operating structure divided the various divisions into working groups while permitting them to interrelate as working parts of an ever-more diverse organization.

Moving into the 1990s Menasha continued to expand and innovate, promising later additions to its already complex operating structure. In 1991 the corporation began marketing fully automated core preparation systems at various North American mills, such as the Blandin Paper Co.'s Grand Rapids, Minnesota, mill. It was estimated that, before Menasha's plan, fewer than 12 of roughly 726 paper mills in the United States and Canada had fully automated core preparation systems to prepare winding machines for consistency in quality, diameter, and length of paper rolls.

In the 1990s the corporation expected continued growth, as reflected by the 8,500-square-foot expansion and remodeling of its Neenah Printing prepress department in May of 1992. In addition, new federal labeling laws, scheduled for May of 1994, ushered in new business. Under the new regulations, food labels were to indicate precise amounts of fat, saturated fat, cholesterol, carbohydrate, and protein, as well as the percentage of recommended daily diet represented in those figures. While labelers like Menasha faced the problem of redesigning labels to accommodate much more information in much less space, they also looked forward to possible benefits of increased demand for new labels. Though many labelers anticipated increased business, most remained diplomatically even-tempered. "I don't think we're sitting here salivating," said Patricia Mulvey, marketing manager of the Mid America Division of Menasha Corporation in a January, 1993, article for *Packaging* magazine. With or without business from new labels, Menasha's history of growth and diversification could hardly be labeled anything other than successful.

Principal Subsidiaries: Land & Timber Division; Wood Fibre Division; Appleton Manufacturing Division; Molded Products Division; Poly-Hi Division; Thermotech Division; Traex Division; Color Division; Mid America Division; Neenah Printing Division; Convoy Plant; LEWISystems Division; Special Products Division; Menasha Packaging Division; Paperboard Division; Printed Systems Division; Murfin Division; Menasha Transport, Inc.

Further Reading:

Cox, Jackie, "Automated Core Prep Systems Are Expanding into North American Mills," *American Papermaker,* October 1991, p. 22.

"Custom P-S Labels Hit Target, Win Awards," *Packaging,* June 1992, p. 69.

Demetrakakes, Pan, "Packaging Field Gears Up for New Labeling Rules," *Packaging,* January 1993, p. 3.

Dunn, Richard L., "Custom-Designed Plastic Pallets Reduce Costs, Errors," *Plant Engineering,* April 10, 1986, p. 58.

Geist, Al, "Logging Has Potential in Interior," *Alaska Journal of Commerce,* sec. 1, p. 7.

Menasha Corporation, Press Release Kit, Neenah: Menasha Corporation, 1993.

"Packagers Enjoy Better Choices and Savings under New Common Carrier," *PR Newswire,* March 29, 1991.

"Reputation, Not Ads, Woos Customers," *Discount Store News,* December 18, 1989, p. 213.

"Tsutsunaka to Sell Menasha Products," *Japan Economic Journal,* November 16, 1985, p. 21.

Whitehead, Sandra, "On the Prowl for Growth Opportunities," *Corporate Report Wisconsin,* January 1991, sec. 1, p. 10.

—Kerstan Cohen

Merry-Go-Round Enterprises, Inc.

3300 Fashion Way
Joppa, Maryland 21085
U.S.A.
(410) 538-1000
Fax: (410) 676-5577

Public Company
Incorporated: 1970
Employees: 9,895
Sales: $761.1 million
Stock Exchanges: New York
SICs: 5651 Family Clothing Stores

Founded in Baltimore, Maryland, in 1968 as a trendy boutique selling only blue jeans, Merry-Go-Round Enterprises, Inc. (MGRE) has grown to become one of the leading retailers of contemporary fashion for men and women age 15 to 35. MGRE operates nearly 1,000 retail stores in 39 states, almost all of which are found in enclosed shopping malls. The original Merry-Go-Round chain and its sister stores, Dejaiz, Attivo, and Cignal, offer a wide range of high-fashion clothing from prom gowns to denim trousers. Due to astute financial practices and a keen ability to capitalize on up-and-coming fashion trends, MGRE has shown a consistent rise in revenues virtually since its incorporation as a public company in 1983.

The first Merry-Go-Round boutique was founded by boyhood chums Leonard Weinglass and Harold Goldsmith. Although Weinglass remains chairman of the board (Goldsmith passed away in 1991), he ceased to be involved in the company's daily business operations during the 1970s. Many operations were taken over by Michael Sullivan, who was hired as chief financial officer in 1974. Under Sullivan's direction, MGRE began to officially implement its long-standing policy of capitalizing on short-lived but profitable clothing fads, opening stores in the enclosed shopping malls that sprang up throughout the United States in the 1970s and 1980s.

In the early 1970s, store interiors were all black, and clothing was held in bins or by metal chains. As trends and styles changed, Merry-Go-Round also changed, and by the 1990s store interiors were brightened with neon and chrome, reflecting the tastes of the younger generation. Despite these cosmetic changes, the underlying market strategy of capitalizing on fashion fads remained constant. Over the years, Merry-Go-Round

and its sister stores have created their own market niche by positioning themselves as purveyors of trendy clothing. MGRE has remained financially secure through a combination of conservative business practices, intelligent acquisitions, and a keen ability to spot fashion trends.

Merry-Go-Round's first fashion coup was to sell prewashed patchwork denim jeans in 1974, which immediately became a hit among fashion-conscious youth and helped boost the company out of a recession. The company was also the first to place an order with Bugle Boy, a manufacturer of casual sportswear destined to become popular among teenagers. In 1977 Merry-Go-Round began capitalizing on the disco craze ignited by the movie *Saturday Night Fever* by selling silk shirts and three-piece polyester suits. When the movie *Urban Cowboy* was released, Merry-Go-Round stores began carrying Western wear and suede jackets with fringe on the sleeves. MGRE's buyers began closely studying the cable television channel MTV (Music Television) shortly after its debut in the late 1970s. From that point on, MTV became the source of many designs introduced in Merry-Go-Round stores. When pop star Michael Jackson appeared on MTV wearing a red leather jacket with 27 zippers, Merry-Go-Round sold more than 50,000 similar jackets at $29 each. Similarly, when the lead singer in the rock band Def Leppard performed in a video sporting a Union Jack sweatshirt with cut-off sleeves, a new fad was born. Merry-Go-Round sold over 40,000 copies of the sweatshirt at $15 each.

Cashing in on fashion trends is considered a risky business, but in 1979, MGRE realized that it was best not to tamper with its seemingly precarious formula for success. Fearing that the economic recession would hurt the high-end fashion business, Merry-Go-Round stores began selling less expensive, less fashionable clothing. Net income fell almost three quarters to $570,000, down from over $2 million in 1978. "We found out that customers weren't all that price-conscious," Sullivan told *Forbes* magazine in 1984. "They were more interested in fashion." Accordingly, Merry-Go-Round discontinued its lower priced merchandise and returned to selling more clothing that followed trends set by rock and roll and other media stars.

In 1982 MGRE opened two new clothing chains. Ship 'N Shore Showcase Shops, a woman's clothing chain, offered medium-priced sportswear—designed for a more conservative clientele of working women—manufactured by General Mills' Ship 'N Shore division. Another chain, DJ's Fashion Center for Men, offered a wider selection of male fashions than traditional Merry-Go-round stores and was aimed at attracting a clientele of fashion-conscious men, a group that had been previously underserved in most shopping malls.

Sullivan was promoted from chief financial officer to chief executive officer in the early 1980s. Under his direction, the rapidly expanding MGRE was subdivided into three divisions. The largest division was comprised of the Merry-Go-Round chain, numbering close to 200 stores. The second-largest, called the Menz division, housed the fast-growing DJ's chain, while the third-largest housed Ship 'N Shore Showcase Shops.

In July of 1983, with annual sales of $75.5 million and a net income of $3.5 million, or 88 cents a share, MGRE went public. By 1984 net income had jumped 108 percent to $7.3 million, or

$1.79 a share. MGRE owned 247 stores in 29 states: 204 Merry-Go-Round stores, 33 DJ's Fashion Centers for Men, and 10 Ship 'N Shore Showcase Shops.

MGRE continued its expansion in the mid-1980s, opening between 20 and 25 new stores annually. Much of MGRE's growth was through purchasing and renovating unsuccessful clothing chains. "If we can find an attractively priced clothing chain of 15 to 20 stores with suitable locations, we would probably acquire that chain and convert it to our type of operations," Sullivan told Barron's in 1984. MGRE soon added to its Menz division Attivo, a clothing chain selling young men's fashion. Despite growing sales in its Menz division, MGRE's earnings dropped in 1986 and 1987. This was primarily due to a sluggish woman's clothing market, which affected sales in the Ship 'N Shore division. In response to the poor performance of Ship 'N Shore's conservative apparel, MGRE replaced the chain with Cignal, a new retail operation selling high-priced European-style men's and women's sportswear.

In 1987 MGRE was ranked 34th on Forbes list of the 200 best small companies in America, with a five-year average return on equity of 29.1 percent. The company continued expanding its profitable Menz division, buying the 28-unit sportswear chain Casey & Osh in 1988 to convert into a new chain of Attivo stores. Also that year, the Merry-Go-Round division made its first foray into the Manhattan market, opening a 3,500-square-foot store in the East Village. Including the Casey & Osh acquisition, the number of MGRE stores grew to 459 by March of 1988.

One of MGRE's most innovative concepts, Boogies Diner, a combination restaurant and clothing store was introduced in a Chicago test market in 1989 and went national with the opening of a Washington, D.C., store in 1990. Boogies Diner was the brainchild of MGRE founder and chief executive officer Leonard Weinglass, whose colorful personality, it has been conjectured, was the basis for the character Boogie in the 1982 movie Diner. Weinglass had privately opened a Boogies in Aspen, Colorado, and given the idea to MGRE free of charge. "We want to be on the cutting edge of things for young people, and we think this is it," Sullivan told the Washington Post. "This is retail overlaid by a theater aspect. The diner brings in people who would not normally be attracted by the retail and the retail attracts the diners." Contingent upon the success of the Washington store, the company planned to open other Boogies Diners in New York, Los Angeles, and Las Vegas.

A New York Times profile in 1990 attributed MGRE's success, in part, to strong inventory tracking and management as well as to the continuity of the company's top management. Paul D. Levine, Stuart M. Lucas, and Ken Rodriguez, heads of MGRE's Merry-Go-Round, Menz, and Cignal divisions, respectively, began as store clerks in the 1970s. "There's a lack of buying talent in the young men's business, and they seem to have it," a retail analyst said of the three men.

Under Lucas, MGRE launched I.O.U., its first private label. The I.O.U. brand offers reasonably priced casual clothing aimed at a teenage market. By 1990 the label accounted for 25 to 30 percent of MGRE's annual sales. I.O.U. tee-shirts, shorts, and sweatshirts were so popular that a number of counterfeit goods

were manufactured and sold. In 1992 MGRE filed suit against United Outlet Centers, New York-based discount stores, alleging that the chain manufactured and sold a number of counterfeit I.O.U. goods. The two companies settled out of court for an undisclosed amount of money and a promise from United Outlets not to violate the trademark again.

In 1991 MGRE was caught in a minor race relations scandal when a customer noticed that sales clerks at all MGRE stores were noting customers' race on the backs of all personal checks. A front-page story about the company's tactic appeared in the Boston Globe, on April 3, 1991. The following day, MGRE announced that it was discontinuing the practice. Company officials issued an apology but defended their position by stating that the noting of race on the backs of checks was "solely for identification purposes, in the event the check did not clear."

Profits continued climbing as the number of stores owned by MGRE grew to 600 by March of 1990. Share prices soared from approximately $6 to almost $27 dollars in just 18 months. However, a decision by Weinglass and a "key partner" to sell $32 million of their MGRE stock in 1989 and another $43.8 million in 1990 caused strong speculation among the investment community that MGRE's heady growth was cooling. Market analysts predicted that once MGRE's recent outlet acquisitions reached the sales levels of older stores, double-digit growth would be difficult to sustain.

MGRE's impressive profit growth continued unabated through the fiscal year ending February 1, 1992. Profits for that year fell 39 percent, caused in part by a slow-down in the women's clothing market and deep discounting during the Christmas season. In response, MGRE initiated a number of measures to improve financial results. Among them were a 45 percent cut in salaries for top officers, a 7 percent reduction in inventory, and careful control of business expenses. At the company's annual meeting, Sullivan outlined a ten-year plan to boost business through expansion, increasing the number of MGRE stores from 900 to 1,800.

True to plan, MGRE purchased the Worth retail chain of 88 NET Work women's clothing stores in June of 1992 for an undisclosed price. MGRE retained the NET Work name but added a line of men's clothing to the pre-existing line of moderately-priced women's wear. Within two weeks of the Worth purchase, MGRE entered into negotiations to purchase three units of the Baltimore-based Hamburgers clothing chain. The company also opened two Boogies Diners and a prototype Merry-Go-Round Fashion Cafe, that year, with the Las Vegas location breaking company records for sales volume.

In August of 1992 MGRE stock posted an upturn after a positive recommendation from Kidder Peabody & Co. Financial results for that year were mixed, however; Net sales increased by only 15 percent, even though the number of stores increased by 20 percent. MGRE continued its expansion in 1993, purchasing the 476-store chain of Chess King/Garage men's clothing stores from Melville Corp. for an undisclosed amount. Market experts seemed confident of MGRE's chances for success through the rest of 1990s. As one analyst put it,

Merry-Go-Round Enterprises, Inc., "is as good as anybody at identifying what's hot, getting it to the store, and selling it."

Further Reading:

Andrews, Edmund L., "Turning Short-Lived Fads Into Steady Growth," *New York Times,* June 10, 1990, p. F5.

Byrne, John A., "Weird," *Forbes,* February 13, 1984, p. 92.

Swisher, Kara, "The Fun Is Just Beginning for Merry-Go-Round," *Washington Post,* May 31, 1990 p. E1; "Diner-Clothing Store to Open," *Washington Post,* November 29, 1990, p. B1.

Troxell, Thomas N. Jr., "Rock 'n' Retailing," *Barron's,* June 18, 1984, p. 48.

Weber, Joseph, "Why Is 'Boogie' Making Tracks?," *Business Week,* June 25, 1990, p. 29.

—Maura Troester

Microdot Inc.

P.O. Box 3001
Fullerton, California 92634-3001
U.S.A.
(714) 871-1550
Fax: (714) 680-0175

Private Company
Incorporated: October 30, 1950 as the Felts Corporation
Employees: 4,500
Sales: $500 million
SICs: 3452 Bolts, Nuts, Rivets & Washers; 3496
    Miscellaneous Fabricated Wire Products

Microdot traces its history to a small fastener manufacturer based in southern California called the Felts Corporation. Established on October 30, 1950, the Felts company turned out a narrow line of clips, nuts and bolts, and tiny cable connectors. These connectors, used in miniaturized hearing aids, are what set the company apart from other manufacturers. At the time, hearing aid cords were unable to withstand frequent bending and often broke off. Felts, however, had developed a durable flexible cord that proved so resistant to breakage that it came with a three-year guarantee. This small market provided the company with an entree into the electronics industry. And, as a trend emerged to miniaturize electronic devices, the demand for ever smaller components began to rise.

Felts took on larger supply contracts in 1955, providing fastening devices to auto manufacturers and electronic components to the emerging aerospace industry. On November 28 of that year Felts became Microdot Incorporated, adopting its new name from one of the company's popular product lines.

On January 6, 1956, Microdot made use of its growing cash flow by acquiring the business of the Nupro Corporation, another small components manufacturer. In 1960, as the business continued to grow, Microdot absorbed several other companies, including San Diego-based Nacimo Products, Micro-Test Inc. in Santa Clara, and another manufacturer called Lerco Electronics. These acquisitions strengthened Microdot's position in aerospace supply markets, which consisted mainly of special computer components and advanced instrumentation.

While it was one of the largest manufacturers of its kind, Microdot remained highly specialized. Further diversification required additional acquisitions, for which the company had insufficient capital. Therefore, in 1960, Microdot went public, later gaining a listing on the American Stock Exchange. In January 1961, now capitalized for further external expansion, Microdot acquired the Spectralab Instruments Company, a leading manufacturer of telemetry instruments based in Monrovia, California. A month later the company took over Owens Laboratories' line of strain gage power supplies and control equipment. Microdot's move into instrumentation devices cleared the way for a bolder presence in that market. In March of 1962, the company purchased Varec, Inc. for $1.9 million. Based in nearby Compton, California, Varec was a leading designer and manufacturer of liquid control gauges, tank-venting equipment and other liquid storage products.

This new emphasis by Microdot on industrial control systems turned out to be highly fortunate. Only months later, President Kennedy delivered his famous speech on space exploration in which he challenged the nation to put a man on the moon and return him safely to Earth, and to accomplish this historic task before the end of the decade. The nation's aerospace industry was charged with developing the systems that would fulfill Kennedy's dream. Grumman built lunar modules, McDonnell Aircraft and North American built the command ships, Martin made the space suits, and companies such as Boeing, Lockheed, and Northrop built launch rockets and other systems.

The race to the moon created plenty of room for subcontractors such as Microdot. With the heavy reliance on liquid fuel systems, as well as water and other liquid controls, Microdot found itself performing a crucial role in the space program. While it took several years for space-related projects to dominate the controls segment of Microdot's business, this demand provided the necessary drive for the company to continue expanding.

In March of 1965, Microdot purchased a 51 percent interest in the White Lighting Company. It increased this share to 65 percent two months later, paying slightly more than $400,000. Microdot was able to provide the lightweight power sources that White required for its line of commercial fluorescent lighting fixtures. That same month Microdot took over Lincoln Dynamics, Inc. This company, whose name was subsequently changed to Microdot Magnetics, dealt mainly with magnet-operated control devices.

The architect of Microdot's rapid growth was a lawyer named Robert S. Dickerman. Originally an advisor to Microdot, Dickerman was drawn deeply into the company's operations. In 1958 he was persuaded to abandon his law practice altogether and join Microdot as president and full-time director. At the time of Microdot's public share offering in 1960, Dickerman was chair of the corporation. Recognizing an opportunity to capitalize on the growth of the instrumentation industry, Dickerman decided to achieve growth rapidly through a series of acquisitions.

Fortunately for the companies Microdot took over, much of the research, manufacturing, and administrative structures of these companies was left untouched. Dickerman believed that synergy alone would provide Microdot with the greatest benefit, and that efficiencies through the elimination of job redundancies could be handled in time.

In fact, Microdot marked sales of only $2 million in 1960, with average sales per employee of $12,000. By 1966, sales had climbed to $15.2 billion and sales per employee was in excess of $21,000. In wider terms, Microdot had grown at a rate of 30 percent each year since it went public.

Dickerman's acquisition strategy also succeeded in drastically changing the company's customer profile. Once dependent on military contracts for more than 90 percent of its sales, commercial projects had grown to half of Microdot's business by 1967. This type of transformation, at a time of rapidly escalating military spending, proved nearly impossible for other companies that were caught in a similar situation.

The primary reason for Microdot's growth in industrial and commercial markets was its acquisition of White Lighting. Consolidated into Microdot from the day it was taken over, the White operations initially stumbled. After its first year, when it contributed more than $1 million to Microdot's total sales, White began to lose money. An effort to immediately cut costs led to the elimination of several unprofitable product lines and the consolidation of several managerial and administrative functions. In all, annual expenditures were reduced by $100,000 and a degree of profitability was restored.

With the Gemini space program in full swing, preparations for Apollo under way, and a booming business with defense contractors, Microdot saw demand for a range of new products. The company introduced seven new product lines, including telemetry calibration devices, pressure transducers, turbine flow meters, and solid state component connectors. These added more than $800,000 to Microdot's annual sales, and helped to make up for the sputtering performance of the commercial sector.

Through its spate of acquisitions, Microdot collected a network of five small factories, concentrated mostly in and around Los Angeles. However, one of these facilities, part of White Lighting, was located in Hialeah, Florida. In addition to Varec and Microdot Mechanics, which the company operated as separate subsidiaries, Microdot operated joint venture companies in Britain and Belgium that manufactured industrial control devices.

Strong sales of about $140 million set the stage for several new acquisitions during 1967. Microdot purchased the Dynisco instrument division of the Abex Corporation in April. This company manufactured heat and pressure transducers, further strengthening Microdot's position in this market. In June, the company acquired the Meyers Company, a manufacturer of metal eyeglass frame and other optical components based in Glendale, California.

By far, however, Microdot's most important acquisition occurred in October, when it absorbed the operations of the Kaynar Manufacturing Company, located in Fullerton, California. Kaynar, a privately owned company founded by Frank A. Klaus, made a line of lightweight self-locking metal fasteners for aerospace and other industrial customers. Because its sales were almost as great as Microdot's, the acquisition represented a virtual doubling of the company's size overnight.

The external growth program continued unabated through 1968. During March and April, Microdot added the businesses of Aircraft Threaded Products and Adams Supply, both suppliers of fastening devices, primarily for aerospace industries. In November, the company acquired Jutco, Inc., a Los Angeles-based manufacturer of molded cables and aircraft support harnesses. During 1969, Microdot took over Drawn Metal Products, and later merged its operations with the Vare Corporation, a steel products company based in Greenwich, Connecticut.

This expansion became unwieldy for Microdot leadership. Under Bob Dickerman, white collar employment ballooned into a classic managerial morass. Progressively dragged down by an increasingly stifling bureaucracy, Microdot's directors turned to the head of Vare, Rudolph Eberstadt, Jr. Eberstadt built Vare from an anemic steel products company—Republic Industrial, which he inherited from his father in 1961—into a major manufacturer of steel moulds. Although an engineer by training, Eberstadt proved highly successful in the business of turning around his steel finishing company. By 1967 the company was sound enough to acquire Valley Mould & Iron, an ingot mould maker. Their subsequent merger yielded Vare, a conglomeration of the names Valley and Republic. While many steel companies were converting to continuous casting, a significant but declining market remained for ingot moulds. As one of the few companies remaining in the business, Vare earned a substantial income from older steel mills that still relied on the obsolete product.

Aware of the fate that would befall his company if he did not diversify immediately, Eberstadt turned to Microdot. By combining operations, he could continue to draw down his steel mould business while channeling profits from the dying trade into Microdot's acquisition funds. Unfortunately, in combining Microdot and Vare, the company's board preserved Dickerman's position and responsibilities on the West Coast, while entrusting Eberstadt with a separate position of authority in Greenwich. This impossible state of affairs ended when the board persuaded Dickerman to retire.

Finally able to place the company under a single vision, Eberstadt began to selectively disassemble those parts of the company that were no longer strategic core businesses of Microdot. In 1973, Microdot sold off Wiley Manufacturing, a crane-making operation, and Clyde Iron Works, a fabricated steel business, and began to wind down several other operations. Not among these, however, was the still-profitable ingot mould business. In fact, the company opened a second mould plant in Chicago. This, combined with two other plants at Cleveland and Hubbard, Ohio, afforded Microdot a leading position in the market, supplying 40 percent of all ingot moulds sold in the United States.

While continuing to draw a profit from these operations, Microdot began to channel further investment into electronic systems and fasteners, including a new line of products intended to meet federal standards for auto safety. Microdot was a leading manufacturer of devices that sounded an alarm in new car models when drivers and passengers failed to fasten their seat belts. Ironically, the company's position in this growing market was due to Bob Dickerman's idea to acquire Malco Manufacturing and the Kent Corporation, both electronic terminal connector manufacturers, in 1971. A similar acquisition attempted under Eberstadt for a similar component manufacturer called Elco Corporation, hit a snag in March, 1973, when a federal judge blocked Microdot from buying more than 50 percent of the company, ostensibly on antitrust grounds.

While Microdot continued to adjust its operations to take advantage of new and emerging markets, Eberstadt succeeded in placing the company on firmer financial ground. Microdot's accounting practices, which he described as ''incomprehensible'' upon joining the company, had given way to simpler schedules that allowed the chief executive to make more enlightened decisions. However, these procedures also clarified Microdot's position in the industry to observers who were on the hunt for a good strong company to take over. On December 3, 1975, Eberstadt was blindsided by a surprise bid for Microdot from the General Cable Corporation. The bid offered $17 for each share of Microdot which, at the time, was trading at under $12. Apparently deeply offended that his life's work could be merely purchased out from under him, Eberstadt launched a vigorous attack on General Cable and the corporate culture of hostile acquisition. He ran a series of newspaper ads calling the practice unethical, immoral, and harmful to business, and implored other corporate leaders to voice their outrage to those who profited from it: commercial and investment banks.

Surprisingly, Eberstadt got a response. By telephoning other executives, he persuaded many to support his campaign. He charged that General Cable's chair R. P. Jensen launched the bid only to protect his annual bonus, that Morgan Stanley was lobbying for a buyout, and that brokers were hungry for commissions. All these allegations were denied, and the $17 per share offer stood. Microdot (and, later, General Cable) amended its rules to require greater voting majorities to fend off hostile takeovers. On December 8, Microdot's board advised shareholders to reject the offer.

As General Cable began to build momentum for its offer, Eberstadt made a highly unusual—and desperate—move. He proposed that Microdot liquidate; literally, to sell off all its businesses and close. This, he maintained, would provide shareholders with more than $17 per share. Eberstadt then filed suit against Irving Trust, the lead bank in General Cable's bid, charging that the company breached nondisclosure rules and provided General Cable with information while working for Microdot.

Faced with certain defeat on his proposal to dissolve Microdot, as well as his lawsuits, and unable to prevent General Cable from going ahead with its tender offer, Eberstadt began searching for a friendly suitor. He asked another investment banker, Goldman Sachs, to invite bids from other companies. If nothing else, Eberstadt was determined to deny his company to General Cable.

Goldman Sachs quickly turned up Ben Heineman, president of Chicago-based Northwest Industries, the parent company of interests spun off from the Chicago & Northwestern Railroad Company. Heineman's company offered to purchase Microdot for $21 per share, a price General Cable refused to match. Thus, in April of 1976, Microdot shareholders tendered 83 percent of their shares to Northwest, effectively foiling General Cable's bid. Eberstadt later told the *Wall Street Journal,* ''If we had to be acquired, Northwest was the best people to go with.'' But it was far from a victory for Rudy Eberstadt who, after 16 years as

the chair of his own company, refused to be a mere division manager. Shortly after Northwest took control of Microdot, Eberstadt resigned from the company and was succeeded by Larry Blackmon, Microdot's head of operations.

Events were no easier for those who remained with Microdot. While Heineman insisted that Microdot be run autonomously, managers were no longer free to make decisions on their own authority. Instead, an entire layer of management was added to Microdot merely for the purpose of reporting monthly operating statistics to Northwest.

A few months later, when Northwest completed its takeover of Microdot, it had paid a total of $81.5 million for the company. However, Heineman's company began to suffer greatly under the stress of its widely varied business, which included Acme Boot, Lone Star Steel, and General Battery, as well as BVD underwear, a range of food products, and a chemical manufacturer. While business remained strong at Microdot, Northwest was forced to divest several of its businesses.

In 1984, after selling off Northwest's Buckingham Foods business to Beatrice, serious losses at Lone Star Steel prompted Heineman to sell Microdot. Rather than returning Microdot to public ownership or selling it to another company, Northwest elected to turn the company over to a group of senior managers at the division, led by Richard P. Streubel. Streubel's group took control of Microdot for $121 million. While this represented a $40 million profit for Northwest, it was still reportedly $20 million less than the company's book value. But under the circumstances, Heineman's financially distressed company was in no position to hold an auction. Eventually, Northwest itself became the prime takeover target of a number of leveraged buyout artists and later was acquired by Chicago financier Bill Farley.

Microdot, however, virtually disappeared from public view. As a private company it was no longer obliged to issue an annual report or publish its financial statistics. In addition, the company halted news releases to the media and avoided press coverage.

Extreme changes were taking place within Microdot. The company sold off its automobile-related companies and concentrated instead on aerospace markets. As a result of the Reagan Administration's armament and Strategic Defense Initiative programs, this segment was growing faster than any other industrial market. In the process of this reorientation of the business, Microdot reduced the number of its manufacturing facilities from 20 to only six, including one in Britain. Microdot thus emerged with only two operating divisions, an Interconnect Systems group and Aerospace Fastening Systems group.

Despite the retrenchment of Reagan's defense programs during the Bush and Clinton administrations, in the early 1990s Microdot remained concentrated in promising aerospace markets, where civilian and scientific, as well as military, resources are likely to be directed in future years, regardless of corporate and government budget restraints.

Principal Subsidiaries: Microdot Aerospace Ltd. (UK); Interconnect Systems Division; Aerospace Fastening Systems Group.

Further Reading:

Campanella, Frank, "Streamlining to Pay Off in Peak Net at Microdot," *Barron's,* November 26, 1973, pp. 26–28.

Johnson, Robert, "Northwest Industries Starts to Restructure by Selling Microdot Unit for $121 Million," *Wall Street Journal,* January 4, 1984, p. 8.

Koshetz, Herbert, "Microdot, to Combat Bid, Plans a Liquidation Vote," *New York Times,* January 6, 1976, p. 37.

Margolies, Susan, "Takeover Trauma: Microdot Officials Find Jobs Dull after Firm Is Sold to Big Company," *Wall Street Journal,* pp. 1–30.

Microdot Inc. Profile, Fullerton, CA: Microdot Inc.

"Microdot Inc. to Sue Irving Trust over Role in Proposed Take-Over," *Wall Street Journal,* January 21, 1976, p. 10.

"Microdot's Directors Urge Rejection of Bid by General Cable Corp.," *Wall Street Journal,* December 8, 1975, p. 11.

"Northwest Industries Wins 83% of Common in Microdot Tender Bid," *Wall Street Journal,* March 5, 1976, p. 21.

Rattner, Steven, "Microdot Sounds Alarm on Take-Over Attempts," *New York Times,* December 22, 1975, pp. 47–48.

Rolland, Louis J., "Microdot Methodology," *Financial World,* September 6, 1967, pp. 20–21.

"What's in a Name?," *Forbes,* June 15, 1975, p. 60.

"Wider Markets a Boon to Microdot, Help Spark Rapid Gain in Earnings," *Barron's,* November 15, 1965, p. 25.

—John Simley

Minnesota Mining & Manufacturing Company (3M)

3M Center
St. Paul, Minnesota 55144-1000
U.S.A.
(612) 733-1110
Fax: (612) 737-2759

Public Company
Incorporated: 1929
Employees: 87,015
Sales: $13.88 billion
Stock Exchanges: New York Pacific Chicago Tokyo Paris
  Amsterdam Swiss German
SICs: 2672 Paper Coated and Laminated, nec; 2678
  Stationery Products; 2891 Adhesives and Sealants; 3086
  Plastics Foam Products; 3089 Plastics Products, nec; 3291
  Abrasive Products; 3695 Magnetic and Optical Recording
  Media; 3841 Surgical and Medical Instruments; 3842
  Surgical Appliances and Supplies; 3843 Dental Equipment
  and Supplies; 3844 X-Ray Apparatus and Tubes; 3845
  Electromedical Equipment; 3861 Photographic Equipment
  and Supplies

The largest manufacturer in Minnesota, the 29th largest industrial company in the United States, and a member of the Dow Jones ''30,'' Minnesota Mining & Manufacturing Company (officially abbreviated as 3M) is Wall Street's epitome of high-tech/low-tech business and solid blue chip performance. Its daunting inventory of some 60,000 products runs the gamut from Post-it Notes and Scotch tape to floppy disks and transdermal patches of nitroglycerin. Its equally daunting global presence extends to subsidiary companies in 57 countries and markets in more than 200, as well as net sales from international operations of $7 billion, fully half of the company's total revenue. 3M owes its formidable strength to its unusual corporate culture, which comfortably fosters innovation and inter-departmental cooperation, backed by a massive research & development budget, which in 1992 exceeded $1 billion. Because of this, 3M ranks as a leader in—and in many cases a founder of—a number of important technologies, including flexible magnetic media, pressure sensitive tapes, sandpaper, protective chemicals, synthetic casting materials, reflective materials, and premium graphics. The company is divided into three major sectors: Industrial and Consumer ($5.2 billion in 1992 sales);

Information, Imaging, and Electronic ($4.6 billion); and Life Sciences ($4 billion).

3M was formed in 1902 in Two Harbors, Minnesota, a thriving village on the shores of Lake Superior, by five entrepreneurs in order to mine the rare mineral corundum and market it as an abrasive. The ill-planned venture—sparked by a flurry of other forms of mining operations in northeastern Minnesota—nearly bankrupted the company, for its mineral holdings turned out to be not corundum but low-grade anorthosite, a virtually useless igneous rock. This unsettling discovery (by whom or when is unclear) was never disclosed in the company records and, for whatever reason, did not deter the owners from establishing a sandpaper factory in Duluth, another more or less ill-fated scheme that placed the company further in jeopardy (3M faced a host of abrasives competitors in the East and was soon forced to import a garnet inferior to that owned by domestic manufacturers, which resulted in a lower quality product).

In May 1905 a principal investor named Edgar B. Ober, determined to save the company, convinced friend and fellow St. Paul businessman Lucius Pond Ordway to join with him in rescuing 3M from almost certain demise by paying off $13,000 in debt and pumping in an additional $12,000 in capital. Together Ordway and Ober purchased 60 percent of the company; over the next several years, Ordway, a self-made millionaire, spent an additional $250,000 on a company that had yet to produce a profit, and Ober, who proceeded to oversee 3M, went without a salary. Ordway's continued backing, despite a strong desire to cut his losses early on and his decision to move the firm to St. Paul in 1910, ensured 3M's eventual health during the boom years following World War I.

However, of greatest significance to both the company's foundation and future were the hirings in 1907 and 1909 of William L. McKnight and A. G. Bush. Former farmhands trained as bookkeepers, the two worked as a team for well over 50 years and developed the system that helped make 3M a success. McKnight ran 3M between 1916 and 1966, serving as president from 1929 to 1949 and chairman of the board from 1949 to 1966. He created the general guidelines of diversification, avoiding price cuts, increasing sales by 10 percent a year, high employee morale, and quality control that fueled the company's growth and created its unique corporate culture. In some ways, the sales system overshadowed the guidelines. McKnight and Bush designed an aggressive, customer-oriented brand of salesmanship. Sales representatives, instead of dealing with a company's purchasing agent, were encouraged to proceed directly to the shop where they could talk with the people who used the products. In so doing, 3M salesmen could discover both how products could be improved and what new products might be needed. This resulted in some of 3M's early innovations. For instance, when Henry Ford's newly motorized assembly lines created too much friction for existing sandpapers, which were designed to sand wood and static objects, a 3M salesman went back to St. Paul with the news. 3M devised a tougher sandpaper, and thus captured much of this niche market within the growing auto industry. Another salesman noticed that dust from sandpaper use made the shop environment extremely unhealthy. Around the same time, a Philadelphia ink manufacturer named Francis G. Okie wrote McKnight with a request for mineral grit samples. According to Virginia Huck, ''McKnight's handling of Okie's request changed the course of 3M's history. He could have explained to Okie that 3M didn't sell bulk mineral. . . . Instead, prompted by his curiosity, McKnight instructed 3M's Eastern Division sales manager, R. H. Skillman, to get in touch with Okie to find out *why* he wanted the grit samples.'' The reason soon became clear: Okie had invented a waterproof, and consequently dust-free, sandpaper. After purchasing the patent and then solving various defects, 3M came out with WetorDry sandpaper and significantly expanded its business, eventually licensing two other manufacturers, Carborundum and Behr-Manning, to keep up with demand. It also hired the inventor as its first full-time researcher. This marked the creation of one of the nation's first corporate research and development divisions.

Sending salesmen into the shops paid off a few years later in an even more significant way, by giving 3M its first non-abrasives product line. In 1923 a salesman in an auto body painting shop noticed that the process used to paint cars in two tones worked poorly. He promised the painter that 3M could develop an effective way to prevent the paints from running together. It took two years, but the research and development division invented a successful masking tape—the first in a line of pressure-sensitive tapes that now extends to over 900 varieties. The invention of Scotch tape, as it came to be called and then trademarked, established 3M as a force for innovation in American industry. Taking a page from its sandpaper business, 3M immediately began to develop different applications of its new technology. Its most famous adaptation came in 1930, when some industrious 3M workers found a way to graft cellophane, a Du Pont invention, to adhesive, thus creating a transparent tape.

Transparent Scotch tape, now a generic commodity, provided a major windfall during the Depression, helping 3M to grow at a time when most businesses struggled to break even. Another salesman invented a portable tape dispenser, and 3M had its first large-scale consumer product. Consumers used Scotch tape in a variety of ways: to repair torn paper products, strengthen book bindings, mend clothes until they could be sewn, and even remove lint. By 1932 the new product was doing so well that 3M's main client base shifted from furniture and automobile factories to office supply stores. During the 1930s, 3M funnelled some 45 percent of its profits into new product research; consequently, the company tripled in size during the worst decade American business had ever endured.

3M continued to grow during World War II by concentrating on understanding its markets and finding a ''niche'' to fill, rather than shifting to making military goods, as many U.S. corporations did. However, the war left 3M with a need to restructure and modernize, and not enough cash on hand to do so. To meet its building needs, in 1947 3M issued its first bond offerings. Its first public stock offering, coupled with its tremendous growth rate, attracted additional attention to 3M. In 1949, when President McKnight became chairman of the board (with A. G. Bush also moving from daily operations to the boardroom), it marked the end of a tremendous era for 3M. Under McKnight, 3M had grown almost twentyfold. By its fiftieth year, it had surpassed the $100 million mark and was employing some 10,000 people.

Such growth could not be ignored. Now that 3M was publicly traded, investment bankers took to recommending it as a buy, business magazines sent reporters to write about it, and other companies tried to figure out how 3M continued to excel. McKnight's immediate successor as president, Richard Carlton, encapsulated the company's special path to prosperity with the phrase: ''we'll make any damn thing we can make money on.'' Yet the 3M method involved a great deal more than simply making and selling. Its métier had been, and continues to be, finding uninhabited markets and then pursuing to fill them relentlessly with high-quality products. Therefore, research and development received money that most companies spent elsewhere—most companies still did not have such departments by the early 1950s—and the pursuit for ideas was intense.

Carlton kept the company focused on product research (today, 3M rewards its scientists with Carlton Awards), which led to another innovation in the 1950s, the first dry-printing photocopy process, ThermoFax. 3M breezed through the 1950s in impressive fashion, with 1959 marking the company's 20th consecutive year of increased sales. Yet, for all its growth and diversity, 3M continued to produce strong profits from its established products. In a way, this was almost to be expected, given 3M's penchant for being in ''uninhabited'' markets. As noted by John Pitblado, 3M's president of U.S. Operations, ''almost everything depends on a coated abrasive during some phase of its manufacture. Your eyeglasses, wrist watches, the printed circuit that's in a TV set, knitting needles . . . all require sandpaper.''

In the 1960s 3M embarked on another growth binge, doubling in size between 1963 and 1967 and becoming a billion-dollar company in the process. Existing product lines did well, and 3M's ventures into magnetic media provided excellent returns. One venture, the backdrops used for some of the spectacular scenes from the 1968 movie *2001: A Space Odyssey,* earned an Academy Award. During the 1970s a number of obstacles interfered with 3M's seeming odyssey of growth. Among these were the resignations of several of the company's top executives when it was revealed that they had operated an illegal slush fund from company money between 1963 and 1975, which included a contribution of some $30,000 to Richard Nixon's 1972 campaign. Sales growth also slowed during the decade, particularly in the oil crunch of 1974, ending 3M's phenomenal string of averaging a 15 percent growth rate every five years. 3M responded to its cost crunch in characteristic fashion: it turned to its employees, who devised ways for the company to cut costs at each plant.

The company also had difficulties with consumer products. Particularly galling was the loss of the cassette tape market, which two Japanese companies, TDK and Maxell, dominated through engaging in price cutting. 3M stuck to its tradition of abandoning markets where it could not set its own prices, and backed off. Eventually, the company stopped making much of its magnetic media, instead buying from an overseas supplier and putting the 3M label on it (3M instead focused attention on data storage media for the computer market, in which it continues as a world leader). The loss of the cassette market was not overwhelming: revenues doubled between 1975 and 1980, and in 1976 3M was named one of the Dow Jones Industrial 30.

Unfortunately, price cutting was not the only problem confronting 3M as it entered the 1980s. Major competitors seemed to face the company on all fronts: the niches of decades past seemed extinct. When Lewis Lehr became company president in 1981, he noted that "there isn't a business where we don't have to come up with a new technology." He promptly restructured 3M from 6 divisions into 4 sectors: Industrial and Consumer, Electronic and Information Technologies, Graphic Technologies (later renamed Imaging and combined with Information and Electronic), and Life Sciences, containing a total of some 40 divisions. He also established a goal of having 25 percent of each division's earnings come from products that did not exist five years before. Lehr's concern was not to keep the company going, for 3M was still well respected, with a less than 25 percent debt-to-equity ratio and reasonable levels of growth. Shareholders, too, had little to complain about, for 1986 marked the 18th consecutive year of increased dividends. Rather, Lehr wanted to ensure that 3M would continue to develop new ideas. The major product to come out of the 1980s was the ubiquitous Post-it, a low-tech marvel created by Art Fry.

Despite its gargantuan size, the company maintains a distinctively entrepreneurial environment and, through one of its several legendary "rules," allows its employees to spend up to 15 percent of company time on independent projects, a process called "bootlegging" or "scrounging." As *In Search of Excellence* authors Thomas J. Peters and Robert H. Waterman, Jr., have written, because heroes abound at 3M, because scrounging is encouraged, because failure is okay, because informal communications are the norm, because overplanning and paperwork are conspicuously absent, because of these and a half-dozen more factors "functioning in concert—over a period of decades," innovation works at 3M.

For the future, the company may be expected to increase its global stature (in May 1993 it began construction of a $21 million electrical components factory in Malaysia); adopt a more aggressive marketing posture (in January 1993 it introduced Scotch Brite Never Rust scouring pads and planned a $9 million ad campaign targeted at Brillo and SOS users); and continue its massive R&D spending (the new, leading corporate rule, under CEO L. D. DeSimone, is *30* percent of sales from products introduced in the last *four* years). In the long run, 3M has little to worry about. A near fixture on *Fortune*'s annual list of the most admired companies in America, 3M is that most prized of conglomerates: a perennial money-maker with the innovative culture and managerial drive to ensure that it remains so.

Principal Subsidiaries: Media Networks, Inc.; National Advertising Co.; Riker Laboratories, Inc.; Sarns, Inc.; 3M Argentina S.A.C.I.F.I.A.; 3M Australia Pty. Ltd.; 3M Oesterreich GmbH (Austria); 3M Belgium S.A./N.V.; 3M do Brazil Limitada; 3M Canada Inc.; 3M A/S (Denmark); 3M Health Care Limited (England); 3M United Kingdom P.L.C.; Suomen 3M Oy (Finland); Laboratories Riker, S.A. and Moser 3M S.A. (France); 3M France, S.A.; 3M Deutschland GmbH (Germany); Kettlehack Riker Phrama GmbH (Germany); 3M Far East Limited (Hong Kong); 3M Hungaria Kft. (Hungary); 3M Italia Finanziaria S.p.A. (Italy); 3M Health Care Limited (Japan); 3M Mexico S.A. de C.V.; 3M Nederland B.V. (Netherlands); 3M Norge A/S (Norway); 3M Puerto Rico, Inc.; 3M Singapore Private Limited; 3M South Africa (Proprietary) Limited; 3M Espana, S.A.; 3M Svenska AB; 3M 9East) AG; 3M (Schweizland) AG (Switzerland); 3M Manufacturera Venezuela, S.A.; Eastern Heights State Bank of St. Paul (99%); Sumitomo 3M Limited (Japan; 50%).

Further Reading:

Dubashi, Jagannath, "Technology Transfer: Minnesota Mining & Manufacturing," *Financial World,* September 17, 1991, pp. 40–1.

"3M: New Talent and Products Outweigh High Costs," *Financial World,* February 18, 1992, p. 19.

Goldman, Kevin, "Scouring-Pad Rivals Face 3M Challenge," *Wall Street Journal,* January 11, 1993, p. B5.

Houston, Patrick, "How Jake Jacobson Is Lighting a Fire under 3M," *Business Week,* July 21, 1986, pp. 106–07.

Huck, Virginia, *Brand of the Tartan: The 3M Story,* New York: Appleton-Century-Crofts, 1955.

Kelly, Kevin, "3M Run Scared? Forget About It," *Business Week,* September 16, 1991, pp. 59, 62.

Larson, Don, *Land of the Giants: A History of Minnesota Business,* Minneapolis: Dorn Books, 1979.

Mattera, Philip, "Minnesota Mining and Manufacturing Company," *World Class Business: A Guide to the 100 Most Powerful Global Corporations,* New York: Henry Holt and Company, 1992, pp. 465–67.

Meyers, Mike, "3M Reports 9% Increase in Net Income on Worldwide Sales Gain of 2.3 Percent," *Star Tribune,* May 4, 1993, p. 1D.

Mitchell, Russell, "Masters of Innovation: How 3M Keeps Its New Products Coming," *Business Week,* April 10, 1989, pp. 58–63.

Moskowitz, Milton, et al, "3M," *Everybody's Business: A Field Guide to the 400 Leading Companies in America,* New York: Doubleday, 1990.

Our Story So Far: Notes from the First 75 Years of 3M Company, St. Paul, MN: 3M Public Relations Department, 1977.

Peters, Thomas J., and Robert H. Waterman, Jr., *In Search of Excellence,* New York: Harper and Row, 1982.

3M Annual Reports, St. Paul, MN: 3M, 1951, 1990–1992.

"3M: 60,000 and Counting," *The Economist,* November 30, 1991, pp. 70–1.

Weiner, Steve, "A Hard Way to Make a Buck," *Forbes,* April 29, 1991, pp. 134–35, 137.

—Jay P. Pederson

Modine Manufacturing Company

1500 DeKoven Avenue
Racine, Wisconsin 53403
U.S.A.
(414) 636-1200
Fax: (414) 636-1361

Public Company
Incorporated: 1916
Employees: 5,348
Sales: $570,839 million
Stock Exchanges: NASDAQ
SICs: 3714 Motor Vehicle Parts and Accessories; 3443
    Fabricated Plate Work (Boiler Shops); 3585 Refrigeration
    and Heating Equipment

Modine Manufacturing Company is an independent, worldwide leader in heat transfer technology serving vehicular, industrial, commercial, and building markets. Modine develops, manufactures, and markets heat transfer products for use in various automotive original equipment manufacturer applications, and for sale to the automotive aftermarket as well as a wide range of heating, ventilating, and air-conditioning markets.

Modine Manufacturing Company was the brainchild of Arthur B. Modine, who graduated from the University of Michigan, Ann Arbor, in 1908 with a degree in engineering and became involved in a Chicago-based radiator repair business where he began experimenting with various radiator designs. In 1912 A. B. Modine moved to Racine, Wisconsin, and became a principle partner in Perfex Radiator (a predecessor to a company Modine Manufacturing would later acquire), where Modine was actively involved in research, testing, and design of radiators. Following a business disagreement with a silent partner at Perfex over how that company should be managed and capitalized, Modine decided to establish his own company.

A. B. Modine founded Modine Manufacturing in 1916 to make radiators for farm tractors. Modine became president and treasurer of the company, which opened a one-room office adjacent to a small workshop in Racine. Soon after opening his office, Modine developed the company's first major product—the Spirex farm tractor radiator—a radiator core with a spiral fin put in the radiator cells which helped with the product's heat transferability.

In December 1916, Modine filed for a patent (issued seven years later) on his Spirex radiator and, in 1917, Modine's radiator was literally called into service by the United States when it became standard equipment on World War I artillery tractors. By the end of 1918, the majority of leading tractor manufacturers were using the company's radiators.

In 1921 Modine Manufacturing entered the field of commercial building heaters after A.B. Modine developed a unit heater—a product enabling buildings to be heated without extensive ductwork—by putting a fan behind an automotive radiator and attaching the assembly to factory steam pipes in order to supply heat. During the early 1920s Modine Manufacturing tried to market its Spirex radiator to Ford Motor Company, but because of the way the radiator's frame was designed, the Spirex was unsuitable for automobiles. By 1925 though, A. B. Modine had designed an automotive radiator, called the Turbotube, which helped Modine Manufacturing land its first major automotive contract that year when Ford adopted the radiator as standard equipment for the Model T. Ford quickly became Modine's principle customer and its major source of income, a role the auto maker would play in Modine's operations for the next 55 years.

Modine Manufacturing received a patent for its unit heater in 1928. That same year the company—boasting a wide mix of automotive, truck, and tractor customers—went public, issuing 100,000 shares of stock on the Chicago (later the Midwest) Stock Exchange. The October 1929 stock market crash did little to affect company sales that year, which climbed to a record $5.5 million. But the following year sales dipped below $4 million and by 1932, when revenues had plunged below $1 million, Modine Manufacturing suffered what would be its last annual loss, of $165,000.

By the early 1930s Modine Manufacturing had moved into the home-heating field and was offering a line of convection heaters for homes, including models targeting large, upscale houses. In 1932 the company landed a contract to produce radiators for Ford's new V-8 engine, which helped Modine Manufacturing pull out of the recession. Business continued to increase through 1937 and reached a peak for the decade that year when the company recorded $8.5 million in sales.

In 1940 Modine Manufacturing developed a vehicular wind tunnel and after the United States entered World War II, the company's technology was again enlisted by the government, with the wind tunnel used to test combat vehicles. During the war, while the wind tunnel was working on domestic soil, the company's convectors took to the sea, having been adapted to Naval vessels. The company also produced radiators for military tanks, tractors, trucks, and bulldozers during the war.

In 1946 A. B. Modine gave up his post as president and became chair of the board. Walter Winkel, who had been actively running the company since 1936 while A. B. Modine was involved in research and product development, succeeded Modine as president. Two years later Winkel died and C. T. Perkins became president.

Modine Manufacturing benefited from the postwar boom in automobile sales, which helped to push annual revenues above $25 million in 1951. During the 1950s Modine began using aluminum to produce heat exchangers and, with the advent of air conditioning, the company began producing all-aluminum brazed air-conditioning coils for passenger cars and trucks in 1956. That year Modine Manufacturing received a patent for its concentric oil cooler, a device destined to become standard equipment on cars with automatic transmissions.

During the late 1950s and early 1960s the company doubled its product line by securing new automotive contracts and introducing new applications for heat exchangers. In 1958, a smaller, more efficient prototype radiator helped Modine Manufacturing secure a contract to become the sole supplier of radiators for the new Ford Falcon. About the same time Modine began supplying American Motors Corporation with a passenger-car radiator. During the early 1960s, Modine extended its use of heat exchangers for buildings and introduced products for school heating and ventilation systems.

In 1961 Modine Manufacturing received a patent for its Alfuse chemical process, a means of fusing aluminum to aluminum that was used to produce condensers. That same year the company received a patent for its light-weight louvered serpentine radiator fin, which was bonded to radiator tubes in a serpentine fashion—as opposed to a plate-type fin bonded in parallel rows—and improved the efficiency of a radiator's heat transferring ability.

At the end of 1961 A. B. Modine retired from active service with the company he founded, although he remained on the corporate board as a director. C. T. Perkins was named to succeed Modine as chair beginning in 1962.

In 1963 Modine Manufacturing became the prime oil cooler and radiator supplier for Rambler. Ford, during the 1960s, steadily increased its production requirements and Modine responded by producing an ever-growing list of truck radiators, aluminum heat exchangers, and aluminum oil coolers. The increased use of aluminum, which required separate production facilities, as well as the increased business from Ford and other auto makers, found the company facing the need to expand production capabilities. That expansion was led by E. G. Rutherford, who became president in 1963. During the next 11 years Rutherford guided the steady growth of the company, which climbed from $34.5 million in sales to $110 million, while the number of its employees was doubled to 3,500 as production facilities grew from six to 13.

In order to facilitate such growth, in 1967 the company engaged in its first long-term borrowing. A. B. Modine, who was still a director, was adamantly against the company taking on debt, but the company's top management convinced the founder that the loan was necessary in order to accommodate the company's growth.

In 1969 Modine Manufacturing received a patent for its Flora-Guard unit heater for greenhouses. That same year the company made its first acquisition, Schemenauer Manufacturing, a privately-owned Ohio maker of unit ventilators and rooftop air-conditioning units.

In 1971 Modine introduced its BT Unit oil cooler, a more efficient type of cooler named after the British Thermal Unit. Two years later the company received its first patent on a Donut oil cooler, originally designed for John Deere tractors but later finding successful applications on high-performance European automobiles.

Modine Manufacturing had been serving the aftermarket business informally for a number of years and, in 1972, established the subsidiary Modine Auto-Cool to produce and sell complete replacement radiators. In 1974 E. E. Richter was named president and Rutherford began a short stint as chair, before dying unexpectedly the following year and leaving the position vacant.

Beginning in the mid-1970s Modine began diversifying away from automotive radiators and entering new vehicular heat-transfer markets. During this period Modine introduced new products for heavy-duty trucks, as well as construction, industrial, agricultural, and drilling and mining equipment. During the latter half of the decade Modine also expanded its production of oil coolers, as well as its production of condensers and evaporators for vehicle air conditioning.

In 1979 Modine established an international marketing group for export purposes and began leasing a New Berlin, Wisconsin plant in order to manufacture automotive air conditioning condensers. By the end of the 1980 fiscal year annual sales were $200 million and Modine was the leading supplier of air-conditioning condensers for Japanese automobiles imported to the United States.

In 1979, with nearly half of Modine's sales volume going to Ford, the major auto maker decided to begin making its own light-truck radiators—which represented nearly 20 percent of Modine's product volume then. At that time, Modine's top 10 customers accounted for as much as 88 percent of Modine's sales—with much of that being geared to the original equipment automotive market—and with Ford responsible for 40 percent or more of all revenues.

During the 1980s the company made a series of moves to lessen its dependence on the cyclical and recession-prone automotive original equipment market. In 1980 the company made its first aftermarket acquisition, Lake Auto Radiator Manufacturing Company, and entered the market for replacement radiator cores. Sales and earnings dipped slightly for the company's fiscal year ending in March 1980, and in October of that year Modine borrowed $10 million from the Wisconsin Investment Board. Sales continued to fall in the fiscal year 1981 and revenues dropped to $7.4 million, down from $14.4 million two years earlier.

In 1982, after years of research and development, Modine introduced its heavy-duty Beta-Weld radiator—the first radiator to feature welded tube-to-header joints. That same year Modine began manufacturing operations outside the United States and established a joint venture in Canada to produce radiators for the aftermarket. In 1983 the Canadian venture, Ontario Limited, became the company's first wholly owned non-U.S. facility.

In fiscal 1983 Modine's sales followed the "double dip" recession and slid more than $30 million, as profits dropped from $8.7 million to $3.8 million. In late 1983, having weathered the worst of the early 1980s recession, Modine restructured its management into a four-man executive office headed by Richter, as president and chief executive. Alex F. Simpson, Richard T. Savage, and B. K. Jacob were named group vice presidents and members of the executive team. In early 1984, Modine switched its stock listing from the Midwest Stock Exchange to NASDAQ.

During the mid-1980s Modine stepped up its market diversification and international expansion efforts and purchased joint or minority interests in several foreign producers of radiators and other heat exchangers. In 1984 Modine Manufacturing established the Holland joint venture NRF Holding B.V., and took 45 percent ownership in the overseas company designed to produce radiators for automotive aftermarkets and original equipment markets. Another joint venture was established that same year in Austria to produce aluminum condensers and evaporators for sale to European passenger car manufacturers.

In 1984 Modine also began a four-year program of acquiring North American aftermarket companies involved in the radiator core and distribution businesses. Acquisitions in 1984 included West's Radiator, Inc. of Indianapolis, a distributor and retail radiator repair shop, and Beacon Auto Manufacturing Company, Inc., a regional replacement radiator core maker and warehouse distributor.

The additional businesses, along with record auto and truck production and aftermarket sales, helped accelerate sales, which topped $300 million in 1985, while earnings soared to $21.5 million, 50 percent higher than ever. Acquisitions in the 1985 calendar year included Eskimo Radiator Manufacturing Company, and Perfex Radiator Group of McQuay Inc., a heat-transfer business with sales to vehicular and industrial markets, with about $30 million in annual sales.

In 1985 the company also entered a joint venture in Germany with Windhoff G.m.b.H to produce heavy duty vehicular and industrial heat transfer products. That same year Modine established another joint venture in Mexico to produce radiators for the Mexican original equipment market.

The company received a patent on its Beta-Weld technology in 1985 and the following year Modine introduced and received several patents for its PF (parallel flow) family of products. The PF condenser, a passenger car heat-exchanger, was designed to use less refrigerant and to reduce or eliminate the use of freon, a chlorofluorocarbon that damages the ozone layer. In 1986 Modine sued the Allen Group's G & O Radiator for alleged infringement on Modine's Beta welded-radiator technology.

An usually cool summer, increased price competition in radiators for the automotive aftermarket, and the cost of assimilating Perfex into Modine operations contributed to a $1 million dip in earnings in 1986. A $1 million settlement with the Environmental Protection Agency over alleged violations of the Clean Water Act pushed earnings down almost another $1 million in 1987. A lower tax rate in 1987, along with a big boost in sales coming from acquisitions, help put Modine earnings back on the upswing the following year.

During the late 1980s Modine acquired numerous manufacturers and distributors of radiator repair parts in its efforts to reduce dependency on original equipment markets. In 1987 Modine purchased Stuart-Western Inc., a California manufac-

turer and distributor of automotive radiator cores, and Heatex Division of Howden Ltd., a Toronto-based manufacturer of radiators and radiator cores primarily for the Canadian automotive aftermarket. The two acquisitions brought Modine an additional $40 million in annual sales.

Additional acquisitions in 1987 further solidified Modine's growing radiator and radiator core manufacturing and warehousing operations. Added to Modine's operations that year were Durafin Radiator Corporation, Central Radiator, Inc., Carolina Cooling Supply Company, Inc., and Octagon Cooling Systems Distributors, Inc. By 1988, when Modine acquired NAYCO Distributors, Inc., Modine's replacement radiator and radiator core businesses were the fastest growing markets for the company, representing a third of sales volume.

In 1987 Modine established a joint venture in Japan with Nippon Light Metal Ltd. The venture, Nikkei Heat Exchanger Company, was designed to manufacture and sell automotive heat exchangers to original-equipment manufacturers in the Japanese market. The following year Modine acquired complete ownership of Windhoff, G.m.b.H., and in 1989 Modine gained entire control of the joint venture it had established in Holland.

In February, 1989, Richter was named chair and Savage became president and chief operating officer. That same year Modine began a two-year acquisition program designed to expand its heating business and acquired Ted Reed Thermal, Inc., a Rhode Island-based heating equipment manufacturer with annual sales of $10 million. In the fall of 1989 Modine's commercial heating business unveiled a line of gas-fired, separated-combustion unit heaters. The following year Modine acquired Industrial Airsystems Inc., a St. Paul, Minnesota, manufacturer and marketer of heating and ventilating equipment for commercial facilities.

In 1990, Modine—in its largest acquisition ever—purchased the $60 million heat-transfer business of Sundstrand Corporation, a manufacturer of refrigeration and air-conditioning coils, secondary heat exchangers for high-efficiency residential furnaces, and copper and aluminum tubular components with operations in Michigan, Missouri, and Mexico. Sundstrand, which became the commercial products division in Modine's off-highway products group, brought with it customers that included original-equipment manufacturers of residential and commercial air conditioners, commercial refrigeration equipment producers, and residential heating systems producers—all representing new markets for Modine.

After five years litigation, in 1990 Modine received an $18.6 million settlement from the Allen Group over the infringement lawsuit on Modine's Beta-Weld radiator technology. In 1991 Savage assumed the additional duties of chief executive officer when Richter retired from active employment after 44 years with Modine. By the time of the company's 75th anniversary in 1991, Modine's sales totalled nearly $500 million, stemming from more than 50 locations around the world.

In late 1991 Modine filed a lawsuit against two firms with parent companies in Japan—Mitsubishi Motor Sales of America, Inc. and Showa Aluminum Corporation—charging the companies with infringement of Modine's patents on its PF condensers. In April 1992, an International Trade Commission judge ruled in favor of Mitsubishi Motor Sales and Showa Aluminum, interpreting Modine's patent as covering only a narrow range of product types. Modine filed an appeal and, in November 1992, with that appeal still pending, the company announced it had licensed its PF condensers to a third Japanese firm, Nippondenso Company Ltd., a major competitor of Showa Aluminum. The deal added less than $10 million in annual sales. In July of 1993, the U.S. International Trade Commission reversed its earlier ruling, upholding Modine's patent, but excluding the specific condensers used by Showa and Mitsubishi from Modine's patent coverage. Modine planned to appeal the court's exclusion of the subject condensers at the Federal Circuit Court of Appeals for Patents.

During the late 1980s and early 1990s Modine extended its Beta-Weld line of radiators to include new models for off-road construction and a variety of engine packages. Modine also introduced a long-life bus radiator core featuring Beta-Weld technology, and a variety of charge-air coolers for trucks and vehicles with turbocharged or supercharged systems. Modine's expanded product mix, and its continued penetration into markets in heat-transfer businesses, helped the company break the half billion sales level for the first time in fiscal 1992.

Modine entered fiscal 1993 having, since the late 1970s, successfully cut much of its dependence on recession-prone major automobile manufacturers and broadened its share of the replacement radiator business. In its 1992 to 1993 fiscal year, Modine's top 10 customers accounted for only one-third of its sales, down from three-quarters of all sales in 1977 when the company relied heavily on Ford and other major original equipment manufacturers for the bulk of its business. And since 1979, when Ford took its light truck radiator business in-house, Modine has not only diversified its automotive operations, but strengthened its nonautomotive operations as well, specifically in the field of commercial building activities.

But Modine, as noted in a 1992 *Forbes* article, remains "focused" on the business with which it began—heat exchangers. The company expects its cutting-edge leadership in heat-transfer technology—such as that which led to the development of PF condensers, light-weight aluminum radiators and parts, and Beta-Weld radiators—to pay ongoing dividends. To this end, in July of 1993 Modine acquired Längerer & Reich, a German limited partnership that produces charge-air coolers, oil coolers, radiators, and other heat-exchangers for the European market, with sales in 1992 of $120 million. Modine's continuing strategy, which it has followed throughout the duration of its history, is to seek diversification and growth in heat-transfer and closely related fields, both in North America and abroad.

Further Reading:

Byrne, Harlan S., "Modine: Record Share Net Is in Sight," *Barron's,* October 5, 1992.
Byrne, Harlan S., "Modine Manufacturing Co.: Maker of Radiators Puts Its Trust in the "Junk Out There," *Barron's,* May 28, 1990, pp. 53–54.
Carey, David, "Using Its Strengths to Best Advantage," *Financial World,* November 14–27, 1984, pp. 83–84.
Cochran, Thomas N., "Modine Manufacturing Co.: Radiator Maker Loosens Ties to Auto Industry's Cycle," *Barron's,* November 7, 1988, pp. 106–107.
Foran, Pat, "Acquisitions Fire a Hot-Growth Period at Modine Manufacturing," *Milwaukee Business Journal,* August 27, 1990, p. 8.
Gordon, Mitchell, "Modine's Move: Acquisitions, Lower Tax Rate Put Company Back into Record Territory," *Barron's,* June 1, 1987, pp. 61–62.
Modine Manufacturing Company (75th Anniversary) Annual Report 1990–91, Racine, Wisconsin: Modine Manufacturing Company, 1991, p. 6.
Rees, Matt, "Staying Focused," *Forbes,* April 27, 1992, p. 136.

—Roger W. Rouland

▲ NAGASE & CO., LTD.

Nagase & Company, Ltd.

1-17- Shinmachi 1-chome
Nishi-ku
Osaka 550
Japan
(06) 535-2114
Fax: (06) 535-2160

Public Company
Incorporated: December 1917
Employees: 1,860
Sales: ¥599.0 billion (US$4.69 billion)
Stock Exchanges: Tokyo, Osaka
SICs: 5169 Chemicals & Allied Products, Nec; 5198 Paints,
   Varnishes & Supplies

Nagase & Company, Ltd. is Japan's foremost chemical products trading company. The company deals mainly in dyestuffs and chemicals, but also handles a variety of plastics, semiconductor manufacturing materials and equipment, pharmaceuticals, enzymes, medial and dairy farming equipment, abrasives, cosmetics, and the equipment to manufacture them. Nagase is different than other chemical companies in Japan in that the bulk of its products are produced under license from other companies. As a chemical trading company, Nagase merely distributes the finished products of other companies or manufactures those products as a licensee. As a result, Nagase is not required to devote huge sums of money to maintain leading technology labs devoted specifically to the development of new chemical compounds. Instead, these responsibilities fall to the companies for whom Nagase acts as an agent. Their investments in new technology are recovered through sales, and companies such as Nagase are there to facilitate greater sales.

Like many other venerable Japanese companies, Nagase traces its history back more than 160 years. The company was originally established as a small family trading enterprise, dealing mainly in dyestuffs that were used to color fabric. Even then Nagase did not function as a manufacturer of commodities, but as a wholesaler/retailer. While little is known about the founding family, the company was established in Osaka in 1832 at a time when Japan was closed to international relations. Osaka, one of Japan's major pre-industrial centers of commerce, provided an excellent market for Nagase. Many of the area's

industries were based in the production and finishing of textiles. As these industries prospered, so did Nagase's small business.

Decades later, when Japan opened its doors to international commerce, Nagase became acquainted with foreign dyes that contained unusual pigments, derived mostly from unique plants and other organic sources along the trade routes of the Middle East, India, Southeast Asia, and the United States. At the time of the Meiji Restoration in the 1860s, when Japan embraced an effort to modernize and industrialize along Western models, Nagase experienced another period of expansion. As Japanese textile manufacturers adopted more efficient Western production methods, their output increased. This resulted in increased demand for silk and other fabrics and the dyes to color them. The growth of Japan's production capacity enabled the country to export a wide variety of products. One of the most lucrative at the beginning of Japan's industrial period was textile products. The fine quality of the silk, careful construction, and beautiful pure dyes made Japanese fabrics and clothing extremely valuable in trading.

As the production capacity of resource-poor Japan increased, the economy became increasingly mercantilist. Japanese manufacturers now imported the majority of the resources needed to make a product, and then finished the goods and sold them at a value added premium. The same situation existed for Nagase, which in 1900 established business ties with the Chemical Industry of Basle, A.G., now known as Ciba-Geigy Ltd. Nagase imported a variety of products from Ciba, but virtually all were chemicals limited to industrial applications. Ciba, meanwhile, had become involved in manufacturing pharmaceuticals, a few of which Nagase later handled.

By 1917 Nagase had outgrown its heritage as a family company. In order to expand, the company required massive sums of money that could not be satisfied through conventional investment loans. In December of that year the company was formally incorporated. The majority of shares remained in family hands or were purchased by banks and other large corporations.

To establish better ties with emerging chemical industries in the United States, Nagase had set up a sales office in New York City in 1915. From this office, Nagase could better observe developments in the American chemical industry and quickly establish purchase orders and sales agreements for new products. The office marked a major success in 1923 when Nagase established an important trading relationship with Eastman Kodak Company, a manufacturer of chemicals and photographic materials. The importance of Nagase's agency business grew dramatically in 1930 when the company reached an agreement with the Union Carbide Corporation to market that company's products in Japan. A few months later Nagase established a similar agreement with the Swedish chemical concern Aktiebolaget Separator, now known as Alfa Laval AB.

Japanese industry continued to grow at an enormous pace through much of the 1930s as Japanese industrial companies began to exploit the massive natural resources of neighboring countries, such as Korea and Taiwan, which were occupied by Japan. By 1937, however, Japan turned toward military adventurism, by invading China and, ultimately, the rest of Asia. With

Japan on a war footing, called the "quasi-war economy," many of Japan's principal industries came under direct government control. Nagase, a major company in the chemicals industry, was also committed to war production. The primary nature of its business, however, was in trading. A trade embargo from the United States cut off Nagase's supply of American products, and the war in Europe virtually eliminated business with Ciba and other firms located in England and Germany.

But Nagase did manufacture a small quantity of products under license agreements. As long as raw materials were available, the company could remain in production. It managed to stay in business through much of the war, manufacturing coloring agents for military uniforms, flags, camouflage, and clothing. By the end of the war, Nagase was less devastated by bombing than by the complete unavailability of raw materials. The firm was effectively closed even before the armistice was concluded.

The managerial leadership of many companies, primarily the *zaibatsu* conglomerates, were subject to review by war tribunals. Many lost their positions, but few were imprisoned. Nagase, for its small and largely involuntary role in the Japanese war effort, was spared from these investigations. Faced with rebuilding the Japanese economy, many industries picked up where they left off. Once again, the textile industry emerged as an engine of growth for the economy because its factories survived the war and there was both strong domestic and foreign demand for the products. With trade restrictions eliminated, Nagase was able to resume its import agreements with numerous manufacturers. Nagase also rebuilt its non-dye operations, providing crucial chemicals and chemical technologies to a variety of industries, including ferrous and non-ferrous metals manufacturing, paint, and other compound manufacturing. The company's position in this area was strengthened in 1952 when it expanded its agreement with Eastman to include trading contracts with Eastman Chemical Products.

The 1950s were a period of strong growth for Japan's basic heavy industries. Companies in these fields laid the foundation for many new industries, including ship and vehicle manufacturing, electronics, and chemicals. Nagase's role in this period was primarily that of supplier, providing the necessary ingredients for paints and other treatments that finished large machinery. As volume increased, so did the demand for specially engineered products with unusual qualities and tolerances. This gave rise to additional contracts with foreign companies, bringing high-technology compounds and processes to Japan and firmly establishing Nagase's position as a market leader in high-tech chemicals.

Nagase gained a listing on the Osaka stock exchange index in 1964, enabling a wider variety of primarily local private investors to become owners of the company. Five years later Nagase was listed on the larger Tokyo index, and shares in the company were traded nationally and internationally.

In 1968 Nagase concluded an exclusive distributorship with General Electric Company of the United States, handling a variety of that company's products in Japan. Three years later, General Electric and Nagase established a plastics manufacturing joint venture called Engineering Plastics, Ltd. This important agreement was followed by the formation of a special joint venture with Ciba-Geigy in 1970. Nagase re-established its relationship with Ciba-Geigy immediately after World War II, when the Swiss company was divested from the German pharmaceutical combine IG Farben. Ciba remained one of the world's leading chemical engineering companies, and was a major supplier and licenser of Nagase. Nagase established a third joint venture company in 1974, called Landauer-Nagase Ltd. Nagase's partner in the venture was the American company Technical Operations, Inc. (now called Landauer, Inc.).

During the 1970s, Nagase gained a firmer position in the international market as a supplier of proprietary engineered compounds and processes. Foreign offices were no longer established with the single aim of gaining distribution of production rights. Instead, Nagase was now competing in foreign markets as a supplier. The company set up two subsidiaries in 1971, Nagase (Hong Kong) Ltd. and the Nagase America Corporation. The company established another subsidiary, Nagase Singapore (Pte) Ltd. in 1975. In 1980 the company opened an operation in Germany, Nagase Europa GmbH, and a second office in Singapore called Chang Fong Overseas Enterprises (Pte) Ltd. Rounding out its expansion into Southeast Asia, the company established Nagase (Malaysia) Sdn. Bhd. in 1982. Nagase subsequently opened new offices in the United States, Taiwan, Korea, England, Holland, Thailand, Canada, India, and Indonesia.

In 1988 Nagase received an award from the Ministry of International Trade and Industry, Japan's government agency charged with industrial coordination. Nagase was awarded for its contributions to international trade through import promotion. This was an unusual and important commendation in light of Japan's much larger and often maligned export industries.

In 1989 the bulk of Nagase's business was still in the distribution of other company's products, leading to a decision to establish a new Science and Technology Foundation and a Research and Development center at Kobe. These research institutes were dedicated to testing existing processes for improvement and developing new biotechnologies and organically engineered chemicals. This marked an important turn in Nagase's mission; the company was no longer interested in merely handling another company's products. The lead time required to yield such technological breakthroughs is long. In addition, it takes many years to assemble a qualified staff that can properly channel the group's energies toward a successful discovery. The primary focus of the group is the development of organic chemical products.

In 1990 Nagase set up a plastics manufacturing operation in Taiwan called Nagase Wah Lee Plastics. This facility manufactures plastic compounds for several manufacturers in Taiwan that produce computer and electrical appliance casings and other products. In April of 1992 Nagase reintroduced itself to the chemical industry as a "technical information trader," promoting a new group of five subsidiary companies: Nagase Electronic Chemicals, Teikoku Chemical Industries, Nagase Chemicals, Nagase Biochemicals and Nagase Fine Chemical. These companies form the crux of Nagase's effort to pioneer biochemicals and organic compounds.

Nagase remains under the control of the founding family. Shozo Nagase, who oversaw much of the company's expansion during the 1960s and 1970s, serves as chairman. Hideo Nagase, another descendant of the company's founder, is president. Over the course of more than 160 years, Nagase has grown into one of Japan's largest chemical companies. Dyes and pigments for fabric, paper, and detergents comprise ten percent of the company's sales volume, while fine and industrial chemicals—including pharmaceuticals, cosmetics and biochemicals—comprise 38 percent. A further 42 percent of Nagase's sales are derived from plastics used in the automotive and electronics industries. The remainder of Nagase's sales comes from electronics, machinery, medical systems, and cosmetics.

Nagase was one of the first Japanese companies to make the foray into biochemicals. With the practical experience of its manufacturing affiliates and sales operations and the strength of its research institute, Nagase is a leader in these technologies. The company has been successful in laying the foundation for diversification and indigenously developed chemical technologies. In the future, this will enable the company to distance itself from lower-margin license production agreements with other companies and to develop its own more profitable patented products and processes.

Principal Subsidiaries: Nagase Barrel Finishing Systems Co., Ltd.; Nagase Beauty Care Co., Ltd.; Nagase Biochemical Sales Co., Ltd.; Nagase Electronic Equipment Service Co., Ltd.; Na-

gase Elex Co., Ltd.; Nagase Information Development, Ltd.; Nagase Machinery Service Co., Ltd.; Nagase Medicals Co., Ltd.; Nagase Plastics Co., Ltd; Nagase Storage & Distribution Co., Ltd.; Nagase Biochemicals, Ltd.; Nagase Chemicals Ltd.; Nagase-CIBA Ltd.; Nagase Cosmetics Co., Ltd.; Nagase Electronics Chemicals Ltd.; Nagase Fine Chemicals Ltd.; GE Plastics Japan Ltd.; Honshu Rheem Co., Ltd.; Kyoraku Co., Ltd.; Landauer-Nagase Ltd.; Setsunan Kasei Co., Ltd.; Teikoku Chemical Industries Co., Ltd.; Totaku Industries, Inc.; Nagase America Corp.; Nagase California Corp. (USA); Sofix Corp. (USA); Canada Mold Technology Inc.; Nagase & Co., Ltd. (Korea); Nagase (Taiwan) Co., Ltd.; Nagase Wah Lee Plastics Corp. (Taiwan); Nagase (Hong Kong) Ltd.; Nagase (Thailand) Co., Ltd.; Nagase (Malaysia) Sdn. Bhd.; Nagase Singapore (Pte) Ltd.; Chang Fong Overseas Enterprises (Pte) Ltd. (Singapore): Nagase (Europa) GmbH (Germany); Nagase Finance Europe B.V. (Netherlands).

Further Reading:

''Nagase'' (company profile and history), Osaka: Nagase & Company, 1992.
''Nagase & Co., Ltd.,'' *Diamond's Japan Business Directory 1991,* p. 1030.
''Nagase & Co., Ltd.: Financial Data'' Osaka: Nagase & Company, 1992
''Technical Info Trader Adopted as Catchword,'' *Japan Chemical Week,* July 9, 1992.

—John Simley

Nash Finch Company

7600 France Ave. S.
P.O. Box 355
Edina, Minnesota 55435
U.S.A.
(612) 832-0534
Fax: (612) 924-4939

Public Company
Incorporated: 1894 as Nash Brothers
Employees: 11,888
Sales: $2.51 billion
Stock Exchanges: NASDAQ
SICs: 5141 Groceries, General Line; 5142 Packaged Frozen
  Foods; 5143 Dairy Products; 5147 Meats and Meat
  Products; 5148 Fresh Fruits and Vegetables; 5411 Grocery
  Stores

The third largest publicly owned wholesaling firm in the United States, Nash Finch Company serves approximately 5,700 supermarkets in 29 states. In addition, its retail operations, which account for 32 percent of sales, encompass some 89 corporate stores in 13 states. Like Nash's large list of affiliated independent retailers and growing number of super warehouse stores, these outlets—Econofoods, Economart, Food Bonanza, Jack & Jill, Sun Mart Foods, Family Thrift Center, Warehouse Market, and Farm Fresh—feature the private label brands "Our Family" and "Buy 'n Save," which together represent approximately 1,400 dairy, meat, grocery, frozen foods, and health and beauty products. Nash Finch also owns Nash DeCamp Company, a produce marketing subsidiary based in California. Although Nash DeCamp contributes only one percent of overall sales, it is nonetheless considered a valuable asset for its penetration of markets worldwide and its ability to generate as much as five percent of total operating profits.

Nash Finch Company began in 1885 when Vermont native Fred Nash, after traveling west and toiling at several unpromising jobs, invested $400 and established a candy and tobacco shop in Devil's Lake, a Dakota Territory boom town. Nash soon enlisted his two younger brothers, Edgar and Willis, to join him. All three benefited from having worked in their parents' general store back East, and they shared a determination to live frugally so that their business might succeed. By the time North Dakota achieved statehood in 1889, the brothers had opened three addi-

tional stores, suffered the loss of one and severe damage to another from separate fires, and, finally, consolidated their operations in the emerging urban center of Grand Forks.

The year 1889 proved pivotal to the company for two reasons. The first stemmed from the serendipitous arrival in Grand Forks of a boxcar of peaches for which no buyer existed. Although primarily retailers, the Nash brothers had conducted some fruit wholesaling and quickly decided to secure a bank loan for the peaches. The venture was a large gamble—the brothers' only collateral was the Grand Forks store—but it paid off when sales were made to retailers throughout the region. Two years later the Nashes became wholesalers exclusively and earned the distinction of founding both the first and largest of the state's wholesaling firms. The second turning point came when Edgar contracted tuberculosis (then known as consumption) and moved to California for health reasons. While Edgar's new contribution as West Coast fruit buyer aided the growth of the company, a replacement was needed at the Grand Forks headquarters. That person was 14-year-old Harry Finch, who several decades later became president of the company. (A legacy of Finch management continued in the hands of Finch's grandson, Harold B. Finch, Jr., who was the company's chief executive officer and chairman of the board in the early 1990s.)

Although 1896 was overshadowed by the death of Edgar Nash in January, later that year the company celebrated its first expansion beyond North Dakota with the acquisition of the Smith Wholesale Company of Crookston, Minnesota. Harry Finch, still relatively young but now with seven years of experience in clerking and sales, was placed in charge of the Crookston operation, which was renamed Finch-Smith Company. After the turn of the century, Nash Brothers solidified its position as North Dakota's leading wholesaler with the successive purchases of Minot Grocery Company and Grand Forks Mercantile Company. A 1905 partnership forged with a budding Red River Valley produce brokerage named C. H. Robinson—to which Finch was elected vice-president—further broadened Nash's service base. After Nash Brothers acquired control of Robinson in 1913, branch offices were established in Minneapolis, Sioux City, Milwaukee, Chicago, Fort Worth, and virtually everywhere else the parent company had sprouted its own warehouse facilities. Until 1966, C. H. Robinson served as the produce procurement branch of Nash Brothers, because, at that time, the Federal Trade Commission succeeded in limiting Nash's broker-buyer monopoly. Ten years later, C. H. Robinson became independent and has since blossomed into a $935-million concern headquartered in Eden Prairie, Minnesota.

From 1907 to 1918, Nash acquired 54 fruit wholesalers spread throughout the northwestern United States and Canada. Highlights of this era included the establishment in Lewiston, Idaho, of White Brothers and Crum, the company's first fruit growing and shipping venture; the creation of the Randolph Marketing Company in Los Angeles to package citrus fruit; and the formation of Nash DeCamp, which would prove to be one of the company's most prized concerns. By 1919 Nash Brothers had become so vast that it required a more centralized headquarters. The logical choice was Minneapolis, which had developed into the nation's seventeenth largest city, a premier milling center, and the wholesaling hub of the Northwest. According to historian Bruce Gjovig in *Boxcar of Peaches: The Nash Bros. &*

Nash Finch Company, "Although the loss of the Nash Bros. headquarters was a blow to Grand Forks, the move made good business sense. . . . [In] Minneapolis, the Nash Bros. had joined the ranks of the Pillsburys, Cargills, and Hills." Two years later, the firm reincorporated under the name Nash Finch Company and consolidated its more than 60 businesses, which had previously functioned as separate units with independent officers. Canadian operations were united under Nash-Simington Ltd. while C. H. Robinson Company and Nash Shareholders became the corporation's primary subsidiaries. As the corporation's first president, Fred Nash oversaw the complex consolidation process, which was completed in 1925. His death the following year resulted in Harry Finch's elevation to president. Willis Nash remained as corporate treasurer and also served as president of the Nash Company, the Nash family's own investment corporation.

At the onset of the Great Depression in 1929, Nash Finch ranked as one of the foremost food distributors in the Midwest, with sales of more than $35 million. Because of its firm foothold within a recession-proof industry, Nash weathered the 1930s better than most U.S. manufacturers. The only year in which the company failed to turn a profit was 1932, generally considered the worst year of the Depression. During the 1930s, one of the most significant advances for the company came with its large-scale introduction and promotion of the Our Family brand, which had become a symbol of the company's operating philosophy and a favorite of Nash consumers by the 1940s.

During the early 1950s, Nash Finch re-entered food retailing with the purchase of 17 supermarkets in Nebraska. The move proved crucial to the company's future health, for it allowed Nash to remain competitive with much larger food concerns, including Eden Prairie-based wholesaler and retailer Super Valu Stores, Inc. From 1960 to 1969 Nash saw its sales grow from $91 million to $248 million. As the company increasingly diversified within its industry and offered a greater variety of services to its retailers, growth in overall revenues became even more impressive during the 1970s and 1980s. By the mid-1980s, Nash ranked as the nation's tenth largest grocery wholesaler, with sales of $1.3 billion. Its geographic sphere of influence, however, was still confined largely to the rural Midwest, which at the time represented a conspicuously slow-growth market. This, and just a five percent compound increase in earnings over a ten-year period (Super Valu's increase, over the same period, was 23 percent), had perpetuated what Dick Youngblood termed the company's "comparative anonymity." In an effort to improve his company's rankings within the food industry, Chairman Harold Finch, Jr. announced a sweeping expansion plan designed to nearly triple earnings and double revenues by the end of the decade.

The 1985 acquisition of M. H. McLean Wholesaler Grocery Company effectively inaugurated the plan. A North Carolina distribution facility serving approximately 60 Hills Food stores, the McLean Company signified additional wholesale revenues of roughly $100 million. More important, though, was Nash's consonant commitment to the South, with its higher-than-average population growth. A series of purchases, including that of Georgia's second largest food wholesaler as well as that of Colorado's largest wholesaler, highlighted the next few years. Yet, the Nash Finch Company entered the 1990s somewhat

precariously; quick profits had not followed quick expansion. Instances of store closings and margin problems related to three separate acquisitions led to notable charges against shares and, although revenues and book value climbed steadily, net income stagnated in 1988 before it plunged by 27 percent in 1989.

Nonetheless, optimism has predominated at the company and among its shareholders as Finch continues its strategy of achieving expansion through acquisition and improving profitability through broadened services and updated facilities. The early 1990s have been singularly bright for Nash Finch. Following a slight dip in net sales from 1990 to 1991 (during which time profits increased by seven percent), the company topped the $2.5 billion mark in 1992 revenues while posting its highest earnings ever—more than $20 million. Two Mid-Atlantic acquisitions in 1992, Virginia-based Tidewater Wholesale Grocery and a prominent division of Maryland-based B. Green & Company, fortified Nash's position as one of the largest distributors to the U.S. military. That same year, the company sought overseas growth by participating in a group venture to acquire 75 percent of Hungary's largest wholesale food company, Alfa Trading Company. The December 1992 loss of an account with Lunds Inc., a $120-million upscale Minnesota retail chain, seemed hardly to hinder the company; within four months it had reached an agreement to acquire Easter Enterprises, a 16-store chain with sales of $250 million. Headquartered in Des Moines, Easter consists of 11 stores in Iowa, three in Illinois, and two in Missouri. Perhaps the sweetest part of the deal is the lost business that it represents for Easter's former provider, Super Valu. The purchase also serves notice that Nash has no intention of abandoning its bread-and-butter Midwest market, which according to most recent estimates still represents approximately 70 percent of sales. That, no doubt, would be received as welcome news by the company's founder, a pioneering Midwesterner who, in February of 1989, received the high posthumous honor of being inducted into the North Dakota Entrepreneur Hall of Fame.

Principal Subsidiaries: GTL Truck Line Inc.; Nash DeCamp Company; The S. C. Shannon Company; T & H Service Merchandisers Inc.; Thomas & Howard Company of Hickory Inc.; Thomas & Howard Company of Rocky Mount Inc.; Timberlake Grocery Company of Macon Inc.; Virginia Foods of Bluefield Inc.

Further Reading:

Byrne, Harlan S., "Nash Finch Co.: It Puts Recent Acquisition Stumbles Behind It," *Barron's,* March 26, 1990, p. 40.

Cochran, Thomas N., "Nash Finch Co.: A Food Wholesaler Succeeds in the Retail End of the Business," *Barron's,* June 6, 1988, pp. 65–66.

Gelbach, Deborah L., *From This Land: A History of Minnesota's Empires, Enterprises, and Entrepreneurs,* Northridge, CA: Windsor Publications, 1988.

Gjovig, Bruce, *Boxcar of Peaches: The Nash Bros. & Nash Finch Company,* Grand Forks: Center for Innovation & Business Development, 1990.

Kennedy, Tony, "Lunds to Drop Nash Finch in Favor of Fairway Foods," *Star Tribune,* December 23, 1992, p. 3D.

Kennedy, Tony, "Nash Finch Acquires Wholesaler," *Star Tribune,* January 8, 1993, p. 3D.

Lambert, Brian, "Nash Finch Celebrates 100 Years of Business," *Corporate Report Minnesota,* March 1985, p. 19.

Marcotty, Josephine, "Nash Finch to Buy Midwest Supermarket Chain," *Star Tribune,* April 8, 1993, p. 3D.

"Nash Finch Invests in Hungarian Firm," *Star Tribune,* November 18, 1992, p. 3D.

"Nash Finch to Buy 16 Easter Stores," *Supermarket News,* April 12, 1993, p. 4.

"Nash Finch to Buy Supermarkets," *Wall Street Journal,* April 8, 1993, p. B5.

Sansolo, Michael, "Nash Finch: A New Horizon," *Progressive Grocer,* November 1985, pp. 40, 42.

Schafer, Lee, ed., "Super Valu Stores Inc.; Nash Finch Company," *Corporate Report Minnesota,* June 1991, pp. 147–48.

Tosh, Mark, "Nash Finch to Capitalize on Strength," *Supermarket News,* June 1, 1992, p. 9.

Youngblood, Dick, "Grocery Giant Nash Finch Still Keeps a Low Profile," *Star Tribune,* June 9, 1986, pp. 1M, 8M.

Zwiebach, Elliot, "Nash Finch Eyes Southeast Buys as Way of Boosting Profitability," *Supermarket News,* May 27, 1991, p. 52.

—Jay P. Pederson

Nashua

Nashua Corporation

44 Franklin Street
P.O. Box 2002
Nashua, New Hampshire 03061-2002
U.S.A.
(603) 880-2323
Fax: (603) 880-5671

Public Company
Incorporated: 1904 as the Nashua Card, Gummed & Coated
   Paper Co.
Employees: 4100
Sales: $552 million
Stock Exchange: New York
SICs: 2672 Coated and Laminated Paper, not elsewhere
   classified; 7384 Photofinishing Laboratories; 3695
   Magnetic & Optical Recording Media; 5112 Stationery
   and Office Supplies; 3861 Photographic Equipment and
   Supplies

Nashua Corporation in Nashua, New Hampshire, is a medium-sized company that conducts a variety of businesses. Its core enterprises are photofinishing (processing of film), the manufacture and sale of coated products such as thermosensitive paper and adhesive tapes, computer product manufacture (primarily computer disks), and office supplies (toners, fax paper, and remanufactured laser printer cartridges). Nashua has leading market shares in labels and tapes, and has the number one market share in the United States, Canada, and the United Kingdom in mail order photofinishing services.

Nashua had its origins in a gummed paper manufacturing enterprise in Rockport, Massachusetts, that went out of business in 1898. The owner, a farsighted entrepreneur and inventor, Charles H. Crowell, sold his faltering firm that year to Carter, Rice & Company of Boston, which retained him as manager of their new subsidiary, renamed Winthrop Manufacturing Company. In February, 1904, a fire destroyed the plant, which had relocated to south Boston, sending the owners Carter and Rice casting about for a new locale for their subsidiary. They found the Nashua Card and Glazed Paper Company, in Nashua, New Hampshire, which was heavily in debt. That year, when the present-day Nashua Corporation was founded, the bankrupted owners gladly sold their factory to Carter, Rice & Company for $74,000 plus mortgage. The following April, the wholly owned

subsidiary was incorporated as the Nashua Card, Gummed and Coated Paper Company. Besides manufacturing gummed flats, gummed paper, and sock linings, Nashua also continued the product lines of the previous company, namely glazed paper, cardboard, and "surface coated" paper.

The new company slowly modernized. In 1910, a plant telephone was added and new office machinery and boilers were installed. Expansion took place with the addition of a fourth story, the creation of a separate purchasing department, and the construction of a lab, and, at this time, the company hired its first chemist. The foundations for modern research and development were laid early and would become more and more crucial to the company's development.

Nashua added an important new product line in 1907, with the manufacture of waxed paper, an up and coming new invention. A French-American, Henri Sevigne, had invented a waxed paper bread wrapper as a young man in the 1880s. More and more bakers adopted the handy item for loaves of bread and Nashua, already specializing in the manufacture of coated paper, seized on this new product, even though it meant paying the inventor a handsome royalty on his license. Soon waxed paper moved out of the bakers' realm into practical, everyday use. For many years it was Nashua's most important commodity. By 1910, Nashua had built the first plant in the country designed solely for the mass production of waxed paper. Business in this consumer item really took off with the invention in 1915 of the automatic bread wrapping machine, first developed at Nashua, which attained the largest market share in the United States of waxed paper bread wrappers.

After 1913, Nashua became an independent, public company, ceasing to be a subsidiary of Carter, Rice & Co., although it still had close links with the corporation. In 1916, at the height of the First World War, the company altered its name to reflect its changed status by eliminating the word "Card," becoming simply the Nashua Gummed & Coated Paper Company.

Business expanded greatly during the war years and, due to rigorous research and development efforts, a new method of coloring was implemented in the coating division, while storage space was increased and a loading platform constructed. The American Tobacco Company became a significant customer at this time. In 1916, Nashua sold 1,500 tons of coated lithographs to the tobacco company, which partly compensated for the war-induced dearth of raw paper necessary for the waxed paper division. By then, waxed paper was being used heavily by chewing gum manufacturers and as lunch wrappers. Despite the raw material and labor shortages, business boomed and a new plant was leased in Middletown, New Hampshire.

After the war, because of the erection of large tariff barriers in the industrialized world, Nashua's management decided to construct their first subsidiary in Canada. In so doing, they evaded the stiff Canadian tariffs on coated products and waxed paper, while continuing to serve their largest foreign market. The Canadian Nashua Paper Company opened its doors in the spring of 1920, specializing in waxed and gummed paper.

Despite the rough recessionary times following the war, Nashua continued to expand. Besides the Canadian subsidiary, in 1921 Nashua bought out the bankrupted National Binding Company of New York City, which started Nashua on the road to becoming an important manufacturer of package sealing and other adhesive products, such as duct tape used in household repairs and in plumbing. The adhesive business became so important for Nashua that the package sealing division was incorporated into a separate, wholly owned company in 1924, the Nashua Package Sealing Company.

Such significant expansion led Nashua's stockholders to agree in 1924 to what then amounted to a huge expenditure for modernization and streamlining of operations—$130,000. The result was a company that wasted less, eliminated duplication, and decreased its overhead expenditures. Part of the modernization efforts showed up in the payment of employees by check instead of cash, which was considered an overdue response to the rash of payroll robberies, of which the Sacco & Vanzetti case had been the most notorious.

The late 1920s were among the company's most prosperous years. New and important product lines were added, such as a "fancy" paper brand called *Nirvana,* popular among women, which came out in 1926 and for many years showed a handsome profit. At this time, the Canadian subsidiary branched out, forming a new company to manufacture milk bottle caps and paper containers for the dairy industry. In 1929, gilt imprints were made for the hat, shoe, pencil-making, and bookbinding industries. "Velour" paper and telegraph tape for Western Union also were profitable. The challenge that the new product cellophane presented to Nashua's waxed paper industry was countered by "artistic" printing on Nashua's waxed paper products, until the company started up its own cellophane division.

Thanks in large part to the strenuous modernization and streamlining efforts of the mid-1920s and continuous product diversification, the Depression of the 1930s did not affect the company seriously. Management calmly adopted the New Deal's increased regulations, even when the mandate to hire 30 percent more employees created some headaches at Nashua. The extra employees came in handy, however, when business once again expanded in 1937 with a large building program that included a separate edifice for administration.

By 1940, the federal government was surveying all factories in the nation to determine how they might contribute to wartime production in the event of hostilities. With America's entry into the war, production for civilian needs virtually ground to a halt. Nashua's advantage was its manufacture of basic necessities, such as adhesives and other coated products that were needed during the war years; in addition, the company entered the unknown arena of gun manufacture, which it discontinued immediately at the war's end.

By then, the number of employees had climbed from a mere 70 in 1907 to 1,500, and annual sales stood at a healthy $13 million, from only $125,000 38 years earlier. Under the company's new president, Vasco Nunez, Nashua adopted new long-range objectives that gave priority to research and development. The traditional product line of colored coated paper was discontinued, and Nashua embarked on a new product line, thermal paper, that remained one of its most important commodities. A new adhesive tape, Rhino corrugators tape, was developed for

corrugated paper, and flat gummed papers also became profitable new products.

Because of the company's broader product lines, its name was altered to Nashua Corporation in 1952. Nine years later, Nashua's office products division was established, which soon began to handle such items as photocopy paper, toners, and developers. The year the office products division was established, Nashua purchased its first European business, Copycat Ltd. of London. From then on, international markets would contribute significantly to sales revenues. Two years later, in 1965, Nashua acquired Paramount Paper Products in Omaha, Nebraska, marking the company's entrance into the increasingly important pressure-sensitive label arena. A year later, Nashua's net sales had climbed to $65 million.

By the 1970s, Nashua had entered into the world of computer products, the manufacture of diskettes having evolved from the company's traditional product lines. But the company was facing increased Japanese competition and declining sales. The "work in quality" business philosophy of W. Edward Deming had gained ground in Japan, and was slowly winning disciples in this country. Nashua's new chair and chief executive officer, William E. Conway, was an early adherent, and in the late 1970s and early 1980s, Conway implemented a 33-hour course for all Nashua employees in which Deming's ideas were introduced and discussed. Nashua then terminated bonus incentives for managers, which Deming criticized as leading to low production targets. Instead, Nashua substituted equitable profit sharing. The implementation of Deming's ideas at Nashua, according to market analysts, led to sales increases and sound financial footing. First evident in the sale of tape, the turnaround became apparent by the mid-1980s in the sale of computer disks, of which Nashua became a leading supplier. The company also acquired mail order photofinishing businesses in the United States and Canada, and subsequently in the United Kingdom in 1990. Nashua then climbed to the number one position in market share in the mail order photofinishing business. Despite the setback of the 1990 to 1991 recession, the company quickly rebounded and in 1992 had a strong financial balance, with a debt of approximately $25 million and equity of $130 million.

Under President and Chief Executive Officer Charles E. Clough, Nashua had four main business divisions in the early 1990s: photofinishing, coated products, office supplies, and computer products. The number one market share in mail order photofinishing in North America and Great Britain, this enterprise consisted of processing film for amateur photographers and offering photo-related products via mail to customers, such as photo imprinted t-shirts and mugs as well as photo albums. This business, which suffered from the 1990 recession, was slowly recovering two years later. Its future looked bright, since mail order photofinishing was 10 to 20 percent more economical than minilab film development.

Nashua's coated products division included the production and marketing of thermal paper, computer labels, carbonless paper, and thermal pressure-sensitive labels as well as adhesive tapes. This division generated almost $200 million in sales revenues, making it Nashua's largest. Labels and tapes, in which Nashua had leading market shares, draw the top share of sales revenues.

A low-energy thermal label developed in the early 1990s as well as a new coating method for duct tape manufacture helped the company maintain its lead. Nashua became the nation's biggest supplier of thermal pressure-sensitive labels to the supermarket industry.

The office supplies division manufactured and marketed toners, developers, and fax and photocopy paper, and remanufactured and sold laser printer cartridges. While this division faced major competitors with huge cash reserves such as the Xerox Corporation and the Eastman Kodak Company, Nashua found its own niche in this growing business. Beyond distributing its office supplies to approximately 250 dealers nationwide, it branched out to distribute to mass merchandisers like K-Mart and various office supply superstores. Remanufactured laser cartridges held the greatest future market potential, with sales of this product nearly doubling on an annual basis because of their competitive price as compared to new cartridges. Remanufactured laser cartridges were also environmentally sound, since they did not end up in the landfill but were refilled with new toner and reused.

Finally, the computer products division produced and marketed magnetic disks used in computer disk drives. The fastest growing segment of this multimillion dollar enterprise (nearly one hundred million dollars in export sales alone) was thin film rigid disks, in which Nashua's market share kept growing.

On the eve of the twenty-first century, Nashua Corporation was just beginning to tap into significant international markets that in 1992 generated approximately 20 percent of its total sales revenues. The company continued to invest heavily in research and product development, approximately $12 million annually. Research and the development of new products and expansion into foreign markets were the strengths of Nashua Corporation, boding well for its future growth.

Principal Subsidiaries: Nashua Cartridge Products, Inc. (Massachusetts); Nashua Photo Inc. (Delaware); Nashua Photo Ltd. (Canada); Nashua Photo Ltd. (England).

Further Reading:

Annual Report, Nashua, New Hampshire: Nashua Corp., 1992.
Cochran, Thomas N., "Nashua Corp.: Its Name Is a Winner on 'Someone Else's Box,' " *Forbes,* July 18, 1988, pp. 61–62.
Henderson, B. A., "Nashua Corp.: Company Report," *Prudential Securities Inc.,* October 19, 1992.
"A History of Nashua Corporation," Nashua, New Hampshire: Nashua Corp., 1968.
Jaffe, Thomas, "The Knock on Nashua (Earnings and Stock Price Recovery)," *Forbes,* April 27, 1992, pp. 418–419.
Linden, Dana Wechsler, "Incentivize Me, Please," *Forbes,* May 27, 1991, pp. 208–212.
Marenghi, Catherine, "Nashua Keeps Quality Flame Burning in Customer Service," *Computerworld,* January 6, 1992, p. 61.
"Nashua Corp. (offers to repurchase 2.75 million common shares)," *New York Times,* May 3, 1990, p. C5(N) and D5(L).

—Sina Dubovoj

NCH Corporation

2727 Chemsearch Blvd.
Irving, Texas 75062
U.S.A.
(214) 438-0211
Fax: (214) 438-0186

Public Company
Incorporated: 1919 as National Disinfectant Company
Employees: 10,477
Sales: $671 million
Stock Exchanges: New York
SICs: 2842 Specialty Cleaning Polishing; 3432 Plumbing
   Fittings and Brass Goods; 2899 Industrial Chemicals; 3452
   Industrial Fasteners; 3089 Plastic Plumbing Specialties

NCH Corporation is a major international marketer of maintenance products, and one of the largest companies in the world to sell such products through direct marketing. NCH's products include specialty chemicals, fasteners, welding supplies, and electronic and plumbing parts. These products are sold through a number of wholly owned subsidiaries, most of which are engaged in the maintenance products business. Subsidiary companies in NCH's Chemical Specialties division produce a diverse array of maintenance chemicals that includes cleaners, degreasers, lubricants, grounds care, housekeeping, and water treatment products. Companies in the Partsmaster group offer a wide variety of items for maintenance and repair, including welding supplies and fasteners. Another group, Plumbmaster, provides plumbing supplies for every level of usage, from residential to industrial. The Safety and Identification Products group makes and sells such items as safety goggles, hard hats, and hearing protection. Other subsidiary groups under the NCH umbrella include Resource Electronics, Cornerstone Direct Marketing, X-Chem Oil Field Chemicals, and Retail Products. NCH has a sales force of about 6,000. Its branch offices and manufacturing plants are located on six continents, and its products are sold in 50 different countries.

National Disinfectant Company, the original incarnation of NCH Corporation, was founded in Dallas, Texas, by Milton P. Levy in 1919. Leadership of the company has remained in the hands of the Levy family to this day. National Disinfectant's original line of products was fairly small; it included a coal tar disinfectant, an insecticide, and a liquid hand soap for institu-

tional use. The company was a small, efficient operation, and orders received in the morning would be delivered in the afternoon of the same day. During the next couple of decades the company's offerings grew. One brand that appeared in the late 1930s was Everbrite, a heavy-duty industrial floor wax. Everbrite has continued to exist in varying forms since then, eventually evolving into a strong multi-purpose cleaner that kills bacteria.

Levy's three sons, Lester A., Milton P., Jr., and Irvin L., were involved in the company's operations from early on, working in the warehouse and shipping areas as teenagers and learning the business from the ground up. When the senior Levy died in 1946, the family was prepared to continue running National Disinfectant. Levy's widow, Ruth, took over as president of the company. Lester Levy was placed in charge of the company's small but growing sales crew. Milton, Jr., began to integrate the development of a sales territory in Austin, Texas, with the completion of his studies there at the University of Texas. Irvin, after working part-time as office manager while he finished school at Southern Methodist University, began developing another sales area in the Dallas-Fort Worth region. In 1947 company sales were $300,000. The Levy's were assisted in running the company by Jack Mann, National Disinfectant's top sales representative since joining the company in the 1920s. Mann, a former vaudeville entertainer and a close friend of Milton, Sr., would stay with the company for 40 years. The company's Mantek chemical division was named after him shortly after his death in 1968.

In the 1950s National Disinfectant began to integrate vertically and to expand its marketing area. The company began to reinvest a sizeable portion of its profits in manufacturing and research facilities in order to decrease its reliance on outside producers for its wares. One important acquisition that was made in the early 1950s was Certified Laboratories. Certified continued to operate as an independent company with its own brand name and its own sales force, but this wholly owned subsidiary was generating over one-fourth of the company's revenue within a few years. By the middle of the decade, National Disinfectant was shipping its products via rail to several points outside of Texas, with new concentrations of customers in Oklahoma, Louisiana, Arizona, and New Mexico. St. Louis was the site of the company's first branch office, established in 1956.

As demand for National Disinfectant's products grew, so did its sales force. A sales management team was created during this period, and the training of new sales representatives became more standardized. National Disinfectant manufacturing plants began to spring up across the United States, first in Texas, and later regional plants appeared in New Jersey, California, Puerto Rico, and Indiana.

In 1960 the company's name was changed to National Chemsearch Corp. in order to better reflect the expansion of its product line beyond disinfectants. National Chemsearch began to go international during the 1960s. Its first overseas sales endeavors were in the Caribbean. Sales efforts soon spread to Canada and to Central and South America. Eventually, the company landed in Europe as well. In 1962 the company's administrative offices, along with laboratories and manufacturing operations, were moved to a new headquarters located in Irving, Texas, a suburb of Dallas. National Chemsearch acquired two more subsidiaries in the first half of the 1960s. Hallmark Chemical Corp., which sold a line of building products, was acquired in 1962. Two years later, the company purchased Lamkin Brothers, Inc., a marketer of vitamin and mineral supplements for livestock.

National Chemsearch offered its stock to the public for the first time in 1965. The Levy family retained control of 70 percent of the stock. By that time, Ruth Levy had retired, and a clear division of labor existed among the three brothers. Lester, chairman of the board, oversaw corporate planning and much of the company's financial dealings. Milton handled production, distribution, and product development as chairman of the executive committee. And company president Irvin was in charge of expanding the company's domestic and foreign sales efforts.

Between 1962 and 1966 National Chemsearch's sales grew at an average rate of 29 percent a year. By the end of that stretch, the company was earning $2.4 million on sales of $25 million. Much of the company's success was attributed to its direct sales methods, which eliminated the need for wholesalers or other intermediaries. By offering a broad range of products to a large number of customers (many of them relatively small shops and plants), National Chemsearch was able to compete favorably with larger companies that were concentrating on selling only very large orders.

By 1967, Chemsearch employed more than 600 sales representatives. None of the company's 40,000 customers accounted for even one percent of its sales. About 60 percent of these customers were industrial or commercial clients; the rest were institutions such as hospitals and schools. The greatest share of sales (over 60 percent) was still coming from cleaning chemicals at that time. Constant research was adding about 20 products a year to the line. Toward the end of the 1960s, the Plumbmaster and Partsmaster divisions were created. The establishment of these divisions meant that the growing number of newly acquired subsidiaries could be grouped according to the nature of their products.

In February of 1969 National Chemsearch stock was listed on the New York Stock Exchange for the first time. In 1970 the company's product line included roughly 250 items, sold under the trade names "National Chemsearch," "Certified," "Mantek," and "Dyna Systems" (fasteners). Turf maintenance supplies, paints and sealers, and sewage treatment chemicals were among the items offered, in addition to the growing list of cleaning chemicals. Sales and profits continued to grow slowly but surely into the early 1970s. By 1971, sales had reached $69 million, with net income of $6.6 million. About 20 percent of the company's revenue was being generated through foreign sales by this time. Among National Chemsearch's acquisitions during this period were P & M Manufacturing Company of Los Angeles in 1970 and the Pennsylvania-based Daniel P. Creed Co., Inc., in 1972. P & M, with annual sales of about $1.5 million in the plumbing maintenance industry, was acquired for 8,686 shares of common stock. Daniel P. Creed, also in the plumbing supply business, was a cash purchase.

By 1973, sales at National Chemsearch had soared to $103 million. About 3,000 sales representatives were hawking the company's products by the middle of the 1970s. In 1977 specialty chemicals accounted for about 90 percent of sales. The remaining 10 percent was derived from the younger segments of the company, including fasteners, plumbing parts, and welding supplies. National Chemsearch's goal of reducing reliance on outside manufacturers had more or less been achieved by this time, as nearly all of the company's specialty chemicals were being fabricated at its own facilities, the exception being its turf maintenance products.

Annual sales doubled again by 1978, breaking $200 million for the first time. The company's name was changed to NCH Corporation that year. As was the case with the previous name change, the intent was to reflect the increasing diversity of the company's wares. NCH's acquisitions around this time included the 1978 purchase of Specialty Products Co., a manufacturer of specialty plumbing items. Specialty Products, based in Stanton, California, had yearly sales of about $4 million. The following year, NCH acquired the domestic assets of American Allsafe Co. This acquisition paved the way for the development of the company's Safety Division, whose mission was to supply items such as eye and head protection gear to the increasingly safety-conscious industrial world. 1979 also marked the launch of Kernite SA, a new trading company set up by NCH in Belgium dealing in chemicals, petrochemicals, and lubricants.

NCH's previously steady growth in sales stalled somewhat in the first half of the 1980s. After reaching a high of $356 million in 1981, sales actually declined in each of the next three years, and did not surpass the 1981 figure until 1986, when $375 million in sales was reported. One obvious reason for this stagnation was a generally sluggish global economy, in which maintenance supplies were easy targets for the cost-cutting efforts of struggling industrial firms. Also, the first-year turnover rate among NCH sales representatives was much higher than usual due to slow sales accompanied by higher gas and car maintenance costs, which are borne by the sales personnel. The size of the sales force was stuck at about 4,000 throughout the first half of the decade.

In 1986 NCH added direct mail, telemarketing, and catalog sales to its arsenal of marketing techniques. Cornerstone Direct was formed for this purpose, offering material handling equipment, first-aid kits, and other industrial supplies. Sales growth returned in the second half of the 1980s, breaking $400 million in 1987 and $500 million in 1988. European operations contributed more and more to the company's sales and income during this period. With sales up and expenses down, NCH's earned income from Europe quadrupled between 1987 and 1989, from $4.8 million to $18.8 million. Another area that expanded significantly in the last few years of the decade was the company's Resource Electronics Division, with the acquisition of three electronic parts distributors between 1988 and 1990.

Sales and income reached new peaks of $677 million and $43 million in 1991, before dropping slightly in 1992. One major cost incurred by the company in 1992 was the restructuring of its Brazilian subsidiary, a downsizing made necessary by the phenomenal rate of inflation and general instability of the Brazilian economy. A new plant was built in Korea in 1992, making it possible to offer a broader range of products in the growing Asian market. Among NCH's acquisitions that year was a line of stainless steel flexible tubing connectors. These new products were marketed under the trade name Aqua-Flo. By the end of fiscal 1992, NCH's plumbing group was offering a total of more than 80,000 different parts. The Resource Electronics group's line had grown to over 40,000 parts by this time as well. The company also expanded its line of retail products, which by this time included Outright brand pet care products, Out! International pet odor eliminators, and Totally Toddler nursery care items. A variety of plumbing and hardware supplies for do-it-yourselfers also became available in retail outlets.

NCH Corporation's major strengths are the diversity and quality of its products, along with the well-planned organization of its huge army of direct sales representatives. The company has a history of choosing its acquisitions carefully, and of investing wisely in its manufacturing and research facilities, a crucial commitment given the competition NCH faces in the industrial supply business from larger corporations. Since NCH managed to thrive during several of the toughest years for industry in recent history, the company's continuing growth in the global market seems likely.

Principal Subsidiaries: Resource Electronics; Cornerstone Direct Marketing; X-Chem Oil Field Chemicals; Certified Laboratories; Hallmark Chemical Corp.; Lamkin Brothers, Inc.; P & M Manufacturing Company; Daniel P. Creed Co., Inc.; Specialty Products Co.; American Allsafe Co.; Kernite SA; Out! International.

Further Reading:

Autry, Ret, "Companies to Watch: NCH Corp.," *Fortune,* June 18, 1990, p. 93.
"National Chemsearch Corp.," *Wall Street Transcript,* August 31, 1970, pp. 21579–21580.
"National Chemsearch Corp.," *Wall Street Transcript,* August 15, 1977, p. 47878.
"NCH Corporation," *Better Investing,* October 1992, pp. 30–31.
"NCH Corporation," *Wall Street Transcript,* February 11, 1985, p. 76825.
NCH Corporation Annual Reports, Dallas, Texas: NCH Corporation, 1989, 1992.
"Specialty Family's Success Formula," *Chemical Week,* May 6, 1975, pp. 75–80.

—Robert R. Jacobson

New Street Capital Inc.

450 Lexington Building
14th Street
New York, New York 10004
U.S.A.
(212) 450-7910

Public Company
Incorporated: 1976 as Drexel Burnham Lambert
   Incorporated
Employees: 20
Sales: $450 million
SICs: 6211 Security Brokers, Dealers and Flotation
   Companies; 8741 Management Services; 6282 Investment
   Advice

Since its incorporation in 1976, Drexel Burnham Lambert Incorporated (reorganized as New Street Capital Inc.), once a little-known, second-tier underwriter, became one of the most widely publicized investment banks in U.S. corporate history. Drexel pioneered the "junk bond" craze of the 1980s and played a leading role in many of the decade's best known corporate takeover bids. At its peak in the early 1980s, Drexel had a firm grip on more than 70 percent of the junk bond market. The company's innovative and aggressive financing strategies made the firm virtually an overnight success, and Drexel became one of Wall Street's most respected, and at times most resented, investment banking houses.

But in 1986, Drexel Burnham Lambert became the center of an investigation by the U.S. Securities and Exchange Commission (SEC) involving insider trading and other illegal trading practices. The firm's role in the scandal took its toll on the company. In the late 1980s, its business declined as quickly as it had been built, and in February of 1990 Drexel declared bankruptcy and liquidated its business. It was the end of an era; the firm emerged from bankruptcy in mid-1992 as New Street Capital Inc.

Drexel Burnham Lambert's roots can be traced back to 1838, when Francis Martin Drexel went into the banking business. His son Anthony took over Drexel and ran it until the 1890s. During the late nineteenth and early twentieth century, Drexel was the Philadelphia arm of J.P. Morgan and Company of New York. The company conducted both commercial and investment banking until 1933, when the Glass-Steagall Act precluded commer-

cial banks from underwriting and dealing in securities. Drexel and Company, like Morgan, followed the commercial banking route.

But in 1940 former Drexel partners Edward Hopkinson, Jr., and Thomas S. Gates, Jr., together with a number of their associates, founded an investment bank. The commercial bank was completely absorbed into the Morgan organization and they acquired the rights to the Drexel name. The new Drexel began with an initial capital investment of $1 million. The firm, although profitable, grew very slowly during its first 15 years, never quite making it to investment banking's first tier. In those days Wall Street played by a strict set of unwritten rules that insured the continued dominance of only a few investment banks. One such practice was "bracketing," which refers to the order of listing participants in the advertisement for an underwriting. The special bracket firms, such as Morgan Stanley, First Boston, and Merrill Lynch, were listed first, then the major bracket firms, then submajors, then regional firms. This hierarchy clearly indicated to issuers and buyers who the most powerful investment banks were. Drexel held close ties to many of the nation's biggest securities issuers, but it ranked one notch below the special firm bracket and was not one of the dominant forces on Wall Street.

In 1965 Drexel merged with Harriman, Ripley and Company to form Drexel Firestone Inc. That arrangement, however, lasted only two years. With its capital dwindling, Drexel Firestone Inc. merged with the very successful, though relatively unknown, Burnham and Company.

Burnham and Company had been built by I. W. "Tubby" Burnham, who founded the company in 1935. Burnham began with $100,000 in capital, $96,000 of which Tubby had borrowed from his grandfather and the founder of I.W. Harper, a Kentucky distillery. Burnham and Company, though very successful, was still a submajor investment bank. By the late 1960s Burnham could see that if he wanted to expand much further he would need to link up with the reputation of a major firm. The ailing Drexel Firestone afforded the opportunity for such a combination. Drexel provided the "white-shoe" image, and Burnham came up with the capital.

Burnham's investment bank had grown substantially over the years, and by 1973 its capital was $44 million—80 percent of the new Drexel Burnham and Company. Tubby Burnham served as chairman of the new company. By focusing on underwriting securities issues of small- and medium-sized companies, Drexel Burnham prospered.

In 1976 Drexel Burnham and Company merged with Lambert Brussels Witter, which was controlled by the Belgian Bank Brussels Lambert. The Lamberts were one of Europe's oldest banking families. Baron Leon Lambert served as a director of the new Drexel Burnham Lambert, Inc., while Tubby Burnham continued as chairman. Burnham's protégé, Robert E. Linton, was president and chief executive officer (CEO).

From the start, Drexel Burnham Lambert concentrated on the leftovers of Wall Street's bigger investment banks, going after smaller companies with less than perfect credit ratings. The company's high-yield (junk) bond department, which would spearhead its climb to the top of the investment banking heap, had the unique talents of Michael Milken. While working on his master's in business administration at Wharton, Milken had discovered that so-called junk bonds—bonds rated BB or lower by Standard and Poor's—had only a slightly higher rate of default than blue chip issues, while their premiums were considerably higher. Milken found that through careful research and selection, a diversified bond portfolio made up of junk bonds would pay interest rates that more than made up for the higher risk. Milken looked at a number of factors that the rating services ignored and paid more attention to a company's future than its past. It was a very successful formula.

In 1978 Milken moved the high-yield bond department to Beverly Hills, a clear indication of his influence inside Drexel as the king of junk bonds. Before 1977 the junk bond market consisted entirely of "fallen angels"—bonds issued by former blue chip companies that had run into financial difficulty and had fallen from grace. In the late 1970s, however, a number of lower credit companies began to issue their own bonds, rated BB or lower. Milken and Drexel Burnham, with their close ties to the institutional investors who liked junk bonds, controlled this rapidly expanding market. Milken's confidence in his ability to distribute high-yield bonds made Drexel actively seek out low-credit issuers. Drexel's first issue was Texas International, followed by Michigan General. As low-credit companies found they could raise capital without having to offer equity shares, the junk bond craze took off. Drexel Burnham Lambert had created a market for first-issue junk bonds.

In the early 1980s Drexel Burnham Lambert continued to tighten its stranglehold on the junk bond market. Investors trusted Milken, who had gathered the most talented group of researchers and traders of any investment bank and paid them well enough to prevent defections. If a company Milken had recommended got into trouble, Milken was on the phone with them getting information and giving advice. Drexel Burnham Lambert was also always willing to make markets for the bonds it underwrote. This built special confidence in the firm, since investors knew they would not get stuck with a bad issue. The policy, combined with Milken's genius for picking winners, made Drexel the hottest investment bank on Wall Street. Although no firm is perfect—Drexel watched the Flight Transportation Company default on a $25 million issue it had underwritten in 1982—Drexel's record was the best of any investment bank.

In 1982 Tubby Burnham stepped down as chairman and was replaced by President and Chief Executive Officer Robert E. Linton. Linton was one of a handful of investment banking executives who had never attended college; he had joined Burnham and Company after his discharge from the Air Force following World War II. Frederick Joseph, formerly head of the company's corporate finance department, took over as president.

Joseph had joined the old Drexel and Burnham in 1974 and had worked closely with Milken assembling an aggressive team in the corporate finance department. Cultivating Drexel's image as an upstart, Joseph once remarked that his firm was loaded with "fat women and ugly men"—not the typical blue-eyed six-footers most people picture as the classic investment banker. Joseph was described as a diplomat in an aggressive business

and was seen as the man who could best coordinate Drexel's West Coast and New York offices. In 1983 Drexel underwrote its first $1 billion junk bond issue, for MCI Communications. Drexel's share of the junk bond market peaked at about 75 percent in 1983 and 1984. At that time, other major investment banks, including Merrill Lynch and Morgan Stanley, were lured into these not-quite-respectable but highly lucrative markets. Drexel maintained its overall superiority, but these companies gradually encroached on its market share.

In the early 1980s Drexel also became increasingly active in mergers and acquisitions, specializing in leveraged buyouts financed by junk bonds. A letter from Drexel saying that it was "highly confident" that financing could be arranged was the go-ahead for many hostile bids, and Drexel became associated with the decade's most notorious corporate raiders. It arranged financing for T. Boone Pickens's unsuccessful run at Gulf Oil in 1983; it helped Carl Icahn try to take over Phillips Petroleum; and it financed Saul Steinberg's bid for Disney Studios. One of the largest leveraged buyouts it arranged was Ted Turner's purchase of MGM/UA for a staggering $1.3 billion.

While junk bonds remained its greatest strength, Drexel had been expanding in other areas as well. In 1984 Drexel acquired the Denver firm Kirchner, Moore, and Company, expanding its expertise in municipal bond financing. Drexel also launched a major effort to enter the mortgage-backed securities markets in 1984. By the mid-1980s Drexel Burnham Lambert ranked solidly among Wall Street's top investment banks.

But at this time Drexel and the junk bond market it had created began to draw some criticism. Critics claimed that many companies were overleveraged, while the media dubbed junk bonds "toxic waste." Although default rates were no higher than before, there was speculation that the collective risk was accumulating and that a major default would soon shake the market. In addition, Drexel Burnham Lambert seemed to be making too much money too fast. Competitors—and the federal government—were inclined to take a closer look at the company.

In May of 1986 the Securities and Exchange Commission charged a Drexel Burnham Lambert managing director, Dennis Levine, with insider trading. When Levine pleaded guilty, a wave of insider charges ensued, including those involving corporate raider Ivan Boesky. Slowly, one of the Wall Street scandals of the century unraveled. The SEC investigated Drexel Burnham Lambert for two years before bringing any charges against the firm, while U.S. attorney Rudolph Guiliani targeted Michael Milken himself. The investigation itself may not have been directly responsible for Drexel's estimated 79 percent drop in earnings in 1987, the same year the stock market crashed, but the cloud over Drexel certainly didn't help business. In spite of the negative publicity, Drexel maintained a 49 percent market share of the junk bond market in 1987, down considerably from the early 1980s but still the biggest single slice of the pie, as junk bonds made up about one-fifth of all new bond issues.

In December of 1988, threatened with racketeering charges that would have allowed seizure of certain Drexel assets and effectively put the firm out of business, Drexel pleaded guilty to six felony charges of illegal trading and paid $650 million in fines. In addition, Drexel agreed to withhold Milken's estimated $200 million compensation for 1988 and remove him from his position as head of the high-yield bond operation. Milken challenged the actions in court, but finally left Drexel in March of 1989, after he was formally charged with 98 counts of wrongdoing, including securities fraud, racketeering, and tax fraud. Milken pleaded not guilty; his defense was expected to center on the notion that a $175 billion market was obviously too big to be controlled by one man.

In April of 1989 Drexel announced it was going to sell its retail operation. Many Wall Street firms had been suffering since the October 1987 stock market crash undermined public confidence in the markets, and Drexel's investigation by the federal government was a double blow to the investment bank's business. In an effort to brighten its tarnished image, Drexel brought in former SEC chief John Shad as chairman in 1989. Shad vowed he would be an active chairman rather than a "window dressing," but just how he planned to restore Drexel Burnham Lambert in the wake of one of the broadest securities scandals of the century was uncertain. And indeed Drexel, which had risen from semi-obscurity in the mid-1970s to achieve annual revenues of $4 billion in the mid-1980s, survived barely more than a month of the new decade: Drexel declared bankruptcy on February 13, 1990.

Although Drexel Burnham Lambert reported $800 million in equity at the end of 1989, it could not pay off $100 million in short-term loans due early in 1990. Drexel had become overly dependent on junk bonds to the detriment of cash flow. Its financial problems were compounded by the "crisis of confidence" precipitated by the firm's ruined reputation.

The SEC adopted new regulations as a result of Drexel's failure, requiring firms with more than $20 million in capital or single-customer accounts in excess of $250,000 to file quarterly disclosures with the government agency. In the ensuing three years, Drexel went from being the first Wall Street investment bank to liquidate since the Great Depression to being the first to endure bankruptcy. The reorganization settled more than $30 billion in claims and established several legal precedents under the guidance of an independent board of directors. Most creditors got from 50 cents to 75 cents of every dollar owed them by Drexel. In the wake of the Drexel collapse, some observers felt that Drexel and Milken should have been punished more severely for the inherently bad investments made with shareholder's money. Others lamented the loss of risk-takers who would invest in medium-sized U.S. companies with no other source of large amounts of capital.

The new incarnation of Drexel, called New Street Capital Inc., was formed under a "loophole" in the federal tax code that permitted companies to change their state of incorporation without having to pay income taxes. New Street maintained its headquarters in New York, but was incorporated in Delaware. The transformation was authorized by bankruptcy Judge Milton Pollack, the Justice Department, the SEC, and the Internal Revenue Service.

Led by new Chairman Robert Shapiro and President and CEO John F. Sorte, New Street had only 20 employees, down from a high of 10,000, and a charter that limited the company's business activities. New Street inherited a portfolio of junk bonds from Drexel totaling $450 million and dumped the former entity's checkered past. New Street's whitewashed reputation allowed it more freedom than Drexel's severely limited purview. The bulk of New Street was owned by Drexel's creditors through a post-bankruptcy trust. Former Drexel employees also held warrants amounting to 20 percent of the new firm. Many predicted that New Street would maintain a low profile, then come under new ownership by the end of the twentieth century. Unresolved lawsuits held up any sale in the meantime.

Further Reading:

Anders, George, "A Shadow of Itself, Drexel Comes Back From Bankruptcy," *Wall Street Journal,* April 30, 1992, p. C1.

Bruck, Connie, *The Predators' Ball: How the Junk Bond Machine Stalked the Corporate Raiders,* New York, NY: Simon & Schuster, 1988.

Hoffman, Paul, *The Dealmakers: Inside the World of Investment Banking,* Garden City, NY: Doubleday, 1984.

Moses, Jonathan M., and Milo Geyelin, "IRS, Many Other Drexel Creditors File Objections to Reorganization," *Wall Street Journal,* February 27, 1992, p. B8.

Sloan, Allan, "How IRS Loophole Helped Drexel Carve Out a New, Clean Identity," *Los Angeles Times,* March 28, 1992, p. D5.

—updated by April S. Dougal

Nike, Inc.

One Bowerman Dr.
Beaverton, Oregon 97005
U.S.A.
(503) 671-6453
Fax: (503) 671-6300

Public Company
Incorporated: 1964 as Blue Ribbon Sports; 1972 as Nike,
  Inc.
Employees: 5,500
Sales: $3.00 billion
Stock Exchanges: NASDAQ New York Pacific
SICs: 3149 Footwear Except Rubber Nec; 2329 Men's/Boys'
  Clothing Nec; Women's/Misses' Outerwear Nec

Founded as an importer of Japanese shoes, Nike, Inc. has grown to be one of the world's largest makers of athletic footwear and apparel. The company has relied on consistent innovation in the design of its products and steady promotion to fuel its growth in both U.S. and foreign markets.

Nike's precursor originated in 1962, a product of the imagination of Philip H. Knight, a Stanford University business graduate who had been a member of the track team as an undergraduate at the University of Oregon. Traveling in Japan after finishing up business school, Knight got in touch with a Japanese firm that made athletic shoes, the Onitsuka Tiger Co., and arranged to import some of its products to the United States on a small scale. Knight was convinced that Japanese running shoes could become significant competitors for the German products that then dominated the American market. In the course of setting up his agreement with Onitsuka Tiger, Knight invented Blue Ribbon Sports to satisfy his Japanese partner's expectations that he represented an actual company, and this hypothetical firm eventually grew to become Nike, Inc.

At the end of 1963, Knight's arrangements in Japan came to fruition when he took delivery of 200 pairs of Tiger athletic shoes, which he stored in his father's basement and peddled at various track meets in the area. Knight's one-man venture became a partnership in the following year, when his former track coach, William Bowerman, chipped in $500 to equal Knight's investment. Bowerman had long been experimenting with modified running shoes for his team, and he worked with runners to improve the designs of prototype Blue Ribbon Sports

(BRS) shoes. Innovation in running shoe design eventually would become a cornerstone of the company's continued expansion and success. Bowerman's efforts first paid off in 1966, when a shoe known as the Cortez, which he had designed, became a big seller.

BRS sold 1,300 pairs of Japanese running shoes in 1964, its first year, to gross $8,000. By 1965 the fledgling company had acquired a full-time employee, and sales had reached $20,000. The following year, the company rented its first retail space, next to a beauty salon in Santa Monica, California, so that its few employees could stop selling shoes out of their cars. In 1967 with fast-growing sales, BRS expanded operations to the East Coast, opening a distribution office in Wellesley, Massachusetts.

Bowerman's innovations in running shoe technology continued throughout this time. A shoe whose upper portion was made of nylon went into development in 1967, and the following year, Bowerman and another employee came up with the Boston shoe, which incorporated the first cushioned mid-sole throughout the entire length of an athletic shoe.

By the end of the decade, Knight's venture had expanded to include several stores and 20 employees, and sales were nearing $300,000. The company was poised for greater growth, but Knight was frustrated by a lack of capital to pay for expansion. In 1971 using financing from the Japanese trading company Nissho Iwai, BRS was able to manufacture its own line of products overseas, for import to the United States. At this time, the company introduced its Swoosh trademark, and the brand name Nike, the Greek goddess of victory. These new symbols were first affixed to a soccer shoe, the first Nike product to be sold.

A year later, BRS broke with its old Japanese partner, Onitsuka Tiger, after a disagreement over distribution, and kicked off promotion of its own products at the 1972 U.S. Olympic Trials, the first of many marketing campaigns that would seek to attach Nike's name and fortunes to the careers of well-known athletes. Nike shoes were geared to the serious athlete, and their high performance carried with it a high price.

In their first year of distribution, the company's new products grossed $1.96 million, and its staff swelled to 45. In addition, operations were expanded to Canada, the company's first foreign market, which would be followed by Australia, in 1974.

Bowerman continued his innovations in running-shoe design with the introduction of the Moon shoe in 1972, which had a waffle-like sole that had first been formed by molding rubber on a household waffle iron. This sole increased the traction of the shoe without adding weight.

In 1974 BRS opened its first U.S. plant, in Exeter, New Hampshire. The company's payroll swelled to 250, and worldwide sales neared $5 million by the end of 1974.

This growth was fueled in part by aggressive promotion of the Nike brand name. The company sought to expand its visibility by having its shoes worn by prominent athletes, including tennis players Ilie Nastase and Jimmy Connors. At the 1976 Olympic

Trials these efforts began to pay off as Nike shoes were worn by rising athletic stars.

The company's growth had truly begun to take off by this time, riding the boom in popularity of jogging that took place in the United States in the late 1970s. BRS revenues tripled in two years to $14 million in 1976, and then doubled in just one year to $28 million in 1977. To keep up with demand, the company opened new factories, adding a stitching plant in Maine and additional overseas production facilities in Taiwan and Korea. International sales were expanded when markets in Asia were opened in 1977 and in South America the following year. European distributorships were lined up in 1978.

Nike continued its promotional activities with the opening of Athletics West, a training club for Olympic hopefuls in track and field, and by signing tennis player John McEnroe to an endorsement contract. In 1978 the company changed its name to Nike, Inc. The company expanded its line of products that year, adding athletic shoes for children.

By 1979 Nike sold almost half the running shoes bought in the United States, and the company moved into a new world headquarters building in Beaverton, Oregon. In addition to its shoe business, the company began to make and market a line of sports clothing, and the Nike Air shoe cushioning device was introduced.

By the start of the 1980s, Nike's combination of ground-breaking design and savvy and aggressive marketing had allowed it to surpass the German athletic shoe company Adidas AG, formerly the leader in U.S. sales. In December of that year, Nike went public, offering two million shares of stock. With the revenues generated by the stock sale, the company planned continued expansion, particularly in the European market. In the United States, plans for a new headquarters on a large, rural campus were inaugurated, and an east coast distribution center in Greenland, New Hampshire, was brought on line. In addition, the company bought a large plant in Exeter, New Hampshire, to house the Nike Sport Research and Development Lab and also to provide for more domestic manufacturing capacity. The company had shifted its overseas production away from Japan at this point, manufacturing nearly four-fifths of its shoes in South Korea and Taiwan. It established factories in mainland China in 1981.

By the following year, when the jogging craze in the United States had started to wane, half of the running shoes bought in the United States bore the Nike trademark. The company was well insulated from the effects of a stagnating demand for running shoes, however, since it gained a substantial share of its sales from other types of athletic shoes, notably basketball shoes and tennis shoes. In addition, Nike benefited from strong sales of its other product lines, which included apparel, work and leisure shoes, and children's shoes.

Given the slowing of growth in the U.S. market, however, the company turned its attention to growth in foreign markets, inaugurating Nike International, Ltd., in 1981 to spearhead the company's push into Europe and Japan, as well as into Asia, Latin America, and Africa. In Europe, Nike faced stiff competition from Adidas and Puma, which had a strong hold on the soccer market, Europe's largest athletic-shoe category. The

company opened a factory in Ireland to enable it to distribute its shoes without paying high import tariffs, and in 1981, bought out its distributors in England and Austria, to strengthen its control over marketing and distribution of its products. In 1982 the company outfitted Aston Villa, the winning team in the English and European Cup soccer championships, giving a boost to promotion of its new soccer shoe.

In Japan, Nike allied itself with Nissho Iwai Corp., the sixth-largest Japanese trading company, to form Nike-Japan Corporation. Because Nike already held a part of the low-priced athletic shoe market, the company set its sights on the high-priced end of the scale in Japan.

By 1982 the company's line of products included more than 200 different kinds of shoes, including the Air Force I, a basketball shoe, and its companion shoe for racquet sports, the Air Ace, the latest models in the long line of innovative shoe designs that had pushed Nike's earnings to an average annual increase of almost 100 percent. In addition, the company marketed more than 200 different items of clothing. By 1983 when the company posted its first-ever quarterly drop in earnings as the running boom peaked and went into a decline, resulting in slowing shoe sales, Nike's leaders were looking to the apparel division, as well as overseas markets, for further expansion. In foreign sales, the company had mixed results. Its operations in Japan were almost immediately profitable, and the company quickly jumped to second place in the Japanese market, but in Europe, Nike fared less well, losing money on its five European subsidiaries.

Faced with an 11.5 percent drop in domestic sales of its shoes in the 1984 fiscal year, Nike moved away from its traditional marketing strategy of support for sporting events and athlete endorsements to a wider-reaching approach, investing more than $10 million in its first national television and magazine advertising campaign. This followed the "Cities Campaign," which used billboards and murals in nine American cities to publicize Nike products in the period before the 1984 Olympics. Despite the strong showing of athletes wearing Nike shoes in the 1984 Los Angeles Olympic games, Nike profits were down almost 30 percent for the fiscal year ending in May 1984, although international sales were robust and overall sales rose slightly. This decline was a result of aggressive price discounting on Nike products and the increased costs associated with the company's push into foreign markets and attempts to build up its sales of apparel.

Earnings continued to fall in the next three quarters, as the company lost market share, posting profits of only $7.8 million at the end of August 1984, a loss of $2.2 million three months later, and another loss of $2.1 million at the end of February 1985. In response, Nike adopted a series of measures to change its sliding course. The company cut back on the number of shoes it had sitting in warehouses, and also attempted to fine-tune its corporate mission by cutting back on the number of products it marketed. It made plans to reduce the line of Nike shoes by 30 percent within a year and a half. In addition, leadership at the top of the company was streamlined, as founder Knight resumed the post of president, which he had relinquished in 1983, in addition to his duties as chairman and chief executive officer, and overall administrative costs were reduced. As part of this effort, Nike also consolidated its research and marketing branches, closing its facility in Exeter, New Hampshire, and cutting 75 of the plant's 125 employees. Overall, the company laid off about 400 workers during 1984.

Faced with shifting consumer interests, as, for instance, the U.S. market moved from jogging to aerobics, the company created a new products division in 1985 to help keep up with changing market demands. In addition, Nike purchased Pro-form, a small maker of weight-lifting equipment, as part of its plan to profit from all aspects of the fitness movement. The company was restructured further at the end of 1985 when its last two U.S. factories were closed and its previous divisions of apparel and athletic shoes were rearranged by sport. In a move that would prove to be the key to the company's recovery, in 1985 the company signed up basketball player Michael Jordan to endorse a new version of its Air shoe, introduced four years earlier.

In early 1986 Nike announced expansion into a number of new lines, including casual apparel for women, a less-expensive line of athletic shoes called Street Socks, golf shoes, and tennis gear marketed under the name "Wimbledon." By mid-1986 Nike was reporting that its earnings had begun to increase again, and that year sales topped $1 billion for the first time. At that time, the company sold its 51 percent stake in Nike-Japan to its Japanese partner, and six months later, at year's end, laid off 10 percent of its U.S. employees at all levels in a cost-cutting move.

Following these moves, Nike announced a drop in revenues and earnings in 1987, and another round of restructuring and cost-cutting ensued, as the company attempted to come to grips with the continuing evolution of the U.S. fitness market from jogging to walking, from aerobics to cross-training—diversified physical workout. Only Nike's innovative Air athletic shoes provided a bright spot in the company's otherwise erratic progress, allowing the company to regain market share from rival Reebok International Ltd. in several areas, including basketball and cross-training.

The following year, Nike branched out from athletic shoes, purchasing Cole Haan, a maker of casual and dress shoes, for $80 million. Advertising heavily, the company took a commanding lead in sales to young people to claim 23 percent of the overall athletic shoe market. Profits rebounded to reach $100 million dollars in 1988, as sales rose 37 percent to $1.2 billion. Later that year, Nike launched a $10 million dollar television campaign around the theme "Just Do It," and announced that its 1989 advertising budget would reach $45 million.

In 1989 Nike marketed several new lines of shoes, and led its market with $1.7 billion in sales, yielding profits of $167 million. The company's product innovation continued, as a basketball shoe with an inflatable collar around the ankle was introduced under the brand name Air Pressure. In addition, Nike continued its aggressive marketing, using ads featuring Michael Jordan and the Mars Blackmon character played by actor-director Spike Lee, the ongoing "Just Do It" campaign, and "Bo Knows" television spots featuring athlete Bo Jackson. At the end of 1989, the company began relocation to its newly constructed headquarters campus in Beaverton, Oregon.

In 1990 the company sued two competitors for copying the patented designs of its shoes, and found itself engaged in a dispute with the U.S. Customs Service over import duties on its Air Jordan basketball shoes. In 1990 the company's revenues hit $2 billion. The company acquired Tetra Plastics Inc., producers of plastic film for shoe soles. That year, the company opened Nike Town, a prototype store selling the full range of Nike products, in Portland, Oregon.

By 1991 Nike's Visible Air shoes had enabled it to surpass its rival Reebok in the U.S. market. In the fiscal year ending May 31, 1991, Nike sales surpassed the $3 billion mark, fueled by record sales of 41 million pairs of Nike Air shoes and a booming international market. Its efforts to conquer Europe had begun to show fruit as the company's business grew by 100 percent in Europe that year, producing over $1 billion in sales and gaining the second-place market share behind the leading German company, Adidas. Nike's U.S. shoe market had largely matured, slowing to five percent annual growth down from 15 percent annual growth from 1980 and 1988. The company began eyeing overseas markets and predicted ample room to grow in Europe. However, Nike's U.S. rival Reebok also saw potential for growth in Europe, and by 1992 European MTV was glutted with athletic shoe advertisements as the battle for the youth market heated up between Nike, Reebok, and their European competitors, Adidas and Puma.

Nike also saw growth potential in its women's shoe and sports apparel division. In February of 1992 Nike began a $13 million print and television advertising pitch for its women's segment, built upon its "Dialogue" print campaign which had been slowly wooing 18-to-34 year old women since 1990. Sales of Nike women's apparel lines Fitness Essentials, Elite Aerobics, Physical Elements, and All Condition Gear increased by 25 percent in both 1990 and 1991 and jumped by 68 percent in 1992.

In July of 1992 Nike opened its second Nike Town retail store in Chicago, Illinois. Like its predecessor in Portland, the Chicago Nike Town was designed to "combine the fun and excitement of FAO Schwartz, the Smithsonian Institute and Disneyland in a space that will entertain sports and fitness fans from around the world" as well as provide a high-profile retail outlet for Nike's rapidly expanding lines of footwear and clothing.

Nike celebrated its 20th anniversary in 1992, virtually debt free and with company revenues of $3.4 billion. Gross profits jumped $100 million in that year, fueled by soaring sales in its retail division which expanded to include 30 Nike-owned discount outlets and the two Nike Towns. To celebrate its anniversary, Nike brought out its old slogan, "There is no finish line." As if to underscore that sentiment, Nike chairman Philip Knight announced massive plans to remake the company with the goal of being "the best sports and fitness company in the world." To fulfill that goal, the company set the ground plans for a complicated yet innovative marketing structure seeking to make the Nike brand into a worldwide megabrand along the lines of Coca-Cola, Pepsi, Sony, and Disney.

Nike continued expansion of its high-profile Nike Town chain, opening outlets in Atlanta, Georgia, in spring of 1993 and Costa Mesa, California, later that year. Also in 1993, as part of its long-term marketing strategy, Nike began an ambitious venture with Mike Ovitz's Creative Artists Agency to organize and package sports events under the Nike name—a move that could lead the company into competition with sports management giants such as ProServ, IMG, and Advantage International.

Nike also began a more controversial venture into the arena of sports agents, negotiating contracts for basketball's Scottie Pippin, Alonzo Mourning, and others in addition to retaining athletes such as Michael Jordan and Charles Barkley as company spokespeople. Nike's influence in the world of sports grew to such a degree that in 1993 the *Sporting News* dubbed Knight the most powerful man in sports.

Critics contend that Nike's influence runs too deep, having its hand in negotiating everything in an athlete's life from investments to the choice of an apartment. But Nike's marketing executives see its as part of a campaign to create an image of Nike not just as a product line but as a *lifestyle,* a "Nike attitude." Marketing ideas under consideration range from the creation of Nike theme park to creating Nike television programs sponsored by Nike products.

Although much of Nike's marketing plan remains in the conceptual stage, its goal after 20 years in the business remained simple: to sell more shoes and clothing. Nike entered into this massive marketing plan with a large supply of financial reserves, a highly polished image, and a strong foothold in both U.S. and European markets. The company has a record of innovative design and savvy promotion. And if it succeeds at enacting its current plan, Nike may well become a household name worldwide.

Principal Subsidiaries: Cole Haan Holdings, Inc.; Tetra Plastics Inc.

Further Reading:

"Fitting the World in Sport Shoes," *Business Week,* January 25, 1982.
Gold, Jacqueline S, "The Marathon Man?," *Financial World,* February 16, 1993, p. 32.
Grimm, Matthew, "Nike Vision," *Brandweek,* March 29, 1993, p. 19.
"Nike Pins Hopes for Growth on Foreign Sales and Apparel," *New York Times,* March 24, 1983.
"Nike Timeline," Beaverton, Oregon: Nike, Inc. 1990.
Tharp, Mike, "Easy-Going Nike Adopts Stricter Controls To Pump Up Its Athletic-Apparel Business," *Wall Street Journal,* November 6, 1984.
"Where Nike and Reebok Have Plenty of Running Room," *Business Week,* March 11, 1991.

—Elizabeth Rourke
updated by Maura Troester

Norton Company

1 New Bond St.
P.O. Box 15008
Worcester, Massachusetts 01615-0008
U.S.A.
(617) 795-5000
Fax: (617) 795-5741

*Private Company, Wholly Owned Subsidiary of Compagnie
  de Saint-Gobain*
Incorporated: 1885 as the Norton Emery Wheel Company
SICs: 3291 Abrasive Products; 3545 Machine Tool
  Accessories

The Norton Company is quite possibly the world's leading producer of grinding wheels and coated and bonded abrasives. It is the leading producer of silicon carbide. From its inception as an offshoot of a small pottery works in Worcester, Massachusetts, in 1885, Norton pioneered the development of new abrasives. It evolved from an owner-operated concern in which the original partners were succeeded by their sons into a modern multinational corporation with manufacturing plants in over 20 countries. In 1989 it was taken over by the French conglomerate Compagnie de Saint-Gobain.

The Norton Company illustrates an interesting characteristic of emerging technologies: they often arise from unexpected quarters. In *Family Firm to Modern Multinational*, Charles W. Cheape's history of Norton, he says, "Manufacturing feli to new people and not to firms like Pike [Company in New Hampshire] and the Cleveland Stone Company that dominated the production of natural abrasives. The older enterprises had merely quarried and shaped their output. They lacked the manufacturing skills and experience required for the new product, including the proper selection of bond and abrasive, their mixture in correct proportions, and their bonding at proper temperatures." All of the skills that Cheape enumerates are skills that a potter would either have or could easily acquire.

Frank Norton had owned a small pottery in Worcester since about 1858. He came from a family of potters in Bennington, Vermont, and had established a partnership with Frederick Hancock. Norton employed his three sons, his son-in-law, and several journeyman potters. The stock in trade of F.B. Norton Stone Ware consisted of stoneware pots, bottles, pitchers, jars, and jugs. In 1873 a depression hit the United States economy, and several of Norton's potters started experimenting with

grinding wheels as a way to generate income. Norton had seen a silicate grinding wheel produced by a company in Detroit, and the story goes that he bet his crew a bucket of beer that they could not duplicate it.

In 1873 a Swedish immigrant potter named Swen Pulson mixed emery with slip clay and fired three wheels at about 2300 degrees in the Norton kiln, one of which vitrified successfully. The clay melted and the emery bonded or fused with it.

Frank Norton was unenthusiastic about the grinding wheels, mainly because he did not want to take a chance on an unproven product with an unknown market. Nevertheless, he patented Pulson's process in 1877 and started production in 1878. The wheels took a back seat to pottery and often were only fired when there were no pottery orders. Frustrated, Pulson left the company. Norton hired another Swede, John Jeppson, to take his place.

Jeppson soon became the acknowledged master at setting kilns and firing emery wheels. As business expanded, Norton hired Walter L. Messer to sell and promote the emery wheels throughout the country. He set up a distribution system that offered huge discounts and extremely easy (to the point of laxness) credit schemes, reasoning that because these wheels were consumed in use, easy terms would attract a loyal clientele. By 1881, largely as a result of Messer's efforts, the company was able to expand and hire more workers. By 1882 Norton's wheel business far surpassed pottery sales, and the company probably produced 10 percent of the entire industry output.

Frank Norton never involved himself in the affairs of the outsiders he had hired to make emery wheels, and the success of the new enterprise caused friction. In 1884, Jeppson, Messer, and Charles Allen, who was brought in to run the business end of the enterprise, offered Norton $10,000 for the entire wheel operation. In consideration of several factors, including ill health and debt, Norton was more than happy to sell. In May 1885 the Norton Emery Wheel Company was incorporated. In order to raise the money and capitalize the new company, the three brought in four new partners—Milton P. Higgins, George I. Alden, Fred H. Daniels, and Horace Young.

The business style of the four owner-operators of the new firm—Jeppson, Allen, Higgins, and Alden—is described by Cheape as follows: "Like New England merchants in the seventeenth century, they believed that business required careful attention, enterprise with close scrutiny and risk avoidance, and growth by reinvestment while maintaining a strong cash reserve." This tension between conservatism and enterprise came to be an established characteristic of the owner-operated company.

In 1886 the partners built a new factory on the outskirts of Worcester, where land was relatively cheap, yet accessible to two rail lines. To hold down costs, they recruited students from Worcester Polytechnic Institute to do the surveying, and in 1886 the partners forewent the yearly dividend. These parsimonious measures enabled the partners to virtually self-capitalize the project. Another indication of the partners' general mindset is apparent upon examination of the lack of compensation the partners bestowed upon themselves in these early days. President Higgins and treasurer Alden were not paid a salary until 1892, when it was clear the company would succeed.

The new kilns at the factory were highly efficient for the time and enabled the company to standardize production. Heat could be controlled to a great extent, allowing the production of wheels with a variety of "grain, grit, and grade" characteristics for different jobs.

Marketing was at least as important as production. The company introduced a numbered grading system and distributed catalogues and pamphlets to customers, explaining in detail the characteristics and uses of each wheel. The permutations of 26 grades, ten faces, 15 thicknesses, 23 diameters, and 21 grits was staggering. By the early 1890s, Norton stocked the largest grinding wheel inventory in the world. In addition, Norton consultants spent whatever time necessary on site to advise on special orders and handle customer questions.

Not only did Norton's sales expand in the United States, where it opened distributorships in Chicago (1897) and New York (1904), but also in Europe. In 1891 Charles Allen negotiated distribution contracts that spread Norton wheels through England, France, Germany, Russia, Austria, Belgium, and Sweden. Sales in Europe are credited with saving the company during the depression of 1893.

By 1900 Norton was the undisputed industry leader. It employed more than 200 people and enjoyed sales of $423,000. The company was profitable each year (including 1893) and paid "conservative" dividends each year (with the exception of 1886, the result of the move). What was not paid out in dividends went into reinvestment and cash reserves. These cash reserves allowed the company to self-finance construction of an office building in the 1890s and an abrasives plant in 1900.

However, the firm's conservatism also had a downside. It sometimes passed up innovation. For example, in 1891 Edward Acheson sent an electric current through a mixture of clay and powdered coke. The resultant crystals, which he dubbed carborundum, scratched glass, and, according to Acheson, diamonds. This new technology opened the way for artificial abrasives: the components of grinding wheels could now be controlled in ways that naturally occurring compounds could not. Norton turned down Acheson's request for financing. Acheson then turned to banker Andrew Mellen for help in forming the Carborundum Company, and by the early 1900s, Acheson's company was Norton's major competitor, with a big head start. It was not until the early 1900s that Norton entered into the realm of artificial abrasives.

In 1900 the company did, however, enter into a partnership with Charles H. Norton (no relation to Frank Norton) and established the Norton Grinding Company. The machine tool business was quite a departure for Norton and was undertaken gingerly. Charles Norton was a machinist who came to the company with an idea for building stationary grinding machines that could replace expensive workmen. What they got in 1901 was a versatile production grinder capable of high volume. Moreover, the grinder was able to work with pieces up to 1200 pounds and had the ability to grind to the unheard of tolerance of .00025 inch. Sales were slow at first because of resistance in the machine shops, although there were some sales to early auto makers. By 1909 Norton Company (it changed its name in 1906

after it began producing artificial abrasives) had loaned the new company some $263,000 in cash, equipment, and services. The company was slow to recoup this investment.

At the turn of the century, Norton was merely the largest enterprise in a tiny industry. Grinding and the use of abrasives was seen primarily as a way of smoothing rough edges, not as a precision tool. That was to change with the popularization of the automobile. Prior to the automobile, it was very rare for a job to require tolerances tighter than .001 inch. A skilled machinist could, with great effort and concentration, achieve that on a lathe. However, automobile engines and other parts, such as crankshafts, required tolerances of .00025 inch, and the metals used were hard steel alloys of carbon, tungsten, nickel, chromium, and vanadium. These could only be tooled efficiently, accurately, and economically by grinding.

This was where Charles Norton's production grinders made all the difference. In 1914 Henry Ford purchased 35 grinders for $30,000. In 1920 Ford is said to have commented that "the abrasive processes are basically responsible for our ability to produce cars to sell for less than a thousand dollars. Were it not for these processes these same cars would cost at least five thousand dollars, if indeed they could be made at all."

In 1927 Norton estimated that 95 percent of an automobile's moving parts required grinding. At that time, the industry bought about 55 percent of Norton Grinding Company's output and had more than 68,000 grinding machines. In fact, the automotive industry had became Norton's biggest customer.

Automobiles, though, were not the only factor in Norton's growth. Norton, like many other companies, received a tremendous boost from World War I. Tanks and airplanes were among the vehicles whose parts required grinding. From a total industry output of $1.3 million in 1899, the abrasives industry reached sales of more than $30 million in 1919, the year in which Norton Grinding Machine merged with the Norton Company. Another factor in Norton's growth was the increase in the size of the machine tool industry to cope with industrial demand. Machine tools had always been a significant user of abrasives.

In the 1920s, however, Norton failed to maintain its role as an innovator in grinding machines. Its piece-by-piece construction of grinders was at odds with the needs of industry. Some products went 28 or more years without significant improvements. It also gave up leadership and business to companies that developed more efficient "centerless" external grinders. In part, this stagnation was due to management's (primarily Jeppson and Higgins, the owner-operators) loyalty to their original product, abrasives. Charles Norton, after all, had been an outsider. And Charles Norton himself opposed the new machines, favoring his own.

In the early 1930s, in an attempt to correct the situation, the company reorganized and redesigned its product line, although resources were withheld from the machine division and put into the construction of abrasives plants. In 1931 Norton purchased the Behr-Manning Company of Watervliet, New York. This company, Norton's first acquisition, added coated abrasives and sandpaper to Norton's line. In fact, these products became the most profitable for Norton well into the 1950s, while the company's grinders and bonded abrasives languished. However, the two companies rarely cooperated or pooled their talents and know-how. Behr-Manning became a leader in the development of belt sanders in the 1930s, although its main competitor, 3M Company, consistently led it in sales. By 1951 the division manufactured more than 30,000 items, with sales of close to $30 million. By the late 1950s, Behr-Manning monthly profits actually outstripped those of the parent company. Behr-Manning was eventually absorbed into Norton.

Overseas expansion, begun in 1891 by Charles Allen, grew slowly and for a long time was mainly concerned with sales. Norton's first foreign plant, the German Deutsche Norton Gesellschaft, was built in 1909. Its production was disrupted by World War I, and after the war Norton was hesitant to upgrade it. Norton did build a plant outside Paris, and established facilities in Canada and Japan in the 1920s. In general, Norton considered these operations peripheral, and in any case, in order to maintain secrecy, all bonds and grains were made and shipped from Worcester.

In 1929 the ten largest abrasives manufacturers formed Durex Abrasives Corporation, whose purpose it was to market American abrasives overseas. Over the years, this expanded Norton's market to a greater degree than it could have accomplished on its own, at least during the initial period. In the 1950s, 1960s, and 1970s, the company built abrasives and other plants throughout the world. By the 1990s, it had about 90 such facilities.

In 1970 Norton was still a family company; the third generation of Jeppsons and Higginses still ran it. However, the need to decentralize authority and bring on competent outsiders to manage the company had been evident since the 1950s and before. Several steps were undertaken. First, the company went public in 1962. This step enabled the company to, among other things, create a bonus plan that would attract professional managers. The company then recruited professional managers to oversee the company. It then diversified into new industries, including the manufacturing of safety products and petroleum and mining tools. Finally, it decentralized authority over the various parts of the business.

Among the companies that Norton acquired in the 1960s was the National Research Corporation (NRC) in Cambridge, Massachusetts. This company was involved in aerospace research and in areas such as the manufacture of transistors and semiconductors, but had also developed such consumer products as frozen orange juice and vacuum lens coatings for binoculars and periscopes. The hope was that the acquisition would push Norton into the consumer market. In fact, NRC began to turn out such products as "space blankets," developed from space suit materials, as well as other profitable items. Its success in these endeavors encouraged further diversification. NRC also helped reorganize Norton's research operations.

By the mid-1960s, the contribution to total sales of abrasives had dropped 15 percent as plastic tubing, vacuum equipment, space blankets, rare metal coatings, and construction equipment contributed an increasing share of the company's revenue. However, by the end of the decade these sales faltered and the firm was forced to borrow for working capital. Fluctuations continued through the 1970s and 1980s, in part because of the cyclical nature of the abrasives industry, but also because of increased competition from European and Japanese manufacturers.

In 1976 Norton acquired the Christensen Company of Salt Lake City, Utah, whose core product was diamond drill bits. Under Norton, Christensen developed a new line of downhole petroleum tools used in ocean exploration. By 1980 Christensen sales had increased 107 percent and contributed 17 percent of sales and 30 percent of Norton's total income.

In March 1990 Norton became the object of an unsolicited takeover bid by the British conglomerate BTR P.L.C. The company offered $1.64 billion to stockholders ($75 per share). After looking at BTR's performance, Norton was determined to remain independent, even filing suit in federal court to prevent BTR representation on the board. However, in April, Compagnie de Saint-Gobain, a French holding company with which it had products in common, made an offer of $1.9 billion ($90 per share), with certain guarantees about how the company would be run. This offer was accepted, and the acquisition was completed in August. Saint-Gobain was founded in 1665 and is one of the world's leading industrial companies. In 1991 it had sales of 75 billion and net income of 2.5 billion.

Norton's 1989 annual report, the last before the takeover, indicated steady rises in sales each year since 1985 to $1.53 billion, with net income of $105 million, the healthiest for Norton in ten years. While sales were down in 1991, Saint-Gobain planned to increase Norton's presence in Europe and the rest of the world through aggressive marketing. It also expanded Norton's role in industrial ceramics and its base product, abrasives, both of which Saint-Gobain saw as vital to its own growth. For example, the company opened a new ceramics plant in Worcester in 1992.

After the acquisition of Norton by Saint-Gobain, the company underwent a legal reorganization in order to bring its various parts into the parent company in a rational way. Saint-Gobain formed a new abrasives branch, made up of Norton Abrasives businesses, and established branch headquarters in Worcester, Massachusetts, the first and only Saint-Gobain branch headquartered outside France. Other, non-abrasive businesses of Norton, such as plastics and ceramics, are being incorporated into the previously existing industrial ceramics branch of Saint-Gobain.

Further Reading:

Cheape, Charles W., *Family Firm to Modern Multinational: Norton Company, a New England Enterprise*, Cambridge, MA: Harvard University Press, 1985.
Greenhouse, Steven, "Saint-Gobain Pushing Worldwide Growth," *New York Times*, April 26, 1990.
Hylton, Richard D., "Norton Board Rejects $1.64 Billion BTR Bid," *New York Times*, March 30, 1990.
"$1.9 Billion Bid Taken By Norton," *New York Times*, April 26, 1990, p. D1.
Prokesch, Steven, "Norton Gets BTR Bid; Stock Soars," *New York Times*, March 17, 1990, p. 33.

—Kenneth F. Kronenberg

NutraSweet Company

1751 Lake Cook Road
Northbrook, Illinois 60015-5222
U.S.A.
(708) 940-9800
Fax: (708) 405-7812

Wholly Owned Subsidiary of Monsanto Company
Incorporated: 1985
Employees: 1,400
Sales: $944 million
SICs: 2869 Industrial Organic Chemicals Nec

NutraSweet, the world's largest manufacturer of the sweetening product known as aspartame, originated as a single product manufactured by the drug company G. D. Searle & Co. Aspartame was discovered in 1965 when a Searle scientist was testing combinations of amino acids for a potential ulcer drug. When the scientist put a finger in his mouth, he found that one of the mixtures, a combination of aspartic acid and phenylalanine, tasted like sugar. Aspartame proved to be 180 times as sweet as sugar, and unlike other artificial sweeteners like cyclamates and saccharin, it did not have a bitter or metallic aftertaste.

Receiving approval to market aspartame from the U.S. Food and Drug Administration (FDA) proved a lengthy process. The FDA approved aspartame in 1974, only to change its mind in 1975 when a psychiatrist claimed it caused brain damage in animals. Further tests showed no evidence of neurological damage. After lengthy studies were completed, aspartame finally received FDA approval in 1981. By that time the sweetener had already received approval in France, Luxembourg, and Belgium and was being sold there.

Searle initially marketed aspartame as a table-top sweetener, packaged in individual serving packets, under the Equal brand name. Aspartame was also used in cereals and desserts under the NutraSweet brand name. The big money in sweeteners was in low-calorie drinks, however, and Searle received approval to include aspartame in carbonated beverages in 1983. By that point aspartame was already being used in 40 products in 22 countries, including soft drinks in Canada. Sales of aspartame reached $74 million in 1982, when Searle decided to create the NutraSweet brand name. It also created a NutraSweet business group to manage the sweetener. One of the group's first moves was an introductory advertising campaign that offered con-

sumers coupons worth five free NutraSweet-containing gumballs. The company received two million coupons in the first year.

Some U.S. soft drink companies were slow to use aspartame because it cost $90 a pound, versus $4 a pound for saccharin, according to an August 1, 1983 article in *Newsweek*. Aspartame also lost its sweetness if stored for long enough in warm temperatures. Blends had a shelf life of about eight months, while products using pure NutraSweet tended to lose their sweetness in about six months. But the beverage market was fiercely competitive, and when manufacturers perceived the use of NutraSweet as a marketing advantage, they began using it in large quantities. Searle allowed some soft drink manufacturers to mix aspartame and saccharin to hold their costs down. In the meantime, Searle worked to increase aspartame production, which could not meet demand anyway. In 1983 construction began on a $100 million aspartame plant in Georgia.

Sales of low-calorie powdered drink mixes using NutraSweet were booming as the entire diet foods sector grew dramatically. Searle's pharmaceutical arm had long been suffering mediocre sales, and NutraSweet's profits were accounting for more and more of its total revenue.

With aspartame becoming a crucial ingredient in the products of other manufacturers, Searle began a campaign to build public recognition for it. When it created the name NutraSweet in 1983, a logo—a red and white swirl—was designed to go along with it. Searle spent $40 million advertising NutraSweet, and got food manufacturers to display the NutraSweet logo on products that used it. The trademark demand was initially unpopular with retailers of products made with Nutrasweet, though some changed their minds when they found that promoting NutraSweet as an ingredient increased demand for their products. Searle's initial ad campaign focused on the number and variety of products that used NutraSweet and the fact that they displayed the red swirl. The move was partly designed to put pressure on soft drink manufacturers and others that used a blend of NutraSweet and saccharin. The firm also wanted to lock up the artificial sweetener market for NutraSweet before its aspartame patent expired in 1992.

In 1985 Searle was bought by Monsanto, which combined the NutraSweet and Equal operations into the NutraSweet Company, a wholly owned subsidiary of Monsanto. NutraSweet sales amounted to over $700 million in 1985.

In 1986, NutraSweet began a $30 million advertising campaign to push the fact that it was made from natural ingredients, not artificial ones like saccharin and cyclamates. The television ads, which featured views of fruits and vegetables, used the theme, "Nature doesn't make NutraSweet, but NutraSweet couldn't be made without it." The print ads, which appeared in major national magazines, focused on the fact that NutraSweet was digested in the same way that fruit or milk are digested.

By 1986 NutraSweet was marketed in over 50 countries, including Germany, where the product had finally been granted approval that year. The company was awaiting approval in France, Spain, and Italy, however, and its patents in several European markets were about to expire. Aware that it was essentially a one-product company, NutraSweet was pouring research dollars into developing new sweeteners and other food products. In the meantime, it received approval from the FDA to use Nutra-Sweet in juice drinks, breath mints, tea beverages, and frozen novelties. These four new product categories had total annual sales of about $6 billion a year, giving NutraSweet huge new market opportunities.

According to *New York Times* contributor Eben Shapiro, when NutraSweet's European patents expired in 1987, the firm took strong competitive measures, cutting prices by over 60 percent, down to $27 a pound. As a result it continued to hold onto most of its market share, though profits in Europe tumbled.

NutraSweet unveiled its first serious attempt at product expansion in January 1988 with an all-natural fat substitute named Simplesse. Simplesse was made of egg whites or milk protein that were heated until they coagulated, then shaped into tiny beads that simulated the texture of fat. The fat-like proteins were discovered in 1979 by a chemist working on alternative uses for the byproducts of cheese making. In 1985, NutraSweet had bought the rights from John Labatt Ltd., a Canadian beer and food concern, and spent another two years perfecting the product.

Simplesse was introduced at a press conference at which the company asserted Simplesse did not need FDA approval since it was made from natural ingredients. The next day, however, the FDA commissioner announced that Simplesse would be seized unless it was submitted for review. NutraSweet chair Robert B. Shapiro quietly announced that Simplesse would be submitted after all. The attempt to skirt FDA review was largely an effort to beat competitors to market. Procter & Gamble had already submitted a fat substitute for review, and others were close behind.

Simplesse had only 15 percent of the calories of fat. When exposed to heat, however, it became tough. It was therefore limited to the $15 billion dairy, cheese, and salad dressing markets. Procter & Gamble's Olestra was a synthetic chemical that had no calories because the body did not digest it. Heat did not change Olestra, and it therefore could be used to cook foods. However, Olestra raised more health concerns than Simplesse, which, like NutraSweet, claimed to be digestible in the manner of the natural ingredients from which it was made. Other Simplesse competition came from products made from starch, though these too could not be heated.

NutraSweet's artificial sweetener market was also hit with increasing competitive pressure. By 1989 Pfizer, Hoechst Celanese Corp. were almost ready with competing products, while Kraft General Foods Group and Procter & Gamble were working on them. NutraSweet had 65 percent of the market, and its years of advertising its red swirl trademark had paid off in high consumer recognition. Its competitors were aware of this, however, and countered with huge advertising budgets of their own. Pfizer spent $30 million on its introductory campaign for its Alitame sweetener, said to be 2,000 times sweeter than sugar. Johnson & Johnson's Sucralose, which was derived from sugar, had the advantage of being stable enough to be used in baked and frozen products.

A potential benefit to NutraSweet's competitors was the dislike many food makers had for the NutraSweet Company. Nutra-

Sweet had acquired a reputation for arrogance as it built its huge business quickly. It had charged premium prices and advertised directly to consumers even though, in its first couple of years, it could not produce enough aspartame to meet demand. Despite criticism over these moves, NutraSweet began marketing Simplesse in similar ways even before it had FDA approval.

The FDA finally approved Simplesse in 1990. By this time, Kraft Foods was well under way in developing a Simplesse-based low-fat mayonnaise. In an attempt to broaden its base, NutraSweet kept the rights to use Simplesse in frozen products for itself. Shortly after the approval of Simplesse, it brought out the Simple Pleasures line of frozen desserts, putting NutraSweet into competition with its own customers. Simple Pleasures ice cream cost as much as premium ice cream and had half the calories and less than 10 percent of the fat. Industry observers reported that its taste was not up to that of premium ice creams like Häagen Dazs. Simple Pleasures was also going up against low-fat frozen yogurt, which had about the same caloric content and was already popular.

Robert E. Flynn became NutraSweet's top executive in 1990, taking on the mission of preventing a drop in earnings when the aspartame patent expired. He immediately began trying to improve relationships with clients. When NutraSweet announced a $20 million ad campaign in 1991, it was targeted to support the products of customers using NutraSweet. Flynn also began cutting NutraSweet prices. Company sales reached $933 million in 1990, but Simple Pleasures reportedly contributed only $12 million of that. Although Simplesse was being approved for use in countries outside the United States, it was falling short of expectations. Kraft, for example, sold back its rights to Simplesse, and brought out its own fat-free mayonnaise. Nutra-Sweet continued working on products using Simplesse, including cheesecake and frostings, and released an ice cream that used Simplesse and NutraSweet. To strengthen the company's bottom line, Flynn stressed reducing the cost of producing aspartame and laid off 12 percent of the firm's 1,700-person work force.

Nevertheless, the firm faced trouble because of its expiring patents. Coca-Cola Co. and Pepsi-Cola Co. reportedly accounted for about 80 percent of NutraSweet's sales. Both were expected to produce aspartame themselves within a few years of the patent expiration, according to Tom Pirko, the president of a food and beverage consulting firm, who was quoted in a 1991 *Advertising Age*. With Simple Pleasures not selling well, Nutra-Sweet finally decided to sell the Niles, Illinois plant where Simple Pleasures products were manufactured. The move improved relations with customers, since NutraSweet resumed its role as an ingredient supplier rather than a potential competitor. NutraSweet instead concentrated on producing a second generation of artificial food ingredients. It worked on methods of eliminating cholesterol and fat from egg yolks and removing high-calorie sucrose from orange juice.

In 1991 NutraSweet announced work on a new product called Sweetener 2000, an artificial sweetener 10,000 times as sweet as sugar. The sweetener was more stable than aspartame, with an indefinite shelf life and the ability to be used in baking. In the meantime, Johnson & Johnson's Sucralose, which was not approved in the United States, seemed to be approaching the market. Despite the prestige of having the NutraSweet logo on its cans, major soft drink companies were expected to consider dropping NutraSweet in favor of Sucralose, which had an indefinite shelf life. The new sweetener would enable the companies to advertise their products as ''new and improved.'' NutraSweet thus found itself in a race to come up with its own new and improved ingredients before decreasing aspartame profits devoured its bottom line. In the early 1990s, the company was a serious competitor in the artificial ingredients arena, but the heady days of the mid-1980s were gone.

Further Reading:

''Aspartame: The Newest Weapon for Diet Soda Rivals,'' *Business Week,* July 18, 1983.

Clark, Matt, ''A Sweet Sugar Substitute,'' *Newsweek,* July 27, 1981.

Dagnoli, Judann, ''NutraSweet Rivals Stirring,'' *Advertising Age,* June 26, 1989.

Kantrowitz, Barbara, ''A Heavyweight Fuss Over the New 'Fake Fat,' '' *Newsweek,* March 5, 1990.

Liesse, Julie, ''Bitter Future for NutraSweet?,'' *Advertising Age,* May 27, 1991, p. 33.

McCann, Joseph E., *Sweet Success: How NutraSweet Created a Billion Dollar Business,* Business One Irwin, Homewood, Illinois, 1990.

O'Neil, Molly, ''First Low-Calorie Substitute for Fats Is Approved by U.S.,'' *New York Times,* February 23, 1990.

Pauly, David, ''Sweet Dreams for Searle,'' *Newsweek,* August 1, 1983.

Petre, Peter, ''Searle's Big Pitch for a Tiny Ingredient,'' *Fortune,* September 3, 1984.

Schiller, Zachary, and James E. Ellis, ''NutraSweet Sets Out for Fat-Substitute City,'' *Business Week,* February 15, 1988.

Shapiro, Eben, ''NutraSweet's Bitter Fight,'' *New York Times,* November 19, 1989.

Therrien, Lois, ''NutraSweet Tries Being More of a Sweetie,'' *Business Week,* April 8, 1991.

—Scott M. Lewis

NVR L.P.

7601 Lewinsville Road, Suite 300
McLean, Virginia 22102
U.S.A
(703) 761-2000
Fax: (703) 761-2030

Public Company
Incorporated: 1980 as NVHomes, Inc.
Employees: 1880
Sales: $730 million
Stock Exchanges: American Stock Exchange (AMEX)
SICs: 6162 Mortgage bankers and correspondents; 6035
   Federal Savings Institutions; 1531 Operative Builders

A holding company that operates through a network of subsidiaries, NVR L.P. (NVR) builds, sells, and finances new single-family dwellings. The company developed more than 4200 units in 1992, making it one of the largest homebuilders in the United States. Aside from the construction of detached houses, which was its primary activity, NVR also built condominiums and townhomes. Although NVR has constructed and financed homes throughout the country, its building operations as of 1993 were active in only eight metropolitan areas, all on the East Coast.

NVR's history is relatively short, but tumultuous. It was founded in 1980 as NVHomes, Inc., by Dwight C. Schar. Between 1973 and 1977 Schar served as vice president and group manager of Ryan Homes, Inc.'s Washington, D.C., operations. From 1969 to 1973 he headed Ryan Homes's land acquisition and development efforts in Ohio, Kentucky, and Indiana. Like Ryan Homes, which was founded in 1948, NVHomes specialized in the construction of single-family homes primarily in the Washington, D.C., area.

By 1983 NVHomes achieved income in excess of $1 million from homebuilding operations on the East Coast. The company continued to grow quickly throughout the early 1980s, doubling its net income each year to nearly $14 million in 1986. In that year, concurrent with its initial public offering of 1980, NVHomes was reorganized into a limited partnership and was renamed NVH L.P.

A few months after becoming a limited partnership, NVH acquired a controlling interest in Ryan Homes, Inc. Before the end of 1987 NVH had acquired all of Ryan, making it a subsidiary of the newly formed NVRyan L.P. holding company. Profits continued to skyrocket in 1987 and 1988, with net incomes exceeding $21.5 and $33.5 million respectively. In 1989 the company shortened its name to NVR L.P.

As the company expanded in the 1980s, an organization evolved that was comprised of nearly 100 subsidiaries. By acquiring and establishing new subsidiaries, NVR was able to provide services relating to construction, land acquisition, home finance, investment advice, and other real estate development activities. Through its network of companies, NVR generated profits from almost every phase of the homebuilding and financing process. The company also branched out regionally, entering markets in Florida, California, Indiana, Kentucky, North Carolina, Ohio, Pennsylvania, and Virginia.

Contributing to the success of NVR and its subsidiaries in the 1980s were several factors that prompted housing industry growth in the early part of the decade. For instance, the demand for new homes in the United States rose significantly in the early and mid-1980s, bolstered by a generally strong U.S. economy. In addition, favorable tax laws pertaining to real estate investments, particularly limited partnerships, were enacted by the presidential administration of Ronald Reagan. These laws made it possible, for example, for limited partners to write off losses incurred from real estate investments against personal income. These developments, in concurrence with the deregulation of some lending institutions in the early 1980s, made it easy for NVR to obtain capital for expansion.

Despite strong growth and healthy profits through 1988, NVR began experiencing severe financial difficulties in 1989. By this time, the demand for new housing was beginning to decrease significantly as the economy fell into recession. In addition, changes in the tax code were making it more difficult for companies like NVR to obtain capital. For example, the Tax Reform of 1986 reduced, over time, the benefits derived from investing in real estate and limited partnerships. The result was over-built housing markets in many regions and the subsequent decrease in demand for new homes that continued through 1991.

Although NVR showed a net income of more than $30 million in 1989, the company was severely distressed going into 1990. The company's homebuilding and land development inventory grew from about $400 million in 1988 to over $600 million at the start of 1990. At the same time, revenues from NVR's construction and development activities plummeted from $1.15 billion in 1988 to about $.9 billion in 1990 and $.6 billion in 1991. In addition, as the development industry slowed, NVR's assets lost much of their market value. As a result of reduced asset values and operating revenues, NVR posted a net income loss of over $260 million in 1990.

In response to the dire market conditions of 1989 and 1990, NVR adopted a comprehensive business reorganization plan in 1990 that was designed to streamline its operations and reduce further losses. The major goals of the plan, which was implemented in 1990 and 1991, were to: restructure homebuilding operations into two product lines—moderately priced and up-scale; reduce homebuilding activity and place all development companies under one management structure; exit all markets except those in the eight mid-Atlantic states in which NVR operated profitably; close several home manufacturing plants; consolidate some finance operations and increase mortgage offerings to customers other than NVR home buyers; and exit speculative land development businesses.

By 1991, NVR maintained two principal business segments: construction and marketing of homes, and financial services, which included both a mortgage and a savings bank. Home construction and marketing activities, NVR's chief source of revenue, was handled through its two primary development companies, Ryan Homes and NVHomes. Ryan Homes, which developed moderately priced single-family units, was responsible for most of NVR's construction activity. NVHomes, on the other hand, concentrated on move-up buyers that were able to purchase relatively high-priced homes yet could not afford custom-built units.

Ryan Homes offered a variety of basic home designs for condominiums, townhomes, and detached houses. In 1992, for instance, it built detached homes ranging from 1,000 to 3,350 square feet in size and from $54,000 to $479,000 in price. The largest homes, which were part of the "Ryan Classics" line, offered amenities such as libraries, sun rooms, cathedral ceilings, hardwood floors, and hot tubs. Although 55 percent of the homes Ryan built in 1992 were detached houses, 35 percent of its dwellings were townhomes. These units ranged from 900 to 2,300 square feet and averaged $127,000 in price. The few condominiums that Ryan built averaged about 1,000 square feet in size and cost an average of $88,200. Although most of its homes were built in the Washington, D.C., area, Ryan also operated in Pennsylvania, New York, North Carolina, and Delaware.

NVHomes developed significantly fewer homes than Ryan, although at a much greater price. For example, the average price of a NVHomes unit in 1992 was $289,100, compared to $137,600 for a Ryan Home development. Because NVHomes catered more heavily to move-up buyers, its homes usually offered four or more bedrooms and at least two and one-half bathrooms. Its larger homes, some priced at more than $600,000, offered luxury amenities such as extra fireplaces and bedrooms, finished basements, and garden rooms. About 30 percent and 12 percent of NVHomes units were townhomes and condominiums, respectively. The company built almost exclusively in the Washington, D.C., metropolitan area.

Both NVHomes and Ryan Homes employed innovative marketing and product delivery techniques to survive in the increasingly competitive market of the early 1990s. For instance, the operations began building homes as they were ordered, rather than by speculation. This was accomplished by first developing a model home in each community being developed. Customers could visit the model home, which also served as a sales center, and choose the floor plan and options that they would like to see integrated into their home. Customers also selected a site within the community. After the neighborhood was fully developed, the model home was also sold. In the case of townhomes and condominiums, construction began only after a significant number of the units in each building had been sold.

Besides building homes as they were ordered, NVR also began to reduce its exposure to risk by not actually purchasing home sites until a customer chose to build on the lot. Instead, after its reorganization, NVR purchased individual options to buy land that were exercised only after home buyers qualified for their mortgages. After the customer qualified, NVR would construct the house using on-site contractors. NVR was able to minimize costs, increase quality, and speed product delivery through its subsidiaries that premanufactured segments of the home in off-site facilities. The ready-made panels were delivered to the site where contractors, under the supervision of NVR representatives, assembled and finished the home. In 1992 NVR completed detached homes in an average of 86 days.

NVR's second principal business activity, financial services, allowed the company to extract greater profits from its homebuilding operations and to generate revenues from unrelated activities. Financial services operations were divided into two functions: thrifts and mortgage banking. In accordance with its goal of streamlining operations and consolidating its finance operations, NVR established NVR Finance in August of 1991. NVR Finance assumed all of the mortgage origination and servicing activities that were formerly conducted by several different divisions. In 1992 NVR Finance arranged financing for approximately 75 percent of NVR's home sales. While NVR's construction activities shrunk regionally, NVR Finance expanded its operations to serve several western states. It also sought to diversify by increasing its share of the retail mortgage market. NVR Finance also provided broker title insurance and title search services for NVR's homebuilding services as well as for third parties.

In the early 1990s NVR continued to operate a thrift institution that it acquired through RFS, one of its subsidiaries. RFS acquired Mclean Federal Savings and Loan Association by merger to form a wholly owned subsidiary called NVRSB. NVRSB provided checking, savings, and lending services, and concentrated in lending for home and automobile purchases as well as other consumer finance loans.

In addition to its thrift and mortgage banking operation, NVR was active in real estate investment trusts and mortgage backed securities operations in the late 1980s. These activities were curtailed following the reorganization plan of 1990.

Despite NVR's attempts to minimize losses by reorganizing and streamlining its operations, falling home prices combined with the continued low demand for new construction proceeded to place the company under severe financial stress in 1991 and 1992. In 1991 NVR built just 3,831 housing units, down almost 27 percent from 5,240 in 1990. Furthermore, total company assets continued to decline, from a peak of $2.4 billion in 1988 to less than $1.6 billion by 1991. Although net income losses decreased in 1991 to -$36.7 from -$260.5 million in 1990, NVR's cash flow was still insufficient to meet its obligations to creditors.

In 1992 NVR developed 10.4 percent more homes than it built in 1991. This increase resulted from an increase in new orders in late 1991 and 1992. The increase in orders, however, was partially offset by a further reduction in the average price of NVR's new homes, which fell from $200,000 in 1991 to

$189,000 in 1992. NVR realized a jump in revenue of about 5.8 percent, or about $37 million. Even an improvement in sales and income in 1992 was not enough to buoy the company, however. Net income remained negative in 1992, at -$3 million, despite a 26 percent jump in gross revenue over 1991 to $818 million.

On April 6, 1992, NVR and some of its homebuilding subsidiaries filed for Chapter 11 bankruptcy. In addition, on December 9, 1992, two of NVR Finance's mortgage banking subsidiaries also filed for bankruptcy. Pursuant to its petition for bankruptcy as well as its default on mostly all of its debts, NVR filed a joint plan of reorganization. The plan was designed to allow NVR to emerge from bankruptcy intact while minimizing losses incurred by NVR creditors. As of April, 1993, NVR was still awaiting approval of the plan by creditors and the bankruptcy court.

In addition to problems related to bankruptcy, including claims and suits filed against NVR as a result of default, NVR was also burdened by litigation related to its homebuilding activities. During the 1980s NVR built about 20,000 townhomes and 2,500 condominiums that may have contained faulty fire retardant plywood in their roofs. In an effort to rectify the situation, NVR spent, as of 1993, about $10.8 million. It also planned to spend an additional $9.4 million in the future. As a result, NVR is suing both the supplier of the plywood and NVR's insurer to recover these losses.

Despite bankruptcy proceedings in 1993, NVR continued to develop homes in the Northeast and to expand its financial services subsidiaries throughout selected regions in the United States. The company was ranked as the sixth-largest developer of single-family homes by *Builder* magazine. As it entered 1993, NVR employed 1,880 people, up from 1,731 at the beginning of 1992. 471 of these employees were company officers and management personnel, 153 were technical and construction personnel, and 678 were administrative workers. 298 people were employed in miscellaneous service and labor jobs.

Record low interest rates, combined with moderate increases in the demand for new construction, indicated that the housing market may have bottomed out in 1990. A slow economic recovery, however, suggested only minor relief for NVR from its financial distress.

Principal Subsidiaries: Ryan Homes, Inc.; NVHomes L.P.; NVR Mortgage Finance, Inc.; NVR Savings Bank; Ryan Mortgage Acceptance Corporation (RYMAC).

Further Reading:

"Builder 100," *Builder,* May 1983.
"Form 10-K: Annual Report Pursuant to Section 13 or 15(d) of the Securities Exchange Act of 1934 for the Fiscal Year Ended December 31, 1992 for NVR L.P.," Washington, DC: Securities and Exchange Commission, 1992.

—Dave Mote

Office Depot Incorporated

2000 Old Germantown Road
Delray Beach, Florida 33445
U.S.A.
(407) 278-4000
Fax: (407) 265-4403

Public Company
Incorporated: 1986
Employees: 9,000
Sales: $1.70 billion
Exchanges: New York
SICs: 5112 Stationery & Office Supplies

Thanks to its 1991 merger with competitor Office Club, Office Depot Incorporated has become the largest discount retailer of office supplies and furniture in North America. In addition to office products, the company also sells computer hardware and electronics designed for small business applications. Office Depot operates over 300 stores, with most of them located in the South, lower Midwest, and Pacific Coast.

Along with rival companies Staples and Office Club, Office Depot was a pioneer in the field of office supplies discount retail. The three companies were founded within months of each other in 1986 in three different corners of the United States—Office Depot in Florida, Staples in Massachusetts, and Office Club in California. All of them saw opportunities in selling office supplies to small businesses at bulk discount rates that had previously been the privilege of larger companies. Since small businesses had never purchased supplies in quantities large enough to receive bulk discounts, they had been at the mercy of conventional retailers who, in the absence of price competition, could sell at manufacturer's suggested retail prices and take markups of as much as 100 percent. Buying directly from manufacturers instead of wholesalers and keeping overhead low, a discount retailer could offer goods from 20 to 75 percent off of full retail. Another trend that proved advantageous for these three companies was the advent of warehouse-style discount retailers in the 1980s; what Price Club had done for general merchandise and what Circuit City had done for consumer electronics, Office Depot, Office Club, and Staples sought to do for ballpoint pens and legal pads.

Office Depot was founded in Boca Raton, Florida, by entrepreneur F. Patrick Sher and two partners. The company opened its first retail store in Fort Lauderdale in October of 1986, and it proved successful enough that two more Office Depot stores appeared in Florida by the end of the year. The company continued to grow rapidly; in 1987 it opened seven more stores in Florida and Georgia and sales topped $33 million. Sher did not have long to savor his success, however, for he died of leukemia scarcely a year after his first store had opened. He was succeeded as CEO by David Fuente, an experienced retail executive whom Office Depot lured away from Sherwin-Williams, where he had been president of the Paint Stores Division.

Under Fuente, Office Depot continued to grow at a breakneck pace, with its success matching the pace of its expansion. The company opened sixteen more stores in 1988, expanding into Kentucky, North Carolina, Tennessee, and Texas. Sales topped $132 million, and Office Depot went public in June with an initial offering of more than 6 million shares at $3.33 per share. Office supply discount retail as a whole was proving wildly successful; although they accounted for only a small fraction of office supply retail sales by the end of the decade, at least one analyst predicted in 1989 that discounters would form the fastest growing specialty-retail segment for several years to come.

Office Depot gained the distinction of being the first of the three original discount chains to turn a profit for a period of four consecutive quarters, which it did during the last two quarters of 1988 and the first two of 1989. The company achieved its success with stores that resembled nothing so much as warehouses; their decor was functional and unassuming—in a style described by a reporter for *Fortune* as "plain pipe rack"—with merchandise stacked floor-to-ceiling on steel shelves. As David Fuente explained it, "Customers pick only from the first six feet of [shelf] space anyway. So we use the area above [for storage]." By 1989, Office Depot stores were averaging $150,000 in sales per week. Of course, lack of concern for the aesthetics of interior design characterized the company's competitors, as well. Office Depot held an edge in that commercial rents were lower in the South than elsewhere in the United States, allowing the company to build exceptionally large stores and still keep overhead costs relatively low.

Office Depot continued to grow dramatically in 1989 and 1990, expanding beyond its regional base in the South into the Midwest. By the end of 1990 the company boasted 122 stores scattered across 19 states and sales of $625 million. Much of that expansion was financed by the sale of 3.6 million shares of stock to Carrefours, a French chain-store concern with subsidiaries throughout Europe.

The office supply discount field became more crowded and competitive in the early 1990s as other companies, including Office Max and BizMart, joined the lucrative industry. With the struggle for market share becoming more vigorous, Office Depot and Office Club decided to merge in 1991. The move solidified Office Depot's position on the Pacific Coast in one swoop by eliminating a major competitor and giving it a substantial number of new stores in a regional market where the company previously had only a slim presence. For its part, Office Club had not fared quite as well as its fellow discounting pioneers; during the four quarters that constituted Office Depot's first profitable one-year period Office Club lost $2.7 million, compared to Office Depot's gain of $5.1 million and Staples's narrower loss of $1.9 million. The merger, therefore, proved advantageous to Office Club as well.

Office Club had been founded in northern California in 1986 by Mark Begelman—previously an executive with British American Tobacco—in partnership with a friend who had been selling office products to Price Club. They reasoned that the same marketing principles that allowed Price Club to retail office supplies at deep discounts would work for stores specializing in that kind of merchandise. The first Office Club store opened in January 1987 in Concord, California. Office Club grew quickly, though not as frantically as Office Depot. By the end of 1987 Office Club had opened five stores. At the time of the merger, it operated 59 stores, most of them in California, and had posted annual sales of $300 million.

The merger was approved by Office Depot shareholders in April of 1991. As a result of the agreement, which entailed a stock swap worth $137 million, Mark Begelman became president and COO of Office Depot, with David Fuente remaining chairman and CEO. Over the next thirteen months, all Office Club stores were either closed or converted into Office Depot outlets and the membership fee that Office Club had been charging its regular customers was dropped.

Even after the merger, Office Depot continued to expand. In June of 1991 it sold another 1.8 million shares of stock to Carrefours to finance expected growth. Aside from the outlets acquired from Office Club, the company opened 57 new stores in 1991. At the end of the year, Office Depot had 229 stores and posted sales of $1.3 billion.

At about the same time, Office Depot saw its sales of office machines, including personal computers, begin to grow by leaps and bounds, and the company began to emphasize this side of its business more strongly. In December of 1992, Begelman claimed in an interview that 10 percent of all fax machines sold in the United States were sold by Office Depot. Store layouts were redesigned so that more machines could be put on display. The company began selling not only PC clones by Packard-Bell and Compaq, but also the real thing—in August 1991 IBM agreed to let Office Depot sell its PS/1 computers—and also Apple's Macintosh Performa line.

In 1992 Office Depot went international, acquiring HQ Office International, the parent company of the Great Canadian Office Supplies Warehouse chain, which operated seven stores in western Canada. HQ Office International had been founded in 1990 by Robert McNulty as a Canadian extension of his unsuccessful California-based HQ Office Supplies Warehouse chain, which was carved up and bought out by Staples and BizMart in 1990. Office Depot immediately replaced the HQ Office International name with its own and began expanding its presence in Canada, opening two stores in Manitoba. Office Depot's entry into the Canadian market set the company up for an eventual confrontation with Business Depot, a small chain based in Eastern Canada, in which Staples holds a minority stake.

In May 1993 Office Depot acquired the office supply operations of contract stationer Wilson Stationery & Printing, a subsidiary of Steelcase Inc. The deal was valued at $16.5 million, and gave Office Depot an entree into the side of the office supply retail business that serves larger companies, rather than the small and mid-sized businesses that had made up its customer base in the past.

Within its first five years, Office Depot grew from a tiny retail firm operating out of a storefront in Boca Raton to a major company with its own headquarters complex. It had also gobbled up one of its most serious competitors. After just seven years, Office Depot became the largest company in a lucrative and rapidly growing retail sector. How long the business can sustain such an amazing rate of growth is open to question, but with markets in the United States that remain largely untapped, a foothold in Canada, and the possibility of ventures in Europe through its link with Carrefours, it is likely that Office Depot's success has yet to approach its highest point.

Principal Subsidiaries: The Office Club, Incorporated; H.Q. Office International, Incorporated

Further Reading:

"The Big Interview: Mark Begelman—Office Depot," *Office Products International,* December 1992.
Caminiti, Susan, "Seeking Big Money in Paper and Pens," *Fortune,* July 31, 1989.
Liebeck, Laura, "Office Depot Ventures Into Canada, Magazine Business," *Discount Store News,* February 3, 1992.
Milstone, Erik, "Office Depot on the Fast Track," *Palm Beach Post,* March 29, 1992.
Selz, Michael, "Office Supply Firms Take Different Paths to Success," *Wall Street Journal,* May 30, 1991.

—Douglas Sun

Oxford Industries, Inc.

222 Piedmont Avenue
Atlanta, Georgia 30308
U.S.A.
(404) 659-2424
Fax: (404) 653-1545

Public Company
Incorporated: 1960 as Oxford Manufacturing Company
Employees: 9,800
Sales: $527.7 million
Stock Exchanges: New York
SICs: 2311 Men's/Boys' Suits and Coats; 2321 Men's/Boys'
    Shirts; 2337 Women's/Misses' Suits and Coats; 2339
    Women's/Misses' Outerwear Nec

Oxford Industries, Inc., one of America's leading apparel manufacturers, has spent most of its history plotting a course for steady growth by providing affordably priced sportswear to retail chains; it later sought to dramatically increase profits by aggressively acquiring higher-end labels and turning out upscale merchandise.

Oxford Industries started as the "temporary" wartime livelihood of Tommy, Sartain, and Hicks Lanier, three Nashville-bred brothers. They had originally joined forces in 1934 by investing in a venture that produced and sold dictaphones and business forms. Business went well and they were able to expand throughout the southeast until 1941, when the onset of World War II brought the supply of their products' component materials to a standstill. The brothers were casting about for an interim investment when, in 1942, a friend pointed them in the direction of Oxford of Atlanta, a small company that merchandised and sold mens' and boys' shirts and slacks, garnering about $1 million in annual sales. Despite the brothers' lack of experience in the apparel business, the three drew upon their sales skills and quickly set about expanding the company.

In 1943 Oxford bought its first manufacturing facility, the Champion Garment Company, in Rome, Georgia, and the company name was promptly changed to the Oxford Manufacturing Company. The limited supply of retail merchandise during the war, coupled with the ability of the Lanier brothers to procure more than the company's allotted amount of material, helped the company immeasurably; according to Sartain, "there was such a shortage of merchandise in those days there was no need for a designer label to sell good. If pants had two legs and the button fly would work, you could sell them."

As the war drew to a close, demand for clothing grew, and Oxford added manufacturing plants in Vidalia and Monroe, Georgia, and Tupelo, Mississippi. The building in Vidalia had originally been used as a bowling alley; for a time the lanes were used as cutting tables. In 1944 the brothers were able to buy out their partners; the "temporary" investment had taken on a life of its own.

After the war one of Oxford's most popular items was a line of slack-suit sets (consisting of a sportshirt and slacks made from the same material, sometimes with a belt from the same material) made from Army surplus twill that were marketed prepackaged in two colors—blue and tan. Over time retailers began to ask for more of one color or another based on consumer demand, and at this point Hicks Lanier decided to return to the dictaphone business. According to Sartain, Hicks felt that "anything this complex is not for me. I'm going back to the dictating machine, where customers only want one model, one size, and one color."

Oxford came out of the postwar recession with a growth strategy that centered on dramatically increasing manufacturing capability and expanding its product lines while maintaining its focus on sportswear. Oxford sought to use its large-scale production force to supply the national retail chains, foremost among them J.C. Penney. By 1950 it had begun to lay the groundwork by opening a new 40,000-square-foot plant in Vidalia, as well as an office in New York City. Throughout the decade expansion of existing plants and the acquisition of nine others greatly increased production strength. The strategy seemed to pay off. In 1950 sales were $3.5 million; by 1954 they had reached $10 million.

High-volume production methods allowed Oxford to provide both branded and unbranded lines, which by this time included mens' suits and sports jackets and womens' apparel as well. Thus it was able to penetrate the national chains—its merchandise appeared in such stores as J.C. Penney, Montgomery Ward, and National Shirt Shops—as well as smaller retailers and mail order companies.

The popularity of the slack-suit set that had fueled the company's early growth began to fade in the 1950s. Oxford expanded into outerwear, denim clothing, and womens' shirts, and in 1956 it began to produce slacks for J.C. Penney. By 1959 sales had reached $29 million (47 percent of this figure from pants sales), and J.C. Penney accounted for 44 percent of Oxford's total business. In that year Oxford bought the Freezer Shirt Corporation, a South Carolina-based manufacturer capable of turning out 36,000 shirts a week.

The advent of the mens' tailored shirt for women, an item first manufactured at the urging of J.C. Penney, broached the womenswear market for the first time. In 1961 Oxford acquired Aansworth Shirt Makers, a womens' sportswear company, and renamed its product line Cos Cob, facilitating penetration into the womenswear market. The growing strength of Oxford's higher-margin womenswear line helped its profit margin during this period of expansion. In 1962 womenswear made up 23 percent of the company's manufacturing volume, yet accounted for 35 percent of the company's earnings.

When Oxford went public in 1960 with an offering of 240,000 class A common shares and began trading on the American Stock Exchange and the Philadelphia and Baltimore stock exchanges, the company had more than 3,000 employees and $31 million in sales.

The years from 1955 to 1963 brought Oxford 18 apparel companies (six in 1963 alone) and a total of 23 plants. In 1963 sales increased $21 million to reach $61 million, and the company's stock split. By 1964 Oxford was listed on the New York Stock Exchange.

One of the men responsible for Oxford's tremendous growth in this period, President Tommy Lanier, was killed in a plane crash near Paris on June 3, 1962, in a disaster that also took the lives of many of Atlanta's civic leaders. Sartain Lanier was thus the last of the co-founding brothers to remain directly involved with Oxford's operations.

Several technological advances greatly changed the business and Oxford was among the first apparel manufacturers to take advantage of them. First was the production process that allowed Dacron and cotton poplin slacks to be sewed without unattractive puckers at the seams—Oxford was the first to master the technique and ran large quantities of this product. Another production advance came with the introduction of "permanent press" material in 1965. The handling of this fabric proved problematic for many manufacturers because of its unique properties. Oxford was one of the first to take advantage of its potential and use it to make mens' and boys' slacks and then womens' shirts, dresses, and sportswear.

When Oxford moved its headquarters into a new 70,000-square-foot site in Atlanta in 1965, the company had grown to include more than 7,000 employees and had topped $81.7 million in net annual sales. Expansion continued with a new 200,000-square-foot plant in Vidalia and a 125,000-square-foot slacks plant and distribution center in Monroe in 1966. Another important development was the 1966 acquisition of Wright Manufacturing Company, a manufacturer and national distributor of mens' slacks that had previously served as an independent contractor.

Although fiscal 1967 brought increased sales of $116.2 million, earnings fell sharply after years of growth (they had more than tripled in the previous five years). A sour retail atmosphere, widespread cutbacks and markdowns of inventories, and increased textile and labor costs (stemming from new minimum wage legislation) all took their toll. Thus, Oxford's 25th anniversary year brought a change in name to Oxford Industries, Inc. and marked the beginning of an intensive reorganization process. Its many sales forces, product lines, and manufacturing plants were seen as too often duplicating efforts. With Sartain Lanier in firm control as both chairman and president, the company set out to respond to changes in the economy and society at large. Oxford shed its marginally profitable businesses in rainwear and outerwear manufacturing. Prices were increased, and the company started to look for ways to lower labor costs. One of its first moves was to lease a plant in Agua Prieta, Mexico, directly across the border from its plant in Douglass, Arizona, in 1968. The minimum wage there was 35 cents an hour.

In 1968 Oxford acquired Lanier Business Products, the office equipment distributor and manufacturer that was a descendant of the Lanier brothers' original business venture. Oxford paid 349,999 shares of class A common stock for Lanier's 1.1 million shares. The strong performance of the business products division—which in 1970 comprised 11 percent of revenue—helped cushion the effects of the apparel divisions' sluggish sales, which were blamed on inflation, rising unemployment, and continuing recession.

The menswear division at this time contributed over 65 percent of volume for Oxford. The cornerstone of its business continued to be sales to Sears Roebuck, J.C. Penney, and Montgomery Ward of branded and unbranded apparel. The popularity of leisure suits was also a factor. The womenswear division, which in 1970 came under the control of John Hicks Lanier, Sartain Lanier's son, sought to make its clothing more fashionable and to this end moved its offices from Atlanta to New York City, the hub of the domestic fashion world.

Sales began to climb again in 1971 and continued to do so throughout the early 1970s. The cost of U.S. labor and the recession that followed the OPEC oil embargo, as well as overarching societal change, radically altered the apparel industry during this period. The large-scale entry of women into the workforce in the 1970s created demand for affordable, office-friendly sportswear, and so Cos Cob in 1974 cast off its lines of separates to capitalize on the demand for coordinates. Another change in the apparel industry centered on the increasing diversity of clothing worn in blue collar occupations. Finally, the increase in white-collar jobs throughout the 1960s and 1970s proved very good for the shirt business. Although the recession of 1974–1975 caused a loss of sales of 2.8 percent, by 1976 apparel sales had increased 15.7 percent to over $230.5 million.

On July 1, 1977, Lanier Business Products was spun off as its own publicly held company and was listed on the New York Stock Exchange. Revenues dropped 29 percent (from $302.3 million in 1976 to $220.5 million in 1977) and Oxford lost 57 percent of its earnings. Oxford returned to focus solely on the apparel business.

That year also brought the ascension of J. Hicks Lanier to the post of president of Oxford. Under his control Oxford sought to enter the 1980s, upgrading its production technology and diversifying its customer base. A computer-operated pattern grading and marking system was introduced in the menswear division in 1976. Computers were also brought in for inventory control and production planning, and some sewing and pressing operations were automated.

In 1978 sales to Sears and J.C. Penney accounted for 55 percent of the company's total sales. The disadvantages of this situation became clear when Oxford saw earnings drop five percent in 1979 as both retailers delayed deliveries on ordered merchandise. Oxford, seen for years as a supplier of "commodities" clothing, sought at this time to broaden its customer base as well as increase sales by venturing into the volatile, higher-margin designer label market.

Perhaps Oxford's most striking success in the designer label market was its first; it sealed an agreement with Ralph Lauren in 1978 to produce a line of all-cotton boys shirts known as Polo for Boys. This arrangement brought Oxford products into such upscale retail establishments as Bloomingdales and Neiman Marcus for the first time. Another major acquisition was the Merona Sport Division of Merona Corporation in 1981. Other labels included Jhane Barnes and Robert Stock.

These efforts brought immediate results. Sales to J.C. Penney and Sears, which in 1978 accounted for 55 percent of sales dropped to 32 percent by 1982, marking an end to Oxford's unhealthy reliance on the two retailers. Designer label sales soared from $4 million in 1980 to $60 million in 1982. Oxford also expanded its private label business by providing merchandise to L.L. Bean, Lands' End, Eddie Bauer, and the Talbots, although private label manufacturing fell from over 80 percent in 1978 to 60 percent in 1983. In 1982 (the year in which Sartain Lanier retired as chairman and his son gained the post) sales increased $100 million over the previous year. In 1983 Oxford became a Fortune 500 company. Profits peaked in 1984 at $25 million.

Oxford's stunning growth ground to a halt in 1985 when earnings dropped 71 percent, to 64 cents a share. Extensive inventories, weak financial controls, and a peak in popularity of its fastest growing labels brought three years of reduced sales. Plants operating below capacity and inventory sell-offs also ate into profits.

Facing growing import strength and a global oversupply of production capacity, Oxford opted for a period of downsizing and restructuring. More merchandise was assembled overseas in such countries as the Dominican Republic and Costa Rica. Some plants in the United States were upgraded with new computer systems and information technologies, while others were closed.

Changes were taking place within the retailers as well. Sears Roebuck temporarily discontinued its mens' tailored clothing line, and J.C. Penney introduced more brand name menswear—these two adjustments taken together cost Oxford $15 million. Oxford also sought to increase distribution at Wal-Mart and Target Stores. Small independent retailers were abandoned and the focus was directed at large chains and department stores. Oxford also proved successful at placing self-contained Polo for Boys "shops" within department stores. These shops were found to increase sales 30 percent to 40 percent per square foot.

Sales began to drop in the apparel market as a whole in 1989 and Oxford responded by paring down lines and reducing inventories. In 1991 the Cos Cob and JBJ lines of womens' sportswear were discontinued, the loss of which cost Oxford $25 million. Also in that year Oxford signed a licensing agreement with Target Stores in which Target was given exclusive rights to design and merchandise the Merona label. By the end of that year Oxford was producing merchandise in 22 countries. Oxford's domestic production was matched by its reliance on offshore production, and it was predicted that an even greater percentage of the company's manufacturing would be shifted overseas. Oxford also repurchased over 2 million shares from 1988 to 1991.

In 1992 J.C. Penney comprised 24 percent of Oxford business, and sales had risen 4.3 percent from the previous year, after three years of reduced sales. Sears expansion of its mens' separates department also proved important, as Oxford was one of its major suppliers. Polo for Boys and Jhane Barnes continued as their strongest labels.

Oxford seems poised to survive the apparel industry convulsions that almost inevitably arise when an oversupply of production capacity becomes apparent. It also sees opportunities for continued growth during this period of industry consolidation through acquisition of cast-offs from other companies and further involvement in the international market.

Further Reading:

"The Designer Look: It's Oxford Industries Stylish Operating Results," *Barron's,* January 18, 1982.

Ettore, Barbara, "Give Ralph Lauren all the Jets He Wants," *Forbes,* February 28, 1983.

Godlenski, Robert, "Oxford Unveil $5M Improvement Plans," *Daily News Record,* October 7, 1980.

"Going Public: Oxford Industries, Private Label Maker, Scores with Designer Lines," *Barron's,* May 9, 1983, p. 56.

Lloyd, Brenda, "Oxford Ready for Recession," *Daily New Record,* October 2, 1990, p. 3.

——, "Men's Fuels Success at Oxford Industries," *Daily News Record,* October 6, 1992, p .6.

MacIntosh, Jeane, "Oxford Seeking New Shirt Brand," *Daily News Record,* November 20, 1992, p. 2.

"Net at Oxford Industries Enjoys More Stylish Look," *Barron's,* May 11, 1968, p. 39.

"Oxford Fiftieth Anniversary," Atlanta: Oxford Industries, Inc., 1992.

"Oxford Industries, Inc., Annual Report," Atlanta: Oxford Industries, Inc., 1992.

"Oxford: A Venture into Designer-Label Clothes Spruces up Earnings by 90 percent," *Business Week,* June 21, 1982, pp. 70–71.

—Cheryl Collins

Foods

P&C Foods Inc.

P.O. Box 4965
Syracuse, New York 13221
U.S.A.
(315) 457-9460
Fax: (315) 453-0353

Wholly Owned Subsidiary of Penn Traffic Co.
Incorporated: 1941 as Cooperative P&C Markets Inc.
Employees: 7,800
Sales: $1.1 billion
SICs: 5411 Grocery Stores

P&C Foods Inc. is a northeastern grocery store chain with 88 P&C Stores and 71 Big M stores. A subsidiary of Penn Traffic Co. of Johnstown, Pennsylvania, it earned more than one billion dollars in 1992. P&C's history began in 1941 when the Grange League Federation (G.L.F.), a farmers' purchasing and marketing cooperative, had a difficult time marketing its products to consumers. The G.L.F. founder, H. E. Babcock, suggested a solution: the missing piece in the G.L.F., which already had farmers and processing facilities (such as flour mills, canneries, and egg auctions), was a retail store.

The Cooperative P&C Markets Inc. had its first board of directors meeting August 29, 1941, in the upstate New York city of Ithaca. The P&C stood for "producers and consumers." Less than six months later, in January, 1942, the first P&C Market opened in nearby Batavia, New York. The opening stirred a lot of local interest since it was the first self-service market in the area. This new concept in marketing offered a complete line of self-service meats, fresh vegetables, and other groceries. Consumers could also rent freezer or cold storage space. Each locker was about six cubic feet. The store offered to hang and age meat for farmers who produced their own meat and then to cut it, wrap it, label it, and deliver it to the individual freezer lockers rented by each farmer. The 24,000-square-foot building rented by the first P&C Market for $125 a month featured a first floor for shopping and a second floor for parking. The store advertised the convenience of being able to drive right in from one of two entrances. The first week of business at P&C brought in $6,000 in sales.

A little more than a year later, a second P&C supermarket was opened in Auburn, New York. That store pulled in $7,500 its first week of business, with consumers spending $2,500 for meat and $1,000 for fresh vegetables and fruits. In response to its success, P&C formed a new cooperative corporation. Farmers and members of other co-ops became members of its board of directors.

P&C expanded quickly in the 1940s. By the end of the decade it had opened 20 more stores and moved its headquarters to the city of Syracuse. During this time, P&C bought Commander Foods' five stores and its warehouse. P&C also marketed canned goods with its own P&C label.

The 1950s brought a shift of population from the cities to the suburbs and P&C responded to this change by building stores in shopping centers in the suburbs. In 1951, P&C's warehouse was destroyed by fire, but service was not interrupted, as suppliers delivered to the individual markets instead of to the warehouse until a store could be closed for use as a warehouse. A year after the fire a new warehouse was completed. The company bought the Netti wholesale division and Big M, a franchise division, as the 1950s came to a close.

For the first decade and a half of its existence, P&C operated as a cooperative with profits returned to the cooperatives. Customers were paid a percentage of the total amount of their cash register receipts for the year. In 1957, P&C ended its cooperative operations by selling shares of stock to the public. To attract and maintain its customer base, P&C offered trading stamps with which customers could purchase merchandise.

During the 1960s, P&C expanded out of New York state, building stores in West Virginia and Pennsylvania. Business was so good that the company had to build a 68,000-square-foot addition to the 150,000-square-foot warehouse it had completed in 1957. The expansion of the warehouse allowed P&C to double its space for frozen foods and become the largest food distributor in the area. P&C sold canned goods and other processed foods, such as coffee, ice cream, flour, dried fruits, and salt, under its own private labels of Sunny Square, Party Club, Country Manor, Penny Curtiss, and Exel. By 1969, P&C had 47 supermarkets, 50 Big M franchises, and eight discount stores. Its sales revenue was more than $100 million.

In 1970, P&C was purchased by an unlikely company, Pneumo Dynamics Corporation, a Boston-based company that manufactured aerospace and defense products. As a subsidiary of Pneumo, P&C continued to expand. In 1971 and 1972 it bought 18 stores in New York, and a chain of 24 stores in New England. In 1979, P&C bought 10 Loblaw grocery stores. By this time, P&C had more than $500 million in sales. It owned 99 P&C supermarkets and 53 Big M stores. P&C also now marketed more than 750 items under its own labels and developed its own advertising department to handle all print and broadcast ads for itself and for clients. It also installed a consumer affairs department.

Supermarkets were becoming bigger, with the average store measuring about 13,000 square feet. The largest store, however, was close to 30,000 square feet. Technology was changing the operations of grocery stores and their warehouses. Computers took the place of cash registers at P&C and other supermarket chains. P&C also installed a state-of-the-art mechanization system in its warehouse, enabling 200 people to handle more than 600,000 cases of food and other products every week.

P&C's parent company, Pneumo, was purchased by Illinois Central Industries (IC) in 1984. This was the first of many changes in P&C's ownership over the next five years. IC had bought Pneumo for its aerospace operations. Although IC also owned Pet Foods and Old El Paso, its strategic plan was to focus on specialty foods, consumer products and services, and aerospace; a grocery store chain did not fit its corporate mission. In 1985, P&C managers, backed by Riordan Freeman & Spogli, a west coast banking firm, and other institutional investors, bought P&C from IC for a reported $125 million. Under the agreement, P&C managers would own 20 percent of the chain. The deal was structured as a leveraged buyout in which a group of investors borrows most of the purchase price and repays that loan with the company's profits or sale of assets.

Within a year, P&C once again sold stock, offering to the public 1.8 million shares valued at between $12 and $14 a share. However, public ownership was short-lived. In 1988, Penn Traffic of Johnstown, Pennsylvania, bought a 90 percent interest in the grocery store chain. Penn Traffic was a food retailer that owned supermarket chains, dairy products stores, and bakeries. Its retail stores included Big Bear, Riverside Markets, Quality Markets, San-Dairy, large dairy processing and ice cream manufacturing operations, bakery operations, Hart Department Stores, and wholesale operations. Penn employed about 25,000 people.

The next year, Penn Traffic had plans to sell P&C to the Grand Union Company, another partially owned subsidiary of Penn Traffic. Grand Union was ready to buy the P&C chain for $89 million, and P&C was to have become a wholly owned subsidiary of Grand Union, of which Penn owned 24 percent. Under the plan, Penn's share of Grand Union would have increased to 40 percent when the sale of P&C was finalized. Penn had decided to sell P&C because Vermont and federal officials found that Penn's ownership of both a Grand Union and a P&C store in some towns violated antitrust laws by reducing competition. The Federal Trade Commission, however, did approve the plans for the Grand Union to buy P&C. Under this buyout plan, P&C would continue to run the upstate New York stores as P&Cs, but its 26 stores in New Hampshire and Vermont and its five in New York would be taken over by Grand Union. The relationship between Grand Union and P&C would have allowed both to purchase goods at reduced prices. The deal did not take place, however. Grand Union was unable to obtain financing because of a decline in the junk bond market. (Junk bonds were high-risk, high-yield investments; they were used heavily during the 1980s to finance corporate takeovers.) Addressing the anti-trust issue, Grand Union and P&C agreed to close a total of 13 grocery stores between them in order to comply with government regulations.

P&C remained a Penn Traffic subsidiary, and the two formed a new kind of bond when Claude Incaudo, president and chief executive officer of P&C, took over as president and CEO of Penn Traffic as well in 1990. The next year, Penn Traffic bought the remaining 10 percent of P&C Markets, giving Penn total ownership. Incaudo ensured that Grand Union and P&C could still work together to secure greater purchasing power.

In 1989 sales for P&C went over the $1 billion dollar mark. Besides 88 stores and 71 Big M's, it had more than 160 wholesale accounts. In the 1990s, P&C faced growing competition from wholesale food clubs and other grocery stores. The average size of its stores grew to between 40,000 and 50,000 feet to accommodate seafood, floral, and bakery departments, larger produce departments, and salad bars. In 1991, P&C opened a pharmacy in one of its stores and planned to introduce pharmacies in other stores as well in order to provide "one-stop shopping."

Wholesale operations were strong, and P&C decided to consolidate its many private label brands into just one label, Sunny Square. P&C also expected to increase its private label items to 1,100 by the end of 1993. Health and beauty products were expected to show the most growth with the addition of toothpastes, vitamins, shampoos, and mouthwashes. P&C was responding to the popularity of private labels with retailers because of their higher profit margin.

P&C also built a new warehouse for perishables in 1992. The facility cost $18 million dollars for 262,000 square feet of refrigerated space for perishable foods such as fruits, vegetables, meats, dairy products, and dry goods. The construction of this warehouse consolidated the company's perishables operations and eliminated transport costs involved in storing goods in separate warehouses.

P&C had a history of keeping pace with new technology. One instance of this was its installation of coupon-scanning devices. P&C stores were the first supermarkets to test The Instant Coupon Machine, an electronic device attached to the grocery shelf to dispense manufacturers' coupons for an item. P&C also experimented with electronic security to scan for shoplifting. Penn Traffic tested video screens at a P&C checkout to display information on coupons while the products were scanned for price. The machine would also be able to dispense manufacturers coupons to match products purchased, thus eliminating the customer's need to clip coupons from the newspaper. Behind the scenes, P&C also utilized state-of-the-art technology with SPACEMAN, a computer-assisted merchandising program to control inventory and help ensure that the right products went to the right stores, thus preventing out-of-stock situations.

P&C markets also put a high value on employee training. Emphasizing the role of teamwork and promoting team building and conflict resolution, P&C's goal was to prevent high and costly employee turnover found throughout the industry. Close to 90 percent of promotions at P&C were within the company, so P&C considered training for entry level jobs to be crucial for its long-term success. About 20 employees a year were selected for management training. Training director James Horton told *Progressive Grocer* that management training cost about $6,000 per employee, but it was money well spent because people who had attended the program tended to stay at P&C. P&C's turnover dropped from about 80 percent in 1988 to only 55 percent in 1991, according to the same article. Management training also included ways to maintain flexible scheduling of employees, since P&C had many employees over the age of 60 and under age 18. P&C began recruiting older workers because of concern about a labor shortage since the teenage population was shrinking and more women were taking full-time jobs.

P&C Foods Inc. celebrated its 50th anniversary in 1992. Having undergone great expansion in its early years and frequent changes of ownership in more recent years, its everyday operations remained quite unaffected and P&C kept its identity. Looking ahead, P&C anticipated that it would continue to adapt to the quickly changing needs and demands of the consumer and the marketplace.

Further Reading:

Elmas, Leslie, "Antitrust Ruling Behind P&C Sale," Syracuse *Herald Journal,* September 8, 1989.

"Grand Union Bid for P&C Cut Short," Syracuse *Herald Journal,* December 21, 1989.

Johnson, Gregory S., "P&C Seeks Unity in Perishables Operations," *Journal of Commerce and Commercial,* July 29, 1992, p. 3B.

Mariani, John, "P&C Buyout Would Bring in Local Ownership," Syracuse *Post Standard,* June 5, 1985.

Muirhead, Greg, "P&C to Expand Its Line of Private-Label Products," *Supermarket News,* December 21, 1992, p. 27.

"P&C Tops $1B in Sales in 1989; CEO Incaudo Now Heading Parent," Syracuse *Post Standard,* February 5, 1990.

A Tradition of Serving: 50 Years, Syracuse, New York: P&C Foods Inc., 1992.

Wold, Marjorie, "Motivating the Masses," *Progressive Grocer,* July 1991, pp. 113–118.

—Wendy J. Stein

P. H. Glatfelter Company

228 South Main Street
Spring Grove, Pennsylvania 17362
U.S.A.
(717) 225-4711
Fax: (717) 225-6834

Public Company
Incorporated: 1906
Employees: 3,200
Sales: $540 million
Stock Exchanges: American
SICs: 2611 Pulp Mills; 2621 Paper Mills

P. H. Glatfelter Company, a producer of high-quality, specialty paper, was founded in 1864 in the rolling hills of south central Pennsylvania. Since the early 20th century it has been an industry leader of uncoated printing paper, used largely in hardback versions of novels and other trade books. Other Glatfelter products have included high-quality recycled paper for trade and reference books, and thin, flax paper for cigarettes as well as religious and financial publications. Guiding the company over the years has been an old-fashioned business philosophy emphasizing long-term goals and fiscal conservatism.

Spring Grove, the home of P. H. Glatfelter Company, was established in 1747 along the Codorus Creek some ten miles north of the Pennsylvania-Maryland border. To the west of the town were the Blue Ridge Mountains, and to the east, beyond the larger town of York, flowed the wide Susquehanna River. The town's original name, Spring Forge, reflected its early industry, an iron forge, which during the American Revolution manufactured supplies for the Continental Army. The forge was in operation until 1851, when Jacob Hauer bought the buildings and converted them into a paper mill.

Some 20 miles southeast, near the Maryland town of Gunpowder Falls, another paper mill, called Loucks, Hoffman & Company, began operations in the 1850s. It was here in 1856 that 19-year-old Philip H. Glatfelter began his first job in the paper trade. Glatfelter—whose wife, Amanda, was the sister of Jacob Loucks—worked in the firm for seven years, and in 1863, at the height of the American Civil War, Glatfelter decided to go into business on his own.

By this time Hauer had died, and his Spring Paper Mill was being sold at an orphan's (probate) court. A printed announcement of the sale mentioned a "tract of land containing about 101 acres . . . a large stone paper mill, a frame machine house, stone stock house, and four tenant houses." The mill itself had two Burnham water wheels propelled by the Codorus Creek, four large-capacity engines, and a 62-inch cylinder paper machine. Glatfelter learned about the mill from Loucks, whose second wife, Mary, was the daughter of Jacob Hauer. On December 23, 1863—one month after President Lincoln's famous speech at nearby Gettysberg—Glatfelter bought the property for $14,000.

Glatfelter's new paper business, initially called Spring Forge Mill, began operations in July of 1864 with a daily capacity of 1,500 pounds. Its first product was newsprint, which Glatfelter made from a pulp of rye straw mixed with a smaller amount of straw and rags collected from various cotton gins along the region's railway lines. This pulp material was retrieved in spacious railcars known as barns. Because at the time Spring Forge itself did not have a railway line, "barns" returning from the cotton gins could get no closer than Jefferson and York, some five and ten miles, respectively, from the mill. When the town changed its name in 1882 to Spring Grove, the company thus became the Spring Grove Mill.

For the first 25 years newsprint continued to be the company's main product, and during this period it made impressive gains in production. From the initial capacity of 1,500 pounds per day, the mill was able to expand to 3,500 pounds in 1873, 60,000 in 1885, and 110,000 by 1895. This increased capacity was made possible by the company's investment in new, modern facilities. In 1874, for example, the mill was moved farther north along the Codorus Creek, and next to it the company constructed a new building costing $200,000 and containing an 82-inch paper machine. Two years later Spring Forge celebrated the opening of its rail line, which ran through the mill's new site.

In 1880 Glatfelter entered into an agreement with Pusey and Jones Company of Delaware to build a 102-inch fourdrinier machine, allowing the mill to produce a considerably wider roll of paper. Named after Henry and Sealy Fourdrinier, who patented an early form of the machine in England in 1806, the fourdrinier machine fed pulp onto a continuous wire belt, shook it to remove excess water, and then pressed and dried the pulp into paper. Glatfelter's new fourdrinier machine was until 1887 the largest in the world, and the extremely wide paper rolls made by the machine helped him gain new customers. In 1887, when the Philadelphia Public Ledger began operating two 94-inch printing presses, Spring Grove Mill was the only business in the country that could supply the paper. The mill also produced paper for a variety of other newspapers in Pennsylvania and Maryland, including the Philadelphia Evening Telegraph.

Soon Glatfelter also changed his pulp-making methods, which would result in a better quality paper. Prior to 1881 the mill mechanically separated the fibers of the raw materials, probably with the use of a grinder. This process, acceptable for newsprint and other paper intended for temporary use, had a number of drawbacks. Mechanical separation tended to fragment and shorten the fibers, thus lessening their ability to bind and make strong paper. Moreover, fragmentation left considerable debris in the pulp, and various remaining chemical constituents caused the paper to grow yellow with age. Even when new, such paper did not have a "high whiteness" and was difficult to bleach.

As a result, Glatfelter began to take note of a new chemical method called the soda process, which enabled a high-quality paper to be made from wood fibers. It was developed in 1851 by Englishman Hugh Burgess, who a few years later immigrated to the United States to set up a paper mill in Pennsylvania. In the soda process, wood chips were boiled in a caustic alkali at a high temperature and pressure; afterward, the separated fibers were washed in water and then bleached. In 1881 Glatfelter built a giant soda-process mill, which was used to make pulp from jack pine, poplar wood, and straw. Straw, however, came to be used in decreasing quantities. By 1885 this new production helped the company surpass $500,000 in total sales, and four years later the number of employees reached 110. With its new pulp-processing method, the company in 1892 was able to make one of its most important changes—the suspension of newsprint production and the subsequent focus on high-quality paper for books, lithographs, and business forms. For this purpose, another soda-process pulp mill was installed in 1895, and by the turn of the century the company had become an industry leader of high-quality uncoated printing paper.

The founder's son, William L. Glatfelter, entered the business in 1887 after graduating from Gettysburg College, and that year he began a long apprenticeship under the guidance of his father. He had already worked at the mill for 19 years when, in 1906, the business was incorporated as P. H. Glatfelter Company. The following year the founder died, and the reins to the company were handed to his son.

President of the company from 1907 to 1930, William Glatfelter oversaw a tremendous increase in production, as well as continued advances in chemically processed wood pulp. In 1918, in order to manage the mill's growing need for wood, he established Glatfelter Wood Pulp Company, a wholly owned subsidiary, with more than 10,000 acres of timberland in southern Maryland. Additional timberland in Maryland and eastern Virginia would eventually boost the acreage to 107,000.

William Glatfelter was responsible for instituting a number of other major projects, many of which were completed in the early 1920s. A new basin for storing up to 50,000 tons of coal—the fuel used to fire the company's high-pressured boilers—was constructed during this period, as was a large indoor loading room, where newly manufactured paper was placed on waiting railroad cars. A tachometer, which measured rotational speed, was attached to all of the company's machines, thus providing a more accurate way to monitor production. Most spectacular was the new fourdrinier paper machine, installed in 1922, which was capable of making rolls of fine paper 170 inches wide. This giant paper machine, designed by Glatfelter engineers and housed in a new building, was the world's first fourdrinier to have an easily replaceable wire belt. Perhaps reflecting these changes, Spring Grove's Main Street, where the company's office building was located, was first paved in 1922.

In 1928, just a year before the great stock market crash, annual production at P. H. Glatfelter Company had reached 50 million pounds, and the number of employees stood at 300. That year,

in keeping with the company's policy of "maintaining a modern, efficient mill," P. H. Glatfelter II, William's son, introduced a new, ten-year modernization program, which included the installation of an even larger, 190-inch fourdrinier machine. As a result, the outlook for the company seemed especially bright, but just two years later conditions noticeably changed for the worse. By 1930 the country was quickly falling into an economic crisis, and sales at P. H. Glatfelter Company and other paper concerns were plummeting. William Glatfelter, moreover, unexpectedly died in April. Unlike many other firms, P. H. Glatfelter Company managed to survive the Depression of the 1930s, and its new president, P. H. Glatfelter II, was even able to complete his modernization program, at a cost of some $2 million. As part of this program, one of the company's pulp mills was refurbished, and its capacity was doubled. When the economy picked up again during World War II, P. H. Glatfelter Company added, among other improvements, new equipment for bleaching paper.

P. H. Glatfelter II, president until January 1, 1970, guided the company through the postwar economic boom and started a new effort at reforestation and environmental stewardship. In 1947 the company set aside 600 acres of land near Fairfield, Pennsylvania, to create the state's first tree farm. Between 1950 and 1962 it spent $1.6 million to build a waste-water treatment plant, and a new 400-ton boiler was installed in 1963 to more efficiently burn a pulp by-product called black liquor. During this time there were also millions of dollars spent on capital improvements for increased production. For example, the company's seventh and eighth paper machines were added in 1956 and 1965, respectively, and between 1964 and 1968 capital expenditures alone were nearly $40 million.

An especially ambitious project was the P. H. Glatfelter Dam, completed in 1965 along a stretch of the Codorus Creek about five miles south of Spring Grove. The dam created a 15-billion-gallon reservoir called Lake Marburg, which was intended to guarantee a reliable water supply for the Glatfelter mill farther downstream. In addition, the reservoir was eventually surrounded by a newly created 3,326-acre Codorus State Park, which included a public swimming pool, and provided opportunities for camping, hiking, horseback riding, and boating. The project cost some $10 million, split equally between P. H. Glatfelter Company and the Pennsylvania Bureau of State Parks.

P. H. Glatfelter II retired in 1970 and his son, P. H. Glatfelter III, became president, a position he held for a decade. An early challenge for the new president was Hurricane Agnes, which hit the eastern seaboard in June of 1972 and created severe floods in Spring Grove. According to P. H. Glatfelter III, the flood "caused more damage and financial loss to the Company than any other single event." Among other notable developments during his tenure was the 1973 decision by Glatfelter employees to join the United Paperworkers International Union, and in 1977 the company received the Isaac Walton League of America Clean Water Award. The company entered a new product line in 1979 with its purchase of Bergstrom Paper Company, a leading manufacturer of recycled printing paper, with mills in Neenah, Wisconsin, and West Carrollton, Ohio. The West Carrollton mill was sold in 1984, but during the 1980s the company rebuilt all three paper machines at the Neenah plant.

Thomas C. Norris, named president in 1980, was the first person outside the Glatfelter family to run the company. His experience with P. H. Glatfelter Company stretched back to 1958, when he took a part-time job in the paper mill at the age of 19. Like his predecessors, Norris oversaw a program of new capital expenditures, including the rebuilding of two paper machines at Spring Grove. Even more significant was the company's 1987, $220-million purchase of Ecusta Corporation, located in Pisgah Forest, North Carolina, which made extremely thin flax paper for the tobacco industry. The purchase of Ecusta doubled the number of Glatfelter employees from 1,700 to 3,400 and provided, along with uncoated and recycled printing paper, the third major underpinning of the company's sales. Uncoated printing paper, however, remained its core product, which by the early 1990s made up some 30 percent of all paper used in the United States for hardcover trade books. Among the many well-known books printed on Glatfelter paper were Norman Mailer's *Harlot's Ghost* (1992), Steven King's *Four Past Midnight* (1990), and Alexandra Ripley's *Scarlett* (1991), the sequel to Margaret Mitchell's *Gone With the Wind,* which in 1936 used Glatfelter paper for the original printing. *Great Books of the Western World,* a multivolume publication of classics, was printed with recycled paper from the Neenah mill.

P. H. Glatfelter Company headed into the 1990s with an exceptionally strong financial base, secured by its remarkable lack of debt. Although P. H. Glatfelter Company has occasionally borrowed money—for example, $179 million in 1987 to complete its acquisition of Ecusta—even this loan was paid off in just two years. The company's strength was also found in its emphasis on specialized, high-quality paper, which was much less affected by recurring business cycles than large-volume, "commodity" paper products. In 1988 Glatfelter's chief financial officer, M. A. Johnson II, explained, "Our emphasis is on profit, not on volume. That's why we continue to be a niche company, one that is competing in areas where we're not banging heads with people who are commodity-oriented." Since the mid-1980s the company has expressed considerable self-confidence in its financial strength by its repurchase of millions of outstanding shares of Glatfelter stock.

With its financial security and its emphasis on specialty products, P. H. Glatfelter Company was able to weather profitably the declining market conditions for paper, which, beginning in 1990, were spurred by industry overproduction. Glatfelter's record sales of $569 million in 1988, $598 million in 1989, and $625 million in 1990 tumbled to $567 million and $540 million, respectively, in 1991 and 1992. Even so, the company still posted a respectable net profit of $56.5 million in 1992, down from a high of $92.9 million in 1989. The company's good health was credited to its old-fashioned, conservative business philosophy, as well as to the able guidance of its president, chief executive officer, and chairman of the board, Thomas Norris, who in 1992 was one of only eleven corporate leaders given *Financial World*'s Silver Award for "superior business leadership and achievement."

Principal Subsidiaries: Ecusta Australia Pty. Limited; Ecusta Fibres Ltd. (Canada); Glatfelter Pulp Wood Company.

Further Reading:

Abelson, Reed, "P. H. Glatfelter Co.," *Fortune,* June 5, 1989, p. 176.
Cauffiel-Zinn, Jan, "The P. H. Glatfelter Company," *The Barker* (in-house magazine of P. H. Glatfelter Company), spring (pp. 12–13), summer (pp. 12–13), fall (pp. 12–13), and winter (pp. 12–13), 1989.
Cochran, Thomas N., "P. H. Glatfelter Co.," *Barron's,* August 29, 1988, pp. 32–33.
Henriques, Diana B., "A Paper Company That Loves Itself," *New York Times,* December 23, 1990, p. F12.
Lipper, Mark, *Paper, People, Progress: The Story of the P. H. Glatfelter Company of Spring Grove, Pennsylvania,* Spring Grove, Pennsylvania: P. H. Glatfelter Company, 1980.
Morris, Kathleen and Elicia Brown, "1992 CEO of the Year Silver Award Winners," *Financial World,* March 31, 1992, p. 34.
P. H. Glatfelter Company Annual Reports, Spring Grove, Pennsylvania: P. H. Glatfelter Company, 1988–92.
"P. H. Glatfelter Co., Spring Grove, Pa.," *1690–1940: 250 Years of Papermaking in America,* Stroudsburg, Pennsylvania: Lockwood Trade Journal Co., 1940, p. 88.

—Thomas Riggs

The Parsons Corporation

100 West Walnut Street
Pasadena, California 91124
U.S.A.
(818) 440-2000
Fax: (818) 440-2630

Private Company
Incorporated: 1944 as Ralph M. Parsons Company
Employees: 8,000
Sales: $1.30 billion
SICs: 8711 Construction & Engineering Services; 8712
  Architectural Services

The Parsons Corporation is one of the world's largest international engineering and construction firms. Serving both government and private clients, the company is involved in a wide range of industries, including petroleum and chemical, mining and metallurgical, transportation, public and civil works, and energy and nuclear power projects throughout the world.

The Parsons Corporation has gone through a number of configurations over the years. Ralph M. Parsons started his namesake company in 1944. Parsons was described in a *New York Times* profile as an "outstanding, self-made engineer" as well as a "first-class salesman" and an "accomplished manager of people." According to the profile, Mr. Parsons first demonstrated his ability to combine engineering and business at the age of 13, when he and his brother opened a garage and machine shop in Amagansett, New York. Parsons went on to study steam and machine design at the Pratt Institute, from which he graduated in 1916. After a brief stint in the Navy, he worked as an aeronautical engineer, before turning his attention to oil refinery engineering. During World War II Parsons formed an engineering partnership that included Stephen D. Bechtel, who later became one of his chief rivals. Finally in 1944 he founded The Ralph M. Parsons Company (RMPCo.) with capital of $100,000.

In 1945 American industry was able to turn to projects that had been delayed by World War II. Within three years RMPCo., having reaped the benefits of such a business climate, grew to more than one hundred employees and expanded its services in architect-engineering, systems engineering, and design. During these first years, RMPCo. constructed plants and facilities for a number of companies, including Shell Chemical Corporation and Standard Oil Company of California. In addition, RMPCo. designed the Pt. Mugu Missile Test Center in California.

In an early major project, RMPCo. designed test facilities for the development of nuclear weapons at Los Alamos, New Mexico, in 1948. The following year, the company began its first overseas project with a water development program that included 125 wells in Taiwan. The company continued these efforts in 1950 with a survey on water resources conducted for the government of India.

During the early 1950s, RMPCo. expanded into the chemical and petroleum industries. The company engineered a sulfur recovery plant—which produced sulfur from hydrogen sulfide—in Baton Rouge, Louisiana, for Consolidated Chemical Industries, Inc. in 1951. During this decade the company also oversaw the construction of a number of refineries for natural gas and petroleum in Turkey and several European nations, including the world's largest in Lacq, France. Also, RMPCo. became involved in a number of advanced aviation projects during the 1950s, including high energy fuel development, programs to develop nuclear-powered aircraft for the U.S. Air Force and Navy, intermediate-range ballistic missiles, and the design of facilities at the National Reactor Test Station in Idaho for nuclear engine development. The company designed underground bulk fuel storage facilities for Strategic Air Command bases all around the world.

The company offered a diverse range of skills to clients, as demonstrated by the high-thrust rocket test station it designed at Edwards Air Force base during the mid-1950s. The station included control facilities, test stands, instrumentation, and laboratories, as well as systems for storing and handling fuel and disposing of hazardous waste. In 1958, the company began the first of many airport projects in the United States and around the world with the design and development of a large terminal in Saudi Arabia. Other international efforts during the late 1950s and early 1960s included additional petroleum refineries in Europe and several in Latin America. In all, RMPCo. provided architect-engineering services for construction facilities worth more than $2 billion between the late 1940s and the late 1950s.

RMPCo. gained some attention as a result of its expansion and numerous projects. One development that brought the company a higher profile, however, had little to do with engineering or construction. In 1958 Parsons purchased a 200-foot yacht, the *Argo*. During the next decade, the company entertained approximately two thousand people on board each year. Not surprisingly, the yacht provided a "great sales advantage," according to Parsons in the *New York Times.*

The purchase of Anaconda-Jurden Associates in 1961 brought significant involvement in mining and metallurgy. Renamed Parsons-Jurden Corporation, the new acquisition had experience in mining facilities around the world. Within the year, a copper concentrator was started in Butte, Montana. In addition to engineering such facilities, Parsons-Jurden was involved in other aspects of metallurgical projects, including geological and mineral surveys and feasibility and market studies.

Throughout the 1960s, RMPCo. continued with the types of projects they had successfully completed in earlier years. The company designed several major petroleum refineries in the

United States and abroad, including a $100 million facility for Atlantic-Richfield in Cherry Point, Washington. New mining projects included an underground copper mine complex located in the Chilean Andes and designed for Cerro Corporation and a comprehensive mineral resources exploration and inventory program for India. RMPCo. also planned an expansion and modernization of Honolulu Airport, designed a terminal for Tunis/Carthage International Airport, and managed the construction of a $110 million airport complex in the Dallas-Fort Worth area. The company received a contract from the Federal Aviation Administration to expand and modernize air traffic control centers.

By the late 1960s RMPCo. had designed one hundred and fifty plants which produced sulfur from hydrogen sulfide. A $60 million natural gas processing plant engineered and constructed by the company in Alberta for Chevron Standard Limited in 1969 included the world's largest single sulfur recovery unit. In addition to these efforts, RMPCo. became involved in an even wider range of activities, some of which were experimental. The company engineered a saline water conversion plant in California and was involved in preliminary efforts to enable the countries of North America to collect unused runoff water in the subarctic. A test site designed and built by the company demonstrated that ballistic missiles could be fired from underground silos. RMPCo. also designed the first "lunar proving ground" to test flight hardware used in the Apollo moon flights.

At that point RMPCo. had become one of the nation's largest engineering and construction firms, with projects totalling $1.2 billion in 1968. In July of the following year, the company went public, selling a combination of stock worth about $7 million. A majority of the stock was sold on behalf of Parsons, who was serving as chairman of the company. Much of the remainder was sold to increase the working capital available for the company. In addition to the stock sale, RMPCo. began to more aggressively explore the possibility of acquiring companies. Parsons noted in the *New York Times* that these new practices represented quite a shift in his approach. He remarked that he would have to move beyond an adage from his childhood, "Never tell your friends where you shoot ducks"; now, he admitted, "We'll have to be more open."

During the early 1970s, RMPCo. did expand. The company acquired a controlling interest in an Australian engineering firm, adding approximately five hundred employees to its Australian operations. RMPCo. also formed a new company to aid in the integration of physical distribution services by providing warehousing, transportation management, and information services. This new company, called National Distribution Services, Inc., was the result of a joint effort between RMPCo., Eastern Airlines, and TRW Inc. In addition to this expansion, RMPCo. restructured its network of offices for improved efficiency. Activities in London were consolidated into one new facility, and a new office was opened in Australia. Finally, Parsons-Jurden moved from New York to Los Angeles, and RMPCo. consolidated its offices from four separate leased buildings in Los Angeles to a new headquarters facility in Pasadena.

Increasing concern with energy sources and pollution in the early 1970s provided opportunities for RMPCo. The company developed several new processes which helped decrease pollu-

tion. The Beavon Sulfur Removal Process reduced air pollution by increasing the amount of sulfur recovered from gases in gas processing plants and petroleum refineries, while the Double Contact/Double Catalysis process, applied in sulfuric acid plants, increased productivity as well as reducing emissions.

However, despite these apparently promising developments, demand for construction services was down in the early years of the decade, and RMPCo.'s revenue fell sharply, from $4.6 million in 1971 to $2.1 million the following year. The company attributed this development to a range of factors, including the unsettled condition of economy, the lack of a coherent energy policy and uncertainty regarding energy requirements and supplies, the lack of government pollution standards, and pressures brought by environmental groups. The slump was short-lived, and by the mid-1970s revenues had begun a rapid and consistent rise. New projects, contracts, and acquisitions contributed to RMPCo.'s growth during these years.

On the international front, the Middle East was the main source of new foreign projects. RMPCo. was involved in the preliminary studies for and the design of Yanbu, a multi-billion dollar industrial city on the Red Sea in Saudi Arabia. In 1976 the joint venture company Saudi Arabian Parsons Limited was founded to help administer projects and pursue other opportunities in the Middle East. Along with another firm, Saudi Arabian Parsons Limited was selected by the government of Saudi Arabia to manage the construction of the new international airport in Jeddah.

That same year RMPCo. began a major domestic undertaking: the company received a contract from the Federal Railroad Administration to manage the design and construction of a five-year, $1.75 billion program to modernize the Northeast Corridor, the passenger railroad route from Boston to Washington, DC. RMPCo. was also involved in several projects with the Department of Energy, including an oil storage program, a synthesis gas plant, and the design of facilities and techniques for the handling of nuclear materials during the nuclear fuel cycle. In addition, Parsons became involved in an increasing number of "mega-projects," large, complex engineering ventures with multi-billion dollar budgets and decades-long schedules. One of Parsons's first such undertakings was a massive oil and gas production facility at Prudhoe Bay in Alaska. This project, the largest undertaken by private industry, required the transportation of hundreds of prefabricated modules to a site 350 miles north of the Arctic Circle.

In 1977 RMPCo. acquired two established engineering firms—De Leuw, Cather & Company of Chicago, and S.I.P., Co., based in Houston. A leading engineering-design firm specializing in transportation systems, De Leuw, Cather & Company was involved in the Northeast Corridor railroad project as well as other ventures. Robert B. Richards, president and chairman of De Leuw, Cather—which retained its own corporate identity and management—was made a vice president of RMPCo. S.I.P., Inc. and provided RMPCo. with a strategic location: the Gulf Coast area, the site of much of the nation's petroleum, chemical, and gas processing industries.

Partly as a result of these acquisitions, and in an attempt to maximize the potential for future growth, RMPCo. management proposed a major reorganization of the company. Approved by shareholders on September 19, 1978, the reorganization divided RMPCo. into two separate corporations, although both were still owned by the same stockholders. In the United States, The Parsons Corporation was incorporated in Delaware as a holding company for RMPCo., De Leuw, Cather & Company, and S.I.P., Inc. Early in 1979 Parsons Constructors, Inc. (PCI), a new subsidiary intended to provide increased construction capability, was added to The Parsons Corporation. Shares of RMPCo. stock were converted to shares of The Parsons Corporation automatically at a one-to-one ratio. The company's management hoped that this restructuring would increase flexibility, aid growth, and make it easier to add subsidiaries.

On the international side, the plan was designed to improve the company's competitive position and provide tax savings. As a result of the reorganization, RMP International, Limited, was incorporated in the Cayman Islands. Shareholders of The Parsons Corporation received shares of RMP International, Limited, on a one-for-one basis. The shares of the two new corporations were required to be traded together.

In the years immediately following the reorganization, The Parsons Corporation continued to grow and to experience increasing revenue. In 1980, for example, Parsons was involved in almost 270 projects in 31 different countries. Revenue increased 25 percent in 1980 over the 1979 figure, and new records were established again in 1981 and 1982, when revenue reached $1.2 billion. William E. Leonhard, Chairman, President, and CEO of The Parsons Corporation summed up the company's strategy this way: "The key to our continuing strength is a basic policy of providing engineering, construction, and related services, a business we fully understand, while diversifying both geographically and in terms of the industries we serve."

In 1984, after fifteen years as a public company, Parsons began to explore the possibility of returning to private status. According to *Business Week,* provisions of the 1984 tax law made the purchase of companies by employee stock ownership plans particularly attractive. An additional reason for the move was offered by Marion Gordon, a Parsons spokesperson, in the *San Francisco Business Journal,* "If you're not accountable [to shareholders and the public], it gives you more flexibility and the ability to map out big plans without the whole world looking on. This is a competitive industry and operating as a private company can provide a benefit in forming strategy." Chairman Leonhard similarly stated in the *Wall Street Journal* that he supported the plan "so we could be in control of our own destiny."

In October of 1984 The Parsons Corporation returned to private ownership as a result of a $560 million buyout by the Employee Stock Option Plan. Almost immediately questions were raised about the deal, one of the largest such transactions in U.S. history. The U.S. Labor Department investigated charges brought by employee groups that executives who designed the plan benefitted disproportionately, while employees were saddled with debt. The employees also argued that they had no meaningful input in the decision to go private and that they will be excluded from the process of shaping the country's future. In addition, some retirement experts expressed concern about the loss of a profit-sharing program of diversified stocks and bonds. Finally, the corporation was the target of several lawsuits. One suit, brought by employees in 1985, claimed that the purchase was a "breach of fiduciary responsibility, misuse of corporate assets, and a termination of predecessor plans," according to the *Wall Street Journal.* Five years later, however, a federal court upheld the buyout.

Despite the difficulties resulting from the buyout, Parsons, now the largest 100 percent employee-owned company of its kind in the United States, continued to adapt and prosper. The company benefitted from an increasing trend toward privatization, providing services to municipal governments in Chester County, Pennsylvania, for example. In addition, while opportunities in the Middle East decreased in the early 1990s, Parsons increasingly turned its attention to Asian markets.

Principal Subsidiaries: AUS-MAIN Clean Air Technologies, Ltd.; Barton-Aschman Associates, Inc.; Engineering-Science, Inc.; Harland Bartholomew & Associates, Inc.; Latinoamericana de Ingenieria, S.A. de C.V. (Mexico); Parsons Construction Services, Inc.; Parsons Constructors Inc.; Parsons De Leuw, Inc.; Parsons Development Company; Parsons Engineering GMBH (Germany); Parsons Environmental Services, Inc.; Parsons International Limited (Philippines); Parsons Main, Inc.; Parsons Overseas Company; Parsons Pacific Corporation (Korea); Parsons Polytech Inc. (Japan); Parsons S.I.P. Inc.; Proyeparsons, C.A. (Venezuela); The Ralph M. Parsons Company; The Ralph M. Parsons Company Limited (England); Saudi Arabian Parsons Limited; Steinman Boynton Gronquist & Birdsall.

Further Reading:

"And at Parsons This Week," *Business Week,* October 1, 1984, p. 50.

Downey, Kirsten E., "Vulnerable San Francisco Builder Takes Stock, Goes Public," *San Francisco Business Journal,* September 2, 1985, p. 1.

Foust, Dean, "Turning to the Private Sector," *Philadelphia Business Journal,* December 29, 1986, p. 1.

Gottschalk, Earl C., Jr., "Parsons's Acquisition by Employee Stock Plan Raises Some Questions about Who Benefitted," *Wall Street Journal,* January 29, 1985, p. 4.

O'Malley, John, "Certified Grocers of California Top Private Sector List," *Los Angeles Business Journal,* August 31, 1987, p. 17.

The Parsons Corporation Annual Report, Pasadena, CA: The Parsons Corporation, 1978–1983.

"Parsons Employees Sue Firm and Others over Recent Buyout," *Wall Street Journal,* May 21, 1985, p. 24.

"Ralph M. Parsons Co. Went Public Last Week," *Chemical Week,* August 2, 1969, p. 10.

Ralph M. Parsons Company, Annual Reports, Los Angeles: Ralph M. Parsons, 1969–1972, 1976–1977.

"Ralph M. Parsons Creates Two, New Corporate Entities," *Engineering News-Record,* September 28, 1978, p. 15.

Stone, Irving, "Architect-Engineers Build for Aviation," *Aviation Week,* October 8, 1956, pp. 62–64, 67, 69.

Williams, Fred. "Parson's Buy-Out Upheld," *Pensions and Investments,* July 23, 1990, p. 24.

Wright, Robert A. "Parsons, A Canny Hunter, *New York Times,* December 5, 1969, pp. 67, 73.

—Michelle L. McClellan

Perini Corporation

73 Mt. Wayte Ave.
Framingham, Massachusetts 01701
U.S.A.
(508) 875-6171
Fax: (508) 820-2530

Public Company
Incorporated: 1918 as B. Perini and Sons Inc.
Employees: 4,625
Sales: $1.07 billion
Stock Exchanges: AMEX
SICs: 1542 Nonresidential Construction Nec; 1622 Bridge,
  Tunnel & Elevated Highway; 1623 Water, Sewer, &
  Utility Lines; 6552 Subdividers & Developers Nec; 8711
  Engineering Services.

Ranked in the top ten percent on *Engineering News Record*'s
1992 list of the top 400 contractors, Perini Corporation services
the public and private sectors in construction and real estate
development from its world headquarters in Framingham, Massachusetts. Perini has built some of the America's most intrigu-
ing and challenging structures, including the Massachusetts
Turnpike Extension—the largest highway contract awarded in
the 1960s—the Trump Taj Mahal Casino Resort in Atlantic
City, New Jersey, and the expansion of the La Guardia Airport
in New York. Perini's construction capabilities span the globe
and include nearly every type of contracting and construction
management. "They don't do the easy stuff," construction
industry analyst Walter Kirchenberger told the *Providence
Business News.* "They specialize in the tough stuff—bridges,
tunnels and very difficult inner-city projects."

Perini Corporation is organized by function in three general
divisions: heavy construction, general construction, and real
estate development. Heavy construction, which focuses on the
United States' infrastructure, such as mass transit systems,
highways, and bridges, and water-treatment facilities, is
Perini's specialty. General construction, including correctional,
commercial, sports, and recreational facilities, is carried out by
Perini Building Company, Inc., a wholly owned subsidiary.
Real estate development takes place under the Perini Land and
Development Company, a wholly owned subsidiary, along with
Paramount Development Associates, Perini Land and Develop-
ment Company's local Massachusetts subsidiary. In addition,

international work is executed through Perini International, a
division of Perini Corporation, and West Virginia mine reclamation projects are done through Pioneer Construction, Inc., a
Perini Corporation subsidiary. Four consecutive years of record
growth and profits in the national and international construction
portions of the company strengthened Perini's financial record
into the 1990s, despite a decline in real estate profitability in that
same period.

Perini Corporation grew out of the hard work of Italian immigrant Bonfiglio Perini. In 1892, five years after he emigrated
from Gotolengo, Italy, where he had been a stone mason,
Bonfiglio Perini won contracts to build waterworks projects in
the eastern United States. One of his first large contracts was a
20-mile bluestone wall in the Catskill Mountains of New York,
which historian Bob Steuding praised in *Constructor* as "a
majestic project when you think about it, a giant piece of
sculpture." Bonfiglio Perini also built one of the nation's first
hot-mixed asphalt highways in 1917 in Rhode Island. In 1918
Bonfiglio Perini brought his sons officially into his business by
incorporating the company as B. Perini & Sons, Inc. Upon
Bonfiglio Perini's death in 1924, four of his ten children took
control of the company. Louis Perini acted as president, Joseph
as treasurer, Ida as secretary, and Charlie, the youngest, eventually became vice-president of equipment. They continued their
father's tradition of hard work, setting new paving records in
1930 on the Boston-Worcester Turnpike, their first million-
dollar contract.

In the 1950s the company name changed to Perini Corporation.
This decade was a period of tremendous growth for the company—especially internationally. Perini built the world's largest uranium ore concentrator for Consolidated Denison Mines
Ltd. in Ontario, Canada. To secure the company's growth as a
large-scale contractor, Louis Perini developed path scheduling—a way of routing project needs—to ensure project efficiency. Louis "was an absolute demon when it came to productivity," his son David Perini told *Constructor.* He was "always
looking for a way to do things faster and better." The company
quest for efficiency and productivity effected Perini's engineers. By the 1950s, entry-level engineers were prepared for
future leadership roles in the company by a 36-month training
program that gave them experience in all aspects of construction. The training program, David Perini noted in *Constructor,*
was "probably the most important program in the company,
because these young engineers are the feedstock, the people
who will lead Perini one day." The program continued into the
1990s.

Perini Corporation offered stock to the public in 1961. The
company continued its reputation as a large-scale contractor
throughout the 1960s, building the 750-foot high Prudential
Center in Boston, the world's tallest building outside of New
York at the time, and the Calima Hydroelectric Project in
Columbia, South America, which was a 3 million cubic-yard
earthfill dam with 35,000 feet of tunnel.

In 1972 the third generation of Perinis assumed control of the
company when David Perini took over his father Louis's position as president and chairman. David was well prepared to
assume the role; he joined the firm as assistant to general
counsel in 1962 after finishing his law degree at Boston Col-

lege, and served as vice president, general counsel, and vice-chairman before taking over the top position. Even though David had gained much academic knowledge, Louis served as his role model. "Dad ate and slept the construction business," David told *Constructor*. David remembered that the *Engineering News Record* wrote that "more than a little bit of the heart went out of the construction industry" when Louis Perini passed away. In 1991 the U.S. Army Corps of Engineers Historical Foundation posthumously honored Louis as one of the top contractors in the engineering and construction industry.

Under David Perini's control, Perini concentrated on growth. The company outgrew the second-floor Framingham storefront headquarters that it had occupied since the 1920s and moved to the company's old equipment shops, which it transformed into a modern office building that included a courtyard and sun deck along the Sudbury River. Perini expanded its business operations through investing and acquiring interest in other companies. After the 1974 merger of a Perini-owned Canadian pipeline subsidiary with Wiley Oilfield Hauling, Ltd., Perini gained control of 74 percent of Majestic Contractors Ltd., a Canadian pipeline construction company. This company built section two of the Trans-Alaska Pipeline, which consisted of 82 miles of heavy pipe built above ground and 67 below. In the same year, Perini acquired Mardian Construction Co. of Phoenix, Arizona. After a troubled venture in open-highway construction, the company began in the 1980s to focus on acquiring firms whose specialties, such as civil works and large-scale urban construction, meshed well with the existing Perini businesses. "Most kinds of construction require a certain degree of specialization. It's generally not a good idea to work in someone else's backyard," Kirchenberger noted in the *Providence Business News*. Perini acquired R. E. Dailey & Co. of Detroit, Michigan in 1980, and Loomis Construction Co. of New Mexico in 1984.

In the 1980s, Perini took steps to reorganize its real estate activities. In 1984 the company made its real estate investment division a separate entity called Perini Investment Properties Inc. Perini Corporation and Perini Investment Properties Inc. were autonomous organizations trading under different names on the American Stock Exchange, but David Perini served as chairman and major stockholder for each. By the mid-1980s, Perini's real estate activities were confined to its wholly owned subsidiary, Perini Land and Development Company, which owned and managed commercial, residential, and industrial properties. As early as 1957, Perini had begun its investment in developmental property with 5,500 acres in West Palm Beach, Florida. By 1988 Perini Land and Development Company had developed 35 percent of West Palm Beach with housing, commercial development, and entertainment facilities. The Villages of Palm Beach Lakes, a 1,400-acre property holding 4,000 residences, offices, retail shops, golf courses, and more than 7,000 people, "has become one of the most profitable projects" for the company, according to the *Palm Beach Post*. Throughout the early and mid-1980s, David Perini told the *Business Worcester*, "our real estate development operations made the major contribution to our overall results." Perini's real estate profits peaked in 1987 due to ten consecutive years of record earnings in Perini Land and Development Company's five real estate markets: Arizona, California, Florida, Georgia, and Massachusetts. Its holdings in Florida contributed the most toward profits.

Perini Land and Development Company ensured the appeal of their real estate through unique marketing techniques. Eager to attract buyers in Golden Gateway Commons, its eight-year-old condominium project in San Francisco, California, Perini Land and Development Company hired the Mulhauser and Young advertising agency to craft a fresh approach. Starting with a new name and logo, Mulhauser and Young promoted the 1,254-unit project as a neighborhood. The most influential aspect of the marketing campaign, however, was a direct mail campaign that included cans of spaghetti, a bar of chocolate in the shape of the new logo, and a shopping bag that listed the neighborhood shopping attractions. Moreover, Perini Land and Development Company advertised in the real estate and business sections of the Sunday *San Francisco Examiner and Chronicle* and the western edition of the *Wall Street Journal,* instead of the traditional trade and consumer press.

Perini's real estate success slowed in late 1988 as the real estate industry slumped, and by the early 1990s this portion of the company accounted for only five percent of corporate revenues. But as the company incurred losses in its real estate investments, the company's construction divisions began to report record earnings. The construction business grew to be the most significant contributor to profits in the early 1990s. Reacting to this shift in trends, Perini consolidated its general construction divisions into the Perini Building Company Inc. in December of 1991 to further penetrate the nationwide building market. The consolidation was designed to allow Perini to take advantage of its name recognition; until that time Perini's acquisitions had acted independently. The Loomis, Mardian, and R. E. Dailey companies were united into the Perini Building Company in name, but continued to operate from their existing offices. Eastern U.S. Division headquarters are located in Framingham, Massachusetts, Western U.S. Division headquarters in Phoenix, and Central U.S. Division headquarters in Detroit. Perini gathered the construction division's executive, administrative, and operational functions into the corporate structure, which centralized decision-making and project allocation.

Perini reorganized its heavy construction division in that same period. The heavy construction division had extensive experience in building mass transit systems like the San Francisco Bay Area Rapid Transit system, and in building infrastructure projects like the Tunnel and Reservoir Plan in Chicago. Perini targeted the infrastructure market for growth into the year 2000 because, according to materials published by the company, "over 40 percent of the nation's bridges are rated deficient, and roughly the same percentage of highway miles are in poor or fair condition." Anticipating the need for future efficiency, Perini divided the heavy construction division into two operating entities, the Metropolitan New York Division and the U.S. Heavy Division. The Metropolitan New York Division handled contracts in New York and other large eastern cities, such as Baltimore and Washington D.C., while the U.S. Heavy Division was responsible for work throughout the rest of the United States.

Perini International's projects made significant contributions to Perini earnings beginning in 1985. The international division has worked in 20 countries, primarily on the construction of U.S. embassies. The division has erected U.S. embassy buildings in Zaire, Gabon, Brazil, and Paraguay. In 1992 the division continued to build for the U.S. Department of State in Djibouti and Venezuela, for the U.S. Air Force in Egypt, and for the National Oil Company in Morocco. The division also began efforts to expand into new overseas markets, focusing initially on Mexico and Latin America.

A source of past success and future growth for Perini is the joint venture. Forming joint ventures is one way that Perini has diversified its operations, won large infrastructure contracts, built its reputation, and shared its financial risk. Executive vice-president of construction Thomas Dailey said in *Perini: Second Century* that Perini's "shared sense of purpose has enabled our joint venture partnerships to be successful, and to contribute to our growth and reputation." Perini began working with other firms beginning in the 1890s, and relationships forged during World War II allowed the company to expand into Australia, Canada, India, and South America. Some projects that Perini contributed to through joint ventures were the Trans-Alaskan Pipeline, the North River Water Pollution Control Project in New York City, and the Trump Taj Mahal Casino Resort.

In 1988 Perini sought further growth through a joint venture in the hazardous waste cleanup market. The company joined with Ashland Technology and Versar Inc. to form Perland Environmental Technologies Inc., which provides scientific, environmental engineering and construction services for hazardous-waste management and cleanup. Perini controlled 90 percent of Perland Environmental Technologies in 1991. That year Perland won a $19 million award to work on the New Bedford harbor Superfund site in Massachusetts. Perland positioned itself to take advantage of the market growth by seeking out projects that would expand its expertise. It has worked on soil stabilization, incineration, and groundwater treatment at Superfund sites in Michigan. Perini expected Perland to contribute significantly to profits, noting that the hazardous waste-cleanup market grew 15 percent in the early 1990s, and that the company expected the market to expand to $5 billion per year by 2000.

In the early 1990s company management, anticipating Perini's future growth, initiated a plan called Mission 2000 to attempt to anticipate the company's needs in the year 2000. Teamwork between company divisions, subsidiaries, trade organizations, and through joint venture partnerships was cited as "a prerequisite for success." Allying Perini with companies whose specialties enhance Perini's work will help the company remain competitive. Given the goal of working with companies that work in similar fields, Perini sold its share of the pipeline company, Majestic Contractors, Ltd., in early 1993 because Majestic's core business did not mesh well with Perini's other divisions. The resultant divisions and subsidiaries could all work together through internal joint ventures. One such internal joint venture between the Eastern U.S. Building Division and the U.S. Heavy Division allowed Perini to work on a $190 million project at the Deer Island residuals treatment facility in Boston, which included building sludge and gas storage tanks.

Perini's competitiveness, noted David Perini in a company publication, will be enhanced by the company's participation in public/private ventures, which include prisons, health centers, sports arenas, and toll roads. Public/private ventures are projects which traditionally have been paid for with taxes but are increasingly being funded by private investors. Project development vice-president Robert Band explained in a company publication that "public/private ventures leverage future revenues generated by projects such as toll roads, lease-back prisons and sports arenas, and present them as the credit in the financial transaction." Tolls, rent monies, and ticket sales supplement or even replace tax dollars in these projects. Band called Perini's public/private venture approach, which includes project design, finance arrangement, and a guaranteed maximum construction cost, "the project delivery system of the future." The company used this approach when it built the Somerset County Prison in Pennsylvania, which allowed the state to lease the prison for 20 years instead of purchasing it outright.

In addition to securing its reputation through new projects and joint ventures, Perini has been concerned with maintaining a company supportive of its employees' needs. Concerned about the rights of nonsmokers in the mid-1980s, Perini constructed smoking lounges that had large fans to draw out smoke to accommodate its employees who smoked. Vice-president of human resources Douglas Mure said that "we were ahead of the game," when the EPA declared passive smoke a carcinogen. Perini emphasized safety as well as health by giving an annual President's Award for safety. The company also employed a retired Occupational Health and Safety Administration (OSHA) inspector to inspect facilities weekly and paid foremen to go to safety meetings. "If they come to [the meetings], have no recordable injuries for the week, pass a safety inspection and give their crews a 'tool-box talk' on safety, they win a $50 bond," according to the *Rochester Business Journal*.

Even though Perini regards itself as a family-owned business, it recognized the advantages of employee ownership in a company. In 1992 the company revised its all-cash bonus plan for top executives and operating management to include 60 percent common stock and 40 percent cash. The cash savings will be invested in company growth and the stock awards will "promote stock ownership among many employees," vice-president of finance James Markert relayed to the *Wall Street Journal*. The adjustment will effect about 100 of the company's 2,000 employees.

Anticipating growth into Perini's second century of business, the company planned to double its construction operations by expanding its work in infrastructure, environmental and general building markets. The company decided to stay in the real estate business but to reduce its level of investments. In his 1992 message to stockholders, David Perini focused on Perini's reputation. He noted that "a company and its reputation are like a building. They take much longer to build than to demolish. Build your image and reputation and do nothing to damage your good name."

Principal Subsidiaries: Perini Building Company, Inc.; Pioneer Construction, Inc.; Perini International Corporation; Perini Land and Development Company; Paramount Development Associates, Inc.; Perland Environmental Technologies, Inc. (90%).

Further Reading:

Fortin, Frank, "Perini Has Deep Roots in State," *Providence Business News* (Rhode Island), September 12, 1988.

Herring, Ben L., "Perini: Quality Construction Since 1892," *Constructor,* December, 1990, pp. 63–65.

Perini Corporation Annual Report, Framingham, MA: Perini Corporation, 1992.

Perini: Second Century, Vols. 1–2, Framingham, MA: Corporate Relations Department, Perini Corporation, 1992.

"Perini Corp.: Cash Bonus Plan Revised to Consist of 60% Stock," *Wall Street Journal,* March 19, 1992, sec. C, p. 15.

Phelps, Richard, "Perini Posts Big Numbers," *Business Worcester* (Massachusetts), June 13, 1988.

Robbins, Jonathan, "Perini Loses $17.9M in '85; Outlook Appears Brighter For '86," *Middlesex News* (Framingham, MA), February 22, 1986.

Saef, Scott, "Linstroth to Leave Perini Co.," *Palm Beach Post* (Florida), April 9, 1988.

Weinberg, Neil, "Perini Returning Construction Group to Corporate Fold," *Middlesex News* (Framingham, MA), July 10, 1992.

Young, Jill, "Chocolate Logos, Spaghetti in Recipe to Market Condos," *San Francisco Business Times,* February 15, 1988.

—Sara and Tom Pendergast

Peter Kiewit Sons' Inc.

1000 Kiewit Plaza
Omaha, Nebraska 68131
U.S.A.
(402) 342-2052
Fax: (402) 271-2829

Private Company
Incorporated: 1941 as Peter Kiewit Sons' Co.
Employees: 2,900
Sales: $2.02 billion
SICs: 1221 Bituminous Coal & Lignite—Surface; 1541
    Industrial Buildings & Warehouses; 1542 Nonresidential
    Construction Nec; 1611 Highway & Street Construction;
    1622 Bridge, Tunnel & Elevated Highway; 1623 Water,
    Sewer & Utility Lines; 1629 Heavy Construction Nec;
    4813 Telephone Communications Except Radio

Peter Kiewit Sons' Inc. is one of the largest construction and
mining companies in the United States. Although considered to
be one of the major producers of coal in the nation, Kiewit's
primary source of revenue comes from its general contracting
business. Construction accounts for over 80 percent of its sales,
followed by mining and telecommunications. A closely held,
employee-owned company that has eschewed publicity
throughout its existence, Kiewit nevertheless has gained notoriety and enjoyed considerable success by constructing many of
the country's highways, bridges, dams, tunnels, public utility
facilities, and defense installations.

The roots of Kiewit stretch back to 1884 when Peter Kiewit, the
son of Dutch immigrants who had settled in Iowa, struck out on
his own and opened a masonry business in Omaha, Nebraska.
By 1912 two of Kiewit's six children, George and Ralph, had
joined the business, and the company became Peter Kiewit &
Sons. Having added general contracting to its business, Peter
Kiewit & Sons completed small construction projects for
Omaha residences and businesses. After the death of the elder
Kiewit in 1914, George and Ralph took control of the company,
changing its name to Peter Kiewit's Sons.

By 1920, the youngest of the Kiewit children, also named Peter,
left Dartmouth College in his freshman year and joined the
company as a foreman. After several years the young Kiewit—
who would eventually run one of the largest construction companies in the nation—began estimating, bidding, and supervis-

ing entire projects. He landed the first million dollar contract for
the company, the construction of Omaha's Livestock Exchange
Building.

In 1930 Peter Kiewit suffered the obstruction of a blood vessel
resulting from the chronic inflammation of his veins—a condition called phlebitis. His doctors informed him that he would be
a semi-invalid for the rest of his life. Meanwhile family members began to pull out of the company, a move begun by George
Kiewit in the mid-1920s. It appeared that the Kiewit legacy—
nearly 50 years old—was at an end as Peter Kiewit remained
confined to a hospital bed for nine months. The next year,
however, only a few months after leaving the hospital, Peter
Kiewit formed a new company, named in honor of his father,
Peter Kiewit Sons'.

With total assets of roughly $100,000, Kiewit decided to ex-
pand into heavy construction, hoping to win contracts for the
construction of highways, bridges, dams, and tunnels. The first
of Kiewit's many gambles, the decision proved to be fortuitous.
By moving in the direction of heavy construction, Kiewit placed
the company in a position to win many of the large construction
projects that characterized the construction industry of the
1930s.

Kiewit's first project in this arena—a Texas road-building contract—was not a tremendous success. He was unable to complete the work on schedule and had spent half of his working
capital by the time the job was completed. The project was a
valuable learning experience, however. By the time President
Franklin D. Roosevelt's New Deal public works program began
soliciting bids for Public Works Administration projects,
Kiewit had honed his bidding and scheduling abilities. During
this era of increased, federally-supported construction, Kiewit's
projects included a canal and reservoir for the Loup River
Public Power and Irrigation District in Nebraska and a similar
project near the North Platte river. The budget for these two
contracts exceeded $3 million.

The profits gained through Public Works Administration projects during the 1930s had provided a stable foundation for the
company, although by 1940, with crews working in seven or
eight states, Kiewit was still considered a small contracting
company. It had, however, assembled a cadre of young men
with the ability to undertake projects of formidable scope. This
pool of talent proved valuable during the construction boom
ignited by World War II, which provided the economic stimulus
to dramatically increased Kiewit's size. Its first large defense
project was the construction of the cantonments at Fort Lewis,
Washington, for $8 million. This initial foray into defense
contracts, the first of many to be awarded to Kiewit, was
followed by the construction of Camp Carson in Colorado for
$43 million, and military installations in Alaska for $35 million.
In all, Kiewit completed nearly $500 million worth of World
War II projects, placing the company among the nation's biggest builders.

The end of the war did not signal the end of Kiewit's involvement in military contracts, though. In 1950 the U.S. Corps of
Army Engineers approached Kiewit for assistance in a joint
venture to construct bomber and housing installations in Greenland. Known as "Operation Blue Jay," the project required the

importation of 5,000 workers to build the facilities that later became Thule Air Force Base. In 1952 Kiewit was awarded a $1.2 billion Atomic Energy Commission contract to build a uranium plant in Portsmouth, Ohio. The project, which at that time represented the largest construction contract the government had ever given a single builder, demonstrated the strides Kiewit had made since its first experience with heavy construction in Texas 20 years earlier. The plant was completed six months ahead of schedule for $268 million below the original estimate. By the end of the decade, Kiewit had gained a reputation as the contractor able to build large facilities, no matter where they might be located. In 1958 the U.S. Army awarded Kiewit a $5 million contract to build Alaska's first nuclear facility. A year later Kiewit crews began the construction of two radar stations on the Greenland ice cap for a $13 million U.S. Defense Department contract.

Multi-million dollar contracts had quickly become the norm for Kiewit, but the company still continued to take on smaller jobs. While the massive uranium plant in Ohio was being constructed, another Kiewit crew worked in Wyoming to complete a $2,000 paving contract. It was Peter Kiewit's reasoning that the smaller projects provided excellent training for his project supervisors. A mistake made on a small project could prove costly, but a mistake made on a multi-million dollar project could prove disastrous. Accordingly, young supervisors were initially given smaller contracts to oversee. If they demonstrated the ability to successfully complete a project on schedule and, preferably, under the estimated budget, they were then given the opportunity to undertake larger contracts.

Kiewit believed in giving his project mangers almost full control over their projects, but by no means did he allow the reins of the company to be taken completely out of his hands. To ensure that Kiewit projects were progressing on schedule, he would often travel to job sites and supervise the proceedings from a distance through binoculars. A competitive atmosphere was created in which employees could quickly rise to the upper echelon of Kiewit management, and especially productive employees were rewarded with Kiewit stock. Peter Kiewit's approach to the construction business and to his employees, aside from striking some as overbearing, produced remarkable results. Under his watchful eye, the company had evolved from a small, family-operated business into a giant in the construction industry.

By the 1960s, the company had developed into an almost self-subsistent organization. Kiewit owned over 40 corporations involved in nearly every facet of enterprise related to construction and day-to-day operations. Global Surety & Insurance Co. handled the medical and health policies for Kiewit employees, while another company provided them with life insurance. Other subsidiaries leased earth-moving equipment and quarried rock and gravel, while still others mined coal to supply public utility facilities. By subcontracting and supplying much of its own construction operations, Kiewit was able to schedule different phases of a project and limit cost overruns. Consequently, the bidding for contracts could be done much more precisely and, as a result, profits were increased.

Unlike the early 1930s when few companies were capable of fulfilling the large-scale Public Works Administration con-

tracts, by the mid-1960s, the competition for large construction contracts had become fierce. Although many cities required the construction of urban transportation systems, highways, bridges, tunnels, and public utility facilities, the volume of work was outpaced by the number of heavy construction companies vying for the contracts. This increased competition placed even more importance on the ability of a construction company to bid a price that would win and still earn a profit. Often construction companies were forced to bid at cost, then hope that the price of materials would drop sufficiently to realize a profit.

Kiewit, however, had learned through trial and error how to make the gamble of estimating a project less risky. Groups of Kiewit engineers were known to occupy entire floors of hotels near possible job sites while they astutely figured costs. Kiewit had suffered serious losses in some of its ventures, as evidenced by the company's construction of a dam and power facilities in California's Sierra Nevada mountains for the Sacramento Municipal Utility District. A miscalculation in the amount of soil needed to be excavated from the site eventually caused the project to be completed nearly a year behind schedule and millions of dollars over budget. However, such experiences served as lessons for future projects, and the wisdom built up over the past 30 years allowed Kiewit to remain in the black during a time when many big construction companies lost money.

Construction projects during the 1960s continued to focus on areas in which Kiewit had expertise. The U.S. Air Force awarded the company a $68 million contract in 1961 for the construction of Minuteman intercontinental ballistic missile launch bases near Minot Air Force Base in North Dakota. The same year Kiewit, along with four other general contracting companies, won a $40 million contract to construct a 300-mile paved highway in Afghanistan for the U.S. Army Corps of Engineers. Two years later Kiewit shared, in another joint venture, a $51 million contract for the construction of the Wells hydroelectric dam on the Columbia River in Washington State. Among other projects, Kiewit crews completed an $80 million contract for the Portage Mountain Dam in Vancouver, British Columbia, and a section of Toronto's subway system. In addition, Kiewit also undertook extensive construction of federal highways during the 1960s, winning contracts for more than half a billion dollars over a five year period—twice as much as any other contractor.

In 1962 Peter Kiewit, who normally shied away from publicity, surprised many observers by purchasing the World Publishing Co., publisher of the *Omaha World-Herald,* Omaha's daily newspaper. Vying with newspaper magnate Samuel I. Newhouse, Kiewit sought to keep ownership of the newspaper in Omaha. In a last minute bid, Kiewit offered $400,000 more than Newhouse and purchased the newspaper, its production plant, television station KETV—an Omaha affiliate of the American Broadcasting Association—and a medical building, for $40.5 million.

In 1970, Kiewit's coal mining operations experienced a boom in production. Growing public concern over air pollution had persuaded utility and manufacturing companies to seek cleaner burning types of coal. The low sulphur content of the coal mined by Big Horn Mining Co.—a Kiewit subsidiary located in a small Wyoming town aptly named Kleenburn—generated less pollution and became a highly sought-after variety of coal. Before air pollution became a general concern, Big Horn had shipped a few carloads at a time, but by the early 1970s three trains were shipping 60 to 65 cars of coal each week to such utility companies as Chicago's Commonwealth Edison Co. and Kansas City Power & Light Co. Kiewit's rate of coal production was further augmented when another of its subsidiaries, Rosebud Coal Sales Co., signed a joint agreement to mine low sulphur coal in Montana. Producing over 5 million tons of coal annually, Rosebud Coal supplied steam-electric generating plants in the Rocky Mountain and Midwest areas. The company gained an even greater share of the coal market in 1976, when Black Butte Coal Co., a joint venture with Rocky Mountain Energy, landed contracts to supply three million tons of coal annually to Idaho Power & Light Co. for 25 years, and to Commonwealth Edison Co. for 20 years.

In addition to experiencing dramatic growth in its coal mining concerns, Kiewit's construction operations continued to garner business. In 1971 the company was awarded a $50 million contract by the U.S. Army to begin preliminary work on building facilities at Malmstrom Air Force Base in Montana for the Safeguard anti-ballistic missile program. A year later, the army awarded an additional $110.9 million for the project, which entailed the construction of a wide array of facilities, including roads, fences, buildings, and a complex of underground concrete and steel missile silos. In 1978 Kiewit won yet another contract from the army for $245.3 million to build a powerhouse at the Bonneville lock and dam in Washington State.

In 1979, after nearly half a century of presiding over the operations of Peter Kiewit Sons', Peter Kiewit died. His immediate successor, Robert Wilson, died soon after of heart surgery complications, and Walter Scott, Jr. was named chairman, president, and chief executive that same year. The son of Kiewit's first chief engineer, Scott had joined Kiewit as an engineer after he graduated from Colorado State University.

Scott quickly took over where Peter Kiewit had left off by landing two giant contracts. The first was for the $426 million Ft. McHenry tunnel under Baltimore's harbor—the largest highway-building contract ever awarded at that time—while the second involved the construction of $400 million worth of facilities for the Washington Public Power Supply System. After this initial success, Scott directed the company toward several other large contracts during the early 1980s, including a $208 million dam and hydroelectric plant for Canada's Saskatchewan Power Corp. and a $129 million hydroelectric plant for the Alaska Power Authority.

By 1983, however, high interest rates had begun to severely limit the number of large public building projects. The U.S. Army Corps of Engineers, a major customer of Kiewit's throughout its existence, had not initiated any civil projects in the previous four years. Sensing the growing trend away from giant construction projects, Scott began to lead Kiewit toward further diversification and the pursuit of smaller construction jobs. That year the company acquired Empire Savings, Building & Loan Association—the largest state-chartered savings and loan in Colorado—for $65 million. The following year Kiewit and financier David H. Murdock purchased Continental Group Inc., a packaging, forest products, insurance, and energy concern, for $2.75 billion. Kiewit initially owned 80 percent of Continental, but fully acquired the company in 1985 after purchasing Murdock's stake. Continuing to diversify, Kiewit purchased Life Insurance Co. of Virginia the following year for $557 million, augmenting the insurance holdings of the former Continental Group, now renamed KMI Continental Inc.

After enlarging the breadth of its investments, the company was reorganized in 1986 to better reflect the more diverse nature of its businesses. Peter Kiewit Sons' Inc., as the parent company, would provide management, administrative, and financial services to its three business groups: Kiewit Construction Group, Kiewit Mining Group, and Kiewit Holdings Group.

By the end of the decade, roughly two-thirds of Kiewit's sales came from Continental Can Co., the major packaging component of the Continental Group acquisition. But Kiewit had sold off many of Continental's subsidiaries for a considerable profit, and as the company entered the 1990s it searched for a purchaser of its remaining unrelated holdings. Kiewit found a buyer for Continental Can in 1991, and the company returned to a more concentrated pursuit of its specialty—construction. By 1993 the average construction contract was for $5.3 million, with a typical year bringing in 200 to 300 contracts.

As the builder of over $2 billion worth of America's highways, in addition to the many dams, tunnels, public utility facilities, and military installations that dot the country, Kiewit has left an indelible mark on the American landscape. While contracting for construction projects entails considerable risk, especially for larger projects, Kiewit—one of the country's oldest and most experienced heavy construction companies—can draw upon its past to build toward the future.

Principal Subsidiaries: Kiewit Construction Group Inc.; Kiewit Diversified Group Inc.; Kiewit Mining Group Inc.

Further Reading:

Bettner, Jill, "The Ultimate Meritocracy," *Forbes,* August 1, 1983, pp. 106–107.
" 'Black Diamond' Boom: Kleenburn Coal Mines Enjoys Demand Surge," *The Wall Street Journal,* January 7, 1970, p. 10.
Hughes, Kathleen A., "Continental Group Inc. Approves Offer of $2.75 Billion from Kiewit, Murdock," *The Wall Street Journal,* July 2, 1984, p. 3.
"Kiewit Is Key Player in High-Stakes Purchase," *Engineering News-Record,* July 12, 1984, p. 59.
McCarthy, Michael J., "Combined International to Buy Insurer," *The Wall Street Journal,* February 14, 1986, p. 7.
Meyers, Harold B., "The Biggest Invisible Builder in the World," *Fortune,* April 1966, pp. 147–200.
"Peter Kiewit: A Biography," *The Explosives Engineer,* May 1954, p. 68.
"Peter Kiewit Sons' Inc. Revamps Management in a Reorganization," *The Wall Street Journal,* January 15, 1986, p. 38.
"Small Is Beautiful," *Fortune,* December 31, 1990, pp. 111–112.

—Jeffrey L. Covell

Petrie Stores Corporation

70 Enterprise Avenue
Secaucus, New Jersey 07094
U.S.A.
(201) 866-3600
Fax: (201) 866-5483

Public Company
Incorporated: 1932
Employees: 17,500
Sales: $1.4 billion
Stock Exchanges: New York
SICs: 5621 Women's Clothing Stores; 5632 Women's
   Accessory and Specialty Stores; 5699 Miscellaneous
   Apparel and Accessory Stores

Petrie Stores Corporation, a major retailer of women's apparel, operates stores under a variety of names, including Petrie's, Winkelman's, Stuarts, M.J. Carroll, Rave, and G&G. Since its incorporation, the retailer has been dominated by the ambition and personality of its founder, president, chairman, and chief executive officer, Milton J. Petrie, who made his fortune by running a company that catered to teenagers for more than half a century.

Milton Petrie was raised in Salt Lake City, Utah, the son of a Russian immigrant who ran several clothing shops. His father went bankrupt while Milton Petrie was young, and Milton worked various jobs until he saved enough money to open a small hosiery shop called Red Robin in Cleveland, Ohio, in 1927. He began to expand, and in 1932, backed by a loan from the Reconstruction Finance Corporation and four silent partners, Petrie Stores Corporation was incorporated in New York. Petrie expanded his stores into a small chain and added other apparel items, and sales soon reached $7 million. By 1937, however, the Great Depression and Petrie's too-ambitious expansion forced him into bankruptcy. Petrie lost most of his stores and was obliged to buy out his partners for $37,500, a debt that took more than three years to pay off.

Petrie forged ahead, determined to succeed, though his aversion to debt led him to move cautiously. Early on, Petrie concentrated on opening shops in downtown areas. As retail activity moved away from Main Street, Petrie sought out space in strip malls, opening shops in centers concentrated in the Midwest.

With the dawn of the age of the shopping mall, Petrie moved aggressively to take full advantage of those controlled environments, where teenagers came to congregate.

From the beginning, Petrie courted young women by providing budget-priced apparel. Under the names Petrie's, Marianne, and Stuarts, Petrie Stores worked by the same guidelines throughout their history. Stores were open six days a week. Advertising was considered unnecessary as the shops relied on their low prices and the closed environment of the shopping center to lure customers. The shops did not deliver or make alterations, and merchandise consisted of in-house brands. Petrie Stores concentrated on turning over and moving inventory quickly. If goods failed to sell, they were soon marked down to make room for something else. Business was largely conducted via cash, and Petrie kept prices low to lure free-spending adolescents. Referring to his target customers, Petrie told *Forbes,* "These girls. They'll live on hot dogs so they can spend their money on clothes. You can't beat a market like that."

Petrie also kept overhead low by leasing, rather than buying, space. He was known as a bare-knuckles real estate negotiator who would threaten when necessary to keep rent low. His stores were invariably staffed by women; he admitted his philosophy in *Forbes:* "With a woman, you are likely to have someone who is supplementing her husband's income, or a divorcee, and you get a helluva girl. To get the comparable person, you would have to pay the man more."

Petrie's belief that female staffers were an asset to the company extended to corporate headquarters, where women dominated senior management years before such practices became commonplace. Hilda Kirschbaum Gerstein, for example, started her career with Petrie at the age of 16 as a clerk hired the first day the first Petrie store opened in 1927. For years as vice-president and then as president (she eventually became vice-chair in 1982), she ran the company's day-to-day operations, while Petrie concentrated on negotiating the lease agreements that were such a crucial factor in Petrie Stores' success. Dorothy Fink Stern and Jean Roberts, longtime vice-presidents, also started out with Petrie in the early days. For years they were among the highest ranking women in the business, yet their salaries were always modest, less than their male counterparts at the company. "The girls," as Petrie referred to them, kept their eyes on merchandising and store operations. Petrie was quoted as saying that he believed a big part of Petrie Stores' success had been its reliance and recognition of women in management.

By 1958 Petrie Stores comprised a 77-shop chain with $17 million in annual sales, yet no detail proved too small to escape Petrie's attention. His unswerving cost-consciousness led Petrie to accumulate much capital as he steadfastly refused to acquire long-term debt in the name of expansion. By 1968, although Petrie's company had more than 150 stores and $76.8 million in sales, he had saved so much cash that the Internal Revenue Service (IRS) wondered whether these reserves had "accumulated beyond the reasonable needs of business."

In 1960 Petrie used half of his $5 million in capital to acquire a position as the largest outside stockholder of one of his major competitors, Lerner Stores. Lerner had been pressuring his suppliers, so Petrie bought a stock position to try to force a merger. Lerner's owner, Rapid-American Corporation, disliked the notion and instead tendered for Lerner. Petrie thus doubled his investment, and funds were used to aid expansion.

By the late 1960s increased sales and rising earnings fueled aggressive expansion. In fiscal 1973 Petrie Stores had grown to number 250 and sales reached $169 million; earnings had risen from 66 cents a share in 1968 to $2.02 in 1973. Despite the accumulation of cash, Petrie remained hesitant to diversify, declining to carry larger sizes or maternity clothing. Rapid growth continued through the 1970s, and by 1980 net income had grown at a compounded annual rate of 26 percent on 19 percent sales growth. Petrie Stores' peak year proved to be 1979, when profits set a record of $52 million on $446 million in sales.

By the late 1970s the fast-paced growth of the previous decade came to a halt, however. A major factor was the steep increase in shopping-center rental rates due to rising energy costs and interest rates. Petrie was able to manoeuver around this by buying existing stores with long-term leases having lower rental rates; yet he had to borrow money to do it. Many of these stores were family-run business that were bailing out during the economic downturn of the early 1980s. This period was marked by a string of acquisitions: Joseph R. Harris in 1979; G&G Shops in 1980; Franklin Stores in 1981; Hartfield Stores and Ranch Shops in 1982; Whitney Stores in 1983; and Petrie's largest purchase, the 400-store Miller-Wohl chain, which he bought for $270 million in 1984. In 1985 Winkelman Stores was purchased for $11 million in cash and $7.2 million in Petrie Stores shares; a 25 percent interest in Paul Harris Stores was also acquired. With the spate of acquisitions, sales increased but profits stalled.

Petrie's other major investment was in Toys "R" Us, the shares of which the company had started purchasing in 1978; by 1980 Petrie Stores had a 23 percent stake in the hugely successful retailer. That company's striking gains helped cushion Petrie Stores' balance sheet as profits began to fall. In 1987 the earnings garnered from the Toys "R" Us stock accounted for 80 percent of Petrie Stores earnings. The following year Petrie reduced the company's position in Toys "R" Us from 26 percent to 14 percent by redeeming $199.4 million worth of the stock's convertible debentures to pay off company debt. Under accounting rules, Petrie Stores was then unable to include its profits from Toys "R" Us stock on its income statement.

In 1986 earnings began to slide, even as sales continued to grow. Some pointed to Petrie's reluctance to diversify his large spaces—which averaged 10,000 feet—into other kinds of stores. Petrie's advancing age and continued tight grip worried investors, who were concerned that his staying power as well as that of his top lieutenants (Gerstein was 76, Roberts was 71, and Stern was 69) had become a liability in a volatile retail environment dominated by rapidly changing fashions. Some analysts felt that the stores and the merchandise needed updating, while others pointed to Petrie's lack of professional managers with whom to share power.

Milton Petrie's attempts, but ultimate failure to find a successor also worried Wall Street. In 1982 Michael Boyle, who had been an executive at Federated Stores, was brought in to become president and chief executive officer. Two months later Boyle departed with a $5 million termination settlement. In 1986 Petrie hired his 24-year-old grandson Matthew Miller with the stated intention of having him eventually fill his chair; within two years Miller had resigned without explanation. There was speculation that it was the absence of someone to whom to pass the reins, especially within his family, that kept Petrie from showing up at the office. None of his children had taken an interest in the business, and other relatives had not worked out. "My mother made me hire everybody, and they were all over the place, ruining the business," Petrie told *Forbes.* "Eventually I got rid of them."

Petrie responded by starting to renovate stores (a five-year plan started in 1987 cost $240 million) and update merchandise. Long-term debt accrued to finance his early 1980s expansion was reduced. And, Petrie finally saw the wisdom in entering the larger-sized clothing market. He had passed up the opportunity to buy the large-sized clothing chain Lane Bryant in the early 1980s because he had thought growth potential was lacking in that market; he came to regret that decision. The Plus size stores brought a significant share of earnings, and management accelerated the pace of new store openings.

Petrie Stores' depressed earnings did not keep the personal worth of Milton Petrie—who owned 60 percent of Petrie Store stock—from reaching more than $1 billion in 1987. His empire had grown to 1,600 stores with $1.2 billion in sales. Petrie, who had gone bankrupt at age 35, was a billionaire at age 85.

Earnings dropped to a 20-year low in 1990 as the apparel industry as a whole took a hit in the economic downturn. Petrie continued to add new stores, though high prices for retail space in the major malls was seen as a reason Petrie turned to downtown locations and strip malls. Petrie Stores shed the ailing Paul Harris Stores, which had filed for bankruptcy in February of 1991.

As Petrie Stores moved through the 1990s, analysts and investors looked to the time when Milton Petrie would not have final say over the business. It was feared that the same qualities that had brought the company such outstanding success—tenacious ambition, tight-fisted management, and strong-willed personalities—were in later years keeping the stores from making much-needed changes. A newfound consumer appreciation of value and the waning of the popularity of designer labels, however, placed Petrie Stores Corporation in the position of having kept one step ahead of the market—by remaining constant.

Principal Subsidiaries: G&G Shops, Inc.; Winkelman Stores, Inc.

Further Reading:

Barmash, Isadore, "The Acquisition Kings of Women's Wear," *New York Times,* March 31, 1985.

Berman, Phyllis, and Kathy Murray, "A Special Case," *Forbes,* October 24, 1988, pp. 128–32.

"But We Never Make a Deal," *Forbes,* December 1, 1976, pp. 38–39.

McCoy, Frank, ''Is Petrie's Tight Grip Strangling His Stores?,'' *Business Week,* August 8, 1988, p. 28.

Rudnitsky, Howard, ''Retailing Through Intimidation,'' *Forbes,* November 9, 1981, pp. 50–57.

Savitz, Eric J., ''Storing Up Value: Why Bargain Hunters Are Attracted to Petrie Stores,'' *Barron's,* October 9, 1989, p. 13.

Serwer, Andrew E., ''Don't Forget Your Exit Strategy,'' *Fortune,* November 30, 1992, p. 83.

''Thrifty Petrie Courts the Teenage Girl and Makes a Fortune,'' *Investor's Reader,* October 22, 1969, pp. 12–14.

—Cheryl Collins

Potlatch

Potlatch Corporation

P.O. Box 193591
San Francisco, California 94119
U.S.A.
(415) 576-8800
Fax: (415) 576-8832

Public Company
Incorporated: 1903 as Potlatch Lumber Company
Employees: 7,400
Sales: $1.33 billion
Stock Exchanges: New York Pacific Midwest
SICs: 2431 Millwork; 2621 Paper Mills; 2631 Paperboard
   Mills; 2671 Coated and Laminated Paper, Nec

Potlatch Corporation—a manufacturer of wood products, printing paper, and other pulp-based products—has its roots in the mountainous, evergreen forests of northern Idaho. Established there in 1903, it has since grown to be a national, billion-dollar enterprise, with more than 1.5 million acres of timberland in Idaho, Arkansas, and Minnesota. High-quality coated paper, oriented strand board, and, on the West Coast, private label tissue have been among its most successful products in the late 20th century.

The early history of Potlatch is closely tied to the more general history of the U.S. logging industry. In the United States logging began in New England, where forests were cleared, often carelessly, to make room for the country's first towns and farms and to provide lumber for buildings, fuel, and furniture. Once thought to be a virtually inexhaustible resource, these forests were virtually depleted by the mid-1800s, and logging companies thus began to spring up in the midwest, especially in the "North Woods" of Wisconsin, Michigan, and Minnesota. By the 1890s much of these vast midwestern pine forests were also cleared, forcing lumbermen to look south and to the far northwest for new regions of forested land.

Also in the 19th century the railroads were spreading their tracks to the outer edges of the nation. The Utah Northern extended its line in 1874 just across the southern Idaho border and several years later began to lay additional tracks to reach the mining communities farther north. By 1883 Northern Pacific had built a line from St. Paul, Minnesota, to Tacoma, Washington, which wound its way through such towns in northern Idaho as Bonner's Ferry and Sandpoint. Without the railroads to carry logs and lumber products, dreams of harvesting Idaho's evergreen forests would never have been realized.

As the railroads brought settlers to the western frontier, stories of the land's riches were carried back east. Northern Idaho, cut off from the southern part of the state by the deep gorge of the Salmon river, was largely uncharted, but many midwestern timbermen began to hear of the area's towering stands of white pine and other valuable trees. Frederick Weyerhaeuser of St. Paul, Minnesota—a powerful lumber capitalist and one of the founders of Potlatch—saw an exhibit of Idaho timberland at Chicago's 1893 World's Fair, and it was he who led the charge of midwest lumber companies to the northwest. He did this with the help of the "Weyerhaeuser syndicate," a group of midwestern businessmen who had long worked together to secure timber for their individual mills. In 1900 his syndicate bought an astonishing 900,000 acres of timberland in the Pacific Northwest, thus forming Weyerhaeuser Timber Company, and that year Weyerhaeuser himself toured on horseback northern Idaho's stands of white pine. Soon the syndicate was buying additional northwest timberland from railroads, state auctions, and homesteaders, and other midwestern companies, trusting Weyerhaeuser's judgment, quickly followed.

In northern Idaho's Palouse, Potlatch, and Elk river basins, thousands of acres of timberland were being purchased by midwestern companies, but most went to just two men—William Deary of Northland Pine Company, a firm established by the Weyerhaeuser syndicate, and Henry Turrish of Wisconsin Log & Lumber Company. Although competitors, Deary and Turrish were by 1902 buying land together, in part for convenience but also to keep land prices lower. The owners of Northland and Wisconsin Log & Lumber soon recognized the value of this collaboration, and the following year they decided to merge their Idaho timberland under a new firm, which they called Potlatch Lumber Company. When the company was formed it owned more than 100,000 acres, but it quickly gained additional land, as well as two mills, when it bought nearby Palouse River Lumber Company and Codd Lumber Company in 1903 and 1904, respectively.

Backed with an initial $3 million in capital, Potlatch Lumber Company was established with great hopes but with little recognition of the difficulties posed by the area's rugged environment. Its name—derived from the northwest Indian word *patshatl,* which referred to an elaborate ceremony of gift-giving—was selected because the Potlatch River cut through the company's land. The first president of Potlatch was Weyerhaeuser's son, Charles, and the vice president was Turrish, but the dominant personality of the company was Deary, who was appointed general manager. One of the first goals of Potlatch was to plan and build a magnificent new sawmill, which Deary decided to place along the Palouse river about 15 miles north of Moscow, Idaho. Opened on September 11, 1906, the structure was some 300 feet long, 100 feet wide, and 70 feet tall, and its giant Corliss engine gave the mill an annual capacity of 135 million board feet. Production began with 125 employees.

To house these employees, the company decided to build a town on two hills overlooking the sawmill. By the mill's opening day there were already 128 completed homes, and soon there was also a hotel, two churches, a large general store, and an elementary and high school. Called Potlatch, this attractive, well-designed town was a great source of pride for the company but also a considerable drain on funds. The company continued to own and maintain the town until the 1950s.

Another major investment by the early company was its 45-mile railroad line, which, when completed in 1907, ran from Palouse, Washington, east through Potlatch and other towns, ending in Bovill, Idaho. It was used to carry logs from the company's timberland to the new mill, as well as to transport finished lumber to connecting railroads at Palouse and Bovill.

Despite its high-quality timber, modern sawmill, and new railway, the early years of the Potlatch Lumber Company were disappointing and often marked by losses. The first dividend was not paid until 1911, and even that was just 3 percent, a low figure in the high-risk lumber business. A few years later the company was paying 10 percent, but the average dividend from 1903 to 1923—when the company's holdings had reached some 170,000 acres—was just 3.6 percent. Before his death in 1914, Frederick Weyerhaeuser reportedly said the company was appropriately called Potlatch because he had given it so much money with little return. Other Idaho timber companies had similarly poor records.

The company's tree cutting policy contributed to this shaky financial picture. Instead of selectively cutting the area's white pine, ponderosa pine, and Douglas fir—the species most in demand—the company cut all trees in its path, even those, such as tamarack, that often cost more to harvest than sell. Other problems included the company's high capital costs (for the railway, mill, and town), rugged terrain and inaccessible timber areas, deep winter snow, the relatively few trees per acre, and heavy state taxes. The 1914 opening of the Panama Canal had an especially harsh impact on Potlatch and other Idaho timber companies. Before the canal's opening, Potlatch benefited from cheaper rail costs than those paid by its Pacific coast rivals, who were hundreds of miles farther from the major eastern markets. After 1914 companies located on the Pacific coast were able to send their timber to these markets by boat, at a cost one-third cheaper than rail, thus undercutting the price of lumber sold by Potlatch and other Idaho timber firms.

As early as 1926 the entire northwest lumber industry was suffering from overproduction and declining prices. When the Great Depression hit the country in 1929, causing a precipitous drop in new building construction, Potlatch found itself facing potential bankruptcy, as did northern Idaho's other major timber companies, Clearwater and Edward Rutledge, which had been established in 1900 and 1902, respectively, by the Weyerhaeuser syndicate. The Clearwater mill was located just south of Potlatch in the town of Lewiston, while the mill of Edward Rutledge was found farther north in Coeur d'Alene.

After considerable debate among stockholders, the financial crisis was resolved by merging the three companies into an organization called Potlatch Forests, Inc. The new corporation, headquartered in Lewiston, was headed initially by John Philip Weyerhaeuser, Jr., a grandson of Frederick Weyerhaeuser, and later, in 1935, by the older Rudolph M. Weyerhaeuser, one of the founder's sons. Effective April 29, 1931, the merger did not remove the companies' common problem of a weak market but

did provide for better efficiency. Some timber in the Clearwater land, for example, could be more cheaply taken to the Potlatch mill. Expensive machinery could be shared between the three concerns. The merger also allowed for a more ambitious attempt at selective cutting, which Clearwater had begun in 1929. The goal of selective cutting was to fell only mature or diseased trees, allowing the younger, healthy ones to stand for future generations of logging. Reforestation, however, did not begin until 1954.

Despite these gains, the Depression remained a difficult period for Potlatch, which was forced to cut its prices and the wages of its workers. The Coeur d'Alene mill was closed for some time beginning in 1932, and that year its operations in the town of Potlatch were open only to ship lumber held in storage. Losses were reported in all but two years of the 1930s, resulting in a total deficit of $8,740,000 for the decade. During this period, however, the company did develop an important new product, Pres-to-logs, a slow-burning, virtually smokeless fuel made of compressed sawdust, wood chips, and splinters. The logs were ideal for fireplaces located in homes or on railcars, where smoke had to be kept to a minimum. A first in the industry, Pres-to-logs were made by a process involving extreme heat, high pressure, and moisture.

World War II brought increased demand for lumber to build houses, military camps, and other facilities for soldiers, and Potlatch, benefiting from booming lumber orders, gained badly needed profits. From 1940 to 1945 the company's after-tax profits surpassed $5 million, of which $1.2 million were placed in a reserve fund for future upgrading of its mills and machinery and for introducing new products. By the war's end, the company was poised for strong, sustained growth, which would be overseen by George F. Jewett, a grandson of the founder, who became president of Potlatch in 1946. Three years later Jewett was elected the company's first chairman of the board, a position that was later filled by Edwin Weyerhaeuser Davis, another grandson, in 1957 and then by Benton R. Cancell in 1962.

The company's profitable postwar era was distinguished by its large number of new products. The first to be introduced was veneer, or thin sheets, of white pine, which Potlatch hoped would be popular for home paneling. To make this product, giant logs of white pine had to be peeled and then made into rolls. In 1949, after three years of developing the process, the company began making white pine veneer, but the project quickly came to be too expensive and problematic. By 1952 the operations were successfully converted to make a different product, plywood, which was made from layers of Douglas fir, white pine, ponderosa pine, or larch.

An especially important new product for Potlatch was paperboard—a thick paper with a variety of uses, such as making milk cartons and other containers. To manufacture the product, the company in 1950 built a new bleach kraft pulp and paper mill, located in Lewiston, which was the first in the United States to produce bleached paperboard from sawmill residue. Within the next few years Potlatch introduced "Lock-Deck" laminated decking, "Pure-Pak" cartons for milk, and additional paperboard items, such as paper plates and meat trays. By the early 1960s the company had also purchased a mill for folding paperboard and entered a new line of products by acquiring

Clearwater Tissue Mills, Inc.

To obtain the raw materials for these new products, Potlatch began to expand its timber reserves. In 1956 it merged with Southern Lumber Company, an Arkansas firm founded by the Weyerhaeuser syndicate in 1882. With the subsequent purchase of Bradley Lumber Company, also located in Arkansas, Potlatch controlled more than 100,000 acres of Arkansas timberland, mostly of southern yellow pine, oak, and other hardwoods. Directing its sights to Minnesota, Potlatch merged in 1964 with another Weyerhaeuser creation, Northwest Paper Company, a producer of printing and writing paper. Established in 1898, Northwest owned about 220,000 acres of forested land in Minnesota, where jack pine, aspen, red pine, and balsam fir were the most common species. With these mergers, Potlatch had become a national company, and the small town of Lewiston subsequently proved to be a difficult place from which to manage its new holdings. As a result, the company's headquarters were moved to San Francisco in 1965, and a few years later, in 1973, the company changed its name from Potlatch Forests, Inc., to Potlatch Corporation.

By 1971, when Richard B. Madden became chairman of the board, the company had diversified into some 20 separate product lines—including modular housing and corrugated boxes—and its sales had reached $356 million. Potlatch was also investing millions of dollars to reduce its air and water pollution. Not simply taking over the reins, Madden spent much of his first year developing what became the company's guiding business philosophy: "Potlatch will be a company characterized by a growing profit and reasonable rate of return that is achieved by talented, well-trained, and highly motivated people. It will be a company that is properly supported by a sound financial structure and will feature a keen sense of social responsibility."

Using this simple statement, Madden then initiated an intensive review of the company's many components. The result was a decision to sell off its less profitable activities and to concentrate on just four product lines: wood products (lumber, plywood, and particle board), printed papers, pulp and paperboard, and tissue products. Moreover, the company decided to focus on "higher-value-added" products, or those that had a relatively high value compared with the cost of the raw materials. Such products tended to be less affected by recurring business cycles. In printed papers, for example, Potlatch concentrated on high grades of coated paper, the type commonly used for annual reports or advertising brochures.

Beginning in the mid-1970s and extending into the 1980s and 1990s, the company combined these shifting priorities with a new program of capital expenditures. In 1981, for example, Potlatch built in Minnesota the first U.S. plant to make oriented strand board (OSB). An alternative to plywood, OSB was a multilayered board made from strands of aspen "oriented" in various directions; the strands were held together by a mixture of wax and resin and compressed under intense heat. By 1991 the company was making more than a billion square feet of OSB in two varieties: Oxboard, with five layers, and Potlatch Select, with three. Although capital projects were curtailed during the recession of the early 1980s, by the late 1980s

Potlatch was again spending large sums of money to retool its plants and machinery. Projects completed by the early 1990s included a $40-million upgrade of the Lewiston sawmill and log processing center; a $400-million modernization of the Lewiston pulp and paperboard mill; a new, $27-million lumber mill in Warren, Arkansas; and, as part of a $107-million upgrade of its tissue operations, a new "twin wire" tissue machine in Lewiston. Beginning in 1993 Potlatch was also constructing a new tissue complex in North Las Vegas, Nevada, to service the southwestern market.

This program of capital expenditures was reflected in the company's skyrocketing sales and healthy profit margins. Total sales jumped from $356 million in 1971, the year Madden became chairman of the board, to $504 million in 1975, $820 million in 1980, $950 million in 1985, and $1.33 billion in 1992, when profits reached $78.9 million. In the early 1990s earnings were highest in its wood products, such as lumber and oriented strand board, and, owing to difficult market conditions, considerably lower in printing paper and pulp and paperboard.

As it moved toward the end of the century, Potlatch was largely insulated from one of the most difficult problems facing the forest-products industry—logging bans on federal land. Bans were especially a concern in northwest forests, where extensive restrictions were proposed to protect a number of threatened species, most notably the spotted owl but also the grizzly bear and salmon. Unlike many other companies in the industry, Potlatch relied little on federal forests for its raw materials, most of which came from the company's 1.5 million acres of timberland in Idaho (641,000), Arkansas (512,000), and Minnesota (316,000). Virtually none of its Idaho land, moreover, contained the endangered spotted owl. The company's large forest holdings, along with its continued focus on manufacturing high-quality products, encouraged some analysts to project strong growth for Potlatch Corporation, despite general problems within the forest-products industry.

Further Reading:

Blackman, Ted, "Team Concept Involves Crews in All Aspects of Mills," *Forest Industries,* November 1991, p. 14.
Hidy, Ralph W., *Timber and Men: The Weyerhaeuser Story,* New York: MacMillan Company, 1963.
Koncel, Jerome A., "Potlatch Keeps It Simple to Achieve Solid Successes," *American Papermaker,* June 1990, pp. 26–29.
McCoy, Charles, "Potlatch Corporation Expects Earnings Recovery to Take Root: Concern's Timber Holdings Are Largely Immune to Spotted-Owl Controversy," *Wall Street Journal,* April 13, 1992, p. B4.
Mehlman, William, "Leverage, Spotted Owl Seen Pulling Hard for Potlatch," *The Insiders' Chronicle,* August 19, 1991, pp. 1, 14–15.
Nelson, Warren and Marc Lerch, "Potlatch Mill Saves Energy Costs by Using Wide-Gap Heat Exchanger," *Pulp and Paper,* March 1990, pp. 212–13.
Petersen, Keith C., *Company Town: Potlatch, Idaho, and the Potlatch Lumber Company,* Pullman, Washington: Washington State University Press, 1987.
Potlatch Corporation Annual Reports, San Francisco: Potlatch Corporation, 1988–92.

—Thomas Riggs

The Procter & Gamble Company

One Procter & Gamble Plaza
Cincinnati, Ohio 45202
U.S.A.
(513) 983-1100
Fax: (513) 983-2060

Public Company
Incorporated: 1890
Employees: 79,000
Sales: $24.08 billion
Stock Exchanges: New York Cincinnati Amsterdam Paris
    Basel Geneva Lausanne Zürich Frankfurt Antwerp
    Brussels Tokyo
SICs: 2844 Toilet Preparations; 2840 Soap, Cleaners &
    Toilet Goods; 2676 Sanitary Paper Products; 2045
    Prepared Flour Mixes & Doughs; 2079 Edible Fats &
    Oils, Nec; 2095 Roasted Coffee

Few companies have influenced American lifestyles as much as The Procter & Gamble Company (P & G). Committed to remaining the leader in its markets, P & G is one of the most aggressive marketers and largest advertisers in the world. Many innovations that are now common practices in corporate America—including extensive market research, the brand-management system, and employee profit-sharing programs—were first developed at Procter & Gamble.

In 1837 William Procter and James Gamble formed Procter & Gamble, a partnership in Cincinnati, Ohio, to manufacture and sell candles and soap. Both men had emigrated from the United Kingdom. William Procter had emigrated from England in 1832 after his woolens shop in London was destroyed by fire and burglary; Gamble came from Ireland as a boy in 1819 when famine struck his native land. Both men settled in Cincinnati, then nicknamed "Porkopolis" for its booming hog-butchering trade. The suggestion for the partnership apparently came from their mutual father-in-law, Alexander Norris, who pointed out that Gamble's trade—soap making—and Procter's trade—candle making—both required use of lye, which was made from animal fat and wood ashes.

Procter & Gamble first operated out of a storeroom at Main and Sixth streets. Procter ran the store while Gamble ran the manufacturing operation, which at that time consisted of a wooden kettle with a cast-iron bottom set up behind the shop. Early each morning Gamble visited houses, hotels, and steamboats collecting ash and meat scraps, bartering soap cakes for the raw materials. Candles were Procter & Gamble's most important product at that time.

Procter & Gamble was in competition with at least 14 other manufacturers in its early years, but the enterprising partners soon expanded their operations throughout neighboring Hamilton and Butler counties. Cincinnati's location on the Ohio River proved advantageous as the company began sending its goods downriver. In 1848 Cincinnati was also linked to the major cities of the East via rail, and Procter & Gamble grew.

Around 1851, when P & G shipments were moving up and down the river and across the country by rail, the company's famous moon-and-stars symbol was created. Because most people were illiterate at this time, trademarks were used to distinguish one company's products from another's. Company lore asserts that the symbol was first drawn as a simple cross on boxes of Procter & Gamble's Star brand candles by dock hands so that they would be easily identifiable when they arrived at their destinations. Another shipper later replaced the cross with an encircled star, and eventually William Procter added the familiar 13 stars, representing the original 13 U.S. colonies, and the man in the moon.

The moon-and-stars trademark became a symbol of quality to Procter & Gamble's base of loyal customers. In the days before advertising, trademarks were a product's principal means of identification, and in 1875 when a Chicago soap maker began using an almost-identical symbol, P & G sued and won. The emblem, which was registered with the U.S. Patent Office in 1882, changed slightly over the years until 1930, when Cincinnati sculptor Ernest Bruce Haswell developed its current form.

During the 1850s Procter & Gamble's business grew rapidly. In the early part of the decade the company moved its operations to a bigger factory. The new location gave the company better access to shipping routes and stockyards where hogs were slaughtered. In 1854 the company leased an office building in downtown Cincinnati. Procter managed sales and bookkeeping and Gamble continued to run the manufacturing. By the end of the decade, the company's annual sales were more than $1 million, and Procter & Gamble employed about 80 people.

Procter & Gamble's operations were heavily dependent upon rosin—derived from pine sap—which was supplied from the South. In 1860, on the brink of the Civil War, two young cousins, James Norris Gamble and William Alexander Procter (sons of the founders), traveled to New Orleans to buy as much rosin as they could, procuring a large supply at the bargain price of $1 a barrel. When wartime shortages forced competitors to cut production, Procter & Gamble prospered. The company supplied the Union Army with soap and candles, and the moon and stars became a familiar symbol with Union soldiers.

Although Procter & Gamble had foreseen the wartime scarcities, as time wore on, its stockpile of raw materials shrank. In order to keep up full production the company had to find new ways of manufacturing. Until 1863 lard stearin was used to produce the stearic acid for candle making. With lard expensive and in short supply, a new method was discovered to produce the stearic acid using tallow. What lard and lard stearin was available was instead developed into a cooking compound. The same process was later adapted to create Crisco, the first all-vegetable shortening. When P & G's supply of rosin ran out toward the end of the war, the company experimented with silicate of soda as a substitute, which later became a key ingredient in modern soaps and detergents.

After the war Procter & Gamble expanded and updated its facilities. In 1869 the transcontinental railroad linked the two coasts and opened still more markets to Procter & Gamble. In 1875 the company hired its first full-time chemist to work with James Gamble on new products, including a soap that was equal in quality to expensive castile soaps, but which could be produced less expensively. In 1878 Procter & Gamble's White Soap hit the market and catapulted P & G to the forefront of its industry.

The most distinctive characteristic of the product, soon renamed Ivory soap, was developed by accident. A worker accidently left a soap mixer on during his lunch break, causing more air than usual to be mixed in. Before long Procter & Gamble was receiving orders for "the floating soap." Although the office was at first perplexed, the confusion was soon cleared up, and P & G's formula for White Soap changed permanently.

Harley Procter, William Procter's son, developed the new soap's potential. Harley Procter was inspired to rename the soap by Psalm 45: "all thy garments smell of myrrh, and aloes, and cassia, out of the ivory palaces whereby they have made thee glad." Procter devoted himself to the success of the new product and convinced the board of directors to advertise Ivory. Advertising was risky at the time; most advertisements were placed by disreputable manufacturers. Nevertheless, in 1882 the company approved an $11,000 annual advertising budget. The slogan "99^{44}/$_{100}$% pure" was a welcome dose of sobriety amidst the generally outlandish advertising claims of the day. Procter, committed to the excellence of the company's products, had them analyzed and improved even before they went to market. This practice was the origin of P & G's superior product development. Procter believed that "advertising alone couldn't make a product successful—it was merely evidence of a manufacturer's faith in the merit of the article."

The success of Ivory and the ability of Procter & Gamble to spread its message further through the use of national advertising caused the company to grow rapidly in the 1880s. In 1886 P & G opened its new Ivorydale plant on the edge of Cincinnati to keep up with demand. In 1890 James N. Gamble hired a chemist, Harley James Morrison, to set up a laboratory at Ivorydale and improve the quality and consistency of Procter & Gamble's products. P & G soon introduced another successful brand: Lenox soap. Marketed as a heavier-duty product, the yellow soap helped P & G reach sales of more than $3 million by 1889.

The 1880s saw labor unrest at many American companies, including Procter & Gamble, which experienced a number of strikes and demonstrations. Thereafter, the company sought to avert labor problems before they became significant. Behind P & G's labor policies was a founder's grandson, William Cooper Procter. William Cooper Procter had joined the company in 1883 after his father, William Alexander Procter, requested that he return from the College of New Jersey (now Princeton

University) just one month before graduation to help with the company's affairs. Procter learned the business from the ground up, starting in the soap factory.

In 1885 the young Procter recommended that the workers be given Saturday afternoons off, and the company's management agreed. Nevertheless, there were 14 strikes over the next two years. In 1887 the company implemented a profit-sharing plan in order to intertwine the employees' interests with those of the company. Although the semiannual dividends were received enthusiastically by employees, that enthusiasm rarely found its way back into the work place. The next year William Cooper Procter recommended tying the bonuses to employee performance, which produced better results.

In 1890 Procter & Gamble incorporated, with William Alexander Procter as its first president. Two years later the company implemented an employee stock-purchase program, which in 1903 was tied to the profit-sharing plan. By 1915 about 61 percent of the company's employees were participating. The company introduced a revolutionary sickness-disability program for its workers in 1915, and implemented an eight-hour workday in 1918. Procter & Gamble has been recognized as a leader in employee-benefit programs ever since.

Meanwhile, new soaps, including P & G White Naphtha, which was introduced in 1902, kept P & G at the forefront of the cleaning-products industry. In 1904 the company opened its second plant, in Kansas City, Missouri, followed by Port Ivory on Staten Island, New York. In 1907 William Cooper Procter became president of the company after his father's death.

Procter & Gamble soon began experimenting with a hydrogenation process which combined liquid cottonseed oil with solid cottonseed oil. After several years of research, Procter & Gamble patented the procedure, and in 1911 Crisco was introduced to the public. Backed by strong advertising budget, Crisco sales took off.

World War I brought shortages, but Procter & Gamble management had again foreseen the crisis and had stockpiled raw materials. William Cooper Procter was also active in the wartime fund raising effort.

During the 1920s the flurry of new products continued. Ivory Flakes came out in 1919. Chipso soap flakes for industrial laundry machines were introduced in 1921. In 1926 Camay was introduced and three years later Oxydol joined the P & G line of cleaning products. The company's market research became more sophisticated when F. W. Blair, P & G chemist, began a six-month tour of U.S. kitchens and laundry rooms to assess the effectiveness of Procter & Gamble's products in practical use and to recommend improvements. After Blair returned, the economic-research department under, D. Paul Smelser, began a careful study of consumer behavior. Market research complemented Procter & Gamble's laboratories and home economics department in bringing new technology to market.

Soon after Richard R. Deupree became president of the company in 1930, synthetic soap products hit the market. In 1933 Dreft, the first synthetic detergent for home use, was introduced, followed by the first synthetic hair shampoo, Drene, in 1934.

Further improvements in synthetics resulted in a host of new products years later.

In 1931 Neil McElroy, a former promotions manager who had spent time in England and had an up-close view of Procter & Gamble's rival Unilever, suggested a system of "one man—one brand." In effect, each brand would operate as a separate business, competing with the products of other firms as well as those of Procter & Gamble. The system would include a brand assistant who would execute the policies of the brand manager and would be primed for the top job. Brand management became a fixture at Procter & Gamble, and was widely copied by other companies.

The Depression caused hardship for many U.S. corporations as well as for individuals, but Procter & Gamble emerged virtually unscathed. Radio took Procter & Gamble's message into more homes than ever. In 1933 Procter & Gamble became a key sponsor of radio's daytime serials, soon known as "soap operas." In 1935 Procter & Gamble spent $2 million on national radio sponsorship, and by 1937 the amount was $4.5 million. In 1939 Procter & Gamble had 21 programs on the air and spent $9 million. That year P & G advertised on television for the first time, when Red Barber plugged Ivory soap during the first television broadcast of a major league baseball game.

In 1940 Procter & Gamble's packaging expertise was given military applications when the government asked the company to oversee the construction and operation of ordinance plants. Procter & Gamble Defense Corporation operated as a subsidiary and filled government contracts for 60-millimeter mortar shells. Glycerin also became key to the war effort for its uses in explosives and medicine, and Procter & Gamble was one of the largest manufacturers of that product.

After World War II the availability of raw materials and new consumer attitudes set the stage for unprecedented growth. Procter & Gamble's postwar miracle was Tide, a synthetic detergent that, together with home automatic washing machines, revolutionized the way people washed their clothes. The company was not ready for the consumer demand for heavy-duty detergent when it introduced the product in 1947; within two years Tide, backed by a $21 million advertising budget, was the number-one laundry detergent, outselling even the company's own Oxydol and Duz. Despite its premium price, Tide remained the number-one laundry detergent into the 1990s. In 1950 Cheer was introduced as bluing detergent, and over the years other laundry products were also marketed: Dash in 1954, Bold in 1965, Era in 1972, and Solo in 1979.

The 1950s were highly profitable for the company. In 1955, after five years of research, Procter & Gamble firmly established itself in the toiletries business with Crest toothpaste. Researchers at the company and at Indiana University developed the toothpaste using stannous fluoride—a compound of flourine and tin—which could substantially reduce cavities. In 1960 the American Dental Association endorsed Crest, and the product was on its way to becoming the country's number-one toothpaste, nudging past Colgate in 1962.

Procter & Gamble began acquiring smaller companies aggressively in the mid-1950s. In 1955 it bought the Lexington, Kentucky–based nut company W. T. Young Foods, and ac-

quired Nebraska Consolidated Mills Company, owner of the Duncan Hines product line, a year later. In 1957 the Charmin Paper Company and the Clorox Chemical Company were also acquired.

In 1957 Neil McElroy, who had become Procter & Gamble president in 1948, left the company to serve as secretary of defense in President Dwight D. Eisenhower's cabinet. He was replaced by Howard Morgens who, like his predecessor, had climbed the corporate ladder from the advertising side. In 1959 McElroy returned to Procter & Gamble as chairman and remained in that position until 1971, when Morgens succeeded him. Morgens remained CEO until 1974.

Morgens oversaw Procter & Gamble's full-scale entry into the paper-goods markets. A new process developed in the late 1950s for drying wood pulp led to the introduction of White Cloud toilet paper in 1958, and Puffs tissues in 1960. Procter & Gamble's Charmin brand of toilet paper was also made softer.

Procter & Gamble's paper-products offensive culminated in the 1961 test marketing of Pampers disposable diapers. The idea for Pampers came from a Procter & Gamble researcher, Vic Mills, who was inspired while changing an infant grandchild's diapers in 1956. The product consisted of three parts: a leak-proof outer plastic shell, several absorbent layers, and a porous film that let moisture pass through into the absorbent layers, but kept it from coming back. Test market results showed that parents liked the diapers, but disliked the 10¢-per-Pamper price. Procter & Gamble reduced the price to 6¢ and implemented a sales strategy emphasizing the product's price. Pamper's three-layer design was a phenomenal success, and within 20 years disposable diapers had gone from less than 1 percent to more than 75 percent of all diapers changes in the United States. Procter & Gamble improved the technology over the years, and added a premium brand, Luvs, in 1976.

In the 1960s Procter & Gamble faced charges from the Federal Trade Commission that its Clorox and Folgers acquisitions violated antitrust statutes. In a case that found its way to the Supreme Court, Procter & Gamble was finally forced to divest Clorox in 1967. The Folgers action was dismissed after Procter & Gamble agreed not to make any more grocery acquisitions for seven years, and coffee acquisitions for ten years.

In the late 1960s public attention to water pollution focused on phosphates, a key group of ingredients in soap products. After initial resistance, Procter & Gamble, along with other soap makers, drastically reduced the use of phosphates in its products.

In 1974 Edward G. Harness became chairman and CEO of Procter & Gamble and the company continued its strong growth. Many familiar products were improved during the 1970s, and new ones were added as well, including Bounce fabric softener for the dryer in 1972 and Sure antiperspirant and Coast soap in 1974.

In 1977, after three years of test marketing, Procter & Gamble introduced Rely tampons, which were rapidly accepted in the market as a result of their "super-absorbent" qualities. In 1980, however, the Centers for Disease Control (CDC) published a report showing a statistical link between the use of Rely and a rare but often fatal disease known as toxic shock syndrome (TSS). In September 1980 the company suspended further sales of Rely tampons, taking a $75 million write-off on the product.

Ironically, P & G was able to capitalize on the resurgence of feminine napkins after the TSS scare. The company's Always brand pads quickly garnered market share, and by 1990 Always was the top sanitary napkin, with over one-fourth of the market.

In 1981 John G. Smale became CEO of Procter & Gamble. He had been president since 1974. Smale led the company further into the grocery business through a number of acquisitions, including Ben Hill Griffin citrus products. The company also entered the over-the-counter (OTC) drug market with the 1982 purchase of Norwich-Eaton Pharmaceuticals, makers of Pepto Bismol and Chloraseptic. The company completed its biggest purchase in 1985, with the acquisition of the Richardson-Vicks Company for $1.2 billion, and bought Dramamine and Metamucil from G. D. Searle & Company. These purchases made Procter & Gamble a leader in the over-the-counter drug sales.

In 1985, unable to squelch perennial rumors linking Procter & Gamble's famous moon-and-stars logo to Satanism, the company reluctantly removed the logo from product packages. The logo began to reappear on some packages in the early 1990s, and the company continues to use the trademark on corporate stationary and on its building.

During fiscal 1985, Procter & Gamble experienced its first decline in earnings since 1953. Analysts maintained that Procter & Gamble's corporate structure had failed to respond to important changes in consumer shopping patterns and that the company's standard practice of extensive market research slowed its reaction to the rapidly changing market. The mass-marketing practices that had served Procter & Gamble so well in the past lost their punch as broadcast television viewership fell from 92 percent to 67 percent in the mid-1980s. Many large companies responded to the challenge of cable TV and increasingly market-specific media with appropriately targeted "micro-marketing" techniques, and Procter & Gamble was forced to rethink its marketing strategy. In the late 1980s Procter & Gamble diversified its advertising, reducing its reliance on network television. Computerized market research including point-of-sale scanning also provided the most up-to-date information on consumer buying trends.

In 1987 the company restructured its brand-management system into a "matrix system." Category managers became responsible for several brands, making them sensitive to the profits of other Procter & Gamble products in their areas. Procter & Gamble brands continued to compete against one another, but far less actively. The restructuring also eliminated certain layers of management, quickening the decision-making process. The company became more aware of profitability than in the past. A company spokesperson summed it up for *Business Week:* "before it had been share, share, share. We get the share and the profits will follow." In the later 1980s, Procter & Gamble was no longer willing to settle just for market share.

In the late 1980s health-care products were one of the fastest-growing markets as the U.S. population grew both older and more health conscious. To serve this market, Procter & Gamble's OTC drug group, which had been built up earlier in the decade, entered a number of joint ventures in pharmaceuticals. Procter & Gamble teamed up with the Syntex Corporation to formulate an OTC version of its best-selling antiarthritic, Naprosyn. Cooperative deals were also struck with the Dutch Gist-Brocades Company for its De-Nol ulcer medicine; UpJohn for its anti-baldness drug, Minoxidil; and Triton Bioscience and Cetus for a synthetic interferon.

In September 1988 Procter & Gamble made its first move into the cosmetics business with the purchase of Noxell Corporation, maker of Noxema products and Cover Girl cosmetics, in a $1.3 billion stock swap. Procter & Gamble also planned to further develop its international operations. In 1988 the company acquired Blendax, a European health- and beauty-care goods manufacturer. The Bain de Soleil sun care-product line was also purchased that year. By 1989 foreign markets accounted for nearly 40 percent of group sales, up from 14 percent in 1985.

P & G's brand equity was threatened by the weak economy and resultant consumer interest in value in the late 1980s and early 1990s. This value orientation resulted in stronger performance by private labels, especially in health and beauty aids. Private labels' market share of that segment grew 50 percent between 1982 and 1992, to 4.5 percent.

To combat the trend, P & G inaugurated "Every Day Low Pricing" (EDLP) for 50 to 60 percent of its products, including Pampers and Luvs diapers, Cascade dish soap, and Jif peanut butter. The pricing strategy was good for consumers, but was compensated for with lower promotion deals for wholesalers. Some retailers objected to P & G's cut in promotional kickbacks to the point of actually dropping products, but others welcomed the value-conscious positioning. P & G redirected the money it saved from trade promotions for direct marketing efforts that helped bring coupon and sample programs to targeted groups for brands with narrow customer bases like Pampers, Clearasil, and Oil of Olay.

In the 1990s Procter & Gamble also hopped on the so-called "green" bandwagon of environmental marketing. It reduced packaging by offering concentrated formulations of products in smaller packages and refill packs on 38 brands in 17 countries.

While P & G expanded its presence in OTC drugs, it also divested holdings in some areas it had outgrown. In 1992 the corporation sold about one-half of its Cellulose & Specialties pulp business to Weyerhaeuser Co. for $600 million. While vertical integration had benefitted P & G's paper products in the past, the forestry business had become unprofitable and distracting by the 1990s. The corporation also sold an Italian coffee business in 1992 to focus on a core of European brands. P & G hoped to introduce products with pan-European packaging, branding, and advertising to capture more of the region's well-established markets.

Principal Subsidiaries: The Procter & Gamble Distributing Company; The Procter & Gamble Manufacturing Company; The Procter & Gamble Paper Products Company; The Procter & Gamble Cellulose Corporation; The Folger Coffee Company; Norwich Eaton Pharmaceuticals, Inc.; Richardson-Vicks Inc.; Procter & Gamble A.G. (Switzerland); Procter & Gamble Benelux (Belgium); Procter & Gamble Inc. (Canada); Procter &

Gamble Espana, S.A. (Spain); Procter & Gamble France; Procter & Gamble GmbH (Germany); Procter & Gamble Italia, S.p.A. (Italy); Procter & Gamble Limited (U.K.); Procter & Gamble de Mexico, S.A. de C.V.; Procter & Gamble Philippines, Inc.; Procter & Gamble de Venezuela, C.A.

Further Reading:

Endicott, R. Craig, "100 Leading National Advertisers; Top 100 Take It on the Chin, Feel Biggest Drop in 4 Decades," *Advertising Age,* v. 63, September 23, 1992, 1–28, 29–72.
"The House that Ivory Built: 150 Years of Procter & Gamble," *Advertising Age,* August 20, 1987.
Johnson, Bradley, "Retailers Accepting P&G Low Pricing," *Advertising Age,* v. 63, June 22, 1992, 36.
Kirk, Jim, "The New Status Symbols; New Values Drive Private-Label Sales," *Adweek* (Eastern Ed.), v. 33, October 5, 1992, 38–44.
Lawrence, Jennifer, "Jager: New P&G Pricing Builds Brands," *Advertising Age,* v. 63, June 29, 1992, 13, 49.
——, "Laundry Soap Marketers See the Value of 'Value!,' " *Advertising Age,* v. 63, September 21, 1992, 3, 56.
Levin, Gary, "P&G Tells Shops: Direct Marketing Is Important to Us," *Advertising Age,* v. 63, June 22, 1992, 3, 35.
Lief, Alfred, *It Floats: The Story of Procter & Gamble,* New York: Rienhart & Company, 1958.
Miller, Cyndee, "Moves by P&G, Heinz Rekindle Fears that Brands Are in Danger," *Marketing News,* v. 26, June 8, 1992 1, 15.
"Procter's Gamble," *Economist,* v. 324, July 25, 1992, 61–62.
Schisgall, Oscar, *Eyes on Tomorrow: Evolution of Procter & Gamble,* Chicago: J. G. Ferguson Publishing Co., 1981.
Weinstein, Steve, "Will Procter's Gamble Work?," *Progressive Grocer,* v. 71, July 1992, 36–40.
"Weyerhaeuser Is Set to Acquire Pulp Assets from Procter & Gamble," *Corporate Growth Report,* August 31, 1992, 6212.
Wilsher, Peter, "Diverse and Perverse," *Management Today,* July 1992, 32–35.

—Thomas M. Tucker
updated by April S. Dougal

Pulte Corporation

33 Bloomfield Hills Pkwy., Ste. 200
Bloomfield Hills, Michigan 48304
U.S.A.
(313) 647-2750
Fax: (313) 433-4598

Public Company
Incorporated: 1956 as William J. Pulte, Inc.
Employees: 2,350
Sales: $1.37 billion
Stock Exchanges: New York
SICs: 1521 General Contractors—Single-Family Houses;
   6162 Mortgage Bankers & Loan Correspondents

Pulte Corporation, organized as a holding company with dozens of subsidiaries, is one of the largest home builders and financial services providers in the United States. The company originated when William J. Pulte built his first house in Detroit, Michigan, in 1950. He incorporated his home building activities in 1956 under the name William J. Pulte, Inc. Over the years, 115,000 families have purchased Pulte homes, including single-family residences, townhouses, condominiums, and duplexes. Pulte offers a wide variety of home models and customers can vary the model's style by choosing from a number of facades and interior options.

In 1961 the company had one subdivision in Detroit; by 1969 it had 12 active subdivisions in six states. The company recorded $5 million in sales in 1964. That figure nearly tripled by 1967, and sales exceeded $20 million by 1968. Pulte entered the Washington, D.C., market in 1964, the Chicago market in 1966, and the Atlanta market in 1968. On March 4, 1969, William J. Pulte, Inc. was reincorporated through a merger with American Builders, Inc. of Colorado Springs, Colorado. The newly formed Pulte Home Corporation became a publicly owned company and 200,000 shares of common stock were issued. The reorganization allowed Pulte entry into the low-cost Federal Home Administration (FHA) and Veterans Administration (VA) housing market. At the same time, Pulte opened its first subdivision of medium-priced homes (to sell in the FHA and VA mortgage market) and began its first subdivision in the state of Virginia. The company also built high-priced conventionally mortgaged homes, student apartments, and turnkey multi-family housing. To control its construction costs, it implemented a computerized critical path program.

During 1970 Pulte evolved from its status as primarily a supplier of high-priced single family homes to a supplier of single family homes across price ranges. For the first time, the company's sales of low- and medium-priced houses exceeded those of high-priced houses in both sales dollars and units. The company completed and delivered 1,000 housing units for the first time, reaching $31.2 million in sales. The company also increased its capital base by selling preferred convertible stock for the first time.

In the early 1970s Pulte architects developed the first Quadrominium project, a single building that resembled large, custom-built, high-priced homes, but contained four separate two-bedroom units with separate entrances and garages. Pulte opened its first Quadrominiums in Chicago in 1971, providing buyers with homes for less than $20,000. To increase quality control and shorten the time period between the first rough carpentry work and the closing in of a house against the weather, Pulte started to make extensive use of component parts. It used prebuilt trusses; prefinished cabinets, windows, and doors; and factory-built floor and wall sections.

The company extended its presence into new housing markets and continued to grow during the 1970s and 1980s. Even as national housing starts and deliveries declined, Pulte's sales increased to nearly 5,000 units in 1980. It ranked first of all on-site builders in the United States in revenues and in homes delivered in 1985.

One of Pulte's first financial services companies was the Intercontinental Mortgage Company, founded in 1972. Later renamed ICM Mortgage Corporation (ICM), the wholly owned subsidiary provided customers with home mortgage financing and thus made Pulte housing units more attractive to homebuyers. (Over half of all Pulte homebuyers financed through ICM in 1992.) ICM services included originating mortgage loans, placing loans with permanent investors, and servicing loans as an agent for investors. ICM posted its third consecutive year of increasing volume in 1992 as it began to focus on origination of "spot" loans for other than Pulte buyers, development of core business relationships with local real estate brokerage professionals, and refinancing activities.

Other Pulte financial services companies included Pulte Financial Companies, Inc. (PFCI), which was the parent company of several bond issuing subsidiaries, and First Line Insurance Services, Inc. (First Line), which provided customers (principally Pulte homebuyers) with convenient and competitively priced insurance-related services to protect their new homes and financial security. In operation since 1981, PFCI subsidiaries engaged in the acquisition of mortgage loans and mortgage backed securities principally through the issuance of long-term bonds. First Line was established in 1987.

On September 17, 1987, PHM Corporation was incorporated and became the publicly held parent holding company of the Pulte Home Corporation group of companies, which became the wholly owned subsidiary of Pulte Diversified Companies, Inc. In 1988 home sales were flat and one of Pulte's financing subsidiaries filed for Chapter 11 protection due to foreclosure losses. PHM saw a good opportunity to expand its financial services operations by taking advantage of the federal government's Southwest Plan to purchase five insolvent Texas savings and loan institutions. Under the plan, the government offered excellent purchase terms, assumed the risk for any loans that went bad, and gave tax benefits for any losses generated. The acquisitions included two newly incorporated Federal Savings and Loan Insurance Corporation (FSLIC) insured institutions, First Heights, fsa, and Heights of Texas, fsb. For $45 million, and with the assistance of the FSLIC, the company acquired substantially all of the five thrifts' assets of $1.3 billion and their business operations and assumed certain of their liabilities. Since Pulte was basically responsible only for loans made after the takeover, it was the Government National Mortgage Association's responsibility when one of the thrifts defaulted on a mortgage servicing contract only a month after the takeover. The $2.4 billion portfolio was Ginnie Mae's largest single default to date.

Heights of Texas merged into First Heights in July 1990 and consolidated operations under the name Heights of Texas, a federal savings bank (First Heights). Throughout 1991, the bank sold off home loans and securities not guaranteed against loss by the government, repaid high priced liabilities, and made other transactions in anticipation of eventually being removed from government backing. The effect was an increase in core capital ratio. By 1992 First Heights had grown to 28 branches that offered a full range of deposit and loan services to retail and small business customers, and it had approximately $2 billion in assets.

The homebuilding industry is traditionally one of the hardest hit by fluctuations in the economy. Factors that affect the housing market include national and world events that impact consumer confidence and changes in interest rates; property taxes, energy prices, and other costs associated with home ownership; federal income tax laws; and government mortgage financing programs. PHM realized that a conservative financial philosophy, combined with delivery of good products, was not enough to assure that the company's more than 35 years of consecutive profitability would continue; in 1989 the company launched the Pulte Quality Leadership (PQL) proactive initiative. PQL was a process to involve every employee, supplier, and subcontractor in devising ways to continuously improve all aspects of the company's operations and assure its continued success. Since the company was already a decentralized organization, PQL further empowered divisions and subsidiaries to adapt products, services, and business strategies to meet the needs of local markets.

Under the PQL process, Pulte had more than 150 teams in the field working on improvements and innovations that would benefit the corporation's diverse companies. Active councils represented each of Pulte's major disciplines: sales and marketing, land management, construction, and finance. Senior managers from every business unit joined to form the seven task teams of the National Quality Council (NQC) in 1990.

PQL training stressed the concept of "Seven Voices" that must be heard and understood to become integral to decision-making. They were the voices of customers, employees, suppliers, competitors, internal systems, communities, and shareholders. The NQC developed the Customer Satisfaction Measurement System, a communication link with new homebuyers that provided feedback on the expectations of customers nationwide. The system measured quality and satisfaction relative to expectations.

The Construction Council developed performance requirements for nearly 200 distinct processes involved in building a house. The council also implemented a comprehensive "building science" program that was the first in the industry. These initiatives fundamentally changed the way the company viewed the entire construction process. For example, in Charlotte, Pulte decided to complete garage slabs, driveways, walks, stairs, and rough grading far earlier in the construction process so Realtors and brokers could show the houses to prospective customers even in bad weather. The new practice contributed to the company's local success and growth during challenging market conditions. Additionally, the subcontractors liked the ease of entry and cleanliness of the job sites and customers were able to view their homes more conveniently. Pulte's Chesapeake Operations converted to a screw system to attach gypsum and subfloors. The new system reduced drywall cracks, nail pops, and floor squeaks—three of the most frequently occurring problems in a new home. It also solved service problems that usually showed up after the customer moved in.

The Land Council changed the procedure Pulte Corporation used to acquire land. Instead of using the traditional industry "price and terms" philosophy, the corporation started to choose land based on an understanding of what targeted customers wanted and where they wanted to live. For instance, Pulte integrated 280 homesites with a large preserve of wetlands, streams, fields, and forests in suburban Baltimore. Boy Scouts, public school groups, and other civic organizations joined in planning and building hiking trails, bird houses, and other enhancements. The community received much praise, including designation by the Urban Wildlife Institute as an "Urban Wildlife Sanctuary."

Because of the PQL initiative, ICM Mortgage Corporation switched from issuing traditional mortgage coupon books to a monthly mailing of mortgage statements. The innovation added costs up front, but reduced the number of calls to customer service, improved late charge collections, and decreased delinquencies because the system encouraged customers to communicate problems earlier.

During the economic downturn of the early 1990s, Pulte continued to enjoy record sales and profits in spite of weakened housing and troubled financial markets, enjoying the highest sales and profit per employee of any firm in the industry. While the country had the lowest number of housing starts since World War II during 1991, PHM Corporation enjoyed a 37 percent increase in earnings. The company was able to compete on the basis of reputation, price, location, design, and quality of its homes. It had more than 150 active subdivisions within 25 markets in the Mid-Atlantic, Central, Southeast, and Southwest geographic areas. Pulte Home Corporation attained its first $1 billion year in 1992, with a unit volume of more than 8,000.

Pulte was ready to respond to changing home design preferences and life-styles. Jean Halliday wrote in *Crain's Detroit*

Business that "homes have changed more over the past two years than they had over the previous 10, according to Robert Halso, president of Pulte Homes of Michigan Corp." The typical home design before the 1990s was for a family of four. But " 'people don't have to move, they want to move; so you have to give them what they want,' Halso said. 'The '90s is certainly a time to delight your customer—satisfying them is not enough, because there's so much competition.' " The company established four different buyer profiles for which it designed homes: the traditional family; the single person; the empty nester; and the extended family. The last profile included parents with children starting college or with children in their 20s still living at home. To suit their customers' life-styles and wishes, Pulte home designs decreased formal areas to provide space for larger kitchens with fireplaces, bigger family rooms, and master suites; and ranches gave way to two-story Cape Cods.

PHM Corporation was renamed Pulte Corporation on July 1, 1993, to capitalize on the public's recognition of the Pulte name. PHM Corporation was not widely known outside of financial circles, while Pulte had name recognition and identification throughout the geographic areas in which the company's subsidiaries marketed their products and services. It was thought that the change would decrease confusion, potentially increase awareness of the company and its subsidiaries' products and services, and help it in its financing.

Pulte Corporation, because of the geographic diversity of its operations, complementary lines of business, and established status as a leader in its industries, appears in a good position to continue to be a successful and profitable company through the 1990s.

Principal Subsidiaries: Pulte Home Corporation; Pulte Home Credit Corporation; First Heights Bank, fsb; ICM Mortgage Corporation; Pulte Financial Companies, Inc.

Further Reading:

Benoit, Ellen, "PHM: Transactions Speak Louder . . .," *Financial World,* May 16, 1989, p. 16.
Drummond, James, "Sweet Deal," *Forbes,* September 18, 1989, pp. 96, 98.
Halliday, Jean, "No Credit Problem Here: PHM Expected To Add Market Share," *Crain's Detroit Business,* March 16, 1992, p. 2.
——, "Pulte Aims at More Buyers," *Crain's Detroit Business,* March 2–8, 1992, p. 13.
Pulte Corporation Annual Reports, Bloomfield Hills, MI: Pulte Corporation, 1969, 1970, 1975, 1985, 1990–92.

—Doris Morris Maxfield

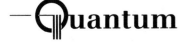

Chemical Corporation

Quantum Chemical Corporation

99 Park Avenue
New York, New York 10016
U.S.A.
(212) 949-5000
Fax: (212) 551-0307

Public Company
Incorporated: 1924 as National Distillers Products
    Corporation
Employees: 8,850
Sales: $2.3 billion
Stock Exchanges: New York
SICs: 2869 Industrial Organic Chemicals, Nec; 5984
    Liquefied Petroleum Gas Dealers; 1311 Crude Petroleum
    and Natural Gas; 1321 Natural Gas Liquids; 3081
    Unsupported Plastics Film and Sheet; 2821 Plastics
    Materials and Resins; 2800 Chemicals and Allied
    Products; 2911 Petroleum Refining; 3080 Miscellaneous
    Plastics Products; 8640 Chemical Industry; 8731
    Commercial Physical Research; 5172 Petroleum Products,
    Nec

Quantum Chemical Corporation (prior to 1988, the National Distillers and Chemical Corporation) is one of the largest U.S. producers and marketers of propane gas petrochemicals—industrial chemicals derived from petroleum refining. The company's USI Division is the country's largest manufacturer and marketer of polyethylene, in which it holds the number one market share, 17 percent, with Dow and Carbide running second and third. Polyethylene is a highly popular plastic that is used, for instance, in milk and detergent jugs, ketchup bottles, film packaging, and snack food bags. The chief raw material in the manufacture of this substance is ethylene, and Quantum Chemical's ethylene "cracker" in La Porte, Texas, is one of the largest in the world. The company is also the largest producer of ethanol—or, industrial alcohol—with a 39 percent market share. Other industrial chemicals produced by the company, acetic acid and vinyl acetate monomer, command the second-largest market share. The small but growing polypropylene business of the early 1990s was becoming significant, especially with the oversupply of polyethylene.

Suburban Propane, the company's second major division and core business, is a distributor and marketer of propane gas for more than 350,000 vehicles in the United States; the chemical is used for home and water heating, cooking, and clothes drying. Quantum Chemical is the largest propane retailer in the nation, dispensing approximately 700 million gallons of propane to 379 locations.

While Quantum Chemical consists of two principal industries, chemicals and propane, this has been true only as of 1988. In January of that year, the company's stockholders adopted the name "Quantum" to underscore the company's commitment to these two industries. Prior to 1988, the firm was identified with the hard liquor and wine businesses as well as many others. A unique characteristic of Quantum Chemical has been its unusual metamorphosis from a diverse company and major liquor dealer into a highly focused firm that has virtually nothing in common with its origins.

Quantum Chemical's history could be said to consist of three histories: that of the original founding company—National Distillers Products Corporation—and those of Quantum Chemical's two principal divisions, USI Chemical and Suburban Propane. The oldest of the three, National Distillers, disappeared and was replaced in 1988 by a new name and identity. Nonetheless, as National Distillers evolved, it had branched out into both the chemical and propane industries.

Quantum Chemical's founding father, Seton Porter, was president of National Distillers Products from the year of the company's establishment, 1924, until 1933. The Great Depression years of the 1930s were extremely trying for the nearly bankrupted company, whose origins as a thriving hard liquor concern stretched back to 1902. Later in the decade, the Prohibition Act, which President Woodrow Wilson vetoed because it was "unenforceable" and "would lead to crime," was passed by Congress over his veto, and sent to the states to be ratified as the Eighteenth Amendment in 1919.

The Distilling Company of America—parent of National Distillers—did not go under, as did so many other liquor concerns with the onset of Prohibition. In 1924 it reorganized as a company that, with a new name and image, could survive and await the turn of events. Headed by Porter, stockholders of National Distillers Products approved the decision to manufacture and market sacramental wine for religious services as well as medicinal and industrial alcohol. The latter would prove to be the company's first step in the relatively new, and soon to be expansive, industrial chemicals industry.

The National Distillers Products Corporation survived the lean Prohibition years, and President Porter was making plans for a resumption of the liquor trade well before the Twenty-First Amendment repealing Prohibition was ratified by a majority of the states in 1933. From then on, the National Distillers Products Corporation took off, expanding vigorously in one of the worst years of the Depression. It acquired Sunny Brook Distilling Company in Louisville, Kentucky, followed by the Overhold Distilling Company with its two plants in Pennsylvania. 1935 and 1936 saw the purchase of Old Crow distillery and a 70 percent interest—which was later expanded to 100 percent in 1986—in John de Kuyper & Son Company. Acquisitions and expansion did not cease even during the stressful years of World War II, when, in addition to a Canadian distillery, a rum concern was purchased in Puerto Rico for the very considerable sum of $647,000.

The World War II years saw the advent of the petrochemical industry. The dearth of raw materials put pressure on industry to find new uses for by-products that were previously discarded as waste. Polyethylene plastic was "discovered" during the war years to be an excellent insulator for wiring, while such staples as industrial alcohol found increasing usefulness in the food and drug industries, especially in packaging.

Emerging from the war with its identity as an alcohol producer intact, National Distillers nonetheless saw a future in industrial chemicals and quickly branched out into this emerging industry. By 1957 the company had so committed itself to industrial chemicals that stockholders altered the company name that year to National Distillers and Chemical Corporation to reflect the change.

The major reason for the name change was National Distillers' acquisition of US Industrial Chemicals, Inc. in 1950, the current USI Division of Quantum Chemical Corporation. US Industrial Chemicals, which would change the identity and future of National Distillers, was one of the largest and oldest industrial chemical concerns in the nation. It was incorporated in 1906, the year U.S. President Theodore Roosevelt's progressive-minded Congress passed a law eliminating the traditional liquor tax on alcohol used for industrial and medicinal purposes. Thus encouraged, the US Industrial Alcohol Company (USIA) was incorporated in West Virginia and boomed thereafter.

USIA was slowly overtaking the Germans' lead in the chemical business, especially after World War I. In 1919 the company became a global leader in the industrial chemical industry when its Curtis Bay plant in Baltimore opened, the first anhydrous—no water—alcohol processing facility in the world. By 1938 the Baltimore plant was pioneering the manufacture of cellulose acetate—a plastic used especially in yarn, textiles and photographic film. During the war, great pressure was felt by USIA's research and development personnel to create new industrial chemicals as well as find new uses for such staples as industrial alcohol. One important result was the manufacture of polyethylene, a plastic that would become increasingly indispensable in the postwar years.

At the end of World War I, USIA changed its name to US Industrial Chemicals, Inc., and was successfully pioneering the manufacture of synthetic alcohol from ethylene. Merger talks were proceeding with National Distillers, a longtime producer of industrial alcohol. After the acquisition of USI in 1951, National Distillers became one of the nation's leading manufacturers and pioneers of industrial chemicals derived from petroleum refining.

Several years after the merger, the world's largest anhydrous alcohol plant was built in Tuscola, Illinois, followed in 1969 by the world's largest plant producing vinyl acetate monomer—a chemical used in the production of paints, adhesives, coatings, and many other products—which was located in Houston. With USI's 1984 purchase of ARCO petroleum company's polyethylene plant in Port Arthur, Texas, followed two years later by its merger with Enron Chemical Company, USI became the largest polyethylene producer in the nation.

The year before the ARCO acquisition, 1983, National Distillers and Chemical Corporation had acquired for $273 million Suburban Propane, the largest marketer of propane in the nation, with distribution outlets in 36 states. Suburban Propane's unusual history began in the 1920s, when founder Mark Anton moved out to a New Jersey suburb that lacked gas for cooking and heating. Prompted by his wife's nostalgia for her former gas range, the resourceful Anton discovered a company that produced liquified petroleum gas, or propane, and sold equipment to install the gas in homes. Delighted by having gas for cooking and heating at relatively little cost and effort, Anton wondered whether other families in the suburbs would choose gas over electric. The demand for propane gas, which hitherto had been considered a useless byproduct of petroleum production, was astounding. In 1945 the Suburban Propane Gas Company was incorporated, business was expanded nationally, and by the time the National Distillers and Chemical Corporation purchased Suburban Propane in 1983, its annual sales had climbed to $1 billion (from only $43 million in 1960). Its distribution network had reached virtually every state in the nation. Suburban Propane owned its own pipelines, oil fields, and petroleum wells and was a very predictable, steady business.

The two "halves" of Quantum Chemical Corporation were thus in place by 1983. With so much of the company's business derived from the chemical and petrochemical industries, there ensued a period of reflection and discussion on the future identity and mission of the National Distillers and Chemical Corporation.

By the mid-1980s, Quantum Chemical was not only the largest producer of polyethylene (as well as a major producer of other petrochemicals, including polypropylene, acetic acid, and vinyl acetate) and biggest distributor of propane, but had become the country's largest manufacturer of blankets and was still a major distiller of hard liquor and wines. The post-World War II years had witnessed further expansion into the liquor and wine fields, as well as film processing, fertilizer production, tire valve manufacture, the insurance business and, already mentioned, the manufacture of blankets.

After several years of assessment, stockholders in 1987 approved the adoption of the company's new name, "Quantum," reflecting their dedication to science and to scientific research and development. All businesses unrelated to this mission were sold one by one, including the company's sizeable liquor concerns, for a total of $684 million. Part of this new orientation was the expansion of research facilities, as the Allen Research Center in Cincinnati—headquarters of Quantum Chemical's USI Division. Constructed in 1991, it employs more than 200 research scientists, making it the one of the largest chemical research teams of any chemical corporation in the world.

Under Chairman John Hoyt Stookey, Quantum Chemical became a leader in the petrochemical and propane businesses, which is not without its problems. The majority of Quantum Chemical's sales are derived from its petrochemical products, primarily polyethylene, polypropylene, ethyl alcohol, acetic acid, and vinyl acetate, but is by no means limited to these. These industrial chemicals, byproducts of petroleum production, are used in a seemingly endless array of products: everything made of plastic is derived from industrial chemical production. Because of this enormous, substantial demand for plastics of all kinds, competition for this lucrative market is intense. The recession of the 1990s also presented financial difficulties for all chemical industries, including that of Quantum Chemical, and as a result several plants that had been built during the prosperous 1980s were forced to close. Similarly, with the outbreak of the Persian Gulf War in 1991, the price of ethylene, the essential raw material for many petrochemicals, skyrocketed for Quantum Chemical as for other major chemical firms. As a result of war and recession, a glut of polyethylene forced down the price of this useful commodity.

There also existed the threat of adverse weather conditions, especially affecting propane gas demand, which plunges in warmer winter weather. Another problem for Quantum Chemical was the expense of meeting increasing federal, state, and local environmental regulations, all of which were not without enormous cost. The company met environmental challenges by committing itself to a strategy of voluntary goals that include a 90 percent reduction in the release of carcinogens into the atmosphere by 1999 and a 50 percent reduction of all non-carcinogenic chemicals by 1995. Further, as a founding member of the American Plastics Council, the USI Division of Quantum is committed to recycling, also good for business. Recycled plastic reduces the dependency on foreign oil and is cheap and widely accepted by consumers. A huge new plastic recycling plant was constructed in 1992 for this purpose in Heath, Ohio.

Propane distribution is a far less volatile business than chemicals, the only fluctuation being the weather rather than economic or political conditions. In its infancy during the Depression, Suburban Propane was churning handsome profits. Nevertheless, because of the serious effects of the recession and the Gulf War on the chemical side of Quantum Chemical, Suburban Propane underwent major cost-cutting and streamlining as well as a redoubling of its efforts to secure more new customers.

While the problems facing Quantum Chemical—which was to be merged with Hanson PLC in September of 1993, pending shareholder approval—were very real, the company is well poised to meet the future. Despite some plant closures, Quan-

tum Chemical has, according to market analysts, among the most efficient plants in the world. Cost-cutting and streamlining have resulted in a minimum of job losses but a savings of $25 million a year. The company's exports and foreign market opportunities were expanding. The slack in the polyethylene market could well be overcome by the increasing use of methanol-based fuel in automobiles: Quantum Chemical is a major methanol producer and marketer. Finally, the demand for plastic continued to grow, and new uses were constantly being found. Developing countries were significant users of plastic but were producing little of it; as one of the oldest and most highly evolved of present day chemical companies, Quantum Chemical Corporation stood to benefit.

Further Reading:

Anton, Mark J., *Suburban Propane Gas Corporation; the Development of a Selectively Positioned Energy Company,* New York: Newcomen Society in North America, 1982, pp. 5–20.

Kiesche, Elizabeth S., "Quantum Leaps Into the Plastics Recycling Movement," *Chemical Week,* February 13, 1991.

Leaversuch, R. D., "Quantum Probes New Polyolefin Technology," *Modern Plastics,* July 1990, pp. 19–20.

McMurray, Scott, "Quantum Chemical Shares Expected to Post Long-Term Rebound, Bullish Analysts Say," *Wall Street Journal,* September 24, 1992, p. C2(W); p.C2(E).

"National Distillers Products Corp.," *Fortune,* November 1933, pp. 32–39 and 112–116.

Pilaro, Joseph F., "Quantum Chemical Corporation Statement," *Business Week,* April 1, 1992, p. 1.

Plishner, Emily S., "Quantum Fights Back From the Brink," *Chemical Week,* February 26, 1992, pp. 22–24.

"Profile of Quantum Chemical Corporation, USI Division," Quantum Chemical Corporation, 1993.

Quantum Chemical Corporation annual reports, 1987 and 1992.

"Quantum Leap," *Forbes,* March 2, 1992, p. 14.

Roberts, J. E., "Major Chemicals Industry—Industry Report," *Merrill Lynch Capital Markets,* January 4, 1993.

Shapiro, Lynn, "Methanol Surge Fuels Quantum, Georgia Gulf," *Chemical Marketing Reporter,* August 31, 1992, p. 8.

Stookey, J. H., "Quantum Chemical Corporation—Company Report," *New York Society of Security Analysts,* May 27, 1992.

—Sina Dubovoj

R. H. Macy & Co., Inc.

151 West 34th Street
New York, New York 10001
U.S.A.
(212) 695-4400
Fax: (212) 629-6814

Private Company
Incorporated: 1919
Employees: 60,000
Sales: $6.35 billion
SICs: 5311 Department Stores; 5632 Women's Accessory &
Specialty Stores

R. H. Macy & Co., Inc. operates through three department store
groups: Macy's East, Macy's West and I. Magnin. The groups,
in turn, operate approximately 133 stores that collectively occupy some 30 million square feet of space, located in 17 states.
Macy also operated 70 specialty stores, 12 inventory closeout
centers, and had interests in shopping centers. However, the
company's dramatic bankruptcy filing in January, 1992 led to
the closing of 66 stores by July, 1993. Macy stores target the
middle-to-higher-priced market, offering women's, men's, and
children's clothing and accessories; housewares; home furnishings; and furniture.

Rowland H. Macy made his fifth attempt at opening a retail
store in Manhattan in 1858. His previous four attempts with
similar stores had failed resoundingly, culminating, with the
demise of his shop of Haverhill, Massachusetts, in his bankruptcy. Although Macy's store was situated far north of the
traditional retail market, the store on Sixth Avenue near Four-
teenth Street sold a healthy $85,000 worth of merchandise
within one year.

Macy instituted a cash-only policy not only for customers but
for himself as well. No Macy's inventory was purchased on
credit, and no Macy's credit account was issued until well into
the 1950s. This was unusual in a day when most stores routinely
sold on credit. He maintained each product's assigned price, so
customers could routinely estimate how wide to draw the purse-
strings. The new store benefited from his advertising and promotion skills as well as his product line instincts. By 1870,
when sales broke $1 million, a stable clientele could purchase
not only dry goods, but items like men's hosiery and ties, linens

and towels, fancy imported goods, costume jewelry, silver, and
clocks.

Macy's son was not interested in the retail business, so Macy
passed ownership into other hands. In 1860 he hired his cousin
Margaret Getchell to do bookkeeping at the store, and she
subsequently married a young Macy's salesman, Abiel T.
LaForge. Macy increased LaForge's responsibilities, and eventually chose him as heir to half his store. The other half went to
Macy's nephew, Robert M. Valentine.

Valentine and LaForge became the proprietors when the
founder died unexpectedly in 1877 on a buying trip in France.
LaForge died soon after. Valentine bought LaForge's share, and
attempted to continue the family succession by bringing in
LaForge's relative, Charles Webster. When Valentine died,
Webster married his widow, and brought in his brother-in-law,
Jerome B. Wheeler. In 1887, however, Webster bought Wheeler
out, becoming the sole proprietor of a thriving business, which
he felt he could not perpetuate single-handedly.

Searching for a partner, Webster approached the Straus family,
who for 13 years had leased space in Macy's to operate a
chinaware department, the store's most profitable section. In
1887 it generated almost 20 percent of the store's sales. The
Strauses eagerly accepted Webster's offer, the partnership culminating many years' work and launching the family into a
social role comparable to that of the Rothschilds in Europe.
Lazarus Straus, the family's patriarch, emigrated in 1852 from
Germany to the United States, dissatisfied with Germany's collapsed 1848 revolution. After several years as a peddler, he was
able to send for his wife and four children. The family developed a successful general store in Talbotton, Georgia, then
moved to New York City in 1867 after the end of the Civil War.
Lazarus Straus bought a wholesale chinaware-importing firm
and brought his sons Isidor, Nathan, and Oscar into the business, renaming the company L. Straus and Sons.

Lazarus Straus died only a year after buying into Macy's but his
sons carried on the business. Under the new partnership,
Macy's matched and outpriced its rivals, including A. T. Stew-
arts, Hearn's, and Siegel & Cooper. Macy's sales rose to $5
million within a year, and subsequently continued to grow by 10
percent annually. The Straus brothers introduced their odd-price
policy, now used virtually everywhere in U.S. retailing. Charging $4.98 instead of $5.00, the store motivated consumers to
buy in quantity in order to accumulate substantial savings. Following in Macy's footsteps, the Strauses brought in line after
line of new merchandise—Oriental rugs, ornate furniture, lavish stationery, new-style bicycles, even pianos. They also instituted the store's depositor's accounts, in which shoppers could
make deposits with the store and then charge purchases against
them. This, in effect, provided Macy's with interest-free loans,
and was a forerunner of installment buying and layaway plans.

In 1896 Charles Webster sold his half interest in Macy's to the
Strauses, ending the founding family's line of ownership. Jesse,
Percy, and Herbert Straus, Isidor's sons, urged their father to
relocate the store to its Herald square location at 34th Street and
Broadway in 1902. The giant new store cost $4.5 million, but
funds were easily raised on the Straus family's good name, built
upon the success of Macy's and the independently operated

Abraham & Straus, acquired in Brooklyn in 1893.

No modern convenience was lacking in the Herald Square store. It was equipped with newly designed escalators, pneumatic tubes to move cash or messages, and an air exhaust system that provided the store with a constant supply of fresh air. Macy's spacious building had ample fitting rooms, accommodation desks, an information counter, and comfortable rest rooms. Macy's had a fleet of comparison shoppers who checked out other stores' prices to be sure Macy's merchandise was competitively priced. Sales pushed to $11 million within a year of the move. Called the world's largest store, Macy's Herald Square thrilled tourists and locals alike.

After his father's death, Isidor Straus had emerged as the family patriarch, and remained, among the sons, the most interested in the store. Nathan gradually developed more as a philanthropist than a businessman, and Oscar, after taking a law degree, disregarded the business in favor of politics. Isidor and his wife, Ida, were among the passengers on the ill-fated voyage of the *Titanic*. After their deaths in 1912, Isidor's sons Jesse, Percy, and Herbert bought out Nathan's interest in Macy's and ceded their interests in Abraham & Straus to Nathan. Nathan, thus, became the sole owner of Abraham & Straus.

As it did most of its products, Macy's sold books at substantially below their wholesale price—25 percent below. In 1909 a book publishers' association sued Macy, charging that the price-cutting hurt their copyright value. The Strauses countersued, claiming that the group constituted an illegal trust under the Sherman Antitrust Act. The publishers responded by cutting Macy off completely. The Strauses, however, obtained stock through other channels—wholesalers, transshippers, or other retailers who had overstocked; they even cut deals directly with authors. The U.S. Supreme Court decided in Macy's favor in 1913, but the controversy made it even tougher for the store to acquire well-known brands in any product line, prompting Macy's to develop its own private labels.

When World War I ended in 1918, sales were up to $36 million, twice that of 1914. Macy's began its expansion into other cities, acquiring substantial interests in LaSalles & Koch Co. in Toledo, Ohio, in 1923 and Davison-Paxon-Stokes Co. in Atlanta, Georgia, in 1925. In subsequent years the balance of stock in both companies was acquired. In the 1920s Macy's began the tradition of sponsoring New York City's Thanksgiving Day parade. The public relations impact of the event went national when two major television networks began to cover the parade in 1952. Just before the Great Depression, Macy's bought L. Bamberger & Co. of Newark, New Jersey, a division that would later lead a renaissance for Macy's. In the 1940s, it added stores in San Francisco, California, and Kansas City, Missouri. By the late 1940s, Macy's was not only the world's largest store but the United States's largest department store chain.

Jack I. Straus, Jesse's son, became chairman of Macy's in 1940. He had grown up with the store, having been present at age two at the Herald Square opening. He realized that the family line was thinning, and began training and promoting outsiders into the top executive positions in the firm. Over the years the Strauses would gradually lessen their holding in the company, but the family remained at the helm of Macy's until the 1980s,

when Edward S. Finkelstein, a manager hired by Macy's in 1948, led the company into an entirely new phase.

Straus passed the chairmanship of Macy's on to Robert (Bobby) Weil, his sister's son, as the 1940s ended. Weil beefed up Macy's advertising campaign, billing the store as the "community" store. Nevertheless, as the postwar economy picked up, New Yorkers no longer craved the bargains that were Macy's stock in trade, and did more shopping at other stores. Macy's stock fell from $3.35 per common share in fiscal 1950 to $2.51 in fiscal 1951. Further problems lay ahead.

In 1931 the Federal Fair Trade Law had allowed suppliers of certain products to specify a minimum retail price in order to stabilize the depression-era economy. With the exception of Korvettes, Macy's competitors—Abraham & Straus, Gimbel Brothers, Bloomingdale's, and B. Altman—abided by these minimums. In 1952, however, Schwegmann Brothers, a New Orleans, Louisiana, drugstore chain, contested the law and won its case. The reversal of the 20-year-old practice of price fixing undercut Macy's strategy. Macy's had undersold its competitors with its 6 percent-less-for-cash policy, but now that fixed minimum prices were not protected by law, all retailers could lower their prices without fear of being sued by suppliers.

Weil decided to combat this by cutting Macy's prices even further. The huge Herald Square store proved to have several weaknesses—while no one could match the giant's prices across the board, Gimbel could undersell Macy's in pharmaceuticals; Gertz of Long Island, New York, in books; and Bloomingdale's in stationery and menswear. In 1952 Macy's posted the first year of loss in its history. Its battle plan was outmoded; Macy's fumbled in directions it had previously ignored, instituting charge accounts and catering more to its suppliers.

While the flagship store struggled with image problems, a renaissance began in another division: Bamberger's of New Jersey. David L. Yunich took the helm of the decaying urban store in Newark in 1955. During his eight years of guidance, Bamberger's mushroomed, opening in suburbs all over New Jersey. The chain's annual sales rose from $82 million to $500 million, its profits being among the highest in the nation and topping even those of the mammoth New York division. Herbert L. Seegal and his protege Finkelstein came to Bamberger's in 1962 to step up its growth, using new customer-oriented merchandising. Instead of buying whatever suppliers offered, Bamberger's bought the top of the line in any new group of goods, and featured that in the most glamorous displays Bamberger's customers had ever seen. The technique garnered notice not only within Macy's but from top executives of other chains as well. The store began its push out of New Jersey to the south and west in 1968, and by the 1980s had three times as many stores as in the late 1960s. Bamberger's of New Jersey's sales for the fiscal year ending July 31, 1981, were $799 million; with Macy's California and New York divisions, it formed a powerful triad generating 86 percent of Macy's sales.

Macy's had acquired the old O'Connor, Moffat Co. store as its first California outpost in 1945. It was renamed and made Macy's flagship in San Francisco's then-posh Union Square. Like other urban retail centers, however, Union Square and its surrounding complement of chic shops, including I. Magnin,

Liberty House, the Emporium, Bonwit Teller, Gumps, and a host of others, fell victim to urban decay in the 1960s. Finkelstein was sent to bail out Macy's California in 1969. Macy's upgraded its image, aiming its product lines at a more well-heeled buyer. The transformation of California's 12 stores helped Macy's surpass most of its competitors, leaving it as one of the top three retailers, along with the Emporium and I. Magnin.

Finkelstein was brought back to the East in 1974 to work on the Herald Square store. He trimmed off such departments as pharmaceuticals, major appliances, sporting goods, and toys in which the store could not compete. Macy's put an end to its concentration on household durable goods, departments that got heavy competition from Korvettes and Sears as well as local department stores. In place of the discontinued departments, inventories were increased and presentations were refined in certain departments, including linens and domestics, furniture, menswear, and jewelry.

Finkelstein remodeled about 35 percent of the space in New York's 16 stores, including the Herald Square store, which benefitted from the installation of the Cellar in 1976. Macy's basement, which had been a no-frills depository for bargain merchandise, was transformed into a sparkling esplanade of airy specialty shops offering gourmet foods, yard goods, stationery, baskets, and contemporary housewares. Geared to a trend-conscious consumer, the cross between a European boulevard and a chic suburban mall also offered frequent cooking demonstrations, an old-fashioned apothecary, and a pottery shop complete with a working potter at the wheel. The Cellar caused such a stir that Bloomingdale's hastily installed a similar group of boutiques, although Bloomingdale's management claimed its conception predated the Cellar's opening. The revitalized Macy's had its biggest holiday season ever in 1976, and increased its annual earnings greatly from the previous year.

The chinks in Macy's formidable front were minor; competitors claimed that Macy's modern image was tarnished by its refusal to accept major credit cards. In addition, Macy's as a corporation lacked diversity. It operated only department stores, while most other similarly sized operations had diversified into specialty stores. Macy's eventually began development of such stores in the early 1980s.

In 1978 Finkelstein was promoted from president to chairman of Macy's New York division. The Macy Miracle, as it was called, gained momentum as annual sales soared between the years 1979 and 1982. In 1982 corporate sales gains of 20.1 percent topped the industry, and Macy's surpassed its major competitors in operating profit per square foot.

While other stores were consolidating departments under fewer buyers, Macy's added more buyers, encouraging them to find unique products. Stores were overstocked by 10 percent to 20 percent, so that unpredicted buying surges could be accommodated. It hired many executives for its training program, up to 300 per year in larger divisions. In 1984 Macy's had its best year ever. Sales rose 17.2 percent to $4.07 billion from 1983's $3.47 billion, which was up 16.4 percent from the previous year. At each of its 96 stores, Macy's averaged after-tax

profits of $2.31 million. During 1984 Macy's common stock soared in value.

The year 1985 was tough for most retailers, including Macy's. For the year, sales were $4.37 billion, up 6.4 percent from the previous year, but net income dropped almost 15 percent from $221.8 million to $189.3 million. The increase in sales was small compared to steady gains of 12 percent to 17 percent in the previous four years. Sales costs had risen, due to an increased advertising push, and to new staff training programs.

By 1984 Macy's bulky inventories had gotten out of hand. Inventories were 35 percent larger than in 1983. Prices were slashed, but the store could not seem to get rid of its excess. The store continued to build stock instead of eliminating it, miscalculating the buying force of the public; other stores were reducing their inventories. Finkelstein had attempted to expand his private-label lines; he kept the prices too high, however, to attract buyers. Finkelstein's vigilant management had never slipped before; the uncharacteristic miscalculation worried analysts. Wall Street began to waver in its praise. Macy's had the second-best year in its history in 1985, but the radical drops were not taken kindly in an institution that had been on a steady upward incline for over a decade.

Mergers and acquisitions abounded in the retail industry in 1985. A company with a weak profit record was a likely target because that performance pushed its stock value down, and a change in management could improve it. Although Macy's ten-year profit history was phenomenal, the recent questions from analysts were pushing Macy's stock prices down, and Finkelstein worried about a hostile takeover. In addition, he felt that his best executives were being lured to other stores. Rapid growth and subsequent compensation had satisfied his players over the past ten years, but now the store approached a plateau. Finkelstein had to do something to restore the company's vitality.

Finkelstein's solution was to lead the top 350 executives in a leveraged buyout of Macy's, at $70 per share, not much above a recent market high. He saw ownership and the subsequent share in profits as a way to motivate employees. Some shareholders objected, and one even filed suit, but the offer was sufficiently attractive that they eventually agreed. As for the Straus family, patriarch Jack was outraged, but in effect he had relinquished ownership long ago. In 1924 the Straus family had total ownership; by the 1960s, it was down to 20 percent; and by the 1980s, the family held only about a 2 percent interest in the chain. Its attachment to the store could not stop management from executing the biggest takeover of a retailer at that time and the first leveraged buyout of a major retail chain.

The year after the buyout, Macy's stores did so well that the chain could almost report a net profit, despite the debt service on the heavy borrowing needed to fund the buyout. In 1988 Macy's added further to its debt, however, by purchasing Federated's Bullocks and Bullocks-Wilshire and the I. Magnin chains. The $1 billion expenditure weighed heavily on company finances, but a confident Macy stocked stores with merchandise in anticipation of a strong holiday season in 1989. The economic recession of the late 1980s, however, had lowered consumer demand for the entire retailing industry, and sales during the holidays proved disappointing. Moreover, when a troubled major competitor, the Campeau retailing empire, ran huge sales to increase its cash flow, Macy had to follow suit. Burdened with an overstocked inventory that was selling too slowly, coupled with high spending on expensive promotions, Macy saw its earnings for the holiday season drop 50 percent.

Factoring companies that finance manufacturers' shipments to retailers tightened credit for those who did business with Macy, but the company was able to show that it was managing its cash flow through financial maneuvering that allowed Macy to get additional monies from major stockholders. In addition, the company sold two subsidiaries, Macy Credit Corp. and Macy Receivables Funding Corp. to General Electric Capital Corp. for $100 million, relieving the company of $1.5 billion in debt. Several months later, Macy completed the sale of its equity interest in the Valley Fair Shopping Center in San Jose, California.

The company, however, still had $4 billion in long-term debt, and in early 1990 rumors of bankruptcy started to circulate. The rumors persisted throughout the year and on December 4, 1990, Finkelstein took out a full-page ad in the trade journal *Women's Wear Daily* to quash them once and for all. Once again the store looked forward to holiday sales to boost cash flow, and once again there were heavy promotions and discounting to spur consumer demand. But the recession had persisted, consumer confidence was low, and sales were again below expectations. Sales throughout 1991 continued to be slow and Macy sustained further losses. Still another disappointing holiday season made it increasingly difficult for Macy to service its debt. To further cut its deficit, Macy's bought back $300 million of its bonds for less than 50 percent of their face value.

However, the poor retail climate combined with ineffective merchandising, diminishing public image, and lack of management focus led to further revenue losses. In early 1992 Macy announced an indefinite delay in paying its suppliers. A last minute effort by investor Laurence Tisch to buy $802 million of outstanding stock did not win creditor support. The final blow came on January 27th when Macy declared bankruptcy. By April, Finkelstein had been replaced by Myron E. Ullman III and Mark S. Handler.

The new co-executives devised a five-year business plan that included reducing the advertising budget from over 4 percent of sales to under 3 percent, fewer one-day sales, more-focused promotions, fewer private-label items, improved customer service, and a new computerized inventory management system. Store expansion continued, however, and in August of 1992, a new department store was opened in Mall of America in Minneapolis, the company's first in the Minnesota area. Later in the year a new Bullock's department store was opened in Burbank, California, and new I. Magnin stores replaced existing department stores in Phoenix and San Diego.

By early 1993, the plan had begun to show its effectiveness as Macy showed its first profit—$147.7 million—since filing for bankruptcy. Moreover, sales during the 1992 holiday season were better than expected, reaching $1.2 billion, while revenue was 3.8 percent higher than the previous year. Even with these promising results, however, Macy continued to rid itself of unprofitable operations. In March of 1993 the company announced that it would close 11 stores with low growth potential. The latest store closings included five department stores in Connecticut, New Jersey, and California, and six I. Magnin specialty stores in Seattle and cities in California.

Continuing its marketing strategy of reaching out to consumers in new ways, Macy announced in June of 1993 that it was planning to start a 24-hour television home shopping channel. Orders and customer service would be provided by the Home Shopping Network Inc. That month brought more promising news—sales of $1.34 billion for the quarter were 5.8 percent higher than the same period the previous year. In addition, sales in stores open at least one year increased 3.1 percent. Macy's cash flow was $28.5 million in the quarter, exceeding the requirements of its bank loans by about $6.5 million. Industry analysts reported that the strategy of increasing productivity and cutting costs, in spite of the continued poor economy on the coasts, was beginning to pay off for Macy. With these indicators of Macy's strengthened performance, the company hoped to end its bankruptcy by early 1995.

Principal Subsidiaries: Macy's Northeast Inc.; Macy's California Inc.; Macy's South Inc.; Bullock Inc.; I. Magnin Inc.; R. H. Macy Overseas Finance N.V.; Funding Corp.; Macy Receivables Master Servicing Corp.

Further Reading:

Barmash, Isadore, *Macy's for Sale,* New York: Weidenfeld & Nicolson, 1989.
Chakravarty, Subrata N., "Survivor on 34th St.," *Forbes,* August 6, 1990, p. 10.
Macy's New York 125th Anniversary: 1858–1983, New York: R. H. Macy & Co., Inc., 1983.
"Macy's Plans to Close Additional 11 Stores with Layoffs of 1,500," *Wall Street Journal,* March 2, 1993, p. B4.
Peterson, Thane, "Macy's is Trimmed in Red," *Business Week,* December 30, 1991, p. 48.
Pomice, Eva, "Macy's Hopes for Santa Claus," *U.S. News and World Report,* December 3, 1990, pp. 60–62.
R. H. Macy & Co., Inc. Annual Report, New York: R. H. Macy & Co., Inc., 1992.
R. H. Macy & Co., Inc. Quarterly Report, New York: R. H. Macy & Co., Inc., May 1, 1993.
"R. H. Macy Shows Profit for Five Weeks, Its First Since Bankruptcy-Law Filing," *Wall Street Journal,* February 2, 1993, p. B3.
Strom, Stephanie, "Home Shopping to Get Work for Macy Channel," *New York Times,* June 8, 1993, p. D5; "Macy shows Gain in Sales, Cash Flow," *New York Times,* June 12, 1993.
Zinn, Laura, "Prudence on 34th St.," *Business Week,* November 16, 1992, p. 44.
Zinn, Laura, and Christopher Power, "It's Too Soon to Write Macy's Obituary," *Business Week,* December 17, 1990, p. 27.

—Elaine Belsito
updated by Dorothy Kroll

Raychem Corporation

300 Constitution Drive
Menlo Park, California 94025-1164
U.S.A.
(415) 361-3333
Fax: (415) 361-7911

Public Company
Incorporated: 1957 as Raytherm Corporation
Employees: 11,000
Sales: $1.30 billion
Stock Exchanges: New York
SICs: 3678 Electronic Connectors; 3082 Unsupported Plastics
    Profile Shapes; 3567 Industrial Furnaces & Ovens; 3357
    Nonferrous Wiredrawing & Insulating; 3676 Electronic
    Resistors; 3613 Switchgear & Switchboard Apparatus

Raychem Corporation is one of the world's largest producers of industrial electronics components, serving such industries as aerospace, automotive, construction, consumer electronics, medical, and telecommunications, and generating annual sales in excess of one billion dollars. For many of its products, it is the leading supplier; for some, it is the only supplier. Raychem operates in a global economy, with manufacturing, sales, or research and development facilities in 40 countries, offering thousands of products in some 85 countries. In 1992, more than 60 percent of Raychem's sales and over 50 percent of its employees were outside the United States. Raychem is ranked among the *Fortune* 500 companies and is one of the top 100 U.S. companies in research and development spending, topping $128 million in 1992. Raychem manufactures over 50,000 different products, each of which is based on some advanced technology likely invented by the company itself.

The Raychem story begins with its founder, Paul Cook, a chemical engineer. A graduate of the Massachusetts Institute of Technology, Cook moved from the East Coast to the San Francisco Bay Area in the early 1950s to work at the Stanford Research Institute. While working at the institute, Cook saw potential in a relatively new branch of science at that time—radiation chemistry—which uses high energy electrons to alter the molecular structure of polymers. The name Raychem derives from this early technology in radiation chemistry that launched the company and still guides most of its research.

Cook used radiation chemistry to create Raychem's first commercial products: lightweight, rugged wire and cable for aircraft, and shortly thereafter, heat-shrinkable tubing. To make heat-shrinkable tubing, crosslinked plastic tubing is heated, then expanded and cooled in the expanded state. When heated again, the crosslinking forces the tubing to shrink to its original size. This phenomenon would prove to have many applications, including sealing splices in electric wiring harnesses and providing protective coatings on metal brake-line tubing. Developing innovative technologies with broad applications became the hallmark of Raychem.

For more than three decades, Raychem grew at an average rate of 25 percent per year, fueled by its reputation as a leading innovator of new technologies. Since the inception of the company, its goals have never wavered. In a 1990 interview with Cook, published in the *Harvard Business Review,* he discussed the Raychem philosophy—to develop core technologies and interpret them to serve the marketplace. Cook explained, "Then we draw on those core technologies to proliferate thousands of products in which we have a powerful competitive advantage and for which our customers are willing to pay lots of money relative to what it costs us to make them. Think about that. If you can pioneer a technology, use it to make thousands of products, sell those products at high price-to-cost relationships to tens of thousands of customers around the world, none of which individually is that important to you, you wind up with an incredibly strong market position. That philosophy hasn't changed for 33 years."

In that same 1990 interview, Cook said that in the first few years of Raychem, they were just learning what radiation chemistry could do, and within four years, they had generated virtually every idea behind the products they're selling today, including ones the company has been working to develop since that time. "Ten years ago, after we began work on conductive polymers, we identified a market for all the manifestations of the technology that totaled $747 million a year. We made our '747 list' and began working through it. At the time, it was a $5 or $10 million business. Today we're up to $150 million a year. So, we still have a long way to go," said Cook.

However, it is Raychem's philosophy toward competition and its efforts to make its own products obsolete that really sets the company apart from its rivals. Cook's philosophy was that the best way to compete was to avoid competition altogether by developing technologies that rivals couldn't touch—products that were more, not less, complicated to design and manufacture. He wanted products with small annual revenues, but he wanted lots of them. Cook declared in *Harvard Business Review* that "it takes a lot of confidence to believe that you can master a technology, stay ahead of everybody else in the world, capture markets based on that technology, obtain broad patent coverage, and then end up with a strong profit margin in a protected business." While other companies might develop a technology and then try to find ways to make its products a little better, a little cheaper, or a little more sophisticated, Raychem's approach was to determine if there were whole new ways to solve the problem—ways that might cut costs in half, or triple performance. Approaching the business in this manner, there was always the potential for making its own products obsolete, but inventing new technologies could also circumvent competition.

Pioneering new technologies is exactly what Raychem has succeeded in doing, applying those technologies in a myriad of industries. In the automotive arena, high-performance Raychem components were used in passenger vehicles for harnessing and circuit protection, and heaters produced by Raychem warmed diesel lines in cold weather. Components manufactured by Raychem were also used worldwide by telephone companies and cable television firms to connect, seal and protect copper, fiber optic, and coaxial connections. Water and gas utilities and pipeline companies utilized Raychem's heat-shrinkable products to reduce damage and protect pipeline systems.

In addition Raychem wire and cable interconnection systems could be found in aircraft, military installations, missile systems, and spacecraft, while the company's cable accessories were used extensively by the electrical distribution industry to help provide reliable power distribution by protecting cables from environmental hazards. In the medical arena, Raychem forged an alliance with United States Surgical Corporation, a fast-growing surgical equipment firm, to provide components for surgical instruments utilized in laparoscopic surgery, a minimally invasive technique used in gall bladder removal, hernia repair, and many other procedures.

Raychem was organized into three primary business segments in order to target the various markets in which the company operated and to foster a continuing entrepreneurial spirit, despite the company's size. The electronics business segment was established to provide the aerospace, automobile, computer, defense and medical industries with such products as electronic interconnection systems, heat-shrinkable insulation, circuit protection devices, computer touchscreens, and fiber optic cables. The industrial business segment served such areas of business as electric utility plants and environmental protection systems. The third segment of Raychem's business provided cable products and accessories to the telecommunications industry.

However, it was the fiber optics field that offered Raychem the greatest opportunity to boost it sales. Through the company's Raynet subsidiary, more than ten years of research and development in fiber optics technology, and an investment of over $150 million, has brought Raychem to the brink of becoming a leader in fiber optics applications for the home. In the not so distant future, advances in optics and electronics will create a society where optical fiber can be delivered to the home as cheaply as copper wire—establishing fiber optic highways between homes and businesses that will allow two-way information, entertainment, and electronic distributions, and creating a market potentially worth billions of dollars.

In the late 1970s, Raychem was wildly successful in the telecommunications industry as a supplier of splice closures which protected splices in the copper cables running from local telephone company offices to homes. It was one of the fastest growing segments of Raychem's business. Even then, Raychem management had only a glimmer of the potential of fiber optics, but began experimenting with the technology.

Eventually, Raychem turned its endeavors to local telephone companies and launched a major research effort. The goal was to develop a system for hundreds of residential telephone subscribers to share optics and electronics resources, creating economies of scale and drastically lowering the cost of delivering fiber optics to the home. This would be an entirely new core technology for Raychem. They set about hiring some of the best electrical engineers and physicists in the field and amassed a team that grew from 10 to 350 people in just three years. It was at this time that the Raynet subsidiary was established. An alliance was formed with BellSouth, a regional telephone company that invested $25 million in the fiber optics project. Raynet's efforts paid off with development of the Loop Optical Carrier (LOP) system that delivers fiber from local telephone companies to the home. But getting there was no easy feat for Raychem. While fiber optics had huge potential, research and development required much of Raychem's capital—it took $150 million to get Raynet on its feet. Subsequently, in 1992, Raynet won a $40 million contract from Deutsche Bundespost Telekom to begin commercial deployment of a fiber optic telephone system in Germany's eastern region. Raychem even began to sell to the Chinese telecommunications industry through a joint venture with Shanghai Cable Works. The project marketed products in a country where telephone density was low and opportunities for expansion of infrastructure were vast.

Using technology based on manipulation of the unique properties of chemicals, polymers and metals, Raychem has developed thousands of products affecting our daily lives from behind the scenes. With the company's philosophy and track record for technological innovation, Raychem is positioned to be a strong global competitor in the future.

Principal Subsidiaries: Sigmaform Corporation; Raynet Corporation; Bentley Harris France S.A. (France); Raychem Limited (U.K.); Raychem N.V. (Belgium); Raychem Pontoise S.A. (France); Raychem Canada Ltd. (Canada); Raychem (Australia) Pty, Ltd.; K.K. Raychem (Japan); Raychem A.G. (Switzerland); Raychem DISC, Inc.; Raychem International, Ltd. (Cayman Islands); Raychem International Manufacturing Corp.; Raychem Manufacturing Corp.; Raychem Middle East Intl., E.C. (Bahrain); Raychem S.A.I.C. (Argentina); Raychem GmbH (Germany); Raychem Products, Inc.; Raychem Industries, Inc.; Raychem Productos Irradiados, Ltda. (Brazil); Raychem Gesellschaft m.b.H. (Austria); Raychem Ltd.; Raychem A/S (Denmark); Raychem Aktie Bolag (Sweden); Raychem Inter-America, Inc.; Raychem International Corp.; Raychem S.P.A. (Italy); Raychem Singapore Pte. Ltd. (Singapore); Raychem S.A. (Spain); SHG-Strahlenshemie Holding GmbH (Germany); Walter Rose GmbH & Co. KG (Germany).

Further Reading:

Corporate Capabilities, Menlo Park, CA: Raychem Corporation.
Kindel, Stephen, ''Sandcastles: Running Raychem Like a Business May be Robert Saldich's Toughest Challenge,'' *Financial World,* October 2, 1990, p. 48.
Raychem Corporation Annual Report, Menlo Park, CA: Raychem Corporation, 1992.
''Raychem: Taking Stock,'' *San Francisco Business Times,* April 30–May 6, 1993, p. 28.
Taylor, William, ''The Business of Innovation: An Interview With Paul Cook,'' *Harvard Business Review,* March-April 1990, pp. 96–106.

—Kathie Levine

Rouge Steel Company

3001 Miller Road
P.O. Box 1699
Dearborn, Michigan 48121-1699
U.S.A.
(313) 323-9001
Fax: (313) 323-2270

Private Company
Incorporated: 1989
Employees: 3,200
Sales: $1.13 billion (1989)
SICs: 3312 Blast Furnaces & Steel Mills; 3316 Cold-
  Finishing of Steel Shapes

The Rouge Steel Company began as an integral part of Henry Ford's sprawling River Rouge automobile plant, built during the 1920s. The steelmaker remained a lucrative division of Ford until the early 1980s, when it lost profitability due to economic recession and a troubled U.S. auto market. In 1982 Ford Motor Company converted its steel division to form a wholly owned subsidiary. Sold to Marico Acquisition Corporation in 1989, Rouge Steel is currently the eighth-largest steelmaker in the United States, commanding five percent of the flat rolled domestic steel market with a steelmaking capacity of 3.2 million tons.

Rouge Steel grew out of Henry Ford's vision of an industrial facility that would bring together the various elements of his automobile production process. Envisioning a manufacturing plant that would transform raw materials into completely finished products, he developed the world's first vertically integrated factory complex.

In 1915 Ford stood on the Rouge's future site and declared it the perfect site to integrate iron-making facilities with his moving assembly line: "It's right here where we stand. Up in northern Michigan and Minnesota are great iron ore deposits. Down in Kentucky and West Virginia are huge deposits of soft coal. Here we stand, half way between, with water transportation to our door. You will look the whole country over but you won't find a place that compares with this." Ford began to acquire coal mines, and a battery of coking ovens were installed on the Rouge site. Coal was shipped into the Rouge by means of the Rouge River as well as by rail. The first of the Rouge's giant furnaces—the largest of its kind in the world at that time—was

finished in May 1920. Blast furnace "A" was blown in on its inaugural run when Ford's grandson, two-and-a-half-year-old Henry II, struck a match to ignite the furnace's coke charge. "B" blast furnace was added in 1922.

Steel was first made at the Rouge in 1923 with an electric furnace, and plans were made for furnaces with much greater production capacities. Ford, working with technical experts from the Morgan Construction Company of Worcester, Massachusetts, began developing large open hearth furnaces as well as blooming mills, rolling mills, and other steel-finishing equipment. Ford placed the development of the Rouge's steel facilities in the charge of John Findlater, who developed them in cooperation with Philip Haglund and Harry Hanson. Two years later, the Rouge's steel-making facilities were operational and the first "heat," or batch, of steel was poured on June 21, 1926. In that year the Rouge produced 321,476 tons of ingot steel, and output was doubled within three years. By 1929 the manufacturing complex covered almost 1,200 acres of land, 350 of which were taken up by the Rouge's steel-making facilities.

The Ford Steel Division continued to expand the Rouge's steelmaking capacity, adding a third blast furnace—furnace "C"—in 1948. Though steel-making technologies remained virtually unchanged, new furnaces and mills were added to Rouge's steel finishing operations during the 1960s. A move was made toward the consistent expansion of Rouge's use of scrap steel. In 1964 two basic oxygen furnaces were installed, making use of seventy-five percent "hot metal" from the blast furnaces and twenty-five percent scrap.

In 1976 two electric arc furnaces (EAFs) were added to Rouge's operations, capable of producing 850,000 tons of steel per year. The EAF facility, unlike the older blast furnace and basic oxygen furnace combinations, worked in a one-stage process that used only high-grade scrap steel. The EAF operation allowed Rouge a high level of flexibility and prepared the company for sudden increases in demand. The new equipment also allowed the company to maintain production during the periodically necessary process of re-lining the blast furnaces.

Rouge Steel moved into the 1970s with state-of-the-art equipment and, as a result, a vastly increased steel-making capacity. The company's outlook was bright: its principal customer, Ford Motor, was doing exceptionally well in the early years of the decade. However, a series of poor decisions by Ford management (including Henry Ford II's decision to cancel the development of a sub-compact model to replace the disastrous Pinto model) and an increasingly competitive U.S. auto market brought about a period of change in Rouge Steel's operations.

Compact cars became increasingly popular during the fuel crunch of the late 1970s, and a surge in small imports from Japan intensified competition for car buyers. The combined effects of Rouge Steel's increased steel capacity, import competition, and Ford's shift to smaller vehicles put Rouge's operation in the red.

In an effort to increase profitability, Ford gave Rouge Steel the unprecedented task of selling fifty percent of its production on the open market. Rouge had previously sold over eighty-five percent of its steel to Ford, and subsequently had little experience in more competitive markets. On January 1, 1982, chairman of Ford Motor Philip Caldwell announced Ford's conversion of its Ford Steel Division to the Rouge Steel Company. "The new subsidiary will provide additional operating and financial flexibility for future growth of steel operations," Caldwell said. "The establishment of Rouge Steel is the first step in a new Ford plan to view its various businesses as independent entities." Shortly afterward, Ford placed Rouge Steel on the market.

In the summer of 1982, a consortium of Japanese companies under the leadership of Nippon Kokan (NKK) began negotiations with Ford for the purchase of Rouge Steel. NKK wanted to buy seventy-five percent of Rouge at a purchase price of several hundred million dollars, and the Japanese firm had proposed a multi-million dollar modernization plan that would include installation of a high-tech continuous steel casting system and a galvanizing operation. Talks between Ford and NKK collapsed in 1983, however, because the Japanese wanted to reduce Rouge's labor costs. Workers at Rouge Steel—organized under the UAW rather than the U.S. Steelworkers because of Rouge Steel's origin within Ford Motor—maintained an hourly rate of pay almost $5 higher than the U.S. industry standard.

Following the failed talks with NKK, officials at UAW Local 600 began to negotiate with Ford over proposed wage reductions at Rouge Steel. Philip Caldwell had announced that Ford Motor was suffering its worst economic downturn since the Great Depression: in the four years preceding 1983, Ford had lost $2.1 billion and had eliminated 67,000 workers from a workforce of 158,000. Clearly, operations at the Rouge had to change, and meetings between Caldwell and UAW Local 600 president Michael Rinaldi in the summer of 1983 resulted in wage and benefit reductions for Rouge Steel workers. In return, Ford agreed to spend $300 million for a new continuous casting system and an electro-galvanizing facility and rebuild a coke oven battery. The agreement proved to be a watershed in Rouge Steel's history.

Over the next three years, Ford began an intensive program of investment in new equipment for the steelmaker. Over $300 million worth of improved technologies were purchased, including a rebuilt coke-oven battery, a sophisticated continuous casting system, and an electro-galvanizing operation which was opened as a joint venture between Rouge and U.S. Steel, dubbed Double Eagle. The new galvanizing operation was capable of producing 700,000 tons of galvanized sheet metal per year for use in automotive factories, the largest such operation in the world.

Installation of the continuous caster was a landmark event, and brought Rouge back into a competition with other U.S. steelmakers. The new facilities reduced the cost of producing slab steel by $40 per ton as well as increasing the quality of the steel produced. The system was installed in cooperation with Hitachi Zozen officials as technical advisor.

In 1986 Rouge Steel president Paul Sullivan commented in an interview with *Automotive News* that "It's sad, but the truth is steel technology has left the U.S. We're no longer leaders, but followers. All the new equipment made in the U.S. today is based on technology that either originated with or was refined

by the Japanese." This turn of events was ironic: Henry Ford had envisioned a continuous casting operation as early as the 1920s, according to company historian Alan Nevins. In his official company history, entitled *Ford: Expansion and Challenge,* Nevins wrote: "Just as [Ford] had modified the methods of manufacturing iron, he meant to improve the making of steel. He was convinced that a flow of production could be established. For example, he envisaged open hearth operations as continuous, raw materials being added from time to time, and the molten metal drawn off as needed and made directly into castings." The Rouge, however, waited almost seventy years for such a system to be installed.

Along with heavy investment in new equipment, Ford spent $10 million in 1986 on an innovative re-training program for 232 employees: the Rouge workers were given 30 weeks of instruction in the use and maintenance of the continuous casting equipment, and core groups were sent to steel plants in Japan to train with experienced operators. Another group of Rouge employees worked with LTV of Cleveland, Ohio, and their continuous casting equipment. Most of the re-trained employees had been working with traditional steelmaking methods for up to fifteen years and the training they received stressed flexibility. "The idea was to have a crew in which anybody could do anything," Hivens A. Gill told *Iron Age* magazine. In order to achieve that flexibility, more traditional UAW work classifications had to be relaxed to provide for only two classes of maintenance workers: mechanical and electrical.

In 1988 Rouge Steel finished its fiscal year in the black for the first time in over a decade, and by the end of the year, almost seventy percent of the steelmaker's output was produced in their new continuous casting facility. Improved relations between the Rouge's management and UAW leaders in conjunction with the success of Rouge Steel's updated casting and galvanizing facilities enhanced the steelmaker's position in the highly competitive U.S. market, particularly in the Midwest's aging Rust Belt. Rouge continued to re-invest in upgraded equipment during 1988 and 1989, with $100 million spent in 1988 alone. The company improved the quality of their steel with the purchase of a ladle metallurgical/re-heating facility and an innovative vacuum de-gassing operation, and improved the efficiency of their existing equipment by computerizing hot strip mill controls to improve consistency and installing enhanced equipment on different mill processes. Rouge also converted their powerhouse boilers to permit the use of both coal to natural gas in an effort to reduce power costs. The improved steel-making technologies and worker training at the Rouge made the company more productive than ever before in its history: Rouge Steel produced 69 percent more steel in 1988 than it produced thirty years earlier.

Rouge Steel was still up for sale in 1988, despite the turnaround in the company's balance sheets. David Blackwell, president of Rouge Steel in 1988, commented that "Ford has recognized that steel is not their area of expertise and they have determined that steel is not a core part of their business." Ford's decision to sell the plant was based on the assessment that Rouge would be a stronger company and a better supplier as an independent entity. Talks between Ford and interested buyers continued.

On December 15, 1989, the Marico Acquisition Corporation acquired eighty percent of Rouge Steel's stock from the Ford Motor Company, and Marico merged with Rouge Steel. Marico, headed by Carl Valdiserri, former executive vice- president of Weirton Steel Corporation, had been formed in 1989 for the express purpose of gaining equity ownership of the Rouge. In addition to Valdiserri, Worthington Industries, Inc.—a Columbus, Ohio–based steel fabricator—gained a strategic equity interest in Rouge Steel. As part of its investment in Rouge Steel, Worthington agreed to a long-term purchase agreement to buy a minimum of fifty percent of its flat-rolled requirements. The deal assured Rouge an opportunity to increase its business as well as guaranteeing Worthington a dependable long-term steel supply at competitive prices. Ford retained an equity interest in Rouge Steel and continued to purchase between thirty and forty percent of the steelmaker's total annual output.

Rouge Steel entered the 1990s in a favorable position, considering the weakened condition of the U.S. steelmaking industry. Paul Sullivan, head of Rouge Steel from 1983 to 1986 had called Rouge "a beleaguered company in a distressed industry." With Ford's purchase of up-to-date casting facilities, new labor contracts between the UAW and Rouge's management, and the completion of an extensive modernization of the company's mills in 1988, Rouge Steel had pulled itself from a fifteen-year decline in profitability and efficiency to become an ambitious player in the American steel industry.

Principal Subsidiaries: Double Eagle Steel Coating Company (50%); Rouge Complex Powerhouse (60%); Eveleth Taconite Company (85%).

Further Reading:

Dougherty, Mary Beth, "Rouge Steel Is Out of the Red," *Iron Age,* October 1988.
"Ford Seeks to Trim Labor Costs at Rouge," *Iron Age,* May 20, 1983.
"Ford Trying to Sell Rouge Steel to NKK," *Iron Age,* August 11, 1982.
Kertesz, Louise, "The Man of Steel," *Automotive News,* June 16, 1986.
Lippert, John, "The Rouge Reborn," *Detroit Free Press Magazine,* January 8, 1989.
"Rouge Steel Will Spend $100 Million on New Equipment," *Iron Age,* December 1987.
"Rouge's Workers Were Ready for the First Cast," *Iron Age,* March 1987.
Samways, Norman L., "Rouge Steel: A Major Independent Strip Producer," *Iron and Steel Engineer,* April 1984.
——, "Rouge Steel Enters the 1990's," *Iron and Steel Engineer,* April 1991.
Versical, David, "Resurrected Rouge to Turn First Profit in Decade," November 2, 1987.

—Thomas Bohn

Roussel Uclaf

35 Boulevard de Invalides
75007 Paris
France
(1) 40 62 40 62
Fax: (1) 40 62 49 49

The company is 54.5% owned by Hoechst A. G. and 40%
  owned by the French State
Incorporated: 1961
Employees: 16,551
Sales: FFr 14.81 billion (US$2.51 billion)
SICs: 2834 Pharmaceutical Preparations; 5122 Drugs,
  Proprietaries & Sundries; 2879 Agricultural Chemicals
  Nec; 2861 Gum & Wood Chemicals.

Roussel Uclaf is one of France's most important pharmaceutical companies and among the world's leading diversified pharmaceutical groups. The multinational corporation was the center of controversy in the late 1980s and early 1990s due to its nationalization and the growing presence of foreign concerns on the domestic market, in addition to the company's abortifacient, RU 486. However, Roussel Uclaf remains a source of pride for the French despite the fact that Hoechst A.G., a German company, holds a major interest in the French firm.

In 1920 Dr. Gaston Roussel established the Institut de Sérothérapie Hémopoiétique (I.S.H.) for the production of Hémostyl. Later he directed the fledgling company toward the area of chemotherapy. The 1928 establishment of the Laboratoires Français de Chimiothérapie and of U.C.L.A.F. (Société des Usines Chimiques des Laboratoires Français) strengthened the company in this area. Over the course of the next several years the company grew through acquisition and expansion. Subsidiaries in Mexico, Brazil, and Argentina began operation and a second factory in France at Vertolaye was acquired.

Upon Dr. Gaston Roussel's death in 1947, Jean-Claude Roussel, the founder's son, took over the leadership of the growing company. Although already well established both in France and abroad, Roussel Uclaf's vast expansion subsequent to the founder's death is attributed to his son's business acumen. As a successful industrialist, Jean-Claude Roussel managed the company virtually by himself and expanded operations into a diverse array of businesses. These included such widely disparate activities as chemicals and aviation. The chemical operations are now organized into Nobel-Bozel, a distinct arm of the group's activities.

By 1961 production demands required the company to restructure its operations. To streamline various scientific, industrial and commercial operations, the Roussel Uclaf Group was formed as the subsidiary holdings of the Roussel Uclaf Company. Today the Roussel Uclaf Group engages in such diverse activities as health care, agricultural products, bulk chemicals and consumer products.

Jean-Claude Roussel continued his single-handed management of the company until a 1968 vacation in the south of France where he was introduced to a senior Hoechst director. The successes of the family enterprise had become a source of pride for the French population. This encounter, however, inspired Roussel to pursue a policy to "Europeanize" his company. The result of this meeting led to the West German company purchasing a 43 percent stake in the Chimio holding company which controlled Roussel Uclaf.

This agreement represented an historical undertaking; never before had two private European companies cooperated under the auspice of the Common Market. Despite the implications such a purchase held for the French pharmaceutical industry, Roussel reassured the French government that certain agreements would protect the market from ever completely losing the industry to a foreign company. These agreements provided the French government with authority to decide on the future sale of shares, and also stipulated that Hoechst would never attempt to enlarge its holdings. In addition, it was also agreed that Roussel himself would never sell his personal holdings.

Roussel Uclaf's association with the large West German concern proved useful to both parties. Both companies' chemical operations benefitted by the establishment of the joint venture Nobel-Hoechst Chimie. Furthermore, the association enabled the French company to make use of Hoechst's marketing structure in the Far East and in North America as well as to form its own marketing company within Germany. Hoechst, on the other hand, benefitted from Roussel's successful research in the area of steroids. By far the most beneficial aspect of this partnership, however, was the development of products through joint research. In 1969, Claforan, a third-generation antibiotic, represented the joint efforts of these two companies. Launched in the European, U.S., and Japanese markets, the drug generated over $100 million in 1982.

Yet the original agreement established between the two companies was destined to change. An unfortunate chain of events allowed Hoechst to gain a majority interest in its French partner. In 1972 Jean-Claude Roussel and several company executives were travelling in a helicopter manufactured by Roussel Uclaf's aviation division. En route to Roussel's summer home the helicopter hit a cable line, killing all the passengers aboard.

The Roussel family, still a major shareholder, was suddenly faced with the disposition of Jean-Claude's estate. Since most of Roussel's estate was intimately connected with the activities of Roussel-Nobel, this posed financial problems. In order to remedy these extenuating circumstances, a number of immediate changes went into effect. A five-man executive team called the "collegiate management" took over all decision making responsibilities formerly held by Roussel. It has been suggested that this structure afforded the German company greater influence over Roussel Uclaf's activities.

Soon after this restructure took effect, the Roussel family announced that financial demands to meet the disposition of the estate compelled them to sell a large amount of voting stock in Chimio. This announcement came at a time of renewed debate on nationalizing the French pharmaceutical industry. With the election awarding victory to a socialist government, the communist minister of health, Jack Ralite, spoke in favor of including Roussel in a nationalized industry. At the same time the French ministry was attempting to find "French solutions" to solve the growing problem of foreign company takeovers. Thus, to keep Roussel Uclaf "French" the government solicited the aid of Rhone-Poulenc, France's largest chemical concern, and Elf-Aquitaine, the state-controlled chemical company. Neither company, however, expressed interest in the purchase of the Roussel shares of stock.

Although the resulting sale found the French government gaining half the seats on the company's supervisory board as well as increasing its holdings in the company to 33 percent, the purchasing party was neither a competing French company nor the state. Instead, Hoechst had increased its holdings to 51 percent. Many people reacted to this state of affairs with disappointment; foreign participation in the French pharmaceutical industry now surpassed 50 percent and drugs patented by international concerns accounted for over 75 percent of all pharmaceuticals on the domestic market.

Notwithstanding the turn of events, the government's solution represented a pragmatic approach to limit the costs of its expensive program of nationalization. At the same time, Hoechst benefitted from Roussel's research in agricultural products and the French company continued to benefit from their partner's marketing organization. Some 65 percent of Roussel's total sales in 1981 came from overseas markets, a figure that was greatly supported by Hoechst's marketing organization. Furthermore, joint research and development would enhance the already successful area of antibiotics.

To appease those members of the French population that opposed Hoechst's increased holdings, the French government issued a statement to the effect that it would eventually increase its interest in Roussel Uclaf; in 1982 the government succeeded in acquiring a 40 percent share. Throughout these proceedings the management of Hoechst maintained that Roussel would always remain an independent entity. One major exception to this occurred with the 1974 creation of a joint subsidiary in the United States.

Roussel's growth subsequent to the agreement was impressive. In 1975 the company diversified into the perfume industry with the purchase of a major interest in Parfums Rochas. Several years later Roussel entered the sunglass industry through the purchase of a French company and Foster Grant, the American manufacturer. In addition, Roussel Laboratories, the subsidiary established in the United Kingdom during the 1930s, had grown into a preeminent British concern.

Total research and development expenditures in 1983 amounted to over $110 million which represented a 22 percent increase over the previous year. The company entered the field of biotechnology through the creation of a genetic engineering unit. Using biochemical fermentation, Roussel's Romainville Centre is said to be the greatest molecular biosynthesis installation in the world. Here the company concentrates on the production of vitamin B12, antibiotics, and veterinary products. At two other sites, one in France and one in Brazil, the company is engaged in multistage synthesis through chemical fermentation. Here corticosteroids and norsteroids are produced.

In addition to these products Roussel manufactured a broad array of successful pharmaceuticals and chemical products. Surgam, an anti-inflammatory drug, garnered strong sales for Roussel, and Rythmodan, a cardiac rhythm regulator, accounted for 58 percent of the world sales for this type of pharmaceutical. The company also manufactured Deltamethrin, an active ingredient in a biodegradable group of products found in agricultural insecticides. This group is said to be the most powerful but least toxic of all agricultural products on the market. When Roussel Uclaf purchased Wellcome plc's environmental health business in 1991, it became a principal player in the worldwide environmental health insecticide industry, manufacturing products for the household, lawn and garden, public health, grain storage, and timber protection markets.''

Roussel Uclaf began preparing for the unified European market in the early 1990s by consolidating its drug production at the main manufacturing facility at Compiegne, France. Modernization and economizing measures were also prescribed by consultants who examined the corporation in the early years of the decade. The company's pharmaceutical division stumbled in 1992, when sales dropped almost 12 percent. Roussel Uclaf's health, agroveterinary, and chemical units picked up the slack, and sales at the end of the year totaled FFr 14.81 billion, a gain of more than 2.5 percent on the year.

Roussel Uclaf grew more widely known in the 1990s for its development of the so-called "abortion pill," RU 486. The drug was developed by Dr. Etienne-Emile Baulieu and announced in 1982. After six years of clinical tests involving 17,000 women, the French government announced that the controversial drug would be made available for public use. When religious leaders in France protested the drug, Roussel quickly removed it from the market, but doctors from around the world petitioned the French government to force Roussel to distribute RU 486. In 1989 the drug was made available to all of France's abortion clinics and hospitals. One hundred thousand Frenchwomen used it successfully over the next several years. These favorable results convinced both Sweden and Britain to license RU 486, but other countries waited for the United States to make a decision on the drug.

The administrations of successive U.S. Presidents Ronald Reagan and George Bush banned RU 486 from the United States beginning in 1989. Enactment of the ban may have been premature—although distribution of the drug in America had the potential to generate $1 billion in revenues for the company, Roussel resisted licensing to that country for fear of the country's politically-charged atmosphere surrounding abortion. In the early 1990s, no American drug company had come forward to license the drug for the same reason. But 1993 brought a new American president and a new policy regarding RU 486. The Clinton Administration cleared the way for testing in 1992, and that April Roussel licensed RU 486 to the U.S. Population Council, a nonprofit organization headquartered in New York City.

Although the drug is most frequently associated with abortion, European research has shown that RU 486 may be indicated as a treatment for endometriosis, a leading cause of female infertility. The drug's hormone-blocking attributes may also help treat breast cancer and Cushing's syndrome, a life-threatening metabolic disorder. It has even been indicated for such varied conditions and diseases as diabetes, brain cancer, and obesity.

While RU 486 captured the media's attention in the early 1990s, Roussel's primary products included new antibiotics sold under the tradenames Rulid, Claforan, Orelox, and Oflocet. Deltamethrin, Rythmodan, and Surgam continued to contribute significantly to the company's sales. In addition Roussel conducted further research in such diverse areas as cardiovascular diseases, nervous system disorders, dermatology, psychotropics, and infectious diseases. Furthermore, Roussel's activities outside the area of human health care, including veterinary medicines, consumer goods, chemicals, and agricultural products, continued to produce successful products. The French company's penetration of foreign markets has been very successful with Japan and the United States representing major market thrusts. Overall, the association between Roussel and Hoechst has been mutually beneficial and both companies appear satisfied with the arrangement.

Principal Subsidiaries: Application des Matières Plastiques S.A., Sté d' (SAMP); Applications Scientifiques et Medicales S.A., Sté d' (SAMS); Applications Tehniques de l'Oest S.A. (ATO); Centramite de Courtage, Sté; Collectorgane S.A.; Distriphar S.A.; Distrivet S.A.; Farquimia S.A. (Argentina); Grupo Roussel México S.A.; Immobilière du 3 Square Desaiz S.A.; Laboratoires Cassenne S.A.; Laboratoires Cassenne Takeda S.A.; Laboratoires Diamant S.A.; Laboratoires Lutsia S.A.; Les Laboratoires Roussel & Cie. S.N.C.; Les Laboratoires Roussel S.A.; Parfums Rochas S.A.; Procida S.A.; Union Chimique Continentale S.A.; Albert Roussel Pharma GmbH (Germany); Albert Roussel Pharma GmbH (Austria); Roussel SA (Belgium); Ruckor SA (Belgium); Cooper Mac Dougall et Robertson (Belgium); Roussel Laboratories Ltd (Great Britain); Roussel Uclaf Environmental Health Ltd (Great Britain); Roussel BV (Netherlands); Sochiphar BV (Netherlands); Roussel Nordiska AB (Sweden); Sofir SA (Switzerland); Roussel Iberica SA (Spain); Laboratorios Hosbon SA (Spain); Hoechst Roussel Veterinaria AIE (Spain); Roussel Hellas SA (Greece); Roussel Italia SpA; Roussel Pharma SpA; Roussel Hoechst Agrovet SpA (Italy); Biochimica Opos SpA (Italy); Camillo Corvi SpA (Italy); Roussel Portugal Ltda; Roussel Laboratories Pty Ltd (South Africa); Sofaco SA (Ivory Coast); Roussel Cameroun SARL; Societe Africaine d'Investissements et de Participations SA (Morocco); Roussel Diamant Maroc SA (Morocco); Sotrachimm SA (Morocco); Roussel Senegal SARL; Roussel Tunisie SA; Roussel Argentina SA; SARSA (Brazil);Larec Ltda (Equador); Roussel Centro America SA (Guatemala); CARUSA (Guatemala); Laboratorios Helios SA (Mexico); Equipos Agricolas Helios SA (Mexico); Laboratorios Larpe SA (Peru); Roussel de Venezuela SA; Roussel Uclaf Australia Pty Ltd; Tianjin Roussel Uclaf Pesticide Co Ltd (China); Roussel Korea Co Ltd (South Korea); Roussel Uclaf Hong Kong ltd; Roussel India ltd; Nippon Roussel Co Ltd (Japan); Nippon Uclaf Co Ltd (Japan); Roussel Morishita Co Ltd (Japan); Roussel NZ ltd (New Zealand); Roussel Vietnam SARL; Hoechst Roussel Canada INc.; Roussel Canada INc; Roussel Uclaf Holdings Corporation; Roussel Corporation; Hoechst Roussel Pharmaceuticals Inc.; hoechst Roussel Agri-Vet Cy (U.S.A.); Roussel Uclaf Corporation (U.S.A.); Granutec Inc. (U.S.A.).

Further Reading:

Jackson, Debbie, "Roussel Uclaf Study Calls for Sweeping Changes," *Chemicalweek*, May 29–June 5, 1991, p. 16.
Smolowe, Jill, "New, Improved and Ready for Battle," *Time*, June 14, 1993, pp. 48–51.

—updated by April S. Dougal

RPM Inc.

2628 Pearl Road
P.O. Box 777
Medina, Ohio 44258
U.S.A.
(216) 273-5090
Fax: (216) 273-5061

Public Company
Incorporated: 1947 as Republic Powdered Metals, Inc.
Employees: 3,000
Sales: $625.7 million
Stock Exchanges: NASDAQ
SICs: 2851 Paints & Allied Products; 5198 Paints, Varnishes
& Supplies

RPM Inc. ranks among the United States' top five paint and allied products manufacturers, with markets in over 75 countries around the world. It is one of only 19 public companies on Gene Walden's list of the *100 Best Stocks to Own in the World,* and by 1992 had raised dividends 19 consecutive times. *Financial World* has recognized RPM as one of the best managed companies in America, awarding it three consecutive Bronze Awards for executive leadership. Recognition was also extended to the company's products when RPM was chosen to provide corrosion control coatings for the restoration of the Statue of Liberty in the mid-1980s.

Headquartered in the small city of Medina, Ohio, RPM has recorded over 46 consecutive years of growth in sales and earnings. It is operated as a holding company, but all its businesses focus on the specialty coatings and chemicals markets. Recent success has been based on a strategy of growth through acquisitions, which has expanded the holding company to include 38 operating companies in the United States, Canada, Holland, Belgium, and Luxembourg. These additions have led RPM activities to group their activities into five primary markets: industrial waterproofing and general maintenance; industrial corrosion control; specialty chemicals; consumer do-it-yourself; and consumer hobby and leisure. The industrial and specialty chemical markets account for 60 percent of RPM's sales.

RPM founder Frank C. Sullivan had built a successful career as a sales executive with a Cleveland paint manufacturer, but decided to move out on his own in 1947. He started the company, then called Republic Powdered Metals, Inc. in 1947 in a garage on Cleveland's west side with a $20,000 investment. The company manufactured a single product called Alumanation. This heavy-duty protective coating has endured as one of RPM's biggest sellers.

Sullivan's original goal was to create and sell industrial maintenance products—to waterproof, rustproof, and protect existing structures. In order to carry out that goal, he concentrated on attracting talented workers, then provided them with a constructive atmosphere in which to develop their abilities. These original goals remain a high priority at RPM. In addition, financial success during Republic Powdered Metals's first ten years was driven by a management team whose members would spend their entire business lives working at RPM. As late as 1987, eight of the ten men were still active in the management of the company. RPM's leadership has long been lauded as one of the most successful and experienced in the coatings industry.

In its first year Republic Powdered Metals achieved $100,000 in revenues, and by 1957 the company had reached the $2 million mark. By 1961 Republic Powdered Metals's sales had outgrown its production capabilities, and a new plant was build in Gliroy, California. That year, Tom Sullivan joined his father's company, advancing to executive vice president in 1965.

As domestic sales grew year after year, RPM turned its attention to the international marketplace. Success in that arena came quickly, and the effort was rewarded with increasing profits and President Lyndon Johnson's "E" Award for excellence in export expansion in 1964. That year was a turning point for RPM. Frank Sullivan and his management team realized that, to continue to grow and prosper, they had to choose between selling out or going public. In 1964 they chose to go public, and offered 1,000 shares of stock at eight dollars per share, but purchasers were limited to Ohioans until the first national stock offering in 1969. RPM's headquarters were moved to Medina, a small community 25 miles south of Cleveland, that year.

This infusion of capital enabled RPM to make its initial acquisition in 1966. The purchase of the Bondex Company of St. Louis, Missouri, brought RPM into the realm of consumer products with the only nationwide line of household patch and repair products. That first purchase also established many of the criteria for RPM's future acquisitions. The company sought to purchase low-volume, high-margin niche companies that were performing well—as Tom Sullivan pronounced in the *Cleveland Enterprise* in 1992, "We don't do turnarounds." Each product was expected to match RPM's gross profits of 40 percent. A hallmark of the Sullivans' system was that a prospective acquisition have an enthusiastic management team in place, since those leaders would continue the administration that had drawn RPM's attention in the first place. RPM has also focused on companies that do not rely on Original Equipment Manufacturers (OEM). That way, RPM and its operating companies are not as sensitive to market fluctuations and economic downturns. Most of RPM's products augment existing equipment and industrial facilities, avoiding the cyclical nature of companies that rely on new construction or sales of capital goods. Finally, RPM looked for "synergism" with its existing product lines, encouraging the leaders of each operating company to find products or technologies that might compliment the products of their colleagues.

RPM's success was tragically disrupted in 1971 with the unexpected death of Frank C. Sullivan on August 18. The shock precipitated a crisis situation: according to Frank's son and successor, Tom, the elder Sullivan had been ''the individual most closely identified with [RPM].'' As the new chairman, president, and chief executive officer, Tom feared that the company would lose its credibility along with its leader.

To fend off such speculation RPM was incorporated as a holding company under which Republic Powdered Metals, Bondex, and any new acquisitions would operate as wholly-owned subsidiaries with a large degree of independence in their daily operations. Since 1972, that ''hands off'' approach has become a model for all RPM's acquisitions and a strategy envied by other large corporations. Jerry J. Dombick, an industry analyst, praised RPM's ''mutual fund of businesses'' in a 1993 *Chemical Week* article.

During the years from 1968 to 1977, RPM's sales grew from $7 million to $57 million annually, but the ten-year period was, in the words of the 1987 annual report, ''a real test for the RPM management team.'' The challenge came from outside the company; between 1972 and 1974 the Dow Jones Industrial Average lost almost half of its value. RPM's stock dropped from a high of 23 to 8 points, in spite of continuously growing sales and earnings.

Despite that brief, but dramatic, downturn, RPM acquired a dozen companies over the course of the 1970s, including Maharam Fabric—later renamed Design/Craft Fabrics—Proko Industries Inc., and Thibaut Wallcoverings. In 1977, RPM purchased all of Alox Corp.'s stock, thereby acquiring that producer of rust corrosion inhibitors and adding Alox's $5 million annual sales to the balance sheet. The purchase of Maharam Fabric, a Chicago designer and distributor of decorative non-apparel fabrics for the construction industry, had added another $10 million in sales to RPM's bottom line.

Later in 1977 RPM announced an offering of 860,000 common shares, which helped to finance the decade's many acquisitions. The stock was issued in November, and sold out the same day. Before the decade was out, RPM acquired Dean & Barry Co., a 77-year-old Columbus-based manufacturer of paints and protective coatings. Before the 1970s' flurry of acquisitions was ended, Mohawk products, a well-known brand in the furniture touch-up industry, and Mameco International, a Cleveland manufacturer of urethane sealants, flooring systems, and coatings, were also added. Founded in 1913, Mameco brought sales of $10 million annually to the growing list of RPM subsidiaries.

With all of the acquisitions came increased responsibilities, and in 1978 Tom Sullivan and the board of directors decided to divide his leadership role into two positions: president/chief operating officer and chairman/chief executive. Sullivan recommended his longtime associate and executive vice president, James A. Karman for the president's position. The two met at Miami (of Ohio) University and worked together for 16 years before the formation of the holding company. From that point forward, Karman oversaw RPM's daily operations, while Sullivan concentrated on acquisitions and public relations.

In the 1970s and 1980s RPM's exports grew, complemented by overseas licensees and joint ventures that accounted for $50 million in annual sales by 1987. From 1976 to 1985, the company's sales compounded 330 percent, fueled primarily by astute acquisitions. At that time 80 percent of RPM's products fell into the industrial category, while the balance was consumer-oriented. Between 1978 and 1987, RPM divested $50 million in weaker margin operations, and sales grew from $57 million to $300 million. During this period, RPM added several consumer-oriented subsidiaries, and its operating companies concentrated on the development of consumer products in several categories: household, automotive aftermarket, and hobby and leisure.

In mid-1983 RPM ventured into the Eurobond markets to finance numerous acquisitions during the decade. ''Eurobond'' designates securities sold in countries that do not utilize the currency of the bond's denomination. They were attractive to RPM and many other large corporations for several reasons: better rates; less expensive legal, printing, and underwriting costs; and more favorable terms.

In 1980, RPM purchased all assets of Haartz-Mason Inc., a Boston manufacturer of synthetic rubber products, which added sales of about $8 million per year to the list. Euclid Chemical Co., a 1984 acquisition, brought a leading manufacturer of liquid and powder concrete additives into RPM's product lineup. Founded in 1910, Euclid Chemical had about 40 employees and estimated sales of $12 million in 1984. Testor Corporation, a Rockford, Illinois, maker of glue and paints for hobbyists, was purchased from Jupiter Industries Inc. that same year. Founded in 1929, Testor was the world's best-known hobby and craft trademark. The company earned national attention in the mid-1980s when it released a 12-inch plastic replica of the top secret F-19 Stealth fighter jet. Aside from the free publicity, the incident helped to illustrate the high degree of autonomy and responsibility enjoyed by the presidents of RPM's operating companies—Testor's president took all press inquiries, and few news reports mentioned Testor's relationship to RPM.

Westfield Coatings Corp., manufacturer of specialized high-performance coatings for the paper, wood, and metals industries, was purchased in January 1985. A stock offer of 700,000 shares at $15.50 each was made in connection with the Westfield acquisition. Later that year, RPM acquired Carboline Co. from Sun Co. Inc., which put the company at the forefront of specialized corrosion-control products. As RPM's largest acquisition, Carboline expanded RPM's product lines to include specially-formulated corrosion-control products used to maintain nuclear reactors. The St. Louis company was one of only a few manufacturers in this exclusive industry, a key factor in its acquisition by RPM. Other Carboline products for the energy, chemical, paper and pulp, and highway industries were manufactured at factories in Ohio, Louisiana, California, and Wisconsin.

RPM returned to the Eurobond market in 1986 for $30 million at just 5.75 percent. The sale helped finance capital investments in manufacturing facilities worldwide and the continued high rate of acquisitions throughout the 1980s. That same year RPM acquired American Emulsions Co. of Dalton, Georgia, a manufacturer of specialty coatings and chemicals for the textile, carpet, and paper industries with annual sales of $10 million. The addition of William Zinsser & Co. of Somerset, New Jersey, brought more consumer items to RPM's roster of products. The company was the leading U.S. manufacturer of primer-sealers, shellac finishes, and special wallcoverings for the professional and do-it-yourself markets, and its brand of edible glazes for candy and pharmaceutical applications was the leading one in those fields. Craft House Corp., a maker of craft, hobby, and toy products with $20 million in annual sales, further expanded RPM's do-it-yourself business in 1987. Chemical Specialties Manufacturing Corp., Baltimore, was a producer of coatings, cleaners, and additives for the carpet, textile, and floor care market that was added in 1988.

National interest in RPM developed in the mid-1980s. The company had been ranked among *Dun's Business Month'* s top five "dividend achievers" for 1983 through 1986 and cited as one of *Fortune'* s ten fastest-growing dividends. But despite this recognition, many institutional investors remained largely unaware of RPM's achievements. However, when RPM's stock price fell from 17 to 10 after the "Black Monday" stock market crash on October 19, 1987, analysts noted that the bulk of RPM's 14,000 individual shareholders kept buying, while other individual investors were scared off. Due to this loyalty the stock was able to recover within the same year.

One reason for the neutralization of the crash was related to the U.S. government's national public health advisory regarding the carcinogen radon. On September 12, 1988, the federal government advised all homeowners and renters nationwide to test for radon gas. Later that fall, RPM became one of the first companies to announce the development of a radon barrier system. The Bondex Radon Blocking System, a non-toxic, water-based sealant designed to protect homes and other buildings from radon gas seepage, was produced by Bondex International in 1989. RPM's stock took its sharpest jump in history after the disclosure concerning the five-step radon sealant.

Unfortunately, with increased investor and analyst attention came takeover speculation. Using some of RPM's own acquisition criteria—an attractive growth record and superior leadership—some analysts hypothesized in the late 1980s that RPM was ripe for acquisition by one of the chemical industry's giant corporations. They often emphasized RPM's 53 percent debt-to-total capitalization ratio, which some industry analysts criticized as too high. Sullivan downplayed the threat, noting the early 1990s low interest rates and the high operating returns of RPM's acquisitions.

The younger Sullivan's business acumen has not only been highlighted by acquisitions, but by divestments as well, especially since 1983. During the ten-year period ending in 1993, RPM sold off businesses accounting for $100 million in sales. Such divestments usually followed a product's move from a niche market to a commodity. For example, when Firestone entered the ethylene propylene diene monomer (EPDM) roofing membrane market in the early 1980s, prices plunged over 75 percent, from 70 cents per square foot to 17 cents per square foot. As a result RPM sold off the EPDM operation, even after sinking $10 million into product development.

The recession of the early 1990s did not slow RPM's acquisition or earnings pace. While the economic downturn made many of the 1980s' winners into losers, the worst it has done to RPM is to slow its growth rate. And it was during this time that RPM made its first venture into the high-quality marine paint market with its second-largest acquisition. Kop-Coat, Inc., of Pittsburgh, had a diverse line of coatings products under the Wolman, Pettit, Woolsey, and Z-Spar brand names and $55 million in annual sales.

RPM also entered into a joint venture in 1990 with Holderbank Franciere Glaris S.A. of Switzerland, one of the world's largest producers of cement. The arrangement involved the sale of 50 percent of Euclid Chemical Co. to Holderbank's special materials division, Holderchem. The following year saw the expansion of RPM's European influence with the purchase of Rust-Oleum's Netherlands and French operations. The activities complimented RPM's previous forays into Belgium and Luxembourg and gave the company increased access to the world's markets.

In 1991 RPM became the dominant player in fluorescent colorant markets with the purchase of Cleveland's Day-Glo Color Corp. The increased popularity of fluorescent colors in the 1990s saw them applied to plastics, textiles, paints, and inks. Day-Glo constituted about 40 percent of that growing industry. Later that year, RPM acquired Martin Mathys, a manufacturer of specialty protective coatings for the building maintenance and construction industry. Martin Mathys was founded in 1845, and had distribution throughout the European marketplace by the time it joined RPM's roster. In June of 1993 RPM also acquired Dynatron/Bondo Corporation of Atlanta, Georgia, which manufactured and marketed products for professional and consumer use in the automotive aftermarket.

RPM's sturdy portfolio has been carefully positioned for continued growth, and as the United States began to emerge from the economic slump of the early 1990s, RPM's consumer products have been strong performers. In terms of industrial products, Tom Sullivan expected the corrosion control segment to experience further growth. Historically, the company has demonstrated an ability to grow during good times and bad, with one of the best records in American industry. RPM has sailed through raw materials shortages, runaway inflation, record-high interest rates, and several post-World War II recessions with much success, as evidenced by 46 consecutive years of rising earnings and sales, ranking RPM among America's best companies.

Principal Subsidiaries: Alox Corporation; American Emulsions Co., Inc.; H. Behlen & Bro., Inc.; Bondex International, Inc.; Bondex International Ltd. (Canada); Carboline Company; Chemical Coatings, Inc.; Chemical Specialties Mfg. Corp.; Consolidated Coatings Corporation; Craft House Corporation; Day-Glo Color Corporation; Design/Craft Fabric Corporation; Dynatron/Bondo ACEuclid Chemical Co. (50%); Floquil-Polly S Color Corp.; Haartz-Mason, Inc.; Kop-Coat, Inc.; Label Systems Corp.; Mameco International, Inc.; Martin Mathys, N.V. (Belgium); Mohawk Finishing Products, Inc.; Mohawk Finishing Products Ltd. (Canada); PCI Industries, Inc.; Paramount Technical Products, Inc.; Radiant Color N.V. (Belgium); RPM/Belgium, N.V.; RPM/France, S.A.; RPM/Luxembourg, S.A.;

RPM/Netherlands, B.V.; RPM International, Inc.; RPM World Travel, Inc.; Republic Powdered Metals, Inc.; Sentry Polymers, Inc.; Talsol Corporation; Testor Corporation; Richard E. Thibaut, Inc.; Westfield Coatings Corp.; Wisconsin Protective Coatings Corp.; Wm. Zinsser & Co., Inc.

Further Reading:

"A Star Performer That the Pros Have Overlooked," *Business Week,* July 29, 1985, p. 68.
Bendix, Jeffrey, "RPM Stirs It Up!" *Cleveland Enterprise,* Summer 1992.
Byrne, Harlan S., "RPM Inc.: It's a Good Bet to Extend Its Long String of Earnings Gains," *Barron's,* February 5, 1990, pp. 57–8.
Gerdel, Thomas W., "Medina Firm is Top Corporate Achiever in Dividend Payout," *Plain Dealer* (Cleveland), December 10, 1983, p. 2C.
Gleisser, Marcus, "RPM Splits Stock, Hikes Dividend for 19th Straight Year," *Plain Dealer* (Cleveland), October 10, 1992, p. 1F.
Karle, Delinda, "Medina Firm's Radon Sealant Excites Investors," *Plain Dealer* (Cleveland), October 3, 1988, p. 5B.
Keische, Elizabeth S., "RPM On a Roll," *Chemical Week,* January 27, 1993, p. 51.
Koshar, John Leo, "Burgeoning RPM Reorganizes," *Plain Dealer* (Cleveland), September 30, 1978, p. 4D.
Marcial, Gene G., "Has This Outfit Found a Miracle for Oil Spills?" *Business Week,* May 22, 1989, p. 150.
Maturi, Richard J., "Finance: Not Just For Giants," *Industry Week,* October 5, 1987, pp. 34–5.
"Metals Firm Chief Frank Sullivan Dies," *Plain Dealer* (Cleveland), August 19, 1971.
"Page From Father's Book Led to Successful Acquisitions," *Plain Dealer* (Cleveland), September 18, 1986, p. 15B.
"Profit Protector: RPM's Winning Streak Left Unbroken by Economy's Slump," *Barron's,* August 8, 1983, pp. 42–3.
"Radon Gas Sealant Rings Stock Bells for Medina's RPM," *Plain Dealer* (Cleveland), September 24, 1988, p. 10C.
"The Radon Scare Has RPM Glowing," *Business Week,* October 17, 1988, p. 102.
"Revving Up: RPM Inc.'s Sales Speed Ahead With a Boost From Carboline Co." *Barron's,* December 9, 1985, p. 68.
"RPM Becomes Major Player With Purchase of Day-Glo," *Plain Dealer* (Cleveland), August 31, 1991, p. 1F.
"RPM Called Safe as Nest Egg; Dividends, Stock Grow Yearly," *Plain Dealer* (Cleveland), September 18, 1986, pp. 14B, 15B.
"RPM Chairman Predicts More Good Years," *Plain Dealer* (Cleveland), October 31, 1985, p. 6B.
RPM, Inc. Annual Report, Medina, OH: RPM, Inc., 1987.
Yerak, Rebecca, "Lessons Learned the Hard Way Give Local Executives Business Savvy," *Plain Dealer* (Cleveland), March 1, 1992, pp. 1E, 3E.

—April S. Dougal

Russell Corporation

P.O. Box 272
Alexander City, Alabama 35010
U.S.A.
(205) 329-4000
Fax: (205) 329-5045

Public Company
Incorporated: 1902 as the Russell Manufacturing Company
   of Alexander City
Sales: $899 million
Employees: 16,000
Stock Exchanges: New York
SICs: 2329 Men's & Boys' Clothing, Nec; 2321 Men's &
   Boys' Shirts; 2231 Broadwoven Fabric Mills, Wool; 2253
   Knit Outerwear Mills

From humble origins in a small Alabama town in 1902, Russell Corporation has evolved into the country's premier designer, manufacturer, and marketer of athletic and leisure wear clothing for men and women. In 1992 Russell Corporation was awarded a five–year contract to serve as the exclusive producer and marketer of athletic uniforms for most Major League baseball teams. The company is America's largest producer of athletic uniforms and has the number one market share in the fleece screen printing business.

Founder Benjamin Russell was only 25 when he bought six knitting machines from R. A. Almond in 1902. Russell, a struggling lawyer in Birmingham, Alabama, was anxious to return home to Alexander City and open his own business. With borrowed money, he incorporated the Russell Manufacturing Company in 1902, remaining its president until he died in 1941. Russell's knitting machines, 12 sewing machines, and 12 employees were crammed into a 50 by 100 foot wooden building. Because of the lack of electricity, Russell Manufacturing Company relied on steam for power. At the end of the first year of production, the company turned out 150 items of clothing per day. Though first year profits were disappointing, the entrepreneurial young owner envisioned his plant expanding into all aspects of the garment making business.

Russell's dream was slowly realized and profits grew steadily in the following years. Six years after opening his plant, Russell acquired spinning frames, allowing the company to produce its own yarn. Several years later, it could bleach its own cloth.

Electricity came to the plant in 1912, and two years later a second yarn plant went into operation.

Demand for cloth and yarn shot up dramatically during World War I, during which time the company expanded and prospered. When the war ended, the ensuing recession left the company unaffected because the demand for yarn continued. In response, the company added workers and plants. Also at this time, the Russell Mill School was established for educating the children of employees and for adult programs. The company's fourth yarn plant began operation in 1921, and in early 1927 a weaving operation was installed. By the end of the year Russell Manufacturing Company could dye its own cotton and yarn, coming close to realizing Benjamin Russell's ambition of making his company a completely vertical or "fiber to fabric" operation.

Until 1932, however, fabric still had to be sent to other U.S. plants for finishing. Despite the company's profit losses during the Great Depression, Benjamin Russell decided to expand his business. The worst year of the Depression, 1932, turned into a milestone year for the 30-year-old company; it acquired full finishing operations, thereby becoming one of the few fully vertical fabric factories in the world. That same year Benjamin Russell's son Benjamin C. Russell established an athletics division called the Southern Manufacturing Company. Its first products were football jerseys sold to a sporting goods distributor in New York. In 1938 the company's first screen printing developed for the printing of names, numbers, and designs on athletic uniforms. In 1960 the Southern Manufacturing Company was renamed the Russell Athletic Division. No one in 1932 would have guessed that this unobtrusive sideline would alter the company's identity from that of a domestic fabric manufacturer to a global leader in the sportswear industry.

Civilian textile manufacturing declined during the World War II because of enormous government clothing contracts that strained the company. By war's end, machinery was badly in need of repair because replacement materials had been difficult to obtain during the war years. In addition the company's founder, Benjamin Russell, had died at the outset of World War II. His son Benjamin C. Russell took over the helm during the difficult but prosperous war years, but died prematurely of pneumonia in 1945. Another Russell son, Thomas Dameron Russell, succeeded to the helm. By the time he stepped down as president 23 years later, the company had become a leading manufacturer of athletic and leisure wear and exited the fashion clothing manufacturing business.

In the 1950s sporting and leisure wear had not yet caught on with the general public. With two domestic recessions, the company was hard hit by falling sales and growing competition, and expansion was temporarily impeded. Changes in the clothing industry, however, helped Russell rebound. By the early 1960s, T-shirts had become acceptable garb for both sexes. In the late 1960s the unisex trend in clothing strengthened while comfortable, leisure clothing became popular in the early 1970s. These trends served to Russell's advantage. In 1966 a new sewing plant was established in Montgomery, Alabama (the first Russell plant to be built outside of Alexander City). Four years later, the Athletic Division had expanded so much that a separate plant became necessary. The company went public in 1963. The firm, whose name had altered in 1962 to

Russell Mills, Inc., would be a public stock-holding company in which the Russell and insiders family would continue to own approximately 32 percent of the stock.

In 1968 Eugene C. Gwaltney became president of Russell Mills (which in 1973 would alter its name to the current Russell Corporation). That year company sales stood at $51 million. During Gwaltney's term in office, plant expansion continued. The company's screen printing facilities were enlarged and it acquired a yarn manufacturing plant in northeast Georgia in 1977. In the mid 1970s Russell opened a new distribution center in Alexander City. All operations at this ultramodern facility, such as storage retrieval, shipping, and goods reception, were fully automated and consolidated. At the same time, new buildings went up to house operations including data processing, personnel, and security. By 1981, with the consolidation of knitting into one plant, Russell could boast the most modern knitting facilities in the world. Expansion into Florida and south Alabama took place after 1982, the year Eugene Gwaltney was elected chairman of the board and was succeeded as president by Dwight L. Carlisle.

In 1989 Russell Corporations's test and evaluation mill was constructed at a cost of $6 million. This was an innovative facility in which new machinery was evaluated before purchase, avoiding the interruptions in operations implicit in tests during the production process. By 1990 the company owned and operated 13 sewing plants outside of Alexander City and employed 15,000 workers. Since 1976 sales revenues had increased by 13 percent annually. With the acquisition of two subsidiaries, Quality Mills in North Carolina and Cloathbond Ltd. in Scotland, in 1988 and 1989 respectively, the company had become a global contender in the sportswear industry.

According to market analysts, a key to the company's success is its aggressive technological modernization. In a five year period ending in 1992, the company invested more than a half billion dollars in capital expenditures which translated into approximately 15 percent of annual sales—far higher than the industry's average of eight percent. In addition, the company spends at least three percent of sales revenues on print and television advertising. In both 1980 and 1990 *Textile World* cited Russell Corporation as the "Model Mill" of the year. Another reason for the company's success is research and development. In 1992 an innovative new material that prevents pilling, NuBlend, was introduced in Russell's *Jerzees* line of sportswear and won accolades from the leisure wear industry. Partly because NuBlend is the preferred fabric for screen printers, Russell holds the top market share in the fleece screen printing business at 30 percent.

Under President and Chief Executive Officer John C. Adams, approximately 80 percent of Russell Corporation's sales are derived from its principal divisions, Athletic, Knit Apparel, Fabrics, and its major U.S. subsidiary, Cross Creek Apparel, Inc. (formerly Quality Mills). The company is the biggest manufacturer of athletic uniforms in the nation. Russell's contract to manufacture uniforms for Major League Baseball teams also stipulates that the company holds the exclusive right to manufacture and market replicas of major league uniforms, T-shirts, and shorts. This has put the company in an advantageous position in relation to its main rival, Champion, Inc., the supplier of uniforms to the NBA teams. The Knit Apparel Division produces the *Jerzees* brand of active wear, such as T-shirts, fleece, knit shorts and tank tops, which are sold to specialized retailers and large merchandisers such as Wal-Mart.

North Carolina's Cross Creek Apparel, Inc. produces the Cross Creek Pro Collection, such as casual knit shirts and rugbys, that are sold mainly in golf pro shops, and Cross Creek Country Cottons, purchased by screen printers and embroiderers for resale. The remainder of Russell's sales revenues are derived from the Fabrics Division, which manufactures and markets lightweight cotton material for sale to clothing manufacturers, and from its European subsidiary, Russell Corp. UK Ltd. in Scotland. This subsidiary is also a vertical establishment that manufactures and markets a full line of Russell clothing, from the cotton fiber to the finished product, for the European market.

By the early 1990s, the company was approaching $1 billion in sales. While technological modernization and continuous research have redounded to the firm's success, that achievement would be less if the company had not turned to overseas markets. With the acquisition of Cloathbond, Inc. in 1989 (now Russell Corp UK Ltd.), Russell Corporation has a foothold in the expanding European market. In 1992 alone, Russell's international sales increased 40 percent over 1991, a figure expected to rise in the coming years. Also in 1992, the company established a small wholly owned subsidiary in Mexico which markets Russell active wear for the growing Mexican and South American markets.

Industry observers believe that the one of the keys to Russell Corporation's growth is the expanding international market. As one of the oldest companies producing athletic wear, Russell is poised to fill such international demand for American type sportswear.

Principal Subsidiaries: Cross Creek Apparel, Inc. (Mt. Airy, North Carolina); Russell Corp. UK Ltd. (West Lothian, Scotland).

Further Reading:

"Annual Report," Alexander City: Russell Corporation, 1991, 1992.
Esquival, J. R., "Russell Corporation, Company Report," *Shearson Lehman Bros., Inc.,* February 5, 1993.
Leibowitz, David S., "Finding Value in Small Town America (Russell and Dean Foods' Stocks)," *Financial World,* February 2, 1993, p. 86.
Miller, Andy, "Russell Hopes to Score with Baseball Apparel," *Atlanta Constitution,* January 21, 1992, sec. D., p. 1.
"Russell's All Star Line-up: Managing for the Distance; Russell Manufacturing Tops Technology Curve," *Textile World,* June 1990, pp. 40–64.
Saunders, Thomas B., "A History of Russell Corporation," Alexander City: Russell Corporation, 1990.
Smarr, Susan L., "Looking at the Big Picture," *Bobbin,* February 1990, pp. 60–64.
Welling, Kathryn M., "Out of Fashion Buys: An Analyst Cottons Up to Selected Apparel Stocks," *Barron's,* July 9, 1990, pp. 12–13, 28–29, 50.

—Sina Dubovoj

RYLAND

The Ryland Group, Inc.

11000 Broken Land Parkway
Columbia, Maryland 21044-3562
U.S.A.
(410) 715-7000
Fax: (410) 715-7196

Public Company
Incorporated: 1967 as The James P. Ryan Company
Employees: 3,200
Sales: $1 billion
Stock Exchanges: New York
SICs: 1521 General Contractors Single Family Houses; 6162
    Mortgage Bankers and Correspondents; 6159
    Miscellaneous Business Credit Institutions; 8370
    Construction & Related Industries; 5250
    Telecommunications Systems; 8120 Retail Banking
    Services

The Ryland Group, Inc., is the third-largest home building and mortgage-finance business in the United States. A company with sales of over $1 billion in 1992, Ryland is unusual in its geographical range and diversity, building homes in seventeen states and in over forty markets. The firm's two principal divisions, Ryland Homes (RH) and Ryland Mortgage Company (RMC), service all of the prospective home buyer's needs, from home building to mortgage loan assistance. Since its founding in 1967, the company has built well over 100,000 homes, with current prices ranging from $60,000 to more than $500,000.

The company was originally named after its founder, James P. Ryan, an energetic real estate entrepreneur who established the James P. Ryan Company in Columbia, Maryland, in 1967. Columbia was a new, planned community of 220 single-family-homes situated mid-way between Washington, D.C., and Baltimore, Maryland. Ryan created the name "Ryland Homes" when he chanced upon a sign that was supposed to say "Maryland," but on which the first two letters had been covered; "Ryland" struck him as the ideal name for his homes.

Operating in a dynamic and highly volatile housing market, Ryland developed a marketing strategy targeted toward the middle class or up-and-coming middle class: homes were built with only brand-name construction materials and appliances and sold in the middle range, starting at $20,000. Ryland sought to be a highly focused home building business rather than a development company speculating in land dealing or the development of "raw" land. In its first year of operation, the company concluded forty-eight sales and made a modest profit of $12.7 million.

In 1971 the company went public and changed its name to The Ryland Group, Inc. That same year Ryland broke ground on another planned community, Peachtree City, outside of Atlanta, Georgia. Here Ryland Homes, with their careful attention to detail, frequent inspections at crucial phases of building, and use of only premium brand name materials and appliances (Anderson windows, Armstrong floor coverings, Owens Corning Fiberglass, General Electric stoves and refrigerators), struck a balance between cost, quality, and choice that was extremely popular with consumers. The customer could select from fifteen different floor plans and from a variety of different housing styles that often reflected regional tastes. Ryland also was building a variety of homes, from single-family dwellings to townhomes (the "townhome" concept was pioneered by Ryland) to condominiums, just as the last was growing in popularity. Ryland's building venture prospered, and more than 75 percent of its employees became stockholders.

The next several years saw further expansion into Texas. Ryland manufacturing centers, initially called Ryland Building Systems (later integrated into the Ryland Homes division in 1992), were also constructed at this time, providing preassembled, factory supervised home building components to the home site. By 1977 Ryland had penetrated the Midwestern market as well as the Philadelphia area, and had completed its 10,000th home. A mere eight years later, in 1985, Ryland celebrated the completion of its 50,000th home.

The purchase in 1978 of Crest Communities in Cincinnati, Ohio, launched Ryland's mortgage operations, modestly begun through Crest's subsidiary Crest Financial Services. From there Ryland Mortgage Company grew to become one of the nation's largest mortgage-finance companies, offering a full range of mortgage financing with branches in eighteen states. In 1981, with the acquisition of Guardian Mortgage Company, RMC introduced full loan servicing. By the early 1990s, RMC was handling more than $2 billion in mortgage loans on an annual basis. In 1982 RMC formed Ryland Acceptance Corporation (which became a wholly owned subsidiary of RMC in 1987), an administrator and distributor of mortgage-backed securities.

During the 1990s Ryland entered the booming Florida and California home building markets. In the latter, the M. J. Brock Corporation, with divisions in Los Angeles and Sacramento, was acquired in 1986. Ryland homes were marketed in California under the Brock or Larchmont Homes labels, and by the early 1990s 40 percent of the company's business derived from southern California. At that time, however, the savings and loans scandal and the recession of the early 1990s struck California especially hard and moderated returns from land investment in the Golden State.

Fortunately, at the same time Ryland was expanding in California, it was also vigorously penetrating markets in Arizona, Colorado, Georgia, and North and South Carolina. In 1987 Ryland crossed the $1 billion mark in revenues; that same year founder James P. Ryan retired from the board of directors. In

1989 Ryland established the Cornerstone Title Company, a wholly owned subsidiary of RMC in Columbia, Maryland, that administered real estate closings.

Market analysts gave Ryland credit for its geographical diversity, which enabled the company to compensate for difficulties in California and other local markets experiencing periodic difficulties. Ryland expanded into the Midwest as well as expanding its activities in the Southwest.

With mortgage interests declining during the recession, Ryland Mortgage Company had record profits, derived largely from entering the ''spot loan'' origination market. The savings and loans crisis, which culminated in the federal government taking over the ailing financial institutions and selling off their assets one by one, also became and advantage for RMC. Ryland's powerful mortgage servicing division, one of the largest in the country, benefitted from the federal government's assumption of mortgage servicing contracts when S & L home mortgages were taken over by the government; by the early 1990s, they comprised approximately 50 percent of RMC's mortgage servicing portfolio.

With the worst of the recession over by 1993, the company was stronger than ever. The housing market had recovered completely, with the exception of California and Florida. Thanks to Ryland's geographical diversity and its conservative business philosophy, it had not only weathered the recession (earnings climbed a phenomenal 191 percent between 1991 and 1992) but, unlike many of its competitors, company finances were in the black. Annual revenues still topped $1 billion. The company's four manufacturing centers, which produce the basic materials (lumber and trim) for all Ryland homes except those in the western states, were working over capacity. Ever attuned to the marketplace, the company shifted its marketing strategy in the 1990s to larger homes that do not necessarily cater to first time home buyers. The average price of a Ryland home has climbed to over $150,000, with resulting larger profit margins.

In February 1991, Ryland Homes was asked to build single-family housing units in Israel because of that country's massive influx of immigrants from Russia. Unlike Israeli stone houses, which take an average of eighteen months to build, Ryland homes could be assembled in a matter of weeks. Eventually, 1,300 housing shells were carefully packed in crates for assembling in Israel. In so doing, Ryland became the biggest American manufacturer of Israeli homes, earning a profit of $13

million, and currently has the strongest overseas market base among its domestic competitors, the two biggest being Centex and the PHM Corp.

Also in 1991 the company formed a new subsidiary, Ryland Trading Ltd., to specialize in building Ryland homes for the overseas market, with a particular eye toward market opportunities in Eastern Europe and the former Soviet Union. The federal government even contributed $400,000 in two grants to Ryland Trading Ltd. to encourage it to study housing-market opportunities and the construction of housing factories in the former Soviet Union.

The result was the first U.S. housing project in newly renamed St. Petersburg, Russia, which had not seen the completion of new private housing in over seventy years. In 1992 Ryland, in a joint venture with Russian companies, began a housing settlement outside of the city consisting of American-style homes priced at $150,000 and up. The homes were targeted toward the increasingly large contingent of foreign businessmen and women in Russia. In a very short time Ryland Trading Ltd. had also expanded its joint-venture portfolios with Mexico, Spain, Turkey, and Senegal.

Principal Subsidiaries: Ryland Mortgage Company; Ryland Trading Ltd.

Further Reading:

Allen, B., ''Housing Snapshots—Industry Report,'' *Oppenheimer & Co., Inc.,* September 25, 1992.
Annual Report: The Ryland Group, Inc., 1972, 1973, 1992.
Blumenthal, Robyn G., ''Ryland Group Inc. Indicates Net Rose in Third Quarter,'' *Wall Street Journal,* October 12, 1992, p. B6A (E).
Fink, Ronald, ''Ryland Group: the Contracyclical Developer?'' *Financial World,* March 3, 1992, p.15.
Kaplan, Peter, ''Ryland Leads Home Builders in Work Abroad,'' *Baltimore Business Journal,* February 21, 1992, sec. 1, p. 3.
Nejmeh, G. A., ''Ryland Group—Company Report,'' Shearson Lehman Brothers, Inc., June 8, 1992.
Snow, Katherine, ''Russian Houses to Carry 'Made in USA' Label,'' *Business Journal–Charlotte,* September 21, 1992, sec. 1, p. 1.
Wells, Melanie, ''Builders Still Falling as Market Hits Bottom (Washington Area Residential Real Estate Market),'' *Washington Business Journal,* September 2, 1991, p.13 (1).
Wexler, Joanie M., ''Ryland Ties Proprietary Platforms into Backbone,'' *Computerworld,* May 18, 1992, pp. 51, 80.

—Sina Dubovoj

Safety-Kleen Corp.

1000 North Randall Road
Elgin, Illinois 60123
U.S.A.
(708) 697-8460
Fax: (708) 468-8500

Public Company
Incorporated: 1963
Employees: 6,800
Sales: $794.54 million
Stock Exchange: New York
SICs: 4953 Refuse Systems

Safety-Kleen Corp. is the world's largest provider of parts cleaner services and the world's largest recycler of automotive and industrial hazardous waste fluids, providing a variety of services to small quantity generators of waste solvents and other hazardous and non-hazardous liquid wastes. The company collects liquid wastes from automotive repair outlets, industrial plants, dry cleaners, and other waste generators and processes and recovers those contaminated fluids for reuse or use in another manner.

Safety-Kleen traces its roots to a Wisconsin inventor named Ben Palmer who designed the Safety-Kleen parts washer, a device that helped remove grease from auto parts. While working in his family's sand and gravel business during the 1950s, Palmer was inspired to come up with a safer means of cleaning automotive parts than the standard and somewhat dangerous method of washing parts in gasoline. In 1954 Palmer developed his first parts-washing device, a sink with a nonflammable fire cover placed on top of a barrel containing a parts-washing solvent. Palmer attached a hose and spigot to the sink, which was used to pump cleaning solution into the sink. Beneath the sink Palmer placed a screening filter, allowing the part-washing solvent, once screened, to be reused in a relatively dirt-free condition.

By 1959 Palmer had received an initial patent for his parts washer and sold a few of his machines to other gravel pit businesses. He then left his native Milwaukee area to market his invention in New Orleans and Chicago. With minimal sales success, Palmer, who was still assembling his own machines, returned to Milwaukee during the early 1960s. He leased his parts washers to local businesses and periodically serviced those machines, removing used solvent and adding a clean solution. By the mid-1960s Palmer had 100 customers.

In 1967 Gene Olson, a Wisconsin businessman, discovered one of Palmer's parts washers in a local service station and thought the under-marketed device represented a gold mine. Olson offered Palmer $100,000 for his Safety-Kleen business and the inventor accepted the offer. In order to make the business more profitable, Olson expanded service areas around the Milwaukee area, franchised his business to independent operators outside of Wisconsin, and established minimum service intervals. But the marketing efforts, which boosted Safety-Kleen's customer base to 400, were not enough to keep the parts washer operation afloat and within a year the company was nearly bankrupt.

In 1968 Olson sold Safety-Kleen to Chicago Rawhide Manufacturing Company, an Elgin, Illinois-based manufacturer of automotive bearing shaft seals for the original equipment market. Chicago Rawhide, seeking to diversify into the automotive replacement market, paid Olson $25,000 in cash and assumed Safety-Kleen's $160,000 worth of debt. Donald W. Brinckman, a Chicago Rawhide vice-president who helped engineer the Safety-Kleen deal, became president and chief executive of the new Chicago Rawhide subsidiary.

In order to avoid competitor duplication of the Safety-Kleen washer, which held only a loose patent, and also to avoid unwanted competition in a yet developed market for parts washer services, Brinckman devised a marketing plan designed to quickly push Safety-Kleen into the national arena. The plan divided the country into seven regions for marketing purposes. Newly-recruited regional managers were trained in the Minneapolis-St. Paul, Minnesota, area just a few months after Safety-Kleen was acquired in preparation for a national rollout of services. The managers leased service centers, rented trucks, hired route drivers and sales help, and established branch routes in a matter of weeks before moving on to their own respective regions. Following a similar formula in other major market areas, Safety-Kleen established a network of 130 branch facilities within three years.

The Safety-Kleen business—which literally created its own industry—was targeted to help sell Chicago Rawhide's replacement wheel seals by placement of route drivers throughout the United States and provision of a regular customer service that could become an inroad for selling seals. Safety-Kleen's initial activities included placement of its parts washer free of charge at an auto or retail repair business; it then collected a fee to remove and replace the dirty solvent.

Safety-Kleen was the first company to provide other companies with solvent disposal services, which became a major selling point. Seeking to avoid direct disposal of waste solvents, in 1969 Allan Manteuffel, a Safety-Kleen chemical engineer, began experimenting with ways to recycle used solvents. That same year Safety-Kleen purchased and began conversion of a former oil storage plant; by 1970 the company was processing solvents at its first recycling center.

Safety-Kleen entered the international arena in 1970 when it began establishing service routes in Canada. By October 1971 Safety-Kleen had placed 75,000 machines on 132 routes in 42 states and two Canadian provinces. That same year the company added a computerized control center in Elgin to manage customer records and automatically generate lists of needed service calls. The company also converted a second oil storage plant into a recycling center in Reedley, California. With annual sales topping $7.4 million in 1971, the company became profitable for the first time.

In 1972 Safety-Kleen began introducing allied products that its service representatives could regularly offer to established customers. Safety-Kleen's first allied product, an oil filter produced outside the company and offered exclusively by Safety-Kleen, debuted in September 1972 and was followed by a cream hand cleaner one year later. In December 1972 Safety-Kleen utilized trade magazines to launch the company's first major advertising drive, which targeted service station and automobile garage operators.

In 1973 Safety-Kleen established its first overseas operations and began to do business in England. That same year the company constructed a new Wisconsin parts cleaner production facility to replace a much smaller factory it had been leasing. In 1974 a recycling center in Clayton, New Jersey, opened.

The expansion of Safety-Kleen's business during the early 1970s drove the company to devise a branch system, with each branch encompassing several service and sales routes. Much like a franchise system without any required initial investment on the part of the branch manager, the branch system rewarded the success of individual branch operators by giving managers a stake in the company at a cost for route trucks and sales help. The branch manager was also responsible for sale representatives' commissions.

The Safety-Kleen formula for sales growth paid off and by 1974 the company had placed 125,000 washers and grown from a local work force of ten to an international operation with more than 700 employees. In October 1974 Safety-Kleen, which never delivered the seal sales expected of it, was spun off as an independent corporation. Brinckman was named president of Safety-Kleen and Russell A. Gwillim, president of Chicago Rawhide, assumed the position of chairman of Safety-Kleen. Four days after the spinoff, Safety-Kleen moved into its new Elgin headquarters, adjacent to the Chicago Rawhide office.

In December 1974 Safety-Kleen set up shop in Germany, but the language barrier resulted in recruiting problems and growth remained slow there throughout the 1970s. In 1975 Safety-Kleen opened recycling centers in Denton, Texas, and Lexington, South Carolina. The company's five recycling centers completed Safety-Kleen's national "closed loop" recovery system, which followed waste fluids throughout their existence and recovered them for re-use. The recycling centers began paying more than environmental dividends in 1973, following the onset of the OPEC Oil Embargo and the accompanying rise in gas prices and the cost of new solvent.

In 1976 Safety-Kleen opened a new, state-of-the-art recycling plant in Elgin and two years later began recycling immersion cleaner solvent. By the mid-1970s Safety-Kleen was processing more than 15 million gallons of used mineral spirits solvent annually, with 70 of every 100 gallons of solvent delivered to customers as recycled liquid.

During the mid-1970s Safety-Kleen introduced a number of allied products, including a powdered concrete floor cleaner that was the first company-made allied product, a wiper blade, a carburetor cold parts cleaner, an aerosol spray choke and carburetor cleaner, and a Safety-Kleen broom. In 1977 Safety-Kleen introduced a wheel seal cabinet service.

Safety-Kleen continued to target industrial customers, introducing a number of allied services during the mid-1970s. In 1976 the company introduced its immersion cleaner service, which cleaned gum-and-varnish encrusted automotive parts, and two years later Safety-Kleen debuted a customer-owned machine service (COMS). COMS—aimed at customers who originally purchased parts washers from Ben Palmer as well as customers who owned parts cleaning machines made by other firms—opened up industrial markets by providing a service for all sizes and brands of parts washers.

In 1978 Safety-Kleen entered the Australian market and two years later established a recycling center there. In April 1979 Safety-Kleen went public with an initial over-the-counter offering of 265,000 shares. Proceeds from the stock offering allowed Safety-Kleen to polish off its $4 million debt to Chicago Rawhide.

During the late 1970s Safety-Kleen began test marketing a restaurant filter cleaning business and in mid-1979, after establishing a regional restaurant filter cleaning business around the Elgin area, Safety-Kleen opened an automated filter cleaning plant in Elk Grove Village, Illinois; similar plants opened a year later in New Jersey and California. Overseas, United Kingdom parts washer placements nearly doubled in the late 1970s. In 1980 Safety-Kleen absorbed its chief United Kingdom competitor, Greaseater, Ltd., a two-year-old firm that had modeled its operations on Safety-Kleen's business.

Safety-Kleen entered the 1980s with more than six domestic recycling centers and over 200 branch facilities, including more than 160 branches in the United States. By 1980 Safety-Kleen was the world's largest solvent recycler, processing more than 25 million gallons of mineral solvents a year. In addition, the company's recycling efforts had been expanded to include restaurant exhaust grease filters and Safety-Kleen route vans and trucks, which the company regularly rebuilt.

Safety-Kleen's business profile shifted during the early 1980s as the industrial market replaced the automotive repair market as the company's targeted core business. The move towards the industrial market was encouraged in part by U.S. Environmental Protection Agency (EPA) regulations that took effect in 1980 and labeled used solvents as hazardous material. Fortunately for the company, its recycling process was recognized as a safe means of disposal of solvents.

By 1980 Safety-Kleen's German business was still losing money, so in April 1981 the German operation was sold to a local businessman who continued to provide Safety-Kleen services for customers as a licensee, paying the company royalties on his revenues. Australian operations flourished, though, and in 1981 a branch office was established in New Zealand.

In 1981 Safety-Kleen enhanced its service to restaurants with the introduction of its Fire-Shield restaurant filter. That same year the company began bulk solvent sales to industrial customers and launched a national collection and recycling business. Safety-Kleen debuted its auto body shop buffing pad service following its 1980 acquisition of American Impacts Corporation, a service company that recycled buffing pads used in high-luster lacquer finishing. Safety-Kleen's sales—pushed upward by diversification and increased industrial sales—rose to $134.8 million in 1981 and the company made the "Fortune 1000" list.

In 1983 the company made a secondary public offering and was listed on the New York Stock Exchange. The following year Safety-Kleen entered Puerto Rico, after licensing Puerto Rico Oil Company (PROICO) to market Safety-Kleen services.

In November 1984 the U.S. Resource Conservation and Recovery Act was expanded to include small-quantity waste generators, which included thousands of Safety-Kleen customers. That same year the company debuted a plan to target dry cleaner businesses, especially small firms in need of help to comply with EPA regulations, which had made dry cleaner solvent a hazardous waste. The dry cleaner service, which included the collection, recovery, and recycling of dry cleaner solvent, was the company's first major experience handling hazardous waste through its branch system and helped to firmly establish Safety-Kleen as an environmental service company.

By 1985 the company had extended its operations to include the acquisition and recycling of large volumes of hazardous waste streams, which were collected and sent directly to recycling centers. The wastes from these customers were recycled and sold, or blended into fuels for industrial use. Safety-Kleen also prepared EPA-approved legal manifests for other companies, which made Safety-Kleen entirely responsible for the life span of the solvent it provided. In order to accommodate the increasing amounts of waste solvent it was handling, in 1985 Safety-Kleen established its first regional accumulation center for small-quantity-generator hazardous waste and within two years a dozen such accumulation centers were in place.

In 1985 Safety-Kleen introduced a paint refinishing service, providing businesses with a machine designed to clean paint spray guns and trap the solvent and paint residue. Like other closed loop solvent services, the paint refinishing service used the company's branch and recycling center system to collect, store, recycle, and produce clean solvent.

As a result of its foreign start-up experiences in Germany, Safety-Kleen resolved to enter non-English-speaking countries only through joint ventures. The first such venture, SOPIA, was created in 1985 through a 50–50 partnership with Primagaz Company, France's largest independent supplier of liquified gases. Within a few years SOPIA had established branches in France, Belgium, and Italy. In 1985 Safety-Kleen also began a test joint venture in Japan and a year later Safety-Kleen and the Spanish firm Armero-Johnsen created the Spanish joint venture CODISA. Through CODISA, Safety-Kleen entered Portugal in 1987.

Between 1985 and 1987 Safety-Kleen made three strategic acquisitions designed to expand its technological base and broaden the types of fluids the company could recycle. In 1985 the company acquired Custom Organics, a privately-owned

recycler of solvents and chemical wastes for the electronics industry. In 1986 Safety-Kleen enhanced its restaurant services through the acquisition of Phillips Manufacturing Company, a vapor-degreaser operation. One year later Safety-Kleen purchased McKesson Envirosystems, a solvent-refining company with plants in Kentucky, Illinois, and Puerto Rico. McKesson's ability to process flammable wastes provided Safety-Kleen with new inroads to industrial markets; it increased the company's ability to handle large quantities of wastes and produce supplemental fuels for cement kilns.

Capitalizing on its expanding capabilities, in 1987 Safety-Kleen launched its fluid recovery service, designed to remove and treat small-and-medium-sized quantities of industrial waste. The service included collection of 55-gallon drums of industrial fluid wastes, which were recycled or processed as part of the company's new supplemental fuels program. In 1987 Safety-Kleen also entered the oil recovery services business after the acquisition of the Canadian firm Breslube Enterprises, North America's leading re-refiner of lubricating oils. Like other Safety-Kleen businesses, the oil recovery service was designed to take advantage of the company's branch network in the collection of used oil, destined to be re-refined into lubricating oils or processed into industrial fuels.

In 1987 Safety-Kleen's revenues leaped 31 percent for the company's biggest percentage gain in 12 years. Net income rose 24 percent and Safety-Kleen became the first American company to post 17 straight years of earnings growth of more than 20 percent.

In 1988 Safety-Kleen entered Ireland after acquiring Greaseaters of Ireland (renamed Safety-Kleen of Ireland). One year later the company established joint ventures in Korea and Taiwan that solidified Safety-Kleen's foothold in the Pacific Rim area.

In 1988 Safety-Kleen sold its restaurant services business after it concluded that the operation no longer fit the company's emerging profile as an industrial waste handler. That profile was enhanced the following year through the acquisition of Solvents Recovery Service of New Jersey, Inc. (SRS), a processor of heavy-duty industrial solvent wastes.

In 1989 Safety-Kleen began construction of both a new re-refining oil plant in East Chicago, Indiana, and the company's first European solvent recycling plant in Dinnington, England. Record expenditures were allocated to expand the company's oil and solvent recovery services, and for the first time in 20 years Safety-Kleen's earnings, which rose only eight percent in 1989, showed less than a 20 percent increase. Gwillim retired at the end of 1989 and Brinckman assumed the additional duties of chairman.

Safety-Kleen entered the 1990s seeking to expand its foreign operations and take advantage of the proposed unification of the European Economic Community. In 1990 Safety-Kleen reached agreements to acquire entire control of Safety-Kleen operations in Belgium, France, and Italy, and started licensee operations in Hong Kong, Israel, Singapore, and Taiwan. That same year Safety-Kleen acquired complete control of Breslube and purchased its German licensee's operation. In 1991 Safety-Kleen acquired Orm Bergold Chemie, Germany's largest solvent recycler. One year later Safety-Kleen purchased Niemann Chemie, a leading provider of parts cleaner services to German automotive repair outlets, and acquired complete control of its Spanish licensee's business in exchange for the sale of Safety-Kleen's 50 percent ownership in Portuguese operations.

Safety-Kleen's nearly-untarnished environmental record was smudged during the early 1990s after the company agreed to pay a $1.3 million settlement to the state of California, which had charged the company with 89 alleged violations of the state's hazardous waste laws. Safety-Kleen neither admitted to nor denied the charges. In 1992 a Safety-Kleen internal inspection found that the company had exceeded its authorized waste storage capacity and was illegally storing three million gallons of hazardous waste fluids at its Puerto Rico facilities. The company was later fined $1.4 million by the U.S. EPA.

In 1991 the company opened its new East Chicago oil recycling facility, billed as the world's largest re-refining plant, with a capacity to process more than 100 million gallons of oil annually. But the oil recovery business, banking in part on an unrealized expectation that lubricating oils would join the federal government's list of hazardous wastes, met with a sluggish economy and a slow start.

Safety-Kleen was ranked among the Fortune 500 companies in 1991, despite the company's first ever drop in annual earnings. The company's payout of two large EPA fines, as well as lower-than-anticipated oil re-refining sales, led to a second drop in earnings the following year. Between 1990 and 1992, then, Safety-Kleen's net income fell from $55 million to $45 million, despite continued record revenue totals.

In March 1993 John G. Johnson, Jr., a former Arco Chemical Company executive, was named president, while Brinckman remained chairman and chief executive. The company moved towards the close of 1993 predicting that its oil recovery services and European operations would be profitable by the end of that year. The company's plans beyond 1993 called for further expansion of European branches, which were expected to increase in number from 55 in 1993 to 75 or 80 by 1997. Looking towards the future, Safety-Kleen—with infrastructure in place to expand both at home and overseas, a near-spotless record of tremendous earnings growth, and still no nationwide competition in its home country—appeared likely to move back into record territory as it rolled into the mid-1990s.

Further Reading:

Bowman, Jim, *"Waste Not" . . . The Safety-Kleen Story*, Chicago, IL: J.G. Ferguson Publishing Company, 1989, 152 p.
Cook, James, "What have you done for me tomorrow?" *Forbes*, February, 19, 1990.
Fish, Dwight, "Kleanliness Is Next to Nothing on Earth," *Business People Magazine*, December, 1991, Section 1, p. 22.
Jackson, Cheryl, "Safety-Kleen facility refines oil recovery," *Chicago Tribune*, July 10, 1991, Section 3, pp. 1, 4.
Murphy, H. Lee, "Oil Recovery: Slippery Slope for Safety-Kleen, *Crain's Chicago Business*, June 22, 1992, p. 41.
Palmer, Jay, "Pay Dirt: Safety-Kleen, After a Mild Skid, on Track Again," *Barron's*, October 21, 1991, pp. 17–20.
Sherrod, Pamela, "Safety-Kleen now remains only in CEO's debt," *Chicago Tribune*, March 30, 1987, Section 4, p. 11.
Young, David, "Green's also the color of money," *Chicago Tribune*, November 17, 1991, pp. 16–18.

—Roger W. Rouland

SSS Seagate

Seagate Technology, Inc.

920 Disc Drive
Scotts Valley, California 95066
U.S.A.
(408) 438-6550
Fax: (408) 438-4127

Public Company
Incorporated: 1979
Employees: 43,000
Sales: $2.86 billion
Stock Exchanges: NASDAQ
SICs: 3572 Computer Storage Devices; 3674 Semiconductors
& Related Devices

Seagate Technology, Inc., is the world's leading independent manufacturer of rigid magnetic disks and disk drives for computers. The company pioneered the downsizing of mainframe hard disk drives, making them affordable for personal computers. Seagate commands about 30 percent of the market in 2.5, 3.5, and 5.25-inch drives, with foreign sales making up about 35 percent of its revenues.

Seagate was established in 1979 in Scotts Valley, California, by a group of businesspeople, including Alan Shugart who had been an engineer with Memorex for four years, following eighteen years at IBM. Seagate was his second start-up after having founded Shugart Associates, the company that made floppy disk drives a standard feature on personal computers. When Shugart Associates was sold to Xerox a year later, Shugart was forced out. Of Seagate's group of four cofounders, another significant member was Tom Mitchell. He had come from Commodore, where he had served as general manager of Commodore business machines, and had previously worked at Bendix, Fairchild Camera, and Honeywell. Shugart became president and CEO of the new company, while Mitchell started out as senior vice president of operations.

Hard disks are made of one or more magnetic-coated aluminum platters. Data is stored on, retrieved from, and erased off the rapidly rotating disk by a mechanical arm, which moves across the disk. The whole mechanism is called the disk drive, or hard drive, and the technology for the sealed unit, which is also known generically as a Winchester disk, is Seagate's basic product. Hard disk technology allows the storage of more data than a floppy disk, and does it at a faster rate.

Unlike larger mainframe computers, personal computers were originally built with only a floppy disk drive and without hard drives. Therefore, the market was open for an independent company like Seagate to manufacture hard drives and sell them directly to the computer manufacturers. They in turn would incorporate the drives into their personal computers as add-on features. Seagate's first client was IBM in 1980, just as the latter was about to introduce its personal computers, which would set the standard for the industry. Seagate's first product, a 5.25-inch hard drive, was very successful. By 1982, with sales of $40 million, Seagate had captured half of the market for small disk drives. The company went public in September of 1981, with an initial stock offering of three million common shares.

Seagate made a name for itself by producing the least expensive disk drives in the industry, largely due to Mitchell's successful efforts to procure component parts from vendors at the lowest possible prices. In 1983 Mitchell replaced Shugart as president, though the latter remained chairman and CEO. Mitchell also took on the new position of chief operating officer to direct day to day operations, while Shugart oversaw planning.

By 1984 sales had shot up to $344 million as Seagate became the world's largest producer of 5.25-inch disk drives, with three-quarter's of the company's shipments going to IBM. Then in mid-1984 the computer industry entered a slump, and the average price for a wholesale 10-megabyte disk drive fell from $430 to $320 in a matter of days. A number of factors contributed to the situation, including a slowing in the growth of personal computer sales, industry-wide falling prices, a glut of disk drive competitors, and rising costs of producing the new generation of drives. Diminished growth of personal computer sales came just as the disk-drive companies were squeezing the last profits from their older product lines. These difficulties were intensified for Seagate, with its reliance on IBM's business, when that company reduced orders and began demanding lower prices. Thus, Seagate's sales for the first quarter of fiscal 1985, at $50.6 million, were half of what they had been for the last quarter of fiscal 1984. Annual sales for fiscal 1985 declined 38 percent to $215 million.

Mitchell immediately began looking into ways of manufacturing the drives even more cheaply. Realizing that disk drives, as a commodity product, would become subject to price pressures, he had already decided to begin relocating Seagate's manufacturing operations overseas where labor costs were lower, and the pressures resulting from cutbacks forced quick implementation of the move. In July of 1984, 900 of the 1,600 employees in Scotts Valley were laid off, as component production shifted to Singapore. By December most of its drives were being produced there, and plans were underway to open another plant in Thailand. In so doing, Seagate successfully followed the Japanese strategy of using less expensive Southeast Asian labor in manufacturing, which had allowed Japanese companies to dominate the floppy disk drive market. Now, however, with the high value of the Japanese yen, Seagate was able to undercut the prices of Fujitsu, Hitachi, NEC, Toshiba, and others, and dominate the hard disk market.

At the same time, Mitchell made one outlet of sales more secure by extending credit to a small but important client, CMS. The latter was buying stripped-down IBM personal computers, furnishing them with Seagate drives and selling them to retailers at bargain prices. Thus, while Seagate's revenues fell temporarily in 1984–85, the company managed to stay profitable.

Seagate was faced with another problem in the fall of 1984—the replacement of its 10-megabyte drives, which were becoming obsolete as higher capacity drives appeared on the market. Mitchell saw an opportunity to outmaneuver a rival, Computer Memories, which was already providing disks with greater memory, but less reliability, to IBM. He promised IBM a shipment of 20 prototype high-capacity, high-reliability drives by December, before Seagate had even finished designing them. Working long hours, Seagate engineers pulled it off. Although mass quantities could not be delivered by March as originally promised, IBM was satisfied and placed orders for tens of thousands of the disk drives.

Seagate also sought to diversify its clientele in order to be less vulnerable to fluctuations in demand. Seagate began marketing more to value-added resellers (VARs), dealers that package stripped-down computer components and software and resell them as specialized systems. By 1987 such dealers came to represent 47 percent of Seagate's clients, up from zero in 1983, while sales to IBM fell to 24 percent. In that year a deal was also signed to supply drives to Hewlett-Packard, among other new personal computer makers. To expand sales internationally, Seagate set up a European headquarters in Versailles, France, in 1987.

Beginning in 1985 Seagate experienced a phenomenal rise in sales, hitting $1 billion in revenue by 1987, with a record $115.3 million in profits. This reflected the rapid growth of the market for hard drives in desk-top computers. In 1984 only 15–20 percent of personal computers had hard drives, while this figure had reached 70 percent by 1987, according to analyst Ronald Elijah at Robertson, Colman & Stephans. As the market grew, Seagate was able to maintain its dominant share by keeping its prices down. It had reduced the costs of storing data by 95 percent since it first went into business.

However, Seagate's concentration on efficient production, while allowing technological innovation to take a back seat, made it vulnerable to the boom and bust cycles of the rapidly changing high technology industry. In 1987 computer manufacturers started demanding the smaller 3.5-inch drives earlier than anticipated. IBM, which was purchasing 30 percent of Seagate's 5.25-inch drives, was now planning to manufacture some of its own 3.5-inch drives. As a consequence, Seagate's profits declined by 39 percent during this product transition period in the second half of 1987, and profits remained low into 1988.

Seagate introduced six models of its first 3.5-inch drives that spring, although 5.25-inch drives continued to dominate its sales. The company had added 32,000 square feet to its Singapore plant, where the 3.5-inch disk drives were made. Meanwhile, it expanded operations in Thailand beyond the manufacture of components and sub-assembling to include the complete assembly process and testing of disk drives. More significantly, Seagate began investing greater amounts on research and development in 1987, double the amount of the previous year, by issuing $250 million in debentures. The company established a

new research and development facility in Boulder, Colorado, in addition to the one at its headquarters in Scotts Valley.

The market's growth was less than anticipated, however, and revenue for fiscal 1988 declined 50 percent from the previous year, while inventories of 5.25-inch disks piled up. Seagate blamed the problem on industry-wide overproduction, while Shugart moved quickly to lay off nearly 2,200 employees in Singapore and the United States. The company barely stayed in the black for fiscal 1989.

Although Seagate remained the undisputed leader in market share, ups and downs in the demand for the personal computer market were a serious concern. Thus, Seagate's next move was to gain entry into the market for the high capacity drives used in mainframes, by purchasing Control Data's disk-drive subsidiary, Imprimis, in June of 1989. In addition, the $450 million acquisition nearly doubled Seagate's sales, to $2.4 billion for fiscal 1990, larger than all its U.S. competitors—Conner Peripherals, Maxtor, Micropolis, and Quantum—combined.

Seagate also had an edge on its competitors in its ability to provide consistently lower priced products, because the company manufactured its own disk drive components. In plants throughout the United States and in Asia, Seagate turned out motors, precision recording heads, and other parts. While the company built many of these factories itself, key component suppliers were also acquired by Seagate. In 1987 the company purchased Integrated Power Semiconductors, Ltd. of Scotland—a long-time Seagate supplier—and Aeon, a Brea, California-based producer of substrates to make thin film magnetic recording media.

On the other hand, Seagate continued to lag behind the competition when it came to introducing new technology. "Seagate has never been that interested in getting products out of the lab first. We wait until we've squeezed every penny of cost out of a product before we bring it to market," Shugart explained in *Forbes* in 1991. "But the product cycles are getting shorter and shorter. Now we can't afford to wait." The latest product on the market was a 2.5-inch disk drive for laptop and notebook computers. Seagate introduced the drive in November of 1990, only five months behind competitor Conner Peripherals, as compared with a delay of a year for the 3.5-inch drives.

Mitchell's emphasis on high volume manufacturing over product innovation was one of the points of contention that led him to resign under pressure from the board in September of 1991. Shugart then reasserted his role in running the company by giving up his position as chairman and assuming the posts of president and chief operating officer vacated by Mitchell. Gary Filler, former vice chairman, replaced Shugart as chairman. This change in management came on the heels of a disappointing fiscal year with revenues down 42 percent, and the layoff of another 1,650 workers.

Firmly in charge again, Shugart pursued a strategy of turning out new products as soon as they were designed. He also began focusing on higher profit margins and specific markets, contrary to Mitchell's goal of general large-volume sales. One of Shugart's first products in this regard was the 1480 disk drive introduced at the end of 1991. This 425-megabyte, 3.5-inch drive was successfully targeted at the high-end workstation and minicomputer markets, where profit margins were greater. Seagate beat the competition by introducing the product first, then continuing to outsell its rivals.

Seagate's profits rebounded beyond expectations in early 1992 as sales of lower priced, high-end personal computers took off amid vendor price wars. At the same time, Seagate also benefited from the current PC owner trend toward buying new higher capacity drives to run more powerful programs. The company's large market share ensured that such upswings in personal computer demand would have a definite effect on its sales.

Shugart in turn pumped those profits into more research and development and strategic investments. In early 1993 Seagate invested $65 million in a factory in Londonderry, Northern Ireland, which doubled its capacity to produce a key part used its hard drives. In addition, Seagate acquired a 25 percent stake in the Sundisk Corp.—another manufacturer of computer data storage products—and together the two companies produced data storage systems for portable computers and other handheld electronic devices. In April of that year Seagate signed an agreement with Corning, the glass manufacturer, to provide a new glass-ceramic compound for use in disks. The new material allowed Seagate to reduce the distance between a disk and its magnetic read-write head, which enabled a higher capacity for data.

While Seagate's business continued to be successful through the early 1990s, new developments in data storage technology presented a potential challenge. Magnetic disks were apparently destined to become obsolete, as high-capacity, erasable optical disks became less expensive and faster. In addition, optical technologies without moving parts began to show promise.

However, if the past is any example, when Seagate lacks the latest technology, it will buy the company that has it.

Principal Subsidiaries: Seagate, Inc. (Korea); Seagate Technology (Singapore) Pte., Ltd.

Further Reading:

Brandt, Richard, "Seagate Goes East—And Comes Back a Winner," *Business Week,* March 16, 1987, p. 94.
"Driven Down," *Forbes,* January 9, 1989, p. 115.
Dubashi, Jaganath, "Seagate Technology: Too Soon to Bet?" *Finance World,* July 10, 1990, pp. 19–20.
Fisher, Lawrence M., "Seagate Trips, Industry Cringes," *New York Times,* August 23, 1988, p. D1+.
Larson, Erik, "Decline in Disk-Drive Demand Puts Squeeze on Many Makers," *Wall Street Journal,* December 3, 1984, p. 4.
O'Reilly, Brian, "How Tom Mitchell Lays Out the Competition," *Forbes,* March 30, 1987, pp. 90–96.
Marks, Don, "Seagate Technology," *Datamation,* June 15, 1992, pp. 49–52.
Pitta, Julie, "The Survivor," *Forbes,* July 8, 1991, pp. 94–95.
Richter, Paul, "700 Workers Dismissed at Seagate Plant," *Los Angeles Times,* July 20, 1984, sec. IV, p. 1.
Schmitt, Richard B., "Seagate Technology's Mitchell Resigns as Board Decides to Shift Management," *Wall Street Journal,* September 23, 1991, pp. B4 (W), B8 (E).
"Seagate Technology," *Datamation,* June 15, 1988, p. 106.
"Seagate Technology Names New President," *New York Times,* August 9, 1983, p. D2 (L).
"Seagate Technology Posts 40% Drop in Net for Fiscal First Period, *Wall Street Journal,* October 14, 1987, p. 49 (E).
Yamada, Ken, "Once-Battered Seagate Gains in Computer Price War," *Wall Street Journal,* June 1, 1992, p. B2 (E).

—Heather Behn Hedden

Seattle First National Bank Inc.

701 Fifth Ave.
Seattle, Washington 98124
U.S.A.
(206) 358-3000
Fax: (206) 358-6800

Wholly Owned Subsidiary of BankAmerica Corporation
Incorporated: 1887 as Dexter Horton and Company
Employees: 7,600
Sales: $15.67 billion
SICs: 6021 National Commercial Banks

Seattle First National Bank Inc., the oldest bank in Seattle, operates the largest community banking network in Washington State. A wholly owned subsidiary of BankAmerica Corporation, Seafirst, as it is commonly known, played an integral role in the growth of Seattle and has continued to pioneer innovations in the banking industry into its second century of business.

As the news of great riches in the West spread throughout the East and the Midwest during the first half of the 19th century, those brave enough to endure the hardships of traveling across the country by horse, wagon, or foot began their slow exodus west in search of their fortunes. One of these restless individuals in particular, itching for greater opportunity, was a farmer in Illinois named Dexter Horton. Horton, who had moved to Illinois in 1841 from his birthplace in Schuyler County, New York, had little success working his 80-acre farm. Eleven years spent clearing and tilling the land had resulted in failure and Horton was ready for a change. Talk of greater prospects in the West circulated throughout his community in DeKalb county, and when his neighbors formed a wagon train in 1852, Horton, his wife, and their small daughter joined the 27 other people and headed west.

Initially, Horton's financial condition remained as bleak as it was in Illinois. Arriving in Seattle in 1853 after spending a year in Salem, the capital of the Oregon Territory, Horton found work anywhere he could get it. He chopped wood, operated a logging camp's cook house, worked at a sawmill, and drove a wagon for a former neighbor from DeKalb County. By the following year, Horton, in a partnership with two other Seattle businessmen, began selling merchandise left by visiting ships as payment for Northwest timber. Selling clothes, tools, groceries, and any of the sundry items ship captains would leave as payment, Horton's mercantile business blossomed and his reputation as a person of high integrity became known to the 170 settlers residing in the area. With no bank in town, loggers, mill hands, and many of the gold prospectors and fur trappers in the area turned to Horton for the safekeeping of their valuables. Horton kept the deposits in sacks or pigskin pouches and cached them in various places around his store—the most popular repository being the bottom of a fish barrel. Eventually, Horton's rudimentary banking services gained such popularity that he decided to start a business devoted solely to fulfilling banking needs. In 1870 Horton and his mercantile partner for many years, David Phillips, opened Phillips, Horton and Company with $50,000 of capital.

Two years later, David Phillips died and Horton renamed the bank Dexter Horton and Company. Over the next 20 years the bank thrived. The growth in deposits at Dexter Horton and Company reflected the transformation of Seattle from a small settlement to a legitimate town. In 1882 deposits totaled more than $300,000. Five years later, they had grown to $750,000, and by the end of the decade deposits had topped $2 million. During this same period Seattle's population leapt 1200 percent, from 3,500 to over 42,000.

During these years of robust growth for Horton's bank, two other predecessor banks of Seafirst were founded. In 1882 a private bank, George W. Harris and Company, was formed. Several months after the bank opened, Harris obtained a national charter and the bank was renamed First National Bank of Seattle. The following year, Puget Sound National Bank was founded. These two banks, along with Dexter Horton and Company, would form the nucleus of what would eventually become Seafirst.

In 1893 the years of exponential growth enjoyed by Dexter Horton and Company shuddered to a stop. An economic downturn pulled the nation into a depression, and a consequent bank panic swept across the country. Fearing their money was at risk, hordes of depositors rushed to their banks to withdraw their accounts, causing many banks to close. The banks in Washington state were not excluded from the panic. In a four-year period from 1892 to 1896, the number of banks declined from 173 to 91. Although Horton's bank escaped closure—as did Seafirst's other main predecessors and the newly formed Seattle National Bank—its deposits shrank considerably. In 1892 Dexter Horton and Company boasted deposits of $1.4 million. By 1897 deposits had fallen to $638,000.

The economic slide of the 1890s ended in the Northwest with the discovery of gold along the Klondike River in the Yukon Territory. On July 14, 1897, a steamship arrived in San Francisco with news of the gold strike. Three days later, a group of miners and an Associated Press reporter docked in Seattle with 3,000 pounds of gold. The news spread quickly and the rush for gold began in earnest. As the nearest seaport to the awaiting riches northward, Seattle and its businesses benefited tremendously from the infusion of thousands of gold seekers. Seattle's population doubled to over 80,000 during the 1890s, with a majority arriving after 1897. Each newcomer was a potential depositor and the boost to businesses in the area increased the wealth of the city, which invariably was funnelled through the city's banks. The deposits at Horton's bank rose from the pre-gold rush low of $638,000 to $3.7 million by 1900. While timber had originally attracted settlers to Seattle, the discovery of gold transformed the area from a town enjoying steady growth into a boom city teeming with hopeful fortune seekers. For Horton's bank, the Klondike strike was a defining event in its history. From 1897 and on, both Seattle and the predecessors of Seafirst began the inexorable push toward greater growth.

In the decade to follow, a time during which Seattle's population increased to almost 250,000 and total bank deposits in the area ballooned from $17 million to $80 million, three additional predecessor banks that would figure prominently in the formation of Seafirst were founded. In 1903, a year before Dexter Horton's death, the Union Savings and Trust Company and the Washington Trust Company were organized. Six years later, the Metropolitan Bank opened its doors. These years of growth also witnessed one of the many bank mergers that would characterize the industry for the rest of the century. In 1910, the same year in which Dexter Horton and Company was granted a national charter (becoming Dexter Horton National Bank), the First National Bank of Seattle and the Puget Sound National Bank merged, retaining the Seattle National name, and supplanted Dexter Horton National as the city's largest bank. Dexter Horton National, now headed by a former messenger for the bank, Norval Latimer, responded by affiliating financially with the Washington Trust Company. This did not restore the bank as the area's largest, but did enable it to circumvent banking regulations that barred national banks from engaging in trust business.

The following decade witnessed the outbreak of World War I, and with it came another upsurge in banking activity. Spurred by the sale of Liberty Loans and an increase in foreign trade and its financing, deposits in Seattle's banks nearly doubled to $174 million. Strengthened by the upturn in business, Dexter Horton National expanded its banking services by adding a foreign exchange department and began engaging in investment banking, an area of banking business eschewed by commercial banks before the war. The breadth of services offered by Dexter Horton National increased during the 1920s, and it once again became the area's largest commercial bank in 1924 by merging with the Union National Bank of Seattle. Deposits after the merger totaled $31.8 million.

The decades of phenomenal growth in the Seattle area had, by the 1920s, begun to attract of bankers and businessmen from the East Coast and California. By 1929 Seattle's population had increased to 365,000, making it the nineteenth largest city in the United States, and its port bustled with activity to and from the Orient and Alaska. As the city rapidly shifted toward the era of modern technology and the modern corporation, the demand for capital to effect the transformation was in high demand. Bankers in the East, with larger reservoirs of cash than their Western counterparts, began to court the customers of Seattle banks. Fearing that the financial control of the area would be wrested away from them by outsiders, several of Seattle's bankers discussed a merger as an antidote to the creeping influence from the Eastern financial centers. In 1929 the Dexter Horton National Bank, the Seattle National Bank, and the First National Bank Group, with combined deposits of $96 million, consolidated to become the First Seattle Dexter Horton National Bank. The consolidation created one of the six largest banks on the Pacific Coast and enabled the bank to finance the capital outlays needed by local companies that banks from Chicago and New York had previously funded.

With the new name and solidified resources came an economic disaster far more deleterious than the bank panics of 1893 and 1907. The beginning of the Great Depression in 1929 rocked the nation's economy and caused the closure of numerous banks. From 1929 to 1933, the number of banks in the United States plummeted from 25,586 to 14,771 and deposits shrank from $58.2 billion to $41.6 billion. Washington state banks suffered even greater losses than the national average, but banks in Seattle incurred comparatively smaller—although still severe—losses. The First Seattle Dexter Horton National Bank, which changed its name again in 1931 to First National Bank of Seattle, saw its deposits sink by nearly $27 million from 1929 to 1933. At the same time its loans drop to $22.5 million from $57.7 million. But by 1934, while most of the United States remained mired in the Depression, First National began a steady comeback, recording deposits of $74.9 million by the middle of 1934 and $84.7 million by the end of the year.

As First National recovered from its losses, sweeping national bank reform changed the nature of banking and marking the beginning of a new era. The Banking Act of 1933 guaranteed deposits, limited bank investments, and, most important for the future of First National, allowed banks to open branches. At roughly the same time that the federal government gave its nod to branch banking, Washington state law also legalized the practice. First National quickly absorbed its six affiliated banks and turned them into branches. In the bank's zeal to open more branches and extend its presence to the eastern regions of Washington state, First National consolidated in 1935 with Spokane and Eastern Trust Company, the oldest and largest of the eastern Washington banks. The consolidation, renamed Seattle First National Bank, joined Eastern and Spokane's deposits of $27 million with those of First National's to give Washington state its first bank with over $100 million in deposits. This move also stretched the presence of the Seattle-based bank across the state.

By 1940, through the aggressive acquisition of additional branches, Seafirst had become the largest bank in the Pacific Northwest and one of the 50 largest in the United States. Deposits had grown to over $200 million, and 22 communities outside of Seattle were served by the bank. This growth, however, paled in comparison to the bank's achievements during World War II. Between 1939 and 1945, deposits at Seafirst jumped from $209 million to $679 million. The bank, with 35 branch offices, catapulted into the top 25 of the nation's largest banks.

In the years following the war, Seafirst's growth was hindered by a sluggish economy that chipped away at the bank's deposit level. It would take six years for the bank to surpass its record high in deposits in 1945. From 1945 to 1951, Seafirst added 16 new branches to a banking system that remained the largest in the Pacific Northwest. Throughout the 1950s and 1960s, Seafirst continued to acquire smaller banks and turn them into branches. By 1962 Seafirst had 100 branch offices and deposits of over $1 billion.

After 15 years of feverish growth, Seafirst directors decided to halt further acquisitions and restructure the bank to streamline its operations in the early 1960s. Concerned that the proliferation of branches had created a labyrinthine management structure and that the mounting competition by local banks would begin to erode into its customer base, directors developed a marketing plan to focus the bank's image and reorganize the supervision of its branch operations.

By the end of the 1960s, Seafirst had launched several innovative banking services, expanded internationally, and positioned itself for its next century of business. In 1966 the bank moved its headquarters into a new 50-story building. Seafirst also pioneered the move toward credit cards in Washington state by issuing Firstbank cards in 1966. Other firsts included the introduction of a savings bond as a new time deposit instrument in 1966, the 1967 acquisition of a mortgage lending company as an affiliate, and the installation of automated teller machines in 1968. Seafirst opened a representative office in Tokyo and a wholly owned subsidiary in Switzerland in 1969, representing the company's initial foray into the European funds market.

Once reorganized, Seafirst continued to expand during the 1970s. Under the stewardship of William M. Jenkins, chairman of the bank since 1962, the number of branches grew to 172 and deposits increased to $6.65 billion during the decade. By the early 1980s, Seafirst was the 18th largest bank in the nation. It controlled nearly 40 percent of the Washington market and was roughly twice as large as its nearest competitor. As the bank's regional dominance increased, however, it became the target of union and consumer groups. Critics charged that Seafirst had grown too fast and had adopted deposit and lending policies that discouraged consumer business. Seafirst did charge higher banking service fees than its competition, apparently assuming its position as the leading bank was unassailable.

The dramatic increase in oil prices during the 1970s spawned a multi-billion dollar energy exploration industry with which Seafirst became heavily involved. The bank opened an energy office in 1979 and began granting loans to fund many of the exploration projects. For Seafirst, the success of these projects upon both the discovery and continued high price of oil. When oil prices began to drop in the early 1980s, Seafirst found itself with $1.2 billion in energy loans (representing 17 percent of its total loans). The ramifications were catastrophic. In 1981 the bank posted earnings of over $80 million. The following year, it recorded a loss of $91.3 million. After losing another $133 million in 1983, Seafirst's capital base dropped to approximately $323 million, $37 million lower than its nearest competitor. The future for Seafirst appeared bleak, but the bank was rescued by the infusion of $150 million into its capital base as a result of its acquisition by BankAmerica Corporation in 1983.

Although the acquisition provided immediate relief for Seafirst, full recovery from the imprudent decisions of the 1970s did not occur overnight. Still saddled by its pernicious energy loans, the bank continued to lose money and suffer from a tarnished image. But by the end of the decade, however, Seafirst began recording profits once again. This turnaround was largely due to sweeping operational and marketing changes that restored the public's perception of Seafirst as a consumer-oriented bank. Branch offices were relieved of much of their administrative and processing responsibilities, allowing personnel more time with customers. Seafirst also offered additional services to attract new customers and halt the attrition of existing accounts. In addition banks stayed open until 6 p.m. each weekday and offered Saturday hours, and customers were offered 24-hour service via telephone.

By the early 1990s, Seafirst had shed its negative image, substantially increased its customer base, and posted enviable profits. In 1992 the bank's deposits totaled $12.35 billion. It reported a net income of over $233 million, buoyed in part by the absorption of 82 former Security Pacific branches from the 1991 merger of BankAmerica and Security Pacific.

As Seafirst points toward the future, its prospects look bright. Having learned from its mistakes during the 1970s, Seafirst's position as the leading bank in Washington state appears solid. Undoubtedly, the bank will be challenged by changing conditions in the future, but if it continues to meet the needs of its patrons, Dexter Horton's legacy should continue well into the future.

Principal Subsidiaries: Centrum Properties Corporation; DAS Holdings Inc.; Equipment Transfer Corporation; LAD Northwest, Inc.; Seafirst Whitehead Dareco; Leasco of Washington; Seafirst America Corporation; Seafirst Capital Corporation; Seafirst Services Corporation; Seattle-First International Bank

Further Reading:

Asher, Joe, ''Seafirst Expands Card Delivery Systems,'' *ABA Banking Journal,* April 1991, pp. 76–78.
Dunphy, Steven H. ''Did State's Biggest Bank Want To Stay In Big Leagues Too Badly?,'' *Seattle Times,* April 24, 1983, p. C1.
Hollie, Pamela G., ''Seafirst Bank's Image Problem,'' *New York Times,* September 15, 1980, pp. D1, D7.
Paich, Milo R., ''Making Service Quality Look Easy,'' *Training,* February 1992, pp. 32–35.
Scates, Shelby, *Firstbank: The Story of Seattle-First National Bank,* Seattle: Seattle-First National Bank, 1970.

—Jeffrey L. Covell

Smith's Food & Drug Centers, Inc.

1550 South Redwood Rd.
Salt Lake City, Utah 84104
U.S.A.
(801) 974-1400
Fax: (801) 974-1662

Public Company
Incorporated: 1948 as Smith and Son's Market
Employees: 18,000
Sales: $2.65 million
Stock Exchanges: New York
SICs: 5411 Grocery Stores

Smith's Food & Drug Centers, Inc., with 119 stores in Arizona, California, Idaho, Nevada, New Mexico, Texas, Wyoming, and Utah, is a leading regional supermarket chain operating in the intermountain, southwestern, and southern California regions of the United States. The company was originally founded by Lorenzo Smith and his son Dee Smith in 1948 as a one-store grocery business. When Dee Smith took over his father's store in 1958 it was valued at $60,000. Since then, the company has grown into a chain worth more than $1 billion. The company went public in 1989 but still remains in the control of the third generation of the Smith family of Brigham City, Utah. Smith's Food & Drug Centers, open 24 hours, are combination food and drug stores that also offer take-out food, photo processing, and video rentals. Smith's plans to expand its operations into new regions and markets in order to remain a top competitor in the food retailing industry in the 1990s.

The story of Smith's Food & Drug Centers, Inc., can be traced back to 1911 when Lorenzo Smith rented a space for a small grocery market stocking such staples as rice, flour, and dry beans. Smith's store was similar to other stores in Brigham City at that time, and it took Smith about ten years to accumulate enough capital to buy a larger store across the street. The family business, named Smith and Son's Market in 1932, remained afloat during the Great Depression, but growth was virtually nonexistent as many former customers were forced back into subsistence farming. Smith took most of his earnings and purchased property in the area, which was available at rock bottom prices.

In 1942 business picked up after the U.S. Army built a hospital near the Smith market. Dee Smith returned from service in World War I and had worked in various jobs, mainly as a promoter of boxing and wrestling matches. He used these skills to promote the grocery store and was also was instrumental in encouraging his father to modernize and expand the store in the late 1940s. With financial backing from his father, Dee Smith and his partner George C. Woodward opened a 10,000 square foot grocery store, the first of its kind in Brigham City. By the end of World War II, Smith and Son recognized that the neighborhood mom-and-pop store was becoming obsolete. Pent-up spending power from the war was being unleashed, and the dynamic expansion of production led to new demands by the average consumer.

From 1946 until Lorenzo Smith's death in 1958 the company grew exponentially, with Dee Smith leading the aggressive growth campaign. The store was refurbished and expanded by 50 percent, an advanced refrigeration system was installed, and the name was changed to Smith's Super Market. Reopened in December of 1952, the store posted huge sales increases; by 1954 Smith's was able to acquire American Food retail stores, a major grocery wholesaler and the primary supplier of Smith's. Soon after, another major store was opened in Brigham City with four times the space as Smith's Super Market.

These moves by Dee Smith and laid a firm base for expansion. Gross sales quadrupled from 1956 to 1957 and profit rates, although only three percent, were high by industry standards at the time. The purchase of Thiokol Chemical Corporation stock, an important business move, provided the duo with further capital for expansion. Thiokol had opened a plant north of Brigham City and was awarded a large Air Force contract. The investment reaped huge dividends, with the stock increasing in market value more than 12-fold by 1960.

With demand picking up as wages and employment grew in Brigham City, Smith and Woodward launched a growth plan which included large ad campaigns and diversified product selection. Bolstered by increased highway construction that would provide access to residential markets, Smith's was also awarded the concession contract for Morrison-Knudsen Construction Company which was building a causeway in the area and was housing its work force nearby. Smith received concession rights for all services, including groceries, restaurant, and a barber shop, to the residential construction camp. The operation was a guaranteed market and solidly profitable.

By 1958 it appeared that the grocery market in Brigham City was becoming saturated, and Dee Smith was forced to look outside the area to new geographical markets. The 1960s were a time of massive expansion for Smith, but growth was uneven. For instance, its first takeover of a Safeway store in Boise, Idaho ended in failure after the discovery that the previous owner had been doctoring the books. A major success was a contract Smith won to supply concessions to a construction camp for workers who were building Flaming Gorge Dam, a ten year project that would provide stable demand for Smith's products. Smith also opened a new store called Food Giant.

Other successful takeovers followed as Smith expanded into wholesale trade, giving him more control over suppliers and distribution. Woodward purchased three Success Markets in Salt Lake City, and by the early 1970s Smith's had obtained over 160 stores. The pattern was to buy failing stores at low prices, modernize them, and turn them into profitable operations. This strategy gave Dee Smith the needed funds and enabled him to build the large supermarkets that would become the standard in the industry. Although Smith was left with a high debt to assets ratio, his company was leading the industry in the southwest United States and sat on a very profitable base of eight stores which had sales of over $13 million.

But like any successful business, Smith's recognized the need for continued growth to fend off competitors. In January of 1968 Dee Smith announced the purchase of Mayfair Markets, a move that Howard Carlisle referred to in *The Dee Smith Story: Fulfilling A Dream,* as a "million-dollar transaction." By the end of the year Smith had acquired 16 of the Mayfair stores, expanding his empire to 23 stores in several Utah cities. Following a proven strategy, Smith and his associates had purchased the Mayfair stores at bargain prices because they were losing money and, after putting the company in a highly leveraged position (for example, Mayfair's Utah operations lost $1.5 million in 1967 while Smith's total net worth was less than $700,000), eventually turned a profit on them.

Smith achieved this task by reorganizing management, slashing wages, and intensifying work loads. He streamlined the management structure and instituted bonus incentives for managers while, at the same time, cutting salaries. An intensive labor effort was also launched to redecorate and reorganize all of the stores. Sales soared, but the company's profits were being strangled by its heavy debt service load which limited cash flow. Nonetheless, the reorganization campaign left the company in a good position to cut prices. The discount pricing strategy helped revive sagging sales at some of the former Mayfair stores, thus expanding market share.

To further enhance its overall profit margins, Smith acquired its first nonfood business, the Utah-based Souvall Brothers, in 1969. Souvall's sold a diverse line of products—from beauty aids and housewares to yarn—and had sales of $3 million and a considerably higher profit margin than Smith's. This acquisition, according to Carlisle in *The Dee Smith Story,* kept the company afloat during the recession years of the early 1970s.

With the nonfood portion of the business growing faster than the grocery side, the company began experimenting with combination stores, gaining a jump on its competitors and momentum that lasted well into the 1980s. In addition to its many acquisitions, Smith also constructed new stores throughout the late 1960s and early 1970s, building new stores in Ogden, Roy, and Magna, Utah as well as expanding the Souvall warehouse facilities in Salt Lake City. The biggest project was the construction of a 150,000 square foot warehouse and distribution center in Layton, Utah. This facility, centrally located and near major highways, enabled Smith's to provide its own wholesaling and warehousing and gain greater cost and inventory control. Acquisitions had cut into profit margins, however, and coupled with the recession of 1973 and Nixon price controls, the company's cash flow problems threatened to become acute. Thus, the need for external funding sources to finance the new warehousing center in Layton were vital. The public sector stepped in to foot the bill, selling $1.5 million of low interest bonds which would be repaid over 15 years. Subsequently,

Smith's realized huge cost cutting success from its direct control over distribution and wholesaling operations.

By May of 1974, however, the company was back on the acquisition trail, buying up two small chains in the populous and lucrative southern California market. Smith's had acquired 110 stores in seven years and the debt service became immense at a time of recession in the early 1970s. Competition was fierce as one-third of the retail food companies were experiencing losses. Smith's record in the decade ending in 1975 reflects this instability; sales increased 30 fold but profits only multiplied four times due to the company's cash flow problems. A severe financial crises ensued in 1975 which led Smith to develop a new long-term competitive strategy.

After soliciting the advice of consultants and advertising experts, Smith's cut prices furiously and launched a large, general advertising campaign while operating stores under distinct names. Most important, Smith's began further experimentation with the combination superstore, sized at either 31,000 or 45,000 square feet. These changes immediately improved the bottom line of the company.

Smith's achieved further success throughout the 1970s as distribution centers were made more efficient, construction was initiated on new super combination stores, and weaker stores were sold off (notably four of the California stores). Although Dee Smith became more cautious in his acquisitions, he continued his growth through acquisition, acquiring six K-Mart stores. Two of the K-Mart stores were in Albuquerque, representing the company's first foray into the southwest market. The new region was solidly profitable and, in 1978, Smith's bought 23 Foodway stores in New Mexico, the second-largest acquisition in the company's history. Also, for the first time, Smith's had to deal with a unionized work force that went out on strike. After reaching an agreement, however, the stores quickly achieved profitable levels of operations.

Although it continued to acquire stores, Smith's main plan was to continue to expand by building more large combination outlets. The company built a total of 22 stores in 1977 and 1978 and planned an expanded production of the new outlets into the 1980s. Smith's used market research to tap new varieties of products, add more services, and merchandise new products. For instance, Smith's was one of the first retailers to market no-name, generic products—over 200 generic items in addition to name brand items. In 1980 the company began using the slogan "We're not just a food store anymore." The diverse mixture of departments sent sales up by 27 percent in 1978 and cash flow also improved. By 1979 the company was earning a 30 percent rate of profit on its equity.

The recession in the early 1980s only minimally affected the company's profits. During recessionary times, it became much cheaper to purchase failing businesses, and Smith's did just that. Specifically, Smith's purchased a group of eight stores in southern California. By this time about half of Smith's business had been acquisitions. Sales were slow but steady, and in 1983 the company weathered an eleven-week strike by Las Vegas workers. The strike did not prevent Smith's from becoming the second largest privately held supermarket chain by the end of 1983. The California stores, operating under the name Smith's

Food King, were sold in 1985 at a profit of $50 million.

In 1984 Dee Smith's five- and ten-year plans were implemented, but Smith died during the year and left the company to the control of the third generation of Smith sons. The new management team that was assembled nearly doubled sales and profits from 1984 to 1988. Jeff Smith took over for his father as chief executive officer, and under his reign the company has experienced accelerated growth. Dee Smith's plan to "phase out smaller, older conventional stores and superstores and replace them with larger combination food and drug centers" was successfully carried out by his sons despite intense competition. By 1990 76 of the company's 95 stores were combination food and drug stores ranging in size from 45,000 to 84,000 feet. New stores constructed in 1990 and 1991 averaged 72,900 square feet, continuing the modernization plan. The expansionist policy included replacing existing stores and pursuing intense cost-cutting strategies. This was supported by expanding and modernizing the company's warehouse facilities to vertically integrate the processing and distribution of perishable goods; achieve greater in-house warehousing to capitalize on economies of scale; and reorganize its transportation and distribution facilities.

To raise the money necessary to gain a foothold in the highly competitive California market (a planned 60 stores in five years), Smith's management decided to take the company public. Management first created Smith's Management Corporation, which was merged into its wholly owned subsidiary, Smith's Food & Drug Centers. Next, in an effort to keep the company in the Smith family and also foil takeovers, certain classes of stock were designated for ownership solely by the Smith family. The value of the shares skyrocketed initially but stabilized within the year. In the early 1990s chief executive officer Jeff Smith owned or controls 48.2 percent of the voting stock (mainly from shares held in a trust for his mother Ida). The next biggest block, 8.3 percent, was held by the Church of Jesus Christ of the Latter-Day Saints as part of Dee Smith's estate and will be completely liquidated by 1999.

The future competitive position of Smith's Food & Drug Centers depends on both the success of the move into the southern California market and the company's ten-year plan to spend $1.4 billion and open 120 stores with annual sales growth targets of 20 percent. This effort will include a one-million square foot fully integrated distribution facility to warehouse the goods for the region and an average store size is 70,000 square feet.

The California market will be an extremely competitive and some industry analysts expecting price wars. Further, the California stores will be unionized, unlike most of Smith's other stores. Yet there are more people in the southern California region than in all of Smith's other markets combined, and the store can offer competitive prices. The degree of growth realized, however is likely to depend on the state of employment in the region in the next decade and on the outcome the battle with five other chains, such as Von's Grocery Co., Lucky Stores Inc., and Albertson's Inc., which already have over 100 stores each in the region. Smith's predicts it will be able to capture about six percent of the region's market when its first 50 to 60 stores are opened. Although this figure is dwarfed by Smith's 40 percent market share in Salt Lake City and its 35 percent share in Las Vegas, the company has gone head-to-head with Von's, Lucky, and Albertson's in these markets in the past.

Further Reading:

Carlisle, Howard M., *The Dee Smith Story: Fulfilling A Dream,* Brigham City, Utah, Ida Smith, 1992.
Lowenstein, Roger, "Smith's Food & Drug Gets Mixed Reviews As It Enters Big, Crowded Phoenix Market," *Wall Street Journal,* September 28, 1989.
Silverstein, Stuart, "Heating Up the Supermarket Wars," *Los Angeles Times,* September 8, 1991.
Smith's Food and Drug Centers, Inc., "General Fact Sheet," 1993.
"Smith's Food and Drug Centers Reports Increased Sales and Net Income For First Quarter 1993," (press release), April 27, 1993.
"Smith's Scores with One-Hour Photo," *Progressive Grocer,* October, 1992.
Taylor, John H., "Mr. Smith Goes to Riverside," *Forbes,* February 17, 1992.

—John A. Sarich

Sonoco Products Company

North Second Street
Hartsville, South Carolina 29550-0160
U.S.A.
(803) 383-7000
Fax: (803) 339-6076

Public Company
Incorporated: 1899 as Southern Novelty Company
Employees: 16,000
Sales: $1.84 billion
Stock Exchanges: NASDAQ
SICs: 2655 Fiber Cans, Tubes, Drums & Similar Products;
    2421 Sawmills and Planing Mills, General; 2426
    Hardwood Dimension & Flooring Mills; 2499 Wood
    Products, Nec; 2631 Paperboard Mills; 2653 Corrugated
    and Solid Fiber Boxes; 2657 Folding Paperboard Boxes,
    Including Sanitary; 2673 Plastics, Foil and Coated Paper
    Bags; 2675 Die-cut Paper and Paperboard and Cardboard;
    2679 Converted Paper and Paperboard Products, Nec;
    2891 Adhesives and Sealants; 3082 Unsupported Plastics
    Profile Shapes; 3089 Plastics Products, Nec; 3499
    Fabricated Metal Products, Nec

Sonoco Products Co. is one of the largest packaging manufacturers in the world. With 16,000 employees and 250 operations
in 22 countries, Sonoco provides containers and carriers made
of paper, plastic, wood and metal to worldwide industrial and
consumer markets. Among numerous innovations in its nearly
100-year history, Sonoco is noted for pioneering the use of the
plastic ''T-shirt'' grocery sack common in supermarkets and
retail stores and for creating Ultraseal, a closure system for
Crisco shortening cans that eliminated the need for a can
opener.

The company originally manufactured paper cones used by the
textile industry to wind yarn. As the company expanded and
diversified, Sonoco began to manufacture additional products
such as molded plastic cones and tubes, toner cartridges, caulk-
ing cartridges, composite containers (used for refrigerated
dough, frozen juice concentrates and other foods), fiber and
plastic drums used for chemicals and pharmaceuticals, tennis
ball containers, paperboard, packaging forms, and cap seals, to
name a few.

Sonoco had its beginnings in 1890, when Major James L. Coker
and his son, James, Jr., founded the Carolina Fiber Company in
Hartsville, South Carolina, to manufacture pulp and paper from
Southern Pine trees. The enterprise was based on James, Jr.'s
senior thesis, which outlined how to make paper pulp using a
chemical process.

A few years later, after unsuccessful attempts to sell the pulp
commercially, the Cokers decided to use the pulp to make paper
cones for the textile industry. On April 15, 1899, Maj. Coker
and W. F. Smith formed the Southern Novelty Company, with
Coker as the first president. The company ordered a Fourdrinier
paper machine, which was built for $19,050. The machine was
capable of turning out five to eight tons of paper in 24 hours.

One year after its founding, the new company had sales of
$17,000 and net earnings of $2,000. As the 20th century
dawned, the textile industry in the South began to grow and
prosper, and Sonoco's yarn carriers were in high demand. The
advent of new uses for cotton and innovations in high-speed
cotton spinning helped revolutionize the textile industry and
fuel Sonoco's growth. By 1923, when the company changed its
name to Sonoco Products Company, sales were approaching the
one-million mark, and income was nearly $40,000.

Although the First World War and the Great Depression devastated many other businesses, Sonoco continued to thrive and
expand. In 1927 the company grew from one main plant in
Hartsville when it acquired Forney Fiber Company of Jersey
City, New Jersey. Also in the 1920s, Sonoco entered into a joint
venture with a company in Manchester, England. The joint
venture introduced the manufacture of Sonoco-style textile carriers in Manchester, and served as the origin for the Textile
Paper Tube Company, Ltd., which eventually grew to include
five plants in England, one in Ireland, and subsidiaries in Holland, Germany, South Africa, and India. The joint venture in
Manchester was the first of many subsequent international affiliations.

Sales reached $1.6 million in 1930, and profits hit $200,000.
Throughout the 1930s and into the 1940s, Sonoco built additional paper machines and acquired other paper tube companies.
Charles Westfield Coker, the Major's third son, who had been
president since his father's death, passed away in 1931. His son,
James Lide Coker III, was named president of Sonoco while
still in his late 20s. Under James Coker, who held a master's
degree from Harvard Business School, Sonoco flourished. New
plants were set up or acquired in eight new locations, and
Sonoco established a subsidiary in Canada.

It was during this era that man-made fibers were introduced,
changing the textile industry dramatically. Sonoco kept up with
the times and focused on developing new product lines, new
types of finishes on its cones, and faster means of production.
By the end of the 1940s, Sonoco had eight paper machines at the
Hartsville mill.

Sonoco looked south of the border in 1950, and expanded its
international operations by forming Sonoco de Mexico, S.A.
The decade of the 1950s was a period of continued growth and
stability for Sonoco. The company posted sales in 1950 of $18.9
million and income of $1.6 million. Tube operations began in
Indiana, Texas, and California. In 1957 the company acquired

National Paper Co. of Georgia. By the end of the decade, Sonoco had branched into the production of corrugated material.

The 1960s opened on a positive note, with sales at $38 million and income at $2.5 million. In a string of acquisitions in 1960, Sonoco launched operations in Richmond, Virginia, Holyoke, Massachusetts, and Munroe Falls, Ohio. The robust tone set that year continued throughout the decade. In 1961 Sonoco began a spiral tube operation at Ravenna, Ohio, and acquired Industrial Steel and Fibre Ltd. of Terrebonne, Quebec, and Toronto, Ontario. This acquisition took Sonoco into the realm of fiber drums and composite containers (containers with a paper body and metal ends).

James Lide Coker III died in 1961 at the age of 56. His brother, Charles W. Coker—another of the Major's grandsons—became president of the company. Under his leadership, Sonoco started tube operations in Washington, Wisconsin, Missouri, Tennessee, New York, and South Carolina during the 1960s. The company also began manufacturing composite cans in Florida, South Carolina, and Kentucky.

1964 marked a new direction for Sonoco when the company began a business relationship with Showa Products Company of Japan. Further business with Japan would follow two decades later. In 1970 Charles Coker became chairman of the board, and his son Charles, Jr., became president. Sales were $125 million, and income was $6.6 million. That year, Sonoco merged Downingtown Paper Company into its business. Sonoco also acquired a lumber mill in Darlington, South Carolina, and leased timberlands. The company set up tube operations in Puerto Rico in 1971, the same year it acquired a Richmond, California, paper mill from Western Kraft Corporation.

Further diversification occurred in 1972, when Sonoco purchased Paper Stock Dealers, Inc., and Gaston Paper Stock Co., Inc. of Statesville, North Carolina. These acquisitions marked Sonoco's entrance into the wastepaper packing business. The company embarked on another type of new operations in 1973 by starting folding carton and fiber partitions operations in Georgia.

By 1974 Sonoco had 36 U.S. branch plants, and the international division had operations in 11 foreign countries. The company featured six distinct divisions—plastic, paper, forest products, packaging, construction products, partitions, and general products (which included products to the textile industry). Sonoco also operated a waste paper company and a steel fabricating company. Vertical integration was standard, and Sonoco produced its own paper, adhesives, lacquers, and varnishes. From its humble origins of 12 employees in a rented warehouse, Sonoco had grown to number 2,700 people in Hartsville alone.

Tube, composite can, and fiber partition operations began in six states during 1974 and 1975. During America's bicentennial year, 1976, Charles W. Coker, Jr., became the company's chief executive officer. Sonoco was, by this time, one of the top employers in South Carolina.

The latter half of the decade was characterized by continued vigorous expansion. Sonoco Ltd. of Canada opened a new plant in Moncton, New Brunswick. In the United States, Sonoco gained five composite can lines from the American Can Company and started composite can operations in Chicago and St. Louis. The company established Sonoco Containers of Puerto Rico in 1978.

Always evolving, Sonoco in 1979 bought 49 percent interest in the can division of Domtar, Inc., of Canada, closed the folding carton plant in Georgia, and sold folding carton plants in Virginia and Pennsylvania. As the decade closed, Sonoco purchased virtually all of T.P.T. Papierfabrik of Nordhorn, West Germany, and T.P.T. of Nederland, Holland.

The 1980s got off to a fast start on various fronts—Sonoco acquired Alabama-based Baker Industries, Inc., a leading manufacturer of reels for the wire and cable industry, started producing plastic grocery sacks at a Massachusetts plant, and launched a new division at T.P.T. England to make ''Bag-in-Box'' liquitainers. Sales for 1980 reached $490 million and income was reported at $32.5 million.

Sonoco made the Fortune 500 list for the first time in 1981. The company ranked 457th among the top 500 public manufacturing companies in the United States. That same year, Sonoco de Mexico opened a plant in Monterrey, Mexico. The following year, 1982, was one of numerous acquisitions. Sonoco bought Capseals, Ltd., of England, Linear Products of Puerto Rico (later sold) and acquired the Briggs-Shaffner Division, a major producer of textile beams based in Winston-Salem, North Carolina. The company also bought most of Container Corporation of America's composite can division.

In 1983 Sonoco opened a second plastic bag production site in Santa Monica, California. The company bought Robinson Hardwood Corporation to produce furniture squares and opened a new tube production plant in West Chicago. Sonoco Limited of Canada, meanwhile, purchased another Canadian company, Federal Packaging and Partition Co.

Sonoco added a new product to its roster in 1984, when the company began producing plastic motor oil bottles. Tube production was still going strong, and the company added three new tube operations in Menasha, Wisconsin, Cincinnati, Ohio, and Clifton Forge, Virginia. The following year, Sonoco began plastic sack production at a third facility. The company continued to move into the fiber drum business, acquiring Continental Fiber Drum of Stamford, Connecticut, then the top U.S. producer of fiber drums. Sonoco also acquired Fibro Tambor, S.A. de C.V., a Mexican fiber drum business.

By 1986 the company had 150 plants operating on five continents and a total of more than 11,000 employees who produced hundreds of products ranging from the original textile cones to drainage pipe, composite cans, shipping and storage tubes, plastic grocery sacks, and construction tubes for forming round concrete columns. Textiles, formerly 100 percent of the business, had shrunk to about 15 percent. Sonoco had carved a niche for itself in the paper industry by collecting waste paper from about 30 sites, mainly in the South, and recycling it into paperboard. In 1986 the company acquired the West German Ka-Ro Werke and the South Carolina-based American Ka-Ro, producers of plastic tubes and cones. The company also added Mako, B.V., of Maastricht, Holland, to its roster of fiber tube and drum operations.

1987 saw the acquisition of the Consumer Packaging Division of Boise Cascade, then the nation's largest producer of composite cans. In 1988 Sonoco completed construction of its Packaging Development Center in Hartsville and purchased Gunther, S.A., and its subsidiaries, French producers of paperboard, tubes, cores, cones, and protective packaging.

In terms of innovations in packaging, Sonoco teamed up with Procter & Gamble to create Ultraseal, a closure for P&G's composite cans of Crisco solid shortening. The new closure was designed to be "in control"—that is, the consumer didn't have to use a can opener to break the seal. Sonoco developed a tight-sealing membrane with a ring for easy removal. Also in the realm of packaging, Sonoco started a new plastic grocery sack operation in Telford, England, and acquired the Hilex Poly Co., Inc., of Los Angeles, another plastic sack manufacturer.

Another merger occurred in 1989, when Sonoco joined its Petroleum Products Division with the Graham Container Corp. of York, Pennsylvania, a manufacturer of plastic bottles, to form Sonoco Graham Co. Sonoco owned 40 percent of the new company, but by 1990 wanted to sell its share for $60 million. Sonoco eventually sold its 40 percent interest back to Graham in 1991.

A significant feature of 1989 was Sonoco's international activity. The company acquired the Udo Fischer Co. of Maulburg, Germany. The move added to Sonoco's coreboard and tube production capabilities. Also in 1989, Sonoco set up Sonoco Taiwan Ltd., with headquarters in Taipei, and opened a new plant in Taiwan; bought Mygind International, a manufacturer of plastic sacks and produce bags, of Roskilde, Denmark; announced a joint venture with CMB Packaging, for production and marketing of composite cans throughout Europe; and bought Unit Group plc, a British manufacturer of reels. Sonoco also expanded into Argentina.

Sonoco's sales in 1989 were $1.7 billion and income was $103 million, the highest sales and earnings in the company's history. Income per share was $2.36. By the beginning of the 1990s, Sonoco's venture into plastic grocery sacks had richly paid off—plastic sacks accounted for about 65 percent of grocery bags used in U.S. supermarkets, and the company had the largest share of that market. In another area of packaging, Sonoco set up a plant in Georgia to produce intermediate bulk containers. The company made this move in response to consumer demand for packages larger than fiber drums.

By 1989 Sonoco was the largest manufacturer of uncoated recycled cylinder paperboard in the world. The company recycled about a million tons of wastepaper annually, and controlled about 44,000 acres of woodland as part of its corrugating business.

From these peaks in 1989, Sonoco entered the 1990s with more than 15,000 employees at 200 locations around the world. Sixty-five percent of Sonoco's business was in industrial packaging, while the remaining 35 percent was in consumer packaging. By 1991 economic recession had affected every division and operation. It was the second down year in two decades. Sales for the year were $1.7 billion and income was $94.8 million. Sonoco decreased its U.S. work force by six percent and embarked on an extensive restructuring program.

The picture was not completely bleak, however. The joint venture with CMB Packaging in Europe did well, and the bag-in-box liquitainers were expected to be an area of growth for the company. Sonoco's Liquid Packaging Group set up a bag-in-box operation in California in 1991. On the international front, Sonoco's Industrial Products Division set up a joint venture relationship with Showa Marutsutsu Co. Ltd. of Japan to produce film cores. In 1990 Sonoco purchased Lhomme S.A. to become the largest tube producer in Europe. Sonoco also became the largest tube producer in Australia when it bought Rolex, an Australian core and tube manufacturer.

Sonoco continued to pursue innovative packaging. The High Density Film Products group developed the "Enviromate/RCB" sack in 1991, which contained 25 percent post-consumer recycled resin.

By 1992 Sonoco employed approximately 16,000 people worldwide and had 250 operations in 22 countries. Sales reached $1.8 billion, an increase of 8.2 percent over the previous year. Income in 1992 was $43.3 million or $1 per share. Sonoco added to its consumer packaging operations in Mexico, Puerto Rico, Colombia, and Venezuela. The Industrial Products Division made Sonoco the leading producer of tubes and cores in Europe and Australia. By the end of 1992, the work force in the Industrial Products Division had been reduced by 15 percent.

In Asia during 1992, Sonoco opened an office in Singapore for Sonoco Asia and launched a new tube and core production facility in Malaysia.

As Sonoco entered 1993, it acquired Crellin Holding, Inc., a major manufacturer of injection molded products. Crellin provides plastic carriers for textiles and plastic reels for fiber optics, and has nine plants in the United States and one in the Netherlands. Crellin's products represented new industries and a growth opportunity for Sonoco.

Principal Subsidiaries: Paper Stock Dealers, Inc.; Sonoco Asia/Pacific; Sonoco Limited (Canada); Crellin Holding; Showa Products Company, Ltd. (Japan; 20%).

Further Reading:

"Businessman of the Year: Charles W. Coker," *South Carolina Business Journal,* January 1, 1986, Vol. 6, p. 53.
Coker, Charles W., *The Story of Sonoco Products Company,* New York: The Newcomen Society in North America, 1974.
Erickson, Greg, "Peelable Lid Enters Era of Zero Defects," *Packaging,* September 1988, Vol. 33, No. 11, pp. 8–10.
"Graham Completes Acquisition," *Wall Street Journal,* April 2, 1991, Section C, p. 14.
Puffer, Dick, "Sonoco Reports Excellent 1992 Operational Results," *PR Newswire,* January 21, 1993.
——, "Sonoco to Acquire German Tube Manufacturer," *PR Newswire,* November 25, 1992.
The Sonoco Products Company Annual Reports, Hartsville, N.C.: Sonoco Products Company, 1989–1992.
"Sonoco Restructuring to Include Selling its Stake in Venture," *Wall Street Journal,* August 29, 1990, Section C, p. 8.
"Sonoco to Buy Plastics Company," *Florence Morning News,* January 6, 1993.

—Marinell Landa

Southwire Company, Inc.

P.O. Box 1000
Carrollton, Georgia 30119
U.S.A.
(404) 832-4242
Fax: (404) 832-4929

Private Company
Incorporated: 1950 as Southwire Company
Employees: 4,556
Sales: $1.30 billion
SICs: 2448 Wood Pallets & Skids; 3351 Copper Rolling &
Drawing; 3355 Aluminum Rolling & Drawing, Nec; 3357
Nonferrous Wiredrawing & Insulating; 3599 Industrial
Machinery, Nec

Southwire Company is the largest wire and cable maker in the
United States. As a manufacturer of copper and aluminum rod,
wire, and cable for use in the transmission and distribution of
electricity, the company has made significant technological
advances that have been adopted by the worldwide wire and
cable industry. Southwire's Wire & Cable Division, the largest
unit of the company, manufactures more than 1,000 products,
ranging from building and utility wire and cable to cable-in-
conduit products.

The creation of Southwire is a classic example of entrepreneurial spirit facing unfavorable odds and triumphing. Shortly after
graduating from Georgia Institute of Technology, Roy Richards, who ran his father's sawmill by the time he was 14 years
old, started his own business in 1937. Called Roy Richards
Construction Company, it was an extension of his father's
sawmill. Six months after opening his business, the 25-year-old
Richards was awarded a $118,000 Rural Electrification Admin-
istration (REA) contract to set the poles and string the wire for
108 miles of power lines in Georgia.

Although REA officials were somewhat anxious about Richards' young age and lack of experience, his construction of the
Georgia power lines garnered high praise and additional REA
contracts. In fact, Richards' method of setting poles and string-
ing wire had reduced the time it took to build a year's worth of
power lines to three months, a process soon adopted by REA
contractors nationwide. By 1939 Richards' company had strung
3,500 miles of power lines for the REA throughout Georgia and
Alabama, establishing it as the second largest constructor of

power lines for the REA in the nation. Two years later, the
company was awarded its first international contract to construct a power generation station in St. Croix in the Virgin
Islands.

By the time Richards' work was completed in the Virgin
Islands, the Japanese had bombed Pearl Harbor and the United
States had entered World War II. The onset of the war marked a
significant decline in the number of REA contracts offered, so
Richards decided to actively join the war effort and enlisted in
the U.S. Army. Shortly after his return in 1945, Richards landed
a contract to build 500 miles of an electrical transmission line in
Georgia. The war, however, had severely limited the amount of
aluminum wire available. Richards canvassed all of the large
wire manufacturers and was told that he would have to wait a
minimum of three years to receive enough wire to complete his
500-mile project. Faced with either waiting for the aluminum
companies to deliver the wire and losing the contract in Georgia, or manufacturing the wire himself, Richards opted for the
latter. In 1950, with $80,000 in capital and the assistance of a
professor of mechanical engineering under whom he had studied during college, Richards created Southwire Company.

Hiring 12 employees who worked with second-hand machinery
in a 12,000 square-foot building, Richards set up operations to
manufacture copper and aluminum wire for his first customer—
himself. Industry pundits had warned Richards that his remote
location would make the shipping of raw materials too costly
and that the number of skilled labor available in the area could
not support his venture. Richards, however, proved them wrong
and produced his first lot of copper and aluminum wire in four
months. By the end of its second year, Southwire had shipped
five million pounds of wire, amassed $560,000 in sales, and
doubled the size of its manufacturing facility.

Having achieved remarkable results in his first two years of
operation, Richards then began searching for a way to improve
the quality of his wire. Wire is made by winnowing a thicker
stock of aluminum or copper, called a "rod," into a smaller
diameter to reach the desired thickness. Traditionally, segments
of rod were welded together, end to end, to create a continuous
roll that was then compressed and stretched into a strand of
wire. Welding the rods together, however, created a weak wire
and, frequently, a strand of wire would break at the location of
the weld.

Wishing to somehow avoid the inherent weakness that welding
caused, Richards traveled to Italy to investigate a method developed by an Italian industrialist named Illario Properzi for continuously casting and rolling rod. Properzi's casting method had
only been used with commercial grade lead and zinc, and he
was convinced the method would not work with aluminum
electrical wire due to the vastly different metallurgical properties between the metals. Richards nevertheless signed a contract
for the rights to the process, and after a year of experimentation
by Southwire engineers, a machine was developed that would
continuously cast aluminum rod.

Next, Richards sought to make the process applicable to copper
rod, which posed even greater metallurgical problems. After
five years of tests on its own, Southwire entered into an agreement with Western Electric Company, and experiments contin-

ued under the joint venture for several more years. Finally, in 1963, a suitable process was developed. This process, known as the Southwire Continuous Rod (SCR) system, marked a revolutionary advance in wire production technology and immediately began being employed by other wire manufacturers. Eventually, 90 percent of copper rod for electrical wire and cable produced in major industrial countries would be manufactured by continuous casting systems, half of which would be designed and built by Southwire.

After presiding over the successful completion of Southwire's experimentation with copper wire production, Richards began exploring the possibility of constructing his own aluminum smelter to produce the aluminum needed in wire production. Unable to finance the construction on his own, Richards searched for a partner in the venture and by 1967 had signed an agreement with Copper Range Company to build a $90 million plant. A copper strike and other projects Copper Range was involved with, however, forced Copper Range to withdraw from its involvement with the project.

The fact that labor difficulties were partly to blame for the collapse of the negotiations between Southwire and Copper Range must have irritated Richards to some extent. A man who chose to guard both himself and his company from public scrutiny, Richards disapproved of organized labor and went to great lengths to keep its presence from penetrating Southwire. For years, a classic anti-union film, *And Women Must Weep,* was shown on Fridays to inculcate his opinion of the union movement to new Southwire employees. During one particularly contentious incident in the 1960s, Richards reportedly hired private detectives to pose as Southwire employees in order to identify union sympathizers on his payroll.

The frustration over the Southwire-Copper Range agreement, however, was short-lived. In 1968 Southwire and National Steel Corporation agreed to build a 135,000-ton, $200 million aluminum smelter in Kentucky. The joint venture, called National-Southwire Aluminum, became upon its formation the seventh-largest primary aluminum producer in the United States. In a peripheral deal, Richards sold 20 percent of Southwire to National Steel for $25 million, which provided him with the necessary working capital to build his own copper smelter in 1971.

By the late 1960s Southwire had evolved from a business created to supply Richards' construction company with wire into a thriving company that far exceeded the original objectives established for it. With sales of $80 million in 1967, Southwire had two plants fabricating electrical wire and cable in Georgia and one in San Juan, Puerto Rico.

The addition of aluminum and copper smelters helped spawn a decade of dramatic growth in the 1970s. Sales in 1970 stood at $123 million and ballooned to $723 million by 1980. This success was partly attributable to Richards' efforts to vertically integrate the company. In addition to the two smelters, Richards operated a sawmill to make shipping pallets and spools from his own timber, a plastics processing plant to prepare wire installations, and owned a fleet of trucks to transport his products. When the oil crisis in 1973 limited the availability of natural gas supplies for his aluminum smelter, Richards drilled gas and oil wells to mitigate the effects of the energy crisis on his operations.

Not all attempts at achieving vertical integration were successful, however. In 1971 Southwire and National Steel signed an agreement with Earth Sciences Inc. to mine and develop a mineral called alunite as an alternative for another mineral, bauxite, in the production of alumina, the raw material from which aluminum is refined. Traditionally, bauxite had been used, but reports of Soviet scientists working on a process to replace bauxite with alunite persuaded Southwire and its partners to develop an alunite process of their own. With a 25 percent interest in the venture, Southwire built a pilot plant and began mining property owned by Earth Sciences in Utah, Colorado, Arizona, and Nevada. The project was expanded in 1973 and then again two years later, but a solution was never found and the project was abandoned.

Despite this failure, Southwire, by 1976, was the third-largest wire producer in the United States, ranking behind Western Electric and United Technologies' Essex Group. With sales of $400 million, the company had become a major force in the industry, competing with such giant corporations as Anaconda, Kaiser, and Reynolds Metals. Flushed with success on the domestic front, Southwire's international involvement had also grown. By 1976 overseas business had intensified, accounting for 10 percent of the company's revenues. It now had facilities operating in England and Venezuela and had signed a contract to build and manage a $500 million aluminum plant in Dubai, Saudi Arabia.

After a decade of robust growth, Southwire entered the 1980s with optimism, expecting to expand its operations and collect further profits. But the geometric rise in sales during the 1970s plummeted in the early 1980s. After posting record sales of $723 million in 1980, sales the following year dropped to $606 million for a net loss of $9.15 million; in 1983 the company's net loss totaled nearly $30 million. Part of the explanation for the sudden collapse was the deleterious effect the worldwide recession had on the housing and automobile industries, both of which were major customers of Southwire's products. Also, throughout the late 1970s and into the 1980s, Southwire continued to borrow large sums of money, convinced the growth of the 1970s would continue into the 1980s. As the recession pushed interest rates skyward, Southwire's interest payments began to drain its cash flow. Yet, during this economic slide, Richards continued to expand, adding a $30 million copper rod mill in 1981.

By 1984 the end of the recession had extricated Southwire from its financial malaise. Upswings in housing construction and the automobile industry buoyed the company's sales, and the elimination of inefficient and unprofitable operations improved the profitability of the company. Several plants in New Jersey and Puerto Rico were closed, ventures in the steel conduit business were dropped, and Kagan-Dixon-Eldra, a joint venture with an Austrian company to manufacture magnet wire in Arkansas, was abandoned.

In June of 1985 Richards died of bone cancer. Two of his sons, Roy, Jr., and James, assumed the leadership of Southwire, which now—after the streamlining of the early 1980s—posted sales of more than $600 million. With Roy Richards, Jr., as chief executive officer and James Richards as president, Southwire began to diversify its product line to increase its customer base. In 1986 the company acquired a building wire and cable plant in Utah and three years later purchased Hi-Tech Cable Corporation, one of the largest copper wire and cable production facilities in the United States. In 1991 Southwire purchased the remaining 54.5 percent interest in National-Southwire Aluminum originally held by National Steel. Also in 1991 Southwire bought the assets of AT&T Nassau Metals Corporation, from which Gaston Copper Recycling Corporation was formed, making Southwire the largest recycler of copper in the United States. Southwire returned to the conduit business in 1992 with the purchase of Integral Corporation, a manufacturer of cable-in-conduit.

The progress Southwire has made during its history is remarkable, given the circumstances of its creation. Beginning with only a casual understanding of how to manufacture wire, Roy Richards quickly became a leader in the industry and transformed his modest, 12-employee company into one of the premier wire manufacturers in the United States. By 1993 Southwire had 11 wire mills, three smelters, and two cable-in-conduit manufacturing plants. Forty-eight of its Southwire Con-

tinuous Rod systems had been sold worldwide to such countries as China, Thailand, Saudi Arabia, Sweden, and Russia. With another generation of the Richards family leading the company and hoping to build upon the legacy established by their father, future prospects looked favorable for Southwire.

Principal Subsidiaries: Southwire-Furukawa Cable Company.

Further Reading:

''Copper Range, Southwire to Build Jointly $90 Million Aluminum Plant in Kentucky,'' *Wall Street Journal,* October 20, 1967, p. 4.

Cumming, Joseph B., *Roy Richards,* Carrollton, GA: Southwire Company, 1987.

''Earth Sciences Inc.'s Joint Venture Widened,'' *Wall Street Journal,* January 17, 1973, p. 7.

Lauterbach, Jeffrey R., ''Southwire's Empire Builder Struggles to Hang On,'' *Industry Week,* May 2, 1983, pp. 35–38.

''Live Wire,'' *Forbes,* August 1, 1976, p. 26.

''National Steel Slates Aluminum Smelter Venture,'' *Wall Street Journal,* May 9, 1968, p. 6.

''Roy Richards: Money for Good Ideas,'' *Forbes,* May 1, 1967, p. 72.

Southwire Company Corporate History, Carrollton, GA: Southwire Company, 1993.

—Jeffrey L. Covell

Spartan Stores Inc.

850 76th Street S.W.
P.O. Box 8700
Grand Rapids, Michigan 49518
U.S.A.
(616) 878-2000
Fax: (616) 878-2667

Private Company
Incorporated: 1918
Employees: 2,000
Sales: $2.1 billion
SICs: 5141 Groceries—General Line

Among the ten largest wholesalers of grocery and related products in the United States, Spartan Stores, Inc., is owned by over 500 independent supermarkets and supermarket chains in northern Indiana, Ohio, and, primarily, Michigan. In addition to distributing food and non-food items to its retailers from two distribution centers in the Michigan cities of Plymouth and Grand Rapids, the company offers its supermarkets a diverse program of assistance, including accounting, advertising, and insurance services.

Seeking to lower grocery prices by providing greater economies of scale, a group of nearly 100 independent store owners met at the Livingston Hotel in Grand Rapids, Michigan, on December 27, 1917. The meeting had been prompted by a recent increase in competition from emerging national grocery store chains, such as A & P, which were able to provide customers with one-stop shopping and lower prices. By the end of the day, 43 of the grocers decided to form a cooperative whose purchasing power they hoped would help their business. Signing Articles of Incorporation, the grocers formed the Grand Rapids Wholesale Grocery Company. Only 27 bought stock in the corporation.

Stock in the company was privately held. Stores becoming members of the cooperative were required to maintain a stock investment, which could be sold back should a store decide to leave the cooperative. In 1957 the wholesale company changed its name to Spartan Stores, Inc., a name management believed would achieve wide recognition in the area due to the popular association in Michigan between the name Spartan and the state university. The Spartan logo, featuring a warrior of ancient Sparta holding sword and shield, colored in a bright green, was reproduced on labels, grocery bags, and on the sides of the

company's trucks. Although the retailers for whom Spartan acted as distributor did business under different names, the stores were united under this logo, which was displayed on the doors of all Spartan stores and also featured on the neon lit signs of many.

In 1973 Spartan's status changed from that of a cooperative to a Michigan business corporation. During this time the grocery business changed considerably, as the rate at which new products became available and the competition among grocery chains increased. Product volume at the Spartan warehouses also increased dramatically, and a new computerized vending system, known as Big Blue, was installed at the Grand Rapids complex, helping to distribute around 174 million pounds of fresh produce, 115 million pounds of meat, and four million cases of frozen foods in 1984. As both sales and the company's stock, available to businesses and individuals who operated grocery retail outfits, steadily climbed, the wholesaler expanded its membership to 475 stores.

Over the next ten years Spartan also became involved in several humanitarian projects, including sponsorship of several area food bank and youth programs and a golf tournament to benefit the American Cancer Society. The company's most notable community project, however, has been its exclusive sponsorship of the Michigan Special Olympics Summer Games, which it took on in 1984. Spartan's role as sponsor is highly publicized every year through television, radio, and newspapers. Furthermore, Spartan designates around 200 products that are carried by its retailers as Special Olympics items; the products are advertised and five cents from each sale of these items goes to the support and promotion of this annual event. In addition to paying the way for athletes to travel to and participate in the games, Spartan provides printed programs and entertainment, as well as food for the hundreds of volunteers who supervise and officiate the games.

The 1980s were a very productive and successful period for Spartan Stores. Annual sales rose by nearly ten percent through 1989. In 1985 sales reached $1.3 billion, up from $1.2 billion the year before. By 1986 Spartan controlled 20 percent of the Michigan grocery market and its sales had risen to $1.4 billion. That year the company was ranked as Michigan's largest grocery wholesaler, and the 12th largest in the country. Sales steadily increased to $1.7 billion in 1988.

Although financially successful during this time, Spartan began to receive complaints from some of its member stores, who charged that Spartan seemed more interested in maintaining the status quo than fostering communication and cooperation between retailer and distributor. Agreeing that management lacked a vision for the company's continued growth and improvement, the board decided to elect a new president. When Patrick Quinn, formerly a vice-president at the 14-store chain of D & W Food Stores, became Spartan's president and CEO in 1985, he was the third person to fill the post in four years. Quinn was charged with reestablishing positive relationships and developing a specific and detailed long-term plan for the company.

When questioned about his lack of background in retailing, Quinn told *Supermarket News* that "it puts me in a naive position, so I can ask questions that may not have been asked in a long time, such as why something is done a certain way. It causes people to think, reexamine why things are done as they are.'' Quinn proceeded to reexamine nearly every aspect of the company and determined that distribution centers needed expanding, and that both Spartan's data processing system and its policy of owning corporate stores needed further consideration.

Considering himself a ''visible'' manager who would strive to be available and responsive, Quinn pledged to visit stores and warehouses in an effort to establish good relations with employees and become better educated about retailers needs. Quinn's vision for the company was characterized as ''getting back to basics,'' a practice realized through several of his early decisions as Spartan's president. He eliminated the computerized vending system in Spartan's Grand Rapids distribution center when he found numerous bugs in the system and noted the increasing expense of its maintenance. He also brought back the conventional wooden pallet, used to move boxes in and out of the company's truck trailers, when he observed that newer high-tech metal mechanisms were more cumbersome and less reliable. Quinn also stressed the importance of keeping Spartan retailers happy. Toward that end he created the position of a customer service director who, by reporting directly to Quinn, could help improve communication and solve problems in all areas of the business.

In September 1985, hoping to gain more warehouse and office space, Spartan entered negotiations to purchase Eberhard Foods, a Grand Rapids chain of 22 stores. The following month negotiations were indefinitely postponed, however, when Eberhard was faced with a lawsuit filed by union members and employees charging the company with mishandling their stock option plan. Plans to acquire Viking Food Stores Inc. of Muskegon, Michigan, fell through two years later when an agreement could not be reached regarding the purchase price and several other terms.

In 1987 Spartan disclosed plans to sell some of its corporate retail stores. Not only did the company wish to refocus its business as that of wholesale and not retail, but it was also concerned that the role it had assumed in both supplying stores and operating competing stores represented a conflict of interest. Thus, Spartan decided to auction off 80 percent, or 22 of its 25, retail stores. The stores were first offered to Spartan's retail members, and in October of that year, D & W Food Stores, Inc., announced its intention to purchase 6 of the stores. Other stores were bid on by smaller local chains.

Spartan's operations are generally divided into four segments: distribution; insurance sales and underwriting; real estate and finance; and retail stores. As a distributor of groceries and grocery related items, Spartan carries over 46,000 items, including general merchandise and health and beauty care products,

which it receives from suppliers. Spartan makes available to its retailers both nationally advertised brands and Spartan's own private label items. Products reach individual stores via Spartan's fleet of over 300 trucks, one of the largest private fleets in Michigan. Insurance is offered to retailers through Spartan's subsidiaries, which make group health plan programs available for store employees and provide Spartan stores with fire, casualty, liability, and several other types of insurance. Those in the Spartan network who wish to either expand or remodel their stores may petition to borrow funds from Spartan's real estate and financing division. The retail store segment, having been scaled back under Quinn's leadership, consisted of one corporate store in 1993, which was maintained through the company's Valueland subsidiary. In addition to its four main business segments, Spartan offered numerous support services to its retailers including market research, training programs, advertising design and printing, and accounting services.

In the early 1990s, the Spartan board voted to allow individual employees of Spartan Stores, its subsidiaries, and its retailers, as well as certain ''approved shareholders,'' to purchase Spartan stock. In 1992 the company expected to generate more than $27 million from the sale of 175,000 shares of its Class A stock, which would be used for working capital. Quinn was characterized by *Progressive Grocer* magazine as cautiously optimistic in his projections for the company's success in 1993. While planning to expand Spartan's network to include more stores in the midwest, the company faced tough competition from the larger chain supermarkets as well as the challenge of recovering from a national economic recession. Nevertheless, by continuing to reevaluate and improve its procedures and products, while maintaining the image of its stores as unique, local alternatives to the giant supermarket chains, the company expected to see continued growth in sales and earnings.

Principal Subsidiaries: Capistar, Inc.; L & L/Jiroch Distributing Company; United Wholesale Grocery Company; Shield Insurance Services, Inc.; Spartan Insurance Company, Ltd.; Shield Benefit Administrators, Inc.

Further Reading:

Bennett, Stephen, ''Spartan Shows Sporting Spirit,'' *Progressive Grocer,* December 1991, pp. 34–35.
De Santa, Richard, ''Renewing the Spartan Philosophy,'' *Progressive Grocer,* January 1988, pp. 28–36.
Natschke, Patricia, ''Quinn Leads a Spartan Life,'' *Supermarket News,* September 2, 1985, p. 1–1A.
Shellenbarger, Pat, ''Big-Volume Spartan Just Clicks Along,'' *Grand Rapids Press,* April 21, 1985.
Veen, Jeffrey, ''Technology Boosts Spartan Inc. Efforts,'' *Grand Rapids Business Journal,* May 18, 1992, p. 5.
Weinstein, Steve, ''It Won't Be Easy,'' *Progressive Grocer,* January 1993, pp. 36–40.

—Tina Grant

these included its core businesses of manufacturing pulp, paper, and plastic products. The specialty industrial papers division was sold to a group of senior executives in conjunction with a New York investment firm, AEA Investors, Inc. Founded in 1968, AEA Investors was funded and managed by more than 60 current or former chief executive officers of major corporations. The firm usually dealt with non-junk borrowings and tended to leave managements intact. James E. Rogers, former senior vice-president and group executive of James River's Speciality Papers Group, was leading the management team that joined with AEA to make the purchase. The transaction was for cash, preferred stock, and assumption of some mill leases and amounted to $285 million in cash and $52 million in preferred stock. Specialty Coatings Group leased five of the business's 22 mills; the other 17 were included in the purchase cost. Four of the mills were in the United Kingdom, including Smith & McLaurin in Scotland and Portlaoise Plant in Ireland. Final agreement wasn't reached until May 1991. James River Corporation retained 20 percent interest.

From the start, Specialty Coatings' sales were estimated at $625 million. The specialty papers business was strong at that time, but targeted to small markets. The thinking was that it was a business best run by an entrepreneurial group. Speciality Coatings divided itself into seven entities: Custom Papers Group; Graphics Technology International; H. P. Smith; Decorative Specialities International; Otis Specialty Papers; Glory Mill Papers Ltd.; and Smith & McLaurin Ltd.

Graphics Technology supplied microfilm, phototools, coated films, and papers for use with computer printers and drafting media. H. P. Smith made silicone-coated release liners, and Smith & McLaurin made thermal self-adhesive label stock. Otis Specialty manufactured release liner base paper. Decorative Specialties supplied embossed latex saturated paper-book coverings and packaging, sold under proprietary brand names. And Custom Paper Group made filter papers, absorbent products, and other technical papers.

No longer part of the previously $5 billion corporation, Specialty Coatings considered its modest size an asset. Nonetheless, it was launched during a very troubled time for the paper industry. The economy was weak, and the extended recession had bruised the key markets for specialty papers—automobiles, electronics, hard-cover books, and graphic arts. A year after the birth of Specialty Coatings, sales were off from projections by about 10 percent, but it had paid down on its debt, maintained employment, increased its capital expenditure budget, and was running 20 plants. Specialty Coatings invested in new equipment and instrumentation to increase yields and reduce waste. And its profitability was maintained. With each of the company's seven business units operating as stand-alone, decentralized entities, decision making time was shortened.

In April 1992, James River Corporation had announced that it would sell its remaining interest in Specialty Coatings, but this deal depended on Specialty Coatings raising money through a public offering. In May 1992 it was decided to postpone the public stock offering because of unfavorable market conditions. Completion of the stock sale would include four James River mills that Specialty Coatings was still leasing.

Specialty Coatings Inc.

704 East Franklin Street
Richmond, Virginia 23210
U.S.A.
(804) 697-3500
Fax: (804) 697-3535

Wholly Owned Subsidiary of Rexham, Inc.
Incorporated: 1991
Employees: 3,850
Sales: $650 million
SICs: 2672 Coated & Laminated Paper; 6719 Holding Companies

Specialty Coatings Group Inc. was created in 1991 when James River Corporation sold its specialty papers operations to a management-led team of investors. In 1993 Specialty Coatings Group Inc. was purchased by Rexham Inc., a wholly owned subsidiary of Bowater PLC. Rexham planned to absorb the businesses of Specialty Coatings into existing Rexham operations.

The specialty papers division of James River Corporation was made up of seven divisions. One historic element was James River Graphics, which began in 1932 as the Beveridge-Marvellum Company and manufactured decorative metalloid and crystal finished papers. This company's name was changed in 1938 to Plastic Coating Corporation. It thrived despite the Depression, opening a sister division, Technifax, in 1949. Technifax manufactured films and diazo-type materials, as well as an engineering paper. Scott Paper Company bought Plastic Coating Corporation, and its sister division Technifax, in 1965, making it a wholly owned subsidiary. The company changed its name to Scott Graphics, then was acquired in 1978 by James River Corporation, and became James River Graphics. Over the years, James River Graphics grew from a few coating machines to a stable of 15 and employed nearly 1,000 people. It had been profitable throughout its years with James River, though the increase in pulp prices had caused a bit of a profit pinch.

Specialty Coatings Group Inc. came into existence as such in 1990, when James River Corporation announced an extensive restructuring plan that included unloading unprofitable operations and lines that were subject to cyclical downturns. The company sought to focus on businesses in which it had a significant market share and was running cost-effective operations;

At this time, the company was involved in three product segments: imaging products, self-adhesive products and specialty products. Imaging products included a broad range of value-added film and paper products such as those used for high quality color presentations. This division produced precision coated paper and film used for by computers and engineers, and polyethylene-coated base paper for use in the manufacture of monochrome and color photographic papers for commercial, industrial, and consumer markets. Self-adhesive products consisted primarily of release liners—important for use in computer-generated color graphics for fleet and poster advertising—and base papers which are coated with silicone and other materials to form release liners. Release liners are sold to manufacturers of decals, pressure-sensitive labels, and other self-adhesive products. Specialty products included filtration media, abrasive backing, cover-grade paperboard, and absorbent and technical grades which are used in diverse industries including manufacturing, automotive, packaging, and graphic arts. It also included book covering.

In February 1992, Bowater PLC, a British industrial conglomerate, announced its purchase of Speciality Coatings for $434 million. With annual sales of more than $3 billion, Bowater was then Great Britain's largest packaging company, and the purchase would double its coated papers business. The immediate plan was to sell the five leased mills and Custom Paper and absorb the rest of Specialty Coatings into Bowater's U.S. subsidiary, Rexham Inc., based in Charlotte, North Carolina. Rexham operated 41 plants in the United States and Canada, making packaging, printing plastics, coated industrial films, and building products. Bowater acquired Rexham Corporation and its portfolio of custom coating and laminated businesses in 1987. It added Release Technologies, manufacturer of release films and papers, in 1989. SCI's specialty in precision coating of specialist films and papers used in the imaging, graphic, and computer industries seemed a perfect fit for Bowater's strategy, launched in 1990, of developing mass in three areas: health care packaging, personal care packaging, and coated industrial films. SCI would grant Bowater a better balance between coated films and papers and its core packaging and printing activities.

In 1993 Specialty Coatings ranked 471 on the Fortune 500 list, its 1992 sales topping $635 million, and had about 3,300 employees. In April 1993, Specialty Coatings's Richmond headquarters were being eliminated—shifting to Rexham, Inc.'s headquarters in Charlotte.

Further Reading:

"A New Tradition Beckons in Iowa City," *Industry Week,* August 6, 1990.

Abbey, Erin, "James River Plans Local Sale," *Transcript-Telegram,* August 17, 1990, pp. 1,12.

"Bowater," *Wall Street Journal,* February 17, 1993, p. C12.

"Bowater in Big Specialty Coating Business Gain," *Special Paper & Boards Materials & Markets Bulletin,* February 1993, pp. 1,2.

Brennan, Robert, "James River Agrees to Sell Specialty Papers Business," *Wall Street Journal,* March 19, 1991.

Buckley, Neil, "A Revamped Package Is Welcomed in the City," *Financial Times,* February 17, 1993.

Buettner, Michael, "James River Sell-Off to Cut Sales by $1 Billion," *News Leader,* August 17, 1990, p. 1.

Clark, Richard, "SQC Graphics Paint the Picture of Quality Control at Work," *Industrial Engineering,* January 1991, pp. 29–32.

Goodwin, William, "Bank Group Will Help Finance Deal for James River Unit," *American Banker,* March 20, 1991, p. 22.

Greehern, Christopher, "Financial Sources Say James River Buyout Comes at Opportune Time," *Springfield Union,* August 18, 1990.

"James River Completes Sale," *Wall Street Journal,* May 2, 1991, p. C9.

"James River Corp.," *New York Times,* May 2, 1991, p. D3.

"James River Corp.," *Wall Street Journal,* April 15, 1992, p. C12.

"James River Expects $47 Million," *Richmond Times-Dispatch,* February 18, 1993, p. B7.

"James River to Trim Operations," *Easton Express,* August 17, 1990, p. 7.

Kale, Wilford, "Bowater Agrees to Buy Firm Here for $434 Million," *Richmond Times-Dispatch,* February 17, 1993, pp. B9, B14.

Kale, Wilford, "Main Office of SCI Here Is Relocating," *Richmond Times-Dispatch,* April 13, 1993, p. B6.

Osborn Howard, Maria, "Paper Firm Here Delays Offering," *Richmond Times-Dispatch,* June 23, 1992.

Potter, Bruce, "Area Membership on Fortune List up 1," *Richmond Times-Dispatch,* March 31, 1993, pp. B8, B14.

Prospectus: Specialty Coatings International, Inc., May 22, 1992.

"Specialty Coatings Sold for $424 Million," *New York Times,* February 17, 1993, p. D4.

Shackleton, Richard, "Bowater in L295m Call," *Scotsman,* February 17, 1993.

Taper, Neil, "Bowater Makes L295m Cash Call," *Independent,* February 17, 1993.

Tehan, Patricia, "Bowater Surprises the Market With Call to Raise L295m," *Times,* February 17, 1993, pp. 1, 25.

"U.S.-led Buy-Out of Smith & McLaurin," *Scotsman,* September 8, 1990.

Wouters, Jorgen, "James River Paper Mill Has New Owner, New Name," *Sentinel & Enterprise,* May 10, 1991, p. 18.

—Carol I. Keeley

St. Joe Paper Company

1650 Prudential Drive
Suite 400
Jacksonville, Florida
U.S.A.
(904) 396-6600
Fax: (904) 396-4042

Public Company
Incorporated: 1936
Employees: 5,040
Sales: $591.9 million
Stock Exchange: New York
SICs: 2631 Paperboard Mills; 2061 Cane Sugar Except
   Refining

The St. Joe Paper Company is one of the rarest types of companies in existence in America today. Like the Hughes Aircraft Corporation, St. Joe was bequeathed by its principal shareholder to provide operating funds for a charitable institution, in this case the Nemours Foundation. The company was established as a conglomeration of the Florida financial interests of Alfred Irenee duPont, whose will stipulated that, upon his death, the proceeds of his estate be used to support an institution for the rehabilitation and care of crippled children with curable afflictions. While a large portion of the company's shares are publicly traded, a large block remains under the control of this institution.

Alfred duPont was one of five children of Eleuthere Irenee duPont (1829–1877) and Charlotte Henderson (1835–1877). Eleuthere duPont was the great grandson of the American family and founder of the E. I. duPont de Nemours Company. DuPont, noted for its commercial development of gunpowder, later expanded into a wide range of chemical businesses over the years, including plastics, synthetic fibers, and paint. In the process, it ran into numerous managerial difficulties that threatened to ruin the company.

Alfred duPont gained a troublesome reputation as a rebel. At the age of 38, he launched a daring takeover of the financially strapped family company to prevent it from falling into the hands of outside investors. At first the youthful duPont wasn't taken seriously. But when he managed to line up the necessary financing, he was allowed to proceed. In the interest of preserving family control, he convinced his fellow family members to

accept notes in lieu of cash payment for their shares. In doing so, Alfred and his cousins Coleman and Pierre managed to gain control of the sprawling $24 million financial empire with only $2,100 of their own money.

DuPont fell from family grace when he divorced his wife, Bessie Gardner, and quickly remarried his cousin Alicia Bradford. Ostracized for his deplorable morals, Alfred was forced out of the duPont company in 1915.

Alfred fought vigorously to prevent Pierre duPont from taking control of the company in his own 1916 coup d'etat, but eventually lost. As the company prospered on government contracts during World War I, the family battles took their toll on the fragile health of Alicia DuPont. Alfred built the grand Nemours estate for his wife, where he hoped they could enjoy greater solitude. Despite this, Alicia died in 1920. A year later he married Jessie Ball, whose family he had known since 1900, and whose brother Edward became a trusted associate. In 1923, in fact, duPont asked Ed Ball to manage his personal business interests while he vacationed in Florida.

DuPont was an avid observer of the growth in real estate activity in Florida. At the time, Jacksonville was the center of Florida commerce; cities such as Miami and Fort Lauderdale were little more than fishing villages. He persuaded Ball to visit the Florida Panhandle and join him in a hunt for properties. DuPont's quest for a vacation home eventually blossomed into a full-fledged acquisition binge of timber properties. By 1925 duPont owned nearly 100,000 acres, mostly of cut-over forest land where growth was slowly returning. In an effort to develop the economies of these areas, duPont organized the Gulf Coast Highway Association, whose mission was to build roads and develop the transportation infrastructure in northwestern Florida.

Back in Delaware, Pierre duPont, now chair of the duPont Company, accepted a position as the state's tax commissioner. In order to escape the probing eye of his nemesis, Alfred transferred all his holdings, except his Nemours estate, to new corporations that he chartered in Florida.

In search of an occupation beyond land speculator, duPont began building interests in a number of banks, including the Florida National Bank of Jacksonville. This he later built into a statewide network called the Florida National Group of Banks. As the nation fell into the Depression years, duPont was frequently called upon to personally intercede when worried depositors made runs on his banks. Rumors of the banks' imminent failure were put to rest by transfers of duPont's $15 million fortune.

Ball used duPont's fortune and his access to the banks to acquire an additional 240,000 acres of land in 1933. This included properties in Gulf, Bay, Liberty, and Franklin Counties and the city of St. Joe, a dying fishing community of 500 people on St. Joseph Bay, about 150 miles east of Pensacola. Included in this transaction was a sawmill, the Apalachicola Northern Railroad Company, the St. Joseph Telephone & Telegraph Company, the Port St. Joe Dock & Terminal Company, and several other land and development companies.

St. Joe had once been a thriving community of 2,000 people whose livelihood stemmed from timber industries and a profitable resort business. Once known as the "richest and wickedest city in the Southeast," St. Joe fell upon hard times after local timber tracts had been exhausted. By 1910, those who remained depended almost entirely on fishing for a living.

Old St. Joseph was founded in 1835 by a group of land speculators and promoters and there, on December 3, 1838, 57 members of the first Constitutional Convention assembled to draft a charter for Florida to become part of the Union. Just 17 years earlier Florida had been a part of a vast territory owned and governed by Spain. Florida was not, however, admitted into the Union until 1845. It then became the thirty-seventh state of the alliance. When citizens of the original city of St. Joseph requested a new post office some years later, they were obliged to find a new name for the community. They chose Port St. Joe as the town's name, but they called it St. Joe.

Alfred duPont acquired St. Joe at the bottom of the Depression and, in effect, took over a huge collection of declining properties at extremely low prices. His initial aim was to revitalize St. Joe and its paper industry. He began by lining the city's streets with trees, building houses and a new business district, and improving the town's schools and playgrounds. He also pursued construction of a new paper mill to produce newsprint. But when the market for this type of paper appeared weak, he converted the design of the plant to produce kraft, a durable paperboard.

In 1935, with the plant under construction as the city once again bloomed, Alfred duPont died at the age of 71. He entrusted Ed Ball to manage his estate, including an unusual request laid out in his will. Alfred duPont asked that a set amount of proceeds from his assets be used to support his wife and family, and the remainder be dedicated to the support of a new institution dedicated to the treatment of crippled children whose conditions were curable. He made this stipulation with the knowledge that numerous government programs and other charities already existed for the care of incurable cases.

Following these instructions, Ball and duPont's widow chartered the Nemours Foundation in 1936 and, in 1937, began laying plans to establish the treatment facility, the Alfred I. duPont Institute. The small hospital, located in Wilmington, opened in 1940.

After payment of $30 million in taxes, duPont's fortune totalled about $27 million. The bulk of this value came from the estate's seven banks, not St. Joe Paper. But Ball worked diligently to complete duPont's goal of building the company. With the paper-making operation just getting into business, the company's Apalachicola Northern Railroad, operating only a 100-mile line between St. Joe to Chattahoochee, had bleak prospects. Worse yet, the telephone company operated only 167 phones, and most were used by the railroad.

St. Joe Paper was incorporated in 1936, and began operations in 1938 through a joint venture with the Mead Corporation, an Ohio company. Mead operated the company's mill under contract until 1940, when Ball exercised the estate's option to buy out that company's interest. Ball subsequently was appointed president of St. Joe Paper.

With the nation finally emerging from the Depression, demand for packaging began to rise. In addition, corrugated cardboard, a new paperboard product that was lighter and more economical than wooden crating, was quickly gaining popularity. This increase in demand led St. Joe to raise its paperboard production capacity from 300 tons a day to 400 tons.

Shipping gained special importance in 1942. With the United States involved in a two-theater war, the transportation of war material and supplies became a high priority. St. Joe established its own corrugating facilities in 1943, and added a second in an expanded facility in 1945.

After the war, St. Joe Paper became heavily engaged in the manufacture of corrugated shipping containers. A corrugator began operating at Port St. Joe just as the war ended. Box plants in Houston, Texas, and South Hackensack, New Jersey, soon came on stream until, by 1960, 20 container plants were in operation.

St. Joe Paper managed to supply its plants with wood products from land owned by the estate and additional leased acreage. But by 1950, with the company's expansion into the Northeast and Texas, it became necessary to secure additional timberland. To speed growth in the company's cut timber lands, St. Joe Paper established a large nursery where millions of pine saplings were produced. These were later transplanted into the depleted forests and allowed to grow naturally. Despite this accelerated reforestation effort, St. Joe Paper had to purchase pulpwood from other foresters in increasingly larger quantities.

The most immediate problem at St. Joe was the need for water. With a projected tripling of output, the flagship plant would require 35 million gallons of fresh water each day. With well sources exhausted, the company was forced to dig a canal to the Chipola River, 18 miles away. This source crossed beneath several existing streams and the Intracoastal Waterway using 42-inch pipes, drawing water down to St. Joe with simple gravity.

While on a trip to Ireland in 1957, Edward Ball visited National Board and Paper Mills, Limited, at Waterford. The Irish company was in need of a steady supply of raw materials and managerial and technical assistance. Ball proposed that St. Joe Paper operate the Irish plant under contract to its owners. This arrangement was finalized in 1958. Some years later, St. Joe Paper purchased the operation outright.

On January 1, 1961, St. Joe Paper formally acquired the Florida East Coast Railway Company, a bankrupt and dilapidated line that ran between Jacksonville and Homestead, in extreme southern Florida. The acquisition followed more than 20 years of constant opposition from the Atlantic Coast Line, which also sought control of the company.

The Florida East Coast Railway was established in 1885 by Henry M. Flagler, a former partner of John D. Rockefeller. Flagler gradually extended the railroad south from Jacksonville, laying track through the swampy wilderness to Palm Beach. Along the line, he established a string of hotels, which became major tourist attractions for vacationing northerners. By 1895 the line had been extended to Biscayne Bay, where the establishment of the Royal Palm Hotel marked the birth of Miami as a resort city.

After stretching the line to Homestead in 1902, Flagler laid out a preposterous plan to extend the line a further 127 miles, through the Florida Keys to Key West. In addition to capitalizing on the island's tourist distinction as the southernmost point in the United States, Flagler recognized that, unlike Miami, Key West had a deep water port that could serve as a center for international commerce. In 1912, after seven years of construction, the $20 million Overseas Railway, called ''Flagler's Folly,'' was completed. The line crossed 75 miles of open water and marshland, including one seven-mile stretch between two islands in the chain.

In later years, the Florida East Coast Railway built a new spur to Lake Okeechobee, where Flagler established yet another vacation community. This development failed miserably, however, and plunged the company into deep financial straits. In 1931, during the Depression, Flagler's survivors were forced to place the railroad into receivership at the bequest of nervous bond holders.

Flagler's brother-in-law William Kenan worked diligently to restore the road to profitability. On Labor Day in 1935, however, a massive hurricane tore through the Keys causing severe damage to the Overseas Railway. Unable to afford repairs, Kenan sold the line from Homestead to Key West to the state of Florida, which later converted it into a highway.

Ball closely watched the demise of the railway company. With experience in operating St. Joe Paper's own run-down railroad, Ball simply awaited an opportunity to take over the company and have a go at turning it around. In 1941, with approval from the duPont estate, Ball began buying up the Florida East Coast's defaulted bonds, thought to be worthless at the time. After gaining 51 percent of the outstanding bonds, Ball could have taken control of the company. Instead, he was challenged in federal court by Champion McDowell Davis, president of the Atlantic Coast Line Railroad. The court battle went on for 17 years, at an estimated cost of $5 million to each Ball and Davis.

In 1959 the president of Florida East Coast announced his retirement. While the court was unwilling to turn over the railroad to the duPont estate, Ball applied for the railroad's presidency. He succeeded, taking a salary of only $12 per year. Ball consolidated control over the Florida East Coast slowly. First, he instituted a new accounting system that gave him a daily view of the company's finances. Second, he updated and mechanized maintenance practices and rationalized job functions. When St. Joe Paper finally was granted permission to exercise its control over Florida East Coast in 1961, Ball reduced the railroad's headcount from 3,300 to less than 2,200. These changes occurred too quickly for much of the unionized work force, which called a strike against the railroad in 1963. The action enabled Ball to initiate even more drastic changes with Florida East Coast, including the elimination of money-losing passenger service.

By 1964 Ball had the railroad down to fewer than 1,000 employees. The line endured several months of sabotage and other disruptions while the strike persisted, but the company was at long last operating profitably.

In 1966 the Congress enacted legislation, believed directed specifically at the duPont estate, which prohibited charitable trusts from engaging in both banking and nonbanking enterprises. The duPont estate was forced to consider divesting either its network of 30 banks or its St. Joe Paper industrial interests. The estate sold its controlling share in the banks in 1971, and was forced in further action to completely dissolve its interests in the banks in 1973.

Meanwhile, Ed Ball, who continued to serve as a trustee of the duPont estate, used the proceeds of the bank sales to further pay down St. Joe Paper's debt and engage in other acquisitions. Among these was the Talisman Sugar Company, which Ball quickly converted to mechanical processes after taking control in 1972. Four years later, the company purchased a sugar refinery from the Borden Company.

Over the years, Ball consistently reinvested the meager earnings of the Apalachicola and Florida East Coast railroads back into their operations. Although it took many years, Ball successfully rehabilitated both lines from veritable scrap heaps to first class rail carriers. By 1980 the railroad had become a larger, more consistently profitable enterprise than its parent, St. Joe Paper.

The company's tiny St. Joseph Telephone operation grew from 167 telephones into a profitable three-company business through the acquisition of Gulf and Florala Telephone companies and an expanding economy during the 1960s and 1970s. More recently, the company has ventured into the cellular operation in partnership with Centel and Alltel.

During the 1980s, after the passing of Ed Ball, St. Joe Paper maintained the same conservative financial policies towards its operations. Like duPont, Ball established his own charity through the Nemours Foundation, dedicated to the care of the crippled children of Florida. During this period, Jacob Belin and Winfred Thornton, long-time trustees of the estate, gained positions as chair and president, respectively, of St. Joe Paper.

In March of 1990 the duPont trust sold 17 percent of St. Joe Paper's shares to the public, raising $230 million. The sale allowed significant trading of the stock for the first time and won St. Joe a listing on the New York Stock Exchange.

In the early 1990s, many of Florida East Coast Industries' properties were being developed by its wholly owned subsidiary, Gran Central Corporation. Likewise, a large portion of St. Joe's 1,100,000 acres of Florida and Georgia holdings were being planned for development. With these holdings in two of the fastest growing states in the union (Florida ranks number four with a population of over 12 million expected to reach nearly 16 million by the turn of the century), St. Joe's assets are expected to appreciate in value. St. Joe's long-standing policy of reinvesting earnings through a meager dividend payout has reflected in greater shareholder value.

The Florida East Coast railroad operations benefitted greatly from increased traffic required for rebuilding from Hurricane Andrew in 1992. In addition, with the collapse of the Soviet Union, hopes were raised for a change in government in Cuba and a resumption of the once highly profitable trade with the Caribbean nation.

The paper company, the Florida East Coast system, the Alfred I. duPont Testamentary Trust, and The Nemours Foundation now control these interests from a new office building that was constructed by the Florida East Coast Industries in 1988.

Principal Subsidiaries: Apalachicola Northern Railroad; Florida East Coast Railway Company; Florida East Coast Industries; Florida East Coast Railway Company; Gran Central; St. Joseph Telephone and Telegraph Company; Gulf Telephone Company; Florala Telephone Company; St. Joe Communications, Inc.; Talisman Sugar Corporation; St. Joe Container Company; St. Joseph Land and Development Company.

Further Reading:

"Borden Inc. Has Sold Liquid Sugar Refinery and Pickle Operation," *Wall Street Journal,* June 4, 1976, p. 18.

"The Estate of Alfred I. duPont and the Nemours Foundation," published by the Estate of Alfred I. duPont, 1974.

"Indictment Cites 14 Paper Makers for Price Fixing," *Wall Street Journal,* January 26, 1978, p. 3.

"Now, This Is the Way to Run a Railroad," *Business Week,* September 7, 1974, pp. 66–67.

"Perform or Perish," *Forbes,* June 11, 1990, p. 132.

St. Joe Paper Company Annual Report, Jacksonville, Florida: St. Joe Paper Company, 1992.

—John Simley

St. Paul Bank for Cooperatives

375 Jackson St.
St. Paul, Minnesota 55101
U.S.A.
(612) 282-8200
Fax: (612) 282-8201

Federally Chartered Cooperative
Incorporated: 1933
Employees: 63
Assets: $1.76 billion
SICs: 6111 Federal and Federally-Sponsored Credit Agencies

The St. Paul Bank for Cooperatives, a member of the Farm Credit System (FCS), serves approximately 650 agriculturally related cooperative businesses in 25 states. Its greatest concentration of loans is with farm supply, agricultural marketing cooperatives, and rural utility systems in the Upper Midwest and Great Lakes regions, a territory to which it was restricted by charter until the Agricultural Credit Act of 1987 was enacted. Following the passing of this act, St. Paul Bank became one of just two federally chartered co-op banks to forego merging into the National Bank for Cooperatives (CoBank), headquartered in Denver, Colorado. Still, its relationship with CoBank is collaborative, for like other FCS facilities, these banks mutually benefit from the same service organizations, which include the Federal Farm Credit Banks Funding Corporation, the FCS Building Association, the Farm Credit Leasing Services Corporation, and the Farm Credit Council. In addition, St. Paul Bank is a major shareholder of and frequent loan participant with CoBank. The Bank also benefits from its sister relationship with the Farm Credit Bank of St. Paul, which was renamed AgriBank FCB in May of 1992 after its merger with the Farm Credit Bank of St. Louis. Entirely owned by its members, St. Paul Bank is regulated by the Farm Credit Administration (FCA), and it reported outstanding gross loans of $2 billion at the end of 1992.

The St. Paul Bank was chartered on October 12, 1933, the same day on which President Franklin D. Roosevelt's newly appointed Farm Credit System chief, Henry Morganthau, Jr., addressed farm leaders in St. Paul. Roosevelt's FCS initiative called for a central bank and 12 federal district banks spread across the nation, all of which were to help ensure the revitalization of rural economies reeling from the Great Depression. Each district bank would actually be composed of three banks: a

Federal Land Bank (FLB) for real estate lending; a Federal Intermediate Credit Bank (FICB) for lending to production credit associations (who would lend directly to individual farmers); and a Federal Bank for Cooperatives for lending to agricultural cooperatives. The area to be served by the three St. Paul Banks was the seventh federal district. Agriculturally rich, this district included all of Minnesota, North Dakota, Wisconsin, and Michigan, which together were home to approximately one-third of all U.S. cooperatives.

The FCS system as it pertained to St. Paul Bank had its origins in President Theodore Roosevelt's Country Life Commission, which was established in 1908 to bolster both the formation and the financing of cooperatives. This Commission engendered the Federal Farm Loan Act of 1916 and the formation of FLBs but neglected to provide a separate resource for cooperatives. In 1923 FICBs were established by Congress; under limited circumstances, these banks did provide funding for cooperatives, but much more was needed. Then, in 1929, President Herbert Hoover oversaw the passing of the Agricultural Marketing Act and the appointment of a Federal Farm Board. Supplied with a $500 million revolving fund, the Farm Board was designed to encourage the organization and development of large marketing cooperatives. According to St. Paul Bank's 60th anniversary chronicle, "The problems [surrounding the Hoover plan] included the continually failing economy, markets that didn't improve, the folly of top-down organization of cooperatives, the failure to provide for credit for farm supply and other non-marketing cooperatives, and the finite supply of loan funds. The need for a dependable source of credit for all types of farmer cooperatives grew greater than ever." By the time Franklin D. Roosevelt took office, the situation was dire. "Farm foreclosures," wrote Harry T. Gatton and Truman L. Jeffers in *Banking in Minnesota,* "had farmers in Minnesota in an uproar. Threats were made against bankers. Minnesota enacted a two-year moratorium on farm foreclosures. All federal agricultural credit was consolidated in the Farm Credit Administration."

A Tennessee-born agricultural economist named Hutzel Metzger was appointed St. Paul Bank's first president. During his first year he oversaw the approval of 169 loans totaling more than $3 million. Around a third of these loans went to dairy cooperatives, another third to fruit and vegetable concerns, and the remaining third to various other cooperatives, including gas and oil businesses. From the start, St. Paul Bank branched beyond mere lending, helping many of its customers institute double-entry bookkeeping and financial statements, and encouraging all to pay down loan balances early in order to save considerable cash on interest and thus enable future, healthy expansion. A number of banking innovations characterized this early era; one of these was the concept of participation loans, which involved paired financing through small-town banks, most of which had been previously undercapitalized and unable to assist their rural customers.

The advent of World War II caused a resurgence in the national economy and a heightened demand for food production. In a very short period, from October of 1941 to February of 1942, the bank issued funds to 125 cooperatives under the lend-lease program. Financing demands for facility expansion from an increasing number of borrowers continued for the remainder of the war. By the time of Metzger's sudden death in 1951, cooperatives had become far more sophisticated, cost efficient, competitive, and prone to vertical integration.

Following the presidencies of Herbert Knipfel, Lloyd Ullyot, and Oren Shelley, which successfully carried the Bank into the 1970s, Burgee Amdahl took the helm. A particularly dynamic leader, with a background in farming and business analysis, Amdahl directed the growth of St. Paul Bank from 1974 until 1986. During the first half of his tenure, he responded to the huge capital needs of rural electric cooperatives—needs that occasionally exceeded the Bank's entire loan volume—with innovative financing. Consequently, rural utilities now comprise the Bank's largest industry segment, some 32 percent of all active loans. During the 1970s Amdahl also introduced leveraged leases, fixed-rate financing, and credit for international operations.

The 1980s were marked by more difficult, but ultimately more liberating circumstances. In his president's message for 1992, Dennis Johnson wrote: "There were a lot of things about the 1980s one would just as soon forget. The years of all-out production gave way to years of cutbacks and restructuring. The '80s became years of devastating shakeout for many farmers and most rural areas, and years of wrenching adjustments for the businesses that served them." Low return operations were disposed of and joint venture deals were struck by co-ops that had previously competed. The same was largely true of St. Paul Bank and the FCS. In 1980 the FICB of St. Paul and St. Paul Bank for Cooperatives were placed under joint management for the first time, with Amdahl serving as CEO. In 1983 the FLB of St. Paul also merged its management. Such consolidations were common throughout the FCS and presaged the Agricultural Credit Act of 1987. This bill, which came the year following Amdahl's retirement and Larry Buegler's appointment as president, was sweeping in its reforms of the FCS. One of its primary purposes was to remedy the current series of agribusiness problems by increasing the options of FCS cooperative banks (i.e., establishing national charters) while assigning greater control of each bank's direction to its customer-owners.

Although St. Paul Bank declared its wish to operate independently and serve customers on a national basis, its relationship with Farm Credit Bank of St. Paul remained particularly close up until March of 1990, when Johnson was named the co-op Bank's president and CEO (during the interim, Buegler had served as head of both banks). One of the most distinguishing developments of the Bank and its CEOs since that time has been its involvement in international agricultural credit programs. Amdahl is head of one such project in Poland and Buegler is head of another in the Commonwealth of Independent States

(the former Soviet Union). According to Johnson, "although the St. Paul Bank receives no immediate return, we see time invested in Eastern Europe today as a good investment in the future of agriculture and cooperatives." The Bank has also become a participant in a CoBank-led export financing package to the Soviets. In March of 1993, however, Soviet defaults on $500 million in U.S. food loan guarantees caused CoBank, the largest lender involved, to request reimbursement for some $116 million, according to a 1993 *Star Tribune* article.

St. Paul Bank's approach to domestic growth is far less speculative than its international ventures, though still aggressive. While its loan volume is still led by two of its original seventh district states, Minnesota (43.1 percent) and North Dakota (33.8 percent), volume outside the four-state district now accounts for 12.4 percent of the Bank's business, more than Wisconsin and Michigan combined. The Bank's long-term mission, despite its change in status, remains that of 60 years ago: to serve the customer well and make a profit. One of the best ways to gauge St. Paul Bank's success and its ability to serve its customers is through its patronage refunds, which over the last five years have totaled $155 million (1992's patronage business resulted in a 19 percent return on interest and fees paid to the Bank). It is because of such unique benefits, and because of the Bank's longstanding commitment to the agricultural community, that a hybrid, government-sponsored/privately owned enterprise has performed so well since the earliest days of FCS banking.

Further Reading:

"Bank of Cooperatives Names Team," *Star Tribune,* June 20, 1989.
Blade, Joe, "Net Interest Income up at Farm Credit Bank," *Star Tribune,* March 9, 1990, p. 2D.
Crockett, Barton, "Agribank Aims to Cut Costs by Insourcing," *American Banker,* June 30, 1992, p. 3.
Egerstrom, Lee, "Co-op Bank Reports Strong Third Quarter," *Pioneer Press,* November 16, 1988.
Egerstrom, "Net Income Rises Slightly at St. Paul Bank for Co-ops," *Pioneer Press,* February 28, 1991.
Gatton, T. Harry and Truman L. Jeffers, *Banking in Minnesota,* Minneapolis: Minnesota Bankers Association, 1989.
Nelson, Connie, "Dennis Johnson Charts New Course for Bank," *Star Tribune,* October 31, 1988.
"Soviet Food Defaults Pass $500 Million," *Star Tribune,* March 16, 1993, p. 3D.
St. Anthony, Neal, "AgriBank of St. Paul Plans to Merge with Farm Credit Bank of Louisville," *Star Tribune,* June 8, 1993, p. 1D.
St. Paul Bank Annual Report (President's Message on 60th anniversary), St. Paul: St. Paul Bank, 1992.
Wright, Gregory, "Merger Held Beneficial to Farm Credit Industry," *Journal of Commerce and Commercial,* August 29, 1991, p. 6A.

—Jay P. Pederson

State Street Boston Corporation

225 Franklin St.
Boston, MA 02110
U.S.A.
(617) 786-3000
Fax: (617) 654-3386

Public Company
Incorporated: 1792, Union Bank; 1891, State Street Deposit
    and Trust Company; 1960, State Street Boston Financial
    Corporation
Employees: 8,321
Sales: $852.4 million
SICs: 6282 Investment Advice; 6022 State Commercial
    Banks; 8741 Management Services

State Street Boston Corporation is a bank holding company conducting business principally through its subsidiary, State Street Bank and Trust Co. Descended from one of the first banks in America—the Union Bank, which was founded in 1792—State Street is now the nation's largest custodian and trustee for mutual funds and pension funds, responsible for an estimated 40 percent of the more than $1 trillion in securities held by America's mutual funds.

Since the 1970s, State Street has become one of America's banking success stories. Beginning in that period, through a strategy of aggressive diversification and the use of the most advanced technologies, State Street rapidly evolved from a traditional, gentlemanly, old-line Massachusetts financial institution into a global banking powerhouse.

State Street has deep roots in the commercial history of Boston, going back to the days when this city was a bustling shipping port and main business artery for the new republic. In the closing years of the 18th century, a group of prominent Bostonians gathered together to establish a new bank, which would be the third bank in Boston. John Hancock, Massachusetts' first governor, signed the bank's charter on June 25, 1792. The bank, named the Union Bank, was located at the corner of State and Exchange Streets and had as its first president Massachusetts Lieutenant Governor Moses Gill.

At that time State Street was the main thoroughfare in colonial Boston and a significant crossroads in America. Bracketed by the State House at one end and the Long Wharf at the other,

State Street was a center of both commerce and politics. It was here, for instance, that the first public reading of the Declaration of Independence took place. It was also where the famous trial of Captain Kidd took place. And it was on State Street that the first Boston merchant, John Coggan, had set up shop.

State Street was also known as the "Great Street to the Sea," and the economic growth of the new bank was closely tied to Boston's flourishing shipping industry. During that romantic period, sleek clippers criss-crossed Boston Harbor, escorting incoming ships, laden with cargo, to shore. Boston was by the mid-19th century in its heyday as a maritime capital. Some of the wealth from that trade would make its way into the coffers of the bank.

Meanwhile, the lore, mystique, and memorabilia of this colorful shipping past would be ardently celebrated and preserved by Union and, in its later incarnation, State Street, during the more than 200 years of its existence. For instance, ship models, prints, harpoons, and figureheads would adorn the offices of State Street Bank for years. The bank would also publish over two dozen monographs recalling Boston's maritime history. In 1992, the bank's pride in this past would lead it to sponsor Sail Boston, an event that brought a flotilla of elegant boats from all over the world into Boston Harbor. And finally, the bank's logo, a silhouette of a clipper ship, is itself a form of homage.

Many of Boston's merchant princes and community leaders were associated with Union Bank during the first century of its operation. For instance, the bank had real estate deals with such notable local families as the Parkmans, Sargents, and Quincys, and among its early officers was Oliver Wendell, the great-grandfather of Oliver Wendell Holmes.

The bank, located at 40 State Street, had its charter renewed several times, and in 1865, the directors applied for and received a National Charter. At that time, the bank was renamed the National Union Bank of Boston.

Going into the early years of the 20th century, National Union had survived to become the oldest bank in continuous operation in Boston and the second oldest bank in America. During all these years, despite wars and the fluctuating fortunes of the new country, the bank thrived, and it is a mark of its stability that it never failed to declare semi-annual dividends.

On July 1, 1891, National Union would have a new neighbor and banking competitor on State Street. On that day, the State Street Deposit & Trust Company was chartered and began business, with offices in the Exchange Building on State Street. The company was started by a group of directors and officers from the Third National Bank, and it opened for business with a capital of $300,000. Shortly afterward, Third National merged with Shawmut Bank, and State Street became entirely independent. In 1897, the bank's name was shortened to State Street Trust Company.

State Street Trust grew steadily during these early years. From 1900 to 1925, deposits increased from roughly $2 million to over $40 million. In 1900, the company moved into offices in the Union Building, on the corner of Exchange and State Streets. In 1911, the main office moved again to another part of State Street. Five years later, it purchased the assets and good will of the Paul Revere Trust Company. The year 1924 proved an historic turning-point for State Street, though it would take many years before the significance of the event would be fully appreciated. In that year, Massachusetts Investors Trust chose the bank as custodian of the country's first mutual fund.

A year later, National Union Bank merged with State Street and the alliance now fattened deposits at State Street to over $57 million. That same year, State Street moved once again and the new location, 53 State Street was, by coincidence, the site of the company's original location. The interior of this new office was an evocation of Boston history, designed to recall the old countinghouses of Boston merchants during the first part of the 18th century. Traditional oak and wood paneled rooms, reproductions of colonial hanging lanterns, hand-forged wrought-iron grillwork, mullioned windows, and tables and chairs copied from old tavern furniture provided a living time capsule of a bygone era—and made the office something of a local landmark.

The man largely responsible for the bank's devotion to its historic roots—and for much of its steady success during these years—was Allan Forbes. Joining State Street in 1899 shortly after graduation from Harvard, Forbes worked his way up from assistant treasurer to president in 1911, and was, from 1950 until the time of his death in 1955, chair of the board. During his 56-year career at the bank, deposits increased from less than $2 million to $187 million.

The identification of the bank with its maritime past would be one of Forbes's lasting legacies. Early in his career, he began to collect and display historical maritime artifacts in State Street's offices. The bank abounded in ship models, prints, harpoons, and figureheads, part of the Forbes collection. His own office was atmospherically steeped in his antiquarian passion; heavy ceiling beams and a great kitchen fireplace recalled the 17th century, while Forbes himself sat in a great mid-18th century, slat-backed armchair surrounded by ship models, prints, and a great sea chest that served as a drawer for papers. This office has been preserved at the bank's 53 State Street branch.

During these years, State Street's growth was fueled by mergers. One of the more significant of these mergers was with the Second National Bank in 1955. Six years later, State Street incorporated the Rockland-Atlas National Bank, which represented three banks dating from the 1800s—the Webster, Rockland, and Atlas banks—that had consolidated in 1948. In 1960, State Street incorporated as the State Street Boston Financial Corp., a one-bank holding company. Its present title, the State Street Boston Corporation, was adopted in May, 1977.

In 1963, ground was broken for the State Street Bank building, which upon completion in 1966 was the first high-rise office building in downtown Boston. It was also the tallest bank building in New England. In 1964, State Street International opened in New York and, six years later, at the dawn of the 1970s, State Street took its first step into the global market, with the opening of an office in Munich.

The 1970s were a bruising decade for the nation's banks, and State Street was no exception. By the mid-1970s, the bank was suffering from major real estate lending problems. Fortunately, a new chief executive officer, William Edgerly, took control in 1975 and began hammering out an ambitious new strategy to turn the company around. He had already made his mark at the company as an outspoken member of the board of directors. Edgerly brought in new managers to help propel the bank into the direction that it had to go if it was to continue to hold its own in the competitive New England banking community. At that time, the bank had four major lines of business: commercial banking, financial services, investment management, and regional banking. Instead of continuing on its present path, Edgerly decided State Street should move away from its traditional commercial role and, rather than expand its branches, shut them down to concentrate on building up its business in investments, trusts, and securities processing. For one thing, it had an early start in the mutual funds market and was ideally situated to build upon its substantial reputation and assets in that area. State Street pushed aggressively into an area that many banks had shunned—the complex, high-technology processing of asset management, global custody, 401(k) retirement plan accounting, and trusteeship of debt securities based on securitized assets.

At the same time, Edgerly recognized that State Street needed to develop its technology if it was going to create a niche for itself with its data processing and telecommunications abilities. And so the company began investing in a big way—an estimated 25 percent of its operating costs—in technology.

In 1973, the company had already made a key move in developing its technical know-how by buying 50 percent of Boston Financial Data Services and then using the software and data processing company for its shareholder-accounting and customer-service functions. The hardware backbone of State Street's numbers crunching was an IBM-mainframe-based Horizon computer system. Built from thousands of modules loaded into a mainframe, each module in Horizon is designed for a specific task and can be accessed at personal computer workstations, using a variety of software. The technological command post for the company became the bank's data-processing headquarters, an office complex opened in Quincy, Massachusetts, a suburb of Boston, in 1974.

Edgerly, who retired as CEO in 1992, brought the stately Boston bank into the high-tech age, finding his inspiration in IBM and its emphasis on research and development. But then Edgerly himself had a degree in engineering from MIT, as well as his M.B.A. from Harvard, and had come to State Street from a petrochemical firm, Cabot Co., rather than from the banking ranks. At State Street he recruited many top-ranking executives from IBM, and by the early 1990s it was estimated that more than 100 veterans from IBM were serving in senior management positions at State Street. Beyond IBM's devotion to technical innovation, Edgerly also admired the company's aggressive approach to sales, and he designed the State Street Institute based upon a sales training class at IBM. At the school, senior executives are required to teach newcomers.

The timing was right for State Street's new technology-based approach. In 1974, the Employee Retirement Income Security Act (ERISA) was passed and, as a result, companies now had new responsibilities when it came to reporting to the government on their pension plans. Recognizing a window of opportunity, State Street developed software that emphasized more advanced record-keeping abilities. Other software systems were spun off to help report on the financial ebb-and-flow of Ginnie Mae (GNMA) securities, international pension assets, and internationally indexed assets.

Typical of its services, State Street designed Pepsico Inc.'s $350-million 401(k) savings plan. In addition to providing accounting, trust, investment management, and benefit payment services for Pepsico, State Street also created a self-managed system whereby employees can transfer funds and evaluate their accounts daily by telephone.

Meanwhile, State Street has been moving assertively into the international market, establishing business footholds around the world. Its advanced numbers-crunching abilities and telecommunications network provided momentum for this global expansion. By the early 1990s, State Street customers could have direct, interactive computer access to their investment information from anywhere in the world, either through their mainframes or through personal computers in the office. They could design their own integrated global reports using the latest multicurrency accounting systems available.

During the 1980s and 1990s, the company established offices throughout the globe, including Montreal, Toronto, London, Paris, Munich, the Cayman Islands, Dubai, Sydney, Melbourne, Wellington, Hong Kong, Taipei, and Tokyo. An international financial caretaker of pensions, securities, and investments, State Street had become recognized as the largest global custodian in Australia, New Zealand, and Canada and as a leading global custodian in Europe. In 1992, the company was selected as the first non-national custodian of a Swiss pension fund and the first non-Scandinavian custodian bank for a Scandinavian institutional investor. That year, the company opened a treasury center in Luxembourg, which joined the Boston, London, Hong Kong, and Tokyo facilities in providing 24-hour capital market services around the world.

While developing its portfolio of services to companies, State Street has downplayed its traditional lending activity, which has helped it weather the recession and the rash of loan defaults that have battered many New England banks. Lending comprises an estimated 16 percent of State Street's business as compared to 60 percent at many other area banks.

At the same time, State Street's continuing financial health has made it the envy of many banks. The price of State Street stock at the end of 1991 was 17 times what it was 10 years earlier. Investors in State Street earned a total return of 33 percent per year for the decade of the 1980s. *Fortune* magazine ranked

State Street number one in total return to investors during the period spanning 1982 to 1992, in a survey of the 100 largest banks in the United States.

State Street has also been ranked by *Pensions & Investments* as the third largest manager of tax-exempt assets in the United States. By 1992, assets under management at State Street totaled $111 billion. Ranked at the end of 1991 as the 37th largest bank holding company in America, State Street reported $16.5 billion in assets.

Within its regional home base, State Street makes loans, primarily to medium-sized businesses, and provides support for a variety of community-based organizations. These include the Metropolitan Boston Housing Partnership, which has rehabilitated buildings throughout the Boston inner city, and the Boston Private Industry Council, which works to improve the city's public schools. The bank has also awarded grants to creative partnerships in science, finance, and community development.

Meanwhile, the future looks promising. Industry analysts predict that the global custody business will soar by the year 2000, with institutional investors from overseas increasingly investing in this country and more U.S. pension fund managers scouting the world for international prospects. This trend should help State Street solidify its position as a leading worldwide servicer of financial assets.

Principal Subsidiaries: State Street Bank & Trust Co.; State Street Boston Credit Co., Inc.; State Street South Corp.; SSB Investments, Inc.; State Street Global Advisors, Inc.; State Street Global Advisors, U.K., Limited; and Boston Financial Data Services, Inc., (50%)

Further Reading:

Cochran, Thomas N., "State Street Boston Corp.: It Prospers with an Alternative to Conventional Banking," *Barron's,* May 9, 1988, p. 53.
Leander, Tom, "State Street Bucks the New England Odds," *American Banker,* May 29, 1991, p. 1.
Leander, Tom, "State Street Thrives in Businesses Banks Didn't Want," *American Banker,* May 30, 1990, p. 8.
The Log of the State Street Trust Company, Boston: State Street Trust Company, 1926.
Quint, Michael, "Four Formulas for Avoiding the Mess in Banking," *New York Times,* Dec. 23, 1990, sec. 3, p. 4F.
Wilke, John R., "State Street Thrives by Stressing Processing Fees," *Wall Street Journal,* June 25, 1992, p. 3B.

—Timothy Bay

Stinnes AG

Humboldtring 15
45472 Muelheim an der Ruhr
Germany
0208/494-0
Fax: 0208/494-698

Wholly Owned Subsidiary of VEBA AG
Incorporated: 1902 as Hugo Stinnes GmbH
Employees: 34,697
Sales: DM 21 billion
SICs: 8999 Services, Nec; 5171 Petroleum Bulk Stations and
   Terminals; 4412 Deep Sea Foreign Transportation of
   Freight; 5169 Chemicals and Allied Products, Nec; 5211
   Lumber and Other Building Materials; 5052 Coal and
   Other Minerals and Ores; 6120 Wholesale Distribution of
   Fuels, Ores, Metals and Industrial Materials; 6110
   Wholesale Distribution of Agricultural Raw Materials,
   Live Animals, Textile; 7630 Supporting Services to Sea
   Transport; 6220 Dealing in Other Scrap Materials, or
   General Dealers; 8200 Institutions Specializing in
   Insurance Other Than Long-Term.

Stinnes AG, a group of independent divisions consisting of 119
major domestic and 85 foreign companies, is Germany's and
one of Europe's largest transportation and distribution companies. As of 1965 Stinnes AG has been a wholly owned subsidiary of VEBA AG, Germany's largest firm. The Stinnes group's
three principal activities are trading in raw materials, especially
coal and oil; chemical distribution and steel processing; and air,
sea, and land transportation. An increasingly important business
segment of Stinnes is the service industry, from do-it-yourself
building materials, to ownership of the prestigious Hotel Nassauer Hof in Wiesbaden, to providing data processing services.

Stinnes AG has deep roots in modern German history. The
company's founder, Mathias Stinnes, was born in Muelheim in
the Ruhr valley during the time of the French Revolution, when
the German states were heavily fragmented and decentralized. It
is all the more amazing that entrepreneurship could succeed in
an area of Europe where innumerable regional interests competed against one another. Added to this politically and economically unstable environment were the numerous invasions
of the Napoleonic armies that devastated the very region in
which Mathias Stinnes was born.

One of many children of a poor bargeman and his wife, Mathias
was affected deeply by the winds of change buffeting him and
his generation. The democratic ideas of the French Revolution
and Napoleon's forced and short-lived consolidation of the
German states signaled change. The legacy of that brief union
was not lost on the diplomats gathered at the 1815 Congress of
Vienna, who issued a call for a voluntary lifting of trade restrictions on the Rhine, the longest river in western Europe, of which
the Ruhr is a tributary.

With so much change in the air, Mathias Stinnes and his two
brothers did not follow in their father's footsteps, as generations
before them had. Instead of remaining poor laborers, they opted
to hire laborers and go into business for themselves. In 1808
Mathias Stinnes, with the help of his brothers, set up his own
company, named after himself as elder brother, that hauled
goods and raw materials on a boat via the Ruhr.

Stinnes's business grew, despite the community's deep-rooted
distrust of someone who chose to strike out on a path different
from his forefathers. When Mathias died in 1845, his steamboats plied the Ruhr, and he had become the largest private
owner of inland shipping in the fragmented German states.
Unusual for that day and age, he branched out into other businesses: the Ruhr area was rich in coal, and by the time he died,
the Mathias Stinnes company owned shares in 36 mines, four of
which his firm had built. Stinnes's traditional lines of business—trading in raw materials and transportation on inland
waterways—were well established by the 1840s.

Mathias's sons took over the family enterprise in turn, each one
dying at a young age. Despite the succession of political crises
in Germany occasioned by wars of unification as well as the rise
of an organized labor movement, the Stinnes firm continued to
expand. In 1908, 100 years after the company was founded, it
possessed 21 tugs and nine of its own ports along with their
storage facilities, and owned and controlled five mines. By then,
however, a new company had arisen that in time would engulf
the old Mathias Stinnes firm.

Hugo Stinnes, grandson of Mathias Stinnes, was born in 1870.
Dissatisfied with the traditional family business, the 21-year-old
Hugo persuaded his mother to sell her ownership in the firm and
to lend him 50,000 gold marks to start up his own business,
which he incorporated in 1902 as Hugo Stinnes GmbH in Muelheim. He still retained technical management of the Mathias
Stinnes mines, however, and gradually the two companies became indistinguishable.

Hugo Stinnes was a dynamic, forceful, and imaginative entrepreneur whose horizons stretched well beyond the traditional
family enterprises and the customary way of doing things. His
original business—coal mining and transportation—was what
he knew best; from there, however, he went on to found the
biggest business empire that Germany, unified into a centralized
state in 1871, had ever seen.

Even the coal business would change under the farsighted
entrepreneur: in the years before World War I, Hugo Stinnes
entered into a partnership with the much older August Thyssen.
Together, the two established the Muelheimer Bergwerk-
sverein, which took over used mines and made a profit out of
them. Soon Hugo Stinnes's firm had branches of its coal busi-

ness in Great Britain, Italy, and the Russian Empire. He entered the shipping business on his own, and his fleets competed with and would eventually absorb the family fleets. He experimented with recycling gas from coke furnaces and became the foremost promoter of electricity in Germany. Hugo Stinnes tirelessly expanded into new business arenas, not for the mere sake of expansion, but to integrate all of his businesses "vertically," a feat that he would not fully accomplish until after World War I.

Despite the shortages of various raw materials because of the Allied blockade of Germany's ports, Hugo Stinnes GmbH emerged unscathed from the war and with an even bigger portfolio. With the Kaiser in exile and a new democratic government in place, Hugo Stinnes became a member of the Reichstag and thus politically influential. The French occupation of the Ruhr valley, where many of Stinnes's assets, especially mines, were located, convinced him that vertical integration of his business, from raw materials to the finished product—including transporting the finished product and controlling the sources of energy in Germany to complete this process—must be accelerated.

A veritable frenzy of expansion followed, in the course of which Stinnes established a partnership with Stahlwerk Breuningshaus steelworks and proceeded to purchase companies that would fully complement this line of business, such as rolling mills, rivet and wire works, a machine tool factory, and other related companies. In 1920 Hugo Stinnes acquired a mining and foundry business that employed 18,000 workers and joined with Germany's largest manufacturer of electrical equipment and appliances, Siemens, to enter that line of business in a partnership. Interested in new energy sources, especially petroleum, Hugo Stinnes's firm began acquiring oil wells abroad, along with refineries and the ocean vessels necessary for conveying the precious fuel. Shipping and transportation companies were purchased as a matter of course, and with Hugo Stinnes's increasing involvement in politics, his business interests turned to newspaper presses, publishing houses and printing establishments, which his firm acquired in short order. Helping this process of acquisition was the cataclysmic German inflation of the early 1920s; property could be bought for almost nothing.

At the time of his premature death in 1924, not only was Hugo Stinnes Germany's most influential and powerful industrialist, but he was also the owner of the largest firm (in terms of assets and revenues) in the country. Hugo Stinnes GmbH consisted of more than 4,500 businesses and employed tens of thousands of workers.

A year and a half after Hugo Stinnes' death, the company was on the brink of ruin. Profligate sons succeeded him and competed against each other; banks recalled their loans, and finally, son Hugo, Jr., sold half of the company's shares to two American banks in return for a huge loan. Much of the company's assets and property were destroyed during the succeeding war years; immediately afterwards, the Stinnes firm reverted to the control of the Allied occupation authorities. Half of the firm was still owned by banks in the United States.

The Hugo Stinnes company probably would have gone under, its stock sold to the highest bidder—most likely to a foreign company—without the intervention of Heinz P. Kemper. Be-

cause he had no Nazi party affiliation during World War II and had for many years directed an American subsidiary in Germany, the American occupation authority selected him to head Stinnes. As its director, Kemper dismissed Hugo Stinnes, Jr., from the helm, thereby ending the Stinnes family's connection to that firm.

Reviving the company and returning it to prosperity was nearly impossible, especially since its assets were spread throughout Germany and British and French authorities were far less friendly and compromising than the Americans. There was also the urgent matter of repurchasing the half of Stinnes still under American ownership, since the Americans were in a position to make a takeover bid for the other half. Unfortunately, Stinnes finances were in turmoil, and there was no money for repurchase.

The firm began to slowly recoup some of its losses and show a profit, thanks in part to the reform of German currency in 1948 and to the formation of the West German state, or Federal Republic of Germany, in 1949. The company was hardly out of deep water, however. The U.S. Government informed Kemper in the mid-1950s that Stinnes stock held by U.S. banks would be sold to the highest bidder, and Germans would be excluded from bidding. Desperate to save the company, Kemper turned to the German government in Bonn for help. Chancellor Konrad Adenauer gave Kemper a sympathetic hearing. Adenauer in turn had a friendly relationship with U.S. President Dwight D. Eisenhower, who was able to pull enough strings to allow the Germans to participate in bidding for their own stock. The Stinnes company, however, did not possess the required capital—DM 100 million—the likely price of repurchasing the stock. So, the German government intervened once more; Finance Minister Ludwig Erhard worked to set up a consortium of German banks that could provide the necessary loan, all of which would have to be repaid to the last pfennig. In the United States, Kemper successfully outbid his competitors, including some of the most powerful firms in the Common Market, and the Hugo Stinnes firm was once more a wholly German-owned company.

The Marshall Plan for the resurrection of the German economy as well as the economic benefits of West German unification laid the foundations of the German "economic miracle." The Hugo Stinnes company once again became one of Germany's largest transportation and raw material supply companies, with sales in the multi-billion dollar range by the early 1970s. In 1976 the company's name was changed to Stinnes AG, in recognition of the fact that the firm was no longer in the hands of the Hugo Stinnes family, and as a reflection of the traditions of both Mathias Stinnes, the founder, and Hugo Stinnes, the daring entrepreneur. By then, Stinnes AG had joined the VEBA group of companies, Germany's largest firm. In 1965 VEBA had bought 95 percent of Stinnes stock, thus turning the company into a subsidiary. By becoming part of this holding company, Stinnes turned into the biggest transportation company in West Germany, since VEBA sold one of its largest barge lines to Stinnes in return for the Stinnes glassworks and the chemical firm Chemiewerk Ruhroel.

By the early 1990s Stinnes AG had become a multibillion dollar company, operating the largest transportation industry in Europe, and also serving as the owner of Brenntag AG, the largest supplier of petrochemicals on the continent. Headquartered in Mathias Stinnes's home town of Muelheim on the Ruhr, Stinnes has branched out into every continent on the globe, and into every country in Europe, including eastern Europe and Russia. On the eve of the twenty-first century, Stinnes consisted of a multitude of major companies, most of whom concentrate on the three business operations of Stinnes: trading in raw materials, distribution, and transportation. Two-thirds of Stinnes' revenues were derived from foreign markets, and one-third of its over 35,000-member work force were employed by Stinnes businesses outside of Germany.

In the early 1990s Europe's biggest transportation (in terms of land traffic) network was the Schenker Eurocargo group, which merged with Stinnes in 1991. A fleet of trucks and other conveyances—including railroads—transported merchandise throughout Europe, including Eastern Europe. Schenker-Rhenus AG, along with its subsidiaries, employed a total of 20,000 people and was without doubt Stinnes's largest component. Stinnes's Schenker International division was a major air and sea transporter of freight and operated fourteen travel agencies as well. In the trading division, Stinnes Intercarbon was the top supplier and marketer in Europe of coal and its byproducts; also in the trading division, the Stinnes firm Frank & Schulte GmbH processed and supplied ores, minerals, and metals to anywhere in the world via its 20 subsidiaries; in the distribution segment, consisting of approximately six major companies, Brenntag AG was the number one supplier of industrial chemicals to chemical manufacturers and the cosmetics industry throughout Europe. An increasingly important segment of Stinnes business was the service sector, especially home-improvement chain stores. A small but important enterprise was the replacement tire market operated by Stinnes Reifendienst, which held the number one market position in Germany; this Stinnes division also owned more than 200 service stations throughout Germany, the Netherlands, Switzerland, Austria, and Alsace.

Since the unification of East and West Germany, Stinnes, unlike many former West German companies, has been in the forefront of investment and expansion into the former German Democratic Republic. Stinnes was also one of the first West German companies to establish corporate branch offices in the eastern German states and to establish major delivery routes into and out of those states. Brenntag AG opened a major distribution center in Magdeburg in former East Germany and quickly established branches of the firm throughout eastern Germany. Shortly after unification in the fall of 1991, Stinnes's earnings from eastern Germany alone totalled DM 1.5 billion—over US$1 billion.

So hungry was the Eastern European population—which for decades lived under restrictive communist governments—for western goods in the early 1990s, that Stinnes was fortunate to have cultivated strong economic ties long before the fall of communism in eastern Europe and Russia. For one thing, the opening up of the east led to new raw material sources for Stinnes, the largest supplier of raw materials in Europe. Because of this, the Stinnes division Frank & Schulte had a year of record profits during the period of slow worldwide growth in 1991. Ores, minerals, and alloys were increasingly being ob-

tained by Frank & Schulte from its Eastern European markets, which represent the best opportunity for growth for that company. Brenntag opened an important branch in Warsaw and offices in the Prague and Moscow, only the beginning of its full penetration of the Eastern European market. The majority of Stinnes's divisions were racing to develop or extend their business in the east, including Russia, where the future of the vast Stinnes firm seems to lie.

According to a past chairman of Stinnes AG, Guenter Winkelmann, the company could not exist without international markets. For this reason, Stinnes was particularly affected by the recession in North America, Australia, and Great Britain in the early 1990s. At the same time, however, Stinnes, which derived most of its revenues from overseas markets, was entrenched as the global leader in transportation and distribution. Stinnes's transition from a German firm to a multinational company took place nearly 100 years ago. By comparison, many other large companies in Germany and elsewhere were just beginning to branch out overseas. Diverse businesses and international markets were the major strengths of Stinnes AG and crucial components of a global leader looking to maintain its position in the twenty-first century.

Principal Subsidiaries: Internationales Kohle-Trading; Stinnes Intercarbon AG; Stinnes Intercoal GmbH; Stinnes Hansen Coal GmbH; Stromeyer GmbH; Stinnes Kohle-Energie Handelsges. mbH; IKO Industriekohle GmbH & Co. KG; Fechner Gmbh & Co. KG; Stinnes Hansen Coal Company; Intercarbon Pty. Ltd; Agenzia Carboni, S.r.l.; Intercarbon do Brasil Ltd.; Store Norske-Stinnes Intercoal A.S.; Internationales Öl-Trading; Stinnes Interoil AG; VTG Paktank Hamburb GmbH; Stinnes Interoil Inc.; Stinnes Interoil PTE LTD; Stinnes Interoil Italia SRL; Internationales Erze/Mineralien-Trading; Frank & Schulte GmbH; Ferrocarbon GmbH; Fergusson Wild & Company Ltd.; Microfine Minerals Ltd.; F + S Alloys and Minerals Corporation; Miller and Company; Brenntag AG; Brenntag Eurochem GmbH; Brenntag Interchem GmbH; Industick GmbH, Chemische Produkte; Chemische Fabrik Lehrte; Stinnes Mineralölhandel GmbH; Boucquillon N.V.; NBM Nederlandsche Benzol Maatschappij B.V.; B.V.V./H Firma L.J. Volkers; Brenntag France S.A.; Groupe Distribution Chimie, S.A.; Brenntag (U.K.) Ltd.; Brenntag Italia S.p.A.; Brenntag Portugal Produtos Quimicos Lda.; SOCO Chemical Inc.; Textile Chemical Company Inc.; SOCO-Lynch Chemical Corp.; Delta Distributors, Inc.; P.B. & S. Chemical Company, Inc.; Brenntag Interchem Inc.; Brenntag (Taiwan) Co. Ltd.; Southern Inc.; Walter Patz OHG; Stinnes Montanhandel GmbH & Co. KG; Stinnes Stahlhandel GmbH; Hollinde & Boudon GmbH; Bausthl Schöder GmbH; Josef Stangl Eisengroßhandel u. Biegebetrieb GmbH; Michael Friess GmbH; Stinnes Rohrunion GmbH; Stinnes Steel AG; Stinnes BauMarkt AG; Baustoff-Union GmbH & Co. KG; SB-Baustoff-Vertrieb GmbH; Stinnes Reifendienst GmbH; Hofka Sampermans B.V.; Pneu Matti AG; Kautzmann S.A.; Reifen Reiner Ges. mbH; Inter-Union Technohandel GmH; Batavia M. Sawatzky GmbH & Co. KG; Mester Werkzeuge, Werkzeugfabrik GmbH; Interconti Industriekontor GmbH; Gelhard GmbH & Co. KG; Tegro AG; Batvia A/S.; Viktor E. Kern Ges. mbH; Schenker Eurocargo; Biermann-Schenker Portugal Lda.; Bischof Gesellschaft mbH; Exped Holland B.V.; Newexco B.V.; Schenker & Co. AG;

Schenker & Co. A/S; Schenker Danmark A/S; Schenker S.A.; Schenkers Ltd.; Schenker Eurocargo B.V.; Schenker Eurocargo N.V.; Schenker Transport AB; Schenker-Berker A.S.; Schenker Interlogistik AG; Schenker Hellas AG; Schenker Hungaria Kft.; Schenker Italiana S.p.A.; Schenker Norge AS; Schenker Polska Sp.zo.o.; Schenker Witag; Schenker International AG; c & d Luftfracht-System GmbH; Rhenus Air Transport GmbH; Schenkers International Forwarders, Inc.; Schenker of Canada Ltd.; Schenker Panamericana (Mexico) S. De R.L.; Schenker Panamericana (Panama) S.A.; Schenker Panamericana (C.A.) Ltda.; Schenker do Brasil Transportes Internacionais Ltda.; Entra, Engelberg Transport Internacionales. C.A.; Schenker Argentina S.A.; Schenker Colombia S.A.; Schenker & Co. (East Africa) Ltd.; Schenker & Co. (Botsuana) (Pty) Ltd.; Schenker & Co. (S.A.) Pty. Ltd.; Japan Schenker Co. Ltd.; Rhenus Transport International Ltd.; Schenker (H.K.) Ltd.; Rhenus Transport (Singapore) Pte. Ltd.; Schenker Singapore (Pte.) Ltd.; P.T. Trans-Kontinent Utama; Schenker Malaysia Sdn. Bhd; Schenker (Thai) Ltd.; Schenker (H.K.) Ltd.; Denny & Roys Ltd.; Schenker & Co. (Aust.) Pty. Ltd.; Rhenus AG; "Nancyport" Société d'Exploitation du Port de Frouard S.A.; Luxport S.A.; Rhenus AG für Schiffahrt und Spedition; Spoorhaven Stevedoring & Warehousing B.V.; Rhenus Nederland B.V.; Stinnes Reederei AG & Co.; RK Reederei + Spedition; Reederei Jaegers GmbH; Combined Container Service GmbH & Co. KG; Bayerischer Lloyd AG; Bulgar Lloyd GmbH; Deutsch-Ukrainische Verkehrs-GmbH; Rom Lloyd GmbH; DLM Donau-Lloyd-Mat GmbH; Stinnes Antverpia N.V.; Hungaro Lloyd KFT; Bayerischer Lloyd Ltd.; Midgard Deutsche Seeverkehrs AG; Poseidon Schiffahrt OHG; Frachtcontor Junge & Co.; Junge & Co.; Ahlers N.V.; De Baerdemaecker N.V.; Railship GmbH & Co. KG; Transwaggon GmbH; Stinnes-Immobiliendienst GmbH & Co. KG; Hotel "Nassauer Hof" GmbH; Hamburger Hof GmbH & Co.; Hamburger Hof Verischerungs-AG; Stinnes-data-Service GmbH; INAS GmbH; Stinnes-Organisationsberatung GmbH; Stinnes Corporation; Precision National Plating Services Inc.; Transwaggon AG; KKKK A/S.

Further Reading:

The Making of a Business Empire; 175 Years of Stinnes; Portrait of a German Company, Econ Verlag, 1983.
"People in Finance: Hugo Stinnes," *The Banker,* October 1982, pp. 74–75.
Stinnes AG Annual Reports, 1991 and 1992.
"Stinnes AG—Company Report," *DAFSA,* August 1, 1992.
Stinnes, Edmund Hugo, *A Genius in Chaotic Times: Edmund H. Stinnes on his Father, Hugo Stinnes (1870–1924),* Bern: E.H. Stinnes, 1979.
Young, Ian, "Stinnes Agrarchemie Builds Five Centers," *Chemical Week,* February 3, 1993, p. 13.

—Sina Dubovoj

Stouffer Corp.

29800 Bainbridge Road
Cleveland, Ohio 44139
U.S.A.
(216) 248-3600
Fax: (216) 498-1420

Wholly Owned Subsidiary of Nestlé USA, Inc.
Incorporated: 1924
Employees: 4,000
Sales: $1.21 billion
SICs: 2038 Frozen Specialties Nec; 2037 Frozen Fruits,
   Frozen Fruit Juices, and Vegetables.

Stouffer Corp., a subsidiary of Nestlé USA, Inc., is the United States' leading manufacturer and marketer of more than 150 varieties of premium quality frozen prepared foods. Stouffer introduced frozen foods in the 1950s and calorie-controlled products in the 1980s. The company's products include frozen entrees, side dishes, the Lean Cuisine line, and popular French bread pizzas.

The company was founded in 1922, when Abraham and Mahala Stouffer left their creamery business in Medina, Ohio, to open a dairy stand in downtown Cleveland's Arcade Building. The couple offered wholesome buttermilk and free crackers, and soon enjoyed a healthy lunch business. The Stouffers later added fresh-brewed coffee and Mrs. Stouffer's homemade deep-dish Dutch apple pies to the limited menu.

Abraham and Mahala's son Vernon graduated from the Wharton School of Finance at the University of Pennsylvania in 1923 and returned home to help with his parents' growing business. His leadership would propel the family business to unanticipated prominence. The family established its first real restaurant with an investment of just $15,000. Stouffer Lunch opened in 1924 on the corner of East 9th Street and Euclid Avenue in the Cleveland Citizens Building. The restaurant's menu featured four sandwiches priced from 20 to 25 cents.

The family extended its dining concept to Detroit and Pittsburgh by 1929, when a younger son, Gordon, joined the business. Gordon realized that, to attain chain status, the Stouffer restaurants' menus, decor, and ambiance should coordinate. He therefore promoted standard uniforms for waitresses—or "Stouffer Girls" as he called them—and launched the slogan, "Everybody is somebody at Stouffers." The family endeavor was such a success that even the Great Depression did not impede expansion: by 1935, the chain opened its sixth location, and in 1937, it launched its first restaurant in New York City.

The burgeoning company's progress was curtailed by World War II, but growth recommenced in 1946, when Stouffer's opened its first suburban restaurant in Cleveland's Shaker Square neighborhood. Postwar suburbanization spawned Stouffer's first diversification in the company's 23-year history: customers at the Shaker Square restaurant began to ask manager Wally Blankinship to freeze popular menu items for reheating at home.

Blankinship soon realized the potential of frozen food, and began to sell the items in a separate business called the 227 Club. The evolution of Stouffer's frozen foods from a restaurant atmosphere strongly influenced their development. Packaging, for example, focused on entrees, rather than entire meals. And without the concept of mass production driving the business, Stouffer's dishes differed from normal frozen fare in their high quality and abundance of meat and vegetables. The products introduced a premium segment to the frozen food market. Stouffer's volume of frozen food business grew so quickly that, in 1954, the company built a pilot processing plant in downtown Cleveland. That year, the company was officially named Stouffer Foods Corporation.

In 1960, Stouffer made its first venture into the hotel business with the purchase of Fort Lauderdale, Florida's Anacapri Inn. The move gave the company three divisions: Stouffer Hotel Co., Stouffer Foods Corp., and Stouffer Restaurant Co. The restaurant group launched its "top" restaurants in the 1960s. These eateries were located atop skyscrapers in major cities, combining fine dining with a view of the city. By 1973, there were six such restaurants around America.

As more and more women entered the work force after World War II, homemakers had less time to prepare elaborate meals, and demand for convenience foods rose. To meet the increased production requirements, Stouffer constructed a highly automated and modernized frozen food plant in 1968 on a 42-acre site in Solon, Ohio, just south of Cleveland.

In the late 1960s, Stouffer's consumer research showed that families with two or more children constituted a considerable segment of sales volume. Assuming a market for multi-serving packages, Stouffer developed a "Family Casserole" line serving four or more people. But Stouffer's research didn't take trends toward split meals and split menus into account. Split meals are eaten by families with conflicting activities that are unable to eat together. Split menu diners eat at the same time, but not all of the family members eat the same thing. The larger families that purchased Stouffer's products were not necessarily eating multiple packages of a single product, but utilizing the single-serving packages for split meals and menus. Although the Family Casserole line was basically a failure, it did launch frozen lasagna, which became an instant success in single- and double-serving sizes.

The frozen foods division earned the United States National Aeronautics and Space Administration's endorsement when Stouffer's products were chosen to feed Apollo 11, 12, and 14 astronauts while in quarantine after their history-making space voyages. Advertising at the time exploited Stouffer's support of the space program with the tag line, "Everybody who's been to the moon is eating Stouffer's."

Swiss food colossus Nestlé S.A. acquired Stouffer's three divisions in 1973, when Stouffer became a subsidiary of Nestlé's American division, Nestlé Enterprises Inc. Once Stouffer became a member of the Nestlé "family," its sales and earnings figures were no longer figured separately.

The Nestlé investment helped bring about the 1976 acquisition of Borel Restaurant Corp., owner of the upscale Rusty Scupper seafood chain. Under Nestlé, Stouffer also increased its holdings of restaurants with unique dining atmospheres by purchasing Parkers' Lighthouse restaurants, which offered waterfront views.

By the 1980s, the Stouffer Hotel Company had grown into a loose chain of 19 Midwest hotels with $80 million in annual revenues. But unlike Stouffer's other two divisions, the hotel group's image had deteriorated. In 1981, former hotel busboy and ex-Marine William Hulett was appointed to the presidency of the hotel group. Hulett embarked on a revitalization of the hotel chain by terminating its franchising program and liquidating seven struggling franchised holdings. He then began a decade-long acquisitions spree that brought several prestigious hotels into the Stouffer group, including: Washington, D.C.'s Mayflower in 1981, the Waiohai Beach Resort in 1983, the Stanford Court in 1989, and Tampa Bay's historic Vinoy Park Hotel in 1990.

Stouffer Foods had become America's leading manufacturer of premium quality frozen foods by the early 1980s. To meet growing consumer demand, the company increased its production capacity in 1980, building a frozen foods plant in Gaffney, South Carolina.

Noting growing sales of diet foods and drinks in the 1970s, Stouffer Foods began research and development for a product that revolutionized the frozen food industry. Almost a decade of consumer and demographic research directed the brand extension. Focus groups indicated the things that dieters didn't like about low-calorie food: inferior taste, unappealing appearance, meager portions, and lack of variety. Demographic figures indicated smaller, two-income, and single person households, which also influenced the development of the new product.

Stouffer used its findings to develop single-serving frozen entrees with lots of vegetables and extra herbs for flavor. The 300-calorie dishes in ten varieties fit in well with the American Dietetic Association's 1200-calorie-per-day recommendations for women. And since dieters shunned the word "diet," product developers chose the name Lean Cuisine over four other ideas. A white package design conveyed lightness and differentiated the new product from Stouffer's standard "red box" line.

After about a year of test marketing, Stouffer launched Lean Cuisine in 1982 with the company's first public relations efforts: a 24-page booklet entitled "On the Way to Being Lean," and a national tour by nutritionists supporting the product. Consumers ordered more than 300,000 copies of the booklet, and, more importantly, purchased $125 million in Lean Cuisine during its first year of national distribution.

Lean Cuisine sales tripled Stouffer's projections, and the company's share of the $500 million frozen food market jumped from an already-impressive 33 percent to 46 percent. The product benefitted the industry as a whole, too; the single-dish entree category enjoyed its first growth in two years. The only problem generated by Lean Cuisine's phenomenal success was that Stouffer had a difficult time keeping up with demand for the product. In 1982 the company expanded its Gaffney plant by 47 percent, and workers put in six-day weeks there and in Solon to keep stores stocked.

Lean Cuisine quickly overtook predecessor Weight Watchers' frozen entrees, outselling the competitor three-to-one by 1984 and capturing almost half of the American frozen entree market. But not long after that coup, two other rival food companies introduced strong competing products. Kraft General Foods, Inc.'s Budget Gourmet cut into Stouffer's share first with its cost-conscious entrees. ConAgra Inc.'s Healthy Choice did more damage with its line of low-sodium, low-fat frozen entrees. At the same time, H. J. Heinz's Weight Watchers began attaching its name to dozens of products.

By 1987, Weight Watchers, Healthy Choice, and the other competitors had taken their portions of the single-dish frozen dinner market, leaving Lean Cuisine with just 13 percent. The rivalry remained fierce through the late 1980s, when Stouffer's introduced a product that it hoped would regain some of the company's market share. Right Course's low-fat, low-cholesterol formulation seemed to fit in well with the ever-expanding health movement. And, like Lean Cuisine, the product was supported with extensive consumer research. But just 17 months after its introduction, the product was pulled from national distribution. After the overwhelming success of Lean Cuisine, Stouffer's Right Course flopped, earning a meager 1 percent of the frozen entree market. Observers inside and outside the company blamed a variety of factors for the product's failure: high pricing, poor shelf placement, overly exotic dishes, and perhaps most significantly, an inauspicious name. By the end of the decade, ConAgra's Healthy Choice had taken the lead in frozen dinners and entrees, beating Stouffer's basic entrees by just one share point.

Despite an industry-wide surplus of hotel rooms, Stouffer's Hotel division continued to grow under Hulett's direction. By the end of the 1980s, the chain bought the seven-unit Presidente Hotel chain in Mexico, adding to its assembly of resorts in the Caribbean and Hawaii. The hotel group had expanded to number 41 award-winning properties by 1990, with revenues of almost $600 million.

That year, Nestlé acknowledged the close relationship between Stouffer's hotel and restaurant divisions. The June merger of those two companies to form the Stouffer Hospitality Group elevated William Hulett to the presidency of the reorganized division. But just one month later, Nestlé revealed its plans to sell Stouffer's restaurants separately from the hotel chain. Nestlé spokespeople noted that, although most of the restaurants were profitable, they contributed less than 1 percent to the world's largest food concern's 1989 sales of $30.5 billion. The sale was only the beginning of a consolidation effort that returned Stouffer's to the single-business emphasis it had established almost 70 years earlier.

In the early 1990s, Hulett continued to develop Stouffer's hotel group, expanding its holdings in Mexico, the Virgin Islands, and the United States. And when other hotel chains announced rate cuts in the early 1990s, Hulett released nationwide advertisements touting the higher quality and value of Stouffer's accommodations. By 1993, the group's hotels and resorts had, in Hulett's words, "won virtually every major award the travel industry has to offer." For Hulett, premium offers like butler service, exclusive amenities, and exceptional dining justified Stouffer's higher prices.

The chain's success, combined with Nestlé's desire to consolidate in the 1990s, attracted the attention of another large hotel chain, Hong-Kong based New World Development Co. Directed by billionaire Cheng Yu-Tung, New World operated both the Renaissance and Ramada International chains, and arranged to purchase the Stouffer group in 1993 for a reported $1.5 billion.

The reorganization left Stouffer Corp. with frozen foods as its sole business, and its business had become more complicated in the 1990s. Intense competition consumed Stouffer management, and in 1991, a reorganization of the parent company drew attention away from the grueling frozen foods rivalry. That year, Nestlé's 15 food and beverage companies in America were reorganized into six business groups according to products or services. The new U.S. subsidiary was renamed Nestlé USA, Inc. Stouffer Foods corporation became part of the Nestlé Frozen/Refrigerated Food Company, yet maintained a separate identity.

Product introductions were a hallmark of the early years of the decade, when Stouffer's fought aggressively to regain its number one spot from ConAgra's Healthy Choice. HomeStyle Entrees sought a niche at the opposite end of the product line from Lean Cuisine. The brand extension offered 13 traditional "meat and potato" dishes. The introduction of new Family-Size and Party-Size versions of Stouffer's most popular entree lines harkened back to the Family Casserole experiment of the 1960s. The company did not, however, abandon its diet line. Stiff competition from Healthy Choice and Weight Watchers continued, yet the frozen food category as a whole declined by 6 percent in 1990. That year, Stouffer's won the right to print exchange information from Weight Watchers popular diet plan on Lean Cuisine packages, making the Stouffer product equally compatible with Weight Watchers' nutrition guidelines. Stouffer's regrouped in 1991, expanding the Lean Cuisine line to 34 varieties, reducing fat, sodium, and cholesterol, lowering prices, and launching a new national television campaign for "the taste you can love for life."

While most of the frozen food market languished in the early 1990s, one segment that did enjoy growth was that of frozen sweets, especially low-calorie frozen desserts. Lean Cuisine entered this market, dominated by Weight Watchers, with five desserts in 1991 and Lean Cuisine ice milk in 1992.

By early 1992, Stouffer's had regained its lead in frozen foods on the introduction of Lean Cuisine Macaroni and Cheese,

which quickly became a best-selling variety. The Lean Cuisine line was expanded for a second time in the decade with eight new entrees, half of which offered vegetarian alternatives.

That year also saw a major change in Stouffer's product image. In 1992 the company introduced a new logo that replaced the corporate identification used since the 1950s. The new black oval and red slash "seal of quality" was just one part of a package redesign that included a modernization of the typeface, simplification of the ingredients lists, clearer nutritional information, more attractive food images, and a toll-free number for Stouffer's Consumer Information Center. Vernon Stouffer was posthumously inducted into the National Frozen Food Association Frozen Food Hall of Fame in 1992 in recognition of his contributions to the industry.

Stouffer Foods Corp. hoped to break out of the frozen foods slump with the 1993 introduction of its Lunch Express lines. The two sub-brands were associated with Stouffer's standard "red box" and Lean Cuisine lines, but were intended specifically for lunchtime consumption. The total of 24 new products continued the frozen foods trend toward ever-greater market segmentation. The nine or 10 ounce meals could be microwaved in about five minutes, eaten right from the package, and purchased for under $2. Stouffer's hoped that Lunch Express would carve out a new niche for itself and, at the same time, expand the frozen food industry, which had experienced virtually no growth in the 1990s.

Once a family-owned, Midwestern dairy stand, Stouffer Corp. grew to encompass a restaurant chain, an award-winning hotel group, and an internationally-recognized producer of frozen foods. After consolidation in the early 1990s, the company has focused on the business that revolutionized the frozen food industry.

Further Reading:

Canedy, Dana, "Stouffer Hotels Move to Fla. Likely," *Plain Dealer* (Cleveland), April 2, 1993, p. 1E.

Clark, Sandra, "Stouffer Turns in Logo for New 'Seal of Quality,'" *Plain Dealer* (Cleveland), May 5, 1992, p. 2F.

"Lunch Hunch: Stouffer Launches Frozen-food Line for Busy Workers," *Plain Dealer* (Cleveland), February 10, 1993, p. 1G.

Dagnoli, Judann, "Weight Watchers Gaining: Heinz Unit Builds Share as It Leans on Stouffer," *Advertising Age,* July 13, 1987, p. 4.

"Lean Cuisine, Weight Watchers Go Healthy," *Advertising Age,* January 8, 1990, p. 35.

"How Stouffer's Right Course Veered Off Course," *Advertising Age,* May 6, 1991, p. 34.

Funk, Nancy M., "Stouffer Hotels Buys Stake in 6 Properties It Manages in Mexico," *Plain Dealer* (Cleveland), February 28, 1991, p. 2D.

Gleisser, Marcus, "Stouffer Began as Lunch Counter," *Plain Dealer* (Cleveland), July 24, 1990, p. 10A.

"Stouffer's to Hold Line on Downtown Hotel Rates," *Plain Dealer* (Cleveland), June 30, 1992, pp. 1G and 11G.

Hammel, Frank, "Frozen Foods," *Supermarket Business,* September 1992, pp. 115–116 and 160–164.

Higgins, Kevin, "Meticulous Planning Pays Dividends at Stouffer's," *Marketing News,* October 28, 1983, pp. 1 and 20.

Karle, Delinda, "Nestlé to Sell Stouffer's Restaurants," *Plain Dealer* (Cleveland), July 24, 1990, pp. 1A and 10A.

Lloyd, Ann, "The Lean Cuisine Story," *American Demographics,* December 1984, pp. 16 and 46.

Monnett, James G., Jr., "Euclid-E.13th St. Gets Restaurant," *Plain Dealer* (Cleveland), November 22, 1935, p. 28:3.

"Nestlé Merging Stouffer Restaurant, Hotel Firms," *Plain Dealer* (Cleveland), June 12, 1990, p. 8D.

Papazian, Ruth, "Consumer Expenditures Study: Frozen Foods," *Supermarket Business,* September 1990, pp. 154–155, 129.

Scapa, James, "William Hulett, President, Stouffer Hotel Co.," *Restaurant Business,* May 1, 1990, pp. 166–7.

Schiller, Zachary, "No More Fat City for Lean Cuisine," *Business Week,* December 24, 1990, p. 24.

"Historical Backgrounder: Stouffer Foods Corporation," Stouffer Foods Corporation, 1993.

"Stouffer Part of $88 Million Florida Resort," *Plain Dealer* (Cleveland), March 13, 1990, p. 7D.

Warner, Fara, "Lean Cuisine Dips into Frozen Desserts," *Adweek's Marketing Week,* May 27, 1991, p. 10.

"Stouffer Defends Its Lead in Frozen Meals," *Adweek's Marketing Week,* April 20, 1992, p. 7.

Wolff, Carlo, "At Your Service," *Lodging Hospitality,* April 1991, p. 50.

Yerak, Rebecca, "New Entrees, Desserts to Beef Up Stouffer Lean Cuisine," *Plain Dealer* (Cleveland), February 20, 1991, p. 2H.

"FTC: Lean Cuisine Ads on Sodium Deceptive," *Plain Dealer* (Cleveland), October 29, 1991, p. 5F.

—April S. Dougal

Stride Rite Corporation

Five Cambridge Center
Cambridge, MA 02142
(617) 491-8800
Fax: (617) 864-1372

Public Company
Incorporated: 1919 as Green Shoe Manufacturing Company
Employees: 3100
Sales: $586 million
Stock Exchange: New York
SICs: 3149 Footwear except rubber, not elsewhere classified;
　5139 Footwear; 5661 Shoe Stores

Founded in 1919 as Green Shoe Manufacturing Company, Stride Rite has become a major producer of children's shoes and casual footwear. Apart from Stride Rite, its children's line, it also manufactures Keds sneakers and Sperry Top-Sider boat shoes. Beyond its success as a profitable manufacturing company, however, Stride Rite is known for the social innovations that former president and chair Arnold Hiatt has put into place. Stride Rite was the first company to provide on-site day care in 1971, the first to provide a smoke-free work environment, and the first to provide an on-site intergenerational day-care center in 1990. While spending the effort and resources necessary for these innovative workers' benefits, Stride Rite nevertheless achieved impressive growth in sales, income, and investment value throughout the late 1980s and early 1990s.

In 1919, Jacob A. Slosberg founded a small shoe manufacturing company with his partner Philip Green. Initially set up in a converted stables in the Roxbury section of Boston, the Green Shoe Manufacturing Company specialized in making stitch-down shoes (also called welt shoes) for children. The company, employing nearly 100 people, was able to produce between 800 and 1,000 pairs of shoes each day.

Slosberg, who came to the United States from Russia in 1887 at the age of 12, had almost 30 years of experience in the shoe manufacturing industry when he cofounded Green Shoe. Beginning in 1892 he had worked for a series of shoe and shoe machinery manufacturers in Lynn and Beverly, Massachusetts. In those factories he had spent long hours stitching shoes and later dismantling and reassembling shoe machinery. He had then become a foreman at the Thomas Plant Company, a manufacturer of shoe machines, and when Thomas was sold to

United Shoe Machinery, he had joined the Greenberg-Miller Company, a manufacturer of children's shoes in New York. He put the money he had been able to save and the experience he had been able to garner into Green Shoe.

In the early 1920s a disagreement emerged between Philip Green and Slosberg. Some sources say that it involved the quality of the product, which Slosberg was determined to maintain, while others say it was about whether to produce children's shoes or, as Green favored, women's shoes. In any case, in 1924 Green sold his share of the enterprise, which was bought up by Charles B. Strecker, a banker, and his son Seymour.

Green Shoe grew rapidly under Slosberg's direction. The main brand names were Green-flex and Mo-Debs. Because of overcrowding in the converted stables, Slosberg built a new manufacturing facility. Seymour Strecker sold his share of Green Shoe to Slosberg 10 days before the stock market crash of 1929. However, even during the Depression, Green Shoe continued to grow. By the mid-1930s, the company was manufacturing about 3,000 pairs of shoes per day. During hard times, the company gained a reputation for reliability and value.

In 1933 Green Shoe, already seeking a brand name that could unite its entire line, hired Tom Lalonde, a manufacturer of children's shoes, to work in sales. Lalonde owned the name Stride Rite, and Green Shoe bought the name for $1,000 from him, using it for a line of extra support shoes. By 1937 the name was extended to all shoes manufactured by the company.

Jacob Slosberg had two sons, Sam and Charles, who began work at Green Shoe in the early 1920s. Sam eventually went into sales, and Charles took over manufacturing. Charles visited shoe factories in the United States and Europe in order to find ways of streamlining production and distribution without sacrificing quality. He was particularly concerned that the company be able to deliver shoes to outlets in a timely fashion with a minimum of mistakes. To this end, he developed a highly efficient in-stock system. Incoming orders were analyzed immediately. If the items requested were out of stock, production lines were switched over to that product as needed. Workers known as "expediters" hand-carried these orders through the production process. In this way, the company was never "out of stock." This enabled Green Shoe, and for some years Stride Rite, to guarantee that 100 percent of an order would be delivered within 24 hours of the placement of the order.

During World War II, Green Shoe helped develop and manufactured the nurse's field boot and the WAC boot for the Army. Slosberg, who was a member of the War Production Board, used the opportunity to encourage retailers to buy Stride Rite, with the result that the business boomed. The company sold shoes to department stores such as Jordan Marsh, Filene's, and Dayton Hudson in Detroit, all under private store labels.

The years between 1945 and the late 1950s saw the most rapid expansion in the company's history, partly as a result of the postwar baby boom. One of the hallmarks of the company came to be multiple widths in children's shoes. Daily production rose to about 25,000 pairs in 1959. The work force quadrupled, and factory floor space increased seven-fold. In fact, the Stride Rite factory was at the time the largest factory in the United States manufacturing all of a company's products under one roof.

When Jacob Slosberg died in 1953, his sons and son-in-law Martin Landay assumed the management of the company. Samuel became president and Charles treasurer, with the additional duties of managing production, maintenance, and in-stock operation. Landay was named vice president. Charles Slosberg died unexpectedly in 1960.

The 1960s and 1970s saw great changes in the way Green Shoe did business. The company went public in 1960. Then in 1962, the first of several acquisitions greatly expanded the company. That year, Green Shoe acquired the Weber Shoe Company in Tipton, Missouri. Weber became a Green Shoe manufacturing facility. A second factory was built in 1969 in Hamilton, Missouri, to augment Weber's capacity. The Weber acquisition was followed in 1964 by that of the R. J. Potvin Company, in Brockton, Massachusetts. A new warehouse was built there in 1965.

In 1966, with increased capacity and public recognition of its name, Green Shoe became the Stride Rite Corporation. In that year, the company acquired the H. Scheft Company and Stone Shoe Company in Boston and in 1967, Blue Star Shoes, Inc., in Lawrence, Massachusetts. Arnold Hiatt, Blue Star's president, became the first nonfamily member to become president of Stride Rite in 1968. The same year, Orange Shoe Co., in Orange, Massachusetts, was added to Stride Rite. The shoe company that began in 1919 with a capacity of 1000 pairs per day was producing 30,000 in 1969.

This period also saw great changes in the work force at Stride Rite. During the 1960s, African American women in particular joined the Stride Rite work force in great numbers, reflecting the changing population of Roxbury, the neighborhood in which the Boston factory is located. Many of the new employees could work only if they had day-care services for their children. In response to their needs, Stride Rite opened the first company-run day-care center in the United States in 1971.

The idea for the center, conceived by Arnold Hiatt, was initially seen as a charitable gift that would serve the surrounding community only. As Hiatt explained, "The company had had a charitable foundation for some time, but it had limited itself to the traditional kinds of gifts—hospitals, universities, and other very visible community organizations—and had played a relatively passive check-writing role. I felt it was time for us to do something in a more targeted way . . . in our community. At the time our offices and our plant were located in Roxbury, and I thought we ought to do something right there."

Shortly after the center opened in the spring of 1971, it began enrolling employees' children. Hiatt commented: "We're given credit for being a pioneer in employer-supported day care, but our aim was to provide child care for the community, for children of welfare mothers and single-parent households. Shortly after we started, one of our workers approached me and said, 'You're willing to do this for the children in the neighborhood. Why don't you do the same for our children?' And I said fine. And from that day forward we tried to maintain a balance at the center between children from the community and the children of our employees."

Although company headquarters were moved to Cambridge, Massachusetts, in 1983 and the original site was turned into a warehouse, the day-care center continued to service the same number of children as before. (In 1993, the company announced that the Roxbury warehouse would close. However, grants will be made available to community groups to continue providing day-care services.) In addition, a day-care center was opened in Cambridge. The Stride Rite day-care centers, which are modeled in part on the Head Start program, have been studied and adapted by hundreds of companies all over the United States. Stride Rite has looked into providing day-care services to employees at its production and distribution facilities outside of Massachusetts. This effort, however, has been hindered by complications resulting from state regulations regarding child care, although, as of 1993, the company was pursuing the possibility of starting day-care services at a distribution center in Kentucky. There is a day-care center at a Stride Rite factory in Bangkok, Thailand.

During the 1970s, faced with skyrocketing leather prices and competition from low-priced imports, the company decided to change direction. It opened its first Stride Rite Bootery in 1972 and its first Overland Trading Company in 1979. In addition, the company purchased Keds and Sperry Top-Sider from Uniroyal in 1979 for $18 million and $5.7 million respectively. Keds, which had been losing money for Uniroyal, was turned around by 1982, and Sperry became very popular as a result of the "preppie look" fad of the 1980s. In fact, in the early 1980s, Sperry grew at a rate of 80 percent, a growth rate that was described as "unmatched at the moment in the shoe industry" by *Footwear News* in 1982. However, in 1991, sales plummeted 26 percent.

What happened to sales of Top-Siders illustrates a basic Stride Rite marketing approach: in general the company does not try to hitch onto every fad and does not try to associate its name with high profile athletes as do some of its competitors. The success of Top-Siders was unplanned and unexpected. The company seems to have benefited from its origins as a maker of children's shoes. Parents look for reliable quality and value for their children, and the company appears not to stray too far from their expectations.

Studies began to appear in the 1980s that showed that toddlers learned to walk better in shoes than in sneakers and these findings fueled a 31 percent increase in sales of baby shoes in 1986 over 1985. Several of its baby shoes were granted the Seal of Acceptance by the American Podiatric Medical Association in 1989, the only baby shoes to hold that seal. As children's apparel became trendier in the 1980s, Stride Rite responded by changing its marketing, while retaining the basic look and quality of the line itself. By early 1989, Stride Rite had 715 retail units, 70 percent of which were owned by independent dealers. However, the 25 Overland Trading Companies became an independent entity in 1988. Also in 1989, Keds brought out a line of natural fiber sportswear for children, under the name Keds Kids Clothes, and in 1992 it began to market a line of women's clothes, Keds Apparel.

In 1991, Stride Rite founded Stride Rite International as a vehicle for marketing its products in foreign countries. This division markets Stride Rite shoe lines in Europe, Asia, and Latin America.

In 1990, Stride Rite started a new social program. Hiatt, who now was chairman of the company, had read an article in 1986 in the *Wall Street Journal* which detailed problems encountered by families with both child care and elder care responsibilities. After several years of research and with funding from the Stride Rite Charitable Foundation and input from several social agencies and Wheelock College, the company opened its Intergenerational Day-Care Center in 1990. The Center, which is housed at the company's headquarters, has separate areas and activities for seniors and children as well as common areas. According to Karen Leibold, the director of the center, "The relationship between the children and the elders has really exceeded our expectations. We thought we'd need to bring them together very slowly, with a lot of staff direction and with specific projects to do. What we've found is that they're like magnets with each other. . . . Sometimes it can be five minutes at the beginning or the end of the day . . . Sometimes it's waving across the lunchroom at each other. Sometimes it can be an extended period of time, reading books together, or cooking, or making things with blocks or Play-Doh."

Stride Rite has demonstrated that socially conscious policies and profitability can go hand in hand. Net income has risen by $5 to $10 million each year between 1984 and 1991—from $5.4 million to $66 million—and its return on equity exceeded 30 percent between 1989 and 1991. Both of these figures were down slightly in 1992; net income dropped to $61.5 million and equity return to 23.6 percent even though net sales increased. Still, the company appears to understand the employees and customers who make such growth possible. Arnold Hiatt summarized the Stride Rite philosophy: "We don't live in a vacuum. We live in a community. And that community has needs. It is people from the community who buy our products and support our business. It doesn't seem too far-fetched to have an interest in the well-being of that community. We're just broadening the definition of our self-interest."

Principal Subsidiaries: The Keds Corp.; Sperry Top-Sider, Inc.; Stride Rite Children's Group, Inc.; Stride Rite Canada, Ltd.; Stride Rite International Corp.; Stride Rite Sourcing International, Inc.

Further Reading:

From Green Shoe to Stride Rite, Cambridge, MA: Stride Rite Corp.

Keegan, Paul, "Doing the Rite Thing," *Boston,* July 1991.

Morgan, Hal, and Kerry Tucker, *Companies That Care,* New York: Simon and Schuster, 1991.

Olivieri, David, "Progressive Company Profits from Its Steady Pace," *Business Journal,* May 1992.

Van Tuyl, Laura, "Day Care Program Bridges Generations," *Christian Science Monitor,* April 15, 1991.

—Kenneth F. Kronenberg

Superior Industries International, Inc.

7800 Woodley Avenue
Van Nuys, California 91406
U.S.A.
(818) 781-4973
Fax: (818) 780-3500

Public Company
Incorporated: 1969
Employees: 3,500
Sales: $325.31 million
Stock Exchanges: New York
SICs: 3714 Motor Vehicle Parts and Accessories

Founded initially to make radiator bug screens, Superior Industries International, Inc., has grown to be the largest aluminum wheel manufacturer in the world and the principal supplier of cast aluminum wheels to the North American automotive industry. Superior designs, manufactures, and markets automotive products for both the original equipment manufacturer (OEM) market and for the automotive aftermarket, specializing in custom road wheels as well as steering wheel covers, lighting products, and suspension products.

In 1957 Louis L. Borick established Superior Industries International to manufacture and supply popular products for a burgeoning automotive aftermarket. The company set up its headquarters in Van Nuys, California, and Borick, who had become a car fanatic as a teenager after landing a job in a Minnesota auto parts shop, became president and chief executive of Superior.

In 1957 the company debuted its first product, a radiator bug screen, which earned Superior a modest $27,000 in sales its first year. In 1961 the company constructed a new, 25,000-square-foot manufacturing plant in Van Nuys, and the following year it introduced its second major product, safety belts. During the mid-1960s Superior's product line was expanded to include other automotive aftermarket products, such as steering wheel covers, custom steering wheels, and spring and suspension systems.

In 1967 Superior added plating facilities to its manufacturing operations and began producing chrome-plated steel wheels for the automotive aftermarket. Riding on the success of its chrome

wheels, Superior became a public corporation in 1969, offering an initial 320,000 shares of common stock, with the proceeds going toward bank debt. Before its first full decade closed, Superior recorded annual sales of more than $2 million.

In 1970 Superior added low-pressure aluminum casting wheels to its aftermarket product line. The following year the company purchased Industrias Universales Unidas De Mexico, S.A., and used the Mexican company's operations to establish an aftermarket road wheels polishing plant in Tijuana. With operations expanding, Superior's annual sales motored upward to $13.7 million in 1971 and $16.5 million in 1972.

In 1973, in its first major strategic acquisition, Superior paid $1.5 million to acquire Ideal Manufacturing Company, an aftermarket producer of recreational vehicle (RV) accessories—including running boards and RV trailers—with production facilities in Iowa and Canada. But Superior's principal focus during its early years as a corporation was on improving its production standards in order to gear up its aluminum wheels for the OEM market, which offered a consistent customer base and improved profitability through volume sales.

Targeting those sales, Superior's senior vice-president, Raymond C. Brown, made numerous trips to Detroit during the early 1970s in an effort to court major auto makers. In 1973 Brown secured Superior's initial purchase order to supply Ford Motor Company with its first cast aluminum wheel, and a year later the company officially entered the OEM market when its aluminum wheels debuted on Ford's Mustang II.

In 1976 Superior constructed a new corporate headquarters and 300,000-square-foot OEM wheel-making facility in Van Nuys. During the mid-1970s rising gas costs and the need for more fuel-efficient automobiles helped accelerate interest in Superior's light-weight aluminum tires, and in 1976 the company began producing aluminum wheels for Chrysler Corporation and General Motors (GM) passenger cars as well as chrome-plated steel wheels for Dodge trucks. By 1979 Superior was producing OEM wheels for seven car models. Looking to expand its manufacturing capabilities for aftermarket automotive accessories, Superior opened a manufacturing facility in 1979 in Arecibo, Puerto Rico, to produce steering wheel covers and seat belts.

In 1980 Superior's drive toward increased sales hit a major bump when demand for its wheels began sliding along with sales of new Ford and Chrysler vehicles. In April of that year, Superior posted its first-ever quarterly loss, of $1.4 million, and the company suspended payment of its regular quarterly dividend. One month after posting the quarterly loss, Superior announced that Borick and his family, controlling approximately 53 percent of the company, had granted Alumax Inc.—a fabricated aluminum products maker—an option to purchase the Borick family's holdings. But Superior shareholders quickly objected to the deal, and in June of 1980 the proposed sale to Alumax was called off.

While Superior's losses for the year were mounting, in August of 1980 the Canadian government cited the company for dumping—selling goods on an export market at prices below those prevailing in their country of origin—and announced it would impose anti-dumping levies on future imports of Superior's custom steel wheel rims. One month later, in September of 1980, Superior sold Ideal Manufacturing's Canadian interests.

For the first time since going public, Superior posted an annual loss for 1980 of $5.2 million. Automobile production remained in low gear in 1981 and Superior logged its second consecutive annual deficit, with combined losses for the two-year period reaching nearly $10 million. Superior's financial troubles were further complicated in April of 1982, when the company technically defaulted on a provision of its $8.5 million long-term debt coverage loan with Bank of America, which required the company to maintain a certain ratio of debts to assets.

In October of 1982 Superior replaced Bank of America as its primary lender and secured a $20 million, four-year credit arrangement with BT Commercial Corporation. The new agreement supplanted Superior's $5 million credit line and $8.5 million long-term debt coverage with Bank of America and did not carry balance sheet stipulations. By the end of year Superior had reduced its inventories nearly 50 percent and sliced its debt from $17 million to just under $6 million.

Superior's lightened debt load, along with new contracts for 1982 vehicle models, helped the company roll back in the black in 1982 as it earned $2.1 million on sales of nearly $70 million. One of the company's new contracts, with Ford, guaranteed Superior at least 50 percent of the automaker's aluminum wheel production needs, making Superior the largest aluminum wheel supplier for Ford.

With an improved economy and production orders rising, in 1983 Superior purchased an aftermarket plant in Toronto and an OEM aluminum wheel plant in Newmarket, Ontario. On the road to financial recovery, the company resumed payment of stock dividends. The following year sales exceeded $100 million for the first time.

Superior's OEM business continued to expand during the mid-1980s, as the company landed contracts to produce standard equipment wheels for Ford and General Motors cars. Superior's turn toward the profitable OEM market was accelerated by an overall expansion of the aluminum wheel market in the 1980s, when a growing number of car and light truck manufacturers abandoned steel wheels and adopted aluminum wheels as standard equipment.

In 1985 Superior received its first multi-year production contract of any kind, for wheels on 1986, 1987, and 1988 Cadillac vehicles. By the end of 1985, the company that was founded to produce aftermarket products was making nearly three-quarters of its sales to the OEM market.

On the road to its second consecutive year of record sales, in 1986 Superior acquired NT&M Corporation, a privately owned Toronto-based company producing mirrors and taillights, primarily under the Do-Ray label, for the Canadian automotive aftermarket. That same year, Superior acquired a cast-aluminum wheel plant in Fayetteville, Arkansas, which began shipping wheels the following year. Despite a two-month strike at its Iowa RV accessories plant—by a union that covered less than 100 of the company's then-2,000 employees—Superior's earnings rose in 1986 to $8.5 million on sales of nearly $149 million.

Superior's sales rose consistently during the late 1980s, moving from $169.4 million in 1987, to $200.1 million in 1988, to $246.1 million in 1989. Earnings during that time climbed from $9.4 million in 1987 to $16.1 million at the close of the decade. Also during the latter part of the decade, Superior expanded its manufacturing operations and improved the production quality of its wheels in the eyes of key automobile manufacturers. In 1988 Superior earned Ford's top Q-1 quality award. The following year Superior opened a new 200,000-square-feet OEM wheel plant in Rogers, Arkansas, installed state-of-the-art paint room robots in its plants, and earned General Motors Mark of Excellence Award. In 1989 Superior, as a result of newly-secured production contracts, became General Motors largest aluminum wheel supplier.

While Superior's relationship with Ford and General Motors was flourishing in the 1980s, Superior was faced with a demand for aluminum wheels that outstripped supply at a time when Chrysler began seeking price concessions. Superior decided to focus on accommodating Ford and General Motors, and Chrysler's production orders finally slowed to a halt in 1989.

Looking to expand its technology base, Superior entered a joint venture with Alumax Inc.—the company that once had a short-lived option to buy Superior—to use Alumax's patented semi-solid metal technology in the production of aluminum wheels. In 1989 Mazda was added to Superior's customer base after Superior teamed up with Japan's largest wheel producer, Topy Industries, Limited, to supply cast aluminum road wheels for a Mazda light-weight truck. One year later, in an effort to move beyond the status of a domestic wheel manufacturer, Superior's relationship with Topy was extended to an ongoing 50–50 joint venture designed to market and sell Superior-made cast aluminum wheels to Japanese OEM customers in Japan and the United States.

Superior entered the 1990s in a restructuring mode and in 1990 closed its OEM plant in Newmarket, Canada. The Newmarket facility was Superior's oldest and least efficient wheel plant, manufacturing just two of the more than 50 wheel models Superior was producing at the time. The company also took steps in 1990 to rev up the profitability of its aftermarket operations by discontinuing production on several lines where sales and profits had been falling. Superior eliminated its RV/light truck accessory line, and as a result, closed its Oskaloosa, Iowa, plant where those items had been produced. The Oskaloosa facility—the site of a 1986 strike by the company's only union workers—had also been the source of bad publicity. In 1988, as a result of labor strife, the AFL-CIO had placed Superior on its "dishonor roll," as noted in a 1988 *Los Angles Times* article.

Between 1981 and 1990 overall cast aluminum wheel use in the United States increased by more than 500 percent. During the same period Superior continued to capitalize on the growing acceptance of cast aluminum wheels by OEMs, and by 1990 OEM revenues represented 87 percent of the company's business. By 1991 the company was producing wheels for 79 passenger car and light truck models—compared to seven models at the close of the 1970s—while supplying nearly 40 percent of the domestic market for aluminium road wheels through its relationships with Ford and General Motors. In late 1991 Superior paved the way for future sales and secured a six-year deal with General Motors valued at more than $35 million annually.

Gearing up for future production orders, in 1990 Superior completed its fourth OEM wheel plant in Pittsburgh, Kansas. Spanning more than 400,000 square feet, the Pittsburgh plant was billed as the world's largest cast-aluminum road wheel manufacturing facility in the world. In 1991 Superior also opened a new aftermarket plant in West Memphis, Arkansas, which began producing chrome-plated aluminium wheels that same year. In 1992 Superior completed a fifth OEM plant in Johnson City, Tennessee. The 200,000-square-foot facility, which the company labeled as the most technologically advanced wheel plant in the world, cost more than $40 million to construct and represented the first plant Superior built with internally generated funds.

As a result of its increased penetration into Japanese and North American OEM markets, in 1992 Superior's sales grew by more than $50 million and rose to well above $300 million for the first time. Net income increased more than 50 percent in 1992, to $28.6 million, up from $18.2 million a year earlier.

Superior entered 1993 with plans to construct a sixth OEM plant in Chihuahua, Mexico, to serve major automobile manufacturers courting the growing Mexican automobile market. The plant was expected to be operational by 1994. Superior's strategic plans included increased penetration into North American and overseas markets. Through its joint venture with Topy, the company expected to expand its Japanese OEM customer base and possibly extend its joint venture operations into European markets. Superior also appeared well positioned for expansion in North America, where it had been courting the return of Chrysler business since 1990. And through its ongoing work with chrome-plating technology, the company hoped to begin selling OEMs chrome-plated aluminum wheels, which in the past had only been available on the aftermarket because of their low quality and poor durability. Such potential technological innovations, coupled with the fast-paced and growing acceptance and use of aluminum wheels as standard equipment on new vehicles, appeared to suggest that there was much open road ahead for Superior in its drive towards increased profitability.

Principal Subsidiaries: Industrias Universales Unidas de Mexico, S.A. (Mexico); Superior Industries International-P.R., Inc.

Further Reading:

Gordon, Mitchell, ''Hot Wheels: Superior Industries Makes a U-Turn, Races Ahead to Record Results,'' *Barron's,* February 2, 1987, pp. 45–46.
Superior Industries International, Inc., Annual Report, Van Nuys, CA: Superior Industries International, Inc., 1991.
Troxell, Thomas M., Jr., ''Fewer Bumps: Superior Industries on Road to Record Earnings in '84,'' *Barron's,* January 30, 1984, pp. 42, 46.

—Roger W. Rouland

Susquehanna Pfaltzgraff Company

140 E. Market St.
York, Pennsylvania 17401
U.S.A.
(717) 848-5500
Fax: 717-771-1440

Private Company
Incorporated: 1970
Employees: 4,000
Sales: $550 million
SICs: 3269 Pottery Products Nec; 3262 Vitreous China Table
& Kitchenware; 4832 Radio Broadcasting Stations; 4833
Television Broadcasting Stations

Susquehanna Pfaltzgraff Company is a holding company whose
major subsidiary is The Pfaltzgraff Co., an historic American
manufacturer of high quality stoneware and bone china dinnerware that is a leader in its industry. Susquehanna Pfaltzgraff
also includes Susquehanna Radio Corporation and Susquehanna Cable Company.

The name Pfaltzgraff is familiar to millions of American consumers, and is especially known to collectors. It is the oldest
manufacturer of pottery in the United States, growing through
five generations of family management and ownership.
Founded by immigrant German potters in 1811, Pfaltzgraff's
early years are largely unrecorded up until the late 1830s, when
Johann George Pfaltzgraff built a potter's shop in Freystown,
Pennsylvania, at the time an expanding center of cottage
industries.

Pfaltzgraff was joined by a number of relatives from Germany,
and in 1848 the operations were moved to Foustown. Located
near several main highways that facilitated the importation of
blue clay used to make stoneware, as well as the distribution of
the final product, there were also rich farmlands where
Pfaltzgraff found red clay and limestone deposits needed for
earthenware products, in addition to timberlands that provided
the wood necessary for running the kilns. By 1850, the potter's
shop manufactured 16,000 gallons of ware—a measurement for
pottery based on capacity of each piece of ware—made on
hand-powered machinery and using 16 cords of wood for firing
the kiln. Not only a potter, Pfaltzgraff was also a farmer, which
enabled him to anticipate people's pottery needs. Records show
Pfaltzgraff & Son Pottery producing $1,000 worth of pottery in

1870, employing two men and turning wheels by both horse and
hand. Thirty cords of wood were used that year for the 10,000
gallons of ware.

Five of Pfaltzgraff's sons entered the pottery trade, three of
whom left a legacy of salt-glazed products. The process of salt-
glazing entails shoveling common rock salt into a hot kiln in
which ware is baking. The salt vaporizes in the heated air, but
sodium from the salt that hits the clay results in a unique shiny
glaze with a textured surface. The eldest Pfaltzgraff son, John
B., made distinctively witty and casual pieces, with no two pots
decorated the same way, often making novelty items for birth-
days, marriages, and other special occasions. He later diversified, adding coal and cigars to his stoneware business. In 1899
his cigar company had 50 workers, while the Pfaltzgraff Stoneware Company Ltd. employed 30.

In the meantime John's brothers George and Henry really
marked the direction of the company. Both men had operated
their own pottery businesses before deciding to combine forces
in 1889 to launch H.B. & G.B. Pfaltzgraff—the forerunner to
The Pfaltzgraff Co.—located in York, Pennsylvania. The brothers started out with two hard-working horses to mix the clay and
three kilns. For the first time, the company began adapting itself
for mass production and using stencils. At the same time,
George ran a general store and Henry traded horses and worked
in politics.

The company name was shortened to The Pfaltzgraff Stoneware
Company in 1894, just as the third generation of Pfaltzgraffs
was joining the operation. The following year, as the company's
production demands were straining its small plant, more land
was purchased—strategically located near a railroad—and a
larger pottery facility was built. By 1903 two more buildings of
the same size had been added to the plant on Belvidere Street,
which had been more mechanized in order to keep up with mass
production. In 1896 the name was changed again to The
Pfaltzgraff Stoneware Co., Ltd. Between this time and the
1920s, production moved ahead at a strong pace as Pfaltzgraff
produced countless liquor jugs for the healthy liquor trade in
York and the surrounding area. Other products included such
everyday items as crocks, butter jars and churns, as well as
specialty items like chamber pots, mixing bowls and pigeon
nests.

In 1906 the booming Belvidere plant was destroyed by a fire—
rumored to have been started by a recently fired moldmaker—
and the loss was tallied at nearly $27,000. Nonetheless, just a
few weeks after the devastating blaze, the Pfaltzgraffs salvaged
what they could and began building a new plant, thus forming
The Pfaltzgraff Pottery Company. Located near two major rail
lines in West York, the new plant—which is still in operation—
was up and running by the summer of 1906. It was, in fact, a
great improvement on the old, multi-story buildings on
Belvidere, which had not been very efficient. The revived
Pfaltzgraff struggled first with debt and outdated machinery,
then with World War I, but managed to stay in business as other
potteries folded. One steady product that contributed to
Pfaltzgraff's survival was the simple red clay flower pot.

By 1919 Pfaltzgraff's sales and distribution stretched along the
East coast from Maine to Florida, and the following year the

company was doing well enough to add a sixth kiln, in addition to a garage and a machine shop. The flower pots and florist items continued to be a mainstay, comprising more than 73 percent of business in 1927. The 1920s were prosperous for the company, although Pfaltzgraff suffered, along with the rest of the country, during the Great Depression—sales revenue dropped almost 40 percent between 1927 and 1933. Changes in production, as well as an increase in imported pottery, combined with the economic climate to challenge the company. It's notable that during this period Pfaltzgraff began manufacturing an entirely new line of products known as Art Pottery. This was accompanied by experiments in glazes, colors, and shapes, and stoneware production began to slow as such items as the decorated flower pots caught on. Sales dropped, however, and there were difficulties with the railroads—in 1933 the company lost money for the first time.

By 1935 Louis J. Appell, who was married to George Pfaltzgraff's daughter, had purchased the company from his father-in-law, under whom distribution had grown to cover nearly half of the United States. Until he purchased Pfaltzgraff, Appell had not been active in the company, but with 122 workers under his leadership, production and profits grew steadily until World War II. While production in 1941 had increased nearly 34 percent over 1933, it was still almost 31 percent below the level of production in 1927, and the company recorded losses in 1943. By the following year, with Pfaltzgraff's situation showing no signs of improvement, Appell began to consider selling the company. The long Pfaltzgraff history, however, persuaded him to keep it going, and while production did not cease during the war, product lines dwindled. In addition, the level of foreign imports was nearly twice that of domestic production.

In 1946 Appell's son, Louis, Jr., became the fifth generation of Pfaltzgraffs to join the company. Two years later Pfaltzgraff recorded its first profit since 1941, and by the following year business was hearty again. With an improved fiscal condition, Pfaltzgraff was able to update its production facilities and introduce new lines of ware, including one developed for such chain stores as F.W. Woolworth Co. and Montgomery Ward & Co. Also popular around this time were Pfaltzgraff's character mugs and cookie jars. In 1950 a new line of giftware was introduced called Gourmet Royale, later known as the Gourmet line. The following year dinner plates were added to this popular line, and by the mid-1950s such stoneware tabletop items had become the mainstay of the company.

Louis Appell died suddenly in 1951 while serving as president of The Pfaltzgraff Pottery Company, in addition to other Appell family businesses including the Susquehanna Broadcasting Company. Appell's wife briefly headed Pfaltzgraff, which, in 1954, became a division of Susquehanna Broadcasting Company, founded in 1942 to run a radio station. The 1950s proved to be a difficult time for the industry as a whole in the United States. Imports from Japan and Europe, together with tariff rates, formed a combined threat, resulting in a more than 50 percent drop in domestic production between 1947 and 1961. While many potters gave up and closed shop, Pfaltzgraff commissioned freelance designers to develop new products and lines, and worked on developing a nationwide network of sales representatives.

Susquehanna Radio Corporation's president, Arthur William Carlson, was hired by Louis Appell, Jr., in 1961. Susquehanna was running WSBA (AM) in York and WARM (AM) in Wilkes-Barre/Scranton, for which Carlson helped to gain a 40 percent share of the market within 60 days. Three more stations joined the Susquehanna family shortly thereafter, and the group bloomed in the 1960s, adding stations in Providence, Long Island, and Miami. By the early 1990s the company ran 17 radio stations around the country. In 1966 the Susquehanna Cable Company was founded and eventually provided cable television to cities in Pennsylvania, Maine, Rhode Island, Mississippi, Indiana, and Illinois. In addition, Susquehanna Pfaltzgraff was also affiliated with Penn Advertising, Inc., an outdoor advertising company with interests in Pennsylvania, Maryland, and New York.

In the early 1960s Pfaltzgraff introduced such classic lines as Country Casual and Heritage, and by 1964, in order to reflect the diversification away from pottery, the business was renamed The Pfaltzgraff Co. In 1967 a new pattern, Yorktowne—considered the largest-selling tabletop pattern in history—was introduced, though its design of a blue flower on a gray background was borrowed from Pfaltzgraff's 19th century salt-glazed stoneware. Sales of the three dinnerware lines—Gourmet, Heritage, and Yorktowne—accounted for nearly 70 percent of Pfaltzgraff's total sales around this time.

The first Pfaltzgraff plant built in 64 years was constructed in 1970 in order to manufacture a new line of metalware products, including fondue pots and pewter, copper, and tin items designed to complement the stoneware lines. However, all metalware and wood product production was discontinued by the end of the decade as it proved unsuccessful. Instead more money could be made by licensing its designs to manufacturers of household products and other home furnishings. In the early 1970s Pfaltzgraff also shifted away from the gift and specialty stores that had carried the company's products the previous two decades, and began appearing in department stores. This move, along with the introduction of the Village dinnerware line in 1975–1976, created an explosion in sales. Retail store and direct mail activities were also accelerated at this time.

To accommodate increasing demand, Pfaltzgraff bought a production facility in Aspers, Pennsylvania, in 1973, later adding the Bendersville plant, purchased from Continental Ceramics Company. In 1978 a new plant, located in Thomasville, began operating with state-of-the-art technology that still allowed old-style craftsmanship. That same year the company purchased the Trenton, New Jersey-based Stangl Pottery, which had been operating its own retail store, Flemington. While the Stangl plant was not operated, Pfaltzgraff used the store as its third retail outlet. A fourth was opened in 1979 in Fairfax, Virginia, and by 1989 there were more than 20 stores throughout the United States.

The company was reorganized in the mid-1980s, resulting in the formation of the holding company Susquehanna Pfaltzgraff Company, which included The Pfaltzgraff Co., Susquehanna Radio Corp., and Susquehanna Cable Co. At this time imports were once again causing problems for the pottery industry—almost two-thirds of all earthenware sold in the United States in 1981 was a foreign import. Pfaltzgraff responded by aggressively researching market needs and introducing new dinnerware patterns, taking advantage of the growing bridal market and targeting mass retailers and catalog showrooms. In 1989, six of the top fifteen casual dinnerware patterns chosen by brides were Pfaltzgraff's.

To become even more competitive, in 1985 the company invested in a state-of-the-art computer system that displayed three-dimensional images of the products to help with design, modeling, drafting, and machining. In 1988 Pfaltzgraff acquired Treasure Craft, a manufacturer of household ceramic products based in California. The purchase marked the first time the company acquired an operating pottery manufacturer in order to expand. During this same time Pfaltzgraff also acquired the New York-based company Syracuse China, the largest supplier of ceramic dinnerware for institutions, hotels, and restaurants in the United States.

In 1988 William H. Simpson—who had been with the company since 1971—became president and chief operating officer of The Pfaltzgraff Co., while Louis J. Appell, Jr., was the CEO and board chairman, as well as president of the Susquehanna Pfaltzgraff holding company. That year Pfaltzgraff took a decisive step in a new direction and began to manufacture bone china, a risky move for a company best known for its casual dinnerware. It marked the first bone china to be produced in the United States and has been featured in leading department stores across the country. Since its introduction in 1988, Pfaltzgraff's bone china line has grown respectably, taking the company into new markets. While the Pfaltzgraff name garnered a mixed response from consumers who recognized and respected it, but associated the name with informal dinnerware, Pfaltzgraff's bone china items found a toehold in the bridal industry and have done well since.

Over the years, Pfaltzgraff has expanded through licensing and new product lines to create a total home concept with such items as dinnerware, glassware, and home textiles. In the early 1990s Pfaltzgraff reached licensing agreements with Trans Ocean, a top rug supplier; Croscill Home Fashions, for window treatments; and Bess Mfg., a leading supplier of lace table linens. By 1992 the company had more than 30 licensees.

Principal Subsidiaries: The Pfaltzgraff Co.; Susquehanna Cable TV; Susquehanna Radio Corporation.

Further Reading:

"Arthur William Carlson," *Broadcasting,* July 6, 1992, p. 67.

Chase, Marilyn, "Ten Makers of China Tableware Settle with California Over Lead Contents," *Wall Street Journal,* January 18, 1993, p. A7B.

Coady, Cliff, "Redesigning the Dinner Plate," *HFD: The Weekly Home Furnishings Newspaper,* November 2, 1992, pp. 50–78.

Cohan Hollow, Michele, "Bess Inks Pact With Pfaltzgraff," *HFD: The Weekly Home Furnishings Newspaper,* June 22, 1992, p. 40.

Griffin, Marie, "Pfaltzgraff Breaks the Mold, Traditionally," *HFD: The Weekly Home Furnishings Newspaper,* November 5, 1990, p. 84.

Historical Society of York County, *Pfaltzgraff: America's Potter,* York, Pennsylvania: The Pfaltzgraff Company, 1989.

Kehoe, Ann-Margaret, "Pfaltzgraff Giftware Line Bows," *HFD: The Weekly Home Furnishings Newspaper,* April 19, 1993, p. 166.

Nellett, Michelle, "Meet the Generations: Pfaltzgraff," *Gifts & Decorative Accessories,* April 1992, pp. 68, 82.

"Pfaltzgraff's Home Designs," *HFD: The Weekly Home Furnishings Newspaper,* April 27, 1992, p. 114.

Tupot, Marie Lena, "Ceramics: Classically American," *Gifts & Decorative Accessories,* April 1993, p. 56.

Williams, Stanley, "Trans-Ocean Inks Vanderbilt, Pfaltzgraff," *HFD: The Weekly Home Furnishings Newspaper,* February 24, 1992, p. 39.

—Carol I. Keeley

TAMBRANDS

Tambrands Inc.

777 Westchester Avenue
White Plains, New York 10604
U.S.A.
(914) 696-6000
Fax: (914) 696-6161

Public Company
Incorporated: 1936 as Tampax Inc.
Employees: 3,800
Sales: $684.11 million
Stock Exchanges: New York Pacific
SICs: 2676 Sanitary Paper Products

Tambrands Inc. is the world's leading supplier of tampons, with manufacturing facilities in ten countries and sales to women in more than 150 countries. With its Tampax brand tampons on the market since 1936, the company was the first commercial producer of internal menstrual protection. Tambrands' market share in the United States was consistently around the 60 percent mark for many years. Tampax was also the third highest selling health-and-beauty-care brand in the United States behind Tylenol and Crest, according to a company report.

In the mid-1930s disposable sanitary napkins were still new, having been on the market for less than 20 years. Most women probably used external menstrual protection, and many women still made their own reusable pads from cotton rags that were boiled so as to be used again. A small segment of American women probably made their own tampons from cotton strips rolled tight for insertion, but for the most part, internal protection was unheard of.

In 1933 Dr. Earle Haas obtained a patent for a tampon he had devised from compressed surgical cotton. He had sewed a waterproof cord down the length of the absorbent material, and put it in a two-part cardboard tube for insertion. Drugstores and department stores began selling the tampons, but in 1936 Ellery Mann formed Tampax Inc. and bought the rights to produce and market the tampons.

Competitors soon sprang up with their own tampon products. By 1942, there were nine major brands on the market. The arrival of disposable, commercially available tampons stirred discussion about the propriety of using internal protection, and raised medical questions about the safety of tampons. Some

articles in medical journals warned of the risks of infections or irritation from tampons, while other articles declared tampons to be safe and hygienic. By the end of the 1950s, medical testing had diminished, and the few studies still being conducted concluded that tampons were safe.

During the 1950s Tampax solidly established itself as the number one tampon manufacturer. The company launched an education campaign aimed at young girls, potential customers. The educational program provided instruction on menstruation, tips on general health habits, a history of menstrual products, the advantages of Tampax tampons, and instruction on the use of Tampax tampons. The company later printed and marketed a booklet called "Accent on You," dealing with menstruation for young girls. In the early 1980s the company began selling a video version of the booklet. The education program remained an important aspect of Tambrands's marketing strategy into the 1990s.

The 1960s brought a new competitor to the tampon marketplace—Carefree, a non-applicator tampon, made by Personal Products Company. It was not, though, the first tampon without an applicator; Johnson & Johnson, the parent company of Personal Products Company, had been marketing just such a product, called o.b., in Europe since the 1950s. Tampax held onto its sales lead, but Carefree became very popular.

Other competitors entered the market, including Playtex tampons, which came in plastic applicators and, a few years later, in a deodorized version. Competition among tampon makers was intense, but Tampax remained the strong leader. During the 1960s and early 1970s Tampax became one of the most profitable companies on the stock market. It was spending only $8 million to advertise its one product, which had profits of $29 million on sales of less than $120 million.

In 1972 the National Association of Broadcasters lifted a ban on television advertising of tampons, sanitary napkins, and douche products. Tampax refused to advertise on television until 1978. With heavy advertising by other competitors, though, Tampax's market share fell while sales of tampons climbed 244 percent. Playtex and the Procter & Gamble Company took a big share of Tampax's market. Tampax fell from a 70 percent share of the market in the 1960s to a 42 percent share in mid-1980.

Entering the tampon arena with its Rely tampons, Procter & Gamble introduced an innovative design with a tampon made of a new superabsorbent modified cellulose. Rely tampons took 17 percent of the market and shot to number three. Tampax still held the lead, but now owned only a 42 percent share of the market.

Most of the other tampon companies were also using some type of superabsorbent modified cellulose like that found in Rely. And during 1980 hundreds of cases of toxic shock syndrome (TSS) were reported around the country. Many researchers agreed that the risk of contracting this mysterious, often fatal, disease among young women under the age of 30 was related to the use of superabsorbent tampons.

Although the majority of cases occurred among Rely users, the entire tampon industry experienced a drop in sales. Tampax officials said that their company had only five percent of the cases. Since October of 1980, Tampax began including a warning about toxic shock syndrome in every package. Although the company denied that TSS had anything to do with the decision, in 1981, Tampax introduced its "Original Regular" tampon, made from cotton.

Tampax Inc. remained a one-product company, selling only tampons of various absorbencies and sizes, until 1982 when Edwin H. Shutt, Jr., assumed the leadership role from E. Russell Sprague, chief executive since 1976. Tampax Inc. became Tambrands Inc. in 1984, and the change in name seemed to signal a change of direction for the company—diversification. Tambrands had seen how quickly the market could turn: six years earlier, when Procter & Gamble introduced Rely, Tampax's market share dropped substantially. Just as quickly, Procter & Gamble lost its momentum and its market when TSS hit the newsstands. Tambrands also saw that the U.S. market was growing by only one to two percent a year. The only way for the company to expand revenues seemed to be to diversify into other product lines.

The natural move appeared to be the manufacture of external protection products. Tambrands entered the sanitary napkin market with its own brand, Maxithins. But Procter & Gamble was also entering that market. By the end of 1985, Tambrands' Maxithins brand had lost $25 million, and the company did not expect it to begin to make a profit until 1986. Shutt looked for other products that were consistent with the company's profile, and the firm considered a wide range of products—over-the-counter medicines, beauty care, and diapers. It added a hypo-allergenic cosmetics line and also went shopping for over-the-counter diagnostic tools.

The home diagnostic market was worth $300 million and growing rapidly. Tambrands officials figured their company already had a built-in market through its Tampax tampons. Tambrands was impressed by Hygeia Sciences, a company in Cambridge, Massachusetts, that had been developing two enzyme tests. Its pregnancy test was believed to be three times more accurate than any currently on the market. And with its ovulation test, a woman trying to conceive could tell within 12 to 14 hours when she would ovulate. Tambrands bought Hygeia, and together they simplified the tests, making them more "user-friendly." Tambrands projected that with three to five million U.S. women trying for at least a year to get pregnant, First Response would easily earn $50 million to $100 million annually.

Tambrands possessed diversified holdings, as well as tampon manufacturing and distribution operations in foreign countries. In a joint venture with Turkey, Tambrands manufactured sanitary napkins and disposable diapers. In a joint venture with Spain, the company produced sanitary pads, disposable diapers, and other personal care products, as well as tampons. Tambrands' Mexican subsidiary produced tampons, sanitary pads, and pre-moistened baby tissues. A facility in Brazil produced tampons and sanitary napkins.

Unfortunately, Tambrands' diversification efforts did not pay off. Martin Emmett, the new chairman and CEO appointed in April of 1989 after Shutt resigned, reversed the company's direction for the past five years and announced that Tambrands would once again focus on tampons, the business it knew best.

Emmett told *Advertising Age* that Tambrands' entrance into the sanitary napkins and hypo-allergenic cosmetics line "was less successful than we had hoped." He restated that the company would concentrate on developing new tampon products. Emmett pushed Maxithins to a backseat position, with the possibility of selling or discontinuing the line. He cut its advertising budget in half in order to devote more money to marketing the Tampax line.

Emmett announced in December of 1989 that Tambrands would restructure its program plan in order to boost performance and lower costs. He wrote a new mission statement that began, "Our core business is the manufacture and sale of tampons." As part of the plan, Emmett announced he would sell its diagnostics and cosmetic concerns, reduce the work force, and consolidate some facilities and functions in Europe, Canada, and the United States. Emmett sold Physicians Formula Cosmetics, which Tambrands had purchased in 1985 for $8 million, and the First Response pregnancy and ovulation tests, for which Tambrands had paid $47.8 million in early 1987. In 1992 Tambrands sold its Maxithins business to Tranzonic Companies for an undisclosed amount. By the beginning of 1993, Tambrands had divested itself of all non-tampon businesses in the United States and abroad. Emmett also consolidated the company's advertising, giving the entire account to one ad agency, rather having it divided between three agencies as before.

Emmett's restructuring seemed to pay off: in 1992 sales rose. As a result of staff reductions and elimination of two levels of management, Tambrands sold its large headquarters in Lake Success, New York, and moved to smaller offices in White Plains, New York.

Emmett made a company goal of increasing its share of the U.S. market from 60 percent to 65 percent by 1994. To help realize that goal, he instituted a compensation policy for the top 135 managers of the company, which called for them to take much of their pay in the form of bonuses, stock options, and restricted stock. Their earnings for the year were tied to the company's success. This strategy forced managers to look at the whole company rather than only their own department needs. As part of its consolidation plan, Tambrands also announced in 1992 that it would shut down its plant in Canada and consolidate manufacturing in three plants in Maine, New Hampshire, and Vermont. It planned to convert another New England plant into a facility for testing new equipment and developing new products.

Emmett also was able to take advantage of new international opportunities as U.S. trade opened up with China, the Commonwealth of Independent States (formerly the Soviet Union), and other eastern bloc nations. Tambrands and Johnson & Johnson battled over who would be the first to market tampons in the former Soviet Union, a country where even sanitary napkins were scarce. The market there was vast and untapped, and it was estimated that demand would be as high as nine billion units annually for 70 million of the 150 million Soviet women.

Tambrands won the competition with Johnson & Johnson, but dealing with the Soviets was tricky, with miles of red tape to contend with first. Tambrands had started negotiating with the

Soviet Union before the country had disbanded. After the breakup of the Soviet Union, dealing with local partners was still complicated and often frustrating. But the negotiation was worth the effort because of the vast opportunity to reach women who for the most part had been making their own sanitary napkins out of bleached cotton and gauze.

Tambrands' joint venture with the former Soviet Union was called Femtech. It employed local labor and suppliers, keeping costs far below those in the United States. In order to do business, however, Tambrands and other U.S. companies had to add some extras at times. For example, Femtech had to supply forklifts to some of its suppliers. And when Femtech registered a fleet of cars, it had to allow the local police to use the cars every three or four weeks, according to an article in the *Wall Street Journal.*

With the breakup of the Soviet Union, there were also worries that hostilities between republics would lead to trade barriers. Bureaucrats imposed other barriers by requiring signatures from hundreds of officials before approving plant expansion. Most exasperating of all, however, was the confusion over who was in charge of various functions and what agencies to contact for information or negotiations. With shortages of currency, Tambrands created a barter agreement that would have been impossible before the break up. It traded ruble profits from its Tampax plant in the Ukraine to buy a cotton bleachery in St. Petersburg. In 1991 Tambrands' share of Femtech increased from 49 percent to 80 percent, and in 1992 the Ukrainian facility became a wholly owned subsidiary of Tambrands. Tambrands officials considered the operation in the Ukraine to be a solid base from which to reach other Eastern European markets.

Tambrands entered into a joint venture with the People's Republic of China in 1988. In 1992 it increased its share of the joint venture from 60 percent to 80 percent, and established sales offices in four cities to market tampons produced in Shenyang. Like the women of the Soviet Union, Chinese women had rarely purchased commercial menstrual protection products; consequently, Tambrands had to educate its market about tampons in order to sell Tampax. Tambrands estimated that China's population of women of child-bearing age was 335 million, representing a promising market for Tampax tampons.

Tambrands also planned to capture more of the European and Latin American market in the 1990s. It marketed aggressively in Europe, introducing a non-applicator tampon that European women seemed to favor over tampons with an applicator. It also launched a pan-European marketing campaign, eliminating its former country-by-country marketing. It established a European trademark, package design, selling price, and marketing design. In Latin America, tampons represented only a small share of the feminine protection market, but Tambrands saw potential there with its market of 300 million women.

Less than ten years after the toxic shock syndrome outbreak, another health concern flared up—concern about dioxin in tampons. Dioxin is a toxic substance believed to be carcinogenic and is sometimes a by-product resulting from the process of bleaching pulp for paper. The dioxin issue, however, had little impact on tampon sales, and Tambrands claimed that Tampax tampons were safe and had no significant levels of dioxin.

Tambrands continued to dominate the tampon market in the 1990s, devoting resources to education and developing and maintaining brand loyalty. Its domination allowed it to raise prices even when inflation was low. This was an important strategy since unit sales in the United States were rising only about one percent a year. When it was not feasible to raise prices again, the company offered new package sizes. In 1993 the company introduced a 20-tampon package with a higher unit price than the 32-tampon package, but that put the package in the most popular price range of $2.99 to $3.29.

Tambrands plan for the 1990s called for growth primarily in the North American markets during the first third of the decade, in the European market during the second third, and from emerging markets such as China and the former Soviet Union in the last third. CEO Emmett's goal was to reach a 50 percent share of a $3 billion tampon market by the year 2000. To achieve this goal, Tambrands put a great deal of emphasis on education, just as it had since 1936 when founder Ellery Mann traveled to drug stores to tell owners about Tampax tampons and persuaded them to carry the new product in their stores.

Principal Subsidiaries: Tambrands Canada Inc.; Tambrands Ltd. (U.K.); Tambrands Ireland Ltd.; Tambrands France S.A.; Tambrands AG (Switzerland); Industria Corporativa Sanitaria (Mexico); Tambrands GmbH (Germany); Tambrands St. Petersburg (Russia); Tambrands—Ukraine.

Further Reading:

Brown, Paul B., ''Compensation: Tambrands,'' *Financial World,* September 29, 1992, p. 53.
Carrington, Tim, ''International: Ukraine's Women Love These Two Firms,'' *Wall Street Journal,* February 6, 1992, p. A10.
Cullen, Robert, ''One Firm's Agonizing Journey through the Red Tape of Russia,'' *Business Month,* March 1989, p. 24–26.
Dagnoli, Judann, ''Tambrands Plans Overseas Growth,'' *Advertising Age,* March 14, 1989, p. 24.
Dunkin, Amy, ''They're More Single-Minded at Tambrands,'' *Business Week,* August 28, 1989, p. 28.
Friedman, Nancy, *Everything You Must Know about Tampons,* New York: Berkley Books, 1981, pp. 33–59, 105–19.
Joseph, Charles, ''New Soviet Thaw,'' *Advertising Age,* February 29, 1988, p. 8.
Levy, Liz, ''Tampax Goes Green to Skirt Dioxin Scare,'' *Marketing,* June 15, 1989, p. 5.
O'Boyle, Thomas, ''Soviet Breakup Stymies Foreign Firms,'' *Wall Street Journal,* January 23, 1992, p. B1.
Seneker, Harold, ''Test Time for Ed Shutt,'' *Forbes,* December 16, 1985, p. 114.
Stix, David, ''Man with a Mission,'' *Forbes,* April 15, 1992, p. 133.
Tambrands Inc. Annual Reports, White Plains, NY: Tambrands Inc., 1988–92.
Worth, Gretchen, ''At-Home Fertility Lab,'' *Working Woman,* February 1986, p. 60.

—Wendy J. Stein

Tecumseh Products Company

100 East Patterson Street
Tecumseh, Michigan 49286-2041
U.S.A
(517) 423-8411
Fax: (517) 423-8526

Public Company
Incorporated: 1930 as Hillsdale Machine & Tool
Employees: 16,554
Sales: $1.88 billion
Stock Exchanges: NASDAQ
SICs: 3585 Refrigeration & Heating Equipment; 3519
    Internal Combustion Engines, Nec; 3714 Motor Vehicle
    Accessories; 3561 Pumps & Pumping Equipment; 3566
    Speed Changers, Drives & Gears

Tecumseh Products Company manufactures compressors for refrigeration and air conditioning equipment, gasoline engines and automobile transmissions, and pumps and pumping equipment for industrial, commercial, and agricultural use. The second-largest domestic manufacturer of engines for small tractors, snow blowers, and lawn mowers, the company is best known for its compressors, machines that compress freon and other gases used to cool the air. The town of Tecumseh, Michigan, in which the company is headquartered, has since become known as the ''Refrigeration Capital of the World.''

Tecumseh Products was founded by Ray W. Herrick, a master toolmaker who came to prominence in the 1920s in Michigan's growing auto industry. Herrick's reputation as a knowledgeable and highly skilled toolmaker led to his rapid advancement in the industry; he was given supervisory positions and became a friend and adviser to such influential inventors and industrialists as Henry Ford, Harvey Firestone, and Thomas Edison. In 1928 Herrick was asked to help turn around the struggling Alamo Engine Company in the southeastern Michigan town of Hillsdale, where he served until 1933 as factory manager and eventually as director of sales and production. The company continued to decline, however, and, during this time Herrick and a local toolmaker named C. F. (Bill) Sage decided to launch a business of their own, incorporating as the Hillsdale Machine & Tool Company in 1930.

The Hillsdale company manufactured high quality automobile and electric refrigerator parts, as well as small tools and me-

chanical novelties. Also handling orders that Alamo couldn't fill, the Hillsdale company went from grossing $26,000 in sales during its first year of operation to $284,000 by 1933. Initially, two-thirds of the company's stock was owned by Sage and his wife, while Herrick owned the remaining third. However, by 1933 Herrick bought out most of their interest and gained control of the company.

Competition in the manufactured parts industry was fierce in 1933, and Hillsdale soon sought larger production facilities. When Alamo went into receivership that year, Herrick leased its plant for one year, hoping to purchase it at the end of the term. However, the rent paid to Alamo's receivers cut into the Hillsdale company's profits. Furthermore, the Hillsdale company had been founded during the height of the Great Depression, and these early years were characterized by escalating debt and inadequate cash flow. By 1934, Herrick's company was close to bankruptcy.

That year, however, as a result of a concerted effort by Herrick, the Ford Motor Company, private investors, and the city of Tecumseh—located about 60 miles southwest of Detroit—the Hillsdale Tool & Machine Company managed to raise a little over $12,000, with which it acquired a 30,000 square foot abandoned facility in Tecumseh. Changing the company's name to Tecumseh Products, Herrick had the building renovated, borrowed the necessary machinery, and soon began the mass production of automotive and refrigerator parts. The following year the company gained much needed cash flow leverage when Henry Ford helped Herrick secure a line of credit with a Detroit bank.

In 1936 Tecumseh Products began to focus on manufacturing the product on which its reputation would be built: the hermetically sealed refrigeration compressor. Five years earlier, Herrick had been approached by Frank Smith, an engineer interested in selling Herrick his compressor designs. At that time, Herrick had employed Smith as a machinist, agreeing to consider the prototypes that Smith was developing. Over the next few years, engineers Curtis Brown and Jens Touborg joined Smith, and the three eventually formed an engineering business known as Tresco. Tresco worked closely with Tecumseh Products, providing Herrick with designs for inexpensive and reliable refrigeration compressors that rivalled those of the major manufacturers. By the end of the 1930s, Tecumseh Products was producing over 100,000 of these compressors a year.

At the onset of World War II, Herrick shifted the focus of Tecumseh Products to the manufacture of defense materials. The company continued to produce compressors, which had applications in military equipment, while also turning out anti-aircraft projectile casings and precision parts for aircraft engines. By 1942, Tecumseh was mainly producing 40-millimeter shell casings, which it supplied to the U.S. Navy. In April of that year the company received the Navy E award for excellence for its contributions to the war effort; it received several similar awards before the war ended.

In 1945 Herrick's son, Kenneth G. Herrick, returned from the war and went to work for Tecumseh Products as the company resumed its focus on the production of compressors. During this time, competition in the industry intensified, with postwar demand for electric appliances, especially refrigerators, rising dramatically. Becoming known for the high quality of its compressors, as well as for their timely delivery, Tecumseh Products soon emerged as an industry leader. In 1947 a Tecumseh Products compressor was featured in the first window unit air conditioner for the home. By 1950, Tecumseh's sales reached $72 million, and the company was producing over two million compressors a year.

Throughout the 1950s and 1960s Tecumseh Products sought to expand. First it increased its production capacity with the 1950 and 1952 purchases of Universal Cooler Corp. in Marion, Ohio, and the Acklin Stamping Company of Toledo, respectively. Also involved in finding new uses for its products, the company marketed an air conditioning compressor for automobiles in 1953. The following year, Tecumseh's sales reached $124 million, and in 1955 Herrick is reported to have paid nearly five million dollars to purchase Tresco, the engineering business founded by Smith, Brown, and Touborg. At this time, Herrick brought Joseph E. Layton in from the International Harvester company to serve Tecumseh Products as president and chief executive officer. Herrick remained the company's chairperson.

Purchasing two Wisconsin companies in 1956 and 1957—the Lauson Engine Company of New Holstein and Power Products of Grafton—Tecumseh Products claimed two new divisions designated for the production of gasoline engines. These two acquisitions were provided with new, modern equipment and tools in order to begin production of compact, lightweight engines suitable for use in lawn and garden machinery. Also during this time the company began to establish licensees abroad, planning to one day market its products worldwide.

In 1960 Tecumseh Products of Canada, Ltd., was formed as a sales distribution center for compressors manufactured in the United States. This facility was later expanded into a production facility to handle demand for compressors in Canada. Over the next decade the company acquired the Diecast Division of Sheboygan Falls, Wisconsin, and the Peerless Gear & Machine Company, which it designated as a separate division and provided with a new plant to manufacture transaxles, transmissions, and differentials for lawn and garden equipment. Furthermore, the company set up research and development laboratories at Purdue University and in Ann Arbor, Michigan, to support its divisions, employing scientists in the fields of chemistry and metallurgy, as well as mechanical and electrical engineers.

In 1964 Layton died unexpectedly, and William Hazelwood, a divisional vice president, was named president of Tecumseh Products. Hazelwood remained in this position until 1966 when the 76-year-old Herrick gave him the chair, and, retaining a position for himself as vice chairperson, named his son Kenneth as president. Four years later Kenneth Herrick's son Todd came to work for Tecumseh Products, Kenneth ascended to chairperson and CEO, and William MacBeth was named president. By this time the company had manufactured over 100 million compressors and 25 million small engines.

In 1973 Ray Herrick died. Under Kenneth Herrick, Tecumseh Products built compressor and engine plants in Kentucky, Tennessee, and Mississippi, while continuing to add to its product line. For example, the company acquired M. P. Pumps, Inc., of Detroit, which produced pumps used in agricultural, industrial, and marine environments. Submersible pumps, used as sump pumps and in large cooling systems, were introduced in 1980, with the company's purchase of the Little Giant Pump Company in Oklahoma.

Tecumseh Products sought to become an international company in the 1980s, and, over the next ten years, foreign sales, both from exports and through European acquisitions, rose to 15 percent of the company's total sales revenues. In 1981 Tecumseh Products entered into a joint venture with the Italian Fiat Settori Componenti, which resulted in the formation of Tecnamotor S.p.A., a manufacturer and marketer of engines for outdoor power equipment. The following year Tecumseh Products increased its holdings in the Sociade Intercontinental de Compressores Hermeticos SICOM, S.A. SICOM was based in Sao Paulo, Brazil, and served world markets through its manufacture of compressors. Tecumseh Products was further able to form a strong European interest through a 1985 joint venture with L'Unite Hermetique S.A. in Paris, a compressor manufacturer and exporter that Tecumseh Products eventually acquired as a subsidiary. The company's expansion into the international market had mixed results. It gained market share and enjoyed financial success particularly, in the engine sales of Tecnamotor, which it acquired 100 percent ownership of in 1989. This new subsidiary went on to become the largest engine manufacturer of its kind in Europe. Nevertheless, the company experienced a sharp decline in earnings during the late 1980s, which it attributed to the undervalued American dollar and delays in new product development.

In the United States, foreign competition in the production of refrigeration components intensified during the late 1980s and early 1990s. Tecumseh Products, though, continued to experience growth. In 1987 the company introduced a new line of air conditioning compressors for residential use, designed to be both quieter and more energy efficient in compliance with the federal government's National Appliance Energy Conservation Act. In 1989 air conditioning compressors were bolstered by a nationwide heat wave, and the company's net income rose to $82 million, up from $70 million the year before.

The company's interest in some foreign markets, however, suffered due to political instabilities during this time, particularly in China, where compressor sales fell almost to zero during the Tiananmen Square riots, as well as in the Middle East, where export sales were threatened by the Persian Gulf war. In 1992 Tecumseh was given an E Star award by the U.S. Department of Commerce for its commitment to international markets during these difficult times.

As Tecumseh Products entered the 1990s, it featured a broad range of products in several divisions. Refrigeration products, which accounted for more than half of its total sales, included compressors sold to the manufacturers of home cooling systems and appliances, water coolers, vending machines, and refrigerated display cases. Engine products mainly featured aluminum diecast engines of 2 to 12 horsepower used in machinery for both home lawn maintenance and farming. Power train products included transmissions, transaxles, and differentials produced for lawn and garden equipment as well as for recreational vehicles. The pump products division featured a variety of pumps made from cast iron, aluminum, stainless steel, or brass, capable of pumping up to 300 gallons per minute, while the company's submersible pumps division produced pumps for use in clothes washers and carpet cleaners as well as kidney dialysis machines.

In 1992 the company faced a new series of federal regulations designed to protect the environment by imposing restrictions on compressor and engine emissions and banning altogether chlorofluorocarbons (CFCs), which were widely used in refrigeration. As the ban on CFCs neared implementation in the mid-1990s, Tecumseh Products began converting its compressors to operate on alternative refrigerants, which, the company asserted, were available but costly. Furthermore, in joint efforts with the Environmental Protection Agency, Tecumseh Products researched possible improvements to the engine manufacturing process that would lead to less harmful emissions, and also developed new techniques for treating and disposing of contaminated sediments resulting from dangerous industrial wastes being dumped into rivers.

Financially, in March of 1992 the stockholders of Tecumseh Products approved a proposal to reclassify its existing shares as voting Class B stock, while creating a new class of nonvoting Class A common stock. The stockholders were issued one share of the Class A stock for each share they already owned. At the time, Edward Wyatt observed in *Barron's* that ''because 45% of the equity currently outstanding is owned by members of the founding Herrick family, the stock plan will allow them to retain their voting rights while effectively splitting the stock 2-for-1.'' He also observed that the new plan would probably induce analysts to follow the fortunes of Tecumseh Products more closely.

Principal Subsidiaries: Tecumseh Products of Canada, Ltd.; M. P. Pumps, Inc.; L'Unite Hermetique S.A.; Little Giant Pump Company; Sociade Intercontinental de Compressores Hermeticos SICOM, S.A.; Vitrus, Inc.; Tecnamotor S.p.A.

Further Reading:

Dawson, John Harper, *A Biography of Ray W. Herrick,* Adrian, MI: Lenawee County Historical Society, Inc., 1984.
Harris, William B., ''Little, Big-Rich Tecumseh,'' *Fortune,* July 1955, p. 98.
Richards, J., ''EPA and Tecumseh Products Conduct Joint PCB Study,'' *Northeastern Wisconsin Business Review,* September 1992, p. 6.
''Tecumseh Products Co.,'' *Journal of Commerce,* August 14, 1992.
Wyatt, Edward A., ''Here Comes Tecumseh: Renewed Earnings Surge Appears in the Works,'' *Barron's,* March 2, 1992, pp. 17, 22–24.

—Tina Grant

learned about a California company that had registered a similar name, Techrad.

Although Tektronix was still without a specific product or purpose, Vollum decided to build an oscilloscope from spare electronics parts being stockpiled by his partners from post-war government surplus sales. At the time, the Du Mont Company was the leading manufacturer of oscilloscopes, which were indispensable to the rapidly growing electronics industry. Vollum, who had built his first oscilloscope while in college, believed he could design one that was better and would sell for less than half what Du Mont charged. Vollum later told *Forbes* that Du Mont "wanted to fool around with big-time television. They were complacent about their scope."

Vollum completed his oscilloscope in the spring of 1946. It was far more accurate than anything then on the market. Unfortunately, it also was so large that it covered Vollum's entire workbench. He immediately began working on a more compact model, and Murdock brought in another buddy from the Coast Guard, a machinist named Milt Bave, to help with the design. The redesign took 12 months, but in May of 1947 Tektronix sold the first "portable" oscilloscope to the University of Oregon Medical School. The model 511, which became known as the Vollumscope, weighed 50 pounds.

In 1947 Tektronix had sales of $27,000. The next year, sales increased almost tenfold, to $257,000, and the customer list included most of the major electronics research firms in the United States, including Hewlett-Packard, Philco Radio Corporation, RCA Laboratories Division, Westinghouse Electric Company, and AT&T Bell Laboratories. In 1948 Tektronix also sold its first oscilloscope overseas, to the L. M. Ericcson Telephone Company of Sweden. By 1950, Tektronix was manufacturing its seventh generation of oscilloscopes, the model 517. Orders were backlogged six months to a year, and annual sales had exceeded $1 million.

By the early 1950s, Murdock was already beginning to lose interest in managing Tektronix. He took up flying and started an aircraft sales company on the side. Vollum, however, continued to be a driving force within the company. Under his direction, Tektronix began manufacturing its own cathode-ray tubes when it could not get the quality Vollum wanted for his oscilloscopes. Vollum also conceived the idea of a basic oscilloscope that could be adapted with "plug-in" devices, rather than special oscilloscopes for different applications. The plug-in oscilloscopes, introduced in 1954, were an instant success. By 1955, the 530 Series accounted for half the oscilloscopes sold by Tektronix. In 1956 Tektronix passed Du Mont for leadership in the market. Riding the crest of solid-state electronics, Tektronix's revenues grew an astonishing 4,000 percent in the 1950s, to $43 million in sales in 1960.

It was also during the 1950s that "Tek culture" began to take shape. Even before the company was founded, Murdock had insisted that future employees would be treated with respect, everyone would be on a first-name basis, and there would be no perks for executives. Murdock even talked about the ideal size for a company to maintain a casual, family atmosphere—no more than a few dozen people. Although Tektronix paid lower

Tektronix

Tektronix, Inc.

26600 S.W. Parkway
Wilsonville, Oregon 97070-1000
U.S.A.
(503) 627-7111
Fax: (503) 685-4017

Public Company
Incorporated: 1946 as Tekrad, Inc.
Employees: 10,000
Sales: $1.3 billion
Stock Exchanges: New York Pacific
SICs: 3825 Instruments to Measure Electricity; 3577 Computer Peripheral Equipment, Nec

Tektronix, Inc., founded in 1946, is the world's leading manufacturer of oscilloscopes—instruments used to measure and display electrical signals; it held approximately 57 percent of the market in 1992. The Oregon-based company was also the second-largest supplier of all other electronic testing and measuring devices, with more than 1,500 products, and a leading maker of computer display terminals and color printers for computers.

Tektronix was founded by three U.S. Coast Guard veterans and an electronics expert from the U.S. Army Signal Corps. Portland native Melvin Jack Murdock spent World War II as a Coast Guardsman, maintaining radio equipment for the Navy and planning for a career once the war ended. By 1945, he had convinced two friends, Glenn Leland and Miles Tippery, that the three of them should start their own business, although none had an idea exactly what that business should be. They also decided to bring in Charles Howard Vollum, a graduate of Portland's Reed University with a degree in physics who had operated a radio-repair business in the back room of an appliance store Murdock had owned before the war. Vollum was then designing radar sighting devices for the Signal Corps.

In December of 1945 the four servicemen met in Portland to draft articles of incorporation for a broadly defined company that would manufacture, sell, install, repair, "and otherwise handle and dispose of" electronic equipment. They called their company Tekrad, which was incorporated on January 2, 1946. Vollum was president and Murdock vice president. The name was changed to Tektronix, Inc., a month later when they wages than other manufacturers in the Portland area, the company provided medical coverage, profit sharing, and other benefits. There were few unbreakable rules, and engineers were encouraged to pursue their individual interests. Tek culture was praised by management consultants, and Tektronix was cited in the book *The 100 Best Companies to Work for in America.* However, Tek culture was later blamed for some of the company's inability to adjust to competitive changes in the 1980s.

As Tektronix was getting ready to enter the 1960s, which included work on a new 300-acre headquarters campus in Beaverton, Oregon, Vollum convinced the board of directors to appoint Bob Davis as executive vice president. As vice president for manufacturing from 1954 until 1958, Davis had begun to bring some order to the rapidly growing, unstructured Tektronix organization. Restructuring was a necessity, but Vollum had neither the experience nor the inclination to give the business of management the attention it needed. Davis would report to Vollum, but he would have sole responsibility for the day-to-day operation of the company. Initially the appointment of the energetic Davis was greeted as a positive step. But inevitably, "the old scope warriors," as Marshall M. Lee called long-time employees in his book *Winning with People: The First 40 Years of Tektronix,* came to resent the changes.

Despite significant growth under Davis and the formation of the company's first foreign subsidiaries, by 1962, Vollum was persuaded to re-assume control. At the time, Tektronix's future seemed secure. The company went public in 1963, and was listed on the New York Stock Exchange in 1964. The company continued to bring out more advanced testing equipment, and by 1969, Tektronix controlled 75 percent of the world's market for oscilloscopes. Sales had reached $148 million, and Vollum told *Forbes:* "[There] is an ever-expanding market [for oscilloscopes]. Wherever electronics go, the oscilloscope goes."

However, despite its stellar performance and Vollum's optimism, in the late 1960s Tektronix was not a favorite among financial experts. There were growing indications that Tektronix's dependence on basically one product was a dangerous strategy, especially with the growth of computers with internal testing programs that no longer required oscilloscopes. Equally troubling was that Tektronix had little marketing experience, since its principal product, the oscilloscope, had practically sold itself for 25 years by being better and cheaper than the competition. Many analysts felt that an early attempt to diversify into programmable calculators had failed because of a lack of market savvy. There was also the lingering need to bring the entire, free-flowing Tektronix organization under better control.

Earnings fell for the first time in fiscal 1971, by a devastating 34.7 percent. Early in the year employees took unpaid time off to avoid layoffs, but it did not help. That autumn, Tektronix announced the first layoffs in its fast-paced history. Adding to the pain that year was the death of Murdock, who drowned when his seaplane flipped during takeoff on the Columbia River. Murdock had not been active in daily management of the company for many years, but he had stayed on as chairman of the board and was generally regarded as the person who gave Tektronix its strategic vision. Less than two weeks after

Murdock's death, Vollum suffered a heart attack. Vollum recovered, but he resigned as president in 1972.

At the same time, Tektronix was beginning to have some success with graphic display terminals, which would become the company's second-largest revenue producer. In 1964 Tektronix developed a way to retain an image on a cathode ray tube (CRT) for up to 15 minutes, instead of the split second that images normally lasted before they needed to be regenerated. This was a tremendous advance for oscilloscopes, and for several years Tektronix used its discovery only in its own products. But the new technology was also valuable for displaying maps, charts, and other graphics on computer terminals, and in 1969 the company decided to sell CRT terminals for other applications.

Unfortunately, the first terminals, introduced in 1970, were over-engineered and costly. Earl Wantland, then executive vice president who would later succeed Vollum as president, organized an Information Display Group to concentrate on redesigning the terminals to reduce the final cost. For perhaps the first time since Vollum built his 511 oscilloscope, Tektronix was designing a product for a competitive market, rather than creating the most sophisticated gadget with the blind faith that engineers somewhere would buy it. When the terminals reappeared a year later, the price had been cut by 60 percent, from $10,000 to $4,000.

From a marketing perspective, the timing was also better, with the emergence of computer-aiding design in several industries being a perfect fit for the new graphics terminals. By 1975, Tektronix controlled 50 percent of the market, and the $50 million a year in terminal sales represented about 15 percent of the company's total business. Tektronix had rebounded from a dismal start to the 1970s by joining the *Fortune* 500 in 1975. It had $336.6 million in sales, which placed it 457th on the list of the largest industrial companies in the United States.

Tektronix also took a successful step into diversification in 1974 when it acquired the Grass Valley Group, a California company that made electronic systems to provide special effects for television. By 1978, *Forbes* was able to report that Tektronix "has finally begun to alter its image as a one-product company whose basic technology, the cathode ray tube, was about to be obsoleted by the digital revolution." Although the bulk of its business still centered on oscilloscopes, Tektronix was then selling more than 700 products customized to various market segments, including government, education, broadcast television, and computer industries, in addition to the electronics and electrical equipment markets.

Once again, the future looked bright for Tektronix. The company passed the $1 billion mark in sales in 1981. But once again, the marketplace, and this time, the advance of technology, caught the engineering-driven company off guard. Tektronix was slow to switch from making analog test equipment to digital equipment. And when it made the switch, Tektronix found that low-cost Japanese competitors had beaten it to the portable oscilloscope marketplace. The company also was three years late entering the market for color display terminals, which slashed its share of the market for graphics terminals in half, from a high of 51 percent in 1979 to 26 percent in 1983.

Between 1979 and 1984 earnings fell more than 40 percent. The company suffered through more layoffs, and several top executives and engineers left to form competitors such as Mentor Graphics, Graphics Systems Software, and Northwest Instruments. In 1984 *Business Week* reported: "Now Tek must come from behind again, in what is likely to be the most critical recoup in its 38-year history," as the company belatedly entered the market for computer-aided engineering (CAE) work stations. It was a marketplace battle that Tektronix would eventually lose.

In 1982 competitors had begun offering fully integrated CAE work stations, which threatened the market for Tektronix's stand-alone graphics terminals and electronic testing equipment. Heretofore, Tektronix had been content to be a supplier to the computer industry and reportedly had passed on several opportunities to purchase small computer manufacturers, including an upstart Digital Equipment Corporation. In fact, Tektronix engineers had designed a technical work station in the 1970s, but the company never brought it to market. Then in 1984 Tektronix attempted to counter the attack on its core businesses by forming a systems development division. Charles Humble, then a columnist for the *Portland Oregonian,* wrote of Tektronix's 1984 annual report: "It is about a company that is torn between restructuring and testing the waters of the future, and a company that can't give up the security of past successes."

Early in 1985 Tektronix acquired CAE Systems Inc. In April of that year it introduced its first CAE work station. The product line, however, was short-lived. Four months later, the company announced that instead of producing work stations, it would develop software for other manufacturers. That, too, faltered. In 1988 Tektronix sold its CAE operations for $5 million to Mentor Graphics. Estimates of Tektronix's losses in the abortive effort to enter the CAE market ranged from $150 million to $225 million.

Despite annual revenues that had almost doubled in ten years to $1.4 billion, Tektronix also reported its first-ever loss of $16.7 million for fiscal 1988. David Friedley, a marketing-oriented Tektronix division manager, succeeded Wantland as president in November of 1987. He later told *Forbes,* "The first thing we did was stop the bleeding." In addition to getting out of unprofitable business, Friedley eliminated 2,500 jobs at Tektronix over the next two years.

Business Week later reported that Friedley "cut through . . . bureaucracy like a logger through the nearby Oregon timber." But it was not enough. Tektronix returned to modest profitability in 1989, due to stringent cost-cutting and a new line of color printers. But its financial troubles were far from over. By early 1990, the company was again posting losses, and there were rumors that Friedley would be fired, especially since Tektronix stock had fallen in value from $31 a share in 1987 to a 14-year low of $12.75 a share. A financial analyst for Prudential-Bache Securities, Inc., told *Business Week* that meetings with Tektronix "were like watching the grass grow." The anticipated

shake-up came in March of 1990, with the company headed toward a $92.5 million loss (largely due to restructuring) for the fiscal year. Robert Lundeen, a former Dow Chemical Co. executive and Tektronix's chairman of the board, and William Walker, another board member, ousted Friedley and took over operational control of the company.

Citing the need to reverse the financial losses, Lundeen told Portland's *Business Journal,* "I don't think management realized how urgent it was that we get there quickly." Lundeen told *Forbes,* "I'd like the new Tektronix style to be more cosmopolitan," and he complained, "We're still doing things the Beaverton way." Lundeen initiated another 1,300 layoffs. In a blow to its corporate image, Tektronix also transferred more than 1,200 workers from Vancouver, Washington, to Oregon, leaving vacant a 488,000 square foot manufacturing facility in Jack Murdock Park, an industrial center named for the company's co-founder. For years, Tektronix had been the largest employer in Oregon, with a high of more than 24,000 employees in 1981. But by the end of 1991, the company had a work force of about 12,000.

Lundeen ran Tektronix as interim president for six months, until October of 1990 when the company hired Jerome J. Meyer, a former senior executive with Sperry Univac and Honeywell, Inc. Meyer took over a company with stagnant sales, a lack of market focus, and badly in need of restructuring. Tektronix rebounded from a dismal 1990 to post a modest $45 million profit in 1991. Meyer was rewarded by being named chairman of the board as well as president. But when Meyer reported on the results of his first full year at Tektronix, for fiscal 1992, the company was again in a slump. Sales had hit a nine year low, with earnings of about $27 million.

Just prior to Meyer joining the company, Tektronix's market value was falling from about $1.3 billion in 1987 to less than $400 million in 1990, and the company was seen by many analysts as a potential take-over target. In September of 1990 the board of directors adopted an anti-takeover "poison pill," which entitled existing shareholders to purchase stock at half price if an investor acquired more than 20 percent of the company's stock. At the time, Jean Vollum, the widow of co-founder Howard Vollum, who had died in 1986, was the largest single shareholder with about 8.1 percent of the outstanding shares.

In 1992 a group headed by George Soros began buying Tektronix stock. By the fall of 1992, the Soros Group owned about 13.9 percent of the company, and was demanding three seats on the board of directors. In November three new members were added to the board of directors, including Tektronix's president, Delbert W. Yocam. At that time, the Soros Group agreed not to acquire more than 14.9 percent of the company. That agreement was to run through March 15, 1994.

P. C. Chatterjee, a New York financier who represented the Soros Group in dealings with Tektronix, also was openly critical of Meyer, including his decision to move corporate headquarters from the Beaverton campus to Wilsonville, Oregon. In what was viewed by many as another move to satisfy the Soros Group, Tektronix had brought in Yocam, a former Apple Computer executive, to assume the duties of president just days before the 1992 annual meeting. Meyer remained chief executive officer and chairman of the board.

According to a company spokesperson, Yocam's role was to execute strategies shaped by Meyer and to align Tektronix's product portfolio with growth markets. In one of his first moves, Yocam reorganized Tektronix into five business divisions: test and measurement products, television products, television production/distribution products and systems (the Grass Valley Group being responsible for this), graphics printing and imaging products, and network displays and display products. Essentially, each division was structured as its own independent business with full profit and loss responsibility. The idea behind this move was to enable divisions to make timely decisions relative to customer issues, and to put more emphasis on developing new products to meet the customers' needs. In addition, support groups would be better equipped to provide world-class service.

In 1992 and 1993 Tektronix continued to strengthen its management team, recruiting aggressive individuals with proven track records from successful, fast-growing companies. Carl Neun, formerly senior vice president of administration and CFO of Conner Peripherals, joined Tektronix as vice president and CFO. John Karalis, vice president of corporate development, was previously general counsel with Apple Computer and the Sperry Corporation. Daniel Terpack, formerly general manager with Hewlett-Packard, became vice president of test and measurement. And Deborah Coleman, vice president of materials operations, held several vice president positions with Apple Computer before joining Tektronix.

In the fourth quarter of fiscal year 1993, Tektronix took a pretax charge of $150 million for a restructuring that was to accelerate the strategic changes Meyer had mapped out in 1990. As a result, the company reported a net loss for the year of $55 million ($1.83 per share). Without the restructuring charges, net earnings for fiscal year 1993 were $39 million, or $1.30 per share, up 29 percent from 1992. New sales were up for the first time in four years, $1.302 billion compared to $1.297 billion in 1992. The restructuring is viewed by Tektronix management as an investment in the future and is expected to speed up improvements in profitability and allow the company to focus its resources on growth. Under the restructuring, Tektronix will exit non-strategic businesses, consolidate facilities, discontinue older products, and cut employment by eight percent (about 800 jobs) through attrition and layoffs.

Also in 1993 Tektronix reduced administrative costs by $30 million, received a $31 million dividend from Sony/Tektronix, its joint venture company in Japan, and refinanced its debt structure. Regarded by some as long overdue decisions, the latest actions taken by Tektronix have resulted in renewed belief by some analysts that the company is moving in the right direction. Even in the sluggish economy of the early 1990s, the company's performance has been improving.

Principal Subsidiaries: Colorado Data Systems, Inc.; The Grass Valley Group, Inc.; Tektronix Development Company.

Further Reading:

1991 Annual Report, Beaverton, OR: Tektronix, Inc., 1991.

1992 Annual Report, Wilsonville, OR: Tektronix, Inc., 1992.

Benner, Susan, "Life in the Silicon Rain Forest," *Inc.,* June 1984. pp. 112–21.

Brandt, Richard, "Textronix (sic) Atten-hut!," *Business Week,* April 18, 1988, p. 33.

Conner, Margery S., "Good Engineering Decisions Are Key to Improving U.S.'s Competitive Stance," *EDN,* October 1, 1987, pp. 73–80.

Hill, Gail Kinsey, "Tektronix Inc.: Will the Cuts be the Last?," *Business Journal* (Portland, OR), June 4, 1990, p. 2.

Hoj, Robert D., "Turning around 'a Battleship in a Bathtub'," *Business Week,* May 7, 1990, p. 122.

"How To Be Big Though Small," *Forbes,* May 15, 1974, p. 115.

Humble, Charles, "Annual Report from Tektronix Inc. Takes on Defensive Tone," *Portland Oregonian,* August 26, 1984, p. E1.

King, Harriet, " 'High Powered' President for Tektronix," *New York Times,* September 11, 1992.

LaPolla, Stephanie, "New Tektronix Chief Outlines Strategy," *PC Week,* October 26, 1992, p. 163.

Lee, Marshall M., *Winning with People: The First 40 Years of Tektronix,* Beaverton, OR: Tektronix, Inc., 1986.

Manning, Jeff, "Managers Forced to Make Further Cuts at Troubled Tek," *Business Journal* (Portland, OR), February 12, 1990, p. 3.

Manning, "Shake-up Follows Ouster of Tektronix's Friedley," *Business Journal* (Portland, OR), April 30, 1990, p. 1.

Manning, "Tek Officials Deny Plan Is a Response to Takeover Threat," *Business Journal* (Portland, OR), September 3, 1990, p. 2.

Manning, "Tek's Workstation Line to Close If Buyer Not Found in 60 Days," *Business Journal* (Portland, OR), October 15, 1990, p. 1.

Manning, "Tektronix Scopes Out Corporate Reworking," *Business Journal* (Portland, OR), March 25, 1991.

Manning, "Does Soros Group Want to Take Over Tek?," *Business Journal* (Portland, OR), August 17, 1992, p. 1.

Manning, "Tek Gives Soros Advance Cold Shoulder," *Business Journal* (Portland, OR), August 24, 1992, p. 1.

Manning, "Tek Fills Spot with Former Apple Exec," *Business Journal* (Portland, OR), September 14, 1992, p. 1.

Manning, "Tek Heads into Annual Meeting with Intrigue on Agenda," *Business Journal* (Portland, OR), September 21, 1992, p. 4.

Manning, "Golf Junkets May Handicap Tek's Meyer," *Business Journal* (Portland, OR), October 5, 1992, p. 1.

Manning, "Soros, Tek Reach Accord after Nasty Board Control Battle," *Business Journal* (Portland, OR), November 16, 1992. p. 1.

Montgomery, Leland, "The Agony of Jerry Meyer," *Financial World,* December 8, 1992, pp. 24–25.

Olmos, Robert, "Tek Adds 'Job-Sharing' to its List of Worker Benefits," *Portland Oregonian,* January 29, 1978, p. A17.

Painter, John, Jr., "Success of Tektronix, Oregon's Largest Employer, Surprises Founder," *Portland Oregonian,* April 6, 1975, p. A30.

Pratt, Gerry, "Time-Off Experiment Bolsters Tektronix," *Portland Oregonian,* April 23, 1971.

"President for Tektronix Hired from Honeywell," *New York Times,* October 25, 1990.

Pitta, Julie, "Can Dinosaurs Adapt?," *Forbes,* March 4, 1991, p. 122.

"Shedding a One-Product Image," *Business Week,* February 16, 1976, pp. 91–92.

"Selective Success," *Forbes,* June 15, 1969, p. 50.

Sorensen, Donald J., "Fred Meyer, Tektronix Join Elite Billion-Dollar Sales Firms," *Portland Oregonian,* January 6, 1980, p. C7.

Sorensen, "Ex-Tektronix Employees Form Own High-Tech Firms," *Portland Oregonian,* March 8, 1982, p. D7.

"Tektronix: Where One Product Isn't Enough," *Business Week,* August 4, 1973, pp. 65–66.

"Tektronix Cofounder City's '1st Citizen,' " *Portland Oregonian,* February 2, 1974.

Tektronix Corporate Backgrounder, Beaverton, OR: Tektronix Inc., March 1990.

''Tektronix Joins Nation's 'Top 500','' *Portland Oregonian,* May 13, 1976, p. B7.

''Tektronix's Push to Get Back on the Fast-Growth Track,'' *Business Week,* September 17, 1984, pp. 108–10.

Tripp, Julie, ''John Gray to Replace Vollum as Tektronix Chairman,'' *Portland Oregonian,* February 3, 1984.

Wiegner, Kathleen K., ''Life in The Fast Lane,'' *Forbes,* April 3, 1978, p. 57.

Wiegner, '' 'Manufacturing Was an Afterthought,' '' *Forbes,* January 27, 1986, pp. 34–35.

Wiegner, ''Nice Guys Finish Last,'' *Forbes,* June 26, 1989.

Woog, Adam, *Sezless Oysters and Self-Tipping Hats: 100 Years of Invention in the Pacific Northwest,* Seattle, WA: Sasquatch Books, 1991, pp. 209–11.

—Dean Boyer

Texas Industries, Inc.

7610 Stemmons Freeway
Dallas, Texas 75247
U.S.A.
(214) 647-6700
Fax: (214) 647-3878

Public Company
Incorporated: 1951
Employees: 2,700
Sales: $601 million
Stock Exchanges: New York
SICs: 3312 Blast Furnaces and Steel Mills; 3271 Concrete
    Block and Brick

Texas Industries, Inc. (TXI) is a major producer of steel and cement/concrete products for construction. In the steel segment, the company's products include reinforcing bar, structural beams, and merchant quality rounds. Texas Industries' steel operations are carried out by Chaparral Steel Company, an 81 percent-owned subsidiary. Chaparral's raw materials consist largely of scrap steel, much of which is produced by shredder operations at its Midlothian, Texas, steel mill. A major source of the scrap steel for shredding is crushed auto bodies that are purchased on the open market. The bulk of Chaparral's customers are steel service centers, steel fabricators, forgers, and equipment manufacturers. The company's products are used primarily in the construction, railroad, defense, automotive, and energy industries.

TXI's cement/concrete operations produce a variety of construction materials, including cement and aggregates, ready-mix, pipe, block, and brick. The company's Midlothian cement facility is the largest cement plant in Texas, with a capacity of 1.2 million tons. Another cement facility is located in Hunter, Texas, near Austin. About one million tons of finished cement were shipped to outside trade customers by TXI in 1992. The principal marketing area for the company's cement products includes Texas, Louisiana, Colorado, Oklahoma, and New Mexico. TXI's aggregate facilities are located in Texas and Louisiana, where sand, gravel, crushed limestone, and lightweight aggregate are produced. Texas and Louisiana are also home to the company's 29 ready-mix concrete plants, which use a sizeable amount of the cement and aggregates produced at the company's other facilities in their own operations.

Texas Industries, Inc. was formed in 1951 as the successor to the Texas Lightweight Aggregate Company. Texas Lightweight Aggregate Company had been organized in 1946 to meet the increasing postwar demand for construction materials in the southwestern part of the United States. This company had a sales volume of $30,000 in 1947. In 1949, Texas Lightweight Aggregate attracted the attention of Ralph Rogers, the former president of Cummins Diesel Engine Corp., who had recently retired to the Dallas area. Texas Lightweight Aggregate was one of the first companies to burn shale and clay in special rotary kilns, producing a unique building material. Noting the potential of this product, Rogers decided to invest in the company. By 1950, the allegedly retired Rogers was elected company president. The following year, Texas Industries was formed, with Texas Lightweight Aggregate and another firm, Texcrete Co., as its core. Texcrete Co., also formed in 1946, was a maker of concrete products that included pipe, joists, and masonry units. In its first year, Texas Industries earned $35,000 on sales of $217,000.

By 1953, Texas Industries had grown explosively, reporting sales that year of $5.8 million. The company had four main product lines at that time: Haydite, the lightweight expanded clay and shale aggregate that had first interested Rogers; concrete products sold under the Texcrete trade name; ready-mixed concrete, sand, gravel, and crushed stone; and Sakrete, the trade name for its dry-mixed concrete. Haydite was the company's most important early product. Because it was as strong as conventional concrete while 40 percent lighter, Haydite quickly became popular in the building industry. By 1954, TXI had expanded to 28 plants. These included the newly acquired Fort Worth Sand & Gravel Co. and a new Haydite subsidiary, the Oklahoma Lightweight Aggregate Company in Choctaw, 12 miles from Oklahoma City. The company's total of six Haydite plants made it the nation's largest expanded clay or shale lightweight aggregates producer. 1954 also marked the completion of a new research and testing laboratory at TXI's Dallas facility.

TXI continued to grow at a rapid pace through the later part of the 1950s. A nine-month expansion and rebuilding program took place in 1955 and 1956 at the company's Texcrete plant in Dallas. In 1958, TXI acquired all outstanding shares of Texcrete Structural Products Company, which had just finished work on a modern new prestressed concrete plant. The plant's initial output was bridge girders to be used in highway construction. Dallas Lightweight Aggregate Company became a wholly-owned subsidiary of Texas Industries the following year. In 1959, construction began on a new cement plant in Midlothian, Texas, equidistant from Dallas and Fort Worth. The plant, with a capacity of 1.4 million barrels annually, marked TXI's entry into the cement business. The construction of the cement plant provided TXI with its own source of cement, which up to that time had been its biggest expense, and therefore made the company less susceptible to cement shortages. Major improvements were made at other facilities as well before the decade ended. The company's Houston masonry products plant became one of the very first of its kind to be totally automated. In addition, new ready-mix concrete facilities were completed in Fort Worth, New Orleans, and Alexandria, Louisiana.

With the opening of the Midlothian plant in October of 1960, TXI became a vertically-integrated, self sufficient company. By 1963, sales at Texas Industries had reached $27 million, with earnings of over $2 million. The company continued to grow through acquisitions during this period. In 1962, TXI acquired two Dallas area real estate properties, Brookhollow Industrial Park and the Empire Central office community. Two Detroit companies were purchased the following year. The two companies, Cooper Supply Co. and the Harris Concrete and Supply Co., were both in the ready-mix concrete business, a growing industry in Detroit at the time. Cooper was Detroit's leading ready-mix producer, with nine plants. Harris had six plants. Combined, the companies employed 400 workers and added 130 trucks to TXI's fleet. In 1964, TXI launched its first European venture, when its French affiliate, Beton Service de France, acquired a significant interest in France's largest distributor of bulk cement, Societe d'Approvisionnement du Batiment et de Travaux Publics (SABTP). SABTP had recently begun operating its first ready-mix batching plant.

In May of 1967, the addition of a third kiln at the Midlothian cement plant made it the largest cement plant in Texas, with a yearly capacity of 5 million barrels of portland cement. The Athens Brick Company was acquired that year as well. Athens Brick, whose plants were also located in Texas and Louisiana, was a manufacturer of clay products sold throughout the Southwest. 1967 also saw the opening of several new facilities at TXI. Three new sand and gravel plants in Louisiana and Texas went into operation during the year, as did the company's new Span-Deck plant in Dallas, which produced prestressed, hollowcored concrete slabs through mechanized casting. Around the same time, TXI purchased a large limestone deposit in southern California, opening the door to future expansion in that area. Another lightweight aggregate plant was completed the following year, this one in Clodine, a town near Houston. In 1969, TXI entered the modular building construction business (modular buildings are easily assembled, low-cost units made of pre-constructed elements), with the formation of a wholly-owned subsidiary called Isocorp Inc.

By 1970, TXI's sales had reached $79 million. Contributing to this total was a further diversification, the acquisition of TXI Paper Products, a producer of paperboard from waste paper. 1970 also marked the end of Ralph Rogers' tenure as company president, though he retained his position as board chair. The new president was Ralph's son, Robert Rogers. During the first part of the 1970s, concrete represented TXI's most important growth area. The construction of the huge new Dallas-Fort Worth airport was one important reason for the emphasis on concrete. Sales continued to climb steadily, reaching $88 million in 1971. This increase over the previous year took place in spite of a sluggish performance by the Brookhollow subsidiary and the usual start-up glitches at TXI Paper Products. The following year, TXI exercised its option to buy 35 percent of S.A.F.B., its French concrete affiliate. Two years later, TXI Paper Products was sold to Clevepak Corp. for about $11 million.

In 1973, TXI launched Chaparral Steel Co. as a joint venture with Co-Steel International Ltd., a Toronto-based steel company with facilities in Toronto, Minneapolis, and Sheerness, England. The Chaparral plant, located near Midlothian, was designed for the production of rolled steel products, such as reinforcing bars, made from scrap steel. The plant, with an initial production capacity of 220,000 tons, was to employ about 300 workers. Several other new facilities and new subsidiaries were created in the mid-1970s. One of these was the 375,000-ton cement plant at Artesia, Mississippi, built by TXI's United Cement Co. subsidiary, and completed in early 1974. Dolphin Construction, a general contracting company serving Louisiana, was formed that year as well. 1974 also brought the creation of Q/A Corporation, a construction company formed to supply concrete for nuclear power plants. Q/A's first contract was the Waterford III nuclear power plant near New Orleans, a project that called for 250,000 cubic yards of ready-mix concrete over five years. TXI's ability to act as its own contractor in the construction of its new facilities enabled the company to keep costs and construction time to a minimum. In spite of this ongoing expansion, TXI's earnings declined for three straight years, from 1973 to 1975.

This trend was reversed during the second half of the decade, however. By 1977, TXI was producing over 1.5 million tons of cement per year at its five kilns, and was employing over 3,000 people. That year, about 70 percent of the company's revenue and 90 percent of its profits were generated by the cement and concrete business, including aggregates. Real estate activities, mainly the Brookhollow Corp. subsidiary, accounted for nearly 14 percent of net. Around two-thirds of TXI's revenues were coming from its home turf of Texas, with Louisiana and Mississippi contributing the bulk of the remainder. The company's most impressive improvement during the late 1970s came from Chaparral. In 1979, TXI's half interest in Chaparral produced 23 percent of its profit, after losing money only two years earlier. By 1980, the Midlothian cement plant's capacity had been expanded to 1.2 million tons, making it the largest cement plant in its region. During this period, the company's two existing cement plants, Midlothian and Artesia, switched from gas and oil to coal, a less expensive energy source. One important reason for the switch was that half of the fuel needs of the two cement plants could be met by a coal mine in West Texas owned by TXI.

In 1981, a new dry process plant at Hunter, Texas, between Austin and San Antonio, was dedicated. The addition of the Hunter plant brought the company's total cement capacity up to 2.2 million tons. A year later, a new sand and gravel plant in Austin began operations, coinciding with a construction boom in the area. This brought to seven the number of sand and gravel plants operated in Texas by TXI, with a yearly output of 8 million tons of aggregates. 1982 also saw the completion of an expansion project at the Chaparral mill, increasing annual production capacity to one million tons. Brookhollow Corporation, TXI's real estate subsidiary, continued to thrive in the first half of the 1980s, generating record earnings for three years in a row in 1983 through 1985. Production records were set in fiscal 1985 at the company's Hunter and Artesia cement plants as well, reflecting the region's growth in cement consumption during that time.

Late in 1985, TXI purchased Co-Steel's share of Chaparral Steel Co., thereby becoming full owner of that subsidiary. Co-Steel's half interest was purchased for $42 million cash, plus a further payment due in 1990 to be determined based on Chaparral's performance in the interim. With Chaparral in hand, TXI's sales and net earnings soared for the fiscal year ending in May 1986. With Chaparral shipping record quantities (in excess of 1 million tons for the first time), TXI's sales leaped from $344 million in 1985 to $648 million in 1986. Net income grew by 26 percent in that period, from less than $18 million to over $22 million. Much emphasis was placed on cost reduction and efficiency during this time. For example, between 1977 and 1987, the amount of labor required to produce a ton of steel at Chaparral was reduced from 3.3 man-hours to less than 1.5. In the cement/concrete business, the company focused on reducing its fuel costs, the largest expense in cement production. The Midlothian plant started burning fuel derived from waste in November of 1987, saving 20 percent on fuel costs by the following year. Between 1981 and 1988, the company's three cement plants reduced their production costs by 15 percent, while boosting production capacities by 14 percent.

In 1987, Co-Steel purchased 6.3 percent of the outstanding TXI common shares. Shortly thereafter, John Shields, Co-Steel's president and CEO, was named to Chaparral's board of directors. This share was increased to 8.7 percent early in 1988. For fiscal 1988, during exceptionally tough market conditions, TXI turned a modest profit of $11 million on sales of $606 million. By this time Chaparral ranked tenth in size among U.S. steel producers, and was generating a very large portion of TXI's revenue and earnings. In 1990, TXI completed the Chaparral buyout, paying Co-Steel $50 million in cash and an additional 1.2 million shares of stock. The payout brought Co-Steel's holding in TXI up to 22 percent, making it TXI's largest shareholder by a sizeable margin.

With the state of Texas mired deeply in recession, the company's cement/concrete operations lost over $11 million in fiscal 1990. In August of 1990, TXI sold its United Cement Company subsidiary for $43 million. The sale of United Cement was the only thing that kept the company from operating at a loss for fiscal 1991. Dolphin Construction Company was sold off in the first quarter of fiscal 1992. For 1992, TXI returned to profitability, earning $1.9 million on sales of just over $600 million. About two-thirds of the revenue was generated by Chaparral, which started up the new Large Beam Mill during the year. The management of Texas Industries hopes that a continuing emphasis on cost reduction, coupled with a significant economic recovery in the southwestern part of the United States, will help return the company to a more consistently profitable state.

Principal Subsidiaries: Athens Brick Company; Brookhollow Corporation; Creole Corporation; Louisiana Industries, Inc.; Southwestern Financial Corporation; Crestview Corporation; TXI Aggregate Transportation Company; TXI Aviation, Inc.; TXI Cement Company; TXI Structural Products,Inc.; TXI Transportation Company; Chaparral Steel Company (81%).

Further Reading:

Balcerek, Tom, "Co-Steel Gets Payout from Pact," *American Metal Market*, September 6, 1990, p. 2.

"Chaparral Aids Net Gain, Texas Industries Says," *American Metal Market*, July 22, 1986, p. 4.

Gordon, Mitchell, "Solid Footings," *Barron's*, March 17, 1980, p. 47.

Gordon, Mitchell, "Texas Industries Racks Up Solid Advance in Profits," *Barron's*, March 13, 1978, pp. 25–26.

Levine, Sid, "More Construction Aggregate for Austin, Texas," *Pit & Quarry*, April 1984, pp. 30–33.

"Plan Unveiled for New Steel Plant in Texas," *Journal of Commerce*, July 26, 1973, p. 9.

Sapino, Brenda, "Texas Industries Becomes Full Owner," *American Metal Market*, December 3, 1985, p. 4.

Texas Industries, Inc. 1992 Annual Report, Dallas: Texas Industries, Inc., 1992.

"Texas Industries Fairly Valued on Earnings," *Financial World*, October 13, 1971, p. 18.

Texas Industries: 40 Years of Production and Progress, Dallas: Texas Industries, Inc., 1991.

"Texas Industries Spurred by Demand for Lightweight Building Materials," *Barron's*, March 1, 1954, p. 22.

—Robert R. Jacobson

The Thomson Corporation

Toronto Dominion Bank Tower, Suite 2706
P.O. Box 24
Toronto-Dominion Centre
Toronto, Ontario M5K 1A1
Canada
(416) 360-8700
Fax: (416) 360-8812

Public Company
Incorporated: 1977
Employees: 46,400
Sales: $5.98 billion
Stock Exchanges: Toronto Montreal London
SICs: 2711 Newspapers; 2721 Periodicals; 2731 Book
   Publishing; 2741 Miscellaneous Publishing; 7999
   Amusement and Recreation, Nec

A towering media, information, and travel empire, The Thomson Corporation ranks as the fifth-largest and third most profitable publisher in the world, according to *Fortune*'s July 1992 global business survey. Through its three major groups—Thomson Information/Publishing, Thomson Travel, and Thomson Newspapers—the sprawling, markedly decentralized company can lay claim to dozens of definitive trade periodicals, including *American Banker* and *Physicians' Desk Reference;* a number of market-leading niche publishers, including military specialist Jane's Information Group, who together provide over 50,000 individual products; the largest commercial provider of scientific data in the world, the Institute for Science Information; the leading British retail holiday chain (Lunn Poly); the leading British leisure airline (Britannia Airways); the largest collection of regional newspapers in Great Britain; and the largest chain of Canadian and U.S. daily and weekly newspapers, over 200 in all. Founded with a small radio station in the 1930s by Ontario entrepreneur Roy Thomson, the company evolved by Thomson's death, in 1976, into the largest privately owned communications conglomerate in the world, then named The Thomson Organisation (subsumed in 1978 by the public holding company International Thomson Organisation Ltd.). The Thomson Corporation was created in June 1989 by a merger of the Toronto-based Thomson Newspapers Ltd. and International Thomson, to control newspaper, publishing, database, and travel holdings centered principally in the United States, Canada, the United Kingdom, Australia, and Scandina-

via. Control of the company has long rested in the hands of Thomson's son, Kenneth, as well as company president Michael Brown and deputy chairman John A. Tory. Thomson (Canada's richest man and heir of his father's title, Lord Thomson of Fleet) also has a 25 percent stake in the venerable Canadian department store chain Hudson's Bay Co. and an 83 percent interest in Markborough Properties, a real estate development company.

Born in Toronto in 1894, Roy Thomson left school at 14 to become a bookkeeper and, later, branch manager of a cordage company. After a brief, unsuccessful attempt at farming in Saskatchewan, he returned to Ontario in 1920 to establish an automotive parts distributorship, which also proved unsuccessful. Finally, in 1930, Thomson agreed to a franchise arrangement to sell radios in the remote town of North Bay. As Susan Goldenberg reported in *The Thomson Empire:* ''Only someone with Thomson's optimism, stamina and ebullient salesmanship would have accepted such an assignment under the odds he faced. In addition to the Depression and poor radio reception, the single transmitter in North Bay was decrepit.'' Thomson solved the predictable problem of feeble radio sales by opening his own radio station, CFCH, in 1932 on borrowed money. Roy Thomson's avowed ambition was to become a millionaire by the time he was 30 but, nearing the age of 40 now, he was nearly penniless. His decision to capitalize on advertising revenue in his current venture, however, helped him to belatedly achieve his goal several hundred times over. Within two years of CFCH's debut, Thomson had bought additional stations in Kirkland Lake and Timmins. This latter purchase coincided with Thomson's entry into newspaper publishing, another source of advertising revenue and what would soon be the cornerstone of his empire, via the *Timmins Press,* a paper whose offices were in the same building as his newest station. By 1944 his holdings included five newspapers and eight radio stations. Newspapers became Thomson's main concern, while Jack Kent Cooke, with whom he went into partnership in 1940, assumed management of the radio end of the business. Their partnership ended in 1949, just as Thomson began buying newspapers outside Ontario.

In 1952 he bought his first non-Canadian newspaper, the *Independent* of St. Petersburg, Florida, to add to the 12 he already owned. A turning point came in 1953, when Thomson moved to Great Britain, leaving his North American operations under the control of Kenneth, then 30. Thomson's first U.K. acquisition was the *Scotsman,* a prestigious Scottish daily that had been founded in 1817 but was suffering financially. Owning Scotland's leading newspaper put Thomson in an excellent position to make his successful bid for a commercial television franchise covering central Scotland when it became available in 1957. Famous for his frugality as well as for his quotes on the topic of wealth, he called this coup ''a license to print money.'' The enormous profits from Scottish Television (STV) made it possible for him to buy London's leading Sunday paper, the *Sunday Times,* as well as 17 other local newspapers, from the Kemsley family in 1959. This was the first ''reverse takeover'' in U.K. business history. Kemsley Newspapers bought Thomson's STV company in return for Kemsley shares, which gave Thomson majority control of the group and allowed it indirectly to retain STV as well, with 70 percent control of the total business. Later, stricter government controls led to a forced reduction in Thomson's holding and the company sold its remaining interest in 1977.

Presciently, Thomson did not restrict himself to newspapers and television. Thomson Publications, the forerunner of what has become Thomson's largest and most profitable group, Thomson Information/Publishing, was established in 1961 to publish books and magazines. This subsidiary began with the acquisition of the Illustrated London News Company, which owned not only the magazine of that name and the *Tatler,* but also the trade book publisher Michael Joseph. To this base Thomson Publications added in the first half of the 1960s the educational publisher Thomas Nelson & Sons; George Rainbird, specializing in illustrated books; Hamish Hamilton in trade books; and Derwent Publications in scientific and technical information. The company moved into consumer, professional, and business press publishing in the United Kingdom, Australia, and southern Africa. It also revamped the regional newspaper group; launched four newspapers; started new magazines, including *Family Circle* and *Living,* to be distributed only through supermarkets (a novel concept that proved highly successful in the United Kingdom); and started the *Sunday Times* color magazine, which by 1963 was an unqualified success. In addition, Thomson Publications created a paperback imprint, Sphere, in 1966, aiming its titles at confectioners, news agents, and tobacconists rather than established bookshops. This venture suffered losses, in part because it could not secure the paperback rights of books published by other Thomson companies, since most of these had already been bought by rival paperback publishers.

In 1964 Roy Thomson made it clear that Britain rather than Canada was now his base by taking British citizenship and accepting a seat in the House of Lords as Lord Thomson of Fleet, an honor sponsored by prime minister Harold Macmillan. From television, newspapers, books, and magazines, Thomson next extended his empire into the travel business starting in 1965, when foreign travel was just beginning to become a popular activity in Britain. Three existing package tour companies and a small airline, Britannia Airways, were bought and formed the basis for Thomson Travel. After an initial period of good profits, the company encountered intense competition in the early 1970s, which resulted in the failure of several competing companies. Thomson Travel survived as the largest operator due to a reconstruction of its management, organizational, and commercial policies.

In 1972 the group moved into travel retailing with the acquisition of Lunn Poly. Thomson introduced Yellow Pages to the United Kingdom as a long-term profit venture. Once he had won the contract from the Post Office to sell advertising in its telephone directories, Thomson persuaded the agency of the need for a classified directory for all 64 telephone regions. From this enterprise the company learned the constraints and difficulties of working in a commercial venture with a public utility. In 1980 International Thomson relinquished the Yellow Pages contract and started its own local directory operation in partnership with the American firm Dun & Bradstreet.

Thomson had been looking for a national daily newspaper to put together with the *Sunday Times,* and in 1966 he bought the London *Times* and its associated weeklies, *Times Literary Supplement* and *Times Educational Supplement,* from the Astor family. Thomson described the acquisition as the summit of a lifetime's work, and the man who admitted that he was "tighter than any Scot" cheerfully bore the continuing financial losses as his one extravagance. At the time of his death, the *Times'* American counterpart, the *New York Times,* reported that "Lord Thomson poured at least £10 million into rescuing the *Times,* expanding the newspaper's staff, introducing a business supplement, promoting the daily issues, livening up the stolid paper . . . and seeking to give it a new informal style." Yet, "the newspaper itself, now plagued by spiraling newsprint costs coupled with the impact of the stagnating British economy, remains in somber financial shape." It would be left to his son to sell this prized possession. Perhaps even more to his credit than his financial commitment was Roy Thomson's well-known pledge, applicable as much to the *Times* as any of his other holdings, that the editorial support of his newspapers was not for sale to anyone, that the organization's headquarters would not guide the policies of the papers, and that the papers' editors would be free and independent.

In 1971 the Thomson group went into its single most profitable area of business when it joined with Occidental Petroleum, Getty Oil, and Allied Chemical as the sole U.K. partner in a bid for licenses to explore for oil in the North Sea. The consortium's first strike, in 1973, was in the Piper field, containing more than 800 million barrels of oil. Thomson rejected the U.S. partners' offer to buy his 20 percent stake, and his investment turned out even wiser than had been expected when a second strike, in the Claymore field in 1974, brought the consortium another 400 million barrels. Within a decade the International Thomson Organisation was gaining most of its overall profits from North Sea oil on the basis of an initial stake of just $5 million and a series of bank loans using the oil itself as collateral. In 1977 International Thomson showed a trading profit of almost $190 million, compared with less than $20 million in 1971.

When Kenneth Thomson succeeded his father, he inherited control of a $750 million media monolith. British government policy on monopolies prevented expansion of newspaper holdings in the United Kingdom, and exchange controls—since abolished—would have made overseas investment from a base in London very costly. The decision was made to concentrate on expanding in North America by investing oil profits into publications and publishers with proven track records. In 1978 International Thomson Organisation Ltd. (ITOL) was established and corporate headquarters were moved back to Toronto. ITOL's philosophy, according to a 1988 *Forbes* article, became: "Buy the market leader, even in a specialized field, and then you can afford to pay for the acquisition."

In 1979 ITOL's first acquisition in North America was the U.S. college textbook publisher Wadsworth Inc., quickly followed by others in business and professional publishing and information services, such as Callaghan & Company, Van Nostrand Reinhold, Research Publications, and Warren, Gorham & Lamont, as well as numerous business magazines. By 1983, 25 percent of ITOL's sales were to the United States and nearly 20 percent of its work force was employed there. Acquisitions continued over the next several years, bringing in such companies as Gale Research (parent company of St. James Press); American Banker/Bond Buyer; South-Western Publishing Co.; and Mitchell International.

Back in the United Kingdom, Times Newspapers had become a source of continual trouble for the group. By 1978 strikes over pay and conditions were seriously disrupting the publication of both titles. The situation continued to deteriorate until the company suspended publication for 11 months. Not long after the papers' operations resumed, International Thomson gave up the unequal struggle to introduce new technology on terms acceptable to the company and, in 1981, sold the titles to Australian media magnate Rupert Murdoch for £12 million; the trading losses and losses on disposal for the previous year were an estimated US$36 million.

The Canadian company Thomson Newspapers Ltd., which was separate from ITOL, had long restricted itself to owning small Canadian and U.S. newspapers with circulations below 20,000; the strategy was in keeping with Roy Thomson's drive to contain costs while nonetheless being assured of near monopolies in local advertising. During the 1950s under Kenneth Thomson, the group published the largest number of newspaper titles in Canada. In the following decade a bold U.S. acquisition program was launched. In 1967 the company acquired 16 daily and 6 weekly newspapers, mainly from the purchase of The Brush Moore Newspaper, Inc., and was publishing more daily newspapers in the United States than in Canada. By 1974 the group owned more than 100 newspapers.

In 1980 its profile was transformed through the acquisition of FP Publications and its chain of newspapers in most of the big cities of Canada, including Toronto's *Globe & Mail,* which Thomson has tried to turn into a national newspaper along U.K. lines. Soon afterward Thomson closed down one of the FP papers, the unprofitable *Ottawa Journal.* Simultaneously a rival newspaper chain, Southam, closed down its Winnipeg paper and bought Thomson's shares in two newspaper firms in Montreal and Vancouver, while Thomson closed down the FP News Service.

By the 1980s Thomson Travel ranked as the largest inclusive tour operator based in the United Kingdom (about three times the size of its nearest rival), owned the country's biggest charter airline, and was one of the largest travel retailers. Within a few years of entering the U.S. market it became one of the top three U.S. tour operators, although by 1988 it had withdrawn completely in order to concentrate on its activities based in the United Kingdom. This same year Thomson strengthened its U.K. leadership in tour operating, charter airlines, and travel retailing with the acquisition of the Horizon Travel Group, which had been one of its major competitors.

For ITOL, expansion continued throughout the 1980s in Britain and the United States alike. With the 1986 acquisition of South-Western, the largest American publisher of business textbooks for schools and colleges, ITOL became second overall in U.S. college textbook publishing. The following year saw one of ITOL's biggest British purchases, when it acquired Associated Book Publishers (ABP), a group including the legal publisher Sweet & Maxwell and the academic publisher Routledge, Chapman & Hall. ABP represented a major advance for ITOL in legal, scientific, technical, and academic publishing in the United Kingdom, North America, and Australia.

This trend toward what Laura Jereski calls "high-profit publishing niches," was orchestrated by Thomson's right-hand man, Gordon Brunton, and furthered by Michael Brown; both were keenly aware that ITOL's oil holdings were rapidly becoming depleted. The 1986 fall in oil prices dragged the North American petroleum subsidiaries into overall losses and both were sold off in 1987. In 1989 ITOL finalized its move away from oil and gas by selling its remaining British interests. Although the immediate cause was the major accident on the Piper Alpha oil rig in 1988, the longer-term rationale was that the company had been less and less dependent on North Sea oil revenue, which had fallen both absolutely and as a proportion of ITOL's business since its peak in 1982. At that time it had provided about 75 percent of ITOL's profits, but by 1985, when the Scapa field in which it had invested came onstream, this proportion had fallen to just over 50 percent.

By leaving the petroleum industry altogether ITOL was able to concentrate even more resources and attention on its core activities of publishing and information services. In 1988, for instance, Thomson & Thomson launched a database containing over 300,000 trademarks and logos; Mitchell International developed further its involvement in the computerizing of motor car building and repairs; and ITOL acquired 36 free newspapers in Britain. By the end of 1988, after 54 years of growth, Thomson Newspapers was publishing 40 daily and 12 weekly newspapers in Canada, and 116 daily and 24 weekly newspapers in the United States, representing the largest number of daily newspapers of any newspaper publishing group in either country. The daily circulation exceeded three million.

In March 1989, to remain competitive in a dawning era of mega-mergers among media conglomerates (e.g., Time Inc. and Warner Communications Inc. had proposed a landmark merger, which was completed in early 1990), ITOL and Thomson Newspapers announced preparations to merge as The Thomson Corporation, a $4.7 billion entity which began operations a few months later. Thus empowered, the new company then bought the Lawyers Cooperative Publishing Company for $815 million, the largest acquisition ever by a Thomson company. In 1990 Thomson Newspapers purchased five daily newspapers and several associated weekly publications in the United States, its largest ever single purchase. Eight more Canadian local papers and the *Financial Times of Canada* were also bought. Thomson newspapers are now being published in 32 of the 50 American states and in 8 of the 10 Canadian provinces.

From 1990 to 1992, Thomson saw its revenues and profits rise from $5.36 to $5.98 billion; its operating profits, however, stumbled from $726 million to $692 million, before partially rebounding to its current figure of $714 million. Two straight years of double-digit profit declines for Thomson Newspapers, caused by recession-influenced decreases in advertising, explain this recent trend. However, according to Thomson's 1992 Annual Report, U.S. circulation increased slightly and overall market share remained strong. In addition, more than 400 new products were introduced, including the first corporation-generated project, an entertainment weekly entitled *CoverSTORY,* whose circulation, primarily through Thomson newspapers, approached one million. Consequently, the division faces the future optimistically and expects to renew its growth track with the economic recovery.

Writing in 1984, Goldenberg claimed that "The Thomson empire has been in the vanguard among media empires in branching into nonpublishing ventures, but it is a member of the pack, not the leader, in today's mecca for the press lords—information services." Yet, by 1992, Thomson had gone far toward quelling such criticism, for it could now boast ownership of 190 online services, 161 CD-ROM products, and a large number of other software offerings, all part of the Thomson Information/Publishing Group (TIPG). At 44 percent of corporate revenues and 56 percent of operating profits, TIPG has clearly come to represent the vitality and future of the company. Largest of the group's six divisions in profits is International Thomson Publishing (which includes South-Western) and, in sales, Thomson Professional Publishing (which includes Lawyers Cooperative). In April 1992 Thomson accelerated its entry into information services with the $210-million purchase of New York–based JPT Publishing; according to *Publishers Weekly* and Thomson's chief financial officer, the deal was struck primarily to acquire data provider Institute for Scientific Information (ISI). ISI enjoys over 300,000 customers worldwide and is believed to be generating healthy annual profits approaching $15 million.

With its longstanding reputation intact as a bottom line–oriented conglomerate, The Thomson Corporation may be expected, contrary to Goldenberg's thesis, to forge through the 1990s as a leader in its own right. Its financial clout and acquisition savvy, together with its ability to expand market share and profits through organic growth, have made it a true media empire, one founded upon old-fashioned principles but nonetheless guided by the urge to remain a smart performer and front-running competitor.

Further Reading:

Coffey, Michael, "Thomson Pays $210M for Electronic Database, Journals," *Publishers Weekly,* April 20, 1992, p. 6.

Fabrikant, Geraldine, "2 Thomson Companies in a Proposal to Merge," *New York Times,* March 16, 1989, p. D22.

"The Global 500 by Industry (table)," *Fortune,* July 27, 1992, p. 212.

Goldenberg, Susan, *The Thomson Empire,* New York: Beaufort Books, Inc., 1984.

Jereski, Laura, "Profits by the Numbers," *Forbes,* September 19, 1988, pp. 104–06.

"Lord Thomson Dies; Built Press Empire," *New York Times,* August 5, 1976, pp. 1, 32.

Morantz, Alan, "The Power Elite: Kenneth Roy Thomson," *Canadian Business,* November 1989, pp. 49–51.

Moskowitz, Milton, et al, "Thomson," *Everybody's Business: A Field Guide to the 400 Leading Companies in America,* New York: Doubleday, 1990.

Rudolph, Barbara, "Good-bye to All That," *Forbes,* March 2, 1981, p. 108.

Smith, Desmond, "Thomson: Media's Quiet Giant," *Advertising Age,* May 14, 1984, pp. 4, 74.

—Jay P. Pederson and Patrick Heenan

TIMKEN®

THE TIMKEN COMPANY

The Timken Company

1835 Dueber Ave., S.W.
Canton, Ohio 44706-2798
U.S.A.
(216) 438-3000
Fax: (216) 471-3452

Public Company
Incorporated: 1899 as Timken Roller Bearing Axle
 Company
Employees: 16,729
Sales: $1.6 billion
Stock Exchanges: New York
SICs: 3562 Ball and Roller Bearings; 3312 Blast Furnaces
 and Steel Mills.

The Timken Company is the world's largest manufacturer of tapered roller bearings. A tapered roller bearing consists of a set of rolling elements between two concentric rings. The design of these bearings, based on Henry Timken's patents from the late 19th century, allows them to virtually eliminate friction created in hauling heavy loads. Timken bearings are used in a wide variety of industries, including automotive, aerospace, and railroads. MPB Corporation, a wholly owned subsidiary of Timken, produces super-precision and miniature bearings, whose applications include missile guidance systems and computer disk drives. Timken also produces about 1.5 million tons of steel alloy each year, and is the leading manufacturer of Seamless mechanical steel alloy tubing in the world. The Latrobe Steel Company, another wholly owned subsidiary, produces more than 300 grades of steel. Among the uses of Latrobe's products are components for automobile axles and fasteners for space shuttles. While Timken's steel facilities are concentrated in the United States, the company as a whole has operations in 20 countries on 6 continents, totalling 100 plants and offices overall.

Henry Timken founded the earliest form of The Timken Company in St. Louis in 1899. Timken had entered the carriage business as an apprentice 40 years earlier at the age of 16. By the time he was 24, Timken had opened his own carriage shop. In 1877 Timken received the patent for the Timken Buggy Spring, the first of his 13 patents. His spring design became widely used throughout the country, and was produced on a royalty basis by a number of companies. As a result of the spring's success, Timken became well known across the United States, and his carriage business flourished. Around 1895 Timken took an interest in the problems created by friction in wagon design. In 1898 the patent was issued for the Timken tapered roller bearing. The new bearing was a dramatic improvement over the ball bearings and straight roller bearings that had previously been used. The following year, the founder and his two sons, William and Henry (H. H.) Timken, organized the Timken Roller Bearing Axle Company. The company produced axles that used the new bearing in their design.

Within the next couple of years, the axle business began to outgrow its allotted space in the St. Louis carriage plant, and in 1902 the company relocated to Canton, Ohio. Canton was seen as an ideal midpoint between Detroit, home of the automotive industry, and Pittsburgh, a steel-producing city. By that time, the Timkens had recognized the future importance of the automobile, and worked to develop bearings tailored to the needs of that young industry. When Henry Ford introduced the automobile assembly line and the Model T that it produced in 1908, the demand for Timken bearings and axles grew exponentially. In 1909 the Timken brothers broke off the axle division and moved it to Detroit, launching the new Timken-Detroit Axle Company with William Timken as its president. The Canton operation continued to manufacture bearings, and its name was changed to The Timken Roller Bearing Company. By 1909, the year Henry Timken died, the company was turning out over 850,000 bearings a year, and it employed about 1,200 people.

Timken began to produce its own steel in 1915 as a way to ensure an adequate supply for its manufacturing in the face of shortages created by World War I. That year, the company added a steel tube mill to its Canton facilities. A year later a melt shop was added. With the inclusion of these steel works, Timken became the first bearing manufacturer to act as its own supplier of steel for its products. The company was soon producing steel in quantities far greater than its own manufacturing needs. It therefore began marketing its alloy steel to outside buyers, with such companies as the Mack Truck Company among its early regular customers. In 1919 the Industrial Division was organized, taking the place of the company's Farm Implement and Tractor Division. The mission of the Industrial Division was to develop bearings for a wide variety of industrial uses, including electric motors, elevators, and printing presses.

The market for Timken bearings and steel continued to expand quickly throughout the 1920s. In 1920 the company opened the Columbus Bearing Plant, its first facility outside of Canton. The same year, a waste treatment plant was built at the Canton facility. Timken stock went on sale to the public for the first time in 1922, and the company opened an assembly plant in Canada that year. Timken bearings found their way into the railroad industry in 1923, when bearings specially designed by Timken were tested first on an inter-city streetcar running between Canton and Cleveland, and later that year in a boxcar on the Wheeling and Lake Erie Railroad. By 1926, other railroads recognized that the tapered bearings would allow the speed of their trains to increase. A large order was placed by the Chicago, Milwaukee, St. Paul & Pacific railroad for use in its high speed trains, such as the Burlington Zephyr and the Santa Fe Super Chief.

Timken began acquiring smaller companies in the mid-1920s. In 1925 the company purchased the assets of Gilliam Manufacturing Co., a Canton-based roller bearing producer. The Bock Bearing Co. of Toledo, Ohio, was acquired the following year. In 1927 Timken purchased a large interest in British Timken Ltd. from Vickers Ltd., which had been manufacturing Timken bearings and axles under license since 1909. Timken went on to acquire the remainder of the British operation in 1959. The Weldless Steel Company's Wooster, Ohio, piercing mill was purchased in 1928. 1928 also brought the creation of Societe Anonyme Francaise Timken (SAFT), a French subsidiary of British Timken. In 1929 Timken purchased a 177-acre block of land adjacent to the company's existing facilities in Canton, and opened two new plants, the Gambrinus Steel Plant and the Gambrinus Bearing Plant.

In spite of the Depression, Timken continued to grow steadily through the 1930s. During the early 1930s the company developed bearings for propeller drive-shafts, thereby expanding its customer base to include shipbuilders, including the U.S. Navy. In 1932 Timken began manufacturing removable rock bits for construction and mining equipment. The production of the rock bits provided a much needed outlet for the company's steel in the face of a badly depressed steel market. By that year, British Timken had stretched to yet another continent, opening a manufacturing subsidiary in South Africa in 1932. In 1934 William Umstattd became president of Timken, succeeding H. H. Timken, who stayed on as chairman of the board. The company's Mt. Vernon Rock Bit Plant opened the following year. When H. H. Timken died in 1940, his son, H. H. Timken, Jr., became the chairman of Timken's board of directors.

The onset of World War II provided the momentum for Timken's continued growth in the 1940s. To meet increasing wartime demand for its products, Timken opened several new facilities in Ohio during this period. In 1941, for example, the Timken Ordnance Company was built in Canton, where about 80,000 gun tubes were built over the next couple of years. The Zanesville Bearing Plant was opened in 1943. Other new locations included Columbus and Newton Falls. During the war, the company's output more than doubled its previous peak. In 1948 Timken began experimenting with automation, beginning a pilot project at a plant in Bucyrus, Ohio. The project was an instant success, and a brand new plant was built in 1950.

Meanwhile, Timken was the subject of an antitrust suit brought by the Justice Department around the same time. After several levels of appeals, the Supreme Court ruled in 1951 that Timken had conspired with its foreign affiliates (British and French Timken) in restraint of trade. The case, initiated in 1947, came about as a result of agreements between the companies regarding sales territories, price coordination, exchange of exclusive information, and other practices. The court's ruling indicated that a company must compete with other companies in which it holds a substantial interest if that company is not a legal subsidiary.

In 1954 Timken introduced the "AP" bearing, an innovation that would have a great impact on the railroad industry. The "AP" was a preassembled, prelubricated, self-contained bearing that was inexpensive and easily integrated into nearly any type of railroad car. The new bearing was credited with dramatically reducing the number of freight car set-outs. The "AP" bearing was initially produced at Timken's Columbus plant. So quickly did demand for it grow, however, that by 1958, the new Columbus Railroad Bearing Plant was opened. In 1956 the Bucyrus Distribution Center was opened. The Distribution Center was a huge warehouse, from which bearings were shipped to customers throughout the United States, as well as to the company's foreign plants. In 1958 Australia became the fourth continent on which Timken operations took place, with the opening of a bearing plant at Ballarat, Victoria. That year, SAFT was officially merged into Timken, and its name was changed to Timken France. Timken purchased the remaining shares of British Timken the following year.

Around this time, Timken began its expansion into South America. A sales subsidiary was established in Argentina in 1959. 1960 marked the opening of the Sao Paulo Bearing Plant in Brazil. That year, W. Robert Timken (another son of H. H. Timken) replaced Umstattd as company president. Timken's sales continued to grow steadily through the first half of the 1960s, climbing from $240 million in 1961 to $393 million in 1966. In 1963 production began at the company's new Colmar Plant in France. Timken Research, a sprawling research and development center located near the Akron-Canton Airport, was completed in 1966. Railroads continued to grow in importance as customers during this period. By 1968, more than 90 percent of the new freight cars being built used tapered roller bearings, and more than 60 percent of those bearings were made by Timken.

During the second half of the 1960s, Timken's sales levelled off, and net income actually shrank, from $49 million in 1966 to $29 million in 1970. The portion of this income that came from foreign sales tripled between 1967 and 1970. In 1968 a continuous casting plant was added to the company's steelmaking facilities. By 1969, the plant had a capacity of 850,000 tons. The company's Ashland Plant was opened in 1969 as well. Timken had a total of 16 plants in operation by 1971, seven of which were in Ohio. Tapered roller bearings and rock bits accounted for about 80 percent of Timken's revenue that year, with specialty steels generating the rest of the company's sales. At that time, about 35 different types of roller bearings were being produced in over 11,000 sizes at its facilities.

H. H. Timken, Jr., died in 1968, and was succeeded as chairman by his brother W. Robert Timken. The company presidency was assumed by Herbert Markley, who had joined the company as an accountant nearly 30 years earlier. In 1970 the corporation's name was officially shortened to The Timken Company. The following year, the Gaffney Bearing Plant, a highly automated facility in South Carolina, was opened. Timken was hurt in 1970 by strikes at General Motors and in the trucking industry. By 1972, however, sales were once again strong in the automotive industry, which, as a whole, was the purchaser of nearly half of the bearings sold by Timken. As a result, Timken's sales began to grow once again, reaching a company record of $470 million in 1972. In 1974 a wholly owned sales subsidiary, Nihon Timken K.K., was formed in Japan.

W. Robert Timken stepped down in 1975, and was replaced as chairman of the Board by his son, W. R. Timken, Jr. That year Timken acquired Latrobe Steel Company, a Pennsylvania-based producer of specialty steel and alloys. For 1975, Timken was able to post record sales of $804 million, in spite of a terrible year in the automobile industry. In 1978 construction was completed on the company's Canton Water Purification Plant. Timken introduced the UNIPAC bearing in 1979. These pre-lubricated and pre-adjusted bearings made assembly operations much easier for vehicle, industrial machinery, and construction equipment manufacturers. Timken also opened the Lincolnton Bearing Plant that year. The Lincolnton plant, located 50 miles north of Gaffney in North Carolina, featured such advanced automation as driverless trains that transported parts between departments. 1979 also brought about Markley's mandatory retirement as company president. He was succeeded by Joseph F. Toot, Jr., a Timken employee since 1962.

As the 1980s began, Timken was still the dominant force in the American bearing industry, controlling about 25 percent of the U.S. bearings market, and 75 percent of the market for tapered roller bearings. In 1981 the company earned $101 million on sales of $1.4 billion. The 1980s proved to be a difficult decade for Timken, however. The company reported a loss of $3 million in 1982, its first unprofitable year since the Depression. Part of the problem was the flood of cheap bearings entering the United States from Europe and Japan. Nevertheless, Timken did not stop investing in its facilities during this time. In 1983 an expansion project that doubled the size of Timken Research was completed. The company's $450 million Faircrest Steel Plant went into production in 1985. Upon the opening of the plant, which was situated not far from Canton, Timken's steelmaking capacity increased by 50 percent, to 1.5 million tons. In 1986 Timken reorganized its corporate structure, cutting costs by consolidating departments and eliminating personnel. The Rock Bit Division was sold off entirely. A new division, the Original Equipment—Bearings group was formed by combining the Industrial Division with the Automotive and Railroad Divisions. In addition, all Research and Development functions and computer operations were organized into a newly created Technology Center.

After six years of showing little or no profit, Timken rebounded in 1988, earning $65.9 million on net sales of $1.55 billion. During that year offices were opened in Italy, Korea, Singapore, and Venezuela. The following year, a 37-day strike by steelworkers prevented a significant continuation of the rally. Nevertheless, a $1 billion multi-year investment program was launched in 1989 to modernize and expand the company's plants. In 1990 Timken paid $185 million for MPB Corporation, a manufacturer of super-precision bearings (used in sensitive machinery such as aircraft, computer disk drives, and medical equipment) based in Keene, New Hampshire, with annual sales of $120 million.

Timken's sales declined slightly in both 1991 and 1992, largely due to reduced demand caused by the global recession. For 1991, the company recorded a net loss of $36 million. Through an active streamlining program, Timken was able to turn a modest profit of $4.45 million in 1992 without making any gains in sales. In April of 1993 the company announced the formation of a steel sales unit in Europe, its first such steel operation outside of the United States. Efforts to improve manufacturing efficiency and to reduce costs throughout the corporation continued. Construction began on a new bearing plant in Ashboro, North Carolina, in 1993, the same year the company began operations at a steel parts plant in Eaton, Ohio. Latrobe Steel planned to open a new facility in Franklin, Pennsylvania, in 1994.

The Timken Company is widely recognized as a well-run company that manufactures products of the highest quality. Because this status has been achieved to a large degree by a willingness to invest heavily in research and facility modernization, it seems likely that Timken will be able to fight off any challengers that might arise in its own industry. The most serious challenges that the company faces are those that arise from its dependence on the health of the many different industries whose companies integrate Timken bearings and steel into their own products.

Principal Subsidiaries: Latrobe Steel Company; MPB Corporation.

Further Reading:

Byrne, Harlan S., "Timken Co.: It Spends Big to Compete in Global Bearings Market," *Barron's,* August 6, 1990, pp. 31–32.
"From a Lost Law Fight, a $4-Million Market," *Business Week,* November 5, 1955, pp. 62–63.
"Great-Grandpa Can Smile Again," *Forbes,* May 28, 1990, pp. 226–28.
History of the Timken Company, Canton, OH: The Timken Company, 1990.
McManus, George J., "Timken Steers Its Own Course—Successfully," *Iron Age,* May 10, 1976, pp. 33–40.
"Must Affiliates Compete?," *Business Week,* April 28, 1951, p. 25.
"Recession Buying Speeds Timken's Automatic Look," *Business Week,* September 20, 1958, pp. 160–62.
"The Road Points Only Up," *Forbes,* June 1, 1968, p. 66.
Thomas, Dana L., "Rough to Smooth," *Barron's,* March 6, 1972, p. 3.
The Timken Company 1992 Annual Report, Canton, OH: The Timken Company, 1992.
"Timken Rolling at Fast Clip," *Financial World,* February 14, 1973, p. 20.
"Timken: Rolling Up Gains," *Financial World,* September 22, 1971, p. 7.
"Timken: Well-Prepared for Future Shocks," *Sales and Marketing Management,* January 17, 1977, pp. 40–42.
Weiss, Gary, "Timken's Folly?," *Barron's,* November 25, 1985, p. 13.
"Why Timken's 'Stability' Will Save Its Bottom Line," *Business Week,* May 17, 1982, pp. 107–08.

—Robert R. Jacobson

TrammellCrowCompany

Trammell Crow Company

3500 Trammell Crow Center
2001 Ross Avenue
Dallas, Texas 75201
U.S.A.
(214) 979-5100
Fax: (214) 979-6040

Private Company
Incorporated: 1948
Employees: 2400
Sales: $1.60 billion
SICs: 6500 Real Estate Services; 6512 Building Operators -
   Nonresidential; 6519 Lessors of Real Property; 6531 Real
   Estate Agencies and Services; 6711 Holding Companies

Trammell Crow Company, the largest real estate company in
the world, built its reputation by developing properties. In the
early 1990s, however, the company began specializing in real
estate services such as property and asset management, construction management, marketing, and investment advisement.
Through the inspiration of its founder, Trammell Crow, the
company has developed over 3000 projects comprising over
300 million square feet of commercial space. In addition, the
company managed over 240 million square feet of commercial
space in 1993, more than any other organization in the world.

Born in Dallas in 1914, Crow was influenced by a highly
religious and disciplined household. He and his parents, along
with his six brothers and sisters, struggled through the Great
Depression. Despite hardship, Crow emerged from his youth
with great self-confidence and what some of his colleagues
called a transparent sincerity and optimism. One of Crow's
favorite aphorisms was that people can't do much about the
hand that they are dealt in life, but there are a lot of different
ways they can play their cards. For instance, despite little formal
education, he was an avid reader and was constantly acquiring
knowledge, eventually receiving three honorary doctorates.

Crow gained valuable experience in the Navy where he managed a material procurement program during World War II. It
was here that he learned accounting and financial skills that
would serve him later as a business man. He left the Navy in
1946 and served a short stint as a grain dealer. It was during this
time that he got a taste of development by building a grain

elevator. Crow began developing real estate full-time until
1948, at the age of 33.

Crow's first significant deal was the development of warehouse
space for the Ray-O-Vac company. This opportunity launched
him into a successful industrial real estate development business that flourished in the fast-paced, post-war economy. While
Crow continued to develop warehouse space, he started branching out into retail and office developments in the 1950s. The
Hartford Insurance Building was among Crow's first office
developments.

As the real estate development environment remained lucrative
throughout the 1950s and 1960s, Crow also began to branch out
regionally. His alliances with Frank Carter and Ewell Pope,
both of Georgia, helped him to expand his warehouse development activity in Atlanta. Crow eventually became active in
retail projects in Atlanta including the Peachtree Center, which
transformed the downtown area. From Atlanta, Crow progressed into other southern states and also began experimenting
with developments in some western states.

Although Crow built a reputation for high quality development
deals and projects, one of the greatest reasons for the success of
the company was his innovative approach to personnel management. Crow believed that his associates should be his partners,
not his employees. In fact, Crow considered himself a partner
working with the other employees of his organization. Crow
envisioned himself and his associates working together, sharing
the risks and rewards of the enterprise. In appraising job applicants, Crow would try to determine if the candidate was the kind
of person that he would like to see walk into a room, or have a
beer with. Next, Crow would determine whether or not the
applicant was smart and would work hard.

Part of the partnership arrangement consisted of compensation
based mostly on performance. Partners basically functioned as
independent developers working under the Trammell Crow
umbrella. They received a negligible base salary, but received
part ownership in the projects that they developed. The organization was less of a company than it was a network of individuals. This approach, however, allowed both Crow and his partners to reap huge rewards. Many of Crow's employees became
millionaires.

By the late 1960s, the Trammell Crow Company had 7 national
offices employing a few dozen people and representing about
100 partnership arrangements. The company was beginning to
establish a significant portfolio of real estate holdings, which
was another factor that distinguished Trammell Crow from
many other developers. Rather than develop a property and sell
it, as many other companies in the industry normally did,
Trammell Crow retained ownership of many of the projects in
which he was involved, enabling him to lease the development.
This meant that Crow and his partners were continually increasing their revenue base and their assets.

Although most of his projects were in the Dallas area, by 1970
Crow had developed properties throughout many parts of the
United States. He had also ventured, with considerable success,
into residential development. At this time, however, he began
looking to other parts of the world, particularly Europe, for new
opportunities. Crow participated in several projects in Switzer-

land, Spain, Germany, Brussels, Italy, and France in the 1970s. Despite some success, the construction and development atmosphere in Europe proved too restrictive for Crow and his associates. Crow also built projects in parts of Asia, the Middle East, and Australia. As in Europe, these projects lacked the profitability available in the U.S. market. In addition to the questionable viability of foreign real estate markets, Crow began facing financial problems at home in the mid-1970s. As a result, Crow eventually abandoned most of his activities abroad so that he could concentrate on his U.S. operations.

As the development market continued to boom during much of the late 1960s and early 1970s, the Trammell Crow organization blossomed into a huge network of partnerships which developed and operated commercial real estate projects throughout much of the United States. In fact, by the mid-1970s Crow had nearly 200 employees in 15 offices representing about 600 partnership arrangements, approximately 150 of which were "in-house" partners.

Despite continued success through 1973, the petals began to fade as the American economy had begun to falter and the Crow organization became unwieldy. The energy crisis, combined with stagflation, caused a depression in the development industry. Crow's massive decentralized network of partnerships proved inadequate to deal with the new business environment.

Oblivious to the economic problems, the Crow partners continued to borrow heavily and build as long as capital existed to develop new properties. In 1973 Crow initiated $400 million worth of projects. The Crow family fortune grew to over $110 million and Trammell Crow Company assets exceeded $1.5 billion. To finance the highly leveraged operations, Crow himself signed notes totalling more than $500 million for his approximately 650 individual companies. Crow was also expanding into other ventures, including farming. Part of the reason for the apparent mismanagement was that partners in the company were unaware of what the other partners were doing, or of the overall financial condition of the organization.

By 1974 Crow, at age 60, was facing serious financial duress and negative company cash flow. In 1975 Crow had to ask his senior partners to liquidate some of their assets to help relieve some of the massive debt that was burdening the company. Financial problems, which persisted in 1975 and 1976 and nearly caused the demise of the company, prompted Crow to begin a reorganization of the company. He relied on Don Williams, his up-and-coming protégé, to assist in the formulation of a new plan that would make the Trammell Crow enterprise more like a company. The plan called for a centralized management structure to handle strategy, financial reporting, and leadership for the partners.

Though the company struggled to survive through 1976, the following year saw a rebirth of the Trammell Crow organization. The new company was separated into Trammell Crow Residential Companies (TCRC) and Trammell Crow Company (TCC), which represented commercial development. Also in 1977 Williams was named president and CEO. In the meantime Crow began to again concentrate on new developments and completed one of his premier properties in 1978, The Anatole Hotel in Dallas. This project was unique for Crow because of his immersion in the project and participation in the details of its design and construction.

Despite a severe recession in the late 1970s and early 1980s the new Crow organization emerged unscathed. While stagflation and unemployment battered most sectors of the U.S. economy, Trammell Crow interests grew. In 1976 Crow interests held assets totaling about $1 billion. By 1982, near the end of the recession, the figure had ballooned to about $3 billion.

Contrary to the early 1980s, the middle part of the decade offered one of the most lucrative and fast-paced real estate environments in U.S. history. Deregulation of lending institutions, an influx of foreign investment dollars, and new tax laws all combined to generate a massive injection of capital into the real estate industry. Despite only moderate increases in demand for new space, development of new commercial properties boomed from less than 700 million square feet in 1982 to a peak of over 1.3 billion in 1985. In that year Crow interests initiated development of over $2.2 billion worth of new properties. The organization's assets skyrocketed to over $13 billion, and by 1986 the company had 90 offices with over 3,500 employees.

While the Crow organization enjoyed massive profits and growth during the mid-1980s, it was also trying to prepare itself for an inevitable industry slowdown like the one that almost crushed the company in the 1970s. Crow hired scores of highly-educated people during the 1980s that had the skills necessary to efficiently manage the company's assets in periods of slower growth. TCC's centralized management also developed a program of identifying and selling certain properties from its portfolio in order to increase liquidity and address changing markets.

Despite efforts to prepare for a development deceleration, the company found itself ill-equipped to deal with an industry depression of a magnitude that few had anticipated. As demand for new properties plummeted in 1988, investment capital also dried up. Massively over-built markets resulted, causing the value of the Trammell Crow Companies' assets to fall as well. The value of new Crow developments fell from $2.2 billion in 1985 to less than $100 million in 1991, as the real estate industry plunged into a protracted depression. In addition, a recessed economy was causing a rise in vacancies which diminished revenues available from Crow's existing projects. For instance, office vacancy rates in Phoenix and Dallas, two of Crow's most active regions, leapt to nearly 30 percent by the early 1990s. Trammell Crow's personal net worth fell over 50 percent from its peak of $1 billion. Furthermore, the company's equity dropped from $1.7 billion in 1986 to $1.3 billion in 1988, while its liabilities rose from $5.9 billion to $7.7 billion.

The Crow organization had grown into a complex web of 1,500 partnerships, joint ventures, and corporations, causing the company to stagger under its heavy debt. Therefore, in 1989 the Trammell Crow Companies, under the increased influence of Williams, reacted to the changed environment. Anticipating a metamorphosis of the entire real estate industry, rather than a cyclical change, the company took drastic measures to avoid bankruptcy and ensure long-term profitability. After compromises with more than 150 of its lenders, Crow reorganized its partnerships. Its partners were no longer active in the building process, although they still held equity interests in some 6,500 projects valued at $9 billion, down from $11.2 billion in 1989. More than half of the 170 partners involved with the company in the late 1980s left. The company eliminated 8 of its 17 regional offices and reduced the number of employees to 2650 by the end of 1989. The company also began offering market rate salaries to its employees, abandoning its old compensation system. It was at this time that Crow, at 75 years of age, began to distance himself from the management of the company.

The shake-out at Crow resulted in several disputes over the ownership of the company assets. For instance, in 1991 TCC sued former Managing Partner Joel Peterson, who had previously been a close associate of both Crow and Williams. TCC claimed that Peterson had not absorbed his share of insolvent debts. Peterson filed a countersuit, accusing Crow and Williams of trying to grab control of TCC assets and the operating company for only pennies on the dollar.

Crow quickly abandoned real estate development as its primary activity and instead turned its attention to real estate management and services. The company sought to parlay its financial management talent, prominence in a large number of markets, and long experience in managing and marketing properties into a formidable service company. In addition to emphasizing the efficient management of the assets which it already controlled, Crow began offering various services to clients that owned and invested in real estate.

Williams organized the new Trammell Crow Company (TCC) into three entities—Regional operating companies that leased and managed Crow holdings; national services; and national operating companies, which included Trammell Crow Ventures, Trammell Crow Asset Services, and Trammell Crow Corporate Services. *Fortune* 500 corporate customers were offered a single point of contact by Trammell Crow Corporate Services for real estate management, construction, acquisition, and tenant representation services. Trammell Crow Ventures provided real estate financing, investment, and consulting services to institutions that were active in real estate. Trammell Crow Asset Services provided asset and portfolio management services for clients that managed real estate investment properties. In marketing its services to potential clients, TCC emphasized three competencies including property management, development services, and project leasing and marketing services.

As revenue from new construction remained flat in the early 1990s, income from services rose to help the organization's bottom line. In 1988 TCC's operating income from real estate services was negative $30 million, an insignificant sum in comparison to income from development activities at the time. By 1991, however, TCC had increased its income from services to over $15 million. Crow ceded its position as the largest developer in the United States, plummeting from first place in 1991 to 15th place by 1992. At the same time, however, Crow remained the largest property manager in the nation. In 1993, TCC managed over 240 million square feet of commercial space.

Part of TCC's new philosophy in the early 1990s was the concept of "seamless quality." This entailed establishing national standards of performance and offering the most comprehensive, state-of-the-art services available. As TCC began to emphasize its management operations, occupancy rates of its properties rose from 85 percent in 1989 to over 90 percent in 1990. During the same period the average industry occupancy rate fell from 80 percent to 74 percent.

Williams hoped to create an "evergreen" company which would profit in both good and bad economic times. The new company philosophy was reflected in the words of Gary Shafer, CEO of the TCC Texas region in 1991. "For 20 years, my job was to build enduring buildings," he said in Business Week, March 2, 1992. "For the next decade, I want to build enduring relationships locally and nationally."

In 1991 TCC was capitalized as a privately held corporation. In 1992, the Dallas-based company developed 2.8 million square feet of new space at a value of $209 million. Its 2,400 employees served 12,000 tenants from 70 offices in the United States, Mexico, Brazil, and the Far East. Furthermore, it managed assets covering all commercial product types, including suburban and high-rise offices, warehouses, service centers, research facilities, and retail centers.

In addition to TCC, in 1993 the Crow family owned interests in several companies that were originally affiliated with Trammell Crow Co. Some of these companies included Wyndham Hotels; Trammell Crow Residential, the nation's largest multi-family developer; and Trammell Crow International, with operations in eight foreign countries.

While TCC was relatively well positioned to compete for a significant piece of the real estate services and management pie, it was entering a highly competitive industry. Like TCC, many other former real estate developers began marketing themselves as service companies in the early 1990s. In addition to regional property management and brokerage firms, many financial institutions were also entering the market. One disadvantage that Crow faced was a conflict of interest with some potential clients. TCC had to convince other property owners to allow TCC to manage their buildings, despite the fact that Crow owned competing properties in the same city.

Principal Subsidiaries: Trammell Crow Asset Management, Trammell Crow Corporate Services.

Further Reading:

"Guess What Trammell Crow is Eating," *Business Week,* March 2, 1992.
Sobel, Robert R., *Trammell Crow, Master Builder: The Story of America's Largest Real Estate Empire,* New York: John Wiley & Sons, 1989.
"Top Developer Survey," *National Real Estate Investor,* January 1993.
"Trammell Crow Blazes a New Trail," *National Real Estate Investor,* December 1991.

—Dave Mote

Triarc Companies, Inc. (formerly DWG Corporation)

6917 Collins Ave.
Miami Beach, Florida 33141
U.S.A.
(305) 866-7771
Fax: (305) 868-3044

Public Company
Incorporated: January 23, 1929 as Deisel-Wemmer-Gilbert
   Corp.
Employees: 17,500
Sales: $995.1 million
Stock Exchanges: OTC
SICs: 2211 Broadwoven Fabric Mills—Cotton; 6794 Patent
   Owners & Lessors; 5172 Petroleum Products Nec; 6719
   Holding Companies Nec

Triarc Companies, Inc., a conglomerate with interests in various
areas such as propane, fast food, and shirt-making, was created
in 1993 as the result of a court-ordered reorganization of the
DWG Corporation. The predecessor company has a long and
unusual history; its activities were consistently overshadowed
by the daring acquisitions of its management. While these
activities led to the demise of that management group, the
companies that comprise Triarc are identical to those under
DWG. Few companies have changed so drastically during their
existence as did the DWG Corporation while still retaining the
same name.

DWG has had, essentially, two very different lives. The company was first established in 1890 as a small Ohio-based partnership. The founders of the Deisel-Wemmer Company (their
full names have disappeared into obscurity) dealt in the importation and manufacturing of cigars. Highly popular during the
early years of the twentieth century, cigars were a common
male accessory that indicated discretion, affluence, and manli-
ness. The cigar trade was a very profitable business, populated
with hundreds of specialty manufacturers.

Deisel-Wemmer was subsequently acquired by an investment
group on January 23, 1929, and changed its name to Deisel-
Wemmer-Gilbert. The new firm continued to operate as a formidable cigar manufacturer, although not on the same scale as
large tobacco companies that maintained stables of several
mass-produced brands. Unable to compete with the marketing

muscle of these large tobacco combines, the Deisel-Wemmer-
Gilbert company was forced to acquire other small competitors
simply to maintain market share. It purchased the brand and
manufacturing operations of Odin cigars in 1930 and the Bernard Schwartz Cigar Corporation in 1939. On May 15, 1946,
the company reduced its cumbersome name to a simple set of
initials, and became the DWG Cigar Corporation. The series of
acquisitions resumed in 1948, when DWG took over the Nathan
Elson Company. In 1955 DWG acquired A. Sensenbrenner &
Sons, and a year later bought out Chicago Motor Club Cigar and
Reading, Pennsylvania-based Yocum Brothers.

By this time, however, the cigar market had weakened substantially. Years of doctors' advisories about the dangers of smoking, the rise of cancer deaths among smokers, and growing
public intolerance with the socially brash habit caused many
men to quit. But perhaps most responsible for the demise of
cigar smoking was the cigarette industry. Convinced that they
should abandon cigars, many men simply switched to cigarettes, which were less obtrusive and carried a less severe health
stigma. In addition, cigarette advertising was feverish during
the 1950s and led smokers to believe that they gained status by
using brands such as Lucky Strike, Chesterfield, and Camel.

The trend toward cigarettes spelled the end for DWG's cigar
operations. Quite gradually, the company began to consider
other lines of business where its wholesale and distribution
skills could be effectively employed. In the mean time, DWG
reorganized its stagnant but still profitable tobacco operations.
The company purchased the M. Trelles company in New Orleans in 1961, and in 1963 formed a new subsidiary in Columbia
to oversee the company's South American buying and processing operations. By this time, several other cigar operations had
been wound up, and the product line was slimmed down. This
process helped to derive new efficiencies from DWG's cigar
business, but also compacted the widely varied operations into a
single unit that could be disposed of quickly and easily.

Ready to plunge into new markets, DWG began purchasing
small stakes in other businesses, including consumer products.
After an attempted takeover of the Allegheny Pepsi bottling
company failed in 1965, the New York Stock Exchange de-
listed DWG from the big board. This removed the final obstacle
that prevented DWG from a wholesale divestment of its cigar
operations. The dying business was sold in one chunk, while
some smaller assets were simply written off. The 1966 sell-off
provided DWG with millions of dollars in new acquisition
capital. In November of 1966—coincident with the company's
adoption of a new name, DWG Corporation—the hunt for new
businesses turned up an unexpected candidate. DWG purchased
a 12 percent share of the National Propane Corporation. Far
removed from the cigar business, National Propane marked a
clean break from DWG's earlier business ventures.

But it was also at this time that a new force behind DWG came
into the picture. Run for decades as a quiet company with a
typical consensus-management leadership, DWG became dominated by an institutional shareholder called Security Management Company, headed by Victor Posner. Posner began in
business at the age of 13, amassing a small pool of capital by
delivering groceries for his father. While still a teenager in the
1930s, Posner began buying run-down houses in his native Baltimore. Reportedly, he realized huge gains on his investments

by reselling the houses to economically depressed urban blacks. Aware that people could more easily afford the homes if he retained ownership of the land, Posner's Security Management Company charged buyers a small amount of rent for the land the houses sat upon. Failure to pay land rent could result in foreclosure. This practice earned Posner the unsavory reputation for being a slumlord. It was this business, however, that formed the basis for Posner's real estate operation and made him a millionaire at an early age.

In 1956, having grown weary of real estate transactions, Posner retired to Sunset Island near Miami. He spent the next ten years without engaging in commercial activity. Posner found a new hobby in 1966, when he began dabbling more actively in the stock market. Familiar with the practice of trading blocks of shares for small profits, Posner now decided to get more deeply involved in the companies he targeted. One of these companies was DWG. Having witnessed DWG's bold but slow transformation from a sleepy cigar company into a corporate raider, Posner saw huge numbers of investors abandon DWG for its failure to maintain a big board listing. From his experience in real estate, he looked upon DWG differently. Rather than seeing a shrinking company in the middle of a huge transition, he saw an undervalued firm with substantial assets.

But for Victor Posner, DWG was more than a great investment. He decided to use the company as an investment vehicle, engineering additional takeovers of other firms through DWG. In January of 1967, Posner used DWG to purchase a controlling share of Wilson Brothers, then a failing shirtmaking concern. Later that year, DWG collected an additional 77 percent of the shares of National Propane. In 1969 DWG acquired 40 percent of the Southeastern Public Service Company, a medium-size utility maintenance and storage company, and the following year increased that holding to more than 50 percent.

DWG became the controlling agent for only half of Posner's empire. He used another company, the vulcanized fiber manufacturer NVF to build up a controlling interest in Pennsylvania-based Sharon Steel Corp., one of the country's largest specialty steel manufacturers.

As Posner grew more active, company presidents across the United States feared that their daily mail would bring a dreaded schedule 13D. This Securities and Exchange Commission (SEC) filing announced that someone had acquired more than five percent of their company's shares. Posner had an unusual talent for inspiring wrath in his dealings. He was often attacked, and frequently sued, for installing himself as chairman and chief executive of companies he had taken over. With the titles came paychecks, and Posner collected reasonable compensation from each of his companies. Collectively, however, Posner was one of the highest paid executives in the country, surpassing the heads of IT&T, Exxon, General Motors, and the Ford Motor Company. Posner also employed his son and two brothers in important positions in his growing corporate empire. In addition, Posner's Security Management Company, the ultimate parent of DWG and NVF, still collected land rent from the homes he sold in Baltimore.

In 1971 the SEC sued Posner for improperly compelling the pension fund of Sharon Steel to invest in Posner properties. Some shareholders lambasted Posner at shareholder meetings and threatened to take him to court. These actions were only occasionally successful. Posner's defense was to simply point to the track record of companies he had taken over. Both DWG and Wilson had been "dead on arrival," yet Posner resuscitated them. Other successful companies such as National Propane, NVF, and Sharon Steel were only marginally profitable before Posner became involved with them. Nonetheless, Posner settled his SEC suit by agreeing not to sit on his companies' pension boards. But this did little to improve his image in the business community. Posner's usual recipe for turning companies around mirrored his strategy with Sharon Steel; after gaining control of the steelmaker in 1969, he eliminated a quarter of the salaried jobs and held whomever remained to ambitious productivity goals. Costs were reduced, and output increased.

By 1976, Posner's Security Management Company controlled 67 percent of DWG's shares. In addition, the parent company held a 44 percent share of NVF and another quasi-investment vehicle, the Pennsylvania Engineering Corporation, a steelmaking equipment manufacturer which Posner acquired in 1966. In turn, DWG held 51 percent of Southeast Public Service Company, 42 percent of Wilson Brothers and, as of 1975, 100 percent of National Propane. Posner's corporate conglomerate held few synergies—particularly within DWG. Through his other companies, Posner bought small shares of Burnup & Simms, a small utility service company, UV Industries, a smelting and mining company, and Foremost-McKesson, a large food and drug company. With these similarly undervalued companies in play, and the 13D form on each president's desk, these companies scrambled to keep Posner out of their boardrooms. Their defense strategies varied. Foremost-McKesson sought out a rival bidder and UV Industries broke up. Even in cases where the companies bought up their own shares, Posner usually emerged with a handsome profit. If he met no resistance, he ended up with yet another undervalued company to turn around.

DWG traded over the counter since it was de-listed by the New York Stock Exchange. Its share value fluctuated, nearly in the penny stock range, between one and four dollars. But for all its accessibility came volatility. The company could double its value in one year or plunge by half. Over the long run, however, businesses such as steel manufacturing and casting and DWG's storage operations were capable of operating with little additional investment beyond basic maintenance. As long as they continued operating, the combination of taxation, inadequate maintenance, and inflation had the effect of liquidating these marginally-performing assets. Posner was allegedly draining them of resources to take advantage of high depreciation on his undervalued properties.

Meanwhile, Posner continued to use DWG to acquire other companies. In 1982 the company took over the Graniteville Company, a textile manufacturer based in South Carolina. In 1984 DWG built up a 25 percent share of Axia Incorporated, and completed a deal in which its Southeastern Public Service subsidiary acquired Royal Crown Cola, the Arby's fast food restaurant chain, a Texas grapefruit grove, and numerous other small companies. Later that year, DWG added the Evans Products fiber group, and in 1985 took over the Fischbach Corp., an electrical contracting business.

This flurry of activity proved to be the undoing of Victor Posner. The acquisition spree and subsequent earnings failures placed DWG deeply in debt. On more than one occasion Posner was forced to seek a financial bailout from one of his backers, Carl H. Lindner. Their friendly relationship came to an abrupt end in 1986 when Posner received his own 13D schedule, indicating that Lindner's American Financial Corporation had acquired warrants for more than 30 percent of DWG's shares. Posner had become a victim in the takeover game. DWG was rich in assets, had steady cash flow and was undervalued. It was exactly the kind of company that Posner himself would target. But rather than exercise his warrants on the beleaguered DWG, Lindner presented Posner with a contract that capped the chairman's salary at $3 million—down from $8.4 million the previous year.

Meanwhile, Posner worked to shore up DWG's balance sheet by disposing of the Foxcroft and Enro shirt groups and the citrus operation, while a $200 million deal for Royal Crown fell through. He also had the benefit of talented outside managers, including Leonard Roberts, whom he hired to run Royal Crown after his acquisition of that company caused Arby's management to resign en masse. He had also placed Harold Kingsmore, a veteran of the Cannon and Avondale textile companies, in charge of Graniteville.

While the threat from Lindner subsided, another far more complex battle emerged. A financier that Posner had retained to pull Sharon Steel out of bankruptcy referred a possible sale of Posner's Fischbach electrical contracting unit to his lawyer, Andrew Heine. When it appeared the deal would go through, Heine suddenly backed out and launched a bid for all of DWG. Once again, Posner was on the defensive. He immediately converted his DWG options into voting shares, but was ordered not to vote them by an Ohio judge.

Heine, through his Granada Investments Company, sued Posner for failing to take his $22 per share bid for DWG seriously. Posner countersued, maintaining that the bid was without merit. In 1991 Posner lost to Heine, whose company was awarded $5.5 million for its expenses. In addition, Judge Thomas D. Lambros, noting court investigations of Posner's compensation and charges of illegal stock trading to acquire Fischbach, appointed three directors to DWG's board, with responsibility for the company's audit, compensation, and intercorporate transactions committees.

By the end of 1991, the three directors appointed by Lambros had presented Posner with a critical report on his dealings with DWG. Posner, with eight solid votes on a board of 13, adjourned meetings to discuss the report. In response, Judge Lambros converted half of Posner's share in DWG into non-voting preferred shares and compelled Posner to sell the remaining common shares. Posner, battered by years of damaging litigation, resigned his chairmanship of DWG in 1992 and walked off with $77 million from his share sales. In return, shareholders agreed to drop their long-standing lawsuits charging the 73-year old raider with plundering DWG. His shares were purchased by the Trian Group, a New York-based investment partnership led by Nelson Peltz and Peter May.

Trian, the parent company of Triangle Wire and Cable, had amassed a series of canning and packaging companies during the 1980s. They sold Triangle Industries, the parent company of American National Can, to Pechiney S.A. for $1.36 billion. This provided the necessary investment capital to purchase DWG. Trian declared that it had no plans to break up DWG or raid its operations for capital to pay down debt. Instead, with good business prospects the partners proposed only to change the name of DWG to Triarc Companies, Inc.

Peltz was named chairman and chief executive officer of Triarc while May was named president and chief operating officer. The new team appointed a series of new heads for the company's subsidiaries. John Carson was put in charge of Royal Crown, Donald Pierce took over at Arby's, Ronald Paliughi headed National Propane, and Douglas Kingsmore was promoted to the top position at Graniteville. The ouster of Victor Posner, the change in management and, perhaps most importantly, the supervision of the company's activities by Judge Lambros did a great deal to shore up DWG's balance sheet and improve share value. These provided an important base for the company as it began its transformation into Triarc.

Principal Subsidiaries: National Propane Corporation; Southeastern Public Service Company (64.9%); Graniteville Company (51%); Home Furnishing Acquisition Corp.; Citrus Acquisition Corp.; Wilson Brothers (54%).

Further Reading:

''Allegheny Pepsi Board Withdraws Approval of Merger with DWG,'' *Wall Street Journal,* July 13, 1965, p. 4.

''DWG Corp.,'' *Moody's Industrial Manual* 1992, pp. 2913–2914.

''DWG Corp.,'' *Wall Street Journal,* February 13, 1991, p. C12.

''DWG Investor Group Sees No Sale of Assets,'' *New York Times,* September 8, 1992, p. C2.

''DWG to Seek the 11% of National Propane it Doesn't Already Hold,'' *Wall Street Journal,* May 30, 1975, p. 29.

''Is Victor Posner Off His Leash?'' *Business Week,* December 30, 1991, p. 39.

''Loosening Posner's Iron Grip,'' *Business Week,* October 22, 1990, p. 104.

''The Man Who Writes His Own Paycheck,'' *Forbes,* March 15, 1974, pp. 55–58.

''Ohio Judge Prevents Posner from Voting New Block in DWG,'' *Wall Street Journal,* May 23, 1989, p. C17.

''Posner Agrees to Quit DWG,'' *New York Times,* October 5, 1992, p. D2.

''Posner Firms to up Axia Stake,'' *American Metal Market,* October 13, 1983, p. 3.

''Posner Set to Reduce DWG Stake,'' *New York Times,* September 4, 1992, p. D3.

''The Posner Touch,'' *Barron's,* November 19, 1979, pp. 4–55.

''Raider vs. Raider: Is Lindner Stalking Posner?'' *Business Week,* June 2, 1986, p. 36.

''There's Action Again in the Posner Suite,'' *Business Week,* March 29, 1976, pp. 108–114.

''Three Sparkling Turnarounds: Can This Really Be Victor Posner?'' *Business Week,* July 27, 1987, pp. 56–57.

''Victor Posner May Soon Taste His Own Medicine,'' *Business Week,* April 10, 1989, pp. 34–36.

''Wall Street Talks,'' *Business Week,* November 4, 1967 p. 130.

—John Simley

The Turner Corporation

375 Hudson St.
New York, New York 10014
U.S.A.
(212)-229-6000
Fax: (212-229-6185)

Public Company
Incorporated: 1984 as The Turner Corporation (Holding Co.)
Employees: 2,700
Sales: $3.14 billion (Total); $2.64 billion (Construction)
Stock Exchange: American Stock Exchange
SICs: 1522 Residential Construction, Nec; 1541 General
  Contractors Industrial Buildings; 1542 Nonresidential
  Construction, Nec; 7389 Business Services, Nec; 8741
  Management Services; 8742 Management Counseling
  Services

Founded in 1902 by Henry C. Turner, a devout Quaker from the eastern shore of Maryland, the Turner Corporation has grown into the leading builder in the United States. It is the largest builder of commercial, industrial, manufacturing, institutional, biotech/pharmaceutical, healthcare, retail, recreational, and government buildings, as well as multi-unit housing and interiors. This award-winning company built many of the most famous buildings in major cities around the nation, among them the John F. Kennedy Memorial Library in Dorchester near Boston, the United Nations Secretariat and Plaza in New York, the Xerox Center in Chicago, and Two Union Square in Seattle. As of mid-1993, the company had won four AGC/Motorola Build America Awards, and from 1985 to 1992 was named number one in Modern Healthcare Magazine's annual design and construction survey. The Turner Corporation has built 20 of the 100 tallest buildings in the world. Its clients are among the world's leading corporations, such as General Motors, Ford, Chrysler, United Airlines, American Airlines, General Electric, and IBM.

The company operates through more than 35 offices in the United States and abroad. It has divisions and subsidiaries located in 97 cities, 22 states, Puerto Rico, Kuwait, the United Arab Emirates, Taiwan, and Belgium. This network of offices enables Turner to function as a local facility as soon as a contract for construction is awarded. In fact, Turner is referred to as "the largest small contractor in America" because of its

system of serving as a local contractor in each community. Turner's president, Harold J. Parmalee said in 1992, "Our roots go very, very deep. We've been in New York City for 90 years, in Philadelphia for 85 years, and in Boston for 76 years. This allows our people to become active citizens of these communities and to work closely with local owners, architects, subcontractors and municipal agencies." Staff members in these offices have an intimate knowledge of local regulatory and review processes, local labor conditions, and strengths and weaknesses of subcontractors, thereby facilitating the construction process.

Another benefit of having ties in a community is that quality is enhanced. According to Chair and Chief Executive Officer Alfred T. McNeill, "People who are building their own community take greater pride in it. Our commitment to quality can be seen in the 75-story First Interstate building in Los Angeles that didn't crack in the earthquake and the Turner-built housing in Florida that remained standing after Hurricane Andrew."

Turner's success has frequently been attributed to its ability to adapt to changing market conditions and construction demands. As the demand for commercial building has declined with world's economic cycles, Turner has been quick to diversify into new markets in the social and public sectors. Thus, Turner has constructed buildings of all types as the market and demand has changed. In addition to the construction of new buildings for niche markets, the company has been involved in expansions and renovations of existing facilities, and in providing services related to construction activities. When poor economic conditions have forced other companies to reduce staff, Turner expanded its services, using its full network of staff and resources to function as a sort of one-stop construction business, providing a full range of services from designing to building to helping with financial matters.

Turner began modestly. After Henry C. Turner graduated as an engineer from Swarthmore College, he worked with the little-known Ransome system of steel-reinforced concrete. Believing that this new method would revolutionize construction, Turner and a partner, D. H. Dixon, purchased the rights to the system for $25,000 and founded Turner Construction Company. In the early 1900s, the company completed the stairways for New York's first subway stations. Industrial contracts soon followed as Turner's reputation for speed and skill grew, and the Ransome system received recognition. Turner's faith in using concrete led the company to adopt the slogan, "Turner for Concrete."

During the years that the nation was involved in World War I, the company received several defense contracts. Volume increased from $6.5 million in 1916 to $35 million in 1918. In 1919, the company received its first international contract. From 1919 to 1922, Turner expanded into new areas and built its first high-rise office building, its first hotel, and its first full-scale stadium.

During the Great Depression of the late 1920s and early 1930s, construction activity declined. Turner's volume fell drastically but the company remained in business while thousands of other contractors were forced to close their doors. Turner was able to continue operations because it shifted its focus from industrial and commercial building to other types of facilities, such as retail stores, churches, and other academic and public buildings.

During World War II, the company once again received defense contracts from the government and was involved in such building projects as a submarine base in Connecticut, Pacific Naval air bases, the Brooklyn Navy Yard Storehouse, and 93 oil tankers for the Alabama Drydock & Shipbuilding Company. During wartime, Turner also managed base facilities for the top-secret village at Oak Ridge, Tennessee, where, without the company's knowledge, the components of the first atomic bombs were being prepared. By 1941, when Henry C. Turner retired, defense work represented 81 percent of the company's business.

After the war, the country started rebuilding programs and Turner received contracts for building academic, commercial, and industrial buildings. Turner built a structure for the Coca-Cola Bottling Co. in New York and was the contractor for the Firestone Library at Princeton University. By 1951, with all this activity, company sales had reached $100 million.

In the 1960s, Turner built high-rise buildings, futuristic airline terminals, and pavilions for the World's Fair, as well as some of the nation's most well-known buildings, such as Lincoln Center, Madison Square Garden, and the U.S. Steel headquarters in Pittsburgh. By the late 1960s there were Turner buildings as far away as Hong Kong. In 1969, the company went public and by 1972 was selling shares on the American Stock Exchange.

By the 1970s, Turner had expanded its foreign offices into such countries as Iran, Pakistan, and Dubai. In the late 1970s and early 1980s, the company continued to build highly visible facilities associated with prestigious names, such as the John F. Kennedy Library in Dorchester in 1979 and the Moscone Convention Center in San Francisco in 1981.

The search for new and different types of markets was especially important during the recessionary years of the late 1980s and early 1990s when the real estate market slumped. Turner continued to expand into niche markets that reflected the scope and range of its experience. For example, in 1989 the company contracted to build a convention center in Columbus, Ohio. In 1990, the company completed the 54-story Mellon Bank Center in Philadelphia, the third tallest building in the city. In 1991, Turner completed construction of the 63-story Society Tower in Cleveland.

In 1992 alone, Turner built 125 projects, including office, retail, airport, industrial, advanced technology, healthcare, justice, residential, educational, science, and recreational facilities. Through diversification into new markets, sales in the commercial sector dwindled, representing only 17 percent of the company's total sales in 1992. Moreover, this volume was mostly for renovation and interiors rather than new construction.

In 1992, a new jointly owned company was developed by Turner and Steiner for acquiring the ongoing business of Turner International, called Turner Steiner International SA (TSI). The domestic company was to retain its responsibility for activities in Japan, North America, Central America, and the Caribbean.

Also in 1992, Turner's policy of moving into the social sector was rewarded when the company became the leading general contractor or construction manager of healthcare facilities, with sales hitting $1 billion. New projects continued to roll in, and Turner was awarded contracts to build University of Chicago Hospitals for their new Center for Advanced Medicine and two new buildings at the New England Medical Center. The company also negotiated construction management contracts at two San Jose area hospitals.

Educational projects were also showing steady growth and were 33 percent higher in 1992 than in 1991. The company was involved in new and renovated educational facilities with local school systems and large public and private colleges and universities. Also, Turner was chosen to manage the seismic upgrade addition and renovations of the Doe and Moffit libraries in San Francisco the same year.

Other projects in 1992 further demonstrated the company's commitment to diversity. Turner built new research and development facilities for companies that wanted to compete internationally. Turner entered into a contract with the biotech/pharmaceutical company Genzyme Corp. for building a quality control/quality assurance laboratory and pharmaceutical manufacturing facilities. The company was also engaged to build a new petroleum additives research facility for Ethyl Corporation. Other work progressed on pharmaceutical projects for Rhone-Poulenc Rorer, Ethicon, Ortho, and Allergan.

Some construction and management contracts for public-funded projects were also awarded in 1992. Contracts were awarded for modernizing and expanding Albany Airport, building the Cleveland Public Library, providing management services for renovations to the New Jersey State House Annex in Trenton, and building a new open-air sports complex in Cleveland.

In keeping with its pursuit of diverse roles in the construction field, Turner contracted its management services at this time as well. Some early management service contracts were made with Hewlett-Packard, the Columbus Convention Center, the University of Washington, and, in partnership with other managers, the new Walt Disney Concert Hall and 2,500-car garage.

Turner also took on the responsibility for both design and construction of a project, as clients sought to save time, money, and staff hours. The design/build projects that were developed from this strategy in 1992 included the Federal Justice Building, Atlanta City Detention Center, and a six-story parking garage at Vanderbilt University in Nashville.

As the recession of the early 1990s persisted with its resulting tight credit market that hampered new building, Turner adopted another strategy. The company took the design/build process one step further and developed the design/build/finance service. Turner assembled teams of facility users, developers, designers, and lenders in agreements that met all the needs of the people involved in the projects. The finance and development was assumed by a third party, a special purpose corporation. Turner arranged these design/build/finance contracts in 1992 with the University of Cincinnati and the Middletown Courthouse in Connecticut.

In the early 1990s, Turner continued to secure contracts with local governments, agencies, and authorities to manage long-term construction programs, such as the Los Angeles County-USC Medical Center replacement facility and the 10-year expansion project at Lambert-St. Louis International Airport.

Expansion into international markets continued as the company focused on projects in Europe, the Middle East, and the Far East as its subsidiaries and affiliates secured contracts from new and existing clients. With TSI, Turner took on several rebuilding projects in Kuwait after the Persian Gulf War, providing in particular reconstruction services for the Kuwait Sheraton Hotel. Other projects with TSI were the Abjar Hotel in Dubai, the Almulla Hospital, New Doha International Airport in Qatar, preconstruction and construction services for office towers in Sri Lanka, and a project in Brussels for Citibank Europe.

As the company looked to the future, it planned to develop more services as a way of satisfying changing client needs. Turner president Parmalee said, "Clients will seek more program management from concept to completion and more overall responsibility."

The company would continue to look for new markets as some sectors showed strength and others showed weakness. Some opportunities were expected to come from expansion in such geographical areas as the Southeast, Southwest, and upper Midwest. Other opportunities were expected to come from new fields such as seismic adaptation and high-strength concrete technology. The specific types of facilities where growth was expected were as varied as in the past, but special emphasis appeared to be in the social service areas. Construction of educational facilities and healthcare facilities in particular was expected to be strong. With its sizeable share of the healthcare market, Turner developed a division called Turner Medical Building Services Inc., located in Phoenix. Growth was also projected for publicly funded projects awarded by federal, state, and local governments for justice facilities. The company even has a division called Correctional Facilities Division located in Portland, Oregon.

Other types of building also were expected to be promising. More construction of research and development facilities was forecasted for biotech and pharmaceutical companies in the Northeast, Mid-Atlantic, and West coast. Turner also anticipates work on public/government buildings such as post offices, airports and libraries, sports and recreational facilities such as stadiums and amusement facilities, as well a future projects such as hotels, religious buildings, and residential condominiums.

Principal Subsidiaries: BFW Construction Co.; The Lathrop Co. Inc.; Service Products Buildings Inc.; Turner Caribe, Inc. (Puerto Rico); Turner International Industries Inc.; Universal Construction Co. Inc.

Further Reading:

"Concrete and Steel Unite," *ENR,* July 19, 1990, pp. 30–32.
"Constructor," New York: Turner Construction Company, 1992.
Lilly, Stephen, "City Review, Columbus, Ohio," *National Real Estate Investor,* December, 1989, pp. 140–142, 156–157.
"Turner City, 1992," *Turner Corporation Annual Report, 1992,* New York: Turner Corporation, 1992.

—Dorothy Kroll

U.S. Home Corporation

1800 West Loop South
Houston, TX 77027
P.O. Box 2863
Houston, TX 77252-2863
U.S.A.
(713) 877-2311
Fax: (713) 877-2452

Public Company
Incorporated: 1954, as Accurate Construction Co.; 1959, as
    U.S. Home and Development Corp.
Employees: 1,035
Sales: $689.90 million
Stock Exchange: New York
SICs: 1521 General Contractors Single-family Houses; 1531
    Operative Builders; 6162 Mortgage Bankers and
    Correspondents

U.S. Home Corporation is among the nation's top ten builders
of single-family homes. It also develops and sells land and
finished building sites to other builders and provides mortgage
banking services to its customers. About a third of its homes are
designed for first time buyers, a third are move-up, and a third
are retirement and vacation homes. In addition to detached
homes, U.S. Home also builds town houses, duplexes, and
condominiums, although these are a very small percentage of its
business.

The company was founded by Robert H. Winnerman in his
home state of New Jersey and was incorporated in New Jersey
as Accurate Construction Co. on April 27, 1954. The company
became U.S. Home Corporation by merger on September 1,
1959. Headquartered at Perth Amboy, New Jersey, during its
first decade the start-up company's projects were primarily
confined to that state.

Then in 1969 Winnerman began to carry out his expansion
plans after acquiring the necessary capital through a public
stock offering. In February of 1969 U.S. Home offered 315,000
common shares and $4 million convertible debentures and that
June joined the American Stock exchange. Winnerman
attracted investors by proposing to develop a nationwide homebuilding company, in what was then a geographically divided
market, which was to succeed with economies of scale.

The initial acquisition by U.S. Home was the acquisition of
Imperial Homes and Rutenberg Homes owned by Charles and
Arthur Rutenberg. Arthur Rutenberg became president of U.S.
Homes and Charles became chair of the executive and finance
committees of the board. U.S. Home began acquiring one home
builder after another and many building suppliers, such as
lumber and concrete companies as well. Winnerman offered
stock in U.S. Home to builders in exchange for turning over
their company ownership to him. By 1972, there were 23 companies under U.S. Home's control, and it had become the
nation's largest home builder, a position it would hold through
the mid-1980s.

Although Winnerman's argument, that economies of scale
would make it more profitable than its competitors, did not
prove entirely true, the company succeeded nevertheless by
being in the right place at the right time. U.S. Home's national
expansion strategy coincided with a significant growth in the
housing market. Housing starts in 1971 were the greatest in 20
years, with levels surpassing for the first time those of the post-
World War II boom.

That year shareholders voted to change the company's name
from U.S. Home and Development Corp. to U.S. Home Corp.
Five new directors were elected, and the number of common
shares was increased from five to 15 million. In the early 1970s
U.S. Home began to diversify by providing rental units, apartments, and some commercial developments.

One of the disadvantages of growing by acquisition was that the
entrepreneurs who were bought out tended to still want to make
their own decisions and did not fit well into the corporate mold.
The consequence was a high rate of turnover of chief executives, which would consistently plague U.S. Home. The first of
these executive changes involved Arthur Rutenberg, who had
been 50 percent owner of Florida-based Imperial Homes Corp.
and Rutenberg Homes, that state's largest "scattered lot"
builder. These two companies had been U.S. Home's first major
acquisition in 1969. Arthur Rutenberg subsequently became the
president of U.S. Home for a short period, while Winnerman
remained as chair. When Arthur resigned, Charles became president. Eventually, however, a power struggle developed between Charles and Winnerman, and in 1973 Winnerman was
forced to resign, his shares in the company bought out. Under
Charles Rutenberg's chairmanship headquarters were moved
from New Jersey to Clearwater, Florida.

In 1972 Rutenberg decided to purchase 3H Building Corp. of
Chicago, which, unfortunately, proved a bad buy. It lost
$200,000 on sales in its first five months under U.S. Home
ownership. As a result the new subsidiary was considerably cut
down. Losses of 3H contributed to U.S. Home's deficit of $2.98
million for 1974, not only the company's first annual loss, but
also the first quarterly downturn the company had sustained
since going public. At the same time, there were other factors
that contributed to this sudden decline from profits of $12.8
million in 1973. Most significant was the U.S. government's
freeze on subsidized housing. This adversely effected U.S.
Home's Communities Division, which built subsidized housing
in New Jersey and Pennsylvania. Other concurrent problems
included a slowdown in sales due to higher interest rates.
Industry experts said U.S. Home should have secured more

borrowing money ahead of time to forestall the ill effects of interest rate increases. Meanwhile, contributing to lower demand for new homes was the 1973 energy crisis, which prompted consumers to reconsider the commuting expenses of moving to new homes in the suburbs. To top it all off, prices of lumber and other building materials had jumped that year.

In 1977, Rutenberg left the company, having brought in Ben Harrison to serve as president. Harrison resigned in a policy dispute and was replaced as president by Guy Odom, who proceeded to double the size of the company. After Charles Rutenberg's resignation, Guy Odom also replaced him as chief executive officer. In February, 1979 the company moved its headquarters from Florida to Houston, Texas. Here again the company was well positioned to take advantage of the local housing boom, a consequence of the growth in the Texas oil industry. Soon it gained 20 percent of the Houston area market and earned nearly a third of its revenues locally, as the 1981–82 housing recession did not effect this city.

U.S. Home's strategy was to acquire land, develop its own lots, and build on speculation. U.S. Home's aggressive building policy worked well during the 1970s when a high rate of inflation encouraged property purchases as investments. The large purchases of land and its development into subdivided lots, however, made the selling of undeveloped land the main source of U.S. Home's profits for a time after 1980.

By the mid-1980s U.S. Home abandoned its strategy of trying to be in every major U.S. market and shifted to emphasizing profits. Instead of piling up debt, it sought to diversify in less capital-intensive ways. Earlier in the 1980s, it had begun seeking partners for joint-ventures in its successful retirement communities, of which it had six by 1981, primarily in Texas and Florida. In 1983 it joined the ranks of builders who were giving home buyers a special kind of mortgage insurance, which paid principal, interest, tax, and hazard insurance payments for as long as 12 months after the buyer loses his or her job. Around this time U.S. Home was the first homebuilder to use mortgage-backed bonds for financing.

In early 1983 U.S. Home went into the manufactured housing business when it acquired two firms: Brigadier Industries Corp., a manufacturer of mobile homes, for stock valued at $25.5 million, and Interstate Homes, a maker of modular homes. U.S. Home's revenues had topped the $1 billion mark for the first time in 1980. In 1983 sales peaked at $1.152 billion. This was also the year U.S. Home reached its peak in number of homes built—14,028 nationwide.

Odom had initially hoped that the mobile home business would increase marginal profits. However, the ventures ended up losing money, partially due to U.S. Home's initial lack of management experience in this field. His idea was to establish a network of dealers selling U.S. Homes mobile products exclusively. But the dealers preferred the traditional method of handling a broad line of mobile homes supplied by several manufacturers. The mobile home division reported increasing operating losses of $5 million in 1983, $9.7 million in 1984, and $15 million in 1985.

Business overall soured in 1984 when Odom erroneously predicted that interest rates would decline in the election year.

While other builders held back, U.S. Home continued to build beyond sale orders. As interest rates went up slightly, new orders dropped by 30 percent in May. By August that year U.S. Home was stuck with 1,700 completed but unsold homes.

At the same time the company was dealt an especially severe blow in its own backyard, the Houston market. The national housing recession eventually came to affect Houston, and the recovery there lagged behind. More significantly, the Texas oil boom of the 1970s was over, as the price of oil fell and the industry declined. U.S. Home meanwhile had become too dependent on the Houston market, which had accounted for 40 percent of the company's total construction in 1982 with 4,975 new homes. Yet its hold on the Houston metropolitan area had been slipping as other large homebuilders began to enter the increasingly competitive Houston market. The rental sector also emerged as tough competition as a consequence of a 1981 municipal housing law that indirectly encouraged the building of rental units.

During the period between 1983 and 1985 the company had to resort to selling more than 3,000 of its slow moving inventory of homes to the syndicator, Equity Programs Investment Corp. (EPIC). The latter in turn rented out the houses, lowering the value of the neighborhoods, which prompted some home-owning neighbors to sue U.S. Home. This particularly hurt U.S. Home's reputation, since it relied heavily on customer referrals. It sold 2,286 houses at discounts to EPIC in 1984 for a loss of $1.5 million, contributing to a net loss for 1984 of $43.9 million on total sales of $1.1 billion. Another 250 of U.S. Home's projects had to be auctioned off. The company also implemented a program of offering home sales to rental tenants for interest rates 1 percent below the going market rate and accepting the last 12 months rent as part of the purchase price.

Following losses in two straight quarters and indications of a large deficit for the year, Odom resigned in 1984. He turned over his posts of chair and chief executive officer to George Matters, who had been president since 1980. Robert Strudler then became president.

Matters proceeded to cut costs and reduced overhead by about $70 million in 1985. Losses were reduced to $9 million, although sales also declined to $922 million, bringing the company down to second place among the nation's builders. To cut losses the company trimmed operations in several states. It closed operations in markets where business was weak and cut housing and land inventories in all of its markets. It began to withdraw from Amarillo, Texas; Birmingham, Alabama; Oklahoma City and Tulsa, Oklahoma; and Seattle. Chicago operations were reduced substantially. Consolidation eliminated 14 building divisions.

Matters failed, however, to go far enough to cut costs where it was most needed: in the mobile homes division and in the depressed Houston market. Twenty-three of U.S. Home's active subdivisions in Houston were losing money that year. Financial troubles contributed to another executive shakeup. Matters resigned as CEO, replaced by Robert Strudler. Isaac Heimbinder, who had been chief financial officer, took over Strudler's post as president. Matters had been criticized for failing to respond quickly enough to declining housing demand. Strudler and

Heimbinder in turn proceeded to cut U.S. Home's Texas operations in half, reducing the number of subdivisions in which it was operating from 70 to 34. They also finally sold off the failing mobile home business.

The company immediately posted two consecutive profitable quarters and its stock went up at the end of 1986. In 1988, however, U.S. Homes ended a year profitably—for the first time since 1983—with a net income of $5 million on sales of $735 million. This reflected further progress in reducing general, administrative, and selling costs. The company continued to improve its cash flow in 1989, although profits and sales had declined even further to $1.24 million and $675.56 respectively, bringing it down to ninth place in the nation's industry. U.S. Home continued to streamline operations, deploying assets in strong markets in California, Florida, and Denver, while closing them in Albuquerque, Atlanta, and Charlotte and reducing them in Phoenix and Tucson.

Then in 1990 the housing industry entered a recession again, with the lowest level of housing starts since the early 1980s. By early 1991 home values were depressed as much as 30 percent in some areas. Other factors hurting the industry at this time included regulations affecting building suppliers of lumber and cement. Local zoning laws and building codes made housing more expensive as well. U.S. Home based its strategy, in facing these unfavorable conditions, on geographic diversity, low overhead, and low inventories, so as to better withstand the inevitable cycles of the housing industry. The company achieved the lowest number of completed unsold units in 15 years.

The national housing slump and a shortage of credit prompted U.S Home to take an $82.2 million write-off in the fourth quarter of 1990. This comprised provisions for discontinued operations, provisions relating to the disposition of excess land and housing inventories in markets where the company had reduced its operations, and litigation costs. It closed the year with an unprecedented $101.6 million loss. U.S. Home's difficulty in restructuring its debt was also representative of an overall lack of credit for the housing industry, although new house sales picked up again in early 1991.

By spring 1991 U.S Home had been unsuccessful for nearly a year in trying to get a group of 17 banks to restructure its $156 million debt, which had been renewed annually since 1973. In April it filed in a New York court for Chapter 11 bankruptcy protection from creditors. Its objective was to reorganize. At the same time U.S. Home secured $72 million of debtor-in-position financing from General Electric Capital Corp., using its unsecured projects as capital. The company was thus able to continue business as usual.

Despite remaining under bankruptcy protection, U.S. Home managed to increase sales for 1992 to $689.9 million up from $485.3. It completed 5,015 homes, up 39 percent from the previous year, which was the most it had built since 1989. Although the net loss for the year was still high at $21.35

million, this reflected reorganization charges of $50.7 million, and the company had an operating profit of $30 million.

In March 1993 U.S. Home submitted its reorganization plan, offering $165 million in new debt plus stock to settle $297 million in unsecured claims. The plan went into effect, and the company came out of bankruptcy that June upon the selling of $200 million in 10-year high-yield bonds. At the same time it gained additional working capital from another four-year loan from the GE Capital Corporation. The company also named six new directors to its 11-member board. When U.S. Home emerged from Chapter 11, all senior creditors were paid in full and shareholder value was significantly increased from shareholder value at the inception of the bankruptcy. The issuance of public debt simultaneously with the emergence from Chapter 11 is an unprecedented event. The company was able to accomplish this because of its excellent operating performance while in Chapter 11. In 1992 the company earned in excess of $29 million on a 39 percent increase in homes delivered. In 1993 the company's performance continued to improved--operating earnings for the first six months exceeded $17 million.

In mid-1993 U.S. Home was active in 26 metropolitan areas in Florida, California, Arizona, Maryland, Minnesota, New Jersey, Texas, Nevada, Virginia, and Colorado. Project sizes ranged from 50 to 1000 units, and the company was ranked the fourth-largest home builder in the country.

Principal Subsidiaries: U.S. Home Acceptance Corp.; U.S. Home Mortgage Corp.; USH II Corp.; U.S. Home Finance Corp.; U.S. Insurers, Inc.

Further Reading:

Davis, Jo Ellen, "U.S. Home Pays a Big Price for a Turnaround," *Business Week,* November 25, 1985, pp. 114–118.
Donahue, Gerry, "U.S. Home Corporation (Gearing Up for Recovery)," *Builder,* May 1992, p. 217.
Klempin, Raymond, "A Surprising Shakeup at U.S. Home," *Houston Business Journal,* May 26, 1986, p. 1.
"News of Realty: Acquisition Plan," *New York Times,* April 22, 1969, p. 74.
Oneal, Michael and Robert Block, "A Sudden Departure from U.S. Home," *Business Week,* May 26, 1986, pp. 45–46.
Somoza, Kelly F., "U.S. Home Corp. Announces Financial Results," *Business Wire (BWRE),* February 9, 1989.
"U.S. Home: A Cozy Investment?" *Business Week,* March 30, 1987, p. 74.
"U.S. Home's Big Mistake," *Business Week,* January 12, 1974, pp. 44–45.
"U.S. Home Corp.: Chapter 11 Protection Ends as Reorganization Proceeds," *Wall Street Journal,* June 22, 1993, P. B4.
"U.S. Home Files Plan of Reorganization, Posts 4th-Period Loss," *Wall Street Journal,* March 4, 1993, p. B5.
"U.S. Home's Financial Roof Is Leaking," *Business Week,* September 17, 1984, pp. 118–121.
"U.S. Home Gets Ruling on Loan," *Wall Street Journal,* May 16, 1991, p. B12.

—Heather Behn Hedden

United Dominion

United Dominion Industries Limited

Registered Office:
2829 Sherwood Heights Drive
Oakville, Ontario L6J 7R7
Canada
Corporate Headquarters:
2300 One First Union Center
301 South College Street
Charlotte, North Carolina 28202-6039
U.S.A.
(704) 347-6800
Fax: (704) 347-6900

Public Company
Incorporated: 1882 as Dominion Bridge Limited
Employees: 10,700
Sales: $1.7 billion
Stock Exchanges: Toronto New York Montreal
SICs: 3448 Prefabricated Metal Buildings; 3728 Aircraft
    Equipment, Nec

United Dominion Industries Limited provides manufacturing, engineering, and construction services throughout the world. With 53 primary locations in seven countries, the bulk of United Dominion's business is concentrated in three engineering-related markets: industrial equipment, energy, and construction. The company's businesses are organized into three segments: Industrial Products; Engineering Services; and Construction Products and Services. Industrial products manufactured by United Dominion include compaction equipment, machinery for food processing and fluid handling, and aerospace components. The company's BOMAG subsidiary is the world leader in the production and design of landfill compaction equipment. The Engineering Services segment of United Dominion's operations serves the energy market with products related to petroleum and petrochemicals. The company's Litwin group of subsidiaries is prominent in this area, particularly in the design and construction of oil refineries and petrochemical plants. The company's Construction Products and Services segment includes the Varco-Pruden business unit. Varco-Pruden specializes in the design and manufacture of pre-engineered metal buildings systems. Other United Dominion units include Cherry-Burrell Process Equipment, which controls about half the North American scraped-surface heat exchanger market; Menck, a leading manufacturer of pile-driving hammers for oil

drilling; and Ceco Doors, a group of three businesses that produce a broad range of doors for residential, commercial, and industrial use. About three-fourths of United Dominion's sales are generated in the United States and 11 percent in Canada, and the rest come primarily from Europe. The company is controlled by Canadian Pacific Limited, which owns 45.4 percent of United Dominion's common stock.

United Dominion was originally incorporated in 1882 as Dominion Bridge Company, Limited. The company was reincorporated in 1912 under the Companies Act of Canada. As the name suggests, Dominion Bridge was primarily engaged in the building of bridges, specifically the bridges that were required for the completion of the 2,600-mile Canadian transcontinental railroad. From those beginnings, the company diversified in the early part of the 20th century into more of a general engineering firm, capable of handling most types of structural steel work. By the beginning of the 1930s, Dominion Bridge had either formed or acquired several companies. Among these were the National Bridge Company of Canada, Ltd., founded in 1910; Riverside Iron Works, Ltd., of which Dominion Bridge acquired controlling interest in 1928; and Dominion Hoist & Shovel Co., a joint venture with American Hoist & Derrick Co. launched in 1931.

By 1934 all of Dominion Bridge's plants taken together had an annual capacity of 200,000 tons of bridge and structural work. In addition to steel and iron bridges, the company was producing boilers and electric and hand powered traveling cranes, among other things. The company's headquarters and main works were located at Lachine, Province of Quebec, where it had connections with important railways, including the Canadian Pacific. Branches were also operating in Ottawa, Winnipeg, and Toronto, as were fabricating plants in Vancouver, Amherst (Nova Scotia), and Calgary by this time. The company remained primarily a structural steel maker and construction outfit, with nearly all of its properties located in Canada, through the first half of the 20th century. In fact, Dominion Bridge quickly became Canada's largest steel distributor, as well as its leading structural steel company. In 1961 Dominion Bridge acquired the Runnymede Construction Co. and all of its assets. That year, the company also absorbed its former subsidiaries Manitoba Bridge and Engineering Works Ltd., which had been acquired in 1930, and Manitoba Rolling Mill Ltd. Another of the company's subsidiaries, the majority-owned Dominion Engineering Works Ltd., was sold to Canadian General Electric Co. the following year. In 1964 Dominion Bridge merged its Robb Engineering Works subsidiary into the company. Another acquisition made during the 1960s was the Crane division of Provincial Engineering Ltd, purchased in 1967.

As the 1960s drew to a close, a long-term decision was made at Dominion Bridge's executive offices to move the company, by this time based in Montreal and controlled by Algoma Steel (with 43 percent ownership), into the United States. Management determined that the company must diversify beyond the structural steel market, and at the same time escape the uncertainties associated with both the capital goods market and labor situation in Canada. Over the next several years, many of the company's Canadian holdings were sold off to raise money for the purchase of U.S. firms. This move across the border was spearheaded by Kenneth Barclay, then vice-president of finance. Barclay would become chief executive a few years later.

A ten-year plan was put into effect, the goal of which was to reach $1 billion in sales by the end of the 1970s. Dominion Bridge's first significant incursion into the United States was the 1971 acquisition of Varco-Pruden, Inc., of Pine Bluff, Arkansas, by Dominion Bridge's U.S. subsidiary, Dombrico, Inc. Varco-Pruden, which made pre-engineered metal buildings, was purchased from Fuqua Industries, Inc., and had annual sales of about $25 million.

Barclay set up shop in Hanover, New Hampshire, which served as a base of operations for Dominion Bridge's U.S. expansion program. Meanwhile, the acquisitions continued in rapid succession. In 1973 the Dombrico subsidiary purchased Priggen Steel Building Co. of Holbrook, Massachusetts. Two companies were also purchased from Microdot Inc. that year: Wiley Manufacturing Co., a maker of vehicular tunnel tubes, and Clyde Iron Works, which manufactured Whirley cranes. When he became chief executive the following year, Barclay moved to gradually relocate the company's headquarters to Hanover rather than return to the Montreal homestead. Another shopping spree took place in 1975. That year's acquisitions included Morgan Engineering Co., an industrial crane manufacturer based in Alliance, Ohio, from United Industrial Syndicate; Cherry-Burrell, a maker of processing and packaging equipment, purchased from Paxall, Inc.; the Indianapolis-based Insley Manufacturing Co.; and Chicago's DESA Industries, a maker of construction equipment, such as chain saws, power tools, and excavating machines. The purchases were once again made by the company's U.S. subsidiary, which by this time was named AMCA International Corporation. Between 1970 and 1978, Dominion Bridge purchased and absorbed a total of twelve businesses. During roughly the same period, ten major plants and properties that were no longer in the company's long-term plan were sold off, as was its $12 million interest in Canadian General Electric, to raise money for Barclay's acquisition program.

As a result of the acquisition program, Dominion Bridge's sales grew from $168 million in 1970 to $521 million by 1977. That year, Barclay added chairman of the board to his list of titles. Barclay's mentor during this period of diversification and expansion was Royal Little, who had orchestrated a similar process at Textron Inc. over a decade earlier. Little, along with his partner Lon Casler, would seek out and prime companies that Dominion Bridge considered potential acquisition targets. Another company whose agenda for growth had been guided by Little was Amtel, Inc., founded by Little after he left Textron. In 1978, Dominion Bridge acquired Amtel, a diversified steel products and energy services company, for $80 million. The purchase of Amtel, which had sales of over $250 million, was the company's most important of the decade. One-third of Dominion Bridge's $886 million in sales for 1978 was contributed by Amtel.

The company did not stop in its quest for growth after the acquisition of Amtel. In 1979, Dominion Bridge formed a subsidiary to explore business possibilities in the Far East. As the decade drew to a close, the company geared up for another major acquisition. $200 million in cash was raised through the sale of a fabricating facility in Quebec and various debt issues and offerings. Late in 1979, Dominion Bridge was narrowly beaten by Bendix in a bidding war for control of Warner and

Swasey Co., a Cleveland-based manufacturing company. By this time, Dominion Bridge was about 52 percent-owned by Canadian Pacific, mostly through that company's controlling interest in Algoma Steel.

In 1980 Dominion Bridge embarked on another ten-year plan. The sales target of the new plan was $5 billion by 1989. The first move toward the new goal was the 1980 acquisition of Koehring Company for $140 million. The purchase of Koehring, a Wisconsin-based manufacturer of construction equipment, increased Dominion Bridge's sales by about 50 percent. In the long run, however, the acquisition program of the 1980s was not the unqualified success that the 1970s version was. In 1981, Dominion Bridge changed its name to AMCA International Ltd., matching the name of its U.S. subsidiary, AMCA International Corporation, which had for several years already been the true meat of the company. AMCA's first acquisition to go bad was the 1982 purchase of Giddings & Lewis Inc., a Wisconsin machine tool company with sales of nearly $400 million. AMCA paid $310 million for Giddings, which at the time was the fifth-largest company in its industry. Although Giddings & Lewis had always been a strong performer compared to other machine tool operations, it could not escape the beating that the entire American tooling industry took in the 1980s, mainly at the hands of competitors from Germany and Asia. By 1987 AMCA was ready to write off much of its investment in Giddings, and the company was spun off to the public two years after that.

AMCA purchased Chemetron Process Equipment, Inc., a subsidiary of Allegheny International, Inc., in 1983. Chemetron, a manufacturer of food and chemical processing equipment was integrated into AMCA's Cherry-Burrell division. The following year, the company's Dominion Bridge operating unit shared a contract with a British firm for the construction of a special coal harbor in Indonesia, at the island of Sumatra's southernmost point. By 1985 AMCA had sales of $1.6 billion. But the company was losing money. Between 1983 and 1987 AMCA lost $285 million, including the write-off for Giddings & Lewis. William Holland took over as president and chief executive in 1985, with Barclay continuing as chairman. Beginning in 1986, Holland embarked on a mission to pare the company back down to its core engineering-related businesses, eliminating some of the dead weight that was holding down the company's earnings. In 1986 AMCA announced that this restructuring would result in the sale of units that accounted for about $500 million in sales, or about one-third of the company's total. Unable to find a buyer for the company's construction products business, Holland ended up closing that segment down. This resulted in a write-off that erased 20 percent of AMCA's revenue for that year. During 1986 Canadian Pacific bought out Algoma's 34.5 percent holding in AMCA, bringing its own interest in the company to just over 50 percent.

In 1987 Holland replaced Barclay as chairman. He retained his position as chief executive, and Barclay remained on as a director. For that year, AMCA reported a net loss of $188 million on sales of $974 million. The company finally returned to profitability in 1988. During that year, AMCA earned $25 million on sales of nearly $1.3 billion. The company also raised $261 million in 1988 through two offerings of common stock rights. Another important development was the reconsolidation of BOMAG, the company's West German subsidiary and world leader in landfill compaction equipment. AMCA had been trying to unload BOMAG to no avail since 1986. The failure to find a buyer for BOMAG proved fortunate, for in 1989 BOMAG's business improved significantly, bringing in $240 million in sales and a record $25 million in pre-tax profit.

Eager to shake things up after a decade of disappointments, AMCA moved its headquarters from Hanover to Charlotte, North Carolina in 1989. During that year, the company succeeded in selling to the public all of its shares in Giddings & Lewis, which had accounted for $168 million of the company's sales the year before. In 1990 the company's name was changed to United Dominion Industries. A new five-year plan was developed, whose goals included doubling the company's 1989 net income, producing at least 15 percent after-tax return on common equity, and keeping net debt at or below 30 percent of total capital. The strategy by which this was to be accomplished was to concentrate on fewer and larger businesses that were leaders in their markets, or which served a very specific market niche. For 1990 United Dominion earned $26 million on sales of $1.4 billion. That year, the company returned to acquisition mode. Among its purchases was AEP-Span, a maker and distributor of architectural metal roofing and a composite wall product for non-residential construction uses.

In 1991 United Dominion combined the operations of two of its units, Varco-Pruden and Stran (purchased in 1983), both producers of pre-engineered building systems. The Blaine Construction Company was also acquired that year. Although sales dropped off a bit to $1.35 billion for 1991, net income actually increased to $37 million. More acquisitions following at the beginning of 1992, most importantly the Robertson-Ceco Corporation, which included Ceco Door and Robertson Building Products. Bredel Exploitatie B.V., a pump manufacturer in the Netherlands, was also acquired at that time. For 1992 sales jumped to $1.7 billion, largely as a result of these acquisitions. Also contributing to the increase was Litwin Engineers & Constructors, whose sales grew by $200 million from the previous year. BOMAG also had a strong year, quadrupling its 1991 earnings figure.

In May 1992, United Dominion made an offering of 6.5 million shares of common stock. Canadian Pacific's decision not to purchase any of these shares reduced its ownership of United Dominion to 45.4 percent. Later in the year, a public offering was made of debentures exchangeable for United Dominion common stock in 1995. The exchange of all of these debentures would dilute Canadian Pacific's ownership of United Dominion to 17.5 percent, a figure that would no longer indicate "control" of the company. In 1993 the company announced a realignment of its corporate management structure. The new organization aimed to decentralize decision making and in-

crease the autonomy of each business unit within the corporation. Several senior officers were named as presidents of the company's operating units, reporting directly to Holland. Among these appointments were the following: Frank Stevenson became president of compaction equipment operations; I. B. Prude was named to head United Dominion Construction Products and Services; and John MacKay was tapped as president of United Dominion Industrial Products.

As the 1990s continued, United Dominion seemed to have regained the footing that it lost during the previous decade. By narrowing the focus of its program for growth to include the acquisition of only companies that were among the top handful in their specific markets, the chances of another Giddings & Lewis fiasco have been sharply reduced. United Dominion has managed to pull itself together during a period in which the construction industry has not been particularly strong. It would seem that a healthier situation in that industry would create an environment in which United Dominion is virtually guaranteed to thrive.

Principal Subsidiaries: Varco-Pruden; Ceco Doors; Robertson Building Products; United Dominion Construction; Dominion Bridge; Cherry-Burrell Process Equipment; Waukesha Fluid Handling; BOMAG (Germany); Fenn Manufacturing; Litwin Engineers & Constructors; Litwin S.A. (France); MENCK (Germany).

Further Reading:

Cook, James, "Crossing the Border," *Forbes,* November 15, 1977, pp. 85–88.
"Dominion Bridge Co.'s Amca Unit Increases Stake in Amtel to 96%," *Wall Street Journal,* January 6, 1978, p. 18.
"Dominion Bridge Plans Growth," *New York Times,* August 12, 1980, p. D1.
"Dominion Bridge: Poised For a Big Buy," *Business Week,* September 24, 1979, pp. 73–77.
Freeman, Alan, "AMCA Posts Loss of $178.5 Million for Fourth Quarter," *Wall Street Journal,* February 8, 1988, p. 41.
Litvak, I. A. and Maule, C. J., *The Canadian Multinationals,* Toronto: Butterworth & Co. Ltd., 1981, pp. 22, 34.
"Picking Up the Pieces at United Dominion," *Business North Carolina,* January 1991, pp. 57–59.
United Dominion 1992 Annual Report, Form 10-K, and Corporate Profile, Charlotte, North Carolina: United Dominion Industries Limited, 1993.
"Warner-Swasey Takeover Fight's Stakes Increased," *Wall Street Journal,* December 17, 1979, p. 4.
Wessel, David, "AMCA Will Shed Units Representing a Third of Sales," *Wall Street Journal,* July 22, 1986, p. 38.
Williams, Winston, "A Giddings Takeover Likely," *New York Times,* July 12, 1982, p. D1.

—Robert R. Jacobson

Upjohn

The Upjohn Company

7000 Portage Road
Kalamazoo, Michigan 49001
U.S.A.
(616) 323-4000
Fax: (616) 323-6654

Public Company
Incorporated: 1958
Employees: 18,960
Sales: $3.64 billion
Stock Exchanges: New York
SICs: 2834 Pharmaceutical Preparations; 2833 Medicinals
and Botanicals; 2830 Drugs; 0181 Ornamental Nursery
Products; 2048 Prepared Feed, Nec

Upjohn is one of the largest ethical drug manufacturers in the United States. Recognized as a world leader in developing medicines for the treatment of central nervous system diseases, disorders, and injuries, the company also manufactures an extensive line of prescription drugs used in the treatment of conditions including heart disease, cancer, and arthritis. In the last decades of the twentieth century, the company expanded into animal pharmaceuticals and vegetable and agronomic seeds. The company has research, manufacturing, sales, and distribution facilities in more than 200 locations worldwide.

Upjohn's Victorian beginnings coincided with the origin of modern pharmaceuticals. In the nineteenth century, physicians who wanted to prescribe medication for their patients were limited to two unsatisfactory choices: fluid extracts of unstable and varying potency, or drugs in pill form. Although pills were of relatively standard potency, they were so hard that they could be hammered into a board without doing damage to their coating (as one of Upjohn's early advertising gimmicks showed); often such pills did not dissolve in the stomach and were passed by the patient. In 1885 Dr. William Upjohn solved these problems and revolutionized the drug industry when he patented a tedious process for the making of a "friable" pill capable of crumbling under the pressure of an individual's thumb.

The image of Dr. Upjohn's thumb crushing a pill eventually became a trademark of the Upjohn Pill and Granule Co., founded in Kalamazoo in 1886 by Upjohn and his brother Henry. A talent for promoting its products ensured the com-

pany's steady growth through the turn of the century. By 1893 Upjohn could be seen at the Chicago World's Fair distributing souvenirs of its exhibit—an enormous bottle filled with colored pills. In 1903 the company shortened its name to The Upjohn Company. Quinine pills and "Phenolax Wafers" (the first candy laxative) were two of the early and successful products made by Upjohn. By 1924 the extremely popular wafers were bringing in $795,000 a year, or 21 percent of Upjohn's sales revenue.

From the very beginning Upjohn emphasized research and development. In 1913 the company hired its first research scientist, Dr. Frederick W. Heyl. Dr. Heyl proved to be a sound investment for Upjohn. One of his developments, Citro-carbonate, an effervescent antacid, reached sales of $1 million in 1926. Heyl was also responsible for patenting a digitalis tablet called Digitora, which is used in the treatment of heart disease, and which is still sold by Upjohn today.

William Upjohn, who was largely responsible for the firm's early research orientation as well as its entrepreneurial spirit, was an extraordinary man whose interests extended well beyond the bottom line of his company's profit sheet. An avid gardener, he grew 1,000 varieties of peonies (and even wrote a book on them) in addition to the medicinal herbs and flowers he cultivated at his country home in Augusta, Michigan. His interest in horticulture led him to donate a 17-acre park to the city of Kalamazoo and to shorten the workday at Upjohn to seven hours during the summer in order to enable employees to go home and water their lawns.

Dr. Upjohn was also dedicated to improving working conditions for his employees. In 1911 he initiated a soup lunch program; in 1915 he instituted a group life insurance and benefit program. At the time of his death he was working on the development of his farm properties in an attempt to create a type of employment insurance for the people of Kalamazoo, most of whom worked for the Upjohn Company. He served as Kalamazoo's first mayor under a commission–city manager style of government, which he had played a critical role in establishing.

The Upjohn Company's attachment to Kalamazoo has been strengthened by the fact that the company has remained largely a family affair. When William Upjohn, eulogized as "Kalamazoo's First Citizen," died in 1932, the job of running the company fell to his nephew, Dr. Lawrence N. Upjohn. In 1944 Lawrence Upjohn retired and Donald S. Gilmore became president. Gilmore, whose family owned Gilmore Brothers', a huge midwestern department store, was both the step-son and the son-in-law of William Upjohn. Ray T. Parfet, who was president of the company from 1961 until the late 1980s, also married into the family. The company has been so tightly held that until 1968 no one who was not a family member or employee of Upjohn was permitted to sit on its board of directors.

During the 1930s and 1940s, under the guidance of Lawrence Upjohn and later under Gilmore, the company expanded its research and manufacturing facilities and added twelve more research scientists. This expansion paid off when Upjohn became the first to market an adreno-cortical hormone product in 1935. During World War II Upjohn, like many other drug companies, developed a broad line of antibiotics, including penicillin and streptomycin. Upjohn was fortunate enough to be selected by the armed forces to process human serum albumin and penicillin. By 1958 Upjohn was the sixth largest manufacturer of antibiotics, with antibiotic sales of $22.6 million. Two important drugs in the antibiotic field that are produced by the company today are Lincocin, an antibiotic useful for patients who are allergic to certain other antibiotics, and Cleocin Phosphate, an injectable form of clindamycin used in the treatment of life-threatening anaerobic infections. The company also markets tetracycline, erythromycin, and erythromycin ethylsuccinate, under the names Panmycin, E-Mycin, and E-Mycin E. Another antibiotic produced by Upjohn, Trobicin, has proven useful as an alternative to penicillin in the treatment of gonorrhea.

In addition to antibiotics, Upjohn also developed a product called Gelfoam during the period of World War II. A substance made from beef bone gelatin, Gelfoam is a porous, sponge-like material which, when used during surgery, absorbs many times its volume in fluid and is itself absorbed by body tissues. Besides being valuable in surgery, Gelfoam is also useful in the treatment of hemophilia. Manufactured in a powder form that can be swallowed, Gelfoam is used to stop hemorrhaging that occurs in the digestive tract.

In 1957 the Upjohn Company introduced the first oral anti-diabetes agent, called Orinase. Many physicians and patients considered Orinase to be the greatest advancement in the treatment of adult-onset diabetes since insulin. Studies conducted in the 1970s, however, linked the drug with heart disease, and its use was subsequently discouraged by the National Institute of Health. Upjohn produced a line of oral anti-diabetes agents that included Tolinase and the more potent Micronase. In 1992 the company brought out a reformulated version of Micronase called Glynase PresTab. The oral treatment featured a patented design that patients could easily snap in two for a more precise dosage.

During the 1950s Upjohn expanded internationally, allowing it to compete with other large drug manufacturers in foreign markets and fostering further advances in research. In 1949 and 1950, Upjohn joined S. B. Penick & Co. on an expedition to Africa in search of a plant that could provide a less expensive source of cortisone than that used by Merck, who had introduced the drug. While this venture was unsuccessful, the company discovered by accident a type of mold that was capable of fermenting progesterone, the basic building block for cortisone, out of diosgenin. Upjohn was able to capitalize on its discovery by forming a partnership with a Mexican firm, Syntex, who isolated diosgenin from yams. A number of new hormones now available, including the injectable contraceptive Depo-Provera, were made possible by Upjohn's international initiatives.

Depo-Provera, which provides protection against pregnancy for about 90 days, has been marketed in over 80 foreign countries through subsidiaries around the world. Depo-Provera was also approved for the treatment of advanced uterine cancer, and a 1975 study revealed that doctors had prescribed the drug as a contraceptive for some 10,000 women in that year alone. Upjohn encountered difficulty in obtaining FDA approval for the sale of Depo-Provera as a contraceptive in the United States, largely because studies linked it to serious side effects, includ-

ing cancer. Depo-Provera Contraceptive Injection was finally approved for contraceptive use by the USFDA in 1992.

During the 1980s Upjohn continued to expand internationally, forming a new Japanese subsidiary in 1985 while selling its worldwide polymer chemical business to Dow Chemical Co. for $232 million. In 1985 foreign markets accounted for 30 percent of Upjohn's total sales. By the early 1990s, that figure had reached $1.27 billion, or over 33 percent of sales.

The 1980s also witnessed a major challenge in the market for its most lucrative drug, Motrin, which as of 1984 accounted for 40 percent of its earnings. Motrin, an anti-inflammatory agent widely prescribed in the treatment of arthritis and menstrual cramps, was introduced into the United States in 1974 when Boots Pharmaceutical Co. of Britain licensed Upjohn to sell ibuprofen (Motrin's active ingredient). In 1977, however, Boots entered the U.S. market itself, even while continuing to license Upjohn, and in 1981 began a price war by selling the drug at 20 to 30 percent less than Upjohn. By 1984 the companies had extended their battle by producing over-the-counter ibuprofen pills Nuprin and Advil. As a result of this competition, Upjohn's dominant market position eroded: by mid-1984 Boots had gained 25 percent of the market share of prescriptions for ibuprofen.

Despite these setbacks, Upjohn's financial situation during the 1980s was good, with retained earnings and dividends increasing steadily between 1979 and 1985. An important factor in Upjohn's prosperity was the success of its anti-anxiety agent, Xanax, whose sales increased 85 percent in 1985 from $82.2 million to $152.4 million. The drug had brought in over $400 million by the end of the decade, when its sales peaked. Sales revived somewhat in the early 1990s, when the FDA approved Xanax's use in the treatment of panic disorders.

Minoxidil, or Rogaine (as the drug was eventually branded) brought Upjohn much publicity in the late 1980s and early 1990s. Discovered in the mid-1960s and originally intended for the treatment of heart disease, Rogaine was found to produce unwanted hair growth in patients for whom it was prescribed. Upjohn began clinical testing for the drug's effectiveness against baldness in 1977. Although huge demand for this treatment was demonstrated even before its approval, Rogaine did not register the high sales that company executives and industry analysts predicted. When the product was introduced in 1986 patients discovered that Rogaine worked best for men whose hair was just beginning to thin. Even the successful cases, about 10 to 20 percent of the total, faced a life of two-a-day applications. In 1989, after three years of disappointing sales, Upjohn began to sidestep traditional pharmaceutical marketing strategies and go directly to the consumer with an information campaign. That year, the company became one of the world's top three pharmaceutical advertisers, primarily on the $50 million Rogaine push.

The direct campaign brought success for Rogaine (sales increased by more than one-third from 1989 to 1990), but criticism from the FDA, which disapproved of Upjohn's promotional leapfrog over physicians. In 1990 Upjohn began to market a non-prescription-strength version through barbers and hairstylists, and raised ad spending by 17.5 percent. And in

1991 the company began to invite inquiries directly from prospective clients, who would then be referred to a dermatologist or other specialist.

Upjohn's problems with Rogaine were exacerbated by a spate of adverse publicity surrounding the sleep-inducing agent Halcion. The drug was linked in the media and over 100 lawsuits to memory lapses and addiction, and its registration was suspended in 13 countries. Upjohn defended the drug, which was reinstated in two countries by 1992, and the FDA concluded that the drug was safe and effective when used within the context of its labeling. Unfortunately, the drug was scheduled to lose its United States patent in October 1993.

The patent for Micronase also expired in 1992, and three other major Upjohn products were scheduled to lose patent protection in 1993 and 1994, including Xanax and Cleocin, a cholesterol-reducing drug. In order to maintain a measure of the sales that Upjohn expected to lose to generic competitors, the company signed agreements with Geneva Pharmaceuticals, Inc., for the smaller company to market generic versions of the drugs.

Upjohn also worked to speed up its research and development process in the 1990s in order to replace the products it would lose to the generic market. The company received FDA approval of eight New Drug Applications in 1992, and its promising new drug Freedox entered Phase III trials in the United States, Canada, Europe, Australia, and Israel. The drug was among a group of steroids called lazaroids indicated for the treatment of head and spinal cord injuries. Upjohn had an Acquired Immune Deficiency Syndrome (AIDS) treatment in the works at that time as well. The company also tried to increase its presence in over-the-counter medicines with the introduction of Maximum Strength Cortaid, on the heels of FDA approval of 1 percent strength hydrocortisones for non-prescription sale. The approval was expected to increase the hydrocortisone business by at least one-fourth.

In the face of an outcry by the public and the U.S. Congress against large increases in drug prices and record-setting profits for drug companies, Upjohn guaranteed in 1992 to freeze the price of its blood pressure drug, Altace, until the turn of the twenty-first century. The company also voluntarily offered a flat rebate to Medicaid programs.

Consolidation in the ethical pharmaceutical industry in the 1990s brought speculation that Upjohn was too small to compete with its larger rivals. But Upjohn responded to the challenges of the changing global market with sizeable investments in facilities, the divestment of peripheral interests and unprofitable assets, and a small-scale restructuring.

Principal Subsidiaries: Upjohn Inter-American Corp.; Asgrow International Corp.; Asgrow Seed Company; California Health Care Services Inc.; Homemakers Licensing Corp.; Cobb, Incorporated; Centennial Collection Corp.; Asgrow Florida Co.; O's Gold Seed Co. Upjohn also has subsidiaries in the following countries: Argentina, Australia, Brazil, Belgium, Canada, Chile, Columbia, England, France, Greece, Guatemala, Indonesia, Italy, Japan, Korea, Mexico, Netherlands Antilles, Panama, Philippines, Portugal, South Africa, Spain, Sweden, Taiwan, Thailand, Venezuela, and West Germany.

Further Reading:

Begley, Ronald, "Pricing Pressure from Congress," *Chemical Week,* v. 151, August 12, 1992, 26–28.
Benoit, Ellen, "Upjohn: Rip Tide," *Financial World,* v. 158, September 5, 1989, 26–28.
Eaton, Leslie, "The Bald Truth: There's More to Upjohn Than Just Rogaine," *Barron's,* v. 69, January 16, 1989, 13, 26–27.
Hoke, Henry R., "Upjohn's Database Fuels Sales Growth," *Direct Marketing,* v. 54, April 1992, 28–30.
"Pharmacy—A Sharp Decline in Ad Pages," *Medical Marketing & Media,* v. 24, September 20, 1989.
Quickel, Stephen W., "Bald Spot: Upjohn's Hair-Raising Experience with Minoxidil," *Business Month,* v. 134, November 1989, 36–43.
Rosendahl, Iris, "First Aid Is a First-Rate Category in Drugstores," *Drug Topics,* v. 134, August 20, 1990, 77–78.
——, "Topical Hydrocortisones Get 1% Lift from FDA; Promoting First Aid: Cash in on Health-Care Image," *Drug Topics,* v. 136, February 17, 1992, 68–69.
Woodruff, David, "For Rogaine, No Miracle Cure—Yet," *Business Week,* June 4, 1990, 100.

—updated by April S. Dougal

Valassis Communications, Inc.

36111 Schoolcraft Rd.
Westwood Office Park
Livonia, Michigan 48150
U.S.A.
(313) 591-3000
Fax: (313) 591-4503

Public Company
Incorporated: March 1992
Employees: 1,100
Sales: $684.0 million
Stock Exchanges: New York
SICs: 2752 Commercial Printing—Lithographic

Valassis Communications is a relatively young corporation, but it has the distinction of having created the industry of free-standing inserts, the four-color coupon booklets distributed in newspapers. The company's coupons are added mechanically to papers throughout the week, but are carried most prominently in Sunday newspapers, where as many as a dozen separate inserts are common. The inserts appear in single or multiple folded sheets, printed in a full four-color format. As the first and largest company in the business, Valassis controls about 49 percent of the free-standing insert market. Valassis coupons are distributed to more than 54 million American households in more than 370 different newspapers.

The company has its origin in 1969, when George Valassis opened a small sales agency in his home in suburban Detroit. He handled contract printing for numerous products, including computerized form letters. After purchasing his own printing press in 1971, however, he found it difficult to keep the machine in operation due to a lack of business.

In 1972, Valassis decided to solicit coupon advertising from a variety of retail product companies. After locating merchandisers that wished to promote their products with cents-off coupons, he then printed the coupons and purchased distribution arrangements with local newspaper publishers that would insert the coupon sheets in their newspapers. The business proved to be highly successful, as product manufacturers discovered the advantages of cooperative coupon advertising. The inserts were effective at enticing consumers to try virtually any product and, unlike advertising, their influence on buying patterns was highly measurable.

The inserts developed by Valassis were free-standing sheets containing bold four-color promotions. Because each sheet could be divided into eight, ten, 16, and even 24 or more different coupons, each a small advertisement, Valassis could piggyback several different company's promotions on the same printing. This created a need to carefully assign coupon spots, since competing colas or brands of raisin bran, for example, could not be satisfactorily run on the same page. Valassis's solution was to encourage large manufacturers to purchase several coupon spots at once. These companies would place coupons for several nonrelated products, from breakfast cereal to cleanser, thereby creating demand for additional sheets from competitors.

Valassis immediately won business from companies such as General Foods, Procter & Gamble, General Mills, Nabisco, and Kellogg, but, still unable to purchase newspaper distribution rights on an efficient scale, the company lost money for several years as it pioneered a path in the new industry. Undeterred, George Valassis purchased additional printing machinery and increased his sales and production staff to 46 employees. By 1974, circulation of his free-standing inserts had grown to 25 million households on sales of $5.7 million. Finally, in 1976, with virtually the same circulation, sales rose to $11.8 million, nearly double the 1974 circulation. This confirmed to Valassis that manufacturers placed a high value on coupon advertising, and encouraged him to continue efforts to expand the business.

He began replacing his older equipment with newer, state-of-the-art machinery that featured added functionality. This included large, eight-page inserts and an oversize "super page." And, to house the operation, Valassis purchased a new production facility at Livonia, in west suburban Detroit. With sales growth at nearly 40 percent per year, Valassis marked sales of $23.5 million on a circulation of 27.8 million in 1978, and $33.7 million in sales on a circulation of 30 million a year later.

The company's employee roll grew to 193 people in 1979, and additions to staff included a young marketing manager from Procter & Gamble named Dave Brandon. Brandon, who played football at the University of Michigan, found employment at Procter & Gamble after graduation through a recommendation from coach Bo Schembechler. Brandon remained in touch with a former teammate, Larry Johnson, who joined Valassis after marrying George Valassis's daughter. Brandon brought to Valassis a powerful personal style. Although he began in the company performing some low priority jobs, his potential was quickly appreciated. As he ascended to higher levels of management, he developed an open, folksy style within the company, giving personal attention to the human, as well as the business, aspects of Valassis. This atmosphere later won Valassis inclusion in a publication that identifies the best 100 companies for which to work. One component of that atmosphere is an across-the-board employee profit sharing plan that can augment annual salaries by as much as 15 percent.

By 1982 circulation had grown to 38 million—50 percent more than in 1977—and sales had increased to more than $90 million, representing a five-fold increase over the period. This expansion led Valassis to build a second plant at Durham, North Carolina, in 1983, which would enable the company to more easily distribute its materials in southeastern markets. The following year, a third plant was established in Wichita, Kansas.

With the expansion of printing capacity, Valassis's sales more than doubled in 1984, to $200 million. Now in a position to consolidate its market, Valassis bought out its largest competitor, Newspaper Co-op Couponing (NCC). In an effort to streamline operations, Valassis dissolved NCC's free-standing insert operation, and added two new printed promotional products to the operation. Nearing saturation of the free-standing insert business, largely as a result of good expansion and a rise of upstart competitors, Valassis began run-of-press advertising, in which coupon space is reserved on pages of the newspaper itself. The primary market for run-of-press coupons was the typical weekly food section of daily newspapers, again featuring cents-off coupons for a variety of products.

A second extension was specialty printing, including production of brochures, catalogs, posters, and magazine inserts that concentrated on food service and fast-food promotions. More sophisticated specialty printing included scratch and sniff and lottery-style rub-off contests. Primary customers included Pizza Hut, Arby's, McDonald's, and Lens Crafters.

Run-of-press and specialty printing were aggressively promoted as complements to the standard free-standing insert promotion. The success of the formula also propelled Valassis into a new function, that of promotional consultant. Now advertisers could retain Valassis much as they did ad agencies or public relations firms, and receive advice on specific campaigns.

The consolidation of NCC also made Valassis an attractive takeover target. With an extremely strong record of sales growth and a favorable position in a market that included competition only from much smaller companies that lacked the finances of a larger operation, Valassis was discovered by Kerry Packer, chair of Consolidated Press Holdings, an Australian publishing conglomerate. The Australian publishing industry, dominated by a handful of media barons, had been exhausted of virtually all its independents. With few investment opportunities in Australia, Packer and other barons such as Rupert Murdoch and Robert Holmes à Court began shopping for deals in the American and British markets. The acquisition of Valassis in 1986 represented an unusual departure for Packer, who had confined his takeovers mostly to magazines and other periodicals. Rupert Murdoch's company, News Corp, was evidently on the same track as Packer. Valassis's principal competitor in the free-standing insert market in the early 1990s was News America, a subsidiary of New Corp.

After the takeover by Consolidated Press Holdings, George Valassis left the company for retirement. His company, however, benefited from numerous press arrangements made possible by its association with Packer. Sales increased by nearly

$100 million by 1987, to $381 million. Packer placed David Brandon in charge of Valassis. The arrangement, in which Packer maintained a hands-off approach from 12,000 miles away, suited Brandon well. He maintained his folksy style, insisting on personally meeting each new hire. But with the added responsibility came larger compensation. When the private Mr. Brandon's million-dollar-plus salary became known, his relationship with employees suffered somewhat.

Brandon kept Valassis on track and ensured that all sales and growth targets were met. For the most part, this kept Packer content and in Australia, but by 1992, Packer decided the time was ripe to reap the benefit of his investment in Valassis. In March of that year, he engineered the sale of 51 percent of the company's shares to the public. More than 22 million shares were issued through the New York Stock Exchange, yielding Packer's Consolidated Press Holdings a profit of about $900 million. The company continued to trade publicly, but was dominated by Consolidated's 49 percent interest.

Meanwhile, Valassis's business continued to expand. Because more than three-quarters of American households used coupons, they were proven sales aids. In Brandon's words, Valassis's coupon business is analogous to printing money. "We bring it to your home and lay it on your doorstep and say 'use whatever you will.' " But manufacturers' customers are always retailers, rather than consumers. Retail grocery stores stock, on average, 18,000 items, all of which compete for shelf space. As the coupons drive up consumer demand for a product, retailers are "pushed" into distributing—and giving favorable shelf display—to that product.

In the early 1990s, Valassis remained the pioneer and leader in its field, printing more than 2.5 billion inserts annually at its three facilities in Livonia, Durham, and Wichita. In addition to providing coupon and other promotional printing, Valassis offered a range of value-added services in the marketing area, including promotion consulting, design services, sweepstakes planning, and industry research. Valassis was also one of the nation's largest purchasers of newspaper space, maintaining its dominant position in the market through long-standing relationships with publishers, who frequently grant volume discounts.

Further Reading:

History Fact Sheet, Livonia, MI: Valassis Communications, Inc.
Markiewicz, David A., "Clip Job," *The Detroit News,* March 14, 1993.
"Valassis Communications," *The 100 Best Companies to Work for in America,* 1992.
Valassis Communications, Inc. Annual Report, Livonia, MI: Valassis Communications, Inc., 1992
Valassis Communications, Inc.: Leading the Way, Livonia, MI: Valassis Communications, Inc.

—John Simley

The Valspar Corporation

1101 Third Street South
Minneapolis, Minnesota 55415
U.S.A.
(612) 332-7371
Fax: (612) 375-7723

Public Company
Incorporated: 1832 as Valentine and Company
Employees: 2,482
Sales: $683.48 million
Stock Exchanges: AMEX
SICs: 2821 Plastics Materials and Resins; 2851 Paints and
   Allied Products

The Valspar Corporation is the fifth-largest North American manufacturer of paints and coatings, a business it has engaged in for more than 185 years. Its sterling reputation was built on the Valspar varnish, which was unveiled in 1906 as the first coating for wood that retained its clear finish when exposed to water. Nonetheless, until formative mergers with Rockcote Paint Company in 1960 and Minnesota Paints in 1970, Valspar was a relatively small manufacturer with limited possibilities for growth. During the past three decades, however, it has risen to Fortune 500 status and Wall Street favor through an aggressive acquisition campaign in which dozens of smaller paint companies have entered the Valspar fold.

The company is divided into four large business segments— Consumer, Packaging Coatings, Industrial Coatings, and Special Products—that are roughly equal in size. Perhaps its greatest potential lies in packaging coatings for the food and beverage industry, a business it dramatically embraced in 1984 with the $100-million purchase of Mobil Corporation's coatings division; Valspar currently ranks as a leader in this industry, for more than half of all beverage and food containers in the United States feature inner coatings made by Valspar. The company operates 21 manufacturing plants in the United States and Canada, has licensing arrangements throughout the world, and markets such consumer brands as Colony, Magicolor, Valspar, and Enterprise as well as private-label products for Target, Our Own Hardware, and Coast-to-Coast stores.

In 1820 two businessmen in Cambridge, Massachusetts, began the first commercial production of varnishes in the United States, a business that was to become Valspar's forte for more

than a century. Fourteen years earlier, on Boston's Broad Street, Samuel Tuck opened a paint dealership that led directly to the formation of Valspar. Tuck's business, Paint and Color, changed names and hands several times during the next 50 years. With Augustine Stimson's assumption of the Broad Street business and Lawson Valentine's incorporation of Boston varnish manufacturer Valentine and Company in 1832, the formation of Valspar was made possible. These two businesses soon merged to become Stimson & Valentine. In 1855 Otis Merriam joined Stimson & Valentine as the other principal owner; Merriam, interestingly, had for the previous six years been associated with the original varnish plant in Cambridge. Although popularly known as "Varnish Manufacturers," these men also conducted an import and retail trade in paints, oils, glass, and beeswax. Around 1860 Valentine's brother, Henry, joined the firm. By 1866, both Stimson and Merriam had retired and left the Valentine brothers the sole partners in the business, which was then renamed Valentine & Company.

Shortly thereafter, Lawson Valentine made a singularly important decision: he hired a chemist at a time when there were fewer than 100 such specialists in the country; this was a first for the American varnish industry. More important than the creation of the position, however, was the candidate selected for the job. That person was Charles Homer, brother of famed New England artist Winslow Homer and an expert craftsman in the mixing of varnishes. According to the *Valspar History,* he "made varnishes so perfect they could be poured from the can to the back or side of a carriage.... Varnishes that flow out smoothly and evenly, dry perfectly." Following Lawson's relocation of the business to New York City in 1870, the same year in which the firm acquired Minnesota Linseed Oil Co., Valentine & Company began to specialize in vehicle finishing varnishes that were competitive with widely prized English varnishes. At the time, the company operated a West Coast office with Whittier, Fuller & Company (later renamed W. P. Fuller & Company) as its representative. In 1878 Valentine & Company entered the Midwest market via a Chicago branch office. Four years later Henry Valentine succeeded his brother as president and the company renewed its Boston ties by reopening a plant there. By the turn of the century, Valentine & Company had established additional operations in Pennsylvania as well as Paris, and had won dozens of international medals for its high-quality varnishes.

Lawson Valentine's grandson, L. Valentine Pulsifer, joined the company in 1903 after receiving his degree in chemistry from Harvard University. Working under Homer, Pulsifer was allowed to conduct experiments to discover why varnishes always turned white when exposed to water. From Homer's standpoint, the experiments would be edifying, though not otherwise profitable; however, Pulsifer believed that the formula for a clear varnish existed—it simply had yet to be discovered. Three years later Pulsifer produced Valspar, the first clear varnish ever; factory production began within two years, accompanied by promotional stunts designed to highlight the product's unique features. The first such exhibition involved a boiling water test at the Grand Rapids Furniture Show in 1908. The following year, at the New York Motor Boat Show, Valspar and eight of the best competing brands were applied to a submarine in alternating stripes; the vessel was then submerged and "gradually took on the appearance of a sea-going zebra, as the other varnishes whitened and Valspar remained clear.''

For the next few decades the company rode on the coattails of Valspar, supported by a strong national advertising campaign during the 1920s that made the product a household word with the tagline ''the varnish that won't turn white.'' Pulsifer's invention, by virtue of its unparalleled appearance, durability, and ease of application, became a willing participant in a number of historic events. These included Admiral Robert Peary's expedition to the North Pole in 1909, U.S. involvement in World War I, and Charles Lindbergh's nonstop solo flight from New York to Paris in 1927; in each of these cases, Valspar finishes were employed as a protective coating on exposed wood surfaces. The varnishing of airplanes, in particular, became synonymous with Valspar during this period. The unveiling of new products and the acquisition of other paint and varnish manufacturers helped Valentine & Company successfully weather the Great Depression. Among the new products were Super Valspar, Four-Hour Valspar, Val-Oil Clear, Valenite Clear, Valenite Enamels, Three V Floor Varnish, and French Formula Enamel; and among the acquired paint and varnish manufacturers were Con-Ferro Paint and Varnish Company and Detroit-Graphite Company (both acquired in 1930) and Edward Smith & Company (acquired in 1938).

Prior to the stock market crash, in 1927 the seed for another important predecessor to the Valspar Corporation was planted. It was in this year that Ralph J. Baudhuin entered the paint business as a salesman. Within a short time, he helped found the Baudhuin-Anderson Company in Rockford, Illinois. In 1932, the same year that Valentine & Company began to operate as a subsidiary of the newly formed Valspar Corporation, Baudhuin-Anderson became Rockford Paint Manufacturing Company. Four years later, after Ralph Baudhuin had gained sole ownership of the Illinois firm, Rockford Paint was renamed Rockcote Paint Company. During the 1950s Rockcote formed two important subsidiaries. The first, Color Corporation of America, was created to license and sell color systems and related equipment to paint manufacturers; the second, Midwest Synthetics, was formed to develop synthetic resins and resin-based varnishes. Like Valspar, Rockcote also grew by steady acquisitions during this period. By 1958, Baudhuin had taken special notice of Valspar; two years later, he succeeded in merging Rockcote with the old-line firm, then headquartered in Ardmore, Pennsylvania, and consolidated headquarters in Rockford.

Under the direction of the Baudhuin brothers, Ralph and F. J., the 1960s represented a heavy period of growth for Valspar. From the time of the merger until the end of the decade, the company averaged almost two acquisitions per year. Among the businesses purchased were Norco Plastics of Milwaukee, McMurtry Manufacturing of Denver, Keystone Paint and Varnish of Brooklyn, and the Trade Sales Division of Mobil Corporation. Fittingly, the company inaugurated the 1970s with even more phenomenal growth, this time through a historic merger. In June of 1970, privately held Minnesota Paints of Minneapolis, with annual sales of $24 million, merged with Valspar, with annual sales of $27 million. The deal came at a propitious time, for the old Valspar had suffered a loss of $148,500 while Minnesota Paints had posted a gain of $200,000. Furthermore, Minnesota Paints boasted a strong, cash-heavy financial position to support further acquisitions. In the first fiscal year following the merger, earnings were $226,000 on revenues of $47.6 million. Within two years, Valspar's earnings had grown to $1.53 million and it was again ready to expand. The consecutive acquisitions of Phelan Faust Paint, Speed-O-Lac Chemical, Conchemco's Detroit Chemical Coatings, Elliott Paint and Varnish, and Conchemco's Coatings Division increased initial annual revenues by another $74 million during the decade.

Overseeing much of this expansion was C. Angus Wurtele, former president of Minnesota Paints and chairman of Valspar since 1973. At the time of Wurtele's succession approximately 60 percent of Valspar's sales came from its consumer business; the remainder came from industrial coatings. This alignment changed dramatically in the 1980s following the purchase of Mobil's chemical coatings business. Among those setting the stage for this acquisition, unprecedented both in size and nature, was Mike Meyers, who reported in June of 1984 that ''in the last 10 years Valspar's net profits have soared 13-fold, while sales have tripled. However, its formula for prosperity may be about to face a severe test, when Valspar in August is expected to complete the most ambitious acquisition in its history.'' For Valspar the test was unusually challenging, but not severe.

In effect, the company more than doubled in size through a bargain purchase: 1983 revenues for Valspar were $161 million while revenues for the Mobil division were around $180 million. Valspar's profit margin, at six percent, had been leading the industry, while Mobil's coatings margin lagged at just three percent. When Wurtele was asked by Meyers why Mobil was willing to sell, he responded that the Mobil division represented ''less than half of 1 percent of the total corporation.'' In others words, Mobil, with such a minute investment, could well afford to let the business go and Valspar, with such an established track record in the industry, could ill afford to pass it by. Virtually overnight, the deal elevated Valspar from the tenth- to the fifth-largest coatings company in North America. In addition, it gave the manufacturer ready access to potentially high-margin markets, including packaging coatings and industrial metal finishes, which it had previously been unable to capitalize on. By 1986, Valspar had successfully integrated the Mobil operations, thereby proving its adeptness at acquiring even the largest paint and chemical plants and instituting means for improving efficiency and profitability. The buy-low, raise-efficiency strategy has remained particularly effective for the company, for the tactic tends to postpone costly new construction and allow for a greater investment in research and development.

To achieve its standing objective of remaining among the top three participants within any of the markets it seeks, Valspar has prudently divested itself of plants and businesses in recent years. Yet, for much the same reason, Valspar acquisitions still continue apace. In July of 1989 The McCloskey Corporation, with $42 million in sales, was acquired. The purchase was especially significant for the growth of Valspar's resin business, conducted through its McWhorter Inc. subsidiary. In October of 1990 the company acquired certain assets of DeSoto, Inc., which had combined revenues of approximately $45 million. This purchase strengthened the company's market-leading packaging coatings group, and elevated it to a leader in coil and extrusion coatings for the construction industry.

Following the much smaller purchases of container coatings and powder coatings businesses, Valspar acquired Hi-Tek Polymers, Inc., from Rhône Poulenc in May of 1991. The Hi-Tek purchase was among the key factors in Valspar's 18 percent increase in packaging coatings sales for 1992. During that year, the company spent a record $19.6 million on such capital improvements as a new resin manufacturing plant, a new consumer coatings research facility, and various capacity enhancements. In addition, nearly $25 million was spent on research and development and quality process training. In May of 1993 the company announced a definitive agreement to acquire Cargill's Resin Products Division, which had $190 million in revenues for the year ended May 31, 1992. By contrast, Valspar's resin sales then ranged somewhere between $60 to $85 million. According to Susan E. Peterson in the *Star Tribune,* this latest deal "means that Valspar would move up to a solid No. 2 in the resin industry, behind Reichhold Chemicals, a subsidiary of a Japanese firm." If track records mean anything, Valspar should continue to outperform most of its competitors during the remainder of the decade, despite rising materials costs and other potential setbacks. Recurrent market share gains, steady return on equity of 20 percent, compounded stock appreciation over 10 years of 33 percent, and 15 consecutive years of dividend increases all point to Valspar's preeminence as a perennially exciting company in a longstanding and often overlooked industry.

Principal Subsidiaries: Color Corporation of America; Conco Paint Company (50%); Enterprise Companies; McClosky Corporation; McWhorter Inc.; Valspar Inc. (Canada).

Further Reading:

Autry, Ret, "Valspar," *Fortune,* July 16, 1990, p. 75.
Byrne, Harlan S., "Valspar Corp.: A Paint Maker Makes Headway Against Rising Material Prices," *Barron's,* May 8, 1989, pp. 57–58.
Cahill, William, "Fresh Coat: Industrial Business Is New Focus for Valspar," *Barron's,* August 4, 1986, pp. 39–40.
Carlson, Scott, "Smart Acquisitions Brush Up Valspar," *Pioneer Press and Dispatch,* July 17, 1989.
Feyder, Susan, "Valspar Earnings Paint Pretty Picture," *Star Tribune,* February 19, 1990, pp. 1D, 6D.
Meyers, Mike, "Valspar Formula Facing Its Biggest Test," *Minneapolis Star and Tribune,* June 18, 1984, pp. 1M, 4M.
160 Years of Valspar History: 1806–1966, Minneapolis: Valspar Corporation, 1966.
Peterson, Susan E., "Valspar Announces Plan to Buy Cargill Division," *Star Tribune,* May 21, 1993, p. 3D.
"Valspar Winds Up Last Steps to Consolidate Operations," *Corporate Report Minnesota,* April 1973, p. 11.
Walden, Gene, "Valspar Corp.," *The 100 Best Stocks to Own in America,* second edition, Chicago: Dearborn Financial Publishing, 1991.

—Jay P. Pederson

WAL·MART ®
ALWAYS THE LOW PRICE
ON THE BRANDS YOU TRUST.
Always.℠

Wal-Mart Stores, Inc.

702 Southwest 8th Street
Bentonville, Arkansas 72716
U.S.A.
(501) 273-4000
Fax: (501) 273-8650

Public Company
Incorporated: 1969
Employees: 434,000
Sales: $55.48 billion
Stock Exchanges: New York Pacific
SICs: 5331 Variety Stores; 5311 Department Stores

Wal-Mart Stores, Inc., is a national discount department store chain operating primarily in small towns throughout the United States. In 1993 the company had more than 1,900 stores in 45 states and Puerto Rico. Its founder, Samuel Walton, was among the richest people in the United States at his death in 1992.

Walton graduated from the University of Missouri in 1940 with a degree in economics and became a management trainee with J. C. Penney Company. After two years he went into the army. Upon returning to civilian life three years later, he used his savings and a loan to open a Ben Franklin variety store in Newport, Arkansas. In 1950 he lost his lease, moved to Bentonville, Arkansas, and opened another store. By the late 1950s, Sam and his brother J. L. (Bud) Walton owned nine Ben Franklin franchises.

In the early 1960s Sam Walton took what he had learned from studying mass-merchandising techniques around the country and began to make his mark in the retail market. He decided that small-town populations would welcome, and make profitable, large discount shopping stores. He approached the Ben Franklin franchise owners with his proposal to slash prices significantly and operate at a high volume, but they were not willing to let him reduce merchandise as low as he insisted it had to go. The Walton brothers decided to go into that market themselves and opened their first Wal-Mart Discount City in Rogers, Arkansas, in 1962. The brothers typically opened their department-sized stores in towns with populations of 5,000 to 25,000, and the stores tended to draw from a large radius. "We discovered people would drive to a good concept," Walton said in *Financial World* on April 4, 1989.

Wal-Mart's "good concept" involved huge stores offering customers a wide variety of name-brand goods at deep discounts that were part of an everyday-low-prices strategy. Walton was able to keep prices low and still turn a profit through sales volume and an uncommon marketing strategy. Wal-Mart's advertising costs generally came to one-third that of other discount chains; most competitors were putting on sales and running from 50 to 100 advertising circulars per year, but Wal-Mart kept its prices low and only ran 12 promotions a year.

By the end of the 1960s the brothers had opened 18 Wal-Mart stores and owned 15 Ben Franklin franchises throughout Arkansas, Missouri, Kansas, and Oklahoma. These ventures became incorporated as Wal-Mart Stores, Inc., in October 1969.

The 1970s held many milestones for the company. Early in the decade, Walton implemented his warehouse distribution strategy. The company built its own warehouses so it could buy in volume and store the merchandise, then proceeded to build stores throughout 200-square-mile areas around the distribution points. This cut Wal-Mart's costs and gave it more control over operations. It meant that merchandise could be restocked as quickly as it sold, and that advertising was specific to smaller regions and cost less to distribute.

Wal-Mart went public in 1970, initially trading over the counter; in 1972 the company was listed on the New York Stock Exchange. By 1976 the Waltons phased out their Ben Franklin stores so the company could put all of its expansion efforts into the Wal-Mart stores. In 1977 the company made its first significant acquisition when it bought 16 Mohr-Value in Missouri and Illinois. Also in 1977, based on data from the previous five years, *Forbes* ranked the nation's discount and variety stores, and Wal-Mart ranked first in return on equity, return on capital, sales growth, and earnings growth.

In 1978 Wal-Mart began operating its own pharmacy, auto service center, and jewelry divisions, and acquired Hutchenson Shoe Company, a shoe-department lease operation. By 1979 there were 276 Wal-Mart stores in 11 states. Sales had gone from $44 million in 1970 to $1.25 billion in 1979.

Wal-Mart sales growth continued into the 1980s. In 1983 the company opened its first three Sam's Wholesale Clubs and began its expansion into bigger-city markets. Business at the 100,000-square-foot cash-and-carry discount membership warehouses proved to be good; the company had 148 such clubs in 1991, by which time the name had been shortened to Sam's Clubs.

The company continued to grow by leaps and bounds. In 1987 Wal-Mart acquired 18 Supersaver Wholesale Clubs, which became Sam's Clubs. The most significant event of that year, and perhaps the decade, was the opening of Wal-Mart's newest merchandising concept—taken from one originated by a French entrepreneur—that Walton called Hypermart USA. Hypermart USA stores combine a grocery store, a general merchandise market, and services such as restaurants, banking, shoe shines, and videotape rentals in a space that covers more area than six football fields. Prices are reduced as much as 40% below full retail level, and sales volume averages $1 million per week, compared to $200,000 for a conventional-sized discount store.

Dubbed "malls without walls," there were four of these facilities in the United States in 1991.

Making customers at home in such a large-scale shopping facility required inventiveness. The Dallas store had phone hot-lines installed in the aisles for customers needing directions. Hypermart floors are made of a rubbery surface for ease in walking, and the stores offer electric shopping carts for the disabled. To entertain children, there is a playroom filled with plastic balls—an idea taken from the Swedish furniture retailer Ikea.

There have also been wrinkles to work out. Costs for air conditioning and heating the gigantic spaces have been higher than expected. Traffic congestion and parking nightmares have proven a drawback. Customers also have complained that the grocery section is not as well-stocked or maintained as it needs to be to compete against nearby grocery stores. Wal-Mart has tried addressing these problems by, for example, redesigning the grocery section of the Arlington, Texas, store. Wal-Mart has also opened five smaller "supercenters"—averaging around 150,000 square feet—featuring a large selection of merchandise and offering better-stocked grocery sections, without the outside services such as restaurants or video stores.

Wal-Mart has received some criticism for its buying practices. For example, according to *Fortune* (January 30, 1989), sales representatives are given this treatment: "Once you are ushered into one of the spartan little buyer's rooms, expect a steely eye across the table and be prepared to cut your price." Wal-Mart has been known not only for setting the tone with its vendors for buying and selling, but often for only dealing directly with the vendor, bypassing sales representatives. In 1987, 100,000 independent manufacturers representatives initiated a public information campaign to fight Wal-Mart's effort to remove them from the selling process, claiming that their elimination jeopardized a manufacturer's right to choose how it sells its products.

Meanwhile, Wal-Mart's revenues kept going up, and the company has moved into new territory. Wal-Mart enjoyed a 12-year streak of 35% annual profit growth through 1987. In 1988 the company operated in 24 states—concentrated in the Midwest and South—1,182 stores, 90 wholesale clubs, and 2 hypermarts. President and chief executive officer David D. Glass, who had been with the company since 1976, was a key player in Wal-Mart's expansion.

In a move that was part good business and part public relations, Wal-Mart sent an open letter to U.S. manufacturers in March 1985 inviting them to take part in a buy-American program. The company offered to work with them in producing products that could compete against imports. "Our American suppliers must commit to improving their facilities and machinery, remain financially conservative and work to fill our requirements, and most importantly, strive to improve employee productivity," Walton told *Nation's Business* in April 1988. Product conversions—arranging to buy competitively priced U.S.-made goods in place of imports—are regularly highlighted at weekly managers' meetings. William R. Fields, executive vice-president of merchandise and sales, estimated that Wal-Mart cut imports by approximately 5% between 1985 and 1989. Nonetheless, analysts estimated that Wal-Mart still purchased between 25% and 30% of its goods from overseas, about twice as much as Kmart.

Wal-Mart has also been criticized for its impact on small retail businesses. Independent store owners often went out of business when Wal-Mart came to town, unable to compete with the superstore's economies of scale. In fact, Iowa State University economist Kenneth Stone conducted a study on this phenomenon and told the *New York Times Magazine* (April 2, 1989), "If you go into towns in Illinois where Wal-Mart has been for 8 or 10 years, the downtowns are just ghost towns." He found that businesses suffering most were drug, hardware, five-and-dime, sporting goods, clothing, and fabric stores, while major appliance and furniture businesses picked up, as did restaurants and gasoline stations, due to increased traffic.

Wal-Mart has a record of community service, however. It awards a $1,000 scholarship to a high school student in each community Wal-Mart serves. But the company's refusal to stock dozens of widely circulated adult and teen magazines, including *Rolling Stone,* had some critics claiming that Wal-Mart was willfully narrowing the choices of the buying public by bowing to pressure from conservative groups.

In 1990 the company continued to grow, adding its first Wal-Mart stores in California, Nevada, North Dakota, Pennsylvania, South Dakota, and Utah. It also opened 25 Sam's Clubs, of which four were 130,000-square-foot prototypes incorporating space for produce, meats, and baked goods. In mid-1990, the company acquired Western Merchandise, Inc., of Amarillo, Texas, a supplier of music, books, and video products to many of the Wal-Mart stores. Late in 1990 Wal-Mart acquired the McLane Company, Inc., a distributor of grocery and retail products. Early in 1991 The Wholesale Club, Inc., merged with Sam's Clubs, adding 28 stores that were to be integrated with Sam's by year end. Also, Wal-Mart agreed to sell its nine convenience store–gas station outlets to Conoco Inc.

Wal-Mart's expansion continued in 1991, and by 1992 the company opened about 150 new Wal-Mart stores and 60 Sam's Clubs, bringing the total to 1,720 Wal-Mart stores and 208 Sam's Clubs. Some of these stores represented a change in policy for the company, opening near big cities with large populations. Another policy change was instituted by the company when it announced that it would no longer deal with independent sales representatives.

In 1991 Wal-Mart introduced its new store brand, Sam's American Choice, and its first products were beverages, colas, and fruit juices. The beverages were made by Canada's largest private-label bottler, Cott Corp., but the colas were supplied from U.S. plants. Future plans called for the introduction of many different types of products that would match the quality of national brands, but at lower prices.

In 1992 Wal-Mart moved into Mexico, where it entered into a joint venture with Cifra, that nation's largest retailer. The venture developed a price-club store called Club Aurrera which required an annual membership of about $25. Shoppers could choose from about 3,500 products ranging from fur coats to frozen vegetables. Within the year, the joint venture operated three Club Aurreras, four Bodegas discount stores, and one Aurrera combination store.

Expansion in the United States also continued, and from 1992 to 1993, 161 Wal-Mart stores were opened and one was closed.

Another 48 Sam's Clubs and 51 Bud's Warehouse Outlets were also opened. Expansions or relocations took place at 170 Wal-Mart stores and 40 Sam's Clubs. All told, there was a net addition of 34,556,271 square feet of retail space. By 1993, the 1,914 stores included 40 Supercenters in 45 states and Puerto Rico, and 27 Sam's Clubs in 41 states.

In January 1993 Wal-Mart's reputation was shaken when a report on *Dateline* on NBC-TV showed child laborers in Bangladesh producing merchandise for the stores. The program showed children working for 5 cents an hour in a country that lacked child labor laws.

The program further alleged that items made outside the United States were being sold under "Made in USA" signs as part of the company's Buy American campaign instituted in 1985. CEO David Glass appeared on the program saying that he didn't know of any "child exploitation" by the company, but did apologize about some of the signs incorrectly promoting foreign-made products as domestic items.

In April 1993 Wal-Mart introduced another private label, called Great Value. The brand was initially used for a line of 350 packaged food items for sale in its supercenter stores. The proceeds from the company's other private label, Sam's American Choice, were to be channeled into the Competitive Edge Scholarship Fund, which the company launched in 1993 in partnership with some vendors and colleges. In the same year, Wal-Mart started to build an experimental store that would sell products made from recycled materials, in keeping with the company's environmental position of using recycled paper and plastic materials.

The company planned to open 150 new Wal-Mart stores and 65 Sam's Clubs in 1994. About 100 older stores and 25 clubs were to be expanded or relocated, including 40 Wal-Mart stores to be operated as Supercenters. Also planned was the construction of two new full-line distribution centers, two grocery distribution centers, a distribution center to process clothing, and a storage center, as well as the introduction of the first Wal-Mart Supercenters in Monterrey and Mexico City.

Principal Subsidiaries: Kuhn's Big K Stores Corp.; North Arkansas Wholesale Co., Inc.; Wal-Mart Realty Co.; Super Saver Warehouse Club, Inc.; McLane Company, Inc.; The Wholesale Club, Inc.

Further Reading:

Bowermaster, Jon, "When Wal-Mart Comes To Town," *New York Times Magazine,* April 2, 1989.
Fitzgerald, Kate, "Suppliers Rallying Against Negative 'Dateline' Report," *Advertising Age,* January 4, 1993, p. 3, 38.
Kelly, Kevin, "Wal-Mart Gets Lost in the Vegetable Aisle," *Business Week,* May 28, 1990.
Koepp, Stephen, "Make That Sale, Mr. Sam," *Time,* May 18, 1987.
Malkin, Elisabeth, "Warehouse Stores Move Into Mexico," *Advertising Age,* January 18, 1993, p. 13.
"Retailing: Wal-Kart Stores Inc.," *Wall Street Journal,* April 6, 1993, B8.
Saporito, Bill, "Is Wal-Mart Unstoppable?" *Fortune,* May 6, 1991, pp. 50–59.
"Wal-Mart: Will It Take Over the World?," *Fortune,* January 30, 1989.
"Walton's Mountain," *Nation's Business,* April 1988.
Zellner, Wendy, "The Sam's Generation," *Business Week,* November 25, 1991, pp. 36–38.

—Carole Healy
updated by Dorothy Kroll

Walton Monroe Mills, Inc.

P.O. Box 1046
Monroe, Georgia 30655
U.S.A.
(404) 267-9411
Fax: (404) 267-5196

Private Company
Incorporated: 1895
Employees: 5,000 (including Avondale Mills subsidiary)
Sales: $500 million
SICs: 2211 Broadwoven Fabric Mills-Cotton (Primary); 2281
Yarn Spinning Mills

Walton Monroe Mills, Inc., a manufacturer of yarn and undyed fabric, has been managed by the same family since its 1895 origins. Like other venerable mills, Walton Monroe was forced to adapt to an era of foreign competition, new technologies, and industry consolidation ushered in by the 1960s. Unlike many of other smaller mills, Walton Monroe survived the sea of change. After launching an aggressive campaign of capital investment and improved efficiency in the early 1980s, Walton Monroe acquired Dakotah Mills in 1984 and Avondale Mills, Inc., in 1986 to become the 325th largest U.S. private company by 1993.

When George W. Felker, Jr., started Walton Monroe Mills in Monroe, Georgia, in 1895, the textile industry was still in its infancy. Many local investors were unable to complete payment on their stock subscriptions, and the funds necessary to complete the mill had to be borrowed at high interest rates. Nevertheless, the Felker family had roots in the region dating back to 1820, and a combination of social credibility paired with business savvy placed Walton Monroe among the surfeit of mills taking root in the Carolinas and in Georgia.

George W. Felker, Jr., maintained consistent and profitable production of yarn and undyed fabric, establishing Walton Monroe as a fixture in an industry that was still in its formative years. Industrial management was still undeveloped. Felker employed a skeleton staff, running the administrative office virtually alone. He wrote his letters in long hand and copied them into letter copy books for preservation; he inspected, weighed, classified, and purchased all the cotton for production; and he served as a small but effective sales force. He also explored new

generations of mill machinery that expedited automation but often created technical problems in the process.

Walton Monroe business held steady ground well into the 1950s, when Felker began seasoning his son to carry on the family business. George W. Felker III graduated from Georgia Tech with a degree in textile engineering and served in the Army in World War II, achieving the rank of lieutenant colonel and earning the Legion of Merit and five battle stars. After working for textile firms in New York, Boston, and Danville, Virginia, the battle-tried son returned to Monroe to head the family-controlled business as president from 1962 to 1980 and chairman from 1980 to 1992.

He returned home to a new type of battle, as the textile industry was confronting fierce foreign competition, tighter profit margins, and runaway technology in the late 1950s and early 1960s. A 1964 *Textile World* article entitled ''The Mill of Tomorrow'' warned mill owners to heed advancing trends or go out of business. ''Technology today is moving at a swift pace,'' reported the article, ''a pace that doesn't tolerate laggards, shows no mercy to men without vision, scorns those who are less than bold, and grants its rewards only to those who lead the parade of progress.'' The feature delineated nine key goals toward which mills should progress: plant construction that was enclosed, economical, and efficient; plant services that were complete and compact; plant design that was streamlined for efficiency; management that was bold, imaginative, and decisive; yarn manufacturing that was high speed and simplified; fabric manufacturing that was complex and controlled; fibers that were varied, blended, and tailor-made; finishing plants that were speedy, programmed, and automatic; and an economic climate described as sunny and brisk. These were the steps that George W. Felker III took, successfully carrying his company into the 1980s, when yet another wave of challenges confronted the textile industry and yet another Felker son, G. Stephen Felker, was seasoned to continue the family concern.

In 1977 George W. Felker III convinced his son to join as the fourth generation of Felkers heading the company. In a March 1988 *Georgia Trend* article he mused, ''Had I not been able to get Stephen back here, I would have considered selling. Otherwise, I don't know who would have headed it after me.'' In his early years, Stephen Felker seemed an unlikely candidate for head of the family business. As a 1974 graduate of the University of Virginia, he displayed a greater inclination toward teaching literature, admitting greater devotion toward Ernest Hemingway and James Joyce than toward textiles. Nevertheless, after graduation he was hired as a management trainee at Avondale Mills, Inc., a yarn and denim weaver in Sylacauga, Alabama. Company officials were impressed by Felker's relaxed manner, his energy, and his aptitude at understanding the complexities of the industry. He left Avondale on excellent terms and joined his father at Monroe. ''When he was ready to leave here, our vice president of manufacturing reported that if Stephen ever wanted to come back, he'd very much like to have him,'' said John Hudson, division president of Avondale in 1977.

Felker entered the textile industry amidst international trade negotiations of crucial importance. The General Agreement on Tariffs and Trade (GATT) aimed to liberalize world trade in various sectors, including textiles and apparel. Among other measures, GATT moved toward phasing out tariffs and quotas on textiles, alarming many textile manufacturers already threatened by lower-priced imports on the rise. Early GATT agreements, concluded in the early 1960s, resurfaced in 1986 for updating and general revision. Of particular interest to textile manufacturers was the Multi-Fiber Arrangement (MFA), the clause providing the guidelines for bilateral import agreements between countries and the primary means of controlling textile and apparel imports to the United States. Though the MFA was historically revised every three years, the late 1980s brought proposals to replace all existing quotas over a period of 10 to 15 years with a system of global product quotas, creating a so-called global basket that would allow all product imports to grow at a specific rate depending on demand for that product and the importance of that product to its country of origin. A tariff rate quota system would also be introduced, establishing a given rate of duty for a given import; imports in excess of that rate would incur substantially higher tariff rates. The American Textile Manufacturers Institute (ATMI) maintained that such measures would foster a flood of imports that could push many American mills out of business.

More promising prospects surfaced in the North American Free Trade Agreement (NAFTA) that would establish a free trade zone between Canada, the United States, and Mexico, creating one of the world's largest trading blocks with a combined population of 360 million people. According to the agreement's "rule of origin" clause, abatements of duties and quotas of apparel and fabric would apply to such products made from yarn spun in one of the three participating nations. Many textile manufacturers hoped that NAFTA would spur market activity and increase North American competitiveness in world markets.

Stephen Felker became president of Walton Monroe in 1980. During his first three years as CEO, company sales dropped from $30 million to $25 million. In addition, plant equipment was outdated and company coffers were low. "I had three choices," Felker explained in a March 1988 *Georgia Trend* article. "I could sell out. I could sit back and do nothing. Or I could jump and go for it."

In order to carry out the third choice, Felker borrowed $17 million from First National Bank of Atlanta, representing one of the first major loans in the history of Walton Monroe. With an eye on the future, the company invested in equipment that extended beyond immediate needs. New rapiers were installed in a modern, expandable plant. To maximize the versatility already inherent in the machines, the company bought them with four-color capability, even though operations used a pick-and-pick weft-insertion system. The weaving machines all featured programmable dobby motions, even though most current bottomweight apparel and lightweight industrial fabrics were produced with cam motions. The building was also state-of-the-art and designed for future growth. Measuring 85 feet in width with no columns, the construction permitted the doubling of floor space by simple displacement of one exterior wall. Modern amenities included underfloor tunnels to carry lint and waste away from work areas, filters with automatic cleaning capabilities, and a high-velocity, blow-through air-conditioning system. "We built a new plant which can be easily doubled when

the time comes," explained Felker in a May 1985 article in *Textile World.*

Walton Monroe's progressive planning continued in 1984 with the purchase of Dakotah Mills, a North Carolina fabric manufacturer, for $5.5 million. With expanded facilities and its new state-of-the-art machinery, the company was able to vary width, weave, and weight of fabrics. Production was accordingly increased and diversified to include custom-tailored cloth for sport shoe companies, convertible tops for automobile manufacturers, and furniture upholstery, among other products. From 1980 to 1986 sales doubled to $84 million.

In 1986 Walton Monroe greatly expanded and diversified its offering line by acquiring Avondale Mills, Inc., an established manufacturer of denim and yarn, for $165 million. The acquisition startled textile experts because of the novel logistics of a small, privately owned mill like Walton Monroe acquiring a large, publicly owned company like Avondale. Walton Monroe had $84 million in sales, compared with $240 million for the Alabama mill. "When you march out and buy Avondale with the assets of a Walton Monroe, well, that's a helluva maneuver," cited Walter Forbes, CEO of the Signal Thread Co. in a March 1988 *Georgia Trend* article. However impressive, the maneuver was not simple.

Avondale Mills, one of Alabama's oldest and largest textile firms, seemed an unlikely target for takeover until 1985, when the company lost $14 million and saw sales decline 20 percent from a high of $300 million in the early 1980s. Over the course of five strained years, the company went through four CEOs. When the Comer family decided to sell it, Walton Monroe became an attractive client, not only because it shared the family-run, generation-old profile of the traditional southern mill, but because Stephen Felker had worked for Avondale and shared important affinities with the proprietors. Mutual affinities aside, Felker had to come up with the funds before other competitors beat him to it.

In order to finance the purchase, Felker first turned to Drexel Burnham Lambert, where dealings were organized with Dennis Levine, the managing partner later convicted for securities violations involving insider trading on Wall Street. Perceiving that Levine was manipulating negotiations to leave him as a minority partner in Avondale, Felker dropped negotiations. He then turned to First Boston Corp. where a new corporation, AM Acquisition Inc., was formed with 50.1 percent owned by Walton Monroe and 49.9 percent owned by two affiliated entities of First Boston. Formation of AM Acquisition was an important strategic step in winning a three-way bidding war for Avondale. In addition to Walton Monroe, two other firms were actively bidding for the Alabama mill: Spectrum Dyed Yarns of New York, and Dominion Textile Inc., Canada's largest surviving primary textile and fabrics group. Dominion filed a complaint in a federal court in Atlanta against Avondale and Walton Monroe seeking to prevent the agreement. But on March 27, 1986, AM Acquisition purchased 51 percent of Avondale at $28.20 per share and entered into an agreement with the Avondale board to purchase the balance of the company in a cash merger at the same price. With an innovative "bridge" or "mezzanine" financing scheme, Felker arranged to buy back First Boston's 49.9 percent equity position in AM Acquisition as cash flow permitted. "It's always nice to beat the big boys in New York," cited Rod Dowling, manager director/corporate finance for Robinson-Humphrey in an April 14, 1986, article in *Atlanta Business Chronicle*. Dowling was instrumental in thwarting Dominion's hostile countertakeover attempt masterminded by Merill Lynch Pierce Fenner & Smith.

Part of Felker's success stemmed from his ability to gain Avondale's trust. "I believe they had faith I would continue to operate Avondale Mills under its present name with management remaining in place, for the most part," he said in *Atlantic Business Chronicle*. "I want to assure you that the company has a very special place in my heart," Felker said in a July 2, 1986, *United Press* article. It was this trust that enabled AM Acquisition to purchase 39 percent of Avondale stock from a descendant of the mill's founder, former Alabama Governor B. B. Comer, while Dominion arrived at purchasing only one percent.

Felker brought to Avondale the same energy that he used to acquire it. While cutting general and administrative expenses by two-thirds, he pumped $40 million into new machinery. He spread out management authority in mill operations, moving, in his words, "the decision-making process to the lowest level," and cut out layers of inefficient bureaucracy. The Avondale debt was reduced by improved cash flow and financing through the Trust Company Bank of Atlanta.

With the Avondale acquisition, Walton Monroe's employment of about 900 people throughout the Southeast grew to include about 3,700 workers in Alabama, Georgia, North Carolina, and South Carolina. With Avondale, Walton Monroe entered into the denim business and set new sights on fancy, light-weight denims as well as the possibility of other apparel-fabric takeovers. "The real key to Felker's continued success will be how well he weathers the next downturn," said Lam Hardman III, president of Harmony Grove Mills in Commerce, Georgia, in a

March 1988 *Georgia Trend* article. Additionally, Standard & Poor's predicted an upturn in demand for apparel and industrial fabrics with an improving economy in 1993, estimating an increase in earnings for textile manufacturers of 15.0 percent to 20.0 percent for 1993.

Principal Subsidiaries: Avondale Mills, Inc.

Further Reading:

Allgood, Lynn, "Robinson-Humphrey vs. Merrill Lynch," *Atlanta Business Chronicle,* April 14, 1986.
Andrews, Mildred Gwin, *The Men and the Mills,* Macon: Mercer University Press, 1987, p. 288.
"Avondale Mills Seeks Stockholder Approval of Sale," *United Press International,* March 28, 1986, AM Cycle.
"Avondale Shuts Some U.S. Sales Offices; Textile Fabric and Yarn Manufacturer," *Women's Wear Daily,* November 19, 1991, p. 14.
"Avondale Stockholders Approve Merger," *United Press International,* July 2, 1986, AM Cycle.
"Dominion Textile," *New York Times,* April 4, 1986, p. D3.
Engardio, Pete, "How Textile Makers Are Dressing for Success," *Business Week,* July 21, 1986, p. 128.
"George W. Felker III, 77, Headed Family's Woven Textile Mills," *Atlanta Journal and Constitution,* February 24, 1993.
Irby, William G., "The Avondale Mills of Alabama and Georgia," *Textile History Review,* October 1962, pp. 197–204.
Issacs, McAllister, III, "Walton Monroe Weaving: Built for the Future," *Textile World,* May 1985, pp. 54–55.
Levin, Rob, "Stephen Felker: A New Breed Takes Over in Textiles," *Georgia Trend,* March, 1988, sec. 1, p. 32.
"The Mill of Tomorrow," *Textile World,* May 1964, pp. 48–83, 104–06.
"Regulations, Energy Lead Major Problems of the '80s," *Textile World,* December 1980, p. 30.
"Third Suitor Emerges in Fight for Avondale Mills," *Financial Times,* March 13, 1986, p. I35.

—Kerstan Cohen

Wellman, Inc.

1040 Broad Street, Suite 302
Shrewsbury, New Jersey 07702
U.S.A.
(908)-542-7302
Fax: (908) 542-9344

Public Company
Incorporated: 1969
Employees: 3,600
Sales: $828.2 million
Stock Exchanges: New York
SICs: 2824 Organic Fibers—Noncellulosic; 2299 Textile
   Goods Nec; 5093 Scrap & Waste Materials

Founded as a small, family-owned wool company, Wellman, Inc. has grown into a multinational *Fortune* 500 company involved in recycling and the manufacture and marketing of fibers—Wellman's core business—and plastic resins. Wellman has attained leadership positions in these areas through a series of acquisitions and joint ventures. By 1992 Wellman was the nation's largest supplier of anhydrous lanolin, third largest producer of polyester staple and polyester partially-oriented yarn (POY) fibers, and the largest and most advanced recycler of plastics.

Wellman traces its history to the Massachusetts wool combing company Hill & Nichols—later renamed Nichols & Company—established in 1927. In 1954 Nichols & Company organized Wellman Combing Company in Johnsonville, South Carolina, marking the first plant of its kind in that state. Ten years later, seeing an opportunity to move into the burgeoning synthetics market, Wellman began to produce nylon fibers, mainly for use by the carpet industry. This was soon followed by the manufacture of polyester staple fibers, which were usually made into fiberfill to be used in such products as cushions, quilts, pillows, and parkas, as well as nonwoven and industrial applications. The fibers were produced from recycled raw materials converted from fiber and film waste.

Due to the steady growth of the plastics business, it was decided that those operations should be separated from other activities at the Johnsonville facility. Thus the Engineering Resins Division was established in 1968. Using recycled nylon fiber and virgin polymers, the division specifically manufactured nylon engineering resins, which were marketed to industries that included automotive, consumer products, and electrical parts for use in such products as fans, headlight housings, aerosol valves, and lawn and garden equipment.

In order to reflect the changing nature of the firm's business, the Wellman Combing Company was renamed Wellman Industries, Inc. in 1969, while Nichols & Company became Wellman, Inc. Three years later Wellman International Limited (WIL) was established in Mullagh, Republic of Ireland, as a wholly owned subsidiary in order to produce polyester and nylon staple fibers for European markets. These fibers were manufactured from recycled raw materials, in part supplied by, ironically, other European fiber producers with which WIL was competing. The fibers were then exported, mainly to the United Kingdom and Europe.

During the 1970s Wellman's growth was relatively slow since its main business was tied to the inconsistent supply of waste materials picked up from major chemical companies. By 1979, however, the company had begun its steady progression toward becoming a major company with the establishment of a PET—polyethylene terephthalate—soft drink bottle recycling operation in Johnsonville. The opening of the facility came at a time when consumers were becoming much more environmentally aware, which in turn led to a steady supply of waste materials that could be recycled by the company. Wellman rightly forecasted that manufacturers would soon advertise the use of recycled materials in packaging their products. By developing the proprietary technology to recycle PET bottles, the company quickly became a frontrunner in the recycling industry, and eventually the nation's leading recycler. Using empty soda bottles collected from states with bottle deposit laws, collection increased markedly from 1983 to 1990 when 30 states enacted laws either granting tax breaks and loans to postconsumer recycling programs, or had mandated separate collection of recyclable materials.

Sacks Industries, a Clark, New Jersey-based fiber broker and manufacturer of nonwovens, purchased a 50 percent stake in Wellman in 1983. The companies' operations were subsequently merged, and Tom Duff of Sacks Industries was appointed vice president and chief operating officer. Wellman's nonwoven business grew out of Sacks' two plants located in Charlotte, North Carolina, and Commerce California. The Charlotte facility uses polyester fiber to make high-loft bonded battings for the home furnishings industry to use as cushioning and insulating in such products as bedspreads, comforters, and furniture cushions. Production as the Commerce plant utilized green polyester fiber, made from recycled green PET soft drink bottles by the Fibers Division, to make geotextile items. These products were used for soil reinforcement and filtration in various civil engineering applications, including landfill and pond linings, and the stabilization of roads and railroads.

Two years after Wellman and Sacks Industries merged, the two companies were purchased by a group of investors and company mangers in a leveraged buyout. Tom Duff became president and CEO of the newly renamed Wellman, Inc. In June of 1987 the company went public when its stock began trading on the NASDAQ exchange at a price of $10.25 per share. Wellman stock was offered on the New York Stock Exchange the following year at an initial share price of $17.50.

In 1989 Wellman entered into two arrangements that would not only ensure the company of a steady supply of recyclable materials, but a market for the resulting products as well. The first agreement, with Browning-Ferris Industries (BFI), a large waste collector, allowed Wellman to buy all the household plastic the company picked up in curbside programs. The second arrangement was with Constar International Inc., one of the largest PET bottle makers in the nation. Constar buys a great amount of the used PET bottles that Wellman collects, and includes the recycled materials to make new bottles. In the meantime Constar International Inc., one of the largest makers of PET bottles in the United States, agreed to purchase much of Wellman's recycled plastic for use in the manufacture of their bottles. Constar hoped to avoid complaints from environmentalists by using an estimated 25 percent recycled plastic in the bottles. In addition, through a joint venture arrangement Wellman and Constar together acquired four European bottle manufacturers between 1989 and 1990, with facilities in the Netherlands, France, and United Kingdom. Wellstar, said to be the largest PET plastic bottle maker in Europe, sold the bottles and then bought them back for recycling.

Also in 1989 Wellman acquired Fiber Industries Inc. from Hoechst Celanese Corp. Fiber Industries was a leading manufacturer of premium polyester textile fibers sold under the brand name, Fortrel. The company became part of Wellman's Fibers Division, doubling Wellman's asset and revenue base, and positioning the company as a leading producer of polyester fiber. By 1992 activities from the Fiber Industries acquisition represented an estimated 82 percent of the company's total sales. Wellman also had fiber-producing facilities located in Fayetteville, North Carolina, and Darlington, South Carolina. It was estimated in 1992 that Wellman manufactured 26 percent of the nation's staple fiber and 13 percent of its partially-oriented yarn (POY) fibers.

In 1990 construction of Wellman's first international PET bottle recycling plant was completed by WIL in Spijk, Netherlands, in order to manufacture polyester fiber. Later that year Wellman acquired New England CRInc, another move that was meant to facilitate its use of recyclable plastics. New England CRInc was the leader in the design, construction and operation of advanced materials recovery facilities (MRF). The company built the first highly-mechanized U.S. MRF and had exclusive North American rights to a patented German recyclable sortation technology, the Bezner automated materials sortation system. New England CRInc separated and processed commingled recyclables, such as plastic, aluminum and glass containers and paper collected from curbside recycling programs. By 1992 there were 10 full-service MRFs in operation, and the company accounted for about 2 percent of Wellman's total sales.

In 1992 Wellman made two more acquisitions that furthered the company's manufacturing and marketing capabilities. A newly completed polyester fiber plant located in Marion was pur-

chased, in addition to Creative Forming, Inc. (CFI), the largest user of recycled PET in the thermoforming market. CFI custom designed, manufactured, and marketed thermoformed plastic packaging products from virgin and recycled PET and other materials. The purchase of CFI enabled Wellman to enter the high-growth PET packaging market, while providing another means of using the company's virgin and recycled PET materials.

Wellman's acquisition strategy laid the foundation for a 70 percent expansion in its recycling capacity set for early 1994. In addition, capacity for the Wool Division was expanded by almost 40 percent when the company bought the operations of its largest wool top customer in 1992. However, the next year, rather than following its former pattern of acquisitions, Wellman began a multi-year capital investment program to modernize and expand projects at the domestic fiber manufacturing, PET bottle recycling, and PET resin operations.

The key to Wellman's success has been that it supplies much of its own materials at low cost through its various virgin and recycling plastics divisions. Another advantage has been its manufacturing facilities that are flexible enough to adapt to product and market changes, necessary because recycling materials are commodities whose prices are subject to market fluctuations. Given Wellman's past record of creating divisions and subsidiaries that meet the changing needs of manufacturers and consumers, and the nation's increasing attention to the environment, Wellman can be expected to continue its strong growth pattern.

Principal Subsidiaries: Wellman International Limited; New England CRInc; CFI.

Further Reading:

"America's Fastest Growing Companies," *Fortune,* April 22, 1991, pp. 67–76.
Cook, James, "A Perfect LBO Candidate," *Forbes,* October 31, 1988, pp. 74–76.
Feder, Barnaby J., "Profits, and Problems, for Recycler," *New York Times,* January 8, 1991, D1, D5.
The History and Operations of Wellman, Inc., Shrewsbury, NJ: Wellman, Inc., 1993.
Koselka, Rita, "Casey at the Bottling Plant," *Forbes,* August 6, 1990, pp. 88–89.
"Merger To Beef Up Recycling," *Packaging,* January 1993, p. 18.
Nulty, Peter, "Recycling Becomes a Big Business," *Fortune,* August 13, 1990, pp. 81–86.
"PET Industry Reveals Its Changing Face," *Chemical Marketing Reporter,* February 1, 1993, pp. 5, 25.
"Wellman Sets Bottle Resin PET Expansion," *Chemical Marketing Reporter,* January 16, 1993, p. 9.
Wellman, Inc. Annual Reports, Shrewsbury, NJ: Wellman, Inc., 1990, 1991.

—Dorothy Kroll

Wendy's International, Inc.

4288 West Dublin-Granville Rd.
Dublin, Ohio 43107-0256
U.S.A.
(614) 764-3100
Fax: (614) 764-6894

Public Company
Incorporated: 1975
Employees: 42,000
Sales: $3.61 billion
Stock Exchanges: Boston Midwest New York Pittsburgh
SICs: 6794 Patent Owners & Lessors; 5812 Eating Places

Wendy's International, Inc. is one of the top three restaurant chains in the world. The chain has been touted as America's favorite hamburger place for 14 years by *Restaurants & Institution's* "Choice in Chains" annual consumer survey. Wendy's hallmark square hamburgers and homey atmosphere were introduced in Columbus, Ohio, in 1969, and the company has enjoyed phenomenal growth in the quarter-century since that time.

The restaurant was created by R. David Thomas, an adoptee who has credited part of his success to his challenging youth. Thomas was born during the depths of the Great Depression in Atlantic City, New Jersey. His early life was punctuated by tragedy. Abandoned at birth, he was adopted by a Michigan couple, Rex and Auleva Thomas. Auleva died when David was five years old, and his father was forced to move from state to state seeking work as a handyman. Rex remarried three times and moved his family ten times over the next eight years.

David himself entered the world of work at the age of 12 delivering groceries in Knoxville, Tennessee. He lied about his age to circumvent child labor laws, and worked 12-hour shifts to keep his job.

Thomas' adulthood began early. When he was 15, his family moved to Fort Wayne, Indiana, and he started work as a busboy at a local restaurant, the Hobby House. When his family announced another move, Thomas elected to set out on his own, taking a room at the local YMCA. As his work began to demand more time than his education, Thomas gave up on the latter, leaving school after the tenth grade and later enlisting in the army. Trained as a cook in the military, he returned to a job behind the grill of the Hobby House, where he met Lorraine, a waitress—and his future wife.

Thomas entered the restaurant business in earnest in 1956 in partnership with Phil Clauss. Just a few years later, Thomas and Clauss met Colonel Harland Sanders, who offered them Kentucky Fried Chicken (KFC) franchises. Clauss purchased one for Fort Wayne, and the pair broke into the chicken business.

By 1962 Clauss was deep into KFC—he owned four unprofitable franchises in Columbus, Ohio, and needed someone to turn them around. If Thomas could turn the stores' $200,000 deficit into a profit, Clauss promised him a 45 percent share of the Columbus franchises. Against the advice of Colonel Sanders, who had become a mentor, Thomas took the challenge. He cut the menu from 100 items down to just a few—Thomas urged the Colonel to concentrate on chicken alone—improved the chicken "bucket," bartered radio advertising with buckets of chicken, invented KFC's spinning bucket sign, and built four additional locations in less than six years. His earnest, imaginative work paid off—Thomas was promoted to regional operations director of KFC and sold his stake in the Columbus restaurants for $1.5 million in 1968, thereby reaching millionaire status by the age of 35.

Thomas parlayed his windfall into a new venture named after his eight-year-old daughter Melinda Lou, or Wendy, as her brothers and sisters nicknamed her. The first restaurant was located on Broad Street in downtown Columbus, Ohio. Its menu featured made-to-order hamburgers, "secret recipe" chili, french fries, soft drinks and the Frosty frozen dessert. Thomas kept the menu simple to save labor costs, remembering his KFC experience. The Wendy's Old Fashioned Hamburgers decor differed from other fast food joints that abounded with easy-clean vinyl and tiled surfaces. Instead, Thomas put in tiffany-style lamps, bentwood chairs, carpeting, and tabletops embellished with vintage newspaper advertisements. Although his ideas were refreshingly original, some industry experts criticized Thomas' use of expensive fresh beef and noted that the fast food industry seemed overcrowded. With all the criticism, Thomas hoped only for a local chain that would provide his children with summer jobs.

Against all predictions, the business took off immediately. Thomas opened a second location just one year later, and began franchising his idea in 1972. Wendy's soon enlisted franchisees at the rate of ten per month. Thomas added a new wrinkle to the franchising concept, giving geographic licenses, rather than single-store rights. Wendy's also commenced its first advertising campaign that year with locally broadcast "C'mon to Wendy's" spots. The 30-second, animated ads stressed Wendy's superiority through the "Quality is Our Recipe" slogan and featured a red-haired, pig-tailed "Wendy" with dancing hamburgers.

The 1970s heralded phenomenal, and somewhat reckless, growth at Wendy's. By the end of 1974 the chain's net income topped $1 million, and total sales reached almost $25 million. In mid-1975 the business celebrated the opening of its 100th restaurant, and that fall Wendy's opened its first international restaurant, located in Canada. Wendy's went public in 1976 with an offering of one million common shares valued at $28 per share. By the end of the year, shareholders understood that their money fueled growth—Wendy's opened its 500th shop.

The chain's rapid expansion was supported by Wendy's first national advertising campaign in 1977. The effort earned Wendy's another entry in the history books—it became the first chain with less than 1000 restaurants to launch network television commercials. "Hot 'n Juicy" ran for three years and won a Clio Award for creativity, setting the pace for future Wendy's advertising.

Before the decade's end, the restaurant chain set even more records. In 1978, the 1000th Wendy's opened in Springfield, Tennessee, not far from the site of Thomas' first job. By the next year the number of shops had increased by half, and the first European Wendy's opened in Munich, West Germany. In November of 1979 Wendy's celebrated its tenth birthday with many "firsts" to flaunt. Wendy's was the first in its industry to surpass $1 billion in annual sales within its initial ten years, in addition to reaching the 1,000th restaurant opening faster than any of its competitors. It boasted 1,767 sites in the United States, Canada, Puerto Rico, and Europe, and had opened more than 750 restaurants from February 1978 to November 1979, averaging nearly one and one-half each day.

In the early 1980s, growth slowed slightly from that hectic pace, but Wendy's was distinguished from its competitors through celebrated advertising and winning menu additions. "Wendy's Has the Taste," the first ad of the decade, depicted customers and employees singing a catchy jingle. The ad emphasized Wendy's new chicken sandwich and all-you-can-eat salad bar. The chain had introduced its "Garden Spot" in 1979 over Thomas's protestations, becoming the first national restaurant chain to offer salad bars nationwide.

Founder Dave Thomas made his first appearance as Wendy's spokesperson in 1981 in a controversial ad titled, "Ain't No Reason (to go anyplace else)." Customers' use of the idiomatic double negative "ain't no" in the ads generated national attention for the chain, though not all of it favorable. Thomas left his position as chief executive in 1982, taking the title of senior chairman. After working for more than 30 years, Thomas felt that he had earned a break, and was confident that he had hired capable managers to carry on his work.

A recession in the early 1980s, combined with high beef prices and Wendy's explosive—as well as threatening—growth incited the "burger wars." Wendy's moved into the number three spot behind McDonald's and Burger King Corp., fueled by its introduction of a chainwide salad bar, chicken breast sandwiches, and baked potatoes. Burger King and McDonald's responded with unsuccessful menu extensions of their own, then moved to a hard-nosed ad campaign. Burger King fired the first shot, but Wendy's responded with a string of hard-hitting, well-known commercials.

In 1983 Wendy's depicted victims of other hamburger restaurants with "Step Aside," "Park It," and "Frozen Stiff." The ads humorously bemoaned the long waits endured in indoor and drive-up lines for frozen hamburger patties. In 1984 Wendy's agency, Dancer Fitzgerald Sample, teamed up with celebrated commercial director Joe Sedelmaier on a campaign that registered the highest consumer awareness levels in the advertising

industry's history, in addition to captivating judges at the 1984 Clio Awards and winning three of the industry's highest honors. "Where's the Beef?" consisted of four network television spots starring senior citizen Clara Peller. It was voted the most popular commercial in America in 1984. One of the ads, "Parts is Parts," pointed out the difference between the competition's pressed chicken patties and Wendy's chicken breast filet sandwiches.

"Parts" focused on Wendy's true money-makers at that point—hamburger sales actually only comprised 40 percent of the chain's revenues. Much of Wendy's sales growth could be credited to such menu extensions as the grilled chicken sandwich, Garden Spot, and stuffed baked potatoes. These new products and the phenomenal success of the "Where's the Beef?" campaign catapulted Wendy's to a record $76.2 million earnings in 1985.

As one unnamed Wendy's executive confessed in *Barron's*, the management started to believe that everything they touched would "turn to gold." Unfortunately, 1985 marked a summit from which Wendy's quickly plummeted. In 1986 the chain introduced sit-down breakfasts featuring omelettes and French toast. The new breakfasts involved a huge investment of capital and labor, and could not be served quickly enough to fit in with the fast food format. At the same time, McDonald's, Burger King, and Hardee's assaulted Wendy's on the hamburger front.

A kind of domino effect plunged the company toward a $4.9 million loss in 1986. Some of the chain's original franchisees sold their stores to new owners who flouted Wendy's high standards. Others became absentee managers, leaving the day-to-day supervision to employees. As the chain's standards of cleanliness, quality, and service slipped, sales dropped. In response to the falling income, store labor was cut, while the morale of those left plunged, and turnover rates began to explode. By the end of the year, 20 percent of Wendy's restaurants were nearing failure, and franchisees presented the chain's management a vote of no confidence.

The desperate situation brought Dave Thomas out of semi-retirement, and challenged one of Wendy's most successful franchisees to revive the failing business. James W. Near had been one of Dave Thomas's competitors in the late 1960s when they both operated restaurants in Columbus. Practically raised in his father's White Castle hamburger chain, Near built a 50-unit Burger Boy Food-A-Rama chain of his own by the end of the decade. Near had become a Wendy's franchisee in 1974, opening 39 successful restaurants in West Virginia and Florida within four years. In 1978, he sold the restaurants back to Wendy's and established Sisters Chicken & Biscuits as an expansion vehicle for the hamburger chain. Sisters became a subsidiary of Wendy's in 1981 and was sold to its largest franchise owner in 1987.

James Near agreed to take the position of president and chief operating officer on the condition that Dave Thomas would sustain an active role in the company as a spokesman and traveling mentor. Thomas agreed—his new business card read, "Founder and Jim's Right Hand Man." Near's turnaround strategy started with an internal reorganization. Weak stores were eliminated and a new building design lowered the initial franchise investment. Near cut 700 administrative positions and revamped field operations. New programs gave the remaining employees a vested interest in the chain's success—base pay, benefits, and bonuses were raised; an employee stock option called "We Share" made workers shareholders; and standardized training gave all employees a new perspective on their jobs. By 1991, turnover rates had decreased sharply.

With renewed chainwide standards for cleanliness and customer service, Near turned his attention to the menu. Changes were based on several industry trends, including discount pricing, consumer health concerns, and premium menu items. Spurred by the recession of the late 1980s and early 1990s, many fast food chains established discount pricing to appeal to more frugal customers. Wendy's introduced its Super Value Menu in 1989. The daily feature includes seven 99-cent items, allowing it to appeal to thrifty consumers without issuing profit-eating coupons. An expanded salad bar and skinless chicken breast sandwich catered to more health conscious consumers, while the Big Classic, Dave's Deluxe, and Chicken Cordon Bleu specialty sandwiches appealed to Wendy's traditional hearty eaters.

As Near worked to cover all of the menu bases, Dave Thomas returned to the television studio for the promotional push. In 1989 Thomas reappeared in commercials offering customers a special moneyback guarantee if they didn't concur that Wendy's had the best-tasting hamburgers in the industry. The ad was supported by one of the largest testimonial advertising campaigns in television history. Local residents in about 100 U.S. markets pronounced Wendy's burgers best.

"Old Fashioned Guy," the next series of TV spots, featured Thomas declaring, "Our hamburgers are the best in the business, or I wouldn't have named the place after my daughter." The hamburgers might have been the best, but Thomas' performances earned poor ratings from the experts at *Advertising Age,* who said he looked like "a steer in a half-sleeved shirt." Thomas himself admitted that he wasn't an ideal subject—he joked that it took two hours to get the expression "muchas gracias" right for one commercial. Unlike the critics, however, consumers gave Thomas an enthusiastic reception—his promotions have earned Wendy's highest advertising awareness figures since "Where's the Beef?" and have been credited with boosting the chain's turnaround. They have even earned him the designation, "the Colonel Sanders of Wendy's," in reference to the promotional efforts of Thomas' early mentor.

The success of Wendy's revitalization has shown in sales, rejuvenated expansion, and widespread recognition of the accomplishment. Although the chain has not yet achieved the profits it reaped in 1985, sales and earnings increased steadily in the early 1990s to $3.61 billion and $64.7 million respectively for 1992. Despite a lingering recession, Wendy's had outperformed the industry with 24 consecutive months of same-store sales gains. Plans for the future targeted international growth, where opportunities for expansion were infinitely better than those in the saturated American market. The company opened its 4,000th restaurant in 1992, and projected another 1,000 openings by mid-decade.

Near and Thomas have accumulated numerous awards in recognition of the dramatic turnaround at Wendy's. In 1989, Near was given the title of chief executive officer at Wendy's, and he was named chairman and CEO two years later. Near was honored by his colleagues in the restaurant industry when he was named Operator of the Year by *Nation's Restaurant News* and Executive of the Year by *Restaurants & Institutions. Restaurant Business* acknowledged both men's entrepreneurial efforts with its annual Leadership Awards. Thomas also received the Horatio Alger Award, named for the author who popularized the concept of the "self-made man."

Thomas' national celebrity has given him an avenue for the promotion of his favorite cause, adoption. The circumstances of his youth inspired him to create the Dave Thomas Foundation for Adoption in 1992 and made him a natural spokesperson for President George Bush's national initiative, "Adoption Works ... For Everyone." Thomas published his autobiography, *Dave's Way,* in 1991, and pledged all proceeds from its sale to national adoption awareness programs.

As Wendy's "ambassador," Thomas spends most of his time traveling to book promotions, public appearances, and franchises. His promotional work complemented Near's continuing efforts to "grow the company." A new corporate theme, "Do It Right! Performance Pays!" related customer-responsiveness to sales and profits for worker-shareholders. Wendy's goals for the future focus on maintaining the momentum the company has generated in the early 1990s with an emphasis on street-level operations, marketing, and efficient administration.

Principal Subsidiaries: Wendy's Restaurants of Canada, Inc. (Canada); The New Bakery Co. of Ohio, Inc.

Further Reading:

Blyskal, Jeff, "Hot Stuff," *Forbes,* June 4, 1984, pp. 169–71.
Byrne, Harlan S., "Wendy's International: It Is Finally Learning How to Handle Success," *Barron's,* January 7, 1991, pp. 43–44.
Chaudhry, Rajan, "James Near Cleans Up Wendy's," *Restaurants & Institutions,* July 22, 1992, pp. 72–82.
"From Peril to Profit: The Man Who Saved Wendy's," *Success,* February 1992, p. 10.
History of Wendy's Advertising, 1969–1993, Dublin, OH: Wendy's International, Inc., 1993.
Hume, Scott, "Thomas Shines as Wendy's Col. Sanders," *Advertising Age,* August 6, 1990, p. 3+.
James W. Near: Chairman and Chief Executive Officer, Dublin, OH: Wendy's International, Inc., 1993.
Killian, Linda, "Hamburger Helper," *Forbes,* August 5, 1991, pp. 106–107.
Near, James W., "Wendy's Successful 'Mop Bucket Attitude,'" *Wall Street Journal,* April 27, 1992.
R. David Thomas: How Wendy's Founder Worked His Way to Success, Dublin, OH: Wendy's International, Inc. 1993.
Scarpa, James, "RB Leadership Award: R. David Thomas, James W. Near," *Restaurant Business,* May 1, 1992.
Thomas, R. David, *Dave's Way,* New York: Putnam Publishing Group, 1991.
Wendy's International, Inc.: Backgrounder, Dublin, OH: Wendy's International, Inc., 1993.
Wendy's International, Inc.: Historical Highlights, Dublin, OH: Wendy's International, Inc., 1993.

—April S. Dougal

West Point Pepperell

West Point-Pepperell, Inc.

400 West Tenth Street
West Point, Georgia, 31833
U.S.A.
(706) 645-4000
Fax: 706-645-4068

Public Company
Incorporated: 1880 as Pepperell Manufacturing Company
Employees: 21,000
Sales: $1.5 billion
Stock Exchanges: New York
SICs: 2211 Broadwoven Fabric Mills—Cotton; 2221
    Broadwoven Fabric Mills—Manmade; 2299 Textile Goods
    Nec

From humble roots in the South's postwar reconstruction, over the last century West Point-Pepperell, Inc. (WPP) has experienced tremendous growth through the acquisition of other companies and investment in new mills and production development. After taking over many companies, West Point-Pepperell experienced some extreme turbulence when it was taken over itself in a deal involving intricate, and very shaky, manipulations within the world of high finance. Despite the failure of the takeover, the company remains a preeminent manufacturer of sheets, towels, and apparel, encompassing such famous brand names as Martex, Ralph Lauren, and Lady Pepperell. It is the top-selling U.S. producer of domestic bed linens and the number two producer of bath towels.

The roots of West Point-Pepperell go back to Appomattox and the start of the New South. In the wake of the Civil War's devastation, the South looked to industry as the means to rebuild. While southern-grown cotton comprised more than 60 percent of all U.S. exports in 1860, very little of it was being manufactured locally. Most was manufactured in Great Britain or the East. Given the depleted economy of the South and the amount of people eager to work, the road to the New South seemed to be via manufacturing.

In Alabama, in the valley of the Chattahoochee River near West Point, two groups of merchants and planters surveyed their ruined businesses and plantations around 1865 and found they had just enough capital to build two cotton mills. Although poverty engulfed the area, by using the river to generate power and by digging clay from the native soil for the bricks to build

the mills, the groups built two plants at Langdale and River View. The laying of cornerstones of the Alabama & Georgia Manufacturing Company in River View and the Chattahoochee Manufacturing Company in Langdale in 1866 was a cause for great celebration.

The two new companies struggled in their early years with machinery, labor, and capital problems. Then came the economic panic of 1873. Both mills closed until two brothers, Lafayette Lanier and Ward Crockett, both veterans of the confederate army, acquired stock in them and converted production to the fabric used in canvas wagon tops and tents, which was then in great demand. Machinery was modernized. In 1880, the mills were reorganized and renamed the West Point Manufacturing Company. There were eight stockholders and 75 employees.

The company prospered until a disastrous fire struck in 1886, destroying the mill. Fortunately, the company had an alliance with a Boston selling agent who helped raise the capital to rebuild the lost mill. In 1890, West Point was larger than ever, having acquired a new mill and in the process of constructing another. As the railroads came and the West was developed, the demand for textiles skyrocketed. West Point continued to expand by adding mill after mill through the end of the 19th century.

In 1906, Lafayette Lanier's son George stepped in to help his ailing father steer the company. Under George Lanier, who helped to launch the company's second expansion program, another duck mill was built and the company made the transition from water power to electricity. Lafayette Lanier died in 1910 and in time, George Lanier became president, serving the company in this capacity from 1925 until 1948.

George Lanier had brought with him experience in the manufacturing of towels, and so, in 1916, the Fairfax mill was established for this purpose. While World War I was underway the company met demands for army fabrics, but after the war it converted back to the manufacture of towels. In 1928, West Point purchased the business of a Philadelphia manufacturer of terry cloth towels, which brought with it the valuable Martex trademark brand name.

The company entered its third expansion period during the Depression of the 1930s, and continued expanding into the 1940s by acquiring and building additional mills. In 1933, West Point purchased the Dixie Cotton Mills of LaGrange, Georgia, a historic mill that had begun operations in 1897. In 1945 West Point purchased the Boston agency that had helped refinance it after the fire in its mills. The following year, Cabin Crafts Incorporated, a subsidiary of West Point, was established in Georgia and became a pioneer in the tufting industry, making bedspreads, drapes, and rugs. Columbus Manufacturing Company was purchased in 1947. By this time, West Point had started its own research division as well.

Even before West Point was born, its future partner had begun a parallel path. In 1844, a Bostonian engineer took a defunct cotton mill in Biddeford, Maine, and, borrowing the name of a legendary Colonial soldier and merchant, obtained a charter for the Pepperell Manufacturing Company. The company was formally organized in 1850, with another mill along the same river site already under construction. The first bed sheet stamped with the Pepperell name was sold in 1851.

Pepperell had three mills humming by 1866; making shirting, sheets, and jeans for sale domestically and overseas. The company merged with the Laconia Company in 1899, just in time for the slump in New England's textile industry. In 1925, Pepperell began construction on its first Southern mill—the Opelika Mill in Alabama. The Massachusetts Cotton Mills and the Lindale plant of Georgia were acquired in 1926. The same year, one of Pepperell's best known brand names was introduced, a line of sheets called Lady Pepperell. Another mill was built in Opelika and a sales force was organized. In 1930 Pepperell purchased Granite Mills, a producer of fine-combed cotton goods. By 1946, a new, wholly modern finishing plant had been built and a new sheet factory was added shortly after that.

The 1950s were a time of growth and change for both concerns. West Point built new general offices and began manufacturing synthetic fabric in its Shawmut Mill Division. Still headed by the Lanier family, the company observed its 75th anniversary in 1955, began manufacturing carpeting the year after that and, in 1958, reformed its subsidiaries into three operating divisions: Dixie Mill Division, Columbus Mill Division, and Anderson Division. During this same time, Pepperell opened a new sewing plant in Alabama. West Point was still expanding in the early 1960s, building a new mill in Georgia, and acquiring Forrest Mills, Inc. and Velvetone Mills, Inc. in 1962.

In March of 1965, West Point Manufacturing Company and Pepperell Manufacturing Company merged to form West Point-Pepperell, Inc. Within two years, each of its name brands—Carlin, Martex, Lady Pepperell—had its own full line of products for the bed and bath, and other new products and brands were being introduced. In 1968, WPP launched a $16 million program to expand and modernize. Alamac Knitting Mills, Inc. and American Rug and Carpet Company were purchased by 1969.

Alamac became a division of the company and underwent a major expansion. In 1971, J. L. Lanier, Sr., retired as chair and chief executive officer. He was succeeded by John P. Howland. Joseph Lanier, Sr., had joined the company in 1930 when his father, George Lanier, brought him on as an assistant. He eventually succeeded his father as president and chair of the board. Joseph Lanier, Jr., became president of West Point-Pepperell in 1974, serving until turmoil beset the company in the late 1980s.

Throughout the 1970s, WPP continued its climb to becoming one of the world's largest and most versatile producers of textile goods. A huge yarn dye plant was launched in North Carolina; Georgia's Cusseta Plant was acquired and added to WPP's Industrial Fabrics Division; a building, land, and machinery were purchased in Georgia for a yarn manufacturing plant; Mission Valley Mills, Inc. of Texas was acquired in 1972 and a new mill was to be built elsewhere in Texas.

Another thrust of this period was to expand WPP's carpet production. Georgian Carpets was established in 1976. Two years later, WPP purchased nearly all of Ludlow Corporation's carpet manufacturing facilities and related assets. Similarly, the knitting operations—machinery and assets—of the Duplex In-

ternational Division of Reeves Bros., Inc. was purchased in 1978. The $1 billion mark was topped for the first time in 1979. This same year, J. L. Lanier, Jr., having served as president for five years, was elected chair.

The company celebrated record sales and earnings highs in 1980. That year, it had purchased Virginia Crafts, Inc. of Virginia and Tifton Carpet Spinning Operation of Georgia. Economic uncertainties and high interest rates caused a slight drop in sales that year; sales continued to dip slightly in 1982, but net income was up that year. For the previous three years, WPP had invested about $150 million in capital projects, especially spinning and weaving mills, to increase output and improve quality.

Advanced Fabrics, Inc. of Georgia was purchased in 1983. An international division of WPP was formed this same year and a joint venture was put underway with a Belgian firm to market bed and bath products in Europe. With the economy improving, WPP's sales were up slightly. More than half of sales that year were in household fabrics; about 30 percent were apparel. WPP purchased the assets of Bond Cote Systems, a maker of coated industrial fabrics based in Virginia.

It was a few years before the economic upturn was reflected in sales of home items like furniture, carpets, drapes, sheets, and bath towels. WPP's sales remained better than average during the recession, in large part due to its high-fashion home furnishings niche, but earnings stumbled 71 percent in the first half of 1985. Market analysts speculated that this reflected the investment costs of the company's conversion to specialized industrial fabrics.

The company's international division bloomed in 1986 with the purchase of London-based Arthur Sanderson & Son Limited, marketers of decorative furnishing fabrics, wall coverings, and specialty carpets, with operations in the United Kingdom, Canada, and the United States.

In 1986, Cluett, Peabody & Co., Inc. was acquired by WPP as a wholly owned subsidiary. Cluett, like West Point and Pepperell, had its origins in the mid-19th century, in a small business in New York that made detachable collars for men's shirts. In 1889, Cluett had acquired the Arrow brand name for its shirts. Between 1900 and 1931, Arrow shirts, promoted heavily through the ''Arrow Collar Man'' ad campaign, became a rage across the nation. By 1941, sales volume for Cluett products topped the $30 million mark and Cluett began to look to the South for expansion. In the late 1950s Cluett acquired Baltimore-based J. Schoeneman, Inc., a manufacturer of top-selling, high-quality men's and women's clothing. Throughout the following decades, it expanded through acquisitions of textile mills, apparel manufacturers, and distributors, such as the Halston line of men's clothing. When West Point-Pepperell acquired Cluett in 1986, its previous year's sales had been $2.1 billion.

In 1988, WPP made another cornerstone acquisition: J. P. Stevens & Company, a rival in several areas of WPPs business. The purchase included 15 manufacturing plants and such famous designer names as Ralph Lauren and Laura Ashley sheets and towels. This doubled WPP's domestic share of those markets—climbing to about 30 percent of towels and 36 percent of sheets. The purchase also catapulted West Point-Pepperell to the number one spot in the $1.2 billion bed-linen market, and number two, behind Fieldcrest-Cannon, in the $1.2 billion towel market. As growth rate in home furnishings is more or less static, increasing market share is the surest way to increase earnings. Acquiring J. P. Stevens was a coup, but a costly one. The bill of $1.2 billion and nearly doubled WPP's debt ratio.

While the company immediately put unwanted portions of J.P. Stevens on the block—such as automotive and carpeting businesses—the leverage incurred in the transaction made WPP more alluring for raiders. The company represented a number of strong brand names in the apparel field, such as Arrow shirts and Gold Toe hosiery, in addition to its leadership in sheets and towels. WPP's labor force was mostly nonunion and a recent $300 million capital-spending program had brought its facilities up to state-of-the-art efficiency. The debt was just one more ingredient to attract a takeover.

And in fact, within eight months of the purchase, William Farley, then chair of Farley, Inc., a holding company whose crown jewel was Fruit of the Loom, Inc., came into the picture. A former investment banker, Farley was a noted takeover artist who had had great success throughout the 1970s with leveraged buyouts, hooking up with investment banker Drexel Burnham Lambert in 1984. He acquired Fruit of the Loom as part of his 1985 purchase of conglomerate Northwest Industries, Inc.—a billion-dollar acquisition he pulled off with the help of emerging junk-bond specialist, Drexel. Farley then groomed the underwear company into a billion-dollar business.

In 1989, Farley launched a five-month, hostile battle to take over WPP and won. The price tag was $3 billion—much more than initially expected—and the deal complicated. Through the ad hoc entity, West Point Acquisition Corporation, Farley purchased 95 percent of WPP's stock at 20 times the company's 1988 earnings, planning to sell $1.6 billion in junk bonds to repay debt and buy the remaining public shares. But he was unable to raise the money when both the junk bond market and Drexel Burnham, Farley's investment banker, collapsed, and his West Point Acquisition Corporation found itself owing $800 million to banks and $700 million to bondholders.

Farley incurred $2.4 billion of acquisition debt in the purchase and had hoped to negotiate interim financing with a junk-bond offering handled by Drexel. He also planned to sell WPP assets, Cluett Peabody in particular, which he hoped would fetch up to $800 million. While Fruit of the Loom did a booming business, its cash was off limits to holding company Farley, Inc., because of debt-covenant restrictions. WPP was already a very lean company, so cost-cutting wouldn't help.

Conditions for Farley were not favorable. WPP had fought the takeover vigorously. Employees burned Fruit of the Loom underwear in demonstrations. Company attorneys sought the aid of state legislators for anti-takeover legislation. The takeover had been so acrimonious, there was trouble brewing immediately afterward with rank-and-file workers, as well as executives. WPP lost many key players, including the fourth generation of the founding Laniers, and the former head of Stevens' sheet division, who left with the highly profitable Laura Ashley license. Then Drexel lost its magician, Michael R.

Milken, and the junk-bond market began to shudder. At the same time, many of WPP's primary customers were also suffering: Marshall Field and Saks Fifth Avenue were reportedly up for sale; B. Altman was bankrupt and Bloomingdale's was teetering on the brink of bankruptcy. Just at the point in the takeover where everything had to go right, nearly everything went wrong.

Tension was high in early 1990, as Farley continued to struggle to arrange financing to complete the acquisition of WPP. Though it had been announced that Biderman S.A., a French company, would buy Cluett, that deal was dragging and the price kept dropping. Farley had arranged a $1.03 billion bridge loan at inflated interest rates in order to pay interest on debts accrued. Then Drexel, which had been Farley's compass in the deal, filed for Chapter 11 bankruptcy law protection against its creditors. Notes on the bridge loan were due in March of 1990.

At the eleventh hour, Farley secured an extension on his bridge loan. But he was short the $83 million needed to buy the last 5 percent of company shares. In March of 1990, Biderman finally signed on the Cluett sale, but the price was a shockingly low $350 million and without 100 percent ownership, Farley couldn't use proceeds from the Cluett sale to help repay his loans, anyway. Then West Point Acquisition defaulted on a $796 million bank loan and missed bond-holder interest payments. The acquisition vehicle went into default in March of 1990; in August of 1991, Farley agreed to cede—through the vehicle—his hold on 95 percent of WPP.

At the same time, the recession was hurting sales of towels, sheets, and other cornerstone WPP products. After Farley ceded control of the company in a debt-for-equity swap, West Point Acquisition filed for a prepackaged Chapter 11 bankruptcy, meaning it had already won most of its creditors' approval for debt-restructuring, a process much faster than most bankruptcy proceedings. Farley announced he would continue as chair and chief executive officer of WPP. He blamed the junk-bond market collapse, the Gulf War, the recession, and resultant credit crunch for the failure of his acquisition.

In the fall of 1992, West Point Acquisition had been restructured and renamed Valley Fashions Corporation. It had departed from Chapter 11 protection and was moving into the hands of private investors. Holcombe T. Green, Jr., headed up the company. A group of WPP shareholders sued Farley for his failure to complete the takeover, and sought to block the debt-for-equity swap. WPP reported a 5.9 percent drop in sales and a plunge in earnings in early 1993, in part due to reorganization charges and overall loss from discontinued operations.

A new president and chief executive officer was announced in February 1993. Joseph L. Jennings, Jr., claimed that all the company needed was a better sense of direction. In the *New York Times,* he said of WPP, ''They are still the largest bed and bath company in the world. My job is mainly to bring more stability.'' Jennings is related to the Lanier family, founders of West Point.

Principal Subsidiaries: J. P. Stevens & Co., Inc.; West Point-Pepperell Stores, Inc.

Further Reading:

Benoit, Ellen, "West Point-Pepperell: the Victor Spoiled?" *Financial World,* May 31, 1988, p. 8, 11.

Berg, Eric, "Farley Sale of Cluett to French," *New York Times,* March 17, 1990, p. 33.

Berss, Marcia, "Squeezed," *Forbes,* January 8, 1990, p. 48.

Christie, Rick, "West Point-Pepperell Winds Up in Limbo," *Wall Street Journal,* February 21, 1990.

"Farley's Acquisition of Pepperell Runs into Financial Snags," *Wall Street Journal,* January 10, 1990, p. A12.

"Farley Unit Misses Loan Payment," *New York Times,* April 3, 1990, p. D4.

Foust, Dean, "Stevens Cries Double-Cross," *Business Week,* May 2, 1988, p. 35–36.

Greising, David, "Bill Farley Is on Pins and Needles," *Business Week,* September 18, 1989, p. 58–59.

Hayes, Arthur, "Law," *Wall Street Journal,* April 23, 1990, p. B5.

Hopper, Lucien, "West Point-Pepperell," *Financial World,* September 5–18, 1984, p. 6.

Johnson, Robert, "Farley Lags in His Plans to Pay Debt as Cluett Is Sold for a Low-End Price," *Wall Street Journal,* March 19, 1990, p. A4.

Johnson, Robert, "Farley May be Close to Sale of Cluett Unit," *Wall Street Journal,* February 22, 1990, p. C18.

Johnson, Robert, "Farley May Have to Fight Bondholders Over Control of West Point-Pepperell," *Wall Street Journal,* May 30, 1990, p. A5.

Johnson, Robert, "Farley Secures Loan Extension," *Wall Street Journal,* March 15, 1990, p. C15.

Johnson, Robert, "Farley to Surrender Majority Ownership of West Point-Pepperell, Sources Say," *Wall Street Journal,* April 11, 1990, p.A3.

Johnson, Robert, "Feeling Pinch William Farley May Accept Bid," *Wall Street Journal,* May 31, 1990, p. A4.

Johnson, Robert, "William Farley's Quest for Status Threatens to Topple His Empire," *Wall Street Journal,* April 30, 1990, pp. A1, A16.

Laing, Jonathan, "Love that Leverage!," *Barron's,* May 1, 1989, p. 6–33.

Lowenstein, Roger, "Bill Farley Is Bailed Out by Rebounds in His Stock," *Wall Street Journal,* April 16, 1991, pp. C1–C2.

Lowenstein, Roger, "West Point-Pepperell's Shares Look Cheap," *Wall Street Journal,* February 23, 1990, p. C2.

Madden, Stephen, "Georgia on His Mind," *Fortune,* January 30, 1989, p. 191.

Miller, James, "Pepperell Group Is Suing Farley over Takeover," *Wall Street Journal,* March 19, 1992, p. A4.

Miller, James, "William Farley, Ceding Control, Severs His Last Ties to West Point-Pepperell," *Wall Street Journal,* October 26, 1992, p. B6.

Norris, Floyd, "Behind Delay in Farley Deal for West Point-Pepperell," *New York Times,* January 9, 1990, p. D1.

"Pepperell Reports a Deficit," *New York Times,* January 1993, p. 39.

"Pepperell's 3rd-Period Loss Amounts to $179.6 Million," *Wall Street Journal,* January 4, 1993, p. B2.

Rice, Faye, "Looking Homeward for Stocks," *Fortune,* June 10, 1985, pp. 217, 220.

Rublin, Lauren, "The Trader," *Barron's,* February 26, 1990, p. 65.

Schellhardt, Timothy, "Farley to Cede Pepperell Unit's Majority Stake," *Wall Street Journal,* August 6, 1991, p. A2.

Schwartz, Jerry, "West Point-Pepperell Names New President," *New York Times,* February 2, 1993, p. D5.

Taub, Stephen, "Market Watch," *Financial World,* March 17, 1992, p. 14.

"$300 Million Worth of Humility," *Business Week,* August 19, 1991, p. 36.

"West Point-Pepperell Taps Jennings for Posts," *Wall Street Journal,* February 5, 1993, p. B5.

—Carol I. Keeley

WHEATON INDUSTRIES

Wheaton Industries

1101 Wheaton Avenue
Millville, New Jersey 08332
U.S.A.
(609) 825-1400
Fax: (609) 825-0146

Private Company
Incorporated: October 24, 1888 as T. C. Wheaton and Co.;
   1971, as Wheaton Industries
Employees: 6,000
Sales: $530.0 million
SICs: 3221 Glass Containers; 3229 Pressed & Blown Glass
   & Glassware; 3085 Plastic Bottles; 3089 Plastics Products,
   Nec; 3559 Special Industry Machinery, Nec; 6719 Holding
   Companies, Nec

With origins in glass production dating to 1888, Wheaton Industries is known as the largest family-owned producer of glassware in the world. From furnishing laboratory glassware, the company moved into design and production of general laboratory supplies and innovative research equipment ranging from centrifuges to micro-processor controlled bioreactors. With the rise of plastics in the 1950s, the company developed and built the world's first commercial injection blow molding (OEM) machine for plastic, revolutionizing the packaging industry and expanding markets in cosmetics and pharmaceutical packaging. Wheaton Plastic Containers eventually specialized in package and graphics design, engineering and package modeling, and mold design and production. These and other developments required innovative machine design, which itself became a company service. Wheaton's General Machinery Company eventually provided every facet of machine building for glass, plastics, military, and industrial markets. After Wheaton's affiliates were reorganized under the parentage of Wheaton Industries in 1971, the company continued to grow and diversify. By the 1990s, the organization's combined operations provided worldwide services in all areas of packaging, OEM components, production equipment, electronics, and scientific instrumentation.

Wheaton Industries survived a stormy beginning. Construction of a new glass factory in Millville, New Jersey, under the ownership of two entrepreneurs, Mr. Shull and Mr. Goodwin, was delayed by the devastating East Coast blizzard of 1888.

When operations finally got underway, the partners fell behind schedule in production of the glass tubing needed to supply their lamp room. In addition, they were losing market share to Western glass companies prospering under more advantageous fuel costs, easier access to raw materials, and a superior transportation network. In a campaign to raise much-needed capital, the fledgling company borrowed $3,000 from a local pharmacist and physician, Dr. T. C. Wheaton. Attempting to salvage his investment, Dr. Wheaton participated in company planning. His involvement grew rapidly, and on October 24, 1888, he purchased controlling interest in the firm, thereby founding T. C. Wheaton and Co.

The new company grew rapidly to reflect the medical interests of its founder, specializing in homeopathic and screw-cap vials used by scientific laboratories, chemists, perfumers, pharmacists, and physicians. Within a year, a new lamp room had been constructed alongside the factory. It accommodated 13 glass workers, as well as room for sorting, cutting, inspecting, and packing the tubing. In addition, a new shop was constructed for the manufacture of prescription bottles. Presses were designed to supply matching stoppers and other solid ware. Nursing bottles, breast pump glasses, and other druggist supplies were added to the Wheaton line.

In addition to the usual risks of starting a new company, Dr. Wheaton had to contend with fire hazards typical of the glass industry. On November 24, 1889, six of the original factory buildings were lost to the first of numerous fires over the years. Other major fires occurred in 1908, 1912, and 1925.

By June of 1890, Dr. Wheaton had discontinued his private medical practice in order to focus all his energies on developing the glass business. In an early public relations stint, the doctor traveled to the West Coast in the summer of 1890 to establish new contacts. In 1891, his younger brother, Walter Scott Wheaton, opened a sales office in Denver, Colorado. Further contacts were made during Dr. Wheaton's periodic trips to Philadelphia, Boston, and New York, where he opened a sales office in 1892.

In 1892, Dr. Wheaton gambled on substantial growth by investing $10,000 in a plot of land surrounding the existing factory. By 1894, the number two furnace was operational, and in 1896, $14,000 was invested in 12 pot furnaces and a new building constituting the number three factory. These additions were designed to employ approximately 250 new workers and to double production capacity.

Expanding business required new staff, for which Dr. Wheaton had cultivated two outstanding candidates: his two sons. In 1899, Frank H. Wheaton joined the company at a starting salary of $5 per week. Frank's career and education were closely allied with the company. After graduating from Millville High School in the spring of 1898, he studied general business subjects at the Eastman Business College in Poughkeepsie, New York, and took a summer course in chemistry at the Philadelphia College of Pharmacy and Science. These skills were put to immediate use at the family business, where he quickly learned technical and sales skills. By 1903, he was elected to the company board and shortly thereafter assumed the post of secretary and treasurer.

His younger brother, Theodore C. Wheaton, Jr., also joined the family enterprise, concentrating more on public relations and marketing than on production. Theodore was born on September 30, 1888, the year T. C. Wheaton Co. was founded. After finishing his studies at the Worcester Polytechnic Institute in Massachusetts, he served on the domestic front of World War I, primarily in Washington, D.C. He eventually became vice president of the New York sales office of T. C. Wheaton Co. and established valuable business ties over the course of his career.

In the pre-World War I years, the company grew quickly, trying new ventures with varying success. In 1903, Wheaton entered the window glass market, or window lights as they were called at the time. Despite high quality, profits were extremely low, and the company had to allocate profits from its Lamp Room and Bottle Glass Departments to finance the loans on the Window Glass Company. By 1908, the window plant was permanently idled. In 1903, the company also had to contend with the unexpected resignation of two top executives, who started their own glass factory, Millville Bottle Works, working in direct competition with T. C. Wheaton in the areas of medicine bottles and laboratory ware. Wheaton would eventually acquire the firm and use the competitive edge to its own benefit.

The glass industry, and particularly T. C. Wheaton, continued to prosper. When Carl Sandburg visited Millville in 1905, he described the setting in unforgettable terms: "Down in Southern New Jersey they make glass. By day and night, the fires burn on in Millville and bid the sand let in the light. . . . Big, black flumes, shooting out smoke and sparks . . . and bottles, bottles, bottles, of every tint and hue from a brilliant crimson to the dull green that marks the death of sand and the birth of glass."

With the onset of World War I, the "fires burning in Millville" redoubled their heat, as the United States became a chief supplier of war materials. Discontinued importation of German glassware, which had dominated the world market, gave American producers the impetus to prove that their products were at least as competitive. Among the many glassware needs of the war effort, the Chemical Warfare Service of the U.S. Army required specially designed canisters known as L.E.C. bottles. According to a company report, T. C. Wheaton Company produced the only L.E.C. bottles that met the exacting standards of military engineers at the Lakehurst Proving Grounds in New Jersey. After the U.S. declaration of war in 1917, Dr. Wheaton offered President Wilson the company's services in production of "a diversified line of scientific glassware, as glass stopcocks, tube funnels, test tubes, pipettes, ampules, etc., as well as blown bottles for prescriptions and supply bottles for hospital use." The offer helped establish valuable new business opportunities and won a personalized note from the President, thanking Dr. Wheaton for his "generous and patriotic offer."

The post-World War I era marked substantial expansion. Additions to the plant included a new etching facility for perfumery ware, a metal and concrete warehouse for storing chemicals, a new mold room and batch house, sheds for grinding, and other improvements. After a debilitating fire in June of 1925 and the death of Dr. Wheaton's brother, Walter Scott Wheaton, company growth continued unhindered. The company acquired Millville Bottle Works in 1926, gaining its competitor's proprietary line of prescription and medicine bottles and laboratory ware, and establishing T. C. Wheaton Co. as a major player in the laboratory glassware business.

With the advent of the Great Depression, T. C. Wheaton Co. withstood turbulent markets as well as unforeseen changes in personnel. On September 7, 1931, Dr. T. C. Wheaton died, leaving the post of president and chair of the board to Frank H. Wheaton, Sr. That same year, Frank Wheaton, Jr., departed for the Boston University School of Business where he passed a shortened tenure before returning to the family business to work his way up the company ladder from batch mixing assistant to truck driver's helper and, before too long, to manager and ultimately president.

Frank Jr.'s reputation as "New Idea Man," was reinforced by his introduction of automated glass production in the late 1930s. Earlier in that decade, he helped introduce handmade borosilicate glass tubes for select pharmaceuticals (borosilicate glass could be molded into long, narrow tubes without collapsing like standard soda-lime glass). For a short time, the company successfully sold handmade serum containers to Eli Lilly, Parke-Davis, and other pharmaceutical companies. Key competition had developed automated production facilities, however, and Wheaton had to either follow suit or lose business. In 1937, Frank Wheaton, Jr., negotiated with the Hartford-Empire Company to lease a single section semi-automatic machine for the production of perfume bottles. That machine's success prompted further negotiations toward the lease of a four-section I. S. Machine, which would increase the company's productivity to eight times its former level. Though the terms of the lease were restrictive, the machine was installed. By 1938, the factory itself had been automated and the first automatic bottles were produced.

World War II brought a flood of needs that, paired with shortages in iron and steel, prompted innovation and diversification of Wheaton products. On the medical and laboratory front, the company supplied products for the blood serum program, serum containers, Halazone containers (used to purify water on the battlefield), and a wide variety of scientific glassware. Experimentation in material substitutes showed that glass could be used in the place of metal, sometimes with unexpected advantages. Wheaton No-Sol-Vit glass was ground to machinery tolerances and fashioned into three types of glass gages: ring gages, tri-lock gages, and taper lock plug blanks. Glass also replaced metal in many electronic applications, for which Wheaton developed water-resistant glass-to-metal seals sold under the Tronex trademark. The seals were especially useful in radio equipment vulnerable in water-prone combat situations. Wheaton prided itself, among other things, on never missing a single shipment during the war. Nor was it the only party to recognize its competence; in February, 1943, the company was awarded the Army-Navy "E" Award for its provision of war equipment. As new techniques and new machines were designed to meet diverse war needs, Wheaton gained expertise in industrial machine design and construction, one of its new specialties after the war.

At the close of the war, the glass industry saw tremendous surge in demand for new molds and new glass containers on the domestic front. In 1947, under the driving influence of Frank Wheaton, Jr., the Wheaton third generation established a new company, Wheaton Glass Company, designed to function separately but in tandem with the older company. For its initial year and a half, Wheaton Glass manufactured only type I (Borosilicate) glass, due to extremely high demand in the market. Afterwards, the new company shifted to long-run soda lime items.

The 1950s saw the rise of industrial plastic, which was quickly exploited by Wheaton and other companies as a powerful packaging medium. In September of 1950, the company acquired in Mays Landing, the closed grounds of a plant belonging to the Millville Manufacturing Company, comprising 240,000 square feet of floor space. In 1953, Frank Wheaton, Jr., designed a new container for those aerosol products that were chemically incompatible with metal canisters. His solution involved a glass container coated with a polymer product, polyvinyl chloride, manufactured by the Goodrich Company. The result was a nonvolatile, break-resistant container that launched a new company line, Wheaton Plasti-Cote. The company also developed a small injection molding machine to make plastic snap caps, which, along with Plasti-Cote items marked the first products of the Wheaton Plastics Company.

Wheaton Plastics worked quickly to develop automatic machinery that could manufacture plastic containers with the same injection blow mold system used for glass. Around 1950, the company acquired the rights to a Swiss manufacturing process called Novoplast. The company's General Machinery division, with the combined expertise of Ted Wheaton and the engineering group, developed the VB65-1 machine, the first in a series of bigger and faster injection blow molding machines.

By 1950, the T. C. Wheaton Co. office force had outgrown its old site, and plans were drawn up for new facilities that would include expanded central offices as well as new research and visitors centers. The complex, completed in September of 1951, was referred to as "the Pentagon," in reference to its rambling and impressive size.

The 1960s and 1970s marked ever-increasing diversification and the formation of new affiliate companies with various specializations. In 1960 General Mod and Machinery was established, and in 1966, Wheaton Scientific was formed. In the mid-1960s the company entered the consumer products market. In 1964, Central Research and Development was established to service all Wheaton companies, especially the rapidly growing Wheaton Plastics. In February of 1974, Decora was formed to specialize in decorating and labeling operations for glass and plastic containers. In 1975, the Wheaton Cartage Company was established, growing from an in-house carrier to a full-service, national trucking company. In 1977, part of Wheaton's glass operations were transferred to Flat River, Missouri, where fuel costs and transportation facilities were favorable to those in New Jersey. The Flat River Glass Company was thus founded. And in January of 1977, American International Container, Inc. was established to distribute Wheaton and other name brands in Florida, Central and South America, the Caribbean, Europe, Asia, Australia, and Africa. Topping the whirlwind expansion of the 1970s, a new Wheaton R&D Center was appended to the so-called Pentagon in 1979. The massive facility would be a driving engine for continued research and product expansion in the 1980s and beyond.

Despite the rapid speed of change in the 1970s, two developments helped define Wheaton as a unified organization with a distinct place in history. The first development was the 1971 formation of Wheaton Industries, which was thereafter considered the parent company of its numerous divisions. The second development was the 1976 dedication of Wheaton Village, a periodized rendition of the original 1888 glassworks, complete with one of the finest glass museums in the United States. The historical park was the result of careful planning and funding on the part of Frank H. Wheaton, Jr., and associates. In 1968, Mr. Wheaton had helped found the Wheaton Historical Association as the first step in researching the town's past and organizing historical resources. In 1984, the Creative Glass Center of America, an organization working in concert with Wheaton Village, started a fellowship program to select and fund contemporary artists to stay in the vintage glass making facilities and use the resources to innovate. The primary objective was to mix old traditions with new art forms, and to expand the costly facilities beyond the scope of traditional, and less experimental, paperweight making.

Rapid diversification and expansion continued in the 1980s, while foreign competition forced Americans to run leaner businesses. In mid-1980, Wheaton Fine Glass was created to produce high-quality glassware products for the American market. Due to the rising value of the dollar and lower wages in foreign industries, the division yielded no profit and discontinued operations in 1984, followed by the closing of all consumer operations in 1986. Another venture launched in 1983, Carolina Glass Works, also folded under the weight of heavy competition. The operation produced state-of-the-art borosilicate flint glass, and was fully computerized and environmentally controlled to produce what the company called "the world's most precise glass containers." The plant closed in 1985. But Wheaton adapted to the changing market, opening Wheaton Science Plastics in 1987 to manufacture injection-molded and blow-molded plastic products for the laboratory. Additionally, the Wheaton Glass Company completely renovated its Plant I in 1987, installing all the capabilities for advanced glass production that had been lost in the Carolina Glass Works.

The 1980s also marked various milestones in Wheaton's long history. On March 16, 1981, the company celebrated the 100th birthday of Frank Wheaton, Sr. Then in September of 1988, the company celebrated its own centennial, attended by former president Gerald R. Ford and New Jersey Governor Thomas H. Kean, among roughly 7,000 others.

By the 1990s, Wheaton Industries constituted over 30 subsidiaries with worldwide distribution. In September of 1992, Beijing-Wheaton Glass Co., Ltd. realized the first Sino-foreign joint venture to daily produce glass containers for cosmetics, foodstuffs, and other products. That same month, Wheaton Science Products, Inc. signed a marketing and distribution agreement with Endotronics, Inc., a Minneapolis-based company providing cell processing products and health-care and biotechnology services. Endotronics agreed to market Wheaton's Integral Bioreactor System along with its BioPro software throughout the United States and Canada. In December of that same year, Wheaton contracted with Sandretto Industrie, an Italian firm, to assemble a limited number of machines for U.S. distribution. The venture was discontinued due to recession and aggressive competition from the Far East, according to the joint managing director in a December, 1992 *Modern Plastics* article. It nevertheless marked an increasing trend of international cooperation in the 1990s. Wheaton had grown from a family business to a family of businesses, held together by an increasingly cosmopolitan parent.

Principal Subsidiaries: American International Container, Inc.; AMS Wheaton; Wheaton Coated Products; Wheaton Cultural Alliance; C P Packaging, Inc.; Wheaton (Export Sales); General Machinery; Wheaton Glass Products Clean Pack; Glass Warehouse; Wheaton Industrial Molding; Wheaton Injection Molding; Wheaton Instruments; Wheaton International; Wheaton Medical Technologies, Inc.; Wheaton Pharmatech; Wheaton Plastic Products; Wheaton Science Plastics; Wheaton (Science Products); Wheaton Tubing Products.

Further Reading:

"Endotronics, Inc. and Wheaton Science Products, Inc. Announce Marketing and Distribution Agreement," *PR Newswire,* September 1, 1992.

"Frank Wheaton Sr., 102, Dies; Major Manufacturer of Glass," *New York Times,* April 17, 1983, Section 1, Part 1, p. 36.

"How To Manufacture a Menagerie of Glass from Grains of Sand," *Los Angeles Times,* March 17, 1991, p. E5.

Jacobs, Muriel, "Antiques; The Fires Burn on in Millville, Where Glass Lets in Light," *New York Times,* June 22, 1986, Section 11NJ, p. 21.

Malarcher, Patricia, "Crafts: A Wedding of Art and Industry," *New York Times,* February 12, 1984, Section 11NJ, p. 18.

Ozanian, Michael and Tina Russo, "Private Enterprise," *Forbes,* December 14, 1987, p. 150.

Rogers, Jack K., "Sandretto Is Reviewing U.S. Assembly Venture," *Modern Plastics,* December, 1992, vol. 69, No. 13, p. 13.

"Wheaton Glass Works Operational," *Xinhua General News Service,* September 24, 1992, Item No. 0924140.

Wheaton Industries Centennial Newsletter, "100 Years of Pride," Millville: Wheaton Industries, October 1987–February 1989.

"Wheaton Shuts Glass Plant: Cites Import Competition for Losses," *Weekly Home Furnishings Newspaper,* April 30, 1984, Vol. 58, p. 41.

—Kerstan Cohen

INDEX TO COMPANIES AND PERSONS _____

Listings are arranged in alphabetical order under the company name; thus Eli Lilly & Company will be found under the letter E. Definite articles (The) and forms of incorporation that precede the name (A.B. and N.V.) are ignored for alphabetical purposes. Company names appearing in bold type have historical essays on the page numbers appearing in bold. Updates to entries that appeared in earlier volumes are signified by (upd.). The index is cumulative with volume numbers printed in bold type.

SGC. *See* Supermarkets General
Corporation.
SGS, **II** 117
Shabazian, Michael R., **6** 243–44
Shad, John, **II** 409
Shafer, Thomas, **7** 463
Shaffer Clarke, **II** 594
Shaffer, Richard A., **6** 244
Shaftesbury (seventh Earl of), **IV** 118
Shagari, Alhaji Shehu, **IV** 473
Shah, Eddy, **IV** 652
Shah of Iran. *See* Muhammad Reza Shah
Pahlevi (Shah of Iran).
Shakespeare, William, **III** 15; **IV** 671
Shalit, Gene, **I** 344
Shamrock Advisors, Inc., **8** 305
Shamrock Capital L.P., **7** 81–82
Shamrock Holdings, **III** 609; **7** 438
Shamrock Oil & Gas Co., **I** 403–04; **IV**
409; **7** 308
Shanghai Hotels Co., **IV** 717
Shanks, Carroll M., **III** 338–39
Shannahan, John N., **6** 532, 555
Shapiro, Irving, **I** 329–30; **8** 152
Sharbaugh, H. Robert, **I** 631; **IV** 550
Sharbaugh, Robert, **7** 414
Shared Use Network Systems, Inc., **8** 311
Sharon Steel Corp., **I** 497; **7** 360–61; **8**
536
Sharon Tank Car Corporation, **6** 394
Sharp and Dohme Inc., **I** 650
Sharp, Bill, **7** 217
Sharp Corporation, **I** 476; **II** 95–96; **III**
14, 428, 455, 480; **6** 217, 231
Sharp, Henry, **I** 314
Sharp, Sir Eric, **6** 320
Sharp-Hughes Tool Co., **III** 428
Sharples Co., **I** 383
Sharples Separator Co., **III** 418–20
Shasta, **II** 571–73
Shattuck, Frank C., **III** 440
Shattuck, Robert, **III** 440
Shaub, Harold A., **II** 480; **7** 67
Shaver, Clarence H., **III** 763
Shaw, Alexander, **V** 491
Shaw, George, **II** 37
Shaw, H.A., **8** 241
Shaw, Harry A., III, **7** 226
Shaw, John S., **6** 577
Shaw, Neil, **II** 582
Shaw, R. Nelson, **V** 140
Shaw's Supermarkets, **II** 658–59
Shawinigan Water and Power Company, **6**
501–02
Shawmut National Bank, **II** 207
Shea, James, Jr., **III** 506
Shea's Winnipeg Brewery Ltd., **I** 268
Shearson Hammill & Co., **II** 445, 450
Shearson Hayden Stone, **II** 450
Shearson Lehman Bros., **I** 202; **II** 478; **III**
319; **8** 118
Shearson Lehman Bros. Holdings Inc., **II**
398–99, 450
Shearson Lehman Hutton, **II** 399, 451; **III**
119
Shearson Lehman Hutton Holdings Inc.,
II 450–52
Shearson Loeb Rhoades Inc., **II** 398
Shedden, William Ian H., **I** 647
Sheehy, Patrick, **I** 426–27
Sheepbridge Engineering, **III** 495
Sheets, Harold, **IV** 558
Sheffield Banking Co., **II** 333
Sheffield, Bill, **7** 559

Sheffield Motor Co., **I** 158
Sheffield Twist Drill & Steel Co., **III** 624
Sheinberg, Sidney, **6** 162–63
Sheinberg, Sidney J., **II** 144
Shelby Steel Tube Co., **IV** 572; **7** 550
Sheldon, Clifford, **IV** 666
Shell. *See* Shell Transport and Trading
Company p.l.c. *and* Shell Oil Company.
Shell Australia Ltd., **III** 728
Shell BV, **IV** 518
Shell Chemical Co., **IV** 410, 481, 531–32,
540; **8** 415
Shell Co.-Qatar, **IV** 524
Shell Co. of California, **IV** 540
Shell Co. of Portugal, **IV** 504
Shell Coal International, **IV** 532
Shell Development Co., **IV** 540
Shell Mining Co., **IV** 541
Shell Nederland BV, **V** 658–59
Shell of Colombia, **IV** 417
Shell Oil Company, **I** 20, 26, 569; **III**
559; **IV** 392, 400, 531, **540–41**; **6** 382,
457; **8** 261–62
Shell Petroleum Corp., **IV** 540
Shell Pipe Line Corp., **IV** 540
Shell Sekiyu, **IV** 542–43
Shell Transport and Trading Company
p.l.c., **I** 605; **II** 436, 459; **III** 522, 735;
IV 363, 378–79, 381–82, 403, 412, 423,
425, 429, 440, 454, 466, 470, 472, 474,
484–86, 491, 505, 508, **530–32**, 564.
See also Royal Dutch Petroleum
Company *and* Royal Dutch/Shell.
Shell Union Oil Corp., **IV** 531, 540
Shell Western E & P, **7** 323
Shell Winning, **IV** 413–14
Shell-BP Petroleum Development Co. of
Nigeria Ltd., **IV** 472
Shell-Mex, **IV** 531
Sheller Manufacturing Corp., **I** 201
Sheller-Globe Corporation, **I** 201–02
Sheller-Ryobi Corp., **I** 202
Shelley, R. Gene, **II** 87
Shenley Laboratories, **I** 699
Shenstone, Naomi Ann. *See* Donnelley,
Naomi Shenstone.
Shepard, Alan, **I** 79
Shepard, Horace, **I** 539–40
Shepard Warner Elevator Co., **III** 467
Shepard's Citations, Inc., **IV** 636–37
Shepherd, Mark, Jr., **II** 113–14
Sheppard, Allen, **I** 249
Sheppard, Dick, **IV** 711
Shepperd, A.J., **I** 715
Shepperly, Chester E., **III** 707; **7** 292
Sheraton Corp. of America, **I** 463–64, 487;
III 98–99
Sheridan Bakery, **II** 633
Sheridan Catheter & Instrument Corp., **III**
443
Sherix Chemical, **I** 682
Sherman, Clifton W., **IV** 73
Sherman, Frank A., **IV** 73
Sherman, George M., **7** 117
Sherman, Harry W., **II** 507
Sherman, William Tecumseh, **6** 446
Sherrill, Colonel, **II** 644
Sherritt Gordon Mines, **7** 386–87
Sherwell, Chris, **IV** 250
Sherwin, E. D., **V** 712
Sherwin, Henry, **III** 744
Sherwin-Williams Company, **III** 744–46;
8 222, 224
Sherwood, J. D., **6** 595

Sherwood Medical Group, **I** 624; **III**
443–44
Shetterly, Robert B., **III** 20–21
SHI Resort Development Co., **III** 635
ShianFu Optical Fiber, **III** 491
Shibaura Engineering Works, **I** 533
Shibusawa, Eiichi, **I** 265, 502–03, 506; **II**
273; **III** 383; **IV** 320
Shield, Lansing P., **7** 202
Shiely, Vincent R., **8** 71
Shijo, Takafusa, **III** 405
Shiki, Moriya, **II** 59
Shikoku Coca-Cola Bottling Co., **IV** 297
Shikoku Drinks Co., **IV** 297
Shikoku Electric Power Company, Inc.,
V 718–20
Shikoku Information &
Telecommunications Network, **V** 719
Shikoku Machinery Co., **III** 634
Shimada family, **I** 506
Shimada, Mitsuhiro, **I** 63
Shimizu, Norihiku, **III** 552
Shimizu, Tsutomu, **V** 487
Shimkin, Leon, **IV** 671–72
Shimomura, Hikoemon, **V** 41
Shimomura, Shotaro, **V** 41
Shimotsuke Electric Railway Company, **6**
431
Shimura Kako, **IV** 63
Shin Nippon Machine Manufacturing, **III**
634
Shin-Nihon Glass Co., **I** 221
Shinano Bank, **II** 291
Shindo, Sadakazu, **II** 58–59
Shinji, Ichiro, **II** 119
Shinko Electric Co., Ltd., **IV** 129
Shinko Kinzoku Kogyo Ltd., **IV** 129
Shinko Koji K.K., **IV** 129
Shinko Pantec Co. Ltd., **IV** 129
Shinko Pfaudler Co., Ltd., **IV** 129
Shinko Rayon, **I** 363
Shinko Rayon Ltd., **V** 369–70
Shinko Wire Co., Ltd., **IV** 129
Shinn, George L., **II** 403
Shinn, Richard R., **III** 293
Shinriken Kogyo, **IV** 63
Shinwa Tsushinki Co., **III** 593
Shiomi Casting, **III** 551
Shiono, Gisaburo, **III** 60–61
Shiono, Kotaro, **III** 61
Shiono, Motozo, **III** 61
Shiono, Yoshihiko, **III** 61
Shionogi & Co., Ltd., **I** 646, 651; **III**
60–61
Ship 'n Shore, **II** 503
Shipley, Walter V., **II** 252
Shipowners and Merchants Tugboat
Company, **6** 382
Shirai, Takaaki, **III** 592
Shiraishi, Ganjiro, **IV** 161
Shiraishi, Tashiro, **III** 545
Shirakawa, Hiroshi, **III** 756
Shirasu, Jiro, **V** 727
Shirasugi, Kanezo, **I** 586
Shirer, William L., **II** 132; **IV** 672
Shirley, Jon, **6** 258, 260
Shiro Co., Ltd., **V** 96
Shirokiya Co., Ltd., **V** 199
Shirokiya Drapery Shop Co., Ltd., **V** 199
Shiseido Company, Limited, **II** 273–74,
436; **III** 46, 48, **62–64**; **8** 341, 343
Shives, Robert, **I** 132
Shoda, Osamu, **II** 554
Shoda, Teiichiro, **II** 554

INDEX TO INDUSTRIES

Index to Industries

PUBLISHING & PRINTING

REAL ESTATE

RETAIL & WHOLESALE

WASTE SERVICES

NOTES ON CONTRIBUTORS

Notes on Contributors

BAY, Timothy. Free-lance writer and editor. Contributor to the *New York Times,* the *Chicago Tribune,* and *Newsday,* as well as various business and consumer publications.

BELSITO, Elaine. Free-lance writer and editor. Assistant managing editor, *Archives of Physical Medicine and Rehabilitation,* 1988–90.

BOHN, Thomas. Free-lance writer.

BOYER, Dean. Former newspaper reporter; free-lance writer in the Seattle area.

COHEN, Kerstan. Free-lance writer and French translator; editor for *Letter-Ex* poetry review.

COLLINS, Cheryl L. Free-lance writer and researcher.

COVELL, Jeffrey L. Free-lance writer and corporate history contractor.

DOUGAL, April S. Archivist and free-lance writer specializing in business and social history in Cleveland, Ohio.

DUBOVOJ, Sina. History contractor and free-lance writer; adjunct professor of history, Montgomery College, Rockville, Maryland.

FARQUHAR-BOYLE, Allyson S. Analyst, Mercy Health Services, Department of Strategic Planning and Analysis. Author of ''Strategic Planning as a Process,'' *Court Management and Public Administration.*

GRANT, Tina. Free-lance writer and editor.

GRIFFIN, Jessica. Former editor, St. James Press, London. Japanese Investment Manager, Thornton Group, London, 1987–89.

HALL, Janet Reinhart. Free-lance writer.

HEALY, Carole. Free-lance writer. Contributing editor, *Global Press,* 1986–87; has written business and feature articles for the *Washington Post,* the *Chicago Tribune,* and the *Daily Yomiuri* in Tokyo.

HEDDEN, Heather Behn. Business periodical abstractor and indexer, Information Access Company, Foster City, California. Senior staff writer, *Middle East Times* Cairo bureau, 1991–92.

HEENAN, Patrick. Course Tutor, St. Catherine's College, Oxford; Kobe Institute, Japan. Editor, Books Department of Euromoney Publications, 1989–90. Editor of *1992,* 1990.

JACOBSON, Robert R. Free-lance writer and musician.

KEELEY, Carol I. Free-lance writer and researcher; researcher for *Ford Times* and *Discovery.* Contributor to *Chicago* magazine, *Playboy,* the *Reader, Oxford Poetry,* 1987, and *Voices International,* 1989.

KIELTYKA, Carol. Free-lance writer.

KROLL, Dorothy. Business writer, journalist, and industry analyst.

KRONENBERG, Kenneth F. Free-lance writer and editor; writer and editor of English and social studies textbooks; translator of business documents and correspondence from German into English.

LANDA, Marinell. San Francisco–based writer and editor specializing in business and health-care topics.

LEVINE, Kathie. Attorney and free-lance writer and editor based in Mill Valley, California.

LEWIS, Scott M. Free-lance writer and editor; contributing editor, *Option.* Staff editor, *Security, Distributing and Marketing,* 1989–90.

MARTIN, Jonathan. Free-lance writer.

MAXFIELD, Doris Morris. Owner of Written Expressions, an editorial services business; contributor to numerous reference publications; editor of *Online Database Search Services Directory,* 1983–84 and 1988, and *Charitable Organizations in the U.S.,* 1991–92 and 1992–93.

McCLELLAN, Michelle L. Historian specializing in American women's history.

MONTGOMERY, Bruce P. Curator and director of historical collection, University of Colorado at Boulder.

MOTE, Dave. President of information retrieval company Performance Database.

PATTI, Nicholas S. Free-lance writer.

PEDERSON, Jay P. Free-lance writer and editor.

PENDERGAST, Sara. Free-lance writer.

PENDERGAST, Tom. Free-lance writer and Ph.D. candidate in American studies at Purdue University.

RIGGS, Thomas. Free-lance writer and editor.

ROULAND, Roger. Instructor of English at Graceland College, Lamoni, Iowa; free-lance writer whose essays and journalism have appeared in the *International Fiction Review, Chicago Tribune,* and *Chicago Sun-Times.*

ROURKE, Elizabeth. Free-lance writer.

SALTER, Susan. Free-lance writer; contributor to the reference series *Contemporary Authors, Newsmakers,* and *Major Authors and Illustrators for Children and Young Adults.*

SARICH, John A. Free-lance writer and editor. Graduate student in economics at the New School for Social Research.

SCHUSTEFF, Sandy. Marketing and communications consultant; adjunct professor, Lake Forest Graduate School of Management, Lake Forest, Illinois.

SHERMAN, Fran Shonfeld. Free-lance writer. Assistant editor, *Compton's Encyclopedia,* 1986–92; contributing editor, *Britannica Book of the Year,* annual.

SIMLEY, John. Professional researcher and corporate issues analyst. Former research editor for *International Direc-tory of Company Histories;* contributor to *Encyclopedia of Consumer Brands.*

STEIN, Wendy. Free-lance writer and editor. Former managing editor of periodicals department, New Readers Press. Former reporter for *Syracuse Herald-Journal* and *Herald American.*

SUN, Douglas. Assistant professor of English, University of California. Contributor to *Los Angeles Times.*

SWORSKY, Mary F. Editor, American Association of Law Libraries, Chicago; free-lance writer.

TROESTER, Maura. Chicago-based free-lance writer.

TUCKER, Thomas M. Free-lance writer.

TUDAHL, Kim L. Executive Assistant/Travel Consultant, Oriental Tours & Travel, Cambridge, MA. Free-lance writer; contributor to the *Harbus News,* Harvard Business School, and the *Rochester Post-Bulletin.*

WOLF, Gillian. Free-lance writer. Author of "The Ultimate Slingshot," 1989, and "Akh, Odessa!" 1990, both for *Jewish Affairs.*

YOUNG, Shannon. Ph.D. candidate in education, University of Michigan; free-lance writer and editor.